FROMMER'S

COMPREHENSIVE TRAVEL GUIDE

Spain

16th Edition

by Darwin Porter
Assisted by Danforth Prince

MACMILLAN • USA

ABOUT THE AUTHOR

A native of North Carolina, **Darwin Porter** was a bureau chief for the *Miami Herald* when was 21, and later worked in television advertising. A veteran travel writer, he is the author of numerous bestselling Frommer Guides, notably to England, France, Germany, Italy, Spain, and the Caribbean. When not traveling (which is rare), he lives in New York City. He is assisted by **Danforth Prince,** formally of the Paris Bureau of the *New York Times.*

Macmillan Travel
A Simon & Schuster Macmillan Company
1633 Broadway
New York, NY 10019

ISBN 0-02-860053-3
ISSN 1053-2439

Design by Michele Laseau
Maps by Geografix Inc. and Ortelius Design

Special Sales

Bulk purchases (10+ copies) of Frommer's Travel Guides are available to corporations at special discounts. The Special Sales Department can produce custom editions to be used as premiums and/or for sales promotion to suit individual needs. Existing editions can be produced with custom cover imprints such as corporate logos. For more information write to: Special Sales, Simon & Schuster, 1633 Broadway, New York, NY 10019.

Manufactured in the United States of America

CONTENTS

21 Galicia 639

Appendix 664

Index 669

List of Maps

What the Symbols Mean

What Is a Frommer Guide? It's a comprehensive, easy-to-use guide to the best travel values in all price ranges—from very expensive to budget. The one guidebook to take along on any trip.

★ **Frommer's Favorites** Hotels, restaurants, attractions, and entertainments you should not miss.

$ **Super-Special Values** Really exceptional values.

Abbreviations in Hotel and Other Listings

The following symbols refer to the standard amenities available in all rooms:

A/C air conditioning
MINIBAR refrigerator stocked with beverages and snacks
TEL telephone
TV television

The following abbreviations are used for credit cards:

AE American Express
CB Carte Blanche
DC Diners Club
DISC Discover
ER enRoute
JCB (Japan)
MC MasterCard
V Visa

Trip Planning with This Guide

USE THE FOLLOWING FEATURES:

What Things Cost In To help you plan your daily budget

Calendar of Events To plan for or avoid

Suggested Itineraries For seeing the regions or cities

What's Special About Checklist A summary of each region's highlights—which lets you check off those that appeal most to you

Easy-to-Read Maps Walking tours, city sights, hotel and restaurant locations—all referring to or keyed to the text

Fast Facts All the essentials at a glance: currency, embassies, emergencies, safety, taxes, tipping, and more

OTHER SPECIAL FROMER FEATURES

Cool for Kids Hotels, restaurants, and attractions

Did you Know? Offbeat, fun facts

Famous People The country's greats

Impressions What others have said

Invitation to the Reader

In this guide to Spain, I have selected what I consider to be the best of the many fine establishments that I came across while conducting my research. You, too, in the course of your visit to Spain, may come across a hotel, restaurant, shop, or attraction that you feel should be included here; or you may find that a place I have selected has since changed for the worse. In either case, let me know of your discovery. Write to me also if you have any other comments on this edition or suggestions for future editions. Address your letter to:

Darwin Porter
Frommer's Spain, 16th Edition
c/o Macmillan Travel
15 Columbus Circle
New York, NY 10023

Disclaimers

I have made every effort to ensure the accuracy of the prices as well as of the other information contained in this guide. Yet I advise you to keep in mind that prices fluctuate over time and that some of the other information herein may also change as a result of the various volatile factors affecting the travel industry.

Neither the author nor the publisher can be held responsible for the experiences of the reader while traveling.

Safety Advisory

Whenever you are traveling in an unfamiliar city or country, stay alert. Be aware of your immediate surroundings. Wear a money belt and keep a close eye on your possessions. *Be especially careful with cameras, purses, and wallets*—all favorite targets of thieves and pickpockets. Although Spain is a lovely country with friendly and hospitable people, nevertheless you should bear in mind that every society has its criminals. It is therefore your responsibility to exercise caution at all times, in heavily touristed areas no less than in secluded areas (which you should avoid, particularly after dark).

1

Getting to Know Spain

THE ONCE-ACCEPTED ADAGE THAT "EUROPE ENDS AT THE PYRENEES" IS NO LONGER true. Today, the two countries forming the Iberian Peninsula at the southwestern end of the continent, Spain and Portugal, are totally integrated in Europe as members of the European Union, with democratic governments and vibrant economies of their own. In fact, Spain has the fastest-growing economy in the EU; new industries and an expanding infrastructure continue to alter its ancient landscape.

The political changes adopted after the death of Gen. Francisco Franco—Europe's last prewar dictator—in 1975 contributed to a remarkable cultural renaissance, known as *la movida.* This rebirth has transformed Spain's two largest cities—Madrid, the capital, and Barcelona—into major European centers of artistic and intellectual activity. Here, amid some of the world's most innovative architecture, contemporary movements in art, literature, the cinema, and fashion are constantly finding new and original expression; and at night the cafés and bars hum with animated discussions on politics, the economy, society. In every aspect of urban life, a visitor can feel the Spanish people's reawakened self-confidence and pride in their newfound prosperity.

The vitality and excitement of today's Spain have made it a popular place to visit. Indeed, this land of jeweled Moorish palaces, sun-drenched beaches, terraced vineyards, sleepy fishing villages, and the primeval rituals of the *corrida* (bullfight) and the flamenco has become the sophisticated "playground of Europe."

These developments contrast with Spain's unhappy experiences at other periods in this century, particularly during the devastating Civil War of 1936–39 and Franco's long rule that followed. During the Franco years, political and intellectual freedom was limited, and Spain was snubbed by most of Europe.

Earlier in its history, Spain had played a major role in the Mediterranean world. During its golden age (circa 16th century), it was the seat of a great empire. The Spanish monarchy dispatched fleets that conquered the New World, returning with its riches. Columbus sailed to America and Balboa to the Pacific Ocean; Cortés conquered Mexico for glory; and Pizarro brought Peru into the Spanish fold.

The conquistadors too often revealed the negative side of the Spanish character, including an adoption of brutality in the name of honor and glory. These adventurers, however, also embodied the positive side, the belief that the "impossible dream" was possible. No character in the history of this country's literature has better embodied this idealism than Don Quixote, whose tilting at windmills on the plains of La Mancha has served for centuries as a parable of the Spanish soul.

It's difficult to visit Spain without recalling its golden past, for there are many reminders: Those famous "castles in Spain" really do exist. Yet to many visitors, Spain isn't a single country but a series of nations, united the way Yugoslavia used to be. Many groups, especially the Basques, the Cataláns, and the Gallegos in the northeast, are asserting their uniqueness in everything from culture to language. Despite these independence movements, Castile and the south, Andalusia, remain quintessentially Spanish, at least to the foreign visitor.

For beneath regional differences there are certain common national traits, as noted by one observer: "The Spaniards are a fierce, idealistic, generous people, capable of great sacrifice and heroism when driven by their proud and burning passions; but they are also intolerant, dogmatic, and individualistic." Yet to visitors, especially those who are well behaved, they are invariably friendly and gracious hosts, with a fine, southern sense of style; indeed, they are among the most hospitable people in Europe.

Did You Know?

- Spain is the only country on which the United States dropped four hydrogen bombs—it was an accident and they didn't explode.
- The Duchess of Alba, not the Queen of England, is the world's most titled woman.
- In 1945 the body of an earlier Duchess of Alba was exhumed to "prove" that she had not posed for Goya's *Naked Maja* in 1797.
- Spanish artist Pablo Picasso was the world's most prolific painter: 13,500 paintings or sketches, 34,000 illustrations, and 100,000 etchings.
- A Spaniard, Josep Grugués, cooked the world's largest sausage, measuring three miles (5km) long.
- A recent survey revealed that 60% of the Spanish population have no interest in bullfighting.
- The palm was introduced into Europe by Muslim monarch Abderraman I, who planted seedlings on the palace grounds at Córdoba.
- In 1762 Charles III ordered that all nudes in the royal collection be burned. Court painter Anton Raphael Mengs didn't obey, thereby rescuing many masterpieces for posterity.
- Ernest Hemingway himself never ran in the *encierro* (running of the bulls) held during the festival in Pamplona.

They are also, in all their diversity, among the most vibrant and fascinating on earth. In the days of empire, they spread their language and culture throughout vast regions of the world, including most of Central and South America, where Spain still exercises a measure of cultural influence, and parts of Asia.

As the inheritors of a great and ancient civilization dating from before the Roman Empire, Spaniards live in a land as culturally rich as it is geographically varied, with wooded sierras, arid plateaus, and sandy beaches. It is this exciting variety in landscape, as well as in art, architecture, music, and cuisine, that makes Spain one of the top countries in the world to visit. In the number of foreign tourists who make a cultural pilgrimage to its soil, Spain ranks alongside France, Italy, and England.

1 Geography, History & Politics

Geography

Three times the size of Illinois, with a population of 38.5 million, Spain faces the Atlantic Ocean and the Bay of Biscay to the north and the Mediterranean Sea to the south and east. Portugal borders on the west, while the high Pyrenees separate Spain from France and the rest of Europe. The southern coastline is only a few sea miles from the north coast of Africa.

One finds it almost impossible to generalize about Spain because it is composed of so many regions—50 provinces in all—each with its own physical makeup, history, and culture. Although the country may look like a single geographical unit, the topography divides it into many different regions: The Cantabrian Mountains in the

Rias Altas
Ortigueira
Vivero
La Coruña
Ribadeo
Cabo Fisterra
Gijón
GALICIA
Rias Bajas
Noya
Lugo
Oviedo
ASTURIAS
Santiago de Compostela
La Toja
Pontevedra
Orense
CANTABRIA
Túy
León
Cantabrian Mts.
Burgos
ATLANTIC
OCEAN
Valladolid
Zamora
CASTILLA-LEÓN
Salamanca
Alba de Tormes
Ciudad Rodrigo
Ávila
Segovia
PORTUGAL
San Lorenzo de el Escorial
Madrid
COMUNIDAD DE MAD
Chinchón
EXTREMADURA
Cáceres
Trujillo
Toledo
Lisbon
Guadalupe
Badajoz
Mérida
Zafra
CASTILLA - LA MANCH
Sierra Morena
Córdoba
Jaén
Baeza
Isla Cristina
Seville
Carmona
GULF OF CADIZ
ANDALUSIA
Costa de la Luz
Jerez de la Frontera
Granada
Ronda
Málaga
Cádiz
Fuengirola
Nerja
Estepona
Tarifa
Gibraltar
Costa del Sol
STRAIT OF GIBRALTAR
Algeciras
Tangier
Ceuta

0
100 mi
160 km
N
BAY OF BISCAY
FRANCE
Ondárroa
San Sebastián
Bilbao
NAVARRA
Vitoria-Gasteiz
Pamplona
Logroño
Pyrenees
Sos del Rey Católico
Ribeira
Andorra
GULF OF LIONS
Tudela
Tarazona
ARAGÓN
Zaragoza
CATALUNYA
Figueres
Cadaqués
Girona
Calatayud
Lérida
Tossa de Mar
Montserrat
Lloret de Mar
Tarragona
Barcelona
Costa Brava
Sitges
Costa Dorada
COMUNIDAD VALENCIANA
Costa del Azahar
Teruel
Cuenca
Menorca
Balearic Islands
Mallorca
Valencia
Palma
Ibiza
Benidorm
Elche
Alicante
Murcia
Costa Blanca
Lorca
Cartagena
MEDITERRANEAN SEA
Costa Calida

north, those of Cuenca in the east, and the Sierra Morena in the south mark off a high central tableland that itself is cut across by other hills.

THE REGIONS IN BRIEF

The Central Plateau Madrid stands at the center of this plateau, ringed by such cities as Toledo, Segovia, and Salamanca. Stretching southwest to the Portuguese border is Extremadura, arid hilly country.

Andalusia and the Costa del Sol This is the Spanish south, including Córdoba, Seville, Málaga, and Granada. The heartland of traditional and Moorish Spain, this area is famous for its Sierra Nevada mountains and for its beaches.

The Levante This is the name given to the Mediterranean coastline of Murcia and Valencia, the latter region famous for its oranges.

The Northeast and the Balearic Islands Barcelona, the capital of Catalonia, is the gateway to the Costa Brava and to the Balearics (Majorca, Ibiza, and Minorca).

The North This region incorporates Navarre and Aragón; the inland cities of Valladolid, Burgos, and Zaragoza; the Basque country, famous for its cuisine and its summer capital, San Sebastián; and Cantabria, with its attractive beaches.

The Northwest Wrapping around the northern boundary of Portugal, this region includes Galicia, León, and Asturias. The prime attraction is Santiago de Compostela in Galicia.

Andorra This is a separate principality in the Pyrenees.

History & Politics

Dateline

- **13th–6th c. B.C.** Original Iberians enter Spain.
- **11th c. B.C.** Phoenicians settle Spain's coasts.
- **650 B.C.** Greeks colonize the east.
- **600 B.C.** Celts cross the Pyrenees and settle in Spain.
- **6th–3rd c. B.C.** Carthaginians make Cartagena their colonial capital, driving out the Greeks.
- **218–201 B.C.** Second Punic War: Rome defeats Carthage.
- **2nd c. B.C.–2nd c. A.D.** Rome controls most of Iberia. Christianity spreads.

➤

ANCIENT TIMES

Ancestors of the Basques may have been the first settlers in Spain 10,000 to 30,000 years ago, followed, it is believed, by Iberians from North Africa. They, in turn, were followed by Celts, who crossed the Pyrenees around 600 B.C. After many intertribal battles, these groups were melded into a Celtic-Iberian people who inhabited central Spain.

Others coming to the Iberian Peninsula in prehistoric times were the Phoenicians, who took over coastal areas on the Atlantic beginning in the 11th century B.C. Cádiz, originally the ancient Phoenician settlement of Gades, is perhaps the oldest town in Spain. Cartagena was settled by people from the Phoenician city of Carthage. Perhaps half a millennium after the Phoenicians, the Greeks came, lured by the gold and silver found in the peninsula. The Greeks set up colonies before they were conquered by the Carthaginians from North Africa.

Around 200 B.C. the Romans vanquished the Carthaginians and laid the foundations of the present Latin culture. Traces of Roman civilization can still be seen today. By the time of Julius Caesar, Spain

(Hispania) was under Roman law and began a long period of peace and prosperity.

BARBARIAN INVASIONS, THE MOORISH KINGDOM & THE RECONQUEST

When Rome fell in the 5th century, Spain was overrun first by the Vandals and then by the Visigoths from Eastern Europe. The chaotic rule of the Visigothic kings lasted about 300 years, but the barbarian invaders did adopt the language of their new country and tolerated Christianity as well.

Early in the 8th century, Spain attracted the attention of the Moors, who were advancing along the north coast of Africa. In A.D. 711, Moorish warriors led by Tarik crossed over into Spain and conquered the disunited country. By 714 they controlled most of it, except for a few mountain regions such as Asturias. For eight centuries, until 1492, the Moors occupied the land and imprinted their culture on the Spanish people.

The Moors called their new land "al-Andalus," or Andalusia, with Córdoba as the capital. A great intellectual center, Córdoba became the scientific capital of Europe; notable advances were made in agriculture, industry, literature, philosophy, and medicine. The Jews were welcomed by the Moors, often serving as administrators, ambassadors, and financial officers. But the Moors quarreled with one another, and soon the few Christian strongholds in the north advanced south to eventually overpower them.

The Reconquest, the name given to the Christian efforts to rid the peninsula of the Moors, lasted more than 700 years. Intermittent battles between Christians and Moors slowly reduced the size of the Muslim holdings, with Catholic monarchies forming small kingdoms in the northern areas. By the middle of the 13th century, the kingdom of Granada was the only Muslim possession left on the Iberian Peninsula. By the time of Alfonso I of Aragón (1104–34), the final push began to rid the land of Islam. The three powerful kingdoms of Aragón, Castile, and León were joined in 1469, when Ferdinand of Aragón married Isabella of Castile. Catholic Kings, as they were called, launched the final attack on the Moors and completed the Reconquest in 1492 by capturing Granada.

That same year Columbus, the Genoese sailor, landed on the West Indies, laying the foundations of the far-flung empire that brought wealth and power to Spain during the 16th and 17th centuries.

Dateline

- **5th c.** Vandals, then Visigoths, invade Spain.
- **8th c.** Moors conquer most of Spain.
- **10th c.** Córdoba becomes a center of learning under the Moors.
- **1214** More than half of Iberia is regained by Catholics.
- **1469** Ferdinand of Aragón marries Isabella of Castile.
- **1492** Catholic monarchs conquer the last Moorish stronghold, Granada. Columbus lands in the New World.
- **1519** Cortés seizes Mexico. Charles I is crowned Holy Roman Emperor, as Charles V.
- **1556** Philip II inherits throne and launches the Counter-Reformation.
- **1588** England defeats Spanish Armada.
- **1700** Philip V becomes king. War of Spanish Succession follows.
- **1713** Treaty of Utrecht ends war. Spain's colonies reduced.
- **1769** Charles III ascends throne.
- **1808** Napoleon places brother Joseph on the Spanish throne.
- **1813** Wellington drives French out of Spain; the monarchy is restored.
- **1876** Spain becomes a constitutional monarchy.
- **1898** Spanish-American War, with loss of Puerto Rico, Cuba, and Philippines.
- **1923** Primo de Rivera forms military directorate.

➤

Dateline

- **1930** Right-wing dictatorship ends; Primo de Rivera exiled.
- **1931** King Alfonso XIII abdicates; Second Republic is born.
- **1933–35** Falange Party formed.
- **1936–39** Civil War between the governing Popular Front and the nationalists led by Franco.
- **1939** Franco establishes dictatorship, which will last 36 years.
- **1941** Spain technically stays neutral in World War II, but Franco favors Germany.
- **1955** Spain joins the United Nations.
- **1969** Franco names Juan Carlos as his successor.
- **1975** Juan Carlos becomes king.
- **1978** New, democratic constitution initiates reforms.
- **1981** Coup attempt by right-wing officers fails.
- **1982** Socialists sweep to power after 43 years of right-wing rule.
- **1986** Spain joins the European Community (now Union).
- **1992** Barcelona hosts the Summer Olympics, Seville hosts Expo '92.

Under Ferdinand and Isabella, the Spanish Inquisition was created to eradicate all heresy and firmly secure the primacy of Catholicism. Non-Catholics, Jews, and Moors, who had lived in Spain for centuries, were mercilessly persecuted.

In 1492, when given the choice of converting to Christianity or leaving the country, most Jews left, but the majority of Moors remained, converting to Catholicism and becoming known as the Moriscos. (They were nonetheless driven out of Spain in 1609–11, under inexorable pressure from the Inquisition.)

THE GOLDEN AGE & LATER DECLINE

Columbus's voyage to America and the subsequent exploration of that land by the conquistadors launched Spain into its golden age.

In the first half of the 16th century, Balboa discovered the Pacific Ocean, Cortés seized Mexico for Spain, Pizarro took Peru, and a Spanish ship (which had started out under the command of the Portuguese Magellan, who was killed during the voyage) circumnavigated the globe. The conquistadors took Catholicism to the New World and shipped masses of gold back to Spain. The Spanish Empire extended all the way to the Philippines. Spanish ships ruled the seas, and Spanish armies were feared all over Europe.

Charles V, the grandson of Ferdinand and Isabella, was the most powerful prince in Europe—king of Spain and Naples, Holy Roman Emperor and lord of Germany, Duke of Burgundy and the Netherlands, and ruler of the New World territories. But much of Spain's wealth and human resources were wasted in religious and secular conflicts. Spain itself was neglected.

First Jews, then Muslims, and finally Moriscos were driven out—and with them much of the country's prosperity. When Philip II came to the throne in 1556, Spain could indeed boast vast possessions—the New World colonies; Naples, Milan, Genoa, Sicily, and other portions of Italy; the Spanish Netherlands (modern Belgium and the Netherlands); and portions of Austria and Germany—but the seeds of decline had already been planted.

Philip, a fanatic Catholic, devoted his energies to subduing the Protestant revolt in the Netherlands and to becoming the standard bearer for the Counter-Reformation. He tried to return England to Catholicism, first by marrying Mary I ("Bloody Mary") and later by wooing her half sister, Elizabeth I, who rebuffed him. When, in 1588, he resorted to sending the Armada, it was ignominiously defeated; the defeat signaled the decline of Spanish power, which continued through the 17th century.

In 1700 a Bourbon prince, Philip V, became king, and the country fell under the influence of France. Philip V's right to the throne was challenged by a Hapsburg archduke of Austria, thus giving rise to the War of the Spanish Succession. When it ended, Spain had lost Flanders, its Italian possessions, and Gibraltar (still held by the British today).

During the 18th century, Spain's direction changed with each sovereign. Charles III (1759–88) developed the country economically and culturally. Charles IV became embroiled in wars with France, and the weakness of the Spanish monarchy allowed Napoleon to place his brother Joseph Bonaparte on the throne in 1808. Even after Napoleon's defeat, when Spain's rightful kings were restored to the throne, the country continued to decline.

THE 19TH & 20TH CENTURIES

Although Britain and France had joined forces to restore the Spanish monarchy, the European conflicts encouraged the Spanish colonists overseas to rebel. Ultimately, this led the United States to free the Philippines, Puerto Rico, and Cuba from Spain in 1898.

In Spain republican ideas agitated the country throughout the 19th century, and in 1876 it became a constitutional monarchy. But labor unrest, disputes with the Catholic Church, and war in Morocco combined to create political chaos. Conditions eventually became so bad that the Cortés, or Parliament, was dissolved in 1923, and Gen. Miguel Primo de Rivera formed a military directorate. Early in 1930 Primo de Rivera resigned, but unrest continued.

On April 14, 1931, a revolution occurred, a republic was proclaimed, and King Alfonso XIII and his family were forced to flee. Initially the liberal constitutionalists ruled, but soon they were pushed aside by the socialists and anarchists, who adopted a constitution separating church and state, secularizing education, and containing several other radical provisions (for example, agrarian reform and the expulsion of the Jesuits).

The extreme nature of these reforms fostered the growth of the conservative Falangist party (*Falange española*, Spanish Phalanx), modeled after Italy's and Germany's fascist parties. By the 1936 elections, the country was divided equally between left and right, and political violence was common. On July 18, 1936, the army, supported by Mussolini and Hitler, tried to seize power, igniting the Civil War. Gen. Francisco Franco, coming from Morocco to Spain, led the Nationalist (rightist) forces in the two years of fighting that ravaged the country. Towns were bombed and many atrocities were committed. Early in 1939, Franco entered Barcelona and went on to Madrid; thousands of republicans were executed. Franco became chief of state, remaining so until his death in 1975.

Although Franco adopted a neutral position during World War II, his sympathies obviously lay with Germany and Italy. Both countries had helped him attain power, so Spain gave aid to the Axis as a nonbelligerent. This action intensified the diplomatic isolation into which the country was forced after the war's end—in fact, it was excluded from the United Nations until 1955.

Before his death, General Franco selected as his successor Juan Carlos de Borbón y Borbón, son of the pretender to the Spanish throne. After the 1977 elections, a new constitution was approved by the electorate and the king; it guaranteed human and civil rights, as well as free enterprise, and canceled the status of the Roman Catholic Church as the church of Spain. It also granted limited autonomy to several regions, including Catalonia and the Basque Provinces, both of which, however, are still clamoring for complete autonomy.

In 1981 a group of right-wing military officers seized the Cortés and called upon Juan Carlos to establish a Francoist state. The king, however, refused, and the conspirators were arrested. The fledgling democracy overcame its first test. Its second major accomplishment—under the Socialist administration of Prime Minister Felipe González, the country's first leftist government since 1939—was to gain Spain's entry into the European Community (now Union) in 1986.

Further proof that the new Spain was now fully accepted by the international community came in 1992. In that *annus mirabilis,* as many Spaniards regarded it, Spain was designated by the EU as the Cultural Capital of Europe for the year; but more significant, the Summer Olympics were held successfully in Barcelona and a world's fair, Expo '92, was mounted in Seville, in Andalusia.

2 Famous Spaniards

Rodrigo Díaz de Vivar (El Cid) (ca. 1043–99) Known in Spain as Campeador, or "winner of battles," El Cid was immortalized in a 12th-century epic poem bearing his name. After winning battles against the Moors, he was exiled in 1081 and became chief political adviser to the Arabs. Later, reconciling with Castile, he overthrew the Moorish kingdom at Valencia in 1089. Upon his death he left control of Valencia to his wife, who could not hold it.

Manuel de Falla (1876–1946) Famous composer of the opera *La Vida Breve* and the ballet *El Amor Brujo.* In 1907 he moved to Paris, where he was influenced by Claude Debussy and Maurice Ravel. Falla retired to Granada in 1922, writing mostly Spanish folk music and flamenco until 1939, when he moved to Argentina. He died before completing the dramatic cantata *L'Atlantida.*

Antoni Gaudí I Cornet (1852–1926) The most famous name in Catalán architecture, Gaudí studied in Barcelona, developing his talents in the art nouveau style, which is known as modernism in Spain. He designed apartment houses and office buildings along the Passeig de Gràcia between 1905 and 1907. A deeply religious man, he is best remembered for his uncompleted cathedral, Sagrada Familia.

El Greco (1541–1614) Born in Crete and named Doménikos Theotokópoulos, he trained in Italy under Titian. He became one of Spain's greatest artists, painting his masterpiece, *The Burial of Count Orgaz,* in Toledo in 1577.

Isabella La Católica (1451–1504) Better known as Isabella I, this powerful monarch ruled Castile and León. Her greatest accomplishment was financing Columbus's expedition to the New World; she even sold her own jewels to do this. She also launched the Spanish Inquisition against Muslims, Jews, and Protestants, thus tainting her historical reputation and making her one of the most notorious bigots in history.

Moses ben Maimon (Maimonides) (1135–1204) Born to a wealthy Jewish family, Maimonides fled to Morocco when the Almohades invaded Córdoba in 1148. Settling in Egypt, he became the leader of Egyptian Jewry and later court physician to Saladin. He wrote in Hebrew a summary of Jewish oral law entitled *Mishneh Torah* and was also famed for his knowledge of medicine, theology, and philosophy. He wrote *Guide to the Perplexed,* which influenced both Jewish and Christian scholars.

Francisco Pizarro (ca. 1476–1541) A conquistador from Extremadura, he conquered Peru in 1533, using cunning and treachery.

Fray Gabriel Téllez (Tirso de Molina) (1584–1648) Often compared to Shakespeare, he ranked with Lope de Vega and Calderón de la Barca as a dramatist, writing more than 300 plays (the most famous being *El Burlador de Sevilla* and *El Condenado por Desconfiado*).

St. Teresa of Avila (1515–82) A mystic who founded a convent that observed the original rules of the Carmelite Order. After her death in Avila, it is said, a violet and fragrant oil emanated from her tomb. The tomb was opened and one of the brothers cut off her hands, alleging they could work miracles. Relic seekers continued to desecrate her corpse over the years. Pope Gregory XV beatified her in 1622.

Tomás de Torquemada (1420–98) Inquisitor-general to Ferdinand and Isabella. As their confessor, he pushed for the expulsion of the Jews and Moriscos from Spain. At least 2,000 people were executed at his behest. According to legend, Torquemada never ate unless the tongue of a scorpion was placed beside his plate.

Miguel de Unamuno (1864–1936) Of Basque heritage, Spain's greatest scholar became a professor of Greek at the University of Salamanca but was fired for political reasons in 1914. Regaining his position, he was made "rector for life" in 1931 but was fired again in 1936 and died under "house confinement." *Paz en la Guerra,* published in 1897, was considered the first real existential novel. His masterpiece, *The Tragic Sense of Life,* was written in 1913.

3 Some Cultural Background

ART Spain's contributions to art range from the ancient carvings and cave paintings of Altamira (which, sadly, are no longer open to the public) to the works of some of the world's foremost artists.

After El Greco (1541–1614), not Spanish-born but a 40-year resident of the country, the great name of the golden age was Diego Velázquez (1599–1660), court painter to Philip IV and a portraitist of rare skills. Other top artists of the seventeenth century included Ribera, Zurbarán, and Murillo.

During the reigns of Charles III and Charles IV, neoclassical art flourished in Madrid, with Francisco de Goya (1746–1828) at the top of the list. You can view his frescoes depicting Madrid at the Pantéon de Goya (Goya's Tomb) in Madrid.

Among 19th-century painters, Joaquín Sorolla (1883–1923) doesn't enjoy the international reputation he deserves, but his work is displayed in his own museum in Madrid.

Madrid can't claim the Spanish genius of 20th-century art: Pablo Picasso was born in Málaga. But he left Madrid his most famous and controversial work, *Guernica,* which depicts the horrors of the Spanish Civil War. Spain was also the birthplace of Gris, Miró, and Dalí.

To name even the most outstanding Spanish artists and their works would demand more space than allotted, but I urge readers to visit the Prado and the Thyssen-Bornemisza Museum in Madrid, as well as other places in Spain where famous artworks can be seen.

ARCHITECTURE Spanish architecture might well have mirrored that of other European countries had it not been for the Muslims' long dominance of most of the Iberian Peninsula. Because they lived for the present rather than planning and building for the future, their architecture tended to be lavishly decorated on the surface but with a flimsy substructure. Therefore, not many complete examples are left of the monumental Saracenic structures of those centuries. But enough exist, including great mosques, minarets, and palaces, to show the lasting influence of various types of arches, colonnades, reflecting pools, and filigree ornamentation.

The Alhambra at Granada and the Alcázar at Seville are the most outstanding examples of Moorish architecture extant in Spain. Both these complexes evolved during various caliphates and periods of Muslim architecture and Mudejar art. The latter name refers to works fashioned in the Spanish Muslim tradition after the Reconquest, by either Moors or converted Muslims (or their trainees). A Mudejar style is still followed in Spain, especially in the villages, although it only dimly recalls the grandeur of Muslim art of old.

For truly original design, visitors should see the work of the controversial Catalonia-born Antoni Gaudí, especially in Santander and Barcelona.

LITERATURE The epic poetry of the late Moorish period and the popular poems composed by wandering minstrels were followed by romantic ballads and Italian-influenced poetry. The 15th century saw the greater dominance of prose biography, novels, and treatises, these forms continuing into the next century's so-called golden age, which was marked principally by religious and humanist writings, picaresque novels (the protagonist being a *picaro,* or rogue), pastoral novels, histories, books of chivalry, and plays. The most familiar figure to Americans from this era is probably the "Man of La Mancha," Don Quixote, created by Cervantes.

During the Civil War many writers heroically defended the Second Republic—the most famous being Federico García Lorca, Rafael Alberti, Jorge Guillen, and Luís Cernuda.

Five Spaniards have won the Nobel Prize for Literature since it was originated in 1901: the playwrights José Echegaray (1904) and Jacinto Benavente (1922); the poets Juan Ramón Jiménez (1956) and Vicente-Aleixandre (1977); and the novelist José Cela (1989).

MUSIC To North Americans, the best-known Spanish musicians are composer Manuel de Falla, pianist José Iturbi, classical guitarist Andrés Segovia, cellist Pablo Casals, and operatic tenor Plácido Domingo.

The first written music of Spain sprang from the early Christian era, when the liturgy evolved into the Visigothic chant (or Moorish chant). Before the Arab invasion, music was flourishing in Toledo, Zaragoza, and Seville, and it continued as Christian Spain developed hymns and liturgical chants in the monasteries.

The conquerors from Africa brought with them many interesting instruments, including the square tambourine (*adufe* in Spanish), standard tambourine (*panderete*), drum (*atabal*), psaltery (*canón*), and metal castanets (*sonajas de azófar*). During the Renaissance, instrumental music became an important art form. This was specially true of pieces written for an early six-string guitar called the *vihuela,* replaced by the five-string guitar in the 17th century.

Opera, emerging in the 17th century, was strongly influenced by the Italians. But the *zarzuela,* an 18th-century light musical entertainment similar to the Gilbert and Sullivan operettas (later a sort of variety show), was truly Spanish.

DANCE From the lowliest *taberna* to the poshest nightclub, you are likely to hear heel clicking, foot stamping, castanet rattling, hand clapping, and the sound of sultry guitar music. This is flamenco. Its origins lie deep in Asia, but the Spanish gypsy has given it an original and unique style. It is a dance dramatizing inner conflict and pain. Performed by a great artist, flamenco can tear your heart out.

Flamenco has no story line. The leader sets the pace, drawing each of the performers forward. He or she lurks behind and around the group at all times, trying to infuse them with rhythm. It can be contagious, so don't be surprised if you end up with the castanets yourself.

Other regional dances include the *sardana* of Catalonia; the *muineira* of Galicia; and the fiery, colorful dances of León, Castile, and Valencia. The *jota* of Aragón is also renowned. When this dance is presented in a more sensuous Arabic fashion, it is transformed into the *fandango*. The *seguidilla* has much in common with the jota and fandango. Described by Cervantes as the "quicksilver of all senses," the seguidilla gave birth to the *bolero*, popular in the taverns of the 18th and 19th centuries.

Today, the most popular dance (especially in Madrid) is the *sevillana*. In the classic tradition, one or two flamenco guitars accompany the steps, but now anything goes, even a mariachi-like brass band or conga drums. Of course, all these dances end with "*Olé!*"

FIESTAS Every month and every town has a fiesta. Almost all are religiously inspired but combine the religious aspect with such popular entertainments as bullfights, parades, and exhibits.

Fiestas vary. A *romería*, which you may see along the road, is a pilgrimage (often overnight) to a particular historic site; a *verbena*, held in a city or town, is a nighttime festivity, with special emphasis on folk dancing; a *feria* (literally, fair) is a riot of song and dance—and an event dear to the Spanish soul, the most popular being the Feria of Seville.

To find out about fiesta times and locations, get a copy of the *Tourist Calendar*—listing more than 3,000 events—available at tourist offices. For this guide's highlights of the year, see "Spain Calendar of Events" in Chapter 2.

BULLFIGHTS—THE SPECTACLE OF DEATH Many consider bullfighting cruel and shocking. But as Ernest Hemingway pointed out in *Death in the Afternoon*: "The bullfight is not a sport in the Anglo-Saxon sense of the word, that is, it is not an equal contest or an attempt at an equal contest between a bull and a man. Rather it is a tragedy: the death of the bull, which is played, more or less well, by the bull and the man involved and in which there is danger for the man but certain death for the bull." Hemingway, of course, was an aficionado.

When the symbolic drama of the bullfight is acted out, some think it reaches a higher plane. Some people argue that it is not a public exhibition of cruelty at all, but rather a highly skilled art requiring the great human qualities of survival, courage, showmanship, and gallantry.

IMPRESSIONS

I thought that I should never return to the country I love more than any other, except for my own.
—Ernest Hemingway

Three Spaniards, four opinions.
—Old Spanish Proverb

Regardless of how you view it, this spectacle is an authentically Spanish experience and as such has much to reveal about the character of the land and its people.

Season and Tickets The season of the *corridas* (bullfights) lasts from early spring until mid-October or earlier. Fights are held in a *plaza de toros* (bullring), ranging in location from the oldest ring in remote Ronda to the big-time Plaza de Toros in Madrid. Sunday is corrida day in most major Spanish cities, although Madrid and Barcelona may also have fights on Thursday.

Tickets fall into three classifications: *sol* (sun), the cheapest; *sombra* (shade), the most expensive; and *sol y sombra* (a mixture of sun and shade), the medium-price range.

The Fight Itself The corrida begins with a parade. For many viewers, this may be the high point of the afternoon's festivities, as all the bullfighters are clad in their *trajes de luce,* or "suits of light."

Bullfights are divided into *tercios* (thirds). The first is the *tercio de capa* (cape), during which the matador tests the bull with various passes and gets acquainted with him. The second portion, the *tercio de varas* (sticks), begins with the lance-carrying *picadores* on horseback, who weaken, or "punish," the bull by jabbing him in the shoulder area. The horses are sometimes gored, even though they wear protective padding, or the horse and rider may be tossed into the air by the now infuriated bull. The picadores are followed by the *banderilleros,* whose job it is to puncture the bull with pairs of boldly colored darts.

In the final *tercio de muleta* the action narrows down to the lone fighter and the bull. Gone are the fancy capes. Instead, the matador uses a small red cloth known as a *muleta,* which, to be effective, requires a bull with lowered head. (The picadores and banderilleros have worked to achieve this.) Using the muleta as a lure, the matador wraps the bull around himself in various passes, the most dangerous of which is the *natural;* here, the matador holds the muleta in his left hand, the sword in his right. Right-hand passes pose less of a threat, since the sword can be used to spread out the muleta, making a larger target for the bull. After a number of passes, the time comes for the kill, the "moment of truth." A truly skilled fighter may dispatch the bull in one thrust.

After the bull dies, the highest official at the ring may award the matador an ear from the dead bull, or perhaps both ears, or ears and tail. For a really extraordinary performance, the hoof is sometimes added. The bullfighter may be carried away as a hero, or if he has displeased the crowd, he may be chased out of the ring by an angry mob. At a major fight usually six bulls are killed by three matadors in one afternoon.

4 Food & Drink

The food in Spain is varied; the portions are immense, but the prices, by North American standards, are high. Whenever possible, try the regional specialties, particularly when you visit the Basque country or Galicia. Many of these regional dishes, including Andalusian gazpacho and Valencian paella, have transcended their regions and have become great dishes of the world.

Food

MEALS

Breakfast In Spain the day starts with a continental breakfast of coffee, hot chocolate, or tea, with assorted rolls, butter, and jam. A typical Spanish breakfast consists of *churros* (fried fingerlike doughnuts) and a hot chocolate that is very sweet and thick. The coffee is usually strong and black, served with hot milk. Some Americans consider it too strong and bitter for their tastes and therefore ask for instant coffee.

Lunch An important meal in Spain, lunch is comparable to the farm-style noonday "dinner" in America. It usually includes three or four courses, beginning with a choice of soup or several dishes of hors d'oeuvres called *entremeses.* Often a fish or an egg dish is served after this, then a meat course with vegetables. Wine is always on the table. Dessert is usually pastry, custard, or assorted fruit; this is followed by coffee. Lunch is served from 1 to 3:30pm, with "rush hour" at 2pm.

Tapas After the early-evening promenade, many Spaniards head for their favorite *tascas,* or bars, where they drink wine and sample assorted *tapas,* or snacks, such as bits of fish, eggs in mayonnaise, or olives.

Dinner Another extravaganza. A typical meal starts with a bowl of soup, followed by a second course, often a fish dish, and by another main course, usually veal, beef, or pork, accompanied by vegetables. Again, desserts tend to be fruit, custard, or pastries.

Wine is always available. Afterward, you might have a demitasse and a fragrant Spanish brandy. The chic dining hour, even in one-donkey towns, is 10 or 10:30pm. (In well-touristed regions and hardworking Catalonia, you can usually dine by 8pm.) In most middle-class establishments, people dine no later than 9:30pm. The choice is up to you.

Dining Customs Most restaurants in Spain close on Sunday, so be sure to check ahead. Hotel dining rooms are generally open seven days, and there's always a food dispenser open in such big cities as Madrid and Barcelona or such well-touristed areas as the Costa del Sol.

Generally, reservations are not necessary, except at popular, top-notch restaurants.

Some Health/Diet Tips North Americans who plunge wholeheartedly into the Spanish routine may experience digestive trouble, particularly if they also drink more wine than usual. By the third day they will invariably be in the grip of "Toledo belly." To stop this malady, purchase Tanagel, sold in all pharmacies.

Two heavy Spanish meals a day are definitely not recommended. For lighter fare, patronize the cafeterias that are not self-service.

As a final caution, if you do eat a large lunch, don't rush out into the noonday sun for a round of sightseeing. Do as the Spaniard does: Take a siesta. Or you can take your large meal at lunch and have a light snack at a tapas bar in the evening.

THE CUISINE

Soups and Appetizers Soups are usually served in big bowls. Cream soups, such as asparagus and potato, can be fine; sadly, however, they are too often made from

IMPRESSIONS

Now you have two homes.
—Traditional Spanish Farewell

Idiocy proliferates in Spain, from politics to culture.
—Nobel Prize-Winner Cela

powdered envelope soups such as Knorr and Liebig. Served year round, chilled gazpacho, on the other hand, is tasty and particularly refreshing during the hot months. The combination is pleasant: olive oil, garlic, ground cucumbers, and raw tomatoes with a sprinkling of croûtons. Spain also offers several varieties of fish soup—*sopa de pescado*—in all its provinces, and many of these are superb.

In the *paradores* (government-run hostelries) and top restaurants, as many as 15 tempting hors d'oeuvres are served. In lesser-known places, avoid these entremeses, which often consist of last year's sardines and shards of sausage left over from the Moorish Conquest.

Eggs These are served in countless ways. A Spanish omelet, a *tortilla española,* is made with potatoes. A simple omelet is called a *tortilla francesa.* A *tortilla portuguésa* is similar to the American Spanish omelet.

Fish Spain's fish dishes tend to be outstanding and vary from province to province. One of the most common varieties is sweet white hake (*merluza*). *Langosta,* a variety of lobster, is seen everywhere—it's a treat but terribly expensive. The Portuguese in particular, but some Spaniards, too, go into raptures at the mention of barnacles. Gourmets relish their seawater taste; others find them tasteless. *Rape* is the Spanish name for monkfish, a sweet, wide-boned ocean fish with a scalloplike texture. Also try a few dozen half-inch baby eels. They rely heavily on olive oil and garlic for their flavor, but they're great tasting. Squid cooked in its own ink is suggested only to those who want to go native. Charcoal-broiled sardines, however, are a culinary delight—a particular treat in the Basque Provinces. Trout Navarre is one of the most popular fish dishes, usually stuffed with bacon or ham.

Paella You can't go to Spain without trying its celebrated paella. Flavored with saffron, paella is an aromatic rice dish usually topped with shellfish, chicken, sausage, peppers, and local spices. Served authentically, it comes steaming hot from the kitchen in a metal pan called a *paellera.* (Incidentally, what is known in America as Spanish rice isn't Spanish at all. If you ask an English-speaking waiter for Spanish rice, he'll serve you paella.)

Meats Don't expect Kansas City steak, but do try the spit-roasted suckling pig, so sweet and tender it can often be cut with a fork. The veal is also good, and the Spanish *lomo de cerdo,* loin of pork, is unmatched anywhere. As for chicken, it will sometimes qualify for the Olympics because it is stringy and muscular. Spit-roasted chicken, however, often can be flavorful.

Vegetables and Salads Except in summer, Spanish-grown vegetables are not the best, except in top restaurants. In some places fresh green vegetables are hard to come by, and the diner is often served canned string beans, peas, or artichokes. Potatoes are also a staple. Salads are usually fresh, made with crisp lettuce and vine-ripened tomatoes in summer.

Desserts The Spanish do not emphasize dessert. Flan, a home-cooked egg custard, appears on all menus—sometimes with a burnt-caramel sauce. Ice cream appears on nearly all menus as well. But the best bet is to ask for a basket of fresh fruit, which you can wash at your table. Homemade pastries are usually moist and not too sweet. As a dining oddity, many restaurants serve fresh orange juice for dessert. Madrileños love it!

Olive Oil and Garlic Olive oil is used lavishly in Spain. You may not want it in all dishes. If, for example, you prefer your fish grilled in butter, the word is *mantequilla.* In some instances, you'll be charged extra for the butter. Garlic is also an integral part of the Spanish diet, and even if you love it, you may find the Spaniard loves it more than you do and uses it in the oddest dishes.

Drink

Water It is generally safe to drink in all major cities and tourist resorts in Spain. If you're traveling in remote areas, play it safe and drink bottled water. One of the most popular noncarbonated bottled drinks in Spain is Solares. Nearly all restaurants and hotels have it. If you'd like your water with a little kick, then ask for *agua mineral con gas.* Note that bottled water often costs more than the regional wine.

Soft Drinks In general, avoid the carbonated citrus drinks on sale everywhere. Most of them never saw an orange, much less a lemon. If you want a citrus drink, order old, reliable Schweppes. An excellent noncarbonated drink for the summer is called Tri-Naranjus, which comes in lemon and orange flavors. Your cheapest bet is a liter bottle of *gaseosa,* which comes in various flavors. In summer you should also try a drink that I've never had outside Spain, *horchara*—a nutty, sweet milklike beverage made of tubers called *chufas.*

Coffee Even if you are a dedicated coffee drinker, you may find the *café con leche* (coffee with milk) a little too strong. I suggest *leche manchada,* a little bit of strong, freshly brewed coffee in a glass that's filled with lots of frothy hot milk.

Milk In the largest cities you get bottled milk, but it loses a great deal of its flavor in the process of pasteurization. In all cases, avoid untreated milk and milk products. About the best brand of fresh milk is Lauki.

Beer Although not native to Spain, beer (*cerveza*) is now drunk everywhere. Domestic brands include San Miguel, Mahou, Aguila, and Cruz Blanka.

Wine Sherry (*vino de Jerez*) has been called "the wine with a hundred souls." Drink it before dinner (try the topaz-colored *finos,* a very pale sherry) or whenever you drop in to some old inn or bodega for refreshment; many of them have rows of kegs with spigots. Manzanilla, a golden-colored medium-dry sherry, is extremely popular. The sweet cream sherries (Harvey's Bristol Cream, for example) are favorite after-dinner wines (called *olorosos*). While the French may be disdainful of Spanish table wines, they can be truly noble, especially two leading varieties, Valdepeñas and Rioja, both from Castile. If you're fairly adventurous and not too demanding in your tastes, you can always ask for the *vino de la casa* (wine of the house) wherever you dine. The Ampurdan of Catalonia is heavy. From Andalusia comes the fruity Montilla. There are also some good local champagnes (*cavas*) in Spain, such as Freixenet. One brand, Benjamin, also comes in individual-size bottles.

Sangría The all-time favorite refreshing drink in Spain, sangría is red-wine punch that combines wine with oranges, lemons, seltzer, and sugar.

Whisky and Brandy Imported whiskies are available at most Spanish bars but at a high price. If you're a drinker, switch to brandies and cognacs, where the Spanish reign supreme. Try Fundador, made by the Pedro Domecq family in Jerez de la Frontera. If you're seeking a smooth cognac, ask for "103" white label.

5 Recommended Books, Films & Recordings

Books

ECONOMIC, POLITICAL & SOCIAL HISTORY Historically, Spain's golden age lasted from the late 15th to the early 17th century, a period when the country reached the height of its prestige and influence. This era is well surveyed in J. H. Elliot's *Imperial Spain 1469–1716* (New American Library, 1977).

Most accounts of the Spanish Armada's defeat are written from the English point of view. For a change of perspective, try David Howarth's *The Voyage of the Armada* (Penguin, 1981).

The story of the Spanish Inquisition is told by Edward Peters in *Inquisition* (University of California Press, 1990).

One of the best accounts of Spain's earlier history is found in Joseph F. O'Callaghan's *History of Medieval Spain* (Cornell University, 1983).

In the 20th century the focus shifts to the Spanish Civil War, recounted in Hugh Thomas's classic, *The Spanish Civil War* (Harper & Row, 1977). For a personal account of the war, read George Orwell's *Homage to Catalonia* (Harcourt Brace Jovanovich, 1969). The poet García Lorca was killed during the Civil War; the best account of his death is found in Ian Gibson's *The Assassination of Federico García Lorca* (Penguin, 1983).

If you like more contemporary history, read John Hooper's *The Spaniards* (Penguin, 1987). Hooper provides insight into the events of the post-Franco era, when the country came to grips with democracy after years of fascism.

ART & ARCHITECTURE The Moors contributed much to Spanish culture. Their distinct legacy is documented in Titus Burckhardt's *Moorish Culture in Spain* (McGraw-Hill, 1972).

Antoni Gaudí is the Spanish architect who most excites visitors' curiosity. Among the many illustrated books on his work, *Gaudí* (Escudo de Oro's "Collection of Art in Spain," 1990) contains 150 photographs. It is sold at most newsstands along Las Ramblas (Catalan: Les Rambles) in Barcelona.

Spain's most famous artist was Pablo Picasso. The most controversial recent book about the late painter is *Picasso, Creator and Destroyer* by Arianna Stassinopoulos Huffington (Simon & Schuster, 1988).

Spain's other headline-grabbing artist was Salvador Dalí. In *Salvador Dalí: A Biography* (Dutton, 1986), author Meryle Secrest asks: Was he a mad genius or a cunning manipulator?

Andrés Segovia: An Autobiography of the Years 1893–1920 (Macmillan, 1976), with a translation by W. F. O'Brien, is worth seeking out.

Residents of Catalonia truthfully maintain that their unique language, culture, and history have been overshadowed (and squelched) by the richer and better-publicized accomplishments of Castile. Robert Hughes, a former art critic at *Time* magazine, has written an elegant testament to the glories of the capital of this region: *Barcelona* (Knopf, 1992); this book offers a well-versed and often witty articulation of the city's architectural and cultural legacy. According to the *New York Times,* the book is probably destined to become "a classic in the genre of urban history."

Juan de Herrera: Architect to Philip II of Spain, by Catherine Williamson Zerner (Yale University Press, 1994), describes (for the first time in English) the remarkable three-decade partnership between Herrera (1530–97) and his royal patron. Richly illustrated.

Catalán Painting: From the 19th to the Surprising 20th Century, by Joan Ainaud de Lasarte (Rizzoli, 1992), has a title that tells its theme accurately. A lavish volume written by the former director of the Art Museums of Barcelona, it contains more than 100 color plates, from Joan Miró's, *The Farm* to Dalí's nightmarish prefiguration of the Spanish Civil War.

TRAVEL *Cities of Spain,* by David Gilmour (Ivan R. Dee, 1992), is a collection of perceptive essays on nine Spanish cities. Containing more literary background and historical lore than most guidebooks have space to cover, Gilmour ranges from Granada to Santiago de Compostela, from Toledo to Córdoba.

FICTION & BIOGRAPHY Denounced by some as superficial, James A. Michener's *Iberia* (Random House, 1968) remains the classic travelog on Spain. The *Houston Post* claimed that this book "will make you fall in love with Spain."

The most famous Spanish novel is *Don Quixote* by Miguel de Cervantes. Readily available everywhere, it deals with the conflict between the ideal and the real in human nature. Despite the unparalleled fame of Miguel de Cervantes within Spanish literature, very little is known about his life. One of the most searching biographies of the literary master is Jean Canavaggio's *Cervantes,* translated from the Spanish by J. R. Jones (Norton, 1991).

Although the work of Cervantes has attained an almost mystical significance in the minds of many Spaniards, in the words of Somerset Maugham, "It would be hard to find a work so great that has so many defects." Nicholas Wollaston's *Tilting at Don Quixote* (André Deutsch Publishers, 1990) punctures any illusions that the half-crazed Don is only a matter of good and rollicking fun.

The collected works of the famed dramatist of Spain's golden age, Pedro Calderón de la Barca, can be read in *Plays* (University Press of Kentucky, 1985).

The major works of pre–Civil War playwright Federico García Lorca can be enjoyed in *Five Plays: Comedies and Tragicomedies* (New Directions, 1964).

Ernest Hemingway completed many works on Spain, none more notable than his novels of 1926 and 1940, respectively: *The Sun Also Rises* (Macmillan, 1987) and *For Whom the Bell Tolls* (Macmillan, 1988), the latter based on his experiences in the Spanish Civil War. Don Ernesto's *Death in the Afternoon* (various editions) remains the English-language classic on bullfighting.

For travelers to Granada and the Alhambra, the classic is *Tales of the Alhambra* (Sleepy Hollow Press, 1982) by Washington Irving.

The Life of Saint Teresa of Avila by Herself (Penguin, 1987), translated by J. M. Cohen, is reputedly the third most widely read book in Spain, after the Bible and *Don Quixote.* Some parts are heavy going, but the rest is lively.

Isabel the Queen: Life and Times, by Peggy K. Liss (Oxford University Press, 1993), an American historian, is a vividly detailed study. It provides a "spin" on this controversial queen not often taught in Spanish history classes. One of the most influential women in history, the Catholic monarch is viewed as forging national unity through the holy terror of the Spanish Inquisition, which was launched in 1478 and resulted in the expulsion of Jews and Moors from Spain and religious intolerance in general. Even her sponsorship of Columbus, it is suggested, led to "genocide" in the Caribbean.

Films

The first Spanish feature film, *Los Guapos del Parque* (*The Dandies of the Park*), directed by Segundo de Chomón, was released in 1903, seven years after the film industry began in Barcelona.

Film studios opened in Madrid in 1920, and by 1926 Spain was producing some 30 feature films a year. Before World War II the biggest name was Florian Rey, who made both silents and talkies, his most notable work being *Le Aldea Maldita* (*The Damned Village*) in 1929.

After the Civil War and under Franco, Spain produced a lot of mediocre films. Even General Franco, using a pseudonym, wrote a propaganda piece called *Raza* (*The Race*) in 1941.

In the 1950s, Spanish film achieved world recognition, mainly because of two directors, Luís García Berlanga and Juan Antonio Bardem. Both made satirical films about social conditions in Spain, sometimes incurring the government's wrath. During the filming of *Death of a Cyclist*, in fact, Bardem was arrested and imprisoned. Upon his release, he finished the film, which won acclaim at Cannes.

Luís Buñuel became one of the biggest names in Spanish cinema, his films mirroring the social, political, and religious conflicts that tore Spain apart during most of the 20th century. In 1928, Salvador Dalí and Buñuel cooperated on the director's first movie, *Un Chien Andalou* (*An Andalusian Dog*), considered the most important surrealist film. Two years later, sadistic scenes in *L'Age d'Or* (*The Golden Age*)—again written with Dalí's help—led to riots in some movie houses. Buñuel also directed *La Mort en ce Jardin* (*Death in the Garden*) with Simone Signoret (1957). In 1960 he made *Viridiana*, which subsequently won the prize for best picture at Cannes, even though Franco banned the film in Spain.

Today's *enfant terrible* is Pedro Almódovar, whose *Woman on the Verge of a Nervous Breakdown* won an Academy Award nomination in 1990. Ostensibly, the film is the story of a woman's abandonment, but its madcap proceedings deal with everything from spiked gazpacho to Shiite terrorists. An iconoclast like Almódovar, who has publicly declared his homosexuality, flourishes in the contemporary liberal Spain, which abolished censorship in 1977.

Another Almódovar international hit, *High Heels* (1991), is a soap opera involving a highly theatrical and highly emotional film diva who returns to Madrid and the daughter she abandoned years before. Praised by critics for "spanking his favorite ideas until they turn red with pleasure," Almódovar plays with what has been defined as "the theatricality of the real and the authenticity of the theatrical—all in an engagingly funny combination of high and low camp." Almódovar continued his glitz with *Kika* (1994), which he both wrote and directed. His eponymous heroine, Verónica Forqué, a beautician, is full of surprises. For example, she meets her lover-to-be, Ramón, when she's making up his presumably dead corpse. He wakes up and they fall in love—but that's only the beginning of twists and turns in this crazed soap opera.

In 1982 José Luís García became the first Spaniard to win an Oscar for best foreign film with *Volver a Empezar (To Begin Again)*, even though local critics considered the film inferior to his earlier *Asignatura Pendiente (Anticipated Assignation)*. *Volver a Empezar* takes a look at an exiled writer's homecoming to Spain.

One of the biggest box-office hits in Spanish film history (and still available on video) is *El Crimen de Cuenca* (*The Crime in Cuenca*), directed by Pilar Miró, who went on to become "chief of state of television." The film, which details Civil Guard torture, caused a furor when it was released and was suppressed until the coup attempt of 1981.

The Basque problem reached the movie screens in 1983 with *La Muerte de Mikel* (*Michael's Death*), which dramatizes the tortured love story of a young Basque nationalist and a transvestite from Bilbao.

The 36-year dictatorship of Franco imposed on the Spanish arts an anesthetizing effect whose aftermath is being explored cinematically today. One of the best-acclaimed examples is Vicente Aranda's steamily entertaining and psychologically insightful *Lovers* (1992). A dark, melodramatic romance set within the moral void of the Franco era, it charts the changing eddies of a love triangle and the bewitching influence of a slightly over-the-hill temptress.

Hailed by some critics as a variation of the farmer's daughter tale, *Belle Epoque,* directed by Fernando Trueba and written by Rafael Azcona (in Spanish with English subtitles), won the 1993 Oscar as best foreign-language film. It's a hot-blooded human comedy of a handsome innocent, a deserter from the Spanish army in the winter of 1930–31, who is seduced by the four daughters of a droll old painter.

Recordings

CLASSICAL Don Odilo Cunill directs the Cor Monastic de Abadía de Montserrat in *Cants Gregorians de la Missa Per Els Fidels Missa Orbis Factor,* Gregorian chants recorded in the chapel of the monastery at Montserrat.

In the album *Andrés Segovia, España,* the late master plays guitar versions of fandangos and *tonadillas.* In a more classical vein, the same artist plays Bach, Scarlatti, and also music by the Czech composer Benda (1722-95) in *Recital Intimo.*

The Orquesta de Conciertos de Madrid performs Falla's *El Amor Brujo* and *El Sombrero de Tres Picos.* The same group, conducted by Enrique Jorda, can be heard in Albéniz's *Suite Española* and *Dos Piezas Españoles.*

FOLK/ETHNIC Isabel Pantoja, widow of the late bullfighter, sings soulful interpretations of Andalusian ballads in *Se Me Enamora el Alma,* Rocio Jurado renders them smolderingly in *Punto de Partida* and *Canciones de España.*

Carlos Cana performs popular interpretations of Spanish Argentinian tangos, habaneras, and sevillanas on Luna de Abril. In *Canalla,* Antonio Cortés Chiquetete is heard in 19th-century folk melodies. Felipe Campuzano gives piano interpretations of Andalusian folk music in *Cádiz: Andalucía Espiritual.*

Pasodobles Famosos, performed by the Gran Banda Taurina, is popular with older Spaniards, partly for its nostalgia value. This was the music played until very recently at every Spanish gathering, from bullfights to weddings to christenings.

In *Siroca,* Paco de Lucía combines traditional flamenco guitar in its purest form with modern influences, including tangos, *bulerías,* and *tanquillos.* You can also hear Paco de Lucía on *Fantasía Flamenca,* interpreting authentic *flamencas* in a traditional manner. One of his most recent releases, *Zyryab,* is named for the eighth-century Persian musician who brought new musical techniques to Córdoba, including (probably) the basis for the modern guitar.

IMPRESSIONS

I also love the Spaniard, for he is a type in his own right, a copy of no one.
—Stendhal

The brilliance of late virtuoso Narciso Yepes can be heard on *Música Española para Guitarra,* performing traditional favorites.

CONTEMPORARY Ana Belén sings contemporary love ballads in *A la Sombra de un León.*

The pop-music scene offers several popular groups. In Madrid, an outstanding local band is *Radio Futura*; its members have been called the "Einsteins of Spanish rock." Another Madrid band is *Mecano*, whose members are invariably referred to by reviewers as "pretty boys"; the band sells records by the ton. A third group is *Gabinete Caligari* (the name comes from a famous old German movie); the group's music has been described by one critic as "macho Hispano-pop." From Catalonia comes a duo with a unique sound, a band recording rock music as *El Último de la Fila* (The Last in Line).

One of the biggest record sellers in Spain is Joan Manuel Serrat, a singer-songwriter recording more traditional popular music in both Catalán and Castilian.

In Madrid, traditional Spanish music is also offered by singer-songwriter Luís Eduardo Aute, who has thousands of fans in the Spanish-speaking world.

In current Spanish jazz, Tete Montoliu's recordings represent some of the best the country has to offer. All, or most, of these records are available at Spanish music stores in the United States. They are available throughout Spain as well.

2

Planning a Trip to Spain

THIS CHAPTER IS DEVOTED TO THE WHERE, WHEN, AND HOW OF YOUR TRIP—THE advance planning required to get it together and take it on the road.

After they've decided where to go, most people have two fundamental questions. What will it cost? and How do I get there? This chapter will address these and such other important issues as when to go, what entry requirements there are, what alternative travel vacations to consider, what pretrip health precautions to take, what additional insurance coverage to investigate, where to obtain more information about Spain, and so on.

1 Information, Entry Requirements & Money

Sources of Information

At least three months before you go, get in touch with the **Tourist Office of Spain,** 665 Fifth Ave., New York, NY 10022 (☎ **212/759-8822**), which can provide sightseeing information, calendars of events, train/ferry schedules, maps, and much, much more. Elsewhere in the United States, branches of the Tourist Office of Spain are located at: 8383 Wilshire Blvd., Suite 960, Beverly Hills, CA 90211 (☎ **213/658-7188**); Water Tower Place, Suite 915 East, 845 N. Michigan Ave., Chicago, IL 60611 (☎ **312/642-1992**); and 1221 Brickell Ave., Miami, FL 33131 (☎ **305/358-8223**).

Outside the United States, tourist offices include Spanish Tourist Information, 203 Castlereagh St., Suite 21A, P.O. Box 675, Sydney, South Australia, NSW 2000 (☎ **612/264-7966**); the Tourist Office of Spain, 102 Bloor St. West, 14th floor, Toronto, Ontario M5S 1M8 Canada (☎ **416/961-3131**), and the Spanish National Tourist Office, 57-58 St. James's St., London SW1 (☎ **0171/499-0901**).

Other useful sources are newspapers and magazines. To find the latest articles that have been published on your destination, go to your library, ask for the *Readers' Guide to Periodical Literature,* and look under "Spain" or specific cities for listings.

You may also want to contact the State Department for their background bulletins. Write to or call the **Superintendent of Documents, U.S. Government Printing Office,** Washington, DC 20402 (☎ **202/783-3238**).

A good travel agent can also be a good source of information. If you use one, make sure he or she is a member of the American Society of Travel Agents (ASTA). If you get poor service from a travel agent, write to ASTA's **Consumer Affairs Department,** 1101 King St., Alexandria, VA 22314 (☎ **703/739-2782**).

And, finally, the best sources of all are family members, friends, and other travelers who have just returned from your destination.

Entry Requirements

PASSPORTS A valid passport is all that an American, British, Canadian, Australian, or New Zealand citizen needs to enter Spain, and one can be secured as follows. (Australians need a visa–see below.)

In the United States Citizens 18 or older who meet the requirements may obtain a 10-year passport. Applications are available from post offices, court offices, and passport agencies. There are passport agencies in 13 cities—New York; Washington, DC; Stamford, Conn.; Seattle; Philadelphia; San Francisco; New Orleans; Boston; Honolulu; Chicago; Los Angeles; Miami; and Houston.

First-time applicants over 18 pay $65. Youths under 18 are granted a five-year passport. Children under 13 must have a parent or a guardian apply on their behalf; teenagers 13 to 16 must have a parent's or a guardian's permission to apply for a passport. Those under 18 pay a $40 fee ($30 plus a $10 first-time fee).

If your expired passport is 12 or more years old, or if it was granted to you before your 16th year, you must apply in person. Otherwise, you may apply by mail. The old passport must be submitted along with new photographs and a pink renewal form (DSP-82). The fee is $55. Call **202/647-0518** at any time for information.

Your passport application must be accompanied by proof of U.S. citizenship—a certified copy of your birth certificate or naturalization papers or an old passport (provided it's not more than 12 years old). A driver's license or employee ID card with photo is also acceptable. If none of these proofs is available, you may have someone who has known you at least two years (who has ID) accompany you and vouch for your identity. You'll also need two identical and recent color or black-and-white passport-size (2-in. by 2-in.) photographs.

You'll wait the longest to receive your passport between mid-March and mid-September; in winter it usually takes about two weeks by mail. Passports can sometimes be issued quickly in an emergency, provided that you present a plane ticket with a confirmed seat.

In Canada Citizens may go to one of 29 regional offices located in major cities. Alternatively, you can mail your application to the Passport Office, Section of External Affairs, Ottawa, ON, K1A 0G3. Post offices have application forms. Passports cost $35 (Canadian), and proof of Canadian citizenship is required, along with two signed identical passport-size photographs. Passports are valid for five years. For more information, call **800/567-6868** any time.

In Great Britain Citizens may apply at one of the regional offices in Liverpool, Newport, Glasgow, Peterborough, and Belfast, or else in London if they reside there. You can also apply in person at a main post office. Documents required include a marriage certificate or a birth certificate; two photos must accompany the application. The fee is £15, and the passport is good for 10 years.

In Australia Citizens may apply at the nearest post office. Provincial capitals and other major cities have passport offices. Application fees are subject to review every three months. Telephone **02/13-12-32** for the latest information. An adult's passport is valid for 10 years; for people under 18, a passport is valid for five years. Australians must also pay a departure tax stamp costing AUS$20 at a post office or airport; children 11 and under are exempt.

In New Zealand Citizens may go to their nearest consulate or passport office to obtain an application, which may be filed in person or by mail. To obtain a 10-year passport, proof of citizenship is required, plus a fee of NZ$56.25 or NZ$23.30 for children 12 and under.

In Ireland Contact the passport office at Setanta Centre, Molesworth St., Dublin 2 (☎ **01/478-0822**). The charge is IR£45. Applications are sent by mail. Irish citizens living in North America can contact the Irish Embassy, 2234 Massachusetts Ave., NW, Washington, DC 20008 (☎ **202/462-3939**). The embassy can issue a new passport or direct you to one of three North American consulates that have jurisdiction over a particular region; the charge is US$80. If you apply in person, you'll be entitled to a $5 discount.

VISAS Visas are not needed by U.S., Canadian, Irish, or British citizens for visits of less than three months. Citizens of Australia and South Africa do need to obtain a visa and should apply in advance at the Spanish Consulate in their home countries.

CUSTOMS You can take into Spain most personal effects and the following items duty free: two still cameras and 10 rolls of film per camera; one movie camera; tobacco for personal use; one liter each of liquor and wine; a portable radio; a tape recorder; a typewriter; a bicycle; sports equipment; fishing gear; and two hunting weapons with 100 cartridges each.

In the United States Returning to the United States from Spain, American citizens may bring in $400 worth of merchandise duty free, provided that they have not made a similar claim within the past 30 days. Remember to keep your receipts for purchases made in Spain. For more specific guidance, write to the U.S. Customs Service, P.O. Box 7407, Washington, DC 20044, and request the free pamphlet "Know Before You Go."

In Canada For total clarification, Canadians can write for the booklet "I Declare," issued by Revenue Canada Customs Department, Communications Branch, Mackenzie Avenue, Ottawa, ON K1A 0L5. Canada allows its citizens a $300 exemption, and they can bring back, duty free, 200 cigarettes, 2.2 pounds of tobacco, 40 ounces of liquor, and 50 cigars. In addition, they're allowed to mail unsolicited gifts to Canada from abroad at the rate of CAN$40 a day (but *not* alcohol or tobacco). On the package, mark "Unsolicited gift, under $40 value." All valuables you own and take with you should be declared before you depart from Canada on the Y-38 form, including serial numbers. **Note:** The $300 exemption can be used only once a year and then only after an absence of seven days.

In Britain and Ireland Members of European Union (formerly Community), countries do not necessarily have to go through Customs when returning home, provided that their travel was exclusively within the EU. Of course, Customs officers reserve the right to search a traveler if they're suspicious. However, there are certain EU guidelines for returning passengers who can bring in 400 cigarillos, 200 cigars, 800 cigarettes, and 1 kilogram of smoking tobacco.

They can also bring in 20 liters of fortified wine, 90 liters of wine, and 110 liters of beer. Persons exceeding these limits may be asked to prove that excess is either for one's personal use or gifts for friends. For further details on United Kingdom Customs, contact: HM Customs and Excise, Excise and Inland Customs Advice Centre, Dorset House, Stamford Street, London SE1 9NG (☎ **0171/202-4227**).

In Australia The duty-free allowance in Australia is AUS$400 or, for those under 18, AUS$200. Personal property mailed back from Spain should be marked "Australian goods returned," to avoid payment of duty. Upon returning to Australia, citizens can bring in 200 cigarettes or 250 grams of loose tobacco and 1 liter of alcohol. If you're returning with valuable goods you already own, such as foreign-made cameras, you should file Form B263. A helpful brochure, available from Australian consulates or Customs offices, is "Customs Information for All Travellers."

In New Zealand The duty-free allowance is NZ$500. Citizens over 16 years of age can bring in 200 cigarettes (or 250 grams of loose tobacco) or 50 cigars, 4.5 liters of wine or beer, or 1.125 liters of liquor. New Zealand currency does not carry restrictions regarding import or export. A Certificate of Export, listing valuables taken out of the country, allows you to bring them back without paying duty. Most questions are answered in a free pamphlet, "New Zealand Customs Guide for Travellers," available at New Zealand consulates and Customs offices.

Money

CASH/CURRENCY The basic unit of Spanish currency is the **peseta** (abbreviated pta.), currently worth about 7/10 of a cent in U.S. currency. One dollar is worth about 140 pesetas. Coins come in 1, 5, 25, 50, 100, 200, and 500 pesetas. Notes are issued in 500, 1,000, 5,000, and 10,000 pesetas.

All world currencies fluctuate, so you should be aware that the amounts appearing in this book are not exact. Currency conversions are presented only to give you a rough idea of the price you'll pay in U.S. dollars. There is no way to predict exactly what the rate of exchange will be when you visit Spain. Check the newspaper or ask at your bank for last-minute quotations.

The Spanish Peseta

For American Readers At this writing, $1 = approximately 140 ptas. (or 1 pta. = 71¢). This was the rate of exchange used to calculate the dollar equivalents given throughout this edition.

For British Readers At this writing, £1 = approximately 200 ptas. (or 1 pta. = 5p). This was the rate of exchange used to calculate the pound values in the table below.

Note International exchange rates fluctuate from time to time according to a complicated series of political and economic factors, and may not be the same when you travel to Spain. Therefore, this table should be used only as a guide for approximate values.

Ptas.	US$	UK£	Ptas.	US$	UK£
5	.04	.03	1,000	7.10	5.00
10	.07	.05	2,500	17.75	12.50
25	.18	.13	5,000	35.50	25.00
50	.36	.25	7,500	53.25	37.50
75	.53	.38	10,000	71.00	50.00
100	.71	.50	12,500	88.75	62.50
200	1.42	1.00	15,000	106.50	75.00
300	2.13	1.50	17,500	124.25	87.50
400	2.84	2.00	20,000	142.00	100.00
500	3.55	2.50	25,000	177.50	125.00
600	4.26	3.00	27,500	195.25	137.50
700	4.97	3.50	30,000	213.00	150.00
800	5.68	4.00	50,000	355.00	250.00
900	6.39	4.50	100,000	710.00	500.00

Be advised that rates of exchange vary, depending on where you convert your money. Your hotel will offer the worst rate of exchange. In general, banks offer the best rate, but even banks charge a commission for the service.

TRAVELER'S CHECKS Before leaving home, purchase traveler's checks and arrange to carry some ready cash (usually about $250, depending on your habits and needs). In the event of theft, if the checks are properly documented, the value of your checks will be refunded. Most large banks sell traveler's checks, charging fees that average between 1% and 2% of the value of the checks you buy, although some out-of-the-way banks, in rare instances, have charged as much as 7%. If your bank wants more than a 2% commission, call the traveler's check issuers directly for the address of outlets where this commission will cost less.

Issuers sometimes have agreements with groups to sell checks commission free. For example, Automobile Association of America (AAA) clubs sell American Express checks in several currencies without commission.

American Express (☎ toll free **800/221-7282** in the U.S. and Canada) is one of the largest and most immediately recognized issuers of traveler's checks. No commission is charged to members of the AAA and to holders of certain types of American Express credit cards. The company issues checks denominated in U.S. dollars, Canadian dollars, British pounds sterling, Swiss francs, French francs, German marks, and Japanese yen.

What Things Cost in Madrid	US$
Taxi from airport to Puerta del Sol	17.80
Public transportation within the city	.90
Local telephone call	.15
Double room at the Palace (very expensive)	227.20
Double room at Hotel Carlos V (moderate)	71.00
Double room at Hostal Principado (budget)	41.20
Lunch for one, without wine, at Alkalde (expensive)	25.50
Lunch for one, without wine, at Foster's Hollywood (budget)	14.00
Dinner for one, without wine, at El Cabo Mayor (expensive)	32.70
Dinner for one, without wine, at Sobrino de Botín (moderate)	19.90
Dinner for one, without wine, at Gran Café de Gijón (budget)	9.90
Coca-Cola in a restaurant	1.95
Cup of coffee	1.95
Glass of wine or beer	1.80
Admission to the Prado	3.20
Roll of ASA 100 color film, 36 exposures	7.90
Movie ticket	6.50
Theater ticket	6.00

The vast majority of checks sold in North America are denominated in U.S. dollars. For questions or problems that arise outside the U.S. or Canada, contact any of the company's many regional representatives.

Citicorp (☎ toll free **800/645-6556** in the U.S. and Canada, or **813/623-1709,** collect, from anywhere else in the world), issues checks in U.S. dollars, British pounds, German marks, and Japanese yen.

Thomas Cook (☎ toll free **800/223-9920** in the U.S. or **609/987-7300,** collect, from other parts of the world) issues MasterCard traveler's checks denominated in U.S. dollars, French francs, German marks, Dutch guilders, Spanish pesetas, Australian dollars, Japanese yen, and Hong Kong dollars. Depending on individual banking laws in each of the various states, some of the above-mentioned currencies may not be available in every outlet.

Interpayment Services (☎ toll free **800/221-2426** in the U.S. or Canada, or **800/453-4284** from most other parts of the world) sells Visa checks sponsored by Barclays Bank and Bank of America at selected branches around North America. Traveler's checks are denominated in U.S. or Canadian dollars, British pounds, Swiss francs, French francs, German marks, and Japanese yen.

CREDIT CARDS Credit cards are useful in Spain. **American Express, Visa,** and **Diners Club** are widely recognized. If you see the **Eurocard** or **Access** sign on an establishment, it means that it accepts **MasterCard.**

What Things Cost in Salamanca	US $
Taxi from train station to cathedral	3.00
Local telephone call	.15
Double room at Parador Nacional de Salamanca (expensive)	95.90
Double room at Alfonso X (moderate)	82.40
Double room at Mindanao (budget)	24.10
Lunch for one, without wine, at El Botón Charro (moderate)	19.90
Lunch for one, without wine, at Río de la Plata (budget)	14.20
Dinner for one, without wine, at Chez Victor (expensive)	24.40
Dinner for one, without wine, at Parador Nacional de Salamanca (moderate)	22.70
Dinner for one, without wine, at any tapas bar (budget)	7.50
Coca-Cola in a restaurant	1.50
Cup of coffee	1.65
Glass of wine or beer	1.50
Admission to the Universidad museum	1.40
Roll of ASA 100 color film, 36 exposures	6.95
Movie ticket	5.00
Theater ticket	7.50

Credit cards can be lifesavers when you're abroad. With American Express and Visa, for example, not only can you charge purchases in shops and restaurants that take the card, but you can also withdraw pesetas from bank cash machines at many locations in Spain. Check with your credit-card company before leaving home.

Keep in mind that the price of purchases is not converted into your national currency until notification is received in your home country, so the price is subject to fluctuation. If your national currency—be it dollars, pounds, or whatever—declines by the time your bill arrives, you'll pay more for an item than you expected. But those are the rules of the game. It can also work in your favor if your national currency should rise against the Spanish peseta.

CURRENCY EXCHANGE Many hotels in Spain do not accept dollar- or pound-denominated checks; those that do will almost certainly charge for the conversion. In some cases, they'll accept countersigned traveler's checks or a credit card, but if you're prepaying a deposit on hotel reservations, it's cheaper and easier to pay with a check drawn on a Spanish bank.

This can be arranged by a large commercial bank or by a specialist such as **Ruesch International**, 825 14th St., NW, Washington, DC, 20005 (☎ **202/408-1200,** or toll free **800/424-2923**), which performs a wide variety of conversion-related tasks, usually for only $2 U.S. per transaction.

If you need a check payable in pesetas, call Ruesch's toll-free number, describe what you need, and note the transaction number given to you. Mail your dollar-denominated personal check (payable to Ruesch International) to their office in Washington, DC. Upon receiving this, the company will mail a check denominated in pesetas for the financial equivalent, minus the $2 charge. The company can also help you with many different kinds of wire transfers and conversions of VAT (Value-Added Tax, which is known as IVA in Spain) refund checks and also will mail brochures and information packets on request. Britishers can go to Reusch International Ltd., 18 Savile Row, London W1X 2AD (☎ **0171/734-2300**).

2 When to Go—Climate, Holidays & Events

CLIMATE May and October are the best months weatherwise and crowdwise.

In summer it's hot, hot, and hot again, with the cities of Castile (Madrid) and Andalusia (Seville and Córdoba) stewing up the most scalding brew. Madrid has dry heat; the temperature can hover around 84°F in July, 75° in September. Seville has the dubious reputation of being about the hottest part of Spain in July and August, often baking under temperatures that average around 93°.

Barcelona is humid. The temperature in Majorca in high summer often reaches 91°. The overcrowded Costa Brava has temperatures around 81° in July and August. The Costa del Sol has an average of 77° in summer. The coolest spot in Spain is the Atlantic coast from San Sebastián to La Coruña, with temperatures in the 70s in July and August.

(In spite of attempts to change it, August remains the major vacation month in Europe. The traffic from France to Spain becomes a veritable migration, and low-cost hotels are almost fully booked along the coastal areas, with top prices in effect. To compound the problem, many restaurants and shops also decide that it's time for a vacation, thereby limiting the visitor's selections for both dining and shopping.)

Spring and fall are ideal times to visit nearly all of Spain, with the possible exception of the Atlantic coast, which experiences heavy rainfall in October and November.

In winter the coast from Algeciras to Málaga is the most popular, with temperatures reaching a warm 60° to 63°. It gets cold in Madrid, as low as 34°. Majorca is warmer, usually in the 50s but often dipping into the 40s. Some of the mountain resorts experience extreme cold.

Spain's Average Monthly Temperatures

		Jan	Feb	Mar	Apr	May	June	July	Aug	Sept	Oct	Nov	Dec
Barcelona	High (°F)	55	57	60	65	72	78	82	82	77	69	62	56
	Low (°F)	43	45	48	52	57	65	69	69	66	58	51	46
Seville	High (°F)	59	63	69	74	80	90	90	98	90	78	68	60
	Low (°F)	42	44	48	52	56	63	63	67	64	57	50	44
N. Coast	High (°F)	50	55	59	61	66	70	75	75	69	60	55	53
	Low (°F)	39	40	42	43	43	59	59	59	53	45	48	42
Alicante	High (°F)	61	64	68	73	78	84	90	89	83	75	68	63
	Low (°F)	43	43	47	50	55	62	67	68	64	57	50	45

HOLIDAYS Holidays include January 1 (New Year's Day), January 6 (Feast of the Epiphany), March 19 (Feast of St. Joseph), Good Friday, Easter Monday, May 1 (May Day), June 10 (Corpus Christi), June 29 (Feast of St. Peter and St. Paul), July 25 (Feast of St. James), August 15 (Feast of the Assumption), October 12 (Spain's National Day), November 1 (All Saints' Day), December 8 (Immaculate Conception), and December 25 (Christmas).

No matter how large or small, every city or town in Spain also celebrates its local saint's day. In Madrid it's May 15 (St. Isidro). You'll rarely know what the local holidays are in your next destination in Spain. Don't use up all your money, because you may arrive in town only to find banks and stores closed. In some cases intercity bus services are suspended on holidays.

Spain Calendar of Events

Be aware that the dates given below may not always be precise. Sometimes the exact days are not announced until six weeks before the actual festival. Check with the National Tourist Office of Spain (see "Information, Entry Requirements & Money" at the beginning of this chapter) if you're planning to attend a specific event.

January

- **Granada Reconquest Festival,** Granada. The whole of Granada celebrates the taking of the town from the Moors in 1492. The highest tower at the Alhambra is open to the public on January 2. For information, contact the Tourist Office of Granada, Plaza de Mariana Pineda, 10, 18009 Granada (☎ **958/22-66-88**). January 1–2.
- **Día de los Reyes (Parade of the Three Kings),** all over Spain. Parades are held throughout the country on the eve of the Festival of the Epiphany. Various "kings" dispense candies to children. January 6.

- **St. Anthony's Day (La Puebla),** Majorca. Bonfires, dancing, revelers dressed as devils, and other riotous events honor St. Anthony on the eve of his day. January 17.

February

- **Bocairente Festival of Christians and Moore,** Bocairente (Valencia). Fireworks, colorful costumes, parades, and a reenactment of the struggle between Christians and Moors mark this exuberant festival. A stuffed effigy of Mohammed is blown to bits. February 1–15.
- **Carnivales de Cádiz,** Cádiz. The oldest and best-attended carnival in Spain has been called "rampant madness." Costumes, parades, strolling troubadours, and drum beating—it's all fun and games. February 22–March 4.

March

- **Fallas de Valencia,** Valencia. Going back to the 1400s, this fiesta sees the burning of papier-mâché effigies of winter demons. Burnings are preceded by bullfights, fireworks, and parades. March 19.

April

✪ Feria de Sevilla (Seville Fair)

This is the most celebrated week of revelry in all of Spain, with all-night flamenco dancing, merrymaking in casetas, bullfights, horseback riding, flower-decked coaches, and dancing in the streets.
Where: Seville. **When:** Mid-April. **How:** Make hotel reservations very early. For general information, contact the Seville Office of Tourism, Avenida de la Constitución, 21B, 41004 Sevilla (☎ **95/422-14-04**).

✪ Semana Santa (Holy Week)

From Palm Sunday until Easter Sunday, a series of processions with hooded penitents moves to the piercing wail of the saeta, a love song to the Virgin or Christ. Pasos (heavy floats) bear images of the Virgin or Christ.
Where: Seville. **When:** April 8–15. **How:** Make hotel reservations very early. For general information, contact the Seville Office of Tourism, Avenida de la Constitución, 21B, 41004 Sevilla (☎ **95/422-14-04**).

May

- **Festival de los Patios,** Córdoba. At this famous fair residents flamboyantly decorate their patios with cascades of flowers. Visitors wander from patio to patio. First two weeks in May.
- **Romería del Rocio (Pilgrimage of the Virgin of the Dew),** El Rocio (Huelva). The most famous pilgrimage in Andalusia attracts a million people. Fifty men carry the statue of the Virgin nine miles to Almonte for consecration. May 11–14.
- **Jerez Horse Fair,** Jerez de la Frontera. "Horses, wine, women, and song," according to the old Andalusian ditty, make this a stellar event at which some of the greatest horses in the world go on parade. May 13–20.

June

✪ International Music and Dance Festival

In its 45th year (1995), this prestigious program of dance and music attracts international artists who perform at the Alhambra and other venues. It's a major event on the cultural calendar of Europe.

Where: Granada. **When:** Mid-June through first week of July. **How:** Make reservations as early as possible. For a complete listing and to reserve tickets, contact El Festival Internacional de Música y Danza de Granada, Auditorio Manuel de Falla, Paseo de los Mártires, 18009 Granada (☎ **958/220-022**).

- **Corpus Christi,** all over Spain. A major holiday on the Spanish calendar, this event is marked by big processions, especially in such cathedral cities as Toledo, Málaga, Seville, and Granada. June 14.
- **Verbena de Sant Joan,** Barcelona. This traditional festival occupies all Cataláns. Barcelona literally "lights up"—with fireworks, bonfires, and dances until dawn. The highlight of the festival is its culmination at Montjuïc with fireworks. June 24.

★ Festival de Cine de Barcelona

Expanded since 1987, this increasingly prestigious event brings filmmakers from all over Europe. Awards are presented to outstanding films, and screenings of new movies take place. Retrospectives are also presented. **Where:** Barcelona. **When:** June. **How:** Get tickets at Rambla de Catalunya and Carrer Aragó (☎ **93/215-24-24**).

July

- **Festival of St. James,** Santiago de Compostela. Pomp and ceremony mark this annual pilgrimage to the tomb of St. James the Apostle in Galicia. Galician folklore shows, concerts, parades, and the swinging of the *botafumeiro* (a mammoth incense burner) mark the event. Mid- to late July.
- **San Sebastián Jazz Festival,** San Sebastián. Celebrating its 30th year (1995), this festival brings together the jazz greats of the world at the pavilion of the Anoeta Sport Complex. Other programs take place al fresco at the Plaza de Trinidad in the old quarter. Last two weeks in July.

★ Fiesta de San Fermín

Torn from the pages of Ernest Hemingway's novel *The Sun Also Rises,* the "running of the bulls" through the streets of Pamplona is the most popular celebration in Spain. The running is the most photographed event, but the celebration also includes wine tasting, fireworks, and, of course, bullfights. **Where:** Pamplona. **When:** July 7–14. **How:** Make reservations months in advance. ("Papa" Hemingway paid a man a yearly stipend to secure the best tickets and hotel rooms.) For more information, such as a list of accommodations, write the Office of Tourism, Duque de Ahumada, 3, 31002 Pamplona (☎ **948/22-07-41**).

August

- **Santander International Festival of Music and Dance,** Santander. A repertoire of classical music, ballet, contemporary dance, chamber music, recitals, and much more. Most performances are staged at the Plaza de la Porticada. All month. For further information, contact Festival Internacional de Santander, Avenida de Calvo Sotelo, 15, 39002 Santander (☎ **942/210-345**).
- **The Mystery Play of Elche,** Elche. In the 17th-century Basilica of Santa María in Elche (Alicante), this sacred drama is reenacted. It represents the Assumption and the Crowning of the Virgin. Tickets may be obtained from

the Office of Tourism, Passeig de l'Estacío, 03203 Elche (☎ **96/545-27-47**). August 11–15.

- **Feria de Málaga** (Málaga Fair) One of the longest summer fairs in Southern Europe (generally lasting for 10 days), this fair kicks off with fireworks displays and is highlighted by a parade of Arab horses pulling brightly decorated carriages. Participants are dressed in colorful Andalusian garb. Plazas rattle with castanets, and wine is dispensed by the gallon. Usually begins around mid-August.

September

- **Diada,** Barcelona. This is considered the most significant festival in all of Catalonia. It celebrates the glory of autonomy from the rest of Spain, following years of repression under the dictator Franco. Demonstrations and other "flag-waving" events take place. The *senyera,* the flag of Catalonia, is much in evidence. Not your typical tourist fare, but interesting nevertheless. September 11.
- **Cádiz Grape Harvest Festival,** Jerez de la Frontera. The major wine festival in Andalusia (which means Spain as well) honors the famous sherry of Jerez, with five days of processions, flamenco dancing, bullfights, livestock on parade, and, of course, sherry drinking. Mid-September (dates vary).
- **International Film Festival San Sebastián.** The premier film festival of Spain takes place in the Basque capital, often at the Victoria Eugenia Theater, a Belle Epoque extravaganza. Retrospectives are often featured, and weeklong screenings are shown. Second half of September (dates vary).
- **Setmana Cran,** Barcelona. As the summer draws to an end, Barcelona stages week-long *verbenas* and *sardana* dances to honor its patron saint, the Virgin of Merced. Parades, concerts, various theatrical and musical events at venues throughout the city, and even sports competitions mark this event dear to the heart of Catalonia. Bullfights are also part of the festival. Look for the "parade of giants" through the streets, culminating at Placa de Sant Jaume in front of the city hall.

October

- **Mostra de Valencia Film Festival,** Valencia. A week of cinema—complete with homages and retrospectives—is staged at various venues in this Levante city. Tickets and information are available from Palau de la Música, Paseo de la Alameda, 46010 Valencia (☎ **96/360-33-56**). Dates vary.
- **St. Teresa Week,** Ávila. *Verbenas* (carnivals), parades, singing, and dancing honor the patron saint of this walled city. Dates vary.

November

- **All Saints' Day,** all over Spain. This public holiday is reverently celebrated, as relatives and friends lay flowers on the graves of the dead. November 1.

December

- **Día de los Santos Inocentes,** all over Spain. This equivalent of April Fools' Day is an excuse for people to do "loco" things. December 28.

Madrid Calendar of Events

February

- **ARCO** (Madrid's International Contemporary Art Fair) One of the biggest draws in Spain's cultural calendar, this exhibit brings the best in contemporary art from Europe and America. At the Crystal Pavilion of the Casa de Campo, the exhibition presents both regional and internationally known artists. Dates vary.
- **Madrid Carnival.** The carnival kicks off with a big parade along the Paseo de la Castellana, culminating in a masked ball at the Círculo de Bellas Artes on the following night. Fancy-dress competitions last until February 28, when the festivities end with a tear-jerking "burial of a sardine" at the Fuente de los Pajaritos in the Casa de Campo. This is followed that evening by a concert in the Plaza Mayor. Dates vary.

May

★ Fiestas de San Isidro

Madrileños run wild with a 10-day celebration honoring their patron saint. Food fairs, Castilian folkloric events, street parades, parties, music, dances, bullfights, and other festivities mark the occasion.
Where: Madrid. **When:** May 12–21. **How:** Make hotel reservations early. Expect crowds and traffic (beware of pickpockets). For information, write to Oficina Municipal de Información y Turismo, Plaza Mayor, 3, 28014 Madrid.

July

- **Veranos de la Villa.** Called "the summer binge" of Madrid, this summer-long program presents folkloric dancing, pop music, classical music, zarzuelas, and flamenco at various venues throughout the city. Open-air cinema is a feature in the Parque del Retiro. Ask at the various tourist offices for complete details (which change every summer). Sometimes admission is charged, but often these events are free.

August

- **Fiestas of Lavapiés and La Paloma.** These two fiestas—the most traditional in Madrid—begin with the Lavapiés on August 1 and continue through the hectic La Paloma celebration on August 15, the day of the Virgen de la Paloma. Tens of thousands of residents and visitors race through the narrow streets. Apartment dwellers above hurl buckets of cold water onto the crowds below to cool them off. Children's games, floats, music, flamenco, and zarzuelas, along with street fairs, mark the occasion.

September

★ Autumn Festival

Both Spanish and international artists participate in this cultural program, with a series of operatic, ballet, dance, music, and theatrical performances. From Strasbourg to Tokyo, this event is a premier attraction, yet tickets are reasonable, costing from 1,500 ptas. ($10.70) per event.

Where: Madrid. **When:** Mid-Sept to mid-Nov. **How:** Make hotel reservations early and write for tickets to Festival de Otoño, Plaza de España, 8, 28008 Madrid (☎ **34-1/580-25-65**).

3 Health & Insurance

HEALTH PREPARATIONS Spain should not pose any major health hazards. Many travelers suffer from diarrhea, generally caused by the overly rich cuisine—garlic, olive oil, and wine. Take along some antidiarrhea medicine; moderate your eating habits; and, even though the water in most parts of Spain is considered safe, consume mineral water only. Milk and milk products are pasteurized and generally considered safe. The Mediterranean, a horrendously polluted sea, washes up on Spain's shores, and fish and shellfish from it should only be eaten cooked. Try to make sure it is fresh. Sometimes inadequate refrigeration of fish and shellfish, especially in the hot summer months, can lead to what some foreign visitors to Spain call "the Toledo trot," the equivalent of Mexico's "Montezuma's revenge."

Sometimes travelers find that the change of diet in Spain leads to constipation. If this occurs, eat a high-fiber diet and drink plenty of mineral water. Avoid large lunches and dinners with wine. Consult your doctor before you go about taking Colace, a stool softener, or Metamucil.

If you need a doctor, ask your hotel to locate one for you. You can also obtain a list of English-speaking doctors in Spain from the **International Association for Medical Assistance to Travelers (IAMAT),** in the United States at 417 Center St., Lewiston, NY 14092 (☎ **716/754-4883**); in Canada, at 40 Regal Rd., Guelph, ON, N1K 1B5 (☎ **519/836-0102**). Getting medical help in Spain is relatively easy, compared to the situation in many countries, and competent doctors are found within each of the country's widely scattered regions.

If your medical condition is chronic, always talk to your doctor before taking an international trip. He or she may have specific advice to give you. For conditions such as epilepsy, a heart condition, diabetes, and some other afflictions, wear a Medic Alert Identification Tag, which will immediately alert any doctor to the nature of your condition. It also provides the number of Medic Alert's 24-hour hotline, so that a foreign doctor can obtain medical records for you. A lifetime membership costs $35, $45, or $60, depending on your choice of identification. Contact the **Medic Alert Foundation,** P.O. Box 1009, Turlock, CA 95381-1009 (☎ toll free **800/432-5378**).

Take along an adequate supply of any prescription drugs that you need and prescriptions that use the generic name—not the brand name—of the drugs as well. Carry all vital medicines and drugs (the legal kind only) with you in your carry-on luggage, in case your checked luggage is lost.

Also, take your own personal medical kit. Include first-aid cream, insect repellent, aspirin, nose drops, and Band-Aids. If you're subject to motion sickness on a plane or train, remember to bring along motion-sickness medicine as well.

It's also a good idea to take along a good sunscreen, one that has a protection factor high enough to block out most of the dangerous ultraviolet rays of the sun, which can be intense in the south of Spain. In case you do find yourself overexposed to the sun, have some liquid solution of the aloe plant with you for soothing relief.

You aren't required to have any particular inoculations to enter Spain (except for yellow fever if you're arriving from an infected area).

INSURANCE Before purchasing any additional insurance, check your homeowner, automobile, and medical insurance policies. Also check the membership contracts issued by automobile and travel clubs and by credit-card companies. If, after close examination, you feel you still need insurance, consider the following.

Health/Accident Many credit-card companies insure their users in case of a travel accident, provided that a ticket was purchased with their card. Sometimes fraternal organizations have policies that protect members in case of sickness or accidents abroad.

The best policies provide advances in cash or transferrals of funds so that you won't have to dip into your travel funds to settle any medical bills you might incur while away from home.

To submit a claim, you'll need documentation from a medical authority that you did suffer the illness for which you are seeking compensation.

Another option is **Travel Assistance International** by Worldwide Assistance Services, Inc., 1133 15th St. N.W., Suite 400, Washington, D.C., 20005 (☎ **800/821-2828** or **202/331-1596**), which offers on-the-spot medical payment coverage up to $15,000, $30,000, $60,000, or $90,000 for emergency care practically anywhere in the world as well as unlimited medical evacuation and repatriation coverage back to the United States if necessary. For an additional fee, you can be covered for trip cancellation or disruption, for lost or delayed luggage, and for accidental death or dismemberment. Fees are based on the length of your trip and the coverage you select. Prices begin at $52 per person ($72 per family) for a one- to eight-day trip.

Loss/Theft Many homeowner insurance policies cover theft of luggage during foreign travel and loss of documents—your Eurailpass, your passport, or your airline ticket, for instance. Coverage is usually limited to about $500 U.S. To submit a claim on your insurance, you'll need police reports that you did in fact suffer the loss for which you are seeking compensation. Such claims can be filed only when you return from Spain.

Cancellation If you've booked a charter fare, you will probably have to pay a cancellation fee if you cancel a trip suddenly, even if it is due to an unforeseen crisis. It's possible to get insurance against such a possibility. Some travel agencies provide this coverage, and often flight insurance against a canceled trip is written into tickets paid for by credit cards from such companies as Visa and American Express. Many tour operators or insurance agents provide this type of insurance.

Insurers Among the companies offering such health, loss, and cancellation policies are the following:

Travel Guard Internationale, 1145 Clark St., Stevens Point, WI 54481 (☎ **715/345-0505,** or toll free **800/826-1300**), offers a comprehensive travel insurance policy that includes coverage and service ranging from trip cancellation and interruption to medical and 24-hour emergency assistance.

You can also contact **Travelers Insurance Company,** Travel Insurance Division, One Tower Square, 10NB, Hartford, CT 06183-5040 (☎ toll free **800/243-3174** in the U.S.). Travel accident and illness coverage starts at $10 for 6 to 10 days; $500 worth of coverage for lost, damaged, or delayed baggage costs $20 for 6 to 10 days; and trip cancellation goes for $5.50 per $100 worth of coverage (written approval is necessary for cancellation coverage above $10,000).

Mutual of Omaha, Mutual of Omaha Plaza, Omaha, NE 68175 (☎ toll free **800/228-9792**), offers insurance packages priced at $113 and above for a three-week trip. Included in the packages are travel-assistance services, and financial protection against trip cancellation, trip interruption, flight and baggage delays, accident-related medical costs, accidental death and dismemberment, and medical evacuation coverages. Applications for insurance can be taken over the phone for major credit card holders.

Healthcare Abroad (MEDEX), Wallach & Co., 107 Federal St., (P.O. Box 480), Middleburg, VA 22117-0480 (☎ **703/687-3166,** or toll free **800/237-6615**), offers a policy good for 10 to 120 days costing $3 a day, that includes accident and sickness coverage (to the tune of $100,000), medical evacuation, and $25,000 accidental death and dismemberment compensation. Trip-cancellation coverage as well as lost- or stolen-luggage coverage can be written into this policy at a nominal cost.

Access America, 6600 W. Broad St., Richmond, VA 23230 (☎ **804/285-3300,** or toll free **800/284-8300**), has a 24-hour hotline in case of an emergency. It offers a comprehensive travel insurance and assistance package, including medical expenses, on-the-spot hospital payments, medical transportation, baggage insurance, trip-cancellation or -interruption insurance, and collision-damage insurance for a car rental. Their 24-hour hotline connects you to multilingual coordinators who can offer advice and help on medical, legal, and travel problems. Packages begin at $27.

Insurance for British Travelers Most big travel agents offer their own insurance, and will probably try to sell you their package when you book a holiday. Think before you sign. Britain's Consumers' Association recommends that you insist on seeing the policy and reading the fine print before buying travel insurance.

You should also shop around for better deals. You might call **Columbus Travel Insurance Ltd.** (☎ **0171/375-0011** in London) or, for students, **Campus Travel** (☎ **0171/730-3402** in London). If you're unsure about who provides what kind of insurance and the best deal, contact the **Association of British Insurers,** 51 Gresham St., London EC2V 7HQ (☎ **0171/600-333**).

4 What to Pack

Always pack as lightly as possible. Sometimes it's hard to get a porter or a baggage cart at rail and air terminals. And airlines are increasingly strict about how much luggage you can take along, not only as carry-on but also as checked baggage.

It depends on where you are going in Spain and at what time of year, but as a general rule, pack the same clothes that you might wear in the southeastern United States: That is, dress as if you were visiting Virginia or the Carolinas at the same time of year as your trip to Spain. Buildings in Spain tend not to be very well heated, so you might want to take an extra sweater.

Dress is casual in Spain. A jacket and tie are required in only first-class establishments. For special occasions, men should pack a suit. For women, skirts and sweaters, suits, simple dresses, and dress slacks are never out of place.

For sightseeing, casual clothes and comfortable shoes (two pairs) are best. When touring churches and cathedrals, dress appropriately: Head coverings are not required, but you'll be denied entry if you're wearing shorts or have bare shoulders. After sunning at the beach, both men and women should wear a cover-up when on the street. If you plan to visit a casino or nightclub, dress up—casual but chic is best.

Finally, pack only items that travel well. Don't count on being able to get your clothes pressed at hotels, especially budget hotels. Take clothes that you can wash out in your bathroom sink and hang up to dry overnight. Pack a plastic bag for clothes that are still damp when you move on to your next destination.

5 Tips for Special Travelers

FOR THE DISABLED Because of Spain's many hills and endless flights of stairs, getting around this country can be difficult for the disabled. Yet, despite the lack of adequate services, more and more disabled travelers are taking on the challenge of Spain, and conditions are slowly improving.

The newer hotels are more sensitive to the needs of the disabled; and the more expensive restaurants, in general, are wheelchair-accessible. (In Madrid, the capital, there is even a museum designed for the sightless and sight impaired—see the section "More Attractions" in Chapter 5, "What to See and Do in Madrid.") However, since most places have very limited, if any, facilities for the disabled, it would be best to consider an organized tour specifically designed to accommodate the disabled.

For information, contact **MossRehab,** 1200 W. Tabor Rd., Philadelphia, PA 19141 (☎ **215/456-9603**), or **Mobility International USA,** P.O. Box 10767, Eugene, OR 97440 (☎ **503/343-1284**). MossRehab offers information to callers only, while Mobility will mail you an information package. Note, however, that both are information-service agencies, not travel agents.

You may also want to consider joining a tour for visitors with disabilities. To obtain the names and addresses of such tour operators, write to the **Society for the Advancement of Travel for the Handicapped,** 347 Fifth Ave., New York, NY 10016 (☎ **212/447-7248**). Annual membership dues are $45, or $25 for senior citizens and students. Send a stamped, self-addressed envelope.

FEDCAP Rehabilitation Services (formerly Federation of the Handicapped), 211 W. 14th St., New York, NY 10011 (☎ **212/727-4268**), operates summer tours to Europe and elsewhere for its members. Membership costs $6 yearly.

You can also obtain, free, a copy of "Air Transportation of Handicapped Persons," published by the U.S. Department of Transportation, by writing: Free Advisory Circular No. AC12032, Distribution Unit, U.S. Department of Transportation, Publications Division, M-4332, Washington, DC 20590.

For the blind, the best source is the **American Foundation for the Blind,** 15 W. 16th St., New York, NY 10011 (☎ **212/620-2000,** or toll free **800/232-5463**).

Tips for Disabled British Travelers **RADAR** (the Royal Association for Disability and Rehabilitation) 25 Mortimer St., London W1N 8AB (☎ **0171/637-5400**), publishes an annual holiday guide for the disabled, "Holidays and Travel Abroad" (£3.50 in the U.K., £5.26 in Europe, £7 in other destinations). RADAR also provides a number of holiday fact sheets on such subjects as sports and outdoor holidays, insurance, financial arrangements, and accommodations with nursing care for groups or for the elderly. There is a nominal charge for all these publications.

Another good resource is the **Holiday Care Service,** 2, Old Bank Chambers, Station Road, Horley, Surrey RH6 9HW (☎ **01293-774-535,** fax 01293/784-647), a national charity that advises on accessible accommodations for elderly and disabled people. It provides a free reservations service offering discounted rates. Their Holiday Care Awards recognize those in the tourism industry who provide excellent service for people with disabilities.

If you're flying around Europe, the airline and ground staff will help you on and off planes, and reserve seats for you with sufficient leg room. But you must arrange for such assistance *in advance* by contacting your airline.

The **Airport Transport Users Council,** 2/F Kingsway House, 103 Kingsway, London WC2B 6QX (☎ **0171/242-3883**), publishes two free pamphlets: "Flight Plan—A Passenger's Guide to Planning and Using Air Travel," which is packed with information, and "Care in the Air," designed specifically to help the disabled traveler.

FOR SENIORS Many discounts are available for seniors, but often you need to be a member of an association to obtain them.

For information before you go, write for a free booklet, "101 Tips for the Mature Traveler," available from **Grand Circle Travel,** 347 Congress St., Suite 3A, Boston, MA 02210 (☎ **617-350-7500,** or toll free **800/248-3737**).

One of the most dynamic travel organizations for seniors is **Elderhostel,** 75 Federal St., Boston, MA (☎ **617/426-7788**), established in 1975, which operates an array of programs throughout Europe, including Spain. Most courses last around three weeks and represent good value, since they include airfare, accommodations in student dormitories or modest inns, all meals, and tuition. Courses involve no homework, are ungraded, and are often liberal arts–oriented. These aren't luxury vacations, but they're fun and fulfilling. Participants must be at least 60 years old. A companion or spouse must be at least 50 years old.

SAGA International Holidays, 222 Berkeley St., Boston, MA 02116 (☎ toll free **800/343-0273**), runs all-inclusive tours for seniors, preferably 60 and older. Insurance is included in the net price of the tours.

In the United States, the best organization to belong to is the **American Association of Retired Persons,** 601 E St. NW, Washington, DC 20049 (☎ **202/434-AARP**). Members are offered discounts on car rentals, hotels, and airfares. The association's group travel is provided by the AARP Travel Experience from American Express. Tours may be purchased through any American Express office or travel agent, or by calling toll free **800/927-0111.** Flights to the various destinations are handled by the toll-free number as part of land arrangements.

Information is also available from the **National Council of Senior Citizens,** 1331 F St. NW, Washington, DC 20005-1171 (☎ **202/347-8800**), which charges $12 per person or couple, for which you receive a monthly newsletter, part of which is devoted to travel tips. Reduced discounts on hotel and auto rentals are available.

If you're between 45 and 89 and need a travel companion, **Golden Companions,** P.O. Box 754, Pullman, WA 99163 (☎ **208/858-2183**), may provide the answer. A research economist, Joanne R. Buteau, founded this helpful service in 1987 (she's quick to point out, however, that it's not a dating service). Members, who are drawn from various walks of life, meet potential companions through a confidential mail network; once they've "connected," they make their own travel arrangements. Membership for a full year costs $85 per person and entitles you to a bimonthly travel newsletter, "The Golden Gateways."

Another company that caters to solo seniors, 50 years or older, who seek compatible traveling companions is **Tempo Travelers,** 938 N. 70th St., #125, Lincoln, NE 68605. Catering to single, widowed, or divorced travelers, it responds to requests for written information.

Uniworld, 16000 Ventura Blvd., Encino, CA 91436 (☎ **818/382-7820** or toll free **800/733-7820** in the U.S.), specializes in single tours for the mature person. It arranges for you to share an accommodation with another single person or gets you a low-priced single supplement. Uniworld specializes in travel to certain districts of England, France, Spain, Italy, and Scandinavia.

Tips for British Seniors **Wasteels,** Victoria Station, opposite platform 2, London SW1V 1JY (☎ **0171/836-8541**), currently provides an over-60s Rail Europe Senior Card. Its price is £5 to any British person with government-issued proof of his or her age, and £19 to anyone with a certificate of age not issued by the British government. With this card, discounts are sometimes available on certain trains within Britain and the rest of Europe.

FOR SINGLES It's no secret that the travel industry caters to people who are not traveling alone. Double rooms, for example, are usually much more reasonably priced than singles. One company has made heroic efforts to match single travelers with like-minded companions. Founder Jens Jurgen charges $36 to $66 for a six-month listing in his well-publicized records. New applicants desiring a travel companion fill out a form stating their preferences and needs. They then receive a list of people who might be suitable. Companions of the same age or opposite sex can be requested. A bimonthly newsletter averaging 30-plus pages also gives numerous money-saving travel tips of special interest to solo travelers. A sample copy is available for $4. For an application and more information, write to Jens Jurgen, **Travel Companion,** P.O. Box P-833, Amityville, NY 11701 (☎ **516/454-0880,** fax 516/454-0170).

Singleworld, 401 Theodore Fremd Ave., Rye, NY 10580 (☎ **914/967-3334,** or toll free **800/223-6490**), is a travel agency that operates tours for solo travelers. Some, but not all, are for people in their 20s and 30s. Annual dues are $25.

Another agency to check is **Grand Circle Travel,** 347 Congress St., Boston, MA 02110 (☎ **617/350-7500,** or toll free **800/248-3737**), which offers escorted tours and cruises for retired people, including singles.

Since single supplements on tours usually carry a hefty price tag, a way to get around paying the supplement is to find a tour company that allows you to share a room with a hitherto unknown fellow traveler. One company offering a "guaranteed-share plan" for its tours within Spain is **Cosmos** (an affiliate of Globus Tours). Upon your arrival in Spain, a suitable roommate will be assigned to you from among the tour's other participants. The company maintains offices at 5301 S. Federal Circle, Littleton, CO 80123. You can obtain information about its tours through any travel agency.

Tips for British Singles Single people feel comfortable traveling with other singles. A tour operator whose groups are usually composed at least 50% of unattached persons is **Explore, Ltd.** (☎ **01252/344-161**), with a well-justified reputation for offering offbeat tours. Groups rarely include more than 16 participants, and children under 14 are not allowed.

Dedicated independent travelers may want to check out **The Globetrotters Club,** BCM/Roving, London WCIN 3XX, which enables members to exchange information and generally assist each other in traveling as cheaply as possible. Persons wishing to join in the United Kingdom for one year pay £12 for the first year, £9 for each year's renewal.

FOR FAMILIES Advance planning is the key to a successful overseas family vacation.

- If you have very small children, you should discuss your vacation plans with your family doctor and take along such standard supplies as children's aspirin, a thermometer, Band-Aids.
- On airlines, a special menu for children must be requested at least 24 hours in advance; but if baby food is required, bring your own and ask a flight attendant to warm it to the right temperature.
- Take along a "security blanket" for your child (a pacifier, a favorite toy, or a book) or, for older children, something to make them feel at home in different surroundings (a baseball cap, a favorite T-shirt, or some good-luck charm).
- If you're going to be driving anywhere, make advance arrangements for cribs, bottle warmers, and car seats.
- Ask the hotel if it stocks baby food; if it doesn't, take some with you and plan to buy the rest in local supermarkets.
- Draw up guidelines on bedtime, eating, keeping tidy, being in the sun, even shopping and spending—they'll make the vacation more enjoyable.
- Babysitters can be found for you at most hotels, but you should always insist, if possible, that you secure a babysitter with at least a rudimentary knowledge of English.

"Family Travel Times" is a newsletter about traveling with children. The cost is $55 for 10 issues. Subscribers can also call in with travel questions, but only on Wednesday from 10am to 1pm eastern standard time. Contact **TWYCH** (which stands for "Travel with Your Children"), 45 W. 18th St., New York, NY 10011 (☎ **212/206-0688**).

Tips for British Families The best deals for families are often package tours put together by some of the giants of the British travel industry. Foremost among these is **Thomsons Tour Operators.** Through its subsidiary, **Skytours** (☎ **0181/200-8733**), it offers dozens of air/land packages to Spain that have a predesignated number of airline seats reserved for the free use of children under 18 who accompany their parents. To qualify, parents must book airfare and hotel accommodations lasting two weeks or more, and book as far in advance as possible. Savings for families with children can be substantial.

FOR STUDENTS **Council Travel** is America's largest student, youth, and budget travel group, with more than 60 offices worldwide. It also sells publications for young people considering traveling abroad. For a copy of *Student Travels* magazine—which provides information on all Council Travel's services as well as on programs and publications of the Council on International Educational Exchange—send $1 in postage.

Council Travel has offices throughout the United States, including the main office at 205 E. 42nd St., New York, NY 10017 (☎ **212/661-1450**). Call that number to find the location nearest you.

The most commonly accepted form of identification is also an "open sesame" to bargains. An **International Student Identity Card (ISIC)** gets you such benefits as special student airfares to Europe, medical insurance, and many special discounts. In Spain the card secures you free entrance into state museums, monuments, and archeological sights. Domestic train fares in Spain are also reduced for students. The card, which costs only $16, is available at Council Travel offices nationwide, as well as on hundreds of college and university campuses across the country. Proof of student status and a passport-size photograph (2 in. by 2 in.) are necessary. For the ISIC-issuing office nearest you, contact the Council on International Educational Exchange, 205 E. 42nd St., New York, NY 10017 (☎ toll free **800/GET AN ID**).

The **IYHF** (International Youth Hostel Federation) was designed to provide bare-bones overnight accommodations for seriously budget-conscious travelers. For information, contact HI-AYH (Hostelling International/American Youth Hostels), 733 15th St. NW, Suite 840, Washington, DC 20005 (☎ **202/783-6161**). Membership costs $25 annually, except for those under 18, who pay $10, and those 54 or more, who pay $15.

Tips for British Students **Campus Travel,** 52 Grosvenor Gardens, London SW1W 0AG (☎ **0171/730-3402**), provides a wealth of information for the student traveler, ranging from route planning to flight insurance, including railcards.

The International Student Identity Card (ISIC) is an internationally recognized proof of student status that will entitle you to savings on flights, sightseeing, food, and accommodation. It costs only £5 and is well worth the cost. Always show your ISIC when booking a trip—you may not get a discount without it.

Youth hostels are the place to stay if you're a student. You'll need an International Youth Hostels Association card, which you can purchase from the youth hostel store at 14 Southampton St., London WC23 7HY (☎ **0171/836-8541**), or Campus Travel (☎ **0171/730-3402**). Take your passport and some passport-size photos of yourself, plus your membership fee. In England and Wales, the fee is £3 for those under 18 and £9 for those over 18. In Scotland, this is slightly less: £2.50 for those under 18, £6 for everyone else.

The Youth Hostel Association puts together *The Hostelling International Budget Guide,* listing every youth hostel in 31 European countries. It costs ß5.99 when purchased at the Southampton Street store in London. Add 61p postage if it is being delivered within the United Kingdom.

In summer, many youth hostels are full. You should therefore book ahead. In London, you can make advance reservations at the membership department at 14 Southampton St. (see above).

6 Educational/Alternative Travel

Offbeat, alternative modes of travel often cost less and can be an enriching way to travel.

LEARNING VACATIONS An international series of programs for persons over 50 who are interested in combining travel and learning is offered by **Interhostel,** developed by the University of New Hampshire. Each program lasts two weeks; is led by a university faculty or staff member; and is arranged in conjunction with a host college, university, or cultural institution. Participants may stay longer if they wish. Interhostel offers in Spain programs that consist of cultural and intellectual activities, with field trips to museums and other centers of interest. For information, contact the **University of New Hampshire, Division of Continuing Education,** 6 Garrison Ave., Durham, NH 03824 (☎ **603/862-1147,** or toll free **800/733-9753**).

STUDYING SPANISH IN SPAIN Your trip to Spain will be enriched and made easier by a basic understanding of the language.

Salminter, Calle Toro, 34-36, 37002 Salamanca (☎ **23/21-18-08;** fax 23/26-02-63), conducts courses in conversational Spanish, with optional courses in business Spanish, translation techniques, and Spanish culture. Classes contain no more than 10 persons. There are courses of two weeks, one month, and three months at seven progressive levels. The school can arrange housing with Spanish families or in furnished apartments shared with other students. The school can also arrange excursions and walking tours to the surrounding region. For reservations and information, write or fax school officials at the address or number above.

Another good source of information about courses in Spain is the **American Institute for Foreign Study** (AIFS), 102 Greenwich Ave., Greenwich, CT 06830 (☎ **203/869-9090,** or toll free **800/727-2437**). This organization can set up transportation and arrange for summer courses, with bed and board included. It can help you arrange study programs at either the University of Salamanca, one of Europe's oldest academic centers, or the University of Granada.

The biggest organization dealing with higher education in Europe is the **Institute of International Education (IIE),** 809 United Nations Plaza, New York, NY 10017 (☎ **212/883-8200**). A few of its booklets are free; but for $36.95, plus $4 for postage, you can purchase the more definitive *Vacation Study Abroad.* Visitors to New York may use the resources of an Information Center, which is open to the public Tuesday through Friday from 11am to 4pm. The institute is closed on major holidays.

One well-recommended clearinghouse for academic programs throughout the world is the **National Registration Center for Study Abroad (NRCSA),** 823 N. 2nd St., P.O. Box 1393, Milwaukee, WI 53201 (☎ **414/278-0631**). The organization maintains language-study programs throughout Europe, including those within about 10 cities throughout Spain. Most popular are the organization's programs in Seville, Salamanca, and Málaga, where language courses last between four and six hours a day. With lodgings within private homes included as part of the price and part of the experience, tuition begins at around $800 for an intensive two-week language course. Courses of six weeks, eight weeks, a semester, and a full academic year are also available. NRCSA warns that the diplomas awarded by these Spanish schools are not always applicable toward an undergraduate degree at every North American university. (Some colleges will, however, accept successful completion of the curriculums as independent studies.) Courses accept participants from 17 to 80.

A clearinghouse for information on at least nine different Spain-based language schools is **Lingua Service Worldwide,** 2 W. 45th St., Suite 500, New York, NY 10036 (☎ toll free **800/394-5327**). Maintaining information about learning programs in 10 languages in 17 countries outside the United States, it represents organizations devoted to the teaching of Spanish and culture in 11 cities of Spain, including one in the Canary Islands. (It also has affiliates in Mexico, Costa Rica, and Ecuador.)

The **Education Office of Spain,** 150 Fifth Ave., Suite 918, New York, NY 10011 (☎ **212/741-5144**), whose funding comes from the Spanish Ministry of Education, offers information on Spanish-language schools within the universities and privately funded schools of Spain. Information is provided free.

One well-recommended Spain-based language school that manages to combine a resort setting with intensive linguistic immersion is the **Escuela de Idiomas Nerja,** Calle Almirange Farrandiz, 73, 2970 Nerja, Málaga (☎ **52/52-16-87**). Offering sessions of between two and 16 weeks, it charges a basic tuition of 39,000 ptas.

($276.90) for two weeks and 45,700 ptas. ($324.50) for three weeks, with the possibility of adding on supplements for one-on-one instruction. Classes are limited to a maximum of 10 students each.

For more information about study abroad, contact the **Council on International Educational Exchange (CIEE),** 205 E. 42nd St., New York, NY 10017 (☎ **212/661-1450**).

HOMESTAYS **The Friendship Force** is a private, nonprofit organization seeking to foster and encourage friendship among the people of the world. Pioneering homestays in the former Soviet Union, and currently in 52 countries, the organization was nominated for the 1992 Nobel Peace Prize. Group visits are arranged to a host country, where participants spend a week or two with a carefully selected family. For more information, contact The Friendship Force, 57 Forsyth St. NW, Suite 900, Atlanta, GA 30303 (☎ **800/688-6777** or **404/522-9490**).

Servas, 11 John St., New York, NY 10038 (☎ **212/267-0252**), is an international nonprofit, nongovernmental, interfaith network of travelers and hosts whose goal is to help promote world peace, goodwill, and understanding. (Its name means "to serve" in Esperanto.) Servas hosts offer travelers hospitality for two days or more. Travelers pay a $55 annual fee and a $25 book deposit after filling out on application and being approved by an interviewer (interviewers are located across the United States). They then receive Servas directories listing the names and addresses of Servas hosts.

HOME EXCHANGES One of the most exciting breakthroughs in modern tourism is the home exchange, whereby the Diego family of Avila can exchange their home with the Brier family's in North Carolina. Sometimes the family automobile is included. Of course, you must be comfortable with the idea of having relative strangers in your home, and you must be content to spend your vacation in one place.

Home exchanges cut costs. You don't pay hotel bills, and you can also save money by shopping in markets and eating in. One potential problem, though, is that you may not get a home in the area you request. For instance, you might want to stay in Galicia but be offered something in the Valencia area instead.

Intervac, U.S., P.O. Box 590504, San Francisco, CA 94159 (☎ toll free **800/756-HOME**), is part of the world's largest home-exchange network. It publishes three catalogs a year, containing listings of more than 9,000 homes in more than 36 countries. Members contact each other directly. The $62 cost buys all three of the company's catalogs, excluding mailing costs, and provides a listing of your home in one of the three catalogs. Seniors over 62 pay $55. Photos cost $11.

The Invented City, 41 Sutter St., Suite 1090, San Francisco, CA 94104 (☎ **415/673-0347,** or toll free **800/788 CITY**), is another international home-exchange agency. Home-exchange listings are published three times a year—in February, May, and November. The $50 membership fee allows you to list your home, with your own description.

Vacation Exchange Club, P.O. Box 650, Key West, FL 33041 (☎ **305/294-1448,** or toll free **800/638-3841**), will send you four directories a year for $60. You'll be listed in one of the directories.

SADDLING UP IN SPAIN Perhaps there is no better way to see the Spanish countryside than on horseback, and several outfits throughout the land offer this experience. Be advised that the terrain can be rugged and that riders often spend seven to eight hours on the trail. Bed and board, in most cases, is arranged.

Almansur Equestrian Trips, c/o José Luis García Saúllo, Dehesa del Roble, Las Ventas de San Julian, 45568 Toledo (☎ **925/43-04-88**), offers outdoor excursions whose duration ranges from four hours to eight full days in the hills of Extremadura. Lodgings are usually at paradores or first-class hotels.

A well-known equestrian center that leads horselovers through the arid Alpujarras highlands of Granada province is **Cabalgar, Rutas Alternativas,** Bubión, Granada (☎ **958/76-31-35.**) The farm is best known for its weekend treks through the scrub-covered hills of southern and central Spain, although tours of between one and nine days are also available.

EARTHWATCHING IN SPAIN Many travelers appreciate the ability to merge a first-hand exposure to the cultures of Spain with a positive contribution to the ecology and cultural preservation of Europe. Founded in 1971, **Earthwatch,** 680 Mount Auburn St., P.O. Box 403, Watertown, MA 02272 (☎ **617-926-8200,** or toll free **800/776-0188**), is a nonprofit organization that recruits ordinary people to work as paying volunteers for university professors on field expeditions throughout the world. Acting as a clearing house, Earthwatch assigns the volunteers to the projects of their choice for two- to three-week programs. Team members may learn to excavate, map, photograph, observe animal behavior, survey flora and fauna, gather data, make collections, conduct oral-history interviews, assist diving operations, lend mechanical and electronic expertise, record natural sounds, and share all other field chores associated with professional expedition research. Volunteers are almost never specialists in any particular field but interested "intergenerational" participants. Note that only 10% of volunteers are students; many come from widely divergent professional careers, and many are senior citizens. Ongoing Spain-centered projects include participation in monitoring the S'Albufera wetlands on the island of Majorca, studying the food sharing and social interactions of dolphins off the Canary Islands, excavating on Majorca a cluster of Bronze Age villages believed to have been occupied for a longer consecutive period than any other prehistoric site in Western Europe, and researching the remains of another Bronze Age Iberian village near Borja in Aragón. To ensure the smooth running of any particular project, Earthwatch encourages all participants to speak reasonable amounts of English, the *lingua franca* of the organization.

Participation in Earthwatch's two- or three-week Spanish projects involves a tax-deductible contribution of between $1,600 and $2,000, depending on the project, plus airfare to Spain. Living arrangements, as well as all meals and drinks at the organization's Saturday-night beer parties, are provided by Earthwatch.

MONASTIC RETREATS Many people like to visit old monasteries and convents when they travel in Europe, and in Spain it's easy to do so, since many of them have been turned into deluxe *paradores.* But if you want a taste of the true monastic life in a tranquil retreat, you can experience that, too. Most monasteries allow men only, but some accept women as well, and a few take women only. You don't need to be Catholic, but you must respect the peaceful monastic atmosphere and a few easy-to-follow rules. Even though you are free at most retreats to come and go as you please, don't use the monastery as you would a hotel or an inn, that is, as a place to leave your gear while you go off sightseeing.

Accommodations include private rooms with baths, good heating, and modern plumbing, plus healthful meals. You take care of your own bedroom during your stay.

Some of the monasteries and convents charge a small fee for room and board; others request a donation. For more information, contact the **National Tourist Office of Spain,** 665 Fifth Ave., New York, NY 10022 (☎ **212/759-8822**).

COOKING SCHOOLS One organization devoted to training Hispanophiles in the fine art of the nation's cuisine is the **Escuela de Cocina Juan Altimiras,** Plaza de la Incarnación, 2, Madrid (☎ **34-1/547-88-27**). Established by Clara María González de Amezúa in 1973, it offers a series of lectures and demonstrations that benefit even professional chefs.

Alternative/Adventure Specialists in the U.K.

Cycling tours are a good way to see Spain at your own pace. **Alternative Travel Group Ltd.,** 69-71 Banbury Rd., Oxford OX2 6PE (☎ **01865/310399**), organizes walking and cycling holidays, plus wine tours in Spain as well as Italy and France through the scenic countryside and medieval towns of these countries.

The **Cyclists' Tourist Club,** 69 Meadrow, Godalming, Surrey GU7 3HS (☎ **01483/417-217**), charges £24 a year for membership; part of the fee provides for information and suggested cycling routes through Spain and dozens of other countries.

The appeal of hill climbing and hiking, especially in areas of scenic or historic interest, is almost universal. **Waymark Holidays,** 44 Windsor Rd., Slough SL1 2EJ (☎ **01753/516-477**) is known for its walking tours in Europe, some lasting as long as two weeks.

Sherpa Expeditions, 131a Heston Rd., Hounslow, Middlesex TW5 0RD (☎ **0181/577-7187**), also offers treks through off-the-beaten-track regions of Europe and other parts of the world.

Cox & Kings, 45 Buckingham Gate, St. James's Court, London SW1E 6AF (☎ **0171/873-5006**) specializes in unusual, and pricey, holidays around the world. It's the oldest travel agency in the United Kingdom, going back to 1758, when it was established to serve as the paymaster and transport director for the British armed forces in India. In Spain, the company offers organized tours to sites of historic or aesthetic interest, pilgrimage-style visits to sites of religious interest, and visits to the country's legendary horse stables, stud farms, and race tracks. The company's staff is noted for its interest in tours of ecological interest.

You may have read a lot about archaeology tours—but most let you look, not dig. A notable and much-respected exception is **Earthwatch Europe** (☎ **01865/311-600**), whose more than 150 programs are designed and supervised by well-qualified academic and ecological authorities. At any time, at least 50 of these programs welcome lay participants in hands-on experience to preserve or document historical, archeological, or ecological phenomena of interest.

If your field of interest is not covered by any of the tours above, call the London headquarters of the Association of Independent Tour Operators (AITO), 133A St. Margaret's Road, Twickenham, Middlesex TW1 1RG (☎ **0181/744-9280**). It may be able to provide you with the names of tour operators that specialize in travel relating to your particular interest.

7 Getting There

By Plane

Flights from the U.S. East Coast take six to seven hours, depending on the season and the prevailing winds.

THE MAJOR AIRLINES

The airline industry is still undergoing upheavals. For last-minute conditions, including even a rundown on carriers flying into Spain, check with a travel agent or the individual airlines. Here is the current status.

From North America

The national carrier of Spain, **Iberia Airlines** (☎ toll free **800/772-4642**), offers more routes into and within Spain than any other airline. It offers daily nonstop service to Madrid from both New York and Miami. From Miami, Iberia takes off for at least six destinations in Mexico and Central America and dozens of destinations throughout South America as well, in cooperation with its air partner, Ladeco, a well-maintained airline based in Chile. Iberia also flies every day to Madrid from Los Angeles, with a brief stop in Miami. Canadians appreciate Iberia's service from Toronto, through Montreal, to Madrid, which is provided between two and three times a week, depending on the season. Also available are attractive rates on fly-drive programs within Iberia and Europe; these offers can substantially reduce the cost of an air ticket and a car rental as separate transactions.

Iberia's fares are cheapest if you reserve an **APEX** (Advanced Payment Excursion) ticket at least 21 days in advance, schedule your return 7 to 30 days after your departure, and leave and return between Monday and Thursday. From June 1 to September 15, round-trip tickets from New York to Madrid cost $778 midweek ($838 if you travel between Friday and Sunday), plus $23 tax. Round-trip flights from Los Angeles to Madrid during the same season cost $1,018 midweek and $1,078 on weekends, plus tax. Fares, which are subject to change, are lower during off-season. Most trans-Atlantic flights are on carefully maintained 747s and DC-10s, and in-flight services reflect a sophisticated interpretation of Spanish traditions, values, and cuisine. A noteworthy cost-cutting option involves Iberia's EuroPass. Available only to passengers who simultaneously arrange for trans-Atlantic passage on Iberia, it allows passage on any flight within Iberia's European or Mediterranean dominion for $250 for the first two flights and $125 for each additional flight. This is especially attractive for passengers wishing to combine trips to Spain with, for example, visits to such far-flung destinations as Cairo, Tel Aviv, Istanbul, Moscow, and Munich. For details, ask Iberia's phone representative.

Iberia's leading competitor is employee-owned **Trans World Airlines** (☎ toll-free **800/221-2000**), whose trans-Atlantic service into Spain has flourished since 1946. TWA operates separate daily nonstop flights to both Barcelona and Madrid from New York's John F. Kennedy Airport. (At press time, TWA was the only carrier offering nonstop service from North America to Barcelona, although other carriers, including Iberia, hinted of their intentions of adding nonstop service to Barcelona, perhaps by the time of your trip.) TWA's cheapest APEX ticket requires a 21-day advance purchase and a delay of between 7 and 30 days before activating the return portion of your flight. Depending on the day of flight (Monday to Thursday is the least expensive), round-trip passages during high season cost from $778 to $838 from JFK to either Madrid or Barcelona. Changes are permitted in departure dates for $150 each. TWA also offers a limited number of youth fares, which must be arranged three days or less before any particular flight. Available only for passengers 12 to 24 who insist on a minimum of restrictions, youth fares cost from $389 to $419 each way, depending on the day of flight. Note that at TWA, as at each of its competitors, youth fares do not represent any noteworthy financial savings over the price of the APEX ticket described above. They do, however, allow a prolonged sojourn in Spain without the penalties sometimes associated with long-term stays abroad, and are therefore ideal for anyone studying or traveling without fixed itineraries. Like its competitors, TWA offers access to its trip-planning service (in this case, the Getaway Vacation desk), and can arrange fly-drive holidays, land packages at Spanish hotels, and escorted motorcoach tours, depending on a client's needs and priorities.

American Airlines (☎ toll free **800/433-7300**) offers daily nonstop service to Madrid from its massive hub in Miami, with excellent connections from there to the rest of the airline's impressive North and South American network. With a 21-day advance purchase and a scheduled return between 7 and 30 days after your departure, American's least expensive round-trip ticket from Miami to Madrid during high season costs $868 for travel Monday to Thursday and $928 for travel Friday to Sunday. Imposing restrictions that are more flexible than in years gone by, American charges a $150 penalty for any changes in itinerary once you've used the outbound portion of your ticket. American offers a wide choice of fly-drive programs and escorted motorcoach tours, and offers a youth fare for travelers 12 to 24. Priced at $525 each way for travel Monday to Thursday and $550 each way for travel Friday to Sunday, it is not substantially less expensive than the APEX fare described above. It does, however, favor last-minute departures, since its restrictions bypass the usual 21-day advance-booking requirements. The youth fare cannot be reserved more than three days before departure in either direction, and it's always issued with an open—that is, unscheduled—return, allowing maximum flexibility for travelers whose plans and projects might change during the course of their trips.

Delta (☎ toll free **800/241-4141**) maintains daily nonstop service from Atlanta (centerpiece of its worldwide network) to Madrid, with ongoing service (and no change of equipment) to Barcelona. The cheapest tickets require 21 days advance booking, a stay abroad of between 7 and 30 days, and cost—depending on the day of the week—between $848 and $908 round trip to either Madrid or Barcelona. (Many travelers used Delta as a cost-conscious means of landing in one city and departing from the other at the end of their trip.) Delta's Dream Vacation department maintains access to fly-drive programs, land packages, and escorted bus tours through the Iberian peninsula.

Another possibility for trans-Atlantic flights to Spain comes from **United Airlines** (☎ toll free **800/538-2929**). Inaugurated in 1991, these routes fly passengers nonstop every day from Washington, D.C.'s John Foster Dulles Airport to Madrid. With a 21-day advance purchase and a stay abroad of between 7 and 30 days, United charges high-season rates of between $828 and $888 round-trip during the midsummer high season, depending on flight dates. United also offers fly-drive programs, escorted motorcoach tours, and youth fares similar to those of its competitors, charging between $414 and $444 each way for travelers 12 to 24. These are bookable only three days or less prior to departure.

Continental Airlines (☎ toll free **800/231-0856**) offers between six and seven nonstop flights per week, depending on the season, to Madrid from Newark, New Jersey, an airport that many New York residents prefer. Round-trip APEX fares during high season, with restrictions very similar to those of the competitors listed above, range from $778 to $838, plus tax, depending on the days of travel. A youth fare, available to travelers 12 to 25 with a valid student I.D. card, costs between $491 and $516 each way, depending on the day of travel, and must be arranged within three days or less of any departing flight. Likewise, Continental offers discounts of 10% on most of its fares to anyone 62 or older, as well as to a senior citizen's companion, regardless of his or her age. Continental also offers regularly scheduled sales promotions that come and go with the seasons. A recent example charged $299 each way between Newark and Madrid, and required reservations and payment before mid-May for flights that then could be taken throughout the summer months. Although that particular promotion ended just before presstime, watch for equivalent bargains from Continental that might be in effect at the time of your trip.

From Great Britain

British Airways (☎ **0171/897-4000** in London) and Iberia (☎ **0171/437-5622** in London) are the two major carriers flying between England and Spain. More than a dozen daily flights, either on BA or Iberia, depart from London's Heathrow and Gatwick airports. The Midlands is served by flights from Manchester and Birmingham, two major airports that can also be used by Scottish travelers flying to Spain. There are about seven flights a day from London to Madrid and back and at least six to Barcelona (trip time: 2–2½ hours). From either the Madrid airport or the Barcelona airport, you can tap into Iberia's domestic network—flying, for example, to Seville or the Costa del Sol (centered at the Málaga airport). The best air deals on scheduled flights from England are those requiring a Saturday night stopover.

Most vacationing Britons, however, go charter, at least those looking for air flight bargains. Delays are frequent (some may last two whole days and nights) and

Frommer's Smart Traveler: Airfares

1. Shop all the airlines that fly to your destination.
2. Always ask for the lowest-priced fare, not just for a discount fare.
3. Keep calling the airline—the availability of cheap seats changes daily. Airlines would rather sell a seat than have it fly empty. As the departure date nears, additional low-cost seats become available.
4. Ask about frequent-flyer programs when you book a flight.
5. Check bucket shops for last-minute discounts, which may be even greater than their advertised slashed fares.
6. Ask about discounted land arrangements. Sometimes they are cheaper when booked with an air ticket.
7. Ask if standby fares are offered.
8. Fly for free or at a heavy discount as a courier.
9. Look for special promotional fares offered by major carriers or airlines struggling to gain a foothold in the market.

departures are often at inconvenient hours. Booking conditions can also be severe; you should therefore read the fine print carefully and deal only with a reputable travel agent. Stays rarely last a month, and booking must sometimes be made at least a month in advance, although a two-week period is sometimes possible.

Charter flights leave from most British regional airports with a destination in mind (for example, Málaga), bypassing the congestion at the Barcelona and Madrid airports. Figure on saving approximately 10% to 15% on regularly scheduled flight tickets. But check carefully. British Sunday papers are full of charter deals, and a travel agent can always advise what the best values are at the time of your intended departure.

REGULAR FARES If your schedule does not permit you one of the options discussed below, you can opt for a regular fare. Economy class is the cheapest regular fare, followed by business class, and then by first class, the most expensive ticket. In first class, increased amenities are the rule, the food is better, and the seats extend backward into something resembling a bed; drinks are free. You'll also get free drinks and better meals in business class, while in economy class, meals are free but you pay for alcoholic beverages. All three of these fares have one thing in common: You can book them at the last minute and can depart and return when you wish. Of course, you'll pay more for the lack of restrictions.

Most airlines offer a consistently popular APEX (Advance Purchase Excursion) fare that often requires a 14-day advance payment and an obligatory stay of between 7 and 90 days, depending on the carrier. In most cases, this ticket is not completely refundable if you change flight dates or destination, so it pays to ask lots of questions before you book.

OTHER GOOD-VALUE CHOICES Most airlines divide their year roughly into seasonal slots, with the least expensive fares between November 1 and March 14, excluding holidays. The shoulder season (spring and early fall) is only slightly more expensive and includes October, which many veteran tourists consider the ideal time to visit Spain. Summer, of course, is the most expensive time.

Special Promotional Fares Since airlines are deregulated, they offer many promotional fares to Europe. This means that you'll have to have a good travel agent or do a lot of shopping or calling around yourself to learn what's available at the time of your intended trip.

Charter Flights A charter flight is one reserved months in advance for a one-time-only transit to a predetermined destination. For reasons of economy, some travelers choose this option.

Before paying for a charter, check the restrictions on your ticket or contract. You may be asked to purchase a tour package and pay far in advance. You'll pay a stiff penalty (or forfeit the ticket entirely) if you cancel. Charters are sometimes canceled if the tickets don't sell out. In some cases the charter-ticket seller will offer you an insurance policy for your own legitimate cancellation (hospital certificate, death in the family, for example).

There is no way to predict whether a charter or a bucket-shop flight will be cheaper. You'll have to investigate this at the time of your trip.

Among charter-flight operators is **Council Charter**, a subsidiary of the Council on International Educational Exchange, 205 E. 42nd St., New York, NY 10017 (☎ **212/661-0311,** or toll free **800/800-8222**). This outfit can arrange charter seats to most major European cities, including Madrid, on regularly scheduled aircraft.

One of the biggest New York charter operators is *Travac,* 989 Sixth Ave., New York, NY 10018 (☎ **212/563-3303,** or toll free **800/TRAV-800**).

Be warned: Some charter companies have proved unreliable in the past.

Bucket Shops "Bucket shops"—or "consolidators," as they are also called—exist in many shapes and forms. In their purest sense, they act as a clearing house for blocks of tickets that airlines discount and consign during normally slow periods of air travel. Charter operators and bucket shops used to perform separate functions, but today many perform both functions.

Ticket prices vary, sometimes going for as much as 35% off full fare. Terms of payment can be anywhere from 45 days before departure to the last minute.

Bucket shops abound from coast to coast, but just to get you started, here are some recommendations. (Look also for ads in your local newspaper's travel section.)

In New York, try **TFI Tours International,** 34 W. 32nd St., 12th Floor, New York, NY 10001 (☎ **212/736-1140** in New York State, or toll free **800/745-8000** elsewhere in the U.S.).

In the Middle West, explore the possibilities of **Travel Avenue**, 10 S. Riverside Plaza, Suite 1404, Chicago, IL 60606 (☎ toll free **800/333-3335**), a national agency whose headquarters are here. Its tickets are often cheaper than those sold by most shops, and it charges the customer only a $25 fee on international tickets, rather than taking the usual $10 commission from an airline. Travel Avenue rebates most of that back to the customers—hence the lower fares.

In New England, a possibility is **TMI** (Travel Management International), 39 JFK St. (Harvard Square), 3rd Floor, Cambridge, MA 02138 (☎ toll free **800/245-3672**). It offers a variety of discounts, including youth fares and student fares, as well as access to other kinds of air-related discounts. Its destinations include Madrid.

One of the biggest U.S. consolidators is **Travac,** 989 Sixth Ave., New York, NY 10018 (☎ **212/563-3303** or toll free **800/TRAV-800**). It offers discounted seats from points throughout the United States to most cities in Europe, including Madrid, on TWA, United, Delta, and other major airlines.

UniTravel, 1177 N. Warson Rd., St. Louis, MO 63132 (☎ toll free **800/325-2222**), offers tickets to Madrid and elsewhere in Europe at prices that may be lower than what airlines charge if you order tickets directly from them. UniTravel is best suited to providing discounts for passengers who want to get to Europe on short notice.

A final option, suitable for clients with flexible travel plans, is available through **Airhitch,** 2790 Broadway, Suite 100, New York, NY 10025 (☎ toll free **800/326-2009**). You let Airhitch know which five consecutive days you're available to fly to Europe, and Airhitch agrees to fly you there within those five days. It arranges for departures from the East Coast or West Coast, the Midwest, and the Southeast and tries, but cannot guarantee, to fly you from and to the cities of your choice.

Standbys A favorite with spontaneous travelers who have absolutely no scheduled demands on their time, a standby fare leaves them dependent on the whims of fortune—and hoping that a seat will remain open at the last minute. Not all airlines offer standbys.

Going as a Courier This cost-cutting technique has lots of restrictions, and tickets may be hard to come by; so it's not for everybody. Basically, you travel as both an airline passenger and a courier. Couriers are hired by overnight air-freight firms hoping to skirt the often tedious Customs hassles and delays that face regular cargo on the other end. With a courier, the checked freight sails through Customs just as quickly as the passenger's luggage. Don't worry—the courier service is absolutely legal; you won't be asked to haul in illegal drugs, for example. For performing this service, the courier gets a great discount on airfare and sometimes even flies for free.

You're allowed one piece of carry-on luggage only (your usual baggage allowance is used by the courier firm to transport its cargo). As a courier, you don't actually handle the merchandise you're "transporting" to Europe; you just carry a manifest to present to Customs. Upon your arrival, an employee of the courier service will reclaim the company's cargo.

Incidentally, you fly alone, so don't plan to travel with anybody. A friend may be able to arrange a flight as a courier on a consecutive day, but don't count on it. Most courier services operate from Los Angeles or New York, but some operate out of other cities, such as Chicago or Miami.

Courier services are often listed in the *Yellow Pages* or in advertisements in travel sections or newspapers. One such firm is **Halbart Express,** 147–05 176th St., Jamaica, NY 11434 (☎ **718/656-8189** from 10am to 3pm daily). Another is **Now Voyager,** 74 Varick St., Suite 307, New York, NY 10013 (☎ **212/431-1616**). Call daily to speak with someone from 10am to 6pm; at other times you'll get a recorded message.

The **International Association of Air Travel Couriers,** P.O. Box 1349, Lake Worth, FL 33460 (☎ **407/582-8320**), for an annual membership of $35, will send you six issues of its newsletter, "Shoestring Traveler" and about half a dozen issues of "Air Courier Bulletin," a directory of air-courier bargains around the world.

The fee also includes access to the association's 24-hour FAX-ON-DEMAND update of last-minute courier flights available for people willing to travel on short notice. A typical recent offering was a $159 round-trip airfare from the United States to Madrid. Most last-minute flights go out the same day in which they're posted, so you have to have your bag packed.

Rebators To confuse the situation even more, rebators also compete in the low-cost airfare market. These outfits pass along to the passenger part of their commission, although many of them assess a fee for their services. Most rebators offer discounts that range from 10% to 25% (but this could vary from place to place), plus a $25 handling charge. They're not the same as travel agents, although they sometimes offer similar services, including discounted land arrangements and car rentals.

Two rebaters are *Travel Avenue*, 641 W. Lake St., Suite 201, Chicago, IL 60606-3691 (☎ **312/876-6866,** or toll free **800/333-3335**), and *The Smart Traveller*, 3111 SW 27th Ave. (P.O. Box 330010), Miami, FL 33133 (☎ **305/448-3338,** or toll free **800/448-3338**). The Smart Traveller also offers discount tours, hotel packages, and fly-drive packages.

Travel Clubs Another possibility for low-cost air travel is the travel club, which supplies an unsold inventory of tickets offering discounts of 20% to 60%.

After you pay an annual fee, you're given a "hotline" number to call in order to find out what discounts are available. Many discounts become available several days, or sometimes as much as a month, before departure. So you have to be fairly flexible.

Some of the best travel clubs are the following:

Discount Travel International, Ives Building, 114 Forrest Ave., Suite 203, Narberth, PA 19072 (☎ **215/668-7184**), which charges an annual membership of $45.

Moment's Notice, 425 Madison Ave., New York, NY 10017 (☎ **212/486-0500**), which has a 24-hour hotline and charges a yearly fee of $45 per family.

Sears Discount Travel Club, 3033 South Parker Rd., Suite 1000, Aurora, CO 80014 (☎ toll free **800/255-1487**), which offers members, for $49, a catalog (issued quarterly) maps, discounts at select hotels, and a 5% cash bonus on purchases.

Encore Travel Club, 4501 Forbes Blvd., Lanham, MD 20706 (☎ toll free **800/638-8976**), which charges $49 a year for membership and offers 50% discounts at recognized hotels, sometimes during off-peak periods; it also offers substantial discounts on airfare, cruises, and car rentals through its volume-purchase plans. Membership includes a travel package outlining the company's many services, and use of a toll-free telephone number for advice and information.

A Note for British Travelers

A regular fare from the United Kingdom to Spain is considered extremely high, so savvy Britons usually call a travel agent for a "deal"—either a charter flight or some special air-travel promotion. Such a deal is always available, because of great interest in Spain as a tourist destination. If one is not possible for you, then you may find that an APEX (Advance Payment Excursion) ticket is the best way to keep costs trimmed. An APEX ticket must be reserved, of course, in advance. An APEX ticket, on the other hand, offers a discount without the usual booking restrictions. You might also ask the airlines about a "Eurobudget ticket," which comes with restrictions or length-of-stay requirements.

British newspapers are always full of classified advertisements touting "slashed" fares to Spain. A good source is *Time Out*, a magazine published in London. London's *Evening Standard* has a daily travel section, and the Sunday editions of almost any newspaper will run many ads. Recommended companies include **Trailfinders** (☎ **0171/937-5400** in London) and **Avro Tours** (☎ **0181/543-0000** in London), which operate charters.

In London, there are many bucket shops, around Victoria Station and Earls Court, that offer cheap fares. Make sure that the company you deal with is a member of the IATA, ABTA, or ATOL. These umbrella organizations will help you out if anything goes wrong.

CEEFAX, a British television information service, runs details of package holidays and flights to Europe and beyond. Just switch to your CEEFAX channel and you'll find travel information.

Make sure you understand the bottom line on any special deal you purchase. Ask whether all surcharges, including airport taxes and other hidden costs, are cited before committing yourself to purchase. Upon investigation, you may find that some of these "deals" are not as attractive as advertised. Also, make sure you understand what the penalties are if you're forced to cancel at the last minute.

By Train

If you're already in Europe, you may want to go to Spain by train, especially if you have a Eurailpass. Even without a pass, you'll find that the cost of a train ticket is moderate, depending on where you are. Rail passengers who visit from Britain or France should make couchette and sleeper reservations as far in advance as possible, especially during the peak summer season.

Since Spain's rail tracks are of a wider gauge than those used for French trains (except for the TALGO and Trans-Europe-Express trains), you'll probably have to change trains at the border unless you're on an express train (see below). For long journeys on Spanish rails, seat and sleeper reservations are mandatory.

The most comfortable and the fastest trains in Spain are the TER, TALGO, and Electrotren. However, you pay a supplement to ride on these fast trains. Both first- and second-class fares are sold on Spanish trains. Tickets can be purchased in either the United States or Canada at the nearest office of FrenchRail Inc. or from any reputable travel agent. Confirmation of your reservation will take about a week.

If you want your car carried, you must travel Auto-Expreso in Spain. This type of auto transport can be booked only through travel agents or rail offices once you arrive in Europe.

To go from London to Spain by rail, you'll need to change not only the train but also the rail terminus in Paris. In Paris, it's worth the extra bucks to purchase a TALGO express or a "Puerta del Sol" express—that way, you can avoid having to change trains once again at the Spanish border. Trip time from London to Paris is about six hours; from Paris to Madrid, about 15 hours or so, which includes two hours spent in Paris just changing trains and stations. Many different rail passes are available in the United Kingdom for travel in Europe. Stop in at the **International Rail Centre,** Victoria Station, London SW1V 1JY (☎ **0171/834-2345**), or **Wasteels,** 121 Wilton Rd., London SW1V 1JZ (☎ **0171/834-7066**). Either place can help you find the best option for the trip you're planning.

By Bus

Bus travel to Spain is possible but not popular—it's slow. Coach services do operate regularly from major capitals of Western Europe, however, heading for Spain, usually Madrid or Barcelona.

The busiest routes are from London and are run by **Eurolines Limited,** 23 Crawley Rd., Luton LU1 1HX in Bedfordshire (☎ **01582/404511**). The journey from London's Victoria Station to Madrid is provided by two services: Service 180, an express from Victoria Station to Madrid, departs from London daily at 9pm and arrives in Madrid the following day at 9:30pm; Service 181 leaves London at 9pm on Day 1 and arrives in Madrid at 12:30am on Day 3.

Other bus trips can be arranged from London to Barcelona, Alicante, Benidorm, and Marbella.

Julia Tours of Barcelona (☎ **34-3/490-4000** in Barcelona) operates a coach that departs from London's Victoria Station on Monday, Wednesday, and Friday. It leaves London at 10:30am and gets into Barcelona the following morning at 10:15. An English-speaking staff in Barcelona can make reservations for you and supply more details.

By Car

If you're touring Europe in a rented car, you might, for an added cost, be allowed to drop off your vehicle in a major city such as Madrid or Barcelona.

Motor approaches to Spain are across France on expressways. The most popular border crossing is near Biarritz, but there are 17 other border stations between Spain and France. If you're planning to visit the north or west of Spain (Galicia), the Hendaye-Irún border is the most convenient frontier crossing. If you're going to Barcelona or Catalonia and along the Levante coast (Valencia), take the expressway in France to Toulouse, then the A61 to Narbonne, and then the A9 toward the border crossing at La Junquera. You can also take the RN20, with a border station at Puigcerda.

If you're driving from Britain, make sure you have a cross-Channel reservation, as traffic tends to be very heavy in summer. The major ferry crossings connect Dover and Folkestone with Dunkirk. Newhaven is connected with Dieppe, and the British city of Portsmouth with Roscoff. One of the fastest crossings is by Hovercraft from Dover to Boulogne or Calais. It costs more than the ferry, but it takes only about half an hour.

As of 1994, however, you can take the "Chunnel," the underwater Channel Tunnel linking Britain (Folkestone) and France (Calais) by road and rail—a great engineering feat that was first envisioned by Napoleon way back in 1802. Travel time between the English and French highway systems is about one hour.

Package Tours

Some people prefer that a tour operator take care of all their travel arrangements. There are many such companies, each offering transportation to and within Spain, prearranged hotel space, and such extras as a bilingual tour guide and lectures. Many of these tours to Spain include excursions to Morocco or Portugal.

There are many different tour operators eager for a share of your business, but one of the most unusual is **Abercrombie & Kent International, Inc.,** 1520 Kensington Rd., Oak Brook, IL 60521 (☎ **708/954-2944,** or toll free **800/323-7308**), a Chicago-based company established some 30 years ago. Known as a specialist in glamorous tours around the world, it offers deluxe 7-, 12-, and 18-day tours of the Iberian Peninsula by train. Despite all the extras that are included, the tours cost less than any personally arranged tours with equivalent facilities and services.

Abercrombie & Kent's "Great Spain & Portugal Express" tour is a rail trip through the tourist gems of Spain and its historic neighbor, Portugal. Tour participants spend their nights in some of the most elegant *paradores* of Spain. (Run by the government and chosen for their historic and/or cultural interest, these hostelries include some of the most famous castles and medieval monasteries.) Tours depart in May and October; the cost is from $2,570 per person, double occupancy, with single supplements from $420 per person.

American Express Vacations, 300 Pinnacle Way, Norcross, GA 30071 (☎ **404/368-5100,** or toll free **800/241-1700**), offers some of the most comprehensive programs available to Spain, including Madrid as the major stopover.

Sun Holidays, 26 Sixth St., Suite 603, Stamford, CT 06905 (☎ **203/323-1166** or toll free **800/678-4787**), has been specializing in extended vacations for senior citizens since 1980. The company regularly features fully escorted motorcoach tours of Spain and Portugal and pays special attention to retired Americans. Its Florida office is at 7280 W. Palmetto Park Rd., Suite 301, Boca Raton, FL 33433 (☎ **407/243-2057** or toll free **800/243-2057**).

As noted in the section on airlines above, virtually every airline flying across the Atlantic directly to Spain can offer some kind of fly-drive program whereby rental cars are discounted if airfare to Spain is arranged simultaneously. A recommendable company is **Kemwel Car Rental,** 106 Calvert St., Harrison, NY 10528-3199 (☎ **914/835-5555** or toll free **800/678-0678**). As of press time, if you buy a round-trip ticket to Spain from Iberia Airlines, you'll receive a three-day free use of a small rental car (an Opel Corsa) that otherwise would rent for around $59 a day. Included are unlimited mileage, all taxes, and a collision-damage waiver. There are no hidden extras—you pay only for the gasoline you use. The offer is based on at least two passengers, traveling together; single travelers pay a supplement of $35. For additional information, you call Kemwel or **Iberia Airlines** (☎ toll free **800/772-4642**). In shopping around for fly-drives, don't overlook the package deals and options offered by other airlines, such as Delta, American, and Continental.

Welcome Tours Hispanidad, 99 Tulip Ave., Floral Park, NY 11001 (☎ **516/488-4700,** or toll free **800/274-4400**), offers a number of attractive features on its tours. These include car rentals, accommodations at paradores, prepackaged and independent travel options, and "stay-put" land-and-air vacations at resort areas. It offers escorted motorcoach tours as well. Its fly-drive program—called "A la Carte"—allows travel to anywhere in Spain for those wishing to make their own itineraries. Compact budget cars are included in the program. Hotels or apartments can be arranged along the Costa del Sol.

8 Getting Around

By Plane

Three fiscally interconnected airlines operate within Spain: the well-recommended **Iberia** and its smaller cousins, **Aviaco** and **Binter Air.** (For reservations on any of these within the United States, call toll free **800/772-4642.**) By European standards, domestic flights within Spain are relatively inexpensive, and considering the vast distances within the country, flying between distant points sometimes makes sense.

If you plan to travel to a number of cities and regions, Iberia's **"Visit Spain"** ticket, priced between $249 and $299, depending on the season, makes flying even more economical. Sold only in conjunction with a transatlantic ticket and valid for any airport within Spain and the Balearic Islands, it requires that passengers identify in advance up to four different cities that they want to visit and the order of these stops. Restrictions forbid flying immediately back to the city of departure, instead encouraging far-flung visits to widely scattered regions of the peninsula. Only one change within the preset itinerary is permitted once the ticket is issued. The dates and departure times of the actual flights, however, can be determined or changed without penalty once you arrive in Spain. Clients wishing to add any point within the Canary Islands to their itinerary pay an additional surcharge of $50. Also, passengers who want to exceed the predesignated number of stops (four) that are included within the basic ticket can add additional cities to their itineraries for $50 each. Children under 2 travel for 10% of the adult fare, and children 2 to 11 travel for 50% of the adult fare. The ticket is valid for up to 60 days after your initial trans-Atlantic arrival in Spain.

By Train

If you plan to travel a great deal on the European railroads, it's worth securing a copy of the *Thomas Cook European Timetable of European Passenger Railroads.* It's available exclusively in North America from **Forsyth Travel Library,** P.O. Box 2975, Shawnee Mission, KS 66201 (☎ toll free **800/FORSYTH**), at a cost of $24.95, plus $4 postage priority airmail in the United States or plus $5 (U.S.) for shipments to Canada.

The most economical way to travel in Spain is on the **Spanish State Railways (RENFE).** Most main long-distance connections are served with night express trains having first- and second-class seats as well as beds and bunks. There are also comfortable high-speed daytime trains of the TALGO, TER, Corail, and Electrotren types. There is a general fare for these trains; bunks, beds, and certain superior-quality trains cost extra. Nevertheless, the Spanish railway is one of the most economical in Europe, so that in most cases this is the best way to go.

Direct trains connect Madrid with Paris and Lisbon, and Barcelona with Paris and Geneva; and international connections are easily made on the frontiers, at Valencia de Alcantara–Marvâo (Portugal), Irún-Hendaye, and Port Bou–Cerbère (France). There is also a direct express from Algeciras to Hendaye.

RAIL PASSES Spain Flexipass RENFE, the national railways of Spain, offers a discounted rail pass. Spain is crisscrossed with a detailed network of rail lines, connecting most of its large and medium-sized cities into a coherent whole. Hundreds of trains depart every day for points around the country, including the fast TALGO and the more recent AVE trains, which reduce rail time between Madrid and Seville to only 2[1]/2 hours.

Flexipasses are usually chosen by passengers who prefer to stop and savor the cultural riches of Spain's cities for several days between train rides. Flexipasses permit a predesignated number of travel days within a predetermined time block—for example, three or five days in a predesignated block of one month or 10 days in two months. A Spain Flexipass granting 3 travel days in one month costs $185 in first class, $125 in second class; 5 days in one month, $265 in first class, $225 in second class; and 10 days in one month, $470 in first class, $345 in second class.

You must buy these passes in the United States prior to your departure. For more information, consult a travel agent or **Rail Europe, Inc.** (☎ toll free **800/4- EURAIL**).

Eurailpass Many in-the-know travelers take advantage of the great travel bargain known as the Eurailpass, which permits unlimited first-class travel in any country in Western Europe, except the British Isles (good in Ireland). The Eurailpass also entitles you to discounts on some bus and steamship lines. Passes are available for 15 days or as long as three months and are strictly nontransferable.

The pass is sold only in North America. Vacationers in Europe can purchase a 15-day Eurailpass for $498; a 21-day pass costs $648; a one-month pass costs $798; a two-month pass costs $1,098; and a three-month pass costs $1,398. Children under 4 travel free, provided they don't occupy a seat of their own (otherwise, they're charged half fare); children 4 to 12 pay half fare. If you're under 26, you can purchase a **Eurail Youthpass,** which entitles you to unlimited second-class travel for 15 days at $398, for one month at $578, and for two months at $768.

The **Eurail Saverpass** provides discounted 15-day travel for groups of three people traveling continuously together between April and September or two people between October and March. The price of a Saverpass, valid all over Europe and good for first class only, is $430 for 15 days, $550 for 21 days, and $678 for one month.

The **Eurail Flexipass** allows passengers to visit Europe with more flexibility. It is valid in first class and offers the same privileges as the Eurailpass. However, it provides a number of individual travel days that can be used over a much longer period of consecutive days. That makes it possible to stay in one city and yet not lose a single day of travel. The pass entitles you, within a two-month period, to 5 days of travel for $348, 10 days of travel for $560, and 15 days of travel for $740.

With similar qualifications and restrictions, travelers under 26 can purchase a **Eurail Youth Flexipass.** It allows, within a two-month period, 5 days of travel for $255, 10 days of travel for $398, and 15 days of travel for $540.

VINTAGE TRAIN TRAVEL **Al Andalus Expreso** (or simply Al Andalus) is a restored vintage train whose itineraries include some of the most historic destinations in Andalusia.

Accommodations retain the atmosphere and service of the first three decades of this century. The passenger and dining cars are filled with panels of inlaid marquetry, hardwoods, and brass fitting and etched glass that would be found in the Edwardian parlor of a private mansion; beneath the antique veneers, an array of state-of-the-art engineering maintains comfortably high speeds. The train offers fine dining and such amenities as individual showers on wheels.

The Al Andalus consists of 13 carriages, manufactured in Britain, Spain, or France between 1929 and 1930 and collected and restored by railway historians at the Spanish Railway Authority (RENFE). The wagons include two restaurant cars, a games and lounge car, a bar car where live piano music and evening flamenco dances often are presented, five sleeping carriages (one of which once transported the King of England from Calais to the French Riviera), and two shower cars. All carriages (except the shower cars) contain air conditioning and heating.

The cost of accommodations on the Al Andalus is $3,815 for a standard double cabin, $4,468 for a deluxe cabin, $2,215 for a standard single cabin, $5,045 for a double suite, and $2,793 for a single suite.

For reservations, brochures, and additional information, contact **Marketing Ahead,** 433 Fifth Ave., New York, NY 10016 (☎ **212/686-9213**).

By Bus

Bus service in Spain is extensive, low-priced, and comfortable enough for short distances. You'll rarely encounter a bus terminal in Spain. The "station" might be a café, a bar, the street in front of a hotel, or simply a spot at an intersection.

A bus may be the cheapest mode of transportation, but it's not really feasible for distances of more than 100 miles. On long hauls, buses are slow and often uncomfortable. Another major drawback might be a lack of toilet facilities, although rest stops are frequent. Bus travel is best for one-day excursions into the environs of a major tourist center, such as Madrid. In the rural areas of the country, bus networks are more extensive than the railway system, as they go virtually everywhere, connecting every village. In general, a bus ride between two major cities in Spain, such as from Córdoba to Seville, is about two-thirds the price of a train ride.

The 44-mile (70km) trip from Madrid to Toledo costs 510 pesetas ($3.60) one way; the 54-mile (87km) trip from Madrid to Segovia costs 690 pesetas ($4.90) one way.

By Car

A car offers the greatest flexibility while you're touring, even if you limit your explorations to the environs of Madrid. Don't, however, plan to drive in Madrid—it's too congested. Theoretically, rush hour is Monday to Saturday from 8 to 10am, 1 to 2pm, and 4 to 6pm. In fact, it is always busy.

CAR RENTALS Many of North America's biggest car-rental companies, including Avis, Budget, and Hertz, maintain offices throughout Spain. Although several Spain-based car-rental companies will try to entice you to their facilities, letters from readers of previous editions have shown that the resolution of billing irregularities and insurance claims tends to be less complicated with the U.S.-based rental firms.

Avis (☎ toll free **800/331-2112**) maintains about a hundred branches throughout Spain, including about 12 in Madrid, eight in Barcelona, a half-dozen in Seville, and four in the provincial city of Murcia. If you reserve and pay your rental by telephone at least two weeks prior to your departure from North America, you'll qualify for the company's best rate, around $217 per week, with unlimited kilometers included, plus 15% tax, for the company's smallest and least-accessorized car, a Ford Fiesta or Renault 5. Any car picked up at any airport in Spain is subject to an additional tax of about $8. At Hertz, as at its major competitors, prepaid rates do not include the taxes, which are settled in separate transactions once you reach the rental kiosk.

For its smallest car (a Ford Fiesta or Peugeot 106), **Hertz** (☎ toll free **800/654-3001**) also requires prepayment; if a renter has access to a fax machine for the receipt of vouchers, only 24 hours advance notification is necessary. Hertz charges around $160 for a week-long rental, plus a value-added tax of 15% and an $8 airport surcharge, both of which are paid separately on Spanish soil.

Also attractive is **Budget Rent-a-Car** (☎ toll free **800/472-3325**), whose least expensive car costs a bit more than those of its competitors ($195 per week for a Fiat Uno plus 15% VAT and, if applicable, the airport surcharge), but its midpriced cars are often less expensive than Avis's or Hertz's. Budget does not charge a supplement if you drop off its car in another Spanish city, such as Barcelona. But although you may drive a Budget car to another country in Europe, you have to return it to one of the company's drop-off points in Spain.

All three companies require that drivers be at least 21 years of age and, in some cases, not older than 72. To be able to rent a car, you must have a passport and a valid driver's license; you must also have a valid credit card or a prepaid voucher (if neither, you'll be asked to make a substantial cash deposit). An international driver's license is not essential, but you might want to present it if you have one; it's available from any North American office of the American Automobile Association (AAA).

Insurance options at each of the companies are complicated, but it's well worth the trouble to ask questions and understand your options before you depart from home. Some companies will include, for a higher net rate, insurance (both liability and collision damage) and taxes into a car's weekly rental fee. A collision-damage waiver costs $10 to $13 extra per day for most small and medium-size cars. Unless you're covered through independent insurance (such as that provided free by some credit-card companies when their cards are used to pay for a rental), it's usually an excellent idea to accept the extra insurance. In some cases, you might also be offered theft insurance to protect the contents of your rented car. This is available for around 250 ptas. ($1.80) extra per day. Know in advance that filing a claim for stolen goods requires lots of paperwork and, in many cases, a police report. Buy this insurance if it's available and if you think it's necessary, but remember that the best way to *protect against theft* is by emptying your car of all luggage when you're not traveling, or at least locking objects in the car's trunk, away from public view.

GASOLINE Gasoline, or petrol, is easily obtainable—but expensive—throughout Spain, with regular fuel being normally used in rented cars. The average Spanish vehicle gets close to 45 miles per gallon. Arrange an itinerary and set up hotels along the way so that you won't have to empty the tank while looking for a room. Try to leave early in the day to avoid the endless traffic lines that form on major arteries of Spanish cities during rush hours. And remember that you'll get far better mileage if you drive at a steady, reasonable speed.

DRIVING RULES Spaniards drive on the right side of the road. Drivers should pass on the left; local drivers sound their horns when passing another car. Autos coming from the right have the right-of-way.

Spain's express highways are known as *autopistas*, which charge a toll, and *autovías*, which don't. To exit in Spain, follow the *salida* sign, except in Catalonia, where the word is *sortida*. On most express highways, the speed limit is 75 m.p.h. (120kmph). On other roads speed limits range from 56 m.p.h. (90kmph) to 62 m.p.h. (100kmph).

Most accidents in Spain are recorded along the notorious Costa del Sol highway, the Carretera de Cádiz.

If you must drive through a Spanish city, try to do so between 3 and 5pm, when many motorists are having a siesta. Never park your car facing oncoming traffic, as that is against the law. If you are fined by the highway patrol (Guardia Civil de Tráfico), you must pay on the spot. Penalties for drinking and driving are very stiff.

MAPS For one of the best overviews of the Iberian Peninsula (Spain and Portugal), obtain a copy of Michelin map no. 990 (for a folding version) or map no. 460 for the same map in a spiral-bound version. For more detailed looks at Spain, Michelin has series of six maps, nos. 441 to 446, showing specific regions, complete with many of their minor roads.

For extensive touring, purchase *Mapas de Carreteras—España y Portugal*, published by Almax Editores and available at most leading bookstores in Spain. This cartological compendium of Spain provides an overview of the country, and includes road and street maps of some of its major cities as well.

The American Automobile Association (☎ toll free **800/222-4357**) publishes a regional map of Spain that's available free to members at most AAA offices in the United States. Also available free to members is a guide of approximately 60 pages, *Motoring in Europe*, that gives helpful information about road signs and speed limits, as well as insurance regulations and other relevant matters. Incidentally, the AAA is associated with the **Real Automóvil Club de España**, José Abascal, 10, Madrid 28003 (**☎ 34-1/447-3200**). This organization will provide helpful information about road conditions in Spain, including tourist and travel data. It will also provide *limited* road service, in an emergency, if your car breaks down.

BREAKDOWNS These can be a serious problem. If you're driving a Spanish-made vehicle, you'll probably be able to find spare parts, if needed. But if you have a foreign-made vehicle, you may be stranded. Have the car checked out before setting out on a long trek through Spain. On a major motorway you'll find strategically placed emergency phone boxes. On secondary roads, call for help by asking the operator to locate the nearest Guardia Civil, which will put you in touch with a garage that can tow you to a repair job.

By Ferry

Travel by ferry is not normally associated with Spain; however, this method of transportation might be convenient at times. For example, the least expensive way to travel from Spain to Morocco is by ferry connections from the Spanish port of Algeciras. Several other boat links also exist between Spain and Tangier and between mainland Spain and the Spanish enclave in Morocco, Ceuta.

There are also good connections by sea from Málaga (capital of the Costa del Sol) to Tangier, as well as to the Canaries. Many boat and ferry links connect mainland Spain and the Balearics (Majorca, Minorca, and Ibiza).

By Hitchhiking

Even though people still do it and it is technically legal, hitchhiking is not tolerated as much as it used to be. And I don't recommend sticking out your thumb in the presence of the Guardia Civil. Most important, hitchhiking is an increasingly unsafe way to travel for both men and women. Take the bus or train—it's safer, easier, and faster.

Suggested Itineraries

The number of places and sights to see in Spain are staggering. It takes at least two months to see all the major cities, and even that calls for some fast moving. Most of us don't have so much time, however, and will want to get the most out of Spain in a shorter time.

The following cities are particularly worth visiting: Barcelona, Córdoba, Granada, Madrid, Salamanca, Santiago de Compostela, Segovia, Seville, and Toledo.

If You Have One Week

Days 1–2 Spend your first two days in Madrid (one to recover from the flight or drive there, another to see the sights, including the Prado).

Day 3 Leave Madrid and drive south to Aranjuez to see its Palacio Real (Royal Palace), then move on to Toledo for the night.

Day 4 Spend a full day and night in Toledo, seeing its cathedral, El Greco paintings, and Alcázar.

Day 5 Leave Toledo and drive north toward Madrid, taking the bypass west to reach El Escorial, Philip II's giant palace. Spend the night there.

Day 6 Proceed west from El Escorial to the walled city of Ávila for an overnight stay.

Day 7 Leave Ávila and drive northeast toward Segovia to visit its Alcázar and Roman aqueduct. Spend the night there before returning to Madrid. (If time remains the next morning, see the Bourbon summer palace at La Granja before returning to Madrid.)

If You Have Two Weeks

Days 1–2 Spend these days as outlined above.

Day 3 While still based in Madrid, take a trip to Toledo, with a possible stopover in the morning at Aranjuez.

Day 4 Make a morning visit to El Escorial and spend the afternoon at Segovia.

Day 5 Drive south to Córdoba, arriving in time to view its world-famous mosque.

Day 6 Leave Córdoba and drive west to Seville, the capital of Andalusia, for an overnight stay.

Day 7 Go south to the sherry town of Jerez, perhaps pressing on to the Atlantic seaport of Cádiz for the night.

Day 8 Drive on to Algeciras, east of Cádiz, with an afternoon visit to Gibraltar.

Day 9 From either port, you could spend a day in Tangier.

Days 10–11 Bask in the sun at one of the resorts, such as Marbella, along the Costa del Sol.

Days 12–13 Drive inland north to Granada and its Alhambra.

Day 14 Return to Madrid or travel to Málaga and catch a flight there.

If You Have Three Weeks

Days 1–3 Fly directly to Barcelona and spend the first day recovering. The next day see some of the many attractions of Barcelona itself. While still based in Barcelona, make a day's pilgrimage to the Monastery of Montserrat, 35 miles northwest.

Day 4 Drive south along the coast, stopping at Sitges to look at its art museums and have lunch, then head for the ancient Roman city of Tarragona for the night.

Day 5 Leave Tarragona and continue south to Valencia, city of El Cid and paella. Stay overnight there.

Day 6 After exploring Valencia in the morning, continue south to Alicante and explore its old quarter and castle before turning in.

Days 7–8 Leave Alicante and head west over mountain roads to Granada for two nights. You'll spend most of the first day driving there. You can see the Alhambra and Generalife on the second day.

Day 9 Drive south from Granada to the Mediterranean, then head west to Nerja, where you can explore its famous caves. Continue on to Málaga or Torremolinos for one night on the Costa del Sol.

Day 10 The next day travel the Costa del Sol highway (be careful—it's the most dangerous in Spain) until you reach Gibraltar or Algeciras. Stay overnight in either place.

Day 11 Take a trip across the channel to Tangier, spending the night there.

Day 12 After the ferry boat delivers you back to Algeciras, head north for an overnight stopover in Jerez to explore its sherry bodegas.

Days 13–14 Continue north for two nights in Seville, the capital of Andalusia and one of the cities in Spain most preferred by visitors.

Day 15 Drive northeast to Córdoba for the night and a visit to its famed mosque.

Day 16 Proceed north from Córdoba all the way to Toledo for an overnight stop.

Day 17 See what sights you didn't see on Day 16, then head north toward Madrid, bypassing that city and going west to El Escorial, Philip's II's giant palace. Stay overnight.

Day 18 Drive west from El Escorial to the walled city of Ávila for another overnight stay.

Day 19 Leave Ávila and drive northeast toward Segovia to visit its Alcázar and Roman aqueduct. Spend the night there.

Days 20–21 From Segovia, visit the nearby Bourbon palace at La Granja before heading to Madrid for two nights. Visit the Prado and take at least two of the walking tours given in Chapter 5 before returning home.

A Themed Itinerary: St. James's Way

Six centuries ago pilgrims used to make the 500-mile trek from the Pyrenees to the shrine of St. James in Santiago de Compostela. The original route, suggested in the 1130 guidebook *Liber Sancti Jacobi*, can't be followed anymore, so here is a modern-day itinerary from the Basque country to Santiago de Compostela.

Day 1 Cross from the Basque country of France and drive into Spain. Before Irún, cut south on C-133 to Pamplona, the capital of the old kingdom of Navarre and the setting of the famous "running of the bulls" (see "Spain Calendar of Events" earlier in this chapter).

Day 2 After an overnight stay in Pamplona, drive northwest to San Sebastián, a Belle Epoque resort just 12 miles (19km) from the French border.

Day 3 After swimming at the Playa de la Concha and taking in the panoramic view from Monte Iqueldo, continue west to Ondárroa—perhaps the most attractive fishing village in Spain—for lunch. In the afternoon continue west to Guernica, subject of Picasso's famous painting. Guernica lies 52 miles (83km) from San Sebastián. After a visit there, drive to Bilbao for the night.

Days 4–5 After a morning visit to Bilbao, drive west to Santander and relax in the afternoon at El Sardinero beach, 1$^{1}/_{2}$ miles (2$^{1}/_{2}$ km) from the capital. Santander is a resort city of summer festivals. The next day, while still based at Santander, drive 18 miles (29km) southwest to visit Santillana del Mar, a medieval village near the site of the prehistoric cave paintings of Altamira. Return to Santander.

Day 6 Drive west from Santander to Oviedo, capital of the province of Asturias and the center of several excursions. Stay overnight there.

Day 7 Drive all the way from Oviedo to Santiago de Compostela, revered as the burial site of St. James, patron saint of Spain. Spend as much time as you have. There are daily flights to Madrid, plus train and bus service; otherwise, it's a 390-mile (625km) drive.

9 Where to Stay

TYPES OF ACCOMMODATIONS From castles converted into hotels to modern high-rise resorts overlooking the Mediterranean, Spain has some of the most varied hotel accommodations in the world—in widely varying price ranges. Accommodations are broadly classified as follows:

One- to Five-Star Hotels The Spanish government rates hotels by stars. A five-star hotel is truly deluxe with deluxe prices; a one-star hotel is the most modest accommodation officially recognized as a hotel by the government. A four-star hotel offers first-class accommodations; a three-star hotel is moderately priced, and a one- or two-star hotel is inexpensively priced. The government grants stars based on such amenities as elevators, private bathrooms, and air conditioning. If a hotel is classified as a *residencia,* it means that it serves breakfast (usually) but no other meals.

Hostals Not to be confused with a hostel for students, a *hostal* is a modest hotel without services, where you can save money by carrying your own bags and the like. You'll know it's a hostal if a small *s* follows the capital letter *H* on the blue plaque by the door. A hostal with three stars is about the equivalent of a hotel with two stars.

Pensions These boarding houses are among the least expensive accommodations, but you're required to take either full board (three meals) or demipension, which is breakfast plus lunch or dinner. The latter is the best option.

Casas Huespedes & Fondas These are the cheapest places in Spain and can be recognized by the light-blue plaques at the door displaying *CH* and *F*, respectively. These are invariably basic but respectable establishments.

Youth Hostels Spain has about 140 hostels (*albergues de juventud*). In theory, those 25 or under have the first chance at securing a bed for the night, but these places are certainly not limited to young people. Some of them are even equipped for the physically disabled. Most hostels impose an 11pm curfew. For information, write **Red Española de Alberques Juveniles,** Calle José Ortega y Gasset, 71, 28006 Madrid (☎ **34-1/401-13-00**).

Paradores The Spanish government in 1926 launched a series of unique accommodations called *paradores* (state-owned inns) that now blanket the country. Deserted castles, monasteries, palaces, and other buildings have been taken over and converted into hotels. Today there are 86 paradores in all, and they're documented in a booklet called "Visiting the Paradores," which is available at Spanish Tourist offices (see "Information, Entry Requirements & Money" at the beginning of this chapter).

At great expense, modern baths, steam heat, and such have been added to these buildings, yet classic Spanish architecture, where it existed, was retained. Some paradores, however, are in modern buildings. Establishments are often furnished with antiques or at least good reproductions and decorative objects typical of the country.

Meals are also served in these government-owned inns. Usually, typical dishes of the region are featured. Paradores are likely to be overcrowded in the summer months, so advance reservations—arranged through any travel agent—are wise.

The government also operates a type of accommodation known as *albergues:* these are comparable to motels, standing along the roadside and usually built in hotel-scarce sections for the convenience of passing motorists. A client is not allowed to stay in an albergue for more than 48 hours, and the management doesn't accept reservations.

In addition, the government runs *refugios,* mostly in remote areas, attracting hunters, fishermen, and mountain climbers. A final state-sponsored establishment is the *hostería,* or specialty restaurant, such as the one at Alcalá de Henares, near Madrid. Hosterias don't offer rooms; decorated in the style of a particular province, they serve regional dishes at reasonable prices.

The central office of paradores is **Paradores de España,** Requena, 3, 28013 Madrid (☎ **34-1/559-0069**). Travel agents in the United States, Canada, and Britain can also arrange reservations.

SEASONAL & OTHER DISCOUNTS In theory, the maximum rate established by a hotel for its rooms is charged for its better rooms during peak season, but in fact the maximum rate is often in effect all year. At some resorts in the slow season, rates may be lowered by the management to attract business. Always ask for a discount if you sense that business is slow.

If there are three or more in your party, ask for an additional bed in your room. In a single an extra bed usually costs 60% or less than the maximum price for the room; in a double it costs 35% or less.

If you're traveling on a budget, don't expect to roll into a city after dark and secure the bargains—they will already have been grabbed by the early birds.

RENT A PLACE If you rent a home or an apartment, you can save money on accommodations and dining and still take daily trips to see the surrounding area.

Apartments in Spain generally fall into two different categories: *hotel apartamientos* and *residencia apartamientos.* The hotel apartments have full facilities, with chamber service, equipped kitchenettes, and often restaurants and bars. The residencia apartments, also called *apartamientos turisticos,* are fully furnished with kitchenettes but lack the facilities of the hotel complexes. They are cheaper, however.

Companies in the United States arranging such rentals include **At Home Abroad,** 405 E. 56th St., Suite 6H, New York, NY 10022 (☎ **212/421-9165**). It offers deluxe apartments on the Costa del Sol (2–4 bedrooms), which are packaged with self-drive car. The estates on which the apartments are located have swimming pools for the residents, and the beach is at the end of the gardens.

A company that has proved helpful to those seeking to rent houses, condominiums, and private apartments in Spain is **Hometours International, Inc.,** 1170 Broadway, New York, NY 10001 (☎ **212/689-0851** or toll free **800/367-4668**). Most of the agency's Spanish inventory lies in Andalusia, which probably attracts more sunseekers from other parts of Europe than any other region of Spain does. For a modest upfront fee of between $2 and $7, depending on the country or region that interests you, Hometours will send you one or several catalogs listing its offerings there. Units are rented for a minimum of seven days; and for the most part, they lie in white-walled villages in such places as the Ronda Sierras of Andalusia, near the cultural and tourist attractions of Málaga, Gibraltar, and Marbella. Hometours also has a variety of offerings in neighboring Portugal and in Britain, France, Italy, and elsewhere in Europe, as well as in Israel.

Another agency willing to match prospective renters with empty real estate in Spain is **ILC (International Lodging Corp.)**, 300 First Ave., Suite 7C, New York, NY 10009 (☎ **221/228-5900**). The company specializes in rentals of privately owned apartments, houses, and villas, for a period of a week or more. It also offers access to suites in well-known hotels for stays of a week or longer, sometimes at rates lower than those that a traveler may have been given when contacting the hotel directly. (This service especially appeals to families with children and to business travelers intending to stay a month or more.) Rental units, regardless of their size, usually contain a kitchen. The company's listings cover accommodations in Madrid, Barcelona, Seville, and Granada, as well as on the Balearic island of Majorca.

Fast Facts: Spain

Business Hours Banks are open Monday to Friday from 9:30am to 2pm and Saturday from 9:30am to 1pm. Most offices are open Monday to Friday from 9am to 5 or 5:30pm; the longtime practice of early closings in summer seems to be dying out. In restaurants, lunch is usually 1 to 4pm and dinner 9 to 11:30pm or midnight. There are no set rules for the opening of bars and taverns, many opening at 8am, others at noon; most stay open until 1:30am or later. Major stores are open Monday to Saturday from 9:30am to 8pm; smaller establishments, however, often take a siesta, doing business from 9:30am to 1:30pm and 4:30 to 8pm. Hours can vary from store to store.

Climate See "When to Go" earlier in this chapter.

Currency See "Information, Entry Requirements & Money" earlier in this chapter.

Customs See "Information, Entry Requirements & Money" earlier in this chapter.

Driving Rules See "Getting Around" earlier in this chapter.

Drugstores To find a drugstore outside normal hours, check the list of stores open for business posted on the door of any drugstore. The law requires drugstores to operate on a rotating system of hours so that there's always a drugstore open somewhere, even Sunday at midnight.

Electricity Most establishments have 220 volts AC. Some older places have 110 and 125 volts. Carry your adapter with you and always check at your hotel desk before plugging in any electrical appliance. It's best to travel with battery-operated equipment.

Embassies/Consulates If you lose your passport, fall seriously ill, get into legal trouble, or have some other serious problem, your embassy or consulate will probably have the means to provide assistance. These are the Madrid addresses and hours: The United States Embassy, Calle Serrano, 75 (☎ **577-40-00;** metro Núñez de Balboa), is open Monday to Friday from 9:30am to 1pm and 2:30 to 5pm. In addition, there's a consular agency, which can provide limited services, in Fuengirola, near Málaga on the Costa del Sol: U.S. Consular Agency, Centrol Comerical Las Rampas, Fase II, 1, locales 12G7/12G8 Fuengirola, Málaga (☎ **952/474-891**). Office hours are 10am to 1pm Monday through Friday. The Canadian Embassy, Núñez de Balboa, 35 (☎ **431-43-00,** metro Velázquez), is open Monday to Friday from 8:30am to 5pm. The United Kingdom Embassy, Fernando el Santo, 16 (☎ **319-02-00,** metro Colón), is open Monday to Friday from 9am to 2pm and 3:30 to 6pm. The Republic of Ireland has an embassy at Claudio Coello, 73 (☎ **576-35-00,** metro Serrano); it's open Monday to Friday from 10am to 2pm. The Australian Embassy, Paseo de la Castellana, 143 (☎ **579-04-28,** metro Cuzco), is open Monday through Thursday 8:30am to 1:30pm and 2:30 to 5pm, Friday 8:30am to 2pm. Citizens of New Zealand should contact the U.K. Embassy for assistance or advice.

Emergencies The national emergency number for Spain (except the Basque country) is **006;** in the Basque country it is **088.**

Etiquette Women often kiss each other once on both cheeks when they meet. Men extend a hand when introduced; if they are good friends, they will often embrace. In general, women (except young moderns) expect men to open doors for them and to rise when they enter a room. The elderly are often treated with great respect and courtesy.

When it comes to lining up for something—say, for a bus—you should step forward or you may find yourself the last one on.

As a foreign guest, avoid all unfavorable references to Spain. Spanish nationalist pride often asserts itself vigorously in the face of criticism by a foreigner.

Film Negra makes both black-and-white and color film. Valca is another popular brand.

Holidays See "When to Go" earlier in this chapter.

Information See "Information, Entry Requirements & Money" earlier in this chapter, as well as individual city chapters for local information offices.

Language The official language in Spain is Spanish (Castilian, actually), the third most widely spoken language in the world after Chinese and English. Although Spanish is spoken in every province of Spain, local tongues reasserted themselves with the restoration of democracy in 1975. After years of being outlawed during the Franco dictatorship, Catalán has returned to Barcelona and Catalonia, even appearing on street signs; this language and its derivatives are also spoken in the Valencia area and in the Balearic Islands, including Majorca. The Basque language is widely spoken in the Basque region (the northeast, near France), which is seeking independence from Spain. Likewise, the Gallego language has enjoyed a renaissance in Galicia (the northwest). Of course, English is spoken in most hotels, restaurants, and shops. The best phrase book is *Spanish for Travellers* by Berlitz; it has a menu supplement and a 12,500-word glossary of both English and Spanish. Another way of communicating, if you don't speak Spanish, is through a visual translator called Quickpoint, which allows you to communicate by pointing at various pictures. This three-panel brochure contains some 400 color illustrations of such everyday items as a pay phone and gasoline. It costs $6; you can order it by calling **703/548-8794** in the United States or by writing to Gaia Communications Inc., Dept. 102, P.O. Box 239, Alexandria, VA 22313-0239.

Laundry In most top hotels, fill out your laundry and dry-cleaning list and present it to your maid or valet. Same-day service usually costs from 25% to 50% more. To save money, go to a Laundromat; your hotel reception desk can advise you of the nearest one. Sometimes these establishments are self-service; others request that you drop off your laundry and pick it up later. See major cities for listings of Laundromats.

Liquor Laws The legal drinking age is 18. Bars, taverns, and cafeterias usually open at 8am, and many serve alcohol until around 1:30am or later. Generally, you can purchase alcoholic beverages in almost any market.

Mail Air-mail letters to the United States and Canada cost 83 pesetas (60¢) up to 15 grams, and letters to Britain or other EU countries cost 45 pesetas (30¢) up to 20 grams; letters within Spain cost 35 pesetas (20¢). Postcards cost the same rate as letters. Allow about a week for delivery to North America, generally less to the United Kingdom; in some cases, letters take two weeks to reach North America. Rates change frequently, so check at your hotel before mailing anything. As for surface mail, forget it. Chances are that you'll be home before your letter arrives.

Maps See "By Car" under Section 8, "Getting Around," earlier in this chapter. See Chapters 3 and 12 and for specific recommendations of stores in Madrid and Barcelona. If you'd like a map before your trip to plan your itinerary, you can obtain one from Rand McNally, Michelin, or the AAA. These are sold at bookstores all over America. Rand McNally has retail stores at 150 E. 52nd St., New York, NY 10022 (☎ **212/758-7488**); 595 Market St., San Francisco, CA 94105 (☎ **415/777-3131**) and at many other outlets. The U.S. headquarters of Michelin is at P.O. Box 3305, Spartanburg, SC 29304 (☎ **803/599-0850,** or toll free **800/423-0485**).

Newspapers/Magazines Most newsstands along the Gran Vía in Madrid, as well as kiosks at the major hotels, carry the latest edition of the International Herald Tribune or USA Today. Lookout magazine is focused primarily on Spain's Costa del Sol but carries many articles of general interest.

Passports See "Information, Entry Requirements & Money" earlier in this chapter.

Pets It's best to leave them at home. If you don't, you must bring any licenses and proof of vaccinations to your nearest Spanish consulate before you leave. Normally, pets aren't welcome in public places; certain hotels will accept them, however. But these arrangements should be made in advance. Don't forget to check quarantine regulations affecting your animal upon your return. Guide dogs, however, are always excluded from such rigid rules. For the pamphlet "Pets," write the U.S. Customs Service, P.O. Box 7407, Washington, DC 20044.

Police The national emergency number is **006** throughout Spain, except in the Basque country, where it is **088**.

Radio/TV Every television network broadcasts in Spanish, but on radio you can listen to the voice of the American Armed Forces—news, music, sports, and local weather.

Restrooms In Spain they're called aseos and servicios and labeled caballeros for men and damas or señoras for women. If you can't find any, go into a bar, but you should order something.

Safety Whenever you're traveling in an unfamiliar city or country, stay alert. Be aware of your immediate surroundings. Wear a moneybelt and keep a close eye on your possessions. Be particularly careful with cameras, purses, and wallets—all favorite targets for thieves and pickpockets. Pickpockets and purse snatchers flourish throughout Spain. They're particularly active in the large cities, such as Madrid and Barcelona, but also in smaller tourist attractions, such as Sevilla (actually throughout Andalusia, which takes in the Costa del Sol). In the wake of so many robberies, visitors have taken to leaving their passports at the hotel. But here's a Catch-22 situation: Identification checks are common by Spanish police, who are actually cracking down on illegal immigrants. Policemen or plainclothes agents can stop you at any time of the day or night and demand to see your passport. You can be arrested, as many visitors are, when you can't produce yours. Carry your passport with you but carefully conceal it on your body, perhaps in a safety belt.

Taxes The internal sales tax (known in Spain as IVA) ranges between 6.12% and 33%, depending on the commodity being sold. Food, wine, and basic necessities are taxed at 6.12%; most goods and services (including car rentals) at 13%; luxury items (jewelry, all tobacco, imported liquors) at 33%; and luxury hotels at 12%, with budget hotels at 6%.

Telephones If you don't speak Spanish, you'll find it easier to telephone from your hotel, but remember that this is often very expensive because hotels impose a surcharge on every operater-assisted call. In some cases this can be as high as 40% or more. On the street, phone booths (known as cabinas), have dialing instructions in English; you can make locals calls by inserting three five-peseta (5¢) coins for three minutes. In Spain many of the smaller establishments, especially bars, discos, and a few low-cost restaurants, don't have phones. Further, many summer-only bars and discos secure a phone for the season only, then get a new number the next season. Many sightseeing attractions, such as small churches or even minor museums, have no staff to receive inquiries from the public.

Time Spain is six hours ahead of Eastern Standard Time in the United States. Daylight Saving Time is in effect from the last Sunday in March to the last Sunday in September.

Tipping Don't overtip. The government requires restaurants and hotels to include their service charges—usually 15% of the bill. However, that doesn't mean you should skip out of a place without dispensing some extra pesetas. The following are some guidelines:

Your hotel porter should get 50 pesetas (40¢) per bag and never less than 100 pesetas (70¢), even if you have only one suitcase. Maids should be given 100 pesetas (70¢) per day, more if you're generous. Tip doormen 100 pesetas (70¢) for assisting with baggage and 25 pesetas (20¢) for calling a cab. In top-ranking hotels the concierge will often submit a separate bill, showing charges for newspapers and other services; if he or she has been particularly helpful, tip extra.

For cab drivers, add about 10% to 15% to the fare as shown on the meter. However, if the driver personally unloads or loads your luggage, add 25 pesetas (20¢) per bag.

At airports, such as Barajas in Madrid and major terminals, the porter who handles your luggage will present you with a fixed-charge bill, usually 75 to 100 pesetas (50¢–70¢) per bag.

In both restaurants and nightclubs, a 15% service charge is added to the bill. To that, add another 3% to 5% tip, depending on the quality of the service. Waiters in deluxe restaurants and nightclubs are accustomed to the extra 5%, which means you'll end up tipping 20%. If that seems excessive, you must remember that the initial service charge reflected in the fixed price is distributed among all the help.

Barbers and hairdressers expect a 10% to 15% tip. Tour guides expect 200 pesetas ($1.40), although a tip is not mandatory. Theater and bullfight ushers get from 25 to 50 pesetas (20¢ to 40¢).

Tourist Offices See "Information, Entry Requirements & Money" earlier in this chapter. See also specific city chapters.

Visas See "Information, Entry Requirements & Money" earlier in this chapter.

Water See "Food & Drink" in Chapter 1.

3

Getting to Know Madrid

After years of stagnation and repression under Franco, Madrid burst into bloom under King Juan Carlos. The city used to be a place where travelers went with a sense of duty and gloom, largely to see the Prado. That's all changed in the Madrid of today, since the creative explosion—*la movida*—that followed Franco's death in 1975. The city is now sought out as a destination unto itself—a bright, vibrant place in which to have fun.

The social life of Madrid, even more than its organized cultural offering, is intriguing to visitors. It's literally a street scene, with locals enjoying the *terrazas* (open-air cafés) and *tascas* (taverns) and whole families dining at local inns where the tables spill out onto the sidewalks.

Nights are long in Madrid. Long after Londoners have gone to bed, Madrileños are just getting started in the cafés, jazz joints, dance clubs, and certainly the terrazas, which often don't close until dawn. Many club owners will tell you that the crowd doesn't really start pouring in until 2am.

The European Union designated Madrid as the Cultural Capital of Europe for the year 1992, a distinction awarded largely because of *la movida.*

Awards come and go, but the cultural awakening continues, as Madrid continues to maintain a *joie de vivre* in spite of economic difficulties. Profound changes in the capital have occurred in film, music, and fashion, and most definitely painting. Madrid is considered one of the most important centers of art in the world.

Home of the Prado, the city now has as well the private art collection of Baron Thyssen-Bornemisza and the Reina Sofía Art Center, forming a "golden triangle" of museums. A visit to these three museums alone is a good reason to go to Madrid, but there are, of course, other reasons also, many of which are described in Chapter 4, "Where to Stay and Dine in Madrid," and Chapter 5, "What to See and Do in Madrid."

1 Orientation

Arriving

BY PLANE Barajas, Madrid's international airport, lying nine miles east of the center, has two terminals—one international, the other domestic. A conveyor belt connects the two. For Barajas Airport information, call **305-43-72.**

Air-conditioned yellow airport buses take you from the arrival terminal to the bus depot under the Plaza de Colón. You can also get off at stops along the way, provided that your baggage isn't stored in the hold. The fare is 325 ptas. ($2.30), and the buses leave every 15 minutes, either to or from the airport.

If you go into town by taxi, expect to pay 2,500 ptas. ($17.80) and up, plus surcharges (in either direction), for the trip to the airport and for baggage handling. If you take an unmetered limousine, negotiate the price in advance.

BY TRAIN Madrid has three major railway stations: **Atocha,** Avenida Ciudad de Barcelona (☎ **527-31-60**; metro: Atocha RENFE), for trains to Lísbon, Toledo, Andalusia, and Extremadura; **Chamartín,** in the northern suburbs at Augustín de Foxá (☎ **323-21-21,** metro Chamartín), for trains to and from Barcelona, Asturias, Cantabria, Castilre-León, the Basque country, Aragón, Catalonia, Levante (Valencia), Murcia, and the French frontier; and **Estación Príncipe Pío** or Norte, Po. del Rey 30 (☎ **247-00-00;** metro: Norte), for trains to and from northwest Spain (Salamanca and Galicia).

What's Special About Madrid

Museums

- The Prado, the number-one attraction in Spain.
- Thyssen-Bornemisza Museum, named for the baron who collected old masters, then sold them to Spain.
- Centro de Arte Reina Sofía, a modern-art museum with more than 300 works by Spanish masters (Dalí to Miró) and home to Picasso's powerful *Guernica.*
- Museum of Lazaro Galdiano, filled with old masters, many from the golden age.
- Convento de las Descalzas Reales, a 16th-century royal convent with many art treasures.

An Urban Oasis

- Parque del Retiro, a place to relax in the heart of Madrid.

A Literary Shrine

- Casa de Lope de Vega, home of the Shakespeare of the Spanish-speaking world.

Shopping

- El Rastro, an open-air flea market that's best visited on Sunday morning.
- Mercado Puerta de Toledo, a shopping mall with 150 of Spain's most glamorous names.

Events/Festivals

- The *corrida* (bullfight), a spectacle of death, celebrated in art and literature and also condemned. At the Plaza de Toros.
- Fiesta de Sant Isidro, 10 days of fairs, parades, and bullfights honoring the city's patron saint.

Cool for Kids

- Casa de Campo, a festive funpark filled with amusements.

After Dark

- Flamenco, the incomparable Spanish art form, at dozens of late-night clubs.

Architectural Highlights

- Plaza Mayor, the main square of the old town and quintessential Hapsburg Madrid.
- Palacio Real, Philip V's colossal palace with 2,000 opulent rooms.

Warning: When leaving Madrid or taking an excursion, don't wait to buy your rail ticket or to make a reservation at the train station. There may be no tickets left. Go to the principal office of **RENFE,** Alcalá, 44 (☎ **563-02-02;** metro: Banco de España). The office is open Monday to Friday from 9:30am to 8pm.

BY BUS Madrid has at least eight major bus terminals, including the large **Estacíon Sur de Autobuses,** Calle Canarias, 17 (☎ **468-45-11;** metro: Palos de la Frontera). Buses to the environs of Madrid, such as Toledo and Segovia, leave from numerous other stations; it's best to call **580-19-80** for current information about departures.

BY CAR The following are the major highways into Madrid, with information on driving distances to the city:

Highways to Madrid

Route	From	Distance to Madrid
N-I	Irún	315 miles (505km)
N-II	Barcelona	389 miles (622km)
N-III	Valencia	217 miles (347km)
N-IV	Cádiz	388 miles (625km)
N-V	Badajoz	254 miles (409km)
N-VI	Galicia	374 miles (598km)

Tourist Information

The most convenient tourist office is on the ground floor of the 40-story **Torre de Madrid,** Plaza de España (☎ **91/541-23-25;** Metro: Plaza de España); it's open Monday to Friday from 9am to 7pm and Saturday from 9:30am to 1:30pm. Ask for a street map of the next town on your itinerary, especially if you're driving. The staff here can give you a list of hotels and hostals but cannot recommend any particular establishment.

City Layout

MAIN ARTERIES & SQUARES In modern Spain all roads, rails, and telephone lines lead to Madrid. The capital has outgrown all previous boundaries and is branching out in all directions.

Every new arrival must find the **Gran Vía,** which cuts a winding pathway across the city beginning at **Plaza de España**, where you'll find one of Europe's tallest skyscrapers, the Edificio España. On this principal avenue is the largest concentration of shops, hotels, restaurants, and movie houses in the city. **Calle de Serrano** is a runner-up.

South of the avenue lies **Puerta del Sol.** All road distances within Spain are measured from this square. However, its significance has declined, and today it is a prime hunting ground for pickpockets and purse snatchers. Here **Calle de Alcalá** begins and runs for 2½ miles.

Plaza Mayor is the heart of Old Madrid, an attraction in itself with its mix of French and Georgian architecture. (Again, be wary, especially late at night.) Pedestrians pass under the arches of the huge square onto the narrow streets of the old town, where you can find some of the capital's most intriguing restaurants and tascas. On the colonnaded ground level of the plaza are shops, many selling souvenir hats of turn-of-the-century Spanish sailors or officers in the kaiser's army.

The area south of Plaza Mayor—known as *barrios bajos*—merits exploration. The narrow cobblestone streets are lined with 16th- and 17th-century architecture. Directly south of the plaza is the **Arco de Cuchilleros,** a street packed with markets, restaurants, flamenco clubs, and taverns.

The Gran Vía ends at Calle de Alcalá, and at this juncture lies **Plaza de la Cibeles,** with its fountain to Cybele, the mother of the gods, and what has become known as "the cathedral of post offices." From Cibeles, the wide **Paseo de Recoletos** begins a short run to **Plaza de Colón.** From this latter square rolls the serpentine **Paseo de la Castellana,** flanked by expensive shops, apartment buildings, luxury hotels, and foreign embassies.

Back at Cibeles again: Heading south is **Paseo del Prado,** where you'll find Spain's major attraction, the Museo del Prado, as well as the Jardín Botánica (Botanical Garden). The paseo also leads to the Atocha Railway Station. To the west of the garden lies **Parque del Retiro,** once reserved for royalty, with restaurants, nightclubs, a rose garden, and two lakes.

FINDING AN ADDRESS Madrid is a city of grand boulevards that extend for long distances and cramped meandering streets that seem to follow no plan. Finding an address can sometimes be a problem, primarily because of the way buildings are numbered.

On most streets, the numbering begins on one side and runs consecutively until the end, then it resumes on the other side, going in the opposite direction, rather as a farmer plows a field—up one side, down the other. Thus, no.50 could be opposite no. 250. But there are many exceptions to this system of numbering. That's why it's important that you know the cross street as well as the number of the address you're looking for. To complicate matters further, some addresses don't have a number at all. What they have instead is the designation "s/n," meaning "*sin número*" (without number). For example, the address of the Panteón de Goya (Goya's Tomb) is Glorieta de San Antonio de la Florida, s/n (see Chapter 5, "What to See and Do in Madrid").

NEIGHBORHOODS IN BRIEF Madrid can be divided into three principal districts—Old Madrid, which holds the most tourist interest; Ensanche, the new district, often with the best shops and hotels; and the periphery, which is of little interest to visitors.

Plaza Mayor/Puerta del Sol This is the heart of Old Madrid, often called "the tourist zone." Filled with taverns and bars, it is bounded by Carrera de San Jerónimo, Calle Mayor, Cava de San Miguel, Cava Baja, and Calle de la Cruz. From Plaza Mayor, the Arco de Cuchilleros is filled with Castilian restaurants and taverns; more cuevas lie along the Cava de San Miguel, Cava Alta, and Cava Baja. To the west of this old district is the Manzanares River. Muslim Madrid centers on the present-day Palacio de Oriente and Las Vistillas. What is now Plaza de la Paja was the heart of the city and its main marketplace during the medieval and Christian period. In 1617 Plaza Mayor became the hub of Madrid, and it remains nighttime center of tourist activity, more so than the Puerta del Sol.

The Salamanca Quarter Ever since Madrid's city walls came tumbling down in the 1860s, the district of Salamanca to the north has been a fashionable address. Cutting through it is Calle de Serrano, a street lined with stores and boutiques. The U.S. Embassy is also here.

Gran Vía/Plaza de España Gran Vía is the city's main street, lined with cinemas, department stores, and the headquarters of banks and corporations. It begins at the Plaza de España, with its bronze figures of Don Quixote and his faithful Sancho Pancho.

Argüelles/Moncloa The university area is bounded by Pintor Rosales, Cea Bermûdez, Bravo Murillo, San Bernardo, and Conde Duque. Students haunt its famous ale houses.

Chueca This is an old and decaying area north of the Gran Vía. Its main streets are Hortaleza, Infantas, Barquillo, and San Lucas. It is the center of gay nightlife, with many clubs and cheap restaurants. It can be dangerous at night, however, although more police are evident at night.

Castellana/Recoletos/Paseo del Prado Not a real city district, this is Madrid's north-south axis, its name changing along the way. The Museo del Prado and some of the city's more expensive hotels are found here. Many restaurants and other hotels are located along its side streets. In summer the several open-air terraces are filled with animated crowds. The most famous café is the Gran Café Gijón (see Chapter 4).

STREET MAPS Arm yourself with a good map before setting out. The best is published by **Falk,** and it's available at most newsstands and kiosks in Madrid. Those given away free by tourist offices and hotels aren't adequate, as they don't list the maze of little streets.

2 Getting Around

Getting around Madrid is not easy, because everything is spread out. Even many Madrileño taxi drivers are unfamiliar with their own city once they're off the main boulevards.

BY SUBWAY The metro system is easy to learn. The central converging point is the Puerta del Sol. The fare is 125 ptas. (90¢) for a one-way trip. The metro operates from 6am to 1:30am. Avoid rush hours. For information, call **552-49-00.** You can save money on public transportation by purchasing a 10-trip ticket known as a *bonos*—for the metro it costs 600 ptas. ($4.30).

BY BUS A bus network also services the city and suburbs, with routes clearly shown at each stop on a schematic diagram. Buses are fast and efficient because they travel along special lanes. Both red and yellow buses charge 125 ptas. (90¢) per ride.

For 600 ptas. ($4.30) you can also purchase a 10-trip ticket (but without transfers) for Madrid's bus system. It's sold at **Empresa Municipal de Transportes,** Plaza de la Cibeles (☎ **401-99-00**), where you can also purchase a guide to the bus routes. The office is open daily from 8am to 8:30pm.

BY TAXI Even though cab fares have risen recently, they're still reasonable. When you flag down a taxi, the meter should register 155 ptas. ($1.10); for every kilometer thereafter, the fare increases by 70 ptas. (50¢). A supplement is charged for trips to the railway station or the bullring, as well as on Sundays and holidays. The ride to Barajas Airport carries a 325 pta. ($2.30) surcharge and a 160 pta. ($1.10) supplement from railway stations. In addition, there is a 150 pta. ($1.10) supplement on Sundays and holidays, plus a 150 pta. ($1.10) supplement at night. It's customary to tip at least 10% of the fare.

Warning: Make sure that the meter is turned on when you get into a taxi. Otherwise, some drivers will "assess" the cost of the ride, and their assessment, you can be sure, will involve higher mathematics.

Also, there are unmetered taxis that hire out for the day or the afternoon. These are legitimate, but some drivers will operate as gypsy cabs. Since they're unmetered, they can charge high rates. They are easy to avoid, though—take either a black taxi with horizontal red bands or a white one with diagonal red bands instead.

If you take a taxi outside the city limits, the driver is entitled to charge you twice the rate shown on the meter.

To call a taxi, dial **445-90-08,** or **447-51-80.**

BY CAR Driving is a nightmare and potentially dangerous in congested Madrid. It always feels like rush hour in Madrid (theoretically, rush hours are 8 to 10am, 1 to 2pm, and 4 to 6pm Monday to Saturday). Parking is next to impossible, except in expensive garages. About the only time you can drive around Madrid with a minimum of hassle is in hot August, when thousands of Madrileños (as the city's residents are called) have taken their automobiles and headed for Spain's vacation oases. Save your car rentals (see "Fast Facts: Madrid," below) for one-day excursions from the capital. If you drive into Madrid from another city, ask at your hotel for the nearest garage or parking possibility and leave your vehicle there until you're ready to leave.

BY BICYCLE Ever wonder why you see so few people riding bicycles in Madrid? Those that tried were overcome by the traffic pollution. It's better to walk.

ON FOOT This is the perfect way to see Madrid, especially the ancient narrow streets of the old town. If you're going to another district—and chances are that your hotel will be outside the old town—you can take the bus or Metro. For such a large city, Madrid can be covered amazingly well on foot, because so much of what will interest a visitor lies in various clusters.

Fast Facts: Madrid

American Express For your mail or banking needs, you can go to the American Express office at the corner of Marqués de Cubas and Plaza de las Cortés, 2, across the street from the Palace Hotel (☎ **322-55-00;** Metro: Gran Vía). Open Monday to Friday from 9am to 5:30pm and Saturday from 9am to noon.

Area Code For phone calls within Spain, Madrid's area code is **91.** For calls from North America, the country code is **34** and Madrid's code is **1.**

Babysitters Most major hotels can arrange for babysitters, called *canguros* in Spanish. Usually the concierge keeps a list of reliable nursemaids and will contact them for you, provided that you give adequate notice. Rates vary considerably but are fairly reasonable. Although many babysitters in Madrid speak English, don't count on it.

Bookstores Turner's, Genova 3 & 5 (☎ **319-28-67;** metro: Alonso Martínez), has one of the largest collections of English-language books in the city, as well as a good selection of Spanish CDs. Open Monday through Friday from 10am to 8pm and Saturday from 10am to 2pm.

Car Rentals For more information on renting a car before you leave home, see "Getting Around" in Chapter 2. Should you want to rent one while in Madrid, you'll have several choices. In addition to its office at Barajas Airport (☎ **208-85-32**), Avis has a main office downtown at Gran Vía, 60 (☎ **247-20-48**). Hertz, too, has an office at Barajas Airport (☎ **205-84-52**) and another in the heart of Madrid in the Edificio España, Gran Vía, 88 (☎ **248-58-03**). Budget Rent-a-Car maintains its headquarters at Gran Vía, 49 (☎ **247-20-48**).

Climate See "When to Go" in Chapter 2.

Crime See "Safety," below.

Currency Exchange The currency exchange at Chamartín railway station (metro: Chamartín) is open 24 hours and gives the best rates in the capital. If you exchange money at a bank, ask about the minimum commission charged.

Dentist For an English-speaking dentist, contact the U.S. Embassy, Serrano 75 (☎ **577-40-00**); it maintains a list of dentists who have offered their services to Americans abroad. For dental services, consult also Unidad Médica Anglo-Americana, Conde de Arandá 1 (☎ **435-18-23**), in back of Plaza de Colón. Office hours are Monday to Friday from 9am to 8pm and Saturday from 10am to 2pm, although there is a 24-hour daily answering service.

Doctor For an English-speaking doctor, contact the U.S. Embassy, Serrano 75 (☎ **577-40-00**).

Drugstores For a late-night pharmacy, dial **098** or look in the daily newspaper under "Farmacias de Guardia" to learn what drugstores are open after 8pm. Another way to find out is go to any pharmacy, even if it's closed—it will always post a list of nearby pharmacies that are open late that day. Madrid contains hundreds of pharmacies, but one of the most central is Farmacia Gayoso, Arenal 2 (☎ **521-28-60;** Metro: Puerta del Sol).

Embassies/Consulates See "Fast Facts: Spain" in Chapter 2.

Emergencies The following are telephone numbers to call in an emergency: fire, **080;** police **091;** ambulance **734-2554.**

Eyeglasses Glasses are sold and repaired at several branches of Optica 2000, the most central of which is at El Corte Inglés, Princesa 56 (☎ **541-63-14;** Metro: Callao).

Hairdressers/Barbers A good hairdresser for women or men is Galico, Velázquez 89 (☎ **563-47-63;** metro: Núñez de Balboa); it's open Monday to Saturday from 10am to 6pm. Call for an appointment. For men or women, a fine choice is Jacques Dessange, O'Donnell 9 (☎ **435-32-20**); Metro: Príncipe de Vergara). Open Monday to Saturday from 10am to 6:30pm. All the El Corte Inglés department stores have good barbershops (see "Department Stores" under "Savvy Shopping" in Chapter 5).

Holidays See "When to Go" in Chapter 2.

Hospitals/Clinics Unidad Médica Anglo-Americana, Conde de Arandá 1 (☎ **435-18-23**), is not a hospital but a private outpatient clinic, offering the services of various specialists; Metro: Usera. This is not an emergency clinic, although someone on the staff is always available. The daily hours are 9am to 8pm. For a real medical emergency, call **734-25-54** for an ambulance.

Information See "Tourist Information" earlier in this chapter.

Laundry/Dry Cleaning Try a self-service facility, Lavandería Donoso Cortés, Donoso Cortés 17 (☎ **446-96-90;** Metro: Quevedo). Open Monday to Friday from 9am to 7pm and Saturday from 9am to 1pm. A good dry-cleaning service is provided by El Corte Inglés department store at Calle Preciados 3 (☎ **532-18-00;** Metro: Callas), where the staff speaks English.

Libraries A large selection of American magazines and other reading material is available at Washington Irving Center, Marqués de Villamagna 8 (☎ **435-6922;** Metro: Rubén Darío). Open Monday to Friday from 2 to 6pm. The British Cultural Center, Almagro 5 (☎ **337-35-00;** metro: Alonso Martínez), also has a large selection of English-language reading material. Hours are Monday through Friday

Madrid Metro

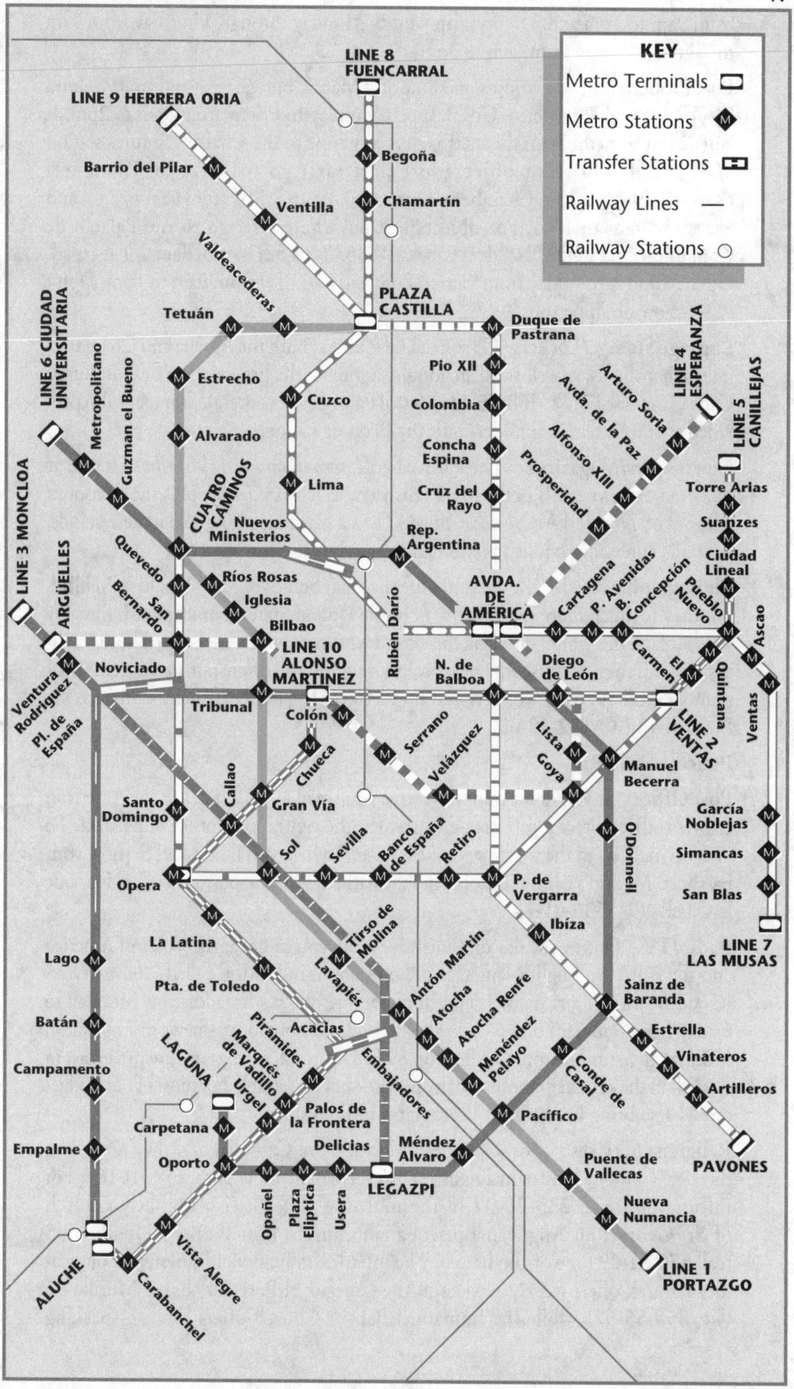

KEY
Metro Terminals
Metro Stations
Transfer Stations
Railway Lines
Railway Stations

LINE 8 FUENCARRAL
LINE 9 HERRERA ORIA
Barrio del Pilar
Begoña
Chamartín
Ventilla
Valdeacederas
Tetuán
PLAZA CASTILLA
Duque de Pastrana
Pio XII
Colombia
Concha Espina
Cruz del Rayo
Estrecho
Alvarado
Cuzco
Lima
LINE 6 CIUDAD UNIVERSITARIA
Metropolitano
Guzman el Bueno
CUATRO CAMINOS
Nuevos Ministerios
Rep. Argentina
LINE 3 MONCLOA
ARGÜELLES
Quevedo
San Bernardo
Ríos Rosas
Iglesia
Bilbao
LINE 10 ALONSO MARTINEZ
Rubén Darío
AVDA. DE AMÉRICA
LINE 4 ESPERANZA
Arturo Soria
Avda. de la Paz
Alfonso XIII
Prosperidad
Cartagena
P. Avenidas
B. Concepción
Pueblo Nuevo
LINE 5 CANILLEJAS
Torre Arias
Suanzes
Ciudad Lineal
Ascao
Ventura Rodríguez
Noviciado
Pl. de España
Tribunal
Colón
N. de Balboa
Diego de León
El Carmen
Quintana
Ventas
LINE 2 VENTAS
Serrano
Velázquez
Lista
Goya
Manuel Becerra
Chueca
Callao
Gran Vía
Santo Domingo
Sol
Sevilla
Banco de España
Retiro
Opera
P. de Vergarra
O'Donnell
García Noblejas
Simancas
San Blas
LINE 7 LAS MUSAS
Ibíza
La Latina
Tirso de Molina
Lavapiés
Antón Martin
Lago
Pta. de Toledo
Atocha
Atocha Renfe
Menéndez Pelayo
Sainz de Baranda
Estrella
Vinateros
Artilleros
Batán
Acacias
Pirámides
Marqués de Vadillo
Embajadores
Conde de Casal
Campamento
LAGUNA
Urgel
Palos de la Frontera
Pacífico
Carpetana
Delicias
Méndez Alvaro
Puente de Vallecas
PAVONES
Empalme
Oporto
LEGAZPI
Opañel
Plaza Elíptica
Usera
Nueva Numancia
Vista Alegre
ALUCHE
Carabanchel
LINE 1 PORTAZGO

9134

from 9am to 1pm and 3 to 6pm (in winter, Monday through Thursday from 9am to 7pm and Friday from 9am to 3pm).

Lost Property If you've lost something on a Madrid bus, go to the office at Alcántra 26 (☎ **401-31-00;** Metro: Goya). Open Monday to Friday from 9am to 2pm. If you've lost something on the metro, go at any time to the Cuatro Caminos station (☎ **552-49-00**). For objects lost in a taxi, go to Plaza de Chamberí (☎ **448-79-26;** metro: Chamberí). Open Monday to Friday from 9am to 2pm and Saturday 9am to 1pm. For objects lost anywhere else, go to the Palacio de Comunicaciones at the Plaza de la Cibeles (☎ **532-93-52;** Metro: Banco de España). Open Monday to Friday from 9am to 2pm and Saturday from 9am to 1pm. Don't call—show up in person.

Luggage Storage/Lockers These can be found at both the Atocha and Chamartín railway terminals, as well as the major bus station at the Estación Sur de Autobuses, Calle Canarias, 17 (☎ **468-45-11;** Metro: Palos de la Frontera). Storage is also provided at the air terminal underneath the Plaza de Colón.

Newspapers/Magazines The Paris-based *International Herald Tribune* is sold at most major newsstands in the tourist districts, as is *USA Today*, plus the European editions of *Time* and *Newsweek. Guía del Ocio*, a small magazine sold in newsstands, contains entertainment listings and addresses, but in Spanish only.

Photographic Needs Kodak and other popular brands of film are sold in Madrid, but they're much more expensive than in the United States. For a Spanish film, try Valca (black and white) or Negra (black and white or color). Ask before photographing in churches or museums because photography is often not permitted. Your photographic needs can be serviced by El Corte Inglés department store at Calle Preciados 3 (☎ **532-18-00**).

Police Dial **091.**

Post Office If you don't want to receive your mail at your hotel or the American Express office, direct it to Lista de Correos at the central post office in Madrid. To pick up mail, go to the window marked "Lista," where you'll be asked to show your passport. Madrid's central office is in "the cathedral of the post offices" at Plaza de la Cibeles (☎ **536-01-11**).

Radio/TV During the day on shortwave radio you can hear the Voice of America and the BBC. An English-language radio program in Madrid called "*Buenos Días*" (Good Morning) airs many useful hints for visitors; it's broadcast on Monday to Friday from 6 to 8am on 657 megahertz. Radio 80 broadcasts news in English on Monday to Saturday from 7 to 8am on 89 FM. Some TV programs are broadcast in English in the summer months. Many hotels—but regrettably not most of our budget ones—also bring in satellite TV programs in English.

Religious Services Most churches in Madrid are Catholic, and they're all over the city. Catholic masses in English, however, are given at Alfonso XIII 165. For information, call **233-20-32** in the morning. The British Embassy Church of St. George, an Anglican/Episcopalian church, is at Núñez de Balboa 43 (call **576-51-09** for worship hours). The interdenominational Protestant Community Church offers weekly services in the Colegio El Porvenir, Bravo Murillo 85 (☎ **858-55-57**); while the Immanuel Baptist Church offers English-speaking services at Hernández de Tajada 4 (☎ **407-43-47**). A Christian Science Church is at Pinilla del Valle 5 (☎ **259-21-25**). You'll find a Jewish synagogue at Balmes 3 (☎ **445-98-35**); services are on Friday at 7:30pm and Saturday at 9:30am.

Restrooms Some public restrooms are available, including those in the Parque del Retiro and on Plaza de Oriente across from the Palacio Real. Otherwise, you can always go into a bar or tasca, but you should order something. The major department stores, such as Galerías Preciados and El Corte Inglés, have good, clean restrooms.

Safety Because of an increasing crime rate in Madrid, the U.S. Embassy has warned visitors to leave valuables in a hotel safe or other secure place when going out. Your passport may be needed, however, as the police often stop foreigners for identification checks. See "Safety" under "Fast Facts: Spain," in Chapter 2 for more details about this requirement. The embassy advises against carrying purses and suggests that you keep valuables in front pockets and carry only enough cash for the day's needs. Be aware of those around you and keep a separate record of your passport number, traveler's check numbers, and credit-card numbers.

Purse snatching is common, and the criminals often work in pairs, grabbing purses from pedestrians, cyclists, and even from cars. A popular scam involves one miscreant's smearing the back of the victim's clothing, perhaps with mustard, ice cream, or something worse. An accomplice pretends to help clean up the mess, while picking all the victim's pockets.

Every car can be a target, parked or just stopped at a light, so don't leave anything in sight in your car. If a vehicle is standing still, a thief may open the door or break a window in order to snatch a purse or package, even from under the seat. Place valuables in the trunk when you park and always assume that someone is watching you to see whether you're putting something away for safekeeping. Keep the car locked while you're driving.

Open Monday to Saturday from 10am to 9pm.

Shoe Repairs In an emergency, go to one of the "Mister Minit" shoe-repair centers at any El Corte Inglés department store. The flagship store of this chain is on the Calle Preciados 3 (☎ **532-18-00**), near the Puerta del Sol (also the metro stop).

Taxes There are no special city taxes for tourists, except for the VAT (central government tax; known as IVA in Spain) levied nationwide on all goods and services, ranging from 6% to 33%. In Madrid the only city taxes are for home and car owners, which need not concern the visitor.

Taxes See "Getting Around" earlier in this chapter.

Telegrams/Telex/Fax Cables may be sent at the central post office building in Madrid at Plaza de la Cibeles (☎ **536-01-11**). To send a telegram by phone, dial **522-20-00.** In Spain it's cheaper to telephone within the country than to send a telegram. You can send telex and fax messages from the same central post office and from all major hotels.

Telephone To make calls in Madrid, follow the instructions in "Fast Facts: Spain" in Chapter 2. However, for long-distance calls, especially transatlantic ones, it may be best to go to the main telephone exchange, Locutorio Gran Vía, Gran Vía 30; or Locutorio Recoletos, Paseo de Recoletos 37–41. You may not be lucky enough to find an English-speaking operator, but you can fill out a simple form that will facilitate the placement of a call.

Transit Information For metro information, call **552-49-00.**

3 Networks & Resources

FOR STUDENTS Contact **TIVE,** Calle José Ortega y Gasset 71 (☎ **347-77-00;** Metro: Lista), which provides data on low-cost transportation in Spain and also Europe. Always check their discounts against those of other airlines to see just how great a reduction you're getting.

FOR GAY MEN & LESBIANS Before you go to Spain, you can order *Spartacus,* the international gay guide ($29.95), from **Giovanni's Room,** 1145 Pine St., Philadelphia, PA 19107 (☎ **215/923-2960**). Gay men headed only for Spain, and not the rest of Europe, might purchase instead *Spartacus International: España Edition* at $19.95. Lesbians, for whom neither of the Spartacus guides is appropriate, might be interested in *Ferrari's Places for Women* at $12.

Madrid is now one of the gay capitals of Europe. Besides Madrid, the major gay centers in Spain are Barcelona, Sítges (virtually the Fire Island of Spain), and Torremolinos on the Costa del Sol (although that resort attracts every known sexual persuasion). Madrid's gay life centers on the **Chueca district,** north of the Gran Vía, where the bar life begins around 11pm and often lasts until dawn.

In Madrid, **Librería El Galeón,** Calle Sagasta 7 (☎ **445-57-38;** Metro: Bilbao), is a gay bookshop, where you can purchase the annual version of *Guía Gay Visado,* containing the most complete list of gay and lesbian entertainment in the country. Hours are Monday through Friday from 9:30am to 1:30pm.

Lesbian life remains much more underground in Spain than does gay male life. However, there is much activity—the problem is in finding it. The best source of information about Madrid is the **Librería de Mujeres** (see below). This feminist bookshop provides much useful data. The best women's entertainment center in Madrid (attracting men, too) is **No Sé Los Digas a Nadie** ("Don't Tell Mama"), recommended in Chapter 5, "What to See and Do in Madrid."

FOR WOMEN The **Women's Medical Hotline** in Madrid is **730-49-01,** receiving calls Monday through Friday from 3:30 to 6:30pm.

A women's center is the **Librería de Mujeres,** Calle San Cristóbal 17 (☎ **521-70-43**), near Plaza Mayor, metro: Puerta del Sol. Poetry readings, concerts, talks, and a good international bookstore with some English-language editions are part of the activities and offerings of this group. Open Monday to Saturday from 10am to 2pm and 5 to 8pm.

4

Where to Stay & Dine in Madrid

IN MADRID THE HORROR DAYS OF FRANCO ARE LONG OVER, AS REFLECTED IN BOTH the hotel and restaurant picture. No more will you get rooms last renovated in 1870 or food that tastes of acidic olive oil left over from the Spanish-American War. Madrid's hotels and restaurants in the 1990s are among the finest in the world, albeit very expensive.

The new Madrid offers more than 50,000 hotel rooms. These range from *grand luxe* bedchambers fit for a prince to bunker-style beds in the hundreds of *hostales* and *pensiones* (low-cost boarding houses) found throughout the city.

As the capital of Spain, Madrid not only showcases its own cuisine, which is basically Castilian, but it offers dozens of restaurants serving regional cuisines from throughout Spain, especially Basque, but also Andalusia and Galicia. Foreign food used to be virtually ignored by Madrileños, who once spoke of their *only* German restaurant. Then a Chinese restaurant opened, then another, and eventually an American restaurant. Now the city has dozens of foreign restaurants, ranging from Indian to Italian to Middle Eastern.

The restaurant repertoire is truly cosmopolitan, as befits a city of Madrid's size and stature. Of course, it can't equal London or New York in that regard, but then what city can? Some of Madrid's restaurants, such as Zalacaín, enjoy stellar reputations around the world, although you'll pay heavily if you dine in Madrid's temples of gastronomy.

If your purse is light and your appetite large, you'll find many family-type dining rooms recommended below, where the *taberna* owner will welcome you with a heaping plate of paella and a carafe of the house wine. If you're traveling with children to Madrid, you'll find the usual array of McDonald's and Burger King outlets.

1 Accommodations

The hotel boom in Madrid has been phenomenal: Three quarters of my recommendations are modern. Yet many guests prefer the landmarks of yesteryear, including those grand old establishments, the Ritz and the Palace (ca. 1910–1912). However, many other older hostelries in Madrid haven't kept abreast of the times. A handful haven't added improvements or overhauled bedrooms substantially since the 1960s.

Traditionally, hotels in Madrid were clustered around the Atocha Railway Station and the Gran Vía. In my search for the most outstanding hotels in the upper brackets, I've almost ignored these two popular, but noisy, districts. The newer hotels have been built away from the center, especially on residential streets jutting off from Paseo de la Castellana. However, bargain seekers will still find great pickings along the Gran Vía and in the Atocha district.

RESERVATIONS Most hotels require at least a day's deposit before they will reserve a room for you. Preferably, this can be accomplished with an international money order or, if agreed to in advance, with a personal check or credit card number. You can usually cancel a room reservation one week ahead of time and get a full refund. A few hotelkeepers will return your money three days before the reservation date, but some will take your deposit and never return it, even if you cancel far in advance. Many budget hotel owners operate on such a narrow margin of profit that they find just buying stamps for airmail replies too expensive by their standards. Therefore, it's most important that you should enclose a prepaid International Reply Coupon with your payment, especially if you're writing to a budget hotel. Better yet, call and speak to the hotel of your choice or send a fax.

If you're booking into a chain hotel, such as a Hyatt or a Forte, you can call toll free in North America and easily make reservations over the phone. Whenever such a service is available, toll-free numbers are indicated in the individual hotel descriptions.

If you arrive without a reservation, begin your search for a room as early in the day as possible. If you arrive late at night, you may have to take what you can get, often for a much higher price than you'd like to pay.

A Note on Making Hotel Reservations The telephone area code for Madrid is 91 if you're calling from within Spain. If you're dialing from North America, the country code is 34 and Madrid's code is 1.

PRICE CLASSIFICATIONS The following prices are for double rooms with private baths. Hotels rated "very expensive" charge from 30,000 pesetas ($213) for a double, although some establishments in this bracket, including the Villa Magna, the Santo Mauro, and the Ritz, can ask twice that price. Hotels judged "expensive" ask from 17,000 to 30,000 pesetas ($120.70–$213) for a double, and "moderate" hotels—at least moderate in the sense of Madrid's hotel price scale—want from a low of 10,000 pesetas ($71) to a high of 17,300 pesetas ($122.80) for a double. Hotels considered "inexpensive"—again, by Madrid's pricing standards—ask for 6,000 pesetas ($42.60) up to 10,000 pesetas ($71) for a double. Any double under 6,000 pesetas ($42.60) is definitely "budget" in today's high-priced Madrid.

Note: All hotels in the "very expensive" and "expensive" categories include private baths with their guest rooms unless otherwise specified. Hotels in the other categories may or may not include baths, and that information is supplied for each entry. Also, breakfast is not included in the quoted rates unless otherwise specified.

A 6% government room tax is added to all rates.

RATINGS Spain officially rates its hotels by star designation—from one to five stars. Five stars is the highest rating in Spain, signaling a deluxe establishment complete with all the amenities and the high tariffs associated with such accommodations.

Most of the establishments recommended in this guide are three- and four-star hotels falling into that vague "middle-bracket" category. Hotels granted one and two stars, as well as pensions (guest houses), are far less comfortable, with limited plumbing and other physical facilities, although they may be perfectly clean and decent places. The latter category is strictly for dedicated budgeters.

PARKING As mentioned, this is a serious problem as so few hotels have garages; many buildings turned into hotels were constructed before the invention of the automobile. Street parking is rarely available, and, even if it is, you run the risk of having your car broken into. If you're driving into Madrid, most hotels (or most police) will allow you to park in front of the hotel long enough to unload your luggage. Someone on the staff will pinpoint the location of the nearest garage in the neighborhood, often giving you a map showing the way. In instances where a hotel has its own parking, charges are given.

Near the Plaza de las Cortés

VERY EXPENSIVE

Hotel Villa Real, Plaza de las Cortés, 10, 28014 Madrid. ☎ **34-1/420-37-67.** Fax 34-1/420-25-47. 115 rms, 19 suites. A/C MINIBAR TV TEL **Metro:** Plaza de la Cibeles.

Rates: 24,000 ptas. ($170.40) single; 31,000 ptas. ($220.10) double; 55,000–65,000 ptas. ($390.50–$461.50) suite. Breakfast 1,350 ptas. ($9.60) extra. AE, DC, MC, V. **Parking:** 1,600 ptas. ($11.40).

Until 1989, the Villa Real was little more than a run-down 19th-century apartment house auspiciously located across a three-sided park from the Spanish Parliament (Congreso de los Diputados) between Puerta del Sol and Paseo del Prado. Its developers poured billions of pesetas into renovations to produce a stylish hotel today patronized by the cognoscenti of Spain. The eclectic facade combines an odd mixture of neoclassical and Aztec motifs, and in front of it wait footmen and doormen dressed in uniforms of buff and forest green. The interior contains a scattering of modern paintings amid neoclassical moldings and details.

Each of the accommodations offers a TV with video movies and satellite reception, a safe for valuables, soundproofing, a sunken salon filled with leather-upholstered furniture, and built-in furniture accented with burlwood inlays.

Dining/Entertainment: The social center is the high-ceilinged formal bar. The hotel's formal Restaurant Europa serves both lunch and dinner, a Spanish and international cuisine, with meals costing from 5,500 ptas. ($39.10).

Services: 24-hour room service, laundry/valet, babysitting, express checkout.

Facilities: Sauna, foreign currency exchange, business center.

★ **Palace,** Plaza de las Cortés, 7, 28014 Madrid. ☎ **34-1/429-75-51,** or toll free **800/221-2340** in the U.S., **800/955-2442** in Canada. Fax 34-1/429-86-55. 487 rms, 31 suites. A/C MINIBAR TV TEL **Metro:** Banco de España or Anton Martín.

Rates: 25,000-32,000 ptas. ($177.50-$227.20) single; 32,000–38,000 ptas. ($227.20-$269.80) double; from 90,000 ptas. ($639) suite. Breakfast 2,400 ptas. ($17). AE, DC, MC, V. **Parking:** 1,600 ptas. ($11.40).

The Palace is known as the "grand *dueña*" of Spanish hotels. The establishment had an auspicious beginning since its inauguration by the late King Alfonso XIII in 1912. Covering a city block, it faces the Prado and Neptune Fountain, in the historical and artistic area, within walking distance of the main shopping center and the best antiques shops. Some of the city's most intriguing tascas and restaurants are only a short stroll away.

Architecturally, the Palace captures the elegant pre-World War I "grand hotel" style, with an emphasis on space and comfort. Even though it is one of the largest hotels in Madrid, it retains first-class service. The hotel is air-conditioned with a formal, traditional lobby. The rooms are also conservative and traditional, boasting plenty of space and large bathrooms with lots of amenities.

Dining/Entertainment: The elegant dining choice is La Cupola, serving Italian specialties along with some of the more famous dishes of the Spanish cuisine. It's decorated in the style of Venice, and meals cost from 6,500 ptas. ($46.20). The Ambigu offers a full buffet costing from 3,950 ptas. ($28) per person, and it's open seven days a week from 12:30pm to 1:30am, serving nonstop. Piano music and other entertainment are featured.

Services: 24-hour room service, laundry/valet, babysitting, express checkout.

Facilities: Foreign currency exchange, business center.

INEXPENSIVE

Hostal Cervantes, Cervantes, 34, 28014 Madrid. ☎ **34-1/429-27-45.** 12 rms (all with bath). **Metro:** Banco de España.

Rates: 5,000 ptas. ($35.50) single; 6,000 ptas. ($42.60) double. No credit cards.

One of Madrid's most pleasant family-run hotels, the Cervantes has been widely appreciated by our readers for years. You'll take a tiny birdcage-style elevator to the immaculately maintained second floor of this stone-and-brick building. Each accommodation contains a bed and Spartan furniture. No breakfast is served, but the owners, the Alfonsos, will direct you to a nearby café. The establishment is convenient to the Prado, Retiro Park, and the older sections of Madrid.

Near the Plaza España

EXPENSIVE

Plaza Hotel, Plaza de España, 8, 28013 Madrid. ☎ **34-1/547-12-00.** Fax 34-1/548-23-89. 266 rms, 40 suites. A/C MINIBAR TV TEL **Metro:** Plaza de España.

Rates: 15,200 ptas. ($107.90) single; 19,000 ptas. ($134.90) double; from 24,000 ptas. ($170.40) suite. Breakfast 1,300 ptas. ($9.20) extra. AE, DC, MC, V. **Parking:** 2,500 ptas. ($17.80).

The Plaza Hotel, built in 1953, could be called the Waldorf-Astoria of Spain. A massive rose-and-white structure, it soars upward to a central tower that's 26 stories high. It is a landmark visible for miles around and one of the tallest skyscrapers in Europe. The hotel's accommodations include both conventional singles and doubles as well as luxurious suites, each of which contains a sitting room and abundant amenities. Each accommodation, regardless of its size, contains a marble bathroom. Furniture is usually of a standardized modern style, in harmonized colors.

MODERATE

Casón del Tormes, Calle del Río, 7, 28013 Madrid. ☎ **34-1/541-97-46.** Fax 34-1/541-18-52. 63 rms (all with bath). A/C TV TEL **Metro:** Plaza de España.

Rates: 7,900 ptas. ($56.10) single; 11,000 ptas. ($78.10) double; 13,900 ptas. ($98.70) triple. Breakfast 600 ptas. ($4.30) extra. MC, V. **Parking:** 1,200 ptas. ($8.50).

The attractive three-star Casón del Tormes is around the corner from the Royal Palace and Plaza de España. Set behind a four-story red-brick facade with stone-trimmed windows, it overlooks a quiet one-way street. The long, narrow lobby contains vertical wooden paneling, a marble floor, and a bar opening into a separate room. Motorists appreciate the public parking lot near the hotel. Laundry service is provided.

On or Near the Gran Vía

MODERATE

Hostal Buenos Aires, Gran Vía, 61, 28013 Madrid. ☎ **34-1/542-01-02.** Fax 34-1/542-28-69. 25 rms (all with bath). A/C TV TEL **Metro:** Plaza de España. **Bus:** 1, 2, or 44.

Rates: 5,000 ptas. ($35.50) single; 7,000 ptas. ($49.70) double. Breakfast 500 ptas. ($3.60) extra. AE, DC, MC, V.

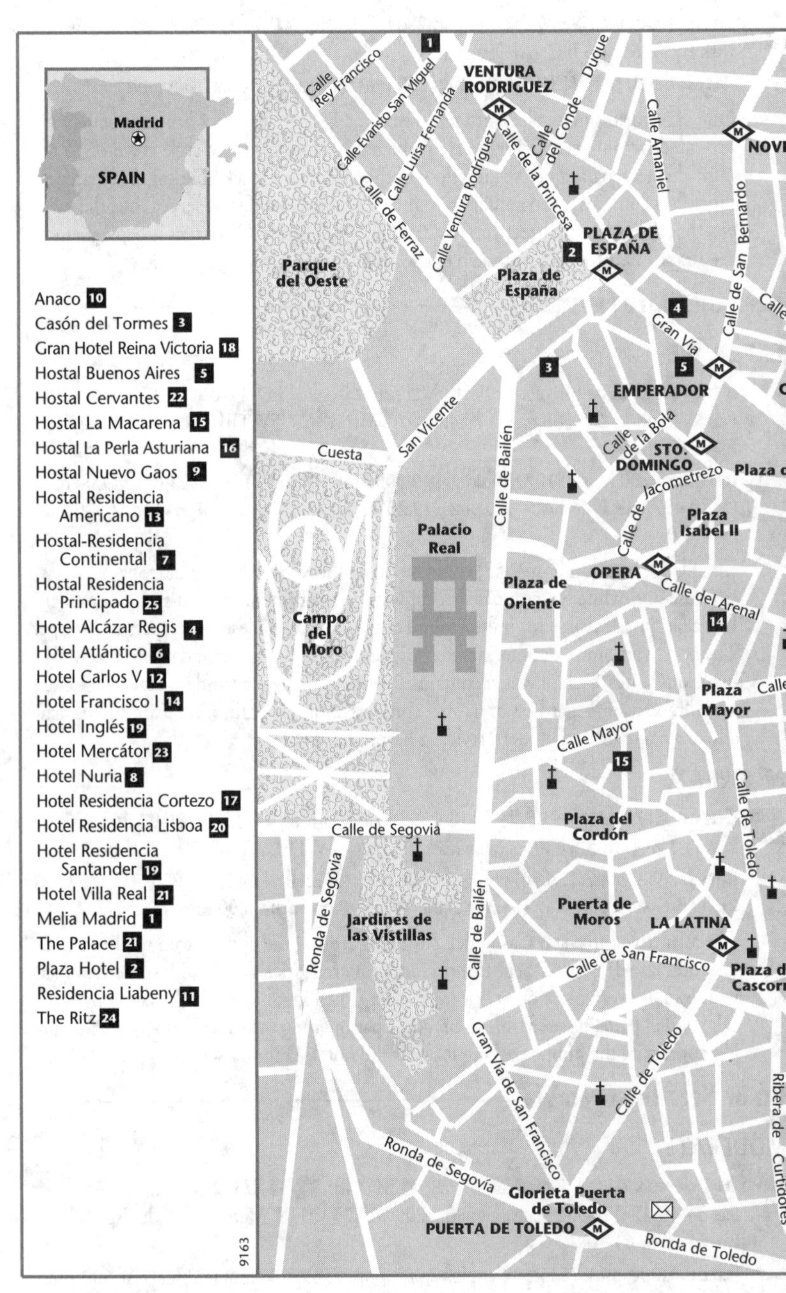
Madrid
SPAIN
Anaco 10
Casón del Tormes 3
Gran Hotel Reina Victoria 18
Hostal Buenos Aires 5
Hostal Cervantes 22
Hostal La Macarena 15
Hostal La Perla Asturiana 16
Hostal Nuevo Gaos 9
Hostal Residencia Americano 13
Hostal-Residencia Continental 7
Hostal Residencia Principado 25
Hotel Alcázar Regis 4
Hotel Atlántico 6
Hotel Carlos V 12
Hotel Francisco I 14
Hotel Inglés 19
Hotel Mercátor 23
Hotel Nuria 8
Hotel Residencia Cortezo 17
Hotel Residencia Lisboa 20
Hotel Residencia Santander 19
Hotel Villa Real 21
Melia Madrid 1
The Palace 21
Plaza Hotel 2
Residencia Liabeny 11
The Ritz 24
9163
Calle Rey Francisco
Calle Evaristo San Miguel
Calle Luisa Fernanda
VENTURA RODRIGUEZ
Calle Ventura Rodríguez
Calle de la Princesa
Calle del Conde Duque
Calle Amaniel
NOVIC
Calle de Ferraz
Parque del Oeste
Plaza de España
PLAZA DE ESPAÑA
Calle de San Bernardo
Gran Vía
EMPERADOR
San Vicente
Cuesta
Calle de Bailén
Calle de la Bola
STO. DOMINGO
Calle de Jacometrezo
Plaza Isabel II
Palacio Real
Plaza de Oriente
OPERA
Calle del Arenal
Campo del Moro
Plaza Mayor
Calle Mayor
Calle de Toledo
Calle de Segovia
Plaza del Cordón
Ronda de Segovia
Jardines de las Vistillas
Puerta de Moros
LA LATINA
Calle de San Francisco
Gran Vía de San Francisco
Ribera de Curtidores
Ronda de Segovia
Glorieta Puerta de Toledo
PUERTA DE TOLEDO
Ronda de Toledo

Accommodations in Central Madrid

Metro Church Post Office Information

To reach this place, you pass through a marble-covered street-floor lobby within a 1955 building, then take the elevator to the second floor. The hostal occupies two floors. One of its best features is a wood-sheathed café/bar that's open 24 hours daily. Bedrooms are comfortable, modern, and clean, with a safety deposit box, balcony, and hairdryer.

Hotel Atlántico, Gran Vía 38, 28013 Madrid. ☎ **34-1/522-64-80,** or toll free **800/528-1234** in the U.S. and Canada. Fax 34-1/531-02-10. 80 rms (all with bath). A/C MINIBAR TV TEL **Metro:** Gran Vía.

Rates (including breakfast): 8,150 ptas. ($57.90) single; 11,350 ptas. ($80.60) double. AE, DC, MC, V.

Refurbished in stages between the late 1980s and 1994, this hotel occupies five floors of a grand turn-of-the-century building on a corner of one of Madrid's most impressive avenues. Established in 1989 as a Best Western affiliate, it offers security boxes in well-furnished bedrooms. The hotel contains an English-inspired bar serving drinks and snacks near the reception area that's open 24 hours a day.

Residencia Liabeny, Salud, 3, 28013 Madrid. ☎ **34-1/532-53-06.** Fax 34-1/532-74-21. 223 rms (all with bath). A/C MINIBAR TV TEL **Metro:** Puerta del Sol, Callao, or Gran Vía.

Rates: 10,000 ptas. ($71) single; 15,000 ptas. ($106.50) double; 19,300 ptas. ($137) triple. Breakfast 900 ptas. ($6.40) extra. AE, MC, V. **Parking:** 1,200 ptas. ($8.50).

This hotel, behind a stone-sheathed rectangular facade, is in a prime location midway between the tourist highlights of the Gran Vía and Puerta del Sol. Named after the original owner of the hotel, it contains seven floors of comfortable, contemporary bedrooms.

INEXPENSIVE

Anaco, Tres Cruces, 3, 28013 Madrid. ☎ **34-1/522-46-04.** Fax 34-1/531-64-84. 39 rms (all with bath). A/C TV TEL **Metro:** Gran Vía, Callao, or Puerta del Sol.

Rates: 5,500–6,500 ptas. ($39.10–$46.20) single; 8,500–9,500 ptas. ($60.40–$67.50) double; 11,475–12,825 ptas. ($81.50–$91.10) triple. Breakfast 500 ptas. ($3.60) extra. AE, DC, MC, V.

A modest yet modern hotel, the Anaco is just off the main shopping thoroughfare, the Gran Vía. Opening onto a tree-shaded plaza, it attracts those seeking a resting place that features contemporary appurtenances and cleanliness. The bedrooms are compact, with built-in headboards, reading lamps, and lounge chairs. A useful tip: Ask for one of the five terraced rooms on the top floor, which rent at no extra charge. The hotel has a bar/cafeteria/restaurant open daily from 7:30am to 2:30am the next morning. English is spoken here. Nearby is a municipally operated garage.

Hostal Nuevo Gaos, Calle Mesonero Romanos, 14, 28013 Madrid. ☎ **34-1/532-71-07.** Fax 34-1/522-70-98. 23 rms (all with bath). A/C MINIBAR TV TEL **Metro:** Callao. **Bus:** 1, 2, or 44.

Rates: 6,200–8,200 ptas. ($44–$58.20) single or double. AE, DC, MC, V.

On the second, third, and fourth floors of a 1930s building just off the Gran Vía, this residencia offers guests the chance to enjoy a comfortable standard of living at moderate rates. The place lies directly north of Puerta del Sol, across the street from the popular flamenco club Torre Bermejas. Breakfast can be taken at a nearby café.

Hotel Nuria, Fuencarral, 52, 28004 Madrid. ☎ **34-1/531-92-08.** Fax 34-1/532-90-05. 80 rms (all with bath). TV TEL **Metro:** Gran Vía or Tribunal. **Bus:** 3, 7, or 40.

Rates (including breakfast): 3,600–4,750 ptas. ($25.60–$33.70) single; 6,250 ptas. ($44.40) double. AE, DC, MC, V.

Hotel Nuria, just three blocks from the Gran Vía, has some bedrooms with especially interesting views of the capital. Furnishings are simple and functional. A bar, restaurant, and TV lounge are available to guests. The hotel was renovated in 1986.

BUDGET

$ **Hostal-Residencia Continental,** Gran Vía, 44, 28013 Madrid. ☎ **34-1/521-46-40.** 29 rms (all with bath). TEL **Metro:** Callao. **Bus:** 1, 2, 36, or 46.

Rates: 3,600 ptas. ($25.60) single; 4,900 ptas. ($34.80) double. Breakfast 500 ptas. ($3.60) extra. AE, DC, MC, V.

Sprawling over the third and fourth floors of Gran Vía, 44, this hostal is a bit more expensive than the other accommodations in the building, but the rooms are comfortable, tidy, and renovated. The desk clerk speaks English. The Continental is in a virtual "casa of budget hotels," a 19th-century building filled exclusively with small hotels and pensions. If no room is available at the Continental, you can ring the doorbells of the other establishments because this "house of hotels" is a good bet for the budget tourist.

Hotel Alcázar Regis, Gran Vía, 61, 28013 Madrid. ☎ **34-1/547-93-17.** 25 rms (none with bath). **Metro:** Plaza de España or Santo Domingo.

Rates: 2,300 ptas. ($16.30) single; 4,000 ptas. ($28.40) double. Breakfast 350 ptas. ($2.50) extra. AE

Conveniently perched on a corner in the midst of Madrid's best shops is this post–World War II building, complete with a circular Greek-style temple as its crown. On

Frommer's Smart Traveler: Hotels

Value-Conscious Travelers Should Take Advantage of the Following:

1. Reductions in rates for rooms without private baths. Usually a room with a shower is cheaper than a room with a private bath, and even cheaper is a room with a basin only.
2. Reductions at some hotels if you pay with cash instead of a credit card.
3. Long-term discounts if you're planning to spend more than one week in Madrid.

Questions to Ask if You're on a Budget:

1. If there's a garage, what is the parking charge? You might want to try to find a parking place on the street (though these are hard to come by).
2. Is there a surcharge for local or long-distance telephone calls? Usually there is, and it can be as high as 40%. Make your calls at the nearest post office instead.
3. Is service included or will it be added to your final bill? Likewise, are all taxes included or will you be billed extra?
4. Is a continental breakfast included in the rate? After a stay of three or four days, the cost of breakfast alone can make a big difference in your final bill.

the building's fifth floor, you'll find long and pleasant public rooms; wood paneling; leaded-glass windows; parquet floors; crystal chandeliers; and high-ceilinged guest rooms, each with hot and cold running water.

Near the Puerta del Sol

EXPENSIVE

Gran Hotel Reina Victoria, Plaza Santa Ana, 14, 28012 Madrid. ☎ **34-1/531-45-00.** Fax 34-1/522-03-7. 187 rms, 9 suites. A/C MINIBAR TV TEL **Metro:** Tirso de Molina or Puerta del Sol.

Rates (including breakfast): 17,000 ptas. ($120.70) single; 22,000 ptas. ($156.20) double; from 28,200 ptas. ($200.20) suite. AE, DC, V. **Parking:** 1,600 ptas. ($11.40).

This establishment is about as important to the legends of Madrid as the famous bullfighter Manolete himself. He used to stay here, giving lavish parties in one of the reception rooms and attracting mobs in the square below when he went out on his balcony for morning coffee. Since the recent renovation and upgrading of this property by Spain's Tryp Hotel Group, it's less staid and more impressive than ever.

Originally built in 1923 and named after the grandmother of the present King of Spain, Juan Carlos, the hotel sits behind an ornate and eclectic stone facade, which the Spanish government protects as a historic monument. Although it's located in a congested neighborhood in the center of town, the Reina Victoria opens onto its own sloping plaza, rich in tradition as a meeting place of intellectuals during the 17th century. Today the area is usually filled with flower vendors, older people catching the rays of the midafternoon sun, and young persons resting between bouts at the dozens of neighborhood tapas bars.

Each of the hotel's bedrooms contains sound-resistant insulation, a safe for valuables, and a private bathroom with many amenities.

Dining/Entertainment: Guests enjoy the hotel's stylish and popular lobby bar, the Manuel Gonzalez Manolete, whose lavishly displayed bullfighting memorabilia and potent drinks add another attraction to an already memorable hotel. The in-house restaurant is El Ruedo.

Services: 24-hour room service, concierge, babysitting.

Facilities: Because of the hotel's position in one of Madrid's most interesting neighborhoods, almost anything is available within a few minutes' walk.

MODERATE

Hotel Carlos V, Maestro Vitoria, 5, 28013 Madrid. ☎ **34-1/531-41-00,** or toll free **800/528-1234** in the U.S. and Canada. 67 rms (all with bath). A/C TV TEL **Metro:** Puerta del Sol or Callao.

Rates: 8,900 ptas. ($63.20) single; 11,200 ptas. ($79.50) double. Breakfast 750 ptas. ($5.30) extra. AE, DC, MC, V.

Hotel Carlos V has long been a Frommer favorite—many faithful readers discovering it in 1967 when this guide was first published as *Spain on $5 a Day.* Some have been returning ever since those days. The seven-story art nouveau building, dating from 1904, has been altered over the years, but the lobby retains its air of elegance. The guest rooms have been upgraded and now contain such amenities as music, personal safes, and modernized bathrooms. What hasn't changed is the unbeatable location:

around the corner from the Galerias Preciados and just a short walk from the Gran Vía and Puerta del Sol.

INEXPENSIVE

$ **Hostal la Macarena,** Cava de San Miguel, 8, 28005 Madrid. ☎ **34-1/365-92-21.** Fax 34-1/364-27-57. 18 rms (all with bath). TEL **Metro:** Puerta del Sol, Opera, or La Latina.

Rates: 3,800 ptas. ($27) single; 6,000 ptas. ($42.60) double; 7,500 ptas. ($53.30) triple; 8,000 ptas. ($56.80) quad. Breakfast 500 ptas. ($3.60) extra. AE, MC, V.

Known for its reasonable prices and praised by readers for the warmth of its reception, this unpretentious, clean hostal is run by the Ricardo González family. Its 19th-century facade, accented with Belle-Epoque patterns, offers an ornate contrast to the chiseled simplicity of the ancient buildings facing it. The location is one of the hostal's assets: It's on a street (an admittedly noisy one) immediately behind Plaza Mayor, near one of the best clusters of tascas in Madrid. Windows facing the street have double windows.

Hotel Francisco I, Arenal, 15, 28013 Madrid. ☎ **34-1/548-43-14.** Fax 34-1/542-28-99. 58 rms (all with bath). TV TEL **Metro:** Puerta del Sol or Ópera.

Rates (including breakfast): 6,300 ptas. ($44.70) single; 8,700 ptas. ($61.80) double. MC, V.

Here you can rent modern, clean rooms. There's a pleasant lounge and a bar, and on the sixth floor you'll find a comfortable, rustically decorated restaurant where a set meal costs around 2,000 ptas. ($14.20). The hotel was considerably modernized in 1993, with the addition of new bathrooms as well as air conditioning in most of the bedrooms. The hotel provides 24-hour room service and laundry and valet service.

$ **Hotel Inglés,** Calle Echegaray, 8, 28014 Madrid. ☎ **34-1/429-65-51.** Fax 34-1/420-24-23. 50 rms (all with bath), 8 suites. TV TEL **Metro:** Puerta del Sol or Sevilla.

Rates: 6,500 ptas. ($46.20) single; 9,500 ptas. ($67.50) double; 13,000 ptas. ($92.30) suite. Breakfast 500 ptas. ($3.60) extra. AE, DC, MC, V. **Parking:** 1,100 ptas. ($7.80).

You'll find the Hotel Inglés on a central street lined with tascas, although the hotel operates its own 24-hour cafeteria. It's perhaps more modern and impersonal than it was when Virginia Woolf made it her address in Madrid. Behind its red-brick facade you'll find unpretentious and contemporary bedrooms, all well maintained. The comfortable armchairs in the TV lounge are likely to be filled with avid soccer fans. The lobby is air-conditioned, although the guest rooms are not. Guests who open their windows at night are likely to hear noise from the enclosed courtyard, so light sleepers beware.

Hotel Residencia Lisboa, Ventura de la Vega, 17, 28014 Madrid. ☎ **34-1/429-98-94.** Fax 34-1/369-41-96. 23 rms (all with bath). **Metro:** Puerta del Sol.

Rates: 4,000 ptas. ($28.40) single; 6,000 ptas. ($42.60) double. AE, DC, MC, V.

The Lisboa, on Madrid's most famous restaurant street, can be a bit noisy, but that's my only complaint. The hotel is a neat, modernized town house with compact rooms and central heating in the cooler months. The staff speak five languages. The Lisboa does not serve breakfast, but it is surrounded by budget dining rooms, cafés, and tascas.

Hotel Residencia Santander, Calle Echegaray, 1, 28014 Madrid. ☎ **34-1/429-95-51.** 38 rms (all with bath). TEL **Metro:** Puerta del Sol.

Rates: 5,600 ptas. ($39.80) single; 7,000 ptas. ($49.70) double. Breakfast 400 ptas. ($2.80) extra. No credit cards.

A snug little hotel just off Puerta del Sol, the Santander is a refurbished 1930 house with adequate rooms, some of which contain TV. Although it's on a teeming street, you might appreciate the nonstop local atmosphere. Restaurants and bars in the area are active day and night.

BUDGET

Hostal la Perla Asturiana, Plaza de Santa Cruz, 3, 28012 Madrid. ☎ **34-1/366-46-00.** 32 rms (all with bath). **Metro:** Puerta del Sol.

Rates: 3,600 ptas. ($25.60) single; 4,900 ptas. ($34.80) double. Breakfast 500 ptas. ($3.60) extra. AE, DC, MC, V.

Ideal for those who want to stay in the heart of old Madrid (one block off Plaza Mayor and two blocks from Puerta del Sol), this small family-run establishment has a courteous staff member at the desk 24 hours a day for security and convenience. You can socialize in the small, comfortable lobby that's adjacent to the reception desk. The bedrooms are clean, with fresh towels supplied daily. Many inexpensive restaurants and tapas bars are nearby.

$ **Hostal-Residencia Principado,** Zorrilla, 7, 28014 Madrid. ☎ **34-1/429-81-87.** 15 rms (all with bath). **Metro:** Sevilla or Banco de España. **Bus:** 5, 9, or 53.

Rates: 4,000 ptas. ($28.40) single; 5,800 ptas. ($41.20) double. AE, MC, V.

The two-star Hostal-Residencia Principado is a real find. Located in a well-kept town house, it is run by a gracious owner who keeps everything clean and inviting. New tiles, attractive bedspreads, and curtains give the guest rooms a fresh look. Safety boxes are provided. For breakfast, you can go to a nearby café. English is spoken.

Hostal Residencia Americano, Puerta del Sol, 11, 28013 Madrid. ☎ **34-1/522-28-22.** 43 rms (all with bath). TEL **Metro:** Puerta del Sol.

Rates: 3,300 ptas. ($23.40) single; 4,700 ptas. ($33.40) double; 7,000 ptas. ($49.70) triple; 8,000 ptas. ($56.80) quad. No credit cards.

Hostal Residencia Americano, on the third floor of a five-floor building, is suitable for those who want to be in Puerta del Sol. Owner/manager A. V. Franceschi has refurbished all the guest rooms, most of them outside chambers with balconies facing the street. Mr. Franceschi promises hot and cold running water 24 hours a day. No breakfast is served.

Near Atocha Station

MODERATE

Hotel Mercátor, Calle Atocha, 123, 28012 Madrid. ☎ **34-1/429-05-00.** Fax 34-1/369-12-52. 89 rms, 3 suites (all with bath). MINIBAR TV TEL **Metro:** Atocha or Antón Martín.

Rates: 8,000 ptas. ($56.80) single; 11,250 ptas. ($79.90) double; 12,500 ptas. ($88.80) suite. AE, DC, MC, V. **Parking:** 1,320 ptas. ($9.40).

Only a three-minute walk from the Prado, Centro de Arte Reina Sofía, and the Thyssen-Bornemisza Museum, the Mercátor draws a clientele seeking a good hotel—

orderly, well run, and clean, with enough comforts and conveniences to please the weary traveler. The public rooms are simple, outfitted in a vaguely modern type of minimalism. Some of the guest rooms are more inviting than others, especially those with desks and armchairs. Twenty-one units are air-conditioned. The Mercátor is a residencia—that is, it offers breakfast only and does not have a formal restaurant for lunch and dinner; however, it has a bar and cafeteria serving light meals, such as *platos combinados* (combination plates). The hotel has a garage and is within walking distance of American Express. Laundry service is provided, plus room service from 7am to 10pm.

Hotel Residencia Cortezo, Doctor Cortezo, 3, 28012 Madrid. ☎ **34-1/369-01-01.** Fax 34-1/369-37-74. 90 rms (all with bath). A/C MINIBAR TV TEL **Metro:** Tirso de Molina.

Rates: 7,950 ptas. ($56.40) single; 11,225 ptas. ($79.70) double. Breakfast 800 ptas. ($5.70) extra. AE, MC, V. **Parking:** 1,000 ptas. ($7.10).

Just off Calle de Atocha, which leads to the railroad station of the same name, the Cortezo is a short walk from Plaza Mayor and Puerta del Sol. The accommodations are comfortable and attractive, with contemporary baths. The beds are springy, the colors are well chosen, and the furniture is pleasantly modern; often there is a sitting area with a desk and armchair. The public rooms match the guest rooms in freshness. The hotel was built in 1959 and last renovated in 1989.

Near Retiro/Salamanca

VERY EXPENSIVE

Park Hyatt Villa Magna, Paseo de la Castellana, 22, 28046 Madrid. ☎ **34-1/576-75-00,** or toll free in North America **800/228-9000.** Fax 34-1/575-95-04. 166 rms, 16 suites. A/C MINIBAR TV TEL **Metro:** Rubén Darío.

Rates: 34,000 ptas. ($241.40) single; 40,000 ptas. ($284) double; from 69,500 ptas. ($493.50) suite. Weekend packages: 2 nights in a single or double room for 40,000 ptas. ($284). Breakfast 2,750 ptas. ($19.50) extra. AE, DC, MC, V. **Parking:** 2,000 ptas. ($14.20).

Considered one of the finest hotels in Europe, the Park Hyatt is faced with slabs of rose-colored granite and set behind a bank of pines and laurels on the city's most fashionable boulevard. It was already a supremely comfortable and elegant modern hotel when Hyatt International took over its management in 1990.

It was originally conceived when a handful of Spain's elite teamed up to create a setting in which their special friends, along with an array of discriminating international visitors, would be pleased to live and dine. They hired an architect, imported a French decorator (whose style has been described as a contemporary version of neoclassicism), planted gardens, and put the staff through an intensive training program.

Separated from the busy boulevard by a parklike garden, its facade has contemporary lines. In contrast, its interior recaptures the style of Carlos IV, with paneled walls, marble floors, and bouquets of fresh flowers. Through the lobby and drawing rooms passes almost every film star shooting on location in Spain.

This luxury palace offers plush but dignified bedrooms decorated in Louis XVI, English Regency, or Italian provincial style. Each has fresh flowers and a TV with video movies and satellite reception (including news broadcasts beamed in from the United States).

Dining/Entertainment: In the lobby-level champagne bar, the bartender can mix any drink you might fancy, while a pianist provides entertainment. The in-house restaurant, the Berceo, serves international food in a glamorous setting. The hotel is known for its summer terraces, Calalú and Berceo, set in gardens. One of them, Calalú, is the only terrace in Madrid where you can enjoy live jazz performed from Tuesday through Saturday.

Services: 24-hour room service, concierge, same-day laundry and dry cleaning, limousine service, babysitting.

Facilities: Business center; car rentals; barber and beauty shop; the boutique "Villa Magna"; availability of both tennis and golf 15 and 25 minutes from the hotel, respectively.

Ritz, Plaza de la Lealtad, 5, 28014 Madrid. ☎ **34-1/521-28-57,** or toll free **800/435-4542** in the U.S. and Canada. Fax 34-1/532-87-76. 158 rms, 24 suites. A/C MINIBAR TV TEL **Metro:** Banco de España.

Rates: 33,000–38,000 ptas. ($234.30–$269.80) single; 43,000–44,000 ptas. ($305.30–312.40) double; from 77,500 ptas. ($550.30) suite. Breakfast 2,000 ptas. ($14.20) extra. AE, DC, MC, V. **Parking:** 2,000 ptas. ($14.20).

This is an international rendezvous point of legendary renown, one of the two most famous hotels in Spain. Its name has appeared in countless pages of Spanish-language tabloids that document the comings and goings of its glamorous guests. Encased in a turn-of-the-century shell of soaring ceilings and graceful columns, it contains all the luxuries and special attentions that world travelers have come to expect of a grand hotel. Billions of pesetas have been spent on renovations since its acquisition in the 1980s by the British-based Forte chain. The result is a bastion of glamor where, despite modernization, great effort was expended to retain the hotel's Belle Epoque character and architectural details.

No other Madrid hotel, except perhaps for the Palace, has a more varied history. One of *Les Grand/Hôtels Européens*, the Ritz was built at the command of King Alfonso XIII, with the aid of César Ritz, in 1908. It looks out onto the big circular Plaza de la Lealtad in the center of town, near the 300-acre Retiro Park, facing the Prado and its extension, the Palacio de Villahermosa, and the Stock Exchange. The Ritz was constructed when costs were relatively low and when spaciousness, luxury, and comfort were the orders of the day. Its facade is classed as a historic monument.

Bedrooms contain fresh flowers, well-accessorized marble bathrooms, and TVs with video movies and satellite reception.

Dining/Entertainment: The hotel maintains a formal dining room decorated in shades of cream, blue, and gold, which is lined with mirrors and 16th-century Flemish tapestries. Its chefs present an international menu featuring a paella which is said to be one of the most elaborate in Madrid. In time-honored Spanish tradition, guests tend to dress up here, sometimes even for breakfast. (Management stresses that this is not a resort hotel.) Guests looking for a more casual eatery usually head for the Terraza Ritz.

Services: 24-hour room service, laundry/valet, express checkout.

Facilities: Car-rental kiosk, business center, foreign currency exchange.

Wellington, Velázquez, 8, 28001 Madrid. ☎ **34-1/575-44-00.** Fax 34-1/576-4164. 280 rms, 10 suites. A/C MINIBAR TV TEL **Metro:** Retiro or Velázquez.

Rates: 19,520 ptas. ($138.60) single; 30,500 ptas. ($216.60) double; from 53,500 ptas.

($379.90) suite. Breakfast 2,100 ptas. ($14.90) extra. AE, DC, MC, V. **Parking:** 2,000 ptas. ($14.20).

The Wellington, with its impressive antique-tapestried entrance, is one of Madrid's more sedate deluxe hotels, built in the mid-1950s but substantially remodeled since. Set within the Salamanca residential area near Retiro Park, the Wellington offers redecorated guest rooms, each with cable TV and movie channels, music, two phones (one in the bathroom), and a guest-operated combination safe. Units are furnished in English-inspired mahogany reproductions, and the bathrooms (one per accommodation) are modern and immaculate, with marble sheathing and fixtures. Doubles with private terraces (at no extra charge) are the most sought-after accommodations.

Dining/Entertainment: An added bonus here is the El Fogón grill room, styled like a 19th-century tavern, where many of the provisions for the typically Spanish dishes are shipped in from the hotel's own ranch. The pub-style Bar Inglés is a hospitable rendezvous. Lighter meals are served in the Las Llaves de Oro (Golden Keys) cafeteria.

Services: 24-hour room service, same-day dry cleaning and laundry.

Facilities: Outdoor swimming pool in summer, garage, beauty parlor.

EXPENSIVE

Emperatriz, López de Hoyos, 4, 28006 Madrid. ☎ **34-1/563-80-88.** Fax 34-1/563-98-04. 170 rms, 1 suite (all with bath). A/C MINIBAR TV TEL **Metro:** Rubén Darío.

Rates: 19,200 ptas. ($136.30) single; 24,000 ptas. ($170.40) double; 40,000 ptas. ($284) suite. Breakfast 1,200 ptas. ($8.50) extra. AE, DC, MC, V. **Parking:** 1,500 ptas. ($10.70) nearby.

This hotel lies just off the wide Paseo de Castellana, only a short walk from some of Madrid's most deluxe hotels, but it charges relatively reasonable rates. Built in the 1970s, it was last renovated in 1993. It contains comfortable and unpretentious bedrooms, each of which has a TV that receives many different European channels and a mixture of both traditional and modern furniture. If one is available, ask for a room on the eighth floor, where you'll get a private terrace at no extra charge. On the premises are a beauty salon, a barbershop, and well-upholstered lounges where you're likely to meet fellow globe-trotting Americans. Laundry and valet service and babysitting also are provided.

Grand Hotel Velázquez, Calle de Velázquez, 62, 28001 Madrid. ☎ **34-1/575-28-00.** Fax 34-1/575-28-09. 71 rms, 75 suites. A/C MINIBAR TV TEL **Metro:** Retiro.

Frommer's Cool for Kids: Hotels

Plaza Hotel (see p. 87) Kids like the rooftop swimming pool and sun terrace so much that it might be hard to get them to leave for the Prado. The Plaza is a landmark, a skyscraper for Madrid.

Novotel Madrid (see p. 98) Children under 16 stay free in their parents' room, where the sofa converts into a comfortable bed. Kids delight in the open-air swimming pool and the offerings of the bountiful breakfast buffet.

Tirol (see p.105) This centrally located three-star hotel is a favorite of families seeking good comfort at moderate price. It also has a cafeteria.

Rates: 15,900 ptas. ($112.90) single; 19,925 ptas. ($141.50) double; from 21,160 ptas. ($150.20) suite. Breakfast 1,200 ptas. ($8.50) extra. AE, DC, MC, V. **Parking:** 1,700 ptas. ($12.10).

Opened in 1947 on an affluent residential street near the center of town, this hotel has a 1930s style art deco facade and a 1940s interior filled with well-upholstered furniture and richly grained paneling. Several public rooms lead off a central oval area; one of them includes a bar area. As in many hotels of its era, the bedrooms vary, with some large enough for entertaining, with a small but separate sitting area for reading or watching TV. All contain piped-in music. This is one of the most attractive medium-size hotels in Madrid, with plenty of comfort and convenience. The in-house restaurant, Las Lanzas, features both international and Spanish cuisine. Parking is available on the premises.

Hotel Alcalá, Alcalá, 66, 28009 Madrid. ☎ **34-1/435-10-60.** Fax 34-1/435-11-05. 153 rms. A/C MINIBAR TV TEL Metro: Príncipe de Vergara.

Rates: 13,500 ptas. ($95.90) single; 7,900 ptas. ($127.10) double. Breakfast 1,000 ptas. ($7.10) extra. AE, DC, MC, V. Parking: 1,400 ptas. ($9.90).

Hotel Alcalá enjoys an enviable position on a busy boulevard near the northern edge of Retiro Park, close to the "Golden Triangle" of art museums, including the Prado. It has tastefully modern guest rooms, each with voluminous draperies, a tile-and-wooden headboard, coordinated colors, a private bathroom, and a TV that receives many different European channels.

Facilities within the hotel include a two-level public lounge dotted with comfortable chairs, the ornate Restaurant Basque, a lower-level coffee shop, an underground garage, and a bright Toledo-red American bar opening off the lounge.

Novotel Madrid, Calle Albacete, 1 (at the corner of Avenida Badajos), 28027 Madrid. ☎ **34-1/405-46-00,** or toll free in North America **800/221-4542.** Fax 34-1/404-11-05. 236 rms. A/C MINIBAR TV TEL **Metro:** Concepción. **Directions:** Exit from the M-30 at Barrio de la Concepción/Parque de las Avenidas, just before reaching the city limits of central Madrid, then look for the chain's trademark electric-blue signs.

Rates: 15,794 ptas. ($112.10) single; 18,550 ptas. ($131.70) double. Children under 16 free in parents' room. Weekend rate: 11,130 ptas. ($79) single or double. Breakfast 1,272 ptas. ($9) extra. AE, DC, MC, V. **Parking:** Free.

Novotel was originally intended to serve the hotel needs of a cluster of multinational corporations with headquarters 1½ miles east of the center of Madrid, but its guest rooms are so comfortable and its prices so reasonable that tourists have begun using it as well. Opened in 1986, it is located on the highway, away from the maze of sometimes confusing inner-city streets, which makes it attractive to motorists.

Bedrooms are designed in a standardized format whose popularity in Europe has made it one of the hotel industry's most notable success stories. Each contains a well-designed bathroom, in-house movies, a radio, a TV, and soundproofing. Each sofa, once its bolster pillows are removed, can be transformed into a comfortable bed where children can sleep. The English-speaking staff is well-versed in both sightseeing attractions and solutions to most business-related problems.

MODERATE

Gran Hotel Colón, Pez Volador, 11, 28007 Madrid. ☎ **34-1/573-59-00.** Fax 34-1/573-08-09. 274 rms (all with bath), 16 suites. A/C MINIBAR TV TEL **Metro:** Sainz de Baranda.

Rates: 11,000-13,000 ptas ($78.10–$92.30) single; 16,000 ptas. ($113.60) double; from 22,000 ptas. ($156.20) suite. Breakfast 900 ptas. ($6.40) extra. AE, DC, MC, V. **Parking:** 1,500 ptas. ($10.70).

West of Retiro Park, the Gran Hotel Colón is a few minutes from the city center by subway. Built in 1966, it offers comfortable yet moderately priced accommodations in one of Madrid's modern hotel structures. More than half of the accommodations have private balconies, and all contain comfortably traditional furniture, much of it built-in.

To top everything off literally, 11 stories up is a rooftop swimming pool where you can sunbathe with a view of Madrid's skyline. Other assets include two dining rooms, a covered garage, and Bingo games. One of the Colón's founders was an accomplished interior designer, which accounts for the unusual stained-glass windows and murals in the public rooms and the paintings by Spanish artists in the lounge.

Hotel Claridge, Plaza Conde de Casal, 6, 28007 Madrid. ☎ **34-1/551-94-00.** Fax 34-1/501-03-85. 150 rms (all with bath). A/C TV TEL **Metro:** Conde Casal.

Rates: 9,950 ptas. ($70.60) single; 12,990 ptas. ($92.20) double. Breakfast 700 ptas. ($5) extra. AE, MC, V. **Parking:** 1,700 ptas. ($12.10) in nearby garage.

This contemporary building, last renovated in 1994, is beyond Retiro Park, about five minutes from the Prado by taxi or subway. The bedrooms are well organized and pleasantly styled: small and compact, with coordinated furnishings and colors. You can take your meals in the hotel's cafeteria and also relax in the modern lounge.

Chamberí

VERY EXPENSIVE

Castellana Inter-Continental Hotel, Paseo de la Castellana, 49, 28046 Madrid. ☎ **34-1/310-02-00,** or toll free **800/327-0200** in the U.S. Fax 34-1/319-58-53. 270 rms, 35 suites. A/C MINIBAR TV TEL **Metro:** Rubén Darío.

Rates: 29,500-33,000 ptas. ($209.50–$234.30) single; 37,000–41,000 ptas. ($262.70–$291.10) double; from 70,000 ptas. ($497) suite. Breakfast 1,700 ptas. ($12.10). AE, DC, MC, V. **Parking:** 1,600 ptas. ($11.40).

Solid, spacious, and conservatively modern, this is one of the more reliable hotels in Madrid. Originally built in 1963 as the then-most-prestigious hotel on this famous boulevard, the Castellana Inter-Continental lies behind a barrier of trees within a neighborhood of apartment houses and luxury hotels. Its high-ceilinged public rooms provide a welcome refuge from the Madrileño heat. They're considered a tribute to the art of Spanish masonry, with terrazzo floors and a large-scale collection of angular abstract murals pieced together from multicolored stones and tiles. Most of the accommodations have private balconies and traditional furniture, each with a color TV with in-house videos and many channels beamed in from across Europe.

Dining/Entertainment: The La Ronda Bar offers drinks near the elegant Los Continentes Restaurant, serving both a creative and Mediterranean cuisine. In addition, El Jardín is a retreat in summer, with candlelit dinners and live soft background music. Good cookery and thrifty prices are found at El Sarracín, yet another restaurant.

Services: There's a helpful concierge and a travel agent who will book theater tickets, rental cars, and airline connections; there are also 24-hour room service, laundry, and babysitting.

Facilities: Kiosks and boutiques, hairdresser/barbershop, business center, top floor gym with sauna and outdoor solarium.

★ **Santo Mauro Hotel,** Calle Zurbano, 36, 28010 Madrid. ☎ **34-1/319-6900.** Fax 34-1/308-5417. 31 rms, 6 suites. A/C MINIBAR TV TEL **Metro:** Rubén Darío or Alonso Martínez.

Rates: 27,000 ptas. ($191.70) single; 52,000 ptas. ($369.20) double; from 60,500 ptas. ($429.60) suite. Breakfast 1,950 ptas. ($13.80) extra. AE, DC, MC, V. **Parking:** 1,950 ptas. ($13.80).

This hotel opened in 1991 within the once decrepit neoclassical walls of a villa that was originally built in 1894 for the Duke of Santo Mauro. Set within a garden and reminiscent of the kind of architecture you'd expect to find in France, it contains a mixture of rich fabrics, art deco art and furnishings, and an impressive number of staff members who exceed the number of accommodations by two to one. Each of the bedrooms contains an audio system with a wide choice of tapes and CDs as well as many coordinated decor notes, which might include curtains of raw silk, Persian carpets, and jewel-toned colors.

Dining/Entertainment: The Belagua Restaurant is reviewed separately in Section 2 of this chapter. An elegant bar is located off the main lobby, and tables are set up beneath the garden's large trees for drinks and snacks.

Services: 24-hour room service, laundry/valet, reception staff trained in the procurement of practically anything.

Facilities: Indoor swimming pool, health club with sauna and massage.

EXPENSIVE

Conde Duque, Plaza Conde Valle de Súchil, 5, 28015 Madrid. ☎ **34-1/447-70-00.** Fax 34-1/448-35-69. 136 rms, 7 suites. A/C MINIBAR TV TEL **Metro:** San Bernardo.

Rates (including breakfast): 19,780 ptas. ($140.40) single; 25,850 ptas. ($183.50) double; 30,600 ptas. ($217.30) suite. AE, DC, MC, V.

The modern three-star Conde Duque, near a branch of the Galerías Preciados department store, opens onto a tree-filled plaza in a residential neighborhood that's near the Glorieta Quevado. The hotel is 12 blocks north of the Plaza de España, off Calle de San Bernardo, which starts at the Gran Vía—the walk to the plaza is too long, but a subway stop is nearby. The guest-room furnishings include built-in modern headboards and reproductions of 19th-century English pieces, plus bedside lights and telephones. Room service is provided 24 hours.

Hotel Escultor, Miguel Angel, 3, 28010 Madrid. ☎ **91/310-42-03.** Fax 91/319-25-84. 17 rms (all with bath), 38 suites. A/C MINIBAR TV TEL **Metro:** Rubén Darío.

Rates: Mon–Thurs, 11,775 ptas. ($83.60) single; 18,200 ptas. ($129.20) doubles and suites. Fri–Sun, 7,975 ptas. ($56.60) single; 9,950 ptas. ($70.60) doubles and suites. Breakfast 1,100 ptas. ($7.80) extra. AE, DC, MC, V. **Parking:** 1,800 ptas. ($12.80) nearby.

Originally built in 1975, this comfortably furnished hotel provides fewer services and offers fewer facilities than others within its category, but it compensates with larger accommodations. Each guest unit has its own charm and contemporary styling—with video films; a private bathroom; and a layout that's well-organized, efficient, and logical.

The hotel is fully air-conditioned, and the staff provides information about facilities in the neighborhood.

Dining/Entertainment: The hotel has a small but comfortable bar that's open nightly from 7pm to 1am, and a traditional restaurant, the Señorio de Erazu, which closes on Saturday at lunchtime and all day on Sunday.

Services: Room service is offered at breakfast only, from 7 to 11am.

Residencia Bréton, Bréton de los Herreros, 29, 28003 Madrid. ☎ **34-1/442-83-00.** Fax 34-1/441-38-16. 56 rms. A/C MINIBAR TV TEL **Metro:** Ríos Rosas.

Rates: 13,500 ptas. ($95.90) single; 18,550 ptas. ($131.70) double. Breakfast 1,000 ptas. ($7.10) extra. AE, DC, MC, V. **Parking:** 1,200 ptas. ($8.50) nearby.

You'll find this modern hotel, well furnished with reproductions of Iberian pieces, on a side street several blocks from Paseo de la Castellana. As a residencia, it doesn't offer a major dining room, but it does have a little bar and breakfast room adjoining the reception lounge. All the guest rooms have wooden beds, wrought-iron electrical fixtures, wall-to-wall curtains, comfortable chairs, and tilework painted with ornate designs in the bathrooms.

Miguel Angel, Miguel Angel, 29–31, 28010 Madrid. ☎ **34-1/442-81-99.** Fax 34-1/442-53-20. 278 rms, 26 suites. A/C MINIBAR TV TEL **Metro:** Rubén Darío.

Rates: Mon–Thurs, 27,350 ptas. ($194.20) single or double. Breakfast 1,800 ptas. ($12.80). Fri–Sun (including breakfast): 13,125 ptas. ($93.20) single; 16,600 ptas. ($117.90) double. Suites from 51,000 ptas. ($362.10) all week. AE, DC, MC, V. **Parking:** 1,800 ptas. ($12.80).

Just off Paseo de la Castellana, Miguel Angel, sleekly modern, opened its doors in 1975 and has been renovated and kept up to date periodically ever since. It has much going for it—ideal location, contemporary styling, good furnishings and art objects, an efficient staff, and plenty of comfort. Behind its facade is an expansive sun terrace on several levels, with clusters of garden furniture that are surrounded by paintings of semitropical scenes.

The soundproof bedrooms contain radios; TVs; color-coordinated fabrics and carpets; and, in many cases, reproductions of classic Iberian furniture.

Dining/Entertainment: The Farnesio bar is decorated in a Spanish Victorian style, and piano music is played beginning at 8pm. A well-managed restaurant on the premises is the Florencia, which serves a set lunch or dinner for 6,000 ptas. ($42.60). Dinner is also served until around 3am in the Zacarias boîte restaurant, where you can dine while watching an occasional cabaret or musical performance.

Services: 24-hour room service, same-day laundry/valet.

Facilities: Indoor heated swimming pool, saunas, hairdressers, and a drugstore. Art exhibitions are sponsored in the arcade of boutiques.

INEXPENSIVE

Hostal Residencia Don Diego, Calle de Velázquez, 45, 28001 Madrid. ☎ **34-1/435-07-60.** Fax 34-1/431-42-63. 58 rms (all with bath). A/C TEL **Metro:** Velázquez.

Rates: 5,800 ptas. ($41.20) single; 7,500 ptas. ($53.30) double; 10,125 ptas. ($71.90) triple. Breakfast 600 ptas. ($4.30) extra. MC, V.

On the fifth floor of a building with an elevator, Don Diego is in a combination residential/commercial neighborhood that's relatively convenient to many of the city monuments. The vestibule contains an elegant winding staircase accented with iron griffin heads supporting its balustrade. The hotel is warm and inviting, filled with leather couches and comfortable, no-nonsense angular but attractive furniture. A bar stands at the far end of the main sitting room. The hotel's cafeteria serves breakfast from 8am and continues to remain open for drinks and snacks throughout the day (until 4pm). From 8pm to midnight daily, you can also order drinks and snacks, especially sandwiches and omelets. Laundry service is provided, and room service is available daily from 8am to midnight.

Chamartín

VERY EXPENSIVE

Eurobuilding, Calle Padre Damián, 23, 28036 Madrid. ☎ **34-1/345-45-00.** Fax 34-1/345-45-76. 420 rms, 100 suites. A/C MINIBAR TV TEL **Metro:** Cuzco.

Rates: 25,000 ptas. ($177.50) single; 32,000 ptas. ($227.20) double; from 40,000 ptas. ($284) suite. Breakfast 1,900 ptas. ($13.50) extra. AE, DC, MC, V. **Parking:** 1,800 ptas. ($12.80).

Even while the Eurobuilding was on the drawing boards, the rumor was that this five-star sensation of white marble would provide, in the architect's words, "a new concept in deluxe hotels." It has long ago lived up to its advance billing, reflecting a high level of taste and design. It is actually two hotels linked by a courtyard, away from the city center but right in the midst of apartment houses, boutiques, nightclubs, first-class restaurants, tree-shaded squares, and the modern Madrid business world.

The more glamorous of the twin buildings is the main one, named Las Estancias de Eurobuilding; it contains only suites, all of which were recently renovated in luxurious pastel shades. Here, drinks await you in your refrigerator. Ornately carved gold-and-white beds, background music, roomwide terraces for breakfast and cocktail entertaining—all are tastefully coordinated. Across the courtyard, the neighbor Eurobuilding contains less impressive—but still very comfortable—single and double rooms, many with views from private balconies of the formal garden and swimming pool below. All the accommodations have TVs with video movies and satellite reception, security doors, and individual safes.

Dining/Entertainment: Le Relais Coffee Shop is suitable for a quick bite, and Le Relais Restaurant offers buffets at both breakfast and lunch. For more formal dining, La Taberna at both lunch and dinner features a selection of Spanish and international cuisine, specializing in seafood and various paella dishes.

Services: Laundry/valet, concierge, 24-hour room service, babysitting.

Facilities: Health club with sauna, outdoor swimming pool.

Melía Castilla, Calle Capitán, Haya, 43, 28020 Madrid. ☎ **34-1/571-22-11,** or toll free **800/336-3542** in the U.S. Fax 34-1/571-2210. 896 rms, 14 suites. A/C MINIBAR TV TEL **Metro:** Cuzco.

Rates: 25,000–30,500 ptas. ($177.50–$216.60) single; 31,000–36,000 ptas. ($220.10–$255.60) double; from 63,000 ptas. ($447.30) suite. Breakfast 1,950 ptas. ($13.80) extra. AE, DC, MC, V. **Parking:** 1,850 ptas. ($13.10).

This mammoth hotel qualifies, along with the above-recommended Palace, as one of the largest in Europe. Loaded with facilities and built primarily to accommodate huge conventions, the Melía Castilla also caters to the needs of the individual traveler. Everything is larger than life here: You need a floor plan to direct yourself around its precincts. The lounges and pristine marble corridors are vast—there are even a landscaped garden and a showroom full of the latest-model cars.

Each twin-bedded room comes with a private bath, a radio, a color TV, and modern furniture. The Melía Castilla is in the north of Madrid, about a block west of Paseo de la Castellana, a short drive from the Chamartín railway station.

Dining/Entertainment: The hotel has a coffee shop, a seafood restaurant, a restaurant specializing in paella and other rice dishes, cocktail lounges, and the Trinidad nightclub. In addition, there's the restaurant/show Scala Melía Castilla.

Services: 24-hour room service, hairdresser/barbershop, concierge, babysitting, laundry/valet.

Facilities: Swimming pool, shopping arcade with souvenir shops and bookstore, saunas, gymnasium, parking garage.

EXPENSIVE

Cuzco, Paseo de la Castellana, 133, 28046 Madrid. ☎ **34-1/556-06-00.** Fax 34-1/556-03-72. 320 rms, 10 suites. A/C MINIBAR TV TEL **Metro:** Cuzco.

Rates: 15,440 ptas. ($109.60) single; 20,550 ptas. ($145.90) double; from 26,000 ptas. ($184.60) suite. Breakfast 1,190 ptas. ($8.40) extra. AE, DC, MC, V. **Parking:** 1,500 ptas. ($10.70).

Popular with businesspeople and tour groups, Cuzco lies in a commercial neighborhood of big buildings, government ministries, spacious avenues, and the main Congress Hall. The Chamartín railway station is a 10-minute walk north, so it's a popular and convenient address.

This 15-floor structure, set back from Madrid's longest boulevard, has been redecorated and modernized many times since it was completed in 1967. The architect of the Cuzco allowed for spacious bedrooms, each with a separate sitting area, video movies, and a private bathroom. The decorator provided modern furnishings and patterned rugs.

There is a bilevel snack bar and cafeteria. The lounge is a forest of marble pillars and leather armchairs, its ambience enhanced by contemporary oil paintings and tapestries. Facilities include free parking, a beauty parlor, a sauna, massage, a gymnasium, and a cocktail bar.

Hotel Chamartín, Agustín de Foxa, Estacíon de Chamartín, 28036 Madrid. ☎ **34-1/323-30-87.** Fax 34-1/733-02-14. 378 rms, 18 suites. A/C MINIBAR TV TEL **Metro:** Chamartín. **Bus:** 5.

Rates: 12,500 ptas. ($88.80) single; 17,300 ptas. ($122.80) double; from 28,000 ptas. ($198.80) suites. Breakfast 1,000 ptas. ($7.10) extra. AE, DC, MC, V. **Parking:** 1,200 ptas. ($8.50) in nearby garage.

This brick-sided hotel soars nine stories above the northern periphery of Madrid. It's part of the massive modern shopping complex attached to the Chamartín railway station, although once you're inside your soundproofed room, the noise of the railway station will seem far away. The owner of the building is RENFE, Spain's government railway system, but the nationwide chain that administers it is HUSA Hotels. The hotel lies 15 minutes by taxi from both the airport and the historic core of Madrid and is conveniently close to one of the capital's busiest Metro stops. Especially oriented to the business traveler, the Chamartín offers a currency exchange kiosk, a travel agency, a car-rental office, and a lobby video screen that posts the arrival and departure of all of Chamartín's trains.

A coffee bar serves breakfast daily, and room service is available from 7am to midnight. The hotel restaurant, Cota 13, serves an international cuisine. A short walk from the hotel lobby, within the railway-station complex, are a handful of shops and movie theaters, a roller-skating rink, a disco, and ample parking.

MODERATE

Aristos, Avenida Pío XII, 34, 28016 Madrid. ☎ **34-1/345-04-50.** Fax 34-1/345-10-23. 24 rms (all with bath). A/C TV TEL **Metro:** Pío XII.

Rates: 12,000 ptas. ($85.20) single; 16,000 ptas. ($113.60) double. Breakfast 750 ptas. ($5.30) extra. AE, DC, MC, V. **Parking:** 1,500 ptas. ($10.70).

This three-star hotel is in an up-and-coming residential area of Madrid, not far from the Eurobuilding (see above). Its main advantage is a front garden where you can lounge, have a drink or order a complete meal. The hotel's restaurant, El Chaflán, is frequented by residents of the neighborhood in addition to hotel visitors. Each of the bedrooms has a small terrace and an uncomplicated collection of modern furniture.

Argüelles/Moncloa

VERY EXPENSIVE

Husa Princesa, Serrano Jover, 3, 28015 Madrid. ☎ **34-1/542-35-00.** Fax. 34-1/559-4665. 320 rms, 38 suites. A/C TV TEL **Metro:** Argüelles.

Rates: 24,800 ptas. ($176.10) single; 31,200 ptas. ($221.50) double; from 61,000 ptas. ($433.10) suite. Breakfast 1,950 ptas. ($13.80) extra. AE, DC, MC, V. **Parking:** 2,500 ptas. ($17.80).

Originally built during the mid-1970s and radically renovated after its takeover in 1991 by the nationwide Spanish chain HUSA, the Princesa is a sprawling hotel designed with a series of massive rectangular sections clustered into an angular whole. The concrete-and-glass facade overlooks busy boulevards in the center of Madrid.

The hotel is well patronized by both businesspersons and groups of visiting tourists; each of the bedrooms contains comfortable, contemporary furniture and a modernized bathroom.

Dining/Entertainment: The hotel's restaurant is called Ricón de Argüelles. There is also a bar, the Bar Royal.

Services: 24-hour room service, concierge, babysitting.

Facilities: The interior contains a large assortment of conference rooms, an underground garage, and a hairdressing salon.

EXPENSIVE

Melía Madrid, Princesa, 17, 28008 Madrid. ☎ **34-1/541-8200,** or toll free **800/336-3542** in the U.S. Fax 34-1/541-19-05. 260 rms, 5 suites. A/C MINIBAR TV TEL **Metro:** Rodríguez.

Rates: 25,000 ptas. ($177.50) single; 26,000 ptas. ($184.60) double; from 45,000 ptas. ($319.50) suite. Breakfast 1,200 ptas. ($8.50) extra. AE, DC, MC, V. **Parking:** 1,600 ptas. ($11.40).

Here you'll find one of the most modern yet uniquely Spanish hotels in the country. Its 23 floors of wide picture windows have taken a permanent position in the capital's skyline. Each of the bedrooms is comfortable, spacious, and filled with contemporary furnishings plus a TV with video movies and many channels from across Europe. Most

offer views over the skyline of Madrid. The chalk-white walls dramatize the flamboyant use of color accents; the bathrooms are sheathed in marble.
Dining/Entertainment: Restaurant Princesa is elegant and restful; equally popular is Don Pepe Grill. The cuisine in both restaurants is international and includes an array of Japanese and Indian dishes. There are also three bars and a coffee shop.
Services: 24-hour room service, concierge, babysitting, hairdresser/barber, laundry.
Facilities: A gallery that includes souvenir shops and bookstores, health club with sauna and massage.

MODERATE

Tirol, Marqués de Urquijo, 4, 28008 Madrid. ☎ **34-1/548-19-00.**
Fax 34-1/541-39-58. 97 rms, 4 suites. A/C TEL **Metro:** Argüelles. **Bus:** 2 or 21.
Rates: 7,300 ptas. ($51.80) single; 10,325 ptas. ($73.30) double; 14,390 ptas. ($102.20) suite. Breakfast 535 ptas. ($3.80) extra. MC, V. **Parking:** 1,710 ptas. ($12.10).

A short walk from Plaza de España and the swank Melía Madrid Hotel (see above) is a good choice for clean, unpretentious comfort. A three-star hotel, the Tirol offers only nine singles. Eight of the guest rooms have private terraces. Furnishings are simple and functional. A cafeteria and a parking garage are within the hotel.

2 Dining

It's the custom in Madrid to consume the big meal of the day from 2 to 4pm. After a recuperative siesta, Madrileños then enjoy snacks called *tapas* in hundreds of bars or tascas scattered throughout the capital.

All this nibbling is followed by dinner—more likely a light supper—in a restaurant, usually from 9:30pm to as late as midnight. Many restaurants, however, start serving dinner at 8pm to accommodate visitors from other countries who don't like to dine late.

Madrid restaurant prices shock first-time visitors—that is, at least those who don't live in such expensive cities as Tokyo, Oslo, London, and Paris.

Meals include service and tax (ranging from 6% to 12%, depending on the restaurant) but not drinks, which add to the tab considerably. The restaurants listed below that are categorized as "very expensive" charge from 6,000 pesetas ($42.60) per person for a meal. The restaurants that are rated, "expensive" ask from 4,000 to 6,000 pesetas ($28.40 to $42.60) per person for a meal; "moderate," from 2,000 to 4,000 pesetas ($14.20 to $28.40); and "inexpensive," less than 2,000 pesetas ($14.20) per person.

If you can't afford the prices charged by most first-class restaurants in Madrid, there is a variety of budget dining options to keep your bill down.

Don't overtip. Follow the local custom. Theoretically, service is included in the price of your meal, but it's customary to leave 10% additional.

For more details on dining (such as when and what to eat), see "Food & Drink" in Chapter 1.

Menú del Día and Cubierto Order the *menú del día* (menu of the day) or *cubierto* both fixed-price menus based on what is fresh at the market that day. They are the dining bargains in Madrid, although often lacking the quality of the more expensive à la carte dining. Usually each will include a first course, such as fish soup or hors d'oeuvres, followed by a main dish, plus bread, dessert, and the wine of the house.

You won't have a large choice. The *menú turístico* is a similar fixed-price menu, but for many it's too large, especially at lunch. Only those with large appetites will find it the best bargain.

Cafeterias These are not self-service establishments but restaurants serving light, often American, cuisine. Go for breakfast instead of dining at your hotel, unless it's included in the room price. Some cafeterias offer no hot meals, but many feature combined plates of fried eggs, french fries, veal, and lettuce-and-tomato salad, which make adequate meals, or light fare like hot dogs and hamburgers.

Tapas If you wish, you can dine well at lunch and stop by a tasca for an evening meal of appetizer-size tapas—eggs in mayonnaise, potato omelets, codfish salad, cured ham, Russian salad, octopus in garlic-mayonnaise sauce, grilled mushrooms, stuffed peppers, croquettes, and so forth.

Near the Plaza de Las Cortés

EXPENSIVE

El Espejo, Paseo de Recoletos, 31. ☎ **308-23-47.**

Cuisine: INTERNATIONAL. **Reservations:** Required. **Metro:** Banco de España or Colón. **Bus:** 27.

Prices: Appetizers 950–1,400 ptas. ($6.70–$9.90); main courses 1,650–2,700 ptas. ($11.70–$19.20); *menú del día* 3,500 ptas. ($24.90). AE, DC, MC, V.

Open: Lunch, Sun–Fri 1–4pm; dinner, daily 9pm–midnight.

Here you'll find good-tasting food and one of the most perfectly crafted art nouveau decors in Madrid. If the weather is good, you can choose one of the outdoor tables, served by a battery of uniformed waiters who carry food across the busy street to a green area flanked with trees and strolling pedestrians. I personally prefer a table inside, within view of the tile maidens with vines and flowers entwined in their hair. After entering, you'll find yourself in a charming café/bar, where many visitors linger before walking down a hallway toward the spacious dining room. Dishes include grouper ragoût with clams, steak tartare, guinea fowl with Armagnac, and lean duck meat with pineapple. Profiteroles with cream and chocolate sauce make a delectable dessert.

MODERATE

Edelweiss, Jovelianos, 7. ☎ **521-03-26.**

Cuisine: GERMAN. **Reservations:** Recommended. **Metro:** Sevilla. **Bus:** 5.

Prices: Appetizers 800–1,200 ptas. ($5.70–$8.50); main courses 1,200–2,600 ptas. ($8.50–$18.50); fixed-price menu 1,900 ptas. ($13.50). AE, MC, V.

Open: Lunch, daily 12:30–4pm; dinner, Mon–Sat 8:30pm–midnight. **Closed:** Aug.

Edelweiss is a German standby that has provided good-quality food and service at moderate prices since World War II. Since no reservations are accepted, during peak dining hours the bar is likely to be full of clients waiting for tables. You are served hearty portions of food, mugs of draft beer, and fluffy pastries; that's why there's always a wait. **Tip:** To beat the crowds, go for dinner at un-Spanish hours, say around 9pm, when tables are not at a premium. But even when it's jammed, service is almost always courteous.

You can start with Bismarck herring, then dive into goulash with Spaetzle or Eisbein (pigs' knuckles) with sauerkraut and mashed potatoes, the most popular dish at the restaurant. Finish with the homemade apple tart. The decor is vaguely German, with travel posters and wood-paneled walls. Edelweiss is air-conditioned in summer.

INEXPENSIVE

La Trucha, Manuel Fernandez Gonzalez, 3. ☎ **492-58-33.**

Cuisine: SPANISH/SEAFOOD. **Reservations:** Recommended. **Metro:** Sevilla.
Prices: Appetizers 350–2,600 ptas. ($2.50–$18.50); main courses 950–3,200 ptas. ($6.70–$22.70), *menú del día* 2,800 ptas. ($19.90). No credit cards.
Open: Lunch, Mon–Sat 1-4pm; dinner, Mon–Sat 8pm–midnight. **Closed:** Aug.

With its Andalusian tavern ambience, La Trucha boasts a street-level bar and small dining room—the arched ceiling and whitewashed walls festive with hanging braids of garlic, dried peppers, and onions. On the lower level the walls of a second bustling area are covered with eye-catching antiques, bullfight notices, and bric-a-brac. The specialty is fish, and there's a complete à la carte menu including *trucha* (trout); *verbenas de abumados* (literally, a "street party" of smoked delicacies); a stew called *fabada* ("glorious"; made with beans, Galician ham, black sausage, and smoked bacon); and a *comida casera rabo de toro* (home-style oxtail). No one should miss nibbling on the *tapas variadas* in the bar. If this Trucha turns out to be too crowded, there's another La Trucha at Núñez de Arce, 6 (☎ **532-08-82**).

Near the Plaza de España

EXPENSIVE

Bajamar, Gran Vía, 78. ☎ **559-59-03.**

Cuisine: SEAFOOD. **Reservations:** Recommended. **Metro:** Plaza de España.
Prices: Appetizers 850–3,600 ptas. ($6–$25.60); main courses 1,750–4,500 ptas. ($12.40–$32). AE, DC, MC, V.
Open: Lunch, daily 1–4pm; dinner, daily 8pm–midnight.

Bajamar, one of the best fish houses in Spain, is right in the heart of the city, near Plaza de España. Both fish and shellfish are shipped in fresh daily by air from their points of origin, the prices depending on what the market charges. Lobster, king crab, prawns, soft-shell crabs, and the like are all priced according to weight. There is a large array of reasonably priced dishes as well. The setting is contemporary and attractive, with smooth and professional service. The menu is in English. For an appetizer, I'd recommend half a dozen giant oysters or rover crayfish. The special seafood soup is a most satisfying selection that's a meal in itself. Try also the lobster bisque. Some of the more recommendable main courses include turbot Gallego style, the special seafood paella, and even baby squid cooked in its ink. Desserts are simple, including the chef's custard.

MODERATE

Las Cuevas del Duque, Princesa, 16. ☎ **559-50-37.**

Cuisine: SPANISH. **Reservations:** Required. **Metro:** Ventura Rodríguez. **Bus:** 1, 2, or 42.
Prices: Appetizers 800–3,000 ptas. ($5.70–$21.30); main courses 1,875–3,000 ptas. ($13.30–$21.30). AE, DC, MC, V.
Open: Lunch, daily 1–4pm; dinner, daily 8pm–midnight.

In front of the Duke of Alba's palace, a short walk from Plaza de España, is Las Cuevas del Duque, with an underground bar and a small, 10-table mesón that serves such simple Spanish fare as roast suckling pig, sirloin, lamb cutlet, and a few seafood dishes, including fish cooked in salt. In fair weather a few tables are set outside, beside a tiny triangular garden. Other tables line Calle de la Princesa side and make an enjoyable roost for an afternoon drink.

BUDGET

$ **Vera Cruz,** San Leonardo, 5. ☎ **547-11-50.**

Cuisine: SPANISH. **Reservations:** Not required. **Metro:** Plaza de España.
Prices: Appetizers 350–550 ptas. ($2.50–$3.90); main courses 550–950 ptas. ($3.90–$6.70); fixed-price menu 950 ptas. ($6.70). No credit cards.
Open: Lunch, daily 1–5pm; dinner, daily 8pm–midnight.

Behind Plaza de España, with its landmark Edificio España, you'll find this old standby for hungry budget-minded visitors. It's a simple *económico,* but the food is acceptable and the service polite. The *menú del día* usually includes soup or hors d'oeuvres, followed by a meat or fish dish, then cheese or fruit, plus bread and wine. The Vera Cruz also has daily specials like paella and cocido, a typical Madrid dish made of chick peas, sausage, cabbage, and potatoes.

On or Near the Gran Vía

MODERATE

Arce, Augusto Figueroa, 32. ☎ **522-59-13.**

Cuisine: BASQUE. **Reservations:** Recommended. **Metro:** Colón.

Frommer's Smart Traveler: Restaurants

Value-Conscious Travelers Should Consider the Following:

1. Most budget restaurants offer a *cubierto* or *menú del día.* It's not very adventurous and limited in selections, but in most cases it is at least 30% cheaper than ordering à la carte.
2. Often major restaurants will offer a *menú del día* at lunch—the Madrid equivalent of a businessperson's lunch—but will revert to expensive à la carte listings in the evening. Check the menu offerings posted outside the restaurant.
3. Patronize the *tascas* (local taverns), and order two or three *tapas* (hors d'oeuvres). Most portions are generous, and you can dine for one-quarter of the price you'd pay in most restaurants.
4. Lock for the *platos del días* (daily specials). They're invariably fresh and usually carry a much lower price tag than regular à la carte listings.
5. Ask for the *vino de la casa,* or house wine. This wine is served in a carafe and is only a fraction of the cost of bottled wines.
6. Anything consumed standing up at a counter or sitting on a bar stool is cheaper than food served at a table.
7. Patronize the famous budget restaurant streets of Madrid: Calle del Barco, Ventura de la Vega, and Calle Echegaray.

Prices: Appetizers 1,100–2,850 ptas. ($7.80–$20.20); main courses 2,150–2,850 ptas. ($15.30–$20.20). AE, DC, MC, V.
Open: Lunch, Mon–Fri 1:30–4pm; dinner, Mon–Sat 9pm–midnight. **Closed:** Week before Easter and Aug 15–31.

Arce has brought some of the best modern interpretations of Basque cuisine to the palates of Madrid, thanks to the enthusiasm of owner/chef Iñaki Camba and his wife, Theresa. Within a comfortably decorated dining room designed for the unabashed enjoyment of food without unnecessary decorative frills, you can enjoy simple preparations of the finest available ingredients, where the natural flavors are designed to dominate your taste buds. Examples include a salad of fresh scallops, an oven-baked casserole of fresh boletus mushrooms with few seasonings other than the woodsy taste of the original ingredients, unusual preparations of hake, and seasonal variations of such game dishes as pheasant and woodcock.

La Barraca, Reina 29–31. ☎ **532-71-54.**

Cuisine: VALENCIAN. **Reservations:** Recommended. **Metro:** Gran Vía or Sevilla. **Bus:** 1, 2, or 74.
Prices: Appetizers 650–4,000 ptas. ($4.60–$28.40); main courses 1,800–5,000 ptas. ($12.80–$35.50); fixed-price menu 2,800 ptas. ($19.90). AE, DC, MC, V.
Open: Lunch, daily 1–4pm; dinner, daily 8:30pm–midnight.

La Barraca is like a country inn—right off the Gran Vía. This Valencian-style restaurant is a well-managed establishment recommendable for its tasty Levante cooking. There are four different dining rooms, three of which lie one flight above street level; they're colorfully cluttered with ceramics, paintings, photographs, Spanish lanterns, flowers, and local artifacts. The house specialty is paella *à la valenciana,* made with fresh shellfish, and one of the most expensive items on the menu. The portions are enormous—only the most ravenous will clean out the skillet. House specialties in the appetizer category include *desgarrat* (a salad made with codfish and red peppers), Barraca mussels, and shrimp Orly. In addition to the already recommended paella, you can select at least 16 rice dishes, including rice with duck and rice with conger eel. Main dish specialties include brochette of angler fish and prawns and rabbit with fines herbes. Lemon-and-vodka sorbet makes a good finish.

$ **Casablanca,** Barquillo, 27. ☎ **521-1568.**

Cuisine: SPANISH/CONTINENTAL/AMERICAN. **Reservations:** Required. **Metro:** Alonso Martínez.
Prices: Appetizers 475–1,200 ptas. ($3.40–$8.50); main courses 1,250–2,200 ptas. ($8.90–$15.60). AE, DC, MC, V.
Open: Lunch, daily 1:30–4pm; dinner, daily 9pm–1am.

The theme here, of course, is the famous movie classic, and memorabilia (such as posters of Bogart and Bergman) are scattered over the two levels of its premises. The cuisine served at the umbrella-covered tables is a combination of Spanish, French, Italian, and American. You might begin with leeks in pastry. The chef's specialties include red peppers with smoked salmon, raw salmon marinated in champagne, filet mignon Bogart, and spaghetti vongole prepared with cream and shellfish. Selections from the American cuisine include Maryland-style fried chicken, barbecue spareribs, and chili con carne made Western style—hot. The owner is Dick Angstadt, an American. Casablanca also has a tapas bar.

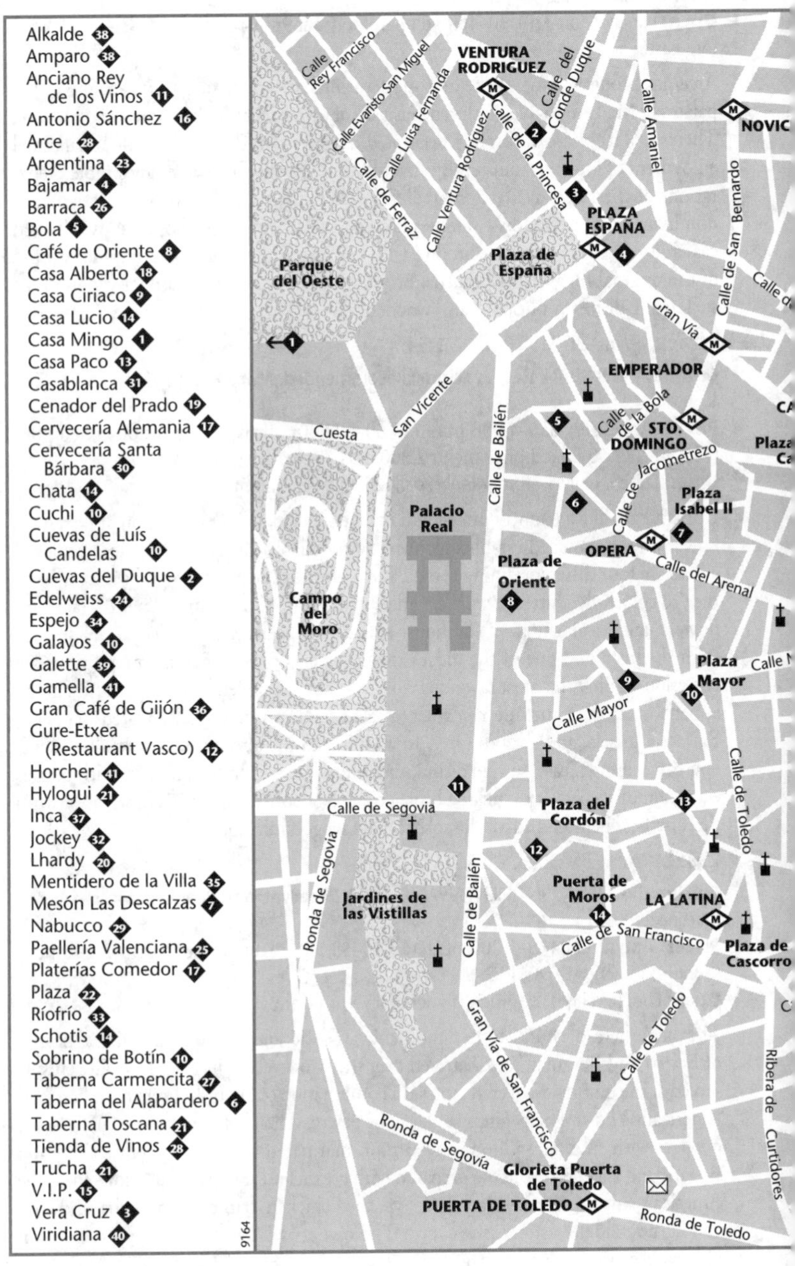

Alkalde 38
Amparo 38
Anciano Rey de los Vinos 11
Antonio Sánchez 16
Arce 28
Argentina 23
Bajamar 4
Barraca 26
Bola 5
Café de Oriente 8
Casa Alberto 18
Casa Ciriaco 9
Casa Lucio 14
Casa Mingo 1
Casa Paco 13
Casablanca 31
Cenador del Prado 19
Cervecería Alemania 17
Cervecería Santa Bárbara 30
Chata 14
Cuchi 10
Cuevas de Luís Candelas 10
Cuevas del Duque 2
Edelweiss 24
Espejo 34
Galayos 10
Galette 39
Gamella 41
Gran Café de Gijón 36
Gure-Etxea (Restaurant Vasco) 12
Horcher 41
Hylogui 21
Inca 37
Jockey 32
Lhardy 20
Mentidero de la Villa 35
Mesón Las Descalzas 7
Nabucco 29
Paellería Valenciana 25
Platerías Comedor 17
Plaza 22
Ríofrío 33
Schotis 14
Sobrino de Botín 10
Taberna Carmencita 27
Taberna del Alabardero 6
Taberna Toscana 21
Tienda de Vinos 28
Trucha 21
V.I.P. 15
Vera Cruz 3
Viridiana 40
9164
Calle Rey Francisco
Calle Evaristo San Miguel
Calle Luisa Fernanda
VENTURA RODRIGUEZ
Calle del Conde Duque
Calle Amaniel
NOVIC
Calle Ventura Rodríguez
Calle de la Princesa
Calle de Ferraz
PLAZA ESPAÑA
Plaza de España
Calle de San Bernardo
Parque del Oeste
Gran Vía
EMPERADOR
Cuesta San Vicente
Calle de Bailén
Calle de la Bola
STO. DOMINGO
Calle de Jacometrezo
Plaza Isabel II
Palacio Real
OPERA
Plaza de Oriente
Calle del Arenal
Campo del Moro
Plaza Mayor
Calle Mayor
Calle de Toledo
Calle de Segovia
Plaza del Cordón
Ronda de Segovia
Jardines de las Vistillas
Puerta de Moros
LA LATINA
Calle de San Francisco
Plaza de Cascorro
Gran Vía de San Francisco
Ribera de Curtidores
Glorieta Puerta de Toledo
PUERTA DE TOLEDO
Ronda de Toledo

Dining in Central Madrid

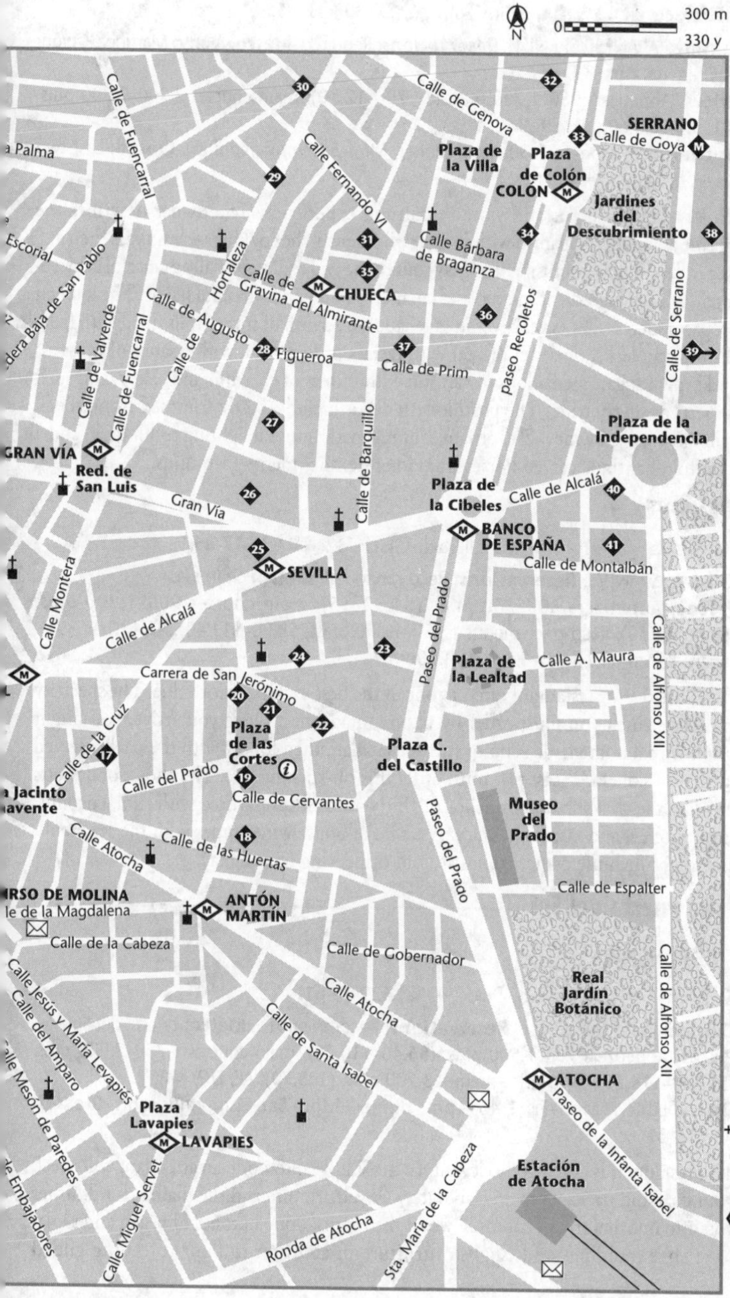

Metro Church Post Office Information

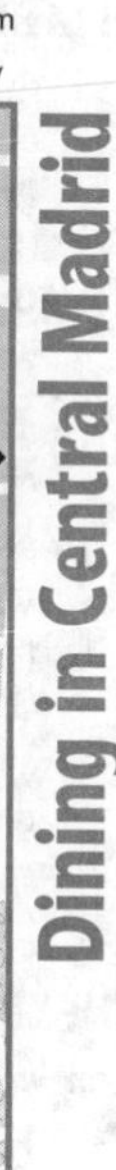

El Mentidero de la Villa, Santo Tomé, 6. ☎ **308-12-85.**

Cuisine: JAPANESE/SPANISH. **Reservations:** Required. **Metro:** Alonso Martínez, Colón, or Gran Vía. **Bus:** 37.
Prices: Appetizers 950–1,700 ptas. ($6.70–$12.10); main courses 2,200–2,900 ptas. ($15.60–$20.60). AE, DC, MC, V.
Open: Lunch, Mon–Fri 1:30–4pm; dinner, Mon–Sat 9pm–midnight. **Closed:** Last two weeks of Aug.

This restaurant is certainly a multicultural experience. The owner describes the cuisine as "modern Spanish with Japanese influence; the cooking technique is French." Regardless of how confusing that may sound, the end result is usually a graceful achievement; as each ingredient in every dish manages to retain its natural flavor. The kitchen prepares such dishes as veal liver in sage sauce, a version of spring rolls filled with fresh shrimp and leeks, noisettes of veal with tarragon, filet steak with a sauce of mustard and brown sugar, médaillons of venison with purées of chestnut and celery, and such desserts as sherry trifle. The postmodern decor includes softly trimmed tromp-l'oeil ceilings, exposed wine racks, ornate columns with unusual lighting techniques, and a handful of antique carved horses from long-defunct merry-go-rounds.

INEXPENSIVE

Paellería Valenciana, Caballero de Gracia, 12. ☎ **531-17-85.**

Cuisine: SPANISH. **Reservations:** Recommended. **Metro:** Gran Vía.
Prices: Appetizers 600–700 ptas. ($4.30–$5); main courses 900–1,200 ptas. ($6.40–$8.50); fixed-price menus 1,250–1,600 ptas. ($8.90–$11.40). AE, MC, V.
Open: Lunch only, Mon–Sat 1:30–4:30pm.

This lunch-only restaurant ranks as one of the best in the city for value. The specialty is paella, which you must order by phone in advance. Once you arrive, you might begin with a homemade soup or the house salad, then follow with the paella, served in an iron skillet. At least two must order this rib-sticking fare. The choice of desserts includes the chef's special pride, razor-thin orange slices flavored with rum, coconut, sugar, honey, and raspberry sauce. A carafe of house wine comes with the set menu, and after lunch the owner comes around dispensing free cognac.

Near the Puerta del Sol

VERY EXPENSIVE

El Cenador del Prado, Prado, 4. ☎ **429-15-61.**

Cuisine: INTERNATIONAL. **Reservations:** Recommended. **Metro:** Puerta del Sol.
Prices: Appetizers 900–1,500 ptas. ($6.40–$10.70); main courses 1,750–2,000 ptas. ($12.40–$14.20); fixed-price menu 13,200 ptas. ($93.70). AE, DC, MC, V.
Open: Lunch, Mon–Fri 1:45–4pm; dinner, Mon–Sat 9pm–midnight. **Closed:** Aug 15–31.

This restaurant is deceptively elegant. In the simple anteroom, an attendant will check your coat and packages in an elaborately carved armoire and the maître d' will usher you into one of a trio of rooms. Two of the rooms, done in tones of peach and sepia, have cove moldings and English furniture in addition to floor-to-ceiling gilded mirrors. A third room, perhaps the most popular, is ringed with lattices and floods of sun from a skylight.

You can enjoy such well-flavored specialties as house-style crêpes with salmon and Iranian caviar, a salad of crimson peppers and salted anchovies, a casserole of snails and oysters with mushrooms, a ceviche of salmon and shellfish, soup studded with tidbits of hake and clams in a potato-and-leek base, sea bass with candied lemons, veal scaloppine stuffed with asparagus and garlic sprouts, and médaillons of venison served with pepper-and-fig chutney. Jackets and ties are recommended for men.

EXPENSIVE

Lhardy, Carrera de San Jéronimo, 8. ☎ **521-33-85.**

Cuisine: SPANISH. **Reservations:** Recommended in the upstairs dining room. **Metro:** Puerta del Sol.

Prices: Appetizers 1,100–2,100 ptas. ($7.80–$14.90); main dishes 3,000–5,000 ptas. ($21.30–$35.50). AE, DC, MC, V.

Open: Lunch, Mon–Sat 1–3:30pm; dinner, Mon–Sat 9–11:30pm. **Closed:** Late July to early Sept.

Lhardy has been considered a Madrileño legend since it opened in 1839 as a gathering place for the city's literati and political leaders. In 1846 it entertained Dumas. Its street level contains what might be the most elegant snack bar in Spain. Within a dignified and antique setting of marble and varnished hardwoods, cups of steaming consommé are dispensed from silver samovars into delicate porcelain cups, and rows of croquettes, tapas, and sandwiches are served to stand-up clients who pay for their food at a cashier's kiosk near the entrance. Cups of consommé cost 119 pesetas (80¢) each, while virtually anything else you select (tapas, sandwiches, pastries, whatever) usually cost around 80 pesetas (60¢) each. The ground-floor deli and takeaway service is open Monday to Saturday from 9am to 9pm; Sunday from 9am to 2:30pm.

The real culinary skill of the place, however, is visible on Lhardy's second floor, where you'll find a formal restaurant decorated in the ornate *belle-époque* style of Isabel Segunda. Specialties of the house include fish, pork and veal, tripe in a garlicky tomato and onion wine sauce, and *cocido*, the celebrated chick-pea stew of Madrid. *Soufflé sorpresa* (baked Alaska) is the dessert specialty.

Platerías Comedor, Plaza de Santa Ana, 11. ☎ **429-70-48.**

Cuisine: SPANISH. **Reservations:** Required. **Metro:** Puerta del Sol.

Prices: Appetizers 1,200–1,800 ptas. ($8.50–$12.80); main courses 4,000–4,500 ptas. ($28.40–$32). AE, DC, MC, V.

Open: Lunch, Mon–Fri 1:30–4pm; dinner, Mon–Sat 9pm–midnight.

One of the most charming dining rooms in Madrid, Platerías Comedor has richly brocaded walls evocative of 19th-century Spain. Despite the busy socializing on the plaza outside, this serene oasis makes few concessions to the new generation in its food, decor, or formally attired waiters. Specialties include beans with clams, stuffed partridge with cabbage and sausage, magret of duckling with pomegranates, duck liver with white grapes, tripe à la Madrid, veal stew with snails and mushrooms, and guinea hen with figs and plumbs. You might follow with passionfruit sorbet.

Frommer's Cool for Kids: Restaurants

Children visiting Spain will delight in patronizing any of the restaurants at the Parque de Atracciones in the **Casa de Campo** (see "Cool for Kids" in Chapter 5). Another good idea is to go on a picnic (see "Picnic Fare & Where to Eat It" later in this chapter).

For a taste of home, there are always the fast-food chains: McDonald's, Burger King, and Kentucky Fried Chicken. Remember, though, that because Spain is a foreign country, everything may have a slightly different taste.

Try taking the family to a local tasca, where children are bound to find something they like from the wide selection of tapas.

Foster's Hollywood (see p. 118) This restaurant has juicy hamburgers, plus lots of fare familiar to American kids.

V.I.P. (see p. 130) This most centrally located member of a chain spread across Madrid, V.I.P. serves fast food, hamburgers, and other foodstuffs that kids go for in a big way, especially the ice-cream concoctions.

MODERATE

Casa Paco, Plaza Puerta Cerrada, 11. ☎ 366-31-66.

Cuisine: STEAK. **Reservations:** Required. **Metro:** Puerta del Sol, Ópera, or La Latina. **Bus:** 3, 21, or 65.

Prices: Appetizers 1,000–1,200 ptas. ($7.10–$8.50); main courses 2,500–3,500 ptas. ($17.80–$24.90); fixed-price menu 3,000 ptas. ($21.30). DC.

Open: Lunch, Mon–Sat 1:30–4pm; dinner, Mon–Sat 8:30pm–midnight. **Closed:** Aug.

Madrileños defiantly name Casa Paco, just beside the Plaza Mayor, when someone has the "nerve" to put down Spanish steaks. They know that here you can get the thickest, juiciest, most flavorsome steaks in Spain, which are priced according to weight. Señor Paco was the first in Madrid to sear steaks in boiling oil before serving them on plates so hot that the almost-raw meat continues to cook, preserving the natural juices. In the Old Town, the two-story restaurant offers three dining rooms for which reservations are imperative. Otherwise, you face a long wait, which you can while away sampling the tapas (hors d'oeuvres) in the tasca in front. Around the walls are autographed photographs of such notables as Frank Sinatra.

Casa Paco isn't just a steakhouse. You can start with a fish soup and proceed to a dish such as grilled sole, baby lamb, *Casa Paco cocido,* or *callos à la madrileña.* You might top it off with one of the luscious desserts, but you can't have coffee here. Paco won't serve it, not necessarily for health reasons but because customers used to be inclined to linger over their cups, keeping tables occupied while people had to be turned away.

INEXPENSIVE

Casa Alberto, Huertas, 18. ☎ 429-93-56.

Cuisine: CASTILIAN. **Reservations:** Recommended. **Metro:** Antón Martín.

Prices: Appetizers 750–1,250 ptas. ($5.30–$8.90); main courses 850–2,250 ptas. ($6–$16). AE, V.

Open: Lunch, Tues–Sun 1–4pm; dinner, Tues–Sat 8:30–midnight.

One of the oldest tascas in the neighborhood, Casa Alberto was originally established in 1827, and has thrived through many different regimes and governments ever since. It lies on the street level of the house where Miguel de Cervantes lived briefly in 1614, and contains an appealing mixture of bullfighting memorabilia, engravings, and reproductions of Old Master paintings. Many visitors opt only for some of the tapas which are continually replenished from platters on the bartop, but there's also a sit-down dining area for more substantial meals. Specialties include fried squid, shellfish in vinaigrette sauce; chorizo in cider sauce; and several versions of baked or roasted lamb.

Mesón las Descalzas, Postigo San Martín, 3. ☎ **522-72-17.**

Cuisine: SPANISH. **Reservations:** Recommended. **Metro:** Callao.
Prices: Appetizers 550–700 ptas. ($3.90–$4.97); main courses 1,600–1,800 ptas. ($11.40–$12.80); fixed-price menu 1,200 ptas. ($8.50). AE, DC, MC, V.
Open: Lunch, daily noon–4pm; dinner, daily 8pm–midnight.

Las Descalzas, a recommended tavern-style restaurant, sits behind a red facade accented with a black metal sign. Inside, you'll be greeted with a massive tapas bar that's often crowded at night. Behind a glass-and-wood screen is the restaurant section, its specialties including kidneys with sherry, *sopa castellana,* seafood soup, Basque-style hake, crayfish, shrimp, oysters, clams, and paella with shellfish. For entertainment, there is folk music.

Retiro/Salamanca

VERY EXPENSIVE

 **La Gamella,** Alfonso XII, 4. ☎ **532-45-09.**

Cuisine: CALIFORNIAN/CASTILIAN. **Reservations:** Required. **Metro:** Retiro. **Bus:** 19.
Prices: Appetizers 1,050–2,200 ptas. ($7.50–$15.60); main courses 2,300–4,200 ptas. ($16.30–$29.80). AE, DC, MC, V.
Open: Lunch, Tues–Sat 1:30–4pm; dinner, Tues–Sat 9pm–midnight. **Closed:** Mid–Aug to mid–Sept.

La Gamella established its gastronomic reputation shortly after it opened several years ago in less imposing quarters in another part of town. In 1988 its Illinois-born owner, former choreographer Dick Stephens, moved his restaurant into the 19th-century building where the Spanish philosopher Ortega y Gasset was born. The prestigious Horcher, one of the capital's legendary restaurants (see below), lies just across the street; the food at La Gamella is better. The design and decor here invite customers to relax in russet-colored, high-ceilinged warmth. Mr. Stephens has prepared his delicate and light-textured specialties for the King and Queen of Spain as well as for many of Madrid's most talked-about artists and merchants, many of whom he knows and greets personally between sessions in his kitchens.

Typical menu items include a ceviche of Mediterranean fish; sliced duck liver in truffle sauce; Caesar salad with strips of marinated anchovies; a dollop of goat cheese served over caramelized endives; duck breast with peppers; and an array of well-prepared desserts, among which is an all-American cheesecake. Traditional Spanish dishes such as chicken with garlic have been added to the menu, plus what has been called "the only edible hamburger in Madrid." Because of the intimacy and the small dimensions of the restaurant, reservations are important.

Horcher, Alfonso XII, 6. ☎ **532-35-96.**

Cuisine: GERMAN/INTERNATIONAL. **Reservations:** Required. **Metro:** Retiro.
Prices: Appetizers 1,100–2,300 ptas. ($7.80–$16.30); main courses 2,500–7,200 ptas. ($17.80–$51.10). AE, DC, V.
Open: Lunch, Mon–Fri 1:30–4pm; dinner, Mon–Sat 8:30pm–midnight.

Horcher originated in Berlin in 1904. In a sudden move prompted by a tip from a high-ranking German officer that Germany was losing the war, Herr Horcher moved his restaurant to Madrid in 1943. The restaurant has continued its grand European traditions, including excellent service, ever since.

Where to start? You might try the seafood mousse or the distinctive wild duck salad. Both the venison stew in green pepper with orange peel and the crayfish with parsley and cucumber are excellent. Other main courses include veal scaloppine in tarragon and turbot with saffron. For dessert, the house specialty is crêpes Sir Holden, prepared at your table, with fresh raspberries, cream, and nuts; or you may prefer a Sachertorte.

Your best chance of getting a seat is to go early. Jackets and ties are imperative for men.

EXPENSIVE

Alkalde, Jorge Juan, 10. ☎ **576-33-59.**

Cuisine: BASQUE/INTERNATIONAL. **Reservations:** Required. **Metro:** Retiro or Serrano. **Bus:** 8, 20, 21, or 53.
Prices: Appetizers 1,000–2,800 ptas. ($7.10–$19.90); main courses 1,800–5,000 ptas. ($12.80–$35.50); fixed-price menu 4,900 ptas. ($34.80). AE, DC, MC, V.
Open: Lunch, daily 1–4:30pm; dinner, daily 8:30pm–midnight. **Closed:** Sun in July–Aug.

Alkalde has been known for decades for serving top-quality Spanish food in an old tavern setting. It's decorated like a Basque inn, with beamed ceilings and hams hanging from the rafters. Upstairs is a large *típico* tavern; downstairs is a maze of stone-sided cellars that are pleasantly cool in summer, although the whole place is air-conditioned.

You might begin with the cream of crabmeat soup, followed by *gambas à la plancha* (grilled shrimp) or *cigalas* (crayfish). Other well-recommended dishes include *mero salsa verde* (brill in a green sauce), trout Alkalde, stuffed peppers, and chicken steak. The dessert specialty is *copa Cardinal.*

★ **El Amparo,** Callejón de Puígcerdá, 8 (at the corner of Jorge Juan). ☎ **431-64-56.**

Cuisine: BASQUE. **Reservations:** Required. **Metro:** Goya. **Bus:** 21 or 53.
Prices: Appetizers 1,500–2,500 ptas. ($10.70–$17.80); main courses 2,900–3,500 ptas. ($20.60–$24.90). AE, MC, V.
Open: Lunch, Mon–Fri 1:30–3:30pm; dinner, Mon–Sat 9–11:30pm. **Closed:** Week before Easter and Aug.

El Amparo, behind the cascading vines on its facade, is one of Madrid's most elegant gastronomic enclaves. It sits beside a quiet alleyway that's close to a bustling commercial section of the center of the city. Inside, three tiers of roughly hewn wooden beams surround elegantly appointed tables where pink napery and glistening silver add cosmopolitan touches of glamour. A sloping skylight floods the interior with sun by day; at night, pinpoints of light from the high-tech hanging lanterns create intimate shadows. A battalion of polite uniformed waiters serves well-prepared nouvelle-cuisine versions of cold marinated salmon with a tomato sorbet, cold cream of vegetable and shrimp soup, bisque of shellfish with Armagnac, ravioli stuffed with seafood, roast lamb chops with garlic purée, breast of duck, ragoût of sole, a platter of steamed fish of the day, roulades of lobster with soy sauce, and steamed hake with pepper sauce.

El Pescador, Calle José Ortega y Gasset, 75. ☎ **402-12-90.**

Cuisine: SEAFOOD. **Reservations:** Required. **Metro:** Lista.

Prices: Appetizers 1,200–3,000 ptas. ($8.50–$21.30); main courses 2,200–4,500 ptas. ($15.60–$32). MC, V.

Open: Lunch, Mon–Sat 1:30–4pm; dinner, Mon–Sat 8:30pm–midnight. **Closed:** Aug.

El Pescador is a well-patronized fish restaurant that has become a favorite of Madrileños who appreciate the more than 30 kinds of fish prominently displayed in a glass case. Many of these are unknown in North America, and some originate off the coast of Galicia. The management air-freights them in and prefers to serve them grilled (*à la plancha*).

You might precede your main course with a spicy fish soup and accompany it with one of the many good wines from northeastern Spain. If you're not sure what to order (even the English translations might sound unfamiliar), try one of the many varieties and sizes of shrimp. These go under the names *langostinos, cigalas, santiaguinos,* and *carabineros.* Many of them are expensive and priced by the gram, so be careful when you order.

Viridiana, Juan de Mena 14. ☎ **523-44-78.**

Cuisine: INTERNATIONAL. **Reservations:** Recommended. **Metro:** Banco.

Prices: Appetizers 1,800–3,000 ptas. ($12.80–$21.30); main courses 2,400–3,600 ptas. ($17–$25.60). No credit cards. **Open:** Lunch, Mon–Sat 1:30pm–4pm; dinner, Mon–Sat 9pm–midnight. **Closed:** August.

This restaurant is praised as one of the up-and-coming new restaurants of Madrid, and known for the creative imagination of its chef and part-owner, Abraham Garcia. Menu specialties are usually contemporary adaptations of traditional recipes, and change frequently according to the availability of the ingredients. Examples include a salad of exotic lettuces served with smoked salmon; guinea fowl stuffed with herbs and wild mushrooms; baby squid with curry served on a bed of lentils; roasted lamb served in puff pastry with fresh basil; carpaccio of beef with a mousseline of white truffles; and a dessert specialty of apple tart flambéed in calvados.

INEXPENSIVE

Gran Café de Gijón, Paseo de Recoletos, 21. ☎ **521-54-25.**

Cuisine: SPANISH. **Reservations:** Needed for restaurant. **Metro:** Banco de España, Colón, or Recoletos.

Prices: Appetizers 390–1,020 ptas. ($2.80–$7.20); main courses 870–3,000 ptas. ($6.20–$21.30); fixed-price menu 1,400 ptas. ($9.90). No credit cards.

Open: Daily 9am–1am (lunch, Mon–Sat 1–4pm; dinner, Mon–Sat 9pm–midnight).

Each of the old European capitals has a coffeehouse that traditionally attracts the literati—in Madrid it's the Gijón, which opened in 1888 in the heyday of the city's Belle Epoque. Artists and writers still patronize this venerated old café, many of them spending hours over one cup of coffee. Hemingway made the place famous for Americans and, in his footsteps in the 1950s, followed such notables as Ava Gardner and Truman Capote. The place has open windows looking out onto the wide paseo, as well as a large terrace for sun worshippers and birdwatchers. Along one side of the café is a stand-up bar, and on the lower level is a restaurant. The set menu consists of two dishes, bread, wine or beer, and dessert—with main dishes varying daily. In summer you can sit in the garden to enjoy a *blanco y negro* (black coffee with ice cream) or a mixed drink.

CHAMBERÍ

Very Expensive

Las Cuatro Estaciones, General Ibéñez Ibero, 5. ☎ **553-63-05.**

Cuisine: INTERNATIONAL. **Reservations:** Required. **Metro:** Guzmán el Bueno.
Prices: Appetizers 1,200–2,800 ptas. ($8.50–$19.90); main courses 2,200–4,500 ptas. ($15.60–$32); fixed-price dinner 6,000 ptas. ($42.60). AE, DC, MC, V.
Open: Lunch, Mon–Fri 1–4pm; dinner, Mon–Sat 9pm–midnight. **Closed:** Aug.

Las Cuatro Estaciones is placed by gastronomes and horticulturists alike among their favorite Madrid dining spots. In addition to superb food, the establishment prides itself on the masses of flowers that change with the season, plus a modern and softly inviting decor. Depending on the time of year, the mirrors surrounding the multilevel bar near the entrance reflect thousands of hydrangeas, chrysanthemums, or poinsettias. Even the napery matches whichever colors the resident botanist has chosen as the seasonal motif. Each person involved in food preparation spends a prolonged apprenticeship at restaurants in France before returning home to try their freshly sharpened talents on the tastebuds of aristocratic Madrid.

Representative specialties include crab bisque, fresh oysters, a petite marmite of fish and shellfish, imaginative preparations of salmon, a salad of eels, fresh asparagus and mushrooms in puff pastry with parsley-butter sauce, a three-fish platter with fines herbes, brochette of filet of beef in pecadillo, and a nouvelle-cuisine version of blanquette of monkfish so tender that it melts in your mouth. The "festival of desserts" includes the specials the chef has concocted that day, a selection of which is placed temptingly on your table.

Inexpensive

Foster's Hollywood, Magallanes, 1. ☎ **448-91-65.**

Cuisine: AMERICAN. **Reservations:** Not required. **Metro:** Quevedo.
Prices: Appetizers 450–600 ptas. ($3.20–$4.30); main courses 600–1,000 ptas. ($4.30–$7.10). AE, DC, MC, V.
Open: Sun–Thurs 1pm–midnight; Fri–Sat 1pm–2am.

When Foster's opened its doors in 1971, it was not only the first American restaurant in Spain, it was one of the first in Europe. Since those early days it has now grown to more than 20 restaurants in Madrid, and has even opened restaurants in Florida. A popular hangout for both locals and visiting Yanks, it offers a choice of dining venues, ranging from "classical club American" to studios, the latter evoking a working movie studio with props. Its varied menu includes Tex-Mex selections, butterfly shrimp, steaks, sandwiches, freshly made salads, and, as its signature product, hamburgers grilled over natural charcoal in many variations. *The New York Times* once reported that it has "probably the best onion rings in the world."

Locations where you can have a direct hook-up to the U.S.A. in Madrid are: Paseo de la Habana, 1 (☎ **564-63-08**); Padre Damián, 38 (☎ **457-36-42**) next to the

Eurobuilding hotel; Apolonio Morales, 3 (☎ **345-10-36**), in the Castellana area; Avenida de Brasil, 14 (☎ **597-16-74**), near the Meliá Castilla hotel; Princesa, 13 (☎ **559-19-14**), near Plaza de España; Velázquez, 80 (☎ **435-61-28**), in the Serrano shopping area; Tamayo y Baus, 1 (☎ **531-51-15**), close to Plaza de Cibeles and the Prado; Plaza Sagrado Corazón de Jesús, 2 (☎ **564-66-50**), next to the National Music Auditorium; Centro Comercial Arturo Soria (☎ **759-73-42**); and Centro Comercial La Vaguada (☎ **738-12-67**).

Jockey, Amador de los Ríos, 6. ☎ **319-24-25.**

Cuisine: INTERNATIONAL. **Reservations:** Required. **Metro:** Colón.
Prices: Appetizers 1,100–6,500 ptas. ($7.80–$46.20); main courses 2,500–6,800 ptas. ($17.80–$48.30). AE, DC, MC, V.
Open: Lunch, Mon–Sat 1–4pm; dinner, Mon–Sat 9–11:30pm. **Closed:** Aug.

For decades this was considered the premier restaurant of Spain, although competition for that title is severe today. At any rate, it is the favorite of international celebrities, diplomats, and heads of state, and some of the more faithful patrons look on it as their own private club. It was, in fact, once known as the "Jockey Club," although the "club" was eventually dropped because it suggested exclusivity. The restaurant, with tables on two levels, isn't overly large. Wood-paneled walls and colored linen provide warmth. Against the paneling are a dozen prints of horses mounted by jockeys—hence the name of the place.

Since Jockey's establishment shortly after World War II, the chef has prided himself on coming up with new and creative dishes. Sheiks from oil kingdoms can still order Beluga caviar from Iran, but others might settle happily for Jockey's goose-liver terrine or slices of Jabugo ham. Cold melon soup with shrimp is soothing on a hot day, especially when followed by grill-roast young pigeon from Talavera cooked in its own juice or sole filets with figs in Chardonnay. Stuffed small chicken Jockey style is a specialty, as is *tripe Madrileña,* a local dish. Desserts are sumptuous, although many people end their meals with the Colombian coffee.

CHAMARTÍN

Very Expensive

Zalacaín, Alvarez de Baena, 4. ☎ **561-48-40.**

Cuisine: BASQUE. **Reservations:** Required. **Metro:** Rubén Darío.
Prices: Appetizers 1,500–5,000 ptas. ($10.70–$35.50); main courses 3,500–4,200 ptas. ($24.90–$29.80). AE, DC, MC, V.
Open: Lunch, Mon–Fri 1:30–3:30pm; dinner, Mon–Sat 9–11:30pm. **Closed:** Week before Easter and Aug.

Outstanding in both food and decor, Zalacaín, which opened in 1973, is reached by an illuminated walk from Paseo de la Castellana and housed at the garden end of a modern apartment complex. In fact, it's within an easy walk of such deluxe hotels as the Castellana and the Miguel Angel. The name of the restaurant comes from the intrepid hero of Basque author Pío Baroja's 1909 novel, *Zalacaín El Aventurero.* Zalacaín is small, exclusive, and expensive. In an atmosphere of an elegant old mansion, you can peruse the menu, perhaps at the rust-toned bar. The walls are covered with textiles, and some are decorated with Audubon-type paintings. Men should wear jackets and ties.

The menu is interesting and varied, often with nouvelle-cuisine touches along with many Basque and French specialties. It might offer a superb sole in a green sauce, but it also knows the glory of grilled pig's feet. Among the most recommendable main dishes are a stew of scampi in cider sauce; crêpes stuffed with smoked fish; ravioli stuffed with mushrooms, foie gras, and truffles; Spanish bouillabaisse; and veal escalopes in orange sauce. For dessert, I'd suggest baked apples stuffed with cinnamon-flavored custard.

EXPENSIVE

Asador Errota-Zar, Corazón de Maria, 32. ☎ **413-52-24.**

Cuisine: BASQUE. **Reservations:** Required. **Metro:** Alfonso XIII. **Bus:** 43.
Prices: Appetizers 850–1,800 ptas. ($6–$12.80); main courses 2,500–3,000 ptas. ($17.80–$21.30). AE, DC, MC, V.
Open: Lunch, Mon–Sat 1–4pm dinner, Mon–Sat 9pm–midnight. **Closed:** Aug.

An Asador is a kind of Spanish restaurant that typically roasts meat on racks or spits over an open fire, and the Errota-Zar is one of Madrid's best. (The technique is said to have been brought to the Basque country by repatriated emigrés who learned it in Argentina and Uruguay a century ago. Since then, the Basques have claimed it as their own and presumably do it better than anyone else.) Asador Errota-Zar, contained behind the stucco-and-stone walls of an antique mill, is managed by Basque-born Segundo Olano and his wife, Eugenia.

You might begin your meal with slices of pork loin, grilled spicy sausage, scrambled eggs with boletus mushrooms, a savory soup made from Basque kidney beans, or red peppers stuffed with codfish. Other dishes include stewed hake with clams in marinara sauce, but the real specialties of the house are the succulent cuts of beef, fish, or pork that are first gently warmed, then seared, then cooked by the expert hand of Sr. Olano himself. The restaurant is at its most interesting when groups of friends arrive, sharing portions of several different appetizers among themselves before concentrating on a main course. The offerings of meat tend to be very fresh but rather limited. The culinary variety here lies in the appetizers.

El Bodegón, Pinar, 15. ☎ **562-31-37.**

Cuisine: INTERNATIONAL/BASQUE. **Reservations:** Required. **Metro:** Rubén Darío.
Prices: Appetizers 800–1,750 ptas. ($5.70–$12.40); main courses 2,200–2,950 ptas. ($15.60–$20.90). AE, DC, MC, V.
Open: Lunch, Mon–Fri 1:30–4pm; dinner, Mon–Sat 9pm–midnight. **Closed:** Holidays and most of Aug.

El Bodegón is imbued with the atmosphere of a gentleman's club for hunting enthusiasts—in the country-inn style. International globe-trotters are attracted here, especially in the evening, as the restaurant is near such deluxe hotels as the Castellana and the Miguel Angel. King Juan Carlos and Queen Sofía have dined here.

Waiters in black and white, with gold braid and buttons, bring dignity to the food service. Even bottled water is served champagne style, chilled in a silver floor stand. There are two main dining rooms—both conservative and oak-beamed.

I recommend cream of crayfish bisque or velvety vichyssoise to launch your meal. Main-course selections include grilled filet mignon with classic béarnaise sauce and venison à la bourguignonne. Other main-course selections include shellfish au gratin Escoffier, quails Fernand Point, tartare of raw fish marinated in parsley-enriched vinaigrette, and smoked salmon. For dessert, try homemade apple pie.

 **El Cabo Mayor,** Juan Ramón Jiménez, 37. ☎ **350-87-76.**

Cuisine: SEAFOOD. **Reservations:** Recommended. **Metro:** Cuzco.
Prices: Appetizers 1,600–3,800 ptas. ($11.40–$27); main courses 2,500–3,900 ptas. ($17.80–$27.70). AE, DC, MC, V.
Open: Lunch, Mon–Sat 1:30–4pm; dinner, Mon–Sat 9pm–midnight. **Closed:** One week in Aug.

In the prosperous northern edges of Madrid, El Cabo Mayor is not far from the city-within-a-city of Chamartín Station. This is one of the best, most popular, and most stylish restaurants in Madrid, attracting on occasion the King and Queen of Spain. The open-air staircase leading to the entranceway descends from a manicured garden on a quiet side street. A battalion of uniformed doormen stand ready to greet arriving taxis. The restaurant's decor is a nautically inspired mass of hardwood panels, brass trim, old-fashioned pulleys and ropes, a tile floor custom-painted with sea-green and blue replicas of waves, and hand-carved models of fishing boats. In brass replicas of portholes, some dozen bronze statues honoring fishers and their craft are displayed in illuminated positions of honor.

Menu choices include paprika-laden peppers stuffed with fish, a salad composed of Jabugo ham and foie gras of duckling, fish soup from Cantabria (a province between the Basque country and Asturias), stewed sea bream with thyme, asparagus mousse, salmon in sherry sauce, and loin of veal in cassis sauce. Desserts include such selections as a mousse of rice with pine-nut sauce.

 **El Olivo Restaurant,** General Gallegos, 1. ☎ **359-15-35.**

Cuisine: MEDITERRANEAN. **Reservations:** Recommended. **Metro:** Plaza de Castilla.
Prices: Appetizers 975–3,650 ptas. ($6.90–$25.90); main courses 2,500–3,500 ptas. ($17.80–$24.90); fixed-price meals 3,850–5,800 ptas. ($27.30–$41.20). AE, DC, MC, V.
Open: Lunch, Tues–Sat 1–4pm; dinner, Tues–Sat 9pm–midnight. **Closed:** Aug and four days around Easter.

Local wits praise the success of a non-Spaniard (in this case, French-born Jean Pierre Vandelle) in recognizing the international appeal of two of Spain's most valuable culinary resources, olive oil and sherry. His likable restaurant, located in northern Madrid near Chamartín Station, pays homage to the glories of the Spanish olive, whose fruit has been praised by cardiologists around the world for its health benefits. Designed in colors whose tones of green and amber reflect the leaves and oil of the olive tree, it is probably the only restaurant in Spain that wheels a trolley stocked with 40 regional olive oils from table to table. From the trolley, diners select one or another variety, a golden puddle of which is offered for taste testing, soaked up with chunks of rough-textured bread that is–according to your taste–seasoned with a dash of salt.

Menu specialties include grilled filet of monkfish marinated in herbs and olive oil and served with black-olive sauce over a compote of fresh tomatoes; and four preparations of codfish arranged on a single platter and served with a pil-pil sauce. (Named after the sizzling noise it makes as it bubbles on a stove, pil-pil sauce is composed of codfish gelatin and herbs that are whipped into a mayonnaiselike consistency with olive oil.) Also popular are thinly sliced roulades of beef stuffed with foie gras of duckling, dredged in flour, and fried in top-quality olive oil. Desserts might be one of several different chocolate pastries or *leche frite* served with an orange sauce. A wide array of reasonably priced Bordeaux and Spanish wines can accompany your meal.

A final note: Many clients deliberately arrive early as an excuse to linger within El Olivo's one-of-a-kind sherry bar. Although other drinks are offered, the bar features more than a hundred brands of *vino de Jerez,* more than practically any other establishment in Madrid. Priced at 300 to 800 ptas. ($2.10–$5.70) per glass, they make the perfect apéritif before a Spanish meal.

MODERATE

O'Pazo, Calle Reina Mercedes, 20. ☎ **553-23-33.**

Cuisine: GALICIAN/SEAFOOD. **Reservations:** Required. **Metro:** Nuevos Ministerios or Alvarado. **Bus:** 3 or 5.

Prices: Appetizers 900–2,400 ptas. ($6.40–$17); main courses 2,100–3,900 ptas. ($14.90–$27.70). MC, V.

Open: Lunch, Mon–Sat 1–4pm; dinner, Mon–Sat 8:30pm–midnight. **Closed:** Aug.

O'Pazo is a deluxe Galician restaurant, considered by local cognoscenti to be one of the top seafood places in the country. The fish is flown in daily from Galicia and much of it is priced by the weight, depending on market quotations. In front is a cocktail lounge and bar, all in polished brass, with low sofas and paintings. Carpeted floors, cushioned Castilian furniture, soft lighting, and colored-glass windows complete the picture. O'Pazo lies north of the center of Madrid, near the Chamartín Station.

The fish and shellfish soup is delectable, although others gravitate to the seaman's broth as a beginning course. Natural clams are succulent, as are *cigalas* (a kind of crayfish), spider crabs, and Jabugo ham. Main dishes range from baby eels to sea snails, from scallops Galician style to a *zarzuela* (seafood and fish casserole).

INEXPENSIVE

Alfredo's Barbacoa, Juan Hurtado de Mendoza, 11. ☎ **345-16-39.**

Cuisine: AMERICAN. **Reservations:** Recommended. **Metro:** Cuzco.

Prices: Appetizers 375–675 ptas. ($2.70–$4.80); main courses 600–1,600 ptas. ($4.30–$11.40). AE, DC, MC, V.

Open: Lunch, Mon–Fri 1–4:30pm, Sat 2–5pm; dinner, Mon–Thurs 8:30pm–midnight; Fri–Sat 8:30pm–1am.

Alfredo's is a popular rendezvous for Americans longing for home-style food other than hamburgers. Al directs his bar/restaurant wearing boots, blue jeans, and a ten-gallon hat; his friendly welcome has made the place a center for both his friends and newcomers to Madrid. You *can* have hamburgers here, but they are of the barbecued variety, and you might prefer the barbecued spareribs or chicken. The salad bar is an attraction. And it's a rare treat to be able to have corn on the cob in Spain.

The original Alfredo's Barbacoa, Lagasca, 5 (☎ **576-62-71**), is still in business, also under Al's auspices. Metro: Retiro.

Chueca

INEXPENSIVE

Taberna Carmencita, Libertad, 16. ☎ **531-66-12.**

Cuisine: SPANISH. **Reservations:** Recommended. **Metro:** Chueca.

Prices: Appetizers 600–1,000 ptas. ($4.30–$7.10); main courses 1,000–3,500 ptas. ($7.10–$24.90); fixed-price menu 1,000 ptas. ($7.10) available only at lunch. AE, DC, MC, V.

Open: Lunch, Mon–Fri noon–5pm; dinner, Mon–Sat 8pm–midnight.

Carmencita, founded in 1840 and exquisitely restored, is a street-corner enclave of old Spanish charm, filled with 19th-century detailing and tilework that witnessed the conversations of a former patron, the poet Federico García Lorca. Meals might include entrecôte with green-pepper sauce, escalope of veal, braised mollusks with port, filet of pork, codfish with garlic, and Bilbao-style hake. Every Thursday the special dish is a complicated version of the famous *cocido* (stew) of Madrid.

BUDGET

$ **La Argentina,** Gravina, 19. ☎ **531-91-17.**

Cuisine: INTERNATIONAL. **Reservations:** Not required. **Metro:** Chueca.
Prices: Appetizers 375–850 ptas. ($2.70–$6); main courses 800–1,250 ptas. ($5.70–$8.90); fixed-price menu 1,200 ptas. ($8.52). No credit cards.
Open: Lunch, Tues–Sun noon–4pm; dinner, Tues–Sat 9pm–midnight. **Closed:** July 25–Aug 31.

La Argentina, set within a building erected in 1941, is run under the watchful eye of owner Andres Rodríguez. The restaurant has only 16 tables, but the food is well prepared, sort of Spanish family style. The best bets are cannelloni Rossini; noodle soup; creamed spinach; and meat dishes, including entrecôte and roast veal. Chicken Villaroy is another special. All dishes are served with mashed or french-fried potatoes. For dessert, have a baked apple or rice pudding. The decor is simple and clean, and you're usually served by one of the two waitresses who have been here for years.

$ **El Inca,** Gravina, 23. ☎ **532-77-45.**

Cuisine: PERUVIAN. **Reservations:** Required on weekends. **Metro:** Chueca.
Prices: Appetizers 550–900 ptas. ($3.90–$6.40); main courses 1,000–1,600 ptas. ($7.10–$11.40); fixed-price menu 2,500 ptas. ($17.80) available at lunch. AE, DC, MC, V.
Open: Lunch, Tues–Sat 1:30–4pm; dinner, Tues–Sat 9pm–midnight. **Closed:** Aug.

For a taste of South America, try El Inca, decorated with Incan motifs and artifacts. Since it opened in the early 1970s, it has hosted its share of diplomats and celebrities, although you're more likely to see families and local office workers. The house cocktail is a deceptively potent *pisco* sour–the recipe comes straight from the Andes. Many of the dishes contain potatoes, the national staple of Peru. The salad of potatoes and black olives is given an unusual zest with a white-cheese sauce. Other specialties are the *ceviche de merluza* (raw hake marinated with onions) and *aji de gallina* (a chicken-and-rice dish made with peanut sauce), a Peruvian favorite.

Nabucco, Calle Hortaleza, 108. ☎ **310-06-11.**

Cuisine: ITALIAN. **Reservations:** Recommended. **Metro:** Alonso Martínez. **Bus:** 7 or 36.
Prices: Pizza 585–725 ptas. ($4.20–$5.10); appetizers 450–700 ptas. ($3.20–$5); main courses 725–1,300 ptas. ($5.10–$9.20). AE, DC, MC, V.
Open: Lunch, Mon–Sat 1:30–4pm; dinner, Mon–Thurs 8:45pm–midnight; Fri–Sat 9pm–1am.

In a neighborhood of Spanish restaurants, the Italian format here comes as a welcome change. The decor resembles a postmodern update of an Italian ruin, complete with trompe-l'oeil walls painted like marble. Roman portrait busts and a prominent bar lend a dignified air. Menu choices include cannelloni, a good selection of veal dishes, and such main courses as osso buco. You might begin your meal with a selection of antipasti, for dessert you can try the chocolate mousse.

Tienda de Vinos, Augusto Figueroa, 35. ☎ **521-70-12.**

Cuisine: SPANISH. **Reservations:** Not accepted. **Metro:** Chueca.
Prices: Appetizers 200–600 ptas. ($1.40–$4.30); main courses 400–800 ptas. ($2.80–$5.70). No credit cards.
Open: Breakfast/lunch, Mon–Sat 9am–4:30pm; dinner, Mon–Sat 8:30pm–midnight.

Officially this restaurant is known as the "Wine Store," but ever since the 1930s Madrileños have called it *El Comunista.* Its now-deceased owner was a fervent Communist, and many locals in sympathy with his political beliefs patronized the establishment. This rather rickety old wine shop, with a few tables in the back, is quite fashionable with actors and journalists looking for Spanish fare without frills. There is a menu, but no one ever thinks of asking for it—just ask what's available. Nor do you get a bill; you're just told how much. You sit at wooden tables and on wooden chairs and benches placed around the walls, which are decorated with old posters, calendars, pennants, and clocks. Start with garlic or vegetable soup or lentils, followed by lamb chops, tripe in a spicy sauce, or meatballs and soft-set eggs with asparagus.

Off the Plaza Mayor

EXPENSIVE

Casa Lucio, Cava Baja 35. ☎ **365-32-52.**

Cuisine: CASTILIAN. **Reservations:** Recommended. **Metro:** Sol or La Latina.
Prices: Appetizers 1,000–2,000 ptas. ($7.10–$14.20); main courses 2,000–3,300 ptas. ($14.20–$23.40). AE, DC, MC, V.
Open: Lunch, Sun–Fri 1–4pm; dinner, daily 9pm–midnight. **Closed:** Aug.

Set on a historic street whose edges once marked the perimeter of Old Madrid, this is a time-honored tasca with all the requisite antique accessories. You'll pass a well-oiled bar accented with dozens of cured hams hanging from hand-hewn beams and see a loyal clientele of sometimes surprisingly well-placed public figures—even perhaps, the king of Spain. You'll be directed to one of two dining rooms on two different floors, each with whitewashed walls, tile floors, and exposed brick. A well-trained staff offers classic Castilian food, which might include *jamón de Jabugo* with broad beans, shrimp in garlic sauce, hake with green sauce, several types of roasted lamb, and a thick steak served sizzling hot on a heated platter, *churrasco de la casa.*

El Schotis, Cava Baja 11. ☎ **365-32-30.**

Cuisine: SPANISH. **Reservations:** Recommended. **Metro:** Sol or La Latina.
Prices: Appetizers 400–750 ptas. ($2.80–$5.30); main courses 1,750–2,400 ptas. ($12.40–$17). Fixed-price menu 3,850 ptas. ($27.30). AE, DC, MC, V.
Open: Lunch, Tues–Sun 1–4pm; dinner, Tues–Sat 9pm–midnight. **Closed:** Two weeks in August.

Set beside one of Madrid's oldest and most historic streets, El Schotis was established in 1962 within a solid stone building with lots of nostalgic garnish. A series of large and pleasingly old-fashioned dining rooms is the setting for an animated crowd of Madrileños and foreign visitors who receive ample portions of conservative, well-prepared vegetables, salads, soups, fish, and above all, meat. Specialties of the house include roasted baby lamb, grilled steaks and veal chops, shrimp with garlic, fried hake in green sauce, and traditional desserts. There's a bar near the entrance for tapas and before- or after-dinner drinks.

Las Cuevas de Luís Candelas, Calle de Cuchilleros, 1. ☎ **366-54-28.**

Cuisine: SPANISH/INTERNATIONAL. **Reservations:** Required. **Metro:** Puerta del Sol.
Prices: Appetizers 550–2,200 ptas. ($3.90–$15.60); main courses 1,200–2,800 ptas. ($8.50–$19.90). AE, DC, MC, V.
Open: Lunch, daily 1–4pm; dinner, daily 7:30pm–2:30am.

Right down the steps from the popular but very touristy Mesón del Corregidor, a competitor restaurant, is the even-better-known Las Cuevas de Luís Candelas, which is housed in a building dating from 1616. The restaurant opened its doors in 1900. It is entered through a doorway under an arcade on the steps leading to the Calle de Cuchilleros, the nighttime street of Madrid, teeming with restaurants, flamenco clubs, and rustic taverns. The restaurant is named after the legendary Luís Candelas, an 18th-century bandit who's sometimes known as the "Spanish Robin Hood." He is said to have hidden out in this maze of cuevas. Although the menu is in English, the cuisine is authentically Spanish. Specialties include the chef's own style of hake. To begin your meal, you might try another house dish, *sopa de ajo Candelas* (garlic soup). Roast suckling pig and roast lamb, as in the other restaurants on the Plaza Mayor, are featured.

MODERATE

Gure-Etxea (Restaurant Vasco), Plaza de la Paja, 12. ☎ **365-61-49.**

Cuisine: BASQUE. **Reservations:** Recommended. **Metro:** La Latina.
Prices: Appetizers 1,200–1,800 ptas. ($8.50–$12.80); main courses 1,500–3,500 ptas. ($10.70–$24.90); fixed-price menu 3,500 ptas. ($24.90). AE, DC, MC, V.
Open: Lunch, Mon–Sat 1:30–4pm; dinner, Mon–Sat 9pm–midnight. **Closed:** Aug.

This restaurant is housed in a stone-walled building that was the convent for the nearby Church of San Andres before the Renaissance. Today, amid a decor enhanced by Romanesque arches, vaulted tunnels, and dark-grained paneling, you can enjoy selections from a small but choice menu. Specialties include vichyssoise, rape (a whitefish) in green sauce, Gure-Etxea's special filet of sole, and *bacalau al pil-pil* (codfish in a fiery sauce).

Los Galayos, Calle Botoneras, 5. ☎ **366-30-28.**

Cuisine: SPANISH. **Reservations:** Recommended. **Metro:** Puerta del Sol.
Prices: Appetizers 450–1,100 ptas. ($3.20–$7.80); main courses 1,100–3,700 ptas. ($7.80–$26.30). AE, MC, V.
Open: Daily 12:30pm–12:45am.

Its position is among the most desirable in all of Spain, on a narrow side street about three steps from the arcades of Plaza Mayor. Set within two separate houses, the restaurant has flourished on this site since 1884. In summer, cascades of vines accent a series of tables and chairs, perfect for tapa-sampling and people-watching, set on the cobblestones outside. Some visitors consider an evening here among the highlights of their trip to Spain.

The ambience inside reflects of Old Castile, which is seen in the accoutrements of several dining rooms with vaulted or beamed ceilings. The Grande family, your multilingual hosts, prepare traditional versions of fish, shellfish, pork, veal, and beef in time-tested ways. Suckling pig, baby goat, and roasted lamb are almost always featured. Naturally, a carafe or bottle of wine goes well.

INEXPENSIVE

El Cuchi, Calle de Cuchilleros, 3. ☎ **366-44-24.**

Cuisine: MEXICAN/SPANISH. **Reservations:** Required.
Metro: Puerta del Sol.
Prices: Appetizers 400–1,350 ptas. ($2.80–$9.60); main courses 900–2,900 ptas. ($6.40–$20.60). AE, DC, MC, V.
Open: Lunch, daily 1–4pm; dinner daily 8pm–midnight.

A few doors down from Hemingway's favorite restaurant (Sobrino de Botín–see later in this chapter), El Cuchi defiantly claims that "Hemingway never ate here." However, just about everybody else has, attracted by both its low prices and its labyrinth of dining rooms. A European link in Mexico's famous Carlos 'n' Charlie's chain, the Madrid restaurant stands off a corner of Plaza Mayor. Ceiling beams and artifacts suggest rusticity. Menu specialties include black-bean soup, ceviche, guacamole, quail Mozambique, "pregnant" trout, and roast suckling pig (much cheaper than that served at Botín). Because after it opens at 1pm, it doesn't close until midnight, you can virtually have lunch as late as you want, or vice versa, dinner as early as you want.

La Chata, Cava Baja, 24. ☎ **366-14-58.**

Cuisine: SPANISH. **Reservations:** Recommended. **Metro:** La Latina.
Prices: Appetizers 1,000–3,000 ptas. ($7.10–$21.30); main dishes 1,500–2,200 ptas. ($10.70–$15.60). V.
Open: Lunch, daily 12:20–5pm; dinner, Mon–Sat 8pm–midnight or 2am.

The cuisine here is Castilian, Galician, and northern Spanish. Set behind a heavily ornamented tile facade, the place has a stand-up tapas bar at the entrance and a formal restaurant in a side room. Many locals linger at the darkly paneled bar, which is framed by hanging Serrano hams, cloves of garlic, and photographs of bullfighters. Full meals might include such specialties as roast suckling pig, roast lamb, *calamares en su tinta* (squid in its own ink), grilled filet of steak with peppercorns, and omelets flavored with strips of eel.

Specialty Dining

TASCA HOPPING

If you think you'll starve waiting for Madrid's fashionable 9:30 or 10pm dinner hour, you've been misinformed. Throughout the city you'll find tascas, bars that serve wine and platters of tempting hot and cold hors d'oeuvres known as tapas: mushrooms, salads, baby eels, shrimp, lobster, mussels, sausage, ham—and, in one establishment at least, bull testicles. Keep in mind that you can often save pesetas by ordering at the bar rather than occupying a table.

El Anciano Rey de los Vinos, Bailén, 19. ☎ **548-50-52.**

Cuisine: TAPAS. **Metro:** Ópera.
Prices: Tapas 95–450 ptas. (70¢–$3.20). No credit cards.
Open: Thurs–Tues 10am–3pm and 5:30pm–11pm.

Lying near the Royal Palace, the bar here is jammed during most of the day with crowds of Madrileños out for a glass (or a carafe) of one of the four house wines, which range from dry to sweet and start at 100 pesetas (70¢) per glass. Beer is also served.

Antonio Sánchez, Mesón de Parades, 13. ☎ **539-78-26.**

Cuisine: SPANISH **Metro:** Tirso de Molina.

Prices: Tapas (in the bar) 200–600 ptas. ($1.40–$4.30); appetizers 200–500 ptas. ($1.40–$3.60); main courses 1,000–1,600 ptas. ($7.10–$11.40); fixed-price menu 1,500 ptas. ($10.70) available at lunch Mon–Fri. MC, V.
Open: Lunch, daily noon–4pm; dinner, Mon–Sat 8pm–midnight.

Named in 1850 after the founder's son, who was killed in the bullring, Antonio Sánchez is full of bullfighting memorabilia, including the stuffed head of the animal that gored young Sánchez. Also featured on the dark paneled walls are three works by the Spanish artist Zuloaga, who had his last public exhibition in this restaurant near Plaza Tirso de Molina. A limited array of tapas, including garlic soup, are served with Valdepeñas wine drawn from a barrel, although many guests ignore the edibles in favor of smoking cigarettes and arguing the merits of this or that bullfighter. A restaurant in the back serves Spanish food with a vaguely French influence.

Cervecería Alemania, Plaza de Santa Ana, 6. ☎ **429-70-33.**

Cuisine: TAPAS. **Metro:** Alonso Martín or Sevilla.
Prices: Beer 95 ptas. (70¢); tapas 100–900 ptas. (70¢–$6.40). No credit cards.
Open: Wed–Thurs and Sun–Mon 10am–12:30am; Fri–Sat 10am–1:30am.

Hemingway used to frequent this casual spot with the celebrated bullfighter Luís Miguel Dominguín—ask the waiter to point out "Hemingway's table." However, it earned its name because of its long-ago German clients. Opening directly onto one of the liveliest little plazas of Madrid, it clings to its turn-of-the-century traditions. Young Madrileños are fond of stopping in for a mug of draft beer. You can sit at one of the tables, leisurely sipping beer or wine, since the waiters make no attempt to hurry you along. To accompany your beverage; try the fried sardines or a Spanish omelet.

Cervecería Santa Bárbara, Plaza de Santa Bárbara, 8. ☎ **419-04-40.**

Cuisine: TAPAS. **Metro:** Ademós. **Bus:** 3, 7, or 21.
Prices: Beer 150–290 ptas. ($1.10–$2.10); tapas 1,000–3,750 ptas. ($7.10–$26.60). No credit cards.
Open: Daily 11am–11pm.

Unique in Madrid, Cervecería Santa Bárbara is an outlet for a beer factory, and the management has spent a lot to make it modern and inviting. Hanging globe lights and spinning ceiling fans create an attractive ambience, as does the black-and-white marble checkerboard floor. You go here for beer, of course: *cerveza negra* (black beer) or *cerveza dorada* (golden beer). The local brew is best accompanied by homemade potato chips or by fresh shrimp, lobster, crabmeat, or barnacles. You can either stand at the counter or go directly to one of the wooden tables for waiter service.

Taberna Toscana, Ventura de la Vega, 22. ☎ **429-60-31.**

Cuisine: TAPAS. **Metro:** Puerta del Sol or Sevilla.
Prices: Glass of wine 100 ptas. (70¢); tapas 500–1,300 ptas. ($3.60–$9.20); No credit cards.
Open: Lunch, Tues–Sat noon–4pm. Dinner, Mon and Wed–Sat 8pm–midnight.
Closed: Aug.

Many Madrileños begin their nightly tasca crawl here. The aura is that of a village inn that's far removed from 20th-century Madrid. You sit on crude country stools under time-darkened beams from which hang sausages, pimientos, and sheaves of golden wheat. The long, tiled tasca bar is loaded with tasty tidbits, including the house specialties: *lacón y cecina* (boiled ham), *habas* (broad beans) with Spanish ham, and *chorizo* (a sausage of red peppers and pork)—almost meals in themselves. Especially delectable are the kidneys in sherry sauce and the snails in hot sauce.

DINING WITH A VIEW

Café de Oriente, Plaza de Oriente, 2. ☎ **541-39-74.**

Cuisine: FRENCH/SPANISH. **Reservations:** Recommended (in the restaurant only). **Metro:** Ópera.
Prices: Café, tapas 850 ptas. ($6), coffee 650 ptas. ($4.60). Restaurant, appetizers 950–2,700 ptas. ($6.70–$19.20), main courses 1,900–2,950 ptas. ($13.50–$20.90). AE, DC, MC, V.
Open: Lunch, daily 1–4pm; dinner, daily 9pm–midnight.

The Oriente is a café-and-restaurant complex, the former being one of the most popular in Madrid. From the café tables on its terrace, there's a spectacular view of the Palacio Real (Royal Palace) and the Teatro Real. The dining rooms—Castilian upstairs, French Basque downstairs—are frequented by royalty and diplomats. Typical of the refined cuisine are vichyssoise, fresh vegetable flan, and many savory meat and fresh-fish offerings; the service is excellent. Most visitors, however, patronize the café, trying if possible to get an outdoor table. The café is decorated in turn-of-the-century style, with banquettes and regal paneling, as befits its location. Pizza, tapas, and drinks (including Irish, Viennese, Russian, and Jamaican coffees) are served.

HEMINGWAY'S ROAST SUCKLING PIG

★ $ **Sobrino de Botín,** Calle de Cuchilleros, 17. ☎ **366-42-17.**

Cuisine: SPANISH. **Reservations:** Required. **Metro:** La Latina or Ópera.
Prices: Appetizers 430–2,400 ptas. ($3.10–$17); main courses 620–3,850 ptas. ($4.40–$27.30); fixed-price menu 3,500 ptas. ($24.90). AE, DC, MC, V.
Open: Lunch, daily 1–4pm; dinner, daily 8pm–midnight.

Ernest Hemingway made Sobrino de Botín famous. In the final two pages of his novel *The Sun Also Rises,* Jake invites Brett there for the Segovian specialty, washed down with Rioja Alta.

By merely entering its portals, you step back to 1725, the year the restaurant was founded. You'll see an open kitchen, with a charcoal hearth, hanging copper pots, an 18th-century tile oven for roasting the suckling pig, and a big pot of regional soup whose aroma wafts across the tables and among the time-aged beams. Your host, Don Antonio, never loses his cool—even when he has 18 guests standing in line waiting for tables.

The two house specialties are roast suckling pig and roast Segovian lamb. From the à la carte menu, you might try the fish-based "quarter-of-an-hour" soup. Good main dishes include baked Cantabrian hake and filet mignon with potatoes. The dessert list features strawberries (in season) with whipped cream. You can wash down your meal with Valdepeñas or Aragón wine, although most guests order sangría.

HOTEL DINING

★ **Restaurant Belagua,** In the Hotel Palacio Santo Mauro, Calle Zurbano, 36. ☎ **319-69-00.**

Cuisine: INTERNATIONAL. **Reservations:** Recommended. **Metro:** Rubén Darío or Alonso Martínez.

Prices: Appetizers 900–2,400 ptas. ($6.40–$17); main courses 1,800–3,800 ptas. ($12.80–$27); fixed-price menu Mon–Thurs 1,800–2,380 ptas. ($12.80–$16.90); fixed-price menu Fri–Sun 2,500 ptas. ($17.80). AE, DC, MC, V.
Open: Lunch, Mon–Sat 1–4pm; dinner, Mon–Sat 8:30–11:30pm. **Closed:** National holidays.

The building that contains this glamorous restaurant was originally created in 1894 as a small palace in the French neoclassical style. In 1991, Catalán designer Josep Joanpere helped transform it into a carefully detailed hotel (the Santo Mauro) which is recommended separately. Part of what emerged from the building's incarnation included this highly appealing postmodern restaurant, which today is considered one of the capital's finest.

Assisted by the well-mannered staff, you'll select from a menu whose inspiration and ingredients change with the seasons. Examples include watermelon-and-prawn salad, light cream of cold ginger soup, haddock baked in a crust of potatoes tinted with squid ink, filet of monkfish with prawn-and-zucchini sauce, and duck with honey and black cherries. There's also a dessert specialty that a waiter will define as a palette of seasonal flavors: Depending on the efforts of the chef, it might include miniature portions of flan with strawberry sauce plus an array of the day's pastries. The restaurant's name, incidentally, derives from a village in Navarre known for its natural beauty.

VEGETARIAN

La Galette, Conde de Aranda, 11. ☎ **576-06-41.**

Cuisine: VEGETARIAN. **Reservations:** Recommended. **Metro:** Retiro.
Prices: Appetizers 350–400 ptas. ($2.50–$2.80); main courses 550–750 ptas. ($3.90–$5.30); fixed–price menu 2,200 ptas. ($15.60). AE, DC, MC, V.
Open: Lunch, Mon–Sat 2–4pm; dinner, Mon–Sat 9pm–midnight.

La Galette was one of Madrid's first vegetarian restaurants, and it remains one of the best. Small and charming, it lies in a residential and shopping area, in the exclusive Salamanca district, near Plaza de la Independenca and the northern edge of Retiro Park. There is a limited selection of meat dishes, but the true allure lies in this establishment's imaginative use of vegetarian fare. Examples include baked stuffed peppers, omelets, eggplant croquettes, and even vegetarian "hamburgers." Some of the dishes are macrobiotic. The place is also noted for its mouth-watering pastries. The same owners in the same building complex also operate La Galette II.

AFTERNOON TEA

The most delightful spot in Madrid for afternoon tea is a sidewalk table at the **Café de Oriente,** overlooking the Royal Palace. See "Dining with a View," above.

LIGHT, CASUAL & FAST FOOD

Chez Lou Crêperie, Pedro Munguruza, 6. ☎ **350-34-16.**

Cuisine: FRENCH. **Reservations:** Required on weekends.
Metro: Plaza de Castilla. **Bus:** 27 or 147.
Prices: Appetizers 500–775 ptas. ($3.60–$5.50); crêpes 600–1,000 ptas. ($4.30–$7.10). No credit cards.
Open: Lunch, Mon–Fri 1:30–4pm; dinner, Mon–Fri 8:30pm–1am.

Near the Eurobuilding in the northern sector of Madrid, Chez Lou stands near the huge mural by Joan Miró, which alone would be worth the trek up here. In this intimate setting, you get well-prepared and reasonably priced French food. The restaurant serves pâté as an appetizer, then a large range of crêpes with many different fillings. Folded envelope style, the crêpes are not tearoom size, and they're perfectly adequate as a main course. I've sampled several variations, finding the ingredients nicely blended yet distinct enough to retain their identity. A favorite is the large crêpe stuffed with minced onions, cream, and smoked salmon. The ham-and-cheese crêpe is also tasty. Your dessert and drink cost extra. Come here if you're seeking a light supper when it's too hot for one of those table-groaning Spanish meals.

La Plaza, La Galería del Prado, Plaza de las Cortés, 7. ☎ **429-65-37.**

Cuisine: SPANISH. **Reservations:** Not required. **Metro:** Sevilla.
Prices: Appetizers 335–660 ptas. ($2.40–$4.70); main courses 1,100–1,800 ptas. ($7.80–$12.80); fixed-price menus 1,100–1,400 ptas. ($7.80–$9.90). AE, MC, V.
Open: Mon–Fri 9am–10pm; Sat 11am–10:30pm.

This restaurant serves as the underground centerpiece of one of Madrid's shopping complexes, La Galería del Prado. Surrounded by thick marble-sheathed walls, its bunker-style position eliminates the possibility of natural sunlight streaming through windows. Nevertheless, it offers an attractive option for light, refreshing meals within an expensive neighborhood near the Prado. Some of its tables overflow into the rotunda of the shopping mall; most diners, however, sit within a glossy series of lattices whose rooms form a garden-inspired enclave near a well-stocked salad bar (visits here are priced according to the portions you take). You might begin with Serrano ham or a mountain-fermented goat cheese, perhaps a homemade pâté. Daily specials include such dishes as ragoût of veal. Platters of pasta also make a zesty way to fill up.

Ríofrío, Centro Colón; Plaza de Colón, 1. ☎ **319-29-77.**

Cuisine: INTERNATIONAL. **Reservations:** Not required. **Metro:** Colón. **Bus:** 5, 6, 14, 27, or 45.
Prices: Appetizers 400–1,700 ptas. ($2.80–$12.10); main courses 950–3,200 ptas. ($6.70–$22.70); sandwiches 460–850 ptas. ($3.30–$6). AE, DC, MC, V.
Open: Daily, noon–1:30am.

Overlooking Madrid's "Columbus Circle," this is a sort of all-purpose place for drinking, eating, dining, or nightclubbing. The least-expensive way to eat here is to patronize one of two self-service cafeterias, where average meals run from 1,000 to 1,500 pesetas ($7.10–$10.70). There's also a large restaurant with an international cuisine, serving meals averaging 3,500 pesetas ($24.90), plus yet another dining room for informal lunches, dinners, snacks, or apéritifs. The spacious glassed-in terrace, open year round, is known for serving some of the best paella in Madrid. Finally, there's even a nightclub, should you desire to make an evening of it. El Descubrimiento serves dinner costing from 4,500 pesetas ($32) that includes not only the meal but a show to follow. Sandwiches are also available throughout the day if you'd like just a light bite in the hot Madrid sun.

CAFETERIAS

V.I.P., Gran Vía, 43. ☎ **411-60-44.**

Cuisine: FAST FOOD. **Reservations:** Not required. **Metro:** Callao.
Prices: Appetizers 450–725 ptas. ($3.20–$5.10); main courses 650–1,200 ptas. ($4.60–$8.50). AE, DC, MC, V.
Open: Daily 9am–3am.

This place looks like a bookstore emporium from the outside, but in back it is a cafeteria serving fast food. You might begin with a cup of soothing gazpacho. There are more than a dozen V.I.P.s scattered throughout Madrid, but this is the most central one. Hamburgers are the rage here.

LOCAL FAVORITES

La Bola, Calle la Bola, 5. ☎ **547-69-30.**

Cuisine: MADRILEÑA. **Reservations:** Required. **Metro:** Plaza de España or Ópera. **Bus:** 1 or 2.
Prices: Appetizers 700–2,000 ptas. ($5–$14.20); main courses 1,200–1,900 ptas. ($8.50–$13.50); fixed-price menu 2,125 ptas. ($15.10). No credit cards.
Open: Lunch, Mon–Sat 1–4pm. Dinner, Mon–Sat 9pm–midnight.

If you'd like to savor 19th-century Madrid, then this *taberna,* just north of the Teatro Real, is an inspired choice. It's one of the few restaurants (if not the only one) left in Madrid that has a blood-red facade; once, nearly all fashionable restaurants were so coated. La Bola hangs on to tradition like a tenacious bull. Time has galloped forward, but not inside this restaurant: The soft, traditional atmosphere; the gentle and polite waiters; the Venetian crystal; the Carmen-red draperies; and the aging velvet preserve the 1870 ambience of the place. Ava Gardner, with her entourage of bullfighters, used to patronize this establishment, but that was long ago, before La Bola became so well known to tourists. Grilled sole, filet of veal, and roast veal are regularly featured. Basque-style hake and grilled salmon also are well recommended. A host of refreshing dishes to begin your meal include grilled shrimp, red-pepper salad, and lobster cocktail.

Casa Ciriaco, Plaza Mayor, 84. ☎ **548-50-66.**

Cuisine: SPANISH. **Reservations:** Recommended.**Metro:** Ópera.
Prices: Appetizers 450–1,500 ptas. ($3.20–$10.70); main courses 1,800–3,500 ptas. ($12.80–$24.90); *menú del día* 1,725 ptas. ($12.20). No credit cards.
Open: Lunch, Thurs–Tues 1–4pm; dinner, Thurs–Tues 8:30pm–midnight. **Closed:** Aug.

Since 1906, this has been a special restaurant in one of the most romantic parts of Old Madrid. It enjoys associations with the Spanish painter Ignacio Zuloaga. The chef features dishes from Navarre and Andalusia, but Castilian specialties predominate on his menu. Gazpacho makes a fine opener, then you can order Navarre-style trout or tender slices of veal.

$ **Casa Mingo,** Paseo de la Florida 2. ☎ **57-79-18.**

Cuisine: SPANISH. **Reservations:** Not accepted. **Metro:** Norte, then a 15-minute walk.
Prices: Main courses 450–1,050 ptas. ($3.20–$7.50). No credit cards.
Open: Daily 10am–midnight.

Casa Mingo has been known for decades for its Asturian cider, both still and bubbly. The perfect accompanying tidbit is a piece of the local Asturian *cabrales* (goat cheese), but the roast chicken is the specialty of the house, with an unbelievable number of helpings served daily. There's no formality here since the customers share big tables under the vaulted ceiling in the dining room. In summer the staff places some tables and wooden chairs out on the sidewalk. In the strictest sense, this is not a restaurant but a bodega/taverna that serves food.

Hylogui, Ventura de la Vega, 3. ☎ **429-73-57.**

Cuisine: CASTILIAN. **Reservations:** Recommended. **Metro:** Sevilla.
Prices: Appetizers 425–900 ptas. ($3–$6.40); main courses 850–1,850 ptas. ($6–$13.10). AE, MC, V.
Open: Lunch, daily 1–4:30pm; dinner, Mon–Sat 9pm–midnight.

Hylogui, a local legend, is one of the largest dining rooms along Ventura de la Vega, but there are many arches and nooks for privacy. One globe-trotting American wrote enthusiastically that he took all his Madrid meals here, finding the soup pleasant and rich, the flan soothing, and the regional wine dry. The food is old-fashioned Spanish home-style cooking.

Taberna del Alabardero, Felipe V, 6. ☎ **547-25-77.**

Cuisine: BASQUE/SPANISH. **Reservations:** Required for restaurant only. **Metro:** Ópera.
Prices: Bar, tapas 450–1,200 ptas. ($3.20–$8.50); glass of house wine 95 ptas. (70¢). Restaurant, appetizers 950–1,600 ptas. ($6.70–$11.40), main courses 1,900–3,100 ptas. ($13.50–$22). AE, DC, V.
Open: Lunch, daily 1–4pm; dinner, daily 9–midnight.

Because of its proximity to the Royal Palace, most patrons visit this little Spanish classic for its selection of tasty tapas, ranging from squid cooked in wine to fried potatoes dipped in hot sauce. Photographs of former patrons, including Nelson Rockefeller and race-car driver Jackie Stewart, line the walls. The restaurant in the rear is said to be one of the city's best-kept secrets. Decorated in typical tavern style, it serves a savory Spanish Basque cuisine with market-fresh ingredients.

LATE-NIGHT DINING

Those famous hamburgers and an array of other dishes are served until 1am at **Foster's Hollywood** (see the previous recommendation under "Chamberí").

PICNIC FARE & WHERE TO EAT IT

On a hot day, do as the Madrileños do: Secure the makings of a picnic lunch and head for Casa de Campo (Metro: El Batán), those once-royal hunting grounds in the west of Madrid across the Manzanares River. Children delight in this adventure, as they can also visit a boating lake, the Parque de Atracciones, and the Madrid Zoo.

Your best choice for picnic fare is **Mallorca,** Velázquez, 59 (☎ **431-99-00;** Metro: Velázquez). This place has all the makings for a deluxe picnic. (For full details, see "Food & Wine" under "Savvy Shopping" in Chapter 5.)

Another good bet is **Rodilla,** Preciados, 25 (☎ **522-57-01;** Metro: Callao), where you can find sandwiches, pastries, and takeaway tapas. Sandwiches, including vegetarian, meat, and fish, begin at 75 pesetas (50¢). It's open Monday through Saturday from 8:30am to 10:30pm and Sunday from 2:30 to 10:30pm.

5

What to See & Do in Madrid

MADRID HAS CHANGED DRASTICALLY IN RECENT YEARS. NO LONGER IS IT FAIR TO say that it has only the Prado and after you see that you should head for Toledo or El Escorial. As you will discover in the pages to come, Madrid has something to amuse and delight everyone.

Suggested Itineraries

If You Have One Day

If you have just arrived in Spain after a long flight, don't tackle too much on your first day. Spend the morning at the **Prado,** one of the world's great art museums, arriving when it opens at 9am (remember, it's closed on Mondays). Have lunch and then visit the **Palacio Real (Royal Palace).** Have an early dinner near the Plaza Mayor.

If You Have Two Days

Spend Day 1 as described above. On Day 2 take a trip to Toledo, where you can visit El Greco's House and Museum, the Santa Cruz Museum, the Church of Santo Tomé, and the Alcázar. Return to Madrid in the evening.

If You Have Three Days

Follow the suggestions for Days 1 and 2. On Day 3 take a one-hour train ride to the Monastery of San Lorenzo del Escorial, in the foothills of the Sierra de Guadarrama. Return to Madrid in the evening.

If You Have Five Days

Follow the suggestions for Days 1 to 3. Day 4 would be a very busy day indeed if you visited the Thyssen-Bornemisza museum in the morning (it opens at 10am), took a walking tour of Medieval Madrid (see below), and visited the Museo Nacional Centro de Arte Reina Sofia in the late afternoon or early evening (it closes at 9pm on most nights). There you can see Picasso's *Guernica* plus other great art of the 20th century. Have dinner once again at one of the many restaurants off the Plaza Mayor. On Day 5 take a trip to **Segovia** in Old Castile. Be sure to see its Alcázar, Roman aqueduct, and cathedral. Sample the region's specialties at lunch and return to Madrid for dinner in the old town.

1 The Top Attractions

★ **Museo del Prado,** Paseo del Prado. ☎ **420-28-36.**

With more than 7,000 paintings, the Prado is one of the most important repositories of art in the world. It began as a royal collection and was enhanced by the Hapsburgs, especially Charles V, and later the Bourbons. In paintings of the Spanish school the Prado has no equal, and on your first visit, concentrate on the Spanish masters (Velázquez, Goya, El Greco, and Murillo).

Most major works are exhibited on the first floor. You'll see art by Italian masters—Raphael, Botticelli, Mantegna, Andrea del Sarto, Fra Angelico, and Correggio. Perhaps the most celebrated Italian painting here is Titian's voluptuous Venus being watched by a musician who can't keep his eyes on his work.

Don't miss the work of El Greco (1524–1614), the Crete-born artist who lived much of his life in Toledo. You can see a parade of "The Greek's" saints, Madonnas, and Holy Families—even a ghostly *John the Baptist.*

In Their Footsteps

Diego Rodriguez de Silva Velázquez (1599–1660). Acclaimed as the greatest painter of the 17th century, who centuries later was to have great influence on Picasso, at age 25 he was made court painter to Philip IV. "I have found my Titian," the king declared. He was a master of atmospheric portraiture, making earth-shattering breakthroughs in use of color and light. His masterpiece, *Las Meninas*, hangs in the Prado. Velázquez painted his greatest works during the last two years of life, including the *Sinners*.

Resting Place A cross at Plaza del Ramal in Madrid marks the site of his burial at the former Church of San Juan.

In the five-star showcase that is the Prado, you'll find a splendid array of works by the incomparable Diego Velázquez (1599–1660). The museum's most famous painting, in fact, is his *Las Meninas*, a triumph in the use of light effects. The faces of the queen and king are reflected in the mirror in the painting itself. The artist in the foreground is Velázquez, of course.

Rubens, who met Velázquez while in Spain, is represented by the peacock-blue Garden of Love and by the **Three Graces**. Also worthy is the work of José Ribera (1591–1652), a Valencia-born artist and contemporary of Velázquez whose best painting is the **Martyrdom of St. Philip.** The Seville-born Bartolomé Murillo (1617–82)—often referred to as the "painter of Madonnas"—has three **Immaculate Conceptions** on display.

The Prado contains one of the world's outstanding collections of the work of Hieronymus Bosch (1450?–1516), the Flemish genius. "El Bosco's" best-known work, **The Garden of Earthly Delights,** is here. You'll also see his **Seven Deadly Sins** and his triptych **The Hay Wagon. The Triumph of Death** is by another Flemish painter, Pieter Breughel the Elder (1525?–69), who carried on Bosch's ghoulish vision.

Francisco de Goya (1746–1828), ranks along with Velázquez and El Greco in the trio of great Spanish artists. Hanging here are his cruel portraits of his patron, Charles IV, and his family, as well as the **Clothed Maja** and the **Naked Maja.** You can also see the much-reproduced **Third of May** (1808), not to mention a series of Goya sketches (some of which, depicting the decay of 18th-century Spain, brought the Inquisition down on the artist) and his expressionistic "black paintings."

Admission: 450 ptas. ($3.20).

Open: Tues–Sat 9am–7pm; Sun and holidays 9am–2pm. **Closed:** Jan 1, Good Friday, May 1, and Dec 25. **Metro:** Banco de España or Atocha. **Bus:** 10, 14, 27, 34, 37, 45, or M6.

★ **Thyssen-Bornemisza Museum,** Palacio de Villahermosa, Paseo del Prado, 8. ☎ **420-39-44.**

Until around 1985, the contents of this museum virtually overflowed the premises of a legendary villa near Lugano, Switzerland. Considered one of the most frequently visited sites of Switzerland, the collection had been laboriously amassed over a period of about 60 years by the Thyssen-Bornemisza family, scions of a shipping, banking, mining, and chemical fortune whose roots began around 1905 in Holland, Germany, and Hungary. Experts had proclaimed it as one of the world's most extensive and valuable privately owned collections of paintings, rivaled only by the legendary holdings of Queen Elizabeth II.

For tax and insurance reasons, and because the collection had outgrown the boundaries of the lakeside villa that contained it, the collection was discreetly marketed in the early 1980s to the world's major museums. Amid endless intrigue, a litany of glamorous supplicants from eight different nations came calling. Among them were Margaret Thatcher and Prince Charles; trustees of the Getty Museum in Malibu, California; the president of West Germany; the Duke of Badajoz, brother-in-law of King Carlos II; even emissaries from Disneyworld in Orlando, Florida, all hoping to acquire the collection for their respective countries or entities.

Eventually, thanks partly to the lobbying by Baron Hans Heinrich Thyssen-Bornemisza's fifth wife, a Spanish-born beauty (and former Miss Spain) named Tita, the collection was awarded to Spain. An agreement that had been born as a nine-year lend-lease arrangement eventually evolved, pending final negotiations, into an outright purchase by the Spanish government for $350 million. Although this amount was far less than the market value of the collection if each painting had been sold individually, controversies over the public cost of the acquisition raged for months throughout every level of Spanish society. Despite the brouhaha, various estimates have placed the value of this collection at anywhere between one and three billion dollars.

To house the collection, an 18th-century building adjacent to the Prado, the Villahermosa Palace, was retrofitted with the appropriate lighting and security devices, and renovated at a cost of $45 million. Rooms are arranged numerically so that by following the order of the various rooms (numbers 1 through 48, spread out over three floors), a logical sequence of European painting can be followed from the 13th through the 20th centuries. The nucleus of the collection consists of 700 world-class paintings. They include works by, among others, El Greco, Velásquez, Dürer, Rembrandt, Watteau, Canaletto, Caravaggio, Frans Hals, Hans Memling, and Goya.

Unusual among the world's great art collections because of its eclecticism, the Thyssen group also contains goodly numbers of 19th- and 20th-century paintings by many of the notable French impressionists, as well as works by Picasso, John Singer Sargent, Kirchner, Nolde, and Kandinsky—artists whose absence within Spanish museums until the von Thyssen acquisition had become increasingly obvious. This museum has attracted many millions of visitors since its long-awaited opening; be prepared for magnificent art and long lines.

Admission: 650 ptas. ($4.60).

Open: Tues–Sun 10am–7pm. **Metro:** Banco de España. **Bus:** 1, 2, 5, 9, 10, 14, 15, 20, 27, 34, 45, 51, 52, 53, 74, 146, or 150.

★ **Museo Nacional Centro de Arte Reina Sofía,** Santa Isabel, 52.
☎ **467-50-62.**

Filling for the world of modern art the role that the Prado has filled for traditional art, the "MOMA" of Madrid (its nickname) reigns without challenge as the greatest repository of 20th-century art in Spain. Set within the echoing, futuristically renovated walls of the former General Hospital, originally built between 1776 and 1781, the museum is a sprawling, high-ceilinged showplace named after the Greek-born wife of Spain's present king. Once designated as "the ugliest building in Spain" by Catalán architect Oriol Bohigas, the building is said to be one of the largest museums, and probably the most security-conscious, in Europe. The design hangs in limbo somewhere between the 18th and the 21st centuries and incorporates a 50,000-volume art library and database; a café; a theater; a bookstore; Plexiglass-sided elevators; and systems that carefully calibrate security, temperature, humidity, and the quality of light surrounding the exhibits.

Special emphasis is paid to the great artists of contemporary Spain: Juan Gris, Dalí, Miró, and Picasso (the museum has been able to acquire a handful of his works). What many critics claim as Picasso's masterpiece, **Guernica,** now rests at this museum after a long and troubling history of traveling. Banned in Spain during Franco's era (Picasso refused to have it displayed there anyway), it hung on world view at New York's Museum of Modern Art. The antiwar piece of art immortalizes the shameful blanket bombing by the German Luftwaffe, fighting for Franco during the Spanish Civil War. Guernica was the cradle of the Basque nation. Picasso's canvas made the Basque town a household name around the world.

An important showplace of 20th-century Spanish art, the museum has also acted as a huge magnet for the relocation within its neighborhood of several new art galleries and cultural institutions that collectively promise to upgrade both the neighborhood and the cultural quality of life of Spain.

Admission: 450 ptas. ($3.20).

Open: Wed–Mon 10am–9pm. **Metro:** Atocha. **Bus:** 6, 14, 26, 27, 32, 45, 57, or C.

★ **Palacio Real (Royal Palace),** Plaza de Oriente, Calle de Bailén, 2. ☎ **248-74-04.**

This huge palace was begun in 1738 on the site of the Madrid Alcázar, which burned to the ground in 1734. Some of its 2,000 rooms—which that "enlightened despot" Charles III called home—are open to the public, while others are still used for state business. The palace was last used as a royal residence in 1931, before King Alfonzo XIII and his wife, Victoria Eugénie, fled Spain.

You'll be taken on a guided tour—say "Inglés" to the person who takes your ticket, so you'll get an English-speaking guide—that includes the Reception Room, the State Apartments, the Armory, and the Royal Pharmacy.

The Reception Room and State Apartments should get priority here if you're rushed. They embrace a rococo room with a diamond clock; a porcelain salon; the Royal Chapel; the Banquet Room, where receptions for heads of state are still held; and the Throne Room.

The rooms are literally stuffed with art treasures and antiques—salon after salon of monumental grandeur, with no apologies for the damask, mosaics, stucco, Tiepolo ceilings, gilt and bronze, chandeliers, and paintings.

In the Armory, you'll see the finest collection of weaponry in Spain. Many of the items—powder flasks, shields, lances, helmets, and saddles—are from the collection of Charles V (Charles of Spain). From here, the comprehensive tour takes you into the Pharmacy.

You may want to visit the **Carriage Museum,** also at the Royal Palace, to see some of the grand old relics used by Spanish aristocrats. Afterward, stroll through the Campo del Moro, the gardens of the palace.

Admission: 500 ptas. ($3.60); Carriage Museum 200 ptas. ($1.40).

Open: Mon–Sat 9am–6pm, Sun 9am–3pm. **Metro:** Ópera or Plaza de España.

Museo de la Real Academia de Bellas Artes de San Fernando (Fine Arts Museum), Alcalá, 13. ☎ **522-14-91.**

An easy stroll from Puerta del Sol, the Fine Arts Museum is located in the restored and remodeled 17th-century baroque palace of Juan de Goyeneche. The collection—

more than 1,500 paintings and 570 sculptures, ranging from the 16th century to the present—was started in 1752 during the reign of Fernando VI (1746–59). It emphasizes works by Spanish, Flemish, and Italian artists. You can see masterpieces by El Greco, Rubens, Velázquez, Zurbarán, Ribera, Cano, Coello, Murillo, Goya, and Sorolla.

Admission: 225 ptas. ($1.60); children free.

Open: Tues–Fri 9am–7pm; Sat–Mon 9am–2:30pm. **Metro:** Puerta del Sol or Sevilla.

Panteón de Goya (Goya's Tomb), Glorieta de San Antonio de la Florida, s/n (no street number). ☎ **542-07-22.**

In a remote part of town beyond the North Station lies Goya's tomb, containing one of his masterpieces—an elaborately beautiful fresco depicting the miracles of St. Anthony on the dome and cupola of the little hermitage of San Antonio de la Florida. This has been called Goya's "Sistine Chapel." Already deaf when he began the painting, Goya labored dawn to dusk for 16 weeks, painting with sponges rather than brushes. By depicting common street life–stone masons, prostitutes, and beggars—Goya raised the ire of the nobility who held judgment until the patron, Carlos IV, viewed it. When the monarch approved, the formerly "outrageous" painting was deemed "acceptable."

The tomb and fresco are in one of the twin chapels (visit the one on the right) that were built in the latter part of the 18th century. Discreetly placed mirrors will help you see the ceiling better.

Admission: 225 ptas. ($1.60).

Open: Apr–Oct, Thurs–Tues 10am–1pm and 4–7pm; winter, Thurs–Tues 10am–2pm and 4–8pm. **Metro:** Norte. **Bus:** 41, 46, 75, or C.

Museo Taurino (Bullfighting Museum), Plaza de Toros de las Ventas, Alcalá, 237. ☎ **255-18-57.**

This museum might serve as a good introduction to bullfighting for those who want to see the real event. Here you'll see the death costume of Manolete, the *traje de luces* (suit of lights) that he wore when he was gored to death at age 30 in Linares's bullring.

Other memorabilia evoke the heyday of Juan Belmonte, the Andalusian who revolutionized bullfighting in 1914 by performing close to the horns. Other exhibits include a Goya painting of a matador, as well as photographs and relics that trace the history of bullfighting in Spain from its ancient origins to the present day.

Admission: Free.

Open: May–Sept, Tues–Fri 9:30am–1:30pm, Sun 10am–1pm. Oct–Apr, Mon–Fri 10am–1pm. **Bus:** 12, 21, 38, 53, 146, M1, or M8.

Museo Lázaro Galdiano, Serrano, 122. ☎ **561-60-84.**

Imagine 37 rooms in a well-preserved 19th-century mansion bulging with artworks—including many by the most famous old masters of Europe. Most visitors take the elevator to the top floor and work down, lingering over such artifacts as 15th-century handwoven vestments, swords and daggers, royal seals, 16th-century crystal from Limoges, Byzantine jewelry, Italian bronzes from ancient times to the Renaissance, and medieval armor.

Two paintings by Bosch evoke his own peculiar brand of horror, his canvases peopled with creepy fiends devouring human flesh. A portrait of Saskia signed by Rembrandt adorns a wall nearby. The Spanish masters are the best represented—El Greco, Velázquez, Zurbarán, Ribera, Murillo, and Valdés-Leal.

Did You Know ?

- Sobrino de Botín, a Hemingway favorite founded in 1725, claims to be the world's oldest restaurant.
- The only public statue anywhere dedicated to the Devil stands in Madrid's Retiro Park.
- A Mexican composer wrote the unofficial anthem "Madrid, Madrid, Madrid" —and he had never been to Madrid.

In Their Footsteps

Francisco José de Goya y Lucientes (1746–1828). One of the greatest artists of all time, Goya became a pupil of Francisco Bayeu in Madrid. In 1773, he married Bayeu's sister. In 1789, he was appointed court painter to King Carlos IV. The works of his early years combined elements of neoclassicism with rococo flamboyance, in contrast to the "black paintings" of his declining years. A mysterious illness in 1794 left him deaf in both ears. The inquisition summoned him in 1803, wanting him to "explain" why he created the first painting in the history of art to show a woman's pubic hair. In Bordeaux, where he died in exile, he created lithography.

Resting Place Panteón de Goya, Madrid (minus his skull, which was missing when his remains were returned from France).

One section is devoted to works by the English portrait and landscape artists Reynolds, Gainsborough, and Constable. Italian artists exhibited include Tiepolo and Guardi. Salon 30—for many, the most interesting—is devoted to Goya and includes some paintings from his "black period," as well as a portrait of the weak Carlos IV and his voluble, amorous queen, Maria Luisa.

Admission: 450 ptas. ($3.20).

Open: Tues–Sun 10am–2pm. **Closed:** Holidays and Aug. **Metro:** Avenida de América. **Bus:** 9, 16, 19, 51, or 89.

★ **Convento de las Descalzas Reales,** Plaza de las Descalzas Reales, s/n. ☎ **248-74-04.**

In the mid-16th century, aristocratic women—either disappointed in love or "wanting to be the bride of Christ"—stole away to this convent to take the veil. Each of them brought a dowry, making this one of the richest convents in the land. By the mid-20th century the convent sheltered mostly poor women. True, it still contained a priceless collection of art treasures, but the sisters were forbidden to auction anything; in fact, they were literally starving. The state intervened, and the pope granted special dispensation to open the convent as a museum. Today the public can look behind the walls of what was once a mysterious edifice on one of the most beautiful squares in Old Madrid.

An English-speaking guide will show you through. In the Reliquary are the noblewomen's dowries, one of which is said to contain bits of wood from Christ's Cross; another, some of the bones of St. Sebastian. The most valuable painting

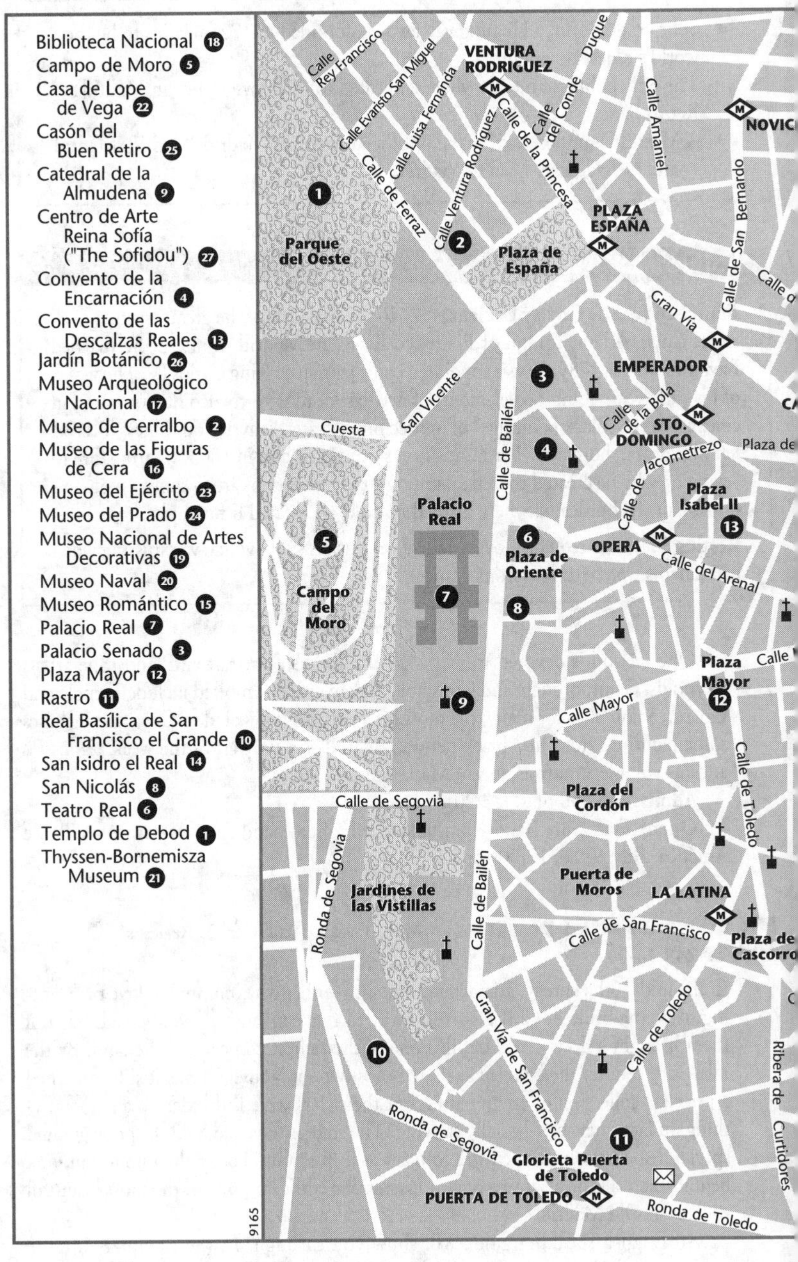
Biblioteca Nacional 18
Campo de Moro 5
Casa de Lope de Vega 22
Casón del Buen Retiro 25
Catedral de la Almudena 9
Centro de Arte Reina Sofía ("The Sofidou") 27
Convento de la Encarnación 4
Convento de las Descalzas Reales 13
Jardín Botánico 26
Museo Arqueológico Nacional 17
Museo de Cerralbo 2
Museo de las Figuras de Cera 16
Museo del Ejército 23
Museo del Prado 24
Museo Nacional de Artes Decorativas 19
Museo Naval 20
Museo Romántico 15
Palacio Real 7
Palacio Senado 3
Plaza Mayor 12
Rastro 11
Real Basílica de San Francisco el Grande 10
San Isidro el Real 14
San Nicolás 8
Teatro Real 6
Templo de Debod 1
Thyssen-Bornemisza Museum 21
Calle Rey Francisco
Calle Evaristo San Miguel
Calle Luisa Fernanda
Calle de Ferraz
VENTURA RODRIGUEZ
Calle Ventura Rodríguez
Calle de la Princesa
Calle del Conde Duque
Calle Amaniel
NOVIC
Calle de San Bernardo
Parque del Oeste
Plaza de España
PLAZA ESPAÑA
Gran Vía
EMPERADOR
Calle de la Bola
STO. DOMINGO
Calle de Jacometrezo
Plaza de
Cuesta San Vicente
Calle de Bailén
Palacio Real
Plaza Isabel II
OPERA
Calle del Arenal
Plaza de Oriente
Campo del Moro
Plaza Mayor
Calle Mayor
Calle de Toledo
Plaza del Cordón
Calle de Segovia
Ronda de Segovia
Jardines de las Vistillas
Puerta de Moros
LA LATINA
Calle de San Francisco
Plaza de Cascorro
Gran Vía de San Francisco
Ribera de Curtidores
Ronda de Segovia
Glorieta Puerta de Toledo
PUERTA DE TOLEDO
Ronda de Toledo
9165

Madrid Attractions 
Metro
Church
Post Office
Information
300 m
330 y
N
Calle de Genova
SERRANO
Calle de Goya
Plaza de la Villa
Plaza de Colón
COLÓN
Jardines del Descubrimiento
Calle de Fuencarral
Calle Fernando VI
Calle Bárbara de Braganza
Calle de Gravina del Almirante
CHUECA
Calle de Hortaleza
Calle de Augusto Figueroa
Calle de Prim
paseo Recoletos
Calle de Serrano
Calle Escorial
Calle Corredera Baja de San Pablo
Calle de Valverde
Plaza de la Independencia
GRAN VÍA
Red. de San Luis
Gran Vía
Calle de Barquillo
Plaza de la Cibeles
Calle de Alcalá
BANCO DE ESPAÑA
SEVILLA
Calle de Montalbán
Calle Montera
Paseo del Prado
Plaza de la Lealtad
Calle A. Maura
Calle de Alfonso XII
Carrera de San Jerónimo
Calle de la Cruz
Plaza de las Cortes
Plaza C. del Castillo
Calle del Prado
Calle de Cervantes
Parque del Retiro
Museo del Prado
Calle Atocha
Calle de las Huertas
Calle de Espalter
ANTÓN MARTÍN
Calle de la Cabeza
Calle de Gobernador
Jardín Botánico
Calle de Santa Isabel
Calle Jesús y María Levapiés
Calle del Amparo
Calle Mesón de Paredes
ATOCHA
Paseo de la Infanta Isabel
Plaza Lavapies
LAVAPIES
Calle Miguel Servet
Calle de Embajadores
Ronda de Atocha
Sta. María de la Cabeza
Estación de Atocha
15
16
17
18
19
20
21
22
23
24
25
26
27

is Titian's *Caesar's Money*. The Flemish Hall shelters other fine works, including paintings by Hans de Beken, and Breughel the Elder. All of the tapestries were based on Rubens' cartoons, displaying his chubby matrons.

Admission: 475 ptas. ($3.40) adults; 250 ptas. ($1.80) children.

Open: Tues–Thurs 10:30am–12:30pm and 4–5:30pm; Fri 10:30am–12:30pm, Sun 11am–1:30pm. **Bus:** 1, 2, 5, 20, 46, 52, 53, 74, M1, M2, M3, or M5. Directions: From Plaza del Callao, off Gran Vía, walk down Postigo de San Martín to Plaza de las Descalzas Reales; the convent is on the left.

Real Fábrica de Tapices (Royal Tapestry Factory), Fuenterrabía, 2. ☎ **551-34-00.**

At this factory, the age-old process of making exquisite (and very expensive) tapestries is still carried on with consummate skill. Nearly every tapestry is based on a cartoon of Goya, who was the factory's most famous employee. Many of these patterns—such as *The Pottery Salesman*—are still in production today. (Goya's original cartoons are in the Prado.) Many of the other designs are based on cartoons by Francisco Bayeu, Goya's brother-in-law.

Admission: 450 ptas. ($3.20).

Open: Mon–Fri 9am–12:30pm. **Closed:** Aug. **Metro:** Menéndez Pelayo. **Bus:** 10, 14, 26, 32, 37, C, or M9.

2 More Attractions

Mainly Museums

Museo Arqueológico Nacional, Serrano, 13. ☎ **577-79-12.**

This stately mansion is a storehouse of artifacts from the prehistoric to the baroque. One of the prime exhibits here is the Iberian statue The Lady of Elche, a piece of primitive carving (probably from the 4th century B.C.), discovered on the southeastern coast of Spain. Finds from Ibiza, Paestum, and Rome are on display, including statues of Tiberius and his mother, Livia. The Islamic collection from Spain is outstanding. There are also collections of Spanish Renaissance lusterware, Talavera pottery, Retiro porcelain, and some rare 16th- and 17th-century Andalusian glassware.

Many of the exhibits are treasures that were removed from churches and monasteries. A much-photographed choir stall from Palencia dates from the 14th century. Also worth a look are the reproductions of the Altamira cave paintings (chiefly of bison, horses, and boars), discovered near Santander in northern Spain in 1868.

Admission: 450 ptas. ($3.20).

Open: Museum, Tues–Sun 9:30am–8:30pm. Caves, Tues–Sun 9:30am–1:30pm. **Metro:** Serrano or Retiro. **Bus:** 1, 9, 19, 51, 74, or M2.

Museo del Ejército (Army Museum), Méndez Núñez, 1. ☎ **522-89-77.**

This museum, in the Buen Retiro Palace, houses outstanding exhibits from military history, including the original sword of El Cid, which Isabella carried when she took Granada from the Moors. In addition, you can see the tent used by Charles V in Tunisia, relics of Pizarro and Cortés, and an exceptional collection of armor. Look for the piece of the cross that Columbus carried when he landed in the New World. The museum had a notorious founder: Manuel Godoy, who rose from relative poverty to become the lover of Maria Luisa of Parma, wife of Carlos IV.

Admission: 125 ptas. (90¢).

Open: Tues–Sat 10am–2pm; Sun 10am–1:30pm. **Metro:** Banco de España.

Museo Municipal, Fuencarral, 78. ☎ **522-57-32.**

After years of restoration, the Museo Municipal displays collections on local history, archeology, and art, with an emphasis on the Bourbon Madrid of the 18th century. Paseos with strolling couples are shown on huge tapestry cartoons. Paintings from the royal collections are here, plus period models of the best-known city squares and a Goya that was painted for the Town Hall.

Admission: 450 ptas. ($3.20).

Open: Tues–Fri 9:30am–8pm; Sat–Sun 10am–2pm. **Metro:** Tribunal. **Bus:** 3, 7, 40, or M10.

Museo Nacional de Artes Decorativas, Calle de Montalbán, 12. ☎ **521-34-40.**

In 62 rooms spread over several floors, this museum near the Plaza de la Cibeles displays a rich collection of furniture, ceramics, and decorative pieces. Emphasizing the 16th and 17th centuries, the eclectic collection includes Gothic carvings, alabaster figurines, festival crosses, elaborate dollhouses, elegant baroque four-poster beds, a chapel covered with leather tapestries, and even kitchens from the 17th century.

Admission: 450 ptas. ($3.20).

Open: Tues–Fri 9am–3pm; Sat–Sun 10am–2pm. **Metro:** Banco de España. **Bus:** 14, 27, 34, 37, 45, or M6.

Frommer's Favorite Madrid Experiences

Tasca Hopping The quintessential Madrid experience and the fastest way for a visitor to tap into the local scene. *Tascas* are Spanish pubs serving tantalizing appetizers (*tapas*). You can go from one to the other, sampling the special dishes and wines in each tavern.

Eating "Around Spain" The variety of gastronomic experiences is staggering: You can literally restaurant hop from province to province—without ever leaving Madrid.

Viewing the Works of Your Favorite Artist Spend an afternoon at the Prado, savoring the works of your favorite Spanish artist, devoting all your attention to his work.

Bargain Hunting at El Rastro Madrid has one of the greatest flea markets in Europe, if not the world. Wander through its many offerings to discover that hidden treasure you've been searching for years.

A Night of Flamenco Flamenco folk songs (*cante*) and dances (*baile*) are an integral part of the Spanish experience. Spend at least one night in a flamenco tavern, listening to the heartrending laments of gypsy sorrows, tribulations, hopes, and dreams.

Outdoor-Café Sitting This is a famous experience for the summertime, when Madrileños come alive again on their *terrazas.* The drinking and good times can go on until dawn. From glamorous hangouts to lowly street corners, the café scene takes place mainly along an axis shaped by the Paseo de la Castellana, Paseo del Prado, and Paseo de Recoletos.

Museo Naval, Paseo del Prado. 5. ☎ **379-52-99.**

The history of nautical science and the Spanish navy, from the time of Isabella and Ferdinand until today, comes alive at the Museo Naval. The most fascinating exhibit is the map made by the *Santa María's* first mate to show the Spanish monarchs the new discoveries. There are also souvenirs of the Battle of Trafalgar.

Admission: Free.

Open: Tues–Sun 10:30am–1:30pm. **Closed:** Aug. **Metro:** Banco de España. **Bus:** 10, 14, 27, 34, 37, 45, or M6.

Museo Romántico, San Mateo, 13. ☎ **448-10-71.**

Attracting those seeking the romanticism of the 19th century, the museum is housed in a mansion decorated with numerous period pieces—crystal chandeliers, faded portraits, oils from Goya to Sorolla, opulent furnishings, and porcelain. Many exhibits date from the days of Isabella II, the high-living, fun-loving queen who was forced into exile and eventual abdication.

Admission: 450 ptas. ($3.20).

Open: Tues–Sat 9am–3pm, Sun 10am–2pm. **Closed:** Aug. **Metro:** Alonso Martínez.

Museo Sorolla, General Martínez Campos, 37. ☎ **410-15-84.**

From 1912, painter Joaquín Sorolla and his family occupied this elegant madrileño town house off Paseo de la Castellana. His widow turned it over to the government, and it is now maintained as a memorial. Much of the house remains as Sorolla left it, right down to his stained paintbrushes and pipes. In the museum wing a representative collection of his works is displayed.

Although Sorolla painted portraits of Spanish aristocrats, he was essentially interested in the common people, often depicting them in their native dress. Don't miss the artist's self-portrait and the paintings of his wife and their son. Sorolla was especially fond of painting beach scenes of the Costa Blanca.

Admission: 450 ptas. ($3.20).

Open: Tues–Sun 10am–3pm. **Closed:** Holidays. **Metro:** Iglesia or Rubén Darío. **Bus:** 5, 16, 61, 40, or M3.

Museo Tiflológico, La Coruña 18. ☎ **571-12-36.**

This museum is designed for sightless and sight-impaired visitors. Maintained by Spain's National Organization for the Blind, it's one of the few museums in the world that emphasize tactile appeal. All the exhibits are meant to be touched and felt; to that end, the museum provides audio tapes, in English and Spanish, to guide the visitor as he moves his hands over the object on display. It also offers pamphlets in large type and Braille.

One section of the museum features small-scale replicas of such architectural wonders as the Mayan and Aztec pyramids of Central America, the Eiffel Tower, and the Statue of Liberty. Another section contains paintings and sculptures created by blind artists, such as Miguel Detrel and José António Braña. A third section outlines the status of blind people throughout history, with a focus on the sociology and technology that led to the development of Braille during the 19th century.

Admission: Free.

Open: Mon–Fri 10:30am–2:30pm.

Real Basilica de San Francisco el Grande, Plaza de San Francisco El Grande, San Buenaventura, 1. ☎ **365-38-00.**

Ironically, Madrid, the capital of cathedral-rich Spain, does not itself possess a famous cathedral—but it does have an important church, with a dome larger than that of St. Paul's in London. This 18th-century church is filled with a number of ecclesiastical works, notably a Goya painting of St. Bernardinus of Siena. A guide will show you through.

Admission: 125 ptas. (90¢).

Open: Tues–Sat 11am–1pm and 4–7pm. **Metro:** La Latina or Puerta del Toledo. **Bus:** 3, 60, C, or M4.

Templo de Debod, Paseo de Rosales. No phone.

This Egyptian temple near Plaza de España once stood in the Valley of the Nile, 19 miles from Aswan. When the new dam threatened the temple, the Egyptian government dismantled and presented it to Spain. Taken down stone by stone in 1969 and 1970, it was shipped to Valencia and taken by rail to Madrid, where it was reconstructed and opened to the public in 1971. Photos upstairs depict the temple's long history.

Admission: Free.

Open: Tues–Fri 10am–1pm and 4–7pm, Sat–Sun 10am–1pm. **Metro:** Plaza de España.

Parks & Gardens

Casa de Campo.

Try to visit these former royal hunting grounds, miles of parkland lying south of the Royal Palace, across the Manzanares River. You can see the gate through which the kings rode out of the palace grounds—either on horseback or in carriages—on their way to the park. The Casa de Campo has a variety of trees and a lake, usually filled with rowers. You can have drinks and light refreshments around the water or go swimming in a municipally operated pool. Children will love both the zoo and the Parque de Atracciones (see "Cool for Kids," below).

Admission: Free.

Open: Daily 8am–9pm. **Metro:** Lago or Batán.

In Their Footsteps

Miguel de Cervantes Saavedra (1547–1616). This reigning figure of Spanish letters led a life filled with more adventure than his fictional characters ever experienced. In 1575 he was captured by pirates and sold into slavery in Algiers. Ransomed at great cost in 1580, he wrote 20 to 30 plays, only 2 of which survived. Joining the Invincible Armada in Seville, he was in great financial trouble and was imprisoned twice in 1590 and 1597. In 1600 he began his tale of a man chasing windmills across the plains of La Mancha, and his *Don Quixote* brought him immortality.

Birthplace Alcalá de Henares.

Favorite Haunt The plains of La Mancha.

Resting Place The Trinitarian Convent in Calle de Cantarranas in Madrid.

Parque del Retiro.

This famous park, originally a royal playground for the Spanish monarchs and their guests, sprawls over 350 acres. The huge palaces that once stood there were destroyed in the early 19th century, and only the former dance hall, the Casón del Buen Retiro (housing the modern works of the Prado) and the building containing the Army Museum remain. The park boasts numerous fountains and statues, plus a large lake. There are also two exposition centers, the Velásquez and Crystal palaces (built to honor the Philippines in 1887), and a lakeside monument, erected in 1922 in honor of King Alfonso XII. In summer the rose gardens are worth a visit, and you'll find several places where you can have inexpensive snacks and drinks.

Admission: Free.

Open: Daily 24 hours (safest 7am–8:30pm). **Metro:** Retiro.

Real Jardín Botánico (Botanical Garden), Plaza de Murillo, 2. ☎ **585-47-00.**

Across Calle de Alfonso XII, at the southwest corner of Retiro Park, the Botanical Garden (founded in the 18th century) contains more than 104 species of trees and 3,000 types of plants. Also on the premises are an exhibition hall and a library specializing in botany.

Admission: 200 ptas. ($1.40).

Open: Daily 10am–8pm. **Metro:** Atocha. **Bus:** 10, 14, 19, 32, or 45.

3 Cool for Kids

Aquápolis, Villanueva de la Canada, Carretera de El Escorial. ☎ **815-69-11.**

Sixteen miles northwest of Madrid lies a watery attraction where the kids can cool off. Scattered amid shops, a picnic area, and a barbecue restaurant are water slides, wavemaking machines, and tall slides that spiral children into a swimming pool below.

Admission: 2,000 ptas. ($14.20) adults; 1,250 ptas. ($8.90) children.

Open: Daily 10am–8pm. **Closed:** Oct–Apr. Transportation: Free bus runs several times a day during park's open hours, leaving Madrid from Calle de los Reyes, next to Coliseum Cinema, on eastern edge of Plaza de España.

Museo de Cera de Madrid (Wax Museum), Paseo de Recoletas, 41. ☎ **319-26-49.**

The kids will enjoy seeing a lifelike wax Columbus calling on Ferdinand and Isabella, as well as Jackie Onassis having champagne at a supper club. The 450 wax figures also include heroes and villains of World War II. Two galleries display Romans and Arabs from the ancient days of the Iberian Peninsula; a show in multivision gives a 30-minute recap of Spanish history from the Phoenicians to the present.

Admission: 750 ptas. ($5.30) adults; 500 ptas. ($3.60) children.

Open: Daily 10:30am–1:30pm and 4–8pm. **Metro:** Colón. **Bus:** 27, 45, or 53.

Parque de Atracciones, Casa de Campo. ☎ **463-29-00.**

The park was created in 1969 to amuse the young at heart with an array of rides and concessions. The former include a toboggan slide, a carousel, pony rides, an adventure into "outer space," a walk through a transparent maze, a visit to "jungleland," a motor-propelled series of cars disguised as a tail-wagging dachshund puppy, and a gyrating whirligig clutched in the tentacles of an octopus named "El Pulpo." The most popular rides are a pair of roller coasters named "7 Picos" and "Jet Star."

The park also has many diversions for adults. See "Evening Entertainment" later in this chapter for details.

Admission: 225 ptas. ($1.60) adults; 75 ptas. (50¢) children under 9. An all-inclusive ticket—good for all rides—is 1,400 ptas. ($9.90).

Open: Apr–June, Tues–Fri noon–9pm; Sat–Sun noon–1am; July–Aug, Tues–Fri 6pm–1am; Sat 6pm–2am, Sun noon–1am; Sept, Tues–Sun (variable hours—call to check before going there); Oct–Mar, Sat noon–8pm (sometimes 9pm), Sun 11am–8pm (sometimes 9pm). **Directions:** Take the Teleférico cable car (see below). At the end of the ride, "microbuses" will take you the rest of the way. Alternatively, take the suburban train from Plaza de España and stop near the entrance to the park (Entrada de Batán).

Planetarium, Parque Tierno Galván, Méndez Alvaro. ☎ **467-34-61.**

This planetarium has a projection room with optical and electronic equipment—including a multivision system—designed to reproduce outer space.

Admission: 375 ptas. ($2.70) adults; 200 ptas. ($1.40) children.

Open: Tues–Sun shows at 11:30am and 12:45, 5:30, 6:45pm, and 8pm. **Closed:** 2 weeks Jan. **Metro:** Méndez Alvaro. **Bus:** 148.

Teleférico, Paseo del Pintor Rosales, s/n. ☎ **541-19-97.**

Strung high above the several of Madrid's verdant parks, this cable car was originally built in 1969 as part of a public fairgrounds (Parque des Atracciones) modeled vaguely along the lines of Disneyland. Today, even for visitors not interested in visiting the park, the *teleférico* retains an allure of its own as a high-altitude method of admiring the cityscape of Madrid. The cable car departs from Paseo Pintor Rosales at the eastern edge of Parque del Oeste (at the corner of Calle Marqués de Urquijo) and carries you high above two parks, railway tracks, and over the Manzanares River to a spot near a picnic ground and restaurant in Casa de Campo. Weather permitting, there are good views of the Royal Palace along the way. The ride takes 11 minutes.

Prices: 300 ptas. ($2.10) one way; 500 ptas. ($3.60) round trip.

Service: Mar–Oct, daily noon–9pm. Nov–Feb, Mon and Thurs–Fri noon–2pm and 4–7pm; Sat–Sun noon–7pm. **Metro:** Plaza de España or Argüelles. **Bus:** 74.

Zoo de la Casa de Campo, Casa de Campo. ☎ **711-99-50.**

This modern, well-organized facility allows you to see the wildlife of Africa, America, Asia, and Europe, with about 2,500 animals on display. Most are in simulated natural habitats, with moats separating them from the public. There's also a petting zoo for the kids and a show presented by the Chu-Lin band.

Admission: 1,240 ptas. ($8.80) adults; 895 ptas. ($6.40) children 3-8; children 2 and under free.

Open: Daily 10am–sunset. **Metro:** Batán. **Bus:** 33. Directions: Exit on the right side for the park, turn left, and walk up to Plaza de España, which takes you directly to the zoo.

4 Special-Interest Sightseeing

For the Literary Enthusiast

Casa de Lope de Vega, Cervantes, 11. ☎ **429-92-16.**

This prolific Madrid-born author dramatized Hapsburg Spain as no one ever had before, earning a lasting position in Spanish letters. A reconstruction of his medieval house stands on a narrow street, ironically named for Cervantes, his competitor for the title of the greatest writer of the golden age of Spain. The dank, dark house is furnished with relics of the period, although one can't be sure that any of the furnishings or possessions actually belonged to this 16th-century genius.

Admission: 200 ptas. ($1.40).

Open: Tues and Thurs 9:30am–3pm, Sat 10am–4pm. **Metro:** Anton Martín.

HEMINGWAY HAUNTS

Chicote, Gran Vía, 12. ☎ **532-67-37.**

Hemingway used Chicote as a setting for his only play, *The Fifth Column.* He would sit here night after night, gazing at the *putas* (it was a famed hooker bar back then) as he entertained friends with such remarks as "Spain is a country for living and not for dying." The bar still draws a lively crowd.

Prices: 850 ptas. ($6) for whisky and soda.

Open: Mon–Sat 1:30pm–3am. **Metro:** Gran Vía.

Museo del Prado, Paseo del Prado. ☎ **420-28-36.**

Of the Prado, A. E. Hotchner wrote in his Papa Hemingway: "Ernest loved the Prado. He entered it as he entered cathedrals." More than any other, one picture held him transfixed, Andrea del Sarto's Portrait of a Woman. (For further details about the Prado, see "The Top Attractions" earlier in this chapter.)

Sobrino de Botín, Cuchilleros, 17. ☎ **366-42-17.**

In the final two pages of his novel *The Sun Also Rises,* Jake invites Brett here for the Segovian specialty, roast suckling pig, washed down with Rioja Alta. In another book, *Death in the Afternoon,* Hemingway told his mythical "Old Lady": "I would rather dine on suckling pig at Botín's than sit and think of casualties my friends have suffered." Since that time, thousands upon thousands of Americans have visited Botín (see Chapter 4 for details). It is a perennial favorite of all visiting Yankees.

For the Architecture Enthusiast

Plaza Mayor.

In the heart of Madrid, this famous square was known as the Plaza de Arrabal in medieval times, when it stood outside the city wall.

The original architect of Plaza Mayor itself was Juan Gómez de Mora, who worked during the reign of Philip III. Under the Hapsburgs, the square rose in importance as the site of public spectacles, including the gruesome autos-da-fé, in which "heretics" were burned. Bullfights, knightly tournaments, and festivals were also staged here.

Three times the buildings on the square burned—in 1631, 1672, and 1790—but each time Plaza Mayor bounced back. After the last big fire, it was completely redesigned by Juan de Villanueva.

Nowadays a Christmas fair is held around the equestrian statue of Philip III (dating from 1616) in the center of the square. On summer nights the Plaza Mayor becomes the virtual living room of Madrid, as tourists sip sangría at the numerous cafés and listen to music, which is often spontaneous. **Metro:** Puerta del Sol.

Puerta de Toledo.

Puerta de Toledo is one of the two surviving town gates (the other is Puerta de Alcalá). Constructed during the brief and unpopular rule of Joseph I Bonaparte, this one marks the spot where citizens used to set out for the former imperial capital of Toledo. On an irregularly shaped square, it stands at the intersection of the Ronda de Toledo and Calle de Toledo. Its original purpose was a triumphal arch to honor Napoleon Bonaparte. In 1813 it became a symbol of Madrid's fierce independence and the loyalty of its citizens to their Bourbon rulers, who had been restored to the throne in the wake of the Napoleonic invasion. **Metro:** Puerta de Toledo.

Walking Tour 1
Medieval Madrid

Start Plaza de la Villa.
Finish Plaza de Puerta Cerrada.
Time 2½ hours.
Best Time Any sunny day.
Worst Times Monday through Saturday 7:30 to 9:30am and 5 to 7:30pm—because of heavy traffic.

The oldest part of the city was a flourishing Muslim area before Madrid became the capital. Begin your tour at:

1. **Plaza de la Villa,** which stands beside Calle Mayor, between the Palacio Real (Royal Palace) and Puerta del Sol. In the center, note the bronze statue of Don Alvaro de Bazán, an admiral under Philip II, best remembered for defeating the Turks at Lepanto.

   With your back to Calle Mayor, on your right you will see the red-brick 17th-century facade of the:

2. **Ayuntamiento de Madrid (Town Hall).** It was originally built as a prison and today houses the Museo Municipal (see "More Attractions" above). On the square's south side rises the depressingly somber stone-and-brick facade of the:

3. **Torre de los Lujanes,** a 15th-century tower whose simple granite entrance is one of Madrid's few remaining examples of Gothic architecture. Beside the tower, behind a Gothic-Mudéjar archway, lies the tomb of Beatriz Galindo, nicknamed La Latina because she taught Latin to the adolescent Isabella I.

   With your back to Calle Mayor, you'll see two narrow streets stretching parallel to one another to the south. Take the one on the left (Calle del Cordón) and walk for about one short block to:

4. **Plaza del Cordón.** (You won't see any street signs here.) You'll find yourself amid a complex of unmarked 16th- and 17th-century municipal buildings that are protected and patrolled by uniformed guards.

   Turn left at the entrance to Plaza del Cordón, walk about 50 feet, and notice the convex, semicircular entrance to the baroque:

5. **Church of San Miguel,** San Justo, 4, built by Giacomo Bonavia in the 18th century. A few steps farther, flanking the right side of the church, is a narrow alley, the Pasadizo del Panecillo, where 17th-century priests distributed bread to hungry paupers. Facing the front of the church is one of the oldest houses in Madrid, a grim, dingy-looking stone building. Look for the heraldic shields carved into its fortresslike facade. Historical sources report that the legendary

Isidro, patron saint of Madrid, worked as a servant in this baronial, now much-faded residence, which today contains private apartments. Its address, although you probably won't see a street sign until you reach the bottom of the hill, is Calle del Doctor Letamendi. Descend this cobblestone street. You'll have to walk back about 10 feet and enter it from an edge of Plaza del Cordón. Follow it one block and cross busy Calle de Segovia.

Turn right and walk about three blocks (the street will now ascend sharply). Look down Costanilla San Pedro, to your left, and notice the Mudéjar tower of the:

6. **Church of San Pedro el Viejo (Old St. Peter's),** which marks the border of Madrid's Muslim quarter. The church's mid–14th-century tower is one of the few remnants of medieval architecture in Madrid. The church itself, however, dates from the 17th century; it was severely looted during the Civil War in 1936. Although the houses in this neighborhood look small, they are considered among the most chic and expensive in Madrid.

Walk one more block uphill along Calle de Segovia until you reach Costanilla San Andrés. Before you turn left into this narrow street, note that to the north of Calle Segovia is:

7. **Plaza de la Cruz Verde,** whose centerpiece is a 19th-century baroque fountain commemorating the end of the Spanish Inquisition. In the background you'll see the back side and the massive brick tower of the:
8. **Iglesia del Sacramento,** where memorial services for soldiers killed in war or by terrorists are performed.

Now ascend the steep cobblestones of the Costanilla San Andrés. Around you is the:

9. **Arab Quarter.** Many buildings that were erected during the past two centuries were built on foundations of Muslim buildings.

Continue on and very shortly you'll reach the triangular and steeply sloping grounds of:

10. **Plaza de la Paja,** whose lovely trees and calm give no hint that this was once the most important produce market in the region. Today the neighborhood waits sleepily in the intense sunlight for night to bring business to the several famous restaurants that ring its perimeter.

To your left as you climb the square is the:

11. **Capilla del Obispo (Bishop's Chapel),** entered from Plaza de la Paja. The mortal remains of San Isidro were interred here from 1518 to 1657. Notice its Renaissance doors. The high altar is considered a masterpiece of Plateresque (the late Gothic style of Castile).

At the top of the square, follow the continuation of the Costanilla San Andrés to the right side of the chapel. You'll discover that it abuts the back of the more imposing:

12. **Church of San Andrés,** Plaza de San Andrés. In one of the most colorful parts of the old town, the church dates from medieval times but was rebuilt in the 17th century. A fire in 1936 destroyed its greatest treasures.

Keep walking and you'll come to the fountains of:

13. **Plaza de los Carros,** the first of four interconnected squares, each with its own name and allure. Descend the steps at the far edge of Plaza de los Carros and turn left onto Plaza de Puerta de Moros.

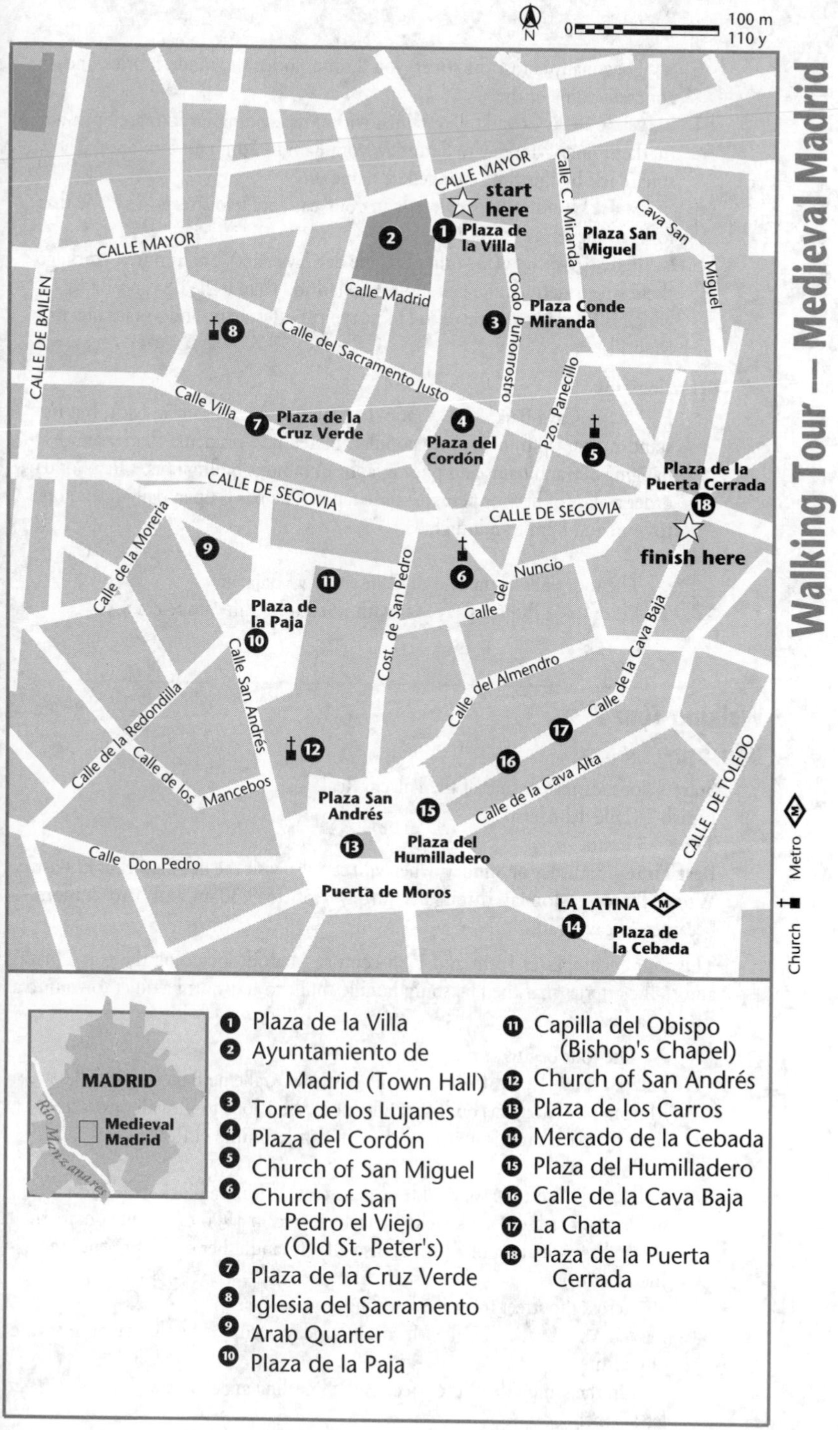

Walking Tour — Medieval Madrid

N
0 100 m
110 y

CALLE MAYOR
start here
1 Plaza de la Villa
2
Plaza San Miguel
Calle C. Miranda
Cava San Miguel
Calle Madrid
Codo Puñonrostro
3 Plaza Conde Miranda
CALLE DE BAILEN
8
Calle del Sacramento Justo
Calle Villa
7 Plaza de la Cruz Verde
4 Plaza del Cordón
Pzo. Panecillo
5
Plaza de la Puerta Cerrada
18
CALLE DE SEGOVIA
finish here
Calle de la Moreria
9
11
Cost. de San Pedro
6
Calle del Nuncio
Plaza de la Paja
10
Calle San Andrés
Calle del Almendro
Calle de la Cava Baja
Calle de la Redondilla
Calle de los Mancebos
12
17
16
Calle de la Cava Alta
CALLE DE TOLEDO
Plaza San Andrés
15
13
Plaza del Humilladero
Calle Don Pedro
Puerta de Moros
LA LATINA
14 Plaza de la Cebada

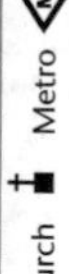

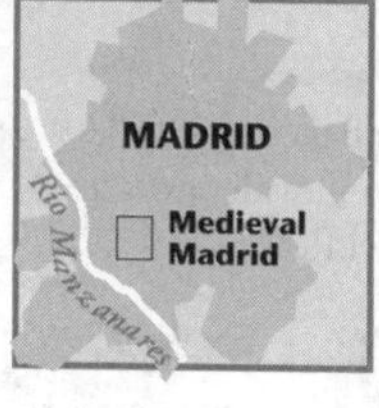

1. Plaza de la Villa
2. Ayuntamiento de Madrid (Town Hall)
3. Torre de los Lujanes
4. Plaza del Cordón
5. Church of San Miguel
6. Church of San Pedro el Viejo (Old St. Peter's)
7. Plaza de la Cruz Verde
8. Iglesia del Sacramento
9. Arab Quarter
10. Plaza de la Paja
11. Capilla del Obispo (Bishop's Chapel)
12. Church of San Andrés
13. Plaza de los Carros
14. Mercado de la Cebada
15. Plaza del Humilladero
16. Calle de la Cava Baja
17. La Chata
18. Plaza de la Puerta Cerrada

Diagonally across the street, you'll soon notice the modern brick-and-concrete dome of the:

14. **Mercado de la Cebada.** Contained within its echoing interior are open-air markets, open Monday to Saturday from 8am to 2pm and 5 to 8pm. The square has by this time changed its name to:
15. **Plaza del Humiliadero.** Directly in your path are two streets. The one that forks to the left is:
16. **Calle de Cava Baja** (the other is Calle de Cava Alta). Six hundred years ago these streets defined the city limits of Madrid. Take Calle de Cava Baja, which is filled with some of the most typical cafés, bars, and restaurants in Madrid.

Refueling Stop

La Chata, Cava Baja, 24 (☎ **366-14-58**), has a restaurant in back, but its stand-up bar up front is more popular. Here, local residents chatter amid hanging Serrano hams and photographs of famous bullfighters. On a hot day, order a glass of beer or perhaps some tapas. The bar is open daily from noon to 5pm and 8pm to midnight.

The tour ends at the end of Calle de Cava Baja, at:

17. **Plaza de la Puerta Cerrada,** with its simple white stone cross.

Walking Tour 2
Hapsburg Madrid

Start Southeastern corner of the Palacio Real.
Finish Calle del Arenal.
Time 3 hours.
Best Time Saturday or Sunday, when you can also visit the flea market of El Rastro.
Worst Times Monday through Saturday 7:30 to 9:30am and 5 to 7:30pm—because of heavy traffic.

This tour encompasses 16th- and 17th-century Madrid, including the grand plazas and traffic arteries that the Hapsburg families built to transform a quiet town into a world-class capital.

The tour begins at the:

1. **Palacio Real (Royal Palace),** at the corner of Calle de Bailén and Calle Mayor. The latter was built by Philip II in the 1560s to provide easy access from the palace to his preferred church, San Jerónimo el Real.
   Walk east on:
2. **Calle Mayor,** on the south side of the street. Within a block, you'll reach a black bronze statue of a kneeling angel, erected in 1906 to commemorate the aborted assassination of King Alfonso XIII (grandfather of the present king, Juan Carlos).
   Across the street from the kneeling angel is the:
3. **Palacio de Abrantes,** Calle Mayor, 86, today occupied by the Italian Institute of Culture.
   On the same side of the street as the kneeling angel, to the statue's left, is the:

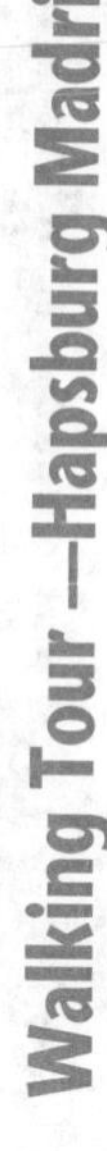

Walking Tour—Hapsburg Madrid

N
0
150 m
165 y
Plaza de Oriente
Teatro Real
OPERA
Jardines del Cabo Noval
Palacio Real
start here
finish here
CALLE DE BAILÉN
Calle San Nicolás
Calle de Vergara
Calle Amnistia
Calle del Arenal
Calle Bordadores
Plaza San Ginés
CALLE MAYOR
Calle C. Miranda
Cava San Miguel
Plaza Mayor
Calle Sal
Calle Zaragoza
Plaza de la Villa
Codo Puñonrostro
Calle Madrid
Plaza C. Miranda
Calle del Sacramento Justo
Calle Villa
Calle de Cuchilleros
Calle Latoneros
Calle Lechuga
CALLE DE SEGOVIA
Cost. de San Pedro
Calle San Andrés
Calle de la Redondilla
Calle del Almendro
Calle de la Cava Baja
Calle de la Cava Alta
CALLE DE TOLEDO
CALLE DE LOS ESTUDIOS
Plaza S. Andrés
Plaza de los Carros
Plaza del Humilladero
Calle Don Pedro
Puerta de Moros
LA LATINA
Plaza de la Cebeda
Carrera San Francisco
Calle Tabernillas
Calle del Humilladero
MADRID
Río Manzanares
Hapsburg Madrid
1 Palacio Real
2 Calle Mayor
3 Palacio de Abrantes
4 Palacio de Uceda
5 Church of San Nicolás
6 Plaza de San Miguel
7 Plaza Mayor
8 Café Bar Los Galayos
9 Calle de Toledo
10 Iglesia de San Isidro
11 Colegio Imperial
12 El Rastro
13 Calle de Segovia
14 Calle de Cuchilleros
15 Calle Bordadores
16 Church of San Ginés
Metro
Church

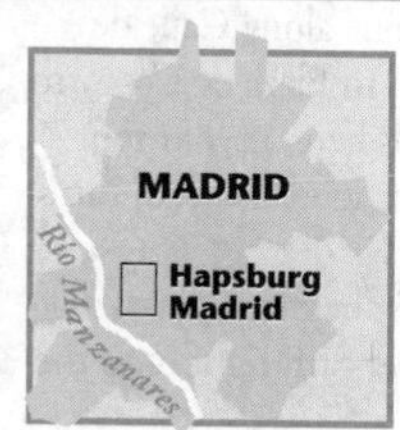

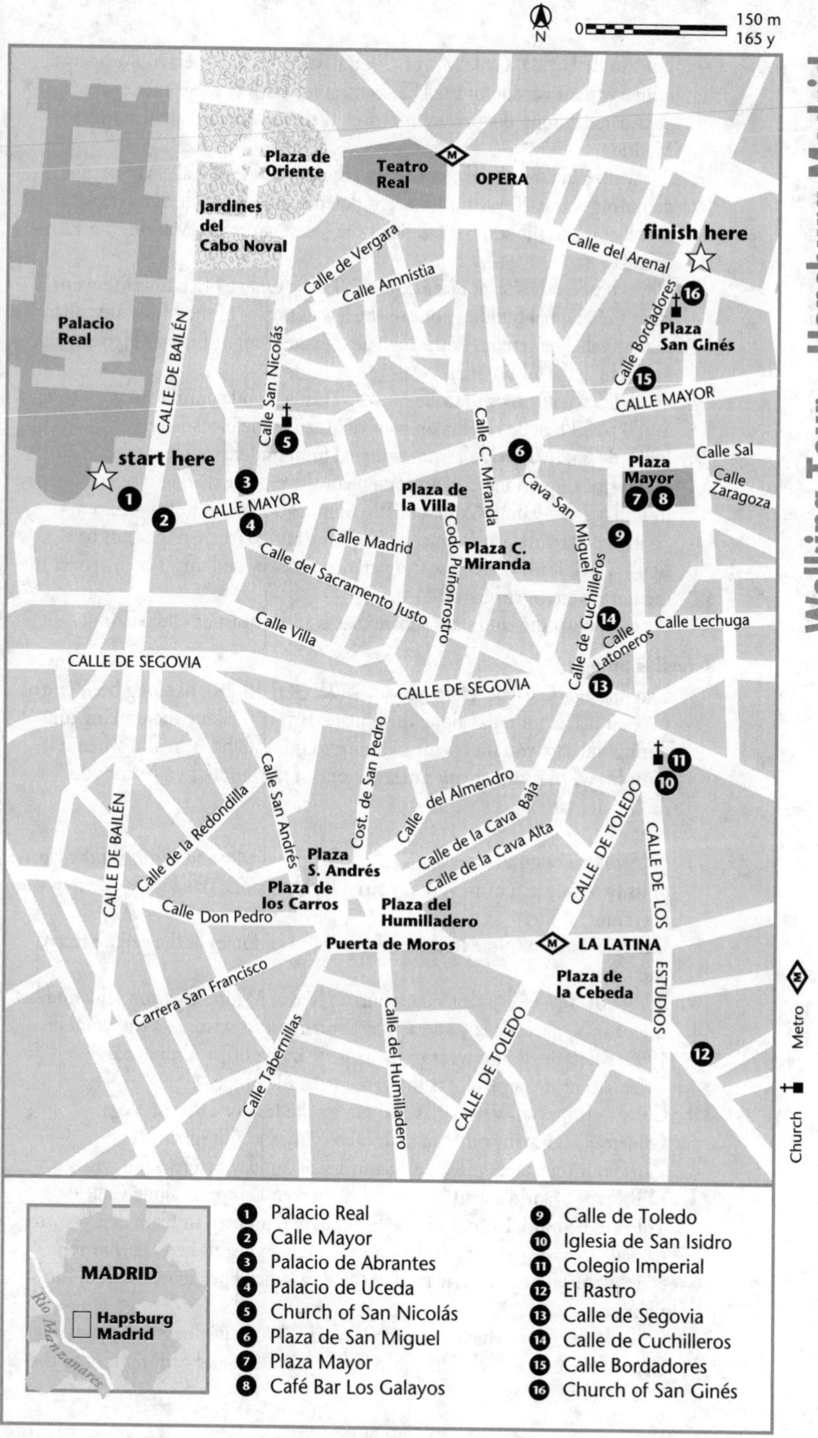

4. **Palacio de Uceda,** Calle Mayor, 79, today the headquarters of the Spanish military (their version of the U.S. Pentagon). Both of these palaces are considered among the best examples of 17th-century civil architecture in Madrid.

   Walk half a block east, crossing to the north side of Calle Mayor and detouring about 20 yards to the left, down narrow Calle de San Nicolás. You'll come to the somber facade of the oldest church in Madrid, the 12th-century:

5. **Church of St. Nicolás,** Plaza de San Nicolás. Only a brick tower remains from the original building, one of the few examples of the Mudéjar style in the capital. The reredos at the high altar is the work of Juan de Herrera, also the architect of El Escorial.

   Retrace your steps to Calle Mayor. Turn left and continue to walk east. You'll pass Plaza de la Villa on your right, and, one block later:

6. **Plaza de San Miguel,** an iron-canopied meat-and-vegetable market. You might stock up on ingredients for a picnic here. (The market is open Monday to Friday from 9am to 2pm and 5 to 8pm, Saturday from 9am to 2pm.)

   Leave Plaza de San Miguel by Ciudad Rodrigo (there might not be a sign), which leads under a soaring granite archway and up a sloping street to the northwestern corner of:

7. **Plaza Mayor,** the landmark square that is at the heart of Old Madrid.

Refueling Stop

Café Bar Los Galayos, Plaza Mayor, 1 (☎ **366-30-28**), has long been one of the best places for tapas along this square. If you're taking the walking tour during the day, you may want to return to this café/bar at night, when it is most lively. In summer you can select one of the outdoor tables for your drinks and tapas.

Stroll through Plaza Mayor, crossing it diagonally and exiting at the closer of its two southern exits. A dingy steep flight of stone stairs leads down to the beginning of the:

8. **Calle de Toledo.** Note in the distance the twin domes of the yellow-stucco–and–granite:

9. **Iglesia de San Isidro,** legendary burial place of Madrid's patron saint and his wife, Santa Maria de la Cadeza. The church lost its status as a cathedral in 1992, when the honor went to the larger Church of La Almudena.

   Adjacent to San Isidro is the baroque facade of the:

10. **Colegio Imperial,** which was also run by the Jesuits. Lope de Vega, Calderón, and many other famous men studied at this institute.

    If your tour takes place on a Saturday or Sunday before 3 pm, visit:

11. **El Rastro,** Madrid's world-famous flea market. Continue along Calle de Toledo, then fork left onto Calle Estudios and proceed to Plaza de Cascorro, named after a hero of the Cuban wars. El Rastro begins here. If your tour takes place Monday to Friday, skip the Rastro neighborhood. Instead, turn right onto:

12. **Calle de Segovia,** which intersects Calle de Toledo just before it passes in front of the Catedral de San Isidro. Walk one block and turn right onto the first street:

13. **Calle de Cuchilleros.** Follow it north past 16th- and 17th-century stone-fronted houses. Within a block, a flight of granite steps forks to the right. Climb the steps (a sign identifies the new street as Calle Arco de Cuchilleros) and you'll pass one of the most famous *mesones* (typical Castilian restaurants) of Madrid, the Cueva de Luís Candelas.

Once again you will have entered Plaza Mayor, this time on the south-western corner. Walk beneath the southernmost arcade and promenade counterclockwise beneath the arcades, walking north underneath the square's eastern arcade. Then walk west beneath its northern arcade. At the northwest corner, exit through the archway onto Calle 7 de Julio. Fifty feet later, cross Calle Mayor and take the right-hand narrow street before you. This is:

14. **Calle Bordadores,** which during the 17th century housed Madrid's embroidery workshops, staffed exclusively by men.

As you proceed, notice the 17th-century brick walls and towers of the:

15. **Church of San Ginés,** Arenal, 15. The church of one of Madrid's oldest parishes owes its present look to the architects who reconstructed it after a devastating fire in 1872.

At the end of this tour, you'll find yourself on traffic-congested Calle del Arenal, at the doorstep of many interesting old streets.

Walking Tour 3
Bourbon Madrid

Start Puerta de Alcalá.
Finish Plaza de Oriente.
Time 3 hours.
Best Times Early morning or late afternoon in summer (or any sunny day in winter).
Worst Times Monday through Saturday 7:30 to 9:30am and 5 to 7:30pm—because of heavy traffic.

By the time the Bourbons came to power in Spain, Madrid was firmly ensconced as a political and cultural center, proud of its role as head of a centralized government. This tour shows off the broad boulevards, spectacular fountains, and interconnected plazas that put Madrid on a par architecturally with other European capitals. Much of this tour goes through neighborhoods planned by Carlos III in the 18th century.

Begin at:

1. **Puerta de Alcalá (Alcalá Gate),** Plaza de la Independencia. One of the grand landmarks of Madrid, the Alcalá Gate was designed by Francesco Sabatini and built from 1769 to 1778. In neoclassical style, it replaced a baroque arch that used to mark the entry into the city; with its five arched passages, it soon became a symbol of the new Bourbon "enlightenment" that swept over Madrid. Today it guards the approach to the major artery leading to northwest Spain and on to France.

Walk west, slightly downhill, along Calle de Alcalá to:

2. **Plaza de la Cibeles,** the most beautiful square in Madrid. In the center of the square is the Fuente de Cibeles, showing the Roman goddess Cybele driving an elaborate chariot pulled by two docile lions, which symbolize elegance and harmony. José Hermosilla and Ventura Rodríguez, architects of Paseo del Prado (see below), designed the fountain. To your left, on the corner of Calle de Alcalá and Plaza de la Cibeles, is the most magnificent post office in Europe, the Palacio de Comunicaciones. Its lavish embellishments give it the air of an ecclesiastical palace. It dates from 1904.

From Plaza de la Cibeles you'll see two monuments—the pink-sided Palacio de Buenavista, the army headquarters of Spain, on the right side of the square; and immediately opposite you on the far side of the square, the Banco de España. You are now at the beginning of the most monumental part of Bourbon Madrid. Promenade beneath the leafy canopy of the:

3. Paseo del Prado, which incorporates two busy one-way streets separated by a wide pedestrian's promenade. Walk south down the world-famed promenade, passing shrubbery, trees, and benches. Paseo del Prado links Plaza de la Cibeles with Plaza del Emperador Carlos V, site of Atocha Train Station, the paseo's southern terminus. It is part of the busy north-south axis of the city. This whole section, called the Salón del Prado, incorporates more world-class art masterpieces than any other area of similar size in the world, not only the Prado but the Thyssen-Bornemisza Museum at Paseo del Prado, 8.

On your left, as you head south toward Plaza de la Lealtad, you'll pass the:

4. Museo Naval, Paseo del Prado, 5. Adjacent to it, behind a gracefully angled row of neoclassical columns, stands the Madrid stock exchange (La Bolsa), dating from the 19th century.

Continue down Paseo del Prado to the:

5. Monument to the Heroes of the Second of May. This 19th-century obelisk, on your left behind a barrier of trees, honors the "unknown soldiers" who fell in the Napoleonic wars of independence.

To your right, a few paces later, is the:

6. Palacio de Villahermosa, Paseo del Prado, 8. This neoclassical palace holds one of the world's greatest artistic bequests, the Thyssen-Bornemisza Museum. In the center of Plaza Canovas del Castillo (also called Plaza de Neptuno) is a fountain dedicated to the Roman god Neptune.

Continue walking south to reach the:

7. Museo del Prado, Paseo del Prado, one of the world's great art museums. The original core of its paintings, which came from royal palaces throughout Spain, were hugely increased in the 19th century by private bequests. Much of the museum's layout results from the efforts of Carlos III in the late 1700s. He commissioned the construction of a neoclassical brick-and-stone palace to house a Natural History Museum, named El Prado de San Jerónimo (St. Jerome's Meadow). It had barely been completed before Napoleon's troops sacked and burned it. Under Ferdinand VII, the museum was restored and finally opened to the public in 1819.

Continue south along Paseo del Prado to the:

8. Jardín Botánico, a fine oasis on a hot day.

Head back up Paseo del Prado, crossing the street. When you reach Plaza Cánovas del Castillo, turn left toward the ancient heart of Madrid along Calle de las Cortes, which leads into:

9. Carrera de San Jerónimo (its name will briefly be Plaza de las Cortés). Walk along the right side. On your left you'll pass the facade of the deluxe Palace

Walking Tour — Bourbon Madrid

1. Puerta de Alcalá (Alcalá Gate)
2. Plaza de la Cibeles
3. Paseo del Prado
4. Museo Naval
5. Monument to the Heroes of the Second of May
6. Palacio de Villahermosa
7. Museo del Prado
8. Jardín Botánico
9. Carrera de San Jerónimo
10. Plaza Canalejas
11. Lhardy
12. Puerta del Sol
13. La Mallorquina
14. Plaza de Isabel II
15. Plaza de Oriente

Post Office Metro

Hotel. Turn around and look behind you for a distant view of the Gothic spire of the Iglesia de San Jerónimo.

Keep walking uphill. On your right you'll pass the Corinthian columns and bronze twin lions, flanking the entrance to the Spanish Parliament, built around 1850. Facing it in a small three-sided park is a statue of Cervantes.

At this point, the street will narrow considerably, funneling itself into:

10. **Plaza Canalejas,** around which sit several late 19th- and early 20th-century buildings. On the left side of the square, notice the twin spires of one of the neighborhood's most whimsically appealing structures. Built around 1920, it was designed as an electric combination of 17th-century styles, including shells, neoclassical obelisks, and heraldic lions holding shields.

Pass along this square back onto Carrera de San Jerónimo, by now a busy, congested, and commercial street lined with stores.

Refueling Stop

Lhardy, Carrera de San Jerónimo, 8 (☎ **521-33-85**), opened its doors in 1839. It soon became the gathering place of Madrid's literati, political leaders, and executives. Today this place has a decor called "Isabella Segundo" and gives off an aura of another era. Upstairs is a restaurant, but for refueling you can stop downstairs, as have thousands of visitors before you, and enjoy a cup of consommé from a large silver samovar; or, in summer, you can refresh yourself with soothing gazpacho. Each cup costs 119 pesetas (80¢). It's open Monday to Saturday from 1 to 3:30pm and 9 to 11:30pm. Closed: Late July to early September.

Continue along Carrera de San Jerónimo to the geographical heart of Spain, the:

11. **Puerta del Sol.** Two-thirds of the way along its half-moon-shaped expanse, you'll come on a small brass plaque from which all the distances in Spain are measured, placed immediately in front of a red-brick municipal building called Comunidade de Madrid, on the southern edge of the square.

Refueling Stop

La Mallorquina, Puerta del Sol, 8 (☎ **521-12-01**), is the most famous pastry shop in Madrid, occupying a position at the southwest corner of Puerta del Sol. It was founded before the turn of the century and became known for one specialty, a Napoletana, filled with cream and studded with almond slices. You can order sandwiches, coffee, and pastries on the ground floor, or you may want to head upstairs, where there's sit-down service. It is open daily from 9am to 9:15pm.

At the far end of Puerta del Sol are two main streets, Calle Mayor and Calle del Arenal, forking off to the right. Take Arenal, passing the red-brick neoclassical facade of the Iglesia de San Ginés on your left.

Within a short distance, you'll come on:

12. **Plaza de Isabel II,** graced with a bronze statue of the 19th-century music-loving queen whose efforts helped construct an opera house for Madrid, the Teatro Real.

Follow the Calle del Arenal, now called Calle Carlos III, around the southern edge of the opera house to:

13. **Plaza de Oriente,** with its view of the Palacio Real (Royal Palace).

Walking Tour 4

Grandeur: Past & Present

Start Gran Vía at Plaza del Callao.
Finish Plaza de la Encarnación.
Time 3 hours.
Best Time Any day except Monday, when the collections are closed.
Worst Times Monday.

The tour begins on the:

1. **Gran Vía,** the major street of central Madrid, at Plaza del Callao. The shop-flanked Gran Vía was opened at the end of World War I, and long before deluxe hotels started to sprout up north on Paseo de la Castellana, the hotels of Gran Vía were the most expensive and elegant in the Spanish capital. The street runs from Calle de Alcalá to Plaza de España and is at the heart of the modern city, with banks, department stores, and office blocks, plus an array of cinemas.

   Begin your promenade at Plaza del Callao, dominated by the Palacio de la Prensa (press), dating from 1924, and the Capitol, the most fashionable-looking building, dating from 1931.

   From the Gran Vía, head west toward Plaza de España. This section of the Gran Vía is considered the most American in inspiration. The architects of the Gran Vía at that time were much influenced by the 1930s style sweeping New York, especially as reflected by the Roxy and Paramount buildings. The Gran Vía comes to an end at the:

2. **Plaza de España,** with its two tower blocks from the 1950s, the Edificio de España and the Torre de Madrid. This vast square, overshadowed by these skyscrapers, is at a hub separating old Madrid from the modern city. Once a military barracks, it is now one of the busiest traffic intersections in Madrid. In the center of the square stands a monument to Cervantes (erected in 1928), with figures of Don Quixote and his faithful Sancho Panza.

   From the square, walk up Calle de la Princesa, turning to your left (south) as you approach Calle de Ventura Rodríguez, where you'll come on one of the esoteric treasure houses of Madrid, the:

3. **Museo Cerralbo,** Ventura Rodríguez, 17 (☎ **547-36-46**). This town house, dripping with the gilt–and–red-velvet romanticism of the 19th century, was once inhabited by the family of the marquís of Cerralbo, who filled its every nook and cranny with decorative bric-a-brac and art treasures. Note the crystal chandeliers and the fashionable, opulently colored glass imported from Venice. The Cerralbo clan were art collectors as well, purchasing well-known works from Zurbarán, Ribera, and El Greco. Especially intriguing is the library and study of the late marquís, preserved just as he left it. Admission costs 250 pesetas ($1.80). It's open Tuesday through Saturday from 9:30am to 2:30pm and on Sunday from 10am to 2pm (**Metro:** Plaza de España or Ventura Rodríguez).

Walking Tour — Grandeur:Past & Present

N
0 200 m
220 y

Calle Amaniel
Calle de San Bernardo
Calle de la Palma
Travesia Conde Duque
Calle de San Bernardino
Calle de la Princesa
TRIBUNAL
NOVICIADO
Calle Jesús del Valle
Calle del Pez
PLAZA DE ESPAÑA
Plaza de España
Calle de San Vicente
GRAN VÍA
Calle de la Luna
Corredera Baja de San Pablo
Calle de Fuencarral
Calle de Hortaleza
Calle de Leganitos
STO. DOMINGO
Calle de Torija
finish here
Calle de la Bola
Cuesta de Sto. Domingo
Plaza de Callao
CALLAO
start here
GRAN VÍA
GRAN VÍA
Plaza Encarnación
Calle del Carmen
Calle Montera
Calle de Bailén
Plaza de Oriente
Calle del Arenal
Calle de Alcalá
Jardines del Cabo Noval
SOL
Puerta del Sol
Calle de San Jerónimo
Calle Mayor

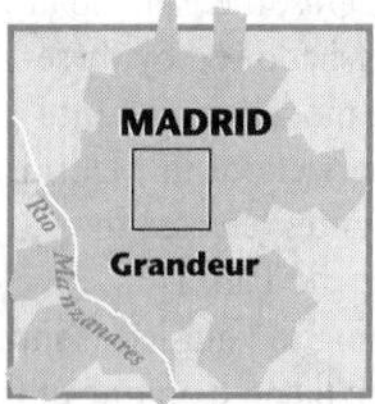

1. Gran Vía
2. Plaza de España
3. Museo Cerralbo
4. Plaza de Oriente
5. Café de l'Oriente
6. Convento de la Encarnación

Metro
Church

9169

Returning to Plaza de España, go to the southeastern corner of the square and head down Calle de Bailén to the semicircular:

4. **Plaza de Oriente,** created in 1840, one of the most famous squares in Spain and the setting of the Palacio Real (Royal Palace). The square was designed to provide a harmonious panoramic vista between the Royal Palace and Puerta del Sol. At the overthrow of the Napoleonic dynasty, work ended and the square was not completed until the reign of Isabella II. An equestrian statue of Philip IV stands in the center of the square, the work, based on drawings by Velázquez, of Italian sculptor Pietro Tacca.

Refueling Stop

Café de Oriente, Plaza de Oriente, 2 (☎ **541-39-74**), gives you a chance to have a drink and tapas with a view of the Royal Palace. The café's entrance is a well-marked doorway set behind shaded sidewalk tables and a turn-of-the-century decor.

From Plaza de Oriente take a tiny side street to the northeast of the square, Calle de Pavia, which will lead to:

5. **Convento de la Encarnación,** Plaza de la Encarnación (☎ **247-05-10**), on one of the most charming squares in Madrid. The convent and adjoining church were completed in 1616. A Spanish-speaking guide will show you around, pointing out the most important ecclesiastical paintings and Ribera's *St. John the Baptist.* Other works include a gory Christ with serpentine hair by Gregorio Fernández. The cloisters are filled with richly decorated chapels, one in the Pompeiian style. Admission is 450 pesetas ($3.20). The convent is open Wednesday and Saturday from 10:30am to 12:30pm and 4 to 5:30pm, and Sunday from 11am to 1:30pm (**Metro:** Ópera).

Walking Tour 5
The Prado in Two Hours

Start Velázquez door (western entrance).
Finish Room 57A.
Time 2 hours.
Best Time At 9am opening.
Worst Time 12:30–3pm (too crowded); Monday, when it's closed.

Considered the most precious cultural institution in all of Spain and the seat of a deep-seated pride in the country's artistic heritage, the Prado places Madrid firmly on the artistic map of Europe. It is also one of the capital's most consistently reliable tourist attractions, as witnessed by the more than two million visitors who shuffle through its corridors every year.

But because of the Prado's *embarras de richesses* (only a third of the collection can be displayed at any given time), you may need some guidance to see at least some of the world-acclaimed masterpieces. You could devote weeks to the Prado, but regrettably many visitors have only two hours. Here's how to make the most of that limited time.

Because the lines there tend to be shorter, I usually prefer to enter via the:

1. **Velázquez door,** the Prado's western (central) entrance, near the larger-than-life bronze statue of the seated artist, Spain's most famous painter. Resolutely

ignoring (for the time being) the riches of the museum's street level, climb to the upper floor, using the building's central (western) staircase, which lies a short distance to the right of the entrance turnstile. At the top of the stairs, walk down the short hall that will deposit you in the museum's famous:

2. **Long Gallery.** Although referred to as a gallery, it is more technically the interconnected series of rooms 24 through 32. Echoing, marble-sheathed, and often very crowded, these rooms are the main traffic artery of the Prado's second showcase floor. Walk south through rooms 28 and 29, admiring the large-scale works by mainly Italian Renaissance painters as you go. Specific artworks will include representations by Raphael, Titian, Tintoretto, and Fra Angelico. The gallery will eventually funnel into an octagonal room (no. 32) that contains:
3. **Oil paintings by Goya,** including his most famous portraits: the cruel depictions of the family of King Carlos IV. You are standing amid the museum's densest concentration of oils by Goya. The best of these lie a few steps to the east. With your back to the previously mentioned Long Gallery, turn left into the long and narrow room 31. At the end of no. 31, turn left into room 22. This and four of its neighbors (specifically, rooms 19 to 23, which lie in a straight, uninterrupted line) contain many of the cartoons (sketches for tapestries) Goya designed for eventual execution by teams of weavers. Walk southward into room 18 to see:
4. **Paintings by Murillo, Ribera, and Zurbarán.** This room, along with its immediate neighbors, rooms 18A and 17A, contains works by Murillo (1617–82), Ribera (1588–1652), and Zurbarán (1598–1664). Each of these artists produced works that are worthy contemporaries of the most-acclaimed artwork ever to emerge from Spain, the:
5. **Paintings by Velázquez.** These lie ahead of you, within about half a dozen rooms whose contents are considered the centerpiece of the Prado. Wander through rooms 16A, 15A, 14, 16, and 13, in any order that appeals to your roving eye. You will probably intuitively gravitate to the Prado's architectural and artistic centerpiece, room 12. Although masterpieces await you on all sides, note in particular *Las Meninas* (*Ladies of the Court*), whose enigmatic grouping has intrigued observers for centuries.

   Now exit from room 12's northern door into room 11, turn left into room 11A, then turn immediately right into rooms 10B and 9B. This series of rooms contains one of Europe's most important collections of:
6. **Paintings by El Greco.** Famous for his nervous depictions of mystical ecstasy, his dramatically lurid colors, and the elongated limbs of his characters (who seem to be physically rising upward to heaven), El Greco was the premier exponent of the late Baroque school of mannerism.

   Time will by now be rushing by. If you choose to prolong your visit, you might want to gaze briefly into rooms 8B, 9, 8, 7, 7A, 8A, and 9A, all of which contain an array of:
7. **Italian Renaissance paintings.** These interconnected rooms lie within a few steps of one another, and each contains more world-class examples of works by such Italian masters as Tintoretto, Titian, and Paolo Veronese.

   Know at this point that you have by now seen—albeit briefly—many of the grandest artworks of the Prado's upper floor. Head quickly for the nearest

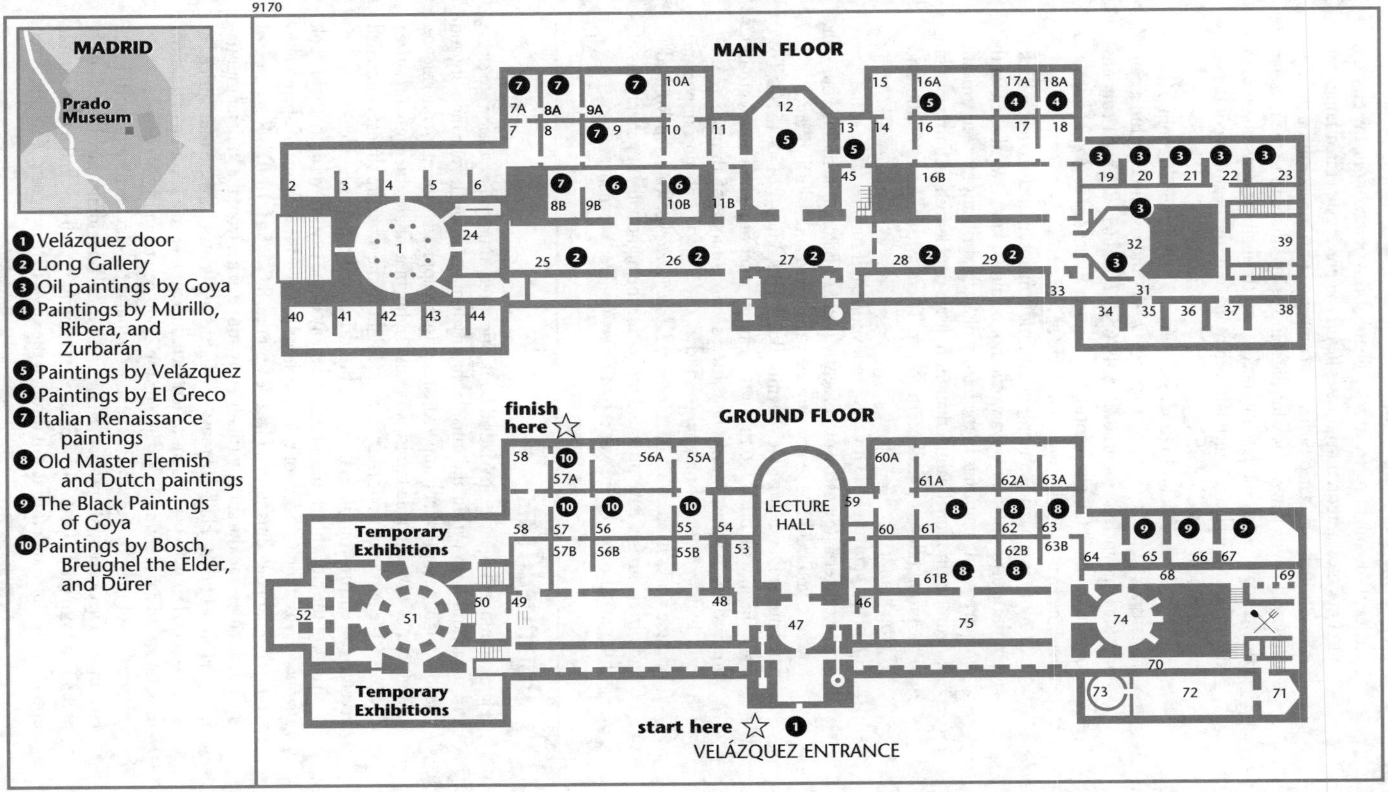

Walking Tour—The Prado in Two Hours

9170

MADRID

Prado Museum

1. Velázquez door
2. Long Gallery
3. Oil paintings by Goya
4. Paintings by Murillo, Ribera, and Zurbarán
5. Paintings by Velázquez
6. Paintings by El Greco
7. Italian Renaissance paintings
8. Old Master Flemish and Dutch paintings
9. The Black Paintings of Goya
10. Paintings by Bosch, Breughel the Elder, and Dürer

MAIN FLOOR

GROUND FLOOR

LECTURE HALL

Temporary Exhibitions

Temporary Exhibitions

finish here

start here

VELÁZQUEZ ENTRANCE

staircase. (You might prefer to ask a guard at this point, but in any event, the museum's most important staircases lie off the previously visited Long Gallery, which—as stated earlier—is comprised of rooms 24 through 32.) Midway along its length, look for the staircase and descend to the museum's ground floor. When you reach it, head south through the very long room 75. Midway down its length, turn left into room 61B, the beginning of the Prado's superb collection of:

8. **Old Master Flemish and Dutch paintings.** These lie within room 61B (famous for Ruben's *Martyrdom of St. Andrew*) and continue within a cluster of rooms that include rooms 62B, 63B, 63, 62, and 61. Room 61 contains some of the most famous paintings in history: Rubens' *The Three Graces* and the somewhat less well known *Judgment of Paris.*

   Your tour is nearing an end, but if time remains, a final excursion back into the artistic vision of Goya would not be amiss. For views of some of the most depressing paintings in the history of Spain, brilliant for their evocation of neurotic emotional pain and anguish, leave the Flemish section by walking to the ground floor's southeastern corner. There, within rooms 65, 66, and 67, you'll find:
9. **The black paintings of Goya.** Refresh yourself, if time remains, at the nearby cafeteria. (Signs are prominently posted.) Before concluding your tour, however, you might be tempted to view the weird and hallucinogenic paintings of Dutch artist Heironymus Bosch ("El Bosco," 1450–1516). To reach them, walk briskly to the northeastern corner of the museum's ground floor, where the artist's works lie scattered among rooms 55 through 57A.
10. **Paintings by Bosch, Breughel the Elder, and Dürer.** The most important of these works is Bosch's *The Garden of Earthly Delights,* whose convoluted and bizarre images have provided fodder for the nightmares of generations of children. Also nearby are works by Rogier Van Der Weyden.

5 Organized Tours

A large number of agencies in Madrid book organized tours and excursions to sights and attractions both within and outside the city limits. Although your mobility and freedom might be somewhat hampered, some visitors appreciate the ease, convenience, and efficiency of being able to visit so many sights in a single efficiently organized day. Also, the hassles of navigating from one sight to the other are almost eliminated because you entrust your itinerary to the bus driver and bilingual guide.

Many of the city's hotel concierges, and many of the city's travel agents, will book anyone who asks for a guided tour of Madrid or its environs with one of Spain's largest tour operators, Pullmantours, Plaza de Oriente, 8 (☎ **541-18-07**). Regardless of their destination and duration, virtually every tour departs from the Pullmantour terminal, at that address. Half-day tours of Madrid include an "artistic tour" priced at 4,300 pesetas ($30.50) per person, which includes entrance to a selection of the city's museums, and a panoramic half-day tour for 2,600 pesetas ($18.50).

Southward treks to Toledo are the most popular full-day excursions outside the city limits. They cost 6,900 pesetas ($49). These tours (including lunch) depart daily at 8:30am from the above-mentioned departure point, last all day, and include ample opportunities for wandering at will through the city's narrow streets. You can, if you wish, take an abbreviated morning tour of Toledo, without stopping for lunch, for 4,470 pesetas ($31.70).

Another popular tour stops briefly in Toledo and continues on to visit both the monastery at El Escorial and the Valley of the Fallen (Valle de los Caídos) before returning the same day to Madrid. With lunch included, this all-day excursion costs 9,410 pesetas ($66.80).

Other worthwhile full-day tours include visits to Segovia and the Bourbon dynasty's 18th-century palace of La Granja costing 5,515 pesetas ($39.20) without lunch and 8,520 pesetas ($60.50) with lunch. A half-day tour of Aranjuez and Chinchón, without lunch, costs 5,200 pesetas ($36.90).

The hop-off, hop-on **Madrid Vision Bus** lets you set your own pace and itinerary. A scheduled panoramic tour lasts a half hour, providing you don't get off the bus. Otherwise, you can opt for an unlimited number of stops, exploring at your leisure. The Madrid Vision makes four complete tours daily, two in the morning and two in the afternoon; on Sunday and Monday buses depart only in the morning. Check with the Madrid tourist office for times of your departure, which are variable. The panoramic tour (without your getting off the bus) costs 560 pesetas ($4); the full-day tour with unlimited stops, 1,050 pesetas ($7.50).

6 Sports & Recreation

Spectator Sports

THE BULLFIGHT

★ **Plaza Monumental de Toros de las Ventas,** Alcalá, 237. ☎ **356-22-00.**

Madrid draws the finest matadors in Spain. If a matador hasn't proved his worth in the major ring in Madrid, he just hasn't been recognized as a top-flight artist. The major season begins during the Fiestas de San Isidro, patron saint of Madrid, on May 15. This is the occasion for a series of fights, during which talent scouts help make up the audience. Matadors who distinguish themselves in the ring are signed up for Majorca, Málaga, and other places.

For tickets to this biggest bullfight stadium in Madrid, go to its box office. Many hotels also have good seats that you can buy. Front-row seats are known as *barreras. Delanteras*—third-row seats—are available in both the *alta* (high) and the *baja* (low) sections. The cheapest seats sold, *filas,* afford the worst view and are in the sun (*sol*) during the entire performance. The best seats are in the shade (*sombra*). Bullfights are held on Sunday and holidays throughout most of the year, and every day during certain festivals, which tend to last around three weeks, usually in the late springtime. Starting times are adjusted according to the anticipated hour of sundown on the day of a performance, usually 7pm from Easter to October, and at 5pm during late autumn and early spring. Late-night fights by neophyte matadors are sometimes staged under spotlights on Saturday around 11pm.

Admission: 600–15,000 ptas. ($4.30–$106.50).

Open: Box office, Fri–Sun 10am–2pm and 5–8pm. **Metro:** Ventas.

HORSE RACING

Hipódromo de la Zarzuela, Carretera de la Coruña, Kilometer 7.8. ☎ **207-01-40.**

There are two seasons—spring (February through June) and fall (mid-September to early December). Races, often six or seven, are generally held on Sunday and holidays (11am), with a series of night races (11pm) held on weekends in July and August. A restaurant and bar are at the hippodrome, which is 11 miles (18km) from the center of Madrid (N-VI).

Admission: 500 ptas. ($3.60).

Directions: Take the free bus that leaves from Moncloa, across from the Air Ministry.

SOCCER

Futbol is played with a passion all year in Madrid. League matches, on Saturday or Sunday, run from September to May, culminating in the annual summer tournaments. Madrid has two teams in the top division.

The *Real Madrid* plays home games at the Estadio Santiago Bernabéu, Concha Espina, 1 (☎ **344-00-52**; metro: Lima). Tickets, which run from 1,500 pesetas ($10.70), can be obtained at the stadium. The Club Atlético de Madrid plays at the Estadio Vicente Calderón, Paseo de la Virgen del Puerto, 67 (☎ **366-47-07**; metro: Pirámides). Tickets are sold at the stadium, costing from 1,500 pesetas ($10.70).

Recreation

FITNESS CENTERS

Although Madrid has scores of gyms, bodybuilding studios, and aerobic-exercise centers, many of them are private. For one open to the public, try Atenas, Victor de la Serna, 37 (☎ **345-16-75**; metro: Colombia). This facility for men and women has an indoor swimming pool, workout equipment, a sauna, and such personal services as massage. It's open Monday to Saturday from 8am to 9:30pm.

JOGGING

Both the Parque del Retiro and Casa de Campo have jogging tracks. For details on how to get there, see below and also refer to "Parks & Gardens" in "More Attractions" earlier in this chapter.

SWIMMING & TENNIS

The best swimming and tennis facilities are found at the Casa de Campo, Avenida del Angel (☎ **463-00-50**; metro: Lago or Batán), a 4,300-acre former royal hunting preserve that lies on the right bank of the Manzanares River. Today it is a public park, serving as a playground for Madrileños.

7 Savvy Shopping

Seventeenth-century playwright Tirso de Molina called Madrid "a shop stocked with every kind of merchandise," and it's true—its estimated 50,000 stores sell everything from high-fashion clothing to flamenco guitars to art and ceramics.

If your time is limited, go to one of the big department stores (see below). They all carry a "bit of everything."

The Shopping Scene

SHOPPING AREAS • The Center The sheer diversity of shops in Madrid's center is staggering. Their densest concentration lies immediately north of Puerta del Sol, radiating out from Calle del Carmen, Calle Montera, Calle Preciados.

• **Calle Mayor & Calle del Arenal** Unlike their more stylish neighbors to the north of Puerta del Sol, shops in this district to the west tend toward the small, slightly dusty enclaves of coin and stamp dealers, family-owned souvenir shops, clockmakers, sellers of military paraphernalia, and an abundance of stores selling musical scores.

• **Gran Vía** Conceived, designed, and built in the 1910s and '20s as a showcase for the city's best shops, hotels, and restaurants, the Gran Vía has since been eclipsed by other shopping districts. Its art nouveau/art deco glamour still survives in the hearts of most Madrileños, though. The bookshops here are among the best in the city, as are outlets for fashion, shoes, jewelry, furs, and handcrafted accessories from all regions of Spain.

• **El Rastro** It's the biggest flea market in Spain, drawing collectors, dealers, buyers, and hopefuls from throughout Madrid and its suburbs. The makeshift stalls are at their most frenetic on Sunday morning. For more information, refer to the "Markets" section, below.

• **Plaza Mayor** Under the arcades of the square itself are exhibitions of lithographs and oil paintings, and every weekend there's a loosely organized market for stamp and coin collectors. Within three or four blocks in every direction you'll find more than the average number of souvenir shops.

On Calle Marqués Viudo de Pontejos, which runs east from Plaza Mayor, is one of the city's headquarters for the sale of cloth, thread, and buttons. Also running east, on Calle de Zaragoza, are silversmiths and jewelers. On Calle Postas you'll find housewares, underwear, soap powders, and other household items.

• **Near the Carrera de San Jerónimo** Several blocks east of Puerta del Sol is Madrid's densest concentration of gift shops, crafts shops, and antiques dealers—a decorator's delight. Its most interesting streets include Calle del Prado, Calle de las Huertas, and Plaza de las Cortés. The neighborhood is pricey—so don't expect bargains here.

• **Northwest Madrid** A few blocks east of Parque del Oeste is an upscale neighborhood that's well stocked with luxury goods and household staples. Calle de la Princesa, its main thoroughfare, has shops selling shoes, handbags, fashion, gifts, and children's clothing. Thanks to the presence of the university nearby, there's also a dense concentration of bookstores, especially on Calle Isaac Peral and Calle Fernando el Católico, several blocks north and northwest, respectively, from the subway stop of Argüelles.

• **Salamanca District** It's known throughout Spain as the quintessential upper-bourgeois neighborhood, uniformly prosperous, and its shops are correspondingly exclusive. They include outlets run by interior decorators, furniture shops, fur and jewelry shops, several department stores, and design headquarters whose output ranges from the solidly conservative to the high-tech. The main streets of this district are Calle de Serrano and Calle de Velázquez. The district lies northeast of the center of Madrid, a few blocks north of Retiro Park. Its most central Metro stops are Serrano and Velázquez.

HOURS AND SHIPPING Major stores are open (in most cases) Monday to Saturday from 9:30am to 8pm. Many small stores take a siesta between 1:30 and 4:30pm. Of course, there is never any set formula, and hours can vary greatly from store to store depending on the idiosyncracies and schedules of the owner.

Many art and antique dealers will crate and ship bulky objects for an additional fee. Any especially large or heavy item, such as a piece of furniture, should probably be sent by ship. Every antiques dealer in Spain maintains lists of reputable maritime shippers. One reliable option is **Emery Ocean Freight** (☎ toll free in the U.S. **800/488-9451**), which maintains branch offices in Barcelona, Alicante, Madrid, Málaga, Bilboa, and Valencia. The main office of their representative in Spain is S.J. Rubert, S.L., (I.T.E. Ltd, c/o Emery) International Freight Forwarding and Customs Agents, Explanada de España #2, Aptdo 8, 03002 Alicante (☎ **96/521-4011**). For more information, either before your departure or when checking the whereabouts of your shipment in transit from Spain, call Emery toll-free in the U.S. at **800/488-9451.**

For most small and medium-size shipments, air freight isn't much more expensive than shipping. **Iberia's Air Cargo Division** (☎ toll free **800/221-6002** in the U.S.) offers air-freight service from Spain to either New York, Miami, or Los Angeles. For shipments from either Barcelona or Madrid to New York, a shipment under 100 kg (220 pounds) costs 760 pesetas ($5.40) per kilo. The per-kilo price goes down as the weight increases, reaching 427 pesetas ($3) per kilo for shipments weighing more than 100 kilos. Regardless of what you ship, there's a minimum charge of 8,500 pesetas ($60.40).

For an additional fee, Iberia or one of its representatives will pick up your package. For a truly precious cargo, ask the seller to build a crate for it. For information within Spain about air-cargo shipments, call Iberia's cargo division at Madrid's Barajas Airport (☎ **91/587-8890**) or at Barcelona's airport (☎ **93/401-3426**).

Remember that your air-cargo shipment will need to clear Customs after it's brought into the United States. This involves some additional paperwork, costly delays, and in some cases a trip to the airport where the shipment first entered the U.S. It's usually easier (and in some cases, much easier) to hire a commercial customs broker to do the work for you. Emery Worldwide, a division of CF Freightways, can clear your goods for around $125 for most shipments, which you'll pay in addition to any applicable duty you owe your home government. For information, you can call toll free **800/323-4685** within the United States.

TAX & HOW TO RECOVER IT If you are a non-EU resident and make purchases in Spain worth more than 82,400 pesetas ($585), you can get a tax refund. (The internal tax, known as VAT in most of Europe, is called IVA in Spain.) Depending on the goods, the rate usually ranges from 6% to 12% of the total worth of your merchandise. Luxury items are taxed at 33%.

To get this refund, you must complete three copies of a form that the store will give you, detailing the nature of your purchase and its value. Citizens of non-EU countries show the purchase and the form to the Spanish Customs Office. The shop is supposed to refund the amount due you. Inquire at the time of purchase how they will do so and discuss in what currency your refund will arrive.

TRADITIONAL SALES The best sales are usually in summer. Called *rebajas*, they start in July and go through August. As a general rule, merchandise is marked down even more in August to make way for the new fall wares in most stores.

DUTY-FREE—WORTH IT OR NOT? Before you leave home, check the regular retail price of items that you're most likely to buy. Duty-free prices vary from one country to another and from item to item. Sometimes you're better off purchasing an item in a discount store at home. If you don't remember prices back home, you can't tell when you're getting a good deal.

BARGAINING The days of bargaining are, for the most part, long gone. Most stores have what is called *precio de venta al público* (**PVP**), a firm retail price not subject to negotiation. With street vendors and flea markets, it's a different story because haggling *à la española* is expected. However, you'll have to be very skilled to get the price reduced a lot, as most of these street-smart vendors know exactly what their merchandise is worth and are old hands at getting that price.

Shopping A to Z

Spain has always been known for its craftspeople, many of whom still work in the time-honored and labor-intensive traditions of their grandparents. It's hard to go wrong if you stick to the beautiful handcrafted Spanish objects—handpainted tiles, ceramics, and porcelain; handwoven rugs; handmade sweaters; and intricate embroideries—the creation of skilled Spanish workers. And, of course, Spain produces some of the world's finest leather. Jewelry, especially gold set with Majorca pearls, represents good value and unquestioned luxury.

Some of Madrid's art galleries are known throughout Europe for discovering and encouraging new talent. Antiques are sold in highly sophisticated retail outlets. Better suited to the budgets of many travelers are the weekly flea markets.

Spain continues to make inroads into the fashion world. Its young designers are regularly featured in the fashion magazines of Europe. Excellent shoes are available, some highly fashionable. But be advised that prices for shoes and quality clothing are generally higher in Madrid than in the United States.

ANTIQUES

These are sold at the flea market (see El Rastro, below) and at the Puerta de Toledo (see "Shopping Malls," below).

Centro de Anticularios Lagasca, Lagasca, 36. No phone.

You'll find about a dozen antiques shops here, clustered into one covered arcade. They operate as individual businesses, although by browsing through each you'll find an impressive assemblage of antique furniture, porcelain, and whatnots. Open Monday to Saturday from 10am to 1:30pm and 5 to 8pm. **Metro:** Serrano or Velázquez.

Centro de Arte y Antigüedades, Serrano, 5. ☎ **576-96-82.**

Housed in a mid-19th-century building are several unusual antiques dealers (and a large carpet emporium as well). Each establishment maintains its own schedule,

Frommer's Smart Traveler: Shopping

1. Read the section on tax refunds (see above). There's red tape, but refunds can mean substantial savings.
2. Tune your haggling skills in the open-air flea market of Madrid (El Rastro). You can come up with good buys with strong, steady, and firm bargaining.
3. If you pay cash, some smaller stores will lower the price.
4. Look for the July and August sales, when merchandise prices are slashed.
5. Don't assume that because a certain product is "made in Spain" that it's cheaper in Spain. It pays to know what something costs at home before you make a substantial purchase.

although the center itself has overall hours. Open Monday to Saturday from 10am to 2pm and 4:30 to 8pm. **Metro:** Retiro. **Bus:** 1, 2, 9, or 15.

ART GALLERIES

Galería Kreisler, Hermosilla, 6. ☎ **431-42-64.**

One successful entrepreneur on Madrid's art scene is Ohio-born Edward Kreisler, whose gallery, now run by his son Juan, specializes in figurative and contemporary paintings, sculptures, and graphics. The gallery prides itself on occasionally displaying and selling the works of artists who are critically acclaimed in and displayed in museums in Spain. Open Monday through Saturday from 10:30am to 2pm and 5 to 9pm. **Closed:** Saturday afternoon July 15 to September 15 and August. **Metro:** Serrano. **Bus:** 27, 45, or 150.

CAPES

Capas Seseña, Cruz, 23. ☎ **531-68-40.**

Founded shortly after the turn of the century, this shop manufactures and sells wool capes for both women and men. The wool comes from the mountain town of Béjar, near Salamanca. Open Monday to Friday from 10am to 1:30pm and 4:30 to 8pm, Saturday from 10am to 1:30pm. **Metro:** Sevilla or Puerta del Sol. **Bus:** 5, 51, or 52.

CARPETS

Ispahan, Serrano, 5. ☎ **575-20-12.**

In this 19th-century building, behind bronze handmade doors, are three floors devoted to carpets from around the world, notably Afghanistan, India, Nepal, Iran, Turkey, and the Caucasus. One section is devoted to silk carpets. In addition, the Art Gallery of the Louvre, Ispahan II, displays both old masters and contemporary art. Open Monday through Saturday from 10am to 2pm and 4:30 to 8:30pm. **Metro:** Retiro. **Bus:** 1, 2, 9, and 15.

CERAMICS

Antigua Casa Talavera, Isabel la Católica, 2. ☎ **547-34-17.**

"The first house of Spanish ceramics" has wares that include a sampling of regional styles from every major area of Spain, including Talavera, Toledo, Manises, Valencia, Puente del Arzobispa, Alcora, Granada, and Seville. Sangría pitchers, dinnerware, tea sets, plates, and vases are all handmade. Inside one of the showrooms is an interesting selection of tiles, painted with reproductions of scenes from bullfights, dances, and folklore. There's also a series of tiles depicting famous paintings in the Prado. At its present location since 1904, the shop is only a short walk from Plaza de Santo Domingo. Open Monday to Friday from 10am to 1:30pm and 5 to 8pm, Saturday from 10am to 1:30pm. **Metro:** Santo Domingo. **Bus:** 1, 2, 46, 70, 75, or 148.

CRAFTS

El Arco de los Cuchilleros Artesania de Hoy, Plaza Mayor, 9 (basement level). ☎ **365-26-80.**

Set within one of the 17th-century vaulted cellars of Plaza Mayor, this shop is entirely devoted to unusual craft items derived from throughout Spain. The merchandise is unusual, one-of-a-kind, and, in most cases, contemporary, and includes a changing array of pottery, leather, textiles, wood carvings, glassware, wickerwork, papier mâché, and silver jewelry. The hardworking owners deal directly with the artisans who produce each item, ensuring a wide inventory of handcrafts that can sometimes contribute profoundly to the aesthetics of any traveler's private home. The staff is familiar with the rituals of applying for tax-free status of purchases here, and speaks several different languages. It's open daily from 11am to 8pm in winter, till 9pm in summer. **Metro:** Puerta del Sol.

DEPARTMENT STORES

El Corte Inglés, Preciados, 3. ☎ **532-18-00.**

This flagship of the largest department-store chain in Madrid sells hundreds of souvenirs and Spanish handcrafts—damascene steelwork from Toledo, flamenco dolls, and embroidered shawls. Some astute buyers report that it also sells glamorous fashion articles, such as Pierre Balmain designs, for about a third less than equivalent items in most European capitals. Services include interpreters, currency-exchange windows, and parcel delivery either to a local hotel or overseas. Open Monday to Saturday from 10am to 9pm. **Metro:** Puerta del Sol.

Galerías Preciados, Plaza del Callao, 1. ☎ **522-47-71.**

Right off the Gran Vía, this is really two stores connected by an underground passageway. Good buys include suede jackets and coats and capes. There is a moderately priced selection of clothing for men, women, and children, with a tailoring department on the second floor where men can have a suit made to order. Also included are a top-floor restaurant and snack bar. Open Monday to Saturday from 10am to 8pm. **Metro:** Callao.

EMBROIDERIES

Casa Bonet, Núñez de Balboa, 76. ☎ **575-09-12.**

The intricately detailed embroideries produced in Spain's Balearic Islands (especially Majorca) are avidly sought for bridal chests and elegant dinner settings. A few examples of the store's extensive inventory are displayed on the walls. Open Monday to Friday from 9:45am to 2pm and 5 to 8pm, Saturday from 10:15am to 2pm. **Metro:** Núñez de Balboa.

ESPADRILLES

Casa Hernanz, Toledo, 18. ☎ **366-54-50.**

A brisk walk south of Plaza Mayor delivers you to this store, in business since the 1840s. In addition to espadrilles, they sell shoes in other styles, as well as hats. Open Monday to Friday 9am to 1:30pm and 4:30 to 8pm, Saturday from 10am to 2pm. **Metro:** Puerta del Sol, Opera, or La Latina.

FANS & UMBRELLAS

Casa de Diego, Puerta del Sol, 12. ☎ **522-66-43.**

Here you'll find a wide inventory of fans, ranging from plain to fancy, from plastic to exotic hardwood, from cost-conscious to lavish. In summer it is open Monday through Saturday from 9:30am to 8pm; in winter, Monday through Saturday from 9:30am to 1:30pm and 5 to 8pm. **Metro:** Puerta del Sol.

FASHIONS FOR MEN

For the man on a budget who wants to dress reasonably well, the best outlet for off-the-rack men's clothing is one of the branches of the Corte Inglés department-store chain (see above). Most men's boutiques in Madrid are very expensive and may not be worth the investment.

FASHIONS FOR WOMEN

Don Carlos, Serrano, 92. ☎ **575-75-07.**

This boutique has a limited but tasteful array of clothing for women (and a somewhat smaller selection for men). Open Monday to Saturday from 10am to 2pm and 5 to 8:30pm. **Metro:** Nuñez de Balboa.

Herrero, Preciados, 16. ☎ **521-29-90.**

The sheer size and buying power of this popular retail outlet for women's clothing make it a reasonably priced emporium for all kinds of feminine garb. An additional outlet lies on the same street, at no. 7 (same phone). Open Monday to Saturday from 10:45am to 2pm and 4:30 to 7pm. **Metro:** Puerta del Sol or Callao.

Jesús de Pozo, Almirante, 28. ☎ **531-66-76.**

The fabrics are beautiful and the garments expensive, but when they make you look gorgeous, it may be worth it. Open Monday to Saturday from 10am to 1:30pm and 5 to 8pm. **Metro:** Banco de España.

Modas Gonzalo, Gran Vía, 43. ☎ **547-12-39.**

This boutique's baroque, gilded atmosphere evokes the 1940s, but its fashions are strictly up to date, well made, and intended for stylish adult women. No children's garments are sold. Open Monday to Saturday from 10am to 1:30pm and 4:30 to 8pm. **Metro:** Callao or Puerta del Sol.

FLEA MARKETS

El Rastro, Plaza Cascorro and Ribera de Curtidores.

Foremost among markets is El Rastro (translated as either flea market or thieves' market), occupying a roughly triangular district of streets and plazas a few minutes' walk south of Plaza Mayor. Its center is Plaza Cascorro and Ribera de Curtidores. This market will delight anyone attracted to a mishmash of fascinating junk interspersed with bric-a-brac and paintings. But thieves are rampant here (hustling more than just antiques), so secure your wallet carefully, be alert, and proceed with caution. Open Tuesday to Sunday from 9:30am to 1:30pm and 5 to 8pm. **Metro:** La Latina. **Bus:** 3 or 17.

FOOD & WINE

Mallorca, Velázquez, 59. ☎ **431-99-09.**

Madrid's best-established gourmet shop opened in 1931 as an outlet selling a pastry called *ensaimada,* and this is still one of the store's most famous products. Tempting arrays of cheeses, canapés, roasted and marinated meats, sausages, and about a dozen kinds of pâté—these accompany a spread of tiny pastries, tarts, and chocolates. Don't overlook the displays of Spanish wines and brandies. A stand-up tapas bar is always clogged with clients three deep, sampling the wares before they buy larger portions to take home. Tapas cost from 250 to 500 pesetas ($1.80–$3.60) per ración (portion). Open daily from 9am to 9pm. **Metro:** Velásquez.

HATS & HEADGEAR

Casa Yustas, Plaza Mayor, 30. ☎ **366-50-84.**

Founded in 1894, this extraordinary hat emporium is very popular. Want to see yourself as a Congo explorer, a Spanish sailor, an officer in the kaiser's army, or even Napoleon? Open Monday to Friday from 9:45am to 1:30pm and 4:30 to 8pm, Saturday from 9:45am to 1:30pm. **Metro:** Puerta del Sol.

LEATHER

Loewe, Gran Vía, 8. ☎ **522-68-15.**

Since 1846 this has been the most elegant leather store in Spain. Its gold-medal–winning designers have always kept abreast of changing tastes and styles, but the inventory still retains a timeless chic. The store sells luggage, handbags, and jackets for men and women (in leather or suede). Open Monday to Saturday from 9:30am to 8pm. **Metro:** Banco de España.

MUSICAL INSTRUMENTS

Real Musical, Carlos III, no. 1. ☎ **541-30-07.**

You'll find the best selection here—everything from a Spanish guitar to a piano, along with string and wind instruments. The place also has excellent Spanish records and sheet music. Open Monday to Friday from 9:30am to 2pm and 5 to 8pm, Saturday from 10am to 2pm. **Metro:** Ópera.

PERFUMES

Perfumería Padilla, Preciados, 17. ☎ **522-66-83.**

This store sells a large and competitively priced assortment of Spanish and international scents for women. They also maintain a branch at Calle del Carmen, 78 (same phone). Both branches are open Monday to Saturday from 9:45am to 8:30pm. **Metro:** Puerta del Sol.

Urguiola, Mayor, 1. ☎ **521-59-05.**

Located at the western edge of the Puerta del Sol, this time-tested shop carries one of the most complete stocks of perfume in Madrid—both national and international brands. It also sells gifts, souvenirs, and costume jewelry. Open Monday to Saturday from 10am to 8pm. **Metro:** Puerta del Sol.

PORCELAIN

Lasarte, Gran Vía, 44. ☎ **521-49-22.**

This store is an imposing outlet for Lladró porcelain, devoted almost exclusively to its distribution. The staff can usually tell you about new designs and releases the Lladró company is planning for the near future. Open Monday to Friday from 9:30 to 8pm, Saturday from 9:30am to 2pm. **Metro:** Callao.

SHOPPING MALLS

Galería del Prado, Plaza de las Cortes, 7.

Spain's top designers are represented in this marble-sheathed concourse below the Palace Hotel. It opened in 1989 with 47 different shops, many featuring *moda joven* (fashions for the young). Merchandise changes with the season, but you will always find a good assortment of fashions, Spanish leather goods, cosmetics, perfumes, and jewelry. You can also eat and drink in the complex. The entrance to the gallery is in front of the hotel, facing the broad tree-lined Paseo del Prado across from the Prado itself. Open Monday to Saturday from 10am to 9pm. **Metro:** Banco de España or Atocha.

Mercado Puerta de Toledo, Puerta de Toledo.

One of Spain's most upscale, ambitious, and architecturally unusual shopping malls is the Mercado Puerta de Toledo, with 150 of the most glamorous names in Spain housed in a slightly run-down neighborhood just southeast of the historic center. Antiques and name-brand fashions especially are featured here, an unusual contrast for a building that once served as Madrid's central fish market; it rises five floors above a sunny courtyard. You won't go hungry between shopping binges because of the many restaurants, tapas bars, and cafés within its premises. Each of the shops is open Monday to Saturday from 10am to 8:30pm. **Metro:** Puerta de Toledo.

8 Evening Entertainment

Madrid abounds with dance halls, tascas, cafés, theaters, movie houses, music halls, and nightclubs. You'll have to proceed carefully through this maze, as many of these offerings are strictly for the residents or for Spanish-speakers.

Because dinner is served late in Spain, nightlife doesn't really get under way until after 11pm, and it generally lasts until around 3am—Madrileños are so fond of prowling around at night that they are known around Spain as *gatos* (cats). If you arrive at 9:30pm at a club, you'll probably find that you have the place all to yourself.

In most clubs a one-drink minimum is the rule: Feel free to nurse one drink through the entire evening's entertainment.

In summer Madrid becomes a virtual free festival because the city sponsors a series of plays, concerts, and films. Pick up a copy of the *Guía del Ocio* (available at most newsstands) for listings of these events. This guide also provides information about occasional discounts for commercial events, such as the concerts that are given in Madrid's parks. Also check the program of *Fundación Juan March,* Calle Castello, 77 (☎ **435-42-40; Metro:** Nuñez de Balboa), which frequently stages free concerts.

Flamenco in Madrid is geared mainly to tourists with fat wallets, and nightclubs are expensive. But since Madrid is preeminently a city of song and dance, you can often be entertained at very little cost—in fact, for the price of a glass of wine or beer, if you sit at a bar with live entertainment.

Like flamenco clubs, discos tend to be expensive, but they often open for what is erroneously called "afternoon" sessions (from 7 to 10pm). Although discos charge entry fees, at an "afternoon" session the cost might be as low as 300 pesetas ($2.10), rising to 2,000 pesetas ($14.20) and beyond for a "night" session—that is, beginning at 11:30pm and lasting until the early-morning hours. Therefore, go early, dance until 10pm, then proceed to dinner (you'll be eating at the fashionable hour).

Nightlife is so plentiful in Madrid that the city can be roughly divided into the following "night zones."

Plaza Mayor/Puerta del Sol The most popular areas from the standpoint of both tradition and tourist interest, they can also be dangerous, so explore them with caution, especially late at night. They are filled with tapas bars and *cuevas* (drinking "caves"). Here it is customary to begin a tasca crawl, going to tavern after tavern, sampling the wine in each, along with a selection of tapas. The major streets for such a crawl are Cava de San Miguel, Cava Alta, and Cava Baja. You can order *pinchos y raciones* (tasty snacks and tidbits).

Gran Vía This area contains mainly cinemas and theaters. Most of the after-dark action takes place on little streets branching off the Gran Vía.

Plaza de Isabel II/Plaza de Oriente This is another area much frequented by tourists. Many restaurants and cafés flourish here, including the famous Café de Oriente.

Chueca Embracing such streets as Hortaleza, Infantas, Barquillo, and San Lucas, this is the gay nightlife district, with many clubs. Cheap restaurants, along with a few female striptease joints, are also found here. This area can also be dangerous at night, so watch for pickpockets and muggers. As of late, there has been greater police presence at night.

Argüelles/Moncloa For university students, this part of town sees most of the action. Many dance clubs are found here, along with ale houses and fast-food joints. The area is bounded by Pintor Rosales, Cea Bermúdez, Bravo Murillo, San Bernardo, and Conde Duque.

The Performing Arts

There are within Madrid a number of theaters, opera companies, and dance companies. To discover where and when specific cultural events are being performed, pick up a copy of *Guía del Ocio* for 85 pesetas (60¢) at any city newsstand. The sheer volume of cultural offerings might stagger you; for concise summary of the highlights, see below.

Tickets to dramatic and musical events usually range in price from 700 to 2,000 pesetas ($5–$14.20), with discounts of up to 50% granted on certain days of the week (usually Wednesday and early performances on Sunday).

The concierges at most major hotels can usually get you tickets to specific concerts, if you are clear about your wishes and needs. He or she will, of course, charge a considerable markup, part of which will be passed along to whichever agency originally booked the tickets. You'll save money if you go directly to the box office to buy tickets. In the event your choice is sold out, you may be able to get tickets (with a considerable markup) at **Localidades Galicia** at Plaza del Carmen (☎ **531-27-32; Metro:** Puerta del Sol). This agency also markets tickets to bullfights and sports events. It is open Tuesday to Sunday from 10am to 1pm and 4:30 to 7:30pm.

Here follows a grab bag of nighttime diversions that might amuse and entertain you. First, the cultural offerings:

MAJOR PERFORMING-ARTS COMPANIES

For those who speak Spanish, the **Companía Nacional de Nuevas Tendencias Escénicas** is an avant-garde troupe that performs new—often controversial—works by undiscovered writers. On the other hand, the **Compañía Nacional de Teatro Clásico,** as its name suggests, is devoted to the Spanish classics, including works by the ever-popular Lope de Vega or Tirso de Molina.

Among dance companies, the national ballet of Spain—devoted exclusively to Spanish dance—is the **Ballet Nacional de España.** Their performances are always well attended. The national lyrical ballet company of the country is the Ballet Lírico Nacional.

Madrid's opera company is the **Teatro de la Opera,** and its symphony orchestra is the outstanding **Orquesta Sinfónica de Madrid**. The national orchestra of Spain—

widely acclaimed on the continent—is the **Orquesta Nacional de España,** which pays particular homage to Spanish composers.

THEATER

Madrid offers many different theater performances, useful to you only if your Spanish is very fluent. If it isn't, check the **Guía del Ocia** for performances by English-speaking companies on tour from Britain or select a concert or subtitled movie instead.

In addition to the major ones listed below, there are at least 30 other theaters, including one devoted almost entirely to children's plays, the **Sala la Bicicleta,** in the Ciudad de los Niños at Casa de Campo. Dozens of other plays are staged by nonprofessional groups in such places as churches.

Teatro Calderón, Atocha, 18. ☎ **369-14-34.**

This is the largest theater in Madrid, with a seating capacity of 1,700. It's known for its popular revues, performances of popular Spanish plays, and flamenco. **Metro:** Tirso de Molina.

Prices: Tickets 900–3,000 ptas. ($6.40–$21.30).

Teatro de la Comedia, Príncipe, 14. ☎ **521-49-31.**

This is the home of the Compañía Nacional de Teatro Clásico. Here, more than anywhere else in Madrid, you're likely to see performances from the classic repertoire of great Spanish drama. Closed on Thursday and in July and August. **Metro:** Sevilla. **Bus:** 15, 20, or 150.

Prices: Tickets 1,000–1,500 ptas. ($7.10–$10.70).

Teatro Español, Príncipe, 25. ☎ **429-62-97.**

The company is funded by Madrid's municipal government, its repertoire a time-tested assortment of great and/or favorite Spanish plays. **Metro:** Sevilla.

Prices: Tickets from 1,300 ptas. ($9.20).

Teatro María Guerrero, Tamayo y Baus, 4. ☎ **319-47-69.**

Also funded by the government, it works in cooperation with the Teatro Español (see above) for performances of works by such classic Spanish playwrights as Lope de Vega and García Lorca. The theater was named after a much-loved Spanish actress. **Metro:** Banco d'España or Colón.

Prices: Tickets: 900–2,000 ptas. ($6.40–$14.20).

CLASSICAL MUSIC

Auditorio Nacional de Música, Príncipe de Vergara, 136. ☎ **337-01-00.**

Sheathed in slabs of Spanish granite, marble, and limestone and capped with Iberian tiles, this hall is the ultramodern home of both the National Orchestra of Spain and the National Chorus of Spain. Standing just north of Madrid's Salamanca district, it ranks as a major addition to the competitive circles of classical music in Europe. Inaugurated in 1988, it is devoted exclusively to the performances of symphonic, choral, and chamber music. In addition to the Auditorio Principal (Hall A), whose capacity is almost 2,300, there's a hall for chamber music (Hall B), as well as a small auditorium (seating 250) for intimate concerts. **Metro:** Cruz del Rayo.

Prices: Tickets 1,500–4,000 ptas. ($10.70–$28.40).

The Major Concert/Performance Halls

Auditorio Nacional de Música, Príncipe de Vergara, 136. ☎ **337-01-00.**

Auditorio del Real Conservatorio de Música, Plaza Isabel II. ☎ **337-01-00.**

Centro Cultural de la Villa, Plaza de Colón. ☎ **532-57-62.**

Teatro Calderón, Atocha, 18. ☎ **369-14-34.**

Teatro de la Comedia, Príncipe, 14. ☎ **521-49-31.**

Teatro Español, Príncipe, 25. ☎ **429-62-97.**

Teatro María Guerrero, Tamayo y Baus, 4. ☎ **319-47-69.**

Auditorio del Parque de Atracciones, Casa de Campo.

The schedule of this 3,500-seat facility might include everything from punk-rock musical groups to the more highbrow warm-weather performances of visiting symphony orchestras. Check with Localidades Galicia to see what's on at the time of your visit (see "The Performing Arts" above). **Metro:** Lago or Batán.

Auditorio del Real Conservatorio de Música, Plaza Isabel II. ☎ **337-01-00.**

This is one of the home bases of the Spanish Philharmonic Orchestra, which presents its concerts between September and May. When it's not performing, the space is sometimes lent to relatively unknown musical newcomers, who perform at admission-free concerts. The auditorium also presents concerts by chamber-music ensembles visiting from abroad. Containing only about 400 seats, the hall is sometimes sold out long in advance, especially for such famous names as Plácido Domingo. **Metro:** Opera.

Prices: Tickets 1,500–7,500 ptas. ($10.70–$53.30).

Fundación Juan March, Castelló, 77. ☎ **435-42-40.**

This foundation sometimes holds free concerts at lunchtime. The advance schedule is difficult to predict, so call for information. **Metro:** Núñez de Balboa.

BALLET

Centro Cultural de la Villa, Plaza de Colón. ☎ **573-57-62.**

Spanish-style ballet is presented at this cultural center. Tickets go on sale five days before the event of your choice, and performances are usually presented at two evening shows (8 and 10:30pm). **Metro:** Serrano or Colón.

Prices: Tickets, depending on event, 1,200–4,000 ptas. ($8.50–$28.40).

FLAMENCO

Café de Chinitas, Torija, 7. ☎ **559-5135.**

Known throughout Madrid as one of the best flamenco clubs in town, the Café de Chinitas is set one floor above street level in a 19th-century building midway between the Ópera and the Gran Vía.

It features an array of (usually) gypsy-born flamenco artists from Madrid, Barcelona, and Andalusia, whose acts and performers change about once a month. You can arrange for dinner before the show, although many Madrileños opt for dinner somewhere else, and then arrive just for drinks and the flamenco. Open Monday to Saturday, with dinner served from 9 to 11pm, and the show lasting from 10:30pm to 2am. Reservations are recommended. **Metro:** Santo Domingo. **Bus:** 1 or 2.

Admission: Dinner and show 8,000 ptas. ($56.80); cover charge for show without dinner (but with one drink included) 3,900 ptas. ($27.70).

Corral de la Morería, Morería, 17. ☎ **365-84-46.**

In the old town, the Morería—meaning "where the Moors reside"—sizzles with flamenco. Strolling performers, colorfully costumed, warm up the audience around 11pm; a flamenco show follows, with at least 10 dancers. It's much cheaper to eat somewhere else first, paying only the one-drink minimum. Open daily from 9pm to 3am. **Metro:** La Latina or Puerta del Sol.

Admission: One-drink minimum 3,800 ptas. ($27); 9,500 ptas. ($67.50) with dinner.

Zambra, in the Hotel Wellington, Velásquez, 8. ☎ **435-49-28.**

Since 1986, some of the best flamenco singers and dancers of Spain appear here every night in front of enthusiastic audiences. Reservations are a good idea. If no one answers the telephone, call the reception desk at the Hotel Wellington (☎ **575-44-00**). Open Monday to Saturday from 9:30pm to 3am; show at 10:15pm. **Metro:** Velázquez.

Prices: 3,750 ptas. ($26.60) show; 9,500 ptas. ($67.50) show and dinner.

Teatro Nuevo Apolo, Plaza de Tirso de Molina, 1. ☎ **369-14-67.**

The Nuevo Apolo is the permanent home of the renowned Antología de la Zarzuela company. It is on the restored site of the old Teatro Apolo, where these musical variety shows were performed since the 1930s. Prices and times depend on the show. The box office is open daily from 11:30am to 1:30pm and 5 to 8pm; show times vary. **Metro:** Tirso de Molina.

Prices: Usually 2,500 ptas. ($17.80).

Teatro Lírico Nacional de la Zarzuela, Jovellanos, 4. ☎ **429-82-25.**

Near Plaza de la Cibeles, this theater of potent nostalgia produces ballet and an occasional opera in addition to zarzuela. Show times vary. **Metro:** Sevilla.

Prices: 1,100–4,500 ptas. ($7.80–$32).

The Club & Music Scene

CABARET

Madrid's nightlife is no longer steeped in prudishness, as it was (at least officially) during the Franco era. You can now see glossy cabarets and shows with lots of nudity.

Las Noches De Cuple, La Palma, 51. ☎ **533-71-15.**

If you don't mind going to bed at sunrise, you might enjoy this updated version of a once-celebrated Madrileño cabaret. Its entrance is on a narrow crowded street. Inside, in a long room with a vaulted ceiling and a tiny stage, Señora Olga Ramos conducts an evening of Iberian song. The charm of her all-Spanish act is increased by the discreet humor of an octogenarian accompanist with an ostrich-feather tiara and a fuchsia-colored boa. Open Monday to Saturday from 9:30pm to 2:30am; shows at midnight. Drinks begin at 1,100 ptas. ($7.80); dinner from 7,500 ptas. ($53.30). **Metro:** Noviciado.

Admission: One-drink minimum 3,000 ptas. ($21.30).

Scala Melía Castilla, Calle Capitán Haya, 43 (entrance at Rosario Pino, 7). ☎ **571-44-11.**

Madrid's most famous dinner show is a major Las Vegas–style spectacle, with music, water, light, and color. The program is varied—you might see international or

Spanish ballet, magic acts, ice skaters, whatever. Most definitely you'll be entertained by a live orchestra. It is open Monday through Saturday from 8:30pm to 3am. Dinner is served beginning at 9pm; the show is presented at 10:30pm. The show with dinner costs 8,500 pesetas ($60.40), and if you partake you don't have to pay the admission charge below, as it's included in the show/dinner price. Reservations are needed. **Metro:** Cuzco.

Admission (including first drink): 4,700 ptas. ($33.40).

JAZZ

Café Berlin/Oba-Oba, Jacometrezo, 4.

This place is really two clubs in one. In the basement is Oba-Oba (☎ **531-06-40**), whose specialty is Caribbean- and Brazilian-inspired jazz, to which an animated clientele dances the lambada, the salsa, and an occasional pasadoble. Upstairs, the Café Berlin (☎ **531-08-10**) has live jazz. Open daily from 6pm to 4 or 5am. Drinks begin at 750 ptas. ($5.30). **Metro:** Callao.

Café Central, Plaza del Angel, 10. ☎ **468-08-44.**

Off the Plaza de Santa Ana, beside the famed Gran Hotel Victoria, the Café Central has a vaguely art deco interior, with an unusual series of stained-glass windows. Many of the customers read newspapers and talk at the marble-top tables during the day, but the ambience is far more animated during the nightly jazz sessions. Open Monday to Thursday from 1pm to 1:30am, Friday to Sunday from 1pm to 2:30am; live jazz is offered daily from 10pm to 2am. Drinks begin at 400 pesetas ($2.80). **Metro:** Antón Martín.

Admission: Cover charge, Mon–Thurs 500 ptas. ($3.60); Fri–Sun 600 ptas. ($4.30)—but prices vary depending on show.

Café Populart, Calle Huertas, 22. ☎ **429-84-07.**

This club is known for its exciting jazz groups, who encourage the audience to dance. It specializes in Brazilian, Afro-bass, reggae, and "new African wave" music. When the music starts, the prices of drinks are nearly doubled. Open daily from 6pm to 4 or 5am. Beer is 350 ptas. ($2.50), whisky is 650 ptas. ($4.60)—when live music isn't playing. **Metro:** Antón Martín or Sevilla. **Bus:** 6 or 60.

Calalú, Park Hyatt Villa Magna, Paseo de la Castellana, 22. ☎ **576-75-00.**

Calalú, run by what many view as the city's most elegant deluxe hotel, is the only terrace in Madrid where you can enjoy live jazz performed Tuesday through Saturday. The relaxed atmosphere comes alive with melodic rhythms ranging in sound from New Orleans to Brazil. It's a warm and vibrant place to enjoy an evening with friends, tropical drinks, and tasty food. Calalú offers different kinds of Cajun-style apéritifs and a variety of appetizers to go with your drinks. Waiters are outfitted in black trousers, white shirts, bow ties, and bowler hats. Potted palms, subdued lighting, and intimate table lamps create the illusion of a tropical island in the center of Madrid. Open daily from 10pm to 2am. **Metro:** Rubén Darío.

Admission: Drinks from 900 ptas. ($6.40).

Clamores, Albuquerque, 14. ☎ **445-79-38.**

With dozens of small tables and a huge bar in its dark and smoky interior, Clamores is the largest and one of the most popular jazz clubs in Madrid. Established in the early 1980s, it has thrived because of its changing venues of American and Spanish jazz bands who have appeared here. The place is open daily from 6pm to around 3am, but jazz is presented only Tuesday to Saturday. On those nights, performances begin at 11:30pm with an additional show every Saturday night at 1:30am. Cover charges vary with the popularity of the act, but usually range from 500 pesetas ($3.60) to 800 pesetas ($5.70). There are no live performances on Sunday or Monday nights, when the format is recorded disco music and there's no cover charge. Regardless of the night of the week you consume them, drinks begin at around 700 pesetas ($5) each. **Metro:** Bilbao.

Whisky Jazz, Diego de León, 7. ☎ **561-11-65.**

Madrid's leading jazz center, Whisky lies off the Calle de Serrano near the American Embassy. There is no number on the oak door. The memorabilia on the walls reveal a reverence for jazz—letters and faded photographs of the greats from New Orleans, Kansas City, and Chicago. Jazz groups appear frequently; otherwise, the management plays jazz recordings. Open Monday to Saturday from 9pm to 3:30am. Drinks are 1,000 pesetas ($7.10). **Metro:** Nuñez de Balboa.

Admission: 1,000 ptas. ($7.10).

DANCE CLUBS

The Spanish dance club takes its inspiration from those of other Western capitals. In Madrid most clubs are open from around 6pm to 9pm, reopening around 11pm. They generally start rocking at midnight or thereabouts.

Archy, Calle Marqués de Riscal, 11. ☎ **308-31-62.**

In the cellar of an old apartment building, this art deco–style dance club is fashionable as of this minute. If you're a woman, it's best to show up looking like a young Cher if you'd like to join what Madrileños call *gente guapa* (the beautiful people). Leave your T-shirts and jeans back in the hotel room or else the security guards may not let you in. There's also an elegant restaurant and pub here. Hours are from 9pm to 5am daily. Drinks range from 790 to 1,200 pesetas ($5.60–$8.50). **Metro:** Colón.

Admission: No cover.

Joy Eslava, Arenal, 11. ☎ **366-37-33.**

This former movie theater has been converted into a high-tech nightspot that's filled with an array of lights and sound equipment. Comfortable chaise longues are scattered throughout for those who don't feel like dancing. It's slightly more expensive on weekends, but that's when it's the most fun. Open daily from 11:30pm to 7am. Drinks are 1,200 pesetas ($8.50). **Metro:** Puerta del Sol or Ópera.

Admission: 2,000 ptas. ($14.20).

Vog, Padre Damian, 23. ☎ **350-6444.**

Set in an upscale neighborhood north of Madrid's center, on the street level of a hotel and office grouping known as the Eurobuilding complex, this is one of Madrid's leading nightspots. It prides itself on maintaining an allure for a well-heeled clientele, many of whom show up in expensively chic dresses and jackets and neckties. Suitably dressed newcomers apply for membership in what is almost considered a semi-private club, especially on those evenings when it's reserved for private parties. Open Monday to Saturday from midnight to 5am. Drinks cost 1,800 to 2,300 pesetas ($12.80–$16.30). **Metro:** Colombia or Cuzco.

Admission: Fri–Sat nights 2,000 ptas. ($14.20), otherwise free.

The Bar Scene

PUBS & BARS

BALMORAL, Hermosilia, 10. ☎ **431-41-33.**

Its exposed wood and comfortable chairs evoke a London club. The clientele tends toward journalists, politicians, army brass, owners of large estates, bankers, diplomats, and an occasional literary star. *Newsweek* magazine once dubbed it one of the "best bars in the world." No food other than tapas is served. Open daily from 7:30pm to 2am. Beer is 400 pesetas ($2.80); drinks are from 800 pesetas ($5.70). **Metro:** Serrano.

Balneario, Juan Ramón Jiménez, 37. ☎ **458-24-20.**

Clients enjoy potent drinks in a setting with fresh flowers, white marble, and a stone bathtub that might have been used by Josephine Bonaparte. Near Chamartín Station on the northern edge of Madrid, Balneario is one of the most stylish and upscale bars in the city. It is adjacent to and managed by one of Madrid's most elegant and prestigious restaurants, El Cabo Mayor, and often attracts that dining room's clients for apéritifs or after-dinner drinks. Tapas include endive with smoked salmon, asparagus mousse, and anchovies with avocado. Open Monday to Saturday from noon to 2:30am. Drinks are 550 to 950 pesetas ($3.90–$6.70); tapas are 550 to 1,750 pesetas ($3.90–$12.40). **Metro:** Cuzco.

Bar Cock, De la Reina, 16. ☎ **532-28-26.**

This bar attracts some of the most visible artists, actors, models, and filmmakers in Madrid, among them award-winning Spanish director Pedro Almódovar, although he has his own bar nowadays. The name comes from the word cocktail, or so they say. The decoration is elaborately unique, in contrast to the hip clientele. Open Monday to Saturday from 9pm to 3am; closed December 24 to 31. Drinks are 700 pesetas ($5). **Metro:** Gran Vía.

Los Gabrieles, Echegaray, 17. ☎ **429-62-61.**

Located in the heart of one of Madrid's most visible warren of narrow streets, in a district that pulsates with after-dark nightlife options, this historic bar served throughout most of the 19th century as the sales outlet for a Spanish wine merchant. In the 1980s, its two rooms were transformed into a bar and café, where you can admire lavishly tiled walls with detailed scenes of courtiers, dancers, and Andalusian maidens peering from behind mantillas and fans. Open daily from 1pm to 2:30am. Beer costs 350 pesetas ($2.50). **Metro:** Tirso de Molina.

Hanoi, Hortaleza, 81. ☎ **319-66-72.**

Its setting is stylish and minimalist—stainless steel, curving lines, and sharp angles—and its clients are fun, young, attractive, and articulate. They include a bevy of male and female models who seem to be in constant attendance. The atmosphere is comfortable for both straights and gays. Eight video screens show films from long-defunct TV series, and the music is up to date; there is a small restaurant out back. Open daily from 9:30pm to 3:30am. Drinks begin at 850 pesetas ($6). **Metro:** Alonso Martínez.

Hispano Bar/Buffet, Paseo de la Castellana, 78. ☎ **411-48-76.**

This establishment does a respectable lunch trade every day for members of the local business community, who crowd in to enjoy the amply portioned *platos del día.* These might include a platter of roast duck with figs or orange sauce, or a suprême of hake. After around 5pm, however, the ambience becomes that of a busy after-office bar, patronized by stylishly dressed women and many local entrepreneurs. The hubbub continues on into the night. Open daily from 1:30pm to 1:30am. Full meals at lunchtime cost from around 3,500 pesetas ($24.90), while beer, depending on the time of day you order it, ranges from 250 pesetas ($1.80) to 350 pesetas ($2.50). **Metro:** Nuevos Ministerios.

Mr. Pickwick's, Marqués de Urquijo, 44 (at the corner of Paseo del Pintor Rosales). ☎ **559-51-85.**

For homesick English expatriates, no other establishment in Madrid better captures the pub atmosphere than Mr. Pickwick's, a 10-minute walk from the Plaza de España. Although only a few of the staff speak fluent English, the decor includes everything you would expect in London: framed prints of Dickens' characters, brass hunting horns, and pewter and ceramic beer mugs. Loners can drink at the bar, or you can sit at one of the small tables, sinking into the soft sofas and armchairs. Open daily from 6pm to 1am. Beer begins at 340 pesetas ($2.40); whisky begins at 700 pesetas ($5). **Metro:** Argüelles.

Oliver Piano Bar, Almirante, 12. ☎ **521-73-79.**

Oliver Piano Bar, off the Paseo de la Castellana, is a pub-style hangout for show-biz people, with a good sprinkling of foreign personalities. The bar feels like a drawing room or library, and there are two club rooms, each with its own personality. The first floor has sofas and comfortable armchairs arranged for conversational gatherings. Reached by a curving stairway, the downstairs room is more secluded. On either side of the fireplace are shelves with an eclectic collection of records (you can pick the ones you want played) and books on theater, movies, and painting. Open daily from 4pm to 4am. Beer is 450 pesetas ($3.20); drinks begin at 750 pesetas ($5.30). **Metro:** Chueca. **Bus:** 70.

Palacio Gaviria, Calle del Arenal, 9. ☎ **526-6069.**

Its construction in 1847 was heralded as the architectural triumph of one of the era's most flamboyant aristocrats, the Marqués de Gaviria. Famous as one of the paramours of Queen Isabel II, he outfitted his palace with the ornate jumble of neoclassical and baroque styles that later became known as "Isabelino." In 1993, after extensive renovations, the building was opened to the public as a concert hall for the occasional presentation of classical music, and as a late-night cocktail bar. Ten high-ceilinged rooms now function as richly decorated, multi-purpose areas for guests to wander in, drinks in hand, reacting to whatever, or whomever, happens to be there at the time. (One room is discreetly referred to as the bedroom-away-from-home of the queen herself.) No food is served, but the libations include a stylish list of cocktails and wines. At presstime, talks were underway for the presentation of either disco music or a cabaret, perhaps during the lifetime of this edition, depending on their marketability within the historic setting. Open Sunday through Wednesday 9:30pm to 3am; Thursday 9:30pm to 4am, and Friday and Saturday 9:30pm to 5:30am.

Admission: 1,500 ptas. ($10.70), including first drink. Second drink from 1,000 ptas. ($7.10) to 1,750 ptas. ($12.40). **Metro:** Puerta del Sol or Ópera.

Viva Madrid, Manuel Fernández y González, 7. ☎ **410-55-35.**

A congenial mix of students, artists, foreign tourists, and visiting Yanks crams into its turn-of-the-century interior, where tilework murals and carved animals contribute an undeniable charm. Crowded and noisy, it is a place where lots of beer is swilled and spilled. It's located in a neighborhood of narrow streets near the Plaza de Santa Ana. Open Sunday to Friday from noon to 1am, Saturday from noon to 2am. Beer is 450 pesetas ($3.20); drinks begin at 800 pesetas ($5.70). **Metro:** Antón Martín.

GAY & LESBIAN BARS

Black and White, Gravina (at the corner of Libertad). ☎ **531-11-41.**

This is the major gay bar of Madrid, located in the center of the Chueca district. A guard will open the door to a large room—painted, as you might expect, black and white. There's a disco in the basement, but the street-level bar is the premier gathering spot, featuring drag shows, male striptease, and videos. Old movies are shown against one wall. Open daily from 8pm to 5am. Drinks are 450 pesetas ($3.20). **Metro:** Chueca.

Café Figueroa, Augusto Figueroa, 17 (at the corner of Hortaleza). ☎ **521-16-73.**

This turn-of-the-century café attracts a diverse clientele, including a large number of gay men and lesbians. It's one of the city's most popular gathering spots for drinks and conversations. Open daily from 1pm to 2am. Drinks are 400 pesetas ($2.80); beer is 350 pesetas ($2.50). **Metro:** Chueca.

Cruising, Perez Galdos, 5. ☎ **521-51-43.**

Considered one of the predominant gay bars of Madrid, a center for gay consciousness-raising and gay cruising (as its name suggests), this place has probably been visited at least once by virtually every gay male in Castile. It doesn't get crowded or lively until late at night. Open daily from 10:30pm to 3am. Beer costs from 450 pesetas ($3.20). **Metro:** Chueca.

Duplex, Hortaleza, 64. ☎ **531-37-92.**

Attracting a young crowd of disco-loving gays, straights, and lesbians, this bar contains a modern decor, a disco with recent and very danceable music, and an amply stocked bar. Open Friday and Saturday from 10pm to 5am. Drinks are 800 pesetas ($5.70); beer is 450 pesetas ($3.20). **Metro:** Chueca.

No Sé los Digas a Nadie, Ventura de la Vega, 7. ☎ **420-29-80.**

"Don't Tell Mama" defines itself as a politically correct women's entertainment center, although it seems to attract an almost equal number of men to its two floors, hidden behind a black garage door on this street of budget restaurants. Inside, there is an art gallery, a bar/café, a mostly lesbian staff with information on women's activities in Madrid, and live or recorded music every evening after 11pm. Open Tuesday through Saturday from 9:30pm to 3 or 4am. Drinks range from 350 to 800 pesetas ($2.50 to $5.70). **Metro:** Puerta del Sol, Sevilla, or Antón Martín.

SUMMER TERRAZAS

At the first of the spring weather, Madrileños rush outdoors to drink, talk, and sit at a string of open-air cafés throughout the city. The best ones—and also the most expensive—are along Paseo de la Castellana between Plaza de la Cibeles and Plaza Emilio Castelar, but there are dozens more throughout the city.

You can wander up and down the boulevard, selecting one that appeals to you; if you get bored, you can go on later to another one. Sometimes these terrazas are called chirinquitos. You'll also find them along other paseos, the Recoletos and the Prado, both fashionable areas, although not as hip as the Castellana. For old, traditional atmosphere, the terrazas at Plaza Mayor win out. The terrazas of Plaza Santa Ana also have several atmospheric choices within the old city. Friday and Saturday are the most popular nights for drinking; many locals sit here all night.

CAVE CRAWLING

To capture a peculiar Madrid joie de vivre of the 18th century, visit some mesones and cuevas, many found in the so-called *barrios bajos.* From the Plaza Mayor, walk down the Arco de Cuchilleros until you find a gypsylike cave that fits your fancy. Young people love to meet in the taverns and caves of Old Madrid for communal drinking and songfests. The sangría flows freely, the atmosphere is charged, and the room usually is packed; the sound of guitars wafts into the night air. Sometimes you'll see a strolling band of singing students (*tuna*) go from bar to bar, colorfully attired, with ribbons fluttering from their outfits.

Mesón Austrias. Cava de San Miguel, 11. No phone.

One of several tapas bars just behind Plaza Mayor, Mesón Austrias has a number of sit-down cells stretching off toward a second bar in the rear. Most customers prefer to stand near the front entrance. In winter the favorite spot is in front of the open fireplace in the front room, when a pitcher of sangría is the thing to order. There's often accordion music at night. Open daily from 6:30pm to 1:30am. Beer is 300 pesetas ($2.10); a pitcher of sangría is 1,200 pesetas ($8.50); tapas begin at 550 pesetas ($3.90). **Metro:** Puerta del Sol or Ópera.

Mesón del Champiñón, Cava de San Miguel, 17. No phone.

The bartenders keep a brimming bucket of sangría behind the long stand-up bar as a thirst quencher for the crowd. The name of the establishment in English is Mushroom, and that is exactly what you'll see depicted in various sizes along sections of the vaulted ceilings. A more appetizing way to experience a champiñón is to order a ración of grilled, stuffed, and salted mushrooms, served with toothpicks and accompanied by beer, for 500 pesetas ($3.60). Two tiny, slightly dark rooms in the back are where Spanish families go to hear organ music performed. Unless you want to be exiled to the very back, don't expect to sit down here. Practically everybody prefers to stand. Open daily from 6pm to 2am. Sangría is 1,200 pesetas ($8.50); tapas begin at 500 pesetas ($3.60). **Metro:** Puerta del Sol or Ópera.

Mesón de la Guitarra, Cava de San Miguel, 13. ☎ **559-95-31.**

My favorite cueva in the area, Mesón de la Guitarra is loud and exciting on any night of the week, and it's as warmly earthy as anything you'll find in Madrid. The decor combines terra-cotta floors, antique brick walls, hundreds of sangría pitchers clustered above the bar, murals of gluttons, old rifles, and faded bullfighting posters. Like most things in Madrid, the place doesn't get rolling until around 10:30pm, although you can stop in for a drink and tapas earlier. Don't be afraid to start singing an American song if it has a fast rhythm—60 people will join in, even if they don't know the words. Open daily from 6:30pm to 1:30am. Beer is 175 pesetas ($1.20); wine is from 150 pesetas ($1.10); tapas are 500 to 700 pesetas ($3.60 to $5). **Metro:** Puerta del Sol or Ópera.

Sesamo, Príncipe, 7. ☎ **429-65-24.**

In a class by itself, this cueva, dating from the early 1950s, draws a clientele of young painters and writers with its bohemian ambience. Hemingway was one of those early visitors (a plaque commemorates him). At first you'll think you're walking into a tiny snack bar—and you are. But proceed down the flight of steps to the cellar. Here, the walls are covered with contemporary paintings and quotations. At squatty stools and tables, an international assortment of young people listens to piano music and sometimes folk singing or guitar playing. Open daily from 6:30pm to 2am. A pitcher of sangría (for four) is 1,200 pesetas ($8.50). Beer costs 300 pesetas ($2.10). **Metro:** Sevilla or Puerta del Sol.

More Entertainment

MOVIES Cinematic releases from Paris, New York, Rome, and Hollywood come quickly to Madrid, where an avid audience often waits in long lines for tickets. Most foreign films are dubbed into Spanish, unless they're indicated as VO (original version).

Madrid boasts at least 90 legitimate movie houses (many of which have several theaters under one roof) and many others with adult entertainment only. The premier theaters of the city are the enormous, slightly faded movie palaces of the Gran Vía, whose huge movie marquees announce in lurid colors whichever romantic or adventure *espectáculo* happens to be playing at the moment. For listings, see *Guía de Ocio*, *Guía de Diario 16* (also available at newsstands), or a newspaper.

If you want to see a film while in Madrid, one of the best places is the quadruplex **Alphaville,** Martín de los Heros, 14 (☎ **559-38-36; Metro:** Plaza de España). It shows English-language films with Spanish subtitles. If the film is not too long, there are four daily showings at 4:30pm, 6:30pm, 8:30pm, and 10:30pm. On Saturday and Sunday, there's a midnight show at 12:30am. The complex also includes a bookstore and a café decorated in an art deco style.

For classic revivals and foreign films, check the listings at Filmoteca in the *Cine Doré*, Santa Isabel, 3 (☎ **369-11-25; Metro:** Antón Martín). Movies here tend to be shown in their original language. Tickets cost around 300 pesetas ($2.10). There is a bar and a simple restaurant.

A CASINO The **Casino Gran Madrid** is at Km. 28,300 de la Ctra. Nacional VI-Madrid-La Coruña, Apdo 62, Torrelodones 28250 (☎ **856-11-00**). Even nongamblers sometimes make the trek here from the capital; the casino's many entertainment facilities are considered by some to be the most exciting thing around. Its scattered attractions include two restaurants, four bars, and a nightclub. The casino is open Sunday to Thursday from 2pm to 4am; Friday, Saturday, and holiday evenings from 2pm to 5am. For an entrance fee of 500 pesetas ($3.60), you can sample the action in the gaming rooms, including French and American roulette, blackjack, punto y banco, baccarat, and chemin de fer.

An à la carte restaurant in the French Gaming Room offers international cuisine, with dinners costing from 8,000 pesetas ($56.80). A buffet in the American Gaming Room will cost around 3,000 pesetas ($21.30). The restaurants are open from 9:30pm to 2am. The casino is about 17 miles (27km) northwest of Madrid, along the Madrid–La Coruña N-BI highway. If you don't feel like driving, the casino has buses that depart from Plaza de España, 6, every afternoon and evening at 4:30, 6, 7:30, 9, and 11:30pm. Note that between October and June, men must wear jackets and ties; jeans and tennis shoes are forbidden in any season. To enter, European visitors must present an identity card and non-European visitors must present a passport.

6 Excursions from Madrid

MADRID MAKES AN IDEAL BASE FOR EXCURSIONS BECAUSE IT'S SURROUNDED BY SOME of Spain's major attractions. The day trips listed below to both New Castile and Old Castile range from 9 miles to 100 miles (14km to 161km) outside Madrid, allowing you to leave in the morning and be back by nightfall. In case you choose to stay overnight, however, I've included a selection of hotels in each town.

The satellite cities and towns around Madrid include Toledo, with its El Greco masterpieces; El Escorial monastery, considered the eighth wonder of the world; castles that "float" in the clouds in Segovia; and palaces of the Bourbon dynasty at La Granja: Cuenca, which is actually in La Mancha, is the longest excursion; unless you want to spend a good part of the day getting there and back, you might consider it for an overnight stopover. For a selection of other cities in Old Castile—each of which is better visited on an overnight stopover rather than a day trip from Madrid—refer to Chapter 7, Old Castile, coming up.

Seeing the Environs of Madrid

The speed of the itinerary below can be achieved only by car. Using public transportation would take twice as long. Therefore, if you have only a week and don't have a car, travel by train or bus from Madrid, taking in only the most important attractions: Toledo, El Escorial, Segovia, and Ávila, in that order.

Day 1 Leave Madrid and drive south to Aranjuez, visiting the Bourbon palace and gardens and continuing southwest to Toledo for the night.

Day 2 Explore Toledo and spend the night.

Day 3 In the morning head northwest for Ávila, exploring its attractions in the afternoon. Stay overnight.

Day 4 Drive northeast to Segovia. Visit the city at leisure and stay overnight.

Day 5 Still in Segovia, spend the day at La Granja, then drive through the snowcapped Guadarrama Mountains.

Day 6 Head southeast toward Madrid. Spend the day exploring the monastery of San Lorenzo de El Escorial, with a side trip to the Valley of the Fallen. Stay overnight in El Escorial (limited accommodations) or return to Madrid.

1 Toledo

42 miles SW of Madrid, 85 miles SE of Ávila

GETTING THERE • By Train RENFE trains run here frequently every day. Those departing Madrid's Atocha Railway Station for Toledo run daily from 8:15am to 8:55pm; those leaving Toledo for Madrid run daily from 6:25am to 9:50pm. Traveling time is approximately 90 minutes. For train information in Madrid call **527-31-60;** in Toledo call **22-12-72.**

• By Bus Buses are faster and more direct than trains. Continental Galiano (☎ **22-29-61**) runs about 12 different buses daily. They depart Madrid every half hour daily from 6:30am to 10pm from the lower level of the Estación Sur de Autobuses, Canarías, 17. (Take the Metro to Palos de la Frontera). Buses take about 1¼ hours to complete the trip between Madrid and Toledo and are usually marked "Santa Bárbara" or "Poligano." In Toledo, you'll be deposited at the Estación Sur de Autobuses on the outskirts of central Toledo, where you can either walk into town or else take a city bus.

What's Special About Castile

Great Towns/Villages

- Toledo, El Greco's hometown and religious center of Spain.
- Segovia, "a mirage of medieval Spain."
- Ávila, whose fairy-tale stone walls earned it the following nickname—Castilian "Disneylandia."

An Ancient Monument

- A Roman aqueduct at Segovia, in use for 2,000 years.

Architectural Highlights

- The Cathedral at Toledo.
- The Monastery of San Lorenzo de El Escorial, a mammoth repository of paintings and tapestries.
- The Alcazar at Segovia, the structure that inspired the romantic fantasy of "castles in Spain."
- The *casas colgadas,* cliff-hanging houses of Cuenca.

Grand Palaces

- The Royal Palace at Aranjuez, spring and fall home of the Bourbons.
- La Granja, a miniature Versailles in Castile, summer palace of the Bourbons.

Natural Wonders

- Ciudad Encantada, 25 miles northeast of Cuenca, a "city" created from rocks and boulders.

A Film Location

- The walled city of Ávila, where *The Pride and the Passion* was shot.

A Religious Shrine

- The Convent of St. Teresa at Ávila, dedicated to this much-adored reformer and tireless mystic.

Festivals/Events

- Chinchón's Easter Saturday Passion Play in its ancient Plaza Mayor.
- Toledo's Corpus Christi processions, the most regal in Spain.

• **By Car** Exit Madrid vía Cibeles (Paseo del Prado) and take the N-401 south.

ESSENTIALS Toledo's area code is 925. The tourist information office is at Puerta Nueva de Bisagra (☎ **925/22-08-43**).

If you have only one day for an excursion outside Madrid, go to Toledo—a place made special by its blending of Arab, Jewish, Christian, and even Roman and Visigothic elements. Declared a national landmark, the city that inspired El Greco in the 16th century has remained relatively unchanged in parts of its central core. You can still stroll through streets barely wide enough for a man and his donkey—much less an automobile.

Surrounded on three sides by a loop of the Tagus River, Toledo stands atop a hill overlooking the arid plains of New Castile—a natural fortress in the center of the Iberian Peninsula. It was a logical choice for the capital of Spain, although it lost its political status to Madrid in the 1500s. But Toledo remains the country's religious center, as the seat of the Primate of Spain.

If you're driving, the much-painted skyline of Toledo will come into view about $3^1/_2$ miles (6km) from the city. But the most awesome moment will follow later, when you cross the 14th-century Puente San Martín spanning the Tagus for a view of the city from its other bank. The scene is reminiscent of El Greco's moody, storm-threatened *View of Toledo,* which hangs in New York's Metropolitan Museum of Art. It is said the artist painted that view from a hillside that is now the site of a government-owned parador. If you arrive at the right time, you can enjoy an apéritif on the parador's terrace and watch one of the famous "violet sunsets" of Toledo.

Another Toledan highlight is the **Carretera de Circunvalación,** the route that threads through the city and runs along the Tagus. Clinging to the hillsides are rustic dwellings, the *cigarrales* of the Imperial City, immortalized by 17th-century dramatist Tirso de Molina, who named his trilogy *Los Cigarrales de Toledo.*

What to See & Do

 **Cathedral,** Arcos de Palacio. ☎ **22-22-41.**

Ranked among the greatest of Gothic structures, the cathedral actually reflects a variety of styles because of the more than two and a half centuries that went into its construction, from 1226 to 1493. The portals have witnessed many historic events, including the proclamation of Joanna the Mad and her husband, Philip the Handsome, as heirs to the throne of Spain.

Among its art treasures, the *transparente* stands out—a wall of marble and florid baroque alabaster sculpture overlooked for years because the cathedral was too poorly lit. Sculptor Narcisco Tomé cut a hole in the ceiling, much to the consternation of Toledans, and now light touches the high-rising angels, a *Last Supper* in alabaster, and a Virgin in ascension.

The 16th-century Capilla Mozárabe, containing works by Juan de Borgona, is another curiosity of the cathedral. Mass is still held here using Mozarabic liturgy.

The Treasure Room has a 500-pound 15th-century gilded monstrance—allegedly made with gold brought back from the New World by Columbus—that is still carried through the streets of Toledo during the feast of Corpus Christi.

Other highlights of the cathedral include El Greco's *Twelve Apostles* and *Spoliation of Christ* and Goya's *Arrest of Christ on the Mount of Olives.*

Admission: Cathedral, free; Treasure Room 350 ptas. ($2.50).

Open: July–Aug, Mon–Sat 10:30am–1pm and 3:30–7pm, Sun 10:30am–1:30pm and 4–7pm; Sept–June, Mon–Sat 10:30am–1pm and 3:30–7:30pm, Sunday 10:30am–1:30pm and 4–6pm. **Bus:** 5 or 6.

Alcázar, Calle General Moscardó, 4, near the Plaza de Zocodover. ☎ **22-30-38.**

The Alcázar, located at the eastern edge of the old city, dominates the Toledo skyline. It became world famous at the beginning of the Spanish Civil War, when it underwent a 70-day siege that almost destroyed it. Today it has been rebuilt and turned into an army museum, housing such exhibits as a plastic model of what the fortress looked like after the Civil War, electronic equipment used during the siege, and photographs taken during the height of the battle. A walking tour gives a realistic simulation of the siege. Allow an hour for a visit.

Admission: 150 ptas. ($1.10) adults; children under 9 free.

Open: Tues–Sun 10am–1:30pm and 4–5:30pm (6:30pm July–Sept). **Bus:** 5 or 6.

Museo de Santa Cruz, Miguel de Cervantes, 3. ☎ **22-10-36.**

Today a museum of art and sculpture, this was originally a 16th-century Spanish Renaissance hospice, founded by Cardinal Mendoza—"the third king of Spain"—who helped Ferdinand and Isabella gain the throne. Look for El Greco's *The Assumption of the Virgin.* Goya and Ribera are also represented, along with a display of gold and opulent antique furnishings, Flemish tapestries, and Visigothic artifacts.

Admission: 225 ptas. ($1.60):

Open: Tues–Sat 10am–6:30pm; Sun 10am–2pm; Mon 10am–2pm and 4:30–6:30pm. **Bus:** 5 or 6. **Directions:** Pass beneath the granite archway on the eastern edge of the Plaza de Zocodover and walk about one block.

Casa y Museo del Greco, Calle Samuel Leví, 3. ☎ **22-40-46.**

Located in Toledo's *antiguo barrio judio* (the old Jewish quarter, a labyrinth of narrow streets on the old town's southwestern edge), the House of El Greco honors the great master painter, although he didn't actually live in this house. In 1585 the artist moved into one of the run-down palace apartments belonging to the marquís of Villena. Although he was to live at other Toledan addresses, he returned to the Villena palace in 1604 and remained there until his death. Only a small part of the original residence was saved from decay. In time, this and a neighboring house became the El Greco museum; today it's furnished with authentic period pieces.

You can visit El Greco's so-called studio, where one of his paintings hangs. The museum contains several more works, including a view of Toledo and three portraits, plus many pictures by various 16th- and 17th-century Spanish artists. The garden and especially the kitchen also merit attention, as does a sitting room decorated in the Moorish style.

Admission: 225 ptas. ($1.60) adults; children under 10 free.

Open: July–Sept, Tues–Sat 10am–1:45pm and 3:30–6:45pm, Sun 10am–1:45pm. Oct–June, Tues–Sat 10am–2pm and 3:30–6pm, Sun 10am–1:45pm. Check with the tourist office to see if it's reopened after a restoration. **Bus:** 5 or 6.

Sínagoga del Tránsito, Calle Samuel Leví. ☎ **22-36-65.**

One block west of the El Greco home and museum stands this once-important house of worship for Toledo's large Jewish population. A 14th-century building, it is noted for its superb stucco Hebrew inscriptions, including psalms inscribed along the top of the walls and a poetic description of the Temple on the east wall. The synagogue is the most important part of the **Museo Sefardí (Sephardic Museum),** which was opened in 1971 and contains art objects as well as tombstones with Hebrew epigraphy, some of which are dated before 1492.

Admission: 200 ptas. ($1.40).

Open: Tues–Sat 10am–2pm and 4–6pm; Sun 10am–2pm. **Bus:** 5 or 6.

Monasterio de San Juan de Los Reyes, Calle Reyes Católicos, 21. ☎ **22-38-02.**

Founded by King Ferdinand and Queen Isabella to commemorate their triumph over the Portuguese at Toro in 1476, the church was started in 1477 according to the plans of architect Juan Guas. It was finished, together with the splendid cloisters, in 1504, dedicated to St. John the Evangelist, and used from the beginning by the Franciscan friars. A perfect example of Gothic-Spanish-Flemish style, San Juan de los Reyes has been restored since the damage caused during Napoleon's invasion and after its abandonment in 1835; since 1954 it has been entrusted again to the Franciscans. The

Environs of Madrid

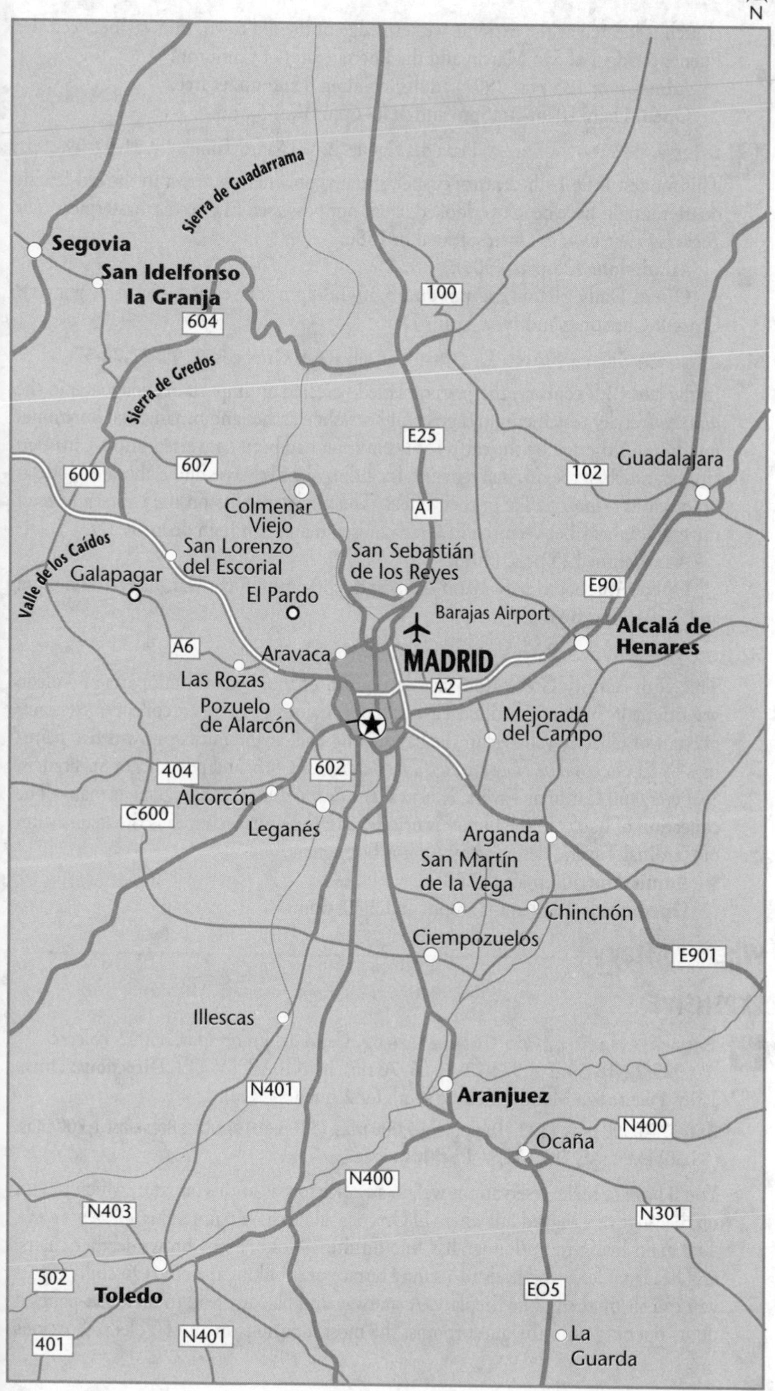

church is located at the extreme western edge of the old town, midway between the Puente (bridge) of San Martín and the Puerta (gate) of Cambron.

Admission: 125 ptas. (90¢) adults; children 8 and under free.

Open: Daily 10am–1:45pm and 3:30–6pm. **Bus:** 5 or 6.

$ **Iglesía de Santo Tomé,** Plaza del Conde, 2, Vía Santo Tomé. ☎ **21-02-09.**

This modest little 14th-century chapel, situated on a narrow street in the old Jewish quarter, might have been overlooked had it not possessed El Greco's masterpiece *The Burial of the Count of Orgaz,* created in 1586.

Admission: 125 ptas. (90¢).

Open: Daily 10am–1:45pm and 3:30–6:45pm (closes at 5:45pm in winter). **Closed:** Christmas and New Year's Day.

Sínagoga de Santa María La Blanca, Calle Reyes Católicos, 2. ☎ **22-72-57.**

In the late 12th century, the Jews of Toledo erected an important synagogue in the *almohade* style, which employs graceful horseshoe arches and ornamental horizontal moldings. Although by the early 15th century it had been converted into a Christian church, much of the original remains, including the five naves and elaborate Mudéjar decorations—mosquelike in their effect. The synagogue lies on the western edge of the city, midway between the El Greco museum and San Juan de los Reyes.

Admission: 125 ptas. (90¢).

Open: Apr–Sept, daily 10am–2pm and 3:30–7pm. Oct–Mar, daily 10am–2pm and 3:30–6pm. **Bus:** 2.

Hospital de Tavera, Paseo de Madrid. ☎ **22-04-51.**

This 16th-century Greco-Roman palace north of the medieval ramparts of Toledo was originally built by Cardinal Tavera; it now houses a private art collection. Titian's portrait of Charles V hangs in the banqueting hall, at the museum owns five paintings by El Greco: *The Holy Family; The Baptism of Christ* and portraits of St. Francis, St. Peter, and Cardinal Tavera. Ribera's *The Bearded Woman* also attracts many. The collection of books in the library is priceless. In the nearby church is the mausoleum of Cardinal Tavera, designed by Alonso Berruguete.

Admission: 500 ptas. ($3.60).

Open: Daily 10:30am–1:30pm and 3:30–6pm.

Where to Stay

EXPENSIVE

★ **Parador Nacional de Conde Orgaz,** Cerro del Emperador, 45002 Toledo. ☎ **925/22-18-50.** Fax 925/22-51-66. 76 rms. MINIBAR TV TEL **Directions:** Drive across Puente San Martín and head south for 2½ miles (4km).

Rates: 10,300 ptas. ($73.10) single; 15,000 ptas. ($106.50) double. Breakfast 1,200 ptas. ($8.50) extra. AE, DC, MC, V. **Parking:** Free.

You'll have to make reservations well in advance to stay at this parador, which is built on the ridge of a rugged hill where El Greco is said to have painted his *View of Toledo.* The main living room/lounge has fine furniture—old chests, brown-leather chairs, and heavy tables—and leads to a sunny terrace overlooking the city. On chilly nights you can sit by the public fireplace. A stairway and balcony lead to dark oak-paneled doors opening onto the guest rooms, the most luxurious in all of Toledo. Spacious and beautifully furnished, they contain private baths and reproductions of regional antique pieces.

Dining/Entertainment: See the restaurant recommendation in "Where to Dine," below.

Services: Room service, laundry/valet.

Facilities: Outdoor swimming pool.

MODERATE

Hostal del Cardenal, Paseo de Recardo, 24, 45005 Toledo. ☎ **925/22-49-00.** Fax 925/22-29-91. 27 rms, 2 suites. A/C TV TEL **Bus:** 2 from rail station.

$ **Rates:** 5,900 pts. ($41.90) single; 9,500 ptas. ($67.50) double; 13,300 ptas. ($94.40) suite. Breakfast 650 ptas. ($4.60) extra. AE, DC, MC, V.

The entrance to this unusual hotel is set into the stone fortifications of the ancient city walls, a few steps from the Bisagra Gate. Inside you'll find flagstone walkways, Moorish fountains, rose gardens, and cascading vines. To reach the hotel, you must climb a series of terraces to the top of the crenellated walls of the ancient fortress. There, grandly symmetrical and very imposing, is the former residence of the 18th-century cardinal of Toledo, Señor Lorenzana. The establishment has tiled walls; long, narrow salons; dignified Spanish furniture; and a smattering of antiques. Each room has a private bath.

Hotel Carlos V, Calle Trastamara, 1, 45001 Toledo. ☎ **925-22-21-00.** Fax 925/22-21-05. 69 rms (all with bath). A/C TEL **Bus:** 5 or 6.

Rates: 7,195 ptas. ($51.10) single; 10,500 ptas. ($74.60) double. Breakfast 645 ptas. ($4.60) extra. AE, DC, MC, V.

This old favorite midway between the Alcázar and the cathedral has a handsome, albeit somber, exterior. It looks more expensive than it is. The rooms are well appointed, and the service is fine. Dining is available, with lunch or dinner costing 2,500 pesetas ($17.80).

Hotel Maria Cristina, Marqués de Mendigorría, 1, 45003 Toledo. ☎ **925/21-32-02.** Fax 925/21-26-50. 60 rms, 3 suites. A/C TV TEL

Rates: 6,995 ptas. ($49.70) single; 10,615 ptas. ($75.40) double; 13,800 ptas. ($98) suite. Breakfast 600 ptas. ($4.30) extra. AE, DC, MC, V. **Parking:** 650 ptas. ($4.60).

Adjacent to the historic Hospital de Tavera and near the northern perimeter of the old town, this stone-sided, awning-fronted hotel resembles a palatial country home. Originally built as a convent and later used as a hospital, it was transformed into this comfortable hostelry in the early 1980s. Sprawling, historic, and generously proportioned, it contains clean and amply sized bedrooms, each attractively but simply furnished and offering a private bath.

Dining/Entertainment: On site is the very large and well-recommended restaurant, El Abside, where fixed-price lunches and dinners begin at 3,000 pesetas ($21.30). There's also a bar.

Services: 24-hour room service, laundry, concierge, babysitting.

Facilities: Tennis courts.

Hotel Pintor El Greco, Alamillos del Tránsito, 13, 45002 Toledo. ☎ **925/21-42-50.** Fax 925/21-58-19. 33 rms (all with bath). A/C TV TEL

Rates: 7,440 ptas. ($52.80) single; 9,300 ptas. ($66) double. Breakfast 650 ptas. ($4.60) extra. AE, DC, MC, V.

In the old Jewish quarter, one of the most tradition-laden and historic districts of Toledo, this hotel was converted from a typical *casa Toledana*, which had once been used as a bakery. With careful restoration, especially of its antique facade, it was converted into one of the Toledo's best and most atmospheric small hotels. The old patio with a fountain was restored, and decoration in both the public rooms and bedrooms is in a traditional Castilian style. Automatic phones, piped-in music, air conditioning, satellite TV, and individual security boxes were added to the immaculately kept bedrooms. At the doorstep of the hotel are such landmarks as the Iglesia de San Juan de los Reyes, Sínagoga de Santa María la Blanca, Sínagoga del Tránsito, Casa y Museo de El Greco, and Iglesia de Santo Tomé.

Hotel Residencia Alfonso VI, Calle General Moscardó, 2, 45001 Toledo. ☎ **925/22-26-00.** Fax 925/21-44-58. 88 rms (all with bath). A/C TV TEL **Bus:** 5 or 6.

Rates: 7,595 ptas. ($53.90) single; 10,900 ptas. ($77.40) double. Breakfast 645 ptas. ($4.60) extra. AE, DC, MC, V.

Although built in the early 1970s, this hotel has been kept up to date. It sits near a great concentration of souvenir shops in the center of the old city, at the southern perimeter of the Alcázar. Inside you'll discover a high-ceilinged, marble-trimmed decor with a scattering of Iberian artifacts, copies of Spanish provincial furniture, and dozens of leather armchairs. There's also a stone-floored dining room, where fixed-price meals cost 2,500 pesetas ($17.80).

INEXPENSIVE

Hotel Residencia Imperio, Calle de las Cadenas, 5, 45001 Toledo. ☎ **925/22-76-50.** Fax 925/25-31-83. 21 rms (all with bath). A/C TV TEL

Rates: 3,700 ptas. ($26.30) single; 5,500 ptas. ($39.10) double. Breakfast 400 ptas. ($2.80) extra. MC, V.

Just off Calle de la Plata, one block west of Plaza de Zocodover, the Imperio is the best bet for those on a tight budget. The rooms are clean and comfortable but small. Most overlook a little church with a wall overgrown with wisteria.

Hotel Maravilla, Plaza de Barrio Rey, 7, 45001 Toledo. ☎ **925/22-33-00.** Fax 925/25-05-58. 18 rms (all with bath). A/C TEL **Bus:** 5 or 6.

Rates: 3,800 ptas. ($27) single; 6,600 ptas. ($46.90) double. Breakfast 500 ptas. ($3.60) extra. AE, MC, V.

If you enjoy hotels with lots of local color, then this little place will please you. It's only one block south of Plaza de Zocodover and opens directly onto its own cobblestone plaza. Semi-modernized in 1971, the building has many bay windows; the bedrooms are modest but adequate, the furnishings so-so. You can hang your laundry on the roof and use an iron in the downstairs laundry room.

Nearby Places to Stay

La Almazara, Carretera Toledo-Argés-Cuerva, KM. 3400, 45080 Toledo. ☎ **925/22-38-66.** 21 rms (all with bath). TEL **Directions:** Follow the road to the Parador of Ciudad Real; then take the C-781 to Cuerva.

Rates: 3,500 ptas. ($24.90) single; 6,000 ptas. ($42.60) double. Breakfast 450 ptas. ($3.20) extra. AE, MC, V.**Closed:** Nov 1–Mar 15. **Parking:** Free.

For readers who have a car or who don't mind one or two taxi rides a day, there are some excellent lodgings across the Tagus. Taking its name from an olive-oil mill that used to stand here, La Almazara offers some of the most offbeat accommodations around. Hidden away in the hills, this old-fashioned country villa, with its own courtyards and vineyards, offers you a rare opportunity to soak up the atmosphere of old Spain, far removed from the pace of city life. It has an exceptional view of Toledo. You may be assigned either a spacious chamber in the main house or a room in the annex. A continental breakfast is served.

Hotel los Cigarrales, Carretera Circunvalacíon, 32, 45000 Toledo. ☎ **925/22-00-53.** Fax 925/21-55-46. 36 rms (all with bath). A/C TEL **Bus:** Chamartín from rail station.

Rates: 3,800 ptas. ($27) single; 5,900 ptas. ($41.90) double. Breakfast 450 ptas. ($3.20) extra. MC, V. **Parking:** Free.

About a mile south of the city center, this hotel offers quiet seclusion. Built in the 1960s in traditional red brick, it looks like a private villa with a garden; the friendliness of the family owners adds to this feeling. Most of the interior is covered with blue and green tiles. The guest rooms are clean, sunny, and decorated with heavy Spanish furniture. Some of the rooms have a terrace with a panoramic view. The dining room offers meals for 1,675 pesetas ($11.90). From the flower-filled terrace of the cozy bar you can see the towers of medieval Toledo.

Where to Dine

MODERATE

Asador Adolfo, La Granada, 6. ☎ **22-73-21.**

Cuisine: SPANISH. **Reservations:** Recommended. **Bus:** 5 or 6.
Prices: Appetizers 650–1,200 ptas. ($4.60–$8.50); main courses 1,850–2,500 ptas. ($13.10–$17.80); fixed-price menus 4,500 ptas. ($32). AE, DC, V.
Open: Lunch, daily 1–4pm; dinner, Mon–Sat 8pm–midnight.

Located less than a minute's walk north of the cathedral, within a warren of narrow medieval streets, Asador Adolfo is considered by many residents to be the finest and most renowned restaurant in Toledo. Sections of the building that contains it were originally built during the 1400s, although recent kitchen renovations have enabled its chefs to prepare many modern variations of traditional Toledo-derived dishes. The ceilings of the several dining rooms are supported by massive beams, and here and there the rooms contain faded frescoes dating from the year of the building's original construction.

The house specialties include different preparations of game dishes, which are said to be among the best anywhere. These might include partridge with white beans, venison, or any of the wild game birds that the region produces in such abundance. Nongame dishes include hake flavored with local saffron and any of a wide array of beef, veal, or lamb dishes. To begin, try the *pimientos rellenos* (red peppers stuffed with pulverized shellfish). The house dessert is marzipan prepared in a wood-fired oven and noted for its lightness.

The restaurant lies at the corner of Calle Hombre de Palo, behind an understated sign.

Casa Aurelio, Calle Sínagoga, 6. ☎ **22-20-97.**

Cuisine: CASTILIAN. **Reservations:** Recommended. **Bus:** 5 or 6.
Prices: Appetizers 600–1,100 ptas. ($4.30–$7.80); main courses 1,90–2,500 ptas. ($1.30–$17.80); fixed-price menu 3,250 ptas. ($23.10). AE, DC, MC, V.
Open: Lunch daily 1–4pm; dinner daily 8–11:30pm.

Established in the late 1940s, Casa Aurelio occupies two separate dining rooms, with two separate entrances, a few feet apart near the northern edge of the cathedral. It's considered one of the restaurant staples of Toledo, offering plentiful food, Castilian ambience, and efficient service. Menu items usually include traditional versions of *sopa castellana*, grilled hake, *lubina à la sal* (whitefish cooked in salt), fresh salmon, roast lamb, and, at certain times of the year, Toledo partridge or roast suckling pig. Note that the main outlet of this restaurant (Calle Sínagoga, 6) is usually closed every Wednesday, although the smaller of the restaurant's two dining rooms (Calle Sínagoga, 1) remains open.

★ **Hostal del Cardenal,** Paseo de Recaredo, 24. ☎ **22-49-00.**

Cuisine: SPANISH. **Reservations:** Required. **Bus:** 2 from the station.
Prices: Appetizers 425–2,200 ptas. ($3–$15.60); main courses 800–2,350 ptas. ($5.70–$16.70); fixed-price menu 2,500 ptas. ($17.80). AE, DC, MC, V.
Open: Lunch, daily 1–4pm; dinner, daily 8:30–11:30pm.

You may want to treat yourself to Toledo's best-known restaurant, owned by the same people who run Madrid's Sobrino de Botín, so beloved by Hemingway. The menu is very similar to that restaurant's. You might begin with "quarter of an hour" (fish) soup or white asparagus, then move on to curried prawns, baked hake, filet mignon, or smoked salmon. Roast suckling pig is a specialty, as is partridge in casserole. Arrive to enjoy a sherry in the bar or in the courtyard.

Parador Nacional de Conde Orgaz, Cerro del Emperador. ☎ **22-18-50.**

Cuisine: CASTILIAN. **Reservations:** Not accepted. **Directions:** Drive across Puente San Martín and head south for 2½ miles (4km).
Prices: Appetizers 1,200–1,500 ptas. ($8.50–$10.70); main courses 2,000–2,600 ptas. ($14.20–$18.50); fixed-price menu 3,600 ptas. ($25.60). AE, DC, MC, V.
Open: Lunch, daily 1–4pm; dinner, daily 8:30–11pm.

Some of the best Castilian regional cuisine is combined here with one of the most panoramic views from any restaurant in Europe. Located in a fine parador, the restaurant is on the crest of a hill—said to be the spot that El Greco selected for his *View of Toledo.* The fixed-price meal might include tasty Spanish hors d'oeuvres, hake, then perhaps either veal or beef grilled on an open fire, plus dessert. If you're dining lightly, try a local specialty, *tortilla española con magra* (potato omelet with ham or bacon). There is a bar on the upper level.

Venta de Aires, Circo Romano, 35. ☎ **22-05-45.**

Cuisine: SPANISH. **Reservations:** Recommended.
Prices: Appetizers 850–1,500 ptas. ($6–$10.70); main courses 1,900–2,500 ptas. ($13.50–$17.80); fixed-price menus 4,500 ($32). AE, DC, MC, V.
Open: Lunch, daily 1–4pm; dinner Mon–Sat 8–11pm.

Just outside the city gates, directly southwest of the Circo Romano (Roman Circus), this restaurant has served Toledo's pièce de résistance—*perdiz* (partridge)—since 1891, when the place was only a little roadside inn. On the à la carte menu, this dish is best eaten with the red wine of Méntrida. For dessert, try the marzipan, an institution in Toledo. On your way out, take note of former President Richard Nixon's entry in the guest book (he dined here in 1963).

INEXPENSIVE

$ El Emperador, Carretera del Valle, 1. ☎ **22-46-91.**

Cuisine: SPANISH. **Reservations:** Recommended. **Bus:** Carretera Valle.
Prices: Appetizers 600–900 ptas. ($4.30–$6.40); main courses 800–1,800 ptas. ($5.70–$12.80); fixed-price menu 1,400 ptas. ($9.90). MC, V.
Open: Lunch Tues–Sun 1–4pm; dinner Tues–Sun 8–11pm.

A modern restaurant on the outskirts of Toledo, southwest of the historic core of the town, near the government parador, El Emperador is reached via an arched bridge. Its terraces overlook the river and the towers of Toledo, while the tavern-style interior has leather- and-wood chairs, heavy beams, and wrought-iron chandeliers. It was established in 1974 by a proud family who still own and manage it today. Service is attentive. The fixed-price menu might include a choice of soup (beef, vegetable, or noodle), followed by a small steak with french fries, then fresh fruit, plus wine.

La Parilla, Horno de los Bizcochos, 8. ☎ **21-22-45.**

Cuisine: SPANISH. **Reservations:** Not accepted. **Bus:** 5 or 6.
Prices: Appetizers 650–950 ptas. ($4.60–$6.70); main courses 1,500–2,200 ptas. ($10.70–$15.60); fixed-price menu 2,300 ptas. ($16.30). AE, DC, MC, V.
Open: Lunch, daily 1–4pm; dinner, daily 8–11pm.

This classic Spanish restaurant, lying within a thick-walled medieval building, stands on a cobbled street near the Hotel Alfonso VI, just east of the cathedral. The menu offers no surprises, but it's reliable. Likely inclusions on the bill of fare are roast suckling pig, spider crabs, Castilian baked trout, stewed quail, baked kidneys, and La Mancha rabbit.

$ Maravilla, Plaza de Barrio Rey, 5. ☎ **22-33-00.**

Cuisine: SPANISH. **Reservations:** Not accepted. **Bus:** 5 or 6.
Prices: Appetizers 650–1,380 ptas. ($4.60–$9.80); main courses 1,300–2,100 ptas. ($9.20–$14.90); fixed-price menus 1,075–1,800 ptas. ($7.60–$12.80). AE, MC, V.
Open: Lunch, Tues–Sun 1–4pm; dinner, Tues–Sun 8–11pm.

Located in the Barrio Rey, a small square off the historic Plaza de Zocodover filled with budget restaurants and cafés that change their names so often it's virtually impossible to keep track, Maravilla offers the best all-round dining bargain. Its kitchen serves a typically Castilian menu, specializing in the famous *perdiz* (partridge) of Toledo but also preparing *cordero asado* (roast lamb).

A TAPAS BAR

Bar Ludeña, Plaza de la Horn Madelena, 13, Corral de Don Diego, 10. ☎ **22-33-84.**

Cuisine: TAPAS. **Reservations:** Not accepted.
Prices: Tapas 250–750 ptas. ($1.80–$5.30). No credit cards.
Open: Thurs–Tues 10am–midnight.

Delectable combinations of tapas are served here to a loyal clientele. Sometimes glasses of wine are passed through a small window to clients who are standing outside enjoying the view of the square. The bar is little more than a narrow corridor, serving *raciones* of tapas that are so generous they make little meals, especially when served with bread. The roasted red peppers in olive oil are especially tasty, along with the stuffed crabs.

Huge dishes of pickled cucumbers, onions, and olives are available. A tiny dining room behind a curtain at the end of the bar serves inexpensive fare.

2 Aranjuez

29 miles S of Madrid, 30 miles NE of Toledo

GETTING THERE • By Train Trains depart about every 20 minutes from Madrid's Atocha Railway Station to make the 50-minute trip to Aranjuez. Trains run less often along the east-west route to and from Toledo (a 40-minute ride). The Aranjuez station lies about a mile outside town. You can walk it in about 15 minutes, but taxis and buses line up on Calle Stuart (two blocks from the city tourist office). The bus that makes the run from the center of Aranjuez to the railway station is marked "N–Z."

• By Bus Buses for Aranjuez depart from Madrid's Estación Sur de Autobuses, Canarias, 17, in Madrid. In Madrid, call 468-45-11 for information. Buses arrive in Aranjuez at the City Bus Terminal, Calle Infantas, 8 (☎ **891-01-83**), in Aranjuez.

• By Car Driving is easy and takes about 30 minutes once you reach the southern city limits of Madrid. To reach Aranjuez, follow the signs to Aranjuez and Granada, taking highway N-IV.

ESSENTIALS The area code for Aranjuez is 91. The tourist information office is at Plaza Puente de Barcas (☎ **91/891-04-27**).

This Castilian town, at a confluence of the Tagus and Jarama Rivers, was the spring and fall home of the Bourbon kings. With its manicured shrubbery, stately elms, fountains, and statues, it remains a regal garden oasis in what is otherwise an unimpressive agricultural flatland known for its strawberries and asparagus.

What to See & Do

Palacio Real, Plaza Palacio. ☎ **891-13-44.**

As you enter the cobblestoned courtyard, you can tell just by the size of the palace that it's going to be spectacular. Ferdinand and Isabella, Philip II, Philip V, and Charles III all made their way through here. The structure you see today dates from 1778 (the previous buildings were destroyed by fire). Its salons show the opulence of a bygone era, room after room of royal extravaganza. Many styles are blended: Spanish, Italian, Moorish, and French. And, of course, no royal palace would be complete without a room reflecting the rage for chinoiserie that once swept over Europe. The Porcelain Salon is also of special interest. A guide conducts you through the huge complex (a tip is expected).

Admission: 600 ptas. ($4.30).

Open: Apr–Sept, Tues–Sun 10am–6:30pm; Oct–Mar, Tues–Sun 10am–5:30pm. **Bus:** Routes from the rail station converge at the square and gardens at the westernmost edge of the palace.

Jardín de la Isla, directly northwest of the Palacio Real. ☎ **891-07-40.**

After the tour of the Royal Palace, wander through the Garden of the Island. Spanish impressionist Santiago Rusiñol captured its evasive quality on canvas, and one Spanish writer said that you walk here "as if softly lulled by a sweet 18th-century sonata." A number of fountain are remarkable: the "Ne Plus Ultra" fountain, the black-jasper fountain of Bacchus, the fountain of Apollo, and the ones honoring Neptune (god of the sea) and Cybele (goddess of agriculture).

You may also stroll through the Jardín del Parterre, located in front of the palace. It's much better kept than the Garden of the Island but not as romantic.

Admission: Free.

Open: Apr–Sept, daily 8am–8:30pm. Oct–Mar, daily 8am–6:30pm.

Casita del Labrador, Calle Reina, Jardín del Príncipe. ☎ **891-13-44.**

The Little House of the Worker, modeled after the Petit Trianon at Versailles, was built in 1803 by Charles IV, who later abdicated in Aranjuez. The queen came here with her youthful lover, Godoy (whom she had elevated to the position of prime minister), and the feeble-minded Charles didn't seem to mind a bit. Surrounded by beautiful gardens, the "bedless" palace is lavishly furnished in the grand style of the 18th and 19th centuries. The marble floors represent some of the finest workmanship of that day, the brocaded walls emphasize the luxurious lifestyle, and the royal john is a sight to behold (in those days, royalty preferred an audience). The clock here is one of the treasures of the house. The *casita* lies half a mile east of the Royal Palace; those with a car can drive directly to it through the tranquil Jardin del Príncipe.

Admission: 400 ptas. ($2.80).

Open: Apr–Sept, Tues–Sun 10am–6:30pm; Oct–Mar, Tues–Sun 10am–5:30pm.

Where to Stay

Hostal Castilla, Carretera Andalucia, 98, 28300 Aranjuez. ☎ **91/891-26-27.**

17 rms (all with bath). MINIBAR TV TEL

Rates: 3,900 ptas. ($27.70) single; 5,100 ptas. ($36.20) double. Breakfast 400 ptas. ($2.80) extra. AE, DC, V.

On one of the town's main streets north of the Royal Palace and gardens, the Castilla consists of the ground floor and part of the first floor of a well-preserved early–18th-century house. Most of the accommodations overlook a courtyard with a fountain and flowers. Owner Joaquin Suarez speaks English fluently. There are excellent restaurants nearby, and the *hostal* has an arrangement with a neighboring bar to provide guests with an inexpensive lunch. This is a good location from which to explore either Madrid or Toledo on a day trip.

Where to Dine

Casa Pablo, Almibar, 42. ☎ **891-14-51.**

Cuisine: SPANISH. **Reservations:** Recommended.

Prices: Appetizers 700–900 ptas. ($5–$6. 40); main courses 1,900–2,500 ptas. ($13.50–$17.80); four-course fixed-price menu 2,700 ptas. ($19.20). MC, V.

Open: Lunch, daily 1–4:30pm; dinner, daily 8pm–midnight. **Closed:** Aug.

An unpretentious and well-managed restaurant near the bus station in the town center, Casa Pablo was established in 1941. At tables set outside under a canopy, you can dine while enjoying the tree-lined street and the red and pink geraniums; in cooler weather you eat either upstairs or in the cozy and clean dining room in the rear. The fixed-price menu includes four courses, a carafe of wine, bread, and service. If it's hot and you don't want a heavy dinner, try a shrimp omelet or half a roast chicken; once I ordered just a plate of asparagus in season, accompanied by white wine. If you want a superb dish, try a fish called *mero* (Mediterranean pollack of delicate flavor), grilled over an open fire.

La Rana Verde, Reina, 1. ☎ **891-32-38.**

Cuisine: SPANISH. **Reservations:** Recommended.
Prices: Appetizers 650–850 ptas. ($4.60–$6); main courses 1,050–2,200 ptas. ($7.50–$15.60); fixed-price menu 2,200 ptas. ($15.60). MC, V.
Open: Daily noon–midnight.

The Green Frog, just east of the Royal Palace and next to a small bridge spanning the Tagus, is still the traditional choice for many. The restaurant looks like a summer house with its high-beamed ceiling and soft ferns drooping from hanging baskets. The preferred tables are in the nooks overlooking the river. As in all the restaurants of Aranjuez, asparagus is a special feature. Game, particularly partridge, quail, and pigeon, can be recommended in season; fish, too, including fried hake and fried sole, makes a good choice. Strawberries are served with sugar, orange juice, or ice cream.

3 San Lorenzo de El Escorial

30 miles W of Madrid; 32 miles SE of Segovia

GETTING THERE • By Train More than two dozen trains depart daily from Madrid's Atocha, Nuevos Ministerios, and Chamartín train stations. During the summer extra coaches are added.

The railway station for San Lorenzo de El Escorial is located about a mile outside of town. The Herranz bus company meets all arriving trains with a shuttle bus that ferries arriving passengers to and from the Plaza Virgen de Gracia, about a block east of the entrance to the monastery.

• By Bus Madrid's Empresa Herranz, Calle Isaac Peral, 10, Moncloa (☎ **543-36-45**), runs about 15 buses daily to El Escorial from the capital. Buses leave passengers at the Plaza Virgen de Gracia, about a block east of the entrance to the monument.

This same company also sells tickets for the single 20-minute trip per day it makes between El Escorial's Plaza Virgen de Gracia and the Valley of the Fallen (see below). A round-trip ticket from El Escorial to this sight costs 565 pesetas ($4). Departure is at 3:15pm; return to El Escorial is at 5:30pm (at 6:15pm in summer).

• By Car Follow the N-VI highway (marked on some maps A8 A-6) from the northwest perimeter of Madrid toward Lugo, La Coruña, and San Lorenzo de El Escorial. After about a half-hour, fork left onto the C-505 toward San Lorenzo de El Escorial. Driving time from Madrid is about an hour.

ESSENTIALS San Lorenzo de El Escorial's area code is 91. The tourist information office is at Floridablanca, 10 (☎ **91/890-15-54**).

Aside from Toledo, the most important excursion from Madrid is the austere Royal Monastery of San Lorenzo de El Escorial. Philip II ordered the construction of this granite-and-slate rectangular monster in 1563, two years after he moved his capital to Madrid. Once the haunt of aristocratic Spaniards, El Escorial is now a resort where hotels and restaurants flourish in summer, as hundreds flock here to escape the heat of the capital. Despite the appeal of its climate, the town of San Lorenzo itself is not very noteworthy. But because of the monastery's size, you might decide to spend a night or two at San Lorenzo—or more if you have the time.

San Lorenzo makes a good base for visiting nearby Segovia and Ávila, the royal palace at La Granja, the Valley of the Fallen—and even the more distant university city of Salamanca.

What to See & Do

Real Monasterio de San Lorenzo de El Escorial, Calle San Lorenzo de El Escorial. ☎ **890-59-02.**

This huge granite fortress houses a wealth of paintings and tapestries and also serves as a burial place for Spanish kings. Foreboding both inside and out because of its sheer size and institutional look, El Escorial took 21 years to complete, a remarkably short time considering the bulk of the building and the primitive construction methods of the day. After his death, Juan Bautista de Toledo, the original architect, was replaced by Juan de Herrera, the greatest architect of Renaissance Spain, who completed the structure in the shape of a gridiron.

Philip II, who collected many of the paintings exhibited here in the New Museums, did not appreciate El Greco and favored Titian instead. But you'll still find El Greco's *The Martyrdom of St. Maurice,* rescued from storage, and his *St. Peter.* Other superb works include Titian's *Last Supper* and Velázquez's *The Tunic of Joseph.*

The Royal Library houses a priceless collection of 60,000 volumes—one of the most significant in the world. The displays range from the handwriting of St. Teresa to medieval instructions on playing chess. See, in particular, the Muslim codices and a Gothic *Cantigas* from the 13th-century reign of Alfonso X ("The Wise").

You can also visit the Philip II Apartments; these are strictly monastic, and Philip called them the "cell for my humble self" in this "palace for God." Philip became a religious fanatic and requested that his bedroom be erected overlooking the altar of the 300-foot-high basilica, which has four organs and whose dome is based on Michelangelo's drawings for St. Peter's. The choir contains a crucifix by Cellini. By comparison, the Throne Room is simple. On the walls are many ancient maps.

The Apartments of the Bourbon Kings are lavishly decorated, in contrast to Philip's preference for the ascetic. The tapestries look like paintings until you examine them closely.

Under the altar of the church you'll find one of the most regal mausoleums in the world, the Royal Pantheon, where most of Spain's monarchs—from Charles I to Alfonso XII, including Philip II—are buried. In 1993, Don Juan de Borbón, the count of Barcelona and the father of King Juan Carlos (Franco "passed over" the count and never allowed him to ascend to the throne) was interred here. Nearby, on a lower floor, is the "Wedding Cake" tomb for children.

Allow about three hours for a visit.

Admission: Comprehensive ticket 800 ptas. ($5.70) adults; 300 ptas. ($2.10) children.

Open: Apr–Sept, daily 10am–7pm; Oct–Mar, daily 10am–6pm.

Casa de Príncipe (Prince's Cottage), Calle Reina, s/n. ☎ **891-03-05.**

This small but elaborately decorated 18th-century palace near the railway station was originally a hunting lodge built for Charles III by Juan de Villanueva. Most visitors stay in El Escorial for lunch, visiting the cottage when it reopens in the afternoon.

Admission: Included in comprehensive ticket to El Escorial, mentioned above.

Open: Tues–Sat 10am–1pm and 3:30–6:30pm.

El Valle de los Caídos (Valley of the Fallen). ☎ **890-56-11.**

This is Franco's El Escorial, an architectural marvel that took two decades to complete, dedicated to those who died in the Spanish Civil War. Its detractors say that it represents the worst of neo-Fascist design; its admirers say they have found renewed inspiration by coming here.

A gargantuan cross that's nearly 500 feet high dominates the Rock of Nava, a peak of the Guadarrama Mountains. Directly under the cross is a basilica in mosaic, completed in 1959. Here José Antonio Primo de Rivera, the founder of the Falange party, is buried. When this Nationalist hero was buried at El Escorial, many, especially influential monarchists, protested that he was not a royal. Infuriated, Franco decided to erect another monument. Originally it was slated to honor the dead on the Nationalist side only, but the intervention of several parties led to a decision to include all the *caídos* (fallen). In time the mausoleum claimed Franco as well; his body was interred behind the high altar.

On the other side of the mountain is a Benedictine monastery that has sometimes been dubbed "the Hilton of monasteries" because of its seeming luxury.

Admission: 400 ptas. ($2.80)

Open: Tues–Sun 10am–7pm (closes at 6pm in winter).

Directions: Drive to the valley entrance, about 5 miles (8km) north of El Escorial in the heart of the Guadarrama Mountains. Once there, drive 3½ miles (6km) west along a dusty road to the underground basilica. **Bus:** Empresa Herranz in El Escorial runs a bus here at 3:15pm, returning at 5:30pm (at 6:15pm in winter); the trip takes 15 minutes. Tour buses from Madrid usually include an excursion to the Valley of the Fallen on their one-day trips to El Escorial. **Funicular:** It extends from near the entrance to the basilica to the base of the gigantic cross erected on the mountaintop above (where there's a superb view). The fare is 250 pesetas ($1.80), and the funicular runs daily from 10:30am to 1:15pm and 4 to 6pm.

Where to Stay

$ **Hostal Cristina,** Juan de Toledo, 6, 28200 San Lorenzo de El Escorial. ☎ **91/890-19-61.** 16 rms (all with bath).

Rates: 4,000 ptas. ($28.40) single; 5,400 ptas. ($38.30) double. Breakfast 350 ptas. ($2.50) extra. MC, V.

An excellent budget choice, this hotel is run by the Delgado family, who opened it in the mid-1980s. About 50 yards from the monastery, it stands in the center of town, offering clean and comfortable rooms. The helpful staff will direct you to their small garden. Since the food is both good and plentiful, many Spanish visitors prefer to book here for a summer holiday. Meals cost from 1,600 pesetas ($11.40).

Hotel Victoria Palace, Calle Juan de Toledo, 4, 28200 San Lorenzo de El Escorial. ☎ **91/890-15-11.** Fax 91/890-12-48. 87 rms. 4 suites (all with bath). TV TEL

Rates: 9,900 ptas. ($70.30) single; 13,750 ptas. ($97.60) double; 25,000 ptas. ($177.50) suite. Breakfast 950 ptas. ($6.70) extra. AE, DC, MC, V. **Parking:** Free.

The Victoria Palace, with its view of El Escorial, is the finest hotel in town, a traditional establishment that has been modernized without losing its special aura of style and comfort. It is surrounded by beautiful gardens and has an outdoor swimming pool. The rooms (some with private terraces) are well furnished and maintained. The rates—reasonable enough, and a bargain for a four-star hotel—also include admission to El Escorial. The dining room serves some of the best food in town, with a meal averaging around 3,500 pesetas ($24.90).

Miranda & Suizo, Calle Floridablanca, 18, 28200 San Lorenzo de El Escorial. ☎ **91/890-47-11.** Fax 91/890-43-58. 48 rms (all with bath). TV

Rates: 6,000 ptas. ($42.60) single; 8,500 ptas. ($60.40) double. Breakfast 500 ptas. ($3.60) extra. AE, DC, MC, V.

On a tree-lined street in the heart of town, within easy walking distance of the monastery, this excellent middle-bracket establishment ranks as a leading two-star hotel. The Victorian-style building has good guest rooms, some with terraces; ten contain TVs. The furnishings are comfortable, the beds often made of brass; sometimes you'll find fresh flowers on the tables. In summer, there is outside dining.

Where to Dine

Charolés, Calle Floridablanca, 24. ☎ **890-59-75.**

Cuisine: SPANISH/INTERNATIONAL. **Reservations:** Required.
Prices: Appetizers 1,075–1,950 ptas. ($7.60–$13.80); main courses 1,450–3,700 ptas. ($10.30–$26.30); fixed-price menu 4,800 ptas. ($34.10). AE, DC, MC, V.
Open: Lunch, daily 1–4pm; dinner, daily 9pm–midnight.

The thick and solid walls of this establishment date, according to its managers, "from the monastic age" and probably pre-date the town's larger and better known monastery of El Escorial. The restaurant contained within was established around 1980, and has been known ever since as the best dining room in town. It has a flower-ringed outdoor terrace for use during clement weather, and a wide choice of menu items based entirely on fresh fish and meats. These include such dishes as grilled hake with green or hollandaise sauce, shellfish soup, monkfish in butter and herb sauce, a succulent charolais of beef with fresh vegetables and herbs, pepper steak, a *pastel* of fresh vegetables with crayfish, and herb-flavored baby lamb chops. Strawberry or kiwi tart is a good dessert choice.

Mesón la Cueva, San Antón, 4. ☎ **890-15-16.**

Cuisine: CASTILIAN. **Reservations:** Recommended.
Prices: Appetizers 850–950 ptas. ($6–$6.70); main courses 1,200–2,200 ptas. ($8.50–$15.60); *menú del día* 3,000 ptas. ($21.30). No credit cards.
Open: Lunch, Tues–Sun 1–4pm; dinner, Tues–Sun 8: 30–11:30pm.

Founded in 1768, this restaurant captures the world of Old Castile, and it lies only a short walk from the monastery. A *mesón típico* built around an enclosed courtyard, "the Cave" boasts such nostalgic accents as stained-glass windows, antique chests, a 19th-century bullfighting collage, faded engravings, paneled doors, and iron balconies. The cooking is on target, and the portions are generous. Regional specialties include Valencian paella and *fabada asturiana* (pork sausage and beans), but fresh trout broiled in butter may be the best of all. The menu's most expensive items are Segovian roast suckling pig and roast lamb (tender inside, crisp outside). Off the courtyard through a separate doorway is La Cueva's *tasca,* filled with Castilians quaffing their favorite before-dinner drinks.

NEAR THE VALLEY OF THE FALLEN

Hostelerie Valle de los Caídos, Valle de los Caídos. ☎ **890-55-11.**

Cuisine: SPANISH. **Reservations:** Not accepted. **Prices:** Appetizers 575–650 ptas. ($4.10–$4.60); main courses 900–1,500 ptas. ($6.39–$10. 70); fixed-price menu 1,200 ptas. ($8.50). No credit cards.
Open: Lunch only, daily 2–4pm.

This restaurant is probably the most likely bet for those heading up into the Valley of the Fallen. Set amid an arid but dramatic landscape halfway along the inclined access road leading to Franco's monuments, and reachable only by car or bus, it's a mammoth modern structure with wide terraces, floor-to-ceiling windows, and a well-established pattern of feeding busloads of foreign tourists. The *menú del día* usually includes such dishes as cannelloni Rossini, pork chops with potatoes, a dessert choice of flan or fruit, and wine.

4 Segovia

54 to 63 miles NW of Madrid; 42 miles NE of Ávila

GETTING THERE • By Train About a dozen trains leave Madrid's Chamartín Railway Station every day and arrive two hours later in Segovia, where you can board bus no. 3, which departs every quarter hour for the Plaza Mayor. The station lies on the Paseo Obispo Quesada, s/n (☎ **42-07-74**), a 20-minute walk southeast of the town center.

• By Bus Buses arrive and depart from the Estacionamiento Municipal de Autobuses, Paseo de Ezequile González, 10 (☎ **42-77-25**), near the corner of the Avenida Fernández Ladreda and the steeply sloping Paseo Conde de Sepúlveda. There are 10 to 15 buses a day to and from Madrid (which depart from Paseo de la Florida, 11; Metro: Norte), and about four a day traveling between Ávila, Segovia, and Valladolid. One-way tickets from Madrid cost around 690 pesetas ($4.90).

• By Car Take the N-VI (on some maps it's known as the A-6) or the Autopista del Nordeste northwest from Madrid, toward León and Lugo. At the junction with Route 110 (signposted Segovia), turn northeast.

ESSENTIALS Segovia's area code is 921. The tourist information office is at Plaza Mayor, 10 (☎ **921/43-03-28**).

Less commercial than Toledo, Segovia, more than anywhere else, typifies the glory of Old Castile. Wherever you look, you'll see reminders of a golden era—whether it's the most spectacular Alcázar on the Iberian Peninsula or the well-preserved, still-functioning Roman aqueduct.

Segovia lies on the slope of the Guadarrama Mountains, where the Eresma and Clamores Rivers converge. This ancient city stands in the center of the most castle-rich part of Castile. Isabella was proclaimed Queen of Castile here in 1474.

The narrow, winding streets of this hill city must be covered on foot to view the Romanesque churches and 15th-century palaces along the way.

What to See & Do

El Alcázar, Plaza de La Reina Victoria Eugenia. ☎ **43-01-76.**

View the Alcázar first from below, at the junction of the Clamores and Eresma Rivers. It is on the west side of Segovia, and you may not spot it when you first enter the city. But that's part of the surprise.

The castle dates back to the 12th century, but a large segment—notably its Moorish ceilings—was destroyed by fire in 1862. Restoration has continued over the years.

Royal romance is associated with the Alcázar. Isabella first met Ferdinand here, and today you can see a facsimile of her dank bedroom: Once married, she wasn't foolish enough to surrender her rights, as replicas of the thrones attest; both are equally proportioned. Philip II also married his fourth wife, Anne of Austria, here.

Walk the battlements of this once-impregnable castle, from which its occupants hurled down boiling oil onto the enemy below. Brave the hazardous stairs of the tower, originally built by Isabella's father as a prison, for a superb view of Segovia.

Admission: 350 ptas. ($2.50) adults; 150 ptas. ($1.10) children 8-14. Children 7 and under free.

Open: Apr–Sept, daily 10am–7pm. Oct–Mar, daily 10am–6pm. **Directions:** Take either Calle Vallejo, Calle de Velarde, Calle de Daoiz, or Paseo de Ronda. **Bus:** 3.

Roman Aqueduct, Plaza del Azoguejo.

This architectural marvel, built by the Romans more than 2,000 years ago, is still used to carry water. Constructed of mortarless granite, it consists of 118 arches, and in one two-tiered section it soars 95 feet to its highest point. The Spanish call it El Puente. It spans the Plaza del Azoguejo, the old market square, stretching nearly 800 yards. When the Moors took Segovia in 1072, they destroyed 36 arches, which were later rebuilt under Ferdinand and Isabella in 1484.

Cabildo Catedral de Segovia, Plaza Catedral, Marqués del Arco. ☎ **43-53-25.**

Constructed between 1515 and 1558, this is supposedly the last Gothic cathedral built in Spain. Fronting the historic Plaza Mayor, it stands on the spot where Isabella I was proclaimed Queen of Castile. Affectionately called *la dama de las catedrales,* it contains numerous treasures, such as the Blessed Sacrament Chapel (created by the flamboyant Churriguera), stained-glass windows, elaborately carved choir stalls, 16th- and 17th-century paintings, including a reredos portraying the deposition of Christ from the cross by Juan de Juni. The cloisters are older than the cathedral, dating from an earlier church that was destroyed in the so-called War of the Communeros. Inside the cathedral museum you'll find jewelry, paintings, and a collection of rare antique manuscripts.

Admission: Cathedral free, cloisters, museum, and chapel room 200 ptas. ($1.40).

Open: Spring and summer, daily 9am–7pm; off-season, daily 9:30am–1pm and 3–6pm.

Iglesia de la Vera Cruz, Carretera de Zamarramala. ☎ **43-14-75.**

Built in either the 11th or the 12th century by the Knights Templars, this is the most fascinating Romanesque church in Segovia. It stands in isolation outside the walls of the old town, overlooking the Alcázar. Its unusual 12-sided design is believed to have been copied from the Church of the Holy Sepulchre in Jerusalem. Inside you'll find an inner temple, rising two floors, where the knights conducted nightlong vigils as part of their initiation rites.

Admission: 125 ptas. (90¢).

Open: Apr–Sept, Tues–Sun 10:30am–1:30pm and 3:30–7pm. Oct–Mar, Tues–Sun 10:30am–1:30pm and 3:30–6pm.

Monasterio del Parral, Calle del Marqués de Villena (across the Eresma River). ☎ **43-23-98.**

The restored "Monastery of the Grape" was established for the Hironymites by Henry IV, a Castilian king (1425–74) known as "The Impotent." The monastery's major art treasure is a large retable (1528) by Juan Rodriguez. A robed monk shows you through.

Admission: Free.

Open: Mon–Fri 10am–1:30pm and 4–7pm. **Directions:** Take Ronda de Sant Lucía, cross the Eresma River, and head down Calle del Marqués de Villena.

Iglesia de St. Martín, Plaza de las Sironas. No phone.

Located in the center of Segovia, this church was once the most outstanding in Old Castile. The porticoes of the 12th-century Romanesque structure are especially striking, but, except for the rare altar, the interior is less interesting. The square on which the church stands, the Plaza de las Sirenas, was modeled after the Piazza di Spagna in Rome. A fountain commemorates the legend of Juan Bravo, the hero of the War of the Communeros against Charles V. Nearby is the 15th-century Mansion of Arias Davila, one of the old houses of the Segovian aristocracy.

Admission: Free.

Open: Apr–Sept, daily 10:30am–1:30pm and 3:30–7pm. Oct–Mar, daily 10:30am–1:30pm and 3:30–6pm.

Where to Stay

Gran Hotel las Sirenas, Juan Bravo, 30, 40001 Segovia. ☎ **921/43-40-11.** Fax 921/43-06-33. 39 rms (all with bath). A/C TV TEL

Rates: 4,000 ptas. ($28.40) single; 6,000 ptas. ($42.60) double. Breakfast 500 ptas. ($3.60) extra. AE, DC, MC, V.

Standing on the most charming old plaza in Segovia, opposite the Church of St. Martín, this hotel was built around 1950, and has been renovated several times since then. It's modest but clean, and decorated in a conservative, traditional style. Each bedroom is well maintained and filled with functional, uncomplicated furniture. No meals other than breakfast are served, but the staff at the reception desk can direct clients to cafés and tascas nearby.

Hotel los Linajes, Dr. Velasco, 9, 40003 Segovia. ☎ **921/46-04-75.** Fax 921/46-04-79. 55 rms, 10 suites (all with bath). TV TEL **Bus:** 1.

Rates: 6,900 ptas. ($49) single; 10,500 ptas. ($74.60) double; from 13,200 ptas. ($93.70) suite. Breakfast 750 ptas. ($5.30) extra. AE, DC, MC, V. **Parking:** 725 ptas. ($5.10).

In the historical district of St. Stephen at the northern edge of the old town stands this hotel, the former home of a Segovian noble family. While the facade dates from the 11th century, the interior is modern except for some Castilian decorations. One of the best hotels in town, Los Linajes offers gardens and patios where guests can enjoy a panoramic view over the city. The hotel also has a bar/lounge, coffee shop, disco, and garage.

Parador de Segovia, Carretera Valladolid, s/n (N-601), 40003 Segovia. ☎ **921/44-37-37.** Fax 921/43-73-62. 113 rms, 7 suites. A/C MINIBAR TV TEL

Rates: 12,000 ptas. ($85.20) single; 15,000 ptas. ($106.50) double; from 22,000 ptas. ($156.20) suite. Breakfast 1,200 ptas. ($8.50) extra. AE, DC, MC, V. **Parking:** 1,000 ptas. ($7.10).

This 20th-century tile-roofed parador sits on a hill two miles northeast of Segovia (take the N-601). It stands on an estate called *El Terminillo,* which used to be famous for its vines and almond trees, a few of which still survive. The guest rooms are deluxe. The vast lawns and gardens contain two lakelike swimming pools, and there is also an indoor pool. Other facilities include saunas and tennis courts. You can eat in the dining room for 3,600 pesetas ($25.60) and up.

Where to Dine

El Bernardino, Cervantes, 2. ☎ **43-32-25.**

Cuisine: CASTILIAN. **Reservations:** Recommended.
Prices: Appetizers 400–2,000 ptas. ($2.80–$14.20); main courses 1,100–2,000 ptas. ($7.80–$14.20); fixed-price menu 2,500 ptas. ($17.80). AE, DC, MC, V.
Open: Lunch, daily 1–4:15pm; dinner, daily 8–11:15pm.

El Bernardino, a three-minute walk west of the Roman aqueduct, is built like an old tavern. Lanterns hang from beamed ceilings, and the view over the red-tile rooftops of the city is delightful. The menú del día might include a huge paella, roast veal with potatoes, flan or ice cream, plus bread and wine. You might begin your meal with *sopa castellana* (made with ham, sausage, bread, egg, and garlic). The roast dishes are exceptional here, including roast suckling pig from a special oven and roast baby lamb. You can also order grilled rib steak or stewed partridge.

Casa Duque, Calle Cervantes, 12. ☎ **43-05-37.**

Cuisine: CASTILIAN. **Reservations:** Recommended.
Prices: Appetizers 575–1,750 ptas. ($4.10–$12.40); main courses 975–1,800 ptas. ($6.90–$12.80); fixed-price menus 1,500–3,800 ptas. ($10.70–$27). AE, DC, MC, V.
Open: Lunch, daily 12:30–5pm; dinner, daily 8–11:30pm.

Duque—the *maestro asador,* as he calls himself—supervises the roasting of the pig, the house specialty, in this *mesón típico* founded in 1895. Waitresses wearing the traditional garb of the mayoress of Zamarramala will serve you other Segovian gastronomic specialties, such as *sopa castellana* or a cake known as *ponche alcázar.* There is a tavern below so that you may enjoy a pre-dinner drink.

José María, Cronista Lecea, 11. ☎ **46-11-11.**

Cuisine: SEGOVIAN. **Reservations**: Recommended.
Prices: Appetizers 400–1,800 ptas. ($2.80–$12.80); main courses 1,200–2,800 ptas. ($8.50–$19.90); fixed-price menu 3,800 ptas. ($27). AE, DC, MC, V.
Open: Lunch daily 1–4pm; dinner daily 8–11:30pm.

This centrally located bar and restaurant, one block east of the Plaza Mayor, serves quality regional cuisine in a rustic stucco-and-brick dining room. Before dinner, locals crowd in for tapas at the bar, then move into the dining room for such Castilian specialties as roast suckling pig, rural-style conger eel, and freshly caught sea bream. Try the cream of crabmeat soup, roasted peppers, salmon with scrambled eggs, house-style hake, filet of sole, or grilled veal steak. For dessert, a specialty is ice-cream tart with a whisky sauce.

La Oficina, Calle Cronista Lecea 10. ☎ **43-16-43.**

Cuisine: CASTILIAN. **Reservations:** Not required.

Prices: Appetizers 650–1,450 ptas. ($4.60–$10.30); main courses 1,600–2,000 ptas. ($11.40–$14.20). Fixed-price menus 1,300–2,000 ptas. ($9.20–$14.20). AE, DC, MC, V.

Open: Lunch Wed–Mon 1–4:30pm; dinner Wed–Mon 7–11:30pm. **Closed:** Three weeks in Nov.

A meal here provides many insights into the traditions and aesthetics of Old Spain. Established in 1893, it has been maintained ever since by three subsequent generations of the original owner's family. As such, it has probably welcomed virtually every resident of Segovia into the thick brick and stone walls that give it its distinctive Castilian flavor. Few changes, other than repairs, seem to have been made to the decor since its founding, a fact which contributes significantly to its charm. Set adjacent to Plaza Mayor, a short walk east of the cathedral, it offers a stand-up bar that is accessible through a separate entrance, where locals usually opt for an apéritif wine or sherry before beginning their meal. The owners have won various awards for the quality of their roast suckling pig, which is prepared and served with suitable pomp and ceremony by the well-trained staff.

★ **Mesón de Candido,** Plaza del Azoguejo, 5. ☎ **42-59-11.**

Cuisine: CASTILIAN. **Reservations:** Recommended.

Prices: Appetizers 700–1,600 ptas. ($5–$11.40); main courses 1,800–2,600 ptas. ($12.80–$18.50); fixed-price menu 2,500 ptas. ($17.80). AE, DC, MC, V.

Open: Lunch, daily 12:30–4:30pm; dinner, daily 8–11:30pm or midnight.

For years this beautiful old Spanish inn, standing on the eastern edge of the old town, has maintained a monopoly on the tourist trade. The oldest part of the building housing the restaurant dates from 1822, and the restaurant has gradually been enlarged since then. The proprietor of The House of Candido is known as *mesonero mayor de Castilla* (the major innkeeper of Castile). He's been decorated with more medals and honors than paella has grains of rice and has entertained everyone from King Hussein to Hemingway. The restaurant's popularity can be judged by the flocks of hungry diners who fill every seat in the six dining rooms. It offers an à la carte menu that includes *cordero asado* (roast baby lamb) and *cochinillo asado* (roast suckling pig).

Mesón el Cordero, Calle de Carmen, 4. ☎ **43-51-96.**

Cuisine: CASTILIAN/IBERIAN. **Reservations:** Recommended.

Prices: Appetizers 400–1,500 ptas. ($2.80–$10.70); main courses 1,400–2,500 ptas. ($9.90–$17.80). AE, DC, MC, V.

Open: Lunch daily 12:30–4:30pm; dinner daily 8–11:30pm.

This restaurant is known throughout the town for the flavorful roasted meats it serves. It was originally built in the 1800s as a Carmelite convent, near the base of the town's Roman aqueduct, although in the 1970s, a pair of hardworking partners added dozens of rustic artifacts and enlarged its premises to create the charming restaurant you'll see today. One noteworthy specialty is roasted suckling lamb (*cordero lechal*) served on the bone and seasoned with fresh herbs that include ample amounts of rosemary and thyme. The wine list includes an array of suitably robust reds from Rioja, Rivera, and southern France.

An Easy Excursion to La Granja

To reach La Granja, 7 miles (11km) southeast of Segovia, you can take a 20-minute bus ride from the center of the city. About 12 buses a day leave from Paseo Conde de Sepulveda at Avenida Fernández Ladreda.

★ **Palacio Real de La Granja,** Plaza de España, 17, San Ildefonso (Segovia). ☎ **47-00-19.**

San Ildefonso de la Granja was the summer palace of the Bourbon kings of Spain, who imitated the grandeur of Versailles in Segovia province. Set against the snow-capped Sierra de Guadarrama, the slate-roofed palace dominates the village that grew up around it (nowadays a summer resort).

The founder of La Granja was Philip V, grandson of Louis XIV and the first Bourbon king of Spain (his body, along with that of his second queen, Isabel de Fernesio, is interred in a mauseoleum in the Collegiate Church). Philip V was born at Versailles on December 19, 1683, which partially explains why he wanted to re-create that atmosphere at Segovia.

At one time a farm stood on the grounds of what is now the palace—hence the totally incongruous name *granja,* meaning "farm" in Spanish.

The palace was built in the first part of the 18th century. Inside you'll find valuable antiques (many in the Empire style), paintings, and a remarkable collection of tapestries of Flemish design and others based on Goya cartoons from the Royal Factory in Madrid.

Most visitors, however, seem to find a stroll through the gardens more to their liking, so allow adequate time for it. The fountain statuary is a riot of gods and nymphs cavorting with abandon, hiding indiscretions behind jets of water. The gardens are studded with chestnuts and elms. A spectacular display follows when the water jets are turned on.

Admission: 600 ptas. ($4.30) adults; 150 ptas. ($1.10) children 5–14. Children 4 and under free.

Open: Apr–May, Mon-Fri 10am–1:30pm and 3–5pm, Sat–Sun 10am–6pm; June–Sept, daily 10am–6pm; Oct–Mar, Mon–Sat 10am–1:30pm and 3–5pm, Sun 10am–2pm.

5 Alcalá de Henares

18 miles E of Madrid

GETTING THERE • By Train Trains travel between Madrid's Atocha or Chamartín station and Alcalá de Henares every day and evening.

• By Bus Buses from Madrid depart from Avenida América, 18 (Metro: América), frequently throughout the day.

• By Car Alcalá lies adjacent to the main national highway (N-11), connecting Madrid with eastern Spain. As you leave central Madrid, follow signs for Barajas Airport and Barcelona.

ESSENTIALS The area code for Alcalá de Henares is 91. The tourist information office is at Callejón de Santa María, 1 (☎ **91/899-26-94**). It will provide a map locating all the local attractions.

History has been unfair to this ancient town, which once flourished with colleges, monasteries, and palaces. When a university was founded here in the 15th century, Alcalá became a cultural and intellectual center. Europe's first polyglot Bible (supposedly with footnotes in the original Greek and Hebrew) was published here in 1517. But during the 1800s the town declined when the university moved to Madrid. Today, however, Alcalá is one of the main centers of North American academics in Spain, cooperating with the Fullbright Commission, Michigan State University, and Madrid's Washington Irving Center. Overall, the city has taken on new life. Commuters have turned it into a virtual suburb, dubbing it "the bedroom of Madrid."

What to See & Do

Museo Casa Natal de Cervantes, Calle Mayor, 48. ☎ **889-96-54.**

Visitors come for the day, mainly to see the birthplace of Spain's literary giant Miguel de Cervantes, the creator of *Don Quixote*, who may have been born here in 1547. This 16th-century Castilian house was reconstructed in 1956 around a beautiful little courtyard that has a wooden gallery supported by pillars with Renaissance-style capitals, plus an old well. The house contains many Cervantes manuscripts and, of course, copies of *Don Quixote*, perhaps one of the most widely published books (in all languages) in the world.

Admission: Free.

Open: Tues–Fri 10:15am–1:45pm and 4:15–6:45pm; Sat–Sun 10:15am–1:45pm.

Colegio Mayor de San Ildefonso, Plaza San Diego. ☎ **885-40-00.**

Adjacent to the main square of town, the Plaza de Cervantes, is the Colegio Mayor de San Ildefonso, where Lope de Vega and other famous Spaniards studied. You can see some of their names engraved on plaques in the examination room. The old university's Plateresque facade dates from 1543. From here you can walk across the Patio of Saint Thomas (from 1662) and the Patio of the Philosophers to reach the Patio of the Three Languages (from 1557), where Greek, Latin, and Hebrew were once taught. Here is the great hall or old examination room (*Paraninfo*), which is now used for special events. The hall has a Mudéjar *artesonado* ceiling. The Paraninfo is entered through a restaurant, Hostería del Estudiante (see "Where to Dine" below).

Admission: 150 ptas. ($1.10).

Open: Tues–Sat, tours (mandatory) at 11am, 11:45am, 12:30pm, 1:15pm, 4pm, 4:45pm, 5:30pm, and 6:15pm.

Capilla de San Ildefonso, Pedro Gumíelz. ☎ **885-40-00.**

Next door to the Colegio is the Capilla de San Ildefonso, the 15th-century chapel of the old university. It also houses the Italian marble tomb of Cardinal Cisneros, the founder of the original university. This chapel also has an *artesonado* ceiling and intricately stuccoed walls.

Admission: Included in tour of Colegio (see above).

Open: See Colegio above.

Where to Dine

Hostería del Estudiante, Calle Colegios, 3. ☎ **888-03-30.**

Cuisine: CASTILIAN. **Reservations:** Recommended.
Prices: Appetizers 800–1,100 ptas. ($5.70–$7.80); main courses 2,400–2,900 ptas. ($17–$20.60); fixed-price menu 3,500 ptas. ($24.90). AE, DC, MC, V.

Open: Lunch, daily 1–4pm; dinner; daily 9–11:30pm. **Closed:** Dinner in July–Aug.

Located within the university complex, this remarkable example of a 1510 building is an attraction in its own right. In the cooler months, if you arrive early you can lounge in front of a 15-foot open fireplace. Oil lamps hang from the ceiling: pigskins are filled with the locally made wine; and rope-covered chairs and high-backed carved settees capture the spirit of the past. Run by the Spanish Parador System, the restaurant offers a tasty (and huge) three-course set-price lunch or dinner featuring such regional specialties as *cocido madrileño,* the hearty stew of Madrid, roast baby lamb, and trout Navarre style. For dessert, try the cheese of La Mancha.

6 El Pardo

8 miles N of Madrid

GETTING THERE • By Bus Local city buses depart every 15 minutes from Madrid's Paseo de Moret (metro: Moncloa).

• By Car Driving can be confusing on the minor roads. Head north from the city limits, following signs to La Coruña, then branch off to the west in the direction of "El Monte de El Pardo."

ESSENTIALS The area code for El Pardo is 91. Spring and fall can be chilly, so dress accordingly. The Manzanares River flows nearby, but there are no convenient rail lines.

After visiting Alcalá de Henares, spend an afternoon in El Pardo. During the Civil War many Spaniards died here, and much of the town was destroyed during the famous advance toward University City. But there's no trace of destruction today, and the countryside, irrigated by the Manzanares River, is lush and peaceful. If possible, go to the top of the hill and take in the view.

What to See & Do

Palacio de El Pardo, Avenida de La Guardia. ☎ **376-15-00.**

A royal residence since medieval times, this was Franco's home until his death, when his body lay in state in front of the palace. When the palace was opened to the public in 1976, it quickly became one of the most popular sights around Madrid. The interior is lavishly furnished with Empire pieces, and Franco's ornate gilt throne reveals his royal pretensions. Many family mementoes are displayed, including an extensive wardrobe; make sure to see the 10 wax dummies modeling Franco's important state uniforms.

Highlights of the 45-minute tour include the Tapestry Room, many of its 18th-century pieces based on cartoons by Goya, Bayeu, Aguirre, and González Ruiz; and the Salon de Consejos, with its 19th-century coved ceiling and—Franco's most prized possession—a 15th-century sideboard that once belonged to Queen Isabella.

Behind the palace stands the 18th-century **Casita del Príncipe (Prince's Cottage),** a small hunting lodge built during the reign of Charles III. It was actually commissioned either by his son, the prince, or by his wife, who often needed trysting places. Designed by architect López Corona, the cottage is lavishly decorated with embroidered silk walls, eight paintings by Lucas Jordán, and Louis XV—and Louis XVI—style furniture. The Casita keeps the same hours as the main palace.

At the **Palacio de la Quinta,** taken over by the Crown in 1745 from the Duke of Arcos, you can view gardens and fountains and explore its elegant interior, where the Museo de Papeles Pintados is installed.

Admission: (including palace, Casita del Príncipe, and Palacio de la Quinta); 400 ptas. ($2.80) adults; 250 ptas. ($1.80) children.

Open: Mon–Sat 9:30am–12:15pm and 3–6pm; Sun 9:30am–1:40pm.

Where to Dine

La Marquesita, avda de la Guardia, 4. ☎ **376-1915.**

Cuisine: CASTILIAN. **Reservations:** Recommended.
Prices: Appetizers 800–1,500 ptas. ($5.70–$10.70); main courses 1,500–2,900 ptas. ($10.70–$20.60); fixed-price menu 3,000 ptas. ($21.30). AE, DC, MC, V.
Open: Lunch daily 1–5pm; dinner, daily 8pm–midnight.

Established in 1926, within a building erected in the 1840s, this restaurant has successfully weathered the passage of several of Spain's most tenacious political regimes. Set on the city's main boulevard, across from the palace gardens of El Pardo, it offers al fresco dining in summer and cozy meals in front of a fireplace in winter. The front room functions as a tasca, where diners traditionally order a Tío Pepe before the beginning of their meal. The decor is that of a typical Castilian tavern, with a charming rusticity and rows of Serrano hams hanging from a beamed ceiling. The house specialties usually involve some presentation of grilled meat or fish, each prepared over glowing coals and flavored with oils and herbs. They usually include roast suckling pig, baby lamb, entrecôte of beef, filets of monkfish or salmon, wild rabbit, and braised venison, in season, with red wine sauce.

7 Chinchón

32 miles SE of Madrid, 16 miles NE of Aranjuez

GETTING THERE • By Bus From Madrid's Place del Condé de Casal, buses run hourly to and from Chinchón, where the terminal is about 300 yards from the center of town. The bus trip takes about an hour each way.

• By Car Drive from Alcalá to Toledo, bypassing Madrid by taking the C-300 in a southwesterly arc around the capital. About halfway there, follow signs to the "Cuevas de Chinchón." Another option is to take the E-901 southeast of Madrid toward Valencia, turning southwest at the turnoff for Chinchón.

ESSENTIALS The area code for Chinchón is 91.

The main attraction of Chinchón is the **cuevas (caves),** where Anis de Chinchón, an aniseed liqueur, is manufactured. You can buy bottles of the liqueur in Plaza Mayor, at the center of town.

Wander along the town's steep and narrow streets, past the houses with large bays and spacious carriageways. Although closed to the public, the 15th-century **Chinchón Castle,** seat of the Condes of Chinchón, can be viewed from outside. The most interesting church, **Nuestra Señora de la Asunción,** dating from the 16th and 17th centuries, contains a painting by Goya.

Where to Stay

Parador de Chinchón, Avenida Generalísimo, 1, Chinchón 28370 Madrid. ☎ **91/894-08-36.** Fax 91/894-09-08. 38 rms (all with bath). A/C MINIBAR TV TEL

Rates: 12,000 ptas. ($85.20) single; 15,000 ptas. ($106.50) double. Breakfast 1,200 ptas. ($8.50) extra. AE, DC, MC, V.

Set near the town center, this hotel lies within the carefully restored 17th-century walls of what was originally built as an Augustinian convent. After a stint as both a civic jail and a courthouse, it was transformed in 1972 into a government-run parador. A team of architects and designers converted it handsomely, with glass-walled hallways opening onto a stone-sided courtyard. The hotel contains two bars and two dining halls, where a filling meal can be ordered for 3,500 pesetas ($24.90). Bedrooms, which are clean, simple, and severely dignified, still manage to convey their ecclesiastical origins. Facilities include an outdoor swimming pool, open in summertime only.

Where to Dine

Mesón Cuevas del Vino, Benito Horteliano, 13. ☎ **894-02-06.**

Cuisine: SPANISH. **Reservations:** Recommended on holidays.
Prices: Appetizers 500–1,500 ptas. ($3.60–$10.70); main courses 1,500–3,500 ptas. ($10.70–$24.90); fixed-price menu 3,200 ptas. ($22.70). No credit cards.
Open: Lunch, Wed–Mon 1:30–4pm; dinner, Wed–Mon 8–11:30pm.

This establishment is famous for its wine cellars, and you can sample the stock at lunch or dinner. Hams, hanging from the rafters, have been cured by the owners, and the flavorful spiced sausages are homemade. Chunks of the ham and sausage cooked in oil, plus olives and crunchy bread are served. The *morteruelo* (warm pâté) is a good beginning, and a popular dessert is *hojuelas* (soft pastry with honey). Specialties include lamb and suckling pig roasted in a wood oven. The wines, or the dry or sweet anisette that is the main export of Chinchón, help make the meal more enjoyable.

Venta Reyes, Ronda de Mediodía, 18. ☎ **894-00-37.**

Cuisine: CASTILIAN/ANDALUSIAN. **Reservations:** Required on holidays
Prices: Appetizers 500–1,500 ptas. ($3.60–$10.70); main courses 1,500–3,500 ptas. ($10.70–$24.90). No credit cards.
Open: Lunch, Wed–Mon 1:30–4pm; dinner, Wed–Mon 8pm–midnight.

With a decor of hanging lamps, tiles, and wicker furniture, this is clearly the most elegant dining choice in the area. In a garden setting, with swans gliding across the pool, Venta Reyes offers romance Sevillian style. In fair weather, you can dine in the garden. Many recipes are based on ancient dishes that have virtually faded from the Spanish culinary repertoire. Game fowl, grown on the premises, is a specialty—for example, partridge prepared Toledan style. Begin with Andalusian gazpacho or fish and shellfish soup, then follow with hen cooked with almonds, garlic, parsley, and saffron. Baked salmon and veal cooked in its own juice are other popular dishes. The savory cuisine is backed up by more than 100 varieties of wine from all the regions of Spain.

8 Ávila

68 miles NW of Madrid, 41 1/2 miles SW of Segovia

GETTING THERE • By Train There are more than two dozen trains leaving daily from Madrid for Ávila, about a 1 1/2- to 2-hour trip each way. Depending on their schedule, trains depart from Chamartín, Atocha, and Príncipe (Norte) railway stations. The 8am train from Atocha, arriving in Ávila at 9:26am, is a good choice, considering all that there is to see. The Ávila station lies at Avenida Portugal, 17 (☎ **22-01-88**), about a mile east of the Old City.

• By Bus Buses leave Madrid daily from Paseo Florida, 11 (Metro: Norte), in front of Norte Railway Station. In Ávila the bus terminal (☎ **22-01-54**) is at the corner of Avenida Madrid and Avenida Portugal, northeast of the center of town.

• By Car Exit Madrid from its northwest perimeter, and head northwest on highway N-VI (A-6), toward La Coruña, eventually forking southwest to Ávila . Driving time is around 1 1/2 hours.

• Taxis You can find taxis lined up in front of Ávila's railway station and at the more central Plaza Santa Teresa. For information, call 21-19-59 or 22-01-49.

ESSENTIALS The Ávila area code is 920. The tourist information office is at Plaza Catedral, 4 (☎ **920/21-13-87**). In case of emergency, dial 091. The police station is at Avenida José Antonio, 3 (☎ **21-11-88**). Bring warm clothes if you're visiting in the early spring.

The ancient city of Ávila is completely encircled by well-preserved 11th-century walls, which are among the most important medieval relics in Europe. The city has been declared a national landmark, and there is little wonder why. The walls aren't the only attraction, however. Ávila has several Romanesque churches, Gothic palaces, and a fortified cathedral.

Ávila's spirit and legend are most linked to St. Teresa, who was born here in 1515. This Carmelite nun, who helped defeat the Reformation and founded a number of convents, experienced visions of the devil and angels piercing her heart with burning hot lances. She was eventually imprisoned in Toledo. Many legends sprang up after her death, including the belief that a hand severed from her body could perform miracles. Finally, in 1622 she was declared a saint.

What to See & Do

Begun on orders of Alfonso VI as part of the general reconquest of Spain from the Moors, the 11th-century ★ **Walls of Ávila,** built over Roman fortifications, took nine years to complete. They average 33 feet in height, have 88 semicircular towers, and more than 2,300 battlements. Among the nine gateways, the two most famous are the St. Vincent and the Alcázar, both on the eastern side. In many respects the walls are best viewed from the west. Whatever your preferred point of view, you can drive along their entire length: 1 1/2 miles (2km).

Convento de Santa Teresa, Plaza de la Santa. ☎ **21-10-30.**

This 17th-century convent and neoclassical baroque church, two blocks southwest of the Plaza de la Victoria, is the site of St. Teresa's birth. It contains a number of relics, including a finger from her right hand. Look also for the fine sculpture by Gregorio Hernández.

Admission: Free.

Open: Daily 9:30am–1:30pm and 3:30–7pm. **Bus:** 1, 3, or 4.

Ávila Catedral, Plaza Catedral. ☎ **21-16-41.**

Built into the old ramparts of Ávila, this cold, austere cathedral and fortress (begun in 1099) bridges the gap between the Romanesque and the Gothic, and, as such, enjoys a certain distinction in Spanish architecture. One local writer compared it to a granite mountain. The interior is unusual, built with a mottled red-and-white stone.

Like most European cathedrals, Ávila's lost its purity of design through the years as new chapels and wings—one completely in the Renaissance mode—were added. A Dutch artist, Cornelius, designed the seats of the choir stalls, also in Renaissance style, and the principal chapel holds a reredos showing the life of Christ by Pedro Berruguete, Juan de Borgoña, and Santa Cruz. Behind the chapel the tomb of Bishop Alonso de Madrigal—nicknamed "El Tostado" ("The Parched One") owing to its brownish color—is Vasco de Zarza's masterpiece. The Cathedral Museum contains a laminated gold ceiling, a 15th-century triptych, a copy of an El Greco painting, as well as vestments and 15th-century songbooks. Note also *The Great Custodia* by Juan de Arfe (1572).

Admission: 200 ptas. ($1.40) adults; 100 ptas. (70¢) children.

Open: May–Sept, daily 8am–1pm and 3–7pm; Oct–Apr, daily 8am–1pm and 3–5pm.

Basilica de San Vicente, Plaza de San Vicente. ☎ **25-52-30.**

Outside the city walls, at the northeast corner of the medieval ramparts, this Romanesque-Gothic church in faded sandstone encompasses styles from the 12th to the 14th century. It consists of a huge nave and a trio of apses. The eternal struggle between good and evil is depicted on a cornice on the southern portal. The western portal, dating from the 13th century, contains Romanesque carvings. Inside is the tomb of St. Vincent, martyred on this site in the 4th century. The tomb's medieval carvings, which depict his torture and subsequent martyrdom, are fascinating.

Admission: 100 ptas. (70¢).

Open: Apr–Sept, Mon–Sat 10am–1pm and 4–7pm; Sun 10:30am–noon. Oct–Mar, Mon–Sat 10am–1pm and 4–6pm; Sun 10:30am–noon.

Monasterio de Santo Tomas, Plaza Granada. ☎ **22-04-00.**

This 15th-century Gothic monastery was once the headquarters of the Inquisition in Ávila. For three centuries it housed the tomb of Torquemada, the first General Inquisitor, whose zeal in organizing the Inquisition made him a notorious figure in Spanish history. Legend has it that after the friars were expelled from the monastery in 1836, a mob of Torquemada-haters ransacked the tomb and burned the remains somewhere outside the city walls. His final-burial site is unknown.

Prince John, the only son of Ferdinand and Isabella, was also buried here, in a sumptuous sepulchre in the church transept. The tomb was desecrated during a French invasion; now, only an empty crypt remains.

Visit the Royal Cloisters, in some respects the most interesting architectural feature of the place. In the upper part of the third cloister, you'll find the Museum of Far Eastern Art, which exhibits Vietnamese, Chinese, and Japanese art and handcrafts.

Admission: 100 ptas. (70¢).

Open: Mon–Sat 10am–1pm and 4–7pm; Sun 4–6pm. **Bus:** 1, 2, or 3.

Carmelitas Descalzas de San José, Las Madres, 4 ☎ **22-21-27.**

Also known as the Convento de las Madres (Convent of the Mothers), this is the first convent founded by St. Teresa, who started the Reform of Carmel in 1562. Two churches are here—the primitive one, where the first Carmelite nuns took the habit; and one built by Francisco de Mora, architect of Philip III, after the saint's death. The museum displays many relics, including, of all things, St. Teresa's left clavicle.

Admission: Museum, 30 ptas. (20¢).

Open: Tues–Sun 10am–1pm and 4–7pm. **Directions:** From Plaza de Santa Teresa and its nearby Church of San Pedro, follow Calle del Duque de Alba for about two blocks.

Where to Stay

Ávila is a summer resort—a refuge from Castilian heat, but the hotels are few in number and the Spanish book nearly all the hotel space in July and August. Make sure to have a reservation in advance. Mesón El Sol y Residencia Santa Teresa (see "Where to Dine," below) also rents rooms.

★ **Gran Hotel Palacio de Valderrábanos,** Plaza Catedral, 9, 05001 Ávila. ☎ **920/21-10-23.** Fax 920/25-16-91. 70 rms, 3 suites. A/C MINIBAR TV TEL Bus: 1, 2, or 3.

Rates: 8,800–9,300 ptas. ($62.50–$66) single; 13,200–14,800 ptas. ($93.70–$105.10) double; 23,100–24,200 ptas. ($164–$171.80) suite. Breakfast 1,000 ptas. ($7.10) extra. AE, DC, MC, V. **Parking:** Free.

Set immediately adjacent to the front entrance of the cathedral, behind an entryway that is considered a marvel of medieval stonework, this is one of the most elegant and historic hotels of Castile. Originally built in the 1300s as a private home by an early bishop of Ávila (and a member of the Valderrábanos family), it contains a once-fortified lookout tower (whose circumference encloses one of the suites), high beamed ceilings, intricately chiseled stonework, and a vivid sense of long-ago Spain. The public rooms contain a somber elegance, with baronial furniture whose tassels and slightly faded upholstery add to the old-fashioned feeling. If at all possible, ask for a bedroom overlooking the cathedral.

Dining/Entertainment: The restaurant El Fogón de Santa Teresa is a high-ceilinged bastion of formality serving traditional Castilian meals. Fixed-price menus cost 3,700 pesetas ($26.30).

Services: Concierge, laundry/valet, babysitting.

Parador Raimundo de Borgoña, Marqués de Canales de Chozas, 2, 05001 Ávila. ☎ **920/21-13-40.** Fax 920/22-61-66. 62 rms, 1 suite. MINIBAR TV TEL

Rates: 6,600–7,200 ptas. ($46.90–$51.10) single; 10,000–11,500 ptas. ($71–$81.70) double; 14,000 ptas. ($99.40) suite. AE, DC, MC, V. **Parking:** 1,000 ptas. ($7.10).

Lying two blocks northwest of Plaza de la Victoria, this parador stands on a ridge overlooking the banks of the Adaja River. Once it was known as the Palace of Benavides, with a history going back to the 15th century. Its facade forms part of the square. The parador takes its name from Raimundo de Borgoña, the former conqueror of Ávila. The palace has a dignified entranceway, and most of its public lounges open onto a central courtyard with an inner gallery of columns. The furnishings are tasteful: a tall stone fireplace, highly polished tile floors, old chests, leather armchairs, paintings, and sculptures. The dining room, with its leaded-glass windows opening onto a terraced garden, serves tasty Castilian dishes. A large three-course dinner costs 3,500 pesetas ($24.90).

$ **El Rastro,** Plaza del Rastro, 1, 05001 Ávila. ☎ **920/21-12-18.** Fax 920/25-00-00. 19 rms (all with bath).

Rates: 4,150 ptas. ($29.50) single; 4,500 ptas. ($32) double. Breakfast 350 ptas. ($2.50) extra. AE, DC, MC, V.

Situated near the junction of Calle Caballeros and Calle Cepadas is the best choice for the bargain hunter. Few tourists know that they can spend the night at this old Castilian inn built into the city walls. The guest rooms are basic and clean. El Rastro is one of my dining recommendations too (see "Where to Dine," below).

Where to Dine

$ **Mesón El Sol y Residencia Santa Teresa,** Avenida 18 de Julio, 25. ☎ **920/22-02-11.** Fax 920/22-41-13.

Cuisine: CASTILIAN. **Reservations:** Recommended. **Bus:** 12.

Prices: Appetizers 700–850 ptas. ($5–$6); main courses 1,200–2,200 ptas. ($8.50–$15.60). No credit cards.

Open: Lunch, daily 1–4pm; dinner, daily 8:30–11:30pm.

You may be distracted by the aromas emanating from the kitchen of the lowest-priced inn in Ávila—a place known for its good food, moderate prices, and efficient service. Full meals could include seafood soup, fried hake, veal with garlic, and house-style flan. The inn also rents 15 simply furnished bedrooms, a single costing 3,900 pesetas ($27.70) and a double going for 6,500 pesetas ($46.20), plus another 400 pesetas ($2.80) for breakfast.

$ **El Rastro,** Plaza del Rastro, 1. ☎ **21-12-19.**

Cuisine: CASTILIAN. **Reservations:** Required on weekends only.

Prices: Appetizers 550–750 ptas. ($3.90–$5.30); main courses 1,200–2,000 ptas. ($8.50–$14.20); fixed-price menu 1,400 ptas. ($9.90). AE, DC, MC, V.

Open: Lunch, daily 1–4pm; dinner, daily 9–11pm.

An old inn built into the 11th-century town walls, El Rastro serves typical Castilian dishes, with more attention given to freshness and preparation than to culinary flamboyance. Roast baby lamb and tender white veal are house specialties. Dessert recipes have been passed down from Ávila's nuns. Try, for example, the *yemas de Santa Teresa* (St. Teresa's candied egg yolk).

9 Cuenca

100 miles (161km) E of Madrid, 202 miles (325km) SW of Zaragoza

GETTING THERE • By Train Trains leave Madrid's Atocha Railway Station about eight times throughout the day, arriving at Cuenca's station at Avenida de la Estación, at the southern edge of the modern city.

• By Bus There are about 4 to 6 buses from both Madrid and Valencia every day. Buses arrive at Calle Fermín Caballero, s/n (☎ **22-11-84** for information and schedules).

• **By Car** Cuenca is the junction for several highways and about a dozen lesser roads that connect it to towns within its region. From Madrid, take the N-III to Tarancon, then the N-400, which leads directly into Cuenca. Driving time from Madrid is 2½ hours.

ESSENTIALS Cuenca's area code is 969. The tourist information office is at Dalmacio García Izcara, 8 (☎ **969/22-22-31**).

This medieval town—once dominated by the Arabs—is a spectacular sight with its *casas colgadas,* the cliff-hanging houses set on multiple terraces that climb up the sides of a ravine. The Júcar and Huécar Rivers meet at the bottom.

What to See & Do

The chief sight of Cuenca is Cuenca itself. Isolated from the rest of Spain, it requires a northern detour from the heavily traveled Valencia-Madrid road. Deep gorges give it an unreal quality, and eight old bridges spanning two rivers connect the ancient parts of town with the growing new sections. One of the bridges is suspended over a 200-foot drop.

Cuenca's streets are narrow and steep, often cobbled, and even the most athletic tire quickly. But you shouldn't miss it, even if you have to stop and rest periodically. At night you're in for a special treat when the casas colgadas are illuminated. Also, try to drive almost to the top of the castle-dominated hill. The road gets rough as you the end, but the view makes the effort worthwhile.

Cathedral, Plaza Pío XII.

Begun in the 12th century, the Gothic cathedral was influenced by England's Norman style. Part of it collapsed in this century, but it has been restored. A national monument filled with religious art treasures, the cathedral is a 10-minute walk from the Plaza Mayor, up Calle Palafox.

Admission: Free.

Open: Daily 9am–1:30pm and 4:30–7:30pm (closes at 6:30pm in winter). **Bus:** 1 or 2.

Museo de Arte Abstracto Español, Calle los Canónigos, s/n. ☎ **21-29-83.**

North of Plaza Mayor, housed in a cliff-hanging dwelling, this ranks as one of the finest museums of its kind in Spain. It was conceived by painter Fernando Zóbel, who donated it in 1980 to the Juan March Foundation. The most outstanding abstract Spanish painters are represented, including Rafael Canogar (especially his *Toledo*), Luís Feito, Zóbel himself, Tápies, Eduardo Chillida, Gustavo Torner, Gerardo Rueda, Millares, Sempere, Cuixart, and Antonio Saura (see his grotesque Geraldine Chaplin and his study of Brigitte Bardot, a vision of horror, making the French actress look like an escape from Picasso's *Guernica*).

Admission: 300 ptas. ($2.10).

Open: Tues–Fri 11am–2pm and 4–6pm; Sat 11am–2pm and 4–8pm; Sun 11am–2pm. **Bus:** 1 or 2.

Where to Stay

$ **Hotel Avenida,** Carretería 39, 16004 Cuenca. ☎ **969/21-43-43.** Fax 969/21-23-35. 49 rms (all with bath or shower). TEL

Rates: 3,200–3,500 ptas. ($22.70–$24.90) single; 4,400–5,200 ptas. ($31.20–$36.90) double. Breakfast 250 ptas. ($1.80) extra. **Parking:** 900 ptas. ($6.40). MC, V.

Considered good value for the money, this hotel lies in Cuenca's modern commercial center, about a block southwest of Parque de San Julian. Built in 1971, and renovated in 1991, it offers tidy rooms with simple amenities, and access to a helpful staff. Only a handful of rooms have air conditioning; the rest are on the shaded side of the building and—at least according to management—don't seem to get very hot. No meals are served other than breakfast, but the staff can direct its clients to the nearby Calle Colón, where many different restaurants in various price ranges are ready, willing, and able to feed foreign visitors. Parking, incidentally, is within a nearby parking lot maintained by Cuenca's municipal government.

Hotel Figón de Pedro, Calle Cervantes, 15, 16004 Cuenca. ☎ **969/23-45-11.** Fax 969/23-11-92. 28 rms (all with bath). TEL

Rates: 3,900 ptas. ($27.70) single; 5,800 ptas. ($41.20) double. Breakfast 500 ptas. ($3.60) extra. AE, DC, MC, V.

Figón de Pedro lies south of the old city, a short walk north of the bus and rail stations and one block south of the landmark Plaza del Generalísimo. The hotel (with elevator) is immaculate but not stuffy, since the staff keeps the atmosphere pleasantly informal. On the second floor you'll find a lounge with TV, and the hotel boasts a country-style dining room, with a tasca in front. Wood beams, fresh linen on the tables, and personal service all make this an inviting place for meals.

Parador de Turismo de Cuenca, Convento de San Pablo, Paseo de la Hoz del Huécar, 16001 Cuenca. ☎ **969/23-23-20.** Fax 969/23-25-34. 61 rms (all with bath). A/C MINIBAR TV TEL

Rates: 12,000 ptas. ($85.20) single; 15,000 ptas. ($106.50) double. Breakfast 1,200 ptas. ($8.50) extra. AE, DC, MC, V. **Parking:** 700 ptas. ($5).

One of the most recently inaugurated paradores in Spain, this government-sponsored hotel occupies the dignified premises of what was originally built, in 1523, as a Dominican monastery. Considered a noteworthy example of late Gothic architecture, it lies on a hillside above Cuenca, about a half-mile northwest of the town's historic center. Opened for business after extensive renovations in 1992, its three-stories contain masses of intricately chiseled 16th-century stonework (some enhanced with glass panels overlooking the river), a church, a severely beautiful cloister, a sense of timeless solidity, and a swimming pool. There's a bar and a high-ceilinged restaurant where fixed-price meals cost 3,500 ptas ($24.90), and two floors of bedrooms which, despite comfortably traditional furniture and modern bathrooms, richly convey their ecclesiastical origins.

Posada de San José, Julián Romero, 4, 16001 Cuenca. ☎ **969/21-13-00.** Fax 969/23-03-65. 30 rms (16 with bath or shower). **Bus:** 1 or 2.

Rates: 1,900–2,200 ptas. ($13.50–$15.60) single without bath or shower; 3,500–4,000 ptas. ($24.90–$28.40) single with bath or shower; 3,500–4,000 ptas. ($24.90–$28.40) double without bath or shower; 6,000–7,800 ptas. ($42.60–$55.40) double with bath or shower. Breakfast 425 ptas. ($3) extra. AE, DC, MC, V.

Posada de San José stands in the oldest part of Cuenca, a short walk north of the cathedral. The 17th-century cells that used to shelter the sisters of this former convent now house overnight guests who consider its views of the old city the best in town. It sits atop a cliff, overlooking the forbidding depths of a gorge. Owners Antonio and Jennifer Cortinas renovated this place into one of the most alluring hotels of the region, with the bar perhaps the most charming of its well-decorated public rooms.

Where to Dine

Mesón Casa Colgadas, Canónigos, 3. ☎ **22-35-09.**

Cuisine: SPANISH/INTERNATIONAL. **Reservations:** Recommended.
Prices: Appetizers 900–1,200 ptas. ($6.40–$8.50); main courses 2,000–3,000 ptas. ($14.20–$21.30); fixed-price menu 3,400 ptas. ($24.10). AE, DC, MC, V.
Open: Lunch, Wed–Mon 1:30–4pm; dinner, Wed–Mon 9–11pm.

One of the most spectacular dining rooms in Spain stands on one of the most precarious precipices in Cuenca. Established in the late 1960s, it occupies a 19th-century house, five stories high, with sturdy supporting walls and beams. Pine balconies and windows overlook the ravine below and the hills beyond. In fact, it's the most photographed "suspended house" in town, and dinner here is worth every *centímo.* The menu includes regional dishes and a wide variety of international cuisine. Drinks are served in the tavern room on the street level, so even if you're not dining here, you may want to drop in for a drink and the view. You'll find the Mesón Casa Colgadas just south of the cathedral and near the Museum of Spanish Abstract Art.

Togar, Avenida República Argentina, 3. ☎ **22-01-62.**

Cuisine: SPANISH. **Reservations:** Not required. **Bus:** 1 or 6.
Prices: Appetizers 550–900 ptas. ($3.90–$6.40); main courses 850–1,850 ptas. ($6–$13.10); fixed-price menu 1,400 ptas. ($9.90). AE, DC, MC, V.
Open: Lunch daily 1–4pm; dinner daily 8–11pm. **Closed:** 1 week in July (dates vary).

Rich with local flavor, and aggressively cost-conscious, this is a simple but likable tasca on the southwestern periphery of town. Established in 1955, and set within an angular building erected the same year, it offers homemade cookery whose inspiration derives from the various regions of Spain. One of the specialties is *revuelto Togar,* an egg, ham, and shrimp dish served with herbs and crusty bread. Also available are well-peppered versions of pork, several kinds of rich soups, and various beef and fish dishes.

An Easy Excursion to Ciudad Encantada

If you're staying over in Cuenca—or otherwise have the time—you can easily visit what its citizens call their ✪ **Ciudad Encantada (Enchanted City),** Carretera de la Sierra, about 25 miles (40km) to the northeast. Storms and underground waters have created a city here out of large rocks and boulders, shaping them into bizarre designs: a seal, an elephant, a Roman bridge. Take CU-912, turning northeast onto CU-913. Ciudad Encantada is signposted.

7

Old Castile

SPAIN OWES MUCH TO CASTILE, ARAGÓN, AND LEÓN, SINCE THESE THREE KINGDOMS helped forge the various regions of the country into a unified whole. Modern Spain was conceived when Isabella of Castile married Ferdinand of Aragón on October 19, 1469. Five years later she was proclaimed Queen of Castile and of León. The Moors were eventually driven out of Granada, the rest of Spain was conquered, and Columbus sailed to America—all during the reign of these two Catholic monarchs.

This proud but controversial queen and her unscrupulous husband fashioned an empire whose influence extended throughout Spain, Europe, and the New World. The power once held by Old Castile shifted long ago to Madrid, but today there are many reminders of its storied past.

The ancient kingdom of León, which was eventually annexed to Castile, embraced three cities: Salamanca, Zamora, and the provincial capital of León. Today the district is known for its many castles.

In Old Castile, I'll cover the inland provincial capital of Valladolid, where Isabella married Ferdinand and where a brokenhearted Columbus died on May 19, 1506. From there I'll move on to Burgos, once the capital of Old Castile. Vivar, a small town near here, produced El Cid, Spain's greatest national hero, who conquered the Moorish kingdom of Valéncia. For other destinations in the region, refer to Chapter 6, "Excursions from Madrid."

Seeing Old Castile

GETTING THERE Old Castile is best explored on overnight trips. Day trips from Madrid are possible, but you'll spend more time getting there and back than you will viewing the monuments in the region's various cities and towns.

The cities of Old Castile lie on fast and frequently serviced rail lines from Madrid. (See individual city listings for information on specific train connections.) Each city is also serviced by buses out of Madrid, which are usually slower than trains.

The only city with a major airport is Valladolid, with flights to and from Barcelona on Monday to Friday.

Driving is easy thanks to the flat region and the good road connections. The main auto route, N-I, goes north from Madrid to the old capital at Burgos, and N-VI heads northwest from Madrid en route to Valladolid.

A SUGGESTED ROUTE Those wishing to see the major capitals of the old provinces should head west from Madrid to Salamanca for two nights. A good part of Day 1 will be spent getting there. On Day 3, head north to León, stopping for lunch at Zamora. Spend Day 4 in León also. On Day 5, cut southeast to Valladolid for a one-night stay, then head northeast to Burgos for another overnight stopover (Day 6). As your week in Old Castile ends, either head back to Madrid or continue northeast to Basque Country.

Ciudad Rodrigo, west of Salamanca, is not worth a special trip, but it makes a convenient overnight stop for those going from Madrid to Portugal.

1 Salamanca

127 miles (204km) NW of Madrid, 73 miles (117km) E of Portugal

GETTING THERE • By Train Only three trains travel directly from Madrid's North Station to Salamanca daily ($3^1/_2$ hours one way), arriving northeast of the center, on the Paseo de la Estación de Ferrocarril (☎ **26-33-33**). More frequent are

What's Special About Old Castile

Towns/Villages

- Salamanca, ancient university city, one of the most beautiful in Europe.
- León, old cathedral city, once the center of Christian Spain.
- Burgos, Gothic city of El Cid, Spain's national hero.

Architectural Highlights

- The university at Salamanca, the oldest in Spain, once the greatest in Europe.
- The cathedral at León, 13th-century early Gothic, known for its stained glass.
- Plaza Mayor, at Salamanca, the most beautiful public square in Spain.
- The cathedral at Burgos; in flamboyant Gothic style, which took 300 years to build.
- Casa de Las Conchas (House of Shells) at Salamanca, dating from the 15th century—facade covered with carved scallops.

Events/Festivals

- La Alberca celebrations at Salamanca (August 15–16), with crowds in folkloric dress converging on the Plaza Mayor.
- Carnival festivities at Ciudad Rodrigo (February), complete with running of the bulls, traditional dances, and costumes.
- National Museum of Sculpture at Valladolid, exhibiting the best of gilded polychrome sculpture.

the rail connections between Salamanca and Ávila and Ciudad Rodrigo (around six trains each per day) and from Valladolid (eight or nine per day).

• **By Bus** There are about 20 buses arriving from Madrid every day. Salamanca's bus terminal is at Avenida Filiberto Villalobos, 71 (☎ **23-22-66**), northwest of the center of town. There are also buses to Salamanca from Ávila, Zamora, Valladolid, León, and Caceres (2 to 13 per day, depending on the point of departure).

• **By Car** Salamanca is not located on a national highway, but there is a good network of roads that converge on Salamanca from such nearby cities as Ávila, Valladolid, and Ciudad Rodrigo. One of the most heavily trafficked highways is the 620, leading into Salamanca from both Barcelona and Portugal. From Madrid, take the N-VI northwest from the capital's periphery, forking off to Salamanca on the N-501.

ESSENTIALS Salamanca's area code is 923. The tourist information office is at Gran Vía, 41 (☎ **923/26-85-71**).

This ancient city, famous for the university founded here by Alfonso IX in the early 1200s, is well preserved, with turreted palaces, faded convents, Romanesque churches, and colleges that once attracted scholars from all over Europe. The only way to explore Salamanca conveniently is on foot. Arm yourself with a map and set out to explore the city. Nearly all the attractions are within walking distance of the Plaza Mayor.

What to See & Do

To start, spend as much time as you can on the ★ **Plaza Mayor,** an 18th-century baroque square acclaimed as the most beautiful public plaza in Spain. No trip to the university city is complete unless you walk through the arcaded shops and feast your eyes on the honey-colored buildings. After this you'll understand why the plaza mayor, a town's main square, is an integral part of Spanish life. If it's a hot day and you want what everybody else in the Plaza Mayor is drinking, stop in a café and order *leche helado,* an icy vanilla-and-almond milkshake that's very refreshing and not too filling.

Even before reaching Plaza Mayor, you may want to stop and admire the facade of the landmark **Casa de las Conchas,** or House of Shells, which appears as you walk north from the Patio de las Escuelas (site of the Universidad de Salamanca; see below) on Calles de Libreros and San Isidro. This much-photographed building is at the corner of Rua Mayor and Calle de la Compañía. This restored 1483 house is noted for its facade of 400 simulated scallop shells. A professor of medicine at the university and a doctor at the court of Isabella created the house as a monument to Santiago de Compostela, the renowned pilgrimage site. The shell represents the symbol of the Order of Santiago.

Catedral Nueva (New Cathedral), Plaza Juan XXII. ☎ **21-74-76.**

The origins of the "new" cathedral date from 1513. It took more than 200 years to complete it, so the edifice represents many styles: It's classified as late Gothic, but you'll see baroque and Plateresque features as well. Churriguera contributed some rococo elements, too. The building has a grand gold-on-beige sandstone facade, elegant chapels, the best-decorated dome in Spain, and bas-relief columns that look like a palm-tree cluster. Unfortunately, its stained glass is severely damaged. The cathedral lies in the southern section of the old town, about five blocks south of Plaza Mayor at the edge of Plaza de Anaya.

Admission: Free.

Open: Daily 10am–2pm and 4:30–7pm. **Bus:** 1.

Universidad de Salamanca, Patio de las Escuelas, 1. ☎ **29-44-00.**

The oldest university in Spain was once considered the greatest in Europe. In front of the Plateresque facade of the building, a statue honors Hebrew scholar Fray Luís de León. Arrested for heresy, Fray Luís was detained for five years before being cleared. When he returned, he began his first lecture: "As I was saying yesterday ..." Fray Luís's remains are kept in the chapel, which is worth a look. You can also visit a dim 16th-century classroom, cluttered with crude wooden benches, but the library upstairs is closed to the public. The university lies two blocks from the cathedral in the southern section of the old town.

Admission: 200 ptas. ($1.40).

Open: Mon–Fri 9:30am–1:30pm and 4:30–6:30, Sat 9:30am–1:30pm and 4:30–6pm, Sun 10am–1pm. **Directions:** Enter from Patio de las Escuelas, a widening of Calle de Libreros.

Catedral Vieja (Old Cathedral), Plaza Juan XXII. ☎ **21-74-76.**

Adjoining the New Cathedral is this older Spanish Romanesque version, begun in 1140. Its simplicity provides a dramatic contrast to the ornamentation of its younger but bigger counterpart. After viewing the interior, stroll through the enclosed cloisters with their Gothic tombs of long-forgotten bishops. The chapels are of special architectural interest. In the Capilla de San Martín, the frescoes date from 1242, and in the Capilla de Santa Bárbara, final exams for Salamanca University students were given. The Capilla de Santa Catalina is noted for its gargoyles.

Admission: 200 ptas. ($1.40).

Open: Apr–Sept, daily 10am–2pm and 4–8pm. Oct–Mar, daily 10am–1pm and 4–6pm. **Bus:** 1.

Museo de Salamanca (Casa de los Doctores de la Reina), Patio de las Escuelas, 2. ☎ **21-22-35.**

Built in the late 15th century by Queen Isabella's physician, this structure, located near the university, is a fine example of the Spanish Plateresque style. The Fine Arts Museum is housed here, boasting a collection of paintings and sculptures dating from the 15th to the 20th century.

Admission: 200 ptas. ($1.40).

Open: Mon–Sat 10am–2pm and 4:30–8pm, Sun 10am–2pm. **Bus:** 1.

Convento de San Esteban, Plaza del Concilio de Trento. ☎ **21-50-00.**

Of all the old religious sites of Salamanca, St. Stephen's Convent is one of the most dramatic. The golden-brown Plateresque facade of this late-Gothic church competes with the cathedral in magnificence. Inside, José Churriguera in 1693 created a high altar that is one of Salamanca's greatest art treasures. The Claustro de los Reyes (Cloisters of the King) is both Plateresque and Gothic in style. The convent lies two blocks east of the New Cathedral on the opposite side of busy Calle San Pablo at the southern terminus of Calle de España (Gran Vía).

Admission: 100 ptas. (70¢).

Open: Mon–Fri 9am–1pm and 4–8pm; Sat–Sun 9:30am–1:30pm and 4–8pm.

Convento de las Dueñas, Plaza del Concillo de Trento. ☎ **21-54-42.**

Across Calle Buenaventura from San Esteban is one of the most popular sights of Salamanca, a former Mudéjar palace of a court official. The cloisters date from the 16th century, and are, in the opinion of some of Spain's architectural critics, the most beautiful in Salamanca. Climb to the upper gallery for a close inspection of the carved capitals, which are covered with demons and dragons, saints and sinners, and animals of every description—some from the pages of *The Divine Comedy.* There is also a portrait of Dante.

Admission: 100 ptas. (70¢).

Open: June–Sept, daily 10am–1pm and 4–7pm, Oct–May, daily 10:30am–1pm and 4–5:30pm.

Casa Museo Unamuno, Calle de Libreros, 25. ☎ **29-44-00.**

The poet and philosopher—and one of the world's most renowned scholars—lived from 1900 to 1914 in this 18th-century home beside the university. Here he wrote many of the works that made him famous. You can see some of his notebooks and his library, along with many personal mementoes, including the small deck of cards he used to play solitaire.

Admission: Free.

Open: Tues–Fri 11am–1:30pm and 4:30–6:30pm; Sat–Sun 10am–2pm. **Closed:** Aug. **Bus:** 1.

IMPRESSIONS

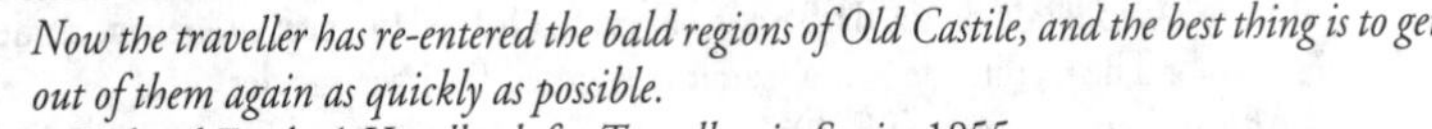

Now the traveller has re-entered the bald regions of Old Castile, and the best thing is to get out of them again as quickly as possible.
—Richard Ford, *A Handbook for Travellers in Spain,* 1855

Where to Stay

EXPENSIVE

Gran Hotel, Plaza Poeta Iglesias, 5, 37001 Salamanca. ☎ **923/21-35-00.** Fax 923/21-35-00. 107 rms, 6 suites. A/C MINIBAR TV TEL

Rates: 10,500 ptas. ($74.60) single; 13,900 ptas. ($98.70) double; 31,800 ptas. ($225.80) suite. Breakfast 1,200 ptas. ($8.50) extra. AE, DC, MC, V. **Parking:** 1,200 ptas. ($8.50).

Because of both its location and the legends that surround it, this hotel has been a favorite since its original construction in 1930. Set on the southeast corner of the Plaza Mayor, it became the traditional favorite of bull breeders and matadors, as well as the literati of this ancient university town. In 1990 the hotel was completely renovated, with modern plumbing and accessories added, but with much of the old-fashioned charm left intact. Each bedroom is well maintained, conservatively dignified, and clean. Castilian-style meals, served à la carte in the hotel's Restaurante Feudal, cost from 3,000 pesetas ($21.30) each.

Parador Nacional de Salamanca, Teso de la Feria, 2, 37008 Salamanca. ☎ **923/26-87-00.** Fax 923/21-54-38. 108 rms. A/C MINIBAR TV TEL

Rates: 10,800 ptas. ($76.70) single; 13,500 ptas. ($95.90) double. Breakfast 1,100 ptas. ($7.80) extra. AE, DC, MC, V. **Parking:** 750 ptas. ($5.30).

Situated just across the Tormes River, this parador with its modern facade opened in the early 1980s, at a point less than a mile south of the historic core. Inside, subtly contrasting shades of polished stone accent the contemporary paintings and leather armchairs of the public areas. Each of the well-furnished and comfortable bedrooms has two or three framed lithographs, as well as a mirador-style balcony and a private bath. Meals in the dining room begin at 3,200 pesetas ($22.70). On the premises are a garden, a parking garage, and an outdoor swimming pool.

MODERATE

Hotel Alfonso X, Toro, 64, 37001 Salamanca. ☎ and fax **923/21-44-01.** 66 rms (all with bath). TV TEL

Rates: 7,800 ptas. ($55.40) single; 11,600 ptas. ($82.40) double. Breakfast 800 ptas. ($5.70) extra. AE, DC, MC, V. **Parking:** 1,200 ptas. ($8.50).

This simple but acceptable hotel rises six floors above its central location, a few steps west of the tourist office, about a five-minute walk from Plaza Mayor. The hotel was converted from an older building around 1970, and renovated in 1990. Guest rooms are conservatively and simply furnished, and relatively well maintained. No meals other than breakfast are served.

Hotel las Torres, Plaza Mayor, 26, at the intersection of Calle Concejo, 37002 Salamanca. ☎ **923/21-21-00.** Fax 923/21-21-01. 42 rms (all with bath), 2 suites. A/C MINIBAR TV TEL

Rates: 8,500 ptas. ($60.40) single; 11,500 ptas. ($81.70) double; 16,000 ptas. ($113.60) suite. AE, DC, MC, V. **Parking:** 1,400 ptas. ($9.90).

Well maintained, dignified, and respectable, this hotel occupies an enviable position near the northwestern corner of Salamanca's largest and most central square, Plaza Mayor. A recent restoration of a historic monument, the hotel has a narrow reception area sheathed with polished marble; a congenial staff; and not overly large but comfortably upholstered and discreetly modern bedrooms. Each contains a well-designed bathroom accented with marble and tile, a safe for a client's valuables, and in many cases, views over the symmetrical grandeur of the plaza outside. There's an unpretentious restaurant on the premises, where full meals begin at around 2,000 pesetas ($14.20). Additional seating spills over beneath the arcades of the plaza, allowing indoor-outdoor dining and lots of opportunities for people-watching.

INEXPENSIVE

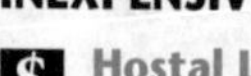

Hostal Laguna, Consuelo, 19, 37001 Salamanca. ☎ **923/21-87-06.** 13 rms (6 with bath).

Rates: 2,700 ptas. ($19.20) double without bath; 3,800 ptas. ($27) double with bath. Breakfast 300 ptas. ($2.10) extra. MC, V.

This unpretentious hotel lies in the center of the historic core of Salamanca, close to both cathedrals and next to the Torre del Clavero. It is also near Plaza Mayor and the university. Its facade is traditional, with distinctive balustrades. The interior has been recently renovated, making for spartan but large, comfortable, and commendable clean doubles.

Hotel Clavero, Consuelo, 21, 37001 Salamanca. ☎ **923/21-81-08.** 28 rms (all with bath). TEL

Rates: 3,000 ptas. ($21.30) single; 4,000 ptas. ($32) double. Breakfast 300 ptas. ($2.10) extra. MC, V.

This modern little hotel near the 15th-century Torre del Clavero enjoys a top-notch location within walking distance of the city's major monuments. Lying just off a small tree-decked plaza, it's usually quiet and peaceful. A recent renovation was carried out, and the bedrooms are tidy, with suitable furnishings, plus a sprinkling of antique reproductions. Dinner costs from 1,200 pesetas ($8.50).

Hostal Mindanao, Paseo de San Vicente; 2, 37007 Salamanca. ☎ **923/26-30-80.** 30 rms (all with bath).

Rates: 2,000 ptas. ($14.20) single; 3,000–3,300 ptas. ($21.30–$23.40) double. No credit cards.

Set within an angular and somewhat nondescript modern building that dates from the early 1980s, this is an unpretentious hostal run by, as you might have guessed, the Mindanao family. It's especially popular with students and, from time to time, their visiting parents. Bedrooms have private baths or showers, but absolutely no frills, and no meals of any kind are served here. Numerous cafés are nearby, however, making a trek out for morning coffee relatively painless. The hotel lies along the southwestern edge of the busy traffic peripheral ringing the town center, within a 12-minute walk of Plaza Mayor.

Where to Dine

★ **Chez Victor,** Espoz y Mina, 26. ☎ **21-31-23.**

Cuisine: CONTINENTAL. **Reservations:** Required.
Prices: Appetizers 850–2,450 ptas. ($6–$17.40); main courses 1,900–3,200 ptas. ($13.50–$22.70). AE, DC, MC, V.
Open: Lunch, Tues–Sun 2–3:30pm, dinner, Tues–Sat 9:30–11:30pm. **Closed:** Aug.

Set within the historic center of town, this is probably the most glamorous and Europeanized restaurant around. Amid a monochromatic and deliberately understated modern decor, you'll enjoy the gastronomic specialties that Victoriano Salvador (known to his clients as Victor) and his wife, Margarit, learned to prepare during the years they lived in France.

Specialties include an array of freshly prepared fish—perhaps a terrine of codfish served with strips of salmon; crabmeat crêpes; a traditional version of roasted lamb; seasonal salad with foie gras and truffle sauce; lamb's brains sautéed in raspberry vinegar; ravioli stuffed with Spanish shellfish; and salmon-and-artichoke stew. Despite the modernity of the cuisine, the portions are ample and well suited to Spanish tastes.

El Botón Charro, Calle Hovohambre, 6-8. ☎ **21-64-62.**

Cuisine: CASTILIAN/INTERNATIONAL. **Reservations:** Not required.
Prices: Appetizers 950–1,300 ptas. ($6.70–$9.20); main courses 1,750–2,500 ptas. ($12.40–$17.80). Fixed-price menu 2,750 ptas. ($19.50). AE, DC, MC, V.
Open: Lunch, daily 1:30–4pm; dinner, Mon–Sat 8:30–midnight.

Considered a well-managed restaurant with some of the best food in town, this establishment has thrived in Salamanca since it was established here in 1975. The building in which it is housed dates from the 1790s. Originally a private house, it lies on a narrow street off Plaza del Mercado, and contains a sampling of artifacts and antiques from the era of its construction. A polite staff prepares several types of grilled meats with well-rehearsed ceremony in the Castilian style. The chef works hard at diversifying into modern and creative interpretations of Spanish cuisine as well. Specific menu choices change with the seasons, but make ample use of autumn and winter game dishes, fresh and exotic mushrooms and asparagus, freshly culled herbs, and fresh seafood.

Río de la Plata, Plaza del Poso, 1. ☎ **21-90-05.**

Cuisine: CASTILIAN. **Reservations:** Recommended.
Prices: Appetizers 950–1,500 ptas. ($6.70–$10.70); main courses 1,500–2,500 ptas. ($10.70–$17.80); *menú del día* 2,000 ptas. ($14.20). MC, V.
Open: Lunch, Tues–Sun 1:30–4pm; dinner, Tues–Sun 8:45pm–midnight.
Closed: July.

This tiny basement restaurant, two blocks south of Plaza Mayor on a small side square formed by the junction of Plaza Poeta Iglesia and Calle San Justo, has thrived since 1958. The kitchen uses fresh ingredients, preparing a traditional *cocida castellana* (Castilian stew), house-style sole, roast baby goat, many varieties of fish, and pungently flavored sausages. The linen is crisply ironed, the service usually impeccable.

An Easy Excursion to Alba de Tormes

Admirers of St. Teresa may want to make the 11-mile (18km) pilgrimage southeast of Salamanca to visit the medieval village of Alba de Tormes. Cross a bridge with 22 arches spanning the Tormes River. Head between the Iglesia de San Pedro and the Basilica de Santa Teresa to Plaza de Santa Teresa, where you will come upon the **Convento de las Carmelitas** and the **Iglesia de Santa Teresa.** The church is a medley of Gothic, Renaissance, and baroque styles. In its marble vault (over the altar) are the ashes of Spain's most beloved saint, St. Teresa of Ávila, who died here in 1582. One of the two reliquaries flanking the altar is said to contain her arm; the other is said to contain her heart. Opposite the entrance door in the rear of the church is a grating through which you can look at the cell in which she died. Pope John Paul II visited Alba de Tormes in 1982 on the occasion of the 400th anniversary of St. Teresa's death. Admission is free. The church is open daily from 9am to 2pm and 4 to 8pm.

2 Ciudad Rodrigo

54 miles (87km) SW of Salamanca, 177 miles (285km) W of Madrid

GETTING THERE • By Train There are five trains per day from Salamanca; the trip takes 1¾ hours. The station is about a 10-minute walk from the center of town.

• By Bus Seven buses per day depart Madrid for Ciudad Rodrigo. The trip takes 1¼ hours from Salamanca, 3½ hours from Madrid.

• By Car The A-620 is the town's main link to both Salamanca and Portugal. Driving time from Salamanca is about 1¼ hours.

ESSENTIALS The area code for Ciudad Rodrigo is 923. The tourist information office is at Arco de Amayuelas, 5 (☎ **923/46-05-61**).

A walled town dating from Roman days, Ciudad Rodrigo is known for its 16th- and 17th-century town houses, built by followers of the conquistadors. It was founded in the 12th century by Count Rodriguez González and today has been designated a national monument. Near the Portuguese frontier, it stands high on a hilltop and is known for the familiar silhouette of the square tower of its Alcázar.

The ramparts were built in the 12th century along Roman foundations. Several stairways lead up to a mile-long sentry path. You can wander these ramparts at leisure and then walk through the streets with their many churches and mansions. It is not one chief monument that is the allure, but rather the city as a whole.

The town's major attraction is its cathedral, **Casco Viejo,** built between 1170 and 1230. It is reached east of Plaza Mayor through Plaza de San Salvador. Subsequent centuries saw more additions. The Renaissance altar on the north aisle is an acclaimed work of ecclesiastical art; look also for the Virgin Portal, at the west door, which dates from the 1200s. For 50 pesetas (40¢), you'll be admitted to the cloisters, which have a medley of architectural styles, including a Plateresque door. Hours are daily from 8am to 7pm.

The **Plaza Mayor** is a showpiece of 17th-century architecture, with two Renaissance palaces. This is the main square of the city.

Your transportation in Ciudad Rodrigo will be your trusty feet, as walking is the only way to "cover" the city. Pick up a map at the tourist office (see above).

Where to Stay

Conde Rodrigo I, Plaza de San Salvador, 9, 37500 Ciudad Rodrigo. ☎ **923/46-14-04.** Fax 923/46-14-08. 35 rms (all with bath). A/C TV

Rates: 4,700 ptas. ($33.40) single; 6,000 ptas. ($42.60) double. Breakfast 400 ptas. ($2.80) extra. AE, DC, MC, V.

Its central location next to the cathedral is one of this two-star hotel's advantages. Behind thick old walls of chiseled stone are simple but comfortable guest rooms, each of which contains a thoughtful bouquet of extras. Full meals in the hotel's popular restaurant go for 1,500 pesetas. ($10.70).

Parador Nacional Enrique II, Plaza del Castillo, 1, 37500 Ciudad Rodrigo. ☎ **923/46-01-50.** Fax 923/46-04-04. 27 rms, 1 suite (all with bath). A/C MINIBAR TV TEL

Rates: 10,000 ptas. ($71) single; 12,500 ptas. ($88.80) double; 15,000 ptas. ($106.50) suite. Breakfast 1,200 ptas. ($8.50) extra. AE, DC, MC, V.

This completely restored building was an embattled castle in the 12th century, constructed by Enrique II of Trastamara on a hill overlooking Río Agueda. The Torre del Homenaje (keep) defines the profile of Ciudad Rodrigo, and once it was the seat of the feudal court. The parador has several gates and what the Spanish call *miradores*—platforms offering panoramic views. Sunset watching is a popular pastime. The Gothic entrance bears the royal coat-of-arms and a plaque in Gothic letters. The facilities include a garden and a foreign exchange. A complete lunch or dinner costs from 3,200 ptas. ($22.70). The food is well prepared, and the service polite.

WHERE TO DINE

$ **Estoril,** Traversia Talavera, 1. ☎ **46-05-50.**

Cuisine: CASTILIAN/BASQUE. **Reservations:** Recommended.
Prices: Appetizers 650–1,500 ptas. ($4.60–$10.70); main courses 1,200–1,800 ptas. ($8.50–$12.80); *menú del día* 1,400 ptas. ($9.90). AE, DC, MC, V.
Open: Lunch, daily 1–4pm; dinner, daily 8:30pm–midnight.

Lying only a short walk from Plaza Mayor, this popular restaurant was established in 1967, within a building constructed that year. Decorated in a typical regional style, with bullfight photographs, it seats you in air-conditioned comfort. Specialties of the house include roasted meats, including roast suckling pig, but with a special emphasis on roasted goat. Seafood is represented in the Basque style here, and other good dishes include scrambled eggs with shrimp, sea bream, and, for the inevitable finish, carmelized custard (flan). Everything is washed down with a variety of regional wines, including Cosechero Rioja.

Mayton, La Colada, 9. ☎ **46-07-20.**

Cuisine: CASTILIAN. **Reservations:** Recommended.
Prices: Appetizers 550–1,200 ptas. ($3.90–$8.50); main courses 800–2,250 ptas. ($5.70–$16); fixed-price menu 1,400 ptas. ($9.90). AE, DC, MC, V.
Open: Lunch, Thurs–Tues 12:30–3:30pm; dinner, Thurs–Tues 7:30pm–12:30am.

Adjacent to Plaza Mayor, within a 17th-century building, Mayton is considered the best restaurant in the city. The walls of the antique and well-preserved bodega in which it stands reverberate with atmosphere and legend. The menu specializes in fresh fish and shellfish. Try the *sopa castellana* (Castilian soup) for an appetizer, followed by *merluza* (hake) in green sauce. You can also order veal, as tender as that of Ávila. The place is air-conditioned.

3 Zamora

40 miles (64km) N of Salamanca, 148 miles (238km) NW of Madrid

GETTING THERE • **By Train** There are four trains to and from Madrid every day and two to and from La Coruña (the trip takes three and six hours, respectively). The railway station is at Calle Alfonso Peña, 3 (☎ **52-19-56**), about a 15-minute walk from the edge of the old town. Follow Avenida de las Tres Cruces northeast of the center of town.

• **By Bus** More than 12 connections a day from Salamanca make this the easiest way to get in and out of town. Travel time between the cities is one hour. There are about six to seven buses a day from Madrid and five to seven buses per day from León. The town's bus station lies a few paces from the railway station, at Calle Alfonso Peña, 3 (☎ **52-12-81**).

• **By Car** Zamora is at the junction of eight different roads and highways. Most of the traffic from northern Portugal into Spain comes through Zamora. Highways headed north to León, south to Salamanca, and east to Valladolid are especially convenient. From Madrid, take the A-6 superhighway northwest toward Valladolid, cutting west on the N-VI and west again at the turnoff onto 122.

ESSENTIALS The area code for Zamora is 980. The tourist information office is at Santa Clara, 20 (☎ **980/53-18-45**).

SPECIAL EVENTS Holy Week in Zamora is a celebration known throughout the country. Street processions, called *pasos,* are considered the most spectacular in Spain. If you plan to visit at this time, secure hotel reservations well in advance.

Little known to North American visitors, Zamora (pronounced "tha-*mor*-a") is perhaps the most representative city of Old Castile, blending ancient and modern, but noted mainly for its Romanesque architecture. In fact, Zamora is often called a "Romanesque museum." A medieval frontier city, it rises up starkly from the Castile flatlands, a reminder of an era of conquering monarchs and forgotten kingdoms.

You can explore Zamora's highlights in about four hours. Stroll along the main square, dusty Plaza Canovas, cross the arched Romanesque bridge from the 1300s, and take in at least some of the Romanesque churches for which the town is known. Many of them date from the 12th century. The cathedral is the best example, but others include **Iglesia de la Magdelena,** Rua de los Francos, and **Iglesia de San Ildefonso,** Calle Ramos Carrión. You might also want to look at **Iglesia de Santa María La Nueva,** Plaza de Santa María, and **Iglesia de Santiago el Burgo,** Calle Santa Clara.

The crowning achievement, however, at the far west end of Zamora, is the **cathedral,** Plaza Castillo o Pio XII, open daily from 11am to 1pm. It is topped by a gold-and-white Eastern-looking dome. Inside, you'll find rich hangings, interesting chapels, two 15th-century Mudéjar pulpits, and intricately carved choir stalls. Later architectural styles, including Gothic, have been added to the original Romanesque features, but this indiscriminate mixing of periods is typical of Spanish cathedrals. Inside the cloister, the Museo de la Catedral possesses ecclesiastical art, historical documents, church documents, and an unusual collection of "Black Tapestries" dating from the 1400s. The cathedral is free but admission to the museum costs 200 ptas. ($1.40).

The cathedral can generally be visited throughout the day. However, the museum is open July through September, daily 11am–2pm and 5–8pm; off-season, Oct–June, daily 9am–2pm and 4–6pm.

Where to Stay

MODERATE

★ **Hostería Real de Zamora,** Cuesta de Pizarro, 7, 49027 Zamora. ☎ or Fax **980/53-45-45.** 15 rms (all with bath). MINIBAR TV TEL

Rates: (including breakfast): 5,255–6,055 ptas. ($37.30–$43) single; 6,925–7,925 ptas. ($49.20–$56.30) double. AE, DC, MC, V. **Parking:** 750 ptas. ($5.30).

Probably the most charming small hotel in town, sporting walls that date from the 1400s, this establishment occupies the long-ago headquarters of Zamora's dreaded Inquisition. (Prior to that, ironically, the site housed a Jewish-owned building reputed to have been the home of the explorer Pizarro.) Today, the outstanding historical features of the building include a Jewish-funded medieval reservoir, a patio that many visitors consider perfect for drinking tea or coffee, and a verdant garden that lies along the city's medieval fortifications. An excellent example of a tastefully modernized aristocratic villa, it stands a few steps to the west of the northern embankment of the city's most photographed bridge, the Stone Bridge. Bedrooms contain simple but solid furnishings and offer safety-deposit boxes.

Dining/Entertainment: The Restaurant Pizarro, with the air of a baronial private dining room, offers three-course fixed-price meals ranging from 2,500 ptas. ($17.80). Adjacent to it is the Restaurant Hostería Real, offering basically the same menu, and a bar.

Services: 24-hour room service, laundry, babysitting.

Facilities: Car rentals.

★ **Parador Turistico de Zamora,** Plaza de Viriato, 5, 49001 Zamora. ☎ **980/51-44-97.** Fax 980/53-00-63. 25 rms (all with bath), 2 suites. MINIBAR TV TEL

Rates: 10,000 ptas. ($71) single; 12,500 ptas. ($88.80) double; suites 14,500 ptas. ($103). Breakfast 1,100 ptas. ($7.80) extra. **Parking:** 600 ptas. ($4.30). AE, DC, MC, V.

The site of this parador has always fulfilled a legendary role within Zamora. Originally fortified as an *Alcazaba* by the Moors during their occupation of Zamora, it was later expanded into a palace during the late middle ages. Most of that original monument was demolished and rebuilt upon its ancient foundations in 1459 by the Count of Alva y Aliste, and today retains the severe, high-ceilinged dignity of its 15th-century Gothic form. Renovated by the Spanish government in the late 1960s, it is today considered one of the most beautiful and desirable paradors in Spain.

Set two blocks south of Plaza Mayor, near the junction of Plaza de Viriato and Calle Ramos Carrión, the parador is richly decorated with medieval armor, antique furniture, tapestries, old mirrors and clocks, and verdant potted plants. In winter, glass partitions close off a large inner patio centered around an antique well, while baronial fireplaces provide much-appreciated warmth. Bedrooms are white walled, clean, and tastefully decorated with conservative furniture.

Dining/Entertainment: The dining room, where dinner costs 3,200 pesetas ($22.70), has been done in a sumptuous rustic style, with a view of the swimming pool and surrounding countryside. There's also a cozy bar (open daily from 12:30 to 11pm).

Services: Room service, laundry/valet, babysitting.

Facilities: Swimming pool.

BUDGET

$ **Hostal Chiqui,** Benavente, 2, 49002 Zamora. ☎ **980/53-14-80.** 14 rms (all with bath).

Rates: 2,200 ptas. ($15.60) single; 3,800 ptas. ($27) double. No credit cards.

If you're looking for a bargain and you don't mind a few minor inconveniences, try this simple second-floor pension. The guest rooms are Spartan but clean, with almost no accessories. No breakfast is served, but cafés are within walking distance. Chiqui lies behind the post office in the northwest section of the old town, near a corner of busy Calle Santa Clara.

Where to Dine

Restaurant París, Avenida de Portugal, 14. ☎ **51-43-25.**

Cuisine: SPANISH/INTERNATIONAL. **Reservations:** Recommended.

Prices: Appetizers 600–1,450 ptas. ($4.30–$10.30); main dishes 1,600–2,600 ptas. ($11.40–$18.50); fixed-price menu 1,600–2,600 ptas. ($11.40–$18.50). AE, DC, MC, V.

Open: Lunch, daily 1:30–4:30pm; dinner, daily 8:30pm–midnight.

This elegantly decorated, air-conditioned restaurant is known for its fish, often made with a regionally inspired twist. Well-prepared specialties include vegetable flan, braised oxtail, Zamora-style clams, and a delectable hake. Most critics rate this restaurant number one in town. It is on the main traffic artery (Avenida de Portugal) that funnels traffic south to Salamanca.

Restaurant Serafín, Plaza Maestro Haedo, 10. ☎ **53-14-22.**

Cuisine: SPANISH. **Reservations:** Not required.

Prices: Appetizers 350–2,000 ptas. ($2.50–$14.20); main courses 1,000–2,750 ptas. ($7.10–$19.50); fixed price menus 1,200–4,600 ptas. ($8.50–$32.70). AE, DC, MC, V.

Open: Lunch, daily 1–4:30pm; dinner, daily 8:30pm–midnight.

At the northeast edge of the old town, about a block south of the busy traffic hub of Plaza Alemania and Avenida de Alfonso IX, this air-conditioned haven with an attractive bar makes a relaxing retreat from the sun. The specialties change with the season but might include seafood soup Serafín, paella, fried hake, Iberian ham, and a savory *cocido* (stew).

Evening Entertainment

Calle Los Herreros, or "Calle de Vinos," contains more bars per square foot than any street in Zamora—about 16 of them in all. Each is willing to accommodate a stranger with a leisurely glass of wine or beer and a selection of tapas. Calle Los Herreros is a narrow street at the southern end of the old town, about two blocks north of the Duero River, within the shadow of the Ayuntamiento Viejo (Old Town Hall), one block south of Plaza Mayor.

4 León

203 miles (327km) NW of Madrid, 122 miles (196km) N of Salamanca

GETTING THERE • By Train León has good rail connections to the rest of Spain—five trains run to Madrid daily from León. The station, Estación del Norte, Avenida de Astorga, 2 (☎ **27-02-02**), lies on the western bank of the Bernesga River. Cross the bridge near Plaza de Guzmán el Bueno. The *rápido* train from Madrid takes five hours, the *talgo* only four.

• By Bus Most of León's buses arrive and depart from the Estación de Autobuses, Paseo Ingeniero Saenz de Miera (☎ **21-10-00**). Three to five buses per day also link León with Zamora and Salamanca, and there are seven per day from Madrid (trip time: $4^1/_2$ hours).

• By Car León lies at the junction of five major highways coming from five different regions of Spain. From Madrid, head northwest from Madrid's periphery on the N-VI superhighway toward La Coruña. At Benavente, bear right onto the N-630.

ESSENTIALS León's area code is 987. The tourist information office is at Plaza de Regla, 4 (☎ **987/23-70-82**).

Once the leading city of Christian Spain, this old cathedral town was the capital of a centuries-old empire that declined after uniting with Castile. León today is the gateway from Old Castile to the northwestern routes of Galicia. It is a sprawling city, but nearly everything of interest to visitors—monuments, restaurants, and hotels—can be covered on foot, once you arm yourself with a good map.

What to See & Do

★ **Catedral de León [Santa Maria de Regla],** Plaza de Regla. ☎ **23-00-60.**

The usual cathedral elements are virtually eclipsed here by the awesome stained-glass windows—some 125 in all (plus 57 *oculi*), the oldest dating from the 13th century. They are so heavy they have strained the walls of the cathedral. Look for a 15th-century altarpiece depicting the Entombment in the Capilla Mayor, as well as a Renaissance *trascoro* by Juan de Badajoz. The nave dates from the 13th and 14th centuries; the Renaissance vaulting is much later. Almost as interesting as the stained-glass windows are the cloisters, dating in part from the 13th and 14th centuries and containing faded frescoes and Romanesque and Gothic tombs; some capitals are carved with starkly lifelike scenes. Visitors can also see a museum containing valuable art and artifacts, including a Bible from the 10th century, notable sculptures, and a collection of romantic images of the Virgin Mary. The cathedral is on the edge of the old city, seven blocks east of the town's most central square, Plaza de Santo Domingo.

Admission: Cathedral, free; cloister and museum, 300 ptas. ($2.10).

Open: Cathedral, daily 8:30am–1:30pm and 4–7pm. Cloisters and museum, Mon–Sat 9:30am–1pm and 4–6:30pm. **Bus:** 4 or 9.

Panteón y Museos de San Isidoro, Plaza San Isidoro, 4. ☎ **22-96-08.**

This church, just a short walk northwest of the cathedral, was dedicated to San Isidoro de Sevilla in 1063 and contains 23 tombs of Leonese kings. One of the first Romanesque buildings in León and Castile, it was embellished by Ferdinand I's artists. The columns are magnificent, the capitals splendidly decorated; covering the vaults are murals from the 12th century. Unique in Spain, the Treasury holds rare finds—a 10th-century Scandinavian ivory, an 11th-century chalice, and an important collection of 10th- to 12th-century cloths from Asia. The Library contains many ancient manuscripts and rare books, including a Book of Job from 951, a Visigothic Bible, and an 1162 Bible, plus dozens of miniatures.

Admission: 300 ptas. ($2.10).

Open: Tues–Sat 10am–1:30pm and 4–6:30pm; Sun 10am–1:30pm. **Bus:** 4 or 9.

Where to Stay

EXPENSIVE

★ **Parador San Marcos,** Plaza de San Marcos, 7, 24001 León. ☎ **987/23-73-00.** Fax 987/23-34-58. 251 rms, 2 suites. A/C TV TEL

Rates: 16,500–22,000 ptas. ($117.20–$156.20) single or double; 42,000 ptas. ($298.20) suite. Breakfast buffet 1,300 ptas. ($9.20) extra. AE, DC, MC, V. **Parking:** Free.

A top tourist attraction, this 16th-century former monastery with its celebrated Plateresque facade is one of the most spectacular hotels in Spain. The government has remodeled it at great expense, installing extravagant authentic antiques and quality reproductions. The old "hostal" used to put up pilgrims bound for Santiago de Compostela, and it still does today. The parador also contains a church with a scallop-shell facade and an archeological museum. The guest rooms are sumptuous, each with private bath. A complete dinner here runs to 3,800 pesetas ($27). The parador is located northwest of the cathedral on the outskirts of the old town, on the east bank of the Bernesga River.

MODERATE

Hotel Quindós, Avenida José Antonio, 24, 24002 León. ☎ **987/23-62-00.** 96 rms (all with bath). TV TEL **Bus:** 4 or 9.

Rates: 5,850 ptas. ($41.50) single; 8,500 ptas. ($60.40) double. Breakfast 580 ptas. ($4.10) extra. AE, DC, MC, V.

This rather functional hotel has been tastefully decorated with modern paintings, which enhance the establishment considerably. The snug, comfortable, and well-maintained rooms are a good value. The hotel offers two restaurants, one with menus typical of Old Castile, another more elegant dining room serving an international cuisine. You can, for example, enjoy fish of the day baked in an oven, sirloin with onion jelly, and marinated pigeon. The Quindós lies three blocks south of Plaza de San Marcos, in the central commercial district in the northwest quadrant of the old town.

BUDGET

$ **Guzmán El Bueno,** López Castrillón, 6, 24003 León. ☎ **987/23-64-12.** 29 rms (20 with bath).

Directions: Walk up Calle Generalísimo from Plaza de Santo Domingo, turning left onto Calle de Cid. López Castrillón is a pedestrian-only street, branching off to the right.

Rates: 1,900 ptas. ($13.50) single without bath, 2,500 ptas. ($17.80) single with bath; 3,000 ptas. ($21.30) double without bath, 4,200 ptas. ($29.80) double with bath. Breakfast 300 ptas. ($2.10) extra. No credit cards.

The cheapest comfortable accommodation in León is the no-frills Guzmán El Bueno, on the second floor of a centrally located boardinghouse. In all, it's a safe destination, widely known among international student travelers, who are drawn to its low prices. Some rooms have phones; all are clean.

This hostal lies on the second floor of a semi-modern, nondescript building without frills of any kind. Favored by student travelers and rock-bottom budgeteers, it's basic, extremely simple, and somewhat anonymous. Still, it appeals because of its low cost and its relative cleanliness. Be warned in advance that the staff speaks only Spanish.

Where to Dine

Albina, Condesa de Sagasta, 24. ☎ **22-19-12.**

Cuisine: FRENCH/SPANISH. **Reservations:** Recommended. **Bus:** 4 or 9.
Prices: Appetizers 700–1,400 ptas. ($5–$9.90); main courses 1,600–2,200 ptas. ($11.40–$15.60); *menú del día* 1,600 ptas. ($11.40). AE, MC, V.

Outside the city center, a 15-minute walk northwest of the cathedral, adjacent to the Parador San Marcos, is this contemporary restaurant much favored by local residents. Within a modern and monochromatic interior, the owner supervises the preparation of fresh fish and meat dishes that are loosely based on French and Spanish models. Signature dishes include *lubina a la sal* (whitefish cooked in a salt crust); filet steak with pepper, carefully seasoned filets of pork, and roast duck in orange sauce. A long wine list is available, and the room is air-conditioned.

Casa Pozo, Plaza San Marcelo, 15. ☎ **22-30-39.**

Cuisine: SPANISH. **Reservations:** Recommended. **Bus:** 4 or 9.
Prices: Appetizers 800–1,000 ptas. ($5.70–$7.10); main courses 1,700–2,800 ptas. ($12.10–$19.90); fixed price menus 2,500–4,500 ptas. ($17.80–$32). AE, DC, MC, V.
Open: Lunch, Mon–Sat 1–4pm; dinner, Mon–Sat 8:30–11:30pm. **Closed:** First two weeks of July; two weeks around Christmas.

Two blocks south of the busy traffic hub of Plaza Santo Domingo and across from city hall, this unpretentious restaurant is a long-enduring favorite with locals who appreciate its unassuming style and flavorful cuisine. Habitués call owner Gabriel del Pozo Alvarez, "Pin," and he's the reason behind the success of the place. Specialties, all made from fresh ingredients, include peas with salty ham, shrimp with asparagus, roast pork or lamb laden with herbs and spices, and a delicate smothered sole known as *estofado*. The restaurant offers an excellent selection of Rioja wines.

Mesón Leonés del Racimo de Oro, Caño Badillo, 2. ☎ **25-75-75.**

Cuisine: CASTILIAN. **Reservations:** Required.
Prices: Appetizers 650–950 ptas. ($4.60–$6.70); main courses 1,600–3,000 ptas. ($11.40–$21.30); fixed price menu 1,500 ptas. ($10.70). AE, MC, V.

Behind Plaza Mayor and beside the cathedral, this bodega is housed in a structure from the early 1700s, and even it was built on older foundations. As such, it is one of the two or three oldest inns in León, and a lot of food and wine have been consumed on this site over the centuries. The building is what the Spanish call a *mesón típico* (house built in the regional style), and its tables overlook a patio. The food is consistently good, with the owner specializing in a regional cuisine—*mollejas con rabo de toro* (oxtail), for example, or "hake (*merluza*) house style." You might begin with an appetizer of Serrano ham or clams, then follow with one of the roast meats, such as roast suckling lamb cooked in a wood-fired clay oven. The service is attentive.

5 Valladolid

125 miles (201km) NW of Madrid; 83 miles (133km) SE of León

GETTING THERE • By Plane Flights to Valladolid land at Vallanubla Airport Highway N-601 (☎ **56-01-62**), a 15-minute taxi ride from the center of town. Aviaco routes daily flights to and from Barcelona and Madrid. The local Aviaco/Iberia office is located at Gamazo, 17 (☎ **30-06-66**).

• By Train Valladolid is well serviced by some two dozen daily trains to and from Madrid (trip time: 4 hours). Other cities with train links to Valladolid include Salamanca (eight trains each per day) and Burgos (11 trains each per day). The train station (Estación del Norte), Calle Recondo, s/n, is about one mile south of the historic center of town, one block southwest of Campo Grande park. The phone number of the railway station is **30-35-18**. There's a RENFE office selling tickets at Divina Pastora, 6 (☎ **21-09-28**). Phone reservations can be made daily from 9:30am to 1:30pm and 4:30 to 7:30pm.

• By Bus The bus station lies within an eight-minute walk of the railway station, at Puente Colgante, 2 (☎ **23-63-08**), at the southern edge of town. There are more than a dozen buses every day to and from Madrid, 2$^1/_2$ hours away. From Zamora, two buses arrive per day (trip time: 40 minutes) and from Burgos 11 buses per day (trip time: 2 hours).

• By Car Valladolid lies at the center of the rectangle created by Burgos, León, Segovia, and Salamanca and is interconnected to each with good highways. From Madrid, driving time is about 2$^1/_4$ hours. Take superhighway A-6 northwest from Madrid, turning north on 403.

ESSENTIALS The area code for Valladolid is 983. The tourist information office is at Plaza de Zorilla, 3 (☎ **983/35-18-01**).

From the 13th century until its eventual decay in the early 17th century, Valladolid was a royal city and an intellectual center that attracted saints and philosophers. Isabella and Ferdinand were married here; Philip II was born here; and Columbus died here on May 19, 1506, broken in spirit and body after Isabella had died and Ferdinand refused to reinstate him as a governor of the Indies.

Valladolid is bitterly cold in winter, sweltering in summer. Today, after years of decline, the city is reviving economically and producing among other things, flour, ironware, and cars. Consequently, it's polluted and noisy, and many of the old buildings have been replaced by utilitarian ones, although there are many attractions remaining.

From the tourist office (see above), you can pick up a map—*plano de la ciudad*—that marks all the major monuments of Valladolid. These attractions can be covered on foot, although you may want to take a taxi to the two most distant points recommended—the Museo Nacional de Escultura and the Museo Oriental.

What to See & Do

Museo Nacional de Escultura (National Museum of Sculpture),

Colegio de San Gregorio, Calle Cadeñas de San Gregorio, I. ☎ **26-79-67.**

Located near Plaza de San Pablo, the museum displays a magnificent collection of gilded polychrome sculpture, an art form that reached its pinnacle in Valladolid. The figures were first carved from wood, then painted with consummate skill and grace to assume lifelike dimensions. See, especially, the works by Alonso Berruguete (1480–1561), son of Pedro, one of Spain's great painters. From 1527 to 1532 the younger Berruguete labored over the altar of the Convent of San Benito—a masterpiece now housed here. In particular, see his *Crucifix with the Virgin and St. John* in Room II and his *St. Sebastian and the Sacrifice of Isaac* in Room III. Works by Juan de Juni and Gregorio Fernández are also displayed.

After visiting the galleries, explore the two-story cloisters. The upper level is florid, with jutting gargoyles and fleurs-de-lis. See the chapel where the confessor to Isabella I (Fray Alonso de Burgos) was buried—and don't miss the gruesome sculpture *Death.*

Admission: 200 ptas. ($1.40).

Open: Tues–Sat 10am–2pm and 4–6pm; Sun 10am–2pm.

Cathedral, Plaza de la Universidad. ☎ **30-43-62.**

In 1580, Philip II commissioned Juan de Herrera, architect of El Escorial, to construct this monument in the city where he was born. When Philip died in 1598, work came to a stop for 18 years. Alberto Churriguera resumed construction, drawing up more flamboyant plans, especially for the exterior, in an unharmonious contrast to the severe lines of his predecessor. The classical, even sober, interior conforms more with Herrera's designs. A highlight is the 1551 altarpiece in the main apsidal chapel, the work of Juan de Juni. Art critics have commented that his polychrome figures are "truly alive." The cathedral is in the heart of the city, east of Plaza Mayor and north of Plaza de Santa Cruz.

Admission: Cathedral, free; museum, 200 ptas. ($1.40).

Open: Cathedral, daily 10am–2pm and 5–8pm. Museum, Tues–Fri 10am–1:30pm and 4:30–7pm; Sat–Sun 10am–2pm.

Iglesia de San Pablo, Plaza San Pablo, 4. ☎ **35-17-48.**

Once a 17th-century Dominican monastery, San Pablo, with its Isabelline-Gothic facade, is very impressive. Flanked by two towers, the main entrance supports levels of lacy stone sculpture. The church lies six blocks north of the cathedral, one block south of busy Avenida Santa Teresa.

Admission: Free.

Open: Daily 7:30am–1pm and 5–9:30pm.

Museo Oriental, Paseo de Filipinos, 7. ☎ **30-68-00.**

Located in the Royal College of the Augustinian Fathers, near Campo Grande park, the museum has 14 rooms: 10 Chinese and 4 Filipino. It has the best collection of Asian art in Spain, with bronzes from the 7th century B.C. to the 18th century A.D.; wooden carvings; 100 fine porcelain pieces; paintings on paper and silk from the 12th century to the 19th; and ancient Chinese coins, furniture, jade, and ivory. In the Filipino section, ethnological and primitive art is represented by shields and arms. Eighteenth-century religious art can be admired in extraordinary ivories, embroideries, painting, and silversmiths' work. Popular art of the 19th century includes bronzes, musical instruments, and statuary.

Admission: 300 ptas. ($2.10); children 9 and under free.

Open: Mon–Sat 4–7pm; Sun 10am–2pm.

Casa de Cervantes, Calle del Rastro, s/n. ☎ **30-88-10.**

Now a museum, this house was once occupied by Miguel de Cervantes, author of *Don Quixote,* who did much of his writing in Valladolid. Here the author remained for the last years of his life; behind its white walls, the house is simply furnished, as it was in his day. It lies half a block south of the cathedral, two blocks north of the city park, Campo Grande.

Admission: 200 ptas. ($1.40).

Open: Tues–Sat 10am–3:30pm; Sun 10am–3pm.

Where to Stay

MODERATE

Felipe IV, Calle de Gamazo, 16, 47004 Valladolid. ☎ **983/30-70-00.** 13 rms (all with bath). A/C TV TEL

Rates: 6,575–8,575 ptas. ($46.70–$60.90) single; 10,825–12,975 ptas. ($76.90–$92.10) double. Breakfast 675 ptas. ($4.80) extra. AE, DC, MC, V. **Parking:** 1,200 ptas. ($8.50).

When it was built, the Felipe IV was considered one of the grandest hotels in the city. Each of its bedrooms was modernized in 1981, guaranteeing its position as one of Valladolid's solidly acceptable establishments. A garage provides parking for motorists. The hotel is south of the busy traffic hub of Plaza de Madrid, a few blocks north of the rail station, near the eastern edge of the city park, Campo Grande.

Hotel Meliá Parque, Joaquin Garcia Morato, 17, 47007 Valladolid. ☎ **983/22-00-00,** or toll free in the U.S. **800/336-3542.** Fax 983/47-50-29. 293 rms (all with bath). A/C TV TEL

Rates: 6,825–7,200 ptas. ($48.50–$51.10) single; 11,000–18,270 ptas. ($78.10–$129.70) double. Breakfast 1,000 ptas. ($7.10) extra. AE, DC, MC, V. **Parking:** 1,200 ptas. ($8.50).

Completed in 1982, this modern chain hotel two blocks west of the rail station lies on the city outskirts. It's popular with business travelers unwilling to negotiate the labyrinth of Valladolid's central streets. The guest rooms are comfortable and functionally furnished—with no surprises and few disappointments. It also provides special rooms and facilities for the disabled. The hotel has a restaurant featuring Castilian meals for 2,650 pesetas ($18.80).

Hotel Old Meliá, Plaza San Miguel, 10, 47003 Valladolid. ☎ **983/35-72-00,** or toll free in the U.S. **800/336-3542** in the U.S. Fax 983/33-68-28. 210 rms, 8 suites. A/C MINIBAR TV TEL

Rates: 10,500 ptas. ($74.60) single; 13,000 ptas. ($92.30) double; 23,500 ptas. ($166.90) suite. Breakfast 1,100 ptas. ($7.80) extra. AE, MC, V. **Parking:** 1,200 ptas ($8.50).

Set in the heart of the historic zone, about five blocks northwest of the cathedral, this is a modern hotel whose original construction in the early 1970s has been upgraded throughout the public rooms with a postmodern gloss. The bedrooms are probably the most comfortable in town, filled with heavy Iberian furniture that seems to suit the hotel's neighborhood.

Dining/Entertainment: There are an in-house restaurant floored with cool slabs of polished stone and a bar.

IMPRESSIONS

Valladolid, sovereign of infirmity. The priest's early death, the maggot's Compostela.
—Guillem de la Gonagal

Services: Room service (available from 7am to 11pm), laundry, babysitting. **Facilities:** Hairdresser/barber.

INEXPENSIVE

Enara, Plaza de España, 5, 47001 Valladolid. ☎ **983/30-03-11.** 25 rms (all with shower). TV TEL

Rates: 4,028 ptas. ($28.60) single; 5,936 ptas. ($42.10) double. Breakfast 300 ptas. ($2.10) extra. AE, MC, V.
Parking: 1,200 ptas. ($8.50) nearby.

About a quarter mile south of the cathedral, near the junction of Avenida 2 de Mayo and Paseo Miguel Iscar, Enara is arguably the best budget accommodation in Valladolid. Its central location is backed up by contemporary, pleasantly furnished guest rooms. There is no restaurant, but a continental breakfast is offered, and you'll be near many low-cost dining rooms and cafés.

Originally built in the 19th century as a private house, it was converted into a hotel in the mid-1970s. Two of its three stories are devoted to simple but well-maintained bedrooms, and the ground floor contains the breakfast area.

Where to Dine

★ **La Fragua,** Paseo de Zorilla, 10. ☎ **33-87-85.**

Cuisine: CASTILIAN. **Reservations:** Recommended.
Prices: Appetizers 900–1,500 ptas. ($6.40–$10.70); main courses 1,400–2,800 ptas. ($9.90–$19.90). AE, DC, MC, V.
Open: Lunch, Tues–Sun 1:30–4pm; dinner, Tues–Sat 8:30pm–midnight.

Amid rustic decor you'll enjoy beautifully prepared Castilian dishes, the best in town, at this restaurant just north of the rail station across busy Paseo de Zorilla. You might begin with spicy sausage, followed by beef, chicken, or lamb, each carefully seasoned and served in a generous portion. A wide variety of fish is imported daily. The huge wine list offers many regional vintages, one of which the steward will choose for you if you request it. Dessert could include a cheese tart or a melt-in-your-mouth chocolate truffle. Owner Antonio Garrote proudly displays his culinary diplomas.

Mesón Cervantes, Rastro, 6. ☎ **30-61-38.**

Cuisine: SPANISH/INTERNATIONAL. **Reservations:** Recommended.
Prices: Appetizers 600–2,000 ptas. ($4.30–$14.20); main course 1,500–2,500 ptas. ($10.70–$17.80). AE, DC, MC, V.
Open: Lunch, Mon–Sat noon–4pm; dinner, Mon–Sat 9am–12:30am. **Closed:** Aug.

This restaurant, regarded by some devotees as the finest in the city, opened in 1973 in a building custom-constructed for that purpose. The owner, Alejandro, works the dining room at Mesón Cervantes, capably complemented in the kitchen by his wife, Julia. Neighborhood residents favor this place for its lack of pretension and its delectable cuisine. Two particular favorites here are sole with pine nuts and seasonal river crabs. Many other fish dishes, including hake and monkfish, are available. Roast suckling pig and roast lamb are also popular. Other specialties include peppers stuffed with crabmeat, tender veal scaloppini "Don Quixote," served with a piquant sauce; and *arroz con liebre* (herb-laden rice studded with chunks of roasted wild rabbit, in season). The restaurant stands beside the Casa de Cervantes, half a mile south of the cathedral.

Mesón Panero, Marina Escobar, 1. ☎ **30-70-19.**

Cuisine: CASTILIAN/INTERNATIONAL. **Reservations:** Required.
Prices: Appetizers 1,100–1,600 ptas. ($7.80–$11.40); main courses 2,100–2,700 ptas. ($14.90–$19.20). AE, DC, MC, V.
Open: Lunch, daily 1:30–4pm; dinner, July–Aug daily 9pm-midnight; Sept–June Mon–Sat 9pm–midnight.

The chef of this imaginative restaurant, Angel Cuadrado, can turn even the most austere traditional Castilian recipes into sensual experiences. Set near the water, this 1960s establishment lures diners with fresh fish, including a succulent brochette of sole and hake with fresh asparagus. Every week brings a featured favorite: *cocida castellana,* the famous regional stew. Roast lamb and suckling pig are also available, plus a selection of well-chosen wines. The Mesón Panero is near the Casa de Cervantes, just a short walk from the tourist office.

6 Burgos

150 miles (242km) N of Madrid, 75 miles (121km) NE of Valladolid

GETTING THERE • By Train Burgos is well connected to Madrid (eight trains per day making the 3- to 5-hour trip), Barcelona (two trains daily, making the 8- to 9-hour run), the French border (nine per day), and Valladolid (eight to nine each per day). The Burgos railway station lies at the terminus of Avenida de Conde Guadalhorce, half a mile southwest of the center. To get there head for the major traffic hub in Plaza Castilla, then walk due south across the Arlazón River. For train information or a ticket, head for the RENFE office in the center of town, at Moneda, 21 (☎ **20-91-31**), about a block northeast of busy Plaza de Santo Domingo de Guzmán.

• By Bus About 10 buses a day make the 3-hour trip up from Madrid, and from Barcelona, four buses per day arrive (trip time: 7 hours). The bus depot in Burgos is at Calle Miranda, 4–6 (☎ **20-55-65**). Calle Miranda intersects the large Plaza de Vega, due south of (and across the river from) the cathedral.

• By Car Burgos is well connected to its neighbors by a network of highways, but its routes to and from Barcelona (six hours away) are especially wide and modern. The road from Barcelona changes its name several times, from the A-2 to the A-68 to the E-4, but it is a superhighway all the way. From Madrid, the highway is fast but less dramatically modern than the route from Barcelona. From Madrid, follow the N-I north for about three hours.

ESSENTIALS The area code for Burgos is 947. The tourist information office is at Plaza Alonso Martínez, 7 (☎ **947/20-31-25**).

Founded in the 9th century, this Gothic city in the Arlazón River valley lives up to its reputation as the "cradle of Castile." Just as the Tuscans are credited with speaking the most perfect Italian, so the citizens of Burgos, with their distinctive lisp ("El Theed" for El Cid), supposedly speak the most eloquent Castilian.

El Cid Campeador, Spain's greatest national hero and immortalized in the epic *El Cantar de Mío Cid,* is forever linked to Burgos. He was born near here, and his remains lie in the city's grand cathedral.

Like all the great cities of Old Castile, Burgos declined seriously in the 16th century, only to be revived later. In 1936, during the Civil War, the right-wing city was Franco's Nationalist army headquarters.

What to See & Do

★ **Catedral de Santa María,** Plaza de Santa María. ☎ **20-47-12.**

Begun in 1221, this cathedral became one of the most celebrated in Europe. Built in diverse styles, predominantly flamboyant Gothic, it took 300 years to complete. The three main doorways are flanked by ornamented 15th-century bell towers by John of Cologne. The 16th-century Chapel of Condestable, behind the main altar, is one of the best examples of Isabelline-Gothic architecture, richly decorated with heraldic emblems, a sculptured filigree doorway, figures of apostles and saints, balconies, and an eight-sided "star" stained-glass window.

Equally elegant are the two-story 14th-century cloisters, filled with fine Spanish Gothic sculpture. The cathedral's tapestries, including one well-known Gobelin, are rich in detail. In one of the chapels you'll see an old chest linked to the legend of El Cid—it was filled with gravel but used as collateral by the warrior to trick money-lenders. The remains of El Cid himself, together with those of his wife, Doña Ximena, lie under Santa María's octagonal lanternlike dome. Finally, you may want to see the elaborate 16th-century Stairway of Gold in the north transept, the work of Diego de Siloé.

The cathedral is across the Arlazón River from the railway station, midway between the river and the Citadel.

Admission: Chapels, cloisters, and treasury, 300 ptas. ($2.10).

Open: Daily 9:30am–1pm and 4–7pm.

Monasterio de las Huelgas, Calle Compás de Adentro. ☎ **20-16-30.**

This cloister outside Burgos has seen a lot of action. Built in the 12th century in a richly ornamented style, it was once "a summer place" for Castilian royalty, as well as a retreat for nuns of royal blood. Inside, the Gothic church is built in the shape of a Latin cross. Despite some unfortunate mixing of Gothic and baroque, it contains much of interest—notably some 14th- and 17th-century French tapestries. The tomb of the founder, Alfonso VIII, and his queen, daughter of England's Henry II, lies in the Choir Room.

Thirteenth-century doors lead to the cloisters, dating from that same century and blending Gothic and Mudéjar styles. Despite severe damage to the ceiling, the remains of Persian peacock designs are visible. The beautiful Chapter Room contains the standard of the 12th-century Las Navas de Tolora (war booty taken from the Moors), while the Museo de Ricas Telas is devoted to 13th-century costumes removed from tombs. These remarkably preserved textiles give a rare look at medieval dress.

The monastery is one mile off the Valladolid Road (the turnoff is clearly marked). From Plaza Primo de Rivera in Burgos, buses for Las Huelgas leave every 20 minutes.

Admission: 400 ptas. ($2.80); free Wed.

Open: Tues–Sat 10:30am–2pm and 4–6:30pm; Sun 10:30am–3pm.

Where to Stay

EXPENSIVE

Hotel Almirante Bonifaz, Vitoria, 22-24, 09004 Burgos. ☎ **947/20-69-43.**
Fax 947/20-29-19. 79 rms. MINIBAR TV TEL

Rates: 7,700 ptas. ($54.70) single; 14,500 ptas. ($103) double; 17,200 ptas. ($122.10) triple. Breakfast 1,100 ptas. ($7.80) extra. AE, DC, MC, V. **Closed:** Dec 24–Jan 7.

Solidly comfortable, modern, and decorated with a contemporary kind of efficiency, this hotel attracts many of the city's visiting businesspeople, who appreciate its low-key charm and central location. The hotel lies two blocks east of the also recommended Condestable Hotel, near the river, within the commercial heart of town. All but a few of the bedrooms are air-conditioned, and all have private baths.

Dining/Entertainment: À la carte Spanish and Castile-inspired meals are served in each of the hotel's restaurants, the most glamorous of which is Los Sauces; less grand are Los Alamos and Los Robles. There's also a bar.

Services: Room service (available from 7am to 10pm), laundry service, babysitting.

Facilities: Car rentals, business center.

Hotel del Cid, Plaza de Santa María, 8, 09003 Burgos. ☎ **947/20-87-15.**
Fax 947/26-94-60. 29 rms, 3 suites. TV TEL

Rates: 7,500 ptas. ($53.30) single; 13,000 ptas. ($92.30) double; 18,000 ptas. ($127.80) suite. Breakfast 950 ptas. ($6.70) extra. AE, DC, MC, V. **Parking:** 1,000 ptas. ($7.10).

Built in 1983 by the Alzaga family, which still owns and operates it, this establishment stands in front of the cathedral and beside their restaurant (recommended below). The hotel is decorated like a 15th-century house, but it boasts 20th-century amenities, including extra-large beds and private baths in all its guest rooms. A laundry and a garage are available.

Hotel Condestable, Vitoria, 8, 09004 Burgos. ☎ **947/26-71-25.**
Fax 947/20-46-45. 85 rms. MINIBAR TV TEL

Rates: 11,400 ptas. ($80.90) single; 14,250 ptas. ($101.20) double. Breakfast 1,000 ptas. ($7.10) extra. AE, DC, MC, V. **Parking:** 1,300 ptas. ($9.20).

Set on the northern bank of the Arlanzón River, a short walk east of the cathedral, this is usually considered the most solidly elegant and best-established hotel in Burgos. Reminiscent from the exterior of a well-constructed masonry fortress and very recently renovated, it contains a modern interior whose furnishings and expanses of marble and stone create a streamlined look. Most of the bedrooms contain off-white walls, lots of light-wood furniture, and a simple kind of comfort; a handful of units still retain the slightly old-fashioned, overstuffed look that made this place a traditional favorite during the early 1960s. All units have a private bath.

Dining/Entertainment: The Restaurant Condestable serves regional and international food in a glossy white setting with pinpointed lighting. A *menú del día* here costs 2,100 ptas. ($14.90). The nearby bar might remind you of a stylish nightclub in Madrid or Barcelona.

Services: Room service (available daily from noon to 4pm and 8 to 11pm), laundry, concierge.

Facilities: Car rentals.

MODERATE

HOTEL FERNÁN GONZÁLEZ, Calera, 17, 09002 Burgos. ☎ **947/20-94-41.**
Fax 947/27-41-21. 84 rms (all with bath). A/C MINIBAR TV TEL

Rates: 7,350 ptas. ($52.20) single; 11,900 ptas. ($84.50) double. Breakfast 625 ptas. ($4.40) extra. AE, DC, MC, V. **Parking:** 850 ptas. ($6).

Set across the River Arlanzón from the soaring bulk of the cathedral, a half-block west of Plaza de Vega, this appealing and unusual hotel incorporates a scattering of Iberian antiques and architectural oddities into its modernized decor. Built in the 1970s, it was last renovated in 1994. Several of the sitting rooms contain grandly vaulted ceilings and noble columns; others are efficiently tiled and streamlined, filled with contemporary leather-covered armchairs and chrome-and-glass tables. The guest rooms are cozy, conservative, and comfortable.

Dining/Entertainment: The hotel's dining room serves traditional Spanish as well as international cuisine priced at 1,300 pesetas ($9.20) for three courses at either lunch or dinner. Bar service is available throughout the several lounges and sitting areas of the street level. There's also a late-night disco.

INEXPENSIVE

$ **Hotel España,** Paseo del Espolón, 32, 09003 Burgos. ☎ **947/20-63-40.** Fax 947/20-13-30. 69 rms (all with bath). TV TEL

Rates: 5,000 ptas. ($35.50) single; 7,500 ptas. ($53.30) double. Breakfast 550 ptas. ($3.90) extra. MC, V. **Closed:** Dec 20–Jan 20.

The best budget choice in town lies a five-minute walk southeast of the cathedral and a block south of Plaza Mayor, on a leafy promenade filled with sidewalk cafés and Castilians taking early-evening strolls. The guest rooms lack style and imagination but are completely comfortable nonetheless. The management is helpful to visitors. When the España is full, they have been known to call other hostelries for stranded tourists. Lunch or dinner here costs 2,000 pesetas ($14.20).

Hotel Norte y Londres, Plaza de Alonso Martínez, 10, 09003 Burgos. ☎ **947/26-41-25.** Fax 947/27-73-75. 50 rms (all with bath). TV TEL

Rates: 4,750 ptas. ($33.70) single; 8,000 ptas. ($56.80) double. Breakfast 575 ptas. ($4.10) extra. AE, MC, V. **Parking:** 1,000 ptas. ($7.10) nearby.

On a pleasant square a short walk northeast of the cathedral, this hotel has traces of faded grandeur with its stained glass, leaded windows, and crystal chandeliers. The building dates from the dawn of the 20th century, and it was converted into a hotel in the 1950s, and has flourished ever since. Bedrooms are of good size, with basic furnishings, and the large bathrooms come equipped with yesterday's finest plumbing. Breakfast is the only meal served.

Where to Dine

The restaurants in the heart of Burgos—surrounding the cathedral—usually feature prices that soar as high as a Gothic spire. Every menu contains the roast lamb and suckling pig known throughout the area, or you might order *entremeses variados,* an appetizer sampler of many regional specialties.

Casa Ojeda, Vitoria, 5. ☎ **20-90-52.**

Cuisine: BURGALESE. **Reservations:** Required.

Prices: Appetizers 750–1,600 ptas. ($5.30–$11.40); main courses 1,800–3,000 ptas. ($12.80–$21.30). AE, DC, MC, V.

Open: Lunch, daily 1:15–4:30pm; dinner, Mon–Sat 9–11:30pm.

This top-notch restaurant combines excellent Burgalese fare, cozy decor, attentive service, and moderate prices. Moorish tiles and low ceilings set an inviting ambience that's enhanced by intimate nooks, old lanterns and fixtures, and intricate trelliswork. Upstairs the restaurant divides into two sections: one overlooking the street and the other, the Casa del Cordón, where Ferdinand and Isabella received Columbus after his second trip to America (1497). À la carte dishes include roast lamb, Basque-style hake, sole Harlequin, and chicken in garlic. A house specialty is *alubias con chorizo y mirocilla* (small white beans with spicy sausages).

Mesón del Cid, Plaza de Santa María, 8. ☎ **20-87-15.**

Cuisine: CASTILIAN. **Reservations:** Required.
Prices: Appetizers 400–1,100 ptas. ($2.80–$7.80); main courses 1,100–2,100 ptas. ($7.80–$14.90); fixed-price menu 3,500 ptas. ($24.90). AE, DC, MC, V.
Open: Lunch, daily 1–4pm; dinner, Mon–Sat 8pm–midnight.

Once the 15th-century private home of the most powerful regional lords, today the Mesón del Cid is a restaurant serving delicious specialties concocted by José López Algaza (known to his clients as Pepín). Menu selections, always fresh, are prepared according to regional traditions. You might be tempted by one of the shellfish soups; roast baby lamb with aromatic herbs; roasted stuffed peppers; the fresh fish brought in daily; or a pork, veal, or chicken dish. Try codfish house style. The restaurant lies on the square flanking the main entrance of the cathedral.

Mesón de los Infantes, Avenida Generalísimo, 2. ☎ **20-59-82.**

Cuisine: CASTILIAN/BASQUE. **Reservations:** Recommended.
Prices: Appetizers 450–1,000 ptas. ($3.20–$7.10); main courses 850–2,200 ptas. ($6.00–$15.60); fixed-price menu 1,800 ptas. ($12.80). AE, DC, MC, V.
Open: Lunch, daily 1–4:30pm; dinner, daily 8pm–midnight.

Just below the gate leading into the Plaza de Santa María, this restaurant serves good food amid elegant Castilian decor. Many of the chef's specialties are based on recipes in use in Castile for centuries. The roast suckling pig is everybody's favorite, and you can also order *cocido* (stew) *Madrileño,* assorted shellfish, river crabs Burgalese style, and beef tail with potatoes. Kidneys are sautéed in sherry, and a wide list of game is often featured, including hare, partridge, rabbit, and pigeon. Grills and roasts are also a crowd pleaser.

Rincón de España, Nuño Rasura, 11. ☎ **20-59-55.**

Cuisine: SPANISH. **Reservations:** Required.
Prices: Appetizers 800–1,200 ptas. ($5.70–$8.50); main courses 1,500–2,200 ptas. ($10.70–$15.60); fixed-price menus 1,500–1,800 ptas. ($10.70–$12.80). AE, DC, MC, V.
Open: Lunch, daily 1–4pm; dinner, daily 8pm–midnight. **Closed:** Tues in winter.

This restaurant, about one block southwest of the cathedral, draws many discerning visitors. You can eat in a rustic dining room or outdoors under a large awning closed off by glass when the weather threatens. The restaurant also offers *platos combinados,* as well as a more extensive à la carte menu. Some special dishes include black pudding sausage from Burgos with peppers, barbecued lamb cutlets with potatoes, and roast chicken with sweet peppers. The food here is good, the portions are large, and the vegetables are fresh.

An Easy Excursion to Santo Domingo de la Calzada

Some 42 miles (67.5km) west of Burgos, and easily visited on a day trip, lies Santo Domingo de la Calzada. The crowning achievement of the town, which grew as a stopover for pilgrims en route to Santiago de Compostela, is the 13th-century **cathedral,** a national landmark. For the most part Gothic in style, it nevertheless contains a hodgepodge of architectural elements—Romanesque chapels, a Renaissance choir, and a freestanding baroque tower. The city is named after St. Dominic, who is buried in the crypt. A centuries-old legend attaches to the cathedral: Supposedly a rooster stood up and crowed after it had been cooked to protest the innocence of a pilgrim who had been accused of theft and sentenced to hang. To this day, a live cock and hen are kept in a cage up on the church wall, and you can often hear the rooster crowing at mass. The cathedral is open daily from 9am to 2pm and 4 to 8:30pm. Motorists can reach Santo Domingo de la Calzada by following either of the traffic arteries paralleling the river, heading east from Burgos Cathedral until signs indicate N-120.

8

Extremadura

THE WESTERNMOST REGION OF SPAIN HAS ALWAYS BEEN KNOWN AS "THE LAND beyond the River Douro." It extends from the Gredos and Gata mountain ranges all the way to Andalusia and from Castile to the Portuguese frontier. A land with a varied landscape, it has both plains and mountains, meadows with holm and cork oaks, and fields of stone and lime. Extremadura (not to be confused with the Portuguese province of Estremadura) includes the provinces of Badajoz and Cáceres.

Ancient civilizations were established here, including those of the Celts, Romans, and Visigoths, but the world knows Extremadura best as the land of the conquistadors. Famous sons included Cortés, Pizarro, Balboa, and many others less well known but also important such as Francisco de Orellana and Hernando de Soto. Many of these men were driven from their homeland by economic necessity, finding it hard to make a living in this dry, sun-parched province. Some sent back money to their native land to finance the building of mansions and public structures that stand today as monuments to their long-ago adventures in the Americas.

Many of Extremadura's previous conquerors have left enduring monuments as well, including, for example, the Roman ruins in Mérida. Arab ruins are found in Badajoz, and medieval palaces stand in Cáceres.

A number of Spaniards come here to hunt. Fishing and water sports are also popular because there are a large number of reservoirs. Horseback riding along ancient trails is another pastime. Since summer is intensely hot here, spring and fall are the best times to visit.

Seeing Extremadura

GETTING THERE Most visitors drive west to Extremadura after visiting Madrid or Toledo. It's also possible to swing northwest from Andalusia and explore the province before heading back to Madrid. The only air link is a small air base at Badajoz (see below).

It's more popular to go by train, however. The main train depots are at Cáceres and Badajoz, with arrivals from Madrid and Seville (stops are made at smaller towns along the way; see individual city or town listings for more details).

There are many bus connections to Mérida, Badajoz, and Cáceres from either Madrid or Seville. Links also exist between Badajoz and Lisbon as well as Córdoba (Andalusia). The small towns of Extremadura are joined by buses to the bigger towns of Cáceres and Badajoz.

If you can afford it, explore Extremadura by car, as you'll see so much more scenery. The east-west run from Madrid to Lisbon (N-V) passes through Trujillo, Mérida, and Badajoz at the frontier. If you're visiting Cáceres from Madrid, travel the N-V to Trujillo (stopover suggested), then cut onto the N-521 to Cáceres. Some of the road connections between the cities or towns of Extremadura are difficult because of poor maintenance. An example is the N-523 linking Cáceres with Badajoz.

A Suggested Route

The itinerary below assumes that you'll start in Madrid or Toledo, driving southwest.

Day 1 Plan an overnight stop at Guadalupe.

Day 2 Explore its monastery in the morning, then head west for Trujillo for the night, wandering at leisure through its old town.

What's Special About Extremadura

Great Towns/Villages

- Guadalupe, a village of great beauty known for its Gothic-Mudéjar monastery.
- Cáceres, a national monument city encircled by old walls.
- Mérida, a miniature Rome, a treasure house of Roman antiquities.
- Zafra, a venerable white-walled town with a medieval castle.

Special Events/Festivals

- Classical Greek and Latin drama performances in June at Mérida's Roman theater.

Architectural Highlights

- The monastery of Guadalupe, dating from the Gothic era and filled with artistic treasures.
- Gothic and Renaissance seignorial mansions at Cáceres, unequaled in all of Spain.
- The Plaza Mayor at Trujillo, with its irregular shape and seignorial mansions.

A Great Museum

- The Museo Nacional de Arte Romano at Mérida, housing the best collection of Roman artifacts in Spain.

Ancient Monuments

- The Teatro Romano at Mérida, built by Agrippa in 24 B.C.
- Mérida's Roman amphitheater, dating from the 1st century B.C., an amphitheater once flooded for "sea battles."

Day 3 Make the short drive west from Trujillo to Cáceres, check into a hotel, see the sights, and spend the night.

Day 4 Drive south to Mérida and spend the night, after exploring its ancient Roman monuments.

Day 5 Those with a day to spare can head south to the town of Zafra for an afternoon's exploration and then an overnight stopover.

Day 6 Either continue southeast to Córdoba and the attractions of Andalusia or make for the border town of Badajoz, crossing into Portugal and driving toward the sights of Lisbon.

1 Guadalupe

117 miles (188km) W of Toledo, 140 miles (225km) SW of Madrid

GETTING THERE • By Train There are no trains coming into Guadalupe.

• By Bus There are two buses every day to and from Madrid's Estación Sur, a three-hour ride away. The road is poor, but the route through the surrounding regions is savagely beautiful. In Guadalupe, the buses park on either side of the street, a few paces uphill from the Town Hall. Phone Empresa Doalde in Madrid (☎ **91/468-76-80**) for schedules.

• **By Car** One narrow highway goes through Guadalupe. Most maps don't give it a number; look on a map in the direction of the town of Navalmoral de la Mata. From Madrid, take the narrow, winding C-401 southwest from Toledo, turning north in the direction of Navalmoral de la Mata after seeing signs for Navalmoral de la Mata and Guadalupe. Driving time from Madrid is between 3 1/2 and 4 1/2 hours, depending on how well you fare with the bad roads.

ESSENTIALS The area code for Guadalupe is 927.

Guadalupe lies in the province of Cáceres, 1,500 feet above sea level. The village has a certain beauty and much local color. Everything of interest lies within a three-minute walk from the point where buses deposit you, at Avenida Don Blas Perez, also known as Carretera de Cáceres.

Around the corner and a few paces downhill is the Plaza Mayor, which contains the Town Hall (which is where many visitors go to ask questions in lieu of a tourist office).

The village is best visited in spring, when the balconies of its whitewashed houses burst into bloom with flowers. Wander at your leisure through the twisting, narrow streets, some no more than alleyways. The buildings are so close together that in summer you can walk in the shade of the steeply pitched sienna-colored tile roofs. The religious-souvenir industry views Guadalupe as one of its major outlets.

What to See & Do

Real Monasterio de Santa María de Guadalupe, Plaza de la Santa María de Guadalupe. ☎ **36-70-00.**

In 1325, a farmer searching for a stray cow reportedly spotted a statue of the Virgin in the soil. In time, this statue became venerated throughout the world, honored in Spain by Isabella, Columbus, and Cervantes. Known as the Dark Virgin of Guadalupe, it is said to have been carved by St. Luke. A shrine was built to commemorate the statue, and tributes poured in from all over the world, making Guadalupe one of the wealthiest foundations in Christendom. You can see the Virgin in a small alcove above the altar.

The church is noted for the wrought-iron railings in its naves. Be sure to see the museum devoted to ecclesiastical vestments and to the choir books produced by 16th-century miniaturists. In the magnificently decorated sacristy are eight richly imaginative 17th-century masterpieces by Zurbarán. The 16th-century Gothic cloister is flamboyant, with two galleries. The pièce de résistance is the stunning Mudéjar cloister, with its brick-and-tile Gothic-Mudéjar shrine dating from 1405; the Moorish fountain is from the 14th century.

Admission: Museum and sacristy, 300 ptas. ($2.10) adults; 100 ptas. (70¢) children 7–14. Children 6 and under free.

Open: June–Sept, daily 8:30am–8:30pm; Oct–May, daily 9am–6pm.

Where to Stay

Hospedería Real Monasterio, Plaza Juan Carlos, 1, 10140 Guadalupe. ☎ **927-36-70-00.** Fax 927/36-71-77. 40 rms (all with bath), 1 suite. A/C TEL

Rates: 4,500 ptas. ($32) single; 6,600 ptas. ($46.90) double; 8,910 ptas. ($63.30) triple; 10,230 ptas. ($72.60) quad; 15,000 ptas. ($106.50) suite. Breakfast 700 ptas. ($5) extra. MC, V. **Closed:** Jan 12–Feb 12.

Once a way station for pilgrims visiting the shrine, the Hospedería used to provide lodging for a small donation. Times have changed, but the prices remain moderate at this two-star hotel in the center of town. Some of the guest rooms contain high-vaulted ceilings. There is a bar. The meals are generally good, and a complete luncheon or dinner goes for 2,350 pesetas ($16.70). Top it off with a home-brewed *licor de Guadalupe.*

Parador Nacional Zurbarán, Marqués de la Romana, 12, 10140 Guadalupe. ☎ **927/36-70-75.** Fax 927/36-70-76. 40 rms (all with bath). A/C MINIBAR TV TEL

Rates: 9,500 ptas. ($67.50) single; 12,000 ptas. ($85.20) double. Breakfast 1,200 ptas. ($8.50) extra. AE, DC, MC, V.

In a scenic spot in the center of the village, the area's most luxurious accommodation is housed in a 16th-century building with a beautiful garden. Queen Isabella once stayed here, and the place often saw meetings between royal representatives and explorers, who signed their contracts here before setting out to the New World. The house is named after Francisco de Zurbarán, the great 17th-century painter who was born in the nearby town of Fuente de Cantos. There is a Zurbarán painting in one of the salons, along with ancient maps and engravings—many of them valuable works of art. Bedrooms are comfortable and partially decorated with reproduction medieval furnishings. In the attractive restaurant, good regional food, both lunch and dinner, is served for 3,500 pesetas ($24.90). Try such local dishes as herb-flavored roast kid or pork Mudéjar style. The facilities include a swimming pool, bar, garage, and tennis court.

WHERE TO DINE

Both of the hotels recommended above also have good restaurants.

Mesón el Cordero, Alfonse/Onceno, 27. ☎ **36-71-31.**

Cuisine: SPANISH. **Reservations:** Recommended.

Prices: Appetizers 400–600 ptas. ($2.80–$4.30); main courses 1,500–2,000 ptas. ($10.70–$14.20). No credit cards.

Open: Lunch, Tues–Sun 1–4pm; dinner, Tues–Sun 7–11pm. **Closed:** Feb.

Miguel and Angelita run Guadalupe's best independent restaurant, named for their specialty, *asado de cordero* (roast lamb flavored with garlic and thyme). You might begin with another of their specialties, *sopas guadalupanas,* then follow with partridge "from the countryside" if you have a taste for game. The house dessert is a creamy custard, *flan casero.*

2 Trujillo

152 miles (245km) SW of Madrid, 28 miles (45km) E of Cáceres

GETTING THERE • By Train There are no trains to Trujillo.

• By Bus There are 14 buses per day to and from Madrid ($3\frac{1}{2}$ and $4\frac{1}{2}$ hours, depending on whether it's local or *expreso*). There are also seven buses running daily from Cáceres, 45 minutes away, and five from Badajoz. Trujillo's bus station, Calle Marqués Albayda (☎ **32-12-02**), lies in the south part of town on a side street that intersects with Calle de la Encarnación.

• **By Car** Trujillo lies at a network of large and small roads connecting it to Cáceres, via the N-521, and both Lisbon and Madrid, via the N-V superhighway. Driving time from Madrid is around four hours.

ESSENTIALS The area code for Trujillo is 927. The tourist information office is at Plaza Mayor (☎ **927/32-06-53**).

Dating from the 13th century, the walled town of Trujillo is celebrated for the colonizers and conquerors born here. Among the illustrious natives were Francisco Pizarro, conqueror of Peru, whose family palace on Plaza Mayor was built with gold from the New World, and Francisco de Orellana, the founder of Guayaquil and the first man to explore the Amazon. Other Trujillano historymakers were Francisco de las Casas, who accompanied Hernán Cortés in his conquest of Mexico and founded the city of Trujillo in Honduras; Diego García de Paredes, who founded Trujillo, Venezuela; Nuño de Chaves, founder of Santa Cruz de la Sierra in Bolivia; and several hundred others whose names are found throughout maps of North, Central, and South America. There is a saying that 20 American countries were "born" here.

Celts, Romans, Moors, and Christians have inhabited Trujillo. The original town, lying above today's modern one, was built on a granite ledge on the hillside. It is centered around the Plaza Mayor, one of the artistic landmarks of Spain. A Moorish castle and a variety of 16th- and 17th-century palaces, manor houses, towers, churches, and arcades encircle the plaza and overlook a bronze equestrian statue of Pizarro by American artists Mary Harriman and Charles Runse. Steep, narrow streets and shadowy little corners evoke bygone times when explorers set out from here on their history-making adventures.

What to See & Do

Plaza Mayor.

The heart of Trujillo, this is one of the outstanding architectural sights in Extremadura and is dominated by a statue honoring Pizarro, who almost single handedly destroyed the Inca civilization of Peru. The statue is an exact double of one standing in Lima. Many of the buildings on this square were financed with wealth brought back from the New World.

The most prominent structure on the square is the **Ayuntamiento Viejo** (Old Town Hall), with three tiers of arches, each tier more squat than the one below.

The **Iglesia de San Martín** stands behind the statue dedicated to Pizarro. This granite church, originally from the 15th century, was reconstructed in the 16th century in Renaissance style. Inside are an impressive nave, several tombs, and a rare 18th-century organ that's still in working condition.

While you are on the square, observe the unusual facade of the **Casa de las Cadenas,** a 12th-century house across which a heavy chain is draped. This was a symbol that Philip II had granted the Orellana family immunity from heavy taxes.

You can then visit the **Palacio de los Duques de San Carlos**, a 16th-century ducal residence turned into a convent. Ring the bell to gain entry any time daily from 9am to 1pm and 3 to 6pm. A donation of at least 100 pesetas (70¢) is appreciated, and a resident will show you around; appropriate dress (no shorts or bare shoulders) is required. The facade has Renaissance sculptured figures, and the two-level courtyard inside is even more impressive.

Extremadura

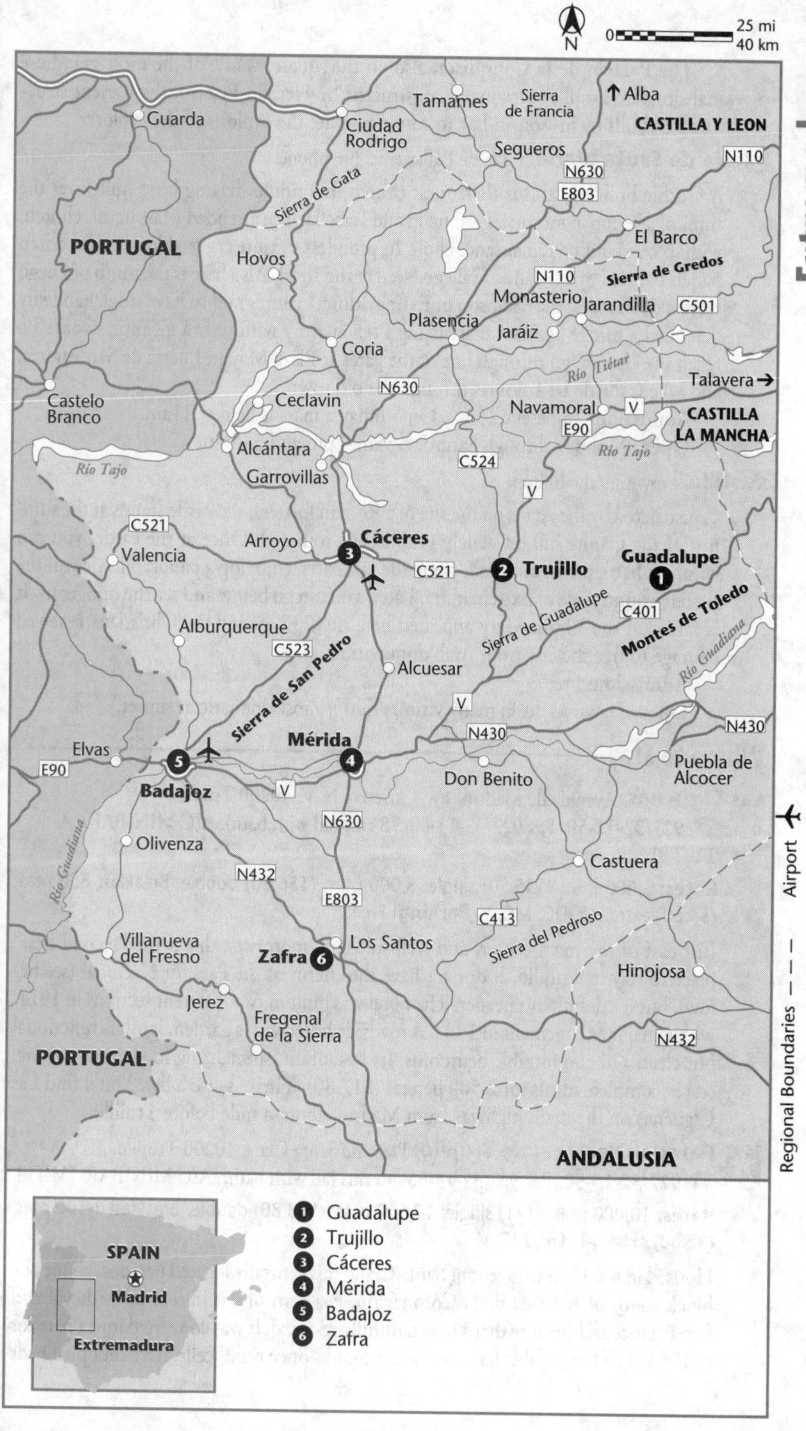

N
0 25 mi
40 km

Alba
CASTILLA Y LEON
Tamames
Sierra de Francia
Guarda
Ciudad Rodrigo
Segueros
N110
N630
E803
Sierra de Gata
El Barco
PORTUGAL
Hovos
N110
Sierra de Gredos
Monasterio
Jarandilla
C501
Plasencia
Jaráiz
Coria
Río Tiétar
Talavera
Castelo Branco
N630
Ceclavin
Navamoral
V
CASTILLA LA MANCHA
E90
Alcántara
Río Tajo
Río Tajo
Garrovillas
C524
V
C521
Cáceres
Arroyo
Valencia
Guadalupe
C521
Trujillo
Sierra de Guadalupe
C401
Montes de Toledo
Alburquerque
C523
Sierra de San Pedro
Alcuesar
Río Guadiana
V
N430
N430
Mérida
Elvas
E90
Puebla de Alcocer
Badajoz
Don Benito
V
N630
Olivenza
Castuera
N432
E803
Río Guadiana
C413
Sierra del Pedroso
Villanueva del Fresno
Los Santos
Zafra
Hinojosa
Jerez
Fregenal de la Sierra
N432
PORTUGAL
ANDALUSIA

Airport
Regional Boundaries

SPAIN
Madrid
Extremadura

1. Guadalupe
2. Trujillo
3. Cáceres
4. Mérida
5. Badajoz
6. Zafra

The **Palacio de la Conquista,** also on the square, is one of the most grandiose mansions in Trujillo. Originally constructed by Hernán Pizarro, the present structure was built by his son-in-law to commemorate the exploits of the explorer.

Iglesia de Santa María, Calle de Ballesteros. No phone.

A Gothic building, this is the largest church in Trujillo, having been built over the ruins of a Moorish mosque. Ferdinand and Isabella once attended Mass in this church, with its outstanding Renaissance choir. Its proudest treasure is a retablo with two dozen panels painted by Fernando Gallego (seen at the altar). Also here is the tomb of Diego García de Paredes, the "Samson of Extremadura," who is said to have singlehandedly defended a bridge against an attacking French army with only a gigantic sword. To reach the church, go through one of the gates at Plaza Mayor, Puerta de San Andrés, and take Calle de las Palomas through the old town.

Admission: 75 pesetas (50¢). On Sunday a mass is held at 11am.

Open: Monday through Saturday, 9am–2pm and 5–8pm.

Castillo, crowning the hilltop.

Constructed by the Arabs on the site of a Roman fortress, the castle stands at the summit of the granite hill on which Trujillo was founded. Once at the castle, you can climb its battlements and walk along the ramparts, enjoying a panoramic view of the austere countryside of Extremadura. Later, you can go below and see the dungeons. It is said that the Virgin Mary appeared here in 1232, giving the Christians renewed courage to free the city from Arab domination.

Admission: Free.

Open: Dawn to dusk; many visitors find it most dramatic at sunset.

Where to Stay

Las Cigüeñas, Avenida de Madrid, s/n, Carretera N-V, 10200 Trujillo.
☎ **927/32-12-50.** Fax 927/32-13-00. 78 rms (all with bath). A/C MINIBAR TV TEL

Rates: 5,000 ptas. ($35.50) single; 8,000 ptas. ($56.80) double. Breakfast 650 ptas. ($4.60) extra. AE, DC, MC, V. **Parking:** Free.

Just east of the town center, and well suited to motorists, this is the "second best" place to stay in Trujillo. It doesn't have the charm of the Parador Nacional (see below), but it's definitely cheaper. The hotel was built in two different sections in 1971, with a major enlargement in 1983. A roadside hotel with a garden, it offers functional but clean and comfortable bedrooms. Its restaurant, specializing in regional cuisine, serves complete meals for 2,500 pesetas ($17.80). There is also a bar. You'll find Las Cigüeñas on the main highway from Madrid, about a mile before Trujillo.

★ **Parador Nacional de Trujillo,** Plaza de Santa Clara, 10200 Trujillo.
☎ **927/32-13-50.** Fax 927/32-13-66. 46 rms (all with bath). A/C MINIBAR TV TEL

Rates: 10,000 ptas. ($71) single; 12,500 ptas. ($88.80) double. Breakfast 1,100 ptas. ($7.80) extra. AE, DC, MC, V.

Housed in the 1533 Convent of Santa Clara, this centrally located parador, about one block south of Avenida de la Coronación, is a gem of Trujillo-style medieval and Renaissance architecture that's now faithfully restored. It was converted into a parador in 1984. The beautifully decorated guest rooms, once nuns' cells, have canopied beds and spacious marble baths. The gardens and fruit trees of the Renaissance cloister are inviting, and there is a swimming pool in the courtyard of a new section that blends with the original convent architecture. You can have breakfast in the old refectory and dinner in what was once a long, vaulted chapel. A three-course Spanish meal costs 3,500 pesetas ($24.90)—try the *caldereta extremena*, a stew made with baby lamb or baby goat.

Where to Dine

Both of the hotels recommended above also have good restaurants that serve regional cuisine.

$ **Mesón la Troya,** Plaza Mayor, 10. ☎ **32-13-64.**
Cuisine: EXTREMADURAN. **Reservations:** Recommended.
Prices: Fixed-price menu 1,700 ptas. ($12.10). V.
Open: Lunch, daily 1–4:30pm; dinner, daily 9–11:30pm.

Locals and visitors alike are drawn to this centrally located restaurant featuring the regional cuisine of Extremadura—and doing the province proud. Have a dry sherry in the bar, which was designed to resemble the facade of a Spanish house. This cozy provincial theme also flows into the dining rooms, with their white walls (decorated with ceramic plates), potted plants, and red tiles. Few people leave hungry after devouring the set menu, with its more than ample portions; food items change daily. Local dishes include *prueba de cerdo* (garlic-flavored pork casserole) and *carne con tomate* (beef cooked in tomato sauce). A table is always reserved for the village priest.

$ **Pizarro,** Plaza Mayor, 13. ☎ **32-02-55.**
Cuisine: EXTREMADURAN. **Reservations:** Recommended.
Prices: Appetizers 600–750 ptas. ($4.30–$5.30); main courses 900–1,650 ptas. ($6.40–$11.70); *menú del día* 1,300 ptas. ($9.20). AE, V.
Open: Lunch, daily 1–4pm; dinner, Wed–Mon 9–11pm.

Locals often cite this centrally located hostal as the best place to go for regional-style Extremaduran cookery. Built in 1864, the inn is set on the town's main square and named for its famous son. We can presume that the cuisine is better than Pizarro might have enjoyed. Regional wines accompany meals that invariably include ham from acorn-fed pigs. You might begin with asparagus with mayonnaise sauce, then follow with *asado de cordero* (roast lamb flavored with herbs and garlic) or Roman-style fried *merluza* (hake). The kitchen's game specialty is *estofado de perdices* (partridge casserole).

3 Cáceres

185 miles (298km) SW of Madrid, 159 miles (256km) N of Seville

GETTING THERE • By Train One regional train per day arrives from Madrid (trip time: 4½ hours), but three faster Talgo trains from Madrid reach Cáceres in 3½ hours. In addition, two regional trains per day arrive from Badajoz (trip time: 2 hours) and one regional train per day from Seville (trip time: 4 hours). The train station in Cáceres is on Avenida Alemania (☎ **22-50-61**), near the main highway heading south (Carretera de Sevilla). A green-and-white bus shuttles passengers about once an hour from the railway and bus stations (they lie across the street from one another;

board it outside the bus station) to the busiest traffic junction in the new city, Plaza de América. From there it's a 10-minute walk to the edge of the old town.

• **By Bus** Bus connections are more frequent than train. From the city bus station, on the busy Carretera de Sevilla (☎ **24-59-54**), buses arrive and depart seven times a day for Madrid and Seville (5 and 4 1/2 hours, respectively). Other buses travel between two and five times a day to and from Guadalupe, Trujillo, Mérida, Valladolid, Córdoba, and Salamanca. For information on reaching the new town from the bus station, see "By Train," above.

• **By Car** Driving time from Madrid is about five hours. Most motorists approach Cáceres from eastern Spain via the N-V superhighway until they reach Trujillo. There, they exit onto the N-521, driving another 28 miles (45km) west to Cáceres.

ESSENTIALS The area code for Cáceres is 927. The tourist information office is on Plaza Mayor (☎ **927/24-63-47**).

A national landmark and the capital of Extremadura, Cáceres is encircled by old city walls and has several seignorial palaces and towers, many financed by gold sent from the Americas by the conquistadors. Allow about two hours to explore the city center.

What to See & Do

The modern city lies southwest of *barrio antiguo,* **Cáceres Viejo,** which is enclosed by ramparts. The heart of the old city lies between **Plaza de Santa María** and, a few blocks to the south, **Plaza San Mateo.** Plaza Santa María, an irregularly shaped, rather elongated square, is one of the major sights. On each of its sides are the honey-brown facades of buildings once inhabited by the nobility.

On the far side of the square rises the **Iglesia de Santa María,** which is basically Gothic in architecture, although the Renaissance era saw the addition of many embellishments. Completed some time in the 1500s, this church is the cathedral of Cáceres, and it contains the remains of many of the conquistadors. It has a trio of Gothic aisles of almost equal height. Look at the carved retable at the high altar, dating from the 16th century. (Insert coins to light it up.)

About 30 towers from the city's medieval walls remain, all of them heavily restored. Originally much taller, the towers reflected the pride and independence of their builders; when Queen Isabella took over, however, she ordered them "cut down to size." The largest tower is at **Plaza del General Mola.** Beside it stands the **Estrella Arco (Star Arch),** constructed by Manuel Churriguera in the 18th century. To its right you'll see the **Torre del Horno,** a mud-brick adobe structure left from the Moorish occupation.

At the highest point of the old city and near its center is the 14th-century **Iglesia de San Mateo** (St. Matthew), which has a Plateresque portal and a rather plain nave (except for the Plateresque tombs, which add a decorative touch). The church lies at the edge of Plaza San Mateo.

Next to it stands the **Casa de las Cigüeñas (Storks' House),** dating from the late 15th century. Its slender tower is all that remains of the battlements. Not open to the public, the building now serves as a military headquarters.

The **Church of Santiago** was begun in the 12th century and restored in the 16th century. It possesses a reredos carved in 1557 by Alonso de Berruguete and a 15th-century figure of Christ. The church lies outside the ramparts, about a block to the north of Arco de Socorro (Socorro East Gate). To reach it, exit from the gate, enter Plaza Socorro, then walk down Calle Godoy. The Church of Santiago is on your right.

La Casa de los Toledo-Montezuma was built by Juan Cano de Saavedra with money from the dowry of his wife, the daughter of Montezuma. The house is set into the northern corner of the medieval ramparts, about a block to the north of Plaza de Santa María.

On the site of the old Alcázar, the **Casa de las Veletas (Weather Vane House),** Plaza de las Veletas (☎ **24-72-34**), with its baroque facade, houses a provincial archeological museum. The building's ancient Moorish cistern, five naves and horseshoe arches, and patio and paneling from the 17th century have been preserved. The museum displays Celtic and Visigothic remains, Roman and Gothic artifacts, and a numismatic collection. Admission is 200 pesetas ($1.40), and the museum is open Tuesday to Saturday from 9:30am to 2:30pm and Sunday from 10:15am to 2:30pm.

Where to Stay

Hotel Alcántara, Virgen de Guadalupe, 14, 10001 Cáceres. ☎ **927/22-89-00.** Fax 927/22-87-68. 67 rms (all with bath). A/C MINIBAR TV TEL

Rates: 6,400 ptas. ($45.40) single; 9,600 ptas. ($68.20) double. Breakfast 800 ptas. ($5.70) extra. AE, DC, MC, V. **Parking:** 800 ptas. ($5.70)

Located in the commercial center of town, this seven-story blandly modern building opened in 1966, and has been renovated at least twice since. It is convenient for exploring the old town. Guest rooms are comfortably furnished and well maintained. The hotel restaurant serves a *menú del día* for 2,500 pesetas ($17.80).

Hotel Extremadura, Avenida Virgen de Guadalupe, 5, 10001 Cáceres. ☎ **927/22-16-00.** Fax 927/21-10-95. 66 rms (all with bath). A/C TV TEL

Rates: 5,500 ptas. ($39.10) single; 8,500 ptas. ($60.40) double. Breakfast 650 ptas. ($4.60) extra. AE, DC, MC, V. **Parking:** Free.

Angular but comfortable, this clean and uncomplicated 1960s hotel offers some of the most straightforward accommodations in town. Located about half a mile southwest of the historic center, in a bustling commercial district, it offers air-conditioned relief from the heat, as well as a much-appreciated swimming pool.

Dining/Entertainment: The hotel's restaurant, Alazán, serves Spanish and international food. There is also a bar.

Services: Room service (available from 7am to midnight), laundry, concierge.

Facilities: Outdoor swimming pool, in-house tour operator/travel agent, car rentals.

Parador de Cáceres, Calle Ancha, 6, 10001 Cáceres. ☎ **927/21-17-59.** Fax 927/21-17-29. 27 rms (all with bath). A/C MINIBAR TV TEL **Parking:** Free on streets.

The finest place to stay in town, this state-operated parador was converted into a hotel in 1989 with a first-class restaurant from a palace constructed here in the 1400s. The parador enjoys a tranquil location and was constructed in a rather severe Extremaduran style, with pristine white corridors, and severely dignified but comfortable bedrooms. The bedrooms are furnished in the regional style. The place is rather stark, with suits of armor placed about, but its patios are quite welcoming. The food is good, with a complete meal costing 3,500 pesetas ($24.90).

Where to Dine

El Figón de Eustaquio, Plaza San Juan, 12. ☎ **24-81-94.**

Cuisine: EXTREMADURAN. **Reservations:** Recommended.
Prices: Appetizers 650–950 ptas. ($4.60–$6.70); main courses 950–2,500 ptas. ($6.70–$17.80); fixed-price menu 1,600 ptas. ($11.40). AE, DC, MC, V.
Open: Lunch, daily 1:30–4pm; dinner, daily 8pm–midnight.

El Figón is a pleasant place that serves local Extremaduran cuisine and has been satisfying locals since 1948. You'll notice the four Blanco brothers who run it doing practically everything. This includes preparing the amazingly varied dishes—for example, honey soup, *solomillo* (filet of beef), and trout Extremaduran style, as well as typical Spanish specialties. The air-conditioned interior has a rustic decor. El Figón lies west of the western ramparts of the old city near the intersection of Avenida Virgen de Guadalupe and Plaza San Juan.

4 Mérida

44 miles (71km) S of Cáceres, 35 miles (56km) E of Badajoz

GETTING THERE • By Train Trains depart and arrive from the RENFE station on the Calle Cardero (☎ **31-81-09**), about half a mile north of the Plaza de España. There are six trains per day to and from Cáceres (the transit requires one hour), five trains per day from Madrid (four hours), six to nine trains to and from Seville (three hours), and eight trains per day to and from Badajoz (one hour).

• By Bus The bus station is on Avenida de la Libertad (☎ **37-14-04**), close to the train station. There are between five to seven buses every day to and from Madrid ($5^1/_2$ hours), six to nine per day to and from Seville (3 hours), five per day to and from Cáceres (2 hours), and eight per day to Badajoz (1 hour).

• By Car Take the N-V superhighway from Madrid or Lisbon. Driving time from Madrid is approximately 5 hours; from Lisbon, about $4^1/_2$ hours. Park in front of the Roman theater and explore the town on foot.

ESSENTIALS The area code for Mérida is 924. The tourist information office is at Pedro María Plano (☎ **924/31-53-53**).

Mérida, known as Augusta Emerita when it was founded in 25 B.C., lay at the crossroads of the Roman roads linking Toledo and Lisbon and Salamanca and Seville. At one time the capital of Lusitania (the Latin name for the combined kingdoms of Spain and Portugal), Mérida was considered one of the most splendid cities in Iberia, ranking as a town of major importance in the Roman Empire; in fact, it was once called a miniature Rome. Its monuments, temples, and public works make it the site of some of the finest Roman ruins in Spain, and, as such, it is the tourist capital of Extremadura. Old Mérida can be covered on foot—in fact, that is the only way to see it. Pay scant attention to the dull modern suburb across the Guadiana River, which skirts the town with its sluggish waters.

What to See & Do

The **Roman bridge** over the Guadiana was the longest in Roman Spain—about half a mile—and consisted of 64 arches. It was constructed of granite under either Trajan or Augustus, then restored by the Visigoths in 686. Philip II ordered further refurbishment in 1610; work was also done in the 19th century. The bridge crosses the river south of the center of Old Mérida, its length increased because of the way it spans two forks of the river, including an island in midstream. In 1993 it was restored and turned into a pedestrian walkway. A semicircular suspension bridge for cars was constructed to carry the heavy traffic and save the bridge for future generations. Before the restoration and change, this bridge served as a main access road into Mérida, watching transportation evolve from hoofs and feet to trucks and automobiles.

Another sight of interest is the old hippodrome, or **Circus Maximus**, which could seat about 30,000 spectators watching chariot races. The Roman masonry was carted off to use in other buildings, and today the site looks more like a parking lot. Excavations have uncovered rooms that may have housed gladiators. The site of the former circus lies at the end of Avenida Extremadura, on the northeastern outskirts of the old town, about half a mile north of the Roman bridge and a 10-minute walk east of the railway station.

The **Arco Trajano (Trajan's Arch)** lies near the heart of the Old Town, beside Calle Trajano, about a block south of the Parador Vía de la Plata. An unadorned triumphal arch, it measures 16 yards high and 10 yards across.

The **Acueducto de los Milagros** is the most intact of the town's two remaining Roman aqueducts, this one bringing water from Proserpina, three miles (5km) away. From the aqueducts, water was fed into two artificially created lakes, Cornalvo and Proserpina. The aqueduct is northwest of the old town, lying to the right of the road to Cáceres, just beyond the railway tracks. Ten arches still stand.

The latest monument to be excavated is the **Temple of Diana** (dedicated to Caesar Augustus). Squeezed between houses on a narrow residential street, it was converted in the 17th century into the private residence of a nobleman who used four of the original Corinthian columns in his architectural plans. The temple lies at the junction of Calle Sagasta and Calle Romero Léal in the center of town.

While in the area, you can also explore the 13th-century **Iglesia de Santa María la Mayor,** Plaza de España. It has a 16th-century chapel and is graced with Romanesque and Plateresque features. It stands on the west side of the square.

★ **Teatro Romano,** José Ramón Melida, s/n. ☎ **31-25-30.**

The Roman theater, one of the best-preserved Roman ruins in the world, was built by Agrippa (Augustus's son-in-law) in 18 B.C. to house an audience of 6,000 people. Modeled after the great theaters of Rome, it was constructed by dry-stone methods, a remarkable achievement. During the reign of Hadrian (2nd century A.D.), a tall stage wall was adorned with statues and colonnades. Behind the stage, visitors of today can explore excavations of various rooms. In July they can enjoy a season of classical plays.

Admission: 200 ptas. ($1.40) adults; children free.

Open: Apr–Sept, daily 8am–9:30pm. Oct–Mar, daily 8am–6pm.

Anfiteatro Romano, Calle José Ramón Melida, s/n. ☎ **31-25-30.**

At the height of its glory, in the 1st century B.C., the amphitheater could seat 14,000 to 15,000 spectators. Chariot races were held here, along with gladiator combats and mock sea battles, for which the arena would be flooded. Many of the seats were placed dangerously close to the bloodshed. You can visit some of the rooms that housed the wild animals and gladiators waiting to go into combat.

Admission: 200 ptas. ($1.40).

Open: Apr–Sept, daily 8am–9:30pm, Oct–Mar, daily 8am–6pm.

Museo Nacional de Arte Romano, Calle José Ramón Melida, s/n. ☎ **31-16-90.**

The museum occupies a modern building adjacent to the ancient Roman amphitheater, to which it is connected by an underground tunnel. It contains more than 30,000 artifacts from Augusta Emerita, capital of the Roman province of Lusitania. Many of the sculptures came from the excavations of the Roman theater and amphitheater. You'll see displays of mosaics, figures, pottery, glassware, coins, and bronze objects. The museum is built of red brick in the form of a Roman basilica.

Admission: 200 ptas. ($1.40) adults; children free.

Open: Tues–Sat 10am–2pm and 4–6pm; Sun 10am–2pm.

Alcazaba, Plaza de España. ☎ **31-25-30.**

On the northern bank of the Guadiana River, beside the northern end of the Roman bridge (which it was meant to protect), stands the Alcázar, known as the Conventual or the Alcazaba. Built in the 9th century by the Moors, who used fragments left over from Roman and Visigothic occupations, the square structure was later granted to the Order of Santiago.

Admission: 200 ptas. ($1.40).

Open: Apr–Sept, Mon–Sat 9am–2pm and 5–7pm; Sun 9am–2pm. Oct–Mar, Mon–Sat 9am–1pm and 3–6pm.

Museo Arqueológico de Arte Visigodo, Plaza de España. ☎ **31-16-90.**

In front of Trajan's Arch is this archeological museum, housing a treasure trove of artifacts left by the one-time conquering Visigoths. Look for the two statues of Wild Men in one of the alcoves.

Admission: Free.

Open: June–Sept, Tues–Sat 10am–2pm and 5–7pm, Sun 10am–2pm; Oct–May, Tues–Sat 10am–2pm and 4–6pm, Sun 10am–2pm.

Where to Stay

$ **Hotel Emperatriz,** Plaza de España, 19, 06800 Mérida. ☎ **924/31-31-11.** Fax 924/31-33-05. 41 rms (all with bath). A/C TEL

Rates: 4,625 ptas. ($32.80) single; 8,425 ptas. ($59.80) double. Breakfast 450 ptas. ($3.20) extra. MC, V.

A former 16th-century palace, the Emperatriz housed a long line of celebrated guests in its day, everybody from Kings Philip II and III of Spain to Queen Isabella of Portugal and Charles V, the Holy Roman Emperor. Its intricate tiled gallery foyer is in the Moorish style. All the guest rooms are functionally furnished and comfortable, but try to get one facing the plaza. Rooms that face the plaza offer unusual views of the occasional storks' nests built on the eaves and cornices of the surrounding buildings.

You can have a complete meal here for 1,300 pesetas ($9.20). Many intriguing specialties from Extremadura are served, including a soothing gazpacho made with white garlic and *tencas fritas* (fried tench), a typical fish of the region. Later you can visit the Emperatriz's nightclub and bar. A garden stands in the center of this good-value three-star hotel, located in the center of town, just north of the ruins of the Alcazaba.

Nova Roma, Súarez Somonte, 42, 06800 Mérida. ☎ **924/31-12-61.** Fax 924/30-01-60. 55 rms (all with bath). A/C TV TEL

Rates: 8,360 ptas. ($59.40) single; 10,450 ptas. ($74.20) double. Breakfast 800 ptas. ($5.70) extra. AE, DC, MC, V. **Parking:** 1,000 ptas. ($7.10).

Lacking the vintage charm of the Emperatriz (see above) or the Parador Vía de la Plata (see below), the 1991 Nova Roma wins hands down for those with more modern taste. Clean, comfortable, and functionally furnished, it is considered a good value for this heavily frequented tourist town. The hotel also runs a reasonably priced restaurant offering a *menú del día* for 1,400 pesetas ($9.90) with many regional dishes. The Nova Roma is west of the Teatro Romano and north of Plaza de Toros (bullring).

★ **Parador Vía de la Plata,** Plaza de la Constitución, 3, 06800 Mérida. ☎ **924/31-38-00.** Fax 924/31-92-08. 82 rms (all with bath). A/C MINIBAR TV TEL

Rates: 14,000 ptas. ($99.40) single; 16,000 ptas. ($113.60) double. Breakfast 1,300 ptas. ($9.20) extra. AE, DC, MC, V.

This parador is in the heart of town, across the street from Plaza de la Constitución, in the former Convento de los Frailes de Jesus (dating from the 16th century). A salon has been installed in the cloister, and a central garden is studded with shrubbery and flowers. Old stone stairs lead to the bedrooms. The place has had a long and turbulent history and was once a prison. In the 1960s two dictators met here: Franco of Spain and Salazar of Portugal. An elevator plummeted to the ground as El Caudillo was entertaining his Portuguese comrade—probably an assassination attempt on either Franco or Salazar (or both). In addition to its bar and garage, the parador has an excellent restaurant, serving both regional and national dishes, with meals costing from 3,500 pesetas ($24.90).

Tryp Medea, Avenida de Portugal, s/n, 06900 Mérida. ☎ **924/37-24-00.** Fax 924/30-01-60. 126 rms (all with bath). A/C MINIBAR TV TEL **Bus:** 4 or 6.

Rates: 9,600 ptas. ($68.20) single; 12,000 ptas. ($85.20) double. Breakfast 1,000 ptas. ($7.10) extra. AE, DC, MC, V. **Parking:** 800 ptas. ($5.70).

Located within a 15-minute walk west of the town's historic center, on the opposite bank of the Guadiana River, this hotel opened in 1993 and was immediately judged the finest hotel in Extremadura. A member of the nationwide Tryp chain, it rises four stories and amply employs white marble within its lobby and bedrooms. Lots of mirrors, stylish post-modern furniture crafted from locally made wrought iron, and many modern accessories decorate the rooms, many of which offer views over the historic core of Mérida. On the premises is an outdoor swimming pool, a health club/gymnasium, squash courts, a sauna, and a helpful, multilingual staff. There's a bar, and the restaurant El Encenar (named after a type of tree that is indigenous to Extremadura) where fixed-price menus average 1,800 pesetas ($12.80).

Where to Dine

In addition to the independent restaurants listed below, the hotels recommended above have good restaurants.

$ **Bar Restaurant Briz,** Félix Valverde Lillo, 5. ☎ **31-93-07.**

Cuisine: EXTREMADURAN. **Reservations:** Not required.
Prices: Appetizers 400–550 ptas. ($2.80–$3.90); main courses 750–1,800 ptas. ($5.30–$12.80); fixed-price menu 1,250 ptas. ($8.90). MC, V.
Open: Lunch, Mon–Sat 1:30–4 pm. Dinner, Mon–Sat 9–11:30 pm.

There is almost universal agreement, even among the locals, that the set menu at Briz represents the best value in town—not only reasonable in price but also very filling. Unprepossessing in its exterior, Briz is known for its Extremaduran regional dishes, and has been feeding locals since 1949. Entrées include lamb stew (heavily flavored) and *perdiz in salsa* (a gamey partridge casserole), which might be preceded by an appetizer of peppery sausage mixed into a medley of artichokes. Peppery veal steak and fried filet of goat are other specialties. Strong, hearty wines accompany the dishes. A meal here will qualify you as an *extremeño.* You'll find Briz across from the post office.

Restaurante Nicolás, Félix Valverde Lillo, 13. ☎ **31-96-10.**

Cuisine: SPANISH. **Reservations:** Recommended.
Prices: Appetizers 750–1,160 ptas. ($5.30–$8.20); main courses 800–2,000 ptas. ($5.70–$14.20); fixed-price menu 2,000 ptas. ($14.20). AE, DC, MC, V.
Open: Lunch, daily 1–5 pm; dinner, Mon–Sat 9 pm–midnight. **Closed:** Sept 7–22.

Transformed from an old, run-down house in 1985, this ranks as one of the most charming restaurants in town. If the lower dining room isn't to your liking, you'll find seating upstairs, as well as a pleasant garden for outdoor repasts. Menu specialties are made with care from fresh ingredients: You might enjoy an array of fresh shellfish; roast baby goat; carefully seasoned roast lamb; and flavorful concoctions of sole, salmon, and monkfish. Roast partridge is the game specialty. Nicolás is located opposite the post office.

5 Badajoz

57 miles (92km) SW of Cáceres, 39 miles (63km) E of Mérida, 254 miles (409km) SW of Madrid

GETTING THERE • By Plane Almost daily flights from Madrid fly into the Aeropuerto de Badajoz, Carretera Madrid-Lisboa, km. 19 (☎ **44-00-16**). On Tuesday and Thursday, there are also flights from Barcelona.

• By Train There are five trains daily from Madrid (a 5-hour trip). Arrivals from Mérida are more frequent, eight trains per day making the 45-minute run. From Cáceres, three trains arrive daily (trip time: 2½ hours). The railway station is situated at the terminus of Carolina Coronado in Badajoz, a 15-minute walk northwest of the center of town.

• By Bus From Madrid there are ten daily buses making the 4-hour drive; from Seville there are five daily buses (4½ hours). From Mérida, there are eight buses daily (45 minutes). The bus station (☎ **25-86-61**) at Badajoz lies at Calzadilla Maestre, south of town. Take bus no. 3 from the station to the town center, the Plaza de España.

• **By Car** Badajoz sits astride the superhighway N-V, which connects Madrid with Lisbon. The E-803 connects it with Seville. Driving time from Madrid is around four hours; from Seville the time is about 3½ hours.

ESSENTIALS The area code for Badajoz is 924. The tourist information office is at Plaza de la Libertad, 3 (☎ **924/22-27-63**).

The capital of Spain's largest province, Badajoz stands on the banks of the Guadiana River near the once-turbulent Portuguese border. A Moorish fortress and an old Roman bridge are two reminders of the past. Sightseeing here is lackluster, but Badajoz does have some local color, provided mainly by its huge ramparts and its narrow medieval streets. Its fortified site is best appreciated if you drive to Badajoz from the north. Park outside and walk into town; along the way you'll pass the 13th-century Gothic cathedral.

Where to Stay

Gran Hotel Zurbarán, Paseo Castelar, s/n, 06001 Badajoz. ☎ **924/22-37-41.** Fax 924/22-01-42. 214 rms (all with bath). A/C TV TEL

Rates: 8,700 ptas. ($61.80) single; 14,500 ptas. ($103) double. Breakfast 1,000 ptas. ($7.10) extra. AE, DC, MC, V. **Parking:** 1,000 ptas. ($7.10).

Set above the heavy ramparts that flank the southern bank of the River Guadiana, this modern but slightly dated four-star hotel enjoys one of the most scenic positions in town, overlooking the welcome verdancy of the Parque de Castelar. The public rooms are decorated with lots of metal trim and a kind of 1970s-era pizzazz, and the guest rooms are comfortably equipped and have been recently remodeled. The service is attentive.

Dining/Entertainment: An in-house restaurant serves à la carte meals for 2,400 pesetas ($17) and up. There are also a bar and disco.

Services: Concierge, laundry, room service, babysitting.

Facilities: Outdoor pool, tennis courts, large garden with stately trees and flowers, in-house news kiosk and bookstore, shopping arcade.

Hotel Lisboa, Avenida de Elvas, 13, 06006 Badajoz. ☎ **924/27-29-00.** Fax 924/27-22-50. 176 rms (all with bath). A/C TV TEL

Rates: 5,600 ptas. ($39.80) single; 7,000 ptas. ($49.70) double. Breakfast 400 ptas. ($2.80) extra. MC, V. **Parking:** 600 ptas. ($4.30).

One of Badajoz's major hotels, this eight-floor establishment is located about a half-mile west of the town center, near the access roads of traffic coming in from Lisbon. Built in 1978, and appealing to many business travelers en route between Madrid and Lisbon, it offers uncomplicated modern rooms with conservative furnishings, and an efficient staff. The hotel contains a bar, a garage, and an economical restaurant where fixed-price meals cost 1,200 pesetas ($8.50) each.

Hotel Río, Adolfo Diaz Ambrona, s/n, 06006 Badajoz. ☎ **924/27-26-00.** Fax 924/27-38-74. 90 rms (all with bath). A/C MINIBAR TV TEL **Bus:** Urbano no. 2 or 6.

Rates: 7,300 ptas. ($51.80) single; 9,750 ptas. ($69.20) double. Breakfast 685 ptas. ($4.90) extra. AE, DC, MC, V. **Parking:** 1,000 ptas. ($7.10).

Near a bridge on the highway connecting Lisbon and Madrid, the Hotel Río offers views of a eucalyptus grove and the river. The amenities include an outdoor pool, a parking garage, a disco pub/restaurant, and a garden; the functional guest rooms are comfortably furnished and well maintained. The hotel attracts many of the Portuguese who come over for the night for "a taste of Spain."

Where to Dine

Aldeberán, Avenida de Elvas, s/n, Urbanización Guadiana. ☎ **27-42-61.**

Cuisine: SPANISH/EXTREMADURAN. **Reservations:** Recommended.

Prices: Appetizers 650–1,450 ptas. ($4.60–$10.30); main courses 2,200–2,850 ptas. ($15.60–$20.20). Fixed-price menu 4,500 ptas. ($32). AE, DC, MC, V.

Open: Lunch, Mon–Sat 1:30–3:45; dinner, Mon–Sat 9–11:45pm.

Established in 1990 within a modern building overlooking the river, on the highway about a mile west of Badajoz' center, Aldeberán is considered one of the best restaurants in town. It prides itself on its Extremaduran origins, having adopted the name of a race of local bulls (*aldeberán*). Although a range of fish and meat dishes are offered, the menu features succulent preparations of pork dishes prepared only from the *pata negra* (black-footed) pigs, which are one of the specialties of the region. Within a dining room accented with natural stone and outfitted in tones of russet and earth, you can order such dishes as *solomillo ibérico*, a tender pork filet carefully seasoned and usually served with spinach; portions of wafer-thin cured ham, served *au naturel* or flavorfully mixed into salads of very fresh greens; hake in green sauce; several different preparations of sole and monkfish; and a signature dessert of ripe peaches flambéed in honey sauce and served with mint-flavored crème fraîche.

Los Gabrieles, Vicente Barrantes, 21. ☎ **22-00-01.**

Cuisine: EXTREMADURAN. **Reservations:** Recommended.

Prices: Appetizers 650–900 ptas. ($4.60–$6.40); main courses 900–1,700 ptas. ($6.40–$12.10); fixed-price menu 990 ptas. ($7). AE, DC, MC, V.

Open: Lunch, Mon–Sat 1:30–4pm; dinner, Mon–Sat 9–11pm.

Los Gabrieles has flourished as the personal domain of three generations of the Palaez family since it was established in 1952 (in a 1900 building) near the cathedral. Today, the granddaughter of the founder concocts well-flavored regional specialties from strictly fresh ingredients in the kitchen, while her husband directs the staff in the turn-of-the-century dining room. Such Extremaduran specialties as roasted partridge, lamb roasted with herbs, soups, stews, omelets, and endless cups of coffee and glasses of wine will happily sate any appetite. One section of the restaurant is devoted to a café and bar, which opens Monday to Saturday around 7:30am and closes long after midnight.

Mesón el Tronco, Calle Muñoz Torrero, 16. ☎ **22-20-76.**

Cuisine: EXTREMADURAN. **Reservations:** Recommended.

Prices: Appetizers 400–700 ptas. ($2.80–$5); main courses 800–1,600 ptas. ($5.70–$11.40); fixed-price menu 1,250 ptas. ($8.90). AE, DC, MC, V.

Open: Lunch, Mon–Sat 1–4pm; dinner, Mon–Sat 8pm–midnight.

You might not suspect the existence here of an attractive restaurant when you encounter the popular bar near the front door, but the excellent tapas will hint at the delicacies available in the back room. The owner offers traditional Extremaduran dishes, as well as a changing repertoire of daily specials. Menu items include gazpacho, *cocido* (stew) of the region, and lamb cutlets, all at affordable prices and served in air-conditioned comfort. Mesón el Tronco is in the center of town, two blocks west of the cathedral.

Easy Excursions

Jerez de los Caballeros makes an interesting journey from either Badajoz (46½ miles [75km] south on the N-432) or Mérida (61½ miles [99km] southwest on the N-360). It's a small town of white houses clustered on a hillside, with the cathedral on the summit. The **birthplace of Balboa,** the first European to discover the Pacific, is nearby—a modest whitewashed house at Capitán Cortés, 10. A statue honors the explorer in one of the town's small squares. Jerez de los Caballeros, with many belfries and towers, including the **Torre Sagrienta** (Bloody Tower), takes its name, traditions, and ambience from the Caballeros del Templo (Knights Templars), who were given the town after it was taken from the Moors in 1230.

Medellín, 25 miles (40km) east of Mérida and 62 miles (100km) east of Badajoz, is the little town where Hernán Cortés, conqueror of Mexico, was born. From the approach you'll see the old whitewashed buildings on the opposite side of the Guadiana River, with the ruins of medieval Medellín Castle dominating the skyline. A 17th-century stone bridge crosses the river into the town, where you'll find a monument to Cortés in the main cobblestoned plaza. From either Mérida or Badajoz, take the N-V superhighway, heading to Madrid, exiting at the C-520, the road into Medellín.

6 Zafra

38 miles (61km) S of Mérida, 107 miles (172km) N of Seville

GETTING THERE • By Train From Seville, there are several trains daily, which pass through Huelva along the way. There are also rail connections from Mérida.

By Bus Buses arrive from Mérida and Seville.

• By Car Zafra lies at the point where the highway from Seville (E-803) splits, heading east to Mérida and Cáceres and west to Badajoz. Driving there is easy. There's also a direct road from Córdoba.

ESSENTIALS The area code for Zafra is 924. The tourist information office is at Plaza de España (☎ **924/55-10-36**).

One of the most interesting stopovers in Lower Extremadura, the white-walled town of Zafra is filled with old Moorish streets and squares. The cattle fair of San Miguel, on October 4, draws cattle breeders from all over the region. The 1457 **castle** of the dukes of Feria, the most important in the province, boasts both a sumptuous 16th-century Herreran patio and the Sala Dorada, with its richly paneled ceiling. The place is now the government parador (see below). You'll want to spend time on the central square, the arcaded 18th-century **Plaza Mayor,** and its satellite, the 16th-century **Plaza Vieja (Old Square).** These are the two most important sights in Zafra, along with the **Nuestra Señora de la Candelaria,** a church with nine panels by Zurbarán, displayed on the retable in a chapel designed by Churriguera. The church, constructed in the Gothic-Renaissance style, has a red-brick belfry. Admission is free. It's open Monday to Saturday from 10:30am to 1pm and 7 to 8:30pm and Sunday from 11am to 12:30pm.

Where to Stay & Dine

Huerta Honda, López Asme, 32, 06300 Zafra. ☎ **924/55-41-00.** Fax 924/55-25-04. 46 rms (27 with bath). A/C MINIBAR TV TEL

Rates: 3,500 ptas. ($24.90) single without bath, 4,720 ptas. ($33.50) single with bath; 5,900 ptas. ($41.90) double with bath. MC, V. Breakfast 600 ptas. ($4.30) extra. MC, V.

Views of the citadel and the old town are to be had from the modern, recently renovated bedrooms of this Andalusian-style hotel in front of the Plaza del Alcázar. There's a disco, as well as a garden and a pretty patio for mid-afternoon drinks. Under the same management, at no. 36 on the same street, is the Restaurant Barbacana, a well-recommended regional restaurant, offering fixed-price menus for 3,500 pesetas ($24.90).

Parador Hernán Cortés, Plaza Corazón de María, 7, 06300 Zafra. ☎ **924/55-45-40.** Fax 924/55-10-18. A/C MINIBAR TV TEL

Rates: 8,800–10,400 ptas. ($62.50–$73.80) single; 11,500–18,000 ptas. ($81.70–$127.80) double. Breakfast 1,100 ptas. ($7.80) extra. AE, DC, MC, V. **Parking:** Free.

This government-run parador—located in a restored castle near the Plaza de España—is named after Cortés, who stayed here with the dukes of Feria before his departure for the New World. The castle was originally built in 1457, on a square plan with four round towers. The interior, beautiful but restrained, contains the chapel of the Alcázar, with an octagonal Gothic dome. In addition to being decorated in splendid taste, the Hernan Cortés is quite comfortable, boasting a patio, a garden, and a swimming pool. The magnificent-looking dining room offers regional meals for 3,500 pesetas ($24.90). Also on the premises are a bar and a large lounge.

9

Andalusia

ANDALUSIA, THE WILD, RUGGED TRACT OF SOUTHERN SPAIN, LIVES UP TO ALL THE clichés you've heard about it: Silvery olive trees sway in the wind; the scent of orange blossoms is everywhere; women wearing mantillas and carnations in their hair run through the narrow streets on fiesta days; and gypsies rattle their castanets in ancient caves.

This once-great stronghold of Muslim Spain is rich in history and tradition, containing some of the country's most celebrated sightseeing treasures: the world-famous Mezquita (mosque) in Córdoba, the Alhambra in Granada, and the great Gothic cathedral in Seville. It also has smaller towns just waiting to be discovered—Úbeda, castle-dominated Jaén, gorge-split Ronda, sherry-producing Jerez de la Frontera, and the gleaming white port city of Cádiz. Give Andalusia at least a week and you'll still have only skimmed the surface of its many offerings.

This dry, mountainous region also embraces the Costa del Sol (Málaga, Marbella, and Torremolinos), a popular strip of Spain that is covered separately in the following chapter. Go to the Costa del Sol for beach resorts, nightlife, and relaxation; visit Andalusia for its architectural wonders and beauty.

Crime alert: Anyone driving south into Andalusia and the Costa del Sol should be wary of thieves. Daylight robberies are commonplace, especially in Seville, Córdoba, and Granada. It is not unusual for a car to be broken into while tourists are enjoying lunch in a restaurant. Some establishments have hired guards (a service for which you should tip, of course). Under no circumstances should you ever leave passports and traveler's checks unguarded in a car.

Seeing Andalusia

GETTING THERE Most air traffic goes into Málaga, capital of the Costa del Sol (see the next chapter), but there are also airports in Córdoba, Granada, Jerez de la Frontera, and Seville. If you want to visit Andalusia (in Spanish "Andalucia," pronounced Andalu*thia*) before heading to the Costa del Sol, and wish to fly, consider Seville as your gateway, since it has the most domestic flights as well as a few international arrivals. Check with Iberia Airlines for information.

Getting to the major cities—Granada, Seville, and Córdoba—by train is the route preferred by most visitors. However, once you're there, buses are often best for travel between smaller towns.

The major cities of Andalusia are connected by bus links to other large cities of Spain, such as Valencia, Madrid, and Barcelona. These are long hauls, however, and the train is more comfortable. Once in Andalusia, the bus becomes the preferred link among the cities of the province. Distances are usually much shorter by bus than by train, and you see more scenery—trains take time going through mountain tunnels.

If you're driving from Madrid, you can take the superhighway N-IV to Andalusia, going by way of Córdoba and Seville, until it ends at Cádiz, an Atlantic seaport. Much of this *autopista* is toll free, except the A-4 from Seville to Cádiz, via Jerez de la Frontera.

A Suggested Route

The itinerary below begins in Madrid, heading south into Andalusia.

Day 1 Stop overnight in Jaén.

Day 2 Explore Jaén in the morning, then drive to Baeza and Úbeda, two of the most charming towns in Andalusia. Return to Jaén for the night.

What's Special About Andalusia

Great Towns/Villages

- Seville, hometown of Carmen, Don Giovanni, and the Barber.
- Córdoba, the monument-filled capital of Muslim Spain.
- Granada, an old Moorish capital, number-one stop on the "romantic pilgrimage" tour of Spain.
- Ronda, an old aristocratic town known for its cliff-hanging houses.

Religious Shrines

- The Spanish Renaissance cathedral at Granada, where Ferdinand and Isabella were buried.
- The grand Gothic cathedral at Seville, ranking in size with St. Peter's in Rome.

Events/Festivals

- Seville's April Fair, the most famous *feria* in Spain—with bullfights, flamenco, and folklore on parade.
- Holy Week in Seville, when wooden figures called *pasos* are paraded through streets by robed penitents.

Ancient Monuments

- The Sinagoga at Córdoba, one of three pre-Inquisition synagogues remaining.
- Giralda Tower at Seville, erected as a minaret in the 12th century.
- Itálica, the ruins of an ancient Roman city northwest of Seville.

Architectural Highlights

- The Mezquita at Córdoba, a mosque dating from the 8th century.
- The Alcázar de los Reyes Cristianos at Córdoba, one of Spain's best examples of military architecture.
- The Alcázar at Seville, a Mudéjar palace built in the 14th century by Pedro the Cruel.
- The Alhambra, a Moorish palace made famous in America by Washington Irving.

Day 3 Drive south from Jaén to Granada and check into a hotel, enjoying a night of gypsy flamenco.

Day 4 Still based in Granada, visit the Alhambra and the Generalife.

Day 5 Go northwest from Granada to Córdoba, arriving in the late afternoon for a visit to the Mezquita.

Day 6 Spend the morning exploring the sights of Córdoba before driving west in the afternoon to Seville. Stay there overnight.

Day 7 Still based in Seville, explore that city's many attractions, including its cathedral and Alcázar.

Day 8 Drive south to Cádiz for an overnight stopover, but en route have lunch and visit one of the sherry bodegas at Jerez de la Frontera.

Day 9 After exploring Cádiz, return to Madrid, or else drive to Algeciras and take the ferry over to Tangier in Morocco. Another alternative is to head east toward Algeciras, stopping at Gibraltar, before planning visits to some of the resort highlights along the Costa del Sol: Marbella, Torremolinos, Málaga, and Nerja.

1 Jaén, Baeza & Úbeda

The province of Jaén, with three principal cities—Jaén, the capital; Baeza; and Úbeda—was discovered by international tourists in the 1960s. For years, visitors whizzed through Jaén on their way south to Granada or bypassed it altogether on the southwest route to Córdoba and Seville. But the government improved the province's hotel outlook with excellent paradores, which now provide some of the finest accommodations in Andalusia.

Jaén

60 miles (97km) E of Córdoba, 60 miles (97km) N of Granada, 210 miles (338km) S of Madrid

GETTING THERE • By Train It's easier to leave Jaén than it is to get there, because trains to Jaén run only from south to north. Northbound trains—including two daily to Madrid's Atocha Railway Station—arrive and depart from Jaén's RENFE station on the Paseo de la Estación (☎ **25-56-07**), north of the center of town. If you're traveling from north to south, however, it isn't quite so easy. Most southbound trains from Madrid, and all trains heading south to Seville and the rest of Andalusia, stop only at a larger railway junction that lies inconveniently in the hamlet of Espeluy, 22 miles (35.5km) to the north. From Espeluy, trains are sometimes funneled a short ride to the east, to the railway junction midway between Linares (31 miles [50km] from Jaén) and Baeza (the Estación de Linares–Baeza). Consult the Jaén tourist office or the railway station for advice on your particular routing.

• By Bus The bus terminal is at Plaza Coca de la Piñera (☎ **25-01-06**), one block south of the central Parque de la Victoria. Either directly or after a transfer at Baeza, 30 miles (48km) to the north, buses travel eight times a day to Granada (2 hours away), 11 times to Úbeda (1½ hours), four times to Córdoba (4½ hours), and three times to Seville (5 hours).

• By Car Four important highways, plus several provincial roads, converge upon Jaén from four directions. Driving time from Madrid is around 5 hours, almost all of which is spent on the N-IV superhighway.

ESSENTIALS The area code for Jaén is 953. The tourist information office is at Arquitecto Bergés, 1 (☎ **953/22-27-37**).

In the center of Spain's major olive-growing district, Jaén is sandwiched between Córdoba and Granada and has always been considered a gateway between Castile and Andalusia. The Christian forces gathered here in 1492 before marching on Granada to oust the Moors.

Jaén's bustling modern section is of little interest to visitors, but the **Moorish old town,** where the narrow cobblestoned streets hug the mountainside, is reason enough to visit. A hilltop castle, now converted into a first-rate parador, dominates the city. On a clear day you can see the snow-covered peaks of the Sierra Nevada.

Jaén, the city, is at the center of a large province of 5,189 square miles (13,491 sq km), framed by mountains: the Sierra Morena to the north, the Segura and Cazorla ranges to the east, and those of Huelma, Noalejo, and Valdepeñas to the south. To the west, plains widen into the fertile Guadalquivir Valley. The landscape is rugged and irregular. Jaén province comprises three well-defined districts: the Sierra de Cazorla, a land of wild scenery; the plains of Bailén, Ajona, and Arjonilla, filled with wheat fields, vineyards, and old olive trees; and the valleys of the tributaries of the Guadalquivir.

WHAT TO SEE & DO

Catedral de Santa María, Plaza de la Catedral. ☎ **27-52-33.**

The formality and grandeur of Jaén's cathedral stand witness to the city's importance in days gone by. Begun in 1555 and completed in 1802, it is a honey-colored blend of Gothic, baroque, and Renaissance styles, but mainly Renaissance. The interior, containing richly carved choir stalls, is dominated by a huge dome. The cathedral museum contains an important collection of historic objects in two underground chambers, including paintings by Ribera. The cathedral stands southwest of the Plaza de la Constitución.

Admission: Cathedral and museum free.

Open: Cathedral, daily 8:30am–1pm and 4:30–8pm (closes at 7pm in winter). Museum, Sat–Sun 11am–1pm. **Bus:** 8 or 10.

Iglesia de la Magdalena, Calle de la Magdalena. ☎ **25-60-19.**

Of the many churches worth visiting in Jaén, La Magdalena is the oldest and most interesting. This Gothic church was once an Arab mosque.

Admission: Free.

Open: Daily 6am–8pm.

Museo Provincial, Paseo de la Estación, 27. ☎ **25-03-20.**

The Provincial Museum's collection includes Roman mosaics; a Mudéjar arch; and many ceramics from the early Iberian, Greek, and Roman periods. On the upper floor is an exhibition of Pedro Berruguete paintings, including *Christ at the Column.* Look also for the Paleo-Christian sarcophagus from Martos. The museum is between the bus and train stations.

Admission: 100 ptas. (70¢).

Open: Tues–Fri 10am–2pm and 4–7pm; Sat–Sun 10am–2pm.

Centro Cultural Palacio de Villardompardo, Plaza de Santa Luisa de Marillac, s/n. ☎ **22-33-59.**

This is a three-in-one attraction, including some former Arab baths (known as *hamman*), a Museo de Artes y Costumbres Populares (folk art and crafts), and a Museo Internacional de Arte Naif (a collection of Naif gathered from all over the world). The opening hours (see below) are the same for all three attractions, and none charges admission.

Underneath the palace, which lies near Calle San Juan and the Chapel of St. Andrew (San Andrés), are the former Arab baths. These represent some of the most important Moorish architecture from the 11th century ever discovered in Spain—in fact, they are considered the most significant ruins of Arab baths in the country. You can visit a warm room, a hot room, and a cold room—the latter having a barrel vault and 12 star-shaped chandeliers. Later you can go upstairs to see the folk art and the Naif collection that opened in 1990.

Admission: Free.

Open: Tues–Fri 10am–2pm and 5–8pm (closes at 7pm in winter); Sat–Sun 10am–4pm. **Directions:** You must go on foot. In the old quarter of Jaén, follow signs indicating either Baños Arabes or Barrio de la Magdalena.

WHERE TO STAY

Parador Castillo de Santa Catalina, Castillo de Santa Catalina, 23000 Jaén. ☎ **953/23-00-00.** Fax 953/23-09-30. 45 rms (all with bath). A/C MINIBAR TV TEL **Directions:** Follow Carretera al Castillo y Neveraol.

Rates: 10,400 ptas. ($73.80) single occupancy of a double; 13,000 ptas. ($92.30) double. Breakfast 1,100 ptas. ($7.80) extra. AE, DC, MC, V. **Parking:** Free.

This castle, three miles (4.8km) to the east on the hill overlooking the city, is one of the government's showplace paradors, and staying here is reason enough to visit Jaén. In the 10th century the castle was a Muslim fortress, surrounded by high protective walls and approached by a steep, winding road. When Christians did approach, the Moors were fond of throwing them over. The castle is still reached by the same road, but the hospitality has improved remarkably. Visitors enter through a three-story-high baronial hallway, and a polite staff shows them to their balconied bedrooms (doubles only), tastefully furnished and comfortable, with spick-and-span tile baths.

Dining at the castle is dramatic—the high-vaulted restaurant looks like a small cathedral with its wrought-iron chandeliers and stone arches, plus a raised hearth and a collection of copper kettles and ceramics. On either side of the lofty room, arched windows open onto a terrace or a fabulous view of Jaén. Lunch or dinner here, at 3,500 ptas. ($24.90), includes typical Jaén dishes—usually made with the olives for which the area is famous—and regional wine.

Xauen, Plaza Deán Mazas, 3, 23001 Jaén. ☎ **953/26-40-11.** 35 rms (all with bath). A/C TV TEL

Rates: 5,000 ptas. ($35.50) single; 7,000 ptas. ($49.70) double. Breakfast 300 ptas. ($2.10) extra. No credit cards. **Parking:** 60 ptas. (40¢) per hour nearby.

Breakfast only is served at this family-run hotel, which opened in 1979, one block west of Plaza de la Constitución. The handcrafted detailing of the building, and its central location, make it an attractive choice. The guest rooms are simply furnished but comfortable. Motorists might have to park far away from the entrance.

WHERE TO DINE

Consider a meal in the luxurious hilltop parador commanding a view of the area (see above). It's one of the best in the area.

The Jockey Club, Paseo de la Estación, 20. ☎ **25-10-18.**

Cuisine: SPANISH. **Reservations:** Required Fri–Sat dinner.
Prices: Appetizers 450–600 ptas. ($3.20–$4.30); main courses 750–1,800 ptas. ($5.30–$12.80); fixed-price menu 2,650 ptas. ($18.80). AE, DC, MC, V.
Open: Lunch, Mon–Sat 12:30–4:30pm; dinner, Mon–Sat 8–11:30pm. **Closed:** Aug.

The leading restaurant in town is the moderately priced Jockey Club, whose owner works hard to maintain a comfortable ambience and a well-prepared cuisine. Main dishes include lotte "Jockey style," Milanese-style rice, salmon with green sauce, and a full range of meats and fish. You'll find the Jockey Club in the center of town, south of Plaza de la Constitución.

Nelson, Paseo de la Estación, 33. ☎ **22-92-01.**

Cuisine: SPANISH. **Reservations:** Required.
Prices: Appetizers 550–825 ptas. ($3.90–$5.90); main courses 1,350–2,100 ptas. ($9.60–$14.90). AE, DC, MC, V.

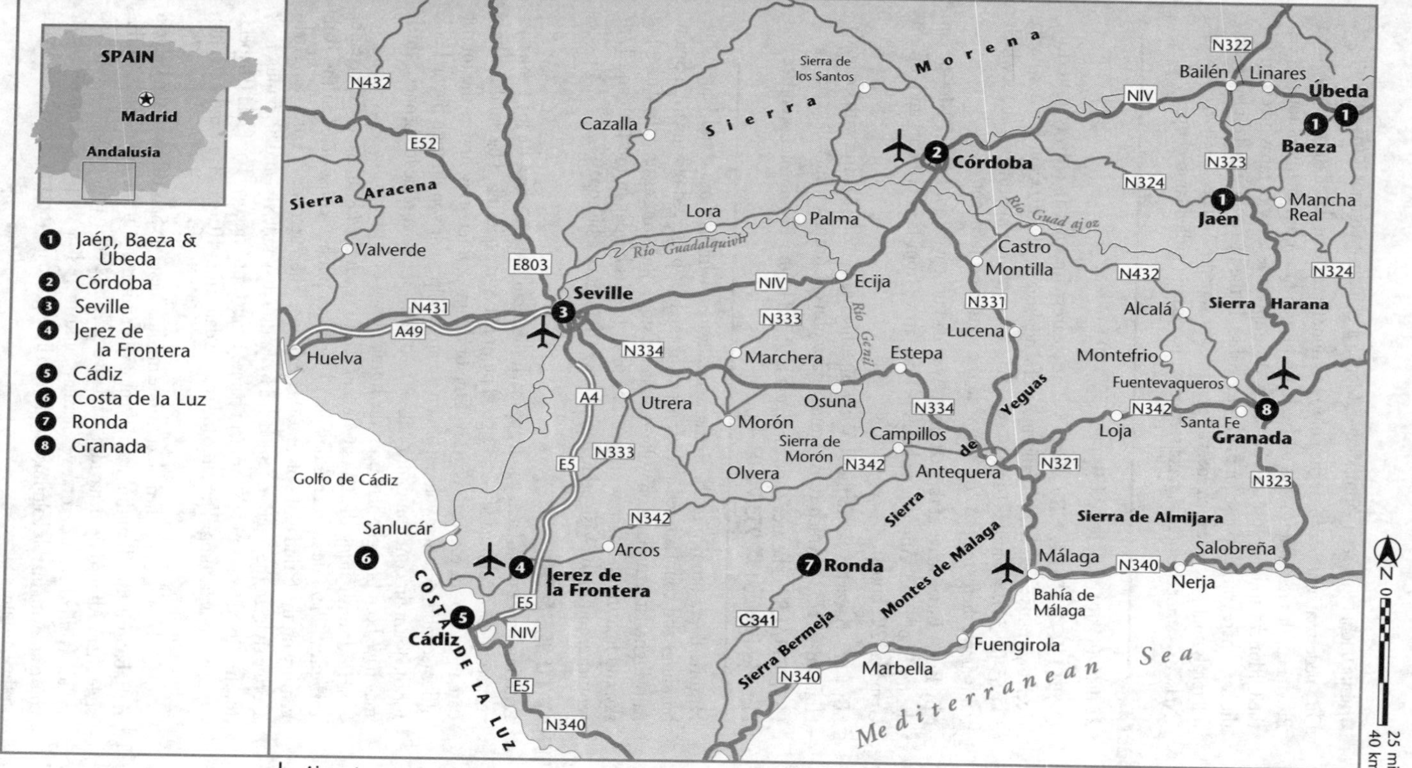

Andalusia: From Córdoba to Granada

Open: Lunch, Mon–Sat 1–4pm; dinner, Mon–Sat 8:30pm–midnight. **Closed:** Aug.

On a pedestrian walkway near the railway station, Plaza de las Batallas, and the Museo Provincial, this restaurant relies on fresh produce and the gruff charm of the owners, the Ordóñez brothers, José and Salvador. An impressive array of tapas greets you at the bar, where you can pause for predinner drinks. In the air-conditioned dining room, full meals might include such specialties as roast goat in the Andalusian style, filet steak "Nelson," escabeche of fish, hake stewed with eels, and grilled lamb chops.

Baeza

28 miles (45km) NE of Jaén, 191 miles (307km) S of Madrid

GETTING THERE • By Train The nearest important railway junction, receiving trains from Madrid and most of Andalusia, is the Estación Linares-Baeza (☎ **65-01-31**), 8½ miles (14km) west of Baeza's center. For information about which trains arrive there, refer to "By Train" in the section on Jaén, above.

• By Bus Buses arrive at the station at Avenida Puche y Pardo, 1 (☎ **74-04-68**) in the north of town. About nine buses per day arrive from Jaén (1 hour) and 8 from Granada (2½ hours).

• By Car Baeza lies east of the N-V, the superhighway linking Madrid with Granada. Highway 321/322, which runs through Baeza, links Córdoba with Valencia.

ESSENTIALS The area code for Baeza is 953. The tourist information office is at Plaza del Pópulo (☎ **953/74-04-44**).

Historic Baeza (known to the Romans as Vilvatia), with its Gothic and Plateresque buildings and cobblestoned streets, is one of the best-preserved old towns in Spain. At twilight, lanterns hang on walls of plastered stone, flickering against the darkening sky and lighting the narrow streets. The town had its heyday in the 16th and 17th centuries, and in the Visigothic period it was the seat of a bishop.

WHAT TO SEE & DO

Entering Baeza from Jaén, you'll approach the main square, **Plaza de los Leones,** a two-story open colonnade—and a good point to begin exploring. The buildings here date in part from the 16th century. One of the most interesting houses the tourist office (see above), where you can obtain a map to help guide you through Baeza. Look for the fountain containing four half-effaced lions, the Fuente de los Leones, which may have been brought here from the Roman town of Cantulo.

Head south along the Cuesta de San Gil to reach the Gothic and Renaissance **cathedral,** Plaza de la Fuente de Santa María (no phone), constructed in the 16th century on the foundations of an earlier mosque. The Puerta de la Luna is in Arab-Gothic style. In the interior, remodeled by Andrés de Vandelvira and his pupils, look for the carved wood and the brilliant painted *rejas* (iron screens). The Gold Chapel is especially outstanding. The cathedral is open daily from 10am to 1pm and 4 to 7pm. Admission is free.

After leaving the cathedral, continue up the Cuesta de San Felipe to the **Palacio de Jabalquinto,** a beautiful example of civil architecture in the flamboyant Gothic style. Juan Alfonso de Benavides, a relative of King Ferdinand, ordered it built. Its facade is filled with decorative elements, and there is a simple Renaissance-style courtyard with marble columns. Inside, two lions guard the stairway, heavily decorated in the baroque style.

WHERE TO STAY

$ **Hotel Juanito,** Plaza del Arca del Agua, s/n, 23400 Baeza. ☎ **953/74-00-40.** Fax 953/74-23-24. 37 rms (all with bath). A/C TV TEL

Rates: 4,400 ptas. ($31.20) single; 5,200 ptas. ($36.90) double. Breakfast 500 ptas. ($3.60) extra. No credit cards. **Parking:** Free.

This establishment, known mainly for its restaurant (see below), is also a suitable choice for an overnight stopover. Built originally in the 1970s, it was renovated and enlarged in 1992. The guest rooms (half of which have a TV) are unpretentious but clean and comfortable. The Hotel Juanito stands on the outskirts of Baeza, toward Úbeda.

WHERE TO DINE

Casa Juanito, Plaza del Arca del Agua, s/n. ☎ **74-00-40.**

Cuisine: SPANISH. **Reservations:** Required Fri–Sat.
Prices: Appetizers 450–800 ptas. ($3.20–$5.70); main courses 1,200–2,450 ptas. ($8.50–$17.40). No credit cards.
Open: Lunch, daily 1–3:30pm; dinner, Tues–Sun 6:30–11:15pm. **Closed:** Nov 1–15.

Owners Juan Antonío and Luisa Salcedo serve regional specialties from Andalusia and La Mancha. Devotees of the "lost art" of Jaén cookery, they revive ancient recipes in their frequently changing "suggestions for the day." Game is served in season, and many vegetable dishes are made with ham. Among the savory and well-prepared menu items are *habas* beans, filet of beef with tomatoes and peppers, partridge in pastry crust, and codfish house style.

$ **El Sali,** Pasaje Cardenal Benavides, 15. ☎ **74-13-65.**

Cuisine: SPANISH. **Reservations:** Not required.
Prices: Appetizers 600–800 ptas. ($4.30–$5.70); main courses 1,000–2,000 ptas. ($7.10–$14.20); fixed-price menu 1,500 ptas. ($10.70). DC, MC, V.
Open: Lunch, daily 1–4pm; dinner, Thurs–Tues 8–11pm. **Closed:** Sept 16–Oct 10.

The setting of this restaurant is a modern building erected in the 1980s in the town center, adjacent to Plaza del Pópulo. Diners in air-conditioned comfort enjoy what many locals regard as the most reasonable set menu in town. The owners serve not only the cuisine of Andalusia but also certain dishes from around Spain. They are known for their fresh vegetables, as exemplified by *la pipirana,* a cold medley of vegetables with tuna, accented with boiled eggs, fresh tomatoes, onions, and spices (only in summer). The atmosphere is relaxed and the service cordial; the portions are generous. You won't leave feeling hungry or overcharged.

Úbeda

6 miles (10km) NE of Jaén, 194 miles (312km) S of Madrid

GETTING THERE • By Train The nearest train station is the Linares-Baeza station (☎ **65-01-31**). For information on trains to and from the station, refer to the Jaén section (see above).

• By Bus There are buses seven times daily to Baeza, less than 6 miles (9.6km) away, and to Jaén. Six buses per day go to the busy railway station at Linares-Baeza, where a train can take you virtually anywhere in Spain. Bus service to and from Córdoba, Seville, and Granada (at least once a day) is also available. Úbeda's bus station lies in the heart of the modern town, on Calle San José (☎ **75-21-57**), where signs will point you on a downhill walk to the *zona monumental.*

• **By Car** Turn off the Madrid-Córdoba road and head east for Linares, then on to Úbeda, a detour of 26 miles (42km).

ESSENTIALS The area code for Úbeda is 953. The tourist information office is at Plaza de los Caídos, 2 (☎ **953/75-08-97**).

A former stronghold of the Arabs, Úbeda, often called the "Florence of Andalusia," is a Spanish National Landmark filled with golden-brown Renaissance palaces and tile-roofed whitewashed houses. The best way to discover Úbeda's charm is to wander its narrow cobblestone streets.

The government long ago created a parador here in a renovated ducal palace—you might stop for lunch if you're pressed for time. Allow time for a stroll through Úbeda's shops, which sell, among other items, leathercraft goods and esparto grass carpets.

The palaces and churches of the city are almost endless. You might begin your tour at the centrally located **Plaza de Vázquez de Molina,** which is flanked by several mansions, including the Casa de las Cadenas, now the Town Hall. For centuries the mansions have been decaying, but many are now being restored. Most are not open to the public.

WHAT TO SEE & DO

Iglesia el Salvador, Plaza de Vázquez de Molina. No phone.

One of the grandest examples of Spanish Renaissance architecture, this church was designed in 1536 by Diego de Siloé. The richly embellished portal is mere window dressing for the wealth of decoration inside the church, including a sacristy designed by Vandelvira and a single nave with gold-and-blue vaulting. Don't miss the many sculptures and altarpieces or the spectacular rose windows.

Admission: Free.

Open: Daily 9am–1pm and 5–7pm.

Iglesia de San Pablo, Plaza 1 de Mayo. No phone.

This church, in the center of the old town, is almost as fascinating as the Iglesia El Salvador. The Gothic San Pablo is famous for its 16th-century south portal in the Isabelline style and its chapels.

Admission: Free.

Open: Daily 9am–1pm and 7–9pm.

Hospital de Santiago, Calle Santiago. No phone.

On the western edge of town, off the Calle del Obispo Coros, stands the Hospital of Santiago, completed in 1575 and still in use. Built by Andrés de Vandelvira, "the Christopher Wren of Úbeda," over the years it has earned a reputation as the "Escorial of Andalusia."

Admission: Free.

Open: Daily 9am–1pm and 5–7pm.

Iglesia de Santa María de Los Reales Alcázares, Arroyo de Santa María. ☎ 75-07-77.

Another intriguing Úbeda church is Santa María de los Reales Alcázares, on the site of a former Arab mosque. The cloisters, with their fan vaulting, are Gothic; the interior, with its tiled and painted ceiling, blends the Gothic and Mudéjar styles. Also inside the church you'll find a gruesome statue of a mutilated Christ. Santa María is in the center of town, opposite the Ayuntamiento (Town Hall).

Admission: Free.
Open: Daily 9am–1pm and 5–7pm.

WHERE TO STAY

Hotel Consuelo, Avenida Ramón y Cajal, 12, 23400 Úbeda. ☎ **953/75-08-40.** Fax 953/75-68-34. 36 rms, 3 suites (all with bath). A/C MINIBAR TV TEL

Rates: 3,000 ptas. ($21.30) single; 5,500 ptas. ($39.10) double; from 7,500 ptas. ($53.30) suite. V. **Parking:** 700 ptas. ($5).

Frankly, if there's room at the parador near the bus station (see below), there isn't much reason for you to go elsewhere. If you must, however, head for this comfortable and utilitarian three-story building across from the Instituto Ensenanza Media. The hotel was built in the late 1960s and renovated in 1991. It doesn't serve breakfast and so its patrons head out for coffee at one of the nearby cafés. The guest rooms are basic but clean.

Hotel la Paz, Calle Andalucía, 1, 23400 Úbeda. ☎ **953/75-21-46.** Fax 953/75-08-48. 58 rms (all with bath), 4 suites. A/C TV TEL

Rates: 5,350 ptas. ($38) single; 6,200 ptas. ($44) double. Breakfast 400 ptas. ($2.80) extra. AE, DC, MC, V. **Parking:** 800 ptas. ($5.70).

Set on a sharply angled street corner in the heart of the commercial district, opposite a statue to a military hero, this seven-story hotel contains comfortably unpretentious bedrooms. Each bedroom is decorated in a simplified Iberian style of dignified wood furniture, with either pure-white or papered walls. Built in 1971, the hotel was renovated in 1994. The street-level El Olivo opens directly onto the sidewalk and does a thriving business with the local community. A *menú del día* served here costs 1,600 ptas. ($11.40). There's also a simple snack restaurant for coffee and drinks, plus a bar. Services include a concierge, laundry, and babysitting; facilities offered are car rentals and a shopping boutique.

★ **Parador Nacional del Condestabe Dávalos,** Plaza de Vázquez de Molina, 1, 23400 Úbeda. ☎ **953/75-03-45.** Fax 953/75-12-59. 31 rms (all with bath), 1 suite. A/C MINIBAR TV TEL

Rates: 11,600 ptas. ($82.40) single occupancy of a double; 14,500 ptas. ($103) double; 17,650 ptas. ($125.30) suite. Breakfast 1,100 ptas. ($7.80) extra. AE, DC, MC, V.

In the heart of town on the most central square, near the Town Hall, stands this 16th-century palace turned parador, which shares an old paved plaza with the Iglesia El Salvador and its dazzling facade. The formal entrance to the Renaissance palace leads to an enclosed patio, encircled by two levels of Moorish arches, where palms and potted plants stand on the tile floors. The guest rooms, doubles only, are nearly two stories high, with beamed ceilings and tall windows. Antiques and reproductions adorn the rooms, and the beds are comfortable.

Before lunch or dinner, stop in at the low-beamed wine cellar, with its stone arches, provincial stools and tables, and giant kegs of wine. Dinner is served in a tastefully decorated ground-floor room where a costumed staff serves traditional Spanish dishes. Lunch or dinner costs around 3,500 ptas. ($24.90), including wine and service.

WHERE TO DINE

The parador (see above) is the best place to dine for miles around. For dinner, try the stuffed partridge or baby lamb chops. The restaurants scattered around Calle Ramón y Cajal are unremarkable.

2 Córdoba

65 miles (105 km) W of Jáen, 260 miles (419km) SW of Madrid

GETTING THERE • By Train Córdoba is a railway junction for routes to the rest of Andalusia and the rest of Spain. There are about five Talgo and TER express trains daily between Córdoba and Madrid (4½ to 5 hours). Other, slower trains (*tranvías*) take 8 or 9 hours for the same transit. There are also 16 trains from Seville every day (1½ hours). The main railway station is on the town's northern periphery, at Avenida de América, 130, near the corner of Avenida de Cervantes. For information, call **49-02-02.** To reach the heart of the old town, head south on Avenida de Cervantes or Avenida del Gran Capitán. If you want to buy a ticket or to get departure times and prices only, you can go to the RENFE office at Ronda de los Tejares, 10 (☎ **47-58-54**).

• By Bus There are several different bus companies, each of which maintains a separate terminal. The town's most important bus terminal is operated by the Alsina-Graells Sur Company, Avenida Medina Azahara, 29 (☎ **23-64-74**), on the western outskirts of town (just west of the gardens beside Paseo de la Victoria).

From the bus terminal operated by Empresa Bacoma, Avenida de Cervantes, 22 (☎ **47-23-52**), a short walk south of the railway station, there are three buses per day to and from Seville (a 2-hour and 3-hour trip, respectively) and five daily buses to Jaén (3 hours). Buses arrive here from Madrid (5½ hours).

• By Car Córdoba lies astride the N-IV connecting Madrid with Seville. Driving time from Madrid is about eight hours; from Seville, it's two to three hours.

ESSENTIALS The area code for Córdoba is 957. The tourist information office is at Calle Torrijos, 10 (☎ **957/47-12-35**). If you're driving, don't think of entering the complicated maze of streets in the old town by car. You'll inevitably get lost and find no place to park.

Ten centuries ago Córdoba was one of the greatest cities in the world, with a population of 900,000. The capital of Muslim Spain, it was Europe's largest city and a cultural and intellectual center. This seat of the Western Caliphate flourished with public baths, mosques, a great library, and palaces. But greedy, sacking hordes have since passed through, tearing down ancient buildings and carting off art treasures. Despite these assaults, Córdoba still retains traces of its former glory—enough to rival Seville and Granada as the most fascinating city in Andalusia.

Today this provincial capital is known chiefly for its mosque, but it abounds with other artistic and architectural riches, especially its domestic dwellings. The old Arab and Jewish quarters are famous for their narrow streets lined with whitewashed homes boasting flower-filled patios and balconies, and it's perfectly acceptable to walk along gazing into the courtyards. This isn't an invasion of privacy: The citizens of Córdoba take pride in showing off their patios as part of the city's tradition. And don't forget to bring along a good pair of walking shoes, as the only way to explore the monumental heart of the city is on foot.

What to See & Do

The Mezquita, now a cathedral, is the principal reason for visiting Córdoba, but the old Alcázar, an ancient synagogue, museums, and galleries will round out your day (see below). There's a lot to absorb, and visitors with more time may want to spend at least two days here.

Don't miss Córdoba's **Roman bridge (Puente Romano)** believed to date from the time of Augustus. It's hardly Roman anymore because none of its 16 supporting arches is original. The sculptor Bernabé Gómez del Río erected a statue of St. Raphael in the middle of the bridge in 1651. The Roman bridge crosses the Guadalquivir River about one block south of the Mezquita.

★ **Mezquita-Catedral de Córdoba,** Calle Cardenal Herrero, s/n. ☎ **47-05-12.**

Dating from the 8th century, the Mezquita was the crowning Muslim architectural achievement in the West, rivaled only by the mosque at Mecca. It is a fantastic labyrinth of red-and-white, peppermint-striped pillars. To the astonishment of visitors, a cathedral sits awkwardly in the middle of the mosque, disturbing the purity of the lines. The 16th-century cathedral, a blend of many styles, is impressive in its own right, with an intricately carved ceiling and baroque choir stalls. Additional ill-conceived annexes later turned the Mezquita into an architectural oddity. Its most interesting feature is the *mihrab,* a domed shrine of Byzantine mosaics that once housed the Koran.

After exploring the interior, stroll through the Courtyard of the Orange Trees, which has a beautiful fountain. The hardy will climb a 16th-century tower built here on the base of a Moorish minaret to catch a panoramic view of Córdoba and its environs.

The Mezquita is south of the train station, just north of the Roman bridge.

Admission: 800 ptas. ($5.70) adults; 400 ptas. ($2.80) children.

Open: Apr–Sept, daily 10am–7pm. Oct–Mar, daily 10am–1:30pm and 3:30–5:30pm.

★ **Alcázar de los Reyes Cristianos,** Amador de los Ríos, s/n. ☎ **47-20-00.**

Commissioned in 1328 by Alfonso XI (The "Just"), the Alcázar of the Christian Kings is a fine example of military architecture. Ferdinand and Isabella governed Castile from this fortress on the river as they prepared to reconquer Granada, the last Moorish stronghold in Spain. Columbus journeyed here to fill Isabella's ears with his plans for discovery.

Located two blocks southwest of the Mezquita, the quadrangular building is notable for powerful walls and a trio of towers—the Tower of the Lions, the Tower of Allegiance, and the Tower of the River. The Tower of the Lions contains intricately decorated ogival ceilings that are considered the most notable example of Gothic architecture in Andalusia.

The beautiful gardens, illuminated at night, and the Moorish baths are celebrated attractions. The Patio Morisco is a lovely spot, its pavement decorated with the arms of León and Castile. Be sure to seek out a distinguished Roman sarcophagus, representative of second- and third-century funeral art. The Roman mosaics are also outstanding—especially a unique piece dedicated to Polyphemus and Galatea.

Admission: 225 ptas. ($1.60) adults; 125 ptas. (90¢) children.

Open: May–Sept, Tues–Sat 9:30am–1:30pm and 5–8pm, Sun 9:30am–1:30pm; Oct–Apr, Tues–Sat, 9:30am–1:30pm and 4–7pm, Sun 9:30am–1:30pm. Gardens illuminated May–Sept 10pm–1am. **Bus:** 3 or 12.

Sinagoga, Calle de los Judíos. No phone.

In Cordoba you'll find one of Spain's few remaining pre-Inquisition synagogues, built in 1350 in the Barrio de la Judería (Jewish Quarter), two blocks west of the northern wall of the Mezquita. The synagogue is noted particularly for its stucco-work; the east wall contains a large orifice where the Tabernacle was once placed (inside, the scrolls of the Pentateuch were kept). After the Jews were expelled from Spain, the synagogue was turned into a hospital, until it became a Catholic chapel in 1588.

Admission: 75 ptas. (50¢).

Open: Tues–Sat 10am–2pm and 3:30–5:30pm; Sun 10am–1:30pm. **Bus:** 3 or 12.

Museo de Bellas Artes de Córdoba, Plazuela del Potro, 1. ☎ **47-33-45.**

As you cross Plazuela del Potro to reach the Fine Arts Museum, notice the fountain at one end of the square. Built in 1557, it is of a young stallion with forelegs raised, holding the shield of Córdoba.

Housed in an old hospital on the plaza, the Fine Arts Museum contains medieval Andalusian paintings, examples of Spanish baroque art, and works by many of Spain's important 19th- and 20th-century painters, including Goya. The museum is east of the Mezquita, about a block south of the Church of St. Francis (San Francisco).

Admission: 250 ptas. ($1.80) adults; children 11 and under free.

Open: June 15–Sept 15, Tues–Sat 10am–2pm and 6–8pm, Sun 10am–1:30pm; Sept 16–June 14, Tues–Sat 10am–2pm and 5–7pm, Sun 10am–1:30pm. **Bus:** 3, 4, 7, or 12.

Museo de Julio Romero de Torres, Plazuela del Potro. ☎ **49-19-09.**

Across the patio from the Fine Arts Museum, this museum honors Julio Romero de Torres, a Córdoba-born artist who died in 1930. It contains his celebrated *Oranges and Lemons.* Other notable works include *The Little Girl Who Sells Fuel, Sin,* and *A Dedication to the Art of the Bullfight.* A corner of Romero's Madrid studio has been reproduced in one of the rooms, displaying the paintings left unfinished at his death.

Admission: 200 ptas. ($1.40).

Open: Daily 10am–1pm and 5–6:45pm.

Museo Municipal de Arte Táurino, Plaza de las Bulas (also called Plaza Maimónides). ☎ **47-20-00.**

Memorabilia of great bullfights are housed here in a 16th-century building in the Jewish Quarter, inaugurated in 1983 as an appendage to the Museo Municipal de Arte Cordobesas. Its ample galleries recall Córdoba's great bullfighters with "suits of lights," pictures, trophies, posters, even stuffed bulls' heads. You'll see Manolete in repose and the blood-smeared uniform of El Cordobés—both of these famous matadors came from Córdoba. The museum is located about a block northwest of the Mezquita, midway between the mosque and the synagogue.

Admission: 200 ptas. ($1.40).

Open: May–Sept, Tues–Sat 9:30am–1:30pm and 5–8pm, Sun 9:30am–1:30pm; Oct–Apr, Tues–Sat 9:30am–1:30pm and 4–7pm, Sun 9:30am–1:30pm. **Bus:** 3 or 12.

Torre de la Calahorra, Avenida de la Confederación, Puente Romano. ☎ **29-39-29.**

Across the river, at the southern end of the Roman bridge, stands the Tower of the Calahorra. Commissioned by Henry II of Trastamara in 1369 to protect him from his brother, Peter I, it now houses a town museum where visitors can walk about on a self-guided tour with headsets. Don't miss the Hall of the Americas. One room houses wax figures of Córdoba's famous philosophers, including Averroës and Maimónides. Other rooms exhibit a miniature model of the Alhambra, at Granada, complete with water fountains; a miniature Mezquita; and a display of Arab musical instruments. Finally, you can climb to the top of the tower for some excellent views of the Roman bridge, the river, and the cathedral/mosque.

Admission: Museum, 350 ptas. ($2.50) adults; 250 ptas. ($1.80) children. Multimedia presentation, 500 ptas. ($3.60) adults, 400 ptas. ($2.80) children.

Open: May–Sept, daily 10am–2pm and 5:30–8:30pm. Oct–Apr, daily 10:30am–6pm. **Bus:** 12.

Museo Arqueológico Provincial, Plaza Jerónimo Páez. ☎ **47-40-11.**

Córdoba's Archeological Museum, two blocks northeast of the Mezquita, is one of the most important in Spain. Housed in a palace dating from 1505, it displays artifacts left behind by the various peoples and conquerors who have swept through the province—Paleolithic and Neolithic items; Iberian hand weapons and ceramics; and Roman sculptures, bronzes, ceramics, inscriptions, and mosaics. Especially interesting are the Visigothic artifacts. The most outstanding collection, however, is devoted to Arabic art and spans the entire Muslim occupation. Take a few minutes to relax in one of the patios, with its fountains and ponds.

Admission: 250 ptas. ($1.80).

Open: Tues–Sat 10am–2pm and 5–7pm, Sun 10am–1:30pm.

Palacio Museo de Viana, Plaza de Don Gome, 2. ☎ **48-22-75.**

The public has seldom had access to Córdoba's palaces, but that's changed with the opening of this museum. Visitors are shown into a carriage house, where the elegant vehicles of another era are displayed. Note the intricate leather decoration on the carriages and the leather wall hangings, some of which date from the period of the Reconquest; there's also a collection of leather paintings. You can wander at leisure through the garden and patios. The palace lies four blocks southeast of Plaza de Colón on the northeastern edge of the old quarter.

Admission: 300 ptas. ($2.10).

Open: June–Sept, Thurs–Tues 9am–2pm; Oct–May, Thurs–Tues 10am–1pm and 4–6pm. **Closed:** First week of June.

A NEARBY ATTRACTION

Ruinas de Medina Azahara, Carretera Palma de Río, km. 8. ☎ **957/32-91-30.**

This place, a kind of Moorish Versailles outside Córdoba, was constructed in the 10th century by Caliph Abd al-Rahman. He named it after the favorite of his harem, nicknamed "the brilliant." Thousands of workers and animals slaved to build this mammoth pleasure palace, said to have contained 300 baths and 400 houses. Over the years the site was plundered for building materials; in fact, it might have been viewed as a "quarry" for the region. Some of its materials, so it is claimed, went to build the Alcázar in Seville. The Royal House, rendezvous point for the ministers, has been reconstructed. The principal salon remains in fragments, though, and you have to imagine it in its majesty. Just beyond the Royal House lie the ruins of a mosque constructed to face Mecca. The Berbers sacked the place in 1013.

Admission: 250 ptas. ($1.80).

Open: Sept 16–May 15, Tues–Sat 10am–2pm and 4–6:30pm, Sun 4–6:30pm; May 16–Sept 15, Tues–Sat 10am–2pm and 6–8:30pm, Sun 6–8:30pm. **Bus:** A bus leaves from the station on Calle de la Bodega, but it lets you off about 2 miles (3.2km) from the site.

SHOPPING

In Moorish times Córdoba was famous for its leather, known as "cordwainer." Highly valued in 15th-century Europe, this leather was studded with gold and silver ornaments, then painted with embossed designs (*guadamací*). Large panels of it often served in lieu of tapestries. Today the industry has fallen into decline, and the market is filled mostly with cheap imitations.

However, one shop in Córdoba continues the old traditions. **Meryan,** Calleja de Las Flores, 2 (☎ **47-59-02**)—one of the most colorful streets in the city—is run by Angel López-Obrero and his two skilled sons. Here, in this 250-year-old building, you can see the artisans plying their craft. Most items must be custom-ordered, but there are some ready-made pieces for sale, including cigarette boxes, jewel cases, attaché cases, book and folio covers, and ottoman covers. Meryan is open Monday to Friday from 9am to 8pm and Saturday from 9am to 2pm.

Where to Stay

Córdoba, at the peak of its summer season, has too few hotels to meet the demand—so reserve as far in advance as possible.

VERY EXPENSIVE

★ **El Conquistador Hotel,** Magistral González Francés, 15, 14003 Córdoba. ☎ **957/48-11-02.** Fax 957/47-46-77. 103 rms, 3 suites. A/C TV TEL **Bus:** 12.

Rates: 12,000 ptas. ($85.20) single; 15,000 ptas. ($106.50) double; from 30,000 ptas. ($213) suite. Breakfast 1,000 ptas. ($7.10) extra. AE, DC, MC, V. **Parking:** 500 ptas. ($3.60).

Built centuries ago as a private villa, the leading hotel of Córdoba was tastefully renovated in 1986 into one of the most attractive hotels in town, with triple rows of stone-trimmed windows and ornate iron balustrades. It sits opposite an unused rear entrance to the Mezquita. The marble-and-granite lobby opens into an interior courtyard filled with seasonal flowers, a pair of splashing fountains, and a symmetrical stone arcade. The quality, size, and comfort of the bedrooms—each with a black-and-white marble floor and a private bath—have earned the hotel four stars, the highest rating of any place in town. But for the added amenities, you also pay more for your room.

Dining/Entertainment: There is no restaurant, but a coffee shop and a bar serve snacks and drinks.

Services: Babysitting, room service, laundry/valet.

Facilities: Garage, sauna, solarium, car-rental facilities.

★ **Hotel Melía Córdoba,** Jardines de la Victoria, 14004 Córdoba. ☎ **957/29-80-66,** or toll free in the U.S. 800/336-3542. Fax 957/29-81-47. 142 rms, 5 suites. A/C MINIBAR TV TEL **Bus:** 12.

Rates: 10,000 ptas. ($71) single; 12,500 ptas. ($88.80) double; 15,000 ptas. ($106.50) suite. Breakfast 1,000 ptas. ($7.10) extra. AE, DC, MC, V. **Parking:** 1,000 ptas. ($7.10).

Originally built in 1955, in one of Córdoba's most desirable positions, the Melía was the first of the town's modern hotels, fulfilling what was regarded as a serious lack of hotel accommodations. Today, it's one of the most visible and prominent hotels in town, especially since a major renovation in 1991 improved much of its infrastructure. The Melía offers a very large lobby, enough distractions and amenities to please most tastes, and an enviable setting at the southwestern tip of the city's best-known park. Its distinguishing feature is its flower-filled terrace. The bedrooms, all with private baths, are cool, contemporary, and comfortable, often with balconies and views over nearby fountains. The cathedral, the historic district, and the modern commercial heart of Córdoba lie within easy walking distance.

Dining/Entertainment: The Palace restaurant serves international food in gracefully modern surroundings. A *menú del día* costs 2,800 ptas. ($19.90). An adjacent bar does an active business with the city's business community.

Services: Laundry/valet, concierge, room service (available from 10am to midnight).

Facilities: Car rentals, shopping, boutiques, outdoor swimming pool.

EXPENSIVE

Hotel Gran Capitán, Avenida de América, 5, 14008 Córdoba. ☎ **957/47-02-50.** Fax 957/47-46-43. 92 rms, 8 suites. A/C TV TEL

Rates: 8,500–10,200 ptas. ($60.40–$72.40) single; 13,200–18,400 ptas. ($93.70–$130.60) double. Breakfast 1,000 ptas. ($7.10) extra. AE, DC, MC, V. **Parking:** 1,500 ptas. ($10.70).

Set about two-thirds of a mile north of the Mezquita, on a broad avenue near the railway station, this efficiently modern hotel is a member of the HUSA chain. The bedrooms are comfortably furnished in a contemporary international style, with tightly soundproofed windows.

Dining/Entertainment: The Restaurant La Reja serves local and international food as part of its three-course, fixed-price lunches and dinners, which cost 2,750 ptas. ($19.50) each. There's also a bar.

Services: 24-hour room service, laundry, concierge, babysitting.

Facilities: Car rentals.

$ **Parador Nacional de la Arruzafa,** Avenida de la Arruzafa, 33, 14012 Córdoba. ☎ **957/27-59-00.** Fax 957/28-04-09. 94 rms. A/C MINIBAR TV TEL

Rates: 12,000 ptas. ($85.20) single; 15,000–18,500 ptas. ($106.50–$131.40) double; 20,250 ptas. ($143.80) triple. Breakfast 1,100 ptas. ($7.80) extra. AE, DC, MC, V. **Parking:** Free.

Lying $2^1/_2$ miles (4km) outside town in a suburb called El Brillante, this parador—named after an Arab word meaning "palm grove"—offers the conveniences and facilities of a luxurious resort hotel at reasonable rates. Occupying the site of a former caliphate palace, it's one of the finest paradores in Spain, with both a view and a swimming pool. The spacious guest rooms have been furnished with fine dark-wood pieces, and some have balconies for eating breakfast or relaxing over a drink. All have private baths.

Dining/Entertainment: Meals in the restaurant cost 3,500 ptas. ($24.90). Try some of the regional specialties, which include *salmorejo* (a chilled vegetable soup that's a variation of gazpacho), stewed oxtail, and a local cake called *pastel cordobés.*

Services: Room service, laundry/valet, babysitting.

Facilities: Swimming pool.

MODERATE

Hotel González, Manríquez, 3, 14003 Córdoba. ☎ **957/47-98-19.** Fax 957/48-61-87. 17 rms (all with bath). A/C TEL

Rates: (including breakfast): 5,350 ptas. ($38) single; 9,360 ptas. ($66.50) double; 17,140 ptas. ($121.70) triple; 14,030 ptas. ($99.60) quad. AE, DC, MC, V. **Parking:** 1,000 ptas. ($7.10).

Within walking distance of the major monuments of Córdoba, the González is a clean, decent hotel. The guest rooms are well kept, functionally furnished, and comfortable.

In the hotel's restaurant, also excellent, you can sample both regional and national specialties. Readers have praised the staff's attitude. One claimed, "They solve problems like magicians, take your car to the parking lot and back, and even teach you Spanish."

Hotel Residencia el Califa, Lope de Hoces, 14, 14004 Córdoba. ☎ **957/29-94-00.** Fax 957/29-57-16. 66 rms (all with bath). A/C TV TEL **Bus:** 12.

Rates (including breakfast): 8,050 ptas. ($57.20) single; 11,500 ptas. ($81.70) double. AE, MC, V. **Parking:** 1,100 ptas. ($7.80).

Attracting mainly a Spanish clientele, this centrally located hotel lies a short walk northwest of the Mezquita. Built in 1974, it rises three floors and is serviced by two elevators. Inside, the hotel has russet-colored marble floors, velour wall coverings, a spacious lounge, and a TV that seems to broadcast soccer matches perpetually. Upstairs, guest rooms are reasonably comfortable and furnished in a functional modern style. In lieu of a restaurant, the hotel maintains a snack bar, where an average meal costs 1,100 ptas. ($7.80). There's also a bar, plus a parking garage.

Hotel Selu, Calle Eduardo Dato, 7, 14003 Córdoba. ☎ **957/47-65-00.** Fax 957/47-83-76. 118 rms (all with bath). A/C MINIBAR TV TEL

Rates: (including breakfast): 6,350 ptas. ($45.10) single; 9,500 ptas. ($67.50) double. AE, DC, MC, V. **Parking:** 1,000 ptas. ($7.10).

In a commercial part of town near Paseo de la Victoria, the Selu was constructed in 1969, in a four-story design, and renovated in 1991. Guests meet a helpful staff near the reception desk, where public rooms have masses of plants, dozens of velvet-covered armchairs, and a huge photograph of the Moorish columns of the Mezquita, which soften the angular lines. The hotel contains functional bedrooms; there's an in-house parking garage. Only breakfast is served.

Sol Gallos, Medina Azahara, 7, 14005 Córdoba. ☎ **957/23-55-00,** or toll free **800/336-3542** in the U.S. Fax 957/23-16-36. 115 rms (all with bath). A/C TV TEL

Rates: 7,950 ptas. ($56.40) single; 9,974 ptas. ($70.80) double. Breakfast 950 ptas. ($6.70) extra. AE, DC, MC, V.

Half a block from a wide, tree-shaded boulevard on the western edge of town, this 1970s hotel stands eight floors high, crowned by an informal roof garden. The comfortable guest rooms have many extra comforts, such as balconies, and the outdoor swimming pool is a pleasure during the summer. The hotel also offers a restaurant, a drinking lounge, and a spacious public lobby.

INEXPENSIVE

Hostal el Triunfo, Corregidor Luís de la Cerda, 79, 14003 Córdoba. ☎ **957/47-55-00.** Fax 957/48-68-50. 58 rms (all with bath). A/C TV TEL **Bus:** 12.

Rates: 3,300 ptas. ($23.40) single; 5,300 ptas. ($37.60) double. Breakfast 450 ptas. ($3.20) extra. AE, DC, MC, V. **Parking:** 1,000 ptas. ($7.10).

Opposite the mosque, a block from the northern bank of the Guadalquivir River, there's a real find—a simple hotel with a formal entranceway, a pleasant white-walled lounge, and comfortable, well-furnished rooms. Built in the late 1970s, the El Triunfo was renovated in 1992. It offers polite and efficient service. The three-floor hotel has no elevator; its only other drawback is that the bells of the Mezquita church may make it difficult for one to sleep.

Hotel Riviera, Plaza de Aladreros, 5, 14001 Córdoba. ☎ **957/47-30-00.** Fax 957/47-60-18. 30 rms (all with bath). A/C TV TEL

Rates: 3,300 ptas. ($23.40) single; 5,500 ptas. ($39.10) double. AE, DC.

The genial owner of this modern hotel is likely to be behind the reception desk when you arrive. His establishment—set on a triangular plaza in a commercial section of town a short walk south of the train station—offers very clean "no-frills" accommodations. Breakfast isn't served, but many cafés are within walking distance.

BUDGET

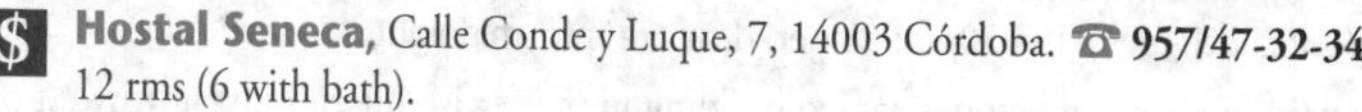

$ **Hostal Seneca,** Calle Conde y Luque, 7, 14003 Córdoba. ☎ **957/47-32-34.** 12 rms (6 with bath).

Rates (including breakfast): 2,050 ptas. ($14.60) single without bath; 3,850 ptas. ($27.30) double without bath, 4,850 ptas. ($34.40) double with bath. No credit cards. **Closed:** Dec 15–Jan 15. **Parking:** 1,000 ptas. ($7.10).

About a 15-minute walk from the train station in the old Jewish quarter, this hotel was built in 1864 on the foundations of a structure dating from the time of the Moorish occupation. You'll enter a garden courtyard where ferns and cascades of vines are set off by blue and yellow tiles. The guest rooms, modest in appointments, are clean and well maintained. Breakfast is the only meal served.

Where to Dine

By all means, shake free of your hotel for at least one meal a day in Córdoba. The restaurants are not just places at which to have a quick bite. Some combine food with flamenco—so make an evening of it.

La Almudaina, Plaza de los Santos Mártires, 1. ☎ **47-43-42.**

Cuisine: SPANISH/FRENCH. **Reservations:** Required. **Bus:** 12.
Prices: Appetizers 800–1,000 ptas. ($5.70–$7.10); main courses 1,500–2,400 ptas. ($10.70–$17); fixed-price menu 3,000 ptas. ($21.30). AE, DC, MC, V.
Open: Lunch, daily 1–5pm; dinner, Mon–Sat 8:30pm–midnight. **Closed:** Sun in Aug.

The owners of this historic restaurant near the Alcázar deserve as much credit for their renovations of a decrepit 15th-century palace as they do for the excellent cuisine produced by their bustling kitchen. Fronting the river in what used to be the Jewish Quarter, La Almudaina is one of the most attractive eateries in Andalusia, where you can dine in one of the lace-curtained salons or on a glass-roofed central courtyard. Specialties include salmon crêpes; a wide array of fish, such as hake with shrimp sauce; and meats, such as pork loin in wine sauce. For dessert, try the not-too-sweet chocolate crêpe.

★ **El Caballo Rojo,** Cardinal Herrero, 28, Plaza de la Hoguera. ☎ **47-53-75.**

Cuisine: SPANISH. **Reservations:** Required. **Bus:** 12.
Prices: Appetizers 850–1,600 ptas. ($6–$11.40); main courses 1,600–3,000 ptas. ($11.40–$21.30). AE, DC, MC, V.
Open: Lunch, daily 1–4:30pm; dinner, daily 8pm–midnight.

This restaurant is the most popular in Andalusia. Within walking distance of the Mezquita in the old town, it is down a long open-air passageway flanked with potted geraniums and vines. Stop in the restaurant's popular bar for a preprandial drink, then take the iron-railed stairs to the upper dining room, where a typical meal might include gazpacho, a main dish of chicken, then ice cream and sangría. (The ice cream, incidentally, is likely to be homemade pistachio.) Try a variation on the usual gazpacho—almond-flavored broth with apple pieces. In addition to Andalusian dishes, the chef offers both Sephardic and Mozarabic specialties, an example of the latter being the monkfish prepared with pine nuts, currants, carrots, and cream. Real aficionados come here for the *rabo de toro* (stew made with the tail of an ox or a bull).

El Churrasco, Romero, 16. ☎ **29-08-19.**

Cuisine: SPANISH. **Reservations:** Required. **Bus:** 12.
Prices: Appetizers 700–1,800 ptas. ($5–$12.80); main courses 1,400–2,800 ptas. ($9.90–$19.90); fixed-price menu 3,000 ptas. ($21.30). AE, DC, MC, V.
Open: Lunch, daily 1–4:30pm; dinner, daily 6:45pm–midnight. **Closed:** Aug.

Housed in an ancient stone-fronted building in the Jewish quarter just northwest of the Mezquita, El Churrasco serves elegant meals in five different dining rooms on two floors. You'll pass a bar and an open grill before reaching a ground-floor dining room that resembles a Moorish courtyard, with rounded arches and a splashing fountain. Upstairs, more formal rooms display the owner's riveting collection of paintings. You can enjoy such specialties as grilled filet of beef with whisky sauce, succulent roast lamb, grilled salmon, and monkfish in a pine-nut sauce—all accompanied by good service—but the signature dish here is the charcoal-grilled pork loin.

Ciro's, Paseo de la Victoria, 19. ☎ **29-04-64.**

Cuisine: ANDALUSIAN. **Reservations:** Recommended.
Prices: Appetizers 800–2,200 ptas. ($5.70–$15.60); main courses 1,700–2,500 ptas. ($12.10–$17.80); fixed-price menu 2,500 ptas. ($17.80). AE, DC, MC, V.
Open: Lunch, daily 1–5pm; dinner, daily 8pm–midnight. **Closed:** Sun in summer.

Once a simple cafeteria, Ciro's has been transformed into an accommodating and comfortably air-conditioned restaurant. The proprietors mix good service with modern and Andalusian-style cuisine. The menu includes such items as a salmon-and-anchovy pudding, stuffed sweet peppers, hake in shrimp sauce, veal in red wine, and an array of dessert sorbets. Ciro's lies directly south of the rail station, about a quarter of a mile northwest of the Mezquita.

Restaurante Da Vinci, Plaza de Los Chirinos, 6. ☎ **47-75-17.**

Cuisine: ITALIAN/INTERNATIONAL. **Reservations:** Required.
Prices: Appetizers 500–750 ptas. ($3.60–$5.30); main courses 995–1,575 ptas. ($7.10–$11.20); *menú del día* 1,795 ptas. ($12.70). MC, V.
Open: Lunch, daily 1:30–4:30pm; dinner, daily 9pm–12:30am.

Situated in a quiet neighborhood a block off the city's main boulevard, Calle Cruz Conde, this ranks as one of the leading restaurants in town. Before heading into the dining room; stop for a drink in the comfortable bar near the entrance, where many guests order from a selection of tempting tapas. Both the cuisine and the decor are a blend of Andalusian, international, and Italian influences, arranged in a curious but pleasing mishmash of traditions. Menu items include a choice of roast meats (veal, pork, beefsteak, and lamb), a choice of pastas and salads, and many kinds of fish and seafood, especially hake, monkfish, squid, and salmon.

Evening Entertainment

Bar Mezquita, Cardenal Herrero, 24. ☎ **47-30-94.**

One of the oldest and coziest bars in Córdoba, Bar Mezquita, on the northern boundary of the mosque, has served beer, wine, and a tasty collection of tapas to a loyal clientele since the early 1800s. The decor, with its Andalusian tiles and battered wooden tables, evokes another era. The bar is open daily from 9am to 3pm and again from 4:30pm to 11pm. Beer ranges from 125–150 pesetas. (90¢–$1.10), tapas from 150–250 pesetas ($1.10–$1.80).

La Canoa, Pasaje Ronda Los Tejares, 18-20. ☎ **47-17-61.**

The rustic interior decorated with wine-barrel tables and Carthusian cellar decor appeals to La Canoa's many customers. A glass of wine or beer here will probably be more of a rapid pick-me-up than something to linger over for hours. You can order a ration of Serrano ham or a hefty platter of cheese if you're hungry. La Canoa, located between the Plaza de Colón and the Paseo de la Victoria, is open Monday to Saturday from noon to 4pm and 8pm to midnight. It's closed for two weeks in August. Tapas range in price from 200 to 1,400 ptas. ($1.40 to $9.90); a beer costs 125 ptas. (90¢).

Casa Rubio, Puerta de Almodóvar, 5. ☎ **29-00-64.**

You must push back a thick curtain to enter this dimly lit enclave of pre-Franco Spain. Once inside, you'll find a gruff but accommodating welcome at the rectangular bar or in one of a pair of rooms partially covered with Andalusian tiles. My preferred place is within a plant-festooned inner courtyard, where iron tables and a handful of chairs wobble only slightly on the uneven flooring. Casa Rubio is open Thursday through Tuesday from 6:30am to midnight. Wine costs from 75 pesetas (50¢) per glass; an order of tapas will range from 100–300 pesetas (70¢–$2.10).

3 Seville

341 miles (549km) SW of Madrid, 135 miles (217km) NW of Málaga

GETTING THERE • By Plane From Seville's San Pablo Airport, Calle Almirante Lobo (☎ **451-61-11**), Iberia flies several times a day to and from Madrid (and elsewhere via Madrid). It also flies several times a week to and from Alicante, Grand Canary Island, Lisbon, Barcelona, Palma de Mallorca, Tenerife, Santiago de Compostela, and (once a week) Zaragoza. The airport lies about 6 miles (9.6km) from the center of the city, along the highway leading to Carmona.

• By Train Train service into Seville is now centralized into the Estación Santa Justa, Avenida Kansas City, s/n (☎ **441-41-11** for information, **901-33-111** for reservations). Bus no. 70 at this train station takes you to the bus station at Prado de San Sebastián, and bus EA runs to and from the airport. The high-speed Tran de Alta Velocidad (TAV) has reduced travel time from Madrid to Seville to 3¼ hours. Ten trains a day connect Seville and Córdoba; the AVE train takes 50 minutes and a *talgo* takes 1½ hours. Three trains a day run to Málaga, taking 3 to 4 hours, depending on the train; there are also three trains per day to Granada (4 to 5 hours).

• By Bus Although Seville confusingly has several satellite bus stations servicing small towns and nearby villages of Andalusia, most buses arrive and depart from the city's largest bus terminal, on the southeast edge of the old city, at Prado de San Sebastián, Calle José María Osborne, 11 (☎ **441-71-11**). From there, buses from several different companies make frequent runs to and from Córdoba (2½ hours), Málaga (3½ hours), Granada (4 hours), and—three buses daily—Madrid (8 hours).

• By Car Several major highways converge on Seville, connecting it with all the rest of Spain and Portugal. Driving time from Madrid is about eight hours. During periods of heavy holiday traffic, the N-V from Madrid through Extremadura (which, at

Mérida, connects with the southbound E-803) is usually less congested than the N-IV through eastern Andalusia.

Sometimes a city becomes famous for its beauty and romance, and Seville, the capital of Andalusia, is such a place. It is indeed the most charming of Spanish cities.

Don Juan and Carmen—aided by Mozart and Bizet—have given Seville a romantic reputation. Perhaps because of the acclaim of *Don Giovanni* and *Carmen,* not to mention *The Barber of Seville,* debunkers have risen to challenge this reputation. But if a visitor can see only two Spanish cities in a lifetime, they should be Seville and Toledo.

All the images associated with Andalusia—orange trees, mantillas, lovesick toreros, flower-filled patios, and castanet-rattling gypsies—come to life in Seville. But it's not just a tourist city; it's a substantial river port, and it contains some of the most important artistic works and architectural monuments in Spain.

Unlike most Spanish cities, Seville has fared rather well under most of its conquerors—the Romans, Arabs, and Christians. Pedro the Cruel and Ferdinand and Isabella held court here. When Spain entered its 16th-century golden age, Seville funneled gold from the New World into the rest of the country. Columbus docked here after his journey to America.

Be warned, however, that driving here is a nightmare: Seville was planned for the horse and buggy rather than for the car, and nearly all the streets run one way toward the Guadalquivir River. Locating a hard-to-find restaurant or a hidden little square might require patience and even a little luck.

FAST FACTS

American Express The American Express office in Seville is operated by Viajes Alhambra, Teniente Coronel Seguí, 6 (☎ **421-29-23**), north of Plaza Nueva.

Area Code The area code for Seville is 95.

Bus Information The Central Bus Station, Prado de San Sebastián, Calle José María Osborne, 11 (☎ **441-71-11**), is the place to go for bus information.

Business Hours Most banks in Seville are open Monday to Friday from 9am to 2pm and on Saturday from 9am to noon. (Always conceal your money before walking out of a bank in Seville.) Shops are generally open Monday to Saturday from 9:30am to 1:30pm and 4:30 to 8pm. Most department stores are open Monday to Saturday from 10am to 8pm.

Consulates The U.S. Consulate is at Paseo de las Delicias, 7 (☎ **423-18-83**). The Canadian Consulate is on the second floor at Avenida de la Constitución, 30 (☎ **422-47-52**). The United Kingdom Consulate is at Plaza Nueva, 8 (☎ **422-88-75**).**Hospital** For medical emergencies, go to the Hospital Universitario y Provincial, Avenida Doctor Fedriani, s/n (☎ **437-84-00**).

Information The tourist office, Oficina de Información del Turismo, Avenida de la Constitución, 21B (☎ **95/422-14-04**), is open Monday to Saturday from 9:30am to 7:30pm.

Laundry Lavandería Robledo, Calle Sánchez Bedoya, 18 (☎ **421-81-32**), is open Monday to Friday from 10am to 2pm and 5 to 8pm and Saturday from 10am to 2pm.

Police The police station is located on Avenida Paseo de las Delicias (☎ **461-67-76**).

Post Office The post office is at Avenida de la Constitución, 32 (☎ **421-95-85**). Hours are Monday to Friday from 9am to 8pm, Saturday from 9am to 1pm.

Seville

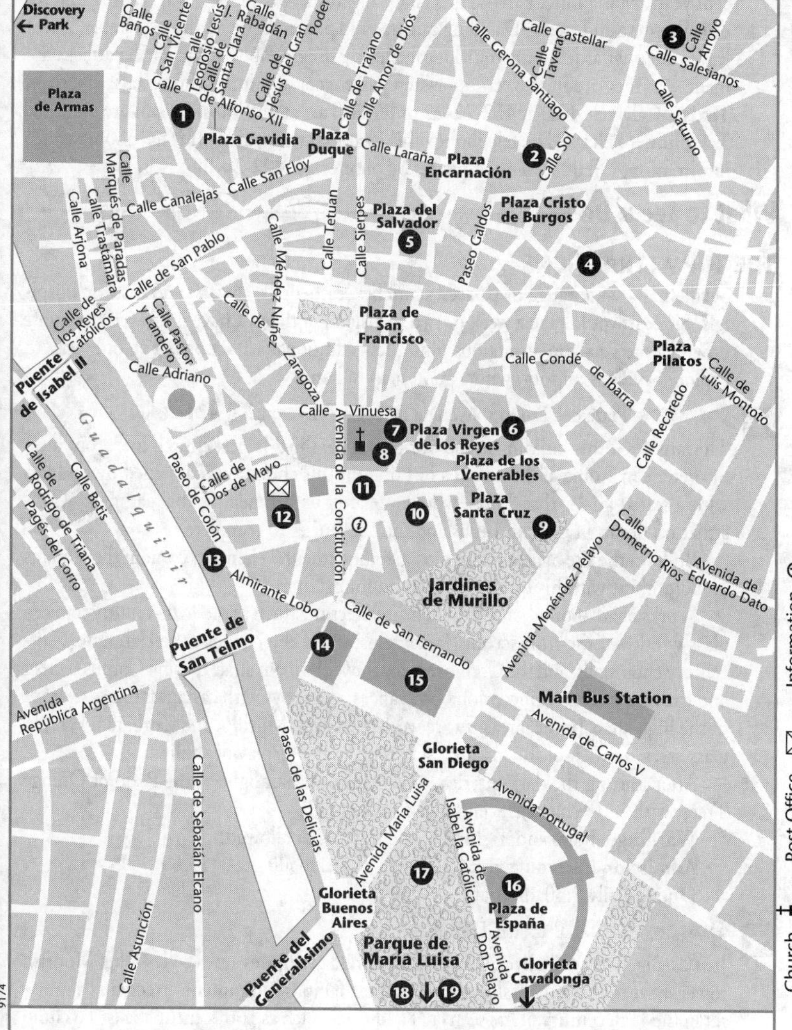

9174

- Alcázar 10
- Barrio de Santa Cruz 6
- Casa de Pilatos 4
- Catedral 8
- Convento Santa Paula 3
- Hospital de la Santa Caridad 12
- Jardines de Murillo 9
- La Giralda Tower 7
- Museo Arqueológico 19
- Museo de Arte Contemporaneo 11
- Museo de Artes y Costumbres Populares 18
- Museo de Bellas Artes 1
- Palacio de San Telmo 14
- Parque de María Luisa 17
- Plaza de España 16
- Réal Fábrica de Tabacos 15
- San Pedro 2
- San Salvador 5
- Torre de Oro 13

Safety With massive unemployment, the city has been hit by a crime wave in recent years. María Luisa Park is especially dangerous, as is the highway leading to Jerez de la Frontera and Cádiz. Dangling cameras and purses are especially vulnerable. Don't leave cars unguarded with your luggage inside. Regrettably, some daring attacks are made—as they are in U.S. cities—when passengers stop for traffic signals.
Taxis Call Tele Taxi at **462-22-22** or Radio Taxi at **458-00-00.** Cabs are metered.
Telephone/Telex The telephone office is at Plaza Gavidia, 7 (for telephone service information, call **003**). To send wires by phone, call **422-20-00.**

What to See & Do

THE TOP ATTRACTIONS

Seville has a wide range of palaces, churches, cathedrals, towers, and historic hospitals. Since it would take a week or two to visit all of them, I have narrowed the sights down to the very top attractions plus a few additional attractions. The only way to explore Seville is on foot, with a good map in hand.

★ **Catedral,** Plaza del Triunfo, Avenida de la Constitución. ☎ **421-28-00.**

The largest Gothic building in the world, and the third-largest church in Europe after St. Peter's in Rome and St. Paul's in London, this church was designed by builders with a stated goal—that "those who come after us will take us for madmen." Construction began in the late 1400s and took centuries to complete.

Built on the site of an ancient mosque, the cathedral claims to contain the remains of Columbus, with his tomb mounted on four statues.

Works of art abound, many of them architectural, such as the 15th-century stained-glass windows, the iron screens (rejas) closing off the chapels, the elaborate 15th-century choir stalls, and the Gothic reredos above the main altar. During Corpus Christi and the Immaculate Conception observances, altar boys with castanets dance in front of the high altar. In the Treasury are works by Goya, Murillo, and Zurbarán; here, in glass cases, a touch of the macabre shows up in the display of skulls.

After touring the dark interior, emerge into the sunlight of the Patio of Orange Trees, with its fresh citrus scents and chirping birds.

Warning: Shorts and T-shirts are definitely not allowed.

Admission (including visit to Giralda Tower): 500 ptas. ($3.60).

Open: Daily 9:30am–8pm.

★ **Giralda Tower,** Plaza del Triunfo.

Just as Big Ben symbolizes London, La Giralda conjures up Seville—this Moorish tower, next to the cathedral, is the city's most famous monument. Erected as a minaret in the 12th century, it has seen later additions, such as 16th-century bells. To climb it is to take the walk of a lifetime. There are no steps—you ascend an endless ramp. If you make it to the top, you'll have a dazzling view of Seville. Entrance is through the cathedral.

Admission: Free with admission to cathedral above.

Open: Same hours as the cathedral; see above.

★ **Alcázar,** Plaza del Triunfo, s/n. ☎ **422-71-63.**

This magnificent 14th-century Mudéjar palace, north of the cathedral, was built by Pedro the Cruel. It is the oldest royal residence in Europe still in use: On visits to Seville, King Juan Carlos stays here. From the Dolls' Court to the Maidens' Court through the domed Ambassadors' Room, it contains some of the finest work of Sevillian artisans. In many ways, it evokes the Alhambra at Granada. Ferdinand and Isabella, who at one time lived in the Alcázar and influenced its architectural evolution, welcomed Columbus here on his return from America. On the top floor, the Oratory of the Catholic Monarchs has a fine altar in polychrome tiles made by Pisano in 1504.

The well-kept gardens, filled with beautiful flowers, shrubbery, and fruit trees, are alone worth the visit.

Admission: 600 ptas. ($4.30).

Open: Tues–Sat 10:30am–5pm; Sun 10am–1pm.

El Parque de Los Descubrimientos (Discovery Park), Isla de la Cartuja. ☎ **446-16-16.**

On the 540-acre island of La Cartuja in the Guadalquivir River, site of Expo '92, the government opened a theme park in 1993. Eight new bridges now join the island to Seville. The theme park itself takes up 168 acres of the site and incorporates some of the more acclaimed attractions at Expo. Among them are the Pavilion of Navigation, tracing the history of maritime exploration from its beginnings to the present; the Pavilion of Nature, containing flora and fauna from all over the world; and eight other pavilions, representing the autonomous regions of Spain.

Puerto de Indias is the re-creation of a 15th-century port, with small shops and evocative taverns, along with silversmiths, cobblers, welders, and other tradespersons. Replicas of Christopher Columbus's ships in 1492, the *Pinta*, *Niña*, and *Santa María*, are docked here. The Children's Park has a host of entertainment, including puppet shows and water slides.

The audiovisual offerings are said to equal or top those of any theme park in the world. The computer-controlled Digital Planetarium, for example, housed in the Pavilion of the Universe, is the only one of its kind in the world—images are projected onto a 60-foot dome, taking viewers on a ride through the universe.

Buses, cable cars, a monorail, catamarans, trolley cars, and rowboats are some of the transportation available to haul visitors around. Other facilities and attractions include concerts, plays, dance clubs, two parades and a circus daily, a lazer-sound show with fireworks, 12 foodstalls, 15 family restaurants, 7 tapas bars, and two deluxe restaurants.

Admission: "Strolling ticket" 500 ptas. ($3.60), giving access to the parks and its gardens; "super ticket" 4,000 ptas. ($28.40) adults, 3,000 ptas. ($21.30) children, giving access to the pavilions.

Open: June 7–Oct 12, Tues–Thurs, park 8pm–2am, pavilions 8pm–midnight; Fri–Sat, park 11:30am–4am, pavilions 8pm–midnight; Sun, park 11:30am–1am, pavilions noon–8pm. Apr 25–June 6 and Oct 13–Dec 21, Thurs, park 8pm–2am, pavilions 8pm–midnight; Fri–Sat, park 11:30am–2am, pavilions noon–8pm; Sun, park 11:30am–midnight, pavilions noon–8pm. Dec 22–Apr 24, Fri–Sat, park 11:30am–midnight, pavilions noon–8pm; Sun, park 11:30am–midnight, pavilions 11:30am–midnight. **Bus:** C2 from the center of Seville.

Hospital de la Santa Caridad, Calle Temprado, 3. ☎ **422-32-22.**

This 17th-century hospital is intricately linked to the legend of Miguel Manara, portrayed by Dumas and Mérimée as a scandalous Don Juan. It was once thought that he built this institution to atone for his sins, but this has been disproved. The death of Manara's beautiful young wife in 1661 caused such grief that he retired from society and entered the "Charity Brotherhood," burying corpses of the sick and diseased as well as condemned and executed criminals. Today the members of this brotherhood continue to look after the poor, the old, and invalids who have no one else to help them.

Nuns will show you through the festive orange-and-sienna courtyard. The baroque chapel contains works by the 17th-century Spanish painters Murillo and Valdés-Leál. As you're leaving the chapel, look over the exit door for the macabre picture of an archbishop being devoured by maggots.

Admission: 200 ptas. ($1.40).

Open: Mon–Sat 10am–1pm and 3:30–6pm; Sun 10:30am–12:30pm.

Torre del Oro, Paseo de Cristóbal Colón. ☎ **422-24-19.**

The 12-sided Tower of Gold, dating from the 13th century, overlooks the Guadalquivir River. Originally it was covered with gold tiles, but someone long ago made off with them. Recently restored, the tower has been turned into a maritime museum, Museo Náutico.

Admission: 100 ptas. (70¢).

Open: Tues–Fri 10am–2pm; Sat–Sun 10am–1pm.

Casa de Pilatos, Plaza Pilatos, 1. ☎ **422-50-55.**

This 16th-century Andalusian palace of the dukes of Medinaceli recaptures the splendor of the past, combining Gothic, Mudéjar, and Plateresque styles in its courtyards, fountains, and salons. According to tradition, this is a reproduction of Pilate's House in Jerusalem. Don't miss the two old carriages or the rooms filled with Greek and Roman statues. The collection of paintings includes works by Carreño, Pantoja de la Cruz, Sebastiano del Piombo, Lucas Jordán, Batalloli, Pacheco, and Goya. The palace lies about a seven-minute walk northeast of the cathedral on the northern edge of Barrio de Santa Cruz, in a warren of labyrinthine streets whose traffic is funneled through the nearby Calle de Aguiles.

Admission: 1,000 ptas. ($7.10).

Open: Daily 9am–7pm.

Archivo General de Indias, Avenida de la Constitución, s/n. ☎ **421-12-34.**

The great architect of Philip II's El Escorial outside Madrid, Juan de Herrera, was also the architect of the old Lonja (Stock Exchange), located next to the cathedral. Construction on the building lasted from 1584 to 1598. In the 17th century it was headquarters for the Academy of Seville, which was founded in part by the great Spanish artist Murillo.

In 1758, during the reign of Charles III, the building was turned over for use as a general records office for the Indies. That led to today's Archivo General de Indias, said to contain some four million antique documents, even letters exchanged between patron Queen Isabella and explorer Columbus (he detailing his discoveries and impressions). These very rare documents are locked in air-conditioned storage to keep

IMPRESSIONS

Seville doesn't have an ambiance. It is ambiance.
—James A. Michener

Seville is a pleasant city, famous for oranges and women.
—Lord Byron

them from disintegrating. Special permission has to be acquired before examining some of them. Many treasure hunters come here hoping to learn details of where Spanish galleons laden with gold went down off the coast of the Americas. On display in glass cases are fascinating documents in which the dreams of those early explorers come alive again.

Admission: Free.

Open: Mon–Fri 10am–1pm.

Museo Provincial de Bellas Artes de Sevilla, Plaza del Museo, 9. ☎ **422-18-29.**

This lovely old convent off Calle de Alfonso XII houses one of the most important Spanish art collections. A whole gallery is devoted to two paintings by El Greco, and works by Zurbarán are exhibited; however, the devoutly religious paintings of the Seville-born Murillo are the highlights. An entire wing is given over to macabre paintings by the 17th-century artist Valdés-Leál. His painting of John the Baptist's head on a platter includes the knife—in case you didn't get the point. The top floor, which displays modern paintings, is less interesting.

Admission: 250 ptas. ($1.80).

Open: Tues–Sun 9am–3pm. **Bus:** 21, 24, 30, or 31.

MORE ATTRACTIONS

☆ BARRIO DE SANTA CRUZ What was once a ghetto for Spanish Jews, who were forced out of Spain in the 15th century in the wake of the Inquisition, is today the most colorful district of Seville. Near the old walls of the Alcázar, winding medieval streets with names like Vida (Life) and Muerte (Death) open onto pocket-sized plazas. Flower-filled balconies with draping bougainvillea and potted geraniums jut out over this labyrinth, shading you from the hot Andalusian summer sun. Feel free to look through numerous wrought-iron gares into patios filled with fountains and plants. In the evening it's common to see Sevillians sitting outside drinking icy sangría under the glow of lanterns.

Although the district as a whole is recommended for sightseeing, seek out in particular the **Casa de Murillo (Murillo's House),** Santa Teresa, 8 (☎ **421-75-35**). Bartolomé Esteban Murillo, the great Spanish painter known for his religious works, was born in Seville in 1617. He spent his last years in this house in Santa Cruz, dying in 1682. Five minor paintings of the artist are on display. The furnishings, though not owned by the artist, are period pieces. Admission is 250 pesetas ($1.80), and the house is open Tuesday through Saturday 10am to 2pm and 6 to 8pm.

In Their Footsteps

Ferdinand II of Aragón (1452–1516). A cruel and unfair ruler, Ferdinand married Isabella of Castile in 1469, and the two became known in history as *Los Reyes Católicos.* They ran Spain as an absolute monarchy and disliked anything that wasn't Catholic. They expelled the Moors from Granada, conquered Navarre, and financed Columbus's expeditions, although Ferdinand broke many promises to the explorer. With Isabella, he produced a daughter who was insane. Upon the death of Isabella, he claimed the throne of Castile. In 1505 he married Germaine of Foix.

Favorite Haunt The Alcázar at Seville.

Resting Place Capilla Real in Granada.

To enter the Barrio Santa Cruz, turn right after leaving the Patio de Banderas exit of the Alcázar. Turn right again at Plaza de la Alianza, going down Calle Rodrigo Caro to Plaza de Doña Elvira. Use caution when strolling through the area, particularly at night; many robberies have occurred here.

PARQUE MARÍA LUISA This park, dedicated to María Luisa, sister of Isabella II, was once the grounds of the Palacio de San Telmo, Avenida de Roma. Its baroque facade visible behind the deluxe Alfonso XIII Hotel, the palace today houses a seminary. The former private royal park is now open to the public.

Running south along the Guadalquivir River, the park attracts those who want to take boat rides, walk along paths bordered by flowers, jog, or go bicycling. The most romantic way to traverse it is by rented horse and carriage, but this can be expensive, depending on your negotiation with the driver.

In 1929 Seville was to host the Spanish American Exhibition, and many pavilions from other countries were erected here. The worldwide depression put a damper on the exhibition, but the pavilions still stand.

Exercise caution while walking through this park. Many muggings have been reported.

PLAZA DE ESPAÑA The major building left from the exhibition at the Parque María Luisa (see above) is a half-moon-shaped structure in Renaissance style, set on this landmark square of Seville. The architect, Anibal González, not only designed but supervised the building of this immense structure; today it is a government office building. At a canal here you can rent rowboats for excursions into the park; or you can walk across bridges spanning the canal. Set into a curved wall are alcoves, each focusing on characteristics of one of Spain's 50 provinces, as depicted in tile murals.

PLAZA DE AMÉRICA Another landmark Sevillian square, Plaza de América represents city planning at its best: Here you can walk through gardens planted with roses, enjoying the lily ponds and the fountains and feeling the protective shade of the palms. And here you'll find a trio of elaborate buildings left over from the world exhibition that never materialized—in the center, the home of the government headquarters of Andalusia; on either side, two minor museums worth visiting only if you have time to spare.

The **Museo Arqueológico Provincial,** Plaza de América, s/n (☎ **423-24-01**), contains many artifacts from prehistoric times and the days of the Romans, Visigoths, and Moors. It's open Tuesday to Sunday from 10am to 2pm. Admission is 250 pesetas ($1.80). **Bus:** 30, 31, or 34.

Also opening onto the square is the **Museo de Artes y Costumbres Populares,** Plaza de América, s/n (☎ **423-25-76**), displaying folkloric costumes, musical instruments, *cordobán* saddles, weaponry, and farm implements that document the life of the Andalusian people. It's open Tuesday to Saturday from 9:30am to 2:30pm. Admission is 250 pesetas ($1.80). It's closed in August.

REAL FÁBRICA DE TABACOS When Carmen waltzed out of the tobacco factory in the first act of Bizet's opera, she made its 18th-century original in Seville world famous. The old tobacco factory was constructed between 1750 and 1766, and a hundred years later, it employed 10,000 *cigarreras,* of which Carmen was one in the opera. (She rolled her cigars on her thighs.) In the 19th century, these tobacco women made up the largest female work force in Spain. Many visitors arriving today, in fact, ask guides to take them to "Carmen's tobacco factory." The building, the second largest in Spain and located on Calle San Fernando near the city's landmark luxury hotel, the Alfonso XIII, is still there. But the Real Fábrica de Tabacos is now part of the Universidad de Sevilla. Look for signs of its former role, however, as reflected in the bas-reliefs of tobacco plants and Indians over the main entrances. You'll also see bas-reliefs of Columbus and Cortés. Then you can wander through the grounds for a look at student life, Sevillian style. The factory is directly south of the Alcázar gardens.

Where to Stay

During Holy Week and the Seville Fair, hotels often double, even triple, their rates. Price increases are often not announced until the last minute. If you're going to be in Seville at these times, arrive with an iron-clad reservation and an agreement about the price before checking in.

VERY EXPENSIVE

★ **Hotel Alfonso XIII,** San Fernando, 2, 41004 Sevilla. ☎ **95/422-28-50,** or toll free within the U.S. and Canada **800/221-2340.** Fax 95/421-60-33. 130 rms, 18 suites. A/C MINIBAR TV TEL

Rates: 27,000 ptas. ($191.70) single; 38,000 ptas. ($269.80) double; from 75,000 ptas. ($532.50) suite. Breakfast 2,200 ptas. ($15.60) extra. AE, DC, MC, V. **Parking:** 2,000 ptas. ($14.20).

Set at the southwestern corner of the gardens that front Seville's famous Alcázar, in the historic heart of town, this is one of the three or four most legendary hotels in Spain. Built as an aristocratic shelter for patrons of the Iberoamerican Exposition of 1929 and named after the then-king of Spain, it reigns as a superornate and superexpensive bastion of glamour. Built in the Mudéjar/Andalusian revival style, it contains hallways that glitter with handpainted tiles, acres of marble and mahogany, antique furniture embellished with intricately embossed leather, and a floor plan and spaciousness that are nothing short of majestic. The hotel is owned by the Italian-based hotel chain CIGA.

Dining/Entertainment: The San Fernando restaurant offers Italian and continental cuisine, with meals costing from 5,000–6,000 pesetas ($35.50–$42.60). A lobby bar features midday coffee amid potted palms and memorials to another age, its blue, white, and yellow tiles reflecting the colors of Seville.

Services: 24-hour room service, laundry/valet, concierge, car rentals with or without drivers, babysitting.

Facilities: Spectacular garden, designed in the Andalusian style; outdoor pool; tennis courts; shops; arcade-enclosed courtyard with potted flowers and splashing fountain.

EXPENSIVE

Hotel Inglaterra, Plaza Nueva, 7, 41001 Sevilla. ☎ **95/422-49-70.** Fax 95/456-13-36. 116 rms. A/C TV TEL

Rates: Jan–Feb, June–Aug, Nov–Dec, 10,880 ptas. ($77.20) single; 13,600–25,000 ptas. ($96.60–$177. 50) double; Mar and May, Sept–Oct, 12,800 ptas. ($90.90) single; 16,000–30,000 ptas. ($113.60–$213) double; Apr, 16,000 ptas. ($113.60) single; 22,000–35,000 ptas. ($156.20–$248.50) double. Breakfast 750 ptas. ($5.30) extra. AE, DC, MC, V. **Parking:** 1,000 ptas. ($7.10).

Established in 1857 and since modernized into a comfortably glossy contemporary design, this eminently respectable hotel lies a five-minute walk southwest of the cathedral, occupying one entire side of a palm-fringed plaza. Much of its interior is sheathed with acres of white or gray marble, and the furnishings include ample use of Spanish leather and floral-patterned fabrics. Despite their modernity, the bedrooms nonetheless evoke old-fashioned touches of Iberian gentility.

Dining/Entertainment: One floor above street level, overlooking the mosaic pavements of Plaza Nueva, the hotel's sunny restaurant serves well-prepared fixed-price meals from a frequently changing international menu for 3,000 pesetas ($21.30) each. There's also an in-house cocktail lounge that seems favored by local businesspeople.

Services: 24-hour room service, laundry/valet service, concierge, babysitting.

Facilities: Car-rental facilities.

Hotel Melía Sevilla, Doctor Pedro de Castro, 1, 41004 Sevilla. ☎ **95/442-26-11,** or toll-free in the U.S. 800/336-3542. Fax 95/442-16-08. 361 rms, 5 suites. A/C MINIBAR TV TEL

Rates: 13,350 ptas. ($94.80) single; 16,650 ptas. ($118.20) double; from 25,000 ptas. ($177.50) suite. Breakfast 1,500 ptas. ($10.70) extra. AE, DC, MC, V. **Parking:** 1,350 ptas. ($9.60).

Located a short walk east of the Plaza de España, near the Parque María Luisa, this is probably the most elegant, tasteful, and international of the modern skyscraper hotels of Seville. A member of the Melía chain, it incorporates acres of white marble as well as several dozen shopping boutiques and private apartments into its L-shaped floor plan. The guest-room decor is contemporary and comfortable, and each unit offers a private bath. The Melía was a favorite of the planners of the massive Expo Fair, which transformed the face of both Seville and Andalusia.

Dining/Entertainment: The Giralda Restaurant serves three-course fixed-price lunches and dinners for 3,500 pesetas ($24.90). There's also a large and stylish piano bar, Corona, plus an informal coffee shop, Las Salinas.

Services: 24-hour room service, laundry, babysitting on request.

Facilities: Business center, car rentals, outdoor swimming pool with a section reserved for children, sauna, arcade of shops and boutiques, several flowering outdoor terraces.

Hotel Tryp Colón, Canalejas 1, 41001 Sevilla. ☎ **95/422-29-00.** Fax 95/422-09-38. 204 rms, 14 suites. A/C MINIBAR TV TEL

Rates: 14,400 ptas. ($102.20) single; 18,000 ptas. ($127.80) double; 42,200 ptas. ($299.60) suite. Breakfast 1,500 ptas. ($10.70) extra. AE, DC, MC, V. **Parking:** 2,200 ptas. ($15.60).

Set about a quarter-mile northwest of the Giralda and about two blocks southeast of the Fine Arts Museum (Museo Provincial de Bellas Artes), this hotel is probably Seville's closest rival—in prestige and architectural allure—to the legendary Alfonso XIII. Originally built around the turn of the century and overhauled in 1988, it retains such features as a massive stained-glass dome stretching over the lobby, staircases worthy of a Spanish baron, formal service, and all the niceties of a good expensive hotel. The bedrooms, all with private baths, are conservative and plushly traditional, some of the finest in town.

Dining/Entertainment: El Burladero restaurant serves three-course fixed-price lunches and dinners costing from 4,100–4,500 pesetas ($29.10–$32). See separate recommendation. There's also a bar that seems to be favored by visiting bullfighters, journalists, and politicians.

Services: 24-hour room service, concierge, babysitting, laundry/valet.
Facilities: Sauna, car-rental facilities, shopping boutiques.

★ **Radisson Principe de Asturias Plaza Hotel Sevilla,** Isla de la Cartuja, 41018 Sevilla. ☎ **95/446-22-22,** or toll-free in the U.S. **800/333-3333.** Fax 95/446-04-28. 285 rms, 18 suites. A/C MINIBAR TV TEL

Rates (including breakfast): Mon–Thurs 15,000 ptas. ($106.50) single; 19,000 ptas. ($134.90) double; 60,000 ptas. ($426) suite; Fri–Sun 8,500 ptas. ($60.40) single; 12,000 ptas. ($85.20) double; 30,000 ptas. ($213) suite. AE, DC, MC, V. **Parking:** Free.

Named after the son and designated heir of King Juan Carlos I, Don Felipe de Borbón, Principe de Asturias (his title is something akin to Britain's Prince of Wales), this hotel was expressly built to house the surge of visitors at the Seville Expo of 1992. The only hotel located at the former site of Expo itself, facing the Guadalquivir River, it lies a five-minute taxi ride from the center of Seville. It was designed in three hypermodern ring-shaped modules, each four stories tall. Each is interconnected by passageways leading to the public rooms. Designated as a five-star luxury hotel, this Radisson was reserved during Expo for visiting dignitaries and heads of state. Its designers intended its perpetual use, at the end of the party, as one of the city's most visible hotels—sort of a modern-day counterpart to the Alfonso XIII (which was designed for use by dignitaries during Seville's International Exposition of 1929).

Dining/Entertainment: The Restaurant Colón serves gourmet versions of regional cuisine. The lobby bar and the Cartura Bar offer soothing libations, sometimes to live piano music.

Services: 24-hour room service, concierge, laundry/valet, limousine pickups, babysitting.

Facilities: Business center, conference facilities, outdoor swimming pool, in-house florist, shops, currency exchange, car rentals, trilingual TV channels, health club with sauna, massage, gymnasium, squash courts.

MODERATE

Bécquer, Calle Reyes Católicos, 4, 41001 Sevilla. ☎ **95/422-89-00.** Fax 95/421-44-00. 120 rms. A/C TV TEL **Bus:** 21, 24, 30, or 31.

Rates: 7,500 ptas. ($53.30) single; 10,000 ptas. ($71) double. Breakfast 750 ptas. ($5.30) extra. AE, DC, MC, V. **Parking:** 1,000 ptas. ($7.10).

A short walk from the action of the Seville bullring (Maestranza) and only two blocks from the river, the Bécquer lies on a street of cafés where you can order tapas (appetizers) and drink Andalusian wine. The Museo de Bellas Artes (previously recommended) also lies nearby. Built in the 1970s, the hotel was enlarged and much renovated in the late 1980s. Guests register in a wood-paneled lobby before being shown to one of the bedrooms, which are functionally furnished, well kept, and reasonably comfortable. All have private baths. Only breakfast is served, but you'll find a bar and lounge, as well as a garage.

Hotel Alcázar, Menéndez y Pelayo, 10, 41004 Sevilla. ☎ **95/441-20-11.** Fax 495/442-16-59. 99 rms. A/C TV TEL.

Rates: 6,000 ptas. ($42.60) single; 10,000 ptas. ($71) double. Breakfast 250 ptas. ($1.80) extra. AE, DC, MC, V. **Parking:** 1,000 ptas. ($7.10).

On the wide and busy Boulevard Menéndez y Pelayo, across from the Jardines de Alcázon, this pleasantly contemporary hotel is sheltered behind a facade of brown brick.

Built in 1964, the hotel was last renovated in 1991. Slabs of striated gray marble cool the reception area in the lobby, next to which you'll find a Spanish restaurant and bar. Above, three latticed structures resemble a trio of *miradores.* The medium-size guest rooms have functional modern furniture and private baths.

Hotel Doña María, Don Remondo, 19, 41004 Sevilla. ☎ **95/422-49-90.** Fax 95/421-95-46. 60 rms. A/C TV TEL.

Rates: Jan–Feb and July–Aug, 7,000 ptas. ($49.70) single; 12,000–15,000 ptas. ($85.20–$106.50) double; Mar 27–Apr 4 and Apr 17–Apr 25, 16,000 ptas. ($113.60) single; 24,000–29,000 ptas. ($170.40–$205.90) double; rest of the year, 10,000 ptas. ($71) single; 16,000–21,000 ptas. ($113.60–$149.10) double. Breakfast 1,000 ptas. ($7.10) extra. AE, DC, MC, V. **Parking:** 1,200 ptas. ($8.50).

Its location a few steps from the cathedral creates a dramatic view from the Doña María's rooftop terrace. Staying at this four-star hotel represents a worthwhile investment, partly because of the tasteful Iberian antiques in the stone lobby and upper hallways. The ornate neoclassical entryway is offset with a pure-white facade and iron balconies, which hint at the building's origin in the 1840s as a private villa. Amid the flowering plants on the upper floor, you'll find a swimming pool ringed with garden-style lattices and antique wrought-iron railings. Each of the "one-of-a-kind" bedrooms offers a private bath and is well furnished and comfortable, although some are rather small. A few have four-poster beds, others a handful of antique reproductions. Light sleepers might find the noise of the church bells jarring. Breakfast is the only meal served.

Residencia y Restaurant Fernando Iii, San José, 21, 41001 Sevilla. ☎ **95/421-77-08.** Fax 95/422-02-46. 157 rms. A/C TV TEL

Rates: 8,784 ptas. ($62.40) single; 10,980 ptas. ($78) double. Breakfast 890 ptas. ($6.30) extra. AE, DC, MC, V. **Parking:** 1,000 ptas. ($7.10).

You'll find the Fernando III on a narrow, quiet street at the edge of the Barrio Santa Cruz, near the northern periphery of the Murillo Gardens. Its vast lobby and baronial dining hall are reminiscent of a luxurious South American hacienda; meals are served for 2,300 pesetas ($16.30). The building is modern, constructed around 1970 with marble and hardwood detailing; it is coolly and sparsely furnished with leather chairs, plants, and wrought-iron accents. Many of the accommodations—medium in size, comfortably furnished, and well maintained—offer balconies filled with cascading plants; all have private baths. There are a TV salon and a paneled bar.

INEXPENSIVE

Hostal Residencia Ducal, Plaza de la Encarnación, 19, 41003 Sevilla. ☎ **95/421-51-07.** Fax 95/422-89-99. 51 rms (all with bath). A/C TEL

Rates: 4,500 ptas. ($32) single; 6,500 ptas. ($46.20) double. Breakfast 350 ptas. ($2.50) extra. AE, DC, MC, V.

In this fairly modern hotel the guest rooms are modest but comfortable, with provincial and utilitarian furnishings and central heating for those Sevillian winters. A continental breakfast can be brought to your room, but no other meals are served. The location, near El Corte Inglés department store, is handy to many specialty shops.

Hotel América, Jesús del Gran Poder, 2, 41002 Sevilla. ☎ **95/422-09-51.** Fax 95/421-06-26. 100 rms (all with bath). A/C MINIBAR TV TEL

Rates: 7,000 ptas. ($49.70) single; 9,500 ptas. ($67.50) double. Breakfast 600 ptas. ($4.30) extra. AE, DC, MC, V. **Parking:** 2,000 ptas. ($14.20) nearby.

Built in 1976 and partially renovated in 1994, this hotel contains rather small bedrooms but keeps the place spick-and-span. Superior features include wall-to-wall carpeting and, in winter, an individual heat control that works. Relax in the TV lounge or order a drink in the Duque Bar. Near the hotel is a parking garage for 600 cars. There isn't a major restaurant, but the América does offer a tearoom, cafeteria, and snack bar. The hotel is set on the northern side of the Plaza del Duque. One of Spain's major department stores, El Corte Inglés, opens onto the same square.

Residencia Murillo, Calle Lope de Rueda, 7–9, 41004 Sevilla. ☎ **95/421-60-95.** Fax 95/421-96-16. 57 rms (all with bath). TEL

Rates: 4,000 ptas. ($28.40) single; 7,000 ptas. ($49.70) double. Breakfast 400 ptas. ($2.80) extra. AE, DC, MC, V.

Tucked away on a narrow street in the heart of Santa Cruz, the old quarter, the Residencia Murillo (named after the artist who used to live in this district) is almost next to the gardens of the Alcázar. Inside, the lounges harbor some fine architectural characteristics and antique reproductions; behind a grilled screen is a retreat for drinks. Many of the rooms I inspected were cheerless and gloomy, so have a look before checking in. Like all of Seville's hotels, the Murillo is in a noisy area.

You can reach this residencia from the Menéndez y Pelayo, a wide avenue west of the Parque María Luisa, where a sign will take you through the Murillo Gardens on the left. Motorists should try to park in Plaza de Santa Cruz. Then walk two blocks to the hotel, which will send a bellhop back to the car to pick up your suitcases. If there are two in your party, station a guard at the car, and if you're going out at night, call for an inexpensive taxi to take you instead of strolling through the streets of the old quarter—it's less romantic but a lot safer.

BUDGET

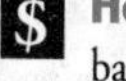

Hostal Goya, Mateus Gago, 31, 41004 Sevilla. ☎ **95/421-11-70.** 20 rms (12 with bath).

Rates: 3,655 ptas. ($26) single without bath; 5,620 ptas. ($39.90) double with bath. Mar 24–Apr 30, 4,240 ptas. ($30.10) single, 6,890 ptas. ($48.90) double. Breakfast 350 ptas. (2.50) extra. No credit cards.

Its location in a narrow-fronted town house in the oldest part of the barrio is one of the Goya's strongest virtues. The building's gold-and-white facade, ornate iron railings, and picture-postcard demeanor are all noteworthy. Bedrooms are cozy and simple, without phones or TVs. Guests congregate in the marble-floored ground-level salon, where a skylight floods the couches and comfortable chairs with sunlight. Breakfast is the only meal served. Reserve well in advance.

NEARBY

Hacienda Benazuza, Calle Virgen de las Nieves, s/n, 41800 Sanlúcar la Major, Seville. ☎ **95/570-3344.** Fax 95/570-3410. 26 rooms (all with bath), 18 suites. A/C MINIBAR TV TEL **Directions:** From Seville, follow the signs for Huelva, and head south on the A49 highway, exiting from it at exit no. 6.

Rates: Mon–Thurs, 24,000 ptas. ($170.40) single; 31,000 ptas. ($220.10) double. Fri–Sun, with two-night minimum stay required, 17,600 ptas. ($125) single, 22,000 ptas. ($156.20) double. Mon–Thurs breakfast 1,500 ptas. ($10.70) extra, Fri–Sun, breakfast free. Suite 40,000–90,000 ptas. ($284–$639) seven days a week, plus breakfast. AE, DC, MC, V. **Parking:** Free. **Closed:** July 15–Sept 1.

Set on a hillside above the agrarian hamlet of Sanlúcar la Mayor, 12 miles south of Seville, this legendary manor house is surrounded by 40 acres of olive groves and its own farmland. Its ownership has been a cross-section of every major cultural influence that has swept through Andalusia since its foundations were laid in the 10th century by the Moors. After the Catholic conquest of southern Spain, the site became a much-feared stronghold of the fanatically religious *Caballeros de Santiago.* Later, during the 18th and 19th centuries, it was developed as the country seat of an aristocratic family known for the fearlessness of the bulls they bred for *corridas* throughout the Hispanic world. (The chapel and olive press they built are now two of the hotel's showpieces.)

In 1992 the property was bought by Basque-born entrepreneur Rafael Elejabeitia, who, after spending many millions of pesetas, transformed the premises into one of Andalusia's most charming hotels. Careful attention was paid to preserving the ancient Moorish irrigation system whose many reflecting pools nourish the gardens. All but a few of the bedrooms lie within the estate's main building, and each is individually furnished with Andalusian antiques and Moorish trappings, representative of the original construction.

Dining/Entertainment: The most formal of the hotel's three restaurants is La Alguería, where first-class service and Andalusian and international cuisine culminate in "surprise menus" priced at 5,500 pesetas ($39.10) each. El Patio is an indoor-outdoor affair overlooking the estate's red-brick patio and palm trees. Meals average around 3,500 pesetas ($24.90). (Both of the above are open daily for lunch and dinner, and are open to nonresidents who reserve in advance.) A lunch buffet beside the swimming pool, where everyone seems to show up in bathing suits and jewelry, is offered in La Alberca for around 2,000 pesetas ($14.20) per person.

Services: Room service, and a concierge well trained to procure almost anything.

Facilities: Tennis courts with a resident pro, paddle tennis courts, a golf range. A mini-museum of Andalusian agriculture lies within an antique building originally designed as an olive press. Many other sporting options lie within driving distance, and can be arranged by the concierge staff.

Where to Dine

VERY EXPENSIVE

★ **Egaña Oriza,** San Fernando, 41. ☎ **422-72-11.**

Cuisine: BASQUE/INTERNATIONAL. **Reservations:** Required.

Prices: Appetizers 1,000–2,100 ptas. ($7.10–$14.90); main courses 2,200–2,900 ptas. ($15.60–$20.60); three-course fixed-price menu 5,000 ptas. ($35.50). AE, DC, MC, V. **Open:** Restaurant, lunch, Mon–Fri 1:30–3:30pm; dinner, Mon–Sat 9–11:30pm. Bar, daily 9am–midnight. **Closed:** Aug.

Set within the conservatory of a restored mansion adjacent to Murillo Park is Seville's most stylish restaurant. Much of its reputation stems from its role as one of the few game specialists in Andalusia—a province that is otherwise devoted to seafood. The restaurant was established by Basque-born owner and chef José Mari Egaña, who managed to combine his passion for hunting with his flair for cooking his catch. Many of the raw ingredients that go into the dishes presented on the menu were trapped or shot within Andalusia, a region whose potential for sports shooting is underutilized, according to Sr. Egaña . The view from the dining room encompasses a garden and a wall that formed part of the fortications of Muslim Sevilla.

The availability of many specialties depends on the season but might include fresh vegetable soup studded with morsels of confit of duck, gazpacho with prawns, steak with foie gras in grape sauce, casserole of wild boar with cherries and raisins, quenelles of duck in a potato nest with apple purée, stewed mountain sheep cooked with figs, rice with stewed thrush, and woodcock flamed in Spanish brandy. The wine list provides an ample supply of hearty Spanish reds to accompany any of these dishes. Dessert might feature a chocolate tart slathered with freshly whipped cream. Sr. Egaña's wife, Mercedes, runs the establishment's two-story dining room.

EXPENSIVE

El Burladero, in the Hotel Tryp Colón, Canalejas, 1. ☎ **422-29-00**

Cuisine: CONTINENTAL. **Reservations:** Recommended.
Prices: Appetizers 600–1,800 ptas. ($4.30–$12.80); main courses 1,800–3,600 ptas. ($12.80–$25.60); fixed-price menu 4,100–4,500 ptas. ($29.10–$32). AE, DC, MC, V.
Open: Lunch, daily 1–4pm. Dinner, daily 9–11pm. **Closed:** Aug.

Set within one of Seville's most prominent hotels, this restaurant is awash with the memorabilia and paraphernalia of the bullfighting trade. The wall tiles that decorate parts of the interior were removed from one of the pavilions at the 1929 Seville World's Fair, and the photographs adorning the walls are a veritable history of bullfighting. (The restaurant, incidentally, is named after the wooden barricade—*el burladero*—behind which bullfighters in an arena can escape from the charge of an enraged bull.) The restaurant boasts a popular bar where a wide assortment of Sevillanos meet and mingle before their meals.

Menu specialties include upscale interpretations of local country dishes, with an attractive mix of items from other regions of Spain as well. Examples include *bacalao al horno con patatas* (baked salt cod with potatoes and saffron sauce);roasted shoulder of lamb stuffed with a deboned bull's tail and served in a richly aromatic sauce; clams with white kidney beans; a local version of *cocido*, a boiled amalgam of sausages, meats, chickpeas, and vegetables; and a stew of eel meat heavily laced with garlic and spices. Dishes from other parts of Europe might include truffled filet steak in puff pastry, duck liver, and salmon cooked in lemon-flavored dill sauce.

MODERATE

La Albahaca, Plaza de Santa Cruz, 12. ☎ **422-07-14.**

Cuisine: SPANISH. **Reservations:** Recommended.
Prices: Appetizers 1,000–1,700 ptas. ($7.10–$12.10); main courses 2,500–3,000 ptas. ($17.80–$21.30); fixed-price menu 3,500 ptas. ($24.90). AE, DC, MC, V.
Open: Lunch, Mon–Sat 1–4pm; dinner, Mon–Sat 8pm–midnight.

Located on a prominent square in the Old Barrio de Santa Cruz, this restaurant with an open-air terrace offers a limited but savory menu that has become a favorite of Sevillians. Specialties include a salad of carpaccio of codfish with fresh asparagus and herbs, seafood soup, shellfish bisque, grilled lamb chops, partridge braised in sherry, salmon in papillote, and chocolate pudding for dessert. The restaurant is in an antique seignorial home built in 1929.

Casa Robles, Calle Alvarez Quintero, 58. ☎ **456-32-72.**

Cuisine: ANDALUSIAN. **Reservations:** Recommended.
Prices: Appetizers 750–1,800 ptas. ($5.30–$12.80); main courses 1,200–2,200 ptas. ($8.50–$15.60). Fixed-price menu 2,500 ptas. ($17.80). AE, DC, MC, V.
Open: Lunch, daily 1–4:30pm; dinner, daily 8pm–1am.

Praised by local residents as well as by temporary visitors, this restaurant began its life as an unpretentious bar and bodega in 1954. Over the years, thanks to a staff directed by owner-chef Juan Robles and his children, it developed into a courteous but bustling restaurant scattered over two floors of a building a short walk from the cathedral. Amid an all-Andalusian decor, you can enjoy such dishes as fish soup in the Andalusian style, *lubina con naranjas* (whitefish with Sevillana oranges), hake baked with strips of Serrano ham, veal steak prepared "in the style of Seville," and many kinds of fresh fish. The dessert list is long, diverse, and very tempting.

$ **Enrique Becerra,** Gamazo, 2. ☎ **421-30-49.**

Cuisine: ANDALUSIAN. **Reservations:** Recommended.
Prices: Appetizers 600–1,500 ptas. ($4.30–$10.70); main courses 1,500–2,000 ptas. ($10.70–$14.20). AE, DC, MC, V.
Open: Lunch, Mon–Sat 1–5pm; dinner, Mon–Sat 8pm–midnight.

On my latest rounds, this restaurant off Plaza Nueva and near the cathedral provided one of my best meals. The restaurant takes its name from its owner, a smart and helpful host, who installed it in a late–19th-century building. A popular tapas bar and Andalusian dining spot, it offers an intimate setting and a hearty welcome that leaves you with the feeling that your business is really appreciated. While perusing the menu, you can sip dry Tío Pepe and nibble herb-cured olives with lemon peel. The gazpacho here is among the city's best, and the sangría is served ice cold. Specialties include hake *real,* sea bream Bilbaon style, and a wide range of meat and fish dishes. Many vegetarian dishes are also featured.

La Isla, Arfe 25. ☎ **421-26-31.**

Cuisine: SPANISH/ANDALUSIAN. **Reservations:** Recommended.
Prices: Appetizers 900–2,000 ptas. ($6.40–$14.20); main courses 2,000–3,000 ptas. ($14.20–$21.30) AE, DC, MC, V.
Open: Lunch, Tues–Sun 1–5pm; dinner, Tues–Sun 8pm–midnight. **Closed:** August.

Set within two large dining rooms designed in Andalusian fashion (thick plaster walls, tile floors, and taurine memorabilia), this air-conditioned restaurant was established shortly after World War II and has done a thriving business ever since. Its seafood is trucked or flown in from either Galicia, in northern Spain, or Huelva, one of Andalusia's major ports, and is almost always extremely fresh. Menu items include *merluza à la primavera* (hake with young vegetables); *solomillo à la Castellana* (grilled beefsteak with strips of Serrano ham); chicken croquettes, shellfish soup, and *rape à la marinera.* The restaurant lies a short walk from the cathedral, within a very old building erected, the owners say, on foundations laid by the ancient Romans.

Mesón Don Raimundo, Argote de Molina, 26. ☎ **421-29-25.**

Cuisine: SPANISH. **Reservations:** Recommended.
Prices: Appetizers 600–2,500 ptas. ($4.30–$17.80); main courses 1,500–2,500 ptas. ($10.70–$17.80). AE, DC, MC, V.

Open: Lunch, daily noon–5pm; dinner, daily 7pm–midnight.

Once a 17th-century convent, this is an attractively furnished restaurant whose entrance lies at the end of a flower-lined alleyway in the center of the Barrio de Santa Cruz. The interior contains lots of brick, terra cotta, and carved columns, which support the beamed or arched high ceilings. Your meal might include fish stew or one of six kinds of soup (including one with clams and pine nuts), then fresh grilled king shrimp, a casserole of partridge in sherry sauce, or wild rabbit casserole. Some of the recipes were adapted from old Arab-Hispanic cookbooks. In winter the central fireplace imparts a warm glow to the antique copper and wrought-iron art objects; in summer the place is comfortably air-conditioned.

Río Grande, Betis, 70. ☎ **427-39-56.**

Cuisine: ANDALUSIAN. **Reservations:** Required. **Bus:** 41 or 42.
Prices: Appetizers 900–2,000 ptas. ($6.40–$14.20); main courses 1,800–2,400 ptas. ($12.80-$17); fixed-price menu 3,500 ptas. ($24.90). AE, DC, MC, V.
Open: Lunch, daily 1–5pm; dinner, daily 8pm–1am.

This classic Sevillian restaurant is named for the Guadalquivir River, which its panoramic windows overlook. It sits against the bank of the river near Plaza de Cuba in front of the Torre del Oro. Some diners come here just for a view of the city monuments. A meal might include stuffed sweet pepper *flamenca*, fish-and-seafood soup seaman's style, the chef's fresh salmon, chicken-and-shellfish paella, bull tail Andalusian, and garlic-chicken Giralda. You can also have a selection of fresh shellfish that's brought in daily. Large terraces contain a snack bar, the Río Grande Pub, and a Bingo room. You can often watch sports events on the river in this pleasant (and English-speaking) spot.

INEXPENSIVE

$ **Hostería del Laurel,** Plaza de los Venerables, 5. ☎ **422-02-95.**

Cuisine: ANDALUSIAN. **Reservations:** Recommended.
Prices: Appetizers 350–1,150 ptas. ($2.50–$8.20); main courses 550–1,850 ptas. ($3.90–$13.10). AE, DC, MC, V.
Open: Lunch, daily 1:30–4pm; dinner, daily 7:30pm–midnight.

Located in one of the most charming buildings on tiny, difficult-to-find Plaza de los Venerables in the labyrinthian Barrio de Santa Cruz, this hideaway restaurant has iron-barred windows stuffed with plants. Inside, amid Andalusian tiles, beamed ceilings, and more plants, you'll enjoy good regional cooking. Many diners stop for a drink and tapas at the ground-floor bar before going into one of the dining rooms. The hostería is attached to a three-star hotel.

$ **La Raza,** Isabel la Católica, 2. ☎ **423-38-30.**

Cuisine: ANDALUSIAN. **Reservations:** Recommended.
Prices: Appetizers 750–1,200 ptas. ($5.30–$8.50); main courses 1,200–2,000 ptas. ($8.50–$14.20). AE, DC, MC, V.
Open: Lunch, daily 1–4pm; dinner, daily 8–11:30pm.

A terrace restaurant in Parque María Luisa, La Raza is known both for its setting and its Andalusian tapas. Begin with gazpacho, then go on to one of the meat dishes. On Friday and Saturday there is often music to entertain guests, many of whom are American and Japanese tourists.

Pizzeria San Marco, Calle Mesón de Moro 6. ☎ **421-4390.**

Cuisine: ITALIAN. **Reservations:** Recommended.

Prices: Appetizers 350–700 ptas. ($2.50–$5); main courses 490–1,375 ptas. ($3.50–$9.80). MC, V.

Open: Lunch, Tues–Sun 1:30–4:30pm; dinner, Tues–Sun 8:30pm–12:30am.

Despite the informality implied by its name, this is actually a well-managed restaurant with sit-down service and bilingual waiters. Pizza is only one of the many items featured on the menu, and often is relegated to a secondary role, as clients usually opt for any of several kinds of pastas, salmon salads, duck in orange sauce, osso buco, chicken parmesan, and several forms of scaloppini. There's also a congenial corner for drinking, named Harry's Bar in honor of grander role models in Venice or elsewhere.

Despite the allure of the food, the real interest of the place is its setting. It lies within what was originally built, more than a thousand years ago, as an Arab bathhouse. Its interior reminds some visitors of a secularized mosque, despite the presence of a modern wing added around 1991 in anticipation of increased business from Seville's Expo celebration. The establishment lies within the Barrio de Santa Cruz, on an obscure side street running into Calle Mateus Gago.

SPECIALTY DINING—FAST FOOD

Lying directly east of the cathedral, **Cervecería Giralda,** Calle Mateus Gago (☎ **422-74-35**), is one of the least expensive dining spots near the cathedral, Alcázar, and Giralda Tower. Residents and tourists alike eat here. You can make a meal from the selection of tapas (appetizers), ranging from 175–500 pesetas ($1.20–$3.60), or order one of the *platos combinados* (combination plates), ranging from 800–1,200 pesetas ($5.70–$8.50). The place is open daily from 9am to midnight.

On the same street, **Pizzeria El Artesano,** Calle Mateus Gago, 9 (☎ **421-38-58**), also lures in customers near the cathedral. Here the feature is an Andalusian version of pizza costing 525–725 ptas. ($3.70–$5.10). Daily hours are 12:30pm to 1am.

Lying on the "opposite side" of the Guadalquivir, away from the throngs of tourists, is the Barrio de Triana. This used to be its own little village community until Seville burst its seams and absorbed it. It still is the place to go to escape the high food tariffs on the cathedral side of the river.

El Puerto, Betis, s/n (☎ **427-17-25**), stands next door to the famed Río Grande restaurant. It has a multilevel al fresco terrace opening onto the river. You can get fresh seafood here, but the special buy is the chef's *cubierto* (menu of the house), costing 450–850 pesetas ($3.20–$6); tapas range from 200–700 pesetas ($1.40–$5). At the cafeteria bar, you serve yourself; inside is an inexpensive restaurant with waiter service. It's open Tuesday to Sunday; lunch is served from 1 to 4pm and dinner from 8pm to midnight. (It's closed in January.) Bus: 41 or 42.

Another way to keep costs trimmed is to eat at one of the tapas bars recommended below under "Evening Entertainment." Portions, called *raciones*, are usually generous, and many budget-minded tourists often eat standing at the bar, making a full meal out of two orders of tapas.

Evening Entertainment

FLAMENCO

When the moon is high in Seville and the scent of orange blossoms is in the air, it's time to wander the alleyways of Santa Cruz in search of the sound of castanets. Or take a taxi to be on the safe side.

★ **El Patio Sevillano,** Paseo de Cristóbal Colón, 11. ☎ **421-41-20.**

In central Seville on the riverbank between two historic bridges, El Patio Sevillano is a showcase for Spanish folksong and dance, performed by exotically costumed dancers. The presentation includes a wide variety of Andalusian flamenco and songs, as well as classical pieces by composers such as Falla, Albéniz, Granados, and Chueca. From March through October, there are three shows nightly, beginning at 7:30pm, 10pm, and 11:45pm. There are only two shows from November through February, beginning nightly at 7:30 and 10pm. Drinks average 1,000 pesetas ($7.10).

Admission: 3,200 ptas. ($22.70).

A SEVILLE DISCO

El Coto, Luis Montoto, 118. ☎ **457-62-03.**

Popular and often crowded, El Coto is located in the basement of the Hotel Los Legreros in the center of Seville (the modern part of town). The club is open daily from 7:30 to 10:30pm and 11:30pm to 5am.

Admission (including one drink): 1,500 ptas. ($10.70).

DRINKS & TAPAS

La Alicantina, Plaza del Salvador, 2. ☎ **422-61-22.**

What is reported to be the best seafood tapas in town are served against a decor in the typical style of Seville utilizing glazed tiles. Both the bar and the sidewalk tables are always filled to overflowing. The owner serves generous portions of clams marinara, fried squid, grilled shrimp, fried codfish, and clams in béchamel sauce. La Alicantina, located about five blocks north of the cathedral, is open daily from noon to 3:30pm and 7 to 11:30pm. Tapas range upward from 300 pesetas ($2.10).

Casa Roman, Plaza des los Venerables. No phone.

Tapas are said to have originated in Andalusia, and this old-fashioned bar, incongruously named Roman, looks as if it has been dishing them up since day one. Definitely include this place on your tasca-hopping through the old quarter. At the deli counter in front you can make your selection; you might even pick up the fixings for a picnic in the Parque María Luisa. The Casa Roman is in the Barrio de Santa Cruz. Open Monday to Friday from 9am to 3pm and 5:30pm to 12:30am; Saturday and Sunday it's open 10am to 3pm and 6:30pm to 12:30am. A glass of wine usually runs 135 pesetas ($1); tapas are priced from 500 pesetas ($3.60).

Modesto, Cano y Cueto, 5. ☎ **441-68-11.**

At the northern end of Murillo Gardens, opening onto a quiet square with flowerboxes and an ornate iron railing, Modesto serves fabulous seafood tapas. The bar is air-conditioned, and you can choose your appetizers just by pointing. Upstairs there's a good-value restaurant, offering a meal for 1,800 pesetas ($12.80), including such dishes as fried squid, baby sole, grilled sea bass, and shrimp in garlic sauce. Modesto is open daily from 8pm to 2am. Drinks average 200 pesetas ($1.40); tapas are priced from 200 pesetas ($1.40).

El Rinconcillo, Gerona, 40. ☎ **422-31-83.**

El Rinconcillo has a 1930s ambience, partly because of its real age and partly because of its owners' refusal to change one iota of the decor—this has always been one of the most famous bars in Seville. Actually, it may be the oldest bar in Seville, with a history going back to 1670. Amid dim lighting, heavy ceiling beams, and iron-based, marble-topped tables, you can enjoy a beer or a full meal along with the rest of the easy-going clientele. The bartender will mark your tab in chalk on a well-worn wooden countertop. El Rinconcillo is especially known for its salads, omelets, hams, and selection of cheeses. Look for the art nouveau tile murals. El Rinconcillo is at the northern edge of the Barrio de Santa Cruz, near the Santa Catalina Church. It's open Thursday to Tuesday from 1pm to 3am. A complete meal will cost around 2,000 pesetas ($14.20). A beer goes for 110 pesetas (80¢).

A SPECIAL BAR

Arabes, Abades, 1. ☎ **421-50-96.**

A converted mansion in the Barrio de Santa Cruz has been turned into a rendezvous that has been compared to "a living room in a luxurious movie set." One member of the Spanish press labeled it "wonderfully decadent, similar to the ambience created in a Visconti film." In the heart of the Jewish ghetto, it evokes the style of the Spanish Romantic era. The house dates from the 19th century, when it was constructed around a central courtyard with a fountain. Drinks and low-key conversations are the style here, and since its opening in 1980 all the visiting literati and glitterati have put in an appearance. Young men and women in jeans also patronize the place, enjoying the comfort of the sofas and wicker armchairs.

The ingredients of a special drink called *aqua de Sevilla* are a secret, but I suspect sparkling white wine, pineapple juice, and eggs (the whites and yolks mixed in separately, of course). Classical music is played in the background. Take a taxi to get here at night, as it might not be safe to wander late along the narrow streets of the barrio. In summer, it's open daily from 9pm to 4am; in winter, hours are daily from 8pm to 2:30am. Drinks are priced from 800 pesetas ($5.70).

Easy Excursions

CARMONA

An easy hour-long bus trip from the main terminal in Seville, Carmona is an ancient city dating from Neolithic times. Twenty-one miles (34km) east of Seville, it grew in power and prestige under the Moors, establishing ties with Castile in 1252.

Surrounded by fortified walls, Carmona has three Moorish fortresses, one a parador and, the other two, **the Alcázar de la Puerta de Córdoba** and **Alcázar de la Puerta de Sevilla.** The top attraction is **Seville Gate,** with its double Moorish arch, opposite St. Peter's Church. Note too, **Córdoba Gate** on Calle Santa María de Gracia, which was attached to the ancient Roman walls in the 17th century.

The town itself is a virtual national landmark, filled with narrow streets, white-washed walls, and Renaissance mansions. **Plaza San Fernando** is the most important square, with many elegant 17th-century houses. The most important church is dedicated to **Santa María** and stands on the Calle Martin López. You enter a Moorish ablutionary patio before exploring the interior with its 15th-century white vaulting.

A **Roman necropolis and amphitheater** at Jorge Bonsor contain the remains of a thousand families who lived in and around Carmona 2,000 years ago. On site is an archeological museum offering 45-minute tours Tuesday through Saturday from 10am to 2pm and 4 to 6pm; Sunday 10am to 2pm; admission is 250 pesetas ($1.80). Of the two important tombs, the Elephant Vault consists of three dining rooms and a kitchen. The other, the Servilia Tomb, was the size of a nobleman's villa. If you're driving to Carmona, exit from Seville's eastern periphery onto the N-V superhighway, following the signs to the airport, then to Carmona on the road to Madrid. The Carmona turnoff is clearly marked.

Where to Stay and Dine

★ **Casa de Carmona,** Plaza de Lasso, 1, 41410 Carmona (Sevilla). ☎ **95/414-33-00,** or **212/686-9213** for reservations within North America. Fax 95/414-37-52. 15 rms (all with bath), 15 suites. A/C MINIBAR TV TEL

Rates: 14,000 ptas. ($99.40) single; 17,000–22,000 ptas. ($120.70–$156.20) double. Add about 30% for Feria de Sevilla and Easter (Semana Santa). Breakfast 1,600 ptas. ($11.40) extra. AE, MC, V. **Parking:** Free.

Considered one of the most elegant and intimate hotels in Andalusia, this plushly furnished hideaway was originally built as the home of the Lasso family during the 1500s. Several years ago, a team of entrepreneurs added the many features required for a luxury hotel, all the while retaining the marble columns, massive masonry, and graceful proportions of the building's original construction. Set at the edge of the village, the hotel offers an outdoor swimming pool with a flowering terrace, an inner courtyard covered against the midsummer heat with a canvas awning, and a small exercise room. The most visible public room still maintains vestiges of its original function as a library. Each bedroom is a cozy enclave of opulent furnishings, with a distinct decor theme inspired by ancient Rome, medieval Andalusia, or Renaissance Spain.

On the premises is a restaurant whose tables are set up outdoors. Its culinary inspiration derives from modern interpretations of Andalusian and international cuisine, with meals served daily from 1 to 4pm and from 9 to 11:30pm and priced from around 3,500 pesetas ($24.90) each, without wine.

★ **Parador Nacional Alcázar del Rey Don Pedro,** Alcázar, s/n, 41410 Carmona (Sevilla). ☎ **95/414-10-10.** Fax 495/414-17-12. 63 rms (all with bath). A/C MINIBAR TV TEL

Rates: 12,000 ptas. ($85.20) single; 16,000 ptas. ($113.60) double. Breakfast 1,200 ptas. ($8.50) extra. AE, DC, MC, V. **Parking:** Free.

Finding this parador amid the narrow Carmona streets that wind in and out of the ancient fortifications is part of the establishment's charm. By following strategically located signs, you'll see it clinging by diagonal stilts to the rock face of a forbidding cliff. After parking in the shadows of a medieval courtyard, you'll enter one of the most attractive paradors in Spain, built around an Andalusian patio whose monumental fountain is ringed with Moorish columns, potted geraniums, and intricate tiles. A hallway crafted from brick, stone, and wooden beams leads to a lattice-shaded breakfast room where views of the surrounding fertile farmland stretch for miles.

The parador, open since 1976, contains comfortable bedrooms with rustically detailed accessories. In most rooms, French doors open onto panoramic views. Special features include a flower garden, a tile-roofed gazebo, and a beautiful swimming pool set with herringbone patterns of blue and white tiles. A snack bar, 16 tile-roofed cabañas for toilet facilities and changing rooms, and rosebushes surround it. Fixed-price meals are served in the stone-vaulted restaurant. Two different *menús del día* are featured, one at 3,500 pesetas ($24.90) and another at 2,600 pesetas ($18.50).

ITÁLICA

Lovers of Roman history will flock to Itálica (☎ **95/439-27-84**), the ruins of an ancient city 5½ miles (9km) northwest of Seville, on the major road to Lisbon, near the small town of Santiponce.

After the battle of Ilipa, Publius Cornelius Scipio Africanus founded Itálica in 206 B.C. Two of the most famous of Roman emperors, Trajan and Hadrian, were born here. Indeed, master builder Hadrian was to have a major influence on his hometown. In his reign the **amphitheater,** the ruins of which can be seen today, was among the largest in the Roman Empire. Lead pipes that carried water from the Guadalquivir River still remain. A small museum displays some of the Roman statuary found here, although the finest pieces have been shipped to Seville. Many mosaics, depicting beasts, gods, and birds, are on exhibit, and others are constantly being discovered. The ruins, including a Roman theater, can be explored for 250 pesetas ($1.80). The site is open April through September, Tuesday through Saturday, from 9am to 6:30pm and on Sunday from 9am to 3pm. From October through March, it's open Tuesday through Saturday from 9am to 5:30pm and on Sunday from 10am to 4pm.

If you're driving, exit from the northwest periphery of Seville, following the signs for highway E-803 in the direction of Zafra and Lisbon. But if you don't have a car, take the bus marked "Calle de Santiponce" leaving from Calle Marqués de Parada near the railway station in Seville. Buses depart every hour for the 30-minute trip.

4 Jerez de la Frontera

54 miles (87km) S of Seville, 368 miles (592km) SW of Madrid, 21 miles (34km) NE of Cádiz

GETTING THERE • By Plane Iberia and Aviaco offer flights to Jerez every Monday through Friday from Barcelona and Zaragoza; daily flights from Madrid; and several flights a week to and from Valencia, Tenerife, Palma de Mallorca, and Grand Canary Island. No international flights land at Jerez. The airport lies about 7 miles (11km) northeast of the city center (follow the signs to Seville). There's an Iberia ticketing and information office conveniently located in the center of Jerez at Plaza del Arenal, 2 (☎ **33-43-00**).

• By Train Trains from Madrid arrive daily (the trip takes 9 to 11 hours). The railway station in Jerez lies at Plaza de la Estación (☎ **34-23-29**), at the eastern end of Calle Medina.

• By Bus Bus connections are more frequent than train connections, and the location of the bus terminal is also more convenient. You'll find it on Calle Cartuja, at the corner of the Calle Madre de Díos, a 12-minute walk east of the Alcázar. About 18 buses arrive daily from Cádiz (1 hour away) and three per day travel from Ronda (3 hours). Seven buses a day arrive from Seville (1½ hours). Phone **34-10-63** for more information.

• By Car Jerez lies on the highway connecting Seville with Cádiz, Algeciras, Gibraltar, and the ferryboat landing for Tangier, Morocco. There's also an overland road connecting Jerez with Granada and Málaga.

ESSENTIALS The area code for Jerez de la Frontera is 956. The tourist information office is at Calle Alameda Cristina, 7 (☎ **956/33-11-50**). To reach it from the bus terminals, take Calle Medina to Calle Honda and continue along as the road turns to the right. The English-speaking staff can provide directions, transportation suggestions, open hours, and so on for any bodega you might want to visit. You will also be given a map pinpointing the location of various bodegas.

The charming little Andalusian town of Jerez made a name for itself in England for the thousands of casks of golden sherry it shipped there over the centuries. With origins going back nearly 3,000 years, Jerez is nonetheless a modern, progressive town with wide boulevards, although it does have an interesting old quarter. Busloads of visitors pour in every year to get those free drinks at one of the bodegas where wine is aged and bottled.

The town is pronounced both "Her-*ez*" and "Her-*eth*," in Andalusian and Castilian, respectively. The French and the Moors called it various names, including Heres and Scheris, which the English corrupted to Sherry.

WHAT TO SEE & DO

☆ TOURING THE BODEGAS Jerez is not surrounded by vineyards, as you might expect. The vineyards lie to the north and west of Jerez, within the so-called "Sherry Triangle" between the towns of Jerez, Sanlúcar, de Barrameda, and El Puerto de Santa María (the latter two on the coast). This is where the best quality *albariza* soil is to be found, the highest quality containing an average of 60% chalk, which is ideal for the cultivation of grapes used in sherry production, principally the white *Palomino de Jerez.* The ideal time to visit is September. However, visitors can count on the finest in hospitality all year round, since Jerez is widely known for the warm welcome it bestows.

There must be more than a hundred bodegas in and around Jerez, where you can not only see how sherries are made, bottled, and aged, but also get free samples. Among the most famous brands are Sandeman, Pedro Domecq, and González Byass, the maker of Tío Pepe.

On a typical visit to a bodega, you'll be shown through several buildings in which sherry and brandy are manufactured. In one building, you'll see grapes being pressed and sorted; in another, you'll see them being bottled; in a third, you'll see thousands of large oak casks. Then it's on to an attractive bar where various sherries—amber, dark gold, cream, red, sweet, and velvety—can be sampled. If either is offered, try the very dry La Ina sherry or the Fundador brandy, one of the most popular in the world.

Warning: These drinks are more potent than you might expect.

Most bodegas are open Monday to Friday only, from 10:30am to 1:30pm. Regrettably, many of them are closed in August; many do reopen by the third week of August to prepare for the wine festival in early September.

Of the dozens of bodegas you can visit, the most popular are listed below. Some of them charge an admission fee and require a reservation.

A favorite among British visitors is **Harveys of Bristol,** Calle Arcos, 57 (**☎ 48-34-00**), which doesn't require a reservation. An English-speaking guide leads a two-hour tour year-round, except for the first three weeks of August. You should visit at noon Monday through Friday, paying an admission of 250 pesetas ($1.80).

You'll definitely want to visit **Williams & Humbert Limited,** Nuño de Cañas 1 (**☎ 33-31-00**), which offers tours from noon to 1:30pm Monday through Friday, charging 300 pesetas ($2.10). Their premium brands include the world famous Dry Sack Medium Sherry, Canasta Cream, Fino Pando, and Manzanilla Alegría, in addition to Gran Duque de Alba Gran Reserva Brandy.

Another famous name is **González Byass,** Manuel María González, s/n, (☎ **34-00-00**); admission is 300 pesetas ($2.10), and reservations are required. Equally famous is **Domecq,** Calle San Ildefonso, 3 (☎ **33-19-00**), requiring a reservation and charging no admission.

THE DANCING HORSES OF JEREZ A rival of sorts to Vienna's famous Spanish Riding School is the ★ **Escuela Andaluza del Arte Ecuestre (Andalusian School of Equestrian Art),** Avenida Duque de Abrantes, 11 (☎ **31-11-11**). In fact, the long, hard schooling that brings horse and rider into perfect harmony originated in this province. The Viennese school was started with Hispano-Arab horses sent from this region, the same steeds you can see today in Jerez. Every Thursday at noon, crowds come to admire the Dancing Horses of Jerez as they perform in a show that includes local folklore. Admission is 2,250 pesetas ($16) for adults and 825 pesetas ($5.90) for children. **Bus:** 18.

A NEARBY ATTRACTION Since many people go to Jerez specifically to visit a bodega, August or weekend closings can be very disappointing. If this happens to you, make a trip to the nearby village of **Lebrija,** about halfway between Jerez and Seville, $8^1/_2$ miles (14km) west of the main highway. Lebrija, a good spot to get a glimpse of rural Spain, is a local winemaking center where some very fine sherries originate. At one small bodega, that of Juan García, you are courteously escorted around by the owner. There are several other bodegas in Lebrija, and the local citizens will gladly point them out to you. It's all very casual—lacking the rigidity and formality attached to the bodegas of Jerez.

Where to Stay

EXPENSIVE

Hotel Avenida Jerez, Avenida Alcalde Álvaro Domecq, 10, 11405 Jerez de la Frontera. ☎ **956/34-74-11.** Fax 956/33-72-96. 90 rms, 5 suites. A/C TV TEL

Rates: 6,000 ptas. ($42.60) single; 11,000 ptas. ($78.10) double; 15,000 ptas. ($106.50) suite. AE, DC, MC, V. **Parking:** 900 ptas. ($6.40).

Set very close to the commercial heart of Jerez, this hotel occupies a modern balconied structure of seven stories. Inside, cool floors of polished stone, leather armchairs, and a variety of potted plants create a restful haven. The bedrooms are discreetly contemporary and decorated in neutral colors, with big windows, comfortable beds, and private baths.

Dining/Entertainment: The hotel maintains a pleasant and unpretentious cafeteria providing coffee-shop–style snacks and platters of Spanish food priced at from 650–2,000 pesetas ($4.60–$14.20) each. There's also a bar.

Services: Room service (available daily from 8am to midnight), babysitting, concierge, laundry/valet.

Facilities: Car-rental desk.

★ **Hotel Royal Sherry Park,** Avenida Alcalde Álvaro Domecq, 11 Bis, 11405 Jerez de la Frontera. ☎ **956/30-30-11.** Fax 956/31-13-00. 170 rms, 3 suites. A/C MINIBAR TV TEL

Rates: 11,200–15,600 ptas. ($79.50–$110.80) single; 14,900–19,500 ptas. ($105.80–$138.50) double; 20,000–30,000 ptas. ($142–$213) suite. Breakfast 1,100 ptas. ($7.80) extra. AE, DC, MC, V.

Especially noted for its setting within a palm-fringed garden and for its large swimming pool whose tiled edges attract many of its sun-loving residents, this is considered one of the best modern hotels in Jerez. Located on a wide and verdant boulevard north of the historic center of town, it contains a marble-floored lobby; efficiently modern public rooms; and simple but comfortable bedrooms, all with private bath. The uniformed staff lays out a copious breakfast buffet and serves drinks at several hideaways both indoors and within the garden.

Dining/Entertainment: El Abaco Restaurant, which spills over onto an outdoor terrace, serves flavorful international cuisine in fixed-price lunches and dinners costing 2,750 pesetas ($19.50). A bar with a good selection of sherries and whiskies lies nearby.

Services: Room service (available daily from 8am to midnight), laundry/valet, concierge, babysitting.

Facilities: Outdoor swimming pool, car rentals, shopping boutiques.

MODERATE

$ **Hotel Ávila,** Ávila, 3, 11140 Jerez de la Frontera. ☎ **956/33-48-08.** Fax 956/33-68-07. 32 rms (all with bath). A/C TV TEL

Rates: 4,000–5,000 ptas. ($28.40–$35.50) single; 6,000–8,000 ptas. ($42.60–$56.80) double. Breakfast 400 ptas. ($2.80) extra. AE, DC, MC, V. **Parking:** 900 ptas. ($6.40) nearby.

One of the better bargains in Jerez, the Ávila is a modern, three-story building, erected in 1968 and renovated in 1987. In the commercial center of town, it lies near the post office and Plaza del Arenal. Inside, its bedrooms are clean, comfortable, and well maintained.

Hotel Serit, Higueras, 7, 11402 Jerez de la Frontera. ☎ **956/34-07-00.** Fax 956/34-07-16. 35 rms (all with bath). A/C TV TEL

Rates: 4,500 ptas. ($32) single; 6,800 ptas. ($48.30) double. Breakfast 450 ptas. ($3.20) extra. AE, DC, MC, V. **Parking:** 800 ptas. ($5.70).

The modern three-star Hotel Serit, lying near Plaza de la Angustias, offers bedrooms that are well furnished and comfortable—all at a good price. There's a pleasant bar downstairs, plus a modern breakfast lounge. Laundry and room service are provided.

Where to Dine

El Bosque, Alcalde Álvaro Domecq, 26. ☎ **30-33-33.**

Cuisine: SPANISH/INTERNATIONAL. **Reservations:** Required.
Prices: Appetizers 700–1,900 ptas. ($5–$13.50); main courses 1,800–2,500 ptas. ($12.80–$17.80). AE, DC, MC, V.
Open: Lunch, Mon–Sat 1:30–5pm; dinner, Mon–Sat 9pm–midnight.

Lying less than a mile northeast of the city center, the city's most elegant restaurant was established just after World War II. A favorite of the sherry-producing aristocracy, it retains a strong emphasis on bullfighting memorabilia, which make up most of the decoration.

You might order the excellent *rabo de toro* (bull's-tail stew); grilled monkfish brochette; or one of the numerous beef, pork, chicken, and fish dishes. The lemon mousse makes a soothing choice for a dessert, and the restaurant maintains a fine wine list.

$ **Gaitán,** Calle Gaitán, 3. ☎ **34-58-59.**

Cuisine: ANDALUSIAN. **Reservations:** Recommended.

Prices: Appetizers 675–1,995 ptas. ($4.80–$14.20); main courses 850–2,300 ptas. ($6–$16.30). AE, DC, MC, V.

Open: Lunch, daily 1–4:30pm, dinner, Mon–Sat 8:30–11:30pm.

This small restaurant near Puerta Santa María is owned by Juan Hurtado, who has won acclaim for the food served here. Surrounded by walls displaying celebrity photographs, you can enjoy such Andalusian dishes as garlic soup, various stews, duck à la Sevillana, and fried seafood. For dessert, the almond tart is a favorite.

Restaurante Tendido 6, Calle Circo, 10. ☎ **34-48-35.**

Cuisine: SPANISH. **Reservations:** Required.

Prices: Appetizers 550–1,600 ptas. ($3.90–$11.40); main courses 1,400–2,400 ptas. ($9.90–$17). AE, DC, MC, V.

Open: Lunch, Mon–Sat 1–4pm; dinner, Mon–Sat 8–11:30pm.

This combination restaurant and tapas bar has loyal clients who come from many walks of life. The chef creates a dignified regional cuisine that includes grilled rump steak; fish soup; and a wide array of Spanish dishes, including Basque and Castilian. The Tendido is on the south side of Plaza de Toros.

A TAPAS BAR

La Venecia, Calle Larga, s/n. ☎ **33-72-94.**

Opened in 1949 within a 19th-century building, this place has been the preferred choice of generations of *Jerezanos* as the tasca at which to imbibe their sherry. In a somewhat gruff but friendly atmosphere, it is also one of the best places in Jerez to go for tapas, which include meatballs, croquettes, meat-stuffed peppers, or even a bowl of stew. You can make an entire meal of these tapas and do so relatively inexpensively, as they're priced from 175–300 pesetas ($1.20–$2.10). La Venecia is open Monday to Saturday from 7:30am to 11pm.

Easy Excursions

MEDINA SIDONIA

This survivor of the Middle Ages is one of the most unspoiled hillside villages of Spain, about 29 miles (46.5km) east of Cádiz and 22 miles (35.5km) southeast of Jerez de la Frontera. Motorists from Jerez should follow the 440 southeast.

A village that time forgot, Medina Sidonia has cobblestoned streets, tile-roofed white buildings dotting the hillside, a Gothic church, a Moorish gate, and steep alleyways traveled by locals on donkeys. The Arab influence is everywhere. The surrounding countryside is wild and seldom visited. The pockets of fog that sometimes settle over the land will make you think you're on the Yorkshire moors.

From Medina Sidonia, it's a 2½-hour drive to the port city of Algeciras, or you can take the Jerez road back to Seville.

ARCOS DE LA FRONTERA

Twenty miles (32km) east of Jerez de la Frontera, this old Arab town—now a National Historic Monument—was built in the form of an amphitheater. Sitting on a rock and surrounded by the Guadalete River on three sides, it contains many houses that have been hollowed out of this formation. From the old city, there's a high-in-the-clouds view that some visitors consider without rival on the Iberian Peninsula.

The city is filled with whitewashed walls and narrow winding streets that disappear into steps. It holds a lot of historical interest and has a beautiful lake complete with paddleboats and a Mississippi riverboat.

The most exciting attraction is the **view from the principal square,** the Plaza del Cabildo, a rectangular esplanade overhanging a deep river cleft. You can see a Moorish castle, but it is privately owned and cannot be visited by the public. You can, however, visit the main church, located on the main square—the **Iglesia de Santa María,** constructed in 1732, a blend of Gothic, Renaissance, and baroque. Its western front—and its most outstanding architectural achievement—is in Plateresque style. The second major church of town, **Iglesia de San Pedro,** standing on the northern edge of the old barrio (quarter), at the far end of the cliff, is known for its 16th- and 18th-century tower. This church, which grew up on the site of a Moorish fortress, owns works by Zurbarán and Murillo, among others. Check with the tourist office (see below) about gaining admission to these churches, as they are often closed for security reasons. Several art thefts have occurred in the area.

Even if you don't succeed in gaining entrance to the churches, it is reason enough to visit Arcos merely to wander its alleys and view its ruins from the Middle Ages. If you have to return to wherever you're going for the night, stay at least long enough to have a drink in the patio of the parador (recommended below) and take in that monumental view.

Because there is no train service to this little bit of paradise, take the bus from Seville, Cádiz, or Jerez de la Frontera. From Jerez, motorists should follow the 342 east until they see the turnoff for Arcos.

The area code for Arcos de la Frontera is 956. The tourist information office is at Cuesta de Belén (☎ **956/70-22-64**).

Where to Stay and Dine

Parador Casa del Corregidor, Plaza de España, s/n, 11630 Arcos de la Frontera, ☎ **956/70-05-00.** Fax 956/70-11-16. 24 rms (all with bath). A/C MINIBAR TV TEL

Rates: 8,800 ptas. ($62.50) single; 13,000 ptas. ($92.30) double. Breakfast buffet 1,100 ptas. ($7.80) extra. AE, DC, MC, V. **Parking:** Free.

The best place to stay is this government-run parador, in a restored palace in the heart of the old quarter. Built in the 1700s, it was the palace and government seat of the king's magistrate (*corregidor*) in Arcos. From the balconies, there are views of the Valley of Guadalete with its river, plains, and farms. In good weather you can take your meals (try the pork with garlic) on one of these balconies; lunch or dinner costs 3,500 pesetas ($24.90). The decor consists of tiles and antiques. The bedrooms are handsomely furnished and beautifully maintained; perhaps you'll be assigned the one where Charles de Gaulle once stayed.

5 Cádiz

76 miles (122km) S of Seville, 388 miles (625km) SW of Madrid

GETTING THERE • By Train Trains arrive at Cádiz from Seville (a 1½- to 2½-hour trip), Jerez de la Frontera (45 minutes), and Algeciras (3 hours away). The train station is located on Avenida del Puerto (☎ **25-43-01**), on the southeast border of the main port.

• **By Bus** Passengers in transit to or from Madrid usually require a transfer in Seville. Buses in Cádiz arrive at two separate terminals. From Seville (11 per day; 1 1/4 hours); Jerez de la Frontera (8 per day), Málaga, Córdoba, and Granada, buses arrive at the Estación de Comes terminal, Plaza de la Hispanidad, 1 (☎ **21-17-63**), on the north side of town, a few blocks west of the main port. Far less prominent is the terminal run by the Transportes Los Amarillos, Avenida Ramón de Carranza, 31 (☎ **28-58-52**), several blocks to the south, which runs frequent buses to several nearby towns and villages, most of which are of interest only for local residents and workers.

• **By Car** Cádiz is connected to Seville via a wide and fast highway (it's a one-hour drive) and to the other cities of the Mediterranean coast by a road that can at times be busy, especially during weekends and holidays.

ESSENTIALS The area code for Cádiz is 956. The tourist information office is at Calderón de la Barca, 1 (☎ **956/21-13-13**).

The oldest inhabited city in the Western world, founded in 1100 B.C., this now modern, bustling Atlantic port is a kind of Spanish Marseille, a melting pot of Americans, Africans, and Europeans who are docking or passing through. The old quarter teems with local life, little dives, and seaport alleyways through which sailors from many lands wander in search of adventure. But despite its thriving life, the city does not hold major interest for tourists, except for the diverse cultural strains that have helped shape it. Phoenicians, Arabs, Visigoths, Romans, and Carthaginians all passed through Cádiz and left their cultural imprints. Throughout the ages this ancient port city has enjoyed varying states of prosperity, especially after the discovery of the New World.

At the end of a peninsula, Cádiz separates the Bay of Cádiz from the Atlantic, so from numerous sea walls around the town, you have views of the ocean. It was here that Columbus set out on his second voyage.

What to See & Do

Despite its being one of the oldest towns in Europe, Cádiz has few remnants of antiquity. It is still worth visiting, however, especially to wander through the old quarter, which retains a special charm.

Plaza de San Juan de Dios is the most ideal place to sit at a sidewalk café and people watch in the shadow of the neoclassical **Isabellino Ayuntamiento** (Town Hall), with its outstanding chapter house. The **Oratory of San Felipe Neri,** where the Cortés (Parliament) met in 1812 to proclaim its constitution, has an important Murillo (*Conception*) and a history museum. Admission is free, and it's open August through June, daily from noon to 2pm and 5 to 7pm. The **Hospital de Mujeros** (Women's Hospital) has a patio courtyard dating from 1740 and a chapel with El Greco's *Ecstasy of St. Francis.*

Museo de Cádiz, Plaza de Mini, s/n. ☎ **21-43-00.**

This museum, now fully restored, contains one of Spain's most important Zurbarán collections, as well as paintings by Rubens and Murillo (including the latter's acclaimed picture of Christ). The archeology section displays Roman, Carthaginian, and Phoenician finds, while ethnology exhibits include pottery, baskets, textiles, and leather works.

Admission: 250 pesetas ($1.80).

Open: Tues–Sun 9:30am–2pm.

Catedral de Cádiz, Plaza Catedral. ☎ **28-61-54.**

This magnificent 18th-century baroque building by architect Vicente Acero has a neoclassical interior dominated by an outstanding apse. The tomb of Cádiz-born composer Manuel de Falla lies in its splendid crypt; music lovers from all over the world come here to pay their respects. Haydn composed *The Seven Last Words of Our Savior on the Cross* for this cathedral. The treasury/museum contains a priceless collection of Spanish silver; embroidery; and paintings by Spanish, Italian, and Flemish artists.

Admission: 175 ptas. ($1.20) adults; 100 ptas. (70¢) children.

Open: Mon–Sat 10am–1pm.

Where to Stay

Cádiz has a number of budget accommodations, some of which are quite poor. However, for moderate tabs you can afford some of the finest lodgings in the city. Note that rooms are scarce during the February carnival season.

Hotel Atlántico, Duque de Nájera, 9, 11002 Cádiz. ☎ **956/22-69-05.** Fax 956/21-45-82. 147 rms (all with bath), 6 suites. A/C MINIBAR TV TEL

Rates: 10,000 ptas. ($71) single; 12,500–17,000 ptas. ($88.80–$120.70) double; 24,500 ptas. ($174) suite. Breakfast 1,100 ptas. ($7.80) extra. AE, DC, MC, V. **Parking:** 700 ptas. ($5).

Actually a modern resort hotel, this national parador is built on one of the loveliest beaches of the Bay of Cádiz, at the western edge of the old town. The white six-story building has a marble patio, a salon decked out in rattan and cane, and bedrooms that feature balconies with tables and chairs for relaxed ocean viewing. The Atlántico's own swimming pool is surrounded by palm trees. The hotel also boasts a bar and a dining room known for its superb Andalusian cuisine, particularly the seafood. Meals cost from 3,500 pesetas ($24.90).

$ **Regio 1,** Ana de Viya, 11, 11009 Cádiz. ☎ **956/27-93-31.** Fax 956/25-30-09. 44 rms (all with bath). TV TEL

Rates: 4,000 ptas. ($28.40) single; 7,500 ptas. ($53.30) double. Breakfast 525 ptas. ($3.70) extra. AE, DC, MC, V. **Parking:** Free at the nearby Regio 2.

Built in 1978, this hotel rises six stories above a location about a block inland from the harbor and Paseo Marítimo. Bedrooms are simple but airy and comfortable. About half contain air conditioning. Breakfast is the only meal served. The overflow from this hotel is sometimes directed to the hotel's slightly more expensive twin, the Regio 2 (see below), with whom it shares a parking lot.

Regio 2, Andalucía, 79, 11008 Cádiz. ☎ **956/25-30-08.** Fax 956/25-30-09. 45 rms (all with bath), A/C TV TEL

Rates: 4,500 ptas. ($32) single; 8,500 ptas. ($60.40) double. Breakfast 525 ptas. ($3.70) extra. **Parking:** Free.

Business was successful enough in the late 1970s to justify the construction of this five-story twin of an already existing hotel, the Regio 1 (see above). Run by the same management, and sharing some of their staff and amenities in common, it was built in 1981, lies about 200 yards from its twin, and contains air conditioning in each of its simple but pleasant bedrooms. Both lie within a very short walk from the ocean.

Where to Dine

El Faro, Calle San Felix, 15. ☎ **21-10-68.**

Cuisine: SEAFOOD. **Reservations:** Recommended.
Prices: Appetizers 550–1,800 ptas. ($3.90–$12.80); main courses 1,800–4,200 ptas. ($12.80–$29.80). Fixed-price menu 2,100 ptas. ($14.90) AE, DC, MC, V. **Open:** Lunch, daily 1–4:30pm; dinner, daily 8:30–midnight.

Unless you're a devotee of seafood, this might not be your preferred restaurant in Cádiz: There's only a limited selection of meat, and a simple *menú del día* that is favored by local fisherfolk, but the main emphasis is on the array of fresh fish and shellfish available within its large dining room. (There's an additional, much smaller room to the side, usually reserved for groups of local *compadres.*) Established in 1964, and considered the favorite restaurant of many frequent visitors, El Faro occupies the white-walled premises of one of the simple houses near the harborfront in Cádiz's oldest neighborhood. Menu items include fried lamb chops and beefsteak and a long list of seafood, such as seafood soup, roulades of sole with spinach, hake with green sauce, lotte with strips of Serrano ham, lobster, and monkfish.

Evening Entertainment

La Boîte, Edificio Isecotel, Paseo Marítimo, s/n. ☎ **26-13-16.**

Most discos around Cádiz come and go with the season, but this one has operated longer than many of its competitors, attracting with recorded music, and air-conditioning. La Boîte draws a large crowd of Andalusian youth. In the old town on an avenue running alongside Playa de la Victoria, it's open nightly from 10pm to 6am. A beer costs 500 pesetas ($3.60). Entrance costs range from 600–700 pesetas ($4.30–$5).

El Manteca, Mariana de Pineda, 66. ☎ **21-36-03.**

This establishment's decor recalls the bullfight, as does that of many places in Cádiz. Homemade tapas are served, many made with fresh seafood. El Manteca is open Tuesday to Saturday from 8:30am to 10pm; Sunday and Monday, hours are 8:30am to 4pm. Wine costs from 125 pesetas (90¢); tapas from 250–600 pesetas ($1.80–$4.30). **Bus:** 2 or 6.

6 Costa de La Luz

Isla Cristina, one of the coast's westernmost cities, lies 34 miles (55km) W of Huelva, 403 miles (649km) SW of Madrid; Tarifa, at the opposite end of the coast, lies 59 miles (95km) SE of Cádiz, 429 miles (691km) SW of Madrid

GETTING THERE • By Train Huelva, the coast's most prominent city, is serviced by train from Seville (two hours away). From Huelva, trains continue on to Ayamonte and the rest of the Portuguese Algarve.

• By Bus Buses run from Seville several times a day. From Seville, connections can be made to all parts of Spain. From Huelva, about eight buses a day depart for Ayamonte and the Portuguese frontier.

• By Car Huelva is easily reached in about an hour from Seville, 55 miles (88.5km) to the east, via a broad and modern highway, the E-01.

ESSENTIALS The area code for the Costa de la Luz is 959. The tourist information office is in Huelva at Avenida de Alemania, 12 (☎ **959/25-74-03**).

West of Cádiz, near Huelva and the Portuguese frontier, lies the rapidly developing Costa de la Luz (Coast of Light), which hopes to pick up the overflow from Costa del Sol. The Luz coast stretches from the mouth of the Guadiana River, forming the boundary with Portugal, to Tarifa Point on the Straits of Gibraltar. Dotting the coast are long stretches of sand, pine trees, fishing cottages, and lazy whitewashed villages.

The Huelva district forms the northwestern half of Costa de la Luz. The southern half stretches from Tarifa to **Sanlúcar de Barrameda,** the spot from which Magellan, in 1519, embarked on his voyage around the globe. Columbus also made this his home port for his third journey to the New World. Sanlúcar today is widely known in Andalusia for its local sherry, Manzanilla, which you can order at any of the city's wine cellars (bodegas). If you make it to Sanlúcar, you'll find the tourist information office at Calzada de Ejército, Paseo Marítimo (☎ **956/36-61-10**), just one block inland from the beach. Do not count on a great deal of guidance, however. To travel between the northern and southern portions of Costa de la Luz, you must go inland to Seville, since no roads go across the Coto Doñana and the marshland near the mouth of the Guadalquivir.

At **Huelva** a large statue on the west bank of the river commemorates the departure of Christopher Columbus on his third voyage of discovery; and about 4$^1/_2$ miles (7.2km) up on the east bank of the Tinto River, a monument marks the exact spot of his departure. His ships were anchored off this bank while they were being loaded with supplies.

South of the Huelva is the **Monasterio de la Rabida,** Palos de la Frontera (☎ **35-04-11**), in whose little white chapel Columbus prayed for success on the eve of his voyage. Even without its connections to Columbus, the monastery would be worth a visit for its paintings and frescoes. A guide will show you around the Mudéjar chapel, and a large portion of the old monastery, which is open daily from 10am to 1pm and 4 to 7pm. Admission is free, but donations are accepted. The monastery lies on the east bank of the Tinto. Take bus no. 1 from Huelva.

Where to Stay & Dine

Ayamonte was built on the slopes of a hill on which a castle stood. It is full of beach high-rises, which, for the most part, contain vacation apartments for Spaniards in July and August. Judging by their license plates, most of these visitors come from Huelva, Seville, and Madrid, so the Costa de la Luz is more Spanish in flavor than the overrun and more international Costa del Sol.

Ayamonte has clean, wide, sandy beaches, and the waves, for the most part, are calm. Portions of the beaches are even calmer because of sand bars some 55 to 110 yards from the shore, which become virtual islands at low tide. The nearest beaches to Ayamonte are miles away at Isla Canela and Moral.

Accommodations are severely limited along Costa de la Luz in summer, so it's crucial to arrive with a reservation. You can stay at a government-run parador east of Huelva in Mazagón (see below); or at Ayamonte, near the Portuguese frontier. Where you are unlikely to want to stay overnight is in the dreary industrial port of Huelva itself.

Parador Nacional Costa de la Luz, El Castillito, 21400 Ayamonte. ☎ **959/32-07-00.** Fax 959/32-07-00. 54 rms (all with bath). A/C MINIBAR TV TEL **Directions:** From the center of Ayamonte, signs for the parador will lead you up a winding road to the hilltop, about 1/2 mile southeast of the center.

Rates: 8,000 ptas. ($56.80) single; 10,000 ptas. ($71) double. Breakfast 1,100 ptas. ($7.80) extra. AE, DC, MC, V. **Parking:** Free.

The leading accommodation in Ayamonte, this parador opened in 1966 and was completely renovated in 1991. Commanding a sweeping view of the river and the surrounding towns along its banks—don't miss the memorable sunsets here—the parador stands about 100 feet above sea level on the site of the old castle of Ayamonte. Built in a severe modern style, with Nordic-inspired furnishings, it numbers among its facilities a swimming pool, a garden, central heating, a dining room, and a bar. Good regional meals cost from 3,500 pesetas ($24.90). Try, if it's featured, *raya en pimiento* (stingray with red pepper); *calamar relleno* (stuffed squid) is another specialty.

Parador Nacional Cristóbal Colón, Carretera de Matalascañas, s/n, 21130 Mazagón. ☎ **959/53-63-00.** Fax 959/53-62-28. 43 rms (all with bath), 1 suite. A/C MINIBAR TV TEL **Directions:** Exit from Magazón's eastern sector, following the signs to the town of Matalascañas. Take the coast road (highway 442) to the parador.

Rates: 11,600 ptas. ($82.40) single; 14,500 ptas. ($103) double; 20,000 ptas. ($142) suite. Breakfast 1,100 ptas. ($7.80) extra. AE, DC, MC, V. **Parking:** Free.

One of the best accommodations in the area is 14 miles (24km) from Huelva and 3 1/2 miles (6km) from the center of Mazagón. A rambling 1960s structure, the parador has comfortable guest rooms with balconies and terraces overlooking a tranquil, expansive garden and pine groves that slope down to the white-sand beach of Mazagón. Swimmers and sunbathers can also enjoy the large pool. The dining room features two *menús del día*, a Spanish one at 3,200 pesetas ($22.70) and a strictly Andalusian regional one at 3,500 pesetas ($24.90).

7 Ronda

63 miles (101km) NE of Algeciras, 60 miles (97km) W of Málaga, 91 miles (147km) SE of Seville, 367 miles (591km) S of Madrid

GETTING THERE • **By Train** There are three trains daily from Málaga (2 hours), one per day from Seville (3 1/2 hours), and three per day from Granada (3 1/2 hours). Most rail routes into Ronda require a change of train in the railway junction of Bobadilla, several miles to the northeast. Ronda's railway station lies in the western edge of the new city, on the Avenida Andalucía (☎ **287-16-73**).

• **By Bus** There are four buses daily between Ronda and Seville (a 2 1/2 hour drive), and five per day from Málaga (2 1/2 hours). The bus station in Ronda lies on the western edge of the new town, at Avenida Concepción García Redondo, 2 (☎ **87-22-64**).

• **By Car** Five highways converge on Ronda from all parts of Andalusia. All five head through mountainous scenery, but the road south to Marbella, through the Sierra Palmitera, is one of the most winding and dangerous. Driving time to Marbella, depending on your nerves and the traffic, is between 1 and 1 1/2 hours.

ESSENTIALS The area code for Ronda is 95. The tourist information office is at Plaza de España, 1 (☎ **95/287-12-72**).

This little town, high in the Serranía de Ronda Mountains (2,300 feet above sea level), is one of the oldest and most aristocratic places in Spain, but the main tourist attraction is the 500-foot **gorge,** spanned by a Roman stone bridge, Puente San Miguel, over the Guadelevín River. On both sides of this "hole in the earth" are cliff-hanging houses, which look as if—with the slightest push—they would plunge into the chasm.

Ronda is an incredible sight. The road there, once difficult to navigate, is now a wide highway with guard rails. The town and the surrounding mountains were legendary hideouts for bandits and smugglers, but today the Guardia Civil has almost put an end to that occupation.

The gorge divides the town into an older part, the Moorish and aristocratic quarter, and the newer section south of the gorge, built principally after the Reconquest. The old quarter is by far the more fascinating; it contains narrow, rough streets, and buildings with a marked Moorish influence (watch for the minaret). After the lazy resort living of Costa del Sol, a side excursion to Ronda, with its unique beauty and refreshing mountain air, is a tonic.

Ronda is great for the explorer. Local children may attach themselves to you as guides. For a few pesetas it might be worth it to "hire" one, since it's difficult to weave your way in and out of the narrow streets.

What to See & Do

The still-functioning **Baños Arabes** are reached from the turnoff to Puente San Miguel. Dating from the 13th century, the baths have glass roof-windows and hump-shaped cupolas. They are generally open Tuesday to Sunday from 10am to 2pm if restoration has been completed. Admission is free, but you should tip the caretaker who shows you around.

The **Palacio de Mondragón,** El Campillo, was once the private home of one of the ministers to Charles III. Flanked by two Mudéjar towers, it now has a baroque facade. Inside are Moorish mosaics. Posted hours are daily from 8am to 2pm, but be advised that the place is often closed. Admission is free.

The **Casa del Rey Moro,** Marqués de Parada, 17, is misnamed. The House of the Moorish King was actually built in the early 1700s. However, it is believed to have been constructed over Moorish foundations. The interior is closed, but from the garden you can take an underground stairway, called La Mina, which leads you to the river, a distance of 365 steps. Christian slaves cut these steps in the 14th century to guarantee a steady water supply in case Ronda came under siege.

On the same street you'll see the 18th-century **Palacio del Marqués de Salvatierra.** Still inhabited by a private family, this Renaissance-style mansion is open for guided tours. Tours depart every 30 minutes, provided that half a dozen people are present. It's open Monday to Wednesday and Friday and Saturday from 11am to 2pm and 4 to 6:30pm, Sunday from 11am to 1pm. Admission is 200 pesetas ($1.40).

Ronda has the oldest bullring in Spain. Built in the 1700s, **Plaza de Toros** is the setting for the yearly Goyesque Corrida in honor of Ronda native son Pedro Romero, one of the greatest bullfighters of all time. If you want to know more about Ronda bullfighting, head for the **Museo Taurino,** reached through the ring. It is open June through September daily from 10am to 7pm; October through May, daily 10am to 2pm. Admission is 200 pesetas ($1.40).

Exhibits document the exploits of the noted Romero family. Francesco invented the killing sword and the *muleta,* and his grandson, Pedro (1754–1839), killed 5,600 bulls during his 30-year career. Pedro was the inspiration for Goya's famous

Tauromaquia series. There are also exhibits devoted to Cayetano Ordóñez, the matador immortalized by Hemingway in *The Sun Also Rises.*

A NEARBY ATTRACTION Near Benaoján, **Cueva de la Pileta (☎ 16-72-02)**, 15 1/2 miles (25km) southwest of Ronda, plus a 1 1/4 mile (2km) hard climb, has been compared to the Caves of Altamira in northern Spain, where prehistoric paintings were discovered toward the end of the 19th century. In a wild, beautiful area known as the Serranía de Ronda, this cave was discovered in 1905 by José Bullón Lobato, grandfather of the present owners. More than a mile in length and filled with oddly and beautifully shaped stalagmites and stalactites, the cave was found to contain five fossilized human and two animal skeletons.

In the mysterious darkness, prehistoric paintings have been discovered, depicting animals in yellow, red, black, and ochre, as well as mysterious symbols. One of the highlights of the tour is a trip to the "chamber of the fish," containing a wall painting of a great black seal-like creature about three feet long. This chamber, the innermost heart of the cave, ends in a precipice that drops vertically nearly 250 feet.

In the valley just below the cave lives a guide who will conduct you around the chambers, carrying artificial light to illuminate the paintings. Plan to spend at least an hour here. Hours are April through October daily from 9am to 1pm and 4 to 7pm; off-season, daily 10am to 2pm and 4 to 6pm. Admission, including the one-hour tour, is 500 pesetas ($3.60).

You can reach the cave most easily by car from Ronda, but those without private transport can take the train to Benaoján. The cave, whose entrance is at least 4 miles (6.5km) uphill, is located in the rocky foothills of the Sierra de Libar, midway between two tiny villages: Jimera de Libar and Benaoján. The valley that contains the cave is parallel to the valley holding Ronda, so the town of Ronda and the cave are separated by a steep range of hills, requiring a rather complicated detour either to the south or north of Ronda, then a doubling back.

Where to Stay

MODERATE

Hotel Don Miguel, Villanueva, 8. **☎ 95/287-77-22.** Fax 95/287-83-77. 20 rms. A/C TV TEL

Rates: 5,500 ptas. ($39.10) single; 9,000 ptas. ($63.90) double. Breakfast 375 ptas. ($2.70) extra. AE, DC, MC, V. **Parking:** Free. **Closed:** Jan 10–24.

From the narrow street that gives it access, this hotel presents a severely dignified white-fronted facade very similar to that of its neighbors. From the back, however, the hotel looks out over the river gorge of a steep ravine, which adds drama to those bedrooms which overlook it. Set a few steps east of Plaza de España, and composed of several interconnected houses, it offers a vine-strewn patio above the river, a warmly modernized interior accented with exposed brick and varnished pine, and simple but comfortable bedrooms. The establishment's restaurant, Don Miguel, is recommended separately (see below).

Hotel Reina Victoria, Paseo Dr. Fleming, 25, 29400 Ronda. **☎ 95/287-12-40.** Fax 95/287-10-75. 86 rms (all with bath), 2 suites. A/C TV TEL

Rates: 8,500 ptas. ($60.40) single; 13,000 ptas. ($92.30) double; 20,000 ptas. ($142) suite. Breakfast 900 ptas. ($6.40) extra. AE, DC, MC, V. **Parking:** Free.

On the eastern periphery of town, a short walk from the center, this country-style hotel was built in 1906 by an Englishman in honor of his recently departed monarch, Queen Victoria. It's near the bullring, with terraces that hang right over a 490-foot precipice. Hemingway frequently visited the hotel, suggesting that it was ideal for a honeymoon "or if you ever bolt with anyone." But the Reina Victoria is known best as the place where poet Rainer Maria Rilke wrote *The Spanish Trilogy.* His third-floor room has been set aside as a museum, with first editions, manuscripts, photographs, and even a framed copy of his hotel bill. A life-size bronze statue of the poet stands in a corner of the hotel garden.

Bedrooms are big, airy, and comfortable, some with complete living rooms containing sofas, chairs, and tables. Many also have private terraces with garden furniture. The beds are sumptuous, and the bathrooms boast all the latest improvements.

Dining here can be recommended. The food is well prepared, and a set meal costs 3,000 pesetas ($21.30).

$ **Hotel Residencia Polo,** Mariano Soubirón, 8, 29400 Ronda. ☎ **95/287-24-47.** Fax 95/287-24-49. 33 rms (all with bath). TV TEL

Rates: 6,000 ptas. ($42.60) single; 9,350 ptas. ($66.40) double. Breakfast, 550 ptas. ($3.90) extra. AE, DC, MC, V.

In the commercial, modern heart of Ronda, near a large shopping arcade, the Polo is run with professionalism. Its accommodations are pleasantly—not elegantly—decorated and maintained. Bedrooms are spacious, with even the closets and private bathrooms large enough for your needs. The hotel has a bar and restaurant and also offers room service.

BUDGET

Hostal Residencia Royal, Virgen de la Paz, 42, 29400 Ronda. ☎ **95/287-11-41.** 25 rms (all with bath). A/C TEL

Rates: 3,950 ptas. ($28) single; 4,900 ptas. ($34.80) double. AE, DC, MC, V.

An adequate stopover for those who want to spend the night in the modern section of town, the Residencia Royal stands near the old bull arena. Each of the basic guest rooms is reasonably comfortable; rooms in the rear, however, tend to be noisy. No breakfast is served, but clients head for any of the town's several cafés for their morning caffeine.

Where to Dine

Don Miguel Restaurant, Plaza de España, 3. ☎ **95/287-10-90.**

Cuisine: ANDALUSIAN. **Reservations:** Not required.
Prices: Appetizers 400-1900 ptas. ($2.80–$13.50); main courses 900–2,400 ptas. ($6.40–$17). AE, DC, MC, V.
Open: Lunch, Thurs–Tues 12:30–4pm; dinner, Mon–Tues and Thurs–Sat 7:30–11pm.
Closed: Jan 10–24.

At the end of the bridge, facing the river, this restaurant allows visitors views of the upper gorge. It has enough tables set outside on two levels to seat 300 people, and in summer this is a bustling place. The food is good, the restrooms are clean, and the waiters are polite and speak enough English to get by. There is also a pleasant bar for drinks and tapas. Try one of the seafood selections or the house specialty, stewed bull's tail. The restaurant is run by the also recommended Hotel Don Miguel (see above).

$ **Mesón Santiago,** Marina, 3. ☎ **95/287-15-59.**

Cuisine: SPANISH. **Reservations:** Not required.
Prices: Appetizers 600–1,200 ptas. ($4.30–$8.50); main courses 900–2,000 ptas. ($6.40–$14.20); fixed-price menu 1,200 ptas. ($8.50). AE, DC, MC, V.
Open: Lunch only, daily noon–5pm.

Santiago Ruíz Gil operates one of the best budget restaurants in Ronda, serving lunch only. A three-course *menú del día,* with bread and wine, is not a bad deal, considering the price. If you order from the *especialidades de la casa,* count on spending more. Try the *caldo de cocido,* a savory stew with large pieces of meat cooked with such vegetables as garbanzos and white beans, almost a meal in itself. You might also like the tongue cooked in wine and served with potato salad. All the servings are generous. The more expensive à la carte menu is likely to include partridge, lamb, mountain trout, and regional meats. Fresh asparagus and succulent strawberries are also available in season. Mesón Santiago is located near Plaza del Socorro.

Pedro Romero, Virgen de la Paz. ☎ **287-10-61.**

Cuisine: SPANISH/ANDALUSIAN. **Reservations:** Required on day of *corrida.*
Prices: Appetizers 575–2,200 ptas. ($4.10–$15.60); main courses 950–2,400 ptas. ($6.70–$17). AE, DC, MC, V.
Open: Lunch, daily 12:30–4pm; dinner, daily 8–11pm.

Named after Francisco Romero, who codified the rules of bullfighting, this restaurant attracts aficionados of that sport. In fact, it stands opposite the ring and gets extremely busy on bullfighting days, when it's almost impossible to get a table. While seated under a stuffed bull's head, surrounded by photographs of young matadors, you might begin your meal with the classic garlic soup.

8 Granada

258 miles (415km) S of Madrid, 76 miles (122km) NE of Málaga

GETTING THERE • By Plane Iberia flies to Granada once or twice daily from Barcelona and Madrid; several times a week from Palma de Mallorca; three times a week from Valencia; and every Thursday from Tenerife in the Canary Islands. Granada's airport lies 10 miles (16km) west of the center of town, dial **22-75-92.** A convenient Iberia ticketing office lies two blocks east of the cathedral, at Plaza Isabel la Católica, 2. (☎ **22-75-92**). A shuttle bus departs several times daily, connecting this office with the airport.

• By Train Two trains connect Granada with Madrid's Atocha Railway Station daily (taking 6 to 8 hours). Trains run three times per day from Seville (4 hours). Many connections to the rest of Spain are funneled through the railway junction at Bobadilla, a 2-hour ride to the west. The train station lies at Calle Dr. Jaime García Royo, s/n (☎ **23-34-08**), at the end of Avenida Andaluces.

• By Bus Most of Granada's long-distance buses arrive and depart from the Baccona Company's terminal, Avenida Andaluces, 12 (☎ **28-42-51**). Buses arrive from Barcelona four times a day, from Valencia five times a day, and from Madrid four times a day. Buses from closer destinations in Andalusia arrive at the Alsina Graells Company's terminal, Camino de Ronda, 97 (☎ **25-13-58**), a small street radiating out from the larger Calle Emperatriz Eugenia. Buses arrive from Almeria seven times a day; from Córdoba seven times a day; from Málaga about a dozen times a day; and from Seville about eight times a day. Bus no. 11 services both stations.

• **By Car** Granada is connected by superhighway to both Madrid, Malága, and Seville. Driving time from Madrid is about eight hours. Many sightseers prefer to make this drive in two days, rather than one. If that is your plan, Jaén makes a perfect stop-over.

ESSENTIALS • Area Code The area code for Granada is 958.

Information The tourist information office is at Plaza de Mariana Pineda, 10 (☎ **958/22-66-88**).

• **City Layout** Granada lies 2,200 feet above sea level. It sprawls over two main hills, the Alhambra and the Albaicín, and it is crossed by two rivers, the Genil and the Darro.

The Cuesta de Gomérez is one of the most important streets in Granada. It climbs uphill from Plaza Nueva, the center of the modern city, to the Alhambra. At Plaza Nueva the east-west artery, Calle de los Reyes Católicos, goes to the heart of the 19th-century city and the towers of the cathedral. The main street of Granada is the Gran Vía de Colón, the principal north-south artery.

Calle de los Reyes Católicos and the Gran Vía de Colón meet at the circular Plaza de Isabel la Católica, graced by a bronze statue of the queen offering Columbus the Santa Fe agreement, which granted the rights to the epochal voyage to the New World. Going west, Calle de los Reyes Católicos passes near the cathedral and other major sights in the "downtown" section of Granada. The street runs to Puerta Real, which is the commercial hub of Granada, with many stores, hotels, cafés, and restaurants.

This former stronghold of Moorish Spain, in the foothills of the snowcapped Sierra Nevada range, is full of romance and folklore. Washington Irving (*Tales of the Alhambra*) used the symbol of this city, the pomegranate (*granada*), to conjure up a spirit of romance. In fact, the name probably derives from the Moorish word *Karnattah.* Some historians have suggested that it comes from Garnatha Alyehud, the name of an old Jewish ghetto.

Washington Irving may have helped publicize the glories of Granada to the English-speaking world, but in Spain the city is known for its ties to another writer: Federico García Lorca. Born in 1898, this Spanish poet and dramatist, whose masterpiece was *The House of Bernarda Alba,* was shot by soldiers in 1936 in the first months of the Spanish Civil War. During Franco's rule García Lorca's works were banned in Spain, but happily that situation has changed and he is once again honored in Granada, where he grew up.

What to See & Do

Try to spend some time walking around Old Granada. Plan on about three hours to see the most interesting sights.

The **Puerta de Elvira** is the gate through which Ferdinand and Isabella made their triumphant entry into Granada in 1492. It was once a grisly place, with the rotting heads of executed criminals hanging from its portals. The quarter surrounding the gate was the Arab section *(morería,)* until all the Arabs were driven out of the city after the Reconquest.

One of the most fascinating streets in Granada is **Calle de Elvira,** west of which the Albaicín, or old Arab quarter, rises on a hill. In the 17th and 18th centuries, artisans occupied the shops and ateliers along this street and those radiating from it. Come here if you're looking for antiques.

Perhaps the most-walked street in Granada is **Carrera del Darro,** running north along the Darro River. It was discovered by the Romantic artists of the 19th century; many of their etchings (subsequently engraved) of scenes along this street were widely circulated, doing much to spread the fame of Granada throughout Europe. You can still find some of these old engravings in the musty antiques shops. Carrera del Darro ends at **Paseo de los Tristes (Avenue of the Sad Ones),** so named for the funeral cortèges that used to go by here on the way to the cemetery.

On Calle de Elvira stands the **Iglesia de San Andrés,** begun in 1528, with its Mudéjar bell tower. Much of the church was destroyed in the early 19th century, but inside are several interesting pieces of art, both paintings and sculptures. Another old church in this area is the **Iglesia de Santiago,** constructed in 1501 and dedicated to St. James, patron saint of Spain. Built on the site of an Arab mosque, it was damaged in the 1884 earthquake that struck Granada. The church contains the tomb of architect Diego de Siloé (1495–1563), who did much to change the face of Granada.

Despite its name, the oldest square in Granada is **Plaza Nueva,** which, under the Muslims, was the site of the "bridge of the woodcutters." The Darro River was covered over here, but its waters still flow underneath the square (which in Franco's time was named Plaza del General Franco). On the east side of the Plaza Nueva is the 16th-century **Iglesia de Santa Ana,** built by Siloé. Inside its five-nave interior you can see a Churrigueresque reredos and coffered ceiling.

★ **Alhambra,** Palacio de Carlos V. ☎ **22-75-27.**

Later enriched by Moorish occupants into a lavish palace, the Alhambra was originally constructed for defensive purposes on a hilltop's rocky outcropping above the Darro River. The modern city of Granada was built across the river from the Alhambra, about half a mile from its western foundations.

When you first see the Alhambra, you may be surprised by its somewhat somber exterior. You have to walk across the threshold to discover the true delights of this Moorish palace. Tickets are sold in the office next to the uncompleted palace of the Hapsburg king Charles V. Enter through the incongruous 14th-century Gateway to Justice. Most visitors do not need an expensive guide but will be content to stroll through the richly ornamented open-air rooms, with their lacelike walls and their courtyards with fountains. Many of the Arabic inscriptions translate as "Only Allah is conqueror."

The most-photographed part of the palace is the Court of Lions, named after its highly stylized fountain. This was the heart of the palace, the most private section, where the sultan enjoyed his harem. Opening onto the court are the Hall of the Two Sisters, where the favorite of the moment was kept, and the Gossip Room, a factory of intrigue. In the dancing room in the Hall of Kings, entertainment was provided nightly to amuse the sultan's party. Eunuchs guarded the harem but apparently not very well—one sultan, according to legend, beheaded 36 Moorish princes here because one of them was suspected of having been intimate with his favorite.

You can see the room where Washington Irving lived (in the chambers of Charles V) while he was compiling his *Tales of the Alhambra*—the best known of which is the legend of Zayda, Zorayada, and Zorahayda, the three beautiful princesses who fell in love with three captured Spanish soldiers outside "La Torre de las Infantas."

Irving credits the French with saving the Alhambra for posterity, but in fact they were responsible for blowing up seven of the towers in 1812, and it was a Spanish soldier who cut the fuse before more damage could be done. When the Duke of

Wellington arrived a few years later, he chased out the chickens, the gypsies, and the transient beggars who were using the Alhambra as a tenement and set up housekeeping here himself.

Charles V may have been horrified when he saw the cathedral placed in the middle of the great mosque at Córdoba, but he is responsible for architectural meddling here, building a Renaissance palace at the Alhambra—although it's quite beautiful, it's terribly out of place. Today it houses the **Museo Bellas Artes en la Alhambra** (☎ **22-48-43**), open Monday to Friday from 10am to 2pm. It also shelters the **Museo Hispano-Musulman en la Alhambra** (☎ **22-62-79**), devoted to Hispanic-Muslim art.

Admission: Comprehensive ticket, including Alhambra and Generalife (below), 625 ptas. ($4.40); Museo Bellas Artes, 250 ptas. ($1.80); Museo Hispano-Musulman, 250 ptas. ($1.80). Illuminated visits, 625 ptas. ($4.40). Because of the overwhelming crowds, there is a chance you might not be admitted, as the government is forced to limit the number of people who can enter. Your best bet is to go as early as possible, but, even then, some people arriving at 10am may not be admitted until 1:30pm. If you arrive after 4pm, it is unlikely you'll get in at all.

Open: Mar–Oct, daily 9am–8pm; floodlit visits daily 10pm–midnight. Nov–Feb, daily 9am–6pm, floodlit visits daily 8–10pm. **Bus:** 2. **Directions:** Many visitors opt for a taxi or bus no. 2. But some hardy souls enjoy the uphill climb from the cathedral, Plaza de la Lonja, to the Alhambra (signs indicate the winding roads and the steps that lead there). If you decide to walk, enter the Alhambra via the Cuesta de Gomérez, which, although steep, is the quickest and shortest pedestrian route. It begins at Plaza Nueva, about four blocks east of the cathedral, and goes steeply uphill to Puerta de las Granadas, the first of two gates to the Alhambra. The second, another 200 yards uphill, is Puerta de la Justicia, which accepts 90% of the touristic visits to the Alhambra. Here you'll find a large parking lot, lots of gypsies willing and able to guide you (or pick your pocket), lines of taxis, and some souvenir and refreshment stands.

★ **Generalife,** Alhambra, Cerro de Sol. ☎ **22-75-27.**

The sultans used to spend their summers in this palace (pronounced hay-nay-rahl-*ee*-fay), safely locked away with their harems. Built in the 13th century to overlook the Alhambra, the Generalife depends for its glory on its gardens and courtyards. Don't expect an Alhambra in miniature: The Generalife was always meant to be a retreat, even from the splendors of the Alhambra. This palace was the setting for Irving's story of the prince locked away from love.

Admission: Comprehensive ticket, including Alhambra and Generalife, 625 ptas. ($4.40), see above.

Open: See the Alhambra, above. **Directions:** Exit from the Alhambra via Puerta de la Justicia, then circumnavigate the Alhambra's southern foundations until you reach the gardens of the summer palace, where Paseo de los Cipreses quickly leads you to the main building of the Generalife.

★ **Catedral and Capilla Real,** Plaza de la Lonja, Gran Vía de Colón, 5. ☎ **22-29-59.**

This richly ornate Spanish Renaissance cathedral, with its spectacular altar, is one of the country's great architectural highlights, acclaimed for its beautiful facade and gold-and-white decor. It was begun in 1521 and completed in 1714. Behind the cathedral (entered separately) is the flamboyant Gothic Royal Chapel (☎ **22-92-39**), where lie the remains of Queen Isabella and her husband, Ferdinand. It was their wish to be buried in recaptured Granada, not Castile or Aragón. The coffins are remarkably tiny—a reminder of how short they must have been. Accenting the tombs is a wrought-iron grill, a masterpiece. Occupying much larger tombs are the remains of their daughter, Joanna the Mad, and her husband, Philip the Handsome. The cathedral lies in the center of Granada, off two prominent streets, the Gran Vía de Colón and the Calle de San Jerónimo. The Capilla Real abuts the cathedral's eastern edge.

Admission: Cathedral, 250 ptas. ($1.80); chapel, 250 ptas. ($1.80).

Open: Cathedral and chapel, daily 10:30am–1pm and 4–7pm (closes at 6pm in winter).

Albaicín.

This old Arab quarter, on one of the two main hills of Granada, doesn't belong to the city of 19th-century buildings and wide boulevards. It, and the surrounding gypsy caves of Sacromonte, are holdovers from the past. The Albaicín once flourished as the residential section of the Moors, even after the city's reconquest, but it fell into decline when the Christians drove them out. This narrow labyrinth of crooked streets escaped the fate of much of Granada, which was torn down in the name of progress. Fortunately, it has been preserved, as have its cisterns, fountains, plazas, whitewashed houses, villas, and the decaying remnants of the old city gate. Here and there, you can catch a glimpse of a private patio filled with fountains and plants, a traditional elegant way of life that continues.**Bus:** 7 to Calle de Pagés.

Monasterio Cartuja, Carrera Alfacar, s/n. ☎ **20-19-32.**

This 16th-century monastery, off the Albaicín on the outskirts of Granada, is sometimes called "the Christian answer to the Alhambra" because of its ornate stucco and marble and the baroque Churrigueresque fantasy in the sacristy. Its most notable paintings are by Bocanegra, its outstanding sculpture by Mora. The church of this Carthusian monastery was decorated with baroque stucco in the 17th century. Don't miss the 18th-century sacristy, an excellent example of latter-day baroque style. Napoleon's armies killed St. Bruno here, and La Cartuja is said to be the only monument of its kind in the world. Sometimes one of the Carthusian monks will take you on a guided tour.

Admission: 250 ptas. ($1.80).

Open: Daily 10am–1pm and 4–7pm (closes at 6pm in winter). **Bus:** No. 8 from cathedral.

Casa-Museo Federico García Lorca, Virgen Blanca, 6, Fuentevaqueros. ☎ **51-64-53.**

Poet and dramatist Federico García Lorca spent many happy summers with his family here at their vacation home. He had moved to Granada in 1909, a dreamy-eyed schoolboy, and he was endlessly fascinated with its life, including the Alhambra and the gypsies, whom he was later to describe compassionately in his *Gypsy Ballads.* You can look out at the Alhambra from a balcony of the house, which is decorated with green trim and grillwork and filled with family memorabilia, including furniture and portraits. Visitors may inspect the poet's upstairs bedroom and see his oak desk, stained

IMPRESSION

One should remember Granada as one should remember a sweetheart who has died.
—Federico García Lorca

with ink. Look for the white stool that he carried to the terrace to watch the sun set over Granada. The house lies in the Fuentevaqueros section of Granada, near the airport.

Admission: 250 ptas. ($1.80).

Open: Tues–Sun, mandatory guided tours at 10am, 11am, 1pm, 5pm, 6pm, and 7pm.

Casa Museo de Manuel de Falla, Antequeruela Alta, 11. ☎ **22-94-21.**

The famous Spanish composer Manuel de Falla, known for his strongly individualized works, came to live in Granada in 1919, hoping to find a retreat and inspiration. He moved into a *carmen* (local dialect for a small white house) just below the Alhambra, and in time befriended García Lorca. In 1922 on the grounds of the Alhambra, they staged the Cante Jondo Festival, the purest expression of flamenco. Today visitors can walk through the gardens of the man who wrote such works as *Nights in the Gardens of Spain* and see his collection of handcrafts and ceramics, along with other personal memorabilia.

Admission: Free.

Open: Tues–Sat 10am–3pm.

Baños Arabes, Carrera del Darro, 31. No phone.

These Arab baths were called by the Moors the "baths of the walnut tree." Among the oldest buildings still standing in Granada, and among the best-preserved Muslim baths in Spain, they predate the Alhambra. Supposedly Visigothic and Roman building materials went into their construction. It is considered remarkable that they escaped destruction during the reign of the so-called Catholic Kings (Ferdinand and Isabella).

Admission: Free.

Open: Daily 9am–6pm.

Casa de Castril, Museo Arqueológico, Carrera del Darro, 41. ☎ **22-56-40.**

This building has always been considered one of the handsomest Renaissance palaces in Granada. The Plateresque facade of 1539 has been attributed to Diego de Siloé. In 1869 it was converted into a museum with a collection of artifacts found in the area.

Admission: 250 ptas. ($1.80).

Open: Tues–Sat 10am–2pm. **Bus:** 7.

SHOPPING

The Alcaicería, once the Moorish silk market, is next to the cathedral in the lower city. The narrow streets of this rebuilt village of shops are filled with vendors selling

In Their Footsteps

Federico García Lorca (1898–1936). The most written-about Spanish writer since Cervantes, this playwright, poet, and musician was brutally murdered by Nationalist soldiers during the Spanish Civil War. A tortured homosexual born in Granada, he worked in vagabond theater called *La Barraca.* In 1928, he created his masterpiece *Gypsy Ballads.* He visited New York that year and wrote two famous works, *Nueva York* and *The Odes to the King of Harlem. The House of Bernardo Alba* brought him world fame. Lorca today, next to Cervantes, is the most translated Spanish writer of all time.

Favorite Haunt Huerta de San Vicente, Granada.

the arts and crafts of Granada province. For the souvenir hunter, the Alcaicería offers one of the most splendid assortments in Spain of tiles, castanets, and wire figures of Don Quixote chasing windmills. Lots of Spanish jewelry can be found here, comparing favorably with the finest Toledan work. For the window shopper, in particular, it makes a pleasant stroll.

EXPENSIVE

Hotel Alhambra Palace, Peña Partida, 2. 18009 Granada. ☎ **958-22-14-68.**
Fax 958/22-64-04. 131 rms, 13 suites. A/C MINIBAR TV TEL **Bus:** 2.

Rates: 14,115 ptas. ($100.20) single; 17,600 ptas. ($125) double; 27,015 ptas. ($191.80) suite. Breakfast 1,150 ptas. ($8.20) extra. AE, DC, MC, V. **Parking:** Free.

Evoking a Moorish fortress, complete with a crenellated roofline, a crowning dome, geometric tilework, and a suggestion of a minaret, this legendary hotel is a good choice. It was built in 1910 in a sort of Mudéjar Revival style. It sits in a shady, secluded spot, midway up the slope between the Alhambra extras, including private baths. Fixed-price lunches or dinners cost around 3,500 pesetas ($24.90).

Hotel Carmen, Acera del Darro 62, 18009 Granada. ☎ **958/25-83-00.**
Fax 958/25-64-62. 272 rms, 11 suites. A/C MINIBAR TV TEL

Rates: 14,650 ptas. ($104) single; 19,220 ptas. ($136.50) double; 35,000–65,000 ptas. ($248.50–$461.50) suite. Breakfast 1,200 ptas. ($8.50) extra. AE, DC, MC, V. **Parking:** 1,500 ptas. ($10.70).

Located about half a mile south of the cathedral on a wide boulevard central to the city's business district, this 1992 hotel offers good service and clean and decent accommodations, each with its own balcony and private bath. The public rooms include lots of polished marble and comfortable sofas scattered throughout a variety of rooms devoted to reading, card playing or socializing.

Dining/Entertainment: There's a dignified modern restaurant here that serves three-course fixed-price lunches and dinners at 2,500 pesetas ($17.80), as well as a shiny cafeteria for drinks, snacks, and coffee-shop–style food. The Bar Inglés serves drinks amid hardwood paneling, leather upholstery, and patterned fabrics.

Services: Laundry, concierge, babysitting, room service.

Facilities: Disco, car rentals, business center, shopping boutiques, outdoor swimming pool.

Hotel Granada Center, Avenida Fuentenueva, s/n, 18002 Granada. ☎ **958/20-50-00.**
Fax 958/28-96-96. 165 rms (all with bath), 7 suites. A/C MINIBAR TV TEL

Rates: Mon–Thurs 15,000 ptas. ($106.50) single, 18,700 ptas. ($132.80) double. Fri–Sun 7,500 ptas. ($53.30) single; 8,800 ptas. ($62.50) double. Suites 55,000 ptas. ($390.50) throughout the week and weekend. Breakfast 1,200 ptas. ($8.50) extra. **Parking:** 1,300 ptas. ($9.20). AE, DC, MC, V.

One of the most recommendable modern hotels in Granada opened in 1992 adjacent to the University. Its six-story design allowed its architects to create a marble-floored, glass-covered atrium at its center, where elevators rise like glass cages against one wall, and potted plants and armchairs are bathed in natural light from above. Bedrooms are comfortable, monochromatically decorated in neutral tones of beige and earth tones, with ample use of postmodern furniture and slabs of polished stone, especially in the bathrooms. There's a hairdresser and in-house garage, a bar, conference facilities, and a discreetly formal restaurant, Al Zagal, serving Andalusian and international food. Meals begin at around 3,500 pesetas ($24.90).

Hotel Princesa Ana, Constitución 37, 18012 Granada. ☎ **958/28-74-47.** Fax 958/27-39-54. 59 rms, 2 suites. A/C MINIBAR TV TEL

Rates: 11,500 ptas. ($81.70) single; 17,900 ptas. ($127.10) double; 28,500 ptas. ($202.40) suite. Breakfast 1,100 ptas. ($7.80) extra. AE, DC, MC, V. **Parking:** 1,000 ptas. ($7.10).

Set midway between the railway station and the Plaza de Toros, about 1½ miles (2.5km) northwest of the Alhambra, this hotel welcomes guests into an interior sheathed with marble and decorated in tones of soft pink and white. Although it has been supplanted by newer four-star hotels since its construction in 1989, it still maintains a well-managed allure with foreign visitors and business travelers. On the premises are an intimate bar, plus a restaurant (La Princesa Ana) and an uncomplicated cafeteria. Frequent clients do not regret the lack of a swimming pool here because of the resulting cost savings, which are passed on in the form of lower overnight rates.

MODERATE

Hotel Melía Granada, Angel Ganivet, 7, 18009 Granada. ☎ **958/22-74-00,** or toll free in the U.S. **800/336-3542.** Fax 958/22-74-03. 188 rms, 9 suites. A/C MINIBAR TV TEL

Rates: 10,000 ptas. ($71) single; 12,500 ptas. ($88.80) double; 26,300 ptas. ($186.70) suite. Breakfast 1,250 ptas. ($8.90) extra. AE, DC, MC, V. **Parking:** 1,300 ptas. ($9.20).

A modern and efficient place run by the Melía chain, about five blocks southeast of the Ayuntamiento (Town Hall), this hotel offers a comfortable format with welcome air conditioning throughout both the public rooms and guest rooms. Each room contains a private bath. Its street level is punctuated with old-fashioned arcades; once inside, you'll find a glossy and contemporary world of clean comfort, soothing monochromes, and efficient service.

Dining/Entertainment: The restaurant Mulhacen, featuring international cuisine, serves fixed-price lunches and dinners priced at 2,600 pesetas ($18.50). There's also a bar.

Services: 24-hour room service, concierge, laundry service.

Facilities: Sauna and health club, hairdresser/barber, car rentals, shopping boutiques.

Hotel Rallye, Camino de Ronda, 107, 18003 Granada. ☎ **958/27-28-00.** Fax 958/27-28-62. 79 rms (all with bath). A/C MINIBAR TV TEL **Bus:** 1, 5.

Rates: 10,800 ptas. ($76.70) single; 12,500 ptas. ($88.80) double. Buffet-style breakfast 1,250 ptas. ($8.90) extra. AE, DC, MC, V. **Parking:** 1,100 ptas. ($7.80)

Some local residents designate this as one of the best hotels in town, and a relatively good value for the price. Originally built as a three-star hotel in 1964, it was thoroughly upgraded into a four-star format in 1990, and today rises five light-green stories above the neighborhood which surrounds it. It lies within a 15-minute walk of the cathedral, on the northern perimeter of Granada's urban center. Bedrooms are comfortable and well maintained, with light-green and white color schemes. The in-house restaurant, the Rallye, serves well-prepared meals that average around 3,000 pesetas ($21.30) each.

Hotel Saray, Tierno Galván, s/n, 18006 Granada. ☎ **958/13-00-09.** Fax 958/12-91-61. 195 rms (all with bath), 8 suites. A/C MINIBAR TV TEL

Rates (including breakfast): Sept–June, 10,000 ptas. ($71) single; 15,000 ptas. ($106.50) double. July–Aug 7,400 ptas. ($52.50) single, 9,800 ptas. ($69.60) double. Suites 21,000 ptas. ($149.10) throughout the year. AE, DC, MC, V. **Parking:** 1,100 ptas. ($7.80).

Set within a ten-minute walk south of Granada's historic center, this hotel rises seven salmon-colored stories, offering a view of the Sierra Nevada Mountains from some of its upper floors. Built in 1991, it maintains carefully designed bedrooms whose color scheme varies from one floor to another, eventually incorporating Andalusian blues, oranges, and terra-cottas. There's a bar near the reception area, which is sheathed, like many of the other public areas, with pale orange-pink marble, and a lobby-level restaurant, the Saray, where meals usually average around 3,500 pesetas ($24.90) each. The hotel maintains its own outdoor swimming pool for use during the midsummer months.

INEXPENSIVE

Hotel Guadalupe, Alijares, s/n, 18009 Granada. ☎ **958/22-34-24.** Fax 958/22-37-98. 43 rms (all with bath). A/C MINIBAR TV TEL **Bus:** 2.

Rates: 8,420 ptas. ($59.80) single; 10,399 ptas. ($73.80) double. Breakfast 600 ptas. ($4.30) extra. AE, DC, MC, V. **Parking:** Free (if available) on nearby streets.

This four-story building, set beside an inclined road leading up to the Alhambra, stands just above the older and more famous Washington Irving Hotel, which has seen better days. It was built in 1969, but with its thick stucco walls, rounded arches, and jutting beams, it seems older. The last renovation was in 1993. The comfortably furnished bedrooms overlook the Alhambra. There's a fifth-floor à la carte restaurant, plus a pleasant bar in the lobby.

Hotel Residencia Cóndor, Constitución, 6, 18012 Granada. ☎ **958/28-37-11.** Fax 958/28-38-50. 104 rms (all with bath). A/C TV TEL **Bus:** 6, 8, 9, or 10.

Rates: 6,500 ptas. ($46.20) single; 9,800 ptas. ($69.60) double. Breakfast 700 ptas. ($5) extra. AE, DC, MC, V. **Parking:** 1,000 ptas. ($7.10).

The attractive 1987 design of this hotel helps make it one of Granada's best in its price range. It's in the center of town, a five-minute walk from the Alhambra and the cathedral. Many of the pleasant bedrooms have terraces, and all have light-grained contemporary furniture. Breakfast is the only meal served.

Hotel Victoria, Puerta Real, 3, 18005 Granada. ☎ **958/25-77-00.** Fax 958/26-31-08. 66 rms (all with bath), 3 suites. A/C TV TEL

Rates: 7,600 ptas. ($54) single; 10,800 ptas. ($76.70) double; 18,000 ptas. ($127.80) suite. Breakfast 625 ptas. ($4.40) extra. AE, DC, MC, V. **Parking:** 1,300 ptas. ($9.20).

Hotel Victoria, in the heart of Granada, has long been a favorite. Its domed tower and elegant detailing around each window evoke 19th-century Paris. You'll enter a circular salmon-and-cream marble lobby. The upper hallways have intricate geometric tilework, and on the second floor there's an American bar with Ionic columns, as well as an attractively formal dining room. Many of the guest rooms have reproductions of antiques and walls upholstered in shades of terra cotta.

BUDGET

Hotel América, Real de la Alhambra, 53, 18009 Granada. ☎ **958/22-74-71.** Fax 958/22-74-70. 13 rms, 1 suite (all with bath). TEL **Bus:** 2.

Rates: 8,000 ptas. ($56.80) single; 9,000 ptas. ($63.90) double; 13,000 ptas. ($92.30) suite. Breakfast 800 ptas. ($5.70) extra. AE, DC, MC, V. **Closed:** Nov–Feb.

Located within the ancient Alhambra walls, this is one of the small hotels of Granada. Walk through the covered entryway of this former villa into the shady patio that's lively yet intimate, with large trees, potted plants, and ferns. Other plants cascade down the white plaster walls and entwine with the ornate grillwork. Garden chairs and tables are set out for home-cooked Spanish meals. The living room of this homey little retreat is graced with a collection of regional decorative objects; some of the bedrooms have Andalusian reproductions. Meals cost from 2,000 pesetas ($14.20).

Macía, Plaza Nueva, 4, 18010 Granada. ☎ **958/22-75-36.** Fax 958/22-35-75. 44 rms (all with bath). TV TEL

Rates: 4,600 ptas. ($32.70) single; 6,900 ptas. ($49) double. Breakfast 530 ptas. ($3.80) extra. AE, DC, MC, V. **Parking:** 1,300 ptas. ($9.20).

An attractive 1970s hotel at the bottom of the hill leading to the Alhambra, the Macía is a real bargain for what should be a three-star hotel. All the guest rooms have heating and are clean and functional; about half have air conditioning. Breakfast is the only meal served.

Where to Dine

EXPENSIVE

Carmen de San Miguel, Plaza de Torres Bermejas, 3. ☎ **22-67-23.**

Cuisine: INTERNATIONAL. **Reservations:** Recommended.
Prices: Appetizers 750–2,200 ptas. ($5.30–$15.60); main courses 2,000–3,100 ptas. ($14.20–$22); three-course fixed-price *menú del día* 5,475–6,375 ptas. ($38.90–$45.30). AE, DC, MC, V.
Open: Lunch, Mon–Sat 1:30–4:30pm; dinner, Mon–Sat 9–11:30pm.

Set on the sloping incline leading up to the Alhambra, this likable restaurant offers spectacular views over the city center. Proud of its glassed-in dining room and patio-style terrace whose banks of flowers are changed seasonally, the restaurant serves specialties that include *rabo de toro* (stewed oxtail), an array of such fish dishes as grilled hake and well-seasoned zarzuela, and a shoulder of lamb (*paletilla de cordero*) stuffed with pine nuts and herbs. The wines here derive from throughout the country, with a strong selection of riojas.

Parador Nacional San Francisco, Real de la Alhambra. ☎ **22-14-40.**

Cuisine: SPANISH. **Reservations:** Required. **Bus:** 2.
Prices: Appetizers 950–1,500 ptas. ($6.70–$10.70); main courses 1,800–2,400 ptas. ($12.80–$17); fixed-price menu 3,500 ptas. ($24.90). AE, DC, MC, V.
Open: Lunch, daily 1–4pm; dinner, daily 8–11pm.

Even if you can't afford to stay at this luxurious parador—the most famous in Spain—consider a meal here. The dining room is spacious, the service is polite, and you gaze upon the rose gardens and a distant view of the Generalife. The same set menu—which changes daily—is repeated in the evening, although you can always order à la carte.

At this 16th-century convent built by the Reyes Católicos, you get not only atmosphere, but also a cuisine that features regional dishes of Andalusia and Spanish national specialties. Lunch is the preferred time to dine here, because the terrace overlooking the palace is open then. A light outdoor lunch menu of sandwiches and salads can be ordered on the à la carte menu if you don't want to partake of the heavy major Spanish repast in the heat of the day. The lighter meal will cost from 1,800 pesetas ($12.80).

Restaurante Cunini, Plaza de la Pescadería, 14. ☎ **25-07-77.**

Cuisine: SEAFOOD. **Reservations:** Recommended.
Prices: Appetizers 500–1,300 ptas. ($3.60–$9.20); main courses 1,600–2,600 ptas. ($11.40–$18.50); fixed-price menu 2,400 ptas. ($17). AE, DC, MC, V.
Open: Lunch, Tues–Sun noon–4pm; dinner, Tues–Sun 8pm–midnight.

The array of seafood specialties served at Cunini, perhaps a hundred selections, extends even to the tapas served at the long stand-up bar. Many guests move on after a drink or two, to the paneled ground-floor restaurant, where the cuisine reflects the whole of Spain. Meals often begin with soup; such as sopa Cunini or sopa sevillana (with ham, shrimp, and whitefish). Also popular is a deep fry of small fish called a *fritura Cunini,* with other specialties including rice with seafood, zarzuela, smoked salmon, and grilled shrimp. Plaza de la Pescadería is adjacent to the Gran Vía de Colón.

★ **Ruta del Valleta,** Carretera de la Sierra Nevada, Km 5.5, Cenés de la Vega. ☎ **48-61-34.**

Cuisine: ANDALUSIAN/INTERNATIONAL. **Reservations:** Recommended.
Prices: Appetizers 1,500–3,000 ptas. ($10.70–$21.30); main courses 2,500–3,200 ptas. ($17.80–$22.70). Fixed-price menu 4,000 ptas. ($28.40). AE, DC, MC, V.
Open: Lunch, daily 1–4:30pm; dinner, Mon–Sat 8pm–midnight.

Despite its origins in 1976 as an unpretentious roadhouse restaurant, this place rapidly evolved into what is usually acclaimed as the best restaurant in or around Granada. It lies within the hamlet of Cenés de la Vega, about 3½ miles northwest of Granada's center, and contains six dining rooms of various sizes, each decorated with a well-planned mixture of English and Andalusian furniture and accessories. (These include a worthy collection of handpainted ceramics from the region, many of which hang from the ceilings.)

Its owners are a pair of Granada-born brothers, Miguel and José Pedraza, who direct a well-intentioned staff in impeccable service rituals. Menu items change with the seasons, but are likely to include roast suckling pig, roasted game birds such as pheasant and partridge often served with Rioja wine sauce; preparations of fish and shellfish, including lotte with Andalusian herbs and strips of Serrano ham; filet steak in a morel-studded cream sauce; and a dessert specialty of frozen rice pudding on a bed of warm chocolate sauce. The wine list is said to be the most comprehensive in the region.

MODERATE

Chikito, Plaza del Campilio, 9. ☎ **22-33-64.**

Cuisine: SPANISH. **Reservations:** Recommended. **Bus:** 1, 2, or 7.
Prices: Appetizers 650–1,200 ptas. ($4.60–$8.50); main courses 1,600–1,900 ptas. ($11.40–$13.50); fixed-price menu 1,800 ptas. ($12.80). AE, DC, MC, V.
Open: Lunch, Thurs–Tues 1–4pm; dinner, Thurs–Tues 8–11:30pm.

Chikito sits across the street from the famous tree-shaded square where García Lorca met with other members of El Rinconcillo (The Little Corner), a dozen young men considered the best and the brightest in the 1920s, when they brought a brief but dazzling cultural renaissance to their hometown. The café where they met has now changed its name, but it's the same building. The present-day Chikito is both a bar and a restaurant. In fair weather, guests enjoy drinks and snacks on tables placed in the square; in winter they retreat inside to the tapas bars. There is also a complete restaurant facility, offering *sopa sevillana,* shrimp cocktail, Basque hake, baked tuna, ox tail, *zarzuela* (seafood stew), grilled swordfish, and Argentine-style veal steak.

Restaurante Sevilla, Calle Oficios, 12. ☎ **22-88-62.**

Cuisine: SPANISH/INTERNATIONAL. **Reservations:** Recommended.
Prices: Appetizers 750–2,000 ptas. ($5.30–$14.20); main courses 850–2,800 ptas. ($6–$19.90); fixed-price menus 2,800–4,800 ptas. ($19.90–$34.10). AE, DC, MC, V.
Open: Lunch, daily 1–4pm; dinner, Mon–Sat 8–11pm.

Attracting a mixed crowd of all ages, the Sevilla is definitely *típico,* with an upbeat elegance. In the past, you might have seen El Cordobés (when he was Spain's leading bullfighter), Brigitte Bardot, or even Andrés Segovia dining here. Even before them, the place had been discovered by García Lorca, a patron in the 1930s, and Manuel de Falla. My most recent meal here included gazpacho, Andalusian veal, and dessert (selections included caramel custard and fresh fruit), plus bread and the wine of Valdepeñas. To break the gazpacho monotony, try *sopa virule,* made with pine nuts and chicken breasts. For a main course, I recommend the *cordero à la pastoril* (lamb with herbs and paprika). The best dessert is bananas flambé. You can dine inside, where it is pleasantly decorated, or have a meal on the terrace. Sevilla also has a bar. You'll find the place in the center of town opposite the Royal Chapel, near Plaza Isabel la Católica.

INEXPENSIVE

$ **Galerías Preciados,** Carrera del Genil, s/n. ☎ **22-35-83.**

Cuisine: SPANISH. **Reservations:** Not required.
Prices: Fixed-price menu 1,200 ptas. ($8.50). AE, DC, MC, V.
Open: Tues–Sun 10am–8pm.

You can get one of the best lunches in Spain in any Galerías Preciados department store, and the one in Granada is no exception. For shoppers in a rush, it offers an express menu that is a bargain. The meal begins with soup, followed by a main course such as breast of chicken and french fries, and also bread and wine (or beer or mineral water).

$ **Mesón Andaluz,** Calle Elivra, 17. ☎ **25-86-61.**

Cuisine: ANDALUSIAN/INTERNATIONAL. **Reservations:** Not required.
Prices: Appetizers 650–1,200 ptas. ($4.60–$8.50); main courses 950–1,600 ptas. ($6.70–$11.40); fixed-price menus 1,000–2,800 ptas. ($7.10–$19.90). AE, DC, MC, V.
Open: Lunch, Wed–Mon 1–4pm; dinner, Wed–Mon 7:30–11:30pm. **Closed:** Feb.

Two blocks east of the cathedral, the Mesón Andaluz is the best pick on this street of budget restaurants. It's decorated in typical Andalusian style, and you get efficient and polite service along with good inexpensive food. A menu, printed in English, offers selections such as hake stew, rabbit hunter's style, brains Roman style, fried chicken with garlic, and, to finish off, a whisky ice-cream tart.

Mesón Antonio, Ecce Homo, 6. ☎ **22-95-99.**

Cuisine: SPANISH. **Reservations:** Not accepted.
Prices: Appetizers 600–700 ptas. ($4.30–$5); main courses 1,100–1,500 ptas. ($7.80–$10.70). AE, MC, V.
Open: Lunch, Mon–Sat 2–3:30pm; dinner, Mon–Sat 9–10:30pm. **Closed:** July–Aug.

This appealing and unpretentious restaurant, established in 1980, lies one floor above street level within an unassuming 1740s house whose address sometimes requires a bit of looking. (The narrow street on which it's found lies a few steps from the landmark Campo del Príncípe.) You'll traverse a communal patio before climbing a flight of stairs to reach the simply decorated dining room. At least some of the specialties served here are prepared in wood-burning ovens. These might include roasted lamb in local herbs, seafood zarzuela, several different versions of steaks, and such vegetables as fresh asparagus and roasted leeks au gratin.

La Nueva Bodega, Cetti Merlem, 9. ☎ **22-59-34.**

Cuisine: IBERIAN. **Reservations:** Not required.
Prices: *Platos combinados* 800–1,200 ptas. ($5.70–$8.50); fixed-price menu 750 ptas. ($5.30); appetizers 350–850 ptas. ($2.50–$6); main courses 650–1,500 ptas. ($4.60–$10.70). AE, MC, V.
Open: Lunch, daily 1–4pm; dinner, daily 8pm–midnight.

This place seems to be everyone's favorite budget restaurant in Granada. You can enjoy both cafeteria and restaurant service and even order food at the bar, which is cheaper than sitting at a table. The restaurant and cafeteria specialize in platos combinados (combination plates). This doesn't mean that you get everything on one plate. You might be served chicken soup, followed by an omelet, then swordfish Milanese style, along with bread and a simple dessert. In addition, the restaurant offers a fixed-price menu that is both filling and well prepared. Specialties are from not only Andalusia but all of Iberia, including Portugal.

Polinarío, Real de la Alhambra, 3. ☎ **22-29-91.**

Cuisine: SPANISH. **Reservations:** Not required. **Bus:** 2.
Prices: *Platos combinados* 900–1,100 ptas. ($6.40–$7.80); luncheon buffet 1,300 ptas. ($9.20). No credit cards.
Open: Lunch only, daily 10am–4pm; bar daily 9am–7pm.

Although its food is usually considered somewhat ordinary, this simple restaurant is one of only three restaurants within the walled confines of the Alhambra. (Another is the dining room within the local parador, which, while preferable, is also more expensive.) The Polinarío enjoys an enviable position within a very old building across from the Palace of Carlos V, and, as such, does a thriving lunch business every day with participants of organized tours. By the end of a hot day, the luncheon buffet might be a bit fatigued, but the Spanish cooking is adequate, and usually includes a selection of salads, soups, meats, and desserts.

Evening Entertainment

THE GYPSY CAVES OF SACROMONTE These inhabited gypsy caves are the subject of much controversy. Admittedly, they are a tourist trap, one of the most obviously commercial and shadowy rackets in Spain. Still, the caves are a potent enough attraction, if you follow some rules.

Once thousands of gypsies lived on the "Holy Mountain," so named because of several Christians martyred here. However, many of the caves were heavily damaged in the floodlike rains of 1962, forcing hundreds of the occupants to seek shelter elsewhere. Nearly all the gypsies remaining are in one way or another involved with tourism. (Some don't even live here—they commute from modern apartments in the city.)

When evening settles over Granada, loads of visitors descend on these caves near the Albaicín, the old Arab section. In every cave you'll hear the rattle of castanets and the strumming of guitars, while everybody in the gypsy family struts his or her stuff. Popularly known as the *zambra,* this is intriguing entertainment only if you have an appreciation of the grotesque. Whenever a gypsy boy or girl comes along with genuine talent, he or she is often grabbed up and hustled off to the more expensive clubs. Those left at home can be rather pathetic in their attempts to entertain.

One of the main reasons for going is to see the caves themselves. If you're expecting primitive living, you may be in for a surprise—many are quite comfortable, with conveniences like telephones and electricity. Often they are decorated with copper and ceramic items—and the inhabitants need no encouragement to sell them to you.

If you want to see the caves, you can walk up the hill by yourself. Your approach will already be advertised before you get there. Attempts will be made to lure you inside one or another of the caves—and to get money from you. Alternatively, you can book an organized tour, arranged by one of the travel agencies in Granada. Even at the end of one of these group outings—with all expenses theoretically paid in advance—there is likely to be an attempt by the cave-dwellers to extract more money from you. As soon as the zambra ends, hurry out of the cave as quickly as possible. Many readers have been critical of these tours.

During the zambra, refuse to accept a pair of castanets, even if offered under the friendly guise of having you join in the fun. If you accept them, the chances are that you'll later be asked to pay for them. Buying anything in these caves is not recommended. Leave your jewelry at your hotel and don't take more money than you're prepared to lose.

A visit to the caves is almost always included as part of the morning and (more frequently) afternoon city tours offered every day by such companies as **Grana Vision** (☎ **20-98-34**). Night tours of the caves (when the caves are at their most eerie, most evocative, and, unfortunately, most larcenous) are usually offered only to those who can assemble 10 or more persons into a group. This might have changed by the time of your visit, so a phone call to a reputable tour operator, such as Grana Vision, might reveal newly developed options which are available.

FLAMENCO The best flamenco show in Granada is staged at **Jardines Neptuno**, Calle Arabial, s/n (☎ **25-11-12**), nightly at 10:15. The acts are a bit racy, even though they have been toned down considerably for today's audiences. In addition to flamenco, performers attired in regional garb do folk dances and give guitar concerts. The show takes place in a garden setting. There's a high cover charge of 3,000 pesetas ($21.30), but it includes a drink that you can nurse all evening. An additional beer costs 300 pesetas ($2.10). It's best to take a taxi here.

10

The Costa del Sol

NOWHERE IS THE SPANISH TOURIST BOOM MORE EVIDENT THAN ON THE COSTA DEL Sol. The mild winter climate and almost-guaranteed sunshine in summer have made this razzle-dazzle stretch of Mediterranean shoreline a year-round attraction. It begins at the western frontier harbor city of Algeciras and stretches east to the port city of Almería. Sandwiched between these two points is a steep, rugged coastline, with poor-to-fair beaches, set against the Sierra Nevada. You'll find sandy coves, whitewashed houses, olive trees, lots of new apartment houses, fishing boats, golf courses, souvenir stands, fast-food outlets, and a widely varied flora—both human and vegetable.

From June through October the coast is mobbed, so make sure that you've nailed down a reservation. And keep in mind that October 12 is a national holiday—visitors should make doubly sure of their reservations at this time. At other times, innkeepers are likely to roll out the red carpet.

Many restaurants close around October 15 for a much-needed vacation. Remember, too, that many supermarkets and other facilities are closed on Sunday.

Seeing the Costa del Sol

GETTING THERE Visitors to the Costa del Sol arriving by **plane** fly into Málaga on both scheduled and charter flights. This airport offers a network of domestic air links with the rest of Spain.

Málaga is linked by RENFE to **rail** connections from all the major Spanish cities, including Granada, Seville, Barcelona, and Madrid. From Málaga airport, there is local train service to take you to the resort of Fuengirola in the west, stopping at Benalmadena (near Torremolinos) and Los Boliches. These trains run daily every 30 minutes between 6am and 11pm.

It's also possible to take a **bus** to the Costa del Sol from all major cities in Spain. From Málaga, bus links to all satellite resorts are available.

By **car,** the main highway from the north to Andalusia is the N-IV from Madrid to Cádiz, via Córdoba and Seville (see Chapter 9). Once at Cádiz, cut east along the coastal road, the E-25, to Algeciras, where it becomes the E-26, connecting all the resorts along the Costa del Sol. This highway is also known as the Carretera de Cádiz. Establishments along this highway use distances from Cádiz as addresses (for example, Carretera de Cádiz, km 68, means the establishment is 68 kilometers from Cádiz).

A Suggested Route

Allow about six days to explore the Costa del Sol.

Day 1 Begin at Algeciras. During the day, cross over to Gibraltar to see all the main attractions. Stay overnight in Algeciras.

Day 2–3 Leave Algeciras and drive west to Marbella. This will be your only chic stopover on the coast. Enjoy the good beaches, restaurants, bars, and discos.

Day 4 Continue east to Torremolinos for the night. For most of the year, the activity here is like a street festival.

Day 5 Leave Torremolinos and continue east to Málaga for an overnight stopover. Although Málaga is an ancient city, its sights can be covered in a day.

Day 6 Continue east to Nerja, the final overnight stopover, and visit the Cave of Nerja. If you're driving, you can continue your trip along the eastern coast all the way to Valencia and Barcelona. If you must leave, the best transportation links are found by returning west to Málaga.

What's Special About the Costa del Sol

Beaches

- Marbella, with 17 miles (27km) of sandy beaches.
- Torremolinos, with sandy but crowded beaches—try Bajondillo or El Lido.
- Fuengirola, where your best bets are Las Gaviotas, Carrajal, and Santa Amalja.

Great Resort

- Marbella, where glitter and hype reach their pinnacle. Visit the "Golden Mile" strip that's home to the superwealthy.

Great Villages

- Mijas, an Andalusian pueblo.
- Nerja, a fishing village transformed into a resort.

Historic City

- Málaga, former harbor for Moorish kingdom of Granada.

Architectural Highlights

- Marbella's old quarter, around the Plaza de los Naranjos.
- The Alcazaba at Málaga, an 11th-century fortress with a Hispano-Muslim garden.

A Pocket of Posh

- Puerto Banús, with a yacht-clogged harbor for the rich.

Festivals/Special Events

- Málaga's major festivals on religious occasions and its big annual *feria* (fair) in August.
- Marbella's flamenco festival, in the second half of June.

1 Algeciras

422 miles (679km) S of Madrid, 82 miles (132km) W of Málaga

GETTING THERE • By Train The local RENFE office is at Calle Juan de la Cierva (☎ **63-02-02**). From Madrid, there are two trains daily; from Málaga, two daily (running along most of the Costa del Sol, including Marbella and Torremolinos); from Sevilla, three daily; and from Granada, two daily.

• By Bus Various independent bus companies service Algeciras. Empresa Portillo, Avenida Virgen de Carmen, 15 (☎ **65-10-55**), 1½ blocks to the right when you exit the port complex, runs nearly a dozen buses a day along the Costa del Sol to Algeciras from Málaga. It also sends one bus daily from Madrid and two from Granada. To make connections to or from Seville, use Empresa La Valenciana, Viajes Koudubia (☎ **60-34-00**). Six buses a day go to Jerez de la Frontera and Seville. Empresa Comes, Hotel Octavio, Calle San Bernardo (☎ **65-34-56**), sells tickets to La Línea (the border station for the approach to Gibraltar) for 185 pesetas ($1.30) and to Tarifa also for 195 pesetas ($1.40), from which a ferry to Tangier can be arranged.

Costa del Sol

• **By Ferry** Most visitors in Algeciras plan to cross to Tangier in Morocco. From April through October, Monday to Saturday, eight ferries a day leave from the port complex in Algeciras, heading for Tangier; on Sunday, only three a day (in off-season, four a day all seven days). A Class A ticket costs 3,440 pesetas ($24.40) per person, with a Class B ticket going for 2,700 pesetas ($19.20). To transport a car costs from 8,500 pesetas ($60.40) per vehicle (cars aren't transported in stormy weather). Discounts are available: 20% with a Eurailpass, 30% with an InterRail pass, and 50% for children.

• **By Car** The Carretera de Cádiz (E-26) makes the run from Málaga west to Algeciras. If you're driving south from Seville (or Madrid); take highway N-IV to Cádiz, then connect with the 340/E-25 southwest to Algeciras.

ESSENTIALS The area code for Algeciras is 956. The tourist information office is at Juan de la Cierva (☎ **956/57-26-36**).

Algeciras is the jumping-off point for Africa—its only three hours to Tangier or Spanish Morocco. If you're planning an excursion, there's an inexpensive baggage storage depot at the ferry terminal. Algeciras is also a base for day trips to Gibraltar. Check at the Gibraltar Tourist Office, 18-20 Bomb House Lane (☎ **7/742-89**), in Gibraltar, for information. If you don't have time to visit "the Rock," you can view it from Algeciras—it's only six miles (10km) away, out in the Bay of Algeciras.

Where to Stay

Hotel Alarde, Alfonso XI, 4, 11201 Algeciras. ☎ **956/66-04-08.** Fax 956/65-49-01. 68 rms (all with bath). A/C MINIBAR TV TEL

Rates: 5,225–5,776 ptas. ($37.10–$41) single; 8,950 ptas. ($63.50) double. Breakfast 495 ptas. ($3.50) extra. AE, DC, MC, V. **Parking:** 1,000 ptas. ($7.10).

If you want to get away from the port area; consider this three-star hotel near the Parque María Cristina—a central location in a quiet commercial section. The double rooms have balconies and Andalusian-style furnishings. There are a snack bar and a restaurant. During my most recent stay I was impressed with both the staff and the inviting atmosphere.

Hotel Al-Mar, Avenida de la Marina, 2, 11201 Algeciras. ☎ **956/65-46-61.** Fax 956/65-45-01. 192 rms (all with bath), 6 suites. A/C TV TEL

Rates (including breakfast): 4,500–4,900 ptas. ($32–$34.80) single; 8,400–9,200 ptas. ($59.60–$65.30) double; from 13,000 ptas. ($92.30) suite. AE, DC, MC, V. **Parking:** 1,000 ptas. ($7.10).

The three-star Al-Mar, one of the best choices in town, stands near the port, where the ferries embark for Ceuta and Tangier. This large hotel boasts a blue-and-white Sevillian and Moorish decor, as well as three restaurants, a handful of bars, and lots of verdant hideaways. The guest rooms are well maintained, furnished in a slightly Andalusian style. The fourth-floor drawing room provides a panoramic view of the Rock.

Hotel Octavio, San Bernardo, 1, 11207 Algeciras. ☎ **956/65-27-00.** Fax 956/65-28-02. 77 rms (all with bath). A/C MINIBAR TV TEL

Rates: 7,000–8,000 ptas. ($49.70–$56.80) single; 10,000–12,000 ptas. ($71–$85.20) double. Breakfast 800 ptas. ($5.70). AE, DC, MC, V. **Parking:** 1,000 ptas. ($7.10).

Conveniently located in the center of town near the railway station, the Octavio is decorated with reproductions of English antiques, which contrast sharply with the building's angular modern exterior. The guest rooms are nicely furnished and well maintained. International drinks are served at an American-style bar.

Hotel Reina Cristina, Paseo de la Conferencia, 11207 Algeciras. ☎ **956/60-26-22.** Fax 956/60-33-23. 158 rms, 2 suites (all with bath). AC TV TEL

Rates: 7,100–8,900 ptas. ($50.40–$63.20) single; 12,000–15,000 ptas. ($85.20–$106.50) double; from 25,000 ptas. ($177.50) suite. Breakfast 1,500 ptas. ($10.70) extra. AE, DC, MC, V. **Parking:** 1,000 ptas. ($7.10).

Set within its own park on the southern outskirts of the city, a 10-minute walk south of both the rail and bus stations, this hotel reigns without challenge as the best established and most prestigious in town. Built during the heyday of the Victorian era and accented with turrets, ornate railings, and a facade appropriately painted with pastels, the Reina Cristina offers its clientele (many of whom are British) a view of the faraway Rock of Gibraltar. On the premises are a small English-language library; a semitropical garden held in place with sturdy retaining walls; and comfortable, high-ceilinged bedrooms.

Dining/Entertainment: The hotel's two restaurants include La Parilla, where set menus cost 3,000 pesetas ($21.30), and the more formal à la carte Restaurante Andalucía. There's also a bar.

Services: Room service (available daily from 7am to midnight), laundry/valet, concierge, babysitting.

Facilities: Sauna, indoor and outdoor swimming pools.

Where to Dine

Because Algeciras is not distinguished for its restaurants, many visitors prefer to dine at the hotels instead of taking a chance at some of the dreary little spots along the waterfront.

$ **Casa Alfonso,** Calle Juan de la Cierva, 4. ☎ **60-31-21.**

Cuisine: SPANISH. **Reservations:** Not required.

Prices: Appetizers 250–350 ptas. ($1.80–$2.50); main courses 550–1,000 ptas. ($3.90–$7.10); *menú del día* 900 ptas. ($6.40). No credit cards.

Open: Lunch, daily 1–4pm; dinner, daily 8pm–midnight.

Simple and unpretentious, this workaday restaurant was established in 1936 within a building on the southern edge of the city, near the harborfront and the tourist office. Convenient to travelers disembarking from the ferryboats from Morocco, it serves simple *menús del día* and such uncomplicated fare as bean soup, fried fish, beefsteak with potatoes, bread, wine, and fruit. Paella is also available, according to the arrival of the ingredients on the day of your arrival. Unnumbered buses from Cádiz and Seville stop nearby.

2 Tarifa

14 miles (22km) W of Algeciras, 443 miles (713km) S of Madrid, 61 miles (98km) SE of Cádiz

GETTING THERE • By Bus In Algeciras, Empresa Comes, Calle San Bernardo, s/n (☎ **65-34-56**), under the Hotel Octavio, runs buses to Tarifa, several leaving daily for the 45-minute ride depending on the time of year and costing 195 pesetas ($1.40).

• **By Car** Take the Cádiz highway, N-340, west from Algeciras.

ESSENTIALS The area code for Tarifa is 956.

Instead of heading east from Algeciras along the Costa del Sol, I'd suggest a visit west to Tarifa, an old Moorish town that is the southernmost point in Europe. After leaving Algeciras, the roads climb steeply, and the drive to Tarifa is along one of Europe's most splendid coastal routes. In the distance you'll see Gibraltar, the straits, and the "green hills" of Africa—in fact, you can sometimes get a glimpse of houses in Ceuta and Tangier on the Moroccan coastline.

Tarifa, named for Tarik, a Moorish military hero, has retained more of its Arab character than any other town in Andalusia. Narrow cobblestoned streets lead to charming patios filled with flowers. The main square is the Plaza San Mateo.

Two factors have inhibited the development of Tarifa's beautiful three-mile (5km) white beach, the Playa de Lances: It's still a Spanish military zone, and the wind never stops blowing (43% of the time). For windsurfers, though, the strong western breezes are unbeatable. Tarifa is filled with shops renting windsurfing equipment, as well as giving advice about the best locales.

Many visitors also come to see Tarifa's historical past and wander its crumbling ramparts. The town is dominated by the **Castle of Tarifa,** site of a famous struggle in 1292 between Moors and Christians. The castle was held by Guzmán el Bueno ("the Good"). When Christians captured his nine-year-old son and demanded surrender of the garrison, Guzmán tossed the Spanish a dagger for the boy's execution, preferring "honor without a son, to a son with dishonor." Sadly, the castle is not open to the public.

A Nearby Attraction

Fourteen miles (23km) beyond Tarifa lie the ruins of the ancient Roman town of Baelo Claudia, off Rte. N-340 along the Algeciras-Cádiz highway at the km 70.2 point. Follow the country road for four miles (6km) to **Bolonia-El Lentiscal** (☎ **956/68-85-30**), where you will find the ruins. The town was founded in the second century B.C., but the remains are mostly from the first century A.D., under Roman rule, it flourished as a fishing town with a population as high as 4,000. Then it was nearly forgotten for 1,500 years, until the archeological site was discovered shortly before World War I—the excavations are still far from complete. Don't miss the old Roman theater, fish-salting factory, temples, and hot baths, among other attractions. The site is open Tuesday through Saturday, and guided tours take about three quarters of an hour. Visits begin at 10am, 11am, noon, 1pm, 4pm, and 5pm from September 16 through June 30. From July 1 through September, there is an additional tour at 6pm. On Sundays and holidays, tours are conducted only at 10am, 11am, noon, and 1pm. Admission is 250 pesetas ($1.80); EU citizens free.

Where to Stay & Dine

Hotel Balcón de España, La Peña, 2, Carretera Cádiz–Málaga, km 77, 11380 Tarifa. ☎ **956/68-43-26.** Fax 956/68-43-26. 38 rms (all with bath). TEL

Rates (including half board): 8,500–11,500 ptas. ($60.40–$81.70) single; 8,250–15,000 ptas. ($58.60–$106.50) double. AE, MC, V. **Parking:** Free. **Closed:** Nov–Apr 19.

The surrounding park adds a welcome calm to your stay at the Balcón de España, located five miles (8km) north of Tarifa. The hotel offers clean and well-kept accommodations, an outdoor pool, tennis courts, and a riding stable. Some guests prefer to stay in outlying bungalows. In the restaurant, meals are served daily from 1 to 4pm and 8 to 11pm, costing from 3,000 pesetas ($21.30).

Mesón de Sancho, 340 Carretera Cádiz-Málaga, km 94, 11380 Tarifa. ☎ **956/68-49-00.** Fax 956/68-47-21. 45 rms (all with bath). MINIBAR TV TEL

Rates: 5,500 ptas. ($39.10) single; 7,000–9,100 ptas. ($49.70–$64.60) double. Breakfast 500 ptas. ($3.60) extra. AE, DC, MC, V. **Parking:** Free.

Ten miles (16km) southwest of Algeciras and 6.5 miles (10.5km) northeast of Tarifa on the Cádiz road stands this informal hacienda-style inn where you can swim in a pool surrounded by olive trees and terraces. The rooms are furnished in modest but contemporary style, and there is steam heating in the cooler months. In the provincial dining room, with its window walls overlooking the garden, a complete lunch or dinner goes for 1,800 pesetas ($12.80). Meals are available daily from 1 to 5pm and 8pm to midnight.

3 Estepona

53 miles (85km) W of Málaga, 397 miles (639km) S of Madrid, 28 1/2 miles (46km) E of Algeciras

GETTING THERE • By Train The nearest rail links are in Algeciras.

• By Bus Estepona is on the bus route from Algeciras to Málaga.

• By Car Drive east from Algeciras along the 340.

ESSENTIALS The area code for Estepona is 95. The tourist information office is at Paseo Marítimo Pedro Manrique (☎ **95/280-09-13**).

A town of Roman origin, Estepona is a budding beach resort, less developed than Marbella or Torremolinos but perhaps preferable for that reason. Estepona contains an interesting 15th-century parish church, with the ruins of an old aqueduct nearby (at Salduba). Its recreational port is an attraction, as are its **beaches:** Costa Natura, km 257 on the N-340, the first legal nude beach of its kind along the Costa del Sol; La Rada, 2 miles (3km) long; and El Cristo, only 600 yards long. After the sun goes down, stroll along the Paseo Marítimo, a broad avenue with gardens on one side, the beach on the other.

In summer the cheapest places to eat in Estepona are the *merenderos,* little dining areas set up by local fishermen and their families right on the beach. Naturally, they feature seafood, including sole and sardine kebabs grilled over an open fire. You can usually order a fresh salad and fried potatoes; desserts are simple.

After your siesta, head for the tapas bars. You'll find most of them—called *freidurías* (fried-fish bars)—at the corner of the Calle de los Reyes and La Terraza. Tables spill onto the sidewalks in summer, and *gambas à la plancha* (shrimp) are the favorite (but not the cheapest) tapas to order.

Where to Stay

★ **Atalaya Park Golf Hotel & Resort,** Carretera de Cádiz, km 168.5, 29688 Estepona. ☎ **95/288-48-01.** Fax 95/288-57-35. 416 rms (all with bath), 32 suites. A/C MINIBAR TEL

Rates (including breakfast): 15,120 ptas. ($107.40) single; 25,980 ptas. ($184.50) double; from 29,380 ptas. ($208.60) suite. AE, DC, MC, V. **Parking:** Free.

Located midway between Estepona and Marbella, this modern resort complex occupies grounds that by anyone's standards are spectacular. The hotel is the largest, most opulent, and most expensive in and around Estepona. Its bedrooms, furnished in a pristine but rather elegant modern style, are well maintained and inviting. Many guests from North Europe check in here and virtually never leave the grounds until it's time to fly back.

Dining/Entertainment: Three restaurants—each inspired by characters or episodes from Cervantes and each serving Spanish and international food—include the Don Quijote, the Sancho, and La Torre. Several bars are scattered throughout the property, and there is also a disco.

Services: Babysitting, concierge, laundry/valet, breakfast room service.

Facilities: Sauna, health club, solarium, indoor and outdoor swimming pools, car-rental facilities, shopping boutiques, tennis, water sports center, two 18-hole golf courses nearby.

Buenavista, Avenida de España, 180, 29680 Estepona. ☎ **95/280-01-37.** 38 rms (all with bath). A/C TV

Rates: 3,500–4,500 ptas. ($24.90-$32) single; 4,900–5,500 ptas. ($34.80–$39.10) double. AE, MC, V.

In the 1970s this comfortable little residencia rose up five floors to open beside the coastal road. It's recommended for an overnight stopover or a modest holiday. The guest rooms are clean but likely to be noisy in summer because of heavy traffic nearby. Meals, except breakfast, are served; lunch or dinner costs 850 pesetas ($6). Buses from Marbella stop nearby.

Where to Dine

Costa del Sol, Calle San Roque, 23. ☎ **280-11-01.**

Cuisine: FRENCH. **Reservations:** Not needed.

Rates: Appetizers 400–600 ptas. ($2.80–$4.30); main courses 700–1,200 ptas. ($5–$8.50). Fixed-price menus 850–1,480 ptas. ($6–$10.50). AE, MC, V.

Open: Lunch, Tues–Sat noon–4pm; dinner, daily 8–11:30pm.

Its French owners have infused this restaurant with the heart and soul of their native Toulouse, creating an outpost of Gallic charm in the heart of Estepona. Set at the edge of the sea, in a modern building whose interior is outfitted in tones of scarlet and gold, it's the multilingual domain of Jean Wilhelm (who cooks) and his wife Gerdy (who directs the staff in the dining room). Menu specialties derive from the bistro tradition of France, and include onion soup, coq au vin, tournedos béarnaise, mussels in Bordelaise sauce, brochettes of *merou*, and cheese soufflés.

4 Puerto Banús

5 miles (8km) E of Marbella, 486 miles (782km) S of Madrid

GETTING THERE • By Bus Fifteen buses a day connect Marbella to Puerto Banús. **• By Car** Drive east from Marbella along the 340.

ESSENTIALS The area code for Puerto Banús is 95.

A favorite resort for international celebrities, this marine village was created almost overnight in the traditional Mediterranean style. It's a dreamy place, a Disney World creation of what a Costa del Sol fishing village should look like. Yachts can be moored at your doorstep. Along the harborfront you'll find an array of expensive bars and restaurants. Wandering through the quiet back streets, you'll pass archways and patios with grilles.

Where to Stay

Hotel Marbella-Dinamar, Urbanización Nueva Andalucía, Carretera de Cádiz, km 175, 29660 Puerto Banús. ☎ **95/281-05-00.** Fax 95/281-23-46. 112 rms (all with bath), 5 suites. A/C TV TEL

Rates: 9,350–14,550 ptas. ($66.40–$103.30) single; 11,855–18,150 ptas. ($84.20–$128.90) double; 35,750 ptas. ($253.80) suite. Breakfast 1,200 ptas. ($8.50) extra. AE, DC, MC, V. **Parking:** Free.

Distinctly Moorish in flavor and feeling, this striking and exotic resort celebrates the Arab domination of what is today Spanish Andalusia. Set just 400 yards from both the beach and the borders of Puerto Banús's congested center, it was built around 1980 with stark white walls; soaring arches; and a central courtyard containing a large, abstractly shaped swimming pool. Bedrooms offer views of the palm trees beside the pool or of the sea, each featuring two large beds and a simple and airy collection of furniture. The resort offers tennis courts that are floodlit at night, plus easy access to both the casino at the neighboring Hotel Plaza Andalucía and one of the best all-around golf courses along the Costa del Sol. There's also an additional indoor swimming pool suitable for year-round use. Perhaps best of all, the diversions and facilities of Puerto Banús lie within a three-minute walk.

Where to Dine

$ **Dalli's Pasta Factory,** Muelle de Rivera. ☎ **281-24-90.**

Cuisine: PASTA. Reservations: Not accepted.

Prices: Pastas 650–1,050 ptas. ($4.60–$7.50); meat platters 1,300–1,650 ptas. ($9.20–$11.70). No credit cards.

Open: Dinner only, daily 7pm–1am.

The light-hearted, California-inspired philosophy at Dalli's has added a new way to save pesetas in high-priced Puerto Banús. Its specialty is pasta, pasta, and more pasta, which, served with a portion of garlic bread and a carafe of house wine, is more than adequate for the gastronomic needs of many budget travelers. In a setting inspired by either high-tech or art deco (even the owners aren't absolutely certain how to define it), you can order nutmeg-flavored ravioli with spinach filling, *penne all'arrabbiata,* lasagne, and several kinds of spaghetti. More filling are the chicken cacciatore and the scaloppine of chicken and veal. These are served with—guess what?—pasta as a side dish.

The owners, incidentally, are a trio of Roman-born brothers who were reared in England and educated in California.

Don Leone, Muelle Ribera, 45. ☎ **281-17-16.**

Cuisine: INTERNATIONAL. **Reservations:** Recommended.

Prices: Appetizers 750–1,500 ptas. ($5.30–$10.70); main courses 1,950–3,800 ptas. ($13.80–$27). AE, DC, MC, V.

Open: Lunch, daily 1–4pm; dinner, daily 8pm–1am. **Closed:** Nov 21–Dec 21; lunch from late June to mid-Sept.

Many residents in villas around Marbella drive to this dockside restaurant for dinner. Luxuriously decorated, it tends to get crowded at times. Begin with the house minestrone, then follow with a pasta in either Bolognese or clam sauce; lasagne is also a regular. Meat specialties include veal parmigiana and roast baby lamb, while the fish dishes are also worth a try, especially the *fritta mista del pescados,* a mixed fish fry. The wine list is one of the best along the coast.

Red Pepper, Muelle Ribera. ☎ **281-21-48.**

Cuisine: GREEK/INTERNATIONAL. **Reservations:** Recommended.
Prices: Appetizers 550–750 ptas. ($3.90–$5.30); main courses 1,500–4,000 ptas. ($10.70–$28.40). AE, DC, MC, V.
Open: Daily 11am to 1 or 3am.

Run by an exuberant band of Cypriot expatriates, Red Pepper offers an array of Greek and international food in a sunny and sparsely furnished dining room. Selections include Hellenic chicken soup, moussaka, a variety of well-seasoned grilled meats, lots of fish, calf's liver, lamb on a skewer in the Greek fashion, and especially king prawns and lobster, which are the most expensive main courses, as they are priced by the gram. Full meals are usually accompanied by a selection of Greek and Spanish wines. You'll find the place in the center of Paseo Marítimo.

La Taberna del Alabardero, Muelle Benabola, A2. ☎ **281-27-94.**

Cuisine: INTERNATIONAL. **Reservations:** Required.
Prices: Appetizers 1,500–1,800 ptas. ($10.70–$12.80); main courses 2,000–3,200 ptas. ($14.20–$22.70). AE, DC, MC, V.
Open: Lunch, daily 1–4pm. Dinner, daily 8pm–2am. **Closed:** Sun in winter; Jan 15–Feb 15.

This restaurant lies directly on the harborfront, within full view of the hundreds of strolling pedestrians whose numbers seem to ebb and flow like the tides. You can dine inside its big windowed interior; however, you might have more fun at one of the dozens of outdoor tables, where the only clues to the place's uppercrust status are the immaculate napery, well-disciplined waiters, and discreet twinkle of some very expensive jewelry among the blue jeans or formal attire of the prosperous and fashionable clientele. An armada of private yachts bobs at anchor a few feet away. Meals might include crêpes stuffed with chunks of lobster and crayfish, hake and small clams served in a Basque-inspired green sauce, filet of duck's breast with green peppercorns or orange sauce, and a wide array of desserts.

Evening Entertainment

Sinatra Bar, Muelle Ribera, 2. No phone.

Sinatra Bar is a center for people watching. Here residents of the nearby apartments meet for drinks late in the evening. The preferred spot, if the weather is right, is on one of the chairs set out on the sidewalk. Only a few feet away, rows of luxury yachts await your inspection. The tables are usually shared, and piped-in music lets you hear Sinatra's voice. Snacks such as the "Mama-burger" are served throughout the night. Hard drinks range from 500 pesetas ($3.60), with burgers from 450 pesetas ($3.20). Open daily from 9pm to 4am.

Hollywood Bar, Muelle Ribera, 14. ☎ **281-68-12.**

Hollywood Bar offers a place for you to sit and examine the yachts bobbing a few feet away and the pedestrians who may be admiring the boats as much as you are. The green-and-white decor of arched awnings and terra-cotta tiles is focused around a series of collages of the best shots of the Hollywood stars of yesteryear. Monroe and Chaplin mark the entrance to the toilets. Beer begins at 300 pesetas ($2.10) and up. Open daily from 9:30am to 2am.

5 San Pedro de Alcántara

43 miles (69km) W of Málaga, 42 1/2 miles (68km) E of Algeciras

GETTING THERE • **By Bus** Service is every 30 minutes from Marbella.

• **By Car** Take the N-340 west from Marbella.

ESSENTIALS The area code for San Pedro de Alcántara is 95.

Between Marbella and Estepona, this interesting village contains **Roman remains** that have been officially classified as a National Monument. In recent years it has been extensively developed as a resort suburb of Marbella and now offers some good hotel selections.

Where to Stay

Cortijo Blanco, Carretera de Cádiz, km 172, 29670 San Pedro de Alcántara. ☎ **95/278-09-00.** Fax 95/278-09-16. 327 rms (all with bath). A/C TEL

Rates (including half board): 4,400–9,400 ptas. ($31.20–$66.70) single; 6,600–16,600 ptas. ($46.90–$117.90) double. V. **Parking:** Free.

Just a few miles west of Marbella and only 600 yards from the beach, the Cortijo Blanco offers bedrooms overlooking miniature patios overgrown with bougainvillea, canna, and roses. The hotel, built in the Andalusian hacienda style, offers modern accommodations, and a large open-air swimming pool. Lunch is served under a long, covered garden pergola, and dinner is offered in the more formal dining hall, with oil paintings on the walls and tables surrounded by high-backed gilt-and-red Valencian chairs.

Golf Hotel Guadalmina, Hacienda Guadalmina, Carretera N-340, 29670 San Pedro de Alcántara. ☎ **95/288-22-11.** Fax 95/288-54-48. 80 rms (all with bath). A/C MINIBAR TV TEL

Rates: 15,600 ptas. ($110.80) single; 19,990 ptas. ($141.90) double. Breakfast 1,100 ptas. ($7.80) extra. **Parking:** Free.

At this moderately priced, large, country club-type resort, the first tee and the 18th green are both right next to the hotel. The golf course is open to both residents and nonresidents. An informal place, it is really a private world on the shores of the Mediterranean. You reach it by a long driveway from the coastal road; the location is 50 yards from the beach, 8 miles (13km) east of Marbella, and 1 1/4 miles (2km) from the center of San Pedro de Alcántara. Two seawater swimming pools attract those seeking the lazy life; the tennis courts appeal to the athletic. The guest rooms—most opening onto the pool/recreation area and the sea—are attractive in their traditional Spanish style.

The hotel offers two excellent dining choices—one a lunch-only reed-covered poolside terrace overlooking the golf course and the sea, the other an interior room in the main building, with a sedate clubhouse aura. Informality and good food reign.

6 Marbella

37 miles (59km) W of Málaga, 28 miles (45km) W of Torremolinos, 50 miles (80km) E of Gibraltar, 47 miles (76km) E of Algeciras, 373 miles (600km) S of Madrid

GETTING THERE • By Bus Twenty buses run between Málaga and Marbella daily, plus three buses coming in from Madrid and another three buses from Barcelona.

• By Car Marbella is the first major resort as you head east on the N-340 from Algeciras.

ESSENTIALS The area code for Marbella is 95. The tourist information office is at Glorieta de la Fontanilla, s/n (☎ **95/277-14-42**).

Although it's packed with tourists, ranking just behind Torremolinos in popularity, Marbella is still the most exclusive resort along the Costa del Sol—with such bastions of posh as the Marbella Club. Despite the hordes, Marbella remains a pleasant Andalusian town at the foot of the Sierra Blanca. Traces of the past are found in its palatial Town Hall, its medieval ruins, and its ancient Moorish walls. Marbella's most charming area is the **old quarter,** with narrow cobblestoned streets and Arab houses, centering around the Plaza de los Naranjos.

The biggest attractions in Marbella, though, are **El Fuerte** and **La Fontanilla,** the two main beaches. There are other, more secluded beaches, but you need your own transportation to get to them.

A long-ago visitor, Queen Isabella, was said to have exclaimed *"¡Que mar tan bello!"* ("What a beautiful sea!"), and the name remained for posterity.

Where to Stay

Since the setting is so ideal—with pure Mediterranean sun, sea, and sky, plus the scent of Andalusian orange blossoms in the air—some of the best hotels along the Costa del Sol are found in Marbella.

VERY EXPENSIVE

Hotel Don Carlos, Jardines de las Goldondrinas, Carretera de Cádiz, km 192, 29600 Marbella. ☎ **95/283-11-40,** or toll free 800/223-5652 in the U.S. and Canada. Fax 95/283-34-29. 223 rms, 15 suites. A/C MINIBAR TV TEL

Rates: 9,000—21,100 ptas. ($63.90–$149.80) single; 12,000–26,000 ptas. ($85.20–$184.60) double; 29,000–96,500 ptas. ($205.90–$685.20) suite. Breakfast from 1,200 ptas. ($8.50) extra. AE, DC, MC, V. **Parking:** Free.

One of the most dramatically alluring hotels along the coastline, the Don Carlos rises on a set of angled stilts above a pine forest. Between the hotel and its manicured beach, considered the best in Marbella, are 130 acres (53 hectares) of award-winning gardens replete with cascades of water, a full-time staff of 22 gardeners, and thousands of subtropical plants. There's far more to this hotel than the modern tower that rises above the eastern edge of Marbella. Its low-lying terraces and elegant eating and drinking facilities attract high-powered conferences from throughout Europe as well as individual nonresident diners from along the Mediterranean coast. Each of the accommodations has its own lacquered furniture, private bath done in honey-colored marble, and satellite TV.

Dining/Entertainment: You can dine amid splashes of bougainvillea beside an oversized swimming pool that's bordered with begonias and geraniums or in La Pergola, where ficus and potted palms decorate the hundreds of lattices. A hideaway, Los Naranjos, has a sun-flooded atrium with mosses and orange trees. The grand piano on the marble dais provides diverting music. Fixed-price meals here go for 4,800 pesetas ($34.10). Meals in the other restaurants, including grills and elaborate buffets in the semi-outdoor beachfront cabaña, cost about half as much.

Among the bars scattered around the various terraces and marble-lined hideaways of the public rooms, the most popular offers an English-inspired decor of exposed hardwoods, a panoramic view of the sea, plenty of sofas, a dance floor, and a musical trio.

Services: 24-hour room service, laundry, babysitting.

Facilities: Three swimming pools, use of five golf courses nearby, saunas, gym, tennis courts. Water sports cost extra.

Hotel Puente Romano, 2½ miles (4km) west of Marbella at Carretera de Cádiz, km 167, 29600 Marbella. ☎ **95/277-01-00.** Fax 95/277-57-66. 142 rms, 67 suites. A/C MINIBAR TV TEL

Rates: 27,500 ptas. ($195.30) single; 34,700 ptas. ($246.40) double; from 40,500 ptas. ($287.60) suite. Breakfast 1,700 ptas. ($12.10) extra. AE, DC, MC, V. **Parking:** Free.

This hotel was originally built as a cluster of vacation apartments, a fact that influenced the attention to detail and the landscaping that surrounds it. In the early 1970s, a group of entrepreneurs transformed it into one of the most unusual hotels in the south of Spain, sitting close to the frenetic coastal highway midway between Marbella and Puerto Banús.

If you're wondering who your fellow guests might be, you may be interested to know that the King of Spain, Barbra Streisand, Björn Borg, Stevie Wonder, Julio Iglesias, various Kennedys, and the President of Ireland have all enjoyed the pleasures of this establishment.

Once inside the complex, guests wander through a maze of arbor-covered walkways. Along the route, they pass cascades of water, masses of vines, and a subtropical garden.

Each of the Andalusian-Mediterranean style accommodations is a showcase of fabrics, accessories, and furniture, boasting a semisheltered balcony with flowers, a private bath, and an electronic safe.

Dining/Entertainment: Nestled amid the lushness are well-upholstered indoor/outdoor bars and restaurants. Three of these overlook a terra-cotta patio bordered at one end by the stones of a reconstructed Roman bridge, the only one of its kind in southern Spain. There is also a nightclub.

Services: 24-hour room service, laundry/valet, babysitting.

Facilities: The edges of the free-form swimming pool are bordered by trees and vines and a drain-away waterfall, which makes it look something like a Tahitian lagoon. There are also a sandy beach with water sports, tennis courts, a cluster of boutiques, a gym, a sauna, and a solarium.

Marbella Club, Carretera de Cádiz, km 178, 29600 Marbella. ☎ **95/277-13-00.** Fax 95/282-98-84. 76 rms, 24 suites, 10 bungalows. A/C MINIBAR TV TEL

Rates: 27,000 ptas. ($191.70) single; 35,000–38,000 ptas. ($248.50–$269.80) double; 45,000–84,000 ptas. ($319.50–$596.40) suite; bungalows 97,000–240,000 ptas. ($688.70–$1,704). Breakfast 1,600–2,100 ptas. ($11.40–$14.90) extra. AE, DC, MC, V. **Parking:** Free.

Until a handful of equally chic hotels were built along the Costa del Sol, the Marbella Club reigned almost without equal as the exclusive hangout of the world's commercial and genealogical aristocracy. Among its first guests when it opened in 1954 were actress Merle Oberon and novelist Leon Uris, and since then the names and titles on its roster of famous guests could have kept a society columnist busy for months. Established on land originally owned by the father of Prince Alfonso von Hohenlohe, the resort sprawls over a landscaped property that slopes from its roadside reception area down to the beach. Composed of small, ecologically conscious clusters of garden pavilions, bungalows, and small-scale annexes (none of which is higher than two stories), the Marbella basks amid some of the most well-conceived gardens along the coast. Rooms have private balconies or terraces. Today, its clientele is discreet, international, elegant, and appreciative of the resort's small scale and superb service.

Dining/Entertainment: The Marbella Club Restaurant moves from indoor shelter to an outdoor terrace according to the season. (For more information, refer to "Where to Dine," below.) A bar is located within the garden nearby.

Services: 24-hour room service, babysitting, laundry/valet, massage, concierge well-versed in the arrangement of almost anything.

Facilities: There are two swimming pools and a beach with a lunch restaurant. Golf can be arranged nearby. Tennis courts are available within a two-minute walk at the Marbella Club's twin resort, Puente Romano.

Melía Don Pepe, Finca Las Merinas, 29600 Marbella. ☎ **95/277-03-00,** or toll free in the U.S. **800/336-3542.** Fax 95/277-99-54. 204 rms, 18 suites. A/C MINIBAR TV TEL

Rates: 22,200–25,900 ptas. ($157.60–$183.90) single; 32,800 ptas. ($232.90) double; from 55,000 ptas. ($390.50) suite. Breakfast 1,500 ptas. ($10.70) extra. AE, DC, MC, V. **Parking:** Free.

Melía Don Pepe occupies six acres (2 hectares) of tropical gardens and lawns between the coastal road and the sea. Its well-furnished bedrooms, with private baths and wall-to-wall carpeting, face either the sea or the Sierra Blanca mountains. The facilities are so vast that you could spend a week here and not use them all.

Dining/Entertainment: The hotel has lounges, bars, and restaurants. La Farola grill provides international à la carte cuisine, with meals costing from 5,500 pesetas ($39.10).

Services: 24-hour room service, laundry/valet, babysitting.

Facilities: Four swimming pools, tennis courts, health club, Swedish sauna, bridge clubroom, boutiques, yacht harbor along beach, golf course.

★ **Los Monteros,** Carretera de Cádiz, km 187, 29600 Marbella. ☎ **95/277-17-00.** Fax 95/282-58-46. 169 rms, 10 suites. A/C MINIBAR TV TEL

Rates (including breakfast): 25,000 ptas. ($177.50) single; 32,000 ptas. ($227.20) double; from 55,000 ptas. ($390.50) suite. AE, DC, MC, V. **Parking:** Free.

Los Monteros, 400 yards from a beach and 4 miles (6km) east of Marbella, is one of the most tasteful resort complexes along the Costa del Sol. Situated between the coastal road and its own private beach, it attracts those seeking intimacy and luxury. No cavernous lounges exist here; instead, many small public rooms, Andalusian/Japanese in concept, are the style. The hotel offers various salons with open fireplaces, a library, and terraces. The bedrooms are brightly decorated, with light-colored lacquered furniture, private baths, and terraces.

Dining/Entertainment: The hotel has a bar and four restaurants on different levels that open onto flower-filled patios, gardens, and fountains. Within the precincts, Grill El Corzo is one of the finest grill rooms along the coast. The grill, done up in Toledo red, is on the first floor. Wall-size scenic murals form a background for tables that are bedecked with bright cloths and silver candlesticks. Soft, romantic music is played nightly. The cuisine is a pleasing combination of French and Spanish, with meals costing from 6,000 pesetas ($42.60).

Services: 24-hour room service, babysitting, laundry/valet.

Facilities: Guests can use the nearby 18-hole golf course, Río Real, for free. Also included are several swimming pools, a beach club with a heated indoor swimming pool, 10 tennis courts, 5 squash courts, a riding club and school—plus a fully equipped gymnasium with sauna, massage, and Jacuzzi.

Andalucía Plaza, Urbanización Nueva Andalucía, 29660 Apartado 21, Nueva Andalucía Marbella. ☎ **95/281-20-00.** Fax 95/281-47-92. 289 rms, 20 suites. A/C MINIBAR TV TEL

Rates (including American breakfast): 9,000–15,000 ptas. ($63.90–$106.50) single; 13,000–20,000 ptas. ($92.30–$142) double; 17,500–27,000 ptas. ($124.30–$191.70) suite. AE, DC, MC, V. **Parking:** Free.

Originally built in 1972, the Andalucía Plaza is a resort complex on a grand scale. On the mountain side of the coastal road between Marbella and Torremolinos, twin five-story buildings are linked by a reception lounge and formal gardens. On the sea side is the hotel's beach club. The public rooms are spacious and lavishly decorated. Equally luxurious are the guest rooms, all with private baths and furnished with reproductions in the classic Castilian manner. The hotel is on more than a 300-foot strip of sand, 4 miles (6km) west of the center of Marbella, a 10-minute walk from Puerto Bánus.

Dining/Entertainment: The Cordova restaurant serves upscale international meals, with a fixed-price menu costing 3,850 pesetas ($27.30). The Bar Toledo, primarily a watering hole, offers light snacks and suppers. The in-house casino is discussed under "Evening Entertainment," below.

Services: 24-hour room service, concierge, babysitting, laundry.

Facilities: The hotel's beach club includes a 300-foot strip of sand, with adjacent sunbathing terraces, tennis courts, two saunas, a gymnasium, an open-air swimming pool, and an enclosed all-weather pool. About half a mile away, there's a 1,000-berth marina, where the hotel will arrange the rental of a vessel for deep-sea fishing.

Hotel El Fuerte, El Fuerte, s/n, 29600 Marbella. ☎ **95/286-15-00.** Fax 95/282-44-11. 261 rms, 2 suites (all with bath). A/C MINIBAR TV TEL

Rates: 8,400–9,200 ptas. ($59.60–$65.30) single; 11,400–17,200 ptas. ($80.90–$122.10) double; 27,900–33,400 ptas. ($198.10–$237.10) suite. Breakfast 1,200 ptas. ($8.50) extra. AE, DC, MC, V. **Parking:** 600 ptas. ($4.30).

The largest and most recommendable hotel in the center of Marbella, with a balconied and angular facade that's divided into two separate six-story towers, El Fuerte is set directly on the waterfront. Originally built in 1957, it added a wing in 1987 and was last renovated in 1994. Catering to a sedate clientele of conservative northern Europeans, it offers a palm-fringed swimming pool set across the street from a sheltered lagoon and a wide-open beach. The hotel offers a handful of terraces, some shaded by flowering arbors, that provide hideaways for quiet drinks. Inside, the public rooms contain a wide variety of tilework, certain sections of which were culled from much older buildings. Bedrooms are contemporary, with piped-in music and terraces.

The hotel offers a coffee shop plus a restaurant serving a *menú del día* for 3,392 pesetas ($24.10). The facilities for leisure activities include the above-mentioned swimming pool, a floodlit tennis court, a health club, and two squash courts.

Hotel Guadalpín, Carretera, 340, Cádiz-Málaga, km 179, 29600 Marbella. ☎ **95/277-11-00.** Fax 95/277-33-34. 110 rms (all with bath). TEL

Rates: 4,450–6,550 ptas. ($31.60–$46.50) single; 6,300–9,400 ptas. ($44.70–$66.70) double. Breakfast 455 ptas. ($3.20). AE, DC, MC, V. **Parking:** Free.

This three-star 1960s hotel is right on the coast, only 300 yards from the beach and a mile from the center of Marbella. Guests can relax around the two swimming pools or walk along the fir-lined private pathway to the Mediterranean. The dining room has large windows that overlook the patio, while the ranch-style lounge boasts round marble tables and leather armchairs. A *menú del día* in the hotel restaurant costs 1,850 pesetas ($13.10). There's also a bar. Most accommodations have two terraces, a living room, and a bedroom furnished in "new ranch" style and centrally heated during the cooler months.

INEXPENSIVE

$ **Residencia Finlandia,** Finlandia, 12, 29600 Marbella. ☎ **95/277-07-00.** 11 rms (all with bath). TEL

Rates: 3,000–3,500 ptas. ($21.30–$24.90) single; 3,500–6,360 ptas. ($24.90–$45.20) double. Breakfast 400 ptas. ($2.80) extra. AE, DC, MC, V.

Situated in the Huerta Grande, a peaceful residential section, the 1970s Finlandia is only a five-minute walk from the center of the old quarter and 200 yards from the beach. It's clean and well run, with spacious guest rooms and contemporary furnishings. Your bed will be turned down at night.

Residencia Lima, Antonio Belón, 2, 29600 Marbella. ☎ **95/277-05-00.** Fax 95/286-30-91. 64 rms (all with bath). TEL

Rates: 6,360 ptas. ($45.20) single; 7,950 ptas. ($56.40) double. Breakfast 425 ptas. ($3) extra. AE, DC, MC, V.

Tucked away in a residential section of Marbella, right off the N-340 and near the sea, this hotel is more secluded than the others nearby. The modern eight-story structure features bedrooms with Spanish provincial furnishings and private balconies.

Residencia San Cristóbal, Ramón y Cajal, 3, 29600 Marbella. ☎ **95/277-12-50.** Fax 95/286-20-44. 96 rms (all with bath). A/C TV TEL

Rates: 3,675–6,250 ptas. ($26.10–$44.40) single; 5,400–8,600 ptas. ($38.30–$61.10) double. Breakfast 450 ptas. ($3.20) extra. AE, MC, V.

In the heart of Marbella, 200 yards from the beach, this 1960s five-story hotel has long, wide terraces and flower-filled windowboxes. The guest rooms have walnut headboards, individual overhead reading lamps, and room dividers separating the comfortable beds from the small living-room areas. An added plus is the private terrace attached to each room—a perfect spot to enjoy the continental breakfast that's the only meal served here.

El Rodeo, Victor de la Serna, s/n, 29600 Marbella. ☎ **95/277-51-00.** Fax 95/282-33-20. 100 rms (all with bath). TEL

Rates: 3,800–5,500 ptas. ($27–$39.10) single; 5,000–7,750 ptas. ($35.50–$55) double. Breakfast 475 ptas. ($3.40) extra. AE, DC, MC, V.

Even though this modern hotel stands just off the main coastal road of Marbella, within walking distance of the bus station, the beach, and the old quarter—it is quiet and secluded. The facilities in the seven-story structure include a swimming pool, terrace, sunbathing area, solarium, and piano bar. Two elevators whisk you to the sunny, spacious second-floor lounges with country furnishings; there's also a bar with tropical bamboo chairs and tables. Continental breakfast is the only meal served in the cheerful breakfast room. The bedrooms are functional, with several shuttered closets, lounge chairs, and white desks. Although the hotel is open all year, the highest rates are charged from April 1 to October 31.

BUDGET

$ **Hostal El Castillo,** Plaza San Bernabé, 2, 29600 Marbella. ☎ **95/277-17-39.** 26 rms (all with bath).

Rates: 1,700 ptas. ($12.10) single; 3,500 ptas. ($24.90) double. No credit cards.

At the foot of the castle in the narrow streets of the old town, this small budget hotel opens onto a minuscule triangular area used by the adjoining convent and school as a playground. There's a small, covered courtyard, and the second-floor bedrooms have only inner windows. The Spartan guest rooms are scrubbed clean and contain white-tile baths. No morning meal is served, and not one word of English is spoken.

$ **Hostal Munich,** Calle Virgen del Pilar, 5, 29600 Marbella. ☎ **952/77-24-61.** 18 rms (all with bath). TEL

Rates: 2,995 ptas. ($21.30) single; 4,275 ptas. ($30.40) double. Breakfast 450 ptas. ($3.20) extras. No credit cards.

Set back from the street and shielded by banana and palm trees, this unassuming three-story hostal is just a short walk from the water and the bus station. Some guest rooms have balconies, and all are simply furnished and well kept. A continental breakfast is the only meal served. The homey lounge and breakfast room are warm and inviting.

Where to Dine

EXPENSIVE

★ **La Fonda,** Plaza Santo Cristo, 9-10. ☎ **277/25-12.**

Cuisine: INTERNATIONAL. **Reservations:** Required.

Prices: Appetizers 1,300–1,800 ptas. ($9.20–$12.80); main courses 1,700–2,900 ptas. ($12.10–$20.60). AE, DC, MC, V.

Open: Dinner only, Mon–Sat 8–11:30pm.

Considered both a gem of 18th-century Andalusian architecture and a gastronomic citadel of renown, La Fonda is the Costa del Sol extension of one of the most famous restaurants in Europe, the Madrid-based Horcher's. (For more information on that restaurant, refer to Chapter 4.) La Fonda was the outgrowth of a simple inn, which had been originally created by interconnecting a trio of town houses in Old Marbella. Today, a central patio with a murmuring fountain, a series of colonnaded loggias, carefully chosen Andalusian *azulejos* (glazed tiles), beamed ceilings, open fireplaces, grill-covered windows, and checkerboard-patterned marble floors have been respectfully maintained. What is new, however, is the professionalism and sophistication.

Some of the most beautiful (and some of the richest) personalities in Europe come here regularly for long and languid dinners. The cuisine is international, and so is the crowd. Menu specialties change about every four months but might include fish terrine with herb sauce, avocado pancakes with prawns, guinea fowl or partridge, coq au vin, blanquette de veau, and chicken Kiev.

★ **La Hacienda,** Urbanización Hacienda Las Chapas, Carretera de Cádiz. km 193. ☎ **283-11-16.**

Cuisine: INTERNATIONAL. **Reservations:** Recommended.

Rates: Appetizers 1,200–1,800 ptas. ($8.50–$12.80); main courses 2,200–3,200 ptas. ($15.60–$22.70); fixed-price menu 6,500 ptas. ($46.20). AE, DC, MC, V.

Open: Summer, dinner Wed–Sun (plus Mon in Aug) 8:30–11:30pm. Winter, lunch Wed–Sun 1–3:30pm; dinner Wed–Sun 8:30–11:30pm. **Closed:** Nov 15–Dec 20.

La Hacienda, a tranquil choice 8 miles (13km) east of Marbella, enjoys a reputation for serving some of the best food along the Costa del Sol. In cooler months you can dine in the rustic tavern before an open fireplace; however, in fair weather, meals are served on a patio partially encircled by open Romanesque arches. The chef is likely to offer foie gras with lentils, lobster croquettes (as an appetizer); and roast guinea hen with cream, minced raisins, and port. An iced soufflé finishes the repast quite nicely.

★ **Marbella Club Restaurant,** The Marbella Club, Carretera de Cádiz, km 178. ☎ **277-13-00.**

Cuisine: INTERNATIONAL. **Reservations:** Recommended.

Rates: Lunch buffet 5,300 ptas. ($37.60) per person; dinner appetizers 1,100–2,500 ptas. ($7.80–$17.80); dinner main courses 1,900–4,500 ptas. ($13.50–$32). AE, DC, MC, V.

Open: Lunch, daily 1–3:30pm; dinner in summer, daily 9pm–12:30am; dinner in winter, daily 7:30–11:30pm.

Much of this establishment's charm derives from the willingness of the staff to move its venue onto a flowering terrace, whenever the weather justifies it. Lunch is traditionally a buffet served under an open-sided pavilion. Teams of formally dressed waiters frequently replenish a groaning table for a clientele featuring the rich and famous. Dinners are served amid blooming flowers, flickering candles, and the strains of live music—perhaps a Spanish classical guitarist, a small chamber orchestra playing 19th-century classics, or the tones of a South American vocalist. Menu items change with the season but include an international array inspired by the cuisines of Europe.

Villa Tiberio, Carretera de Cádiz; km 178.5. ☎ **277-17-99.**

Cuisine: ITALIAN. **Reservations:** Recommended.

Prices: Appetizers 750–2,000 ptas. ($5.30–$14.20); main courses 1,200–2,300 ptas. ($8.50–$16.30) AE, MC, V.

Open: Dinner only, Mon–Sat 7:30pm–midnight.

Villa Tiberio's proximity to the upscale Marbella Club (a five-minute walk away) ensures a flow of visitors from that hotel's elite confines. Set within what was originally built as a private villa during the 1960s, it serves what might be the most innovative Italian food in the region. Owned by the Morelli brothers, gregarious proprietors of restaurants as far away as London, it was established in 1990, and today it attracts the many north European expatriates living nearby.

Appetizers include grilled eggplant stuffed with onions, mushrooms, and tomatoes; slices of thinly sliced smoked beef with fresh avocados and oil-and-lemon dressing; prawn crêpes au gratin; a "fungi fantasia," composed of a large wild mushroom stuffed with seafood and lobster sauce; and any of a wide array of pastas. Especially tempting is the *pappardelle alla Sandro*—large flat noodles studded with chunks of lobster, tomato, and garlic. Other versions come with cream, caviar, and smoked salmon. Main dishes include grilled monkfish with prawns and garlic butter, grilled filets of pork or veal with mushroom-and-cream sauce, and osso buco. Live music sometimes accompanies a meal here.

MODERATE

Hostería del Mar, Cánovas del Castillo, 1. ☎ **277-02-18.**

Cuisine: MEDITERRANEAN. **Reservations:** Recommended.
Prices: Appetizers 700–875 ptas. ($5–$6.20); main courses 1,700–2,100 ptas. ($12.10–$14.90). AE, MC, V.
Open: Lunch, Mon–Sat 1–4pm; dinner, Mon–Sat 7:30pm–midnight.

Hostería del Mar lies at the beginning of the bypass road that runs beside the Hotel Melía Don Pepe. Its cuisine is known throughout the region as being both delicious and highly unusual. The Hostería has been called the most consistently good restaurant in the region—a judgment with which many loyal clients agree.

The dining room is decorated in shades of fern green and cream and accented with wooden columns, a floor colored blue and terra-cotta, decorative ceiling beams, and handpainted porcelain. In summer, a tree-shaded patio is also set with tables. Meals might include calves' sweetbreads in mustard sauce; clams stuffed with ratatouille; roast duck with a sauce made from roasted figs and cassis; Catalán-style shrimp with chicken; deboned leg of baby lamb prepared for two diners; a casserole of monkfish with white wine sauce, clams, and fresh asparagus; and stuffed quails with spinach, mushrooms, and pâté. The sumptuous desserts include a selection of cold soufflés.

$ **Mesón del Museo,** Plaza de Los Naranjos, 11. ☎ **282-3332.**

Cuisine: SWEDISH/INTERNATIONAL. **Reservations:** Recommended.
Prices: Appetizers 800–1,200 ptas. ($5.70–8.50); main courses 1,000–2,800 ptas. ($7.10–$19.90). AE, MC, V.
Open: Dinner only, Mon–Sat 7:30–11:30pm. **Closed:** Two weeks in August.

Mesón del Museo bears its name because of its location on the upper floor of an 18th-century building that contains one of the oldest art and antiques galleries in Marbella. Although its dining room is decorated with Iberian accessories and Andalusian antiques, its menu is partially Swedish—the inspired result of the partnership of Stockholm-born Hans Jöhncke and his Chilean wife, Valeska. Menu items include smoked or marinated salmon served with mustard sauce and creamed spinach; beef Stroganoff; versions of Swedish meatballs with gravy and mashed potatoes; and top-quality sirloin filet prepared in at least five different versions. (Variations on the theme include versions served with béarnaise, green pepper, madeira, or cabrales (a Spanish blue cheese) sauce, as well as filets stuffed with truffles and/or foie gras.) Desserts might include a homemade and very succulent pear tart with vanilla sauce.

Santiago, Duque de Ahumada, 5. ☎ **277-43-39.**

Cuisine: SEAFOOD. **Reservations:** Required.
Prices: Appetizers 750–3,000 ptas. ($5.30–$21.30); main courses 1,200–3,200 ptas. ($8.50–$22.70). AE, DC, MC, V.
Open: Lunch, daily 12:30–5pm; dinner, daily 7pm–midnight.

As soon as you enter Santiago, the bubbling lobster tanks give you an idea of what's in store. The decor, the tapas bar near the entrance, and the summertime patio join with fresh fish dishes to make this one of the most popular eating places in town. On my most recent visit, I arrived so early for lunch that the mussels for my mussels marinara were just being delivered. The fish soup is well prepared, well spiced, and savory. The sole in champagne comes in a large serving, and the turbot can be grilled or sautéed. On a hot day, the seafood salad, garnished with lobster, shrimp, and crabmeat and served with a sharp sauce, is especially recommended. For dessert, I suggest a serving of Manchego cheese.

INEXPENSIVE

La Gitana, Buitrago, 2. ☎ **277-66-74.**

Cuisine: INTERNATIONAL. **Reservations:** Recommended.
Prices: Appetizers 500–900 ptas. ($3.60–$6.40); main courses 1,100–2,100 ptas. ($7.80–$14.90). AE, MC, V.
Open: Dinner only, daily 8–11:45pm.

La Gitana, on a narrow street in the old pueblo off Plaza de los Naranjos, offers popular rooftop dining. It specializes in barbecued meats, including honey-glazed chicken, spareribs, sirloin steak, and even lamb. Other dishes, such as fresh fish, are also available.

$ **Mesón del Pasaje,** Pasaje, 5. ☎ **277-12-61.**

Cuisine: CONTINENTAL. **Reservations:** Required.
Prices: Appetizers 550–650 ptas. ($3.90–$4.60); main courses 1,100–1,700 ptas. ($7.80–$12.10). AE, MC, V.
Open: Dinner only, Mon–Sat 7:30–11:30pm. **Closed:** Nov to mid-Dec.

A well-run restaurant in an old house in the ancient quarter, just off Plaza de los Naranjos, this *mesón* is a maze of little dining rooms. Since word is out that the food is the best in the old town—for the price—the place invariably fills up. *You* can fill up on one of the excellent pastas, which are most reasonable, or try the well-prepared, but more expensive, seafood and meat selections. The place offers charm and good value.

$ **La Tricyclette,** Buitrago, 14. ☎ **277-78-00.**

Cuisine: INTERNATIONAL. **Reservations:** Not required.
Prices: Appetizers 400–1,350 ptas. ($2.80–$9.60); main courses 750–1,800 ptas. ($5.30–$12.80); fixed-price menu (Oct–May only) 1,500 ptas. ($10.70). AE, MC, V.
Open: Dinner only, Mon–Sat 7:30pm–midnight.

One of the more popular dining spots in Marbella, this restaurant is in a converted 18th-century home—courtyard and all—located on a narrow street in the old quarter near Plaza de los Naranjos. Sofas in the bar area provide a living-room ambience, and a stairway leads to an intimate dining room with an open patio that is delightful in the warmer months. Perhaps start with crêpes with a soft cream-cheese filling or grilled giant prawns, then move on to a delectable main dish such as roast duck in beer, filet steak with green-pepper sauce, or calves' liver cooked in sage and white wine. The wine list is extensive and reasonably priced.

A NEARBY PLACE TO DINE

El Refugio, Carretera de Ojén C337. ☎ **288-10-00.**

Cuisine: SPANISH. **Reservations:** Not required.
Prices: Appetizers 550–750 ptas. ($3.90–$5.30); main courses 1,400–2,000 ptas. ($9.90–$14.20); fixed-price menu 2,550 ptas. ($18.10). AE, DC, MC, V.
Open: Lunch, Tues–Sun 1–4pm; dinner, Tues–Sat 8–11pm.

If the summer heat has you down, retreat to the Sierra Blanca, just outside Ojén, where motorists come to enjoy both the mountain scenery and the cuisine at El Refugio, lying 12½ miles (20km) up in the hills north of Marbella. Meals are served in a rustic dining room, with an open terrace for drinks. Specialties include local versions of various spicy regional sausages, roast pork, roast chicken, grilled steaks, and in season local pheasant. The lounge has an open fireplace and comfortable armchairs, along with a few antiques and Oriental rugs.

Evening Entertainment

A MARBELLA TASCA CRAWL

There's no doubt about it—the best way to keep food costs low in Marbella is to do what the Spaniards do: Eat your meals in the tapas bars. You get plenty of atmosphere, lots of fun, good food, and low costs. Order a first course in one bar with a glass of wine or beer, a second course in another, and on and on as your stamina and appetite dictate. You can eat well in most places for around 600 pesetas ($4.30); and tascas are found all over town.

FLAMENCO

Ana María, Plaza del Santo Cristo, 4–5. ☎ **286-07-04.**

The elongated tapas bar here is often crowded with locals, and a frequently changing collection of singers, dancers, and musicians perform everything from flamenco to popular songs. Ana María is open daily from 11pm to 4am; it's closed in November and on Monday from December through March. Drinks run about 1,000 ptas. ($7.10).

Admission: 2,200 ptas. ($15.60).

GAMBLING

Casino Nueva Andalucía Marbella, Hotel Andalucía Plaza, Urbanización Nueva Andalucía. ☎ **281-40-00.**

Set six miles (10km) west of Marbella, near Puerto Banús, this casino lies on the lobby level of the previously recommended Andalucía Plaza Hotel. The designers carefully incorporated traffic flows between the facilities of the hotel and the jangle and clatter of the casino. Unlike the region's competing casino at the Hotel Torrequebrada, the Nueva Andalucía does not offer cabaret or nightclub shows. The focus, instead, is on gambling, which the mobs of visitors from northern Europe perform with abandon. Individual games include French and American roulette, blackjack, punto y banco, craps, and chemin de fer.

You can dine before or after gambling in the Casino Restaurant, which is raised a few steps above the gaming floor, for about 4,000 pesetas ($28.40) per person, excluding wine. Jackets are not required for men, but shorts and T-shirts will be frowned on. The casino is open daily from 8pm to either 4 or 5am. La Caseta Bar offers flamenco shows at 11pm on Friday and Saturday nights. Entrance is free but drinks cost from 1,500 pesetas ($10.70).

Admission: Casino 600 ptas. ($4.30) and the presentation of a valid passport.

7 Fuengirola & Los Boliches

20 miles (32km) W of Málaga, 64½ miles (104km) E of Algeciras, 356½ miles (574km) S of Madrid

GETTING THERE • By Train From Torremolinos, take the Metro at La Nogalera station (under the RENFE sign). Trains depart every 30 minutes.

• By Bus Fuengirola is on the main Costa del Sol bus route from either Algeciras in the west or Málaga in the east.

• By Car Take the N-340 east from Marbella.

ESSENTIALS The area code for Fuengirola and Los Boliches is 95. The Tourist Information Office is at Avenida Jesús Santos Rein, 6 (☎ **95/246-74-57**).

The twin fishing towns of Fuengirola and Los Boliches lie halfway between the more famous resorts of Marbella and Torremolinos. The promenade along the water stretches some 2½ miles (4km) with the less developed Los Boliches just half a mile from Fuengirola.

The towns don't have the facilities or drama of Torremolinos and Marbella. Except for two major luxury hotels, Fuengirola and Los Boliches are cheaper, though, and that has attracted a horde of budget-conscious European tourists.

On a promontory overlooking the sea, the ruins of **San Isidro Castle** can be seen. The **Santa Amalja, Carvajal,** and **Las Gaviotas beaches** are broad, clean, and sandy. Everybody goes to the big **flea market** at Fuengirola on Tuesdays.

Where to Stay

Byblos Andaluz, Urbanización Mijas Golf, 29640 Fuengirola. ☎ **95/246-30-50.** Fax 95/247-67-83. 144 rms (all with bath), 3 suites. A/C MINIBAR TV TEL

Rates: 20,000–24,000 ptas. ($142–$170.40) single; 25,000–33,500 ptas. ($177.50–$237.90) double; from 47,000 ptas. ($333.70) suite. Buffet breakfast 1,800 ptas. ($12.80) extra. AE, DC, MC, V. **Parking:** Free.

This luxurious resort is in a golf club setting three miles (5km) from Fuengirola and six miles (10km) from the beach. The grounds contain shrubbery, a white minaret, Moorish arches, tile-adorned walls, and an orange-tree patio inspired by the Alhambra grounds. Two 18-hole golf courses designed by Robert Trent Jones, tennis courts, spa facilities, a gymnasium, and swimming pools bask in the Andalusian sunshine. The health spa is housed in a handsome classic structure, Mijas Thalasso Palace.

The rooms and suites are elegantly and individually designed and furnished in the Roman, Arabic, Andalusian, and rustic styles. Private sun terraces and lavish bathrooms add to the comfort.

Dining/Entertainment: The dining choices here include Le Nailhac, with its French gastronomic offerings; El Andaluz, with its regional and Spanish specialties; and La Fuente, with its dietetic cuisine. The San Tropez Bar opens onto a poolside terrace, and live entertainment is often presented here.

Services: Laundry/valet, babysitting, room service.

Facilities: Health club, sauna, solarium, two outdoor pools, three indoor pools, two golf courses, tennis.

Florida, Paseo Marítimo, s/n, 29640 Fuengirola. ☎ **95/247-61-00.** Fax 95/258-15-29. 116 rms (all with bath). TV TEL

Rates: 3,600–5,700 ptas. ($25.60–$40.50) single; 6,200–8,600 ptas. ($44–$61.10) double. Breakfast 575 ptas. ($4.10) extra. AE, DC, MC, V. **Parking:** Free.

There is a semitropical garden in front of the Florida, and guests can enjoy refreshments under a wide, vine-covered pergola. Most of the comfortable guest rooms have balconies overlooking the sea or mountains. The floors are of tile, and the furnishings, particularly in the lounge, make much use of plastic. It's a ten-minute walk from the train station.

$ **Hostal Sedeño,** Don Jacinto, 1, 29640 Fuengirola. ☎ **95/247-47-88.** 30 rms (all with bath).

Rates: 2,225–3,200 ptas. ($15.80–$22.70) single; 3,180–3,750 ptas. ($22.60–$26.60) double. No credit cards.

The Sedeño is three minutes from the beach, in the heart of town. Its modest lobby leads to a larger lounge furnished with antiques and reproductions. You pass a small open courtyard where stairs go up to the second- and third-floor balconied but basic bedrooms. These overlook a small garden with fig and palm trees, plus a terrace. There is no restaurant and not even breakfast is served.

Las Pirámides, Paseo Marítimo, 29640 Fuengirola. ☎ **95/247-06-00.** Fax 95/258-32-97. 280 rms (all with bath), 40 suites. A/C MINIBAR TV TEL

Rates (including breakfast): 7,925–10,475 ptas. ($56.30–$74.40) single; 10,450–13,650 ptas. ($74.20–$96.90) double; 13,950–16,050 ptas. ($99–$114) suite. AE, MC, V. **Parking:** 1,000 ptas. ($7.10).

This resort, much favored by clients and travel groups from northern Europe, is divided into two 10-story towers capped with pyramid-shaped roofs, from which the complex takes its name. It's a citylike compound, set about 50 yards from the beach, with seemingly every kind of divertissement: flamenco shows on the large patio; a cozy bar and lounge; traditionally furnished sitting rooms; a coffee shop; a poolside bar; and a gallery of boutiques and tourist facilities, such as car-rental agencies. All the guest rooms have slick modern styling, as well as terraces. Room service is provided, as are laundry/valet services and babysitting.

Where to Dine

MODERATE

Casa Vieja, Avenida de Los Boliches, 27, Los Boliches. ☎ **258-38-30.**

Cuisine: FRENCH. **Reservations:** Recommended.

Prices: Fixed-price three-course lunch (Sat–Sun only) 1,550 ptas. ($11); dinner appetizers 555–1,650 ptas. ($3.90–$11.70); main dinner courses 1,175–2,350 ptas. ($8.30–$16.70). AE, MC, V.

Open: Lunch, Sat–Sun 12:30–3pm; dinner, Tues–Sun 7:30–11pm.

Set within the thick stone walls of a cottage that was originally built in the 1870s for a local fisherman, this restaurant lies on the main street of Los Boliches, a short walk east of the center of Fuengirola. Owned and managed by London-born Jon Adams, the establishment is a favorite of the expatriate community living among the nearby hills. A flowering patio is available for outdoor dining, and there's a cozy bar for chatting with the owner. Menu items include a subtly flavored terrine of oxtail, fresh vegetable soup, king prawns, tournedos with béarnaise sauce, suprême of salmon, gratin of sole in puff pastry, guinea fowl with cumin and honey-glazed turnips, duck breast with creamy foie-gras sauce, and turbot in white-wine sauce. The house's special dessert is a tarte tatin, an upside-down tart inspired by France, served with fresh cream and ice cream.

INEXPENSIVE

Don Pe', De la Cruz, 19, Fuengirola. ☎ **247-83-51.**

Cuisine: CONTINENTAL. **Reservations:** Recommended for dinner.

Prices: Appetizers 325–800 ptas. ($2.30–$5.70); main courses 750–2,100 ptas. ($5.30–$14.90). AE, DC, MC, V.

Open: Dinner only, Mon–Sat 7pm–midnight.

The name of this charming restaurant originated in 1984 as Don Perignon, but after a lawsuit by the famous champagne-maker, the owners abbreviated its name to its present form. In hot weather, visitors at Don Pe' dine in the courtyard, where the roof can be adjusted to allow in light and air. In cold weather, a fire within the hearth illuminates the heavy ceiling beams and rustic accessories. The menu features a selection of game dishes: medallion of venison, roast filet of wild boar, and duck with orange sauce. The ingredients are imported from the forests and plains of Andalusia. Don Pe' lies off the Avenida Ramón y Cajal.

El Paso, Calle Francisco Cano, 39, at Los Boliches. ☎ **247-50-94.**

Cuisine: MEXICAN. **Reservations:** Recommended.

Prices: Appetizers 375–850 ptas. ($2.70–$6); main courses 1,000–1,950 ptas. ($7.10–$13.80). MC, V.

Open: Dinner only, daily 7pm–midnight.

The building that contains El Paso was originally built a century ago as a canning factory for sardines, with a row of fishermen's cottages nearby. Today, this is one of the neighborhood's busiest Mexican restaurants, where a splashing fountain enlivens an outdoor patio rich with blooming flowers. (There are additional tables set up inside.) By far the most popular drink here is a frothy margarita, which might be followed by your choice of tacos, burritos, frijoles, fajitas, and guacamoles. The chef's specialty is barbecue meats. Be alert to the number of drinks you consume, however, since the bill seems to mount quickly once you begin.

Monopol, Palangreros, 7. ☎ **247-44-48.**

Cuisine: INTERNATIONAL. **Reservations:** Recommended.

Prices: Appetizers 390–1,100 ptas. ($2.80–$7.80); main courses 990–2,550 ptas. ($7–$18.10); fixed-price menus 1,150–3,990 ptas. ($8.20–$28.30). AE, MC, V.

Open: Dinner only, Mon–Sat 7pm–midnight. **Closed:** Aug.

Set in the heart of town, near both the beach and Fuengirola's post office, this cozy restaurant is the domain of German-born Paul Wartman and his wife, Barbal. Since 1981, Monopol has catered to a varied European clientele, many of whom appreciate the culinary specialties of their respective homelands. The building was constructed about a century ago, and although it's not graced with an open-air courtyard, the restaurant offers a quartet of rustically decorated dining rooms and a wine list including a fine assortment of Riojas. House specialties include a ragoût of chicken with mango and curry cream, filets of lamb saddle with rosemary, magret of duck with lentils, and filet strips in a *fines herbes* sauce.

Restaurant Tomate, El Troncon, 19. ☎ **246-35-59.**

Cuisine: INTERNATIONAL. **Reservations:** Recommended.
Prices: Appetizers 350–725 ptas. ($2.50–$5.10); main courses 650–1,990 ptas. ($4.60–$14.10). AE, MC, V.
Open: Dinner only, Tues–Sun 7pm–midnight.

One of the most gastronomically sophisticated restaurants in town presents the best culinary traditions of northern and southern Europe. Set within the heart of Fuengirola, in a century-old town house whose dining space was recently added on in back, Tomate is the creative statement of German-born Michael Lienhoop. Meals might include dishes from Spain (gazpacho or filet of hake floating on a lake of mustard-flavored cream-and-herb sauce), France (langoustines Provençales), Germany (sauerkraut with an assortment of smoked meats or pork in a sauce of red wine and mushrooms), and Scandinavia (a selection of marinated herring and marinated salmon with dill sauce).

8 Mijas

18½ miles (30km) W of Málaga, 363 miles (584km) S of Madrid.

GETTING THERE • **By Bus** There's frequent bus service from the terminal at Fuengirola.

• **By Car** At Fuengirola, take the Mijas road north.

ESSENTIALS The area code for Mijas is 95.

Just five miles (8km) north of coastal road N-340, this village is known as "White Mijas" because of its marble-white Andalusian-style houses. Mijas is at the foot of a sierra near the turnoff to Fuengirola, and from its lofty height, 1,476 feet above sea level, you get a panoramic view of the Mediterranean.

Celts, Phoenicians, and Moors preceded today's intrepid tourists in visiting Mijas. The town itself—not any specific monument—is the attraction. The easiest way to get around its cobblestoned streets is to rent a burro taxi. If you find Mijas overrun with souvenir shops, head for a park at the top of Cuesta de la Villa, where you'll see the ruins of a **Moorish fortress** dating from 833. If you're in Mijas for a fiesta, you'll be attending events in the country's only square bullring.

Where to Stay

★ **Hotel Mijas,** Urbanización Tamisa, 2, 29650 Mijas. ☎ **95/248-58-00.** Fax 95/248-58-25. 100 rms (all with bath), 3 suites. TV TEL

Rates: 8,000–10,000 ptas. ($56.80–$71) single; 10,000–12,000 ptas. ($71–$85.20) double. Suite 20,000–24,000 ptas. ($142–$170.40). Breakfast 1,200 ptas. ($8.50) extra. AE, DC, MC, V. **Parking:** Free.

One of the most charming hotels on the Costa del Sol was built in the 1970s on steeply sloping land in the center of town. Designed in a four-story, Andalusian-inspired block of white walls, wrought-iron accents, and flowering terraces, it features sweeping views over the Mediterranean from most of its public areas and accommodations. Throughout, the style is sun-flooded, comfortable, and Andalusian, and the staff is tactful and hardworking. The in-house tavern is accented with enormous kegs of wine, while the lounge is the setting for live music on some evenings, performed amid Iberian antiques and a collection of unusual fans. A fixed-price meal in the restaurant costs 2,500 ptas. ($17.80). The hotel's facilities include tennis courts, a swimming pool, a sauna, a gymnasium, a boutique, facilities for games of lawn bowling, a hairdresser, and a barber. If you have an aversion to climbing stairs, ask for a room on one of the lower floors, because there is no elevator.

Where to Dine

Club El Padrastro, Paseo del Compás. ☎ **248-50-00.**

Cuisine: INTERNATIONAL. **Reservations:** Recommended.
Prices: Appetizers 450–1,475 ptas. ($3.20–$10.50); main courses 975–2,400 ptas. ($6.90–$17); fixed-price menus 1,175–2,215 ptas. ($8.30–$15.70). AE, DC, MC, V.
Open: Lunch, daily 12:30–4pm; dinner, daily 7–11pm.

Part of the fun of dining at El Padrastro is reaching the place. You go to the cliff side of town and, if you're athletic, walk up 77 steps; if you're not, take the elevator to the highest point. Once you get there, you'll discover that El Padrastro is the town's best dining spot, offering international cuisine on its terraces with their panoramic views of the Mediterranean coast. You can choose whether to eat inexpensively or elaborately. If it's the latter, make it chateaubriand with a bottle of the best Spanish champagne. If you stick to regional dishes, you'll save money.

$ **Restaurante El Capricho,** Los Caños, 5. ☎ **248-51-11.**

Cuisine: INTERNATIONAL. **Reservations:** Recommended.
Prices: Appetizers 400–875 ptas. ($2.80–$6.20); main courses 1,400–2,100 ptas. ($9.90–$14.90); fixed-price lunch 1,000 ptas. ($7.10). AE, DC, MC, V.
Open: Lunch, Thurs–Tues 12:30–4pm; dinner, Thurs–Tues 7–11:30pm. **Closed:** Nov 15–Dec 15.

El Capricho, located in what was once an 1850s private home in the town center, draws a large English-speaking clientele, and the varied menu is geared to their tastes. Appetizers include prawn cocktail, Serrano ham, omelets, corn on the cob, soups, and salads. Among the main dishes are sole and trout, grilled swordfish, chicken Kiev, shish kebab, steak Diane, fiery hot shrimp pil-pil, and flambéed meats. You might prefer the paella Mijeña, which is excellent. Desserts range from flambéed concoctions to baked Alaska. The wine list offers good choices, including the house Valdepeñas.

9 Torremolinos

9 miles (14km) W of Málaga; 76 miles (122km) E of Algeciras; 353 miles (568km) S of Madrid

GETTING THERE • By Plane Torremolinos is served by the nearby Málaga airport.

- **By Train** There are frequent departures from the terminal at Málaga.
- **By Bus** Buses run frequently between Málaga and Torremolinos.
- **By Car** Take the N-340 west from Málaga or the N-340 east from Marbella.

ESSENTIALS The area code for Torremolinos is 95. The tourist information office at La Nogalera, 517 (☎ **95/238-15-78**). In winter the weather can get chilly, so pack accordingly.

This Mediterranean beach resort is the most famous in Spain. It's a gathering place for international visitors, a melting pot of Europeans and Americans. Many relax here after a whirlwind tour of Europe—the living's easy, the people are fun, and there are no historical monuments to visit. Thus the sleepy fishing village of Torremolinos has been engulfed in a cluster of cement-walled resort hotels. Prices are on the rise, but it nevertheless remains one of Europe's vacation bargains.

Where to Stay

EXPENSIVE

Aloha Puerto Sol, Calle Salvador Allende, 45, 29620 Torremolinos. ☎ **95/238-70-66,** or toll free in the U.S. **800/336-3542.** Fax 95/238-57-01. 430 rms (all with bath) A/C MINIBAR TV TEL

Rates: (including buffet breakfast): 6,143–9,408 ptas. ($43.60–$66.80) single; 7,000–13,550 ptas. ($49.70–$96.20) double. AE, DC, MC, V.

Heralded as one of the most modern hotels along the Costa del Sol when it was built in 1972, this hotel stands on the seashore in the residential suburb of El Saltillo, on the southwestern edge of Torremolinos, beside the coastal road leading to Marbella. Away from the noise of the town center, it offers spacious rooms, each of which is defined by the hotel as a mini-suite. Each faces the sea, the Benalmádena marina, or the beach, and each contains a separate sitting area.

Amid all the accessories of a resort, guests are given a choice of two restaurants and four bars. The most popular lunchtime option is a poolside buffet, where each diner pays 1,500 ptas. ($10.70) for an all-you-can-eat medley of meats, salads, and seafood. Many guests spend their days near the two swimming pools, one of which is heated. Spanish evenings at El Comodoro, one of the several bars on the premises, last well into the early morning hours.

Don Pablo, Paseo Marítimo, s/n, 29620 Torremolinos. ☎ **95/238-38-88.** Fax 95/238-37-83. 443 rms. A/C MINIBAR TV TEL

Rates: (including buffet breakfast): 10,350–14,450 ptas. ($73.50–$102.60) single; 13,250–18,350 ptas. ($94.10–$130.30) double. AE, DC, MC, V.

One of the most desirable hotels in Torremolinos is housed in a modern building that's located a minute from the beach and surrounded by its own garden and playground areas. There are two unusually shaped open-air swimming pools, with terraces for sunbathing and refreshments, and a large indoor pool as well. The surprise is the glamorous interior, which borrows heavily from Moorish palaces and medieval castle themes. Arched tile arcades have splashing fountains, and life-size stone statues of nude figures in niches line the grand staircase. The comfortably furnished bedrooms have sea-view terraces and private baths.

The hotel has a full day-and-night entertainment program, including keep-fit classes, dancing at night to a live band, and a disco. Piano music is played in a wood-paneled English lounge, and the hotel has video movies shown on a giant-screen every night. At lunch, a buffet is spread before you.

Hotel Cervantes, Calle las Mercedes, s/n, 29620 Torremolinos. ☎ **95/238-40-33.** Fax 95/238-48-57. 370 rms. A/C TV TEL

Rates: (including breakfast): 7,844–99,540 ptas. ($55.70–$67.70) single; 11,256–14,000 ptas. ($79.90–$99.40) double. Half board 4,500 ptas. ($32) per person extra. AE, DC, MC, V.

The four-star Cervantes is a seven-minute walk from the beach. It has its own garden and is adjacent to a maze of patios and narrow streets of boutiques and open-air cafés. The Cervantes is self-contained, with many facilities—including a sun terrace; a sauna; massage; two pools (one covered and heated); hairdressers; a gift shop; a TV and video lounge; games, such as billiards, table tennis, and darts; and a card room.

The bedrooms have streamlined modern furniture, private baths, piped-in music, safes, TVs, and spacious terraces; many have sea-view balconies.

A restaurant, a bar with an orchestra and entertainment programs, and a coffee shop are among the attractions. A fixed-price lunch for nonresidents costs 2,438 pesetas ($17.30). In midsummer, this hotel is likely to be booked with tour groups from northern Europe.

Melía Costa del Sol, Paseo Marítimo, 19, 29620 Torremolinos. ☎ **95/238-66-77,** or toll free in the U.S. **800/336-3542.** Fax 95/238-64-17. 540 rms, 18 suites. A/C TV TEL

Rates: 6,550–9,550 ptas. ($46.50–$67.80) single; 8,350–11,900 ptas. ($59.30–$84.50) double; 22,500–31,500 ptas. ($159.80–$223.70) suite. Breakfast 700 ptas. ($5) extra. AE, DC, MC, V. **Parking:** Free.

There are two Melía hotels in Torremolinos, both operated by a popular hotel chain in Spain, but this one is preferred by many travelers because of its more central location. It is practically twice the size of the smaller hotel and offers modern and well-maintained guest rooms, each with a private bath. However, the hotel is popular with package-tour groups, and you may not feel a part of things if you're here alone. The facilities include a garden, swimming pool, Thalassotherapy center, shopping arcade, and hairdressing salon. Once a week a free flamenco show is presented to house guests, and on the other six nights there is a pianist who plays for dancing couples.

Melía Torremolinos, Carlota Alessandri, 109, 29620 Torremolinos. ☎ **95/238-05-00,** or toll free in the U.S. **800/336-3542.** Fax 95/238-05-38. 275 rms, 6 suites. A/C TV TEL

Rates: 9,440–12,000 ptas. ($67–$85.20) single; 11,800–15,000 ptas. ($83.80–$106.50) double; 22,000–27,000 ptas. ($156.20–$191.70) suite. Breakfast 950 ptas. ($6.70) extra. AE, DC, MC, V. **Parking:** Free. **Closed:** Nov–Mar.

This is the more luxurious of the two Melía hotels at the resort, but farther removed from the center. The hotel deliberately lowered its official rank from five stars to four stars, which means you can enjoy the amenities and service of a five-star hotel but at lower prices. Rising six floors from a position on the western outskirts of town, on the road to Cádiz, it stands in its own gardens. Bedrooms are generally spacious and always well furnished and maintained; many contain minibars. The public areas were renovated and upgraded in 1993. The hotel features a seemingly endless series of buffets, costing 2,300 pesetas ($16.30) per person. Other facilities include a swimming pool and tennis courts, and flamenco shows are occasionally presented.

Hotel Los Arcos, Carlota Alessandri, 192, 29620 Torremolinos. ☎ **95/238-08-22.** Fax 95/238-02-20. 51 rms (all with bath). A/C TV TEL

Rates (including breakfast): 4,550 ptas. ($32.30) single; 7,900 ptas. ($56.10) double. AE, DC, MC, V.

Built in 1958 as a grand villa evocative of Beverly Hills in the 1920s, this Spanish-style house was remodeled and modernized in the 1990s. Eclectic furnishings are placed throughout. The bedrooms are pleasant, all with balconies and garden views and half with minibars. A complete lunch or dinner is available for 1,260 pesetas ($8.90). The hotel stands 225 yards from the beach and less than a mile (1km) from the town center.

Sidi Lago Rojo, Miami, 1, 29620 Torremolinos. ☎ **95/238-76-66.** Fax 95/238-08-91. 144 rms (all with bath). A/C TV TEL

Rates: 7,500 ptas. ($53.30) single occupancy of double rooms; 9,950 ptas. ($70.60) double. Breakfast 625 ptas. ($4.40) extra, AE, DC, MC, V.

Located in the heart of the fishing village of La Carihuela and the finest place to stay there, Sidi Lago Rojo stands only 150 feet from the beach and has its own gardens, swimming pool, sunbathing terraces, and refreshment bar. It offers studio-style guest rooms, doubles only, tastefully decorated with contemporary Spanish furnishings and tile baths. All the rooms have terraces with views; some have minibars. In the late evening there is disco dancing. The hotel also has a good restaurant, with meals costing 2,000 pesetas ($14.20).

Sol Palomas, Carmen Montes, 1, 29620 Torremolinos. ☎ **95/238-50-00.** Fax 95/238-64-66. 345 rms (all with bath). TEL

Rates (including half board): 3,640–7,265 ptas. ($25.80–$51.60) per person. AE, DC, MC, V.

Originally built during the heyday of Torremolinos' construction boom (1968), this well-managed hotel is one of the town's most attractive, surrounded by carefully tended gardens. Located near the coastal road, a one-minute walk from the beach and a ten-minute walk south of the center of town, it has an Andalusian decor that extends into the bedrooms; a formal entrance; and a clientele of repeat visitors who hail mostly from France, Belgium, and Holland. Each of the rooms contains a private balcony, a tiled bathroom, and furniture inspired by southern Spain. None is air-conditioned, although many clients compensate by opening windows and balcony doors to catch the sea breezes. The hotel boasts a sauna, three swimming pools (one reserved for children), some form of entertainment going on throughout the day and early evening, a handful of shops, a hairdresser, and an unending series of lunchtime and dinner buffets.

INEXPENSIVE

Hostal Los Jazmines, Lido, s/n, 29620 Torremolinos. ☎ **95/238-50-33.** Fax 95/237-27-02. 85 rms (all with bath). TEL

Rates: 3,000–4,700 ptas. ($21.30–$33.40) single; 4,000–5,900 ptas. ($28.40–$41.90) double. Breakfast 330 ptas. ($2.30) extra. AE, MC, V.

On one of the best beaches in Torremolinos, facing a plaza at the foot of the shady Avenida del Lido, this choice for sunseekers is replete with terraces, lawns, and an irregularly shaped swimming pool. Meals are served al fresco or inside the appealing dining room, furnished with Spanish reproductions. A set menu costs 1,500 pesetas ($10.70). The bedrooms, all doubles, seem a bit impersonal, but they have their own little balconies, coordinated colors, and compact baths. From here it's a good hike up the hill to the town center.

Hotel El Pozo, Casablanca, 4, 29620 Torremolinos. ☎ **95/238-06-22.** 28 rms (all with bath). TV TEL

Rates: 4,000 ptas. ($28.40) single; 5,500 ptas. ($39.10) double. Breakfast 325 ptas. ($2.30) extra. DC, MC, V.

This hotel isn't for light sleepers, and it's usually filled with budget travelers, including many students from the north of Europe. It's in one of the liveliest sections of town, a short walk from the train station. The lobby-level bar has an open fireplace, heavy Spanish furniture, cool white tiles, and a view of a small courtyard. From your window or terrace you can view the promenades below. The guest rooms are furnished in a simple, functional style.

$ **Miami,** Aladino, 14, 29620 Torremolinos. ☎ **95/238-52-55.** 27 rms (all with bath). TEL

Rates: 3,340 ptas. ($23.70) single; 5,700 ptas. ($40.50) double. Breakfast 290 ptas. ($2.10) extra. No credit cards.

The Miami, near the Carihuela section, is like one of those Hollywood movie-star homes of the 1920s. It may even bring back silent-screen memories of Vilma Banky and Rod La Rocque. Its swimming pool is isolated by high walls and private gardens. Fuchsia bougainvillea climb over the rear patio's arches. A tile terrace is used for sunbathing and refreshments. The country-style living room contains a walk-in fireplace and abundant brass and copper. The bedrooms are furnished with style, each traditional and comfortable and boasting a balcony. Breakfast is the only meal served.

NEARBY PLACES TO STAY

Where Torremolinos ends and Benalmádena-Costa to the west begins is hard to say. Benalmádena-Costa has long been a resort extension on the western frontier of Torremolinos, and it's packed with hotels, restaurants, and tourist facilities.

★ **Hotel Torrequebrada,** Carretera de Cádiz, km 220, 29630 Benalmádena. ☎ **95/244-60-00.** Fax 95/244-57-02. 317 rms, 33 suites. A/C MINIBAR TV TEL

Rates (including breakfast): 15,300–18,000 ptas. ($108.60–$127.80) single; 19,000–22,500 ptas. ($134.90–$159.80) double; 28,500-31,500 ptas. ($202.40–$223.70) suite. Discounts granted for stays of 5 or more days. AE, DC, MC, V. **Parking:** Free.

In the late 1980s this became one of the largest five-star luxury hotels to rise along the Costa del Sol. Lying three miles (5km) west of Torremolinos, it opens onto its own beach and offers a wide range of facilities and attractions, including one of the largest casinos in Europe and a world-class golf course. In addition, it has an array of restaurants, bars, pools, gardens, a nightclub, a health club, a beach club, and tennis courts—you'll almost need a floor plan to navigate your way around the complex. Nine levels of underground parking accommodate motorists. The hotel is furnished in muted Mediterranean colors, and both antique and modern furniture are used.

The hotel offers handsomely furnished and coordinated bedrooms in two 11-story towers. All accommodations have large terraces with sea views, plus private safes and baths.

A specialty restaurant, Café Royal, overlooks the gardens and the sea, enjoying a five-fork rating for its international cuisine. Meals cost from 5,000 pesetas ($35.50). At garden level, the Pavillion provides buffet and cafeteria service throughout the day. A flamenco show is presented at 11pm on Thursday, Friday, and Saturday, costing 3,500 pesetas ($24.90) including two drinks.

Tritón, Avenida António Machado, 29, 29491 Benalmádena-Costa. ☎ **95/244-32-40.** Fax 95/244-26-49. 196 rms, 10 suites. A/C MINIBAR TV TEL

Rates (including breakfast): 14,800–15,800 ptas. ($105.10–$112.20) single; 19,100–21,000 ptas. ($135.60–$149.10) double; from 39,600 ptas. ($281.20) suite. AE, DC, MC, V. **Parking:** Free.

Less than 2 miles (3km) north of Torremolinos, the Tritón is a beachfront Miami Beach–style resort colony in front of the marina of Benalmádena-Costa. It features a high-rise stack of guest rooms as well as an impressive pool and garden area.

Surrounding the swimming pool are subtropical trees and vegetation, plus thatched sunshade umbrellas. All the rooms have wide windows opening onto sun balconies and private baths.

Among the public rooms are multilevel lounges and two bars with wood paneling and handmade rustic furniture (one has stained-glass windows). For dining, there's the main restaurant with its three-tiered display of hors d'oeuvres, fruits, and desserts; a barbecue grill; plus a luncheon terrace where ferns and banana trees form the backdrop. The Tritón also offers tennis courts, a Swedish sauna, and a piano player in the bar.

Where to Dine

The cuisine in Torremolinos is more American and continental European than Andalusian. The hotels often serve elaborate four-course meals, but you may want to sample the local fast-food offerings. A good spot to try is the food court called **La Nogalera,** the major gathering place in Torremolinos, located between the coast road and the beach. Head down the Calle del Cauce to this compound of modern whitewashed Andalusian buildings. Open to pedestrian traffic only, it features a maze of passageways, courtyards, and patios for eating and drinking. If you're seeking anything from sandwiches to Belgian waffles to scrambled eggs to pizzas, you'll find it here.

AT LA NOGALERA

El Gato Viudo, La Nogalera, 8. ☎ **238-51-29.**

Cuisine: SPANISH. **Reservations:** Not required.

Prices: Appetizers 400-800 ptas. ($2.80–$5.70); main courses 700–1,850 ptas. ($5–$13.10). AE, DC, MC, V.

Open: Lunch, Thurs–Tues 1–4pm; dinner Thurs–Tues 6–11:30pm.

Simple and aimiable, this old-fashioned tavern occupies the street level and the cellar of a building off Calle San Miguel. It offers sidewalk seating for those who prefer it, and a tradition with local diners that dates back to its founding in 1960. The menu includes such dishes as grilled fish; marinated hake; roasted pork, steak, and veal;

calamari with spicy tomato sauce; grilled shrimp; and shellfish or fish soup. The atmosphere is informal, and the staff has grown accustomed over the years to coping with clients from virtually everywhere.

Golden Curry, Calle Guetaria, s/n, La Nogalera, Bloque 6. ☎ **237-4855.**

Cuisine: INDIAN. **Reservations:** Not required.
Prices: Appetizers 400–550 ptas. ($2.80–$3.90); main courses 850–1,400 ptas. ($6–$9.90). AE, MC, V.
Open: Lunch daily 1–4pm; dinner daily 7pm–1am.

Set one floor above street level, in the commercial heart of Torremolinos, this restaurant specializes in traditional Moghul dishes of India, which have been adapted and altered to suit British tastes. The two chefs and the Calcutta-born owner all worked in Indian restaurants in London prior to emigrating to Spain, and today receive a goodly percentage of their business from British holidaymakers. Menu items are served in a single dining room amid a scattering of Indian paintings, and include, among others, chicken Madras; chicken in onion sauce; lamb slow-cooked in spices and served with lentils; and succulent versions of prawns. Vegetarian dishes are also served, the best of which arrive as an array of small dishes which, when several or more are combined, create satisfying meatless meals.

IN THE CENTER

Restaurante Cantón, Plaza de la Gamba Alegre, 22. ☎ **238-21-17.**

Cuisine: CHINESE. **Reservations:** Recommended. **Bus:** 4 to town center.
Prices: Appetizers 195–450 ptas. ($1.40–$3.20); main courses 500–925 ptas. ($3.60–$6.60); fixed-price menus 950 ptas. ($6.70). AE, MC, V.
Open: Lunch, Wed–Mon 1–4pm; dinner, Wed–Mon 7:30pm–midnight.

Near the main shopping center of Torremolinos is one of the resort's most reasonably priced restaurants. Its very popular set menu includes a spring roll, sweet-and-sour pork, beef with onions, steamed white rice, dessert, and a drink. You can also order special combination platters for 500 pesetas ($3.60) and up. Ordering à la carte means partaking of such specialties as chicken with almonds and grilled king prawn Chinese style. The staff is efficient and cordial.

AT LA CARIHUELA

If you want to get away from the brash high-rises and honky-tonks, head to nearby Carihuela, the old fishing village on the western outskirts of Torremolinos, where some of the best bargain restaurants are found. You can walk down a hill toward the sea to reach it.

$ **Casa Prudencio,** Carmen, 41, at La Carihuela. ☎ **238-14-52.**

Cuisine: SEAFOOD. **Reservations:** Recommended.
Prices: Appetizers 550–750 ptas. ($3.90–$5.30); main courses 850–1,800 ptas. ($6–$12.80); fixed-price menu 1,500 ptas. ($10.70). AE, MC, V.
Open: Lunch, Tues–Sun 1–5pm; dinner, Tues–Sun 7:30pm–midnight. **Closed:** Dec 25–Feb 15.

Tops with locals and visitors alike, this seaside restaurant just over a mile (2km) west of the center is the oldest surviving restaurant in the fishing hamlet of Carihuela. It features gazpacho, lentils, shrimp omelets, swordfish, and shish kebab. Try the special paella for a main course, followed by strawberries with whipped cream (in the late spring) for dessert. The atmosphere is cordial, and almost everyone sits together at long tables. If you want to splurge, order *lubina à la sal*—a huge boneless fish packed under a layer of salt, which is then broken open at your table. It makes a singular gastronomical treat.

El Roqueo, Calle del Carmen, 35, at La Carihuela. ☎ **238-49-46.**

Cuisine: SEAFOOD. **Reservations:** Recommended.
Prices: Appetizers 550–850 ptas. ($3.90–$6); main courses 1,400–2,200 ptas. ($9.90–$15.60); fixed-price menus 1,300 ptas. ($9.20). AE, DC, MC, V.
Open: Lunch, Wed–Mon 1–4pm; dinner, Wed–Mon 7pm–midnight. **Closed:** Nov.

Right in the heart of this fishermen's village, El Roqueo, which was established in 1975, makes the perfect place for a seafood dinner near the sea. Begin with the savory *sopa de mariscos* (shellfish soup). Then try a specialty of the chef, fish baked in rock salt; you can also order grilled sea bass or shrimp. Top everything off with a soothing caramel custard for dessert. Some of the more expensive fish courses are priced by the gram, so order carefully.

AT PLAYAMAR

El Vietnam del Sur, Playamar, Bloque, 9. ☎ **238-67-37.**

Cuisine: VIETNAMESE. **Reservations:** Required.
Prices: Appetizers 475–600 ptas. ($3.40–$4.30); main courses 750–1,200 ptas. ($5.30–$8.50). AE, MC, V.
Open: Lunch, Sun 1–4pm; dinner, Thurs–Tues 7pm–midnight. **Closed:** Jan–Feb.

The inexpensive food here is best shared. Chopsticks are the norm as you begin with spring rolls served with mint and a spicy sauce for dipping. The chef's specials include fried stuffed chicken wings and beef with rice noodles. The wine list is short and moderately priced. With an outside dining terrace, the restaurant stands in the Playamar section near the beach.

AT LOS ALAMOS

Frutos, Carretera de Cádiz, km 235, Urbanización Los Alamos. ☎ **238-14-50.**

Cuisine: SPANISH. **Reservations:** Recommended.
Prices: Appetizers 600–1,200 ptas. ($4.30–$8.50); main courses 1,000–2,100 ptas. ($7.10–$14.90); fixed-price menu 1,200 ptas. ($8.50). AE, MC, V.
Open: Lunch, daily 1–4:30pm; dinner, Mon–Sat 8pm–midnight.

Malagueños frequent this place in droves, as they like its good old-style cooking—the cuisine is Spanish with a vengeance. The portions are large and the service is hectic. Diners enjoy the "day's catch," perhaps rape (monkfish), angler fish, or the increasingly rare mero (grouper). Also available are garlic-studded leg of lamb and oxtail prepared in a savory ragoût. Frutos is located next to the Los Alamos service station, $1^1/_4$ miles (2km) from the town center.

AT BENALMÁDENA

★ **Mar de Alborán,** Alay, 5. ☎ **244-64-27.**

Cuisine: BASQUE/ANDALUSIAN. **Reservations:** Recommended.
Prices: Appetizers 750–1,850 ptas. ($5.30–$13.10); main courses 1,600–2,350 ptas. ($11.40–$16.70); *menús del día* 3,500–4,000 ptas. ($24.90–$28.40). AE, DC, MC, V.
Open: Lunch, Sun and Tues–Fri 1:30–3:30pm; dinner, Tues–Sun 8:30–11:30pm. **Closed:** Dec 22–Jan 22.

Decorated in shades of yellow and white, this restaurant offers an elegantly airy decor that seems appropriate for its location near the sea. Within a short walk from the resort's Puerto Marina, it offers a combination of the regional specialties of both Andalusia and the Basque region of northern Spain. Menu items change with the seasons but might include cold terrine of leeks; crabmeat salad; Basque *piperadda* in puff pastry; *piquillos rellenos* (red peppers stuffed with pulverized fish in a sweet pepper sauce); *bacalao* (salted cod) "Club Ranero," served with garlic and red-pepper cream sauce; *kokotxas,* the Basque national dish of hake cheeks in green sauce with clams; anglerfish with prawns; pork filet with béarnaise sauce; duck with apples; and foie gras served with sweet Málaga wine and raisins. In season, the restaurant's game dishes are renowned. Dessert might be a frothy version of peach mousse served with purée of fruit and dark-chocolate sauce.

Marrakech, Carretera de Menalmádena, 1. ☎ **238-21-69.**

Cuisine: MOROCCAN. **Reservations:** Recommended.
Prices: Appetizers 650–850 ptas. ($4.60–$6); main courses 1,200–2,000 ptas. ($8.50–$14.20). AE.
Open: Lunch, Wed–Sat 12:30–4:30pm; dinner, Mon and Wed–Sat 7:30pm–midnight.

Excellent Moroccan cuisine is offered here amid a rather garish decor of tiles and carved plaster. Some of the more famous dishes of the Maghreb served here include couscous; *tagine* (meat pies); and various kebabs, usually made with lamb. The stuffed pastries make a fitting dessert if you're Moroccan; otherwise, you might find them too sweet. Marrakech is located at the western edge of Torremolinos, 1¹/₄ miles (2km) from the town center.

Evening Entertainment

Torremolinos has more nightlife activity than any other spot along the Costa del Sol. The earliest action is always at the bars, which are lively most of the night, serving drinks and tapas (Spanish hors d'oeuvres). Sometimes it seems that in Torremolinos there are more bars than people, so you shouldn't have trouble finding one you like. Note that some of the bars are open during the day as well.

DRINKS & TAPAS

Bar Central, Plaza Andalucía, Bloque 1. ☎ **238-27-60.**

Bar Central offers coffee, brandy, beer, cocktails, limited sandwiches, and pastries—served either inside or on a large, French-style covered terrace. It's a good spot to meet congenial people. Drinks begin at 125 pesetas (90¢) for a beer or 350 pesetas ($2.50) for a hard drink. Bar Central is open Monday to Saturday from 9am to 2am.

Bar El Toro, San Miguel, 32. ☎ **238-65-04.**

Bar El Toro, in the very center of Torremolinos, is for bullfight aficionados. Kegs of beer, stools, and the terrace in the main shopping street make it perfect for drinking a before-dinner sherry or an after-dinner beer. As a special attraction, the staff prepares a bullfight poster, with your name between those of two famous matadors, for 550 pesetas ($3.90). Drinks at your table begin at 175 pesetas ($1.20) for beer or 380 pesetas ($2.70) for a pitcher of sangría. Open daily from 8am to midnight.

La Bodega, San Miguel, 38. ☎ **238-73-37.**

La Bodega relies on its colorful clientele and the quality of its tapas to draw customers, who seem to seek this place out above the dozens of other tascas within this popular tourist zone. You'll be fortunate to find space at one of the small tables, since many clients consider the bar food plentiful enough for a satisfying lunch or dinner. Once you begin to order one of the platters of fried squid, pungent tuna, grilled shrimp, or tiny brochettes of sole, you might not be able to stop. Most tapas cost 175 pesetas ($1.20) to 650 pesetas ($4.60). A beer costs 125 pesetas (90¢). La Bodega's hours are daily from noon to midnight.

DANCE CLUBS & DISCOS

New Piper's Club, Plaza Costa del Sol. ☎ **238-29-94.**

The leading disco in town resembles a subterranean world: Its decor is tongue-in-cheek and suggests the caves at Nerja. Spread over many levels, with connecting ramps and tunnels, it has several dance floors, splashing water in reflecting pools, strobe lighting, and an aggressive set of international records to amuse its packed audience. It's very much the 1960s in aura and ambience. After your first drink, a beer costs 300 pesetas ($2.10). Open nightly from 6 to 10:30pm and 11pm to 4:30am.

Admission (including first drink): Before 10pm, 800 ptas. ($5.70); Sun–Thurs after 11pm, 1,100 ptas. ($7.80); Fri–Sat after 11pm, 1,300 ptas. ($9.20).

El Palladium, Montemar, 68. ☎ **238-42-89.**

Set close to the Hotel Sol Palomas, within a 10-minute walk south of the town center, this well-designed nightclub is one of the most convivial in Torremolinos. The illumination contains strobes and spotlights accompanying a sound system described as loud and distortion free. It's open nightly from 6pm to 4am, with disco music beginning around 10pm. Expect to pay from 350 pesetas ($2.50) for a drink.

Admission: 800 ptas. ($5.70) after 10pm.

THE GAY LIFE

Torremolinos has the largest cluster of gay life along the coast of southern Spain. Several bars huddle together in Pueblo Blanco, which is like a little village of its own. Although much gay and lesbian life also sprawls across La Nogalera, the restaurants there tend to attract a mixed crowd.

Bronx, Edificio Centro Jardín. ☎ **238-73-60.**

The leading gay disco in town is Bronx, where beer goes for 350 pesetas ($2.50). It's open nightly from 10pm to 6am.

Admission: 1,000 ptas. ($7.10).

Men's Bar, La Nogalera, 714. ☎ **238-42-05.**

One of the most popular gay bars in La Nogalera is called simply "Men's Bar." Crowded most nights, it charges 300 pesetas ($2.10) for beer and stays open nightly from 9pm to 5am.

A CASINO

Casino Torrequebrada, Carretera de Cádiz, 266, Benalmádena Costa. ☎ **244-25-45.**

Considered one of the major casinos along the Costa del Sol, this establishment is located on the lobby level of the Hotel Torrequebrada. The Torrequebrada combines a nightclub/cabaret; a restaurant; and an array of tables devoted to blackjack, chemin de fer, punto y banco, and two kinds of roulette.

The nightclub offers year round a flamenco show presented at 11pm on Thursday, Friday, and Saturday nights; in midsummer, there might be more glitz and frequent shows (ask when you get there or call). The casino is open daily from 9am to 4am. Nightclub acts begin at 10:30pm (Spanish revue) and midnight (Las Vegas revue). The restaurant is open nightly from 9:30pm to 2am.

Admission: Casino, 600 ptas. ($4.30). Cabaret/nightclub, 3,500 ptas. ($24.90), which includes two drinks, admission to both shows, and admission to the casino.

10 Málaga

340 miles (547km) S of Madrid, 82 miles (132km) E of Algeciras

GETTING THERE • By Plane None of the several airlines that fly into Spain from North America touches down in Málaga. Transfers are required in either Madrid or Barcelona, although some airlines (such as British Airways) offer nonstop flights to Málaga from other European cities, such as London.

For passengers who opt for a transfer through Madrid, the largest operator, with the greatest number of connections, is **Iberia,** the national airline of Spain. Iberia offers daily nonstop service to Madrid from New York, Miami, Los Angeles, Montreal, and Toronto, as well as nonstop service to Barcelona from New York three times per week. (Passengers interested in arranging flights into Málaga should review the information on the "Visit Spain" program described in Chapter 2.)

As for the frequency of its flights, Iberia offers an even greater selection of itineraries into Málaga through its affiliate airlines, which include Binter, Viva, and Aviaco. Flights on any of these airlines can be booked via Iberia's toll-free reservations line: 800/772-4642.

• By Train Málaga maintains good rail connections with Madrid (at least five trains a day). The trip takes seven hours. Many visitors arrive by train after having explored the Andalusian city of Seville. There are five trains a day connecting Seville with Málaga, a four-hour run. For rail information in Málaga, call RENFE at **95/221-31-22.**

• By Bus Buses from all over Spain arrive at the terminal on the Paseo de los Tilos, behind the RENFE offices. Málaga is linked by bus to all the major cities of Spain, including Madrid (five buses per day), Barcelona (three per day), and Valencia (four per day). Call **95/235-00-61** in Málaga for bus information.

• By Car From the resorts in the west (such as Torremolinos or Marbella), head east along the N-340 to Málaga. If you're in the east at the end of the Costa del Sol (Almería), take the N-340 west to Málaga, with a recommended stopover at Nerja.

ESSENTIALS The area code for Málaga is 95. The tourist information office is at Pasaje de Chinitas, 4 (☎ **95/221-34-45**).

Warning: Málaga has one of the highest crime rates in Spain. The most common complaint is purse-snatching, with an estimated 75% of the crimes committed by juveniles. Stolen passports are also a problem—if it happens to you, contact the U.S. Consulate, Edificio El Ancla, Calle Ramón y Cajal, Apt. 502, in nearby Fuengirola (☎ **95/247-98-91**).

SPECIAL EVENTS The most festive time in Málaga is the first week in August, when the city celebrates its reconquest by Ferdinand and Isabella in 1487. This big **feria** (fair) is the occasion for parades and bullfights. A major tree-shaded boulevard of the city, Paseo del Parque, is transformed into a fairground featuring amusements and restaurants.

Málaga is a bustling commercial and residential center whose economy does not depend exclusively on tourism. Its chief attraction is the mild off-season climate—summer can be sticky.

Málaga's most famous citizen is Pablo Picasso, born here in 1881 at Plaza de la Merced, in the center of the city. The co-founder of cubism, who would one day paint his *Guernica* to express his horror of war, unfortunately left little of his spirit in his birthplace and only a small selection of his work.

What to See & Do

Unlike the rest of the Costa del Sol, Málaga has several historical sites of interest to the average visitor.

Alcazaba, Plaza de la Aduana, Alcazabilla. ☎ **221-60-05.**

The remains of this ancient Moorish palace are within easy walking distance of the city center, off Paseo del Parque (plenty of signs point the way up the hill). The fortress was probably erected in the 9th or 10th century, although there have been later additions and reconstructions. Ferdinand and Isabella stayed here when they reconquered the city. The Alcazaba now houses an archeological museum, with exhibits of cultures ranging from Greek to Phoenician to Carthaginian. With government-planted orange trees and purple bougainvillea making the grounds even more beautiful, the view overlooking the city and the bay is among the best on the Costa del Sol.

Admission: Museum, 30 ptas. (20¢).

Open: Museum, Apr–Sept, Tues–Sat 9:30am–1:30pm and 5–8pm; Sun 10am–2pm. Winter, Tues–Fri 10am–1pm and 5–7pm; Sat 10am–1pm and 5–8pm; Sun 10am–2pm. **Bus:** 4, 18, 19, or 24.

Málaga Cathedral, Plaza Obispo. ☎ **221-59-17.**

This 16th-century Renaissance cathedral in Málaga's center, built on the site of a great mosque, suffered damage during the Civil War. But it remains vast and impressive, reflecting changing styles of interior architecture. Its most notable attributes are the richly ornamented choir stalls by Ortiz, Mena, and Michael. The cathedral has been declared a national monument.

Admission: 100 ptas. (70¢).

Open: Mon–Sat 10am–12:30pm and 4–5:30pm. **Bus:** 14, 18, 19, or 24.

Castillo de Gibralfaro, Cerro de Gibralfaro.

On a hill overlooking Málaga and the Mediterranean are the ruins of an ancient Moorish castle-fortress of unknown origin. It is near the government-run parador and might easily be tied in with a luncheon visit.

Warning: Do not walk to Gibralfaro Castle from town. Readers have reported muggings along the way, and the area around the castle is dangerous. Take the bus (see below).

Admission: Free.

Open: Daylight hours. **Microbus:** H, leaving hourly from cathedral.

Museo de Bellas Artes, San Agustín, 6. ☎ **221-83-82.**

Behind the cathedral, this former Moorish palace houses a modest collection of paintings, including a gallery devoted to native son Pablo Picasso. In addition, it also displays works by Murillo, Ribera, and Morales, along with Andalusian antiques, mosaics, and sculptures.

Admission: 250 ptas. ($1.80).

Open: Mon–Fri 10:30am–1:30pm and 5–7pm; Sat–Sun 10:30am–1:30pm. **Bus:** 4, 18, 19, or 24.

Where to Stay

For such a large city in a resort area, Málaga has a surprising lack of hotels. The best ones in all price ranges are documented below. **Note:** Book well in advance for all the paradores.

EXPENSIVE

Hotel Guadalmar, Urbanización Guadalmar, Carretera de Cádiz, km 238, 29080 Málaga. ☎ **95/231-17-03.** 190 rms. A/C MINIBAR TV TEL

Rates: 9,950 ptas. ($70.60) single; 12,950 ptas. ($91. 90) double. Children under 12 free in parents' room. MC, V. **Parking:** Free.

The Guadalmar is a nine-story resort hotel located two miles (3km) from the center of the city and about one mile (2km) from the airport. The hotel has its own private beach, and all the guest rooms open onto the swimming pool and garden. Each well-furnished accommodation is spacious, with a private sea-view balcony and a private bath. For those traveling with children, there are cribs, babysitters, and special menus available, as well as a playground. Take your meals in the dining room, La Bodega, which opens onto the sea and is decorated in a rustic theme. For dancing to a live combo, go straight to La Corrida, the hotel bar.

Málaga Palacio, Cortina del Muelle, 1, 29015 Málaga. ☎ **95/221-51-85.** Fax 95/221-51-85. 207 rms, 16 suites. A/C MINIBAR TV TEL **Bus:** 4, 18, 19, or 24.

Rates: 11,600 ptas. ($82.40) single; 17,500 ptas. ($124.30) double; 23,650 ptas. ($167.90) suite. Breakfast 950 ptas. ($6.70) extra. AE, DC, MC, V. **Parking:** 1,000 ptas. ($7.10) nearby.

One of the leading hotels in the town center, the Palacio opens directly onto a tree-lined esplanade near the cathedral and the harbor. The 1960s building was constructed flat-iron style, rising 15 stories and crowned by an open-air swimming pool and refreshment bar. Most of the balconies open onto views of the port, and down below you can see turn-of-the-century carriages pulled by horses. The bedrooms are traditionally furnished and have private baths. The street-floor lounges mix antiques with more modern furnishings. Other facilities include hairdressers for both men and women, a cafeteria, and boutiques.

Parador Nacional del Golf, Carretera de Málaga, Torremolinos, 29080 Apartado 324, Málaga. ☎ **95/238-12-55.** Fax 95/238-21-41. 60 rms. A/C MINIBAR TV TEL

Rates: 10,000–11,200 ptas. ($71–$79.50) single; 12,500–14,000 ptas. ($88.80–$99.40) double. Breakfast 1,100 ptas. ($7.80) extra. AE, DC, MC, V. **Parking:** Free.

A tasteful resort hotel created by the Spanish government, this hacienda-style parador is flanked by a golf course on one side and the Mediterranean on another. It's less than two miles (3.2km) from the airport, 6.5 miles (10.5km) from Málaga, and 2.5 miles (4km) from Torremolinos. Each bedroom has a private bath and a private balcony with a view of the golfing greens, the circular swimming pool, or the water. The furnishings are attractive. Long tile corridors lead to the air-conditioned public rooms: graciously furnished lounges, a bar, and a restaurant.

MODERATE

Hotel Los Naranjos, Paseo de Sancha, 35, 29016 Málaga. ☎ **95/222-43-19.** Fax 95/222-59-75. 40 rms (all with bath), 1 suite. A/C MINIBAR TV TEL **Bus:** 11.

Rates: 10,100 ptas. ($71.70) single; 13,500 ptas. ($95.90) double; 19,500 ptas. ($138.50) suite. Breakfast 800 ptas. ($5.70) extra. AE, DC, MC, V. **Parking:** 920 ptas. ($6.50).

Hotel Los Naranjos is one of the more reasonably priced (and safer) choices in the city. Serving breakfast only (which costs extra), this is a well-run and well-maintained hotel lying one mile from the heart of town on the eastern side of Málaga past the Plaza de Torres (bullring). It is near the best beach in Málaga, the Baños del Carmen. The hotel offers guest rooms in contemporary styling, with private baths or showers. The public rooms are decorated in the typical Andalusian style, with colorful tiles and ornate wood carving.

Parador de Málaga-Gibralfaro, Monte Gibralfaro, 29016 Málaga. ☎ **95/222-19-02.** Fax 95/222-19-04. 40 rms (all with bath). A/C MINIBAR TV TEL **Directions:** Take the coastal road, Paseo de Reding, which becomes first Avenida Casa de Pries and then Paseo de Sancha. Turn left onto Camino Nuevo and follow the small signs the rest of the way.

Rates: 10,000 ptas. ($71) single; 12,000 ptas. ($85.20) double. Breakfast 1,200 ptas. ($8.50) extra. AE, DC, MC, V. **Parking:** Free.

Restored in 1994 and slated for a reopening in early 1995, this is one of Spain's oldest, more tradition-laden paradors. It enjoys a scenic location high on a plateau near an old fortified castle, overlooking the city and the Mediterranean, with views of the bullring, mountains, and beaches. Originally a famous restaurant, the parador has been converted into a fine hotel with two dining rooms. The bedrooms, with their own entranceways, have private baths, living-room areas, and wide glass doors opening onto private sun terraces with garden furniture. The rooms are tastefully decorated with modern furnishings and reproduction of Spanish antiques.

INEXPENSIVE

$ **El Cenachero,** Barroso, 5, 29001 Málaga. ☎ **95/222-40-88.** 14 rms (all with bath or shower). **Bus:** 15.

Rates: 2,700 ptas. ($19.20) single with shower; 4,000–4,600 ptas. ($28.40–$32.70) double with shower; 5,000 ptas. ($35.50) double with bath. No credit cards.

Opened in 1969, this modest little hotel is five blocks from the park (near the harbor). All the nicely carpeted guest rooms are different; half have showers, the rest baths. Everything is kept clean. No meals are served here.

Hostal Residencia Carlos V, Cister, 6, 29015 Málaga. ☎ **95/221-51-20.** 50 rms (all with bath). TEL **Bus:** 15 from the rail station.

Rates: 2,682–2,925 ptas. ($19–$20.80) single; 5,300–6,095 ptas. ($37.60–$43.30) double. Breakfast 500 ptas. ($3.60) extra. AE, DC, MC, V. **Parking:** 1,090 ptas. ($7.70)

This hotel has a good central location near the cathedral, as well as an interesting facade decorated with wrought-iron balconies and *miradores.* The lobby is fairly dark, but this remains an old, safe haven. An elevator will take you to your room, furnished in a no-frills style.

$ **Hostal Residencia Derby,** San Juan de Díos, 1,29015 Málaga. ☎ **95/222-13-01.** 16 rms (8 with bath or shower). TEL **Bus:** 15.

Rates: 2,500 ptas. ($17.80) single without bath or shower; 3,000 ptas. ($21.30) single with shower; 3,000 ptas. ($21.30) double without bath or shower; 3,500 ptas. ($24.90) double with shower; 4,000 ptas. ($28.40) double with bath. No credit cards.

The Derby is a real find. This fourth-floor boarding house right in the heart of Málaga, on a main square directly north of the train station, has some rooms with excellent views of the Mediterranean and the port of Málaga. The hostal is quite clean. No breakfast is served.

A NEARBY PLACE TO STAY

La Bobadilla, Finca La Bobadilla, 18300 Loja (Granada), Apartado 53. ☎ **958/32-18-61.** Fax 958/32-18-10. 60 rms, 8 suites. A/C MINIBAR TV TEL **Directions:** From the airport at Málaga, follow the signs toward Granada, but at km 178 continue through the village of Salinas. Take the road marked Salinas/Rute but after two miles (3km) follow the signposts for the hotel to the entrance.

Rates (including breakfast): 18,600–22,800 ptas. ($132.10–$161.90) single; 25,600–35,800 ptas. ($181.80–$254.20) double; from 49,800 ptas. ($353.60) suite. AE, DC, MC, V. **Parking:** Free.

An hour's drive northeast of Málaga, La Bobadilla is the most luxurious retreat in the south of Spain. It is a secluded oasis in the foothills of the Sierra Nevada near the town of Loja, which is 44 miles (71km) north of Málaga. La Bobadilla is a 13-mile (21km) drive from Loja.

The hotel complex is built like an Andalusian village, a cluster of whitewashed *casas* constructed around a tower and a white church. Every *casa* is rented to guests, complete with a roof terrace and balcony overlooking the olive-grove-studded district. Each accommodation is individually designed, from the least expensive doubles to the most expensive King's Suite, the latter with plenty of room for bodyguards. The hotel rents its sumptuous bedrooms to a pampered coterie of international guests. The service here is perhaps the finest in all of Spain.

Set on 1,750 acres (718 hectares) of private unspoiled grounds, the hotel village stands on a hillside, red roofed and white painted, blending in with its landscape. Superb craftsmanship is reflected at every turn, from the wrought-iron gates to the Andalusian fountains. The hotel breeds its own domestic animals and grows much of its own food, including fruit and vegetables.

If you get bored in this lap of luxury, you can always drive to Granada in only an hour. Should you decide to marry your companion at this resort, you'll find a chapel featuring an organ 30 feet high with 1,595 pipes.

Dining/Entertainment: Even the King of Spain has dined at La Finca, which serves both a Spanish national and an international cuisine. Meals cost from 4,500 pesetas ($32). El Cortijo, on the other hand, specializes in a regional cuisine. Concerts, featuring flamenco, are presented on Friday and Saturday nights.

Services: Laundry/valet, room service, massage, babysitting.

Facilities: Two tennis courts, horseback riding, archery, outdoor swimming pool, heated indoor swimming pool, Jacuzzis, Finnish sauna, Turkish steam bath, fitness club.

Where to Dine

VERY EXPENSIVE

Café de Paris, Vélez Málaga, 8. ☎ **222-50-43.**

Cuisine: FRENCH. **Reservations:** Required: **Bus:** 13.
Prices: Appetizers 600–1,800 ptas. ($4.30–$12.80); main courses 1,800–2,500 ptas. ($12.80–$17.80); *menú del día* 3,050 ptas. ($21.70). AE, DC, MC, V.
Open: Lunch, Mon–Sat 12:30–4pm; dinner, Mon–Sat 8:30pm-midnight. **Closed:** Aug 30–Sept 10.

Café de Paris lies at La Malagueta, the district surrounding the Plaza de Toros (bullring) of Málaga. This is the domain of the proprietor and chef de cuisine, José García Cortés, who has worked at many important dining rooms before carving out his own niche. Some critics have suggested that the chef's cuisine is pitched too high for the taste of the average Malagueño patronizing this establishment, at least too high for the pocketbook—particularly when it comes to caviar, game (including partridge), or foie gras, which are often featured on the menu.

Much of the Cortés's cuisine has been adapted from classic French dishes to please the Andalusian palate. Menus are changed frequently, reflecting both the chef's imagination and the availability of produce in the Málaga markets. You might on any given night be served crêpes gratinée (filled with baby eels) or local white fish baked in salt, (it doesn't sound good but is excellent). Meat Stroganoff is made here not with the usual cuts of beef but with ox meat. Save room for the creative desserts: Try, for example, a citrus-flavored sorbet made with champagne. One pleased diner pronounced the custard apple mousse "divine."

Moderate

Antonio Martín, Paseo Marítimo, 4. ☎ **222-21-13.**

Cuisine: SPANISH. **Reservations:** Required. **Bus:** 13.
Prices: Appetizers 900–1,500 ptas. ($6.40–$10.70); main courses 1,750–2,300 ptas. ($12.40–$16.30). AE, DC, MC, V.
Open: Lunch, daily 1–4pm; dinner, Mon–Sat 8pm–midnight.

Although this brick building is close to a busy intersection near the Plaza de Toros, you'll hardly be aware of the traffic outside. Four dining rooms with natural brick walls are clustered under a peaked wooden ceiling. The most rustic of them, the Rincón de Ordóñez, honors one of Spain's top matadors. On the wall is the head of the last bull Ordóñez killed before retiring, and the suit he wore. In summer the shaded harborfront terrace makes an ideal place to dine and, before your meal, you can stop for an apéritif and tapas at the crowded bar at the entrance, which is filled with local residents and taurine memorabilia. Menu items include stewed oxtail, grilled sirloin, kidneys in sherry sauce, leg of baby lamb, grilled salmon, mixed fried fish, grilled red mullet, fresh fried anchovies, shrimp cocktail, and shellfish soup. The service is both fast and attentive.

Parador de Málaga–Gibralfaro, Monte Gibralfaro. ☎ **222-19-02.**

Cuisine: SPANISH. **Reservations:** Not required. **Microbus:** H, by the cathedral.
Prices: Appetizers 650–950 ptas. ($4.60–$6.70); main courses 1,800–2,200 ptas. ($12.80–$15.60). AE, DC, MC, V.
Open: Lunch, daily 1–4pm; dinner, daily, 8:30–11pm.

Government owned, this restaurant sits on a mountainside high above the city and is notable for its view. You can look down into the heart of the Málaga bullring, among other things. Meals are served in the attractive dining room or under the arches of two wide terraces, which provide views of the coast. Featured are hors d'oeuvres parador—your entire table literally covered with tiny dishes of tasty tidbits. Two other specialties are an omelet of chanquetes, tiny whitefish popular in this part of the country, and chicken Villaroi.

Parador Nacional del Golf, Carretta de Málaga, Apartado 324, Málaga. ☎ **238-12-55.**

Cuisine: Appetizers 850–1,700 ptas. ($6–$12.10); main courses 1,600–2,000 ptas. ($11.40–$14.20); fixed-price menu 1,800–2,200 ptas. ($12.80–$15.60). AE, DC, MC, V.
Open: Lunch, daily 1:30–4pm; dinner, daily 8:30–11pm.

This government-owned restaurant has an indoor/outdoor dining room that opens onto a circular swimming pool, golf course, and private beach. The interior dining room, furnished with reproductions of antiques, has a refined country-club atmosphere. Before-lunch drinks at the sleek modern bar tempt golfers, among others, who then proceed to the covered terrace for their Spanish meals.

Refectorium, Calle Cervantes, 8. ☎ **221-89-90.**

Cuisine: SPANISH. **Reservations:** Recommended on weekends and at all bullfights.
Prices: Appetizers 650–1,100 ptas. ($4.60–$7.80); main courses 1,400–1,800 ptas. ($9.90–$12.80). AE, V.
Open: Lunch, daily 1–4pm; dinner, daily 9pm–2am.

Located behind the bullfighting ring of Málaga, this place becomes hectic during any bullfight, filling up with aficionados and, after the fight, often with the matadors themselves. But it can be visited at any time, especially when the pace here is less frantic. The cuisine has an old-fashioned flair, and the servings are generous. The typical soup of the Málaga area is *ajoblanco con uvas* (cold almond soup flavored with garlic and garnished with big muscatel grapes). For a classic opener, try a plate of garlic-flavored mushrooms seasoned with bits of ham. The fresh seafood is a delight, including rape (monkfish) and angler fish; lamb might be served with a saffron-flavored tomato sauce. Desserts are "like mama made," including rice pudding.

INEXPENSIVE

$ **La Manchega,** Marín García, 4. ☎ **222-21-80.**

Cuisine: SPANISH. **Reservations:** Not required. **Bus:** 7 or 9.

Prices: Appetizers 300–500 ptas. ($2.10–$3.60); main courses 550–1,300 ptas. ($3.90–$9.20). No credit cards.

Open: Lunch, daily 11:30am–4:30pm; dinner, daily 7:30–11:30pm.

This restaurant has thrived as a crowded and popular tavern since its establishment in 1954. Set within a building from the 1920s on a popular pedestrian-only street in Málaga's downtown commercial zone, it offers sidewalk tables, a ground-floor bar with tile walls, and a decorator's attempt to create an indoor Andalusian courtyard. A *salon comedor* offers additional space for dining on an upper floor. Menu items include a peppery version of fish soup; shrimp omelets; Málaga-style soup; beans with Serrano ham; snails; eels; and a full array of fish, including grilled shrimp, hake, monkfish, clams, and mussels.

$ **Mesón Danes (Faarup),** Barroso, 7. ☎ **222-74-42.**

Cuisine: DANISH/SPANISH. **Reservations:** Not necessary. **Bus:** 15.

Prices: Appetizers 200–600 ptas. ($1.40–$4.30); main courses 1,095–1,850 ptas. ($7.80–$13.10); *menú del día,* 1,350 ptas. ($9.60). V.

Open: Lunch, Mon–Sat noon–4pm; dinner, Mon–Sat 8–11:30pm. **Closed:** Aug.

Here you can enjoy Danish and Spanish snacks at low prices, with choices including Danish or Spanish soup, fish, and meat. Also available is a special Faarup plate with assorted food. The cheapest *menú del día* represents one of the best food values in Málaga. Mesón Danes is located near the harbor and city center.

$ **Las Trevedes,** in El Corte Íngles Department Store, Andalucía 4. ☎ **230-00-00.**

Cuisine: SPANISH. **Reservations:** Not required. **Bus:** 15

Prices: Appetizers 575–850 ptas. ($4.10–$6); main courses 1,200–1,900 ptas. ($8.50–$13.50). Buffet 1,950 ptas. ($13.80) per person. AE, DC, MC, V.

Open: Lunch only, Mon–Sat 1–4:30pm.

Although it originated as a sales incentive to lure shoppers into Málaga's best-accessorized department store, this restaurant quickly adopted a clientele of its own. Set on the sixth floor of El Corte Inglés, the local branch of the nationwide chain, it offers a buffet table of salads and hot and cold meats and fish, as well as à la carte service. The setting is dignified and comfortable, with a well-trained staff who serve such dishes as green peppers stuffed with shellfish; fillet of pork in a pepper-cream sauce; several kinds of brochettes, and a long list of wines.

Evening Entertainment

DRINKS & TAPAS

Bar Loqüeno, Marín García, 12. ☎ **222-30-48.**

This offers basically the same tapas as its neighbor, La Tasca (see below). The entrance is behind a wrought-iron-and-glass door that leads into a stucco-lined room decorated in a "local tavern style" with a vengeance. There are enough hams, bouquets of garlic, beer kegs, fish nets, and sausages to feed an entire village for a week. There's hardly enough room to stand, and you'll invariably be jostled by a busy waiter shouting "calamari!" to cooks in the back kitchens. Tapas cost from 125 pesetas (90¢) for a potato croquette to 1,600 pesetas ($11.40) for Serrano ham. Hours are daily from 12:30 to 4:30pm and 7:30pm to 1:30am. **Bus:** 15.

La Tasca, Marín García, 1–6. ☎ **222-20-82.**

La Tasca is not the place to go if you're looking for a quiet and mellow tasca where no one ever raises his or her voice. The most famous bar in Málaga, this is really a hole in the wall, but it has style, conviviality, and a large staff crowded behind the bar to serve the sometimes-strident demands of practically everyone in Málaga, many of whom bring their children. You can have a choice of beer from the tap, wine, and an array of tapas. Try the croquettes (*croquetas*) and pungent shish kebabs laced with garlic and cumin. If you see an empty seat, try to commandeer it politely. Otherwise you'll stand in what might be awestruck observation of the social scene around you. Tapas cost from 200 pesetas ($1.40), beer from 115 pesetas (80¢). The bar lies between Calle Larios and Calle Nueva, and it's open daily from noon to 4pm and from 7pm to midnight. **Bus:** 15. Just opposite La Tasca is La Tasca 2, an offshoot restaurant serving a reasonably priced cuisine.

11 Nerja

32 miles (51km) E of Málaga, 104 miles (167km) W of Almería, 340 miles (547km) S of Madrid

GETTING THERE • By Bus Nerja is well serviced by buses from Málaga, at least 10 per day making the 1½-hour trip. If you're coming from Almería in the east, there are four buses a day making the three-hour trip.

• By Car Head along the N-340 east from Málaga or take the N-340 west from Almería.

ESSENTIALS The area code for Nerja is 95. The tourist information office is at Puerta del Mar, 2 (☎ **95/252-15-31**).

Nerja is known for its good beaches and small coves, its seclusion, its narrow streets and courtyards, and its whitewashed flat-roofed houses. Nearby is one of Spain's greatest attractions, the Cave of Nerja (see below).

At the mouth of the Chillar River, Nerja gets its name from an Arabic word, *narixa*, meaning "bountiful spring." Its most dramatic spot is the **Balcón de Europa,** a palm-shaded promenade that juts out into the Mediterranean. The sea-bordering walkway was built in 1885 in honor of a visit from the Spanish king Alfonso XIII in the wake of an earthquake which had shattered part of nearby Málaga. The phrase "Balcón de Europa" is said to have been coined by the king during one of the speeches he made in Nerja praising the beauty of the panoramas around him. To reach the best beaches, head west from the Balcón and follow the shoreline.

A NEARBY ATTRACTION

★ The most popular outing from either Málaga or Nerja is to the **Cueva de Nerja** (Cave of Nerja), Carretera de Maro, C.D. 29787 (☎ **95/252-95-20**), which scientists believe was inhabited from 100,000 to 40,000 B.C. This prehistoric stalactite and stalagmite cave lay undiscovered until 1959, when it was found by chance by a handful of boys. When fully opened, it revealed a wealth of treasures left from the days of the cave dwellers, including Paleolithic paintings. These depict horses and deer, but as of this writing they are not open to the public view. The archeological museum in the cave contains a number of prehistoric artifacts; don't miss walking through its stupendous galleries. The ceiling soars to a height of 200 feet.

The cave is located in the hills near Nerja where there is a magnificent view of the countryside and sea. The cave is open daily from 10:30am to 2pm and from 3:30pm to 6pm. Admission is 400 pesetas ($2.80) for adults, 200 pesetas ($1.40) for children 6–12. Children 5 and under are admitted free.

Nerja Cave–bound buses leave hourly from Muelle de Heredia in Málaga from 7am until 8:15pm. Return buses are also hourly until 8:15pm. The journey takes about one hour.

In July a cultural festival takes place here, which in the past has drawn some of the leading artists, musicians, and dancers around the world, including on occasion, Yehudi Menuhin, Maya Plisetskaya, and the Ballet Bolshoi.

Where to Stay

EXPENSIVE

Hotel Mónica, Playa de la Torrecilla, s/n, 29780 Nerja. ☎ **95/252-11-00.** Fax 95/252-11-62. 234 rms, 1 suite. A/C TV TEL

Rates: 7,000–8,600 ptas. ($49.70–$61.10) single; 10,000–13,500 ptas. ($71–$95.90) double; 15,800 ptas. ($112.20) suite. Breakfast 850 ptas. ($6) extra. AE, MC, V. **Parking**: 2,650 ptas. ($18.80).

Hotel Mónica looks something like a three-pronged propeller if you view it from the air. At ground level as you approach the entrance, you see that it has North African arches and green-and-white panels. This hotel opened in 1986, a four-star establishment in an isolated position about a 10-minute walk from the Balcón de Europa on a low-lying curve of beachfront.

The glistening white marble in the lobby is highlighted with such neobaroque touches as elaborately detailed cast-iron balustrades; curved marble staircases; and bas-reliefs, paintings, and sculptures. Some of the stairwells even contain oversize copies, set in tiles, of the beach scenes of Claude Monet. A nautical theme is carried out in the bar with brass navigational instruments and models of clipper ships and comfortable sofas add to the mood. Both of the hotel's restaurants have outdoor terraces or patios for indoor/outdoor dining. A *menú del día* costs 2,650 pesetas ($18.80). A curved swimming pool was built into a terrace a few feet above the beach. Comfortable bedrooms offer private balconies and private baths.

★ **Parador Nacional de Nerja,** Calle Almuñecar, 8, Playa de Burriana-Tablazo, 29780 Nerja. ☎ **95/252-00-50.** Fax 95/252-19-97. 73 rms. A/C MINIBAR TV TEL

Rates: 9,600–11,200 ptas. ($68.20–$79.50) single; 12,000–14,000 ptas. ($85.20–$99.40) double; 13,500–15,100 ptas. ($95.90–$107.20) suite. Breakfast 1,100 ptas. ($7.80) extra. AE, DC, MC, V. **Parking:** Free.

On the outskirts of town, a five-minute walk from the center of town, this government-owned hotel takes the best of modern motel designs and blends them with a classic Spanish ambience of beamed ceilings, tile floors, and hand-loomed draperies. It's built on the edge of a cliff, around a flower-filled courtyard with a splashing fountain, and its social life centers around a large swimming pool. There is a sandy beach below, reached by an elevator, plus lawns and gardens. The bedrooms are spacious and furnished in an understated but tasteful style, each with a private bath. International and Spanish meals are served in the hotel restaurant, a complete dinner costing 3,500 pesetas ($24.90).

MODERATE

Hotel Balcón de Europa, Paseo Balcón de Europa, 1,29780 Nerja. ☎ **95/252-08-00.** Fax 95/252-44-90. 85 rms (all with bath), 20 suites. A/C TV TEL

Rates: 5,200–8,400 ptas. ($36.90–$59.60) single; 7,450–11,200 ptas. ($52.90–$79.50) double; 14,200–18,500 ptas. ($100.80–$131.40) suite. Breakfast buffet 650 ptas. ($4.60) extra. AE, DC, MC, V. **Parking:** 750 ptas. ($5.30).

Occupying the best position in town at the edge of the Balcón de Europa, this 1970s hotel offers guest rooms with private balconies overlooking the water and the rocks. At a private beach nearby, parasol-shielded tables offer a place for a peaceful vista. The comfortable bedrooms are decorated with modern furniture and terra-cotta floors. There's a private garage a few steps away.

Guests can dine at the fourth floor Restaurant Azul, which offers a panoramic view, or at the beach restaurant, Nautico. An international menu is served. Azul offers a *menú del día* for 2,100 pesetas ($14.90). The Nautico is open only for lunch in winter but for both lunch and dinner in summer. The facilities include a sauna, health club, and solarium; the services include babysitting, laundry, and room service.

BUDGET

Cala-Bela, Puerta del Mar, 8, 29780 Nerja. ☎ **95/252-07-00.** 10 rms (all with bath). TEL

Rates: 2,500–3,500 ptas. ($17.80–$24.90) single; 3,750–5,000 ptas. ($26.60–$35.50) double. Breakfast 400 ptas. ($2.80) extra. AE, DC, MC, V.

Originally built as a private house in 1895, but much modernized since then, this is a well-positioned hotel. Lying only a one-minute walk from the Balcón de Europa, Cala-Bela offers bedrooms opening onto the sea. They may be small, but they're clean—and what a view! The lounge is charming. In the seafront dining room, seated in a bone-white Valencian chair, you are served a fixed-price meal for 1,500 pesetas ($10.70). The food is good, so even if you're not staying at the hotel, you may want to give the restaurant a try. Enjoy the filet of pork in sherry sauce, the chef's paella, grilled crayfish, or trout with cream.

$ **Hostal Mena,** Alemania, 15, 29780 Nerja. ☎ **95/252-05-41.** 14 rms (8 with bath). TV.

Rates: 1,700 ptas. ($12.10) single without bath; 3,000 ptas. ($21.30) double without bath; 3,700 ptas. ($26.30) double with bath. No credit cards.

This century-old little residencia near the Balcón de Europa serves no meals, but there's a lot of charm about the place, including the central hallway whose back walls are lined with hundreds of blue and white Andalusian tiles. The family running the hostal is very helpful. The bedrooms are plain and functional but clean.

Hostal Miguel, Almirante Ferrándiz, 31, 29780 Nerja. ☎ **95/252-15-23.** Fax 95/252-34-85. 9 rms (all with bath).

Rates: 2,500 ptas. ($17.80) single; 3,500 ptas. ($24.90) double. Breakfast 250 ptas. ($1.80) extra. MC, V.

The Miguel is a pleasant, unpretentious inn that contains only nine simply furnished rooms. They're housed in a 19th-century building with iron-rimmed balconies, situated on a quiet back street about a three-minute walk from the Balcón de Europa, and across from the well-known Pepe Rico Restaurant. Breakfast is the only meal served.

Where to Dine

EXPENSIVE

Casa Paco y Eva, El Barrio, 50. ☎ **252-15-27.**

Cuisine: INTERNATIONAL. **Reservations:** Required.
Prices: Appetizers 650–850 ptas. ($4.60–$6); main courses 1,600–2,200 ptas. ($11.40–$15.60). MC, V.

This air-conditioned Andalusian restaurant lies a five-minute walk from the Balcón de Europa. The decor is bright and typically Spanish. The food is excellent, and the owner/chef prepares a varied menu. Some of his special dishes include a *sopa de marisco* (shellfish soup), giant prawns cooked *à la plancha* (grilled) with garlic or else in a whisky sauce, sole cooked in fresh orange sauce, and tender steaks, either grilled or else served with a pepper and cream sauce. You might also try his pheasant cooked with grapes or, in season, his partridge. Finish off with a homemade crème Catalán. The house Rioja wine goes well with most dishes.

Restaurante de Miguel, Pintada, 2. ☎ **252-29-96.**

Cuisine: INTERNATIONAL. **Reservations:** Recommended.
Prices: Appetizers 450–850 ptas. ($3.20–$6); main courses 1,290–1,800 ptas. ($9.20–$12.80). MC, V.
Open: Lunch, Mon–Sat 1–3pm; dinner, Mon–Sat 7–11pm. **Closed:** Feb.

This restaurant was established in 1986 by the son of a Nerja resident. At first it was patronized only by local families hoping for their friend to succeed. Since then, however, mostly because of the excellent food, the place has attracted a devoted coterie of foreign visitors and expatriate residents of the Costa del Sol. It sits in the center of town near the busiest traffic intersection, behind a plate-glass aquarium loaded with fresh lobsters, fish, and shellfish. Its not-very-large air-conditioned interior is one of the most decidedly upscale places in Nerja, with white marble floors, elegant crystal and porcelain, and crisply ironed white napery. The menu lists a full array of international dishes, including cream-of-shrimp soup flavored with cognac, tournedos with a sauce made from goat cheese, sea bass with Pernod and fennel, a wide selection of beef and steak dishes, and concoctions composed from the cornucopia of fish from the aquarium.

Casa Luque, Plaza Cavana, 2. ☎ **252-10-04.**

Cuisine: ANDALUSIAN. **Reservations:** Required.
Prices: Appetizers 475–1,100 ptas. ($3.40–$7.80); main courses 1,100–1,900 ptas. ($7.80–$13.50); *menú degustación* 2,450 ptas. ($17.40). AE, MC, V.
Open: Lunch, Mon–Sat 1–4pm; dinner, Mon–Sat 7:30pm–midnight.

With its impressive canopied and balconied facade, the Casa Luque looks like a dignified private villa, lying near the heart of town. The interior has an Andalusian courtyard, and in summer there is a seaview terrace. Meals might include *pâté maison* with raspberry sauce; shoulder of ham; osso buco; pork filet; hot-pepper chicken

Casanova; grilled meats; or a limited selection of fish, including grilled Mediterranean grouper.

El Colono, Granada, 6. ☎ **252-18-26.**

Cuisine: ANDALUSIAN/FRENCH. **Reservations:** Required.
Prices: Wed and Fri Flamenco shows with fixed-price menus 1,995–2,795 ptas. ($14.20–$19.80); other nights, fixed-price dinner 1,250 ptas. ($8.90); fixed-price lunch 1,250 ptas. ($8.90). No credit cards.
Open: Wed-Mon lunch, noon–3:30pm; dinner, Wed–Mon 8pm–midnight. **Closed:** Nov 15–Dec 20.

A family place for a night of Spanish fun—that's El Colono, near the Balcón de Europa, a three-minute walk from the main bus stop at Nerja. Guitar music and flamenco dancing account for the entertainment highlights, and you can also dine here in a tavern atmosphere, enjoying set menus featuring local specialties. If you just want a glass of wine, you can still enjoy the shows (three per evening, from 8pm until "the wee hours").

Pepe Rico Restaurant, Almirante Ferrándiz, 28. ☎ **252-02-47.**

Cuisine: INTERNATIONAL. **Reservations:** Recommended.
Prices: Appetizers 650–1,050 ptas. ($4.60–$7.50); main courses 1,300–2,100 ptas. ($9.20–$14.90); fixed–price menu 2,800 ptas. ($19.90). DC, MC, V.
Open: Lunch, Wed–Mon 12:30–3pm; dinner, Wed–Mon 7–11pm. **Closed:** Nov 20–Dec 20.

Established in 1966, Pepe Rico is today one of the finest places for food in Nerja. It's housed in a white building with grille windows and little balconies. The rooms open onto a large rear balcony overlooking a flower-filled courtyard. Dining is in a tavern room, half wood paneled, with handmade wooden chairs, plaster walls, and ivy vines—the vines creep in from the patio, where you can order meals al fresco.

The specialty of the day, which might be a Spanish, German, Swedish, or French dish, ranges from almond-and-garlic soup to Andalusian gazpacho, available only in the summer. The list of hors d'oeuvres is impressive—including Pepe Rico salad, smoked swordfish, salmon mousse, and prawns pil-pil (with hot chile peppers). Main dishes include filet of sole Don Pepe, roast leg of lamb, prawns Café de Paris, and steak dishes. Considering the quality of the food, the prices are reasonable.

$ **Restaurant Rey Alfonso,** Paseo Balcón de Europa, s/n. ☎ **252-09-58.**

Cuisine: SPANISH/INTERNATIONAL. **Reservations:** Recommended.
Prices: Appetizers 375–650 ptas. ($2.70–$4.60); main courses 850–2,100 ptas. ($6–$14.90). Fixed-price menu 950 ptas. ($6.70). MC, V.
Open: Lunch, Thurs–Tues 11am–4pm; dinner, Thurs–Tues 7–11pm. **Closed:** Nov.

Few visitors to the Balcón de Europa realize that they're standing directly above one of the most unusual restaurants in town. You enter from the bottom of a flight of stairs that skirts the rocky base of what was originally designed in the late 19th century as a *miradore* (viewing station), which juts seaward as an extension of the town's main square. The restaurant's menu and interior decor don't hold many surprises, but the close-up view of the crashing waves makes dining here worthwhile. Have a drink at the bar if you don't want a full meal. Specialties include *paella valenciana*, Cuban-style rice, five different preparations of sole (from grilled to meunière), several versions of tournedos and entrecôte, beef Stroganoff, *fondue bourguignonne*, crayfish in whisky sauce, and crêpe Suzette for dessert.

11

Valencia & the Costa Blanca

THE THIRD-LARGEST CITY OF SPAIN, VALENCIA, CELEBRATED FOR ORANGES AND paella, lies in the midst of a *huerta*—a fertile crescent of an alluvial plain that's irrigated by a system built centuries ago. As such, the area is a bread basket of Spain, a place where "the soil never sleeps."

For such a major city, Valencia is relatively unexplored by foreigners, but it provides an offbeat adventure for those who decide to seek out its treasures. The town has a wealth of baroque architecture, fine museums, good cuisine, and a proud but troubled history.

The Costa Blanca (White Coast) begins rather unappealingly at Valencia but improves considerably as it winds its way south toward Alicante. The route is dotted with fishing ports and resorts known chiefly to Spanish and other European vacationers. The success of Benidorm, fitting for a long stay, began in the 1960s, when this fishing village was transformed into an international resort. Alicante, the official capital of the Costa Blanca, enjoys a reputation as a winter resort because of its mild climate. Murcia is inland, but it's on the main road to the Costa del Sol, so hordes of motorists pass through it.

Seeing Valencia & the Costa Blanca

GETTING THERE Flying is the best way, with international airports at both Valencia and Alicante. Valencia is the best choice if you want to land in the north, whereas Alicante is better if you'd like to begin in the south along the Costa Blanca.

Many arrive by train, with RENFE offering good service along the Barcelona-Alicante line. The Rápido Talgo Mare Nostrum begins its mid-morning run at the French frontier, getting you to Valencia in six hours. Stay on it for another 2½ hours and you'll be in Alicante. Most train passengers head for Valencia from Barcelona, the trip taking about four hours.

The Costa Levante is also well serviced by buses, with coaches arriving from Madrid and Barcelona, among other cities.

If you're driving, take the A-7 *autopista* (expressway) along the coast to the southern side of Alicante. It's expensive because of high tolls, but you avoid the slow-moving drive on the N-340 through the beach towns. Valencia can also be reached from Madrid via the N-III.

A Suggested Route

Day 1 Begin in Valencia, exploring its ancient monuments.

Day 2 Still based in Valencia, branch out on a day trip. Try going north to the old Roman ruins at Sagunto or south to the rice paddies of La Albufera.

Day 3 Head south along the coast for an overnight stop in Benidorm, a popular beach resort.

Day 4 Make the short drive south to Alicante, where you can explore its monuments.

Day 5 While in Alicante, spend the day exploring the palm groves and the huerta around Elche.

Day 6 Drive to Murcia to see its attractions, which should take you three to four hours, Stay overnight in Murcia.

What's Special About Valencia & the Costa Blanca

Beaches

- Benidorn, with 3½ miles (6km) of beach.
- Alicante, with its Postiguet Beach and balmy Mediterranean climate.

Great Towns/Cities

- Valencia, home of paella and El Cid.
- Elche, a touch of North Africa.

Architectural Highlights

- The Cathedral at Valencia, said to possess the Holy Grail.
- Castillo de Santa Bárbara at Alicante, a fortress dating from the 3rd century B.C.

Ancient Ruins

- Sagunto, outside Valencia, the reason the Second Punic War began.

Natural Sights

- La Albufera, outside Valencia, land of rice paddles and reedbeds.
- The palm grove at Elche, with some 600,000 trees started by Phoenician or Greek seafarers.

Festivals/Special Events

- The mystery play at Elche (August), oldest liturgy performed in Europe.
- The Fallas of San José in Valencia (March), honoring spring's arrival.
- The Holy Week celebration at Murcia, a mile-long procession with 3,000 taking part.

1 Valencia

218 miles (351km) SE of Madrid, 224 miles (361km) SW of Barcelona, 404 miles (650km) NE of Málaga.

GETTING THERE • **By Plane** Iberia flies to Valencia from Barcelona, Madrid, Málaga, and many other destinations. There are also flights between Palma de Mallorca and Valencia. You'll land 9 miles (14.5km) southwest of the city, but bus no. 15 takes you to the terminal, leaving hourly and costing 200 pesetas ($1.40). For flight information, call **350-95-00.** In the city, the office of Iberia Airlines is at Calle Paz, 14 (☎ **352-05-00**).

• **By Train** Valencia is linked to all parts of Spain. The Estación del Norte (North Station) is close to the heart of the city, making it a convenient arrival point. Its information office at Calle Xátiva, 15 (☎ **351-36-12**), is open daily from 7am to 10:30pm. Nine trains from Barcelona arrive daily, both the talgo (which takes four hours and is faster and more expensive) and the rápido (six hours). Eight trains daily connect Madrid to Valencia, the ter (five hours; more expensive) and the rápido (7½ hours). It's also possible to take a train from Málaga on the Costa del Sol (nine hours).

• **By Bus** Valencia's Central Station, Avenida de Ménendez Pidal, 13 (☎ **349-72-22**), is about a 30-minute walk northwest of the city's center, so you take bus no. 8 leaving from the Plaza del Ayuntamiento. Thirteen buses a day run from Madrid (five hours away), 10 buses from Barcelona (five hours), and 30 buses from Málaga (11 hours).

• **By Ferry** You can take a ferry to and from the Balearic Islands. Ferries for Palma de Mallorca depart Monday to Saturday at 11:30pm. The all-night journey (which takes nine hours) lets passengers off the next morning in Majorca. There are also sailings from Valencia to Ibiza at midnight Thursday through Tuesday from June 15 to September 15. Travel agents in Valencia sell these tickets (see American Express, below); or on the day of departure, you can go to the office at the port, Estación Marítima (☎ **367-39-72**), to purchase them. To reach it, take bus no. 4 or 19 from the Plaza del Ayuntamiento.

• **By Car** The easiest route is the express highway (E-15) south from Barcelona. Connections are also made on a national highway, E-901, from Madrid, which lies northwest of Valencia. From Alicante, south of Valencia, an express highway, E-15, connects the two cities. If you're coming from Andalusia, the roads are longer and more difficult and not connected by express highways. You can drive from Málaga north to Granada and cut across southeastern Spain along the 342 which links with the 340 into Murcia. From there, take the road to Alicante for an easy drive into Valencia.

The charms of Valencia—or the lack of them—have been much debated. There are those who claim that the city where El Cid faced the Moors is one of the most beautiful on the Mediterranean. Others write it off as drab, provincial, and industrial. The truth lies somewhere in between.

Set in the midst of orange trees and rice paddies, Valencia seems to justify its reputation as a romantic city more by its past than by its present looks. Hidden between modern office buildings and monotonous apartment houses, remnants of that illustrious past do remain. However, floods and war have been cruel to Valencia, forcing Valencianos to tear down buildings that today would be considered architectural treasures.

Valencia also has a strong cultural tradition. Its most famous son was writer Vicente Blasco Ibañez, best known for his novel about bullfighting, *Blood and Sand,* and for his World War I novel, *The Four Horsemen of the Apocalypse.* Both were filmed twice in Hollywood, with Rudolph Valentino starring in the first version of each. Joaquín Sorolla, the famous Spanish impressionist, was another native of Valencia. You can see his works at a museum dedicated to him in Madrid.

FAST FACTS

American Express The local agency is Duna Viajes, Calle Cirilo Amorós, 88 (☎ **374-15-62**), open Monday to Friday from 9:30am to 2pm and 5pm to 8pm and Saturday from 10am to 2pm.

Area Code The area code for Valencia is **96.**

Buses For information and tickets, go to the red-painted kiosk at Plaza del Ayuntamiento. A ticket for one ride costs 65 pesetas (50¢).

Consulate The U.S. Consulate is at Calle Paz, 6 (☎ **351-69-73**); it's open Monday to Friday from 10am to 1pm.

Emergency Call **091.**

First Aid Assistance is provided at Plaza de América, 5 (☎ **322-22-39**).

Valencia

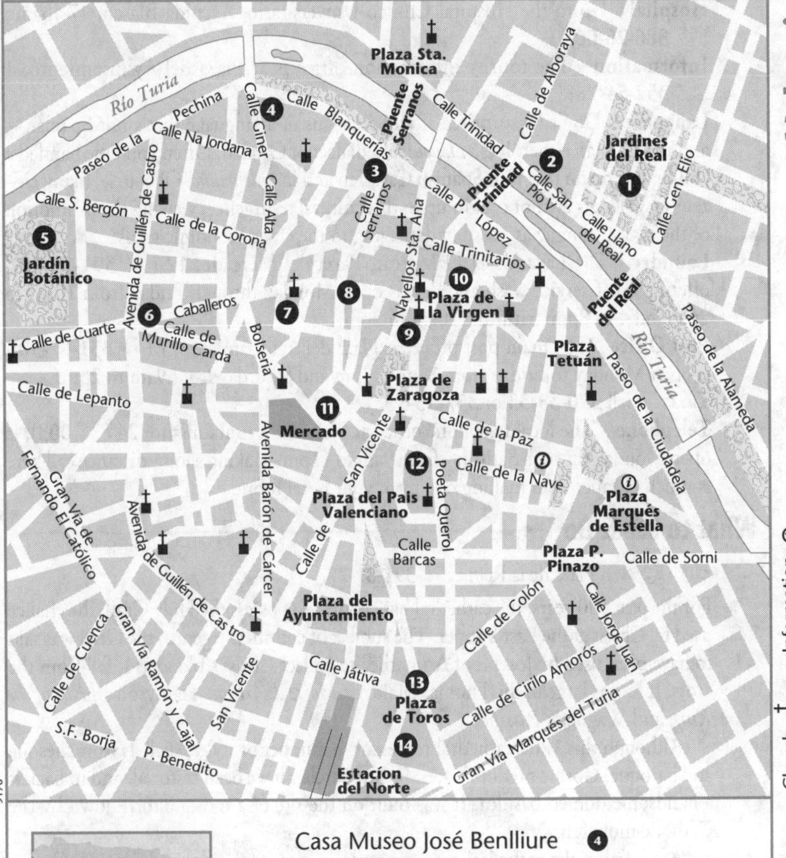

Church
Information

9176

- Casa Museo José Benlliure 4
- Catedral 9
- Jardín Botánico 5
- Jardines del Real 1
- La Longa de la Seda 11
- Museo de Bellas Artes 2
- Museo Nacional de Cerámica 12
- Museo de Paleontológia 10
- Museo Taurino 14
- Palacio de la Generalidad 8
- Plaza de Toros 13
- San Nicolás 7
- Torres de Cuarte 6
- Torres de Serranos 3

Hospital Go to the Hospital Clínico Universitario, Avenida Blasco, 17 Ibañez (☎ **386-26-00**).

Information The tourist information office is at Plaza del Ayuntamiento, 1 (☎ **352-54-78**).

Language Don't be surprised if you see signs in a language that's not Spanish—and not Catalán either. It is *valenciano*, a dialect of Catalán. Often you'll be handed a "bilingual" menu that is in Spanish Castilian and in *valenciano*. Of course, many citizens of Valencia are not caught up in this cultural resurgence, viewing the promotion of the dialect tongue as possibly damaging to the city's economic goals.

Laundry The Lavanderia El Mercat, Plaza del Mercado, 12 (☎ **391-20-10**), offering a self-service wash and dry, is open Monday through Friday from 10am to 2pm and 4 to 8pm, Saturday 10am to 2pm.

Post Office The main post office, at Plaza del Ayuntamiento, 1 (☎ **351-67-50**), is open Monday to Friday from 8am to 9pm and Saturday from 9am to 2pm.

Taxis Call **370-33-33** or **357-13-13.**

Telephone The local telephone office at Plaza del Ayuntamiento, 24 (☎ **003**), is open Monday through Saturday from 9am to 11pm. Making a long-distance call here is much cheaper than making one from your hotel room.

What to See & Do

Catedral (Seu), Plaza de la Reina. ☎ 391-81-27.

For the past 500 years, the cathedral has claimed to possess the Holy Grail, the chalice used by Christ at the Last Supper. The subject of countless legends, the Grail was said to have been used by Joseph of Arimathea to collect Christ's blood as it fell from the cross. It looms large in Sir Thomas Malory's *Morte d'Arthur,* Tennyson's *Idylls of the King,* and Wagner's *Parsifal.*

Although this 1262 cathedral represents a number of styles, such as Romanesque and baroque, Gothic predominates. Its huge arches have been restored, and in back is a handsome domed basilica. It was built on the site of a mosque torn down by the Catholic monarchs.

After seeing the cathedral, you can scale an uncompleted 155-foot-high Gothic tower—known as Miguelete—for a panoramic view of the city and the fertile huerta beyond, or visit the **Museo de la Catedral,** where works by Goya and Zurbarán are exhibited.

Admission: Cathedral, free; Miguelete, 100 ptas. (70¢); Museo de la Catedral, 100 ptas. (70¢).

Open: Cathedral, Mon–Sat 10am–1pm and 4–7pm. Miguelete, Mon–Sat 10:30am–12:30pm and 5–7:30pm; Sun 10:30am–12:30pm. Museo de la Catedral, Mon–Sat 10am–1pm and 4–6pm. Bus: 9, 27, 70, or 71.

Palacio de la Generalidad, Caballeros, 2. ☎ 386-61-00.

Located in the old aristocratic quarter of Valencia, this Gothic palace, built in the 15th and 16th centuries, is one of the most fascinating buildings in Spain, with its two square towers (one of them built as recently as 1952), its carved wooden ceilings and galleries, and its fresco paintings. It now serves as the headquarters of the regional government (Generalidad), and is visited only with the permission of the Gabinete del Presidente de la Generalidad (☎ **386-34-61** before visiting).

Admission: Free.

Open: Mon–Fri 9am–2pm. **Bus:** 5 from railway station.

La Lonja de la Seda, Plaza del Mercado. ☎ **391-36-08.**

This former silk exchange, completed in 1498, is the most splendid example of secular Gothic architecture in Spain. A beautiful building, La Lonja has twisted spiral columns inside and stained-glass windows.

Admission: Free.

Open: Tues–Sat 10am–1:30pm and 5–9pm, Sun 10am–2pm. **Closed:** Holidays. **Bus:** 4, 7, 27, 60, or 81.

Mercado Central, Plaza del Mercado. ☎ **332-10-51.**

Across the street from La Lonja (see above) is one of the most fascinating city markets you'll ever encounter, with about 1,200 stalls. It has everything: dried herbs, homemade soup, black-blood sausage, and plucked chickens. You may never want to shop in a supermarket again. The Mercado Central is in a giant stained-glass building that dates from 1928.

Open: Mon–Sat 8am–2:30pm. **Bus:** 4, 7, 27, 81, or 60.

Museo Nacional de Cerámica, Palacio del Marqués de Dos Aguas, Poeta Querol, 2. ☎ **351-63-92.**

The National Ceramics Museum, the best in Spain, looks like a surrealist decorator's masterpiece: an 18th-century palace of rococo and Churrigueresque elements. It's not surprising that the architect died in an insane asylum. The rooms in this bizarre building compete with the vast collection of ceramics ranging from the 10th to the 20th century. Some are by Picasso. In addition, there is a Gallery of Humorists, with caricatures from Einstein on down, and a carriage display.

Admission: 250 ptas. ($1.80) adults; children free.

Open: Tues–Sat 10am–2pm and 4–6pm; Sun 10am–2pm. **Bus:** 24 or 27.

Museu San Pío (Museu Sant Píus V), San Pío V, 9. ☎ **360-57-93.**

This treasure house of paintings and sculptures, which stands on the north bank of the Turia River, contains a strong collection of Flemish and native Valencian artworks (note particularly those by the 14th- and 15th-century Valencian "primitives"). The most celebrated painting is a 1640 self-portrait by Velázquez, and there is a whole room devoted to Goya. Other artists exhibited include Bosch, Morales, El Greco (*St. John the Baptist*), Ribera, Murillo, Pinturicchio, and Sorolla. Of special interest is a salon displaying the works of contemporary Valencian painters and an important sculpture by Mariano Benlliure. The ground-floor archeological collection encompasses early Iberian, Roman, including an altar to a pagan Roman emperor and early Christian finds.

Admission: Free.

Open: Tues–Sat 10am–2pm and 4–6pm; Sun 10am–4pm. **Bus:** 1, 6, 8, or 11.

Instituto Valenciano de Arte Modern [Viam], Calle Guillén Castro, 118. ☎ **386-30-00.**

This giant complex, costing millions to build, consists of two sites—an ultramodern building and a 13th-century former convent. Its opening launched Valencia into primestatus among the world's art capitals.

The **Julio González Center** is named for an avant-garde Spanish artist whose paintings, sculptures, and drawings form the nucleus of the institute's permanent collection. Much influenced by Picasso, González was a pioneer in iron sculpture.

The other site is the nearby **Center del Carme,** the old convent, with cloisters from both the 14th and the 16th centuries. It contains three halls devoted to changing exhibitions of contemporary art. Other permanent exhibitions include works of Ignacio Pinazo, whose paintings and drawings mark the beginning of modernism in Valencia.

The institute is located on the western edge of the old quarter, near the Torres de Quart.

Admission: 250 ptas. ($1.80) adults; children free.

Open: Julio González Center, Tues–Sun 11am–8pm. Center del Carmen, Tues–Sun noon–3:30pm and 4:30–8:30pm. **Bus:** 5.

Where to Stay

Normally, Valencia maintains year-round hotel prices, but often in July and August if business is slow some hoteliers will lower prices—it always pays to ask. Business drops off in the peak of the hot weather because Valencia becomes less livable and rather uncomfortable owing to the humidity and high temperatures.

EXPENSIVE

Hotel Astoria Palace, Plaza Rodrigo Botet, 5, 46002 Valencia. ☎ **96/352-67-37.** Fax 96/352-8-78. 192 rms, 15 suites. A/C MINIBAR TV TEL **Bus:** 9, 10, 27, 70, or 71.

Rates: Sept–July, 15,500 ptas. ($110.10) single; 19,500 ptas. ($138.50) double; 27,000 ptas. ($191.70) suite; Aug, 7,800 ptas. ($55.40) single; 11,200 ptas. ($79.50) double; 22,000 ptas. ($156.20) suite. Breakfast 1,200 ptas. ($8.50) extra. AE, DC, MC, V. **Parking:** 1,200 ptas. ($8.50) nearby.

Located on a small and charming square in the heart of town, five short blocks south of the cathedral, this modern hotel contains some of the best-furnished public and private rooms in Valencia. A favorite of such Spanish stars as opera singer Montserrat Caballé, bullfighter Manuel Benitez ("El Cordobés"), and an impressive roster of writers and politicians, the Astoria is plush, well-managed, and appealing. Many of the bedrooms overlook a statue of Grecian maidens and swans in the square outside, and each contains a private bath and a tasteful arrangement of dignified and conservative furniture.

Dining/Entertainment: The Vinatea restaurant serves regional and international cuisine as part of three-course fixed-price lunches and dinners at 3,500 to 4,000 pesetas ($24.90 to $28.40) each. There's also a bar.

Services: 24-hour room service, laundry and limousine service, concierge, babysitting.

Facilities: Car rentals, shopping boutiques.

Hotel Reina Victoria, Barcas, 4, 46002 Valencia. ☎ **96/352-04-87.** Fax 96/352-04-87. 97 rms. A/C MINIBAR TV TEL **Bus:** 4, 7, or 27.

Rates: July-Aug, 8,000 ptas. ($56.80) single or double; Sept–June, 10,800 ptas. ($76.70) single; 17,250 ptas. ($122.50) double. Breakfast 1,100 ptas. ($7.80) extra. AE, MC, V. **Parking:** 1,500 ptas. ($10.70).

Although it has lost some of its individualized charm and spit-and-polish luster in recent years, the Reina Victoria has traditionally been considered the most prestigious and architecturally glamorous hotel in Valencia. Built in 1913, and renovated in 1988 under the auspices of a national chain, the hotel has welcomed many distinguished guests, including Alfonso XIII and Queen Victoria (its namesake), Dalí, Manolete, Picasso, Falla, Garcia Lorca, and Miró. Bristling with neoclassical detailing and wrought-iron accents, it overlooks the flower gardens and fountains of Valencia's central square, the Plaza del Pais Valenciano. Bedrooms are furnished with conservative elegance and many modern accessories. The Bar Inglés is a popular rendezvous, and the hotel's restaurant, El Levant, serves international food in a dignified setting. The hotel lies in the heart of town, a five-minute walk from the railway station.

Melía Valencia, Baleares, 2, 46023 Valencia. ☎ **96/337-50-30,** or toll free in the U.S. **800/336-3542.** Fax 96/337-15-72. 322 rms. A/C MINIBAR TV TEL **Bus:** 19, 41, 89, or 90.

Rates: Sept-July, 15,725 ptas. ($111.60) single; 19,950 ptas. ($141.60) double; Aug and Fri–Sat in winter, 8,480 ptas. ($60.20) single; 10,600 ptas. ($75.30) double. Breakfast 1,400 ptas. ($9.90) extra. AE, DC, MC, V. **Parking:** 1,000 ptas. ($7.10).

A 1970s' and well-respected member of one of Spain's largest hotel chains, the Melía Valencia towers over an urban landscape about half a mile southeast of the city's cathedral. Many of the clients here appreciate it for its nearness to the Convention and Concert Hall (Palau de la Música) midway between the Old Town and the Port. The public rooms of the stylish interior are sheathed with marble, rough stone, and tilework, while the bedrooms are sunny, well-maintained enclaves of contemporary comfort and harvest-inspired colors.

Dining/Entertainment: International cuisine is served in the tawny-colored elegance of the well-recommended Restaurant Christina where meals average 4,000 pesetas ($28.40). Nearby, a richly paneled bar with leather sofas and armchairs evokes a private club in England.

Services: 24-hour room service, laundry/valet service, concierge, babysitting.

Facilities: Business center, car-rental kiosk, solarium, outdoor swimming pool set into rooftop garden terrace.

MODERATE

Hotel Inglés, Marqués de Dos Aguas, 6, 46002 Valencia. ☎ **96/351-64-26.** Fax 96/394-02-51. 61 rms (all with bath), 1 suite. A/C MINIBAR TV TEL **Bus:** 31 or 32.

Rates: 9,000 ptas. ($63.90) single; 11,000 ptas. ($78.10) double; 20,000 ptas. ($142) suite. Breakfast 750 ptas. ($5.30) extra. AE, DC, MC, V. **Parking:** 1,500 ptas. ($10.70).

This turn-of-the-century hotel, the former palace of the Duke and Duchess of Cardona, has aged well. In the heart of old Valencia, it stands opposite another Churrigueresque palace. Most of its bedrooms have views of the tree-lined street below and offer old-fashioned comforts. The lounge and dining room have original decorating touches—chandeliers, gilt mirrors, provincial armchairs, and murals. The service is discreet and polite.

INEXPENSIVE

Sorolla, Convento de Santa Clara, 5, 46002 Valencia. ☎ **96/352-33-92.** Fax 96/352-14-65. 50 rms (all with bath). A/C TV TEL

Rates: 5,200–6,600 ptas. ($36.90–$46.90) single; 9,100 ptas. ($64.60) double. AE, MC, V.

In the city center, this 1960s six-story hotel is named after Valencia's most famous artist. The guest rooms have narrow balconies and compact, utilitarian furnishings. Comfort, not style, is the key; everything, however, is clean. No meals are served. To reach the Sorolla, take any bus from the rail station.

BUDGET

$ **Hostal Residencia Bisbal,** Pie de la Cruz, 9, 46001 Valencia. ☎ **96/391-70-84.** 17 rms (all with shower or bath). **Bus:** 8, 27, 29, or 81.

Rates: 2,500 ptas. ($17.80) single with shower; 3,500 ptas. ($24.90) single with bath; 3,800 ptas. ($27) double with shower; 5,000 ptas. ($35.50) double with bath. No credit cards. **Parking:** 1,100 ptas. ($7.80).

Conveniently located in the old city, this husband-and-wife operation has clean and simply furnished rooms. English is spoken. No meals are served, but you'll find many bars and restaurants nearby.

Where to Dine

EXPENSIVE

Eladio, Calle Chiva, 40. ☎ **384-22-44.**

Cuisine: SPANISH/INTERNATIONAL. **Reservations:** Recommended.
Prices: Appetizers 650–1,800 ptas. ($4.60–$12.80); main courses 1,400–3,200 ptas. ($9.90–$22.70). AE, DC, MC, V.
Open: Lunch, Mon–Sat 1–4pm; dinner, Mon–Sat 8:30pm–midnight. **Closed:** Aug.

Borrowing from culinary models he learned during his apprenticeship in Switzerland, Eladio Rodríguez prepares flavorful cuisine based on the season's ingredients. Some clients praise him particularly for his shellfish and fish from Galicia, which might include hake, monkfish, or seawolf, any of which is prepared as simply or as elaborately as you want. (Many clients prefer these grilled simply over charcoal and served with garlic-butter sauce.) Noteworthy are his ragoût of shellfish, anglerfish, and salmon and his recipe for octopus, derived from his native Galicia. The pastries prepared by Eladio's wife, Violette, are a suitable finish. The menu is changed daily, always based on what is fresh and available in any season. The setting is calm and pleasant, accented with touches of marble, oak, and plush upholstery.

 **La Hacienda,** Navarro Reverter, 12. ☎ **373-18-59.**

Cuisine: VALENCIAN/INTERNATIONAL. **Reservations:** Recommended.
Prices: Appetizers 800–1,500 ptas ($5.70–$10.70); main courses 2,000–3,500 ptas. ($14.20–$24.90); *menú del día* 5,000 ptas. ($35.50). AE, DC, MC, V.
Open: Lunch, Mon–Sat 1:30–4:30pm; dinner, Mon–Sat 9pm–1am.

Considered one of Valencia's most luxurious restaurants, the Hacienda caters to a lunch crowd of businesspersons discussing their deals and an evening crowd of conservative locals celebrating a dignified night on the town. In a dining room filled with antique furniture, gilt-framed mirrors, and pastels, you can enjoy the fine service of a time-tested staff, plus such dishes as peppers stuffed with asparagus and exotic mushrooms, lobster with strips of salmon and pink peppercorns, roasted oxtail in the style of Córdoba, cold slices of roast beef with horseradish, filet of duckling with blackberry sauce, and chateaubriand topped with slices of foie gras. To accompany these dishes, the wine steward maintains an assortment of French and Spanish wines. The restaurant lies near the river and Valencia's eastern gate, about two blocks east of the historic center of town.

MODERATE

★ **Galbis,** Marvá, 28-30, ☎ **380-94-73.**

Cuisine: SPANISH. **Reservations:** Recommended.

Prices: Appetizers 850–975 ptas. ($6–6.90); main courses 1,400–1,975 ptas. ($9.90–$14); *menú del día* at lunch 3,320 ptas. ($23.60); *menú del día* at dinner 2,800 ptas. ($19.90). AE, V.

Open: Lunch, Mon–Fri 1–4pm; dinner, Mon–Sat 8:30–11pm. **Closed:** Aug 8–Sept 8.

Bustling, popular, and one of the most consistently crowded in town, this highly visible restaurant serves filling portions of straightforward food in an unmistakably Valencian ambience. You'll pass through a convivial bar area (where the ingredients for much of the day's cuisine might be displayed in a refrigerated case) before heading into the dining room. Specialties include salad of roasted peppers with fresh duckmeat, traditional preparations of hake and anglerfish, roast pork in savory sauce, roasted lamb with Mediterranean herbs, roasted goat in garlic sauce, and a succulent version of peppersteak. Next door, accessible via a separate entrance, the owners have established a simple cafeteria that many diners shun in favor of the better-known original restaurant. It is open as a "day bar" for lunch only Monday through Friday from 7:30am to 5:30pm; on Saturday it is open only in the evening from 8:30pm to 2am. Inexpensive *menús del día* are served in this cafeteria/bar, costing 1,500 pesetas ($10.70) each. However, if someone wants one of the more glamorous—and more expensive items—available in the restaurant, it is available on demand.

El Gourmet, Calle Taquígrafo Martí, 3. ☎ **395-2509.**

Cuisine: SPANISH/INTERNATIONAL. **Reservations:** Recommended.

Prices: Appetizers 450–1,200 ptas. ($3.20–$8.50); main courses 1,500–1,900 ptas. ($10.70–$13.50). Fixed-priced menu 2,500 ptas. ($17.80) AE, V.

Open: Lunch, Mon–Sat 1–3:30pm; dinner, Mon–Sat 9–11:30pm. **Closed:** One week at Easter and August.

This restaurant has welcomed clients since the 1950s. It's known as an honest, straightforward establishment where well-trained waiters serve food that is not overly expensive and the quality is good. Set in the center of Valencia, it offers such dishes as hake with clams; partridge with herbs in puff pastry; oxtail stew; fried filets of veal or pork; scrambled eggs with eggplant and shrimp; and seasonal vegetables.

Palace Fesol, Hernán Cortés, 7. ☎ **352-93-23.**

Cuisine: INTERNATIONAL. **Reservations:** Recommended. **Bus:** 13.

Prices: Appetizers 900–1,500 ptas. ($6.40–$10.70); main courses 1,400–2,200 ptas. ($9.90–$15.60); fixed-price menu 3,000 ptas. ($21.30). AE, DC, MC, V.

Open: Lunch, Tues–Sun, 1–3:30pm; dinner, Tues–Sat 9–11:30pm.

Back in the post–World War I era, the Palace Fesol, known as the "bean palace," became famous for its namesake specialty, lima beans. Today, of course, many more excellent dishes grace the menu, with typical Valencian paella high on the list at lunch. You can also order several chicken dishes served with rice that go under the general name paella, since they are cooked in paella pans. Dinner selections include *zarzuela de mariscos* (shellfish medley), grilled red mullet and baby hake, baby lamb cutlets, and chateaubriand. Photos of film stars, bullfighters, and other celebrities line the walls. The restaurant is cooled by old-fashioned ceiling fans and is decorated with beamed ceilings, lanterns, and a hand-painted tile mosaic.

INEXPENSIVE

Foster's Hollywood, Gran Vía Marqués del Turia, 16. ☎ **395-15-20.**

Cuisine: AMERICAN. **Reservations:** Not required.
Prices: Appetizers 450–600 ptas. ($3.20–$4.30); main courses 600–1,000 ptas. ($4.30–$7.10). AE, DC, MC, V.
Open: Sun–Thurs 1pm–midnight; Fri–Sat 1pm–2am.

This is one of the many, many branches of Foster's which opened its doors in 1971, becoming the first American restaurant in Madrid. It carries its same format of California-style hamburgers to Valencia. Some locals originally encountered problems in eating the hamburgers, as would anyone not familiar with devouring food that is five inches high. Hamburgers weigh in at half a pound, and they vary from simple and unadorned to one with cheese, bacon, and Roquefort dressing; they are served with french fries and salad. The varied menu includes many Tex-Mex selections such as chili con carne, along with steaks, butterfly shrimp, and freshly made salads.

Evening Entertainment

THE PERFORMING ARTS

The **Palau de la Música,** Paseo de la Alameda, 30 (☎ **337-50-20**), is a contemporary concert hall constructed in a dried-out river bed of the Turia. Opened in 1987, it stands within a sort of Hispano-Muslim venue—palm trees, "temples," and reflecting pools—between the Aragón and Angel Custudio bridges. Call to find out the day's program or ask at the tourist office (see "Fast Facts," above). Details of major concerts are also published in the newspapers. Ticket prices vary.

The Bar Scene

Barcas 7, Barcas, 7. ☎ **352-12-33.**

Set among banks and office buildings in the heart of town, directly north of the Estación del Norte, Barcas 7 offers drinks and tapas (including small servings of paella) at the stand-up bar. Conceivably you could visit here for your first cup of coffee at 7am and for your final "nightcap" at 1am. In the evening it often offers live music. Despite the restaurant in back, where beef filet and veal dishes are house specialties, the establishment is more popular as a bar than as a restaurant. Open daily from 7am to 1am, Barcas charges from 400 pesetas ($2.80) for drinks, 250 to 1,100 pesetas ($1.80 to $7.80) for tapas.

Easy Excursions

LA ALBUFERA Eleven miles (17.7km) south of Valencia lies La Albufera, a land of rice paddies and reed beds. The largest wetland along the Mediterranean coast of

Spain, it was called "an agreeable lagoon" in the writings of Pliny the Elder. Sand dunes separate the fresh water from the salt water.

La Albufera has been declared a national park since its lake is home to some 250 species of waterfowl, including a European version of the endangered flamingo. About waist deep at its center, it abounds with such fish as mullet, tench, and eel, still caught by ancient traps. You can rent an *albuferenc* (flat-bottomed boat) from local fishermen, but make sure to negotiate prices beforehand. As you go about the lake, you can see *barracas,* whitewashed houses with thatched and steeply pitched roofs. Some of these *barracas,* which stand on stilts, can be reached only by boat.

La Albufera gave the world paella, and nearly all the restaurants in the area serve this classic dish. Try **Raco de l'Olla,** Carretera de El Palmer, s/n (☎ **96/161-00-72**), eight miles (13km) south of Valencia on the El Saler road near the turnoff to El Palmer. The restaurant was opened in the 1960s and since then has served paella to thousands of visitors from around the world. It is open only for lunch, Tuesday through Sunday, from 10am to 6pm. Meals range from 1,000 to 2,000 pesetas ($7.10 to $14.20), and Visa cards are accepted. It's also customary to stop in the town of El Palmer to order a plate of *alli al pebre* (garlic-flavored eels) before heading north to Valencia or south to Alicante.

SAGUNTO Another popular excursion is to Sagunto, 15 ½ miles (25km) north of Valencia, reached by bus or rail connections. Sagunto is known for holding out nine months against Hannibal's conquering Carthaginian soldiers in 219 B.C. The Iberians set themselves on fire rather than surrender. In time, the Romans discovered the town, and later it was taken by the Visigoths and the Muslims.

Its **Roman ruins** today are just that: ruins. But it makes an interesting stopover. In the 2nd century A.D. it had an amphitheater seating 8,000, in the remains of which theatrical performances are still staged. It also has an old **Acrópolis**—*castillo* (castle)—and the remains of its Moorish walls and ramparts stretch for about a half mile. The letters FORV suggests that a Roman forum once stood on the spot. The **Museo Arqueológico de Sagunto,** Carrer Castell, s/n (☎ **96/266-55-81**), on the hill has artifacts of the early Romans, including some mosaics. Admission is 255 pesetas ($1.80) to the castle, with the museum and theater free. Hours July through September are Tuesday through Saturday 10am to 2pm and 4 to 6pm, Sun 10am to 2pm; October through June, Tuesday through Saturday, 10am–8pm, Sun 10am–2pm.

The best place for food is right at the castle: **L'Ameler,** Calle Subida del Castillo, 44 (☎ **96/266-43-82**). Meals cost 3,000 pesetas ($21.30); it's open Tuesday to Saturday from 1:30 to 4pm and 9:30 to 11pm. You can get both French and Spanish food in the ambience of a *vieja mansion* (old mansion). Try one of the splendid pâtés, salmon casserole, or filet steak with truffle sauce. The terrace provides a fine view.

2 Benidorm

27 miles (43km) NE of Alicante, 84 miles (135km) S of Valencia

GETTING THERE • By Train From Alicante, there are hourly departures for Benidorm.

- **By Bus** Buses from Valencia and Alicante to Benidorm leave almost hourly.
- **By Car** Take the E-15 expressway south from Valencia or north from Alicante.

ESSENTIALS The area code for Benidorm is **96.** The tourist information office is at Avenida Martínez Alejos, 16 (☎ **96/585-13-11**).

Before its 3½ miles (6km) of beach were discovered by tourists, Benidorm was the tiniest of fishing villages. But now summer vacationers pour in apace, and it seems as if a new concrete hotel is being built every day. With its heavy European influence and topless beach, Benidorm has become the most overrun beach town east of Torremolinos. It has both its devotees and detractors.

Where to Stay

Make sure you reserve in advance between mid-June and September—if you arrive without a reservation, you'll be out of luck. During this time most hotel managers often slap the full-board requirement onto their rates. The way to beat this is to book into one of the rare *residencias* in Benidorm, which serve breakfast only.

Don Pancho, Avenida del Mediterráneo, 39, 03500 Benidorm. ☎ **96/585-29-50.** Fax 96/586-77-79. 251 rms (all with bath). A/C TV TEL

Rates: 7,200–11,200 ptas. ($51.10–$79.50) single; 9,000–14,000 ptas. ($63.90–$99.40) double. Breakfast 750 ptas. ($5.30) extra. AE, DC, MC, V.

One of the best hotels in Benidorm, Don Pancho is a high-rise set a short walk from the beach. Its inviting lobby has a Spanish-colonial/Aztec decor, and each of the well-furnished, well-maintained bedrooms opens onto a small balcony. Each room is a double, although can be rented for single use. Facilities include a swimming pool and lighted tennis court.

Gran Hotel Delfín, Playa de Poniente (La Cala), 03500 Benidorm. ☎ **96/585-34-00.** Fax 96/585-71-54. 99 rms (all with bath). A/C TV TEL

Rates: 7,950–10,175 ptas. ($56.40–$72.20) single; 13,250–17,960 ptas. ($94.10–$127.50) double. Breakfast 740 ptas. ($5.30) extra. AE, DC, MC, V. **Parking:** Free. **Closed:** Oct–Mar.

Located about two miles (3km) west of the center of town, away from the traffic-clogged mayhem that sometimes overwhelms the center of Benidorm, this 1960s hotel lies beside the very popular Poniente Beach. It caters to a sun-loving crowd of vacationers who appreciate its airy spaciousness and lack of formality. Bedrooms are sparsely decorated, with masonry floors and much-used furniture, some in a darkly stained Iberian style.

Dining/Entertainment: The in-house restaurant, El Delfín, serves fixed-price *menús del día* for 3,570 pesetas ($25.30) each. There are also two bars, one of which serves drinks near the pool.

Services: Room service (available daily from 7am to 11pm), laundry/valet, concierge, babysitting.

Facilities: Outdoor swimming pool set into large and verdant garden, tennis courts.

Hotel Brisa, Playa de Levante, 03500 Benidorm. ☎ **96/585-54-00.** 70 rms (all with bath). TEL

Rates: July–Aug (with obligatory half board): 8,000 ptas. ($56.80) single; 13,000 ptas. ($92.30) double. Sept–June (including breakfast): 3,500 ptas. ($24.90) single; 7,000 ptas. ($49.70) double. V.

Set immediately opposite one of the town's most popular beaches, this hotel is a five-story modern building with a swimming pool, a small garden, and clean and sunny bedrooms which are simply furnished with sturdy furniture and easy-to-clean tile floors. This is very much a beach hotel, where many of the clients bring uncomplicated wardrobes and, in some cases, their children, in anticipation of langorous mornings and afternoons on the beach. There's at least one bar on the premises, an airy, sunflooded dining room, and, in summer, a large percentage of clients from northern Europe.

$ **Hotel Canfali,** Plaza de San Jaime, 5, 03500 Benidorm. ☎ **96/585-08-18.** Fax 96/585-47-16. 39 rms (all with bath). TEL

Rates (including breakfast): 3,500–5,700 ptas. ($24.90–$40.50) single; 5,000–8,400 ptas. ($35.50–$59.60) double. No credit cards.

A seaside villa between the Playa de Levante and the Playa de Poniente, the Canfali ranks as one of the best small hotels in the town. Originally built in 1950, it was enlarged in 1992. Its position is a scene-stealer—on a low cliff at the end of the esplanade, with a staircase winding down to the beach. The best rooms have balconies with sea views. Although the hotel is spacious and comfortable, its decor is undistinguished, its bedrooms functional. Terraces overlook the sea, a perfect spot for morning coffee.

Hotel Cimbel, Europa, 1, 03500 Benidorm. ☎ **96/585-21-00.** Fax 96/586-06-61. 144 rms (all with bath). A/C TV TEL Bus: 1, 2, 3, 4, or 5.

Rates (including breakfast): 7,100–8,000 ptas. ($50.40–$56.80) single; 15,000–16,000 ptas. ($106.50–$113.60) double. AE, DC, MC, V.

Since this hotel stands on one of the most popular beaches in town, it has appeal for sun worshippers, who step from the lobby virtually onto the sand. The guest rooms are functionally furnished but comfortable. The hotel restaurant serves a *menú del día* for 2,900 pesetas ($20.60). Guests will enjoy the swimming pool and later can order drinks in a *sala des noches*, a nighttime gathering spot where they can listen to disco music.

Where to Dine

I Fratelli, Edificio Principado, Arena, Calle Dr. Orts Llorca, 21. ☎ **585-39-79.**

Cuisine: ITALIAN/INTERNATIONAL. **Reservations:** Recommended.
Prices: Appetizers 500–2,500 ptas. ($3.60–$17.80); main courses 1,100–2,300 ptas. ($7.80–$16.30). AE, DC, MC, V.
Open: Lunch, daily 1–4pm; dinner, daily 7:30pm–midnight. **Closed:** Nov.

Established in 1983, this place is considered the best Italian restaurant along the Costa Blanca by its most diehard devotees. Its menu is similar to that of a trattoria in Italy. Dishes include fresh grilled peppers stuffed with Mediterranean seafood, homemade pastas, grilled meats, saltimbocca, and tempting calorie-laden Italian desserts. You can dine on the terrace or in the air-conditioned dining room.

Pérgola, Acantillado-Edificio Coblanca, 10, Rincón de Loix. ☎ **585-38-00.**

Cuisine: SPANISH/INTERNATIONAL. **Reservations:** Recommended.
Prices: Appetizers 50–1,800 ptas. ($5.30–$12.80); main courses 1,500–2,300 ptas. ($10.70–$16.30). No credit cards.
Open: Lunch, Tues–Sun 1–4pm; dinner, Tues–Sun 7:30–11pm. **Closed:** Dec 15–Feb 1.

Of the many buildings along the seafront at the Playa de Levante, this is the one which is nearest the center of Benidorm. Established in 1979, it offers a sweeping view over the bay, an airy and stylish interior, and a flower-strewn terrace which is open for warm-weather lunches and dinners. Food is skillfully prepared, and includes seafood crêpes with clams, a combination platter of hake with salmon drizzled in crabmeat sauce; stuffed crabs; stewed codfish with a confit of garlic; breast of duck with pears; and rack of beef with mustard sauce.

Tiffany's, Avenida del Mediterráneo, 51. ☎ **585-44-68.**

Cuisine: SPANISH/INTERNATIONAL. **Reservations:** Recommended.
Prices: Appetizers 700–1,800 ptas. ($5–$12.80); main courses 1,900–2,700 ptas. ($13.50–$19.20). AE, MC, V.
Open: Dinner only, daily 8pm–midnight. **Closed:** Jan 10–Feb 10.

One of the town's better restaurants has attracted holidaymakers in Benidorm since the 1970s. Meals are served with a well-rehearsed dignity and the occasional sound of a live pianist, and include food items which change with the seasons and the availability of the ingredients. Your meal might include a roulade of filet of sole stuffed with caviar and shrimp; tournedos "Tiffany" with foie gras and truffles; a choice of fish or veal dishes, and a dessert choice of homemade chocolate éclairs with warm chocolate sauce.

Evening Entertainment

Benidorm Palace, Carretera de Diputación, s/n, Rincón de Loix. ☎ **585-16-60.**

One of the best dance clubs in the region, located in the Rincón de Loix, the Benidorm Palace features the latest music and a large dance floor. There are expansive bars and ample seating. It's open Tuesday to Saturday from 9pm to 2am; closed in January. Drinks run 400 pesetas ($2.80).

Admission: 2,800 ptas. ($19.90).

Casino Costa Blanca, Carretera Nacional, km 114. ☎ **589-27-12.**

Located about 4 1/2 miles (7km) from Benidorm, beside the highway leading to Alicante, this establishment offers gambling in a modern building surrounded by the rolling hills of the Costa Blanca. Most visitors come only to try their hand at roulette (both the French and the American versions), blackjack, and boules. An on-site restaurant, Costa Blanca, serves à la carte Spanish meals from 3,000 pesetas ($21.30) per person every evening from 9pm to 1am. The casino's hours are nightly from 8pm to 4am.

Admission: Casino, 660 ptas. ($4.70). Passports must be presented.

3 Alicante

50 miles (80km) N of Murcia; 25 miles (40km) S of Benidorm; 107 miles (172km) S of Valencia; 259 miles (417km) SE of Madrid

GETTING THERE • By Plane Alicante's Internacional El Altet Airport (☎ **528-50-11**) is 12 miles (19.3km) from the city, usually with two daily flights from Alicante to Madrid. There are about two flights per day from Seville and three to Barcelona. By transferring from one of those three cities, you can reach virtually any place in Europe from Alicante. There are also three flights arriving here weekly from Ibiza and Málaga (on the Costa del Sol). Thirteen buses daily connect the city to the airport, the fare costing 125 pesetas (90¢). The Iberia Airlines ticket office is at Calle C.F. Soto, 9 (☎ **520-60-00**).

• By Train From Valencia, there are five trains a day making the three-hour trip; from Barcelona, five trains a day (11 hours); and from Madrid, six trains a day (nine hours). The RENFE office is at the Estación Término, Avenida Salamanca, s/n (☎ **592-02-02**).

• **By Bus** Different bus lines from various parts of the coast converge at the terminus, Calle Portugal, 17 (☎ **513-07-00**). There is frequent service—almost hourly—from Benidorm (see above) and from Valencia (four hours away). Buses also run from Madrid (a five- to six-hour trip).

• **By Car** Take the E-15 expressway south along the coast from Valencia. The expressway and the N-340 run northeast from Murcia.

• **By Ferry** There are ferry connections four times per day by Transmediterránea, Explanada d'Espanya, 2 (☎ **514-25-51**), to Ibiza (3 hours). Marítima de Formentera offers service to Ibiza and Formentera twice weekly (7 hours to Ibiza, 10 hours to Formentera).

ESSENTIALS The area code for Alicante is 96. The tourist information office is at Explanada d'Espanya, 2 (☎ **96/520-00-00**). The telephone office is at Avenida de la Constitució 10 (☎ **004**), open daily from 9am to 10pm. For medical assistance, go to the Hospital Clínico, Calle Alicante Sant Joan (☎ **590-83-00**). If you need an ambulance, call **521-17-05**; in case of emergency, dial **091**; to reach the city police, call **514-22-22.**

Alicante, capital of the Costa Blanca, is considered by many to be the best all-around city in Spain, since it's popular in both summer and winter. As you walk its esplanades, you almost feel as if you're in Africa: Women in caftans and peddlers hawking carvings from Senegal or elsewhere often populate the waterfront.

What to See & Do

With its wide, palm-lined avenues, this town was made for walking. The magnificent **Explanada d'Espanya,** extending around part of the yacht harbor, includes a great promenade of mosaic sidewalks under the palms. All the boulevards are clean and lined with unlimited shopping facilities, including Alicante's leading department store, Galerías Preciados, where you can find bargains without being trampled by mobs, as in Madrid. Alicante is known for its parks, gardens, and lines of palm trees, and it offers several old plazas, some paved with marble.

The **Castillo de San Fernando** has a panoramic view and can be visited during the day. High on a hill, the more stately **Castillo de Santa Bárbara** (☎ **520-51-00**) towers over the bay and provincial capital. The Greeks called the fort Akra Leuka (White Peak). Its original defenses were probably erected by the Carthaginians in 400 B.C. and were later used by the Romans and the Arabs. The grand scale of this fortress is evident in its moats, drawbridges, tunneled entrances, guardrooms, bakery, cisterns, underground storerooms, hospitals, batteries, powder stores, barracks, the Matanza Tower and the Keep, high breastworks, and deep dungeons. From the top of the castle there's a panoramic view over land and sea (the castle is reachable by road or an elevator that is boarded at the Explanda d'Espanya). Admission is 200 pesetas ($1.40) by elevator. In winter the castle is open daily from 9am to 7pm; in summer it's open daily from 9am to 8pm.

On the slopes of the Castillo de Santa Bárbara is the **Barrio de Santa Cruz.** Lying behind the cathedral and forming part of the **Villa Vieja** (as the old quarter of Alicante is called), it is a colorful section with wrought-iron grilles on the windows, banks of flowers, and a view of the entire harbor.

Alicante isn't all ancient. Facing the Iglesia Santa Maria, the **Museu Colecció Art del Segle XX,** Calle Mayor (☎ **521-45-78**), is housed in the city's oldest building, but contains modern art. Constructed as a granary in 1685, the restored building features works by Miró, Calder, Cocteau, Vasarely, Dalí, Picasso, and Tápies. Notable foreign artists include Braque, Chagall, Giacometti, Kandinsky, and Zadkine. You'll also see a musical score by Manuel de Falla. The museum was formed in 1977 from the donation of a private collection by the painter/sculptor Eusebio Sempere, whose works are also on display. It is open May through September, Tuesday through Saturday, from 10:30am to 1:30pm and 6 to 9pm; October through April, Tuesday through Saturday, 10am to 1pm and 5 to 8pm. Sunday hours year round are from 10am to 1pm. Admission is free.

Just north of the entrance to Santa Bárbara, catch a 58-mile (93km) narrow-gauge train that will take you along the beautiful rocky, beach-lined coast to **Denia,** passing through Villajoyosa, Benidorm, Altea, and 26 other stations, almost all of which are worth a visit. Built by a French company in 1915, the *Limón Exprés* offers departures every Wednesday and Friday at 9:55am. Passengers stop to shop for wicker baskets and they also visit a guitar factory. On the way back to Benidorm, they drink sparkling wine. For more information about these excursions, call **96/585-18-95.**

Now a lively tourist center, Denia stretches from the slopes of a hill to the seashore. It was inhabited by the Greeks, its name deriving from an ancient temple dedicated to the goddess Diana (fragments of the temple are displayed in the early 16th-century Town Hall). You'll also find the remnants of an old Iberian settlement and a great Moorish castle. Denia has fine beaches, and its fishing port is one of the region's best.

San Juan, the largest beach in Alicante, lies a short distance from the capital. It's lined with villas, hotels, and restaurants. The bay of Alicante has two capes, and on the bay is **Postiguet Beach.** The bay stretches all the way to the **Cape of Santa Pola,** a town with two good beaches, a 14th-century castle, and several seafood restaurants.

Where to Stay

EXPENSIVE

Hotel Melía Alicante, Playa de El Postiguet, 03001 Alicante. ☎ **96/520-50-00,** or toll free in the U.S. **800/336-3542.** Fax 96/520-47-56. 535 rms, 10 suites. A/C MINIBAR TV TEL

Rates: 12,700 ptas. ($90.20) single; 15,850 ptas. ($112.50) double; 24,350 ptas. ($172.90) suite. Breakfast 1,300 ptas. ($9.20) extra. AE, DC, MC, V. **Parking:** 1,000 ptas. ($7.10).

Built in 1973 on a spit of landfill jutting into the Mediterranean, midway between the main harbor and the very popular El Postiguet beach, this is a comfortable hotel, so massive in size that it almost dwarfs every other establishment in town. Bedrooms are painted in clear, sunny colors and contain private baths and balconies, usually with sweeping panoramas to either the rows of moored sailboats in the nearby marina or over the beach. The public rooms are contemporary, with lots of marble and a uniformed staff.

Dining/Entertainment: The two in-house restaurants serve à la carte meals at from around 3,300 ptas. ($23.40) pesetas. There are also a bar near the pool and an indoor bar with a piano player, plus a *sala de fiestas* where drinking, conversation, and dancing occur.

Services: Concierge, laundry, 24-hour room service, babysitting.

Facilities: Gymnasium, two outdoor swimming pools.

Hotel Tryp Gran Sol, Rambla Méndez Nuñez, 3, 03002 Alicante. ☎ **96/520-30-00,** or toll free in the U.S. **800/272-8674.** Fax 96/521-14-39. 144 rms, 4 suites. A/C MINIBAR TV TEL

Rates: 7,360 ptas. ($52.30) single; 9,200 ptas. ($65.30) double; 14,950 ptas. ($106.10) suite. Breakfast 925 ptas. ($6.60) extra. AE, DC, MC, V. **Parking:** 1,100 ptas. ($7.80).

Set in the heart of the tourist zone, a block from the beachfront Paseo Marítimo, his 1970 hotel towers conspicuously above almost every other building in town. A member of the widely known Tryp chain, it offers simple and uncomplicated bedrooms with unimaginative but comfortable furnishings, plus private bathrooms accented with tiles and/or marble.

Dining/Entertainment: The Ramblas Restaurant lies adjacent to a popular and comfortable bar. *Menús del día* cost from 1,600 to 1,800 pesetas ($11.40 to $12.80). Both of these are on the building's 26th floor, where big windows offer sweeping views of the town and coastline.

Services: 24-hour room service, laundry service, concierge, babysitter.

Facilities: Car rentals, reading room, game room, TV room, meeting facilities.

MODERATE

Hotel Residencia Covadonga, Plaza de los Luceros, 17, 03004 Alicante. ☎ **96/520-28-44.** Fax 96/521-43-97. 83 rms, 4 suites (all with bath). A/C TV TEL **Bus:** 5, A, B, or D.

Rates: 4,200 ptas. ($29.80) single; 6,900 ptas. ($49) double; from 8,400 ptas. ($59.60) suite. Breakfast 440 ptas. ($3.10) ptas. ($3.40) extra AE, DC, MC, V. **Parking:** 800 ptas. ($5.70).

Convenient to attractions, the railway station, buses, and the airport, the Covadonga also offers comfortable, spacious rooms and good service. The public rooms are large and inviting. There's no restaurant, but you'll find many places to dine nearby.

Palas, Cervantes, 5, 03002 Alicante. ☎ **96/520-92-11.** Fax 96/514-01-21. 40 rms (all with bath). A/C TEL

Rates: 4,900 ptas. ($34.80) single; 8,380 ptas. ($59.50) double. Breakfast 500 ptas. ($3.60) extra. AE, DC, MC, V. **Parking:** 500 ptas. ($3.60).

This charmer has a lot of old-fashioned style. Many guests like its location–near the seafront at the eastern end of the Explanada d'Espanya–along with its personal service. Several public areas are graced with chandeliers and antiques. The bedrooms are pleasantly furnished and well-maintained.

BUDGET

Hotel Residencia San Remo, Navas, 30, 03001 Alicante. ☎ **96/520-95-00.** Fax 96/520-96-69. 28 rms (22 with bath). TEL Bus: B.

Rates: 3,000 ptas. ($21.30) single without bath, 4,000 ptas. ($28.40) single with bath; 4,500 ptas. ($32) double without bath, 5,500 ptas. ($39.10) double with bath. AE, DC, MC, V. **Parking:** 1,500 ptas. ($10.70).

A white-plastered seven-floor building, the San Remo offers clean, unpretentious, comfortable rooms, some with balconies. Breakfast is the only meal served. The welcome is warm, the price right. Room service is provided from 8am to 8pm.

Portugal, Calle Portugal, 26, 03003 Alicante. ☎ **592-92-44.** 18 rms (5 with bath).

Rates: 2,000 ptas. ($14.20) single with sink; 3,500 ptas. ($24.90) double with sink; 4,000 ptas. ($28.40) double with bath. Breakfast 350 ptas. ($2.50) extra. No credit cards. **Parking:** 1,000 ptas. ($7.10).

The Portugal is a two-story hotel, one block from the bus station, about four blocks from the railway station, and a three-minute walk from the harbor. The accommodations, furnished in tasteful modern style, are immaculate.

Where to Dine

The characteristic dish of Alicante is rice, served in many different ways. The most typical sauce is *aïoli,* a kind of mayonnaise made from oil and garlic. Dessert selections offer the greatest variety on the Costa Blanca, with *turrón de Alicante* (Spanish nougat) the most popular of all.

EXPENSIVE

Delfín, Explanada d'Espanya, 14. ☎ **521-49-11.**

Cuisine: MEDITERRANEAN. **Reservations:** Recommended.
Prices: Appetizers 600–1,500 ptas. ($4.30–$10.70); main courses 2,000–2,600 ptas. ($14.20–$18.50); *menú del día* 3,500 ptas. ($24.90). AE, DC, MC, V.
Open: Lunch, daily 1–5 pm; dinner, daily 8pm–midnight.

Set on the town's most visible promenade, this restaurant, established in 1961, offers an upstairs dining room, where hushed service, lots of mirrors, and views over the town's harbor and yacht basin complement the attentive service and culinary style. Menu specialties might include smoked salmon served on toast with a gratin of shrimp, filet steak grilled with goat-cheese topping, sauté of sweetbreads flavored with foie gras and strips of duckmeat, crêpes stuffed with seafood, paella, and an array of tempting pastries rolled from table to table on a trolley.

Restaurante El Jumillano, César Elquezábel, 64. ☎ **521-17-64.**

Cuisine: SPANISH. **Reservations:** Recommended. **Bus:** D or F.
Prices: Appetizers 850–1,300 ptas. ($6–$9.20); main courses 1,950–2,500 ptas. ($13.80–$17.80); fixed-price menu 3,400 ptas. ($24.10). AE, DC, MC, V.
Open: Lunch, Mon–Sat 1–4pm; dinner, Mon–Sat 8pm–midnight.

This was a humble wine bar when it opened in 1936 near the old city. The original wine-and-tapas bar is still going strong, but the food has improved immeasurably. Today the original owner's sons (Juan José and Miguel Pérez Mejías) offer a cornucopia of succulent food, including an array of fresh fish laid out in the dining room on the sun-bleached planks of an antique fishing boat. Many of the menu items are derived from locally inspired recipes. The specialties include a "festival of canapes"; slices of cured ham served with fresh melon; shellfish soup with mussels; Alicante stew; pig's trotters; a savory filet of beef seasoned with garlic; and a full gamut of grilled hake, sea bass, and shellfish.

MODERATE

Nou Manolín, Calle Villegas, 4. ☎ **520-0368.**

Cuisine: REGIONAL/SPANISH. **Reservations:** Recommended.
Prices: Appetizers 250–1,500 ptas. ($1.80–$10.70); main courses 1,700–2,100 ptas. ($12.10–$14.90). AE, DC, MC, V.
Open: Lunch, daily 1–3 pm; dinner, daily 8:30–11:30pm.

When it was established in 1972, the founder of this restaurant named it after an almost-forgotten neighborhood bar (El Manolín) that his grandfather had maintained before the Civil War. The Nou Manolín's street level contains a busy bar area where a cornucopia of food and bottles of wine are positioned for both beauty and ease of access on shelves and from the beamed ceiling. Diners usually gravitate to the upstairs dining room, where tiled walls and uniformed waiters contribute to the ambience of an elegant tasca. Menu items include many kinds of fish cooked in a salt crust, as well as paella, several kinds of stew, fresh shellfish, and a wide selection of Iberian wines.

Restaurant La Dársena, Muelle del Puerto (Explanada d'Espanya). ☎ **520-75-89.**

Cuisine: SPANISH. **Reservations:** Required at lunch.
Prices: Appetizers 750–2,500 ptas. ($5.30–$17.80); main courses 1,400–2,400 ptas. ($9.90–$17); fixed-price menu 3,700 ptas. ($26.30). AE, DC, MC, V.
Open: Lunch, Tues–Sun 1–4pm; dinner, Tues–Sat 8pm–midnight.

At this popular place located off the Explanada d'Espanya, overlooking the harbor, paella is the best choice on the menu. Some 20 other rice dishes are commendable as well—for example, *arroz con pieles de bacalao* (rice with dried codfish). Try the crab soup flavored with Armagnac or the tart made with tuna and spinach.

INEXPENSIVE

Quo Vadis, Plaza Santísma Faz, 3. ☎ **521-66-60.**

Cuisine: SPANISH. **Reservations:** Required.
Prices: Appetizers 800–1,200 ptas. ($5.70–$8.50); main courses 1,300–2,450 ptas. ($9.20–$17.40). AE, DC, MC, V.
Open: Lunch, Tues–Sun 1–5pm; dinner, Tues–Sun 8pm–midnight.

Considered one of the best in town, ever since it opened in 1962, Quo Vadis is located north of the Explanda d'Espanya. You'll first pass through a sidewalk café and popular bar before reaching the air-conditioned dining room. Amid a dignified country decor, you'll be able to watch your food prepared with touches of culinary theater. There's also an intimate terrace, open from May to October. Specialties include a wide array of fresh seafood, such as *lubina à la sal* (a fish encrusted in salt, removed after baking), and flambéed fish, as well as roast suckling lamb. A dessert specialty is *nueces flambé*—whipped cream, ice cream, and chocolate flambéed with Grand Marnier and sprinkled with grated almonds.

4 Elche

13 miles (21 km) SW of Alicante; 35 miles (56km) NE of Murcia; 252 miles (406km) SE of Madrid

GETTING THERE • By Train The central train station is the Estación Parque, Plaza Alfonso XII. Trains arrive almost hourly from Alicante.

- **By Bus** The bus station is at Avenida de la Libertat. Buses travel between Alicante and Elche on the hour.
- **By Car** Take the N-340 highway from Alicante and proceed southwest.

ESSENTIALS The area code for Elche is **96.** The tourist information office is at Passeig de l'Estació (☎ **96/545-27-47**).

Between Alicante and Murcia, the little town of Elche is famous for its age-old mystery play, lush groves of date palms, and shoe and sandal-making. The play is reputedly the oldest dramatic liturgy performed in Europe. On August 14 and 15 for the last six centuries, the ★ **Mystery of Elche** has celebrated the Assumption of the Virgin. Songs are performed in an ancient form of Catalán. Admission is free, but it's hard to get a seat unless you book in advance through the tourist office (see above). The play is performed at the Church of Santa Mariá, dating from the 17th century.

Unless you visit at the time of the mystery play, the town's date palms will hold the most appeal. The palm forest is unrivaled in Europe—some 600,000 trees said to have been originally planted by Phoenician (perhaps Greek) seafarers. The Moors created the irrigation system 1,000 years ago. Stroll through the **Huerto del Cura (Priest's Grove),** open daily from 9am to 6pm, to see the palm garden and collection of tropical flowers and cacti. In the garden look for the Palmera del Cura (Priest's Palm), from the 1840s with seven branches sprouting from its trunk. In the grove you will see one of the most famous ladies of Spain, *La Dama de Elche.* This is a replica, since the original limestone bust (500 B.C.) is on display in the National Archeological Museum in Madrid. It was discovered in 1897.

Where to Stay

Don Jaime, Primo de Rivera, 5, 03203 Elche. ☎ **96/545-38-40.** Fax 96/542-64-36. 64 rms (all with bath). TEL

Rates: 4,240 ptas. ($30.10) single; 6,360 ptas. ($45.20) double. Breakfast 400 ptas. ($2.80) extra. MC, V. **Parking:** 1,750 ptas. ($12.40).

Totally lacking the glamour of the parador Huerto del Cura (see below) and rated only two stars by the government, this hotel near the town center is easy on the purse. Built in 1960, it contains five floors. The well-maintained guest rooms are comfortable rather than stylish. During performances of the *Mystery of Elche,* prices here rise about 25%. There's no restaurant, but there are a number of places to eat nearby.

★ **Huerto Del Cura,** Porta de La Morera, 14, 03200 Elche. ☎ **96/545-80-40.** Fax 96/542-19-10. 70 rms (all with bath), 3 suites. A/C MINIBAR TV TEL

Rates: 9,275–10,250 ptas. ($65.90–$72.80) single; 9,275–11,200 ptas. ($65.90–$79.50) double; 15,500–17,000 ptas. ($110.10–$120.70) suite. Breakfast 1,000 ptas. ($7.10) extra. AE, DC, MC, V. **Parking:** 1,000 ptas. ($7.10).

Huerto del Cura stands in the so-called Priest's Grove, and from your bedroom you'll have lovely views of the palm trees. The privately owned parador consists of a number of cabins in the grove. Although the rates are high, staying here proves a unique experience—everything beautifully furnished and immaculately kept, the service impeccable. A swimming pool under the palms separates the cabins from the main hotel building. There is an attractive bar, and in the upstairs dining room, the four-fork Els Capellans, the food is well prepared and the wine list extensive. Dinner costs around 3,200 pesetas ($22.70).

Where to Dine

Parque Municipal, Paseo Alfonso XIII, s/n. ☎ **545-34-15.**

Cuisine: SPANISH/INTERNATIONAL. **Reservations:** Recommended.
Prices: Appetizers 600–1,000 ptas. ($4.30–$7.10); main courses 1,200–1,800 ptas. ($8.50–$12.80); fixed-price menu 1,200 ptas. ($8.50). MC, V.
Open: Lunch, daily 1–4pm; dinner, daily 8–11pm.

A large open-air restaurant and café right in the middle of a public park, the Parque Municipal is a good place to go for decent food and relaxed service. Many regional dishes appear on the menu; try one of the savory rice dishes as a main course, followed by "cake of Elche." Two specialties here are paella and Mediterranean sea bass, sailor's style.

Restaurante La Finca, Partida de Perleta, 1-7. ☎ **545-60-07.**

Cuisine: SPANISH. **Reservations:** Recommended.
Prices: Appetizers 900–1,800 ptas. ($6.40–$12.80); main courses 1,600–2,000 ptas. ($11.40–$14.20); fixed-price menus 3,500–4,500 ptas. ($24.90–$32). AE, DC, MC, V.
Open: Lunch, Tues–Sun 1–5pm, dinner, Tues–Sat 8:30pm–midnight.

In the campo near the Elche football stadium, three miles (5km) south of town along the Carretera de El Alted, La Finca opened in 1984 and has attracted customers ever since with its good food. The menu changes frequently, based on the season and what's fresh. Both fish and meat are prepared in creative ways, although time-tested recipes are used as well. Try tuna-stuffed peppers, if featured, or veal kidneys with potatoes. Chocolate mousse might be a featured dessert.

5 Murcia

52 miles (83km) SW of Alicante; 245 miles (409km) SE of Madrid; 159 miles (256km) SW of Valencia

GETTING THERE • **By Train** From Alicante, 18 trains arrive daily (a 1½-hour trip); from Barcelona, one daily (11 hours); and from Madrid, three daily (5 to 8¼ hours). From the Estación del Carmen, Calle Industria, s/n (☎ **25-21-54**), take bus no. 11 to the heart of the city.

• **By Bus** From Valencia, five buses arrive daily; from Granada, five; and from Seville, three. If you're coming from Almería, there are three connections daily. Buses come into the terminal at Sierra de la Pila. Cal 29-22-11 for information.

• **By Car** Take the N-340 southwest from Alicante.

ESSENTIALS The area for Murcia is 968. The tourist information office is at Alejandro Seiquer, 4 (☎ **968/21-37-16**).

SPECIAL EVENTS The **Holy Week celebration** at Murcia is an ideal time to visit. Its processions are spectacular, with about 3,000 people taking part, and some sculptures of Salzillo (see below) are carried through the streets. Musicians blow horns so big they have to be carried on wheels.

This ancient Moorish city of sienna-colored buildings is an island provincial capital on the main road between Valencia and Granada. It lies on the Segura River.

What to See & Do

Although it suffered much from fire and bombardment during the Spanish Civil War, the city abounds in grand houses built in the 18th century. But the principal artistic treasure is the **cathedral,** Plaza Cardenal Belluga (☎ **21-63-44**), a bastardized medley of Gothic, baroque, and Renaissance. Begun in the 1300s, its bell tower was built at four different periods by four different architects. You can climb the tower for a view of Murcia and the enveloping fertile *huerta* (plain). The Capilla de los Vélez, off the ambulatory, is the most interesting chapel. You can see works by the famous local sculptor, Francisco Salzillo (1707–83), as well as the golden crown of the Virgen de la Fuensanta, patroness of Murcia. To reach the museum, go through the north transept. You can visit it daily from 10am to 1pm and 5 to 7pm for an admission of 150 pesetas ($1.10). The cathedral and bell tower keep the same hours.

The other major sight is the **Museo de Salzillo,** San Andrés, 1 (☎ **29-18-93**). The son of an Italian sculptor father and a Spanish mother, Salzillo won fame with sculptures done in polychrome wood. This museum displays his finest work, plus many terra-cotta figurines based on Biblical scenes. It is open Tuesday through Saturday from 9:30am to 1pm and 4 to 7pm, Sunday from 9:30am to 1pm. Admission is 200 pesetas ($1.40).

Another attraction is the **Museo de Arqueología,** Calle Alfonso, X El Sabio, 7 (☎ **23-46-02**), considered one of the best in Spain. Through artifacts—mosaics, fragments of pottery, Roman coins, ceramics, and various other objects—it traces life in Murcia province from prehistoric times. The two most important collections are devoted to objects from the Hispano-Moorish period of the 12th to the 14th century and to Spanish ceramics of the 17th and 18th centuries. It is open Monday through Friday from 9am to 2pm and 4:30 to 8pm; Saturday from 10am to 1:30pm. Admission is 75 pesetas (50¢).

Where to Stay

Hispano 1, Trapería, 8, 30001 Murcia. ☎ **968/21-61-52.** Fax 968/21-68-59. 46 rms (all with bath). TV TEL **Bus:** 2, 5, 6, or 11.

Rates: 4,800 ptas. ($34.10) single; 6,000 ptas. ($42.60) double. Breakfast 800 ptas. ($5.70) extra. AE, DC, MC, V.

An older version of Hispano 2 (see below), run by the same people, this good-value hotel is still reliable after all these years. It stands right at the cathedral. The well-kept guest rooms are functional and comfortable. The hotel also has a restaurant serving a regional cuisine.

Hotel Conde de Floridablanca, Princesa, 18, 30002 Murcia. ☎ **968/21-46-26.** Fax 968/21-32-15. 60 rms (all with bath), 5 suites. A/C MINIBAR TV TEL **Bus:** 2, 5, 6, or 11.

Rates: 9,600 ptas. ($68.20) single; 12,000 ptas. ($85.20) double; 15,000 ptas. ($106.50) suite. Breakfast 900 ptas. ($6.40) extra. AE, DC, MC, V. **Parking:** 1,200 ptas. ($8.50).

Rising from the center of the Barrio del Carmen, near the cathedral, this hotel is ideally suited for explorations of the old city. Originally built in 1972, it was thoroughly renovated and enlarged in 1992. The building is attractively decorated in a conservatively modern style, and bedrooms are comfortable and appealing. The hotel serves only breakfast but the polite staff will direct clients to several well-recommended local restaurants.

Hotel Hispano 2, Calle Radio Murcia, 3, 30001 Murcia. ☎ **968/21-61-52.** Fax 968/21-68-59. 35 rms (all with bath). A/C MINIBAR TV TEL **Bus:** 2, 5, 6, or 11.

Rates: 9,000 ptas. ($63.90) single; 11,500 ptas. ($81.70) double. Breakfast 900 ptas. ($6.40) extra. AE, DC, MC, V. **Parking:** 1,000 ptas. ($7.10).

The older Hispano 1 (see above) proved so successful that the owners inaugurated this version in the late 1970s. Bedrooms are comfortably furnished. Family run, the hotel restaurant offers well-prepared regional food and tapas.

Hotel Melía 7 Coronas, Paseo de Garay, 5, 30000 Murcia. ☎ **968/21-77-72,** or toll free in the U.S. **800/336-3542.** Fax 968/22-12-94. 150 rms (all with bath). A/C MINIBAR TV TEL **Bus:** 2, 5, 6, or 11.

Rates: July–Aug, 7,000 ptas. ($49.70) single; 9,000 ptas. ($63.90) double; Sept–June 13,000 ptas. ($92.30) single; 16,300 ptas. ($115.70) double. Breakfast 1,300 ptas. ($9.20) extra. AE, DC, MC, V. **Parking:** 1,000 ptas. ($7.10).

Set within a 15-minute walk east of the cathedral, near the gardens abutting the northern edge of the Río Segura, this angular 1971 hotel offers comfortable bedrooms and a cool, refreshing terrace with bar service and a legion of flowering plants. A member of the well-recommended nationwide chain, the hotel is generally regarded as the finest in town.

Dining/Entertainment: The in-house restaurant serves à la carte Spanish and continental meals that begin at 2,500 pesetas ($17.80) for a set menu. There's also a bar.

Services: Concierge, laundry service, babysitting.

Residencia Rincón de Pepe, Plaza de Apóstoles, 34, 30002 Murcia. ☎ **968/21-22-39.** Fax 968/22-17-44. 116 rms (all with bath). A/C TV TEL

Rates: 13,775 ptas. ($97.80) single; 18,000 ptas. ($127.80) double. Breakfast 1,500 ptas. ($10.70) extra. AE, DC, MC, V. **Parking:** 1,250 ptas. ($8.90).

This modern hotel hidden on a narrow street in the heart of the old quarter is attached to a well-known restaurant (see below). Once beyond its entranceway, accented with marble, glass, and plants, you'll discover a good-sized lounge as well as a bar. The comfortable bedrooms are up to date with many built-in conveniences; some have minibars.

Where to Dine

$ **Acuario,** Plaza Puxmaria, 1. ☎ **21-99-55.**

Cuisine: MURCIAN/INTERNATIONAL. **Reservations:** Recommended. **Bus:** 2, 5, 6, or 11.

Prices: Appetizers 700–900 ptas. ($5–$6.40); main courses 1,250–2,000 ptas. ($8.90–$14.20); fixed-price menu 3,000 ptas. ($21.30). AE, DC, MC, V.

Located near the cathedral, this restaurant allows you to dine in air-conditioned comfort. Since it opened in 1987, it has long been known both for its excellent Murcian cuisine as well as a selection of international dishes. Begin perhaps with the pâté of salmon, following with such dishes as *merluza* (hake) in sherry sauce, a tender tournedos, or the chef's specialty, eggplant cooked with Serrano ham and mushrooms. If featured, the lemon soufflé is delectable.

Rincón de Pepe, Plaza de Apóstoles, 34. ☎ **21-22-39.**

Cuisine: SPANISH/INTERNATIONAL. **Reservations:** Recommended. **Bus:** 3, 4, or 8.
Prices: Appetizers 400–3,600 ptas. ($2.80–$25.60); main courses 1,800–3,200 ptas. ($12.80–$22.70). AE, DC, MC, V.
Open: Lunch, daily noon–5pm; dinner, Mon–Sat 8pm–midnight.

Many visitors won't leave town without going to this culinary landmark set up in the mid-1920s. It rates as the best restaurant in town, and you can dine here at a wide range of price levels, depending on what you order. Specialties change frequently, since every effort is made to produce a menu with seasonal variations. You might enjoy a dish such as pig's trotters and white beans, spring lamb kidneys in sherry, or white beans with partridge. The shellfish selection includes Carril clams, a platter of assorted grilled seafood and fish, and grilled red prawns from Aguilas. Among the meat and poultry specialties are roast spring lamb Murcian style and duck in orange sauce.

TAPAS

Good tapas are served at **La Tapa,** Plaza de las Flores (☎ **21-13-17**), daily from 7am to 11pm. In addition to being an interesting end to a walk through the old city (it's located on one of the oldest town squares), La Tapa offers beer on tap as well as its savory selection of tapas starting at 200 pesetas ($1.40). There is a big terrace on which you can enjoy your food and drink.

12

Getting to Know Barcelona

BARCELONA HAS LONG HAD A REPUTATION FOR BEING THE MOST EUROPEAN OF Spanish cities. The third-largest port on the Mediterranean, it rediscovered itself after the long, dark period of the Franco dictatorship, which seemed determined to wipe out a proud Catalonian culture. Barcelona may still be the "second city of Spain" (after Madrid), but it is very much a "first" in certain respects.

Blessed with rich and fertile soil, an excellent harbor, and a hardworking population, Barcelona has always shown a talent for transforming dreams into art and dialog into commerce. It has always been one of Spain's most prosperous cities, with more wealth distributed among greater numbers of people (especially during the 19th century) than anywhere else in Spain.

Barcelona was a powerful and diverse capital when Madrid was still a dusty and unknown Castilian backwater. Exploited by several different empires, Barcelona turned to the Mediterranean for inspiration and linguistic roots, inspired more by the cultures to the east than the arid plains of Iberia.

As if the attractions of Barcelona weren't enough, it stands on the doorstep of some of the great playgrounds and vacation retreats of Europe: the Balearic Islands to the east; the Costa Brava (Wild Coast) to the north and the Pyrenees even beyond; the Penedés wine country; resorts such as Sitges on the Costa Dorada to the south; the old Roman city of Tarragona; and the monastery of Montserrat.

Despite its allure, Barcelona shares the problems of hundreds of other cities—an increasing polarization between rich and poor, a rising rate of delinquency and drug abuse, and an upsetting frequency of crime. In fairness, however, the city authorities have, with some degree of success, managed to combat much of the crime (at least within the tourist zones) in reaction to a rash of negative publicity.

A revitalized Barcelona eagerly prepared and welcomed thousands of visitors as part of the 1992 Summer Olympic Games. But the action didn't end with the games. Barcelona is turning its multimillion-dollar Olympic building projects into permanently expanded facilities for sports and tourism. As its modern $150-million terminal at El Prat de Llobregat Airport gears up to receive 12 million passengers a year, the restructuring of Barcelona is called "Post Olympica"—a race to the 21st century.

1 Some Cultural Background

Barcelona (which was described in the Middle Ages as "the head and trunk of Catalonia") has always thrived on contacts and commerce with countries beyond Spain's borders. From its earliest days, the city has been linked more closely to France and the rest of Europe than to Iberia. And each of the military and financial empires that swept through and across the collective consciousness of Catalonia left its cultural legacy.

ARCHITECTURE Like many other cities in Spain, Barcelona has its share of Neolithic dolmens and ruins from the Roman and Moorish periods. Monuments survive from the Middle Ages, when the Romanesque solidity of no-nonsense barrel vaults (sometimes with ribbing), narrow windows, and a fortified design were widely used. In fact, as early as the 10th century, Catalonian churches were among the first to use the stone barrel vault.

In the 11th and 12th centuries, a religious fervor swept through Europe and pilgrims began to flock through Barcelona on their way west to Santiago de Compostela, bringing with them the influence of French building styles and a need for new and larger churches. The style that developed had softer lines, more ornamentation

What's Special About Barcelona

Museums

- Museu Picasso, Barcelona's most popular attraction, focusing on the artist's early period.
- Fundació Joan Miró at Montjüic, paying tribute to Catalonia's master of surrealism.
- Museu d'Art de Catalunya, with its renowned collection of Romanesque and Gothic art from many small churches.

Architectural Highlights

- The cathedral of Barcelona, begun in 1298, an exemplary monument to Mediterranean Gothic.
- Gaudí's works—surrealistic imagination running rampant, as exemplified by his church La Sagrada Familia.

Districts

- The Barri Gòtic (Gothic Quarter), filled with buildings constructed between the 13th and 15th centuries.
- The Eixample, studded with late 19th- and early 20th-century architecture unequaled in Europe, including many works by Gaudí.

Promenade

- Les Rambles, the single most famous promenade in Spain—five separate sections extending from city's main square to its harbor.

Parks/Gardens

- Montjuïc, the site of the 1992 Summer Olympics, south of the city—with great museums and a recreated Spanish village.
- Parc Güell, a Gaudí dream unfulfilled but a fascinating preview of what might have been.
- Parc de la Ciutadella, former citadel, with everything from a lake and a zoo to a modern art museum.

Panoramas

- Tibidabo Mountain, named for the one where Satan is said to have taken Christ to tempt him with the world—"All this I'll give you."
- The Columbus Monument, with its view of one of Mediterranean's most famous harbors.

(columns with decorative capitals), and an understood freedom for the stone-mason to carve, within limits, in whatever manner he felt the most inspired. This eventually led to a richly ornate, very dignified style called Catalonian Gothic. Appropriate for both civic and religious buildings, it called for ogival (pointed) arches, intricate stone carvings, very large interior columns, exterior buttresses, and large rose windows set with colored glass. One of Barcelona's purest and most-loved examples of this style is the Church of Santa María del Mar, north of the city's harborfront.

The Barcelona that visitors best remember, however, is the Barcelona of modernism, a movement that, from about 1860 to 1910, put the city on the architectural map. From the minds of a highly articulate school of Catalán architects came a blend of Pre-Raphaelite voluptuousness and Catalonian romanticism, heavily laced with a yearning for the curved lines and organic forms easily recognized in nature.

The movement's most visible architect was Antoni Gaudí, who usually preferred a curved over a straight line. The chimneys of his buildings look like half-melted mounds of chocolate twisted into erratic spirals, and his horizontal lines flow, rather than lie, over their vertical supports. Some of Gaudí's most distinctive creations include the Casa Milá, the Casa Batlló, Parc Güell and the neighborhood around it, and the landmark Temple Expiatori de la Sagrada Familia (never completed).

Other modernist architects looked to Romanesque and medieval models for inspiration, particularly the fortified castles and sculpted gargoyles and dragons of the 12th-century counts of Barcelona. Examples include Domènech i Montaner and Puig i Cadafalch, whose elegant mansions and concert halls seemed perfectly suited to the enlightened and sophisticated prosperity of the 19th-century Catalonian bourgeoisie. Fortunately, a 19th-century economic boom neatly coincided with the profusion of geniuses who suddenly emerged in the building business. Some of the elaborately beautiful villas of Barcelona and nearby Sitges were commissioned by entrepreneurs whose fortunes had been made in the fields and mines of the New World.

Contemporary with the buildings designed by the modernist architects was the expansion—first initiated in 1858—of Barcelona into the northern Eixample district. Its gridwork pattern of streets was intersected, in surprisingly modern motifs, with broad diagonals. Though opposed by local landowners, and never manifested with the detail of its original design, it provided a carefully planned and elegant path in which a growing city could showcase its finest buildings.

Consistent with the general artistic stagnation of Spain during the Franco era (1939 to 1975), the 1950s saw a tremendous increase in the number of anonymous housing projects around the periphery of Barcelona. Since the death of Franco, the renaissance of *La Movida* (the movement) has enhanced all aspects of Spain's artistic life; new and more creative designs for buildings are once again being executed.

ART From the cave paintings discovered at Lérida to the giants of the 20th century, such as Picasso, Dalí, and Miró, Catalonia has had a long artistic tradition. It is said to be the center of the plastic arts in Spain.

Barcelona entered the world art pages with its Catalonian Gothic sculpture, which held sway from the 13th to the 15th century and produced such renowned masters as Bartomeu and Pere Johan. Sculptors working with Italian masters brought the Renaissance to Barcelona, but few great Catalonian legacies remain from this period. The rise of baroque art in the 17th and 18th centuries saw Catalonia filled with several impressive examples but nothing worth a special pilgrimage.

In the neoclassical period of the 18th century, Catalonia, and particularly Barcelona, arose from an artistic slumber. Art schools opened in the city and foreign painters arrived, exerting considerable influence. The 19th century produced many Catalonian artists who, it might be said, followed the general European trends of the time without forging any major creative breakthroughs.

The 20th century brought renewed artistic ferment in Barcelona, as reflected by the arrival of Málaga-born Pablo Picasso (the city today is the site of a major Picasso museum). The great surrealist painters of the Spanish school, Joan Miró (who also has a museum in Barcelona) and Salvador Dalí (whose museum is along the Costa Brava, north of Barcelona), also came to the Catalonian capital.

Many Catalán sculptors also achieved acclaim in this century, including Casanovas, Llimon, and Blay. The Spanish Civil War brought a cultural stagnation, yet against all odds many a Catalán artist continued to make bold statements. Tàpies was a major artist of this period (one of the newest museums in Barcelona is devoted to his work). Among the various schools formed in Spain at the time was the neofigurative band, which included such artists as Váquez Díaz and Pancho Cossio. Antonio López, dubbed a hyperrealist, went on to international acclaim.

Today, toward the end of the 20th century, many Barcelona artists are making major names for themselves, and their works are sold in the most prestigious galleries of the Western world.

LITERATURE & LANGUAGE Catalonia, a region lying midway between France and Castilian Spain, is united by a common language, Catalán. The linguistic separateness of the region is arguably the single most important element in the sometimes obsessive independence of its people. Modern linguists attribute the earliest division of Catalán from Castilian to two phenomena: The first was the cultural links and trade ties between ancient Barcina and the neighboring Roman colony of Provence, which shaped the Catalán tongue along Provençal and Languedocian models. The second major event was the invasion of the eastern Pyrenees by Charlemagne in the late 800s and the designation of Catalonia as a Frankish march (buffer zone) between Christian Europe and a Moorish-dominated Iberia.

Contemporaneous with the troubadour tradition of courtly love so popular in Provence and neighboring Languedoc during the 1100s and the 1200s, a handful of courtly minstrels composed similar poems in Catalán and recited them at banquets for the amusement of the lords of Barcelona. By the late 1200s, Catalonia's literature became better defined, thanks to the works of Peter the Ceremonious, Desciot, and Mutaner and to the religious treatises of Arnau de Vilanova. The best-remembered of them all was a socially prominent physician and mystic theologican, a true Renaissance man born 200 years too soon, Ramón Llull. In addition to poetry and the composition of a scientific encyclopedia, he worked in what has been called an early form of the novel, describing a medieval urban landscape filled with what later generations would have labeled bourgeois characters. Llull also coined many words of his own (or recorded existing words for the first time), thereby enriching the Catalán language.

The most prolific period of Catalán literature was the late 1300s and early 1400s, a period critics view as an early articulate expression of the humanism that later swept through the rest of Europe in better-developed forms. Authors from this period include Bernat Metge, Febrer, Ausias March, Ruís de Corella, and Jordi de Sant Jordi. About a century later, Catalán literature received a tremendous boost from the most important and venerated writer in Spanish history, Miguel de Cervantes (1547–1616), who lavishly praised a Catalán epic written about a century before his birth—the chivalric poem *Tirant lo Blanch* by Joanot Martorell.

From about 1500 to about 1810, Catalán literature was severely eclipsed by the brilliant works being written in Castilian. The capital of the Spanish Empire shifted to Madrid, and it was both fiscally and politically expedient to mimic Castilian, rather than Catalán, models. A more cynical view suggests that this era marked the beginning of the suppression of Catalonian culture, with the simultaneous relegation to obscurity of works that otherwise might have been celebrated.

IMPRESSIONS

Although the great adventures that befell me there occasioned me no great pleasure, but rather much grief, I bore them the better for having seen the city [Barcelona].
—Don Quixote

The 19th century, however, brought economic prosperity to a hardworking Catalonia, where the bourgeois middle class enjoyed a financial boom that made it the envy of Spain. Prosperity and the resulting *renaixença* (renaissance) of Catalonian culture produced a form of romanticism exemplified by Jacint Verdaguer and Àngel Guimerà (in dramatics), Milà i Fontanals (in poetry), Narcís Oller (described as a naturalist), and Santiago Rusiñol (a modernist). Writing was considered inappropriate for women at this time, but Catalonia nevertheless produced a female novelist, Caterina Albert, who wrote under the pseudonym Victor Catala.

During the early 20th century, there was a strong emphasis on literary style and form. In the same way that the Parisians applauded the sophistication of Proust, Catalάns read and appreciated such stylists as Eugeni d'Ors and poets such as Carles Riba (*Elégies de Bierville*) and Salvat-Papasseit.

In the 1950s, despite the suppression of the Catalonian language by Franco, such works as *Béarn* by Lorenc Villalonga, *La Plaça del Diamant* by Mercé Rodoreda, and *Els Payesos* by Josep *Plá* were enthusiastically received by international critics.

MUSIC & DANCE The counts of Barcelona, so we are told, were great music lovers, and the Catalán appreciation of music continues to this day. Richard Strauss arrived to dedicate the musical center, the Palau de la Música Catalana, in 1908.

In addition to importing the great talents of Europe for its listening pleasure, the people of Catalonia also create music. Many of their own artists and composers have gone on to international acclaim in their fields, Pablo Casals being the most notable.

But few artistic traditions enjoy the renown of the *sardana*, the national dance of the Catalάns. This is really a street dance, accompanied by *coblas* (brass bands). You can perform a sardana almost anywhere and at any time, provided you get some like-minded people to join you. Age doesn't matter—everybody joins in the spontaneous outburst. The roots of the dance are not known. Some claim that it originated in one of the Greek islands and was brought to Barcelona by seafarers; others say that it came from the Italian island of Sardinia, which would at least account for its name. To see this dance, go to the Plaça de Sant Jaume in the Barri Gótic of Barcelona on a Sunday morning.

2 Orientation

Arriving

BY PLANE During the months prior to the 1992 Olympics, airlines scrambled over one another to provide nonstop transatlantic service into Barcelona. At presstime, however, in noted contrast, most transatlantic passengers were obliged to change aircraft in Madrid before continuing on to Barcelona. The only exception to this rule is **TWA,** which maintains nonstop transatlantic service to Barcelona from New York long after other carriers, including Iberia, dropped out of the race. Passengers originating in such European capitals as London, Paris, and Rome, of course, can fly nonstop to Barcelona, usually on their national airlines, but the majority of passengers, for whatever reason, opt for transit through Madrid. If you don't mind changing aircraft in Madrid, you can get to Barcelona from even the smallest airports of Spain and its offshore islands. For more information on flying into Madrid, refer to "Getting There" in Chapter 2.

Within Spain, by far the most likely carrier is **Iberia**, which offers a string of peak-hour shuttle flights at 15-minute intervals between Madrid and Barcelona. Service from Madrid to Barcelona at less congested times of the day average around one flight every 30 to 40 minutes. Iberia also offers flights into Barcelona from such population centers as Valencia, Granada, Seville, and Bilbao.

Aeropuerto de Barcelona, 08820 Prat de Llobregat (☎ **478-50-00**), the Barcelona airport, lies 7½ miles (12km) southwest of the city. The route to the center of Barcelona is carefully sign-posted. A train runs between the airport and Barcelona's Estació Central de Barcelona-Sants daily between 6:14am to 10:44pm (10:14pm is the last city departure, 6:14am is the first airport departure). The 21-minute trip costs 300 pesetas. ($2.10). If your hotel lies near Plaça de Catalunya, you might opt instead for an Aerobús that runs daily every 15 minutes between 5:30am and 10pm. The fare is 425 pesetas ($3). A taxi from the airport into central Barcelona will cost approximately 2,000–2,500 pesetas ($14.20–$17.80).

Within Barcelona, you can arrange ticketing at one of two Iberia offices. The easiest to find lies a few blocks north of the sprawling Plaça de Catalunya, at Passeig de Gràcia, 30 (☎ **401-33-84** or **301-39-93**); Metro: Passeig de Gràcia.

BY TRAIN A train called Barcelona-Talgo provides rail lines between Paris and Barcelona in 11½ hours. For many other connections from the mainland of Europe, it will be necessary to change trains at Port Bou. Most trains issue seat and sleeper reservations.

Trains departing from the **Estació de Franca,** Avenida Marqués de L'Argentera, s/n (no building number), cover long distances within Spain as well as international routes, carrying a total of 20,000 passengers daily. There are express night trains to Paris, Zurich, Milan, and Geneva. All the international routes served by the state-owned RENFE railway company use the Estació de Franca, including some of its most luxurious express trains, such as the "Pau Casals" and the "Talgo Catalán."

The totally modernized 1929 station includes a huge screen with updated information on train departures and arrivals, personalized ticket dispatching, a passenger attention center, a tourism information center, showers, internal baggage control, a first-aid center, as well as centers for hotel reservations and car rentals. But it is much more than a mere departure point: The station has an elegant restaurant, a cafeteria, a book-and-record store, a jazz club, and even a disco. The Estació de Franca is just steps away from the Ciutadella Park, the Zoo, and the Port and is near Vila Olimpica. Metro: Barceloneta, L3.

From this station you can book tickets to the major cities of Spain: Madrid (three *talgos,* 9 hours; and three *rápidos,* 10 hours), Seville (three per day, 13 hours), and Valencia (10 per day, 4 hours).

RENFE also has a terminal at **Estació Central de Barcelona-Sants,** Plaça de Països Catalanes (Metro: Sants-Estació).

For general RENFE information, call **490-02-02.**

BY BUS Many visitors from mainland Europe arrive by bus, but it's a long, tedious haul. For example, the daily bus from London takes 25 hours; from Paris, 15 hours; and from Rome, 20 hours. For these continental connections in Barcelona, contact **Iberbus,** Paral.lel, 116 (☎ **441-54-94;** Metro: Paral.lel).

Enatcar, Estació del Nord (☎ **245-25-28**), operates five buses per day to Madrid (trip time: 8 hours) and 10 buses per day to Valencia (trip time: 4½ hours). For bus travel to one of the beach resorts along the Costa Brava (see Chapter 16), go to Sarfa, Estació del Nord (☎ **265-11-58**), which operates buses from Barcelona to such resorts as Tossà de Mar. Trip time is usually two hours.

BY CAR From France (the usual road approach to Barcelona), the major access route is at the eastern end of the Pyrenees. You have a choice of the express highway (E-15) or the more scenic coastal road. Be forewarned, however, that if you take the scenic coastal road in July and August, you will often encounter bumper-to-bumper traffic. From France, it is possible to approach Barcelona also via Toulouse. Cross the border into Spain at Puigcerdá (frontier stations are there), near the principality of Andorra. From there, take the N-152 to Barcelona.

From Madrid, take the N-2 to Zaragoza, then the A-2 to El Vendrell, followed by the A-7 motorway to Barcelona. From the Costa Blanca or Costa del Sol, take the E-15 north from Valencia along the eastern Mediterranean coast.

BY FERRY **Transmediterránea,** Avenida Drassanes, 6 (☎ **317-42-62**), operates daily voyages to the Balearic island of Majorca (trip time: 8 hours) and also to Menorca (trip time: 9 hours). In summer, it's important to have a reservation as far in advance as possible, because of overcrowding.

Tourist Information

A conveniently located tourist office is the **Patronat de Turisme,** Gran Vía de les Corts Catalanes, 658 (☎ **93/301-74-43;** Metro: Urquinaona or Plaça de Catalunya). It's open Monday to Friday from 9am to 7pm and Saturday from 9am to 2pm. There's also an office at the airport, **El Prat de Llobregat** (☎ **93/478-47-04**), which you'll pass as you clear Customs. Summer hours are Monday to Saturday from 9:30am to 8pm; off-season hours are Monday to Saturday from 9:30am to 8pm; year round, it's open on Sunday from 9:30am to 3pm.

There's another office at the **Estació Central de Barcelona-Sants,** Plaça Països Catalanes, s/n (☎ **93/491-44-31;** Metro: Sants-Estació). In summer it is open daily from 8am to 8pm; off-season, Monday through Friday from 8am to 8pm and Saturday and Sunday from 8am to 2pm. At these offices, you can pick up maps and information.

City Layout

MAIN SQUARES, STREETS & ARTERIES The **Plaça de Catalunya** (Plaza de Cataluña in Spanish) is the city's heart; the world-famous Rambles (*ramblas* in Spanish) are its arteries. The Rambles begin at the Plaça Portal de la Pau, with its 164-foot-high monument to Columbus and a superb view of the port, and stretch north to the Plaça de Catalunya, with its fountains and trees. Along this wide promenade you'll find bookshops and newsstands, stalls selling birds and flowers, and benches or café tables and chairs, where you can sit and watch the passing parade.

At the end of the Rambles is the **Barri Xinés** (Barrio Chino in Spanish, Chinese Quarter in English), which has enjoyed notoriety as a haven of prostitution and drugs, populated in Jean Genet's *The Thief's Journal* by "whores, thieves, pimps, and beggars." Still considered a dangerous district, it is best viewed during the day, if at all.

Off the Rambles lies **Plaça Reial** (Plaza Real in Spanish), the most harmoniously proportioned square in Barcelona. Come here on Sunday morning to see the stamp and coin collectors peddle their wares.

The major wide boulevards of Barcelona are the **Avinguda** (Avenida in Spanish) **Diagonal** and **Passeig de Colom,** and the elegant shopping street—the **Passeig de Gràcia** (Paseo de Gràcia in Spanish).

A short walk from the Rambles will take you to the 1990s developed **Passeig del Moll de la Fusta,** a waterfront promenade with some of the finest (but not the cheapest) restaurants in Barcelona. If you can't afford the high prices, come here at least for a drink in the open air and take in a view of the harbor.

To the east is the old port of the city, called **La Barceloneta,** dating from the 18th century. This strip of land between the port and the sea has traditionally been a good place for seafood.

The **Barri Gòtic** (Barrio Gótico in Spanish, Gothic Quarter in English) lies to the east of the Rambles. This is the site of the city's oldest buildings, including the cathedral.

North of Plaça de Catalunya, the **Eixample** unfolds. An area of wide boulevards, in contrast to the Gothic Quarter, it contains two major roads leading out of Barcelona, the previously mentioned Avinguda Diagonal and Gran Vía de les Corts Catalanes. Another major area, Gràcia, lies north of the Eixample.

Montjuïc, one of the mountains of Barcelona, begins at Plaça d'Espanya, a traffic rotary. This was the setting for the 1992 Summer Olympic Games and is today the site of Vila Olimpica (see below). The other mountain is Tibidabo, in the northwest, offering views of the city and the Mediterranean. It contains an amusement park.

FINDING AN ADDRESS/MAPS Finding an address in Barcelona can be a problem. The city is characterized by long boulevards and a complicated maze of narrow, twisting streets. Therefore, knowing the street number is all-important. If you see the designation, s/n it means that the building is without a number. Therefore, it's crucial to learn the cross street if you're seeking a specific establishment.

The rule about street numbers is that there is no rule. On most streets, numbering begins on one side and runs up that side until the end, then runs in the opposite direction on the other side. Therefore, number 40 could be opposite 408. But there are many exceptions to this. Sometimes street numbers on buildings in the older quarters have been obscured by the patina of time.

Arm yourself with a good map before setting out. Those given away free by tourist offices and hotels generally aren't adequate, since they don't label the little streets. The best map for exploring Barcelona, published by **Falk,** is available at most bookstores and newsstands, such as those found along the Rambles. This pocket map includes all the streets, with an index of how to find them.

NEIGHBORHOODS IN BRIEF

Barri Gòtic The glory of the Middle Ages lives on here. The section rises to the north of Passeig de Colom, with its Columbus Monument, and is bordered on its east by a major artery, Via Laietana, which begins at La Barceloneta at Plaça d'Antoni López and runs north to Plaça d'Urquinaona. The Rambles are the western border of the Gothic Quarter, and on the northern edge is the Ronda de Sant Pere, which intersects with Plaça de Catalunya and the Passeig de Gràcia. The heart of the quarter is the Plaça de Sant Jaume, which was a major crossroads in the old Roman city. Many of the structures in the old section are ancient, including the ruins of a Roman temple dedicated to Augustus. Antiques stores, restaurants, cafés, museums, some hotels, and bookstores fill the place today. It is also the headquarters of the Generalitat, seat of the Catalán government.

Les Rambles The most famous promenade in Spain, ranking with Madrid's Paseo del Prado, was once a drainage channel. That was long ago filled in, however, much to the delight of today's street entertainers, flower vendors, news vendors, café patrons, and strollers. Les Rambles (L*a*s Rambl*a*s in Spanish) is actually composed of five different sections, each a particular Rambla, with names like Rambla de Canaletes, Rambla dels Estudis, Rambla de Sant Josep, Rambla dels Caputxins, and Rambla de Santa Mònica. The pedestrian esplanade is shaded, as it makes its way from the Plaça de Catalunya to the port—all the way to the Columbus Monument. Along the way you'll pass the Gran Teatre del Liceu, Rambla de Caputxins, 61, at Sant Pau, 1, one of the most magnificent opera houses in the world until it caught fire. Miró did a sidewalk mosaic at the Plaça de la Boqueria. During the stagnation of the Franco era, this street grew seedier and seedier. But the opening of the Ramada Renaissance hotel and the restoration of many buildings have brought energy and hope for the street.

Barri Xinés This isn't "Chinatown," as most people assume from the name—and it never was. For decades it has had an unsavory reputation, known for its houses of prostitution. Franco outlawed prostitution in 1956, but apparently no one ever got around to telling the denizens of this district of narrow, often murky, old streets and dark corners. Petty thieves, drug peddlers, purse snatchers, and other "fun types" form just part of the parade of humanity that flows through the district. Nighttime can be dangerous, so exercise caution. Still, most visitors like to take a quick look to see what all the excitement is about. Just off Les Rambles, the area lies primarily between the waterfront and Carrer de l'Hospital.

Barri de la Ribera Another barrio that stagnated for years but is now long into its renaissance, the Barri de la Ribera lies alongside the Barri Gòtic, going east to Passeig de Picasso, which borders the Parc de la Ciutadella. The centerpiece of this district is the Museu Picasso, housed in the 15th-century Palau Agüilar, Montcada, 15. Numerous art galleries have opened around the museum, and the old quarter is fashionable. Many mansions in this area were built at the time of one of the major maritime expansions and trading explosions in Barcelona's history, principally in the 1200s and 1300s. Most of these grand homes still stand along Carrer de Montcada and nearby streets.

La Barceloneta and the Harborfront Although Barcelona was founded on a seagoing tradition, its waterfront was allowed to decay for years. Today it is alive again and bursting with activity, as exemplified by the 1990s waterfront promenade, Passeig del Moll de la Fusta. The best way to get a bird's-eye view of this section is to take an elevator to the top of the Columbus Monument in Plaza Portal de la Pau.

In the vicinity of the monument were the Reials Drassanes, or royal shipyards, a booming place of industry during Barcelona's maritime heyday in the Middle Ages. Years before Columbus landed in the New World, ships sailed around the world from here, flying the traditional yellow-and-red flag of Catalonia.

To the east lies a mainly artificial peninsula called La Barceloneta (Little Barcelona), formerly a fishing district, dating mainly from the 18th century. It's now filled with seafood restaurants. The blocks here are long and surprisingly narrow—architects planned it that way so that each room in every building fronted a street. Many bus lines terminate at the Passeig Nacional here, site of the Barcelona Aquarium.

Eixample [Ensanche] To the north of the Plaça de Catalunya lies the Eixample, or Ensanche, where avenues form a grid of perpendicular streets cut across by a majestic boulevard, Passeig de Gràcia, a posh shopping street ideal for leisurely promenades. This is the section of Barcelona that grew beyond the old medieval walls. This great period of "extension," or enlargement (*eixample* in Catalàn), came mainly in the 19th century. The area's main traffic artery is Avinguda Diagonal, which links the expressway and the heart of this congested city.

The Eixample possesses some of the most original buildings any architect ever designed—not just those by Gaudí, but by other notable achievers as well. Of course, Gaudí's Sagrada Familia is one of the major attractions of the area, which was the center of Barcelona modernism. This cultural renaissance began in 1814, and reached its greatest heights of expression in the Eixample, where you'll want to walk, perhaps live or dine, while visiting Barcelona.

Montjuïc and Tibidabo These mountains form two of the most enduring attractions of Barcelona. Montjuïc, called Hill of the Jews after a Jewish necropolis there, gained prominence in 1929 as the site of the World's Fair and again in 1992 as the site of the Summer Olympic Games. Its major attraction is the Poble Espanyol (Spanish Village), a five-acre (two-hectare) site constructed for the World's Fair, with examples of Spanish art and architecture displayed against the backdrop of a traditional Spanish village. Tibidabo (1,650 feet) may be where you'll want to go for your final look at Barcelona. On a clear day you can see the mountains of Majorca (the most famous of the Balearic Islands). Reached by train, tram, and cable car, Tibidabo is the most popular Sunday excursion in Barcelona.

Pedralbes Pedralbes is where the wealthy people live, some in stylish blocks of apartment houses, others in 19th-century villas behind ornamental fences, and others still in structures erected during the heyday of modernism. Set in a park, the Palau de Pedralbes, Avinguda Diagonal, 686, was constructed in the 1920s as a gift from the city of Barcelona to Alfonxo XIII, the last king of Spain, who was forced to abdicate (he was the grandfather of today's Juan Carlos). The king fled in 1931 and never made much use of the palace. Today it has a new life, housing a museum of carriages and a group of European paintings called the Colecció Cambó.

Vila Olímpica This seafront property contains the tallest buildings in the city. The revitalized site in the post–Olympic Games era is the setting for numerous showrooms for imported cars, designer clothing stores, and restaurants, as well as business offices. The "village" was the center of the games hosted in 1992 in the Catalonian capital. A regular city is taking shape, complete with banks, art galleries, nightclubs, bars, even pastry shops.

3 Getting Around

DISCOUNTS To save money on public transportation, buy one of the two-card transportation cards, each good for 10 trips; **Tarjeta T-1,** costing 625 pesetas ($4.40), is good for the Metro, bus, Montjuïc funicular, and Tramvía Blau, which runs from the Passeig de Sant Gervasi/Avinguda del Tibidabo to the bottom part of the funicular to Tibidabo. **Tarjeta T-2,** for 600 pesetas ($4.30), is good on everything but the bus.

For stays in Barcelona, ranging from three to five days, you'll save on transportation by purchasing at three-day pass at 1,000 pesetas ($7.10) or a five-day pass at 1,650 pesetas ($11.70). These allow unlimited travel on buses and the Metro system. To make the most use of these, obtain a copy of *Guía del Transport Públic,* distributed free at the tourist office or at the transportation office (see below).

Passes (*abonos temporales*) are available at the office of **Transports Metropolita de Barcelona,** Plaça de Catalunya, open Monday to Friday from 8am to 7pm and Saturday from 8am to 1pm.

To save money on sightseeing tours during the summer, take a ride on **Tourist Bus No. 100,** which passes by a dozen of the most popular sights. You can get on and off the bus as you please and also ride the Tibidabo funicular and the Montjuïc cable car and funicular for the price of a single ticket. Tickets, which may be purchased on the bus or at the transportation booth at Plaça de Catalunya, cost 700 pesetas ($5) for a half day or 1,000 pesetas ($7.10) for a full day.

By Subway Barcelona's underground railway system is called the **Metro.** Consisting of five main lines, it crisscrosses the city more frequently and with greater efficiency than the bus network. Two commuter trains also service the city, fanning out to the suburbs. Service is Monday to Friday from 5am to 11pm, Saturday from 5am to 1am, and Sunday and holidays from 6am to 1am. A one-way fare is 115 pesetas (80¢). The entrance to each Metro station is marked with a red diamond. The major station for all subway lines is Plaça de Catalunya.

By Bus Some 50 bus lines traverse the city, and as always, you don't want to ride them at rush hour. The driver issues a ticket as you board at the front. Most buses operate daily from 6:30am to 10pm; some night buses go along the principal arteries from 10pm to 4am. Buses are color-coded—red ones cut through the city center during the day, and blue ones do the job at night. A one-way fare is 115 pesetas (80¢).

By Taxi Each yellow-and-black taxi bears the letters *SP (servicio público)* on both its front and its rear. A lit green light on the roof and a "Libre" sign in the window indicate that the taxi is free to pick up passengers. The basic rate begins at 250 pesetas ($1.80). Check to make sure you're not paying the fare of a previously departed passenger; taxi drivers have been known to "forget" to turn back the meter. For each additional kilometer in the slow-moving traffic, you are assessed 100 pesetas (70¢). Supplements might also be added—110 pesetas (80¢) for a large suitcase, for instance. Rides to the airport carry a supplement of 325 pesetas ($2.30), and after 10pm and on Saturday, Sunday, and holidays, a supplement of 100 pesetas (70¢) is added. For a taxi, call **330-08-04, 300-38-11,** or **358-11-11.**

By Bicycle Ever wonder why you see so few people riding bicycles in Barcelona? Heavy pollution from traffic and pedestrian-clogged narrow streets of the inner city make riding a bicycle very difficult. It's better to walk.

By Car Driving is next to impossible in congested Barcelona, and it's potentially dangerous. Besides, it is unlikely that you would find a place to park. Try other means of getting around. Save your car rentals for one-day excursions from the Catalonian capital to such places as Sitges and Tarragona in the south, Montserrat in the west, or the resorts of the Costa Brava in the north.

All three of the major U.S.-based car-rental firms are represented in Barcelona, both at the airport and at downtown offices. The company with the longest hours and some of the most favorable rates is **Budget,** Travesera de Gràcia, 71 (☎ **201-21-99**), which is open Monday to Friday without a midday break, from 9am to 7pm. Hours on Saturday and Sunday are 9am to 1pm.

Other contenders include **Avis**, Carrer de Casanova, 209 (☎ **209-95-33**), which is open Monday through Friday 9am–1pm and 4–7pm; and Saturday 8am to 1pm. **Hertz** maintains its office at Tuset, 10 (☎ **217-8076**), open Monday through Friday from 8am to 2pm and 4–7pm; Saturday from 9am to 1pm. Both Hertz and Avis are closed on Sunday, forcing clients of those companies to trek out to the airport to pick up or return their cars.

9177

Barcelona Metro

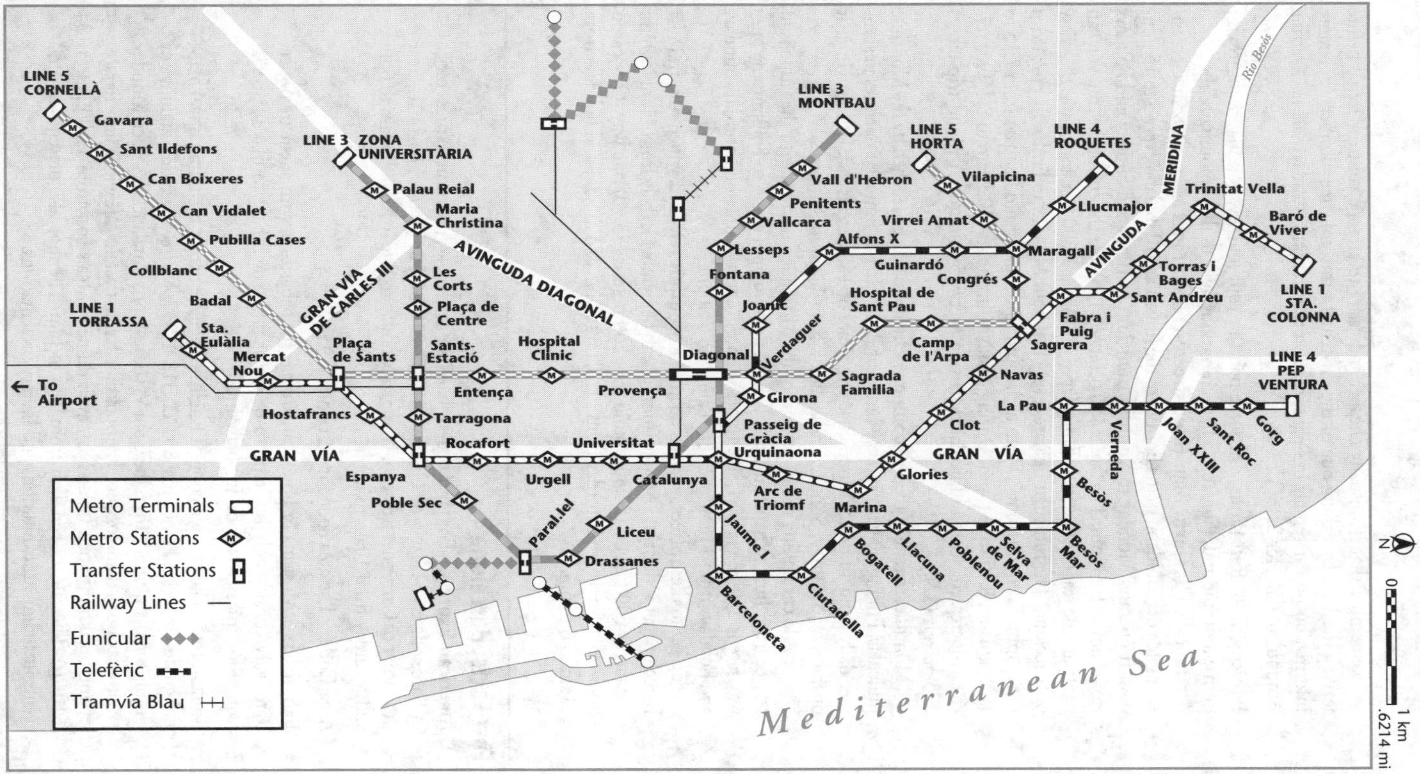

Remember that it's usually cheaper and easier to arrange your car rental before leaving the U.S. by calling one of the car-rental firms' toll-free numbers. For more information on car rentals in Spain, refer to the section on car rentals in "Getting Around" in Chapter 2.

Funiculars & Rail Links At some point in your journey, you may want to visit both Montijuïc and Tibidabo. There are various links to these mountaintops. A train called **Tramvía Blau (blue streetcar)** goes from Passeig de Sant Gervasi/ Avinguda del Tibidabo to the bottom of the funicular to Tibidabo every 3 to 15 minutes. It operates Monday to Saturday from 7am to 10pm and Sunday and holidays from 7am to 10:30pm. The fare is 150 pesetas ($1.10). At the end of the run, you can continue the rest of the way by funicular to the top, at 1,600 feet, for an amazing view of Barcelona. The funicular operates every half hour Monday to Friday from 7:45am to 9:45pm, Saturday from 7:15am to 9:45pm, and Sunday and holidays from 7:15 to 10:15am and 8:45 to 9:45pm. During peak visiting hours (10:15am to 8:45pm) service is increased, with a funicular departing every 15 minutes. A round-trip fare is 275 pesetas ($2).

Montjüic, the site of the 1992 Summer Olympics, can be reached by the Montjuïc funicular, linking up with subway Line 3 at Paral.lel. The funicular operates in summer daily from 11am to 10pm, charging a fare of 150 pesetas ($1.10). In winter it operates on Saturday, Sunday, and holidays from 11am to 8:15pm.

A **cable car** linking the upper part of the Montjuïc funicular with the castle is in service from June to September, daily from noon to 3pm and 4 to 8:30pm; the one-way fare is 250 pesetas ($1.80). In off-season it operates only on Saturday, Sunday, and holidays from 11am to 2:45pm and 4 to 7:30pm.

To get to these places, you can board the **Montjuïc telèferic,** which runs from La Barceloneta to Montjuïc. Service from June to September is daily from 11am to 9pm; the fare is 600 pesetas ($4.30) round trip, 500 pesetas ($3.60) one way. Off-season hours are Monday to Saturday from 11:30am to 6pm and Sunday and holidays from 11am to 6:45pm.

Fast Facts: Barcelona

American Express For your mail or banking needs, the American Express office in Barcelona is at Passeig de Gràcia, 101 (☎ **217-00-70;** Metro: Diagonal), near the corner of Carrer del Rosselló. It's open Monday to Friday from 9:30am to 6pm and Saturday from 10am to noon.

Area Code The area code for Barcelona is **93.**

Babysitters Most major hotels can arrange for babysitters with adequate notice. Rates vary considerably but tend to be reasonable. You'll have to make a special request for an English-speaking babysitter.

Bookstores The best selection of English-language books, including travel maps and guides, is LAIE, Pau Claris, 85 (☎ **318-17-39;** Metro: Plaça de Catalunya or Urquinaona), one block from the Gran Vía de les Corts Catalanes. It's open Monday to Saturday from 10am to 9pm. The bookshop has an upstairs café with a little terrace, serving breakfast, lunch (salad bar), even dinners. Meals cost from 1,500 pesetas ($10.70). The café is open daily from 9am to 1am. The shop also presents cultural events including art exhibitions and literary presentations.

Climate See Chapter 2.

Consulates For embassies, refer to Chapter 2, "Fast Facts: Spain." The U.S. Consulate, at Reina Elisenda, 23, 4th floor (☎ **280-22-27;** Metro: Reina Elisenda), is open Monday to Friday from 9am to 1pm. The Canadian Consulate, Vía Augusta, 125 (☎ **209-06-34;** Metro: Plaça Molina) is open Monday through Friday from 9am to 1pm. The U.K. Consulate, Avinguda Diagonal, 477 (☎ **419-90-44;** Metro: Hospital Clinic), is open Monday through Friday from 9:30am to 1:30pm and from 4 to 5pm; Saturday (from the end of June to early September), 10am to noon. The Australian Consulate is at Gran Vía Carlos III, no. 98, 9th floor (☎ **330-94-96;** Metro: María Cristina), and is open Monday through Friday from 10am to noon.

Currency Exchange Most banks will exchange currency Monday to Friday from 8:30am to 2pm and Saturday from 8:30am to 1pm. A major *oficina de cambio* (exchange office) is operated at the Estació Central de Barcelona-Sants, the principal rail station for Barcelona. It's open Monday to Saturday from 8:30am to 10pm, Sunday from 8:30am to 2pm and 4:30 to 10pm. Exchange offices are also available at Barcelona's airport, El Prat de Llobregat, open daily from 7am to 11pm.

Dentist Call Dr. Angel Salesi, Casanoves, 209, 2nd floor (☎ **200-70-11;** Metro: Guinardo), for an appointment.

Doctors See "Hospitals," below.

Drugstores The most central one is Farmacía Manuel Nadal i Casas, Rambla de Canaletes, 121 (☎ **317-49-42;** Metro: Plaça de Catalunya), open Monday to Friday from 9am to 1:30pm and 4:30 to 8pm, and on Saturday from 9am to 1:30pm. After hours, various pharmacies take turns staying open at night. Pharmacies not open post names and addresses of pharmacies in the area that are open.

Emergencies Fire, **080;** police, **092;** ambulance, **300-20-20.**

Eyeglasses Complete service is provided by Optica 2000, Santa Anna, 2 (☎ **302-12-47;** Metro: Plaça de Catalunya), open Monday through Saturday from 9:30am to 2pm and 4:30 to 8pm.

Hairdresser A few steps from the Rambles, Santos, Santa Anna, 6 (☎ **317-54-87;** Metro: Plaça de Catalunya), is for both *señoras y caballeros.* Located one floor above street level, the shop receives men Tuesday through Saturday from 9am to 2pm and 4 to 8pm, women from 10am to 7pm.

Hospitals Call **255-55-55** for a doctor in a hurry. Barcelona has many hospitals and clinics, including Hospital Clínic, and Hospital de la Santa Creu i Sant Pau, at the intersection of Carrer Cartagena and Carrer Sant Antoni Moria Claret (☎ **347-31-33;** Metro: Hospital de Sant Pau).

International See "Tourist Information," earlier in this chapter.

Laundromats Ask at your hotel for the one nearest you, or try one of the following. *Lavandería Brasilia,* Avinguda Meridiana, 322 (☎ **352-72-05;** Metro: Plaça de Catalunya), is open Monday to Friday from 9am to 2pm and 4 to 8pm, Saturday from 9am to 2pm. Also centrally located is *Lava Super,* Carrer Carme, 63 (☎ **329-4368;** Metro: Liceu, at Les Rambles), which keeps the same hours as the establishment listed above.

Libraries There's an American Studies library with an English-language collection at the Instituto de Estudios Norteamericanos called the Max H. Klein Library,

Vía Augusta, 123 (☎ **200-75-51**), with a large selection of U.S. magazines and newspapers, and circulation reference sections. Open Monday through Friday from 11am to 2pm and 4 to 9pm; closed August. Take the FFCC commuter train to Plaça Molina.

Lost Property To recover lost property, go to Objects Perduts, Ajuntament (ground floor), Plaça de Sant Jaume (☎ **301-39-23;** Metro: Jaume I), Monday to Friday from 9:30am to 1:30pm. If you've lost property on public transport, contact the office in the Metro station at Plaça de Catalunya (☎ **318-52-93**).

Luggage Storage/Lockers The train station, Estacío Central de Barcelona-Sants (☎ **491-44-31**), has lockers for 300–500 pesetas ($2.10–$3.60) per day. You can obtain locker space daily from 7am to 11pm.

Newspapers/Magazines The *International Herald-Tribune* is sold at major hotels and nearly all the news kiosks along the Rambles. Sometimes you can also obtain copies of *USA Today,* or one of the London newspapers, such as *The Times.* The two leading daily newspapers of Barcelona, which often list cultural events, are *El Periódico* and *La Vanguardia.*

Police See "Emergencies," above.

Post Office The main post office is at Plaça d'Antoni López (☎ **318-38-31;** Metro: Jaume I). It's open Monday through Saturday from 9am to 10pm.

Radio/TV If your hotel room has a TV set (unlikely in budget accommodations) or a radio, you can often get Britain's BBC World Service. If you're listening to radio, tune in the Spanish music program, "Segunda Programa," with everything from classical music to jazz—nights only. Otherwise, what you'll see in the TV lounges of most budget hotels are Spanish broadcasts of international soccer and rugby competitions and perhaps a bullfight. Deluxe and some first-class hotels subscribe to CNN. Two national TV channels (1 and 2) transmit broadcasts in Spanish, and two regional channels (3 and 33) broadcast in Catalán. Some private TV channels also broadcast.

Religious Services Nearly all of the churches of Barcelona are Roman Catholic, holding mass on Sunday between 7am and 2pm and 7pm and 9pm. For a mass in English attend the English-speaking Catholic Church of Pedralbes in Avinguda Espluges (☎ **211-41-51**) at 10am each Sunday. Protestant services are held in English every Sunday at 11am and Wednesday at noon at St. George's Anglican/Episcopal Church, Carrer Horacio, 38 (☎ **417-88-67;** Metro: Avinguda Tibidabo).

Restrooms Some public restrooms are available, including those at popular tourist spots, such as Tibidabo and Montjuïc. You'll also find restrooms at the major museums of Barcelona, at all train stations and airports, and at Metro stations. The major department stores, such as Galerías Preciados, also have good restrooms. Otherwise, out on the streets you may be a bit hard-pressed. Sanitation is a bit questionable in some of the public facilities. If you use the facilities of a café or tavern, it is customary to make a small purchase at the bar, even if only a glass of mineral water.

Safety Whenever you're traveling in an unfamiliar city or country, stay alert. Be aware of your immediate surroundings. Wear a moneybelt and keep a close eye on your possessions. Be particularly careful with cameras, purses, and wallets, all favorite targets of thieves and pickpockets; particularly on the world-famous Rambles.

The southern part of the Rambles, near the waterfront, is the most dangerous section, especially at night. Proceed with caution.

Shoe Repairs Simago, Ramble dels Estudis, 113 (☎ **302-48-24;** Metro: Plaça de Catalunya or Liceu), in the basement, is open for repairs Monday through Saturday from 9:30am to 8:30pm.

Taxes See "Shopping" in Chapter 5 for details on VAT.

Taxis See "Getting Around," earlier in this chapter.

Telegrams/Telex These can be sent at the main post office (see above). You can send telex and fax messages at all major and many budget hotels.

Telephone Dial **003** for local operator information within Barcelona. For elsewhere in Spain, dial **009.** Most local calls cost 25 pesetas (20¢). Hotels impose various surcharges on phone calls, especially long distance, either in Spain or abroad. It's cheaper to go to the central telephone office at Fontanella, 4, off the Plaça de Catalunya (Metro: Plaça de Catalunya). The office is open Monday to Saturday from 8:30am to 9pm.

Transit Information For general RENFE (train) information, dial **490-02-02.** For details about airport information, call **478-50-00.**

4 Networks & Resources

FOR STUDENTS When you arrive in Barcelona with your ISIC (International Student Identity Card) or your FIYTO (International Youth Card), you can go to the **Oficina de Turisme Juvenil** (youth travel bureau) at Carrer Calabria, 147 (☎ **483-83-78**). There you can get discounts on air, train, and bus travel, plus other tourist-type services. Hours are Monday to Friday from 9am to 1pm and 4 to 5:30pm.

FOR GAY MEN & LESBIANS For gay men, Barcelona is a mecca for those who practice safe sex. A wide assortment of gay establishments, ranging from discos to saunas, from restaurants to bars, await the visitor. And if you get bored with the gay scene in Barcelona, it's just half an hour by train to the sands of Sitges, the premier gay resort of Europe. For gay men, a source of information is **Front d'Allibrement Gai de Catalunya**, Carrer Villaroel, 63 (☎ **254-63-98;** Metro Urgell), which is found at the corner of Carrer Consell de Cant. For women, inquire about activities at **Grup de Lesbianes Feministes de Barcelona**, Gran Vía de les Corts Catalanes, 549 (☎ **323-33-07;** Metro: Plaça de Catalunya), on the fourth floor.

Another source of information about gay life in Barcelona is provided by **Sextienda**, Rauric, 11 (☎ **318-86-76;** Metro: Liceu). It's open Monday to Saturday from 10am to 8:45pm. This is the premier gay pornography shop in Spain, located on a street with some gay bars. The English-speaking staff will give you a free map pinpointing the bars, restaurants, discos, and other places catering to gay men. It's called *Plano Gay de Barcelona y Sitges,* and it's revised every year.

FOR WOMEN Women traveling alone should avoid the area near the port after dark. See the Plaça Reial during the day, but go elsewhere at night. There have been attacks on women in this area. Women who have been the victim of an attack or rape should call the crisis service—**Information Dona,** Carrer Valància, 302 (☎ **487-80-92;** Metro: Passeig de Gràcia), Monday through Friday from 10am to

2pm. A good women's bookstore with a wide feminist collection (in English too) is **Libreriá de Dones Prolèg,** Carrer Dagueria, 13. Workshops, activities about affairs pertaining to women, and other events are posted here, but you must show up in person—not phone. Hours are Monday through Friday from 10am to 8pm and Saturday 10am to 2pm. Metro: Jaume I.

FOR SENIORS Senior citizens, especially those in their 70s and 80s, increasingly are the victims of crimes worldwide—often committed by young men. Barcelona is no exception. Be especially careful about purse-snatching and pickpockets. However, should an emergency occur, call **Tourist Attention,** Rambles 43 (☎ **301-90-60**), where an English-speaking staff helps victims of crime, especially those needing medical help. They can also help you with temporary documents in case you've lost your originals.

13

Where to Stay & Dine in Barcelona

BARCELONA HOTELS HAVE NEVER BEEN BETTER—NOR AS PLENTIFUL. IN THE WAKE of the 1992 Olympics, old palaces were restored and converted into hotels, and long seedy and tarnished hotels were completely renovated in time for the games. The final result—which should benefit Barcelona visitors until the 21st century, at least—is an abundance of good hotels in all price ranges. Regrettably, the first-class and deluxe hotels are vastly overpriced, in the view of many visitors from less expensive parts of the world. For top-grade comfort, you'll pay—and pay dearly—in the Barcelona of the 1990s.

Safety is an important factor to consider when choosing a hotel in Barcelona. Some of the least expensive hotels are not in good locations. A popular area for the budget traveler is the Barri Gòtic, located in the heart of town. You'll live and eat less expensively here than in any other part of Barcelona. But you should be especially careful when returning to your hotel late at night.

More modern, but also more expensive, accommodations can be found north of Les Rambles and the Barri Gòtic in the Eixample district, centered around the Metro stops Plaça de Catalunya and Universitat. Many of the buildings are in the modernist style (that is, turn-of-the-century art nouveau), and sometimes the elevators and plumbing tend to be of the same vintage. The Eixample is a desirable and safe neighborhood, especially along its wide boulevards. Noise is the only problem you might encounter.

Farther north still, above the Avinguda Diagonal, you'll enter the Grácia area, where you can enjoy Catalán neighborhood life. You'll be a bit away from the main attractions, but they can be reached by public transportation.

For tips on saving money on accommodations, see "Frommer's Smart Traveler: Hotels" in Chapter 4.

Finding a cheap **restaurant** in Barcelona is easier than finding a cheap, safe hotel. There are sometimes as many as eight places per block, if you include *tapas* bars as well as restaurants. Reservations are seldom needed, except in the most expensive and popular places.

The Barri Gòtic offers the cheapest meals. There are also many low-cost restaurants in and around the Carrer de Montcada, site of the Picasso museum. Dining rooms in the Eixample tend to be more formal, more expensive, but less adventurous.

For money-saving dining tips, see "Frommer's Smart Traveler: Restaurants" in Chapter 4.

However, if you're not a budget traveler and can afford to dine in first-class and deluxe restaurants, you'll find in Barcelona some of the grandest culinary experiences in Europe. The widely diversified Catalán cuisine reaches its pinnacle of perfection in Barcelona, and many of the finest dishes feature fresh seafood. But you don't get just Catalán fare here, as the city is also rich in the cuisines of all the major regions of Spain, including Castile and Andalusia. Because of Barcelona's proximity to France, many of the finer restaurants also serve French or French-inspired dishes, the latter often with a distinctly Catalán flavor.

1 Accommodations

Barcelona hotels judged very expensive charge from 28,000 pesetas ($198.80) and up per day for a double room; those considered expensive ask from 17,500 pesetas

($124.30) to 30,000 ptas. ($213) for a double; and those viewed as moderate charge from 12,000–20,000 pesetas ($85.20–$142) for a double. Hotels asking from 6,000–12,000 ptas. ($42.60–$85.20) for a double are considered inexpensive. Anything under 6,000 pesetas ($42.60) for a double is viewed as budget, as least by Barcelona's high-priced standards. In the latter category, you can sometimes find a double for as little as 3,500 pesetas ($24.90) per night.

Many of Barcelona's hotels were built before the invention of the automobile, and even those that weren't rarely found space enough for a garage. When parking is available at the hotel, the price is indicated; otherwise, the hotel staff will direct you to a garage somewhere in the general vicinity. Expect to pay from 1,800 pesetas ($12.80) for 24 hours, you might as well park your car, as you can't see traffic-congested Barcelona comfortably by automobile—rely on your trusty feet and public transportation instead.

The phone and fax numbers for the hotels that follow contain the area code needed to dial from outside Spain. If you're calling from another city or town *within* Spain, dial 93 and then the local number.

Ciutat Vella

"Old City" in Catalán, Ciutat Vella forms the monumental heartland of Barcelona, taking in Les Rambles, Plaça de Sant Jaume, Via Laietana, Passeig Nacional, and Passeig de Colom. It contains some of the city's best hotel bargains which exist in older structures. Most of the glamorous—and more expensive—hotels are in Sur Diagonal (see below).

VERY EXPENSIVE

Le Meridien Barcelona, Rambles, 111, 08002 Barcelona. ☎ **34-3/318-62-00,** or toll free in the U.S. **800/543-4300.** Fax 34-3/301-77-76. 200 rms, 8 suites. A/C MINIBAR TV TEL **Metro:** Liceu or Plaça de Catalunya

Rates: Mon–Fri 23,000 pesetas ($163.30) single; 30,600 pesetas ($217.30) single on executive floor; 32,000 pesetas ($227.20) double; 37,000 pesetas ($262.70) double on executive floor. Sat–Sun, 15,000 pesetas ($106.50) single or double; 26,000 pesetas ($184.60) single or double on executive floor. Suites from 48,000 pesetas ($340.80) all week. Breakfast buffet 2,000 pesetas ($14.20) extra. AE, DC, MC, V.

This is the finest hotel in the old town of Barcelona, as such former guests as Michael Jackson will surely agree. Built in the classic modernist style in 1956, it was called the Hotel Manila. Then it was completely renovated and opened as the Ramada Renaissance in 1988. Finally, in 1991 the Meridien chain took it over. It is a medley of tasteful pastels and tasteful decorating. Its guest rooms are spacious and comfortable, with such amenities as extra-large beds, heated bathroom floors, 18 TV channels, three in-house videos, hairdryers, and two phones in each room; all rooms have double-glazed windows. The Renaissance Club—the executive floor popular with businesspeople—provides extra amenities, including private check-ins.

Dinner/Entertainment: The chic lobby bar, open daily from 7 to 11pm, has live piano music. The main restaurant, Le Patio, serves a fine continental and Catalán cuisine.

Services: 24-hour room service, laundry, concierge.

Facilities: Business center, rooms for the disabled, small gym.

EXPENSIVE

Hotel Colón, Avenida de la Catedral, 7, 08002 Barcelona. ☎ **34-3/301-14-04,** or toll free in the U.S. **800/845-0636.** Fax 34-3/317-29-15. 136 rms, 11 suites. A/C MINIBAR TV TEL **Bus:** 16, 17, 19, or 45.

Rates: 13,750–20,000 ptas. ($97.60–$142) single; 20,500–32,500 ptas. ($145.60–$230.80) double; from 37,000 ptas. ($262.70) suite. Buffet breakfast 1,500 ptas. ($10.70) extra. AE, DC, MC, V.

Blessed with what might be the most dramatic location in Barcelona, immediately opposite the main entrance to the cathedral, this hotel sits behind a dignified neoclassical facade graced with carved pilasters and ornamental wrought-iron balustrades. Inside, you'll find conservative and slightly old-fashioned public rooms; a helpful staff; and guest rooms filled with comfortable furniture and—despite recent renovations—an appealingly dowdy kind of charm. Although not all rooms have views, they all have private baths. The Colon is an appropriate choice if you plan to spend a lot of time exploring the medieval neighborhoods of Barcelona.

Dining/Entertainment: The hotel maintains two well-recommended restaurants, the Grill (for continental specialties) and the Carabela (for Catalán specialties). Three-course fixed-price meals cost 3,300 pesetas ($23.40).

Services: 24-hour room service, laundry/valet, limousine, concierge, babysitting.

Rivoli Ramblas, Rambla dels Estudis 128, 08002 Barcelona. ☎ **34-3/302-66-43.** Fax 34-3/317-50-53. 78 rms, 9 suites. A/C MINIBAR TV TEL **Metro:** Plaça del Catalunya.

Rates: 19,000 ptas. ($134.90) single; 24,000–26,000 ptas. ($170.40–$184.60) double; from 36,000 ptas. ($255.60) suite. Breakfast 1,400–1,900 ptas. ($9.90–$13.50) extra. AE, DC, MC, V.

Set behind a dignified, art deco town house on the upper section of the Rambles, a block south of the Plaça de Catalunya, this recently renovated hotel incorporates many fine examples of avant-garde Catalán design into its stylish interior. The public rooms glisten with polished marble and a pristinely contrived minimalism. The guest rooms are carpeted, soundproof, and elegant. Along with safety-deposit boxes and private baths, the guest rooms boast such electronic amenities as VCRs, radios, and TVs with satellite hookups.

Dining/Entertainment: Le Brut Restaurant serves regional, Spanish, and international dishes. The Blue Moon cocktail bar features piano music and a soothingly high-tech design. A rooftop terrace, decked with flowers and suitable for coffee or drinks, offers a view over the rooftops of one of Barcelona's most architecturally interesting neighborhoods.

Services: 24-hour room service, babysitting, concierge, laundry/valet.

Facilities: Small health club/fitness center, sauna, solarium, car rentals, shopping boutiques.

Moderate

Hotel Lleó, Pelal, 24, 08001 Barcelona. ☎ **34-3/318-13-12.** Fax 34-3/412-26-57. 75 rms (all with bath). A/C MINIBAR TV TEL **Metro:** Plaça de Catalunya.

Rates: 9,000–9,600 ptas. ($63.90–$68.20) single; 12,000 ptas. ($85.20) double. Breakfast 525 ptas. ($3.70) extra. AE, DC, MC, V. **Parking:** 1,800 ptas. ($12.80) nearby.

Solid, well run, and conservative, this hotel occupies the premises of a 1840s building on a busy commercial street in one of the most central neighborhoods in town. Completely renovated in 1992 in time for the Olympics, it offers clean, streamlined, and comfortable bedrooms, each equipped with a lock-box and comfortable, functional furniture. There's a restaurant on one of the upper floors.

Hotel Regencia Colón, Carrer Sagristans, 13-17, 08002 Barcelona. ☎ **34-3/318-98-58.** Fax 34-3/317-28-22. 55 rms (all with bath). A/C MINIBAR TV TEL **Metro:** Urquinaona.

Rates: 7,900-9,200 ptas. ($56.10–$65.30) single; 13,500 ptas. ($95.90) double; 16,000 ptas. ($113.60) triple. Breakfast buffet 1,000 ptas. ($7.10) extra. AE, DC, MC, V.

This stately stone building stands directly behind the more prestigious (and more expensive) Hotel Colón—both lie in the shadow of the cathedral. The formal lobby seems a bit dour, but the well-maintained rooms are comfortable if somewhat small. All have piped-in music. The hotel's location at the edge of the Barri Gòtic is a plus.

Turín, Carrer Pintor Fortuny, 9-11 08001 Barcelona. ☎ **34-3/302-48-12.** Fax 34-3/302-10-05. 60 rms (all with bath). A/C TV TEL **Metro:** Plaça de Catalunya.

Rates: 8,500 ptas. ($60.40) single; 12,900 ptas. ($91.60) double; 13,900 ptas. ($98.70) triple. Breakfast 700 ptas. ($5) extra. AE, DC, MC, V. **Parking:** 1,800 ptas. ($12.80).

This neat and well-run three-star hotel is in a terra-cotta grillwork building located in a shopping district. It offers small, streamlined accommodations with balconies. An elevator will take you to your room. The Turín also offers a restaurant, specializing in grilled meats and fresh fish.

INEXPENSIVE

Granvía, Gran Vía de les Cortes Catalanes, 642, 08007 Barcelona. ☎ **34-3/318-19-00.** Fax 34-3/318-99-97. 50 rms (all with bath). A/C MINIBAR TEL **Metro:** Plaça de Catalunya.

Rates: 8,000 ptas. ($56.80) single; 11,500 ptas. ($81.70) double. Breakfast 600 ptas. ($4.30) extra. AE, DC, MC, V. **Parking:** 2,100 ptas. ($14.90).

A grand hotel on one of the most fashionable boulevards in Barcelona, the Granvía has public rooms that reflect the opulence of the 1860s—chandeliers, gilt mirrors, and French provincial furniture—and a grand balustraded staircase. Although the traditional bedrooms contain interesting antique reproductions, they are comfortable rather than luxurious. The courtyard, graced with a fountain and palm trees, is set with tables for al fresco drinks; in the garden room off the courtyard, continental breakfast is served. Centrally heated in the winter, the hotel has one drawback: the noise. Street sounds might disturb the light sleeper.

Hotel Continental, Rambla de Canaletes, 138, 08002 Barcelona. ☎ **34-3/301-25-70.** Fax 34-3/302-73-60. 36 rms (all with bath). MINIBAR TV TEL **Metro:** Plaça de Catalunya.

Rates (including buffet breakfast): 6,150–9,550 ptas. ($43.70–$67.80) single; 8,300–9,900 ptas. ($58.90–$70.30) double; 9,150–11,450 ptas. ($65–$81.30) triple; 10,850–12,600 ptas. ($77–$89.50) quad. AE, DC, MC, V.

This hotel lies on the upper two floors of a commercial building in a safer section of the upper Rambles. The flowery, slightly faded reception area is clean and accented with 19th-century statues. The rooms are pleasant and modern, and 10 have

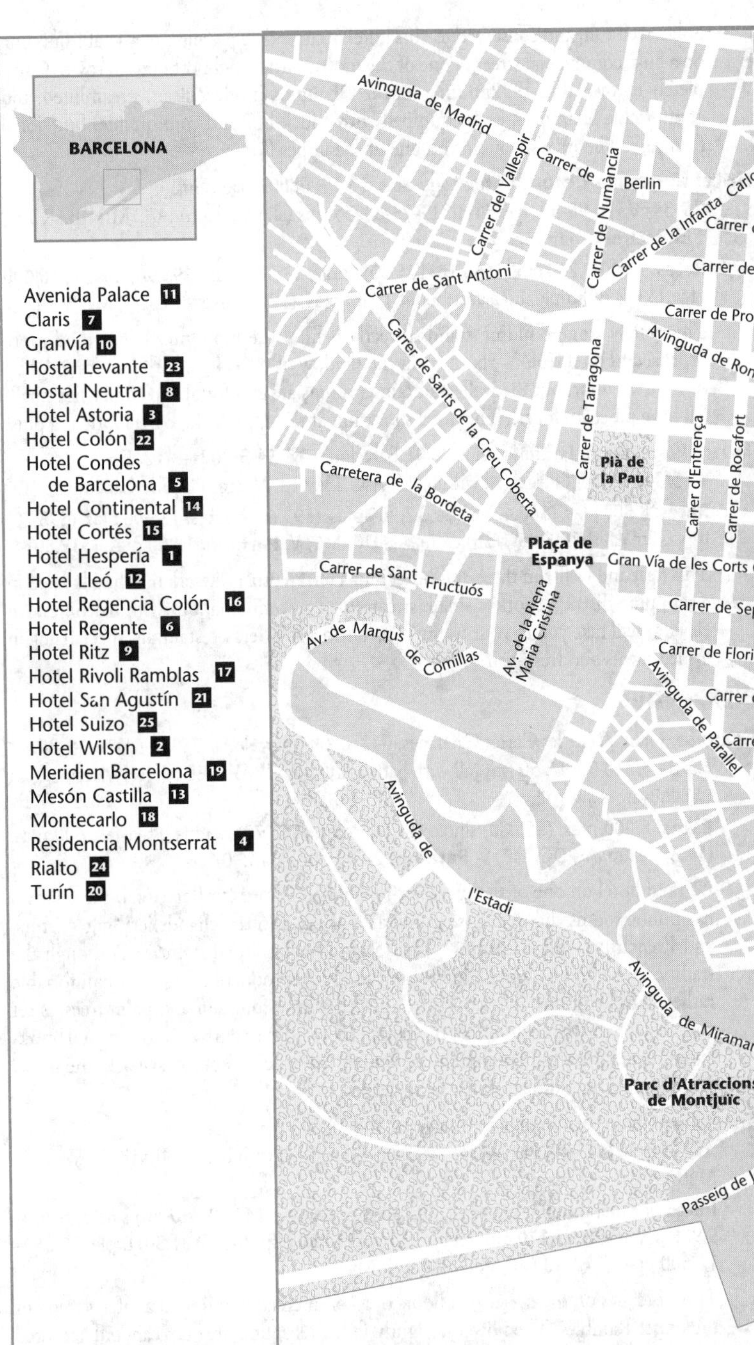
BARCELONA
Avenida Palace 11
Claris 7
Granvía 10
Hostal Levante 23
Hostal Neutral 8
Hotel Astoria 3
Hotel Colón 22
Hotel Condes de Barcelona 5
Hotel Continental 14
Hotel Cortés 15
Hotel Hespería 1
Hotel Lleó 12
Hotel Regencia Colón 16
Hotel Regente 6
Hotel Ritz 9
Hotel Rivoli Ramblas 17
Hotel San Agustín 21
Hotel Suizo 25
Hotel Wilson 2
Meridien Barcelona 19
Mesón Castilla 13
Montecarlo 18
Residencia Montserrat 4
Rialto 24
Turín 20
Avinguda de Madrid
Carrer del Vallespir
Carrer de Berlin
Carrer de Numància
Carrer de la Infanta Carlota
Carrer de Sant Antoni
Carrer de Tarragona
Avinguda de Roma
Carrer de Sants de la Creu Coberta
Carretera de la Bordeta
Pià de la Pau
Carrer d'Entrença
Carrer de Rocafort
Plaça de Espanya
Gran Vía de les Corts Ca
Carrer de Sant Fructuós
Av. de Marqus de Comillas
Av. de la Riena Maria Cristina
Carrer de Florida
Avinguda de Parallel
Avinguda de l'Estadi
Avinguda de Miramar
Parc d'Atraccions de Montjuïc
Passeig de Jose
9178

Accommodations in Central Barcelona

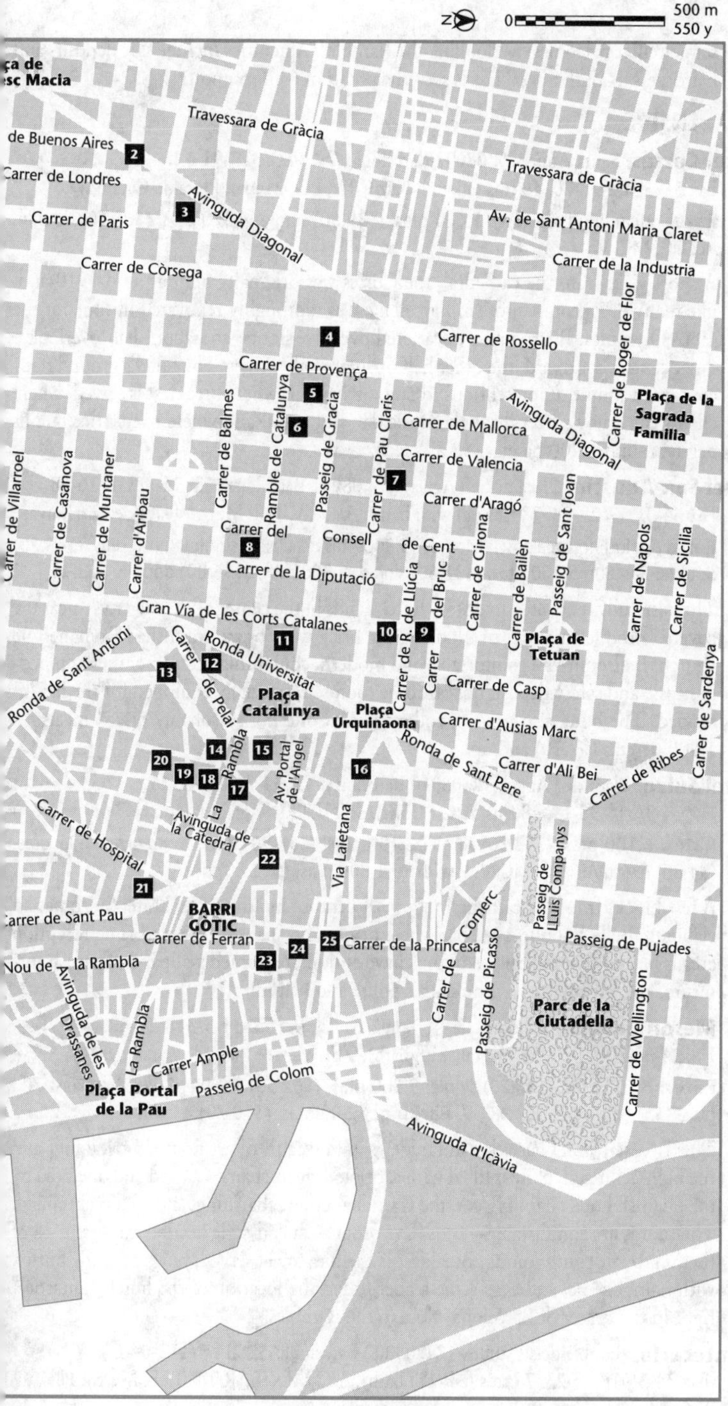

N
0 500 m
550 y

ça de
sc Macia
Travessara de Gràcia
de Buenos Aires
2
Carrer de Londres
Travessara de Gràcia
Avinguda Diagonal
3
Carrer de Paris
Av. de Sant Antoni Maria Claret
Carrer de Còrsega
Carrer de la Industria
4
Carrer de Rossello
Carrer de Provença
Carrer de Roger de Flor
5
Plaça de la
Sagrada
Familia
Avinguda Diagonal
6
Carrer de Mallorca
Carrer de Balmes
Ramble de Catalunya
Passeig de Gracia
Carrer de Pau Claris
Carrer de Valencia
7
Carrer d'Aragó
Carrer de Villarroel
Carrer de Casanova
Carrer de Muntaner
Carrer d'Aribau
Carrer del
Consell
de Cent
8
Carrer de la Diputació
Carrer de Girona
Passeig de Sant Joan
Carrer de Bailèn
Carrer de Napols
Carrer de Sicilia
Gran Vía de les Corts Catalanes
Carrer de R. de Llúcia
Carrer del Bruc
10
9
11
Plaça de
Tetuan
Ronda de Sant Antoni
Carrer de Pelai
Ronda Universitat
12
13
Carrer de Casp
Plaça
Catalunya
Plaça
Urquinaona
Carrer d'Ausias Marc
Carrer de Sardenya
Ronda de Sant Pere
La Rambla
14
15
Av. Portal de l'Angel
Carrer d'Ali Bei
16
20
19
18
17
Carrer de Ribes
Carrer de Hospital
Avinguda de la Catedral
22
Via Laietana
Passeig de LLuis Companys
21
Carrer de Comerc
Carrer de Sant Pau
BARRI
GÒTIC
Carrer de Ferran
25
Carrer de la Princesa
24
Passeig de Pujades
23
Nou de la Rambla
Passeig de Picasso
Parc de la
Ciutadella
Avinguda de les Drassanes
La Rambla
Carrer Ample
Carrer de Wellington
Plaça Portal
de la Pau
Passeig de Colom
Avinguda d'Icàvia

semicircular balconies overlooking the Rambles. Amenities include safe deposits and hairdryers. A buffet breakfast is served daily from 6am to noon.

INEXPENSIVE

Hotel Cortés, Santa Anna, 25, 08002 Barcelona. ☎ **34-3/317-91-12.** Fax 34-3/302-78-70. 46 rms (all with bath). TV TEL **Metro:** Plaça de Catalunya.

Rates (including breakfast): 5,600 ptas. ($39.80) single; 9,370 ptas. ($66.50) double. AE, DC, MC, V.

A short walk from the cathedral, the Cortés was originally built around 1910 and, like many of its competitors in Barcelona, was thoroughly renovated in time for the 1992 Olympics. Bedrooms are scattered over five floors, and about half overlook a quiet central courtyard, the other half open onto the street. The hotel's ground floor contains a simple, unpretentious restaurant and bar, where breakfast is served, where clients can enjoy a beer throughout the day and night, and where fixed-price menus begin around 1,200 pesetas ($8.50) each.

Hotel San Agustín, Plaça de San Agustín, 3, 08001 Barcelona. ☎ **34-3/318-16-58.** Fax 34-3/317-29-28. 77 rms (all with bath). A/C TV TEL **Metro:** Plaça de Catalunya.

Rates (including breakfast): Mon–Fri 5,800 ptas. ($41.20) single; 8,900 ptas. ($63.20) double; Sat–Sun 5,300 ptas. ($37.60) single; 8,000 ptas. ($56.80) double. MC. V.

This tastefully renovated five-story hotel stands in the center of the old city—near the covered produce markets overlooking the brick walls of an unfinished Romanesque church. Bedrooms are comfortable and modern, containing such amenities as piped-in music and safety deposit boxes. Some rooms are specially equipped for the handicapped. The hotel also runs a good restaurant offering reasonably priced meals for 1,000 pesetas ($7.10) and up.

Hotel Suizo, Plaça de l'Angel, 12, 08010 Barcelona. ☎ **34-3/315-41-11.** Fax 34-3/315-38-19. 48 rms. A/C MINIBAR TV TEL **Metro:** Jaume I.

Rates: 6,100 ptas. ($43.30) single; 8,100 ptas. ($57.50) double. Breakfast 675 ptas. ($4.80) extra. AE, DC, MC, V. **Parking:** 1,800 ptas. ($12.80) nearby.

A few blocks from the cathedral in a 19th-century building, the Hotel Suizo has an elaborate Belle Epoque–style bar where drinks and snacks are served. The reception area is pleasantly modern. Bedrooms have antique-patterned wallpaper, Spanish furniture, and private baths. The staff is polite and helpful.

★ **Mesón Castilla,** Valldoncella, 5, 08002 Barcelona. ☎ **34-3/318-21-82.** Fax 34-3/412-40-20. 56 rms (all with bath). TEL **Metro:** Plaça de Catalunya.

Rates: 6,500 ptas. ($46.20) single; 9,500 ptas. ($67.50) double. Buffet breakfast 700 ptas. ($5) extra. AE, DC, MC, V. **Parking:** 1,500 ptas. ($10.70).

This two-star hotel has a lavish facade, with a wealth of art nouveau detailing, and the high-ceilinged lobby is filled with cabriole-legged chairs. Owned and operated by the Spanish hotel chain HUSA, the Castilla is clean, charming, and well maintained. The rooms are comfortable—beds have ornate Catalán-style headboards—and 28 of them have air conditioning. Breakfast is the only meal served, but it is a fine buffet, with ham, cheese, and eggs. One reader found the location of the hotel "fantastic," right in the center of Barcelona, close to the Rambles.

Montecarlo, Ramble dels Estudis, 124, 08002 Barcelona. ☎ **34-3/412-04-04.** Fax 34-3/318-73-23. 76 rms (all with bath). A/C MINIBAR TV TEL. **Metro:** Plaça de Catalunya.

Rates: Mon–Thurs, 7,900 ptas. ($56.10) single, 11,300 ptas. ($80.20) double. Fri–Sun, 6,300 ptas. ($44.70) single, 9,000 ptas. ($63.90) double. Breakfast 850 ptas. ($6) extra. AE, DC, MC, V. **Parking:** 1,800 ptas. ($12.80).

This hotel, set beside the wide and sloping promenade of the Rambles, was originally built around 200 years ago as a opulent and aristocratic private home. In the 1930s, it was transformed into the comfortably unpretentious hotel you'll find today. Each of the bedrooms is efficiently decorated and comfortable, most of them renovated around 1989. Public areas include some of the building's original accessories, with carved doors, a baronial fireplace, and crystal chandeliers.

Rialto, Ferran, 40-42, 08002 Barcelona. ☎ **34-3/318-52-12.** Fax 34-3/315-38-19. 141 rms. A/C MINIBAR TEL **Metro:** Jaume 1.

Rates: 9,880 ptas. ($70.10) single; 10,500 ptas. ($74.60) double. Breakfast 675 ptas. ($4.80) extra. AE, DC, MC, V. **Parking:** 1,800 ptas. ($12.80) nearby.

One of the best choices in the Barri Gòtic, this hotel is part of the Gargallo chain, which also owns the Hotel Suizo. The three-star Rialto is furnished with Catalán flair and style; completely overhauled in 1985, it offers clean, well-maintained, and comfortably furnished guest rooms with private baths. There is a cafeteria.

BUDGET

$ **Hostal Levante,** Baïxada de Sant Miguel, 2, 08002 Barcelona. ☎ **34-3/317-95-65.** 38 rms (7 with bath). **Metro:** Liceu or Jaume 1.

Rates: 2,000 ptas. ($14.20) single without bath; 3,500 ptas. ($24.90) double without bath; 4,500 ptas. ($32) double with bath. No credit cards.

In my opinion, this is one of the nicest and most reasonably priced places to stay in Barcelona. In a quiet, imposing building more than two centuries old, it stands just a short distance from the Plaça de Sant Jaume, in the center of the Barri Gòtic. The units are clean and comfortable, and there is central heating. The staff speaks English. No meals are served.

$ **Hostal Neutral,** Rambla de Catalunya, 42, 08007 Barcelona. ☎ **34-3/487-63-90.** 35 rms (all with bath). TEL **Metro:** Aragón.

Rates: 2,500 ptas. ($17.80) single; 5,000 ptas. ($35.50) double. Breakfast 400 ptas. ($2.80) extra. No credit cards.

An older pension, but very recommendable, the *hostal* has a reputation for its cleanliness and efficiency. As the name suggests, the rooms here are neutral—but comfortable nevertheless. English is spoken.

Sur Diagonal

VERY EXPENSIVE

Barcelona Hilton, Diagonal, 589, 08014 Barcelona. ☎ **34-3/419-22-33,** or toll free within the U.S. and Canada **800/445-8667.** Fax 34-3/322-52-91. 275 rms, 15 suites. A/C MINIBAR TV TEL **Metro:** María Cristina.

Rates: 25,500 ptas. ($181.10) single; 32,000 ptas. ($227.20) double; from 40,000 ptas. ($284) suite. Buffet breakfast 2,000 ptas. ($14.20) extra. AE, DC, MC, V. **Parking:** 1,800 ptas. ($12.80).

Opened in 1990 as one of the most publicized hotels in Barcelona, this five-star property lies in a desirable position on one of the most famous and elegant boulevards.

Dining/Entertainment: The Restaurant Cristal Garden serves well-prepared international and Spanish menus in a relaxed but polished setting. A bar/lounge lies nearby. Night owls head for a popular local disco, Up & Down, a short walk from the hotel.

Services: 24-hour room service, laundry/valet, concierge, translation and secretarial services, express checkout, limousine service, babysitting.

Facilities: The hotel maintains a cooperative relationship with a well-equipped health club half a mile away. Tennis courts are a mile away, and the hotel can arrange golf at a course 16 miles away. Shopping boutiques and a news kiosk are on the premises.

★ **Claris,** Carrer de Pau Claris, 150, 08009 Barcelona. ☎ **34-3/487-62-62,** or toll free in the U.S. **800/888-4747.** Fax 34-3/487-87-36. 106 rms (all with bath), 18 suites. A/C MINIBAR TV TEL **Metro:** Passeig de Gràcia.

Rates: Mon–Thurs, 23,600 ptas. ($167.60) single, 29,500 ptas. ($209.50) double. Suites from 32,500 ptas. ($230.80). Fri–Sun, 13,800 ptas. ($98) single, 16,800 ptas. ($119.30) double. Suites from 21,800 ptas. ($154.80). Breakfast 1,800 ptas. ($12.80) extra Mon–Thurs, free Fri–Sun. AE, DC, MC, V. **Parking:** 1,750 ptas. ($12.40).

Considered one of the most unusual hotels built in Barcelona since the 1930s, this postmodern hotel incorporated vast quantities of teak, marble, steel, and glass with the historically important facade of a landmark 19th-century building (the Verdruna Palace). It opened in 1992, in time for the Barcelona Olympics, in a seven-story format that includes a swimming pool and garden on its roof, a mini-museum of Egyptian antiquities on its second floor, and two restaurants, one of which specializes in different brands of caviar. Each of the bedrooms is painted an iconoclastic shade of blue-violet, and incorporates unusual art objects with state-of-the-art electronic accessories. (Art objects, depending on the inspiration of the decorator, include Turkish kilims, English antiques, Hindu sculptures, Egyptian stonecarvings, and engravings inspired by Napoléon's campaigns in Egypt.) Committed to celebrating many facets of Catalán culture, the hotel's owner and developer, art dealer Jordi Clos, named his hotel after the 19th-century Catalán writer Pau Claris.

Dining/Entertainment: On site is the Restaurant Claris, where fixed-price Catalán meals cost around 5,000 ptas. ($35.50) each. Also on the premises is a restaurant sponsored by the international caviar emporium, Caviar Caspa, where sturgeon eggs from many different distributors compete for gastronomic attention with an array of smoked meats, smoked fish, and bubbly wines. The restaurant's forte is light but elegant lunches and suppers.

Services: Laundry/valet; babysitting; room service.

Facilities: Swimming pool, sauna, foreign currency exchange.

★ **Hotel Ritz,** Gran Vía de les Corts Catalanes, 668, 08010 Barcelona. ☎ **34-3/318-52-00,** or toll free in the U.S. **800/223-1230.** Fax 34-3/318-01-48. 155 rms, 6 suites. A/C MINIBAR TV TEL **Metro:** Arc del Triomf.

Rates: 33,800–52,000 ptas. ($240–$369.20) single; 45,000–62,000 ptas. ($319.50–$440.20) double; suites from 128,000 ptas. ($908.80). Breakfast 2,000 ptas. ($14.20) extra. AE, DC, MC, V. **Parking:** 1,800 ptas. ($12.80).

Acknowledged as the finest, most prestigious, and most architecturally distinguished hotel in Barcelona, the Ritz was built in art deco style in 1919. Richly remodeled during the late 1980s, it has probably welcomed more millionaires, famous people, and aristocrats (with their official and unofficial consorts) than any other hotel in northeastern Spain. One of the finest features is the cream-and-gilt neoclassical lobby, whose marble floors and potted palms are flooded with sunlight from an overhead glass canopy and where afternoon tea is served to the strains of a string quartet. Bedrooms are as formal, high-ceilinged, and richly furnished as you'd expect, sometimes with Regency furniture and bathrooms accented with mosaics and bathtubs inspired by those in ancient Rome.

Dining/Entertainment: The elegant Restaurant Diana serves French and Catalán cuisine amid soaring ceilings, crystal chandeliers, and formally dressed waiters. See separate recommendation. Nearby lies the elegantly paneled Bar Parilla, where music from a grand piano will soothe your frazzled nerves while you enjoy the deep leather upholstery and gilded cove moldings.

Services: 24-hour room service, laundry, limousine service, concierge, babysitting.

Facilities: Business center, car rentals, handful of shopping kiosks and boutiques.

★ **Rey Juan Carlos I,** Avinguda Diagonal, 661, 08028 Barcelona.
☎ **34-3/448-08-08,** or toll free in the U.S. **800-448-8355.** Fax 34-3/448-06-07. 375 rms, 37 suites. A/C MINIBAR TV TEL. **Metro:** Palau Real.

Rates: Mon–Thurs, 27,000 ptas. ($191.70) single, 37,000 ptas. ($262.70) double. Suite 63,000 ptas. ($447.30). Fri–Sun, 13,500 ptas. ($95.90) single, 16,200 ptas. ($115) double. Suite 44,000 ptas. ($312.40). Breakfast 2,100 ptas. ($14.90) extra. AE, DC, MC, V. **Parking:** Free for guests, otherwise 2,100 ptas. ($14.90) per day.

Named for the Spanish king, who attended its opening and who has visited it several times since, this is one of the newest five-star luxury hotels in Barcelona. Opened in 1992, in time for the Olympics, it rises 17 stories from a position at the northern end of the Diagonal, within a prestigious neighborhood known for its corporate headquarters and banks. The design includes a soaring inner atrium, at one end of which a bank of glass-sided elevators glide silently up and down. Bedrooms contain many electronic extras, conservatively comfortable furnishings, and in many cases, views out over Barcelona to the sea.

Dining/Entertainment: The hotel's most elegant restaurant is Chez Vous, a glamorous and panoramic locale with impeccable service and French/Catalán meals priced at around 5,000 ptas. ($35.50) each. Saturday night, a dinner dance offers a live orchestra and set-price menus for around 8,000 ptas. ($56.80) per person. There's also a Japanese restaurant (Kokoro); and the Café Polo, which serves an endless series of

Frommer's Cool for Kids: Hotels

Hotel Colón (see p. 432) Opposite the cathedral in the Gothic Quarter, this hotel has been compared to a country home. Families ask for—and often get—the more spacious rooms.

Hotel Hespería (see p. 443) At the northern edge of the city, this hotel has gardens and a safe neighborhood setting. The rooms are generous enough in size for an extra bed.

Hotel Regente (see p. 442) In a good Eixample location, this renovated hotel has a rooftop terrace with panoramic views and a small swimming pool with sun deck.

buffets at lunch and dinner for 3,300 ptas. ($23.40) per person. The gardens which surround the hotel contain fountains, flowering shrubs, and the Café Terraza.

Services: 24-hour room service, laundry, concierge staff.

Facilities: A swimming pool, health club, jogging track, men's and women's hairdresser, car rental facilities, business center.

EXPENSIVE

Avenida Palace, Gran Vía de les Corts Catalanes, 605 (at the corner of Passeig de Gràcia), 08007 Barcelona. ☎ **34-3/301-96-00.** Fax 34-3/318-12-34. 147 rms, 18 suites. A/C MINIBAR TV TEL **Metro:** Gran Vía.

Rates: 13,500–17,000 ptas. ($95.90–$120.70) single; 20,000 ptas. ($142) double; from 35,000 ptas. ($248.50) suite. Breakfast 1,400 ptas. ($9.90) extra. AE, DC, MC, V. **Parking:** 2,000 ptas. ($14.20).

Set in an enviable 19th-century neighborhood filled with elegant shops and apartment buildings, this hotel lies behind a pair of mock-fortified towers that were built (like the hotel) in 1952. Despite its relative modernity, it evokes an old-world sense of charm, partly because of the attentive staff, scattering of flowers and antiques, and 1950s-era accessories that fill its well-upholstered public rooms. Bedrooms, all with private baths, are solidly traditional and quiet.

Dining/Entertainment: The hotel has an elegantly proportioned dining room, El Restaurant Pinateca, charging 3,000 pesetas ($21.30) for a set menu at lunch and dinner. It is open only Monday through Friday. The bar/lounge contains potted palms, a scattering of interesting antiques, and a sense of graciousness.

Services: Concierge, translation and secretarial services, currency exchange, hairdresser/barber, 24-hour room service, express checkout, babysitting.

★ **Hotel Condes de Barcelona,** Passeig de Gràcia, 73-75, 08008 Barcelona. ☎ **34-3/484-86-00.** Fax 34-3/488-06-14. 181 rms, 2 suites. A/C MINIBAR TV TEL **Metro:** Passeig de Gràcia.

Rates: 23,000 ptas. ($163.30) single; 29,000 ptas. ($205.90) double; 34,000 ptas. ($241.40) suite. Breakfast 1,700 ptas. ($12.10) extra. AE, DC, MC, V.

Located off the architecturally splendid Passeig de Gràcia, this four-star hotel, originally designed to be a private villa (1895), is one of Barcelona's most glamorous. It boasts a unique neomedieval facade, influenced by Gaudí's modernist movement. During recent renovation, just enough hints of high-tech furnishings were added to make the lobby exciting, but everything else has the original opulence. The curved lobby-level bar and its adjacent restaurant add a touch of art deco. All the comfortable salmon-, green-, or peach-colored guest rooms contain marble baths, reproductions of Spanish paintings, and soundproof windows.

Dining/Entertainment: In times past, you might have seen the late Conde de Barcelona, father of King Juan Carlos, passing through on the way for a refreshing snack in the Café Condal, featuring regional dishes. Guests also enjoy the piano bar, including, on occasions, the Baron von Thyssen and his Catalán-born wife, who sold their fabulous art collection to Madrid.

Services: Laundry, babysitting, room service.

Facilities: Outdoor swimming pool.

Hotel Melía Barcelona Sarría, Avinguda Sarría, 50, 08029 Barcelona. ☎ **34-3/410-60-60,** or toll free in the U.S. **800/336-3542.** Fax 34-3/321-51-79. 295 rms, 20 suites. A/C MINIBAR TV TEL **Metro:** Hospital Clínic.

Rates: 20,000 ptas. ($142) single; 26,000 ptas. ($184.60) double; from 40,000 ptas. ($284) suite. Breakfast 2,200 ptas. ($15.60) extra. AE, DC, MC, V. **Parking:** 2,100 ptas. ($14.90).

Located just a block away from the junction of the Avinguda Sarría and the Avinguda Diagonal, right in the modern business heart of Barcelona, this five-star hotel contains some of the most up-to-date hotel amenities in the city. It originally opened in 1976, but most of its bedrooms were remodeled as late as 1993. It offers comfortably upholstered and carpeted bedrooms in a neutral international modern style. The hotel—a member of the Melía nationwide Spanish chain—caters both to the business traveler and the vacationer.

Dining/Entertainment: The hotel restaurant serves both Catalán and international dishes, and a cocktail bar provides not only drinks but piano music six nights a week.

Services: 24-hour room service; concierge; laundry/valet; executive floor; private parking, and babysitting on request.

Facilities: Business center, one of the best-equipped health clubs in Barcelona.

Hotel Princesa Sofía, Plaça de Pius XII, 4, 08028 Barcelona. ☎ **34-3/330-71-11.** Fax 34-3/330-76-21. 481 rms, 24 suites. A/C MINIBAR TV TEL **Metro:** Palau Reial or María Cristina.

Rates: 18,000 ptas. ($127.80) single; 25,000 ptas. ($177.50) double; from 68,000 ptas. ($482.80) suite. Breakfast 1,800 ptas. ($12.80) extra. AE, DC, MC, V. **Parking:** 2,250 ptas. ($16).

Set beside the Avinguda Diagonal, about a block east of the Palau Reial and about two miles (3km) northwest of Barcelona's historic center, the Princesa Sofía is perhaps the busiest, most business-oriented, and most international of the large-volume modern hotels in Barcelona. The hotel was built in 1975 and renovated during the early 1990s. Packed with glamorous grace notes (including a branch of Régine's disco in the basement) and named after the wife of the Spanish monarch, the Princesa Sofía is the venue for dozens of daily conferences and social events. The guest rooms contain comfortable traditional furniture, often with a vaguely English feel.

Dining/Entertainment: Le Gourmet restaurant serves continental and Catalán meals priced from around 5,000 pesetas ($35.50) each, although they could go much higher. L'Emporda is slightly less expensive, and an in-house coffee shop, El Snack 2002, is open 24 hours a day. Also on the premises are two bars, one with live music for dancing.

Facilities: Handful of upscale shopping boutiques, barber/hairdresser, car rentals, amply equipped gym and health club, sauna, indoor and outdoor swimming pools, several well-conceived gardens, extensive conference and meeting facilities, unusually well-managed business center offering translation and secretarial services.

Services: 24-hour room service, laundry/valet, concierge, in-house branch of Iberia Airlines, babysitting.

MODERATE

Hotel Astoria, París, 203, 08036 Barcelona. ☎ **34-3/209-83-11.** Fax 34-3/202-30-08. 114 rms (all with bath). A/C MINIBAR TV TEL **Metro:** Diagonal.

Rates: 13,500 ptas. ($95.90) single; 15,400 ptas. ($109.30) double. Breakfast 975 ptas. ($6.90) extra. AE, DC, MC, V.

One of my favorite hotels, the Astoria has an art deco facade that makes it appear older than it is. The high ceilings, geometric designs, and brass-studded detailings in the public rooms could be Moorish or Andalusian. Each of the comfortable bedrooms is soundproofed; half have been renovated with slick international louvered closets and glistening white paint. The more old-fashioned rooms have warm textures of exposed cedar and elegant, pristine modern accessories.

Hotel Derby/Hotel Gran Derby, Loreto, 21-25, and Loreto, 28, 08029 Barcelona. ☎ **34-3/322-32-15.** Fax 34/410-08-62. 117 rms. 43 suites. A/C TV TEL **Metro:** Hospital Clínic.

Rates: 12,400 ptas. ($88) single; 13,600 ptas. ($96.60) double; 15,000 ptas. ($106.50) single suite; 16,500 ptas. ($117.20) double suite. Breakfast 1,250 ptas. ($8.90) extra. AE, DC, MC, V. **Parking:** 1,800 ptas. ($12.80).

Divided into two separate buildings, these twin hotels (owned and managed by the same corporation) lie in a tranquil neighborhood about two blocks south of the busy intersection of the Avinguda Diagonal and Avinguda Sarría. The Derby offers 117 conventional hotel rooms, while the Gran Derby (across the street) contains 43 suites, many of which have small balconies overlooking a flowered courtyard. (All drinking, dining, and entertainment facilities lie in the larger of the two establishments, the Derby.) A team of English-inspired designers imported a British aesthetic into these hotels, and the pleasing results include well-oiled hardwood panels, soft lighting, and comfortably upholstered armchairs. The guest rooms and suites are less British in feel than the public rooms, outfitted with simple furniture in a variety of decorative styles, each comfortable and quiet.

Dining/Entertainment: Although the hotel does not have a full-fledged restaurant, it contains a dignified but unpretentious coffee shop, The Times, which serves Spanish, British, and international food. The Scotch Bar, an upscale watering hole, has won several Spanish awards for the diversity of its many cocktails.

Services: Concierge, laundry, babysitting.

Hotel Regente, Rambla de Catalunya, 76, 08008 Barcelona. ☎ **34-3/215-25-70.** Fax 34-3/487-32-27. 78 rms. A/C MINIBAR TV TEL **Metro:** Plaça de Catalunya.

Rates: 9,000 ptas. ($63.90) single; 15,000 ptas. ($106.50) double. Breakfast 1,000 ptas. ($7.10) extra. AE, DC, MC, V.

Despite the hotel's extensive renovations, its grand art nouveau facade, famous picture windows, and traditional lobby have been preserved. The Regente's Scotch Bar-Restaurant is elegant, and the rooftop terrace with swimming pool and sun deck provides panoramic views of the area from Montjuïc to the harbor. Situated amid fine shops and restaurants, the hotel is easily accessible to city sights.

BUDGET

Residencia Montserrat, Passeig de Gràcia, 114, 08008 Barcelona. ☎ **34-3/217-27-00.** 39 rms (all with bath). TEL **Metro:** Diagonal. **Bus:** 22, 24, or 28.

Rates: 3,200 ptas. ($22.70) single; 5,000 ptas. ($35.50) double. Breakfast 400 ptas. ($2.80) extra. No credit cards.

The Montserrat lies in one of Barcelona's most desirable central neighborhoods. Although the facade is ornate and handsome, the rooms on the fourth-floor *residencia* are serviceable and clean—but a little drab. Some have terraces.

Norte Diagonal

MODERATE

Hotel Hespería, Los Vergós, 20, 08017 Barcelona. ☎ **34-3/204-55-51.** Fax 34-3/204-43-92. 139 rms. A/C MINIBAR TV TEL **Metro:** Tres Torres.

Rates: Mon–Thurs, 12,560 ptas. ($89.20) single; 14,950 ptas. ($106.10) double. Breakfast 1,250 ptas. ($8.90) extra. Fri–Sun (including breakfast): 7,250 ptas. ($51.50) single; 10,500 ptas. ($74.60) double. AE, DC, MC, V. **Parking:** 1,450 ptas. ($10.30).

This hotel, on the northern edge of the city, a 12-minute taxi ride from the center, is surrounded by the verdant gardens of one of Barcelona's most pleasant residential neighborhoods. Built in the late 1980s, the hotel was renovated before the 1992 Olympics. You'll pass a Japanese rock garden to reach the stone-floored reception area, with its adjacent bar. Sunlight floods the monochromatic interiors of the bedrooms—all doubles, although singles can be rented at the prices above. The uniformed staff offers fine service.

INEXPENSIVE

Hotel Wilson, Avinguda Diagonal, 568, 08021 Barcelona. ☎ **34-3/209-25-11.** Fax 34-3/200-83-70. 57 rms (all with bath), 6 suites. A/C MINIBAR TV TEL **Metro:** Diagonal.

Rates: 8,000 ptas. ($56.80) single; 12,000 ptas. ($85.20) double; from 21,500 ptas. ($152.70) suite. Breakfast buffet 750 ptas. ($5.30) extra. AE, DC, MC, V.

Set in a neighborhood rich with architectural curiosities, this comfortable hotel is a member of the nationwide HUSA chain. The small lobby isn't indicative of the rest of the building, which on the second floor opens into a large and sunny coffee shop/bar/TV lounge. The guest rooms are well kept. Room service and laundry are provided.

Villa Olímpica

EXPENSIVE

Hotel Arts, Carrer de la Marina, 19-21, 08005 Barcelona. ☎ **34-3/221-10-00,** or toll free in the U.S. **800/241-3333.** Fax 34-3/221-10-70. 326 rms, 47 suites. A/C MINIBAR TV TEL. **Metro:** Ciutadella.

Rates: Mon–Thurs 20,000–30,000 ptas. ($142–$213) single or double, suites from 35,000 ptas. ($248.50). Fri–Sun 18,000 ptas. ($127.80) single or double, suites from 25,000 ptas. ($177.50). Breakfast 2,000 ptas. ($14.20) extra Mon–Thurs, free Fri–Sun. AE, DC, MC, V. **Parking:** 2,500 ptas. ($17.80) Mon–Thurs, free Fri–Sun.

This is the only hotel in Europe managed by the luxury-conscious Ritz-Carlton chain, the first of what the company hopes will be a string of hotels across the European continent. It occupies 33 floors of what (at presstime) was the tallest building in Spain, a 45-floor postmodern tower whose upper floors contain the private condomiums of some of Iberia's most gossiped-about aristocrats and financiers. The location is about 1½ miles southwest of Barcelona's historic core, adjacent to the sea and the Olympic Village. Although some rooms were occupied by athletes and Olympic administrators in 1992, the hotel didn't became fully operational until January of 1994, making it Barcelona's newest and most talked-about hotel. Its decor is contemporary and elegant, including a large lobby sheathed in slabs of soft gray and yellow marble, and bedrooms outfitted in pastel shades of yellow or blue. Views from the bedrooms sweep out over the skyline of Barcelona and the Mediterranean. The staff is youthful, well trained, polite, and hardworking, each the product of months of training by Ritz-Carlton.

Dining/Entertainment: Three in-house restaurants include the Newport Room, which pays homage to new American cuisine and the seafaring pleasures of New England; the Café Veranda, a light and airy indoor/outdoor restaurant; and the Goyesca, which serves Spanish food and shellfish in a Catalán setting.

Services: 24-hour room service, business center, laundry, and a concierge staff who can arrange almost anything.

Facilities: A health club is scheduled to open during the lifetime of this edition. Adjacent to the hotel is an upscale cluster of many different luxury boutiques operated by the Japanese retailer, Sogo.

2 Dining

Ciutat Vella

EXPENSIVE

★ **Agut d'Avignon,** Trinitat, 3. ☎ **302-60-34.**

Cuisine: CATALÁN. **Reservations:** Required. **Metro:** Jaume I or Liceu.
Prices: Appetizers 950–2,200 ptas. ($6.70–$15.60); main courses 1,800–4,200 ptas. ($12.80–$29.80). AE, MC, V.
Open: Lunch, daily 1–3:30pm; dinner, daily 9–11:30pm.

Founded in 1962, one of my favorite restaurants in Barcelona is located near the Plaça Reial, in a tiny alleyway (the cross street is Calle d'Avinyó, 8). The restaurant attracts the leading politicians, writers, journalists, financiers, industrialists, and artists of Barcelona—even the king and various ministers of the cabinet, along with the visiting presidents from other countries. Since 1983, the restaurant has been run by Mercedes Giralt and her husband, José Luís Falagan Vazquez. A small 19th-century vestibule leads to the multilevel dining area that has two balconies and a main hall and is evocative of a hunting lodge. You might need help translating the Catalán menu. Specialties are likely to include acorn-squash soup served in its shell; fisherman soup with garlic toast; haddock stuffed with shellfish, sole with *nyoca* (medley of different nuts), large shrimps with *aïoli* (a garlicky mayonnaise sauce), duck with figs, chicken with shrimp, and filet steak in a sherry sauce.

Quo Vadis, Carme, 7. ☎ **302-40-72.**

Cuisine: SPANISH/CONTINENTAL. **Reservations:** Recommended. **Metro:** Liceu.
Prices: Appetizers 790–2,650 ptas. ($5.60–$18.80); main courses 1,450–3,500 ptas. ($10.30–$24.90). Menú del día 3,750 ptas. ($26.60). AE, DC, MC, V.
Open: Lunch, Mon–Sat 1:15–4pm; dinner, Mon–Sat 8:30–11:30pm.

Elegant and impeccable, this is considered one of the finest restaurants in Barcelona. Set within a century-old building near the open stalls of the Boquería food market, it was established in 1967 and has done a discreet but thriving business ever since. Seating is within any of four different dining rooms, each decorated with exposed paneling and a veneer of conservative charm. Menu items include a ragoût of seasonal mushrooms; fried goose liver with prunes; filet of beef with wine sauce; a wide variety of fish, grilled or—in some cases, flambéed; and a wide choice of desserts made with seasonal fruits imported from throughout Spain.

MODERATE

$ **Can Cuelleretes,** Quintana, 5. ☎ **317-64-85.**

Cuisine: CATALÁN. **Reservations:** Recommended. **Metro:** Liceu. **Bus:** 14 or 59.
Prices: Appetizers 750–950 ptas. ($5.30–$6.70); main courses 850–1,600 ptas. ($6–$11.40). DC, V.
Open: Lunch, Tues–Sun 1:30–4pm; dinner, Tues–Sat 9–11pm. **Closed:** July 4–25.

Founded in 1786 as a *pastelería* in the Barri Gòtic, this oldest of Barcelona restaurants still retains many original architectural features. All three dining rooms are decorated in Catalán style, with tile dadoes and wrought-iron chandeliers. The well-prepared food features authentic dishes of northeastern Spain, including sole Roman style, *zarzuela à la marinara* (shellfish medley), *canalones* (cannelloni), and paella. From October to January, special game dishes are available, including *perdiz* (partridge). Signed photographs of celebrities, flamenco artists, and bullfighters who have visited this *casa* decorate the walls.

Can Pescallunes, Carrer Magdalenes, 23. ☎ **318-54-83.**

Cuisine: FRENCH/CATALÁN. **Reservations:** Required for lunch. **Metro:** Urquinaona.
Prices: Appetizers 850–1,200 ptas. ($6–8.50); main courses 1,500–2,100 ptas. ($10.70–$14.90); fixed-price menu 3,500 ptas. ($24.90). MC, V.
Open: Lunch, Mon–Fri 1–3:30pm; dinner, Mon–Fri 8:30–10:30pm.

With the look, feel, and menu of a French bistro, this 10-table restaurant is a short walk from the cathedral. In 1980 it opened its doors in a turn-of-the-century building. An elaborate street lantern marks the entrance. Specialties are *rape* (monkfish) with clams and tomatoes, a smooth vichyssoise, chateaubriand with béarnaise, sole cooked in cider, steak tartare, and dessert crêpes with Cointreau. The specials change daily.

La Cuineta, Paradis, 4. ☎ **315-01-11.**

Cuisine: CATALÁN. **Reservations:** Recommended. **Metro:** Jaume I.
Prices: Appetizers 1,200–4,500 ptas. ($8.50–$32); main courses 1,800–3,000 ptas. ($12:80–$21.30); fixed-price menu 2,500 ptas. ($17.80). AE, DC, MC, V.
Open: Lunch, daily 1–4pm; dinner, daily 8pm–midnight.

A well-established restaurant near the center of the Catalán government, this is a culinary highlight of the Barri Gòtic. The restaurant is decorated in typical regional style and favors local cuisine. The fixed-price menu represents good value, or you can order à la carte. The most expensive appetizer is *bellota* (acorn-fed ham), but I suggest that you settle instead for a market-fresh Catalán dish.

Naviera, Rambla de Canaletes, 127. ☎ **301-92-25.**

Cuisine: CATALÁN. **Reservations:** Not required. **Metro:** Plaça de Catalunya.
Prices: Appetizers 600–1,900 ptas. ($4.30–$13.50); main courses 1,900–2,800 ptas. ($13.50–$19.90). AE, DC, MC, V.
Open: Cervecería daily 9am–2am. Restaurant, lunch daily 2–4pm; dinner daily 8pm–midnight.

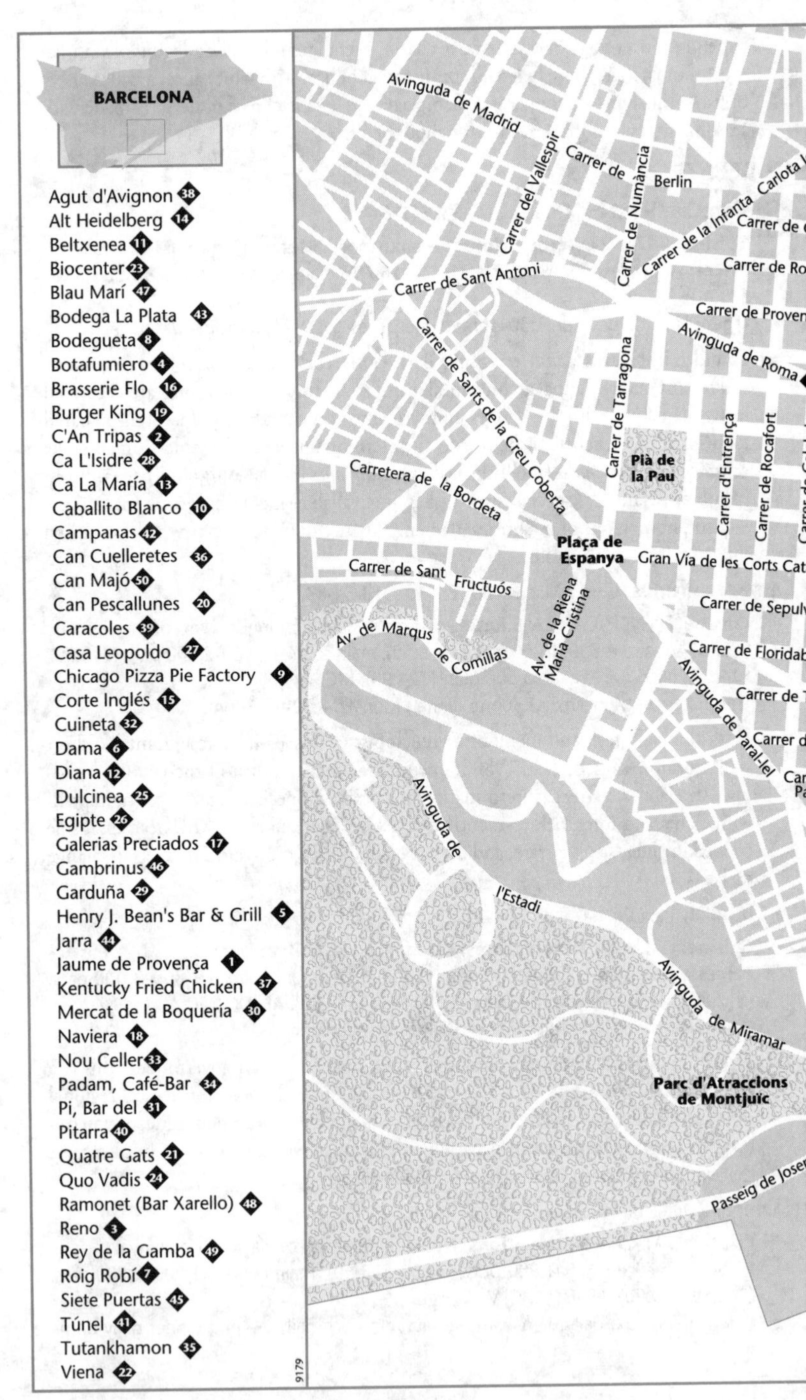
BARCELONA
Agut d'Avignon 38
Alt Heidelberg 14
Beltxenea 11
Biocenter 23
Blau Marí 47
Bodega La Plata 43
Bodegueta 8
Botafumiero 4
Brasserie Flo 16
Burger King 19
C'An Tripas 2
Ca L'Isidre 28
Ca La María 13
Caballito Blanco 10
Campanas 42
Can Cuelleretes 36
Can Majó 50
Can Pescallunes 20
Caracoles 39
Casa Leopoldo 27
Chicago Pizza Pie Factory 9
Corte Inglés 15
Cuineta 32
Dama 6
Diana 12
Dulcinea 25
Egipte 26
Galerias Preciados 17
Gambrinus 46
Garduña 29
Henry J. Bean's Bar & Grill 5
Jarra 44
Jaume de Provença 1
Kentucky Fried Chicken 37
Mercat de la Boquería 30
Naviera 18
Nou Celler 33
Padam, Café-Bar 34
Pi, Bar del 31
Pitarra 40
Quatre Gats 21
Quo Vadis 24
Ramonet (Bar Xarello) 48
Reno 3
Rey de la Gamba 49
Roig Robí 7
Siete Puertas 45
Túnel 41
Tutankhamon 35
Viena 22
Avinguda de Madrid
Carrer del Vallespir
Carrer de Numància
Carrer de Berlin
Carrer de la Infanta Carlota
Carrer de Sant Antoni
Carrer de Rosse
Carrer de Provença
Avinguda de Roma
Carrer de Sants de la Creu Coberta
Carrer de Tarragona
Plà de la Pau
Carrer d'Entrença
Carrer de Rocafort
Carrer de Calabria
Carretera de la Bordeta
Plaça de Espanya
Gran Vía de les Corts Catala
Carrer de Sant Fructuós
Av. de la Riena María Cristina
Carrer de Sepulve
Av. de Marqus de Comillas
Carrer de Floridabla
Avinguda de Paral-lel
Avinguda de l'Estadi
Avinguda de Miramar
Parc d'Atraccions de Montjuïc
Passeig de Josep C
9179

Dining in Central Barcelona

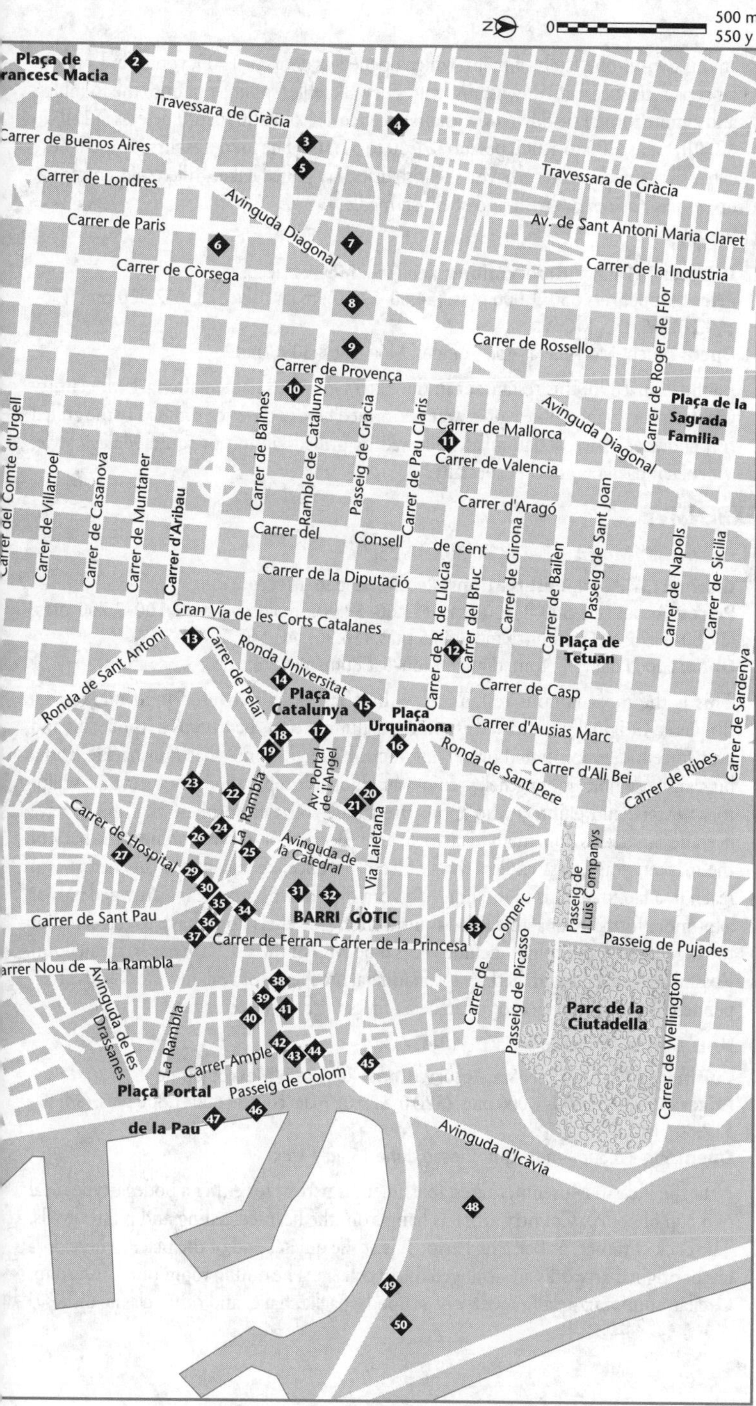

In this two-in-one establishment, which opened its doors in 1905, you'll find a popular cervecería (beerhall) downstairs, with sidewalk tables spilling out onto the Rambles, and a more formal sit-down downstairs. Beer costs from 200 to 400 pesetas ($1.40 to $2.80); tapas, 200 to 1,000 pesetas ($1.40 to $7.10). The food upstairs is much more expensive, especially if you have a shellfish dish. Try grilled hake, grilled sole, entrecôte, or *zarzuela de pescado* (fish-and-shellfish medley).

$ **Pitarra,** Avinyó, 56. ☎ **301-16-47.**

Cuisine: CATALÁN. **Reservations:** Required. **Metro:** Liceu.
Prices: Appetizers 650–1,000 ptas. ($4.60–$7.10); main courses 850–2,000 ptas. ($6–$14.20). AE, DC, MC, V.
Open: Lunch, Mon–Sat 1–4pm; dinner, Mon–Sat 8:30–11pm.

Founded in 1890, this restaurant in the Barri Gòtic was named after a 19th-century Catalán playwright whose works were performed here in the back room. Try the grilled fish chowder or a Catalán salad, followed by grilled salmon or squid Málaga style. Valencian paella is another specialty.

INEXPENSIVE

$ **Garduña,** Morera, 17–19. ☎ **302-43-23.**

Cuisine: CATALÁN. **Reservations:** Recommended. **Metro:** Liceu.
Prices: Appetizers 500–1,400 ptas. ($3.60–$9.90); main courses 1,100–2,700 ptas. ($7.80–$19.20). Fixed-price menu 975 ptas. ($6.90). AE, MC, V.
Open: Lunch daily, 1–4pm; dinner, Mon–Sat 8pm–midnight.

This is the most famous restaurant within Barcelona's covered food market, La Boquería. Originally conceived as a hotel, it eliminated its bedrooms in the 1970s and ever since has concentrated on serving food. Battered, somewhat ramshackle, and a bit claustrophobic, it nonetheless enjoys a fashionable reputation among actors, sculptors, writers, and painters who appreciate a blue-collar atmosphere that might have been designated as bohemian in an earlier era. Because of its position near the back of the market, you'll pass endless rows of fresh produce, cheese, and meats before you reach it, a fact that adds to its allure. You can dine downstairs, near a crowded bar, or a bit more formally upstairs. Food is ultra-fresh (the chefs don't have to travel far for the ingredients) and might include "hors d'oeuvres of the sea," *canalones* (cannelloni) Rossini, grilled hake with herbs, rape marinera, brochettes of veal, filet steak with green peppercorns, seafood rice, or a zarzuela of fresh fish with spices.

$ **Nou Celler,** Princesa, 16. ☎ **310-47-73.**

Cuisine: CATALÁN/SPANISH. **Reservations:** Required. **Metro:** Jaume I.
Prices: Appetizers 300–1,000 ptas. ($2.10–$7.10); main courses 600–1,800 ptas. ($4.30–$12.80). MC, V.
Open: Sun–Fri 8am–midnight. Closed: June 15–July 15.

Near the Picasso Museum, this establishment is perfect for either a bodega-type meal or a cup of coffee. Country artifacts hang from the beamed ceiling and plaster walls. The back entrance, at Barra de Ferro, 3, is at the quieter end of the place, where dozens of original artworks are arranged into a collage. The dining room offers fish soup, Catalán soup, zarzuela (a medley of seafood), paella, hake, and other classic dishes.

Tutankhamon, Rauric, 18. ☎ **412-52-01.**

Cuisine: CATALÁN. **Reservations:** Recommended. **Metro:** Liceu.
Prices: Appetizers 350–650 ptas. ($2.50–$4.60); main courses 750–1,500 ptas. ($5.30–$10.70). AE, MC, V.
Open: Lunch, Wed–Mon 1–4pm; dinner, daily 7:30–1:30am.

A meal at this restaurant will lead prospective diners down some of the oldest alleyways in Barcelona, through a neighborhood rich in ambience, local color, and the not always discreet inventories of an occasional erotic bookstore. Named in honor of the legendary Pharaoh by its Egyptian-born founder, Tutankhamon offers a stylish and contemporary interior with a granite bar, tile floors, and accessories inspired by the Moorish traditions of Andalusia. Menu items include eggplant salads, shish kebabs, many different presentations of grilled fish or steaks, and shrimp.

Sur Diagonal

VERY EXPENSIVE

Beltxenea, Mallorca, 275. ☎ **215-3024.**

Cuisine: BASQUE. **Reservations:** Recommended. **Metro:** Passeig de Gràcia.
Prices: Appetizers: 625–1,700 ptas. ($4.40–$12.10); main courses: 2,500–5,500 ptas. ($17.80–$39.10). *Menú degustación* 6,500–7,000 ptas. ($46.20–$49.70) AE, DC, MC, V.
Open: Lunch Mon–Fri 1:30–4pm; dinner, Mon–Sat 8:30pm–midnight. **Closed:** Two weeks in August.

Set in a building originally conceived in the late 19th century as a modernist apartment building, this restaurant celebrates the nuances and subtleties of Basque cuisine. Within a dignified dining room with parquet floors and nautical accessories, you can enjoy a cuisine that is affected by the inspiration of the chef and the availability of ingredients. Examples include hake served either fried with garlic or garnished with clams and served with fish broth. Roast lamb, grilled rabbit, and pheasant are well prepared and succulent, as are the desserts.

Ca l'Isidre, Les Flors, 12. ☎ **441-11-39.**

Cuisine: CATALÁN. **Reservations:** Required. **Metro:** Parallel.
Prices: Appetizers 1,200–3,000 ptas. ($8.50–$21.30); main courses 2,000–3,800 ptas. ($14.20–$27). AE, MC, V.
Open: Lunch, Mon–Sat 1:30-3:30pm; dinner, Mon–Sat 8:30–11pm. **Closed:** Aug.

This is perhaps the most sophisticated Catalán bistro in Barcelona, drawing such patrons as King Juan Carlos and Queen Sofía. Opened in 1970, it was also visited by Julio Iglesia and the famous Catalán band leader Xavier Cugat. Isidre Gironés, helped by his wife, Montserrat, is known for his market-fresh Catalonian cuisine. Flowers decorate the restaurant, along with artwork, and the array of food is beautifully prepared and served. Try spider crabs and shrimp, a gourmand salad with foie gras, sweetbreads with port and flap mushrooms, or carpaccio of veal Harry's Bar style. Sometimes *espardenyes,* that increasingly rare sea creature, is served here. The selection of Spanish and Catalán wines is excellent.

EXPENSIVE

La Dama, Diagonal, 423. ☎ **202-06-86.**

Cuisine: CATALÁN/INTERNATIONAL. **Reservations:** Required. **Metro:** Provença.
Prices: Appetizers 550–1,800 ptas. ($3.90–$12.80); main courses 1,700–4,000 ptas. ($12.10–$28.40); fixed-price menus 4,750–6,950 ptas. ($33.70–$49.30). AE, DC, MC, V.
Open: Lunch, daily 1–3:30pm; dinner, daily 8:30–11:30pm.

Located one floor above street level in one of the grandly iconoclastic 19th-century buildings for which Barcelona is famous, this stylish and well-managed restaurant serves a clientele of local residents and civic dignitaries with impeccable taste and confidence. You'll take an art nouveau elevator (or the sinuous stairs) up one flight to reach the dining room. The specialties might include roast filet of goat; salmon steak served with vinegar derived from *cava* and onions; confit of duckling; cream-of-potato soup flavored with caviar; a salad of crayfish with orange-flavored vinegar; an abundant seasonal platter of autumn mushrooms; and succulent preparations of lamb, fish and shellfish, beef, and veal dishes. The building that contains the restaurant, designed by the modernist architect Manuel Sayrach, lies three blocks west of the intersection of Avinguda Diagonal and Passeig de Grácia.

Jaume de Provença, Provença, 88. ☎ **430-00-29.**

Cuisine: CATALÁN/FRENCH. **Reservations:** Recommended. **Metro:** Extació-Sants.
Prices: Appetizers 1,400–2,750 ptas. ($9.90–$19.50); main courses 1,950–3,000 ptas. ($13.80–$21.30). AE, DC, MC, V.
Open: Lunch, Tues–Sun 1–4pm; dinner, Tues–Sat 9–11:30pm. **Closed:** Easter week and Aug.

Located a few steps away from the Estació Central de Barcelona-Sants railway station at the western end of the Eixample, this is a small, cozy, and personalized restaurant with a country-rustic decor. The young-at-heart clientele is served by a polite and hardworking staff. Named after its owner/chef Jaume Bargués, it serves modern interpretations of traditional Catalán and southern French cuisine. Examples include a gratin of clams with spinach; a salad of two different species of lobster; small packets of foie gras and truffles; pig's trotters with plums and truffles; crabmeat lasagne; cod with saffron sauce; sole with mushrooms in a port-wine sauce; and a dessert specialty of orange mousse, whose presentation is considered something of an artistic statement in its own right. This establishment, incidentally, was established during the 1940s by Jaume's forebears, who acquiesced to their talented offspring's new and successful culinary theories.

INEXPENSIVE

Ca La María, Tallers, 76. ☎ **318-89-93.**

Cuisine: CATALÁN. **Reservations:** Recommended Sat–Sun. **Metro:** Universitat.
Prices: Appetizers 650–1,000 ptas. ($4.60–$7.10); main courses 950–1,700 ptas. ($6.70–$12.10). AE, DC, MC, V.
Open: Lunch, Tues–Sun 1:30–4pm; dinner, Tues–Sat 8:30–11pm.

This small blue-and-green-tiled bistro (only 18 tables) is on a quiet square opposite a Byzantine-style church near the Plaça de la Universitat. Menu items include roast goat, veal scaloppine, rape (monkfish) in a pimiento-cream sauce, sole with orange, and codfish in a garlic-cream sauce. There are also daily specials that change frequently.

C'an Tripas, Carrer Sagues, 16. ☎ **200-85-40.**

Cuisine: CATALÁN/SPANISH. **Reservations:** Recommended. **Metro:** Diagonal.
Prices: Appetizers 550–850 ptas. ($3.90–$6); main courses 750–1,800 ptas. ($5.30–$12.80); menú del día 1,000 ptas. ($7.10). MC, V.
Open: Lunch, Mon–Fri 1–4pm; dinner, Mon–Sat 9–11pm.

This well-known no-frills budget restaurant has a certain charm, even if it is located on a block of adult nightclubs. It has flourished at this address since 1945. There's sawdust on the floor, the tables are covered with oilcloth, arc lights shine, racks of bottles line the poster-covered walls, and a TV plays in the background. Among the menu choices that might make up a full meal are fish soup, beef with brussels sprouts, brook trout, and Spanish melon. Or sample the most classic dish of Barcelona, the regional stew called *escu della i carn d'olla* (broad beans, sausages, meatballs, and herbs).

Norte Diagonal

VERY EXPENSIVE

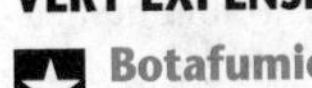

Botafumiero, Gran de Gràcia, 81. ☎ **218-42-30.**

Cuisine: SEAFOOD. **Reservations:** Recommended for dining rooms, not necessary for meals at the bar. **Metro:** Enrique Cuiraga.
Prices: Appetizers 1,500–7,500 ptas. ($10.70–$53.30); main courses 2,500–5,800 ptas. ($17.80–$41.20); fixed-price menus 8,000–9,000 ptas. ($56.80–$63.90). AE, DC, MC, V.
Open: Tues–Sat 1pm–1am; Sun 1–5pm.

Much of the allure of this place comes from the attention to details paid by the white-jacketed staff, who prepare a table setting at the establishment's bar for anyone who prefers to dine there. If you do choose to venture to the rear, you'll find a series of attractive dining rooms outfitted with light-grained panels, white napery, polished brass, potted plants, and paintings by Galician artists. These rooms are noted for the ease with which business deals seem to be arranged over the lunch hour, when international business people often make it their favorite rendezvous. The king of Spain is a frequent patron.

Menu items include some of the most legendary seafood in Barcelona, prepared ultrafresh in a glistening and ultramodern kitchen that's visible from parts of the dining room. The establishment prides itself on its fresh and saltwater fish, clams, mussels, lobster, crayfish, scallops, and several varieties of crustaceans that you may never have seen before. Stored live in holding tanks or in enormous crates near the restaurant's entrance, many of the creatures are flown in every day from Galicia, home of owner Moncho Neira. In contrast to the hundred-or-so fish dishes (which might include zarzuelas, stews, paellas, and grills), the menu contains a listing for only four or five meat dishes, including three kinds of steak, veal, and a traditional version of pork with turnips. The wine list offers a wide array of highly drinkable choices from Galicia and a wide variety of *cavas* from Catalonia.

Neichel, Pedralbes, 16. ☎ **203-84-08.**

Cuisine: FRENCH. **Reservations:** Required. **Metro:** Palau Reial or María Christina.
Prices: Appetizers 1,200–2,500 ptas. ($8.50–$17.80); main courses 2,300–3,800 ptas. ($16.30–$27). AE, DC, MC, V.
Open: Lunch, Mon–Sat 1–3:30pm; dinner, Mon–Sat 9–11pm. **Closed:** Aug 15–Sept 15 and Christmas.

Owned and operated by Alsatian-born Jean Louis Neichel, who has been called "the most brilliant ambassador French cuisine has ever had within Spain," this restaurant serves a clientele whose credentials might best be described as stratospheric. Outfitted in cool tones of gray and pastel, with its main decoration derived from a bank of windows opening onto greenery, Neichel is vastly and almost obsessively concerned with gastronomy—the savory presentation of some of the most talked-about preparations of seafood, fowl, and sweets in Spain.

Your meal might include a "mosaic" of foie gras with vegetables, a salad composed of fresh asparagus, strips of salmon marinated in sesame and served with escabeche sauce, slices of raw and smoked salmon stuffed with caviar, a prize-winning terrine of seacrab floating on a lavishly decorated bed of cold seafood sauce, escalope of turbot served with coulis of sea urchins, fricassée of Bresse chicken served with spiny lobsters, sea bass with a mousseline of truffles, Spanish milk-fed lamb served with the juice of Boletus mushrooms and a *concasse* of tomatoes, a ragôut of sole containing fresh asparagus and Iranian caviar, rack of lamb gratinéed within an herb-flavored pastry crust, and an array of well-flavored game birds obtained in season from hunters throughout Catalonia and France. Both the selection of European cheeses and the changing array of freshly made desserts are nothing short of spectacular.

Reno, Tuset, 27. ☎ **200-91-29.**

Cuisine: CATALÁN/FRENCH. **Reservations:** Required. **Metro:** Diagonal.
Prices: Appetizers 1,000–2,900 ptas. ($7.10–$20.60); main courses 1,200–3,500 ptas. ($8.50–$24.90). AE, DC, MC, V.
Open: Lunch, Sun–Fri 1–4pm; dinner, Sun–Fri 8:30–11:30pm.

Considered one of the finest and most enduring restaurants in Barcelona, Reno boasts an impeccably mannered staff (formal but not intimidating) and an understated modern decor accented with black leather and oversized mirrors. A discreet row of sidewalk-to-ceiling windows hung with fine-mesh lace shelters diners from the prying eyes of those on the octagonal plaza outside. Specialties, influenced by the seasons and by the traditions of France, might include partridge simmered in wine or port sauce, a platter of assorted smoked fish (each painstakingly smoked on the premises), hake with anchovy sauce, filet of sole either stuffed with foie gras and truffles or grilled with anchovy sauce, Catalán-style civet of lobster, roast duck with a sauce of honey and sherry vinegar, and an appetizing array of pastries wheeled from table to table on

Frommer's Cool for Kids: Restaurants

Fast Food Places Burger King (see p.461), The Chicago Pizza Pie Factory (see p. 461), and Kentucky Fried Chicken (see p. 461) are good bets for fast food that the kids will enjoy.

Henry J. Bean's Bar and Grill (see p. 461) This place has sit-down meals that the kids will love.

Dulcinea (see p. 461) This makes a great refueling stop any time of the day—guaranteed to satisfy any chocoholic.

Poble Espanyol (see p. 470) A good introduction to Spanish food. All the restaurants here serve comparable food at comparable prices—let the kids choose what to eat.

a trolley. Dessert might also be one of several kinds of crêpes flambéed at your table. The restaurant, incidentally, was established in 1954 by the father of the present owner.

★ **Via Veneto,** Granduxer, 10-12. ☎ **200-72-44.**

Cuisine: CATALÁN/INTERNATIONAL. **Reservations:** Required. **Metro:** La Bonanova.
Prices: Appetizers 1,680–3,300 ptas. ($11.90–$23.40); main courses 2,200–3,990 ptas. ($15.60–$28.30). AE, DC, MC, V.
Open: Lunch, Mon–Fri 1:15–4pm; dinner, Mon–Sat 8:45–11:30pm.

With a soothing and dignified decor of calming colors and baroque swirls, this restaurant is known for its solid respectability and consistently well-prepared cuisine. Set a short walk from the Plaça de Francesc Macia, it offers such dishes as a tartare of fresh fish with caviar; roasted salt cod with potatoes; veal kidney with truffle sauce; loin of roast suckling pig with baby vegetables of the season; and filet steak served in a brandy, cream, and peppercorn sauce. There's a wide array of wines to accompany any meal. Dessert might be a richly textured combination of melted chocolate, cherries, Armagnac, and vanilla ice cream.

EXPENSIVE

★ **Eldorado Petit,** Dolors Monserdà, 51. ☎ **204-51-53.**

Cuisine: CATALÁN. **Reservations:** Required. **Metro:** Vía Augusta-Sarriá.
Prices: Appetizers 1,000–2,900 ptas. ($7.10–$20.60); main courses 1,500–3,500 ptas. ($10.70–$24.90). AE, DC, MC, V.
Open: Lunch, Mon–Sat 1:30–4pm; dinner, Mon–Sat 9am–midnight.

Located in a former private 19th-century villa, this restaurant serves a Catalán cuisine that's the rage of Barcelona. Very imaginative dishes are offered—brochette of crayfish; lasagne of fresh asparagus and salmon; peppers stuffed with pâté of *rascasse* (Mediterranean fish); and original variations of pork, lamb, and fish dishes. Diners can sit in either the enclosed courtyard or the high-ceilinged champagne-colored dining room.

★ **Florián,** Bertrand i Serra, 20. ☎ **212-46-27.**

Cuisine: CATALÁN. **Reservations:** Required. **Metro:** Tres Torres.
Prices: Appetizers 850–1,650 ptas. ($6–$11.70); main courses 1,400–3,100 ptas. ($9.90–$22). AE, DC, MC, V.
Open: Lunch, Mon–Sat 1–3:30pm; dinner, Mon–Sat 9–11:30pm. **Closed:** Holy Week, two weeks in Aug.

Famous as the domain of one of the classic husband-and-wife teams in Barcelona, this restaurant features a dining room hung with attractive pictures, plus the cuisine of Rosa Grau, who concocts the simple but flavorful house specialties from the kitchen in back. Her husband, Xavier García-Ruano, directs a dining room where calm, polite efficiency and dignity are carefully cultivated. Menu items change with the season but might include a warm salad of freshly grilled sardines, a salad of freshly made warm mozzarella with roasted anchovies, tagliatelle with quailmeat in mustard-flavored vinaigrette, a varied collection of seasonal mushrooms, white beans with shrimp and caviar, and roast beef with cabernet-sauvignon sauce.

★ **Roig Robí,** Séneca, 20. ☎ **218-92-22.**

Cuisine: CATALÁN/FRENCH. **Reservations:** Required. **Metro:** Diagonal.
Prices: Appetizers 850–1,950 ptas. ($6–$13.80); main courses 1,950–3,250 ptas. ($13.80–$23.10). AE, DC, MC, V.
Open: Lunch, Mon–Sat 1–4pm; dinner, Mon–Sat 9pm–midnight.

Excellent food from an imaginative kitchen and a warm welcome keep patrons coming back here. Begin by ordering an apéritif from the L-shaped oaken bar. Then head down a long corridor to a pair of flower-filled dining rooms. In warm weather, glass doors open onto a walled courtyard, ringed with cascades of ivy and shaded with willows and mimosa. Menu items include fresh beans with pine-nut sauce, codfish salad with pintos, lobster salad, ravioli stuffed with spring herbs, three different preparations of hake, chicken stuffed with foie gras, and a cockscomb salad.

MODERATE

Arcs de Sant Gervasi, Santaló, 103. ☎ **201-92-77.**

Cuisine: CATALÁN. **Reservations:** Recommended. **Metro:** Muntaner.
Prices: Appetizers 950–1,400 ptas. ($6.70–$9.90); main courses 1,900–2,400 ptas. ($13.50–$17). AE, DC, MC, V.
Open: Lunch, Tues–Sun 1–4pm; dinner, Tues–Sun 8:30–11:30pm.

North of the old town, Arcs de Sant Gervasi is sleekly decorated with such trappings as black-lacquer chairs. A nearby gallery fills the walls with pictures that are for sale. To begin, try cream-of-crab soup or Palafrugell "black rice." For a main dish, order tender slices of veal served with wild mushrooms in a delectable cognac-flavored sauce; the kid cutlets are also juicy and superb. For dessert, try the scooped-out pineapple filled with chopped fresh fruit and *crema catalana.* The restaurant is open every day of the year.

Moll de la Fusta & Barceloneta

EXPENSIVE

Can Majó, Almirante Aixada, 23. ☎ **221-54-55.**

Cuisine: SEAFOOD. **Reservations:** Recommended. **Metro:** Barceloneta.
Prices: Appetizers 750–1,400 ptas. ($5.30–$9.90); main courses 1,800–3,500 ptas. ($12.80–$24.90); fixed-price menu 6,000 ptas. ($42.60). AE, DC, MC, V.
Open: Lunch, Tues–Sun 1:30–4pm; dinner, Tues–Sun 9–11:30pm. **Closed:** Aug.

Located in the old fishing quarter of Barceloneta, Can Majo attracts many people from the fancier quarters who journey down here for a great seafood dinner. The Suárez-Majo family welcome you; they're still operating a business where their grandmother first opened a bar. Try a house specialty, *pelada* (Catalán for paella), perhaps starting with *entremeses* (hors d'oeuvres), from which you can select barnacles, oysters, prawns, whelks, clams, and crab—virtually whatever was caught that day. The clams with white beans are recommended. The classic all-vegetable gazpacho comes with fresh mussels and shrimp.

MODERATE

Blau Marí, Passeig del Moll de la Fusta. ☎ **310-10-15.**

Cuisine: CATALÁN. **Reservations:** Recommended. **Metro:** Drassanes.
Prices: Appetizers 650–1,400 ptas. ($4.60–$9.90); main courses 950–2,400 ptas. ($6.70–$17). MC, V.
Open: Drinks and snacks, daily 1pm–2 or 3am; lunch, daily 1–4pm; dinner, daily 9pm–midnight.

Set in a low-slung modern building between Barcelona's harborfront and the roaring traffic of the coastal boulevard, this is probably my favorite of the waterside seafood restaurants. Well directed, and staffed with a crew of white-jacketed employees, it's airy, sunny, and relaxed. A Catalán version of bouillabaisse, studded with shellfish, is prepared for two or more. Although formal service is provided, you can have snacks, coffee, or drinks, plus a tasty selection of tapas, throughout the day. It's refreshing to come here in the afternoon and sit out at the *chiringuito* (open-air bar).

Gambrinus, Passeig del Moll de la Fusta. ☎ **221-96-07.**

Cuisine: SEAFOOD. **Reservations:** Required. **Metro:** Drassanes.
Prices: Appetizers 750–1,800 ptas. ($5.30–$12.80); main courses 950–3,500 ptas. ($6.70–$24.90). AE, DC, MC, V.
Open: Daily 10am–2:30am.

Although this restaurant is respected for the well-prepared food served within, much of its fame derives from the enormous statue perched on its roof. Made of polychromed fiberglass by Javier Mariscal (creator of the Olympic mascot in 1992), the statue depicts a giant lobster whose waving tentacles and threatening claws attract looks of amazement from pedestrians and motorists.

Set beside the sea, in a low-slung modern building with lots of glass, the restaurant offers outdoor tables set on a pier, shaded with parasols. Menu items are priced from relatively inexpensive to very expensive, as, for example, anything made with lobster or hard-to-find shellfish. Meals can include such dishes as fish soup, fresh oysters, fried squid, shellfish paella, and various cuts and filets of grilled fish, depending on the day's catch. Many visitors opt for a drink at the boat-shaped bar before or after their meal.

Ramonet (Bar Xarello), Carrer Maquinista, 17. ☎ **319-30-64.**

Cuisine: SEAFOOD. **Reservations:** Recommended. **Metro:** Barceloneta.
Prices: Appetizers 675–2,100 ptas. ($4.80–$14.90); main courses 1,700–3,950 ptas. ($12.10–$28); fixed-price menus 4,200–5,950 ptas. ($29.80–$42.20). AE, DC, MC, V.
Open: Lunch, daily 10am–4pm; dinner, daily 7:30–11:30pm. **Closed:** Aug 15–Sept 15.

Located in a Catalán-style villa near the seaport, this rather expensive restaurant serves a large variety of fresh seafood, and has done so since 1763. The front room, with stand-up tables for seafood tapas, beer, and regional wine, is often crowded. In the two dining rooms in back, lined with wooden tables, you can choose from a wide variety of fish—shrimp, hake, and monkfish are almost always available. Other specialties include a portion of pungent anchovies, grilled mushrooms, braised artichokes, and a tortilla with spinach and beans. Mussels "from the beach" are also sold.

El Túnel, Ample, 33-35. ☎ **315-27-59.**

Cuisine: CATALÁN. **Reservations:** Recommended for lunch. **Metro:** San Jaume.
Prices: Appetizers 750–1,600 ptas. ($5.30–$11.40); main courses 1,200–2,500 ptas. ($8.50–$17.80). AE, DC, MC, V.
Open: Lunch, Tues–Sun 1:30–4pm; dinner, Tues–Sat 9–11:30pm. **Closed:** Apr.

This established and prestigious restaurant features a delectable fish soup, cannelloni with truffles, kidney beans with shrimp, roast kid, fish stew, and filet of beef with peppers. The service is eager, the wine cellar extensive. El Túnel lies close to the general post office.

Specialty Dining

DINING WITH A VIEW

La Balsa, Infanta Isabel, 4. ☎ **211-50-48.**

Cuisine: INTERNATIONAL. **Reservations:** Required. **Transportation:** Taxi.
Prices: Appetizers 700–1,700 ptas. ($5–$12.10); main courses 2,000–2,600 ptas. ($14.20–$18.50); fixed-price lunch 3,000 ptas. ($21.30). AE, DC, V.
Open: Lunch, Tues–Sat 2–3:30pm; dinner, Mon–Sat 9–11:30pm. **Closed:** Holy Week, reduced menu during Aug.

Poised on the uppermost level of a circular tower that was originally built as a water cistern, La Balsa offers a view over most of the surrounding cityscape. To reach it you must climb up to what was originally intended as the structure's rooftop. Glassed-in walls, awnings, and a verdant mass of potted plants create the decor. You're likely to be greeted by owner and founder Mercedes López before being seated. Menu items emerge from a cramped but well-organized kitchen several floors below. (The waiters here are reputedly the most athletic in Barcelona because they must run up and down the stairs carrying steaming platters.) Often booked several days in advance, the restaurant serves such dishes as a salad of broad beans (*judías verdes*) with strips of salmon in lemon-flavored vinaigrette, stewed veal with wild mushrooms, a salad of warm lentils with anchovies, pickled fresh salmon with chives, undercooked magret of duck served with fresh and lightly poached foie gras, and baked hake (flown in frequently from faraway Galicia) prepared in squid-ink sauce.

HOTEL DINING

Restaurant Diana, in the Hotel Ritz, Gran Vía de les Corts Catalanes, 668. ☎ **318-52-00.**

Cuisine: FRENCH. **Reservations:** Recommended. **Metro:** Arc del Triomf.
Prices: Appetizers 1,200–3,000 ptas. ($8.50–$21.30); main courses 1,900–3,500 ptas. ($13.50–$24.90); fixed-price menu Mon–Fri 3,300 ptas. ($23.40); fixed–price menu Sat–Sun 4,500 ptas. ($32). AE, DC, MC, V.
Open: Lunch, daily 1:30–4pm; dinner, daily 8:30–11pm.

At least part of the allure of dining here involves the chance to visit the most legendary hotel in Barcelona. Located on the lobby level of the Ritz, the restaurant is filled with French furnishings and accessories amid a color scheme of gilt and blue. The polite and well-trained staff serves such dishes as seafood salad flavored with saffron; filets of sole layered with lobster; filet mignon braised in cognac, cream, and peppercorn sauce; turbot in white-wine sauce; and a wide array of delectable desserts.

LOCAL FAVORITES

El Caballito Blanco, Mallorca, 196. ☎ **453-10-33.**

Cuisine: SEAFOOD/INTERNATIONAL. **Reservations:** Not required. **Metro:** Hospital Clínic.
Prices: Appetizers 600–1,650 ptas. ($4.30–$11.70); main courses 875–2,900 ptas. ($6.20–$20.60). MC, V.
Open: Lunch, Tues–Sun 1–3:45pm; dinner, Tues–Sat 9–10:45pm. **Closed:** Aug.

This old Barcelona standby, famous for its seafood, has long been popular among locals. The fluorescent-lit dining area does not offer much atmosphere, but the food is good, varied, and relatively inexpensive. The Little White Horse, in the Passeig de Gràcia area, features a huge selection, including rape, mussels marinara, and shrimp with garlic. If you don't want fish, try the grilled lamb cutlets. Several different pâtés and salads are offered. There's a bar to the left of the dining area.

★ $ **Los Caracoles,** Escudellers, 14. ☎ **302-31-85.**

Cuisine: CATALÁN/SPANISH. **Reservations:** Required. **Metro:** Drassanes.
Prices: Appetizers 850–1,400 ptas. ($6–$9.90); main courses 1,800–2,400 ptas. ($12.80–$17). AE, DC, MC, V.
Open: Daily 1pm–midnight.

Set in a labyrinth of narrow cobblestoned streets, Los Caracoles is one of the port's most colorful and popular restaurants—and it has been since 1835. It has won acclaim for its spit-roasted chicken and for its namesake, snails. A long, angular bar is located up front, with a two-level restaurant in back. You can watch the busy preparations in the kitchen, where dried herbs, smoked ham shanks, and garlic bouquets hang from the ceiling. In summer, tables are placed outside. The excellent food features all sorts of Spanish and Catalán specialties. Everybody from who's who of yesterday, from Richard Nixon to John Wayne, has stopped in, and Salvador Dalí was a devoted patron. Today's clientele isn't as legendary, but over the decades people keep coming in hordes to dine at this place.

Casa Leopoldo, Carrer Sant Rafael, 24. ☎ **441-30-14.**

Cuisine: CATALÁN/SEAFOOD. **Reservations:** Required. **Metro:** Liceu.
Prices: Appetizers 950–1,800 ptas. ($6.70–$12.80); main courses 1,600–8,000 ptas. ($11.40–$56.80). AE, MC, V.
Open: Lunch, Tues–Sun 1–4pm; dinner, Tues–Sat 9–11pm. **Closed:** Aug.

An excursion through the seedy streets of the Barri Xinés is part of the experience of coming to this restaurant. At night, though, it's safer to come by taxi. This colorful restaurant (founded in 1939) has some of the freshest seafood in town and caters to a loyal clientele. There's a popular stand-up tapas bar in front, then two dining rooms, one slightly more formal than the other. Specialties include eel with shrimp, barnacles, cuttlefish, seafood soup with shellfish, and deep-fried inch-long eels. Lobster is very expensive.

Els Quatre Gats, Montsió, 3. ☎ **302-41-40.**

Cuisine: CATALÁN. **Reservations:** Required Sat–Sun. **Metro:** Plaça de Catalunya.
Prices: Appetizers 750–1,500 ptas. ($5.30–$10.70); main courses 1,000–2,500 ptas. ($7.10–$17.80); fixed-price menu 1,600 ptas. ($11.40). AE, MC, V.
Open: Lunch, Mon–Sat 1–4pm; dinner, Mon–Sat 9pm–midnight; Café, daily 8am–2am.

A Barcelona legend the Four Cats was the favorite of Picasso and other artists. In their heyday, their works decorated the walls of the avant-garde café on a narrow cobblestoned street near the cathedral. It was the setting for poetry readings by Maragall, piano concerts by Albéniz and Granados, and murals by Ramón Casa.

Today a *tertulia* bar in the heart of the Barri Gòtic, it was long ago restored but retains its fine old look. The fixed-price meal, offered every day but Sunday, rates as one of the best bargains in town, considering the locale. The good food is prepared in an unpretentious style of Catalán cooking called *cuina de mercat* (based on whatever looked fresh at the market that day). The constantly changing menu reflects the seasons. No hot food is served on Sunday.

Siete Puertas (also known as 7 Portes), Passeig d'Isabel II, 14. ☎ **319-30-33.**

Cuisine: SEAFOOD **Reservations:** Required. **Metro:** Barceloneta.
Prices: Appetizers 810–3,320 ptas. ($5.80–$23.60); main courses 1,100–3,380 ptas. ($7.80–$24). AE, DC, MC, V.
Open: Daily 1pm–midnight.

This is a lunchtime favorite for businesspeople and an evening favorite for in-the-know clients who have made it their preferred restaurant in Catalonia. It's been going since 1836. Regional dishes include fresh herring with onions and potatoes, a different paella daily (sometimes with shellfish, for example, or with rabbit), and a wide array of fresh fish, succulent oysters, and a herb-laden stew of black beans with pork or white beans with sausage.

LATE-NIGHT DINING

Brasserie Flo, Jonqueras, 10. ☎ **319-31-02.**

Cuisine: FRENCH/INTERNATIONAL. **Reservations:** Recommended. **Metro:** Urquinaona.
Prices: Appetizers 750–3,000 ptas. ($5.30–$21.30); main courses 1,800–3,600 ptas. ($12.80–$25.60); fixed-price menu 3,000 ptas. ($21.30). AE, DC, MC, V.
Open: Lunch, daily 1–4pm; dinner, daily 8:30pm–1am.

The art deco dining room here has been compared to one on a transatlantic steamer at the turn of the century—it's spacious, palm-filled, comfortable, and air-conditioned. The food isn't overlooked either, and you might begin with fresh foie gras. The specialty is a large plate of choucroute (sauerkraut) served with a steamed hamhock. Also good are the shrimp in garlic, salmon tartare with vodka, and stuffed sole with spinach.

Egipte, Carrer Jerusalem, 3. ☎ **317-74-80.**

Cuisine: CATALÁN/SPANISH. **Reservations:** Recommended. **Metro:** Liceu.
Prices: Appetizers 850–1,500 ptas. ($6–$10.70); main courses 950–2,400 ptas. ($6.70–$17); fixed-price menu 1,200 ptas. ($8.50). AE, MC, V.
Open: Lunch, Mon–Sat 1–4pm; dinner, Mon–Sat 8:30pm–12:30am.

A favorite among the locals, this tiny place, located right behind the central marketplace, jumps day and night. The excellent menu includes spinach vol-au-vent (traditionally served with an egg on top), *lengua de ternera* (tongue), and *berengeras* (stuffed eggplant), a chef's specialty. The ingredients are fresh and the price is right.

TASCAS

Alt Heidelberg, Ronda Universitat, 5. ☎ **318-10-32.**

Cuisine: GERMAN/SPANISH. **Metro:** Universitat.
Prices: Tapas 400–1,100 ptas. ($2.80–$7.80); combination plates 1,000–1,450 ptas. ($7.10–$10.30). No credit cards.
Open: Daily 8am–2am.

Since the 1930s, this has been an institution in Barcelona, offering German beer on tap, a good selection of German sausages, and Spanish tapas. You can also enjoy full meals here—sauerkraut garni is a specialty. A glass of beer costs 235 pesetas ($1.70).

Bar del Pi, Plaça Sant Josep Oriol, 1. ☎ **302-21-23.**

Cuisine: TAPAS. **Metro:** Liceu.
Prices: Tapas 250–550 ptas. ($1.80–$3.90). No credit cards.

Open: Mon–Fri 9am–11pm; Sat 10am–10pm; Sun 10am–9:30pm.

One of the most famous bars in the Barri Gòtic, this establishment lies midway between two medieval squares, opening onto Églésia del Pi. You can sit inside at one of the cramped bentwood tables or stand at the crowded bar. In warm weather, take a table beneath the single plane tree on this landmark square. Tapas are limited; most visitors come to drink coffee, beer, or wine.

Bar Turó, Tenor Viñas, 1. ☎ **200-69-53.**

Cuisine: TAPAS. **Metro:** Muntaner.
Prices: Tapas 300–1,500 ptas. ($2.10–$10.70). No credit cards.
Open: Mon–Sat 9am–1am; Sun 11am–6pm.

Set in an affluent residential neighborhood north of the old town, Bar Turó serves some of the best tapas in town. In summer you can either sit outside or retreat to the narrow confines of the inside bar. There you can select from about 20 different kinds of tapas, including Russian salad, fried squid, and Serrano ham.

Bodega la Plata, Mercè, 28. ☎ **315-10-09.**

Cuisine: TAPAS. **Metro:** Barceloneta.
Prices: Tapas 200 ptas. ($1.40). No credit cards.
Open: Mon–Sat 8:30am–11pm.

Part of a trio of famous bodegas on this narrow medieval street, La Plata occupies a corner building whose two open sides allow richly aromatic cooking odors to permeate the neighborhood. This bodega contains a marble-topped bar and overcrowded tables. The culinary specialty is *raciones* (small plates) of deep-fried sardines (head and all). You can make a meal with two servings of these, coupled with the house's tomato, onion, and fresh anchovy salad.

Bodegueta, Rambla de Catalunya, 100. ☎ **215-48-94.**

Cuisine: TAPAS. **Metro:** Diagonal.
Prices: Tapas 160 ptas. ($1.10). No credit cards.
Open: Mon–Sat 8am–2am.

Founded in 1940, this old wine tavern specializes in Catalán sausage meats. Everything can be washed down with inexpensive Spanish wines.

Café Bar Padam, Rauric, 9. ☎ **302-50-62.**

Cuisine: TAPAS. **Metro:** Liceu.
Prices: Tapas 400–600 ptas. ($2.80–$4.30). No credit cards.
Open: Mon–Sat 7pm–2am.

The tapas served here are derived from time-honored Catalán culinary traditions, but the clientele and decor are modern, hip, and often gay. The café/bar lies on a narrow street in the Ciutat Vella, about three blocks east of the Ramble dels Caputxins. The only color in the black-and-white rooms comes from fresh flowers and modern paintings. Tapas include fresh anchovies and tuna, and cheese platters. Jazz is sometimes featured.

Las Campanas [Casa Marcos], Mercè, 21. ☎ **315-06-09.**

Cuisine: TAPAS. **Metro:** Barceloneta.
Prices: Tapas 250 ptas. ($1.80). No credit cards.
Open: Thurs–Tues noon–2am.

No sign announces its name—from the street Las Campanas looks like a storehouse for cured hams and wine bottles. At a long and narrow stand-up bar, patrons flock here for a *chorizo* (spicy sausage), which is then pinioned between two pieces of bread. Sausages are usually eaten with beer or red wine. The place opened in 1952, and nothing has changed since then. A tape recorder plays nostalgia favorites, everything from Edith Piaf to the Andrews Sisters.

Casa Tejada, Tenor Viñas, 3. ☎ **200-73-41.**

Cuisine: TAPAS. **Metro:** Muntaner.
Prices: Tapas 250–2,000 ptas. ($1.80–$14.20). V.
Open: Daily 10am–2am.

Covered with rough stucco and decorated with hanging hams, Casa Tejada (established in 1964) offers some of Barcelona's best tapas. Arranged behind a glass display case, they include such specialties as marinated fresh tuna, German-style potato salad, five preparations of squid (including one that's stuffed), and ham salad. For variety, quantity, and quality, this place is hard to beat. There's outdoor dining in summer.

Jamón Jamón, Mestre Nicolau, 4. ☎ **209-41-03.**

Cuisine: TAPAS. **Metro:** Muntaner.
Prices: Tapas 1,200–1,600 ptas. ($8.50–$11.40). No credit cards.
Open: Mon–Sat 9am–4pm and 6pm–1am.

Located north of Avinguda Diagonal, near Plaça de Francesc Maria, this establishment has a modern interior of gray granite and chrome, a deliberate contrast to the traditional pork products that are the tasca's specialty. Entire hams from Heulva, deep in the south of Andalusia, are impaled on steel braces, evoking the Spanish Inquisition. The ham is laboriously carved and trimmed before you into paper-thin slices.

La Jarra, Mercè, 9. ☎ **315-17-59.**

Cuisine: TAPAS. **Metro:** Barceloneta.
Prices: Tapas 200–352 ptas. ($1.40–$2.50). No credit cards.
Open: Thurs–Tues 10:30am–1am.

La Jarra occupies a tile-covered L-shaped room that's somewhat bleak in appearance, yet residents claim it is one of the most authentic tapas bars in the old town. You can order a ración of marinated mushrooms or well-seasoned artichokes Rioja style, but the culinary star is the ever-present haunch of *jamón canario* (Canary Island ham), which is carved before your eyes into lean, succulent morsels served with boiled potatoes, olive oil, and lots of salt. It resembles roast pork in flavor and appearance.

Rey de la Gamba, Joan de Borbo, 53. ☎ **221-75-98.**

Cuisine: TAPAS/SHELLFISH. **Metro:** Barceloneta.
Prices: Tapas 800–1,850 ptas. ($5.70–$13.10). V.
Open: Daily 11am–1am.

The name of this place means "king of prawns," but this restaurant could also be called the House of Mussels since it sells more of that shellfish. In the old fishing village of Barceloneta, dating from the 18th century, this place packs them in, especially on weekends. A wide array of seafood is sold, along with cured ham—the combination is considered a tradition.

FAST FOOD & CAFETERIAS

For those travelers who miss good old American food, don't fret—there are plenty of fast-food joints. It may not be as adventurous as trying authentic Spanish cuisine, but you'll definitely please the kids!

Burger King, Rambla de Canaletes, 135 (☎ **302-54-29**); Metro: Plaça de Catalunya), is open Sunday through Friday, 10am to midnight; Saturday 10am to 1am.

Chicago Pizza Pie Factory, Carrer de Provença, 300 (☎ **215-94-15;** Metro: Passeig de Gràcia), offers pizzas for 1,275 to 3,000 pesetas ($9.10 to $21.30), the latter big enough for four. It's open daily from 12:30pm to 1am; happy hour runs from 6 to 9pm.

Viena, Rambla dels Estudis, 115 (☎ **317-1492;** Metro: Plaça de Catalunya), is Barcelona's most elegant fast-food place. Waiters wearing Viennese vests serve croissants with Roquefort for breakfast and, later in the day, toasted ham sandwiches, hamburgers with onions, and pasta with tomato sauce. Meals cost from 900 pesetas ($6.40). Service is Monday through Saturday, 9am to 1am; Sunday, 2pm to 2am.

Kentucky Fried Chicken, Ferran, 2 (☎ **412-51-54**); Metro: Drassanes), is open daily from 11am to midnight. A bucket containing nine pieces of chicken, enough for a meal for two, costs 1,600 pesetas ($11.40).

FOR THE SWEET TOOTH

Dulcinea, Via Petrixol, 2. ☎ **302-68-24.**

Cuisine: CHOCOLATE. **Metro:** Plaça de Catalunya or Liceu.
Prices: Cup of chocolate 275 ptas. ($2). No credit cards.
Open: Daily 9am–1pm and 5–9pm.

At this, the most famous chocolate shop in Barcelona, the specialty is *melindros* (sugar-topped soft-sided biscuits), which the regulars who flock here love to dunk into the very thick hot chocolate—so thick, in fact, that imbibing it resembles eating a melted chocolate bar.

DEPARTMENT-STORE DINING

El Corte Inglés, Plaça de Catalunya, 14 (☎ **302-12-12;** Metro: Plaça de Catalunya), and Avinguda Diagonal, 617 (☎ **332-40-11**), offers combination plates and a buffet, with complete meals for 2,600 pesetas ($18.50).

Getting a table may be more of an adventure in **Galerías Preciados,** Avinguda Portal de l'Angel, 19 (☎ **317-00-00;** Metro: Plaça de Catalunya). Meals cost around 1,400 pesetas ($9.90). Both store restaurants have buffets Monday to Saturday from 12:30 to 4pm.

AMERICAN FOOD

Henry J. Bean's Bar and Grill, La Granada de Penedés, 14-16. ☎ **218-29-98.**

Cuisine: AMERICAN. **Reservations:** Not accepted after 9pm Fri–Sat. **Metro:** Diagonal.
Prices: Appetizers 350–850 ptas. ($2.50–$6); main courses 1,200–1,500 ptas. ($8.50–$10.70). AE, DC, MC, V.
Open: Daily 12:30pm–1:30am.

Food is cheap, plentiful, and savory in this unassuming restaurant filled with Americana. Have a great smokehouse burger or perhaps chili con carne, stuffed mushrooms, nachos, or barbecued baby back ribs. No meal is complete without pecan or mud pie for dessert. Half-price drinks are de rigueur during happy hour, between 7 and 9pm and all night Wednesday.

VEGETARIAN FARE

Biocenter, Pintor Fortuny, 25. ☎ **301-45-83.**

Cuisine: VEGETARIAN. **Reservations:** Not required. **Metro:** Plaça Catalunya.
Prices: Appetizers 450–575 ptas. ($3.20–$4.10); main courses 600–950 ptas. ($4.30–$6.70). Fixed-price menu 975 ptas. ($6.90). No credit cards.
Open: Bar, Mon–Sat 9am–11pm. Food, lunch only, Mon–Sat 1–5pm.

This is the largest and best-known vegetarian restaurant in Barcelona, the creation of Catalán-born entrepreneur Pep Cañameras, who is likely to be directing the service from his position behind the bar in front. Many clients, vegetarians or not, congregate over drinks in the front room. Some continue on for meals in one of two ground-floor dining rooms, whose walls are decorated with the paintings and artworks of the owner and his colleagues. There's a salad bar, an array of vegetarian casseroles, such soups as gazpacho or lentil, and a changing array of seasonal vegetables. No meat and no fish of any kind are served.

PICNIC FARE & WHERE TO EAT IT

The best place in all Barcelona to buy the makings of your picnic is **Mercat de la Boquería,** lying in the center of the Rambles (metro: Liceu). This is the old marketplace of Barcelona. You'll jostle elbows with butchers and fish mongers in bloodied smocks and see saleswomen selling cheeses and sausages. Much of the food is uncooked, but hundreds of items are already prepared and you can even buy a bottle of wine or mineral water.

Now for where to have your picnic. Right in the heart of Barcelona is the **Parc de la Ciutadella** (see "Parks & Gardens" in Chapter 14), at the southeast section of the district known as the Barri de la Ribera, site of the Picasso Museum. After lunch, take the kids to the park zoo and later go out on the lake in a rented rowboat.

It's more scenic to picnic in **Montjuïc,** site of the 1992 Summer Olympics. After your picnic, you can enjoy the amusement park or walk through the Poble Espanyol, a re-created Spanish village.

14

What to See & Do in Barcelona

BARCELONA, LONG A MEDITERRANEAN CENTER OF COMMERCE, IS FAST EMERGING as one of the focal points of European tourism, a role that reached its zenith during the 1992 Summer Olympic Games. Spain's second-largest city is also its most cosmopolitan and avant-garde.

Because its rich historical past extends back for centuries; Barcelona is filled with landmark buildings and world-class museums offering many sightseeing opportunities. These include Antoni Gaudí's Sagrada Familia; the Museu Picasso; Barcelona's Gothic cathedral; and Les Rambles, the famous tree-lined promenade cutting through the heart of the old quarter.

The capital of Catalonia, Barcelona sits at the northeast end of the Costa Brava, Spain's gateway to the Mediterranean. A half-hour flight east will land you in one of the Balearic Islands—Majorca, Ibiza, or Minorca. You can also branch out from Barcelona to one of the cities of historic interest in its environs, including the old Roman city of Tarragona or the monastery at Montserrat.

To begin, however, you will want to take in the artistic and intellectual aura of the unique seafaring city of Barcelona. The people take justifiable pride in their Catalán heritage, and they are eager to share it with you. Many of these sights can be covered on foot, and I have included a number of walking tours.

The multifaceted array of nightlife (Barcelona is a *big* bar town), shopping possibilities, and sports programs are also covered in this chapter, along with some organized tours, special events, and trips to the wine country of Catalonia. It makes for some hefty sightseeing, and you'll need plenty of time to take it all in.

Suggested Itineraries

If You Have One Day

Spend the morning following my walking tour of the **Barri Gòtic,** taking in all of the highlights of this ancient district. In the afternoon visit Antoni Gaudí's unfinished cathedral, **La Sagrada Familia,** before returning to the heart of the city for a walk down Les Rambles. To cap your day, take the funicular to the fountains at Montjuïc or go to the top of Tibidabo for an outstanding view of Barcelona and its harbor.

If You Have Two Days

Spend Day 1 as described above. On Day 2 visit the **Museu Picasso,** which is housed in two Gothic mansions. Then stroll through the surrounding district, the **Barri de la Ribera,** which is filled with Renaissance mansions. Follow this with a ride to the top of the **Columbus Monument** for a panoramic view of the harborfront. Have a seafood lunch at La Barcelonata, and in the afternoon stroll up Les Rambles again. In the afternoon explore Montjuïc and visit the Museu d'Art de Catalunya. End the day with a meal at Los Caracoles, the most famous restaurant in the old city, just off Les Rambles.

If You Have Three Days

Spend Days 1 and 2 as described above. On Day 3, make a pilgrimage to the monastery of **Montserrat** to see the venerated Black Virgin and a host of artistic and scenic attractions. Try to time your visit to hear the 50-member boys' choir.

If You Have Five Days

Spend your first three days as described above. On Day 4 take a morning walk in modernist Barcelona and have lunch on the pier at a restaurant called Moll de la Fusta.

In the afternoon visit Montjuïc again to tour the **Fundació Joan Miró** and walk through the **Poble Espanyol,** a miniature village created for the 1929 World's Fair. On day five take another excursion from the city. If you're interested in history, visit the former Roman city of **Tarragona** to the south. If you want to **unwind on a beach,** head south to Sitges or north to the Costa Brava to Tossà de Mar.

1 The Top Attractions

★ **La Sagrada Familia,** Mallorca, 401. ☎ **455-02-47.**

Gaudí's incomplete masterpiece is one of the more idiosyncratic artworks of Spain—if you have time to see only one Catalán landmark, make it this one. Begun in 1882 and still incomplete at Gaudí's death in 1926, this incredible cathedral—the Church of the Holy Family—rates as one of the bizarre wonders of Spain. The lanquid, amorphous structure embodies the essence of Gaudí's style, which some have described as art nouveau run rampant. Work continues on the structure but without any sure idea of what Gaudí intended. Some say that the cathedral will be completed in the mid-21st century.

Admission: 600 ptas. ($4.30), including a 12-minute video about the religious and secular works of Gaudí. An elevator takes you to the top (about 200 feet) for an additional 150 ptas. ($1.10).

Open: Jan–Feb and Nov–Dec, daily 9am–6pm; Mar–Apr and Oct, daily 9am–7pm; May and Sept, daily 9am–8pm; June–Aug, daily 9am–9pm. **Metro:** Sagrada Familia.

★ **Catedral de Barcelona,** Plaça de la Seu, s/n. ☎ **315-15-54.**

Barcelona's cathedral stands as a celebrated example of Catalonian Gothic. Except for the 19th-century west facade, the basilica was begun at the end of the 13th century and completed in the mid-15th century. The three naves, cleaned and illuminated, have splendid Gothic details. With its large bell towers, blending of medieval and Renaissance styles, beautiful cloister, high altar, side chapels, sculptured choir, and Gothic arches, it ranks as one of the most impressive cathedrals in Spain. Vaulted galleries in the cloister surround a garden of magnolias, medlars, and palm trees; the galleries are further enhanced by forged iron grilles. The historian Cirici called this place the loveliest oasis in Barcelona. The cloister, illuminated on Saturdays and fiesta days, also contains a museum of medieval art. The most notable work displayed is the 15th-century *La Pietat* of Bartolomé Bermejo. At noon on Sunday you can see a *sardana,* the Catalonian folk dance, performed in front of the cathedral.

Admission: Cathedral, free; museum, 25 ptas. (20¢).

Open: Cathedral, daily 8am–1:30pm and 4–7:30pm. Cloister museum, daily 11am–1pm. **Metro:** Jaume I.

★ **Barri Gòtic.**

This is the old aristocratic quarter of Barcelona, parts of which have survived from the Middle Ages. Spend at least two or three hours exploring its narrow streets and squares; start by walking up the Carrer del Carme, east of the Rambles. A nighttime stroll takes on added drama, but exercise extreme caution.

The buildings, for the most part, are austere and sober, the cathedral being the crowning achievement. Roman ruins and the vestiges of 3rd-century walls add further interest. This area is intricately detailed and filled with many attractions that are easy to miss. For a tour of the Barri Gòtic, see Walking Tour 1, later in this chapter.

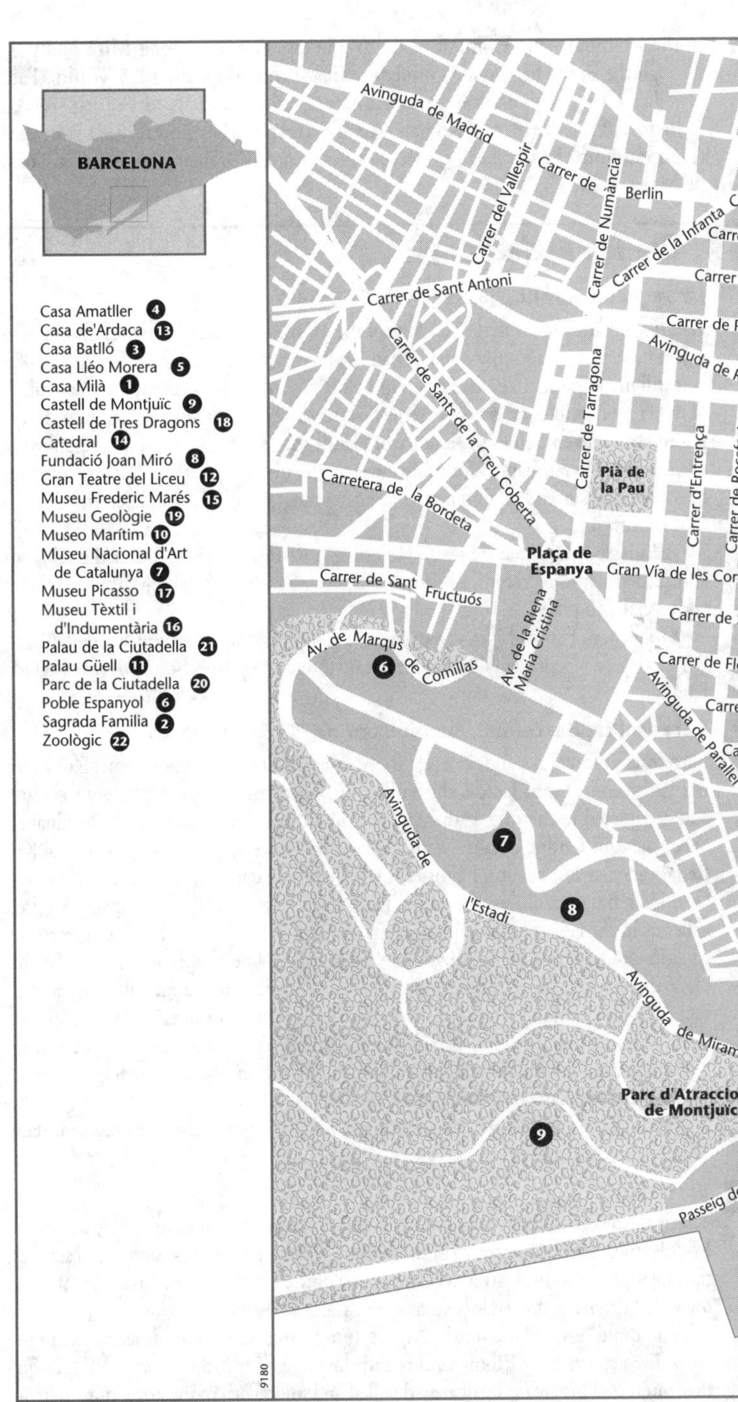

BARCELONA
Casa Amatller 4
Casa de'Ardaca 13
Casa Batlló 3
Casa Lléo Morera 5
Casa Milà 1
Castell de Montjuïc 9
Castell de Tres Dragons 18
Catedral 14
Fundació Joan Miró 8
Gran Teatre del Liceu 12
Museu Frederic Marés 15
Museu Geològie 19
Museo Marítim 10
Museu Nacional d'Art de Catalunya 7
Museu Picasso 17
Museu Tèxtil i d'Indumentària 16
Palau de la Ciutadella 21
Palau Güell 11
Parc de la Ciutadella 20
Poble Espanyol 6
Sagrada Familia 2
Zoològic 22
Avinguda de Madrid
Carrer del Vallespir
Carrer de Berlin
Carrer de Numància
Carrer de la Infanta Carlota
Carrer de Sant Antoni
Carrer de Sants de la Creu Coberta
Carrer de Tarragona
Avinguda de Roma
Carrer d'Entrença
Carrer de Rocafort
Pià de la Pau
Carretera de la Bordeta
Plaça de Espanya
Gran Vía de les Corts C
Carrer de Sant Fructuós
Av. de Marqus de Comillas
Av. de la Riena Maria Cristina
Carrer de Florid
Avinguda de Parallel
Avinguda de l'Estadi
Avinguda de Miramar
Parc d'Atraccions de Montjuïc
Passeig de Jo
9180

Barcelona Attractions

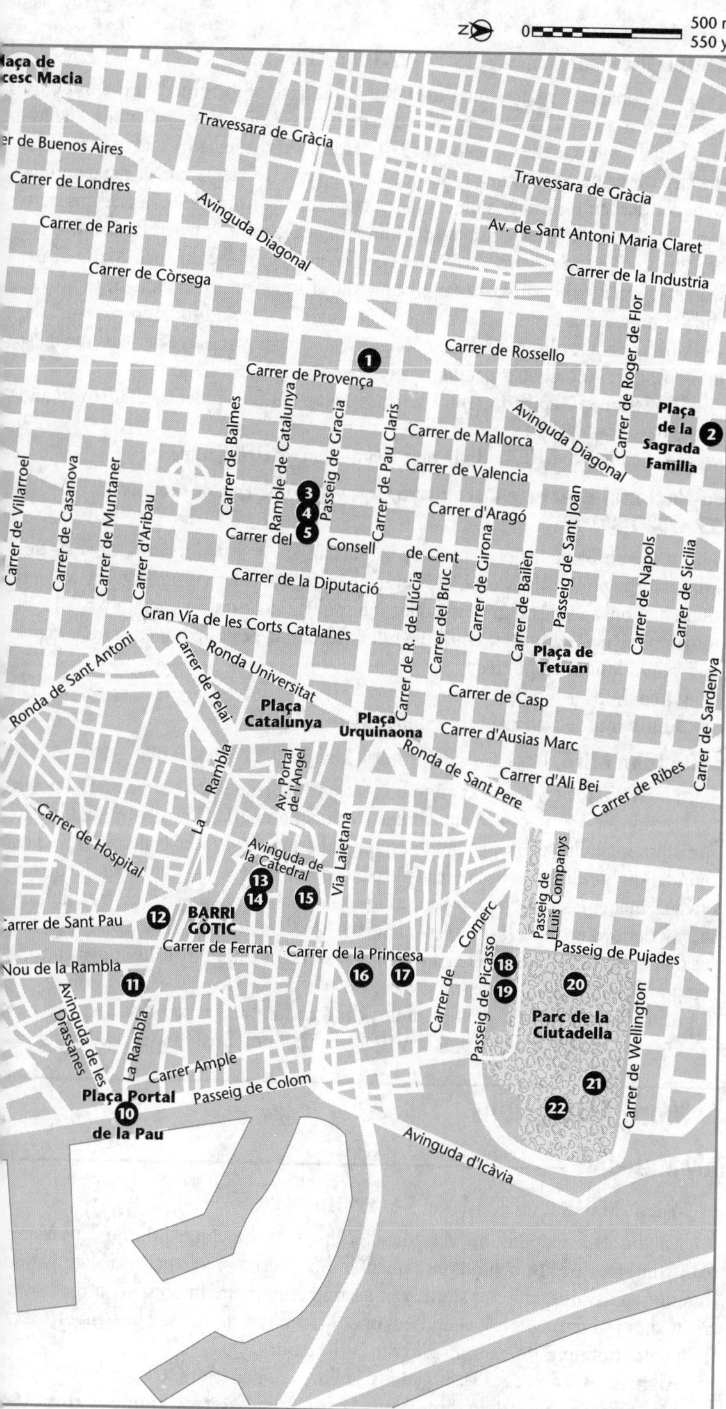

★ **Museu Picasso,** Montcada, 15-17. ☎ **319-63-10.**

Two old converted palaces on a medieval street have been turned into a museum housing works by Pablo Picasso, who donated some 2,500 of his paintings, engravings, and drawings to the museum in 1970. Picasso was particularly fond of Barcelona, the city where he spent much of his formative youth. In fact, some of the paintings were done when Picasso was nine. One portrait, dating from 1896, depicts his stern aunt, Tía Pepa. Another, completed at the turn of the century when Picasso was 16, depicts *Science and Charity* (his father was the model for the doctor). Many of the works, especially the early paintings, show the artist's debt to van Gogh, El Greco, and Rembrandt; a famous series, *Las Meninas* (1957), is said to "impersonate" the work of Velázquez. From his blue period, the *La Vie* drawings are perhaps the most interesting. His notebooks contain many sketches of Barcelona scenes.

Admission: 500 ptas. ($3.60) adults; 250 ptas. ($1.80) students; children 17 and under free.

Open: Tues–Sat 10am–8pm; Sun 10am–3pm. **Metro:** Jaume I.

Museu Nacional d'Art de Catalunya, Palau Nacional, Parc de Montjuïc. ☎ **423-71-99.**

This museum is the major depository of Catalán art, a virtual treasure trove of this important region of the world. However, the national palace is undergoing renovations, and only a small part of its collection is likely to be on view, mainly a series of romanesque wall paintings. Until the full collection is exhibited once more, temporary exhibitions are mounted.

Open: Wed–Mon 9am–9pm.

Admission: Depends on the exhibit. **Metro:** Espayna.

Fundació Joan Miró, Plaça de Neptú, Parc de Montjuïc. ☎ **329-19-08.**

Born in 1893, Joan Miró went on to become one of Spain's greatest painters, known for his whimsical abstract forms and brilliant colors. Some 10,000 works by this Catalán surrealist, including paintings, graphics, and sculptures, have been collected here. The foundation building has been greatly expanded in recent years, following the design of Catalán architect Josep Lluís Sert, a close personal friend of Miró's. An exhibition in a modern wing charts (in a variety of media) Miró's complete artistic evolution from his first drawings at the age of eight to his last works. Temporary exhibitions on contemporary art are also frequently shown.

Admission: 500 ptas. ($3.60) adults; children nine and under free.

Open: Tues–Sat 11am–7pm; Sun 10:30am–2:30pm. **Bus:** 61 at Plaça d'Espanya.

2 More Attractions

Mainly Museums

Museu Frederic Marès, Plaça de Sant Iù, 5-6. ☎ **310-58-00.**

One of the biggest repositories of medieval sculpture in the region is the Frederic Marès Museum, located just behind the cathedral. It's housed in an ancient palace whose interior courtyards, chiseled stone, and soaring ceilings are impressive in their own right, an ideal setting for the hundreds of polychrome sculptures. The sculpture section dates from pre-Roman times to the 20th century.

Admission: 250 ptas. ($1.80) adults; children under 16 free.

Open: Tues–Sat 10am–5pm; Sun 10am–2pm. **Metro:** Jaume I. **Bus:** 16, 17, or 19.

Museu Marítim, Portal de la Pau, 1. ☎ **318-32-45.**

At the edge of the harbor near the southern end of Les Rambles, the Maritime Museum, with its stone-vaulted ceilings, displays figureheads and nautical instruments and artifacts. The most outstanding exhibition here is a reconstruction of *La Galería Real* of Don Juan of Austria, a lavish royal galley. Another special exhibit features a map by Gabriel de Vallseca that was owned by explorer Amerìgo Vespucci. The nautical displays are housed in a 14th-century royal boatyard, called Drassanes Reials.

Admission: 200 ptas. ($1.40) adults; children 14 and under free.

Open: Tues–Sat 9:30am–1pm and 4–7pm; Sun 10am–2pm. **Closed:** Hols. **Metro:** Drassanes.

Museu de la Ciència, Teodor Roviralta, 55. ☎ **212-60-50.**

The Museu de la Ciènia of the "La Caixa" Foundation is one of the most popular in Barcelona, with more than 500,000 people visiting annually. Its modern design and hands-on activities have made it the most important science museum in Spain and a major cultural attraction.

Visitors can touch, listen, watch, and participate in a variety of hands-on exhibits. From the beauty of life in the sea to the magic of holograms, the museum offers a world of science to discover. Watch the world turn beneath the Foucault Pendulum; ride on a human gyroscope; hear a friend whisper from 20 meters away; feel an earthquake; or use the tools of a scientist to examine intricate life forms with microscopes and video cameras.

More than 300 exhibits explore the wonders of science, from optics to space travel to life sciences. In the Optics and Perception exhibits visitors can interact with prisms,

Frommer's Favorite Barcelona Experiences

A Walk Through the Barri Gòtic You'll pass through fifteen centuries of history in one district.

Watching the Sardana The national dance of Catalonia is performed at noon at the Plaça de San Jaume, in front of the cathedral.

A Trip to the Top of Montjuïc This will provide enough amusement to fill three days.

Soaking Up Bar Culture Bars in all shapes and sizes are the chic places to go at night. Barcelona has more bars than any other city in Spain.

Drinking Cava in a Xampanyería Enjoy a glass of bubbly—Barcelona style. The wines are excellent, and Cataláns swear that their cavas taste better than French champagne.

A Tour of Barcelona's Harbor Stroll from the pier in front of the Columbus Monument to the breakwater.

Exploring the Museum Picasso Examine the evolution of a genius from the age of 14.

Marveling at La Sagrada Familia Gaudí's "sand-castle cathedral" is a testimony to the architect's talent and religious belief.

A Trip to Pobla Espanyol This is an artificial village, to be sure, but it gives you a chance to see the architecture of all of Spain without leaving Barcelona.

lenses, and holograms and walk inside a kaleidoscope. In the Living Planet area baby sharks swim, a tornado swirls, and plants magically change their form when touched.

In the Mechanics exhibit, visitors can lift a 40kg weight with little effort. The use of lasers and musical instruments provides a fun way to learn about sound and light waves. Throughout the exhibits, there are computers to help you delve deeper into various topics. Visitors can also walk inside a submarine and make weather measurements in a working weather station. For those who want to explore new worlds, there are Planetarium shows where the beauty of the night sky surrounds the audience. Special programs explore everything from the night sky to exploding supernovas.

Admission: Museum and planetarium, 800 ptas. ($5.70) adults; 600 ptas. ($4.30) children 16 and under.

Open: Tues–Sun 10am–8pm. **Bus:** 17, 22, 58, or 73.

Fundació Antoni Tàpies, Aragó, 255. ☎ **487-03-15.**

When it opened in 1990, this became the third museum in Barcelona devoted to the work of a single artist. In 1984 the Catalán artist Antoni Tàpies set up the foundation bearing his name, and the city of Barcelona donated an ideal site: the old Montaner i Simon publishing house near the Passeig de Gràcia in the 19th-century Eixample. One of the landmark buildings of Barcelona, the brick-and-iron structure was built between 1881 and 1884 by that exponent of Catalán modernism, architect Lluís Domènech i Montaner. The core of the museum is a collection of works by Tàpies (most contributed by the artist himself), covering the different stages of his career as it evolved into abstract expressionism. Here you can see his entire spectrum of mediums: painting, assemblage, sculpture, drawing, and ceramics. His associations with Picasso and Miró are apparent. The largest of all of Tàpies' works is on top of the building itself: a gigantic sculpture made from 9,000 feet of metal wiring and tubing, entitled *Cloud and Chair.*

Admission: 400 ptas. ($2.80) adults; 200 ptas. ($1.40) children.

Open: Tues–Sun 11am–8pm. **Metro:** Passeig de Gràcia.

Museu d'Art Modern, Plaça d'Armes, Parc de la Ciutadella. ☎ **319-57-28.**

This museum shares a wing of the Palau de la Ciutadella with the Catalonian Parliament. Constructed in the 1700s, it once formed part of Barcelona's defenses because it was used as an arsenal. In time it became a royal residence before being turned into a museum early in this century. Its collection of art focuses on the early 20th century and features the work of Catalán artists, including Martí Alsina, Vayreda, Casas, Fortuny, and Rusiñol. The collection also encompasses some 19th-century Romantic and neoclassical works, as well as modernist furniture (including designs by architect Puig i Cadafalch).

Admission: 300 ptas. ($2.10) adults; children 17 and under free.

Open: Wed–Mon 9am–9pm. **Metro:** Arc de Triomf.

Monestir de Pedralbes, Baixada del Monestir, 9. ☎ **203-92-82.**

One of the oldest buildings in Pedralbes (the city's wealthiest residential area) is this monastery founded in 1326 by Elisenda de Montcada, queen of Jaume II. Still a convent, the establishment is also the mausoleum of the queen, who is buried in its Gothic church. Walk through the cloisters, with nearly two dozen arches on each side, rising three stories high. A small chapel contains the chief treasure of the monastery, murals by Ferrer Bassa, who was considered the major artist of Catalonia in the 1300s.

This monastery was considered a minor attraction of Barcelona until 1993 when 72 paintings and 8 sculptures from the famed Thyssen-Bornemisza collection now housed in Madrid went on permanent display here. Among the more outstanding works of art are Fra Angelico's *The Virgin of Humility,* plus 20 paintings from the early German Renaissance period, including works by Lucas Cranach. Italian Renaissance paintings range from the end of the 15th century to the middle of the 16th century, as exemplified by works from Dosso Dossi, Lorenzo Lotto, Tintoretto, Veronese, and Titian. The baroque era is also represented, and such old masters as Rubens, Zurbarán, and Velázquez are displayed.

Admission: 300 ptas. ($2.10) adults; 175 ptas. ($1.20) students and senior citizens; free ages 11 or under.

Open: Tues–Fri and Sun 10am–2pm; Sat 10am–5pm. **Metro:** Reina Elisenda. **Bus:** 22, 63, 64, 75, or 114.

Museu Palau Reial de Pedralbes, Avinguda Diagonal, 686. ☎ **203-75-01.**

Set in a beautiful park, this palace was constructed as a municipal gift to King Alfonso XIII. He didn't get to make much use of it, however, as he was forced into exile in 1931. Many of its furnishings and objets d'art were imported from Italy. Much personal memorabilia of the royal family remains. Some local visitors come here just to walk through the gardens, which have ornamental statues and charming fountains. There's a Museo de las Carrozas on the grounds, with some antique carriages.

Admission: 250 ptas. ($1.80).

Open: Tues–Fri 10am–1pm and 4–6pm; Sat–Sun 10am–1:30pm. **Metro:** Palau Reial.

Palau Reial, Plaça del Rei. ☎ **315-09-57.**

Former palace of the counts of Barcelona, this later became the residence of the kings of Aragón—hence, the name of its plaza (Kings' Square). It is believed that Columbus was received here by Isabella and Ferdinand when he returned from his first voyage to the New World. Here, some believe, the monarchs got their first look at a Native American. Columbus may have been received in the Saló del Tinell, a banqueting hall with a wood-paneled ceiling held up by half a dozen arches. The hall dates from the 14th century. Rising five stories above the hall is the Torre del Reí Martí, a series of porticoed galleries.

Admission: 250 ptas. ($1.80).

Open: Mon 3:30–8pm; Tues–Sat 9am–8pm; Sun 9am–1:30pm. **Bus:** 16, 17, 19, 22, or 45.

Museu d'Història de la Ciutat, Plaça del Rei. ☎ **315-11-11.**

Connected to the Royal Palace (see above), this museum traces the history of the city from its early days as a Roman colony to its role as the city of the 1992 Summer Olympics. The museum is housed in a Catalán-Mediterranean mansion from the 1400s called the Padellás House. Many of the exhibits date from Roman days, with much else from medieval times.

Admission: 300 ptas. ($2.10).

Open: Tues–Sat 10am–2pm and 4–8pm; Sun 10am–2pm. **Bus:** 16, 17, 19, 22, or 45.

Museu Arqueològic de Barcelona, Passeig de Santa Madrona, 39-41. Parc de Montjuïc. ☎ **423-21-49.**

Occupying the former Palace of Graphic Arts, built for the 1929 World's Fair, the Museu Arqueològic reflects the long history of this Mediterranean port city, beginning with prehistoric Iberian artifacts. The collection includes articles from the Greek, Roman (glass, ceramics, mosaics, bronzes), and Carthaginian periods. Some of the more interesting relics were excavated in the ancient Greco-Roman city of Empúries in Catalonia, and other parts of the collection came from the Balearic Islands.

Admission: 200 ptas. ($1.40) adults; children free.

Open: Tues–Sat 9:30am–1:30pm and 3:30–7pm; Sun 9:30am–2pm. **Metro:** Espanya. **Bus:** 55.

Poble Espanyol, Marqués de Comilias, Parc de Montjuïc. ☎ **325-78-66.**

In this re-created Spanish village, built for the 1929 World's Fair, various regional architectural styles—from the Levante to Galicia—are reproduced—in all, 115 life-size reproductions of buildings and monuments, ranging from the 10th through the 20th centuries. At the entranceway, for example, stands a facsimile of the gateway to the walled city of Ávila. The center of the village has an outdoor café where you can sit and have drinks. Numerous shops sell crafts and souvenir items from all of the provinces, and in some of them you can see artists at work, printing fabric and blowing glass. Ever since the 1992 Olympics, the village has offered 14 restaurants of varying styles, one disco, and eight musical bars. In addition, visitors can see an audiovisual presentation about Barcelona and Catalonia in general.

Admission: 650 ptas. ($4.60) adults; children 6 and under free. Audiovisual hall an extra 300 ptas. ($2.10) (children 6 and under free).

Open: Mon 9am–7pm; Tues–Thurs 9am–2pm; Fri–Sat 9am–4pm; Sun 9am–2pm. **Metro:** Espanya, then free red double-decker bus.

Monument à Colom, Portal de la Pau. ☎ **302-52-34.**

This monument to Christopher Columbus was erected at the harborfront of Barcelona on the occasion of the Universal Exhibition of 1888. It is divided into three parts, the first being a circular structure, raised by four stairways (19½ feet wide) and eight iron heraldic lions. On the plinth are eight bronze bas-reliefs depicting the principal feats of Columbus. (The originals were destroyed—the present ones are copies.) The second part is the base of the column, consisting of an eight-sided polygon, four sides of which act as buttresses; each side contains sculptures. The third part is formed by the column itself, Corinthian in style and rising 167 feet. The capital boasts representations of Europe, Asia, Africa, and America—all linked together. Finally, over a princely crown and a hemisphere recalling the newly discovered part of the globe, is a 25-foot-high bronze statue of Columbus himself by Rafael Ataché. Inside the iron column, an elevator ascends to the mirador. From there, a panoramic view of Barcelona and its harbor unfolds.

Admission: 225 ptas. ($1.60) adults; 125 ptas. (90¢) children 4-12. Free, children 3 and under.

Open: Sept 26–Mar 26, Tues–Sat 10am–2pm and 3:30–7pm, Sun and holidays 10am–7pm; Mar 27–May 31, Tues–Sat 10am–2pm and 3:30–8pm, Sun and holidays 10am–8pm; June 1–Sept 25 daily 9am–9pm. **Metro:** Drassanes.

Torre de Collserola, Carretera de Vallvidrera, Turó de la Vilana. ☎ **211-79-42.**

Some city planners considered this the most ambitious building program of the 1992 Olympics. When it was perceived that Barcelona lacked a state-of-the-art television transmitter, a team of engineers whipped up plans for a space-age needle. Completed within 24 months of its initiation, its pinnacle rises 940 feet above the city's highest mountain ridge, the Collserola, beaming TV signals throughout the rest of Europe. Open now as a tourist attraction, the tower offers panoramic views over Catalonia, and an insight into some of the most bizarre engineering in town. Trussed with cables radiating outward to massive steel anchors, the tower perches delicately atop an alarmingly narrow vertical post only 14 feet wide. A high-speed elevator carries visitors from deep inside the mountain (where there's a cafeteria) to an observation platform 1,820 feet above the level of the (very visible) Mediterranean.

Admission: 500 ptas. ($3.60)

Open: Mon–Fri 11am–2pm and 5–7pm; Sat–Sun 11am–7pm. **Transportation:** The city's panoramic funicular carries passengers to a point near the needle's carpark. From there, free minivans make frequent runs up the mountain to the base of the tower.

Parks & Gardens

Barcelona isn't only about dark and stuffy museums. Much of its life takes place outside, in its unique parks and gardens, through which you'll want to stroll.

Parc Güell, Carrer del Carmel. ☎ **424-38-09.**

Begun by Gaudí as a real-estate venture for a wealthy friend, Count Eusebi Güell, a well-known Catalán industrialist of his day, this development was never completed. Only two houses were constructed, but it makes for an interesting excursion nonetheless. The city took over the property in 1926 and turned it into a public park.

One of the houses, **Casa-Museu Gaudí,** Carrer del Carmel, 28 (☎ **284-64-46**), contains models, furniture, drawings, and other memorabilia of the architect. Gaudí, however, did not design the house. Ramón Berenguer took that honor. Admission is 150 pesetas ($1.10). The museum can be visited Sunday to Friday from 10am to 2pm and 4 to 7pm.

Gaudí completed several of the public areas, which today look like a surrealist Disneyland, complete with a mosaic pagoda and a lizard fountain spitting water. Originally, Gaudí planned to make this a model community of 60 dwellings, somewhat like the arrangement of a Greek theater. A central grand plaza with its market below was built, as well as an undulating bench decorated with ceramic fragments. The bizarre Doric columns of the would-be market are hollow, part of Gaudí's drainage system.

Admission: Free.

Open: May–Sept, daily 10am–9pm. Oct–Apr, daily 10am–6pm. **Metro:** Alfonso X.

Tibidabo Mountain

At the top of Tibidabo Mountain, at 1,600 feet, you'll have a panoramic view of Barcelona. The ideal time to visit this summit north of the port (the culmination of the Sierra de Collcerola), is at sunset, when the city lights are on. An amusement park—with Ferris wheels swinging over Barcelona—has been opened here. There's also a church in this carnival-like setting, called Sacred Heart, plus restaurants and mountaintop hotels. From Plaça de Catalunya, take a bus to Avinguda del Tibidabo, where you can board a special bus that will transport you to the funicular. You can hop aboard and scale the mountain.

Admission: Tibidabo funicular 275 ptas. ($2) round trip.

Open: See "Cool for Kids," below, for details on the Parc d'Attraccions.

Montjuïc.

Located in the south of the city, the mountain park of Montjuïc (Montjuch in Spanish) has splashing fountains, gardens, outdoor restaurants, and museums, making for quite an outing. The re-created village, the Poble Espanyol, and the Joan Miró Foundation are also within the park. There are many walks and vantage points for viewing the Barcelona skyline.

The park was the site of several events during the 1992 Summer Olympics. An illuminated fountain display, the Fuentes Luminosas at Plaça de la Font Magica, near the Plaça d'Espanya, is on view from 8 to 11pm every Saturday and Sunday from October to May, and from 9pm to midnight on Thursday, Saturday, and Sunday from June to September.

Open: See individual attractions in the park for various hours of opening. **Bus:** 61 from Plaça d'Espanya or Montjuïc funicular.

Parc de la Ciutadella, at the edge of the Barri de la Ribera.

This is called the Park of the Citadel because it is the site of a former fortress that defended the city. After winning the War of the Spanish Succession (Barcelona was on the losing side), Philip V got his revenge. He ordered that the "traitorous" residential suburb be leveled. In its place rose a citadel. In the mid-19th century it, too, was leveled, though some of the architectural evidence of that past remains in a governor's palace and an arsenal. Today most of the park is filled with lakes, gardens, and promenades, including a zoo (see "Cool for Kids," below) and the Museu d'Art Modern (see "More Attractions," above). Gaudí is said to have contributed to the monumental "great fountain" in the park when he was a student.

Admission: Free.

Open: Apr–Sept, daily 8am–9pm. Oct–Mar, daily 8am–8pm. **Metro:** Ciutadella.

Parc de Joan Miró.

Lying near the Plaça d'Espanya, this park dedicated to Joan Miró, one of the most famous artists of Catalonia, occupies a whole city block. One of Barcelona's 1990s parks and one of its most popular, it is often called Parc de l'Escorxador (slaughterhouse), a reference to what the park used to be. Its main features are an esplanade and a pond from which a sculpture by Miró, *Woman and Bird,* rises up. Palm, pine, and eucalyptus trees, as well as playgrounds and pergolas, complete the picture.

Open: Throughout the day. **Metro:** Espanya.

3 Cool for Kids

The Cataláns have a great affection for children, and although many of the attractions of Barcelona are for adults only, there is an array of amusements designed for the young or the young at heart.

Children from three to seven have their own special place at the **Museu de la Ciència,** Teodor Roviralta, 55 (☎ **212-60-50**). Clik del Nens is a playground of science. Children walk on a giant piano, make bubbles, lift a hippopotamus, or enter an air tunnel. They observe, experiment, and examine nature in an environment created just for them. Special one-hour guided sessions are given daily. See Section 2, "More Attractions," earlier in this chapter, for further details.

Also described in Section 2 is the **Poble Espanyol,** Marqués de Comillas, Parc de Montjuïc (☎ **325-78-66**). Kids compare a visit here to a Spanish version of

Disneyland. Frequent fiestas enliven the place, and it's fun for everybody, young and old.

Parc Zoologic, Parc de la Ciutadella. ☎ **221-25-06.**

Modern, with barless enclosures, this ranks as Spain's top zoo. One of the most unusual attractions is the famous albino gorilla, Snowflake (Copito de Nieve), the only one of its kind in captivity in the world. The main entrances to the Ciutadella Park are via the Passeig de Pujades and Passeig de Picasso.

Admission: Mon–Sat 900 ptas. ($6.40); children under 3 free.

Open: Summer, daily 9:30am–7:30pm. Off-season, daily 10am–5pm. **Metro:** Ciutadella.

Parc d'Attraccions, Parc de Montjuïc. ☎ **441-70-24.**

This place becomes a festival in summer, with open-air concerts and more than three dozen rides for the kiddies. Everything is set against a wide view of Barcelona and its harbor. Children love the nightly illuminated fountain displays and the music.

Admission: 500 ptas. ($3.60); ticket for all rides, 1,700 ptas. ($12.10).

Open: Sept 15–Mar 31, Sat–Sun and holidays, 11am–8pm; Apr 1–June 20, Sat–Sun and holidays, noon–10pm; June 21–Sept 14, Mon–Thurs 6pm–midnight; Fri–Sat 6pm–1am; Sun and holidays noon–11:15pm. **Transportation:** Metro to Paral.lel, then the funicular.

Parc d'Attraccions, Plaça Tibidabo, 3-4, Cumbre del Tibidabo. ☎ **211-79-42.**

On top of Tibidabo, this park combines tradition with modernity—rides from the beginning of the century complete with 1990s novelties. In summer the place takes on a carnival-like setting.

Admission: Ticket for all rides 1,800 ptas. ($12.80); 300 ptas. ($2.10) seniors (65 or older); children under 3 free.

Open: June–Sept, daily 4:30pm–12:30am; May to mid-June, Wed–Sun 4:30–12:30am; off-season Sat–Sun and holidays 11am–8pm. **Transportation:** Ferrocarrils de la Generalitat to Avinguda Tibidabo, then Tramvía Blau, then the funicular.

4 Special-Interest Sightseeing

Architecture

Architecture enthusiasts will find a wealth of fascinating sights in Barcelona. The **Casa Milà,** Passeig de Gràcia, 92 (☎ **487-36-13;** Metro: Diagonal), commonly called La Pedrera, is the most famous apartment-house complex in Spain. Antoni Gaudí's imagination went wild when planning its construction; he even included vegetable and fruit shapes in his sculptural designs. Controversial and much criticized upon its completion, today it stands as a classic example of modernist architecture. The ironwork around the balconies forms an intricate maze, and the main gate has windowpanes shaped like eggs. The rooftop is filled with phantasmagorical chimneys known in Spanish as *espantabrujas* (witch-scarers). Free tours of the famous rooftops are available Tuesday to Saturday at 10 and 11am, noon, and 1pm, but they have to be arranged in advance by calling the number above. From the rooftop, you'll also have a view of Gaudí's unfinished cathedral, La Sagrada Familia.

Casa Lleó Morera, Passeig de Gràcia, 35 (☎ 215-44-77; Metro: Passeig de Gràcia), lying between the Carrer del Consell de Cent and the Carrer d' Aragó, is one of the most famous buildings of the modernist movement. It comprises one of the trio of structures called the Mançana de la Discòrdia (Block of Discord), an allusion to the mythical judgment of Paris. Three of the most famous modernist architects of Barcelona, including Gaudí, competed with their various works along this block. In florid modernist design, the Casa Lleó, designed by Domènech i Montaner in 1905, was considered extremely revolutionary in its day. Perhaps that assessment still stands. Today the building is the headquarters of the business office of Patronato de Turismo (this, however, is not a tourist information center).

Constructed in a cubical design, with a Dutch gable, the **Casa Amatller,** Passeig de Gràcia, 41 (☎ **216-01-75;** Metro: Passeig de Gràcia), was created by Puig i Cadafalch in 1900. It stands in sharp contrast to its neighbor, the Gaudí-designed Casa Batlló. The architecture of the Casa Amatller, actually imposed on an older structure, is a vision of ceramic, wrought iron, and sculptures. Admission to the Gothic-style interior is free and upon request. There are no set hours.

Next door to the Casa Amatller, the **Casa Batlló,** Passeig de Gràcia, 43 (☎ **216-01-12;** Metro: Passeig de Gràcia), was designed by Gaudí in 1905. Using "sensuous" curves in iron and stone, the architect created a lavish baroque exuberance in the facade. The balconies have been compared to "sculptured waves." The upper part of the facade evokes animal forms, and delicate tiles spread across the design. A polychromatic exterior extraordinaire. The downstairs building is the headquarters of an insurance company. Although visitors are not always welcome, many tourists walk inside for a view of Gaudí's interior, which is basically as he designed it. Since this *is* a place of business, be discreet.

Casa de la Ciutat Ayuntamiento, Plaça de Sant Jaume (Metro: Jaume I), originally constructed at the end of the 14th century, is considered one of the best examples of Gothic civil architecture in the Catalán Mediterranean style. Across this landmark square from the Palau de la Generalitat, it has been endlessly renovated and changed since its original construction. Behind a neoclassical facade, the building has a splendid courtyard and staircase. Its major architectural highlights are the 15th-century Salón de Ciento (Room of the 100 Jurors) and the Salón de las Cronicas (Room of the Chronicles), the latter decorated with black marble. The Salón de Ciento, in particular, represents a medley of styles. You can enter the building Monday to Saturday from 9:30am to 1:30pm and 4:30 to 7:30pm; it is closed from mid-December to mid-January.

Olympics

Galeria Olímpico, Passeig Olimpic s/n, lower level. ☎ **93/426-06-60.**

An enthusiastic celebration of Barcelona's Olympic games of 1992, this is one of the few museums in Europe exclusively devoted to sports and sports statistics. Its exhibits include photos, costumes, and memorabilia, with heavy emphasis on the events' pageantry, the numbers of visitors who attended, and the fame the events brought to Barcelona. Of interest to statisticians, civic planners, and sports buffs, the gallery contains audio-visual information about the building programs which prepared the city for the onslaught of visitors, conference facilities, an auditorium, video recordings of athletic events, and archives. It lies within the cellar of the Olympic Stadium's southeastern perimeter, and is most easily reached by entering the stadium's southern gate (Porta Sud).

Admission: 300 ptas. ($2.10).

Open: Apr–Sept, Tues–Sat 10am–2pm and 4–8pm, Sun 10am–2pm. Oct–Mar, Tues–Sat 10am–1pm, 4–6pm, Sun 10am–2pm. **Metro:** Espanya. **Bus:** 9, 13.

Walking Tour 1
The Gothic Quarter

Start Plaça Nova.
Finish Plaça de la Seu.
Time 3 hours.
Best Time Any sunny day.
Worst Time Mon–Sat 7–9am and 5–7pm because of traffic.

Begin at the:

1. **Plaça Nova,** set within the shadow of the cathedral. This is the largest open-air space in the Gothic Quarter and the usual site of the Barcelona flea market. Opening onto this square is the Portal del Bisbe, a gate flanked by two round towers that have survived from the ancient Roman wall that once stood here. From Plaça Nova, climb the incline of the narrow asphalt-covered street (Carrer del Bisbe) lying between these massive walls. On your right, notice the depth of the foundations, which indicates how much the city has risen since the wall was constructed.

   At the approach of the first street, Carrer de Santa Llúcia, turn left, noticing the elegant simplicity of the corner building with its Romanesque facade, the:

2. **Capilla de Santa Llúcia,** open daily from 8am to 1:30pm and 4 to 7:30pm. Its solidly graceful portal and barrel-vaulted interior were completed in 1268. Continue down Carrer de Santa Llúcia a few paces, noticing the:
3. **Casa d'Ardiaca (Archdeacon's House),** constructed in the 15th century as a residence for Archdeacon Despla. The Gothic building has sculptural reliefs with Renaissance motifs. In its cloisterlike courtyard are a fountain and a palm tree. Notice the mail slot, where five swallows and a turtle carved into stone await the arrival of important messages. Since 1919 this building has been home to the **Municipal d'Història de la Ciutat (Municipal Institute of the History of the City).** As you exit the Archdeacon's House, continue in the same direction several steps until you reach the:
4. **Plaça de la Seu,** the square in front of the main entrance to the **Catedral de Barcelona** (see "The Top Attractions," above). Here you can stand and admire the facade of Mediterranean Gothic architecture. On each side of Plaça de la Seu, you can see the remains of Roman walls. After touring the cathedral, exit from the door you entered and turn right onto Carrer des Comtes, admiring the gargoyles along the way. After about 100 paces, you'll approach the:
5. **Museu Frederic Marés** on Plaça de Sant Iú. On the lower floors are Punic and Roman artifacts, but most of the museum is devoted to the works of this Catalán sculptor. Exit through the same door you entered and continue your promenade in the same direction. You'll pass the portal of the cathedral's side where the heads of two rather abstract angels flank the throne of a seated female saint. A few paces farther, notice the stone facade of the:
6. **Arxiu de la Carona d'Aragó,** the archives building of the crown of Aragón. Formerly called Palacio del Lugarteniente (Deputy's Palace), this Gothic building was the work of Antonio Carbonell. On some maps it also appears

as the Palacio de los Virreyes (Palace of the Viceroys). The palace contains medieval and royal documents. Enter its courtyard, admiring the century-old grape vines. Then climb the 11 monumental steps to your left, facing a modern bronze sculpture by a Catalán artist. It represents with a rather abstract dateline and map, the political history and imperial highlights of Catalonia.

As you exit from the courtyard, you'll find yourself back on Carrer dels Comtes. Continue in the same direction, turning left at the intersection of Baixada de Santa Clara. This street, in one short block, will bring you to one of the most famous squares of the Gothic Quarter:

7. **Plaça del Rei.** The Great Royal Palace, an enlarged building of what was originally the residence of the counts of Barcelona, stands at the bottom of this square. Here at the King's Square you can visit both the **Palau Reial** and the **Museu d'Història de la Ciutat** (see "More Attractions," above). On the right side of the square stands the **Palatine Chapel of Santa Agata,** a 14th-century Gothic temple that is part of the Palau Reial. In this chapel is preserved the altarpiece of the Lord High Constable, a 15th-century work by Jaume Huguet.

   Retrace your steps up Baixada de Santa Clara, crossing Carrer dels Comtes, and continue straight to Carrer de la Pietat, which will skirt the semicircular, massively buttressed rear of the cathedral. With the buttresses of the cathedral's rear to your right, pass the 14th-century:

8. **Casa del Canonge (House of the Canon),** opening onto Carrer Arzobispo Irurita, s/n. This building was erected in the Gothic style and restored in 1929; escutcheons from the 15th and 16th centuries remain. Notice the heraldic symbols of medieval Barcelona on the building's stone plaques—twin towers supported by winged goats with lion's feet. On the same façade, also notice the depiction of twin angels. The building today is used as a women's training school, the Escola Professional per a la Doña.

   Continue walking along Carrer de la Pietat, which makes a sudden sharp left. Notice the carved *Pietà* above the Gothic portal leading into the rear of the cathedral. Continue walking straight. One block later, turn left onto Carrer del Bisbe and continue downhill. Your path will lead you beneath one of the most charming bridges in Spain. Carved into lacy patterns of stonework, it connects the Casa del Canonge with Palau de la Generalitat.

   Continue walking until Carrer del Bisbe opens into:

9. **Plaça de Sant Jaume,** in many ways the political heart of Catalán culture. Across this square, constructed at what was once a major junction for two Roman streets, race politicians and bureaucrats intent on Catalonian government affairs. On Sunday evenings you can witness the dance of the sardana, the national dance of Catalonia. Many bars and restaurants stand on side streets leading from this square. Standing in the square, with your back to the street you just left (Carrer del Bisbe), you'll see, immediately on your right, the Doric portico of the **Palau de la Generalitat,** the parliament of Catalonia. With its large courtyard and open-air stairway, along with twin arched galleries, this exquisite work in the Catalonian Gothic style began construction in the era of Jaume I. A special feature of the building is the Chapel of St. George, built in flamboyant Gothic style between 1432 and 1435 and enlarged in 1620 with the addition of vaulting and a cupola with

Walking Tour— Gothic Quarter

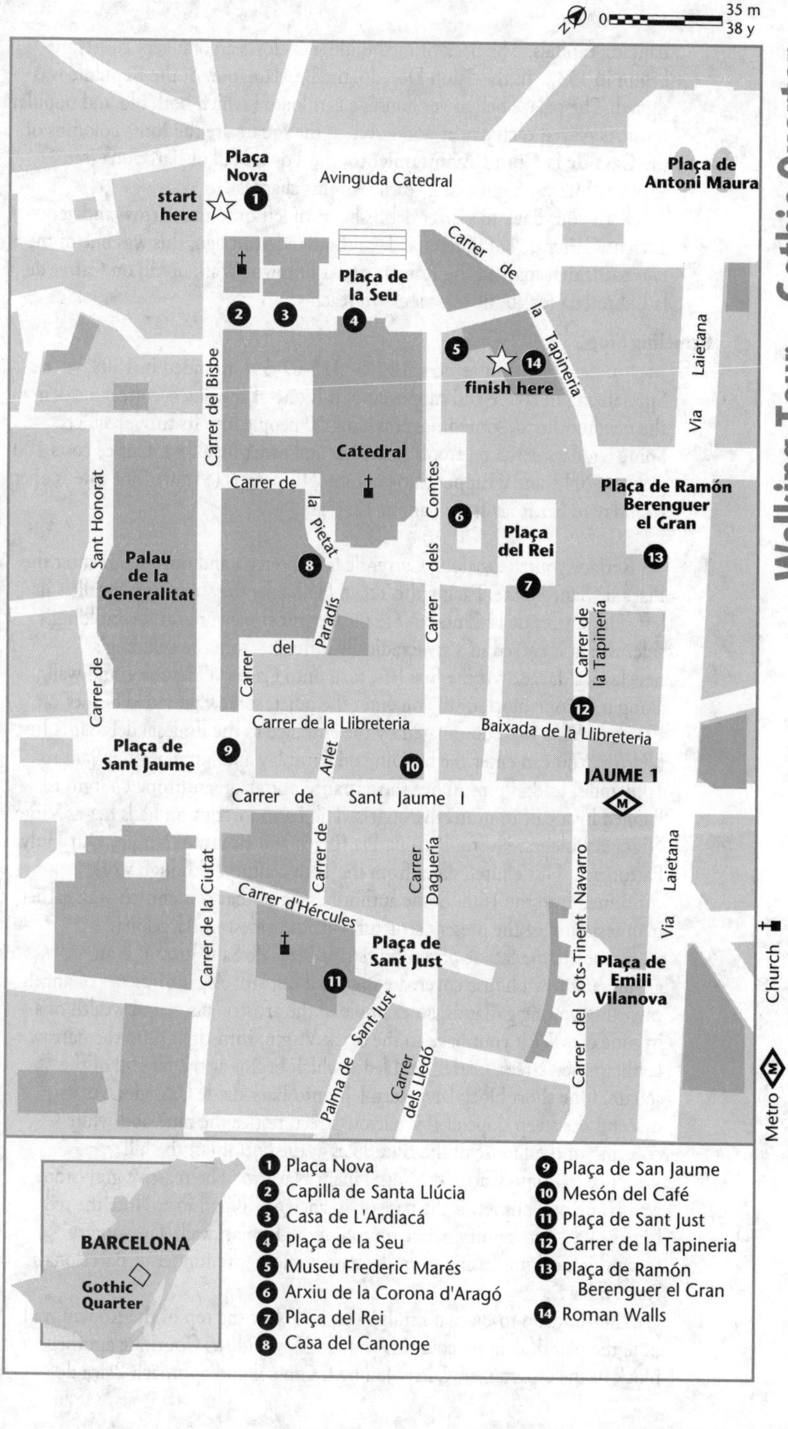

0 35 m / 38 y

Plaça Nova
start here
Avinguda Catedral
Plaça de Antoni Maura
Carrer de la Tapineria
Plaça de la Seu
Carrer del Bisbe
finish here
Via Laietana
Catedral
Carrer de la Pietat
Carrer dels Comtes
Sant Honorat
Palau de la Generalitat
Plaça del Rei
Plaça de Ramón Berenguer el Gran
Carrer del Paradís
Carrer de la Tapinería
Carrer de
Carrer de la Llibreteria
Baixada de la Llibreteria
Plaça de Sant Jaume
Arlet
JAUME 1
Carrer de Sant Jaume I
Carrer de
Carrer Daguería
Carrer de la Ciutat
Carrer d'Hércules
Plaça de Sant Just
Carrer del Sots-Tinent Navarro
Plaça de Emili Vilanova
Palma de Sant Just
Carrer dels Lledó
Church
Metro

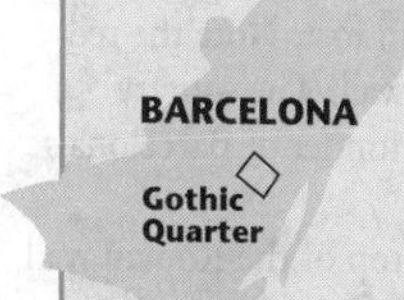

1. Plaça Nova
2. Capilla de Santa Llúcia
3. Casa de L'Ardiacá
4. Plaça de la Seu
5. Museu Frederic Marés
6. Arxiu de la Corona d'Aragó
7. Plaça del Rei
8. Casa del Canonge
9. Plaça de San Jaume
10. Mesón del Café
11. Plaça de Sant Just
12. Carrer de la Tapineria
13. Plaça de Ramón Berenguer el Gran
14. Roman Walls

hanging capitals. The back of the building encloses an orangery courtyard begun in 1532. In the Salón Dorado, the Proclamation of the Republic was signed. The palace bell tower houses a carillon on which both old and popular music is played each day at noon. Across the square are the Ionic columns of the **Casa de la Ciutat/Ayuntamiento,** the Town Hall of Barcelona (see "Special-Interest Sightseeing" earlier in this chapter).

With your back to Carrer del Bisbe, turn left onto the narrow and very ancient Carrer de la Llibreteria. Two thousand years ago, this was one of the two roads that marked the Roman center of town. Walk uphill on Carrer de la Llibreteria for about $1^1/_2$ blocks to reach a:

Refueling Stop

10. Mesón del Café, Llibreteria, 16 (☎ **315-07-54**), founded in 1909. Specializing in coffee and cappuccino, it is one of the oldest coffeehouses in the neighborhood, sometimes crowding 50 people into its tiny precincts. Some regulars perch on stools at the bar and order breakfast. Coffee costs 100 pesetas (70¢), and a cappuccino goes for 210 pesetas ($1.50). The café is open Monday to Saturday from 7am to 12:45am.

Retrace your steps along Carrer de la Llibreteria and once again enter the Plaça de Sant Jaume. Facing the Town Hall, take the street that parallels its left side, Carrer de la Ciutat. Note the elegant stonework on the building's side, which is carved in a style radically different from the building's neoclassical facade. At the first left, turn onto Carrer d'Hercules, and walk along it for one block until you enter the quiet, somewhat faded beauty of:

11. Plaça de Sant Just, dominated by the entrance to the Església dels Sants Just i Pastor. You can enter the building on Saturday and Sunday from 9am to 1pm and 5 to 8:30pm. Above the entrance portal, an enthroned Virgin is flanked by a pair of protective angels. The Latin inscription hails her as Virgo Nigra et Pulchra, Nostra Patrona Pia (Black and Beautiful Virgin, Our Holy Patroness). This church dates from the 14th century, although work continued into the 16th. Some authorities claim that this church—an earlier manifestation of the present structure—is the oldest in Barcelona.

Opposite the facade of the church, at Plaça de Sant Just, 4, is an aristocratic town house covered with faded but still elegant frescoes of angels cavorting among garlands, an example of the artistry, taste, and wealth of a bygone era. With your back to the black Virgin, turn right onto the narrow cobblestoned street, Carrer del Lledo, which begins at the far end of the square. One short block later, turn left onto Baixada de Cassador. As you descend the steep slope of this narrow street, notice the blue-and-white covering of the House of the Blue Tiles at the bottom of the hill.

Turn left onto Carrer del Sots Tinent Navarro. The massive gray-stone wall rising on your left is the base of an ancient Roman fort. Note the red bricks of a 13th-century palace on top of the Roman wall. The solitary Corinthian column rising from the base is another reminder of Barcelona's Roman past.

Continue on to Plaça d'Emili Vilanova. Near the top of the Roman wall, note the pair of delicate columns of a Gothic window. Continue another block to the cross street, Carrer Jaume I. Cross it and approach Plaça de l'Angel. Continue walking to the:

12. Carrer de la Tapineria. In medieval times, this was the street of the shoemakers. In fact, the industry is so entrenched that there is even a museum devoted to footwear, the Museu del Calcat Antic, Plaça Sant Felip Neri, 5 (☎ **307-45-33**). It is open Tuesday to Sunday from 11am to 2pm, with admission at 200 pesetas ($1.40).

In one short block Carrer de la Tapineria leads to:

13. Plaça de Ramón Berenguer el Gran. An equestrian statue dedicated to this hero (**1096–1131**) is ringed with the gravel of a semicircular park whose backdrop is formed by the walls of the ancient Roman fort and, nearby, a Gothic tower.

Traverse the park, crossing in front of the equestrian statue, until you once again reach the edge of the Roman wall as you head toward the park's distant end. There Carrer de la Tapineria will lead you on a path paralleling the ancient:

14. Roman walls, one of Barcelona's most important treasures from its past. The walls, known as *Las Murallas* in Spanish, were constructed between A.D. 270 and 310. The perimeter of the walls was 1,389 yards. They followed a rectangular course, and were built so that their fortified sections would face the sea. By the 11th and 12th centuries, Barcelona had long outgrown their confines. Jaume I ordered the opening of the Roman walls, and the burgeoning growth that ensued virtually destroyed them, except for the foundations you see today.

Continue your promenade, but turn left at the narrow Baixada de la Canonja. A short walk down this cobblestoned alleyway will return you to **Plaça de la Seu,** not far from where you began this tour.

Walking Tour 2
Les Rambles

Start Plaça Portal de la Pau.
Finish Plaça de Catalunya.
Time 1½ hours.
Best Time Any time except midnight to dawn, which might be unsafe.

This most famous promenade in Spain was laid out in the 18th century. Begin at:

1. Plaça Portal de la Pau, with its Columbus Monument, which you can scale for a view of the harbor (see under "More Attractions," above). You can also book a harbor cruise of the port here or even take a horse-and-carriage ride.

With your back to the monument to Columbus, head up Les Rambles, the first of which is the:

2. Rambla de Santa Mònica, where it is recommended that you walk with care late at night, as this Ramble borders the Barri Xinés, long known as a center of drugs, prostitution, and criminal activity. Hookers, pimps, beggars, transvestites, and various immigrants live in this quarter along with some hardworking, respectable poor people. If you have children with you (or even if you don't), you may want to turn right at the Passatge de la Banca and visit the:

3. **Museu de Cera** (☎ **317-26-49**), a wax museum with some 300 figures—past and present—from Barcelona's history. Admission is 750 pesetas ($5.30) for adults and 450 pesetas ($3.20) for children 5 to 11; it's open daily from 11am to 8pm.

Refueling Stop

4. **Café Opera, Les Rambles,** 74 (☎ **317-75-85**). In warm weather, its tables spill out onto the Rambles, but for most of the year clients pack into a narrow stand-up area beside a marble-topped bar or head to the tables in back. Everywhere, reminders of the café's Belle Epoque past sheath the slightly seedy room with its tarnished crystal chandeliers and turn-of-the-century frescoes. International gays mingle with unionists, trade leaders, anarchists, vacationing American students, and French schoolteachers. It is the most famous café along Les Rambles. Waiters in black vests bring beer costing from 200 pesetas ($1.40) or other drinks to the tables either inside or outside. The café is open daily from 9am to 2am.

The next Rambla is the:

5. **Rambla dels Caputxins,** which begins at Plaça del Teatre. This was once the heart of the old theater district, but only the rather bleak Teatro Principal survives. Philip II launched this area on its theatrical career when he granted permission for the construction of a playhouse here to raise money for the city. In the Plaça del Teatre you can see a monument to Serafi Pitarra, considered "the father" of contemporary theater in Catalonia.

Turn left here to reach the:

6. **Museu de les Artes de l'Espectable,** Nou de La Rambla, 3 (☎ **317-39-74**). Also known as the Güell Palace (it was constructed for Gaudí's patron Eusebi Gûell in the 1880s), this is considered one of the masterpieces of Antoni Gaudí. His tastes, although essentially Gothic, show even Moorish influences in this strange building. The main hall is usually open to the public, who can wander in and look about—and up. Its perforated cupola is adorned with broken fragments of ceramic tiles, and crowned with a curious mélange of balustrades, multiform chimneys, and crenels. The building houses theatrical archives containing such items as memoirs of Catalán literary figures, props left over from long-forgotten hits of yesteryear, and antique theater posters. The archives are open Monday to Saturday from 11am to 2pm and 5 to 8pm, charging 200 pesetas ($1.40) for admission.

Walking back to Les Rambles, continue up the promenade but veer right onto Carrer de Colom on the other side of the esplanade, entering the landmark:

7. **Plaça Reial (Royal Square).** At first you'll think you've been transported to Andalusia. Constructed in a neoclassical style during the 19th century, this plaza has palms and elaborate facades, even ocher-painted arcades, and in the center is a fountain dedicated to the Three Graces. The lampposts are attributed to the young Gaudí. You'll see old men sunning themselves on the benches in this square, which was built on the site of a former Capuchin monastery, one of many religious edifices that lined the Rambles until they were suppressed in 1835. Sunday morning brings out a coin and stamp market.

Walking Tour —Les Rambles

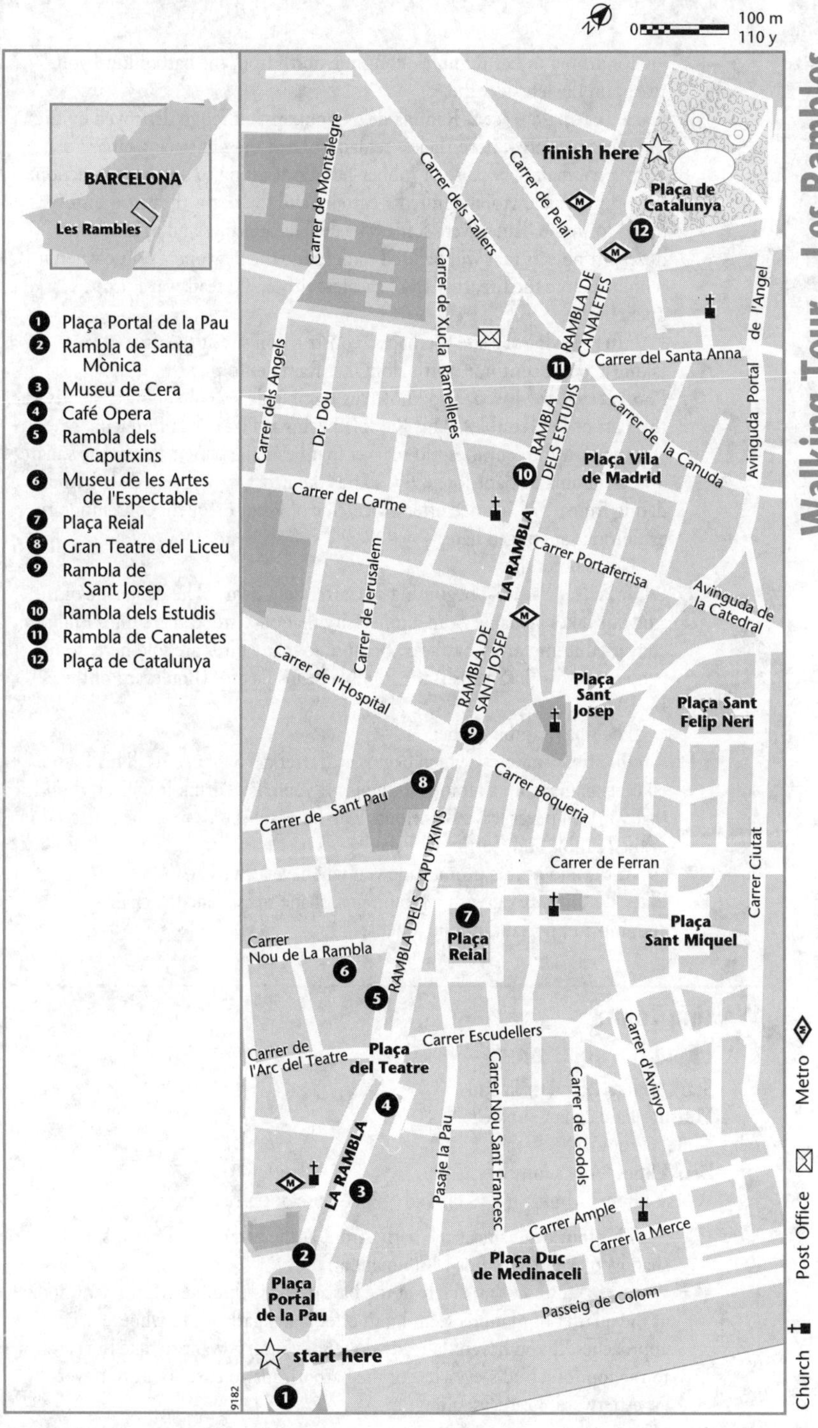

100 m
110 y

1. Plaça Portal de la Pau
2. Rambla de Santa Mònica
3. Museu de Cera
4. Café Opera
5. Rambla dels Caputxins
6. Museu de les Artes de l'Espectable
7. Plaça Reial
8. Gran Teatre del Liceu
9. Rambla de Sant Josep
10. Rambla dels Estudis
11. Rambla de Canaletes
12. Plaça de Catalunya

finish here
Plaça de Catalunya
Carrer de Pelai
Carrer dels Tallers
Carrer de Montalegre
Carrer de Xucla
Ramelleres
RAMBLA DE CANALETES
Carrer del Santa Anna
Avinguda Portal de l'Angel
Carrer dels Angels
Dr. Dou
RAMBLA DELS ESTUDIS
Carrer de la Canuda
Plaça Vila de Madrid
Carrer del Carme
LA RAMBLA
Carrer Portaferrisa
Avinguda de la Catedral
Carrer de Jerusalem
RAMBLA DE SANT JOSEP
Carrer de l'Hospital
Plaça Sant Josep
Plaça Sant Felip Neri
Carrer Boqueria
Carrer de Sant Pau
RAMBLA DELS CAPUTXINS
Carrer de Ferran
Carrer Ciutat
Plaça Reial
Plaça Sant Miquel
Carrer Nou de La Rambla
Carrer Escudellers
Carrer de l'Arc del Teatre
Plaça del Teatre
Carrer d'Avinyo
Carrer Nou Sant Francesc
Carrer de Codols
Pasaje la Pau
LA RAMBLA
Carrer Ample
Carrer la Merce
Plaça Duc de Medinaceli
Plaça Portal de la Pau
Passeig de Colom
start here

9182

Church
Post Office
Metro

Returning to Les Rambles, continue north from the harbor until you reach, on the left side, the:

8. **Gran Teatre del Liceu,** Rambla dels Caputxins, although destroyed by fire in January of 1994, nevertheless remains one of the sightseeing targets of Barcelona, mainly because of rubber-neckers wanting to see the destruction. A workman's blowtorch ignited a curtain, and the rest is theatrical history. Saved from the flames were some 85 valuable paintings and at least three dozen art objects that will be used to decorate the new opera house when it is rebuilt. Before the fire, this 1847 theater with 2,700 seats was Europe's largest opera house.

   After viewing the site (perhaps a construction site at the time of your taking a look), continue north along Les Rambles to the:

9. **Rambla de Sant Josep,** also known as Rambla de les Flors. Flower stands line this part of Les Rambles. This Rambla begins at Plaça de la Boquería, where you can visit the centuries-old market that bears the same name as the square.

   At Rambla de Sant Josep, 99, stands the neoclassical Palau de la Virreina dating from 1778, named after a vicereine of Peru. Frequent contemporary exhibitions are staged here.

   Next comes the:

10. **Rambla dels Estudis,** beginning at Carrer del Carme. The esplanade of the students takes its name from a university that once stood there until Philip V converted it into army barracks. Because so many birds are sold here, some people call this (in Spanish) the Rambla de los Pajaros (Boulevard of the Birds).

    The final Rambla is the:

11. **Rambla de Canaletes,** which begins at Carrer del Santa Anna. This Rambla takes its name from a famous fountain. If you take a drink from it, it is said that you will never leave Barcelona. The fountain stands near the intersection of the Rambla and Carrer del Pelai.

    At the end of this promenade you will have arrived at:

12. **Plaça de Catalunya,** with its fountains, shade trees, benches, chairs—and, most important, public toilet.

Walking Tour 3
Barcelona Harborfront

Start Plaça Portal de la Pau.
Finish Parc de la Ciutadella.
Time 2 hours.
Best Time Any sunny day.
Worst Time Mon–Sat 7–9am and 5–7 because of traffic.

This tour begins near the harborfront at the end of the Rambles in the shadow of the Columbus Monument at:

1. **Plaça Portal de la Pau.** Here at the base of the Columbus Monument, look at the quartet of nymphs seeming to offer laurel garlands to whoever approaches. If you haven't already done so, you may want to take the elevator to the top for a bird's-eye view of the harborfront you are about to traverse.

   Afterward, head east along:

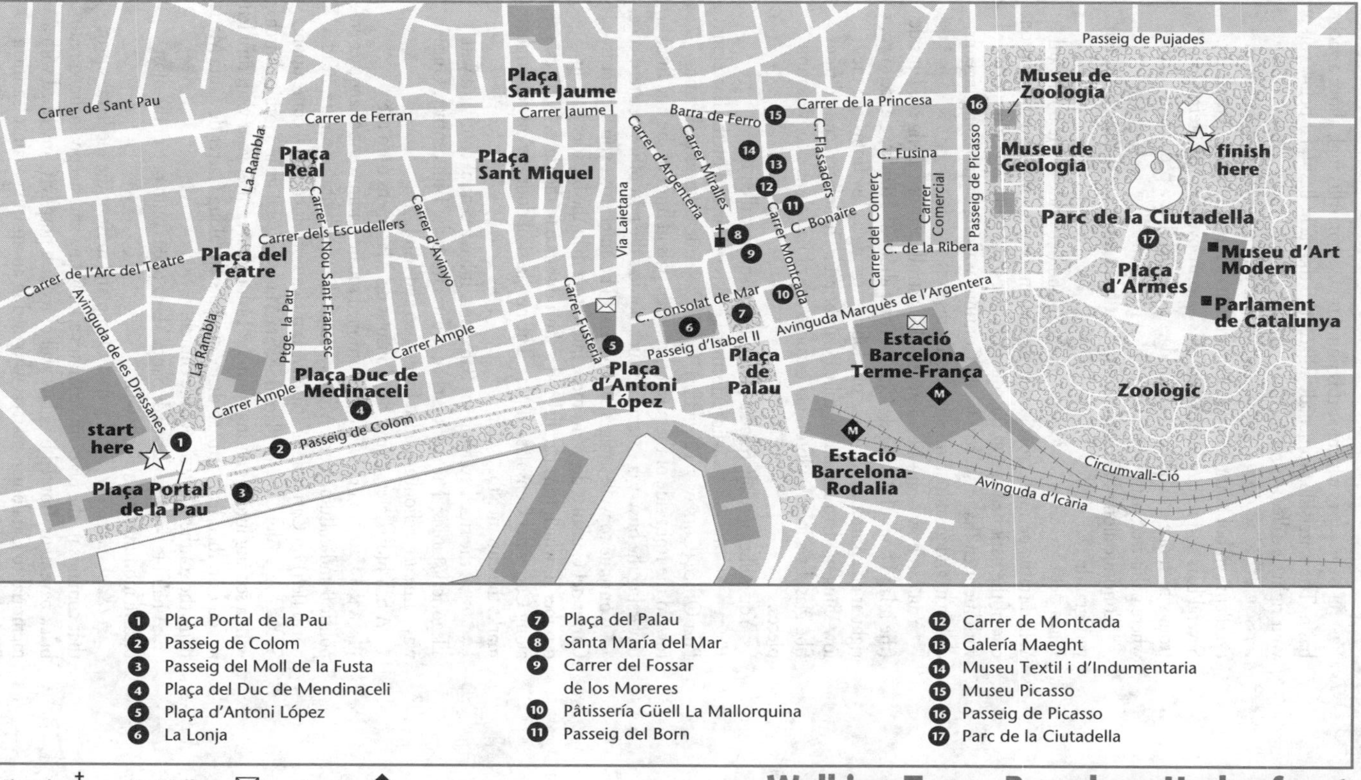

1. Plaça Portal de la Pau
2. Passeig de Colom
3. Passeig del Moll de la Fusta
4. Plaça del Duc de Mendinaceli
5. Plaça d'Antoni López
6. La Lonja
7. Plaça del Palau
8. Santa María del Mar
9. Carrer del Fossar de los Moreres
10. Pâtissería Güell La Mallorquina
11. Passeig del Born
12. Carrer de Montcada
13. Galería Maeght
14. Museu Textil i d'Indumentaria
15. Museu Picasso
16. Passeig de Picasso
17. Parc de la Ciutadella

Church Post Office Metro

Walking Tour—Barcelona Harborfront

2. **Passeig de Colom,** which, at this point, is raised on stilts high above a yacht basin. The waterside promenade adjacent to the yacht basin, far below you on your right, is called:
3. **Passeig del Moll de la Fusta,** originally the timber wharf. It stands as an excellent symbol of the recovery of Barcelona's formerly seedy waterfront. Several bars and restaurants enliven this balcony over the Mediterranean, from which one can descend via bridges to the level of a pedestrian wharf where palm trees arise from the cobbled pavement.

   Continue along Passeig de Colom until you reach the slightly faded but very grand:
4. **Plaça del Duc de Mendinacell,** on the inland (left) side of the boulevard. When traffic permits, cross Passeig de Colom, perhaps resting a moment on one of the park benches in the square, whose focal point is a column ringed with mermen (half fish, half men). Continue walking east, passing pigeons, children, and grandparents sunning themselves.

   You can now begin a brisk seven-block stroll eastward along the left side (the inland one) of Passeig de Colom. After about 2½ blocks, glance to your right at an enormous sculpture of a lobster waving a claw from atop the low-slung modern restaurant called Gambrinus. The lobster, crafted from fiberglass by a local sculptor, has become one of Barcelona's conversation pieces.

   You will eventually reach a monumental square called the:
5. **Plaça d'Antoni López,** whose northern end is dominated by the Barcelona Post Office (Correos y Telegrafos). Cross Carrer de la Fustería, heading toward the front side of the post office, then pass in front of the building, traversing the busy Via Laietana, which borders the post office's eastern edge.

   Continue to walk straight, always east. The quiet street you'll enter is Carrer del Consolat del Mar, more interesting than the broader Passeig d'Isabel II, which runs parallel and a short distance to the right. Walk east along Carrer del Consolat del Mar. The neoclassical doorway on your right marks the entrance to:
6. **La Lonja,** the stock exchange of Barcelona. It has a central courtyard with allegorical statues. The stock exchange dates from the 14th century. Once it was a fine arts school attended by Picasso and Miró.

   A half block later, Carrer del Consolat del Mar opens onto the:
7. **Plaça del Palau,** a gracefully proportioned square reminiscent of another era's political and cultural glory. Midway down the length of this square, head north (left) on Carrer de l'Espasería, at the end of which you'll come upon:
8. **Santa María del Mar,** in Plaça de Santa María, a Catalonian Gothic church with a soaring interior dating from the 14th century. After your visit, turn left as you exit, then left again, so that your footsteps along Carrer de Santa María flank the southern exterior of the church.

   A half block later, Carrer de Santa María opens onto one of the most bizarre monuments in Barcelona:
9. **Carrer del Fossar de los Moreres.** Occupying most of the medieval square that contains it, the plaza incorporates a sprawling and steeply inclined red-brick pavement, fronted by a low wall of reddish porphyry, inscribed with a memorial to Catalonian martyrs who died in an uprising against Castilian Spain in 1714. As you enter the square, note on your left a narrow street leading to the:

Refueling Stop

10. Pâtissería Güell La Mallorquina, Plaça de Les Oiles, 7 (☎ **319-39-83**), established in 1878 in a 16th-century building. Sample the *llunes,* half-moon-shaped pastries filled with almonds and sprinkled with powdered sugar. Or take out an order of *coques,* sprinkled with sugar and topped with pine nuts. All pastries are made on the premises, and the dough is rolled out on marble tables. You can stop in here and buy pastries on Monday and Wednesday through Saturday from 8am to 2pm, and 5 to 8:30pm, Sunday from 8am to 3pm.

Return to the square of the martyrs and continue walking along Carrer de Santa María until you reach the rear of the Church of Santa María del Mar, where you'll notice the massive buttresses. You have arrived at the:

11. Passeig del Born, one of the colorful old squares of Barcelona and the residence of some appealing and nostalgic bars. But this square doesn't come alive until much later at night.

Turn left after one very short block onto Placeta de Montcada, which after about 30 paces becomes more narrow and changes its name to the:

12. Carrer de Montcada, which represents the aristocratic heart of Barcelona during the height of its prestige and power. Notice the semifortified palace at no. 20, which served during the 18th century as the Barcelona residence of the Catalonian ambassador from Great Britain. Also note the nine gargoyles adding visual interest to the fourth and uppermost floor of the palace, whose forbidding exterior seems even more severe because of the narrow street containing it.

A few steps later, on your right, is the:

13. Galería Maeght, Montcada, 25 (☎ **310-42-45**), established by the children of the couple who created one of the most famous museums of modern art in Europe, the Galerie Maeght in St-Paul-de-Vence in France. Many well-known and unknown painters are exhibited under the gallery's brick vaults, and works are for sale. The showrooms are open Tuesday to Saturday from 9:30am to 2pm and 3 to 8pm.

As you leave the gallery, turn right and continue walking until you reach the:

14. Museu de Textil i d'Indumentaria, Montcada, 12 (☎ **310-45-16**), occupying two 13th-century Gothic palaces. Many of the articles in this textile and costume museum are Egyptian and Hispano-Muslim. Textiles range from the Gothic era to the 20th century; many of the garments are liturgical. Summer hours are Tuesday to Sunday from 10am to 2pm and 4:30 to 7pm; off-season hours are Tuesday to Sunday from 9am to 2pm and 4 to 7pm. Admission is 800 pesetas ($2.10).

After exiting the museum, turn left and continue walking until you reach the most visited museum in Barcelona; the:

15. Museu Picasso, Montcada, 15-19 (☎ **319-63-10**), ensconced in two Gothic mansions (see "The Top Attractions," above, for more details). Exit from the museum and turn right along Carrer de Montcada. In one short block, turn right again onto Carrer de la Princesa and walk straight for four blocks, traversing a confusing five-way intersection. You'll soon arrive at the wide and busy Carrer del Comerç, which you should cross. Continue walking along Carrer de la Princesa until it dead-ends at the:

16. **Passeig de Picasso,** designed by architects Amadó and Domènech. A sculpture by Tàpies, *Homage to Picasso,* is the central piece. Cross the Passeig de Picasso and notice the ornate wrought-iron gates guarding the entrance to the:

17. **Parc de la Ciutadella,** which was the site of the 1888 Universal Exposition (see "Parks & Gardens," above, for more details). If you enter the park through its main entrance on the Passeig Lluís Companys, you can still see some of the relics from that great fair. The park is filled with museums, a zoo, and many attractions. Since it covers a large area, these attractions are signposted, and you can follow the directions and take in whatever interests you—or whatever you have time to explore.

Walking Tour 4
Modernist Barcelona

Start Plaça de Catalunya.
Finish Plaça de Catalunya.
Time 2 hours.
Best Time Any sunny day.
Worst Time Mon–Sat 7–9am and 5–7pm because of traffic.

Much of Barcelona's worldwide reputation is based on the architectural works found in the 19th-century Eixample (Ensanche) section, an urban expansion plan dating mostly from 1860. This barrio was filled with a Catalonian art nouveau style of architecture called *modernisme.* Its most famous monument is Antoni Gaudí's Sagrada Familia, his unfinished cathedral. Many other architects worked in this area as well, including Domènech i Montaner, Puig i Cadafalch, and Josep Vilaseca. Most of these buildings are still occupied as businesses and apartments.

Begin your tour at the symbolic center of Barcelona, the sprawling and traffic-clogged:

1. **Plaça de Catalunya,** site of everything from Catalonian song and dance festivals to political protests. This square is a potent symbol of Barcelona's cultural independence from the rest of Spain. Exit onto the plaza's northernmost boulevard, Passeig de Gràcia. Keep the city's largest department store, El Corte Inglés, on your right.

   As you ascend Passeig de Gràcia, you'll be heading north. Walk along its east (right) sidewalk and notice the dozens of bookstands patronized by an avidly literate Catalán market. You'll reach:

2. **Gran Vía de los Corts Catalanes,** a major boulevard intersecting Passeig de Gràcia. Traverse this intersecting boulevard and continue to walk straight to the north to Carrer de la Disputació. Turn right. After going one block east, notice that the 19th-century city planners designed their intersections like miniature plazas, rounding off the edges of each of the corner buildings. Turn left at Carrer de Pau Claris and walk on the east (right) side of the street, heading north. Note in about a half block the private passageway (reserved for residents only) of:

3. **Passatge de Permanyer,** whose wrought-iron gates and sculpted cherubs guard an entrance reserved for the occupants of 19th-century villas and gardens lining either side. (There's likely to be a surly-looking guard blocking

Walking Tour — Modernist Barcelona

your entrance to the gate.) Some consider the Passatge de Permanyer the most charming little street of Barcelona.

Continue walking a few paces to the next boulevard, Carrer del Consell de Cent, where you should go right, crossing it at the Hotel Diplomatic. Walk east along the north (left) side of Carrer del Consell de Cent. At the intersection with Carrer de Roger de Llúria, turn left. Walk one block north. When you reach Carrer d'Aragó, cross it and turn right. A few steps later, you'll see the massively buttressed 14th-century Església de la Concepció, Aragó, 299, which seems to host an elaborate wedding every weekend.

Continue to walk east on Aragó until you reach Carrer del Bruc. Observe the Consell Municipal on Carrer del Bruc's far side. Designed by the noted Catalán architect Pere Falques i Urpi in 1893, it is considered a neighborhood landmark and a good example of Neo-Romanesque Catalonian architecture. Note its wrought-iron gates, the oak-leaf clusters carved into the Romanesque capitals, and the coat-of-arms over the third floor.

Turn left (north) onto Carrer del Bruc, which has dozens of plane trees lining the sidewalk. Search out the massive stones of the building on your right. The entrance to this famous structure is at the next street corner, at the intersection of Carrer de València. The building is the Conservatorio Superior Municipal de Música.

Turn left (heading west) onto Carrer de València. A landmark building stands at:

4. **Carrer de València,** 296, on the street's north (right) side. Considered one of the city's most distinguished examples of wrought ironwork and *modernisme*, it has twin towers, jutting bay windows, and a bit of romantic fantasy—as if an urban château had been crafted with grace and style. Like many other buildings in this neighborhood, it houses private apartments and cannot be visited.

   Continue walking west along Carrer de València until you reach the corner of Carrer de Roger de Llúria, where virtually every building at the intersection is architecturally noteworthy. Turn right onto Carrer de Roger de Lluría and walk one block. At Carrer de Mallorca, detour for half a block to the right to admire the:

5. **Casa Tómas,** Carrer de Mallorca, 291, one of Barcelona's most famous 19th-century buildings. Designed by Domènech i Montaner, it is now the home of a design firm. Retrace your steps for half a block, heading west until you reach Carrer de Mallorca. Across the intersection is the Neo-Byzantine:

6. **Delegación del Gobierno,** Carrer de Mallorca, 278. The tilework here is among the best of its kind in Barcelona. Through an iron fence, you can admire the building's garden as well.

   From your position on Carrer de Mallorca, turn right at Carrer de Roger de Llúria. Within half a block on the right you'll see:

7. **Carrer de Roger de Llúria,** 112, a charming building that's a good example of the many beautiful art nouveau structures whose builders and architects are barely remembered. This particular example contains private apartments. A half block later, turn left on Carrer de Provença. Continue walking straight two blocks, crossing the intersection of Carrer de Pau Claris. One block later, on the right side (at the corner of the Passeig de Gràcia) you'll pass one of the most famous apartment buildings in the world, the:

8. **Casa Milà,** known as La Pedrera (the Quarry). Its serpentine front and "organically" inspired iron balconies represent Gaudí at his most distinctive. (Note that the Casa Milà's address is Carrer Provença, 261–265, or Passeig de Gràcia, 92.) Admire the Casa Milà from both Carrer Provença and Passeig de Gràcia, observing the womblike slabs of chiseled stone. Now, traverse the busy Passeig de Gràcia, stopping on the far (west) side for a view of the building's twisted chimneys, which are the best examples of their highly bizarre kind.

   You will now descend the gentle slope of one of Europe's most famous boulevards, the:

9. **Passeig de Gràcia.** At the first intersection, Carrer de Mallorca, notice the red brick and gray stone of the Hotel Condes de Barcelona, Passeig de Gràcia, 75. Built in 1895 as the private home of a Catalan nobleman, it was designed by the master architect Vilaseca, who used many medieval decorative touches (crenellations, heraldic shields, and palm-shaped columns) that later helped define the modernist movement. Today, rescued from destruction and restored, it is one of Barcelona's best hotels.

   Continue your walk down the western (right) slope of the Passeig de Gràcia.

Refueling Stop

10. **El Drugstore,** Passeig de Gràcia, 71 (☎ **215-70-74**), is a complex with a snack bar and cafeteria, boutiques, record shops, and a tearoom. Combination plates are available, and you can order these plus a wide variety of drinks, sitting out at sidewalk tables if you prefer. It's ideal for people watching. If it's lunchtime, you'll find a *menú del día* offered for only 1,100 pesetas ($7.80). The place stays open 24 hours.

   When you reach Carrer d'Aragó, turn right and walk to the:

11. **Funació Antoni Tàpies,** Aragó, 255, one of Barcelona's 1990s museums (see "More Attractions," above). The building was designed by one of Barcelona's most admired modernist architects, Domènech i Montaner. The façade was not changed during the building's transformation into a museum of modern art.

   Turn left to retrace your steps back to Passeig de Gràcia. As you go downhill along the boulevard, two buildings merit your attention (both are described under "Special-Interest Sightseeing" earlier in this chapter), the:

12. **Casa Amatiller,** Passeig de Gràcia, 41, and the **Casa Batlló,** Passeig de Gràcia, 43, the former by Puig i Cadafalch, the latter by Gaudí.

   After a few more steps, you'll encounter the:

13. **Casa Lléo Morera** (see "Special-Interest Sightseeing" earlier in this chapter), another building by Domènech i Montaner, dating from 1905. Today it houses the Patronato de Turismo. Step inside to admire the vestibule. One block farther at:

14. **Passeig de Gràcia,** 27, is a richly embellished building, with eagles, laurel branches, and floral garlands carved in high relief into the stone.

   Shortly after, after having seen some of the landmark examples of modernisme, you'll find yourself back of the northern edge of the Plaça de Catalunya, where you started.

5 Organized Tours

Pullmantur, Gran Vía de les Corts Catalanes, 635 (☎ **317-12-97**), offers a number of tours and excursions (with English-speaking guides)—in both Barcelona and its environs. For a preview of the city, you can take a morning tour departing from the company's terminal at the above address at 9:30am, taking in the cathedral, the Gothic Quarter, the Rambles, the monument to Columbus, and the Spanish Village. An afternoon tour leaves at 3:30pm, with visits to some of the most outstanding architectural examples in the Eixample, including Gaudí's Sagrada Familia, and a stop at the Picasso Museum. Each of these tours costs 3,600 pesetas ($25.60). Pullmantur also offers full-day tours to the environs of Barcelona. Schedules depend on the season (call for information). The nearest Metro stop to this company is Plaça de Catalunya.

6 Sports & Recreation

BULLFIGHTING The Catalâns of Barcelona do not pursue this "art" with as much fervor as do the Castilians of Madrid. Nevertheless, you may want to attend one of the *corridas.* Bullfights are held from March to September, usually on Sunday at 6:30pm at Plaça de Toros Monumental, Gran Vía de les Corts Catalanes (☎ **245-58-04**). Purchase tickets in advance from the office at Muntaner, 24 (☎ **453-38-21**). Tickets cost from 1,600 pesetas ($11.40).

A FITNESS CENTER The city's most obvious fitness center lies adjacent to the Olympic Stadium, within an indoor-outdoor complex whose main allure is its beautifully designed pair of swimming pools. Built for the 1992 Summer Olympics, the facility contains a health club and gymnasium open to members of the public for 1,000 pesetas ($7.10) for a full day's pass. For the address, opening hours and a description, refer to the Piscina Bernardo Picornell in "Swimming" below.

GOLF One of the city's best courses, **Club de Golf Vallromanas,** Afueras s/n, Vallromanas (Barcelona) (☎ **572-90-64**) lies within a 20-minute drive north of the town center. Nonmembers who reserve tee-off times in advance are welcome to play for a greens fees of 5,750 pesetas ($40.80) on weekdays, and 11,500 pesetas ($81.70) on weekends. The club is open Wednesday to Monday from 8am to 9pm.

JOGGING In the heart of Barcelona, the **Parc de la Ciutadella** (see "Parks & Gardens," in Section 2) is the jogger's favorite. You can also use the paths surrounding Montjuïc.

SQUASH Your best bet is the **Squash Club Barcelona,** Doctor Gregoria Maranon, 17 (☎ **334-02-58;** Metro: Universitat), accepts nonmembers and is open daily from 8:30am to 2am. Squash courts can be rented by anyone for 1,320 ptas. ($9.40) per half hour of play time. There are 14 courts in all. The swimming pool and gym, however, are reserved for members.

SWIMMING Most city residents head out to the beaches of Sitges whenever they feel like swimming, but if you're looking for a not-very-crowded pool, you'll find one at the **Esportiu Piscina DeStampa,** Calle Rosich, s/n, in the Hospitalete district (☎ **334-56-00**). It's open Monday through Friday from 1 to 3pm, and 7 to 9pm; Saturday 10am to 2pm and 4 to 11pm; and Sunday 10am to 1pm. Admission costs 250 pesetas ($1.80).

A much better choice, however, allows you to swim where some of the events of the 1992 Summer Olympics took place, at **Piscina Bernardo Picornell,** Avinguda de Estadi, 30–40, on Montjuïc (☎ **423-40-41**). Set adjacent to the Olympic Stadium, it incorporates two of the best and most state-of-the-art swimming pools in Spain, each custom-built for the 1992 Olympics, and now open to the public Tuesday through Saturday from 7am to midnight, Sunday and Monday from 7am to 8pm. (One pool is outdoors; the other is indoors.) Entrance costs 1,000 pesetas ($7.10), and allows full use throughout the day of whichever pool is in use at the time, the gymnasium, the sauna, and the Jacuzzis. Bus 61 makes frequent runs from the Plaça d'Espanya.

TENNIS The neighborhoods of Barcelona don't contain as many tennis courts as you might have expected from a city of its size. The ones that do exist are organized in often unexpected places, usually within clusters of two or three courts per grouping. Many of them are private; others are associated with hotels or some of the city's schools and universities. One of city's largest clubs is technically private, but sometimes allows qualified players to use their facilities for an hour if the courts aren't busy. The **Open Tennis Club** (also known as Club Open) (☎ **379-42-46**), lies in the village of Castel de Fels, 3½ miles beyond the airport, beside the road leading to Sitges. (Signs will guide you from the highway.) If space is not available at the time of your call, your hotel concierge, the Barcelona tourist office, or the operators at phone line "010" might be able to tell you of other courts that might allow short-term access to non-members.

7 Savvy Shopping

Barcelonans look more to Paris than to Madrid for their fashions and style and, of course, create much of their style themselves. *Moda joven* (young fashion) is all the rage in Barcelona.

If your time and budget are limited, you may want to patronize the two major department stores, El Corte Inglés and Galerías Preciados, for an overview of Catalán merchandise at reasonable prices. Barcelona is filled with boutiques, but clothing is an expensive item here, even though the city has been a textile center for centuries.

Markets (see below) are very popular in Barcelona and are suitable places to search for good buys.

THE SHOPPING SCENE If you're a window shopper, stroll along the **Passeig de Gracìa** from the Avinguda Diagonal to the Plaça de Catalunya. Along the way, you'll see some of the most elegant and expensive shops in Barcelona, along with an assortment of splendid turn-of-the-century buildings and cafés, many with outdoor tables.

Another shopping expedition is to the **Mercat de la Boquería,** Rambla, 101 (☎ **318-25-84**), near Carrer del Carme, open all day. Here you'll see a wide array of straw bags and regional products, along with a handsome display of the food that you are likely to be eating later in a local restaurant: fruits, vegetables (artfully displayed), breads, cheeses, meats, and fish.

In the **old quarter** the principal shopping streets are all five of the Rambles, plus Carrer del Pi, Carrer de la Palla, and Avinguda Portal de l'Angel, to cite only some of the major ones. Moving north in the Eixample are Passeig de Catalunya, Passeig de Gràcia, and Rambla de Catalunya. Going even farther north, Avinguda Diagonal is a major shopping boulevard. Other prominent shopping streets include Bori i Fontesta, Via Augusta, Carrer Muntaner, Travessera de Gràcia, and Carrer de Balmes.

In general, shopping hours are Monday to Saturday from 9am to 8pm. Some smaller shops close from 1:30 to 4pm.

The **American Visitors Bureau,** Gran Vía, 591 (☎ **301-01-50**), between Rambla de Catalunya and Calle de Balmes, will pack and ship your purchases and gifts and even handle excess luggage and personal effects. The company also operates a travel agency here, booking flights and hotel accommodations for those needing it. It's open Monday to Friday from 9am to 1pm and 4 to 7pm, Saturday from 9am to 1pm.

Watch for summer **sales** (*rebajas*) in late July and August. Merchandise is often heavily discounted by stores getting rid of their summer stock before fall.

Shopping A to Z

Barcelona, a city of design and fashion, offers a wealth of shopping opportunities. In general, prices tend to be slightly lower than those in London, Paris, and Rome.

In addition to modern, attractively designed, and stylish clothing, shoes and decorative objects are often good buys. In the city of Miró, Tàpies, and Picasso, art is a major business, and the reason so many gallery owners from around the world come to visit. You'll find dozens of galleries, especially in the Barri Gòtic and around the Picasso Museum. Barcelona is also noted for its flea markets, where good purchases are always available if you search hard enough.

Antiques abound here, but rising prices have put them beyond the means of the average shopper. However, I've listed some shops where you can look, if nothing else. Most shoppers from abroad settle happily for handcrafts, and the city is rich in offerings, ranging from simple pottery to handmade furniture. Barcelona has been in the business of creating and designing jewelry since the 17th century, and its offerings in this field are of the widest possible range—as are the prices.

What follows is only a limited selection of some of the hundreds of shops in Barcelona.

ANTIQUES

Artur Ramón Anticuario, Carrer de la Paella, 25. ☎ **302-59-70.**

One of the finest antiques stores in Barcelona is this three-level emporium with high ceilings and a medieval kind of grace. Set on a narrow flagstone-covered street near Plaza del Pi (the center of the antiques district), it stands opposite a tiny square, the Placeta al Carrer de la Palla, whose foundations were laid by the Romans. The store, which has been operated by four generations of men named Artur Ramón, contains everything from Romanesque works to Picasso. The prices are high, as you'd expect, for items of quality and lasting value. Open Monday to Friday from 9am to 1:30pm and 5 to 8pm, Saturday from 9am to 1:30pm. Metro: Jaume I.

El Bulevard des Antiquaris, Passeig de Gràcia, 55. No central phone.

This 70-unit shopping complex just off one of the town's most aristocratic avenues has a huge collection of art and antiques, assembled in a series of boutiques. There's a café/bar on the upper level. Some boutiques keep "short" hours. Summer hours are Monday to Friday from 9:30am to 8:30pm; winter hours are Monday from 4:30 to 8:30pm and Tuesday to Saturday from 10:30am to 8:30pm. Metro: Passeig de Gràcia.

Urbana, Còrsega, 258. ☎ **218-70-36.**

Urbana sells an array of architectural remnants (usually from torn-down mansions), antique furniture, and reproductions of brass hardware. There are antique and reproduction marble mantlepieces, wrought-iron gates and garden seats, even carved wood fireplaces with the modernist look. It's an impressive, albeit costly, array of merchandise rescued from the architectural glory of yesteryear. Open Monday to Saturday from 10am to 2pm and 4:30 to 8pm. Metro: Hospital Sant Pau.

CAMERAS

Casa Arpi, Rambla dels Caputxins, 40. ☎ **301-74-04.**

This is one of the most famous camera shops in Spain. A multilingual staff will guide you to the best buys in new and used cameras, including familiar brand-name products. The firm also does quality processing, ready within 24 to 48 hours. Open Monday to Saturday from 9:30am to 1:30pm and 4:30 to 8pm. Metro: Liceu.

DEPARTMENT STORES

El Corte Inglés, Plaça de Catalunya, 14. ☎ **302-12-12.**

This is the largest and most glamorous department store chain in Spain. The store sells a wide variety of merchandise, ranging from Spanish handcrafts to high-fashion items, from Spanish or Catalán records to food. The store also has restaurants and cafés and offers a number of consumer-related services, such as a travel agent. It has a department that will arrange for the mailing of purchases back home. Open Monday to Friday from 10am to 8pm and Saturday from 10am to 9pm. Metro: Plaça de Catalunya.

Galerías Preciados, Avinguda Portal de l'Àngel, 19-21. ☎ **317-00-00.**

The other major department store in Barcelona. It has much the same merchandise as El Corte Inglés but with perhaps a larger selection of more cut-rate items. It, too, has a travel agent and a number of other consumer-related services of interest to visitors. There are also catering facilities if you'd like food on the run. Open Monday through Saturday from 10am to 9pm. Metro: Plaça de Catalunya.

DESIGNER HOUSEWARES

Bd Ediciones de Diseño, Mallorca. ☎ **458-69-09.**

Housed in one of the Belle Epoque's most famous buildings, a modernist creation by Llúis Domènech i Montaner, is this showcase of Catalán design. The "Bd" stands for Barcelona design. The emporium's two floors of showrooms contain housewares, furniture, and utilitarian household aids whose unifying element is a style-conscious flair brought to the design. Some of the merchandise, such as chairs, are copies of pieces by such masters as Gaudí. Copies of works by Salvador Dalí are also sold. A catalog shows photographs and prices of everything in inventory; only a fraction of the offerings are displayed in the showrooms. Famous designer names from abroad include Alvar Aalto of Finland and Le Corbusier of France. The store can arrange to ship purchases abroad. Open Monday through Saturday from 10:30am to 1:30pm and 4 to 8pm. Closed in August. Metro: Verdaguer.

Roser-Francesc, Roger de Llúria, 87. ☎ **215-78-67.**

With an inventory scattered over two floors of a narrow storefront in the Eixample district, this establishment is the quintessential boutique. It stocks only a limited selection of casually elegant clothes for both men and women, each chosen carefully with an alert consciousness of what is currently fashionable in Rome, Paris, Düsseldorf, and Los Angeles. Most of the garments are crafted from cotton, and are ideal for such warm-weather resorts as Sitges, a short car ride to the south of Barcelona. Open Monday to Saturday from 10:30am to 8pm. Metro: Urquinaona.

GALLERIES

Art Picasso, Tapineria, 10. ☎ **310-49-57.**

Here you can get good lithographs of works by Picasso, Miró, and Dalí, as well as T-shirts emblazoned with the designs of these masters. Tiles sold here often carry their provocatively painted scenes. Open Monday to Saturday from 9:30am to 8pm and Sunday from 9:30am to 3pm. Metro: Jaume I.

Vincón, Passeig de Gràcia, 96. ☎ **215-60-50.**

Fernando Amat's Vincón is the best in the city, with 10,000 products—everything from household items to the best in Spanish contemporary furnishings. Housed in the former home of artist Ramón Casas, with gilded columns and mosaic-inlaid floors, the showroom is filled with the best Spain has, with each item personally selected because of its quality and craft. The window display alone is worth the trek there: Expect *anything.* Open Monday to Saturday from 10am to 1:30pm and 5 to 8pm. Metro: Passeig de Gràcia.

FABRICS & WEAVINGS

Coses de Casa, Plaça de Sant Josep Oriol, 5. ☎ **302-73-28.**

Appealing fabrics and weavings are displayed in this 19th-century store. Many are handwoven in Majorca (Balearic Islands), their boldly geometric patterns inspired by the Arabs centuries ago. The fabric, for the most part, is 50% cotton, 50% linen; much of it would make excellent upholstery material. Open Monday to Saturday from 9:45am to 1:30pm and 4:30 to 8pm. Metro: Jaume I.

FASHION

Groc, Ramble de Catalunya. ☎ **215-74-74.**

Designs for both women and men are sold here. One of the most stylish shops in Barcelona, it is expensive but filled with high-quality apparel made from the finest of natural fibers. The men's store is downstairs, the women's store one flight up. Open Monday to Saturday from 10am to 2pm and 4:30 to 8pm. Closed in August; the men's department is closed Monday from 10am to 2pm, the women's department is closed Saturday from 4:30 to 8pm. Metro: Plaça de Catalunya.

Sala Parés, Petritxol, 5. ☎ **318-70-20.**

Established in 1840, this is the finest art gallery in the city, recognizing and promoting the work of many Spanish and Catalán painters and sculptors who have gone on to acclaim. The Maragall family has been the "talent" who recognized all this budding talent. Paintings are displayed in a two-story amphitheater, whose high-tech steel balconies are supported by a quartet of steel columns evocative of Gaudí. Exhibitions of the most avant-garde art in Barcelona change about every three weeks. Open Monday to Saturday from 10:30am to 2pm and 4:30 to 8:30pm, Sunday from 11am to 2pm. Metro: Plaça de Catalunya.

GIFTS

Beardsley, Petritxol, 12. ☎ **301-05-76.**

Named after the Victorian English illustrator, this store lies on the same street where the works of Picasso and Dalí were exhibited before they became world famous. The wide array of gifts, perhaps the finest selection in Barcelona, includes a little bit of everything from everywhere—dried flowers, writing supplies, silver dishes, unusual bags and purchases, and lots more. Open Monday to Friday from 9:30am to 1:30pm and 5 to 8pm, Saturday from 10am to 2pm. Metro: Plaça de Catalunya.

LEATHER

Loewe, Passeig de Gràcia. ☎ **216-04-00.**

The biggest branch in Barcelona of this prestigious nationwide leather-goods chain. Everything is top-notch, from the elegantly spacious showroom to the expensive merchandise to the helpful salespeople, who operate out of one of the best-known modernist buildings in the city. The company exports its goods to branches throughout Asia, Europe, and North America. Open Monday to Saturday from 9:30am to 2pm and 4:30 to 8pm. Metro: Passeig de Gràcia.

MARKETS

El Encants antiques market is held every Monday, Wednesday, Friday, and Saturday in Plaça de les Glóries Catalanes (Metro: Glóries) (no specific times—go any time during the day to survey the selection).

The open-air **Mercado Gòtico de Antiquedades (Gothic Antiques Market),** Plaça Nova (☎ **317-19-96;** Metro: Jaume I), takes place next to the cathedral every Thursday, except in August, from 9am to 8pm. Here you can bargain with abandon if you find something that appeals to you.

Coins and postage stamps are traded and sold in **Plaça Reial** on Sunday from 10am to 2pm. The location is off the southern flank of the Rambles (Metro: Drassanes).

A book-and-coin market is held at the **Ronda Sant Antoní** every Sunday from 10am to 2pm (Metro: Universitat).

MUSIC

Casa Beethoven, Rambles, 97. ☎ **301-48-26.**

Probably the most complete collection of sheet music in town can be found here. In a narrow store established in 1920, the collection naturally focuses on the works of Spanish and Catalán composers. Music lovers might make some rare discoveries here. Open Monday to Friday from 9am to 1:30pm and 4 to 8pm, Saturday from 9am to 1:30pm. Metro: Liceu.

PORCELAIN

Kastoria 2, Avinguda Catedra, 6-8. ☎ **310-04-11.**

This large store near the cathedral carries many kinds of leather goods, including purses, suitcases, coats, and jackets. But most people come here to look at its famous Lladró porcelain—they are authorized dealers and have a big selection. Open Monday to Saturday from 10am to 2pm and 3 to 8pm, Sunday from 10am to 2pm and 4 to 7pm. Metro: Plaça de Catalunya.

POTTERY

Artesana I Coses, Placeta de Montcada, 2. ☎ **319-54-13.**

Here you'll find pottery and porcelain from every major region of Spain. Most of the pieces are heavy and thick-sided—designs in use in the country for centuries. Open Monday to Saturday from 10am to 2pm and 4 to 8pm. Metro: Jaume I.

Itaca, Carrer Ferran, 26. ☎ **301-30-44.**

Here you'll find a wide array of handmade pottery, not only from Catalonia but also from Spain, Portugal, Mexico, and Morocco. The merchandise has been selected for its basic purity, integrity, and simplicity. Open Monday to Friday from 10am to 1:30pm and 4:30 to 8pm, Saturday from 10am to 2pm and 5 to 8:30pm. Metro: Liceu.

SHOPPING MALLS

El Bulevard Rosa, Passeig de Gràcia, 55. ☎ **309-06-50.**

In some 100 stores you'll find a wide display of merchandise. Upstairs is the previously recommended antiques gallery, El Bulevard des Antiquaris, with some 70 shops. Open Monday to Saturday from 10:30am to 8:30pm. Metro: Passeig de Gràcia.

Diagonal Center, Avinguda Diagonal, 584. ☎ **209-65-97.**

One of the leading shopping malls of Barcelona, with 60-odd stores displaying a wide range of merchandise. Some of it is geared mainly to local consumers, but casual shoppers from abroad will also find items of interest here to take home. Open Monday to Saturday from 10:30am to 2pm and 4:30 to 8:30pm. Metro: Diagonal.

Poble Espanyol.

This is not technically a shopping mall but a "village" (see "More Attractions," earlier in this chapter) with about 35 stores selling typical folk crafts from every part of Spain: glassware, leather goods, pottery, paintings, and carvings—you name it. Stores keep various hours, but you can visit any time during the day. Transportation: Metro to Espanya; from there, free red double-decker bus to Montjuîc.

STRAW PRODUCTS

La Manuel Alpargaters, Aviño, 7. ☎ **301-01-72.**

In addition to its large inventory of straw products, such as hats and bags, this shop is known mainly for its footwear, called *espadrilles (alpargatas* in Spanish). This basic rope-soled shoe (said to go back 1,000 years) is made on the premises. Some Cataláns wear only espadrilles when performing the sardana, their national dance. To find La Manuel Alpargaters turn off the Rambles at the Carrer Ferran, walk two blocks, and make a right. Open Monday to Saturday from 9:30am to 1:30pm and 4:30 to 8pm. Metro: Jaume I.

UMBRELLAS

Julio Gomez, Rambla de Sant Josep, 104 (also called Rambla de las Flors). ☎ **301-33-26.**

For more than a century, Julio Gomez has rung up umbrella sales here. In a workshop out back, women labor over these unique umbrellas or lace-trimmed silk or cotton parasols. There are also Spanish fans, walking sticks capped with silver, and other memorabilia—all adding up to an evocative piece of nostalgia in shopping. Open Monday to Saturday from 9:30am to 1:30pm and 4 to 8pm. Metro: Liceu.

8 Evening Entertainment

Barcelona comes alive at night—the funicular ride to Tibidabo or the illuminated fountains of Montjuïc are especially popular. In the Franco era the center of club life was the cabaret-packed district near the south of the Rambles, an area incidentally known for nighttime muggings—so use caution if you go there. But the most fashionable clubs long ago deserted this seedy area and have opened in nearly every major district of the city.

Your best source of local information is a little magazine called *Guía del Ocio,* which previews "La Semana de Barcelona" (This Week in Barcelona). It's in Spanish, but most of its listings will probably be comprehensible. The magazine is sold at virtually every news kiosk along the Rambles.

Nightlife begins for Barcelonans with a promenade (*paseo*) along the Rambles in the early evening, usually from 5 to 7pm. Then things quiet down a bit, until a second surge of energy brings out the Rambles crowds again, from 9 to 11pm. After that the esplanade clears out quite a bit.

If you've been scared off by press reports of the Rambles between the Plaça de Catalunya and the Columbus Monument, you'll feel safer along the Rambla de Catalunya, in the Eixample, north of the Plaça de Catalunya. This street and its offshoots are lively at night, with many cafés and bars.

The array of nighttime diversions in Barcelona is staggering. There is something to interest almost everyone and to fit most pocketbooks. For families, the amusement parks are the most-frequented venues. Sometimes locals opt for an evening in the *tascas* (taverns) or pubs, perhaps settling for a bottle of wine at a café, an easy and inexpensive way to spend an evening people watching. Serious drinking in pubs and cafés begins by 10 or 11pm. But for the most fashionable bars and discos, Barcelonans delay their entrances until at least 1am.

Cultural events are big in the Catalonian repertoire, and the old-fashioned dance halls, too, still survive in some places. Although disco has waned in some parts of the world, it is still going strong in Barcelona. Decaying movie houses, abandoned garages, long-closed vaudeville theaters, whatever, have been taken over and restored to become nightlife venues for *movida,* that after-dark movement that sweeps across the city until dawn.

Flamenco isn't the rage here that it is in Seville and Madrid, but it still has its devotees. The city is also filled with jazz aficionados. And, best of all, the old tradition of the music hall with vaudeville lives forever in Barcelona.

SPECIAL EVENTS & DISCOUNTS In the summer you'll have plenty of free entertainment just by walking the streets. You'll see everything from opera to monkey acts. The Rambles are a particularly good place to watch.

There is almost always a **festival** happening in the city, and many of the events can be enjoyed for free. The tourist office can give you details of when and where.

Some **theaters** advertise discount or half-price nights. Check in the weekly *Guía del Ocio.*

The Performing Arts

Culture is deeply ingrained in the Catalán soul. The performing arts are strong here—some, in fact, taking place on the street, especially along the Rambles. Crowds will often gather around a singer or mime. A city square will suddenly come alive on Saturday night with a spontaneous festival—"tempestuous, surging, irrepressible life and brio," is how writer Rose MacCauley described it.

Long a city of the arts, Barcelona experienced a cultural decline during the Franco years, but now it is filled once again with the best opera, symphonic, and choral music.

The **Gran Teatre del Liceu,** Rambla dels Caputxins, was a monument to Belle Epoque extravagance, a 2,700-seat century opera house, one of the grandest theaters in the world. It was designed by Catalán architect Josep Oriol Mestves. In January of 1994, the opera house was gutted by fire, which sent shock waves through Catalonia, many of whose citizens regarded this place as the citadel of their culture. The old Liceu now belongs to the "Bare ruin'd choirs, where late the "sweet birds sang," to borrow from Shakespeare's sonnet. The government of Catalonia has vowed that "the Liceu will be rebuilt–right here, in the same place, and just as it was." Even as Barcelona debates the future of this world-famous opera house, visitors to the city now view its ruins as a sightseeing oddity. Stay tuned for future developments. Metro: Liceu.

CLASSICAL MUSIC

Palau de la Música Catalán, Sant Francest de Paula, 2. ☎ **268-10-00.**

In a city of architectural highlights, this one stands out. In 1908 Lluís Domènech i Montaner, a Catalán architect, designed this structure, including stained glass, ceramics, statuary, and ornate lamps among other elements. It stands today—restored—as a classic example of modernism. Concerts and leading recitals are presented here. The box office is open Monday to Friday from 10am to 9pm, Saturday from 3 to 9pm.

Prices: Ticket prices depend on the presentation.

THEATER

Theater is presented in the Catalán language and therefore will not be of interest to most visitors. However, for those who speak the language, or perhaps who are fluent in Spanish, the following venues are recommended.

Companyia Flotats, Teatre Poliorama, Rambla dels Estudis, 115. ☎ **317-75-99.**

This leading company is directed by Josep Maria Flotats, an actor-director who was trained in the tradition of theater repertory, working in such theaters in Paris as the Théâtre de la Villa and the Comédie-Français. He founded his own company in Barcelona, where he presents both classic and contemporary plays. Metro: Liceu.

Prices: Tickets 1,500–2,500 ptas. ($10.70–$17.80). **Closed:** Aug.

Mercat de Los Flors, Lleida, 59. ☎ **426-18-75.**

Housed in a building constructed for the 1929 International Exhibition at Montjuïc is this other major Catalán theater. Peter Brook first used it as a theater for a 1983 presentation of *Carmen.* Innovators in drama, dance, and music are showcased here, as are modern dance companies from Europe, including troupes from Italy and France. The 999-seat house also has a restaurant overlooking the rooftops of the city. Metro: Espanya.

Prices: Tickets 1,100–2,000 ptas. ($7.80–$14.20).

Teatre Lliure, Montseny, 47. ☎ **218-92-51.**

This self-styled free theater is the leading Catalán-language theater in Barcelona. Once a workers' union, since 1976 the building has been the headquarters of a theater

Major Concert/Performance Halls

Mercat de los Flors, Lleida, 59. ☎ **426-18-75.**

Palau de la Música Catalán, Sant Francest de Paula, 2. ☎ **268-10-00.**

Teatre Lliure, Montseny, 47. ☎ **218-92-51.**

Teatre Poliorama, Rambla dels Estudis, 115. ☎ **317-75-99.**

cooperative. Its directors are famous in Barcelona for the bold presentations here, including works by Bertolt Brecht, Luigi Pirandello, Jean Genêt (who wrote about Barcelona), and even Molière and Shakespeare. New dramas by Catalán playwrights are also presented. The house seats from 200 to 350. Metro: Passeig de Gràcia.

Prices: Tickets 1,100–1,750 ptas. ($7.80–$12.40).

FLAMENCO

El Tablao de Carmen, Poble Espanyol de Montjuïc. ☎ **325-68-95.**

This club provides a highly rated flamenco cabaret in the re-created village. You can go early and explore the village if you wish and even have dinner here. This place has long been a tourist favorite. The club is open Tuesday through Sunday from 8pm to past midnight. During the week, they sometimes close around 1am, often staying open until 2 or 3am on weekends, everything depending on business. The first show is always at 9:30pm, and second show on Tuesday, Wednesday, Thursday, and Sunday at 11:30pm, and on Friday and Saturday midnight. Reservations are encouraged.

Prices: Dinner and show, 7,000 ptas. ($49.70); drink and show, 3,500 ptas. ($24.90).

Tablao Flamenco Cordobés, Les Rambles, 35. ☎ **317-66-53.**

At the southern end of the Rambles, a short walk from the harborfront, you'll hear the strum of the guitar, the sound of hands clapping rhythmically, and the haunting sound of the flamenco, a tradition here since 1969. Head upstairs to an Andalusian-style room where performances take place with the traditional *cuadro flamenco*—singers, dancers, and guitarist. Cordobés is said to be the best showcase for flamenco in Barcelona. Open nightly at 10 and 11:45pm. Reservations are required. Closed in January. Metro: Drassanes.

Prices: Dinner and show, 7,000 ptas. ($49.70); one drink and show, 3,800 ptas. ($27).

The Club & Music Scene

CABARET

Arnau, Avinguda del Paral.lel, 60. ☎ **442-28-04.**

The show includes a great dance troupe with musical numbers, both nostalgic and modern. A little folklore is included, too. It's a warm, family atmosphere that has been going for a century. Open Sunday to Friday from 6:30 to 11pm and Saturday from 10:30pm to 1:15am. Metro: Paral.lel.

Admission (including first drink): 2,500–3,000 ptas. ($17.80–$21.30).

Belle Epoque, Muntaner, 246. ☎ **209-73-85.**

The opulent crystal chandeliers and plush accessories provide an appropriate backdrop for the glamour and glitter. The amplification system plus some of the most advanced lighting tricks in Barcelona add to the quality of the old-time music-hall shows. Open Monday to Saturday from 11pm to 1:30am. Metro: Diagonal.

Admission: Mon–Thurs 4,300 ptas. ($30.50); Fri–Sat 4,800 ptas. ($34.10).

Bodega Bohemia, Lancaster, 2. ☎ **302-50-61.**

This cabaret extraordinaire, off the Rambles, is a Barcelona institution, and everybody who is anybody has been here. The Bodega Bohemia rates as high camp—a talent showcase for theatrical personalities whose joints aren't so flexible but who perform with bracing dignity. Curiously, most audiences fill up with young people, who cheer, boo, catcall, and scream with laughter—and the old-timers on stage love it. The show stretches on forever. In all, it's an incredible entertainment bargain if your tastes lean slightly to the bizarre. Hard drinks cost 1,000 pesetas ($7.10). The street outside is none too safe; take a taxi right to the door. Open daily from 11pm to 4am. Metro: Liceu.

Admission: 1,000 ptas. ($7.10).

DANCE CLUBS & DISCOS

Estudio 54, Avinguda del Paral.lel, 64. ☎ **329-54-54.**

Barcelona's version of the ill-fated and long-defunct Studio 54 in New York rattles and rolls with some of the same energy as its namesake. It lies on the opposite side of the Barri Xinés from the Rambles. Inside, you'll discover several different light and slide shows, and a dance floor that is likely to be filled with some of the more offbeat and energetic members of Barcelona's night scene. Most of the establishment's business is conducted Friday to Sunday from 10:30pm to 4am. It also opens in a somewhat calmer mode for what it defines as "matinees" between 6:30 and 10pm on certain weekdays whose schedules vary from week to week. (At presstime, these matinees were held only Friday to Sunday, although the schedule will probably change before your arrival.) Metro: Paral.lel.

Admission: 1,000 ptas. ($7.10) during disco hours; 500 ptas. ($3.60) during the "matinees."

Up and Down, Numancia Diagonal, 179. ☎ **280-29-22.**

The chic atmosphere of this disco attracts the elite of Barcelona, spanning a generation gap. The more mature patrons, specifically the black-tie, post-opera crowd, head for the upstairs section, leaving the downstairs to the loud music and "flaming youth." Up and Down is the most cosmopolitan disco in Barcelona, with a carefully planned ambience, impeccable service, and a welcoming atmosphere. Every critic who comes here comments on the piquant, sassy antics of the waiters, whose theatricality is part of the carnival-like atmosphere pervading this place. The disco is enhanced by audiovisual techniques; the decor is black and white. Dress can be your own selection, but men must always—regardless of their outfit—wear a tie.

Technically, this is a private club and you can be turned away at the door. The restaurant is open Monday through Saturday from 10pm to 2am, serving meals costing from 4,000 pesetas ($28.40). The disco is open Monday through Saturday from 12:30am to anytime between 5am or 6:30am, depending on business. Drinks in the disco cost 1,600 pesetas ($11.40) for a beer or from 1,800 pesetas ($12.80) for a hard drink. Metro: Sants Estació.

Admission (including first drink): 2,000 ptas. ($14.20).

A DANCE HALL

La Paloma, Tigre, 27. ☎ **301-68-97.**

Those feeling nostalgic may want to drop in on the most famous dance hall of Barcelona. It was young in 1903. The iron for the famed Barcelona statue of Columbus was smelted in La Paloma before it became the dance hall it is today. Remember the fox trot? The mambo? If not, learn about them at La Paloma, where they're still danced, along with the tango, the cha-cha, and the bolero. Tuesday is boxing night: A boxing match actually takes place in a ringed-off area of the dance floor. Live orchestras provide the music for this old hall with its faded but flamboyant trappings, including gilded plaster angels, crystal chandeliers, and opera-red draperies. "Matinees" are from 6 to 9:30pm; night dances are from 11:30pm to 5am. Drinks cost from 800 pesetas ($5.70). Metro: Universitat.

Admission: 300–700 ptas. ($2.10–$5).

The Bar Scene

PUBS & BARS

El Born, Passeig del Born, 26. ☎ **319-53-33.**

Facing a rural-looking square, this place, once a fish store, has been cleverly converted. There are a few tables near the front, but my preferred spot is the inner room, decorated with rattan furniture, ceramic jugs, books, and modern paintings. Music here could be anything from Louis Armstrong to classic rock and roll. Dinner can also be had at the upstairs buffet. The room is somewhat cramped, but there you'll find a simple but tasty collection of fish, meat, and vegetable dishes—all carefully laid out; a full dinner without wine costs around 3,000 pesetas ($21.30). Open daily from 6:30am to 3am. Beer costs 350 pesetas ($2.50). Metro: Jaume I.

Cocktail Bar Boadas, Tallers, 1. ☎ **318-95-92.**

This intimate and conservative bar is usually filled with regulars. Established in 1933, it lies near the top of the Rambles. Many visitors use this place for a predinner drink and snack before wandering to one of the district's many restaurants. You can choose among a wide array of Caribbean rums, Russian vodkas, and English gins—the skilled bartenders know how to mix them all. The place is especially well known for its daiquiris. Open daily from 12:30pm to 2:30am. Drinks are 650 pesetas ($4.60), and beer costs 325 pesetas ($2.30). Metro: Plaça de Catalunya.

Dirty Dick's, Carrer Marc Aureli, 2. ☎ **200-89-52.**

An English-style pub behind an inwardly curving bay window in a residential part of town, Dirty Dick's has an interior of dark paneling and exposed brick, with banquettes for quiet conversation. If you sit at the bar, you'll be faced with a tempting array of tiny sandwiches that taste as good as they look. The pub is set at the crossing of Vía Augusta, a main thoroughfare leading through the district. Open daily from 6pm to 2:30am. Beer costs 400 pesetas ($2.80), and drinks are 600 pesetas ($4.30). Metro: Muntaner.

Pub 240, Aribau, 240. ☎ **209-09-67.**

This elegant bar, which bears absolutely no resemblance to an English pub, is arranged in three sections: a bar, a small amphitheater, and a lounge for talking and listening to music. Rock and South American folk music are played here, and the place is jammed almost every night. Open daily from 5pm to 5am. Drinks are 1,400 pesetas ($9.90).

Admission: 2,300 ptas. ($16.30).

Zig-Zag Bar, Platón, 13. ☎ **201-62-07.**

Favored by actors, models, cinematographers, and photographers, this bar claims to have inaugurated Barcelona's trend for high-tech minimalism in its watering holes. Owned by the same entrepreneurs who developed the state-of-the-art nightclub Otto Zuiz, it offers an unusual chance to see Spain's new *movida* in action. Open nightly from 7:30pm to 2:30am. Beer costs 400 pesetas ($2.80). Metro: Muntaner.

SPECIALTY BARS

Champagne Bars

The growing popularity of champagne bars during the 1980s was an indication of Spain's increasing cosmopolitanism. The Cataláns call their own version of champagne *cava.* In Spanish, champagne bars are called *champanerías,* and in Catalán the name is *xampanyerías.* These Spanish wines are often excellent, said by some to be better than their French counterparts. With more than 50 companies producing cava in Spain and with each bottling up to a dozen different grades of wine, the best way to learn about Spanish champagne is either to visit the vineyard or to sample the products at a xampanyería.

Champagne bars usually open at 7pm and stay open into the wee hours of the morning. Tapas are served, ranging from caviar to smoked fish to frozen chocolate truffles. Most establishments sell only a limited array of house cavas by the glass—you'll be offered a choice of *brut* or *brut nature* (brut is slightly sweeter). More esoteric cavas must be purchased by the bottle. The most acclaimed brands include Mont-Marçal, Gramona, Mestres, Parxet, Torello, and Recaredo.

La Cava del Palau, Verdaguer I Callis, 10. ☎ **310-09-38.**

Located in an old part of Barcelona, this large champagne bar is a favorite of the after-concert crowd (the Palace of Music is just around the corner). Live music is sometimes presented, accompanied by a wide assortment of cheeses, cold cuts, pâtés, and fresh anchovies. Open Monday to Saturday from 7pm to 3:30am. Cava costs 550 pesetas ($3.90). Metro: Urquinaona.

Xampanyería Casablanca, Bonavista, 6. ☎ **237-63-99.**

Someone had to fashion a champagne bar after the Bogart-Bergman film, and this is it. Four kinds of house cava is served by the glass. The staff also serves a good selection of tapas, especially pâtés. The Casablanca is close to the Passeig de Gràcia. Open Sunday to Thursday from 6:45pm to 2:30am and Friday and Saturday from 6:45pm to 3am. Cava costs 500 to 650 pesetas ($3.60 to $4.60), and tapas cost 400 to 800 pesetas ($2.80 to $5.70). Metro: Passeig de Gràcia.

Xampú Xampany, Gran Vía de los Corts Catalanes, 702. ☎ **265-04-83.**

At the corner of the Plaça de Tetuan, this champanería offers a variety of hors d'oeuvres in addition to the wine. Abstract paintings, touches of high tech, bouquets of flowers, and a pastel color scheme create the decor. Open daily from 6:30pm to 3:30am. Cava costs 450 to 500 pesetas ($3.20 to $3.60) per glass. Metro: Girona.

Grand Chic Bars

In Barcelona they speak of a "bar boom"—the weekly entertainment guide, *Guía del Ocio,* has estimated that 500 new bars opened before the 1992 Olympics. A staff writer said, "The city has put her ambition and energy into designing bars and hopping from bar to bar. The inauguration of a new watering hole interests people more than any other social, cultural, or artistic event." The bars are stylish and often avant-garde in design. I'll sample only a few of the better ones, but know that there are literally hundreds more.

Nick Havanna, Roselló, 208. ☎ **215-65-91.**

Its soaring ceiling is supported by vaguely ecclesiastical concrete columns, off which radiate four arms like a high-tech cathedral. There's a serpentine-shaped curve of two different bars upholstered in black-and-white cowhide, plus a bank of at least 30 different video scenes. To keep patrons in touch with world events between drinks, a Spanish-language teletype machine chatters out news events. Some women have admitted to detouring to the men's room for a view of the famous mirrored waterfall cascading into the urinal. This has become one of Barcelona's most-talked-about and most-frequented watering holes. It's hip and happening—so dress accordingly and go late or you'll have the place to yourself. Open daily from 8pm to 5am. Hard drinks cost from 900 pesetas ($6.40) for a whisky and from 600 pesetas ($4.30) for a beer. Metro: Diagonal.

Admission: Sun–Thurs, free; Fri–Sat, 900 ptas. ($6.40), including first drink.

Otto Zuiz Club, Lincoln, 15. ☎ **238-07-22.**

Sheathed in one of the most carefully planned neoindustrial decors in Spain, this nightspot is the last word in hip and a magnet for the city's artists and night people. Facetiously named after a German optician and the recipient of millions of pesetas worth of interior drama, it sits behind an angular facade that reminds some visitors of a monument to some mid-20th-century megalomaniac. Originally built to house a textile factory, the building contains a labyrinth of metal staircases decorated in shades of blue, highlighted with endless spotlights and warmed with lots of exposed wood. On the uppermost floor, a high-tech restaurant serves supper-club food (brochettes, light pastas, and platters of smoked fish) for around 3,000 pesetas ($21.30) for a full meal. Don't even think of showing up here before midnight. Open daily from 11pm to 4:30am. Drinks cost 1,000 to 1,400 pesetas ($7.10 to $9.90). Metro: Passeig de Gràcia or Fontana.

Admission: 2,000 ptas. ($14.20).

Ticktacktoe, Roger de Llúria, 40. ☎ **318-99-47.**

In the Eixample district, this bar/restaurant is one of the most-talked-about rendezvous in the city. The decor is definitely tongue-in-cheek—everything from a marble whale to a bar in the form of a female breast. Frequented by TV personalities, Ticktacktoe draws a fashionable crowd, most of whom are under 35. At the snooker and the billiards tables, regular competitions are held. Open Monday to Saturday from 7pm to 2:30am. Closed from August 15 to 30. Minimum consumption is 500 pesetas ($3.60). Metro: Passeig de Gràcia.

Zsa Zsa, Roselló, 156. ☎ **453-85-66.**

This is a favorite bar with journalists, writers, and advertising executives, who mingle, drink, converse, and make or break deals. A light system creates endlessly different patterns that seem to change with the mood of the crowd. Chrome columns capped with stereo speakers dot the room like a high-tech forest. Open Sunday to Thursday from 7pm to 2:30am and Friday and Saturday from 7pm to 4am. Beer costs 600 pesetas ($4.30), and drinks range from 900–1,600 pesetas ($6.40 to $11.40). Metro: Provença.

Nostalgia Bars

Bar Pastis, Santa Mònica, 4. ☎ **318-79-80.**

Just off the southern end of the Rambles, this tiny bar was opened in 1947 by Carme Pericás and Quime Ballester, two *valencianos.* They made it a shrine to Edith Piaf, and her songs are still played on an old phonograph in back of the bar. If you look at the dusty art in this dimly lit place, you'll see some of Piaf. But mainly the decor consists of paintings by Quime Ballester, who had a dark, rather morbid vision of the world. You can order four different kinds of *pastis* in this "corner of Montmartre." Outside the window, check out the view, usually a parade of transvestite hookers. The crowd is likely to include almost anyone, especially people who used to be called "bohemians"; they live on in this bar of yesterday. Go after 11:30pm. Open Monday, Wednesday, and Thursday from 7:30pm to 2am, Friday and Saturday from 7:30pm to 3am, and Sunday from 6:30pm to 1:30am. Pastis are 300 pesetas ($2.10), beer is 350 pesetas ($2.50), and drinks are 700 pesetas ($5). Metro: Drassanes.

Els Quatre Gats, Montsió, 3. ☎ **302-41-40.**

The Four Cats has been called "the best bar in Barcelona" (see the restaurant listing in Chapter 13). In 1897 Pere Romeu and three of his friends, painters Ramón Casas, Santiago Rusiñol, and Miguel Utrillo, opened a café for artists and writers at the edge of the Barri Gòtic. Early in the history of the café, they staged a one-man show for a young artist, Pablo Picasso, but he didn't sell one painting. However, Picasso stayed around to design the art nouveau cover of the menu. The café folded in 1903, becoming a private club and art school and attracting Joan Miró.

In 1978 two Cataláns reopened the café in the Casa Martí, a building designed by Josep Puig i Cadafalch, one of the leading architects of *modernisme.* The café displays works by major modern Catalán painters, including Tàpies. You can come in to drink coffee at the café, taste some wine, eat a full meal—and even try, if you dare, a potent Marc de Champagne, an *eau de vive* distilled from the local cava. The café is open daily from 8am to 2am. Drinks are 650 pesetas ($4.60), and beer is 250 pesetas ($1.80). Metro: Urquinaona.

Gay and Lesbian Bars

Chaps, Avinguda Diagonal, 365. ☎ **215-53-65.**

Gay residents of Barcelona refer to this saloon-style watering hole as the premier leather bar of Catalonia. But, in fact, the dress code usually steers more toward boots and jeans than leather and chains. Set behind a pair of swinging doors evocative of the old American West, Chaps contains two different bar areas. Open daily 7pm to 3am. Beer is 335 pesetas ($2.40). Metro: Diagonal.

El Convento, Carrer Bruniquer, 59 (Plaça Joanic). No phone.

This may be like no disco you've ever seen. The decoration is like a church, with depictions of the Virgin Mary and even candles adding to the ecclesiastical atmosphere. But the clientele consists of mainly young gay males in a party mood. Often shows and organized parties are presented here. A novelty, to say the least. Hours are daily from midnight to 6am. Drinks cost from 350 pesetas ($2.50) for a beer. Metro: Joanic.

Martin's Disco, Passeig de Gràcia, 130. ☎ **218-71-67.**

Behind a pair of unmarked doors, in a neighborhood of art nouveau buildings, this is one of the more popular gay discos in Barcelona. Within a series of all-black rooms, you'll wander through a landscape of men's erotic art, upended oil drums (used as cocktail tables), and the disembodied front-end chassis of yellow cars set amid the angular surfaces of the drinking and dancing areas. Another bar supplies drinks to a large room where films are shown. Beer costs 450 pesetas ($3.20). Open Sunday to Thursday from midnight to 4:30am and Friday and Saturday from midnight to 5am. Metro: Passeig de Gràcia.

Admission (including first drink): 900–1,300 ptas. ($6.40-$9.20).

Santanassa, Carrer Aribau, 27. ☎ **451-00-52.**

As a welcoming gesture, a plate of cookies and apples is placed at the front door. Up front you'll find a bar, and at the disco in back is a *homo erectus* mural. The clientele is predominantly gay male, but many single women also come here. Open daily from 11pm to 3am. Beer costs 325 pesetas ($2.30). Metro: Universidad.

Admission: Sun–Thurs, free; Fri–Sat (including first drink). 500 ptas. ($3.60).

More Entertainment

MOVIES Recent cinematic releases from Paris, New York, Rome, Hollywood, and even Madrid come quickly to Barcelona, where an avid audience often waits in long lines for tickets. Most foreign films are dubbed into Catalán, unless they're indicated as *VO* (original version). Movie listings are published in *Guía de Ocio,* available at any newsstand along the Rambles.

If you're a movie buff, the best time to be in Barcelona is June and early July for the annual film festival.

A CASINO Midway between the coastal resorts of Sitges and Villanueva, about 25 miles (40km) southwest of Barcelona and about 2 miles (3km) north of Sitges, stands the **Gran Casino de Barcelona,** Sant Pere (San Pedro) de Ribes (☎ **893-36-66**). The major casino in all of Catalonia, it is housed in a villa originally built during the 1800s. Elegant, with gardens, it attracts restaurant clients as well as gamblers. A set menu in the restaurant (reservations recommended) costs 5,000 pesetas ($35.50), and drinks go for around 700 pesetas ($5) each. For admission, you'll pay 550 pesetas ($3.90) and must show your passport. The casino is open year round daily from 5pm to perhaps 5am (closing times vary).

9 Easy Excursions

The major one-day excursions, such as to the monastery of Montserrat or to the resorts north along the Costa Brava, are covered in Chapters 15 and 16. However, if you've got a day to spare, you might also want to consider the following jaunt.

Penedés Wineries

From the Penedés wineries comes the famous cava (Catalán champagne), which can be sampled in the champagne bars of Barcelona. You can see where this wine originates by journeying 25 miles (40km) from Barcelona via highway A-2, Exit 27. There are also daily trains to Sant Sadurní d'Anoia, home to 66 cava firms. Trains depart from Barcelona Sants.

The firm best equipped to receive visitors is **Codorniu,** the largest producer of cava—some 40 million bottles a year. Codorniu is ideally visited by car because of unreliable public transportation. However, it's sometimes possible to get a taxi from the station at Sant Sadurní d'Anoia.

Groups are welcomed at Codorniu (there must be at least four). It's not necessary to make an appointment before showing up. Tours are presented in English, among other languages, and take 1½ hours; they visit some of the 10 miles (16km) of underground cellars by electric cart. Take a sweater, even on a hot day. A former pressing section has been turned into a museum, exhibiting wine-making instruments through the ages. The museum is housed in a building designed by the great modernist architect Puig i Cadafalch.

King Juan Carlos has declared the plant a national historic and artistic monument. The tour ends with a cava tasting. Tours are conducted Monday to Thursday from 8 to 11:30am and 3 to 5:30pm, Friday from 8 to 11:30am. The ideal time for a visit is for the autumn grape harvest. Codorniu is closed in August.

Cardona

Another popular excursion from Barcelona is to Cardona, 60 miles (97km) northwest of Barcelona or 370 miles (596km) northeast of Madrid. Take the N-11 west, then north on Rte. 150 to Manresa. Cardona, reached along Rte. 1410, lies northwest of Manresa, a distance of 20 miles (32km).

The home of the dukes of Cardona, the town is known for its canonical church, **Sant Vicenç de Cardona,** placed inside the walls of the castle. The church was consecrated in 1040. The great Catalán architect Josep Puig i Cadafalch wrote, "There are few elements in Catalán architecture of the 12th century that cannot be found in Cardona, and nowhere better harmonized." The church reflects the Lombard style of architecture. The castle (now the parador—see below) was the most important fortress in Catalonia.

WHERE TO STAY & DINE

Parador Nacional Duques De Cardona, Castillo de Carona, s/n, 08261 Cardona. ☎ **93/869-12-75.** Fax 93/869-16-36. 58 rms (all with bath), 2 suites. A/C TV TEL

Rates: 7,200–8,800 ptas. ($51.10–$62.50) single; 9,000–11,000 ptas. ($63.90–$78.10) double; 13,765–17,600 ptas. ($97.70–$125) suite. Breakfast 1,100 ptas. ($7.80) extra. AE, DC, MC, V. **Parking:** Free.

Sitting atop a cone-shaped mountain that towers 330 feet above Cardona, this restored castle opened as a four-star parador in 1976. Once the seat of Ludovici Pio (Louis the Pious) and a stronghold against the Moors, it was later expanded and strengthened by Guifré el Pilós (Wilfred the Hairy). In the 9th century the palace went to Don Ramón Folch, nephew of Charlemagne. The massive fortress castle proved impregnable to all but the inroads of time, and several ancient buildings in this hilltop complex have been restored and made part of the parador.

The spacious accommodations, some with minibars, are furnished with handcarved wooden canopied beds and woven bedspreads and curtains. The bedrooms command panoramic views. The public rooms are decorated with antique furniture, tapestries, and paintings of various periods. The bar is in a former castle dungeon, with meals served in the lone stone-arched medieval dining room where the counts once took their repasts. Offered on the menu are regional dishes costing 3,500 pesetas ($24.90) for a complete meal. Try the Catalán bouillabaisse, accompanied by wines whose taste would be familiar to the Romans. Service is daily from 1 to 4pm and 8 to 10:30pm.

15

Catalonia

FROM BARCELONA YOU CAN TAKE SEVERAL ONE-DAY EXCURSIONS. THE MOST popular excursion is to the Benedictine monastery of Montserrat, northwest of Barcelona. To the south, the Roman city of Tarragona has been neglected by visitors but is particularly interesting to those who appreciate history, while beach lovers should head for the resort of Sitges.

Catalonia has about six million residents and twice that many visitors annually. It is one of the "playgrounds" of Europe, with its beaches along the Costa Brava (see Chapter 16) and the Costa Dorada, centered around Sitges. Tarragona is the capital of its own province, and Barcelona, of course, is the major center of Catalonia (see Chapters 12 to 14).

The province of Catalonia forms a triangle bordered by the French frontier to the north, the Mediterranean Sea to the east, and the ancient province of Aragón to the west. The northern part is a rugged coastline, whereas the Costa Dorada is flatter, with miles of sandy beaches as well as a mild, sunny climate.

Pilgrims may go to Montserrat for its scenery and religious associations, and history buffs to Tarragona for its Roman ruins, but foreigners and locals alike head for the Costa Dorada just for fun. This seashore, named for its strips of golden sand, extends sometimes unbroken along the coastlines of Barcelona and Tarragona provinces. The most avid beach explorers sometimes traverse the entire coast.

One popular stretch is called La Maresme, extending from Río Tordera to Barcelona, a distance of 40 miles (64.5km). Allow at least 2½ hours to cross it without stopovers. The Tarragonese coastline extends from Barcelona to the Ebro River, a distance of 120 miles (193km); a trip along it will take a whole day. Highlights along this coast include Costa de Garraf, a series of creeks skirted by the corniche road after Castelldefels; Sitges; and Tarragona. One of the most beautiful stretches of the coast is Cape Salou, lying south of Tarragona in a setting of pinewoods.

We'll begin our tour through this history-rich part of Catalonia by going not along the coast but rather inland to the Sierra de Montserrat, which has more spectacular views than any place along the coast. Wagner used it as the setting for his opera *Parsifal*. The serrated outline made by the pinnacles of the sierra's steep cliffs led the Catalonians to call it *montserrat* (sawtooth mountain). It is the premier religious center of Catalonia. Thousands of pilgrims annually visit its monastery with its Black Virgin.

The Monestir de Poblet in Tarragona is the other major monastery of Catalonia. It, too, is a world-class attraction.

Seeing Catalonia

GETTING THERE Barcelona is your gateway to Catalonia. From this city you can consider visiting any of the attractions in the environs, including not only the towns in this chapter, but also the Costa Brava, north of Barcelona (see Chapter 16).

The best way to explore the region is at your leisure by car. Failing that, you can use public transportation. For Sitges and Tarragona, the train is best, but bus connections are also possible. There are both train and bus connections from Barcelona to the monastery at Montserrat.

A SUGGESTED ROUTE • Day 1 From Barcelona visit Montserrat. Return to Barcelona in the evening.

• Day 2 Head south from Barcelona for a day at Sitges. (If you have an extra day, spend it on the beach.) Based in Sitges, you can visit Tarragona. Or you can go to Tarragona and spend the night.

What's Special About Catalonia

Beaches
- Sitges, with miles of golden beaches—from family favorites to nudist spots.

Great Towns/Villages
- Tarragona, one-time home of Julius Caesar.
- Nearby Montblanch, a living museum from the Middle Ages.
- Sitges, a gay resort mecca that was a famous early 20th-century colony for artists and writers.

Ancient History
- The Museum Nacional Arqueològic at Tarragona, with relics from the Roman Empire and a celebrated *Head of Medusa.*
- The Passeig Arqueològic, at Tarragona, a walk along ancient Roman ramparts.

A Pilgrimage Center
- The monastery at Montserrat, legendary home of the Black Virgin, patron saint of Catalonia.

Scenic Views
- The eerie rock formations on the monastery road to Montserrat.

Special Events/Festivals
- The Carnaval at Sitges, celebrated before Lent, complete with floats and fancy dress.

• **Day 3** Head for Tarragona, either as a day trip (from Barcelona) or as an overnight excursion. You'll need all the time you can spare in Tarragona, as it offers many monuments.

1 Montserrat

35 miles (56km) NW of Barcelona, 368 miles (592km) E of Madrid

GETTING THERE • By Train The best and most exciting way to go is via the Catalán railway—Ferrocarrils de la Generalitat de Catalunya (Manresa line), with five trains a day leaving from the Plaça d'Espanya in Barcelona. The central office is at Plaça de Catalunya, 1 (☎ **205-15-15**). The train connects with an aerial cableway (Aeri de Montserrat), included in the rail passage. Expect to spend 2,080 pesetas ($14.80), including the funicular.

• **By Bus** The train with its funicular tie-in has taken over as the preferred means of transport. However, at certain times long-distance bus service is provided by Autocars Julià in Barcelona. Daily service from Barcelona to Montserrat is generally operated, with departures near Estacio Central de Barcelona-Sants, Plaça de Països Catalanes. Contact the Julià company at Carrer Viriato (☎ **490-40-00**).

• **By Car** Take the N-2 southwest of Barcelona toward Tarragona, turning west at the junction with the N-11. The signposts and exit to Montserrat will be on your right. From the main road, it's 9 miles (14.5km) up to the monastery through dramatic Catalán scenery, with eerie rock formations.

ESSENTIALS The area code for Montserrat is 93. The tourist information office is at Plaça de la Creu (☎ **93/835-02-51**).

Avoid visiting Montserrat on Sunday, if possible. Thousands of locals pour in then, especially if the weather is nice. Remember that the winds blow cold at Montserrat. Even in summer, visitors should take along warm sweaters, jackets, or coats. In winter, thermal underwear might not be a bad idea.

What to See & Do

Montserrat, sitting atop an impressive 4,000-foot mountain 7 miles (11km) long and 3.5 miles (5.5km) wide, is one of the most important pilgrimage spots in Spain, ranking with Zaragoza and Santiago de Compostela. Thousands travel here every year to see and touch the 12th-century statue of La Moreneta (The Black Virgin), the patron saint of Catalonia. So many newly married couples flock here for her blessings that Montserrat has become Spain's Niagara Falls.

The 50-member ★ *Escolanía* (boys' choir) is one of the oldest and most renowned in Europe, dating from the 13th century. At 1pm daily you can hear them singing *Salve Regina* and the *Virolai* (hymn of Montserrat) in the Basilica. The Basilica is open daily from 8 to 10:30am and noon to 6:30pm. Admission is free. To view the Black Virgin (12th or 13th century) statue, enter the church through a side door to the right. At the Plaça de Santa María you can also visit the **Museu de Montserrat,** known for its collection of ecclesiastical paintings, including works by Caravaggio and El Greco. Modern Spanish and Catalán artists are also represented (see Picasso's early *El Viejo Pescador*, dating from 1895). Works by Dalí and such French impressionists as Monet, Sisley, and Degas are also shown. The collection of biblical artifacts is also interesting; look for the crocodile mummy, at least 2,000 years old. Charging 300 pesetas ($2.10) admission, the museum is open daily from 10:30am to 2pm and 3 to 6pm.

The nine-minute funicular ride to the 4,119-foot-high peak, Sant Jeroni, makes for an exciting trip. The funicular operates about every 20 minutes in April through October, daily from 10am to 6:40pm. The cost is 700 pesetas ($5) round trip. From the top, you'll see not only the whole of Catalonia but also the Pyrenees and the islands of Majorca and Ibiza.

You can also make an excursion to **Sant Cova (Holy Grotto),** the alleged site of the discovery of the Black Virgin. The grotto dates from the 17th century and was built in the shape of a cross. Many famous Catalán artists, such as Puig i Cadafalch and Gaudí, exhibited religious works on the road to the shrine. You go halfway by funicular but must complete the trip on foot.

The chapel is open April to October, daily from 9am to 6:30pm; off-season hours are daily 10am to 5:30pm. The funicular operates from April to October only, every 15 minutes daily from 10am to 7pm, charging 300 pesetas ($2.10) round trip.

Where to Stay & Dine

Few people spend the night here, but most visitors will want at least one meal. If you don't want to spend a lot, purchase a picnic in Barcelona or ask your hotel to pack a meal.

Abat Cisneros, Plaça de Monestir, 08691 Montserrat. ☎ **93/835-02-01.** Fax 93/828-40-06. 41 rms (all with bath). TV TEL

Rates: 4,600 ptas. ($32.70) single; 7,700 ptas. ($54.70) double. Breakfast 625 ptas. ($4.40) extra. AE, DC, MC, V. **Parking:** 300 ptas. ($2.10).

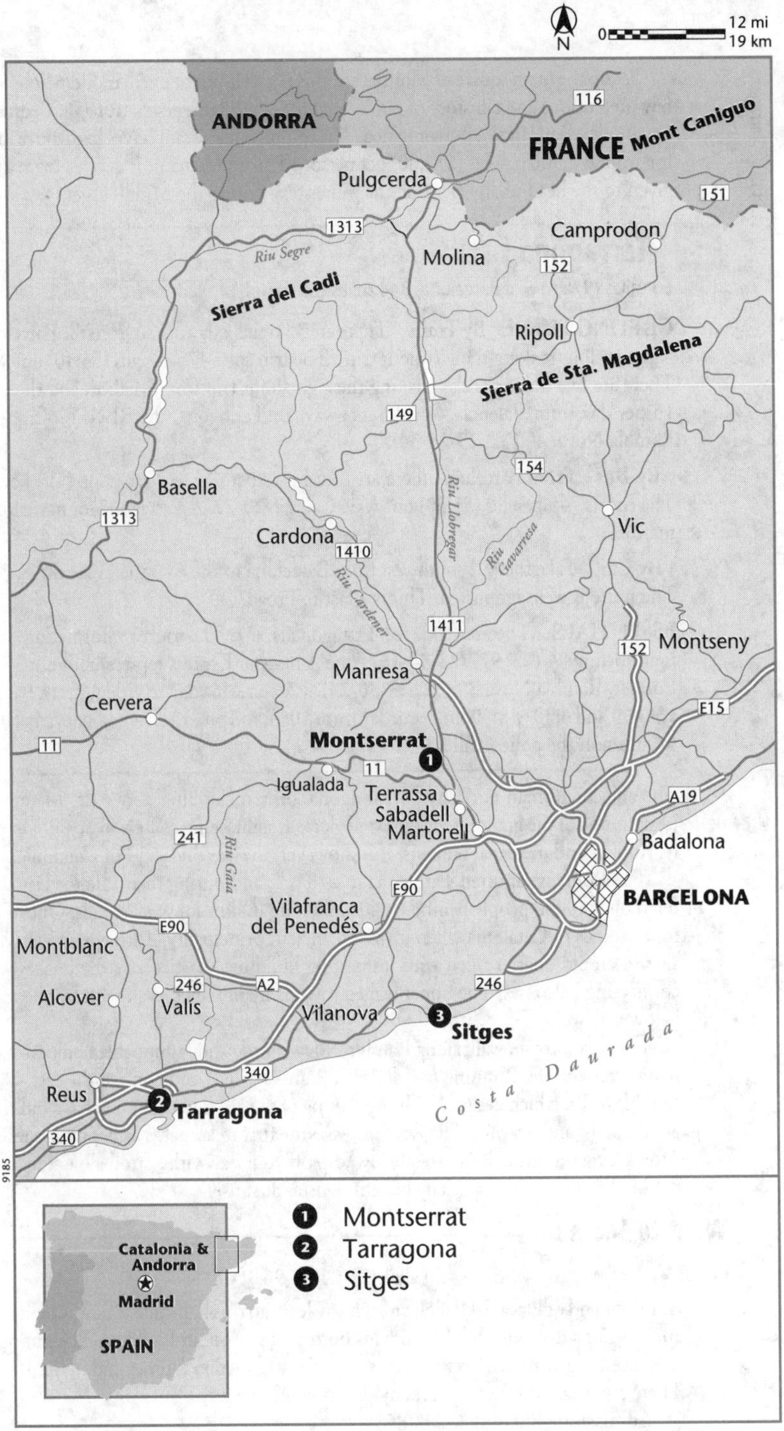

Catalonia

ANDORRA
FRANCE
Mont Caniguo
116
Pulgcerda
151
1313
Camprodon
Riu Segre
Molina
152
Sierra del Cadi
Ripoll
Sierra de Sta. Magdalena
149
154
Basella
Riu Llobregat
Vic
1313
Cardona
Riu Gavarresa
1410
Riu Cardener
1411
Montseny
152
Manresa
Cervera
E15
Montserrat
11
11
Igualada
Terrassa
A19
Sabadell
Martorell
Badalona
241
Riu Gaia
E90
BARCELONA
Vilafranca
del Penedés
E90
Montblanc
246
A2
246
Alcover
Valís
Vilanova
Sitges
340
Reus
Tarragona
Costa Daurada
340

9185

Catalonia & Andorra
Madrid
SPAIN

1. Montserrat
2. Tarragona
3. Sitges

Set on the main square of Montserrat, this is a well-maintained, modern hotel with few pretensions and a history of family management dating back to 1958. Bedrooms are simple, clean, and well-maintained. The in-house restaurant serves fixed-price meals for around 2,500 pesetas ($17.80) per person. The hotel's name is derived from a title given to the head of any Benedictine monastery during the Middle Ages.

2 Tarragona

60 miles (97km) S of Barcelona, 344 miles (554km) E of Madrid

GETTING THERE • By Train There are 32 trains a day to and from the Barcelona-Sants station (making the 1½-hour trip). The trip costs 475 pesetas ($3.40) one way. There are five trains per day making the eight-hour trip from Madrid, and there are 15 per day from Valencia, four hours away. In Tarragona, the RENFE office is at Rambla Nova, 40 (☎ **23-25-34**).

• By Bus From Barcelona, there are four buses per day to Tarragona (1½ hours). The cost is 745 pesetas ($5.30) one way. Call **22-20-72** in Tarragona for more information.

• By Car Take the A-2 southwest from Barcelona to the A-7, then take the N-340. The route is well signposted. This is a fast toll road.

ESSENTIALS The area code for Tarragona is 977. The tourist information office is at Fortuny, 4 (☎ **977/23-34-15**). The American Express representative at Viajes Eurojet, Rambla Nova 30 (☎ **23-36-23**), is open Monday to Friday from 9am to 1:30pm and 4:30 to 8:30pm, Saturday from 10am to 1pm. In an emergency, dial 091; to summon the police, call **23-33-11.**

The ancient Roman port city of Tarragona, on a rocky bluff above the Mediterranean, is one of the grandest, but most neglected, sightseeing centers in Spain. Despite its Roman and medieval remains, it is, however, the "second city" of Catalonia.

The Romans captured Tarragona in 218 B.C. and during their rule the city sheltered one million people behind its 40-mile-long (64km-long) city walls. One of the four capitals of Catalonia when it was an ancient principality, Tarragona today consists of an old quarter filled with interesting buildings, particularly the houses with connecting balconies. The upper walled town is mainly medieval, whereas the town below is newer.

In the new town, walk along Rambla Nova, a wide and fashionable boulevard, the main artery of life. Running parallel with Rambla Nova, and lying to the east, is the Rambla Vella, which designates the beginning of the old town. The city has a bullring, good hotels, and beaches. The Romans were the first to launch Tarragona as a resort. After seeing the attractions listed below, cap off your day with a stroll along the Balcó del Mediterrani, with especially beautiful vistas at sunset.

What to See & Do

Passeig Arqueològic, Plaça del Pallol. ☎ **24-57-96.**

At the far end of Plaça del Pallol, an archway leads to this half-mile walkway along the ancient ramparts, built by the Romans on top of cyclopean boulders. The ramparts have been much altered over the years, especially in medieval times and in the 1600s. There are pleasant views from many points along the way.

Admission: 400 ptas. ($2.80).

Open: July–Sept, daily 10am–midnight. Oct–Mar, Mon–Sat 10am–5:30pm; Sun 10am–3pm. Apr–June, daily 10am–8pm. **Bus:** 1.

Catedral, Plaça de la Seu. ☎ **23-86-85.**

Situated at the highest point of Tarragona is this 12th-century cathedral, whose architecture represents the transition from Romanesque to Gothic. It has an enormous vaulted entrance, fine stained-glass windows, Romanesque cloisters, and an open choir. In the main apse, observe the altarpiece of St. Thecla, patron of Tarragona, carved by Pere Joan in 1430. Two flamboyant doors open into the chevet. The east gallery is the Museu Diocesà, with a collection of Catalán art.

Admission: Cathedral, free; museum, 300 ptas. ($2.10).

Open: Mar 16–June 30, daily 10am–12:30pm and 4–6:45pm; July 1–Oct 15, daily 10am–7pm; Oct 16–Nov 15, daily 10am–12:30pm and 4–6:45pm; Nov 16–Mar 15, daily 10am–1:45pm. **Bus:** 1.

Amfiteatre Romà, Parc del Milagro.

At the foot of Miracle Park and dramatically carved from the cliff that rises from the beach, the Roman amphitheater recalls the days in the 2nd century when thousands of Romans gathered here for amusement.

Admission: 400 ptas. ($2.80).

Open: Apr–Sept, Tues–Sat 10am–8pm; Sun 10am–3pm. Oct–Mar, Tues–Sat 10am–5:30pm; Sun 10am–3pm. **Bus:** 1.

Necròpolis, Passeig de la Independència. ☎ **21-11-75.**

This is one of the most important burial grounds in Spain, having been used by the Christians from the 3rd century through the 5th. It stands outside town next to a tobacco factory whose construction led to its discovery in 1923. While on the grounds, visit the Museu Paleocristià, which contains a number of sarcophagi and other objects discovered during the excavations.

Admission: Necròpolis plus museum 100 ptas. (70¢).

Open: June 16–Sept 15, Tues–Sat 10am–1:30pm and 4:30–8pm, Sun 10am–1:30pm. Sept 16–June 15, Tues–Sat 10am–1:30pm and 4–7pm, Sun 10am–2pm. **Bus:** 1:

Museu Nacional Arqueològic, Plaça del Rei, 5. ☎ **23-62-09.**

The Archeology Museum, overlooking the sea, houses a collection of Roman relics—mosaics, ceramics, coins, silver, sculpture, and more. Don't miss the outstanding *Head of Medusa,* with its penetrating stare.

Admission: 100 ptas. (70¢).

Open: June 16–Oct 15, Tues–Sat 10am–1pm and 4:30–8pm, Sun 10am–2pm. Oct 16–June 15, Tues–Sat 10am–1:30pm and 4–7pm, Sun 10am–2pm. **Bus:** 1.

Where to Stay

EXPENSIVE

Hotel Imperial Tarraco, Paseo de las Palmeras/Rambla Vella, 43003 Tarragona.
☎ **977/23-30-40.** Fax 977/21-65-66. 145 rms, 25 suites. A/C MINIBAR TV TEL **Bus:** 1.

Rates (including breakfast): 13,500–25,000 ptas. ($95.90–$177.50) single; 16,500–31,500 ptas. ($117.20–$223.70) double; 32,500–54,000 ptas. ($230.80–$383.40) suite. AE, DC, MC, V. **Parking:** Free.

Located about a quarter-mile south of the cathedral, atop an oceanfront cliff whose panoramas include a sweeping view of both the sea and the Roman ruins, this hotel is considered the finest in town. Designed in the form of a crescent, it has guest rooms that usually angle out to sea and almost always include small balconies. The accommodations, all with private baths, are furnished with uncomplicated modern furniture. The public rooms contain lots of polished white marble, Oriental carpets, and leather furniture. The staff corresponds well to the demands of both traveling businesspeople and art lovers on sightseeing excursions.

Dining/Entertainment: The hotel contains both a bar and a restaurant. Meals cost from 3,000 pesetas ($21.30).

Services: Room service, laundry, concierge, hairdresser, babysitting.

Facilities: Outdoor pool, tennis courts, pleasant garden.

MODERATE

Hotel Lauria, Rambla Nova, 20, 43004 Tarragona. ☎ **977/23-67-12.** Fax 977/23-67-00. 72 rms (all with bath). A/C TV TEL **Bus:** 1.

Rates: 7,000-9,000 ptas. ($49.70–$63.90) single; 11,000 ptas. ($78.10) double. Breakfast 550 ptas. ($3.90) extra. AE, DC, MC, V. **Parking:** 800 ptas. ($5.70).

Set less than half a block north of the town's popular seaside promenade (Paseo de les Palmeres), beside the tree-lined Rambla, this straightforward three-star hotel offers unpretentious, functional, and clean bedrooms, each of which was recently modernized. For years considered the leading hotel of town until its replacement by other newcomers, it still draws a loyal clientele of repeat visitors. The rooms in back open onto a view of the sea, a garden, and the hotel's swimming pool. Only the public rooms are air-conditioned.

Dining/Entertainment: There is no full-fledged restaurant on the premises, but the staff happily directs clients to nearby eateries. The ground floor contains an informal pizzeria.

Services: Room service (daily 7 am to midnight), laundry, concierge, babysitting.

Facilities: Outdoor swimming pool, bar, car rentals.

Hotel París, Juan Maragall 4, 43003 Tarragona. ☎ **977/23-60-12.** Fax 977/23-86-54. 45 rms (all with bath). TEL **Bus:** 1.

Rates: 5,500 ptas. ($39.10) single; 9,000 ptas. ($63.90) double. Breakfast 600 ptas. ($4.30) extra. AE, DC, MC, V.

Opening onto an attractive landmark square, the Plaça de Berdaguer, this hotel, with simply furnished but clean rooms, rates as one of your best bets. There is no restaurant, but you can order a continental breakfast.

Hotel Urbis, Carrer Reding, 20 bis, 43001 Tarragona. ☎ **977/24-01-16,** or toll free **528-1234** in the U.S. and Canada. Fax 977/24-36-54. 44 rms (all with bath). A/C MINIBAR TV TEL **Bus:** 3.

Rates (including buffet breakfast): 7,575 ptas. ($53.80) single; 10,700 ptas. ($76) double. AE, MC, V. **Parking:** 1,300 ptas. ($9.20).

The rooms at this hotel off the Plaça de Corsini are three-star quality and much improved in recent years, with such added amenities as safes. The hotel also offers a restaurant with an English menu, with meals ranging from 1,000–2,000 pesetas ($7.10–$14.20). The nearby tourist office will give you a map for exploring Tarragona.

INEXPENSIVE

Hotel Astari, Via Augusta, 95, 43003 Tarragona. ☎ **977/23-69-00.** Fax 977/23-69-11. 83 rms (all with bath or shower). TV TEL **Bus:** From station to Via Augusta, No. 3.

Rates: 4,000–5,000 ptas. ($28.40–$35.50) single; 5,500–6,500 ptas. ($39.10–$46.20) double. Breakfast 550 ptas. ($3.90). **Closed:** Oct 31–May 2.

In-the-know travelers in search of peace and quiet on the Mediterranean come to the Astari, which opened its doors back in 1959 and was last renovated in 1992. This five-story resort hotel on the Barcelona road offers fresh and airy, but rather plain accommodations; a swimming pool; and a solarium. The Astari has long balconies and terraces, one favorite spot being the outer flagstone terrace with its umbrella tables set among willows, orange trees, and geranium bushes. There are both a cafeteria and a cocktail lounge. This is the only hotel in Tarragona with garage space for each guest's car.

Nuría, Vía Augusta, 217, 43007 Tarragona. ☎ **977/23-50-11.** Fax 977/24-41-36. 61 rms (all with bath). TEL **Bus:** 1 or 9.

Rates: 3,300 ptas. ($23.40) single; 5,800 ptas. ($41.20) double. Breakfast 475 ptas. ($3.40) extra. MC, V. **Closed:** Nov–Mar. **Parking:** 850 ptas. ($6).

Built near the beach in 1967, this five-floor modern building offers neat, pleasant rooms, most with balconies. You can dine in the sunny restaurant, where a meal goes for 1,350 pesetas ($9.60). The Nuría's specialty is *romesco*, a kind of *zarzuela* (seafood medley).

Where to Dine

$ **Barquet,** Gasometro, 16. ☎ **24-00-23.**

Cuisine: CATALÁN/SEAFOOD. **Reservations:** Recommended.

Prices: Appetizers 450–875 ptas. ($3.20–$6.20); main courses 700–2,000 ptas. ($5–$14.20). Menú del día 950 ptas. ($6.70). MC, V.

Open: Lunch, Mon–Sat 1:30–4pm; dinner, Mon–Sat 8:30–11:30pm. **Closed:** Aug.

Set in the center of town, within a five-minute walk from the cathedral, this restaurant specializes in seafood and shellfish prepared in the Catalán style. It was established in 1950 in the cellar of a relatively modern building, and is today run by the third generation of its original owners. Within a pair of dining rooms, comfortably outfitted in nautical themes, you can enjoy such dishes as *sopa de pescados* Tarragona style; *romesco* (ragoût) of lotte with herbs; a local assemblage of fried finned creatures identified for many hundreds of years as *fideos rossejats*, several different preparations of sole and hake, and, if you're not interested in seafood, a choice of grilled veal, chicken, or beef. A list of Spanish and Catalán wines will complement any meal here. The staff is well-trained, polite, and proud of their Catalán antecedents.

$ **Cafetería Arimany,** Rambla Nova, 43–45. ☎ **23-79-31.**

Cuisine: CATALÁN/INTERNATIONAL. **Reservations:** Not required. Bus: 1.

Prices: Appetizers 500–1,000 ptas. ($3.60–7.10); main courses 1,200–2,100 ptas. ($8.50–$14.90); fixed-price menu 2,000 ptas. ($14.20). AE, DC, MC, V.

Open: Breakfast, daily 8–11am; lunch, daily 1–4pm; dinner, Mon–Sat 7:30–11pm.

When this central and popular cafeteria opens its doors at 8am, visitors and locals alike pour in for breakfast. Others come back for lunch, and some finish with a good-value dinner. You can eat here inexpensively or for more money, depending on your appetite. The shrimp in garlic oil is outstanding. Try the fresh fish of the day, based on the local catch, or else squid cooked Roman style. The dessert specialty is Pau Casals, named after a native Catalonian, the late musician Pablo Casals. It is a chocolate cake served with a hot chocolate sauce. Another bakery specialty is *maginet*, the typical cookie of Tarragona.

Sol-Ric, Via Augusta, 227. ☎ **23-20-32.**

Cuisine: CATALÁN. **Reservations:** Not required.

Prices: Appetizers 650–1,000 ptas. ($4.60–$7.10); main courses 1,800–2,200 ptas. ($12.80–$15.60); fixed-price menu 2,000 ptas. ($14.20). AE, MC, V.

Open: Lunch, Tues–Sat 1–4pm; dinner, Tues–Sun 8:30–11pm. **Closed:** Mid–Dec to mid–Jan.

Many guests remember the service here long after memories of the good cuisine have faded. Dating from 1859, the place has a rustic ambience, replete with antique farm implements hanging from the walls. There are also an outdoor terrace and a central fireplace, usually blazing in winter. The chef prepares oven-baked *dorado* with potatoes, tournedos with Roquefort, seafood stew, and several exotic fish dishes, among other specialties.

Excursions from Tarragona

If you rent a car, you can visit two attractions within a 30- to 45-minute drive from Tarragona. The first stop is the **Monestir de Poblet,** Plaça Corona d'Aragó, s/n, E-43448 Poblet (☎ **87-00-89**), 29 miles (46.5km) northwest of Tarragona, one of the most intriguing monasteries in Spain. Its most exciting features are the oddly designed tombs of the old kings of Aragón and Catalonia. Constructed in the 12th and 13th centuries and still in use, Poblet's cathedral-like church reflects a mixture of Romanesque and Gothic architecture styles. Cistercian monks live here, passing their days writing, studying, working a printing press, farming, and helping to restore the building that suffered heavy damage during the 1835 revolution. Admission to the monastery is 300 pesetas ($2.10) for adults and 100 pesetas (70¢) for children. It's open Monday to Friday from 10am to 12:30pm and 3 to 6pm, Saturday and Sunday from 10am to 12:30pm and 2:35 to 5pm.

About three miles (4.8km) farther, you can explore an unspoiled medieval Spanish town, **Montblanch**. At its entrance, a map pinpoints the principal artistic and architectural treasures—and there are many. Walk. Don't drive along the narrow, winding streets.

3 Sitges

25 miles (40km) S of Barcelona, 370 miles (596km) E of Madrid

GETTING THERE • By Train RENFE runs trains from Barcelona-Sants to Sitges for the 50-minute trip. Call **93/490-02-02** in Barcelona for information about schedules. A round-trip same-day ticket costs 550 pesetas ($3.90). Two trains leave Barcelona per hour.

• By Car Sitges is a 45-minute drive from Barcelona along the C-246, a coastal road. An express highway, the A-7, opened in 1991. The coastal road is more scenic, but it can be extremely slow on weekends because of the heavy traffic, as all of Barcelona seemingly heads for the beaches.

ESSENTIALS The area code for Sitges is 93. The tourist information office is at Carrer Sínis Morera, 1. (☎ **93/811-76-30**).

SPECIAL EVENTS The **Carnaval** at Sitges is one of the outstanding events on the Catalán calendar. For more than a century, the town has celebrated the days prior to the beginning of Lent. Fancy dress, floats, feathered outfits, and sequins all make this an exciting event. The party begins on the Thursday before Lent with the arrival of the king of the "Carnestoltes" and ends with the "Burial of a Sardine" on Ash Wednesday. Activities reach their flamboyant best on Sant Bonaventura, where gays hold their own celebrations.

Sitges is one of the most frequented resorts of southern Europe, the brightest spot on the Costa Dorada. It is crowded in summer, mostly with affluent young northern Europeans, many of them gay. For years the resort was patronized largely by prosperous middle-class industrialists from Barcelona, but those rather staid days have gone; Sitges is as lively today as Benidorm and Torremolinos down the coast, but it's nowhere near as tacky.

Sitges has long been known as a city of culture thanks in part to resident artist, playwright, and Bohemian mystic Santiago Rusiñol. The 19th-century modernist movement largely began at Sitges, and the town remained the scene of artistic encounters and demonstrations long after modernism waned. Sitges continued as a resort of artists, attracting such giants as Salvador Dalí and poet Federico García Lorca. Then the Spanish Civil War (1936–39) erased what has come to be called the "golden age" of Sitges. Although other artists and writers arrived in the decades to follow, none had the name or the impact of those who had gone before.

What to See & Do

The old part of Sitges used to be a fortified medieval enclosure. The castle is now the seat of the town government. The local parish church, called La Punta (the point) and built next to the sea on top of a promontory, presides over an extensive maritime esplanade where people parade in the early evening. Behind the side of the church are the Museu Cau Ferrat and the Museu Maricel (see below).

It is the beaches that attract most visitors to Sitges. They have showers, bathing cabins, and stalls. Kiosks rent such items as motorboats and air cushions for fun on the water. Beaches on the eastern end and those inside the town center are the most peaceful, such as **Aiguadoiç** and **Els Balomins.** The **Playa San Sebastián, Fragata Beach,** and the **"Beach of the Boats"** (under the church and next to the yacht club) are the area's family beaches. Most young people go to the **Playa de la Ribera,** in the west.

All along the coast women can go topless. Farther west are the most solitary beaches, where the scene grows more kinky, especially along the **Playas del Muerto,** where two tiny nude beaches lie between Sitges and Vilanova i la Geltrú. A shuttle bus runs between the cathedral and Golf Terramar. From Golf Terramar, go along the road to the old Guardia Civil headquarters, then walk along the railway. The first beach draws nudists of every sexual persuasion, and the second is almost solely gay. Be advised that lots of action takes place in the woods in back of these beaches.

Beaches aside, Sitges has some interesting museums.

Museu Cau Ferrat, Carrer del Fonollar. ☎ **894-03-64.**

Catalán artist Santiago Rusiñol combined two 16th-century cottages to make this house, where he lived and worked and which upon his death (1931) he willed to Sitges along with his art collection. More than anyone else, Rusiñol made Sitges popular as a resort. The museum collection includes two paintings by El Greco and several small Picassos, including *The Bullfight.* A number of Rusiñol's works are also on display.

Admission: 200 ptas. ($1.40) adults; children free.

Open: Tues–Sat 9:30am–2pm and 4–6pm; Sun 9:30am–2pm.

Museu Maricel, Carrer del Fonallar. ☎ **894-03-64.**

Opened by the king and queen of Spain, the Museu Maricel contains art donated by Dr. Jesús Pérez Rosales. The palace, owned by American Charles Deering when it was built right after World War I, is in two parts connected by a small bridge. The museum has a good collection of Gothic and Romantic paintings and sculptures, as well as many fine Catalán ceramics. There are also three noteworthy works by Rebull and an allegorical painting of World War I by Sert.

Admission: 200 ptas. ($1.40) adults; children free.

Open: Tues–Sat 9:30am–2pm and 4–6pm; Sun 9:30am–2pm.

Museu Romàntic ("Can Llopis"), Sant Gaudenci, 1. ☎ **894-29-69.**

This museum re-creates the daily life of a Sitges landowning family in the 18th and 19th centuries. The family rooms, furniture, and household objects are most interesting. You'll also find wine cellars, and an important collection of antique dolls (upstairs).

Admission: 200 ptas. ($1.40) adults; children free. Free on Sun.

Open: Tues–Sat 9:30am–2pm and 4–6pm; Sun 9:30am–2pm.

Where to Stay

In spite of a building spree, Sitges is unprepared for the large numbers of tourists who flock here in July and August. By mid-October just about everything, including the hotels, restaurants, and bars, slows down considerably or closes altogether.

EXPENSIVE

Hotel Calípolis, Passeig Maritim, 00870 Sitges. ☎ **93/894-15-00.** Fax 93/894-07-64. 164 rms, 6 suites. A/C MINIBAR TV TEL

Rates: 8,400–13,200 ptas. ($59.60–$93.70) single; 10,500–16,500 ptas. ($74.60–$117.20) double; 15,000–23,500 ptas. ($106.50–$166.90) suite. Breakfast 950 ptas. ($6.70) extra. AE, DC, MC, V. **Parking:** 1,500 ptas. ($10.70) (available June 15-Sept 15).

Built in 1964 and renovated at great expense in 1990, this 11-story hotel fits in a gently undulating curve against the resort's beachfront and seaside promenade. Bedrooms contain expansive balconies, individual safes, satellite TV hookups, marble-sheathed bathrooms, and a comfortably conservative decor of contemporary furniture. Most offer sea views; the remainder offer views of the mountains.

Dining/Entertainment: The hotel restaurant includes a flowering outdoor terrace and offers formal service, very crisp linens, and both international and Catalonian specialties. A three-course fixed-price *menú del día* at lunch or dinner costs 1,700 pesetas ($12.10). There's also a bar.

Services: Room service (available from 8am to 11:30pm), concierge, babysitting, laundry/valet.

Facilities: Car rentals, excursions to nearby tennis courts and golf courses, horseback riding, sailing, and trips to nearby historic monasteries can be arranged. The parking lot is available only during the congested summer months; the lot closes when street parking becomes available again in the autumn.

Radisson Hotel Gran Sitges Barcelona, El Puerto de Aiguadolç, 08870 Sitges. ☎ **93/811-08-11,** or toll free in the U.S. **800/333-3333.** Fax 93/894-90-97. 294 rms (all with bath), 13 suites. A/C MINIBAR TV TEL

Rates: Mon–Thurs 17,500 ptas. ($124.30) single, 20,000 ptas. ($142) double. Fri–Sun, 7,500 ptas. ($53.30) single, 12,000 ptas. ($85.20) double. Suites from 30,000 ptas. ($213) throughout the week. Breakfast 1,300 ptas. ($9.20) Mon–Thurs; free Fri–Sun. **Parking:** 1,300 ptas. ($9.20). AE, DC, MC, V.

Designed with steeply sloping sides reminiscent of a pair of interconnected Aztec pyramids, this hotel was built in 1992 as housing for spectators and participants in the Barcelona Olympics. In 1994, its management was taken over by the U.S.-based Radisson chain. Angled to curve around two sides of a large swimming pool, and set a few yards from the beach, the hotel contains a white-marble lobby with what's probably the largest window in Spain overlooking a view of the mountains. Each of the bedrooms is outfitted in shades of blue, and includes a large, furnished veranda for sunbathing, and many of the electronic amenities you'd expect. The in-house restaurant, Norai, charges around 2,500 ptas. ($17.80) for a *menú del día.* Many guests at this hotel are here to participate in any of dozens of conferences and conventions held frequently within the establishment's battery of high-tech convention facilities. It lies within a 15-minute walk east of the center of Sitges, near the access roads leading to Barcelona.

MODERATE

El Galeón, Sant Francesc, 44, 08870 Sitges. ☎ **93/894-06-12.** Fax 93/894-63-35. 45 rms. TEL

Rates (including breakfast): 7,000 ptas. ($49.70) single; 10,500 ptas. ($74.60) double. MC, V. Closed: Oct 20–Apr. **Parking:** 1,000 ptas. ($7.10).

A leading three-star hotel only a short walk from both the beach and the Plaça d'Espanya, this well-styled hostelry blends a bit of the old Spain with the new. The small public rooms feel cozy, while the good-sized guest rooms, accented with woodgrain, have a more streamlined aura. There are a swimming pool and a patio in the rear. Advance reservations are necessary.

Hotel Platjador, Passeig de la Ribera, 35, 08870 Sitges. ☎ **93/894-50-54.** Fax 93/894-63-35. 59 rms. TV TEL

Rates (including breakfast): 7,750 ptas. ($55) single; 11,500 ptas. ($81.70) double. MC, V. **Closed:** Nov–Apr.

One of the best hotels in town, the Platjador, on the esplanade fronting the beach, has comfortably furnished and recently restored guest rooms, all with private baths and many with big French doors opening onto balconies and sea views. There is also a swimming pool. The dining room, facing the beach, is known for its good cuisine, including gazpacho, paella, fresh fish, and dessert flan. For 1,800 pesetas ($12.80) you can enjoy a set menu.

INEXPENSIVE

Hotel El Cid, San José, 19 bis, 08870 Sitges. ☎ **93/894-18-42.** Fax 93/894-6335. 77 rms (all with bath). TEL

Rates (including continental breakfast): 5,000 ptas. ($35.50) single; 8,000 ptas. ($56.80) double. MC, V. **Closed:** Nov–Apr.

El Cid's exterior suggest Castile and inside, appropriately enough, you'll find beamed ceilings, natural stone walls, heavy wrought-iron chandeliers, and leather chairs. The same theme is carried out in the rear dining room and in the pleasantly furnished bedrooms. A fine meal costs 1,800 pesetas ($12.80). The hotel has a top-floor swimming pool and solarium. El Cid lies off the Passeig de Vilanova in the center of town.

$ **Hotel Romàntic de Sitges,** Carrer de Sant Isidre, 33, 08870 Sitges. ☎ **93/894-83-75.** Fax 93/894-81-67. 55 rms (all with shower). TEL

Rates (including breakfast): 6,300–6,900 ptas. ($44.70–$49) single; 9,000–10,000 ptas. ($63.90–$71) double. MC, V. **Closed:** Nov–Mar 15.

Made up of three beautifully restored 19th-century villas, this hotel lies only a short walk from both the beach and the train station. The romantic bar is an international rendezvous and public rooms are filled with artworks. You can have breakfast either in the dining room or in the garden filled with mulberry trees. Overflow guests are housed in a nearby annex, the Hotel de la Renaixença.

Hotel Subur, Passeig de la Ribera, s/n, 08870 Sitges. ☎ **93/894-00-66.** Fax 93/894-69-86. 96 rms (all with bath). A/C MINIBAR TV TEL

Rates (including breakfast): 5,075–6,125 ptas. ($36–$43.50) single; 9,050–11,130 ptas. ($64.30–$79) double. AE, DC, MC, V. **Parking:** 900 ptas. ($6.40).

The first hotel built in Sitges (in 1916), the Subur was later torn down and reconstructed in 1960 and last renovated in 1992. Today, as always, it occupies a prominent position in the center of town on the seafront. Its rooms are well furnished, with balconies opening onto the Mediterranean. The dining room, decorated with fine woods, lays a bountiful table of both regional and international dishes. A *menú del día* costs 1,750 pesetas ($12.40). The hotel remains open all year, even during the cooler months.

$ **Sitges Park Hotel,** Carrer Jesús, 16, 08870 Sitges. ☎ **93/894-02-50.** Fax 95/894-08-39. 85 rms (all with bath). A/C TV TEL

Rates: 5,500 ptas. ($39.10) single; 9,030 ptas. ($64.10) double. Breakfast 700 ptas. ($5) extra. AE, DC, MC, V. **Closed:** Dec–Feb.

Outside, the Sitges Park has an 1880s red-brick facade. Inside, past the desk, a beautiful garden with palm trees and a swimming pool awaits. This, in fact, was once a private villa, owned by a family who made their fortune in Cuba. You'll find a good restaurant downstairs, and you can have your coffee or drinks indoors or outdoors at the café/bar, surveying the landmark Catalán tower on the premises. The hotel is about 50 yards from the bus station.

Where to Dine

EXPENSIVE

El Velero, Passeig de la Ribera, 38. ☎ **894-20-51.**

Cuisine: SEAFOOD. **Reservations:** Required.

Prices: Appetizers 800–1,600 ptas. ($5.70–$11.40); main courses 1,900–3,500 ptas. ($13.50–$24.90); fixed-price menu 2,850 ptas. ($20.20). AE, DC, MC, V.
Open: Lunch, daily 1:30–4pm; dinner, daily 8:30–11:30pm.

This is one of the leading restaurants of Sitges, occupying a position along the beachfront promenade. The most desirable tables are found on the "glass greenhouse" terrace, opening onto the esplanade, although there is a more glamorous restaurant inside. Try a soup such as clam and truffle or white fish, followed by a main dish such as paella marinara (with seafood) or suprême of salmon in pinenut sauce. The restaurant is named after a type of pleasure boat.

MODERATE

$ **Chez Jeanette,** Sant Pau, 23. ☎ **894-00-48.**
Cuisine: CATALÁN. **Reservations:** Recommended.
Prices: Appetizers 550–895 ptas. ($3.90–$6.40); main courses 1,000–2,500 ptas. ($7.10–$17.80); *menú del día* 1,200–1,550 ptas. ($8.50–$11). No credit cards.
Open: Lunch, Thurs–Tues 1–4pm; dinner, Thurs–Tues 7:30–11:30pm. Closed: Dec 20–Jan 15.

A Frenchwoman, Jeanette, established her Catalán-style restaurant here in 1975, and has since died, but her culinary tradition continues. Patrons flock to a rustic atmosphere created by textured stucco walls and a regional tavern decor. Set back on a restaurant-flanked street a short walk from the beach, it draws both straight and gay clients. The food features *platos del día* (plates of the day). From the standard menu, you can order such dishes as onion soup, rape (monkfish) with whisky, and entrecôte with Roquefort sauce. The chef is proudest of his *parilla pescada*, a mixed grill of fresh fish from the Mediterranean.

$ **Els 4 Gats,** Sant Pau, 13. ☎ **894-19-15.**
Cuisine: CATALÁN. **Reservations:** Recommended.
Prices: Appetizers 600–1600 ptas. ($4.30–$11.40); main courses 1,500–2,100 ptas. ($10.70–$14.90). Menú del día 1,700 ptas. ($12.10). AE, DC, MC, V.
Open: Lunch, Thurs–Tues 1–3:30pm; dinner, Thurs–Tues 8:30–11pm. **Closed:** Nov–Mar.

When it was established in the early 1960s as a bar and café, it adopted the name of one of Catalonia's most historic cafés, Els 4 Gats, a Barcelona hangout that had been a favorite of Picasso. By 1968, the newcomer was firmly established as one of the leading restaurants in Sitges, serving a well-received *cocina del mercado* based on whatever was fresh and available that day in the local markets. Within a setting accented with paintings and varnished paneling, you can enjoy fresh grilled fish, garlic soup, lamb cutlets with local herbs, roast chicken in wine sauce, and veal kidneys in sherry sauce. Set on a side street near the sea, the restaurant lies a few steps from the beachfront Passeig de la Ribera.

Fragata, Passeig de la Ribera, 1. ☎ **894-10-86.**
Cuisine: SEAFOOD. **Reservations:** Recommended.
Prices: Appetizers 575–1,800 ptas. ($4.10–$12.80); main dishes 975–3,200 ptas. ($6.90–$22.70). AE, DC, MC, V.
Open: Lunch, daily 1–4pm; dinner, daily 8–11pm.

Although its simple interior offers little more than well-scrubbed floors, tables with crisp napery, and air conditioning, some of the most delectable seafood specialties in town are served here, and hundreds of loyal customers come to appreciate the fresh, authentic cuisine. Specialties include seafood soup, a mixed grill of fresh fish, codfish salad, mussels marinara, several preparations of squid and octopus, plus some flavorful meat dishes such as grilled lamb cutlets.

Mare Nostrum, Passeig de la Ribera, 60. ☎ **894-33-93.**

Cuisine: SEAFOOD. **Reservations:** Required.
Prices: Appetizers 750–950 ptas. ($5.30–$6.70); main courses 1,100–2,200 ptas. ($7.80–$15.60). AE, DC, MC, V.
Open: Lunch, Thurs–Tues 1–4pm; dinner, Thurs–Tues 8–11pm. **Closed:** Dec 15–Feb 1.

This landmark restaurant was established in 1950 during the height of the Franco era, and has flourished ever since. It was built in the 1890s as a private home. The dining room has a waterfront view, and in warm weather tables are placed outside. The menu includes a full range of seafood dishes, among them grilled fish specialties and steamed hake with champagne. The fish soup is particularly delectable. Next door the restaurant's café—resting under a blue beamed ceiling—serves ice creams, milk shakes, sandwiches, a selection of tapas, and three varieties of sangría, including one with champagne and fruit.

La Masía, Paseo Vilanova, 164. ☎ **894-10-76.**

Cuisine: CATALÁN. **Reservations:** Required.
Prices: Appetizers 650–1,000 ptas. ($4.60–$7.10); main courses 850–2,300 ptas. ($6–$16.30); *menú del día* 1,325 ptas. ($9.40). AE, DC, MC, V.
Open: Lunch, daily 1–4pm; dinner, daily 8:30–11:30pm.

The provincial decor complements the imaginative regional specialties for which this place has been known since 1972. They include several preparations of codfish, roast suckling lamb well seasoned with herbs, *pollo a los hijos* ("brother's chicken," a regional dish), a wide array of fresh fish and shellfish, and monkfish with aïoli—the chef's pride. Every Catalonian's favorite dessert is *crème catalán*. If you prefer to dine outdoors, you can sit in the pleasant garden adjacent to the main dining room.

Oliver's, Isla de Cuba, 39. ☎ **894-35-16.**

Cuisine: CATALÁN/INTERNATIONAL. **Reservations:** Required.
Prices: Appetizers 550–1,800 ptas. ($3.90–$12.80); main courses 1,100–2,100 ptas. ($7.80–$14.90). MC, V.
Open: Lunch, Sat–Sun 1–4pm; dinner, Tues–Sun 8pm–midnight.

Lying on the northern fringe of the old town, directly south of the Plaça de Maristany, this angular bistro-style establishment is decorated like a regional tavern with local paintings. It makes a good choice for dinner, unless you insist on being on the beachfront esplanade, five minutes away. The wines are reasonably priced, and the chef features daily specials. Try the grilled salmon, entrecôte flavored with herbs of Provence, grilled goat cutlets, and a daily soup prepared with fresh ingredients of the market. The seafood is excellent; look for the chef's daily specials.

Evening Entertainment

One of the best ways to spend the night in Sitges is to walk the waterfront esplanade, have a leisurely dinner, then retire at about 11pm to one of the open-air cafés for a nightcap and some serious people-watching. Few local dives can compete with "the scene" taking place on the streets.

If you're straight, you'll have to look carefully for a bar that isn't gay. There are so many gay bars, in fact, that a map is distributed pinpointing their locales. Most of them are concentrated on Sant Bonaventura in the center of town, a five-minute walk from the beach (near the Museu Romàntic); there are nine gay bars in this small district alone. If you grow bored with the action in one place, you just have to walk down the street to find another. Drink prices run about the same in all the clubs.

Mediterráneo, Sant Bonaventura, 6. No phone.

This leading—also the largest—gay disco and bar in Sitges has a formal Iberian garden and sleek modern styling. And upstairs in this restored 1690s house just east of the **Plaça d'Espanya,** there are pool tables and a covered terrace. The club, which on a summer night can be filled to overflowing, is open only from May through October, Monday to Thursday, from 10pm to 3am, until 3:30am Friday and Saturday. A beer will cost you 350 pesetas ($2.50), and drinks are 800 pesetas ($5.70).

Ricky's Disco, Sant Pau, 25. ☎ **894-96-81.**

This is the town's most popular straight disco. In business since the 1970s, it is set back from the beach on a narrow little street noted for such favorite restaurants as Els 4 Gats. The music is recorded, and the crowd is international. Don't overlook the comfortable annex high above the dance floor. Open daily from 11:15pm to 5am; closed in November. Drinks run about 900 pesetas ($6.40), and beer costs 400 pesetas ($2.80). Sometimes on midsummer weekends there's a cover charge of 1,500 pesetas ($10.70). Otherwise, it's free.

16

Girona & the Costa Brava

THE COSTA BRAVA (WILD COAST) IS A 95-MILE (153KM) STRETCH OF COASTLINE—the northernmost Mediterranean seafront in Spain—that begins north of Barcelona at Blanes and stretches toward the French border. Visit this area in May, June, September, or October and avoid July and August, when tour groups from Northern Europe book virtually all the hotel rooms.

Undiscovered little fishing villages along the coast long ago bloomed into resort towns. Tossa de Mar is perhaps the most delightful of these. Lloret de Mar is also immensely popular but perhaps too commercial for many tastes. The most unspoiled spot is remote Cadaqués. Some of the smaller villages also make excellent stopovers.

If you want to visit the Costa Brava but simply cannot secure a room in high season, consider taking a day trip by car from Barcelona or booking one of the daily organized tours that leave from that city. Allow plenty of time for driving. In summer the traffic jams can be fierce, the roads between towns difficult and winding.

If you visit the coast in summer without a hotel reservation, you'll stand a fair chance of getting a room in Girona, the capital of the province and one of the most interesting medieval cities in Spain.

Seeing Girona & the Costa Brava

GETTING THERE The main airport serving the Costa Brava is in the provincial capital, Girona, where most of the package tours from northern Europe land. Most North Americans arrive first at Barcelona's Prat de Llobregat Airport, explore that city, then head north for the Costa Brava.

Some parts of the area can be toured using the train. Girona lies on the main rail link between Barcelona and the French frontier. Local train service from Barcelona also covers the coast to the French border, with Figueres the best hub. Coastal resorts reached by train are Blanes in the south and Port Bou in the north (not covered here).

All the small coastal resorts have local bus service. There is, as well, service from both Barcelona and Girona to all the major resorts such as Tossa de Mar.

The north-south *autopista* A-17 is the fastest way to travel the coast by car, but expect high tolls. The N-11 also runs north and south, but it's slower and more crowded. At the coast, the C-253 runs from Blanes to Palamós. You get great views but sometimes dangerous turns and curves. Some of the roads connecting coastal resorts are unclassified.

A Suggested Route

Day 1 Drive north from Barcelona, stopping at the coastal resorts of Lloret de Mar or Tossa de Mar for a two-day stay.

Day 2 While based in Tossa or Lloret, explore the environs if you have a car, or stay and enjoy the joie de vivre of these fun-loving towns. If you're staying at Lloret, go to Tossa to explore its old quarter.

Day 3 Leave Tossa or Lloret and continue to drive along the coast to Figueres to see the Dalí Museum, one of the most popular attractions in Spain. Stay overnight in the gourmet citadel of Figueres, or drive over to Cadaqués on the far eastern coast, where Dalí used to live, and spend the night there.

What's Special About Girona & the Costa Brava

Beaches

- Tossa de Mar—with two sandy beaches and plenty more in the environs, for beach lovers who enjoy a "Cézanne landscape."
- Lloret de Mar—the so-called fun house of the Costa Brava, with the area's longest beach (it's packed).

Great Towns/Villages

- Tossa de Mar, with its battlements and towers, a former hideaway for writers and artists.
- Cadaqués, a select retreat on this rugged coast so beloved by Salvador Dalí.
- Girona, capital of the province, a medieval city with a centuries-old Jewish ghetto.

A Museum

- The Teatre Museu Dalí at Figueres, pure surrealist theater.

Parks/Gardens

- Blanes, where you can wander through gardens originally planted by famed German botanist Karl Faust.

An Ancient Monument

- The Arab baths at Girona—Romanesque civic architecture at its best and the site of many movie backdrops.

Special Events/Festivals

- The International Music Festival at Cadaqués, which attracts some of the world's finest musicians.

Day 4 Drive south again on the N-11 or the A-17 to the provincial capital of Girona. See what you can before nightfall, and the following morning take a walk through the monumental district.

Day 5 Return to Barcelona.

1 Girona

60 miles (97km) NE of Barcelona, 56 miles (90km) S of the French city of Perpignan

GETTING THERE • By Train There are more than two dozen trains per day running between Girona and Barcelona from 6:10am to 10pm, including two *talgos.* Trip time is one to two hours, depending on the train. The one-way cost ranges from 565 to 1,560 pesetas ($4 to $11.10), the latter the price of a talgo ticket. Trains arrive in Girona at the Plaça Espanya (☎ **20-70-93** for information).

• By Bus From the Costa Brava, you can take one of the SARFA buses (☎ **20-17-96** in Girona) to Girona. Three per day depart from Tossa de Mar (see below). Fills de Rafael Mas (☎ **21-32-27** in Girona), another bus company, makes three to five runs per day between Girona and Lloret de Mar. Barcelona Bus (☎ **20-24-32** in Girona), also operates express buses between Girona and Barcelona (or vice versa) at the rate of 4 to 13 per day, depending on the season and demand.

• By Car From Barcelona or the French border, connect with the main north-south route (A-7), taking the turnoff to Girona. From Barcelona, take the A-2 north to reach the A-7.

ESSENTIALS The area code for Girona is 972. The tourist information office is at **Rambla de la Libertat (☎ 972/22-65-75).**

Split by the Onyar River, this sleepy medieval city attracts crowds of tourists darting inland from the Costa Brava for the day.

Founded by the Romans, Girona is considered one of the most important historical sites in Spain. Later, it was a Moorish stronghold. Later still, it reputedly withstood three invasions by Napoleon's troops (1809). For that and other past sieges, Girona is often called La Ciudad de los Sitios (The City of a Thousand Sieges).

For orientation purposes, go to the ancient stone footbridge across the Onyar. From there, you'll have the finest view. Bring good walking shoes, as the only way to discover the particular charm of this medieval city is on foot. You can wander for hours through the **Call,** the labyrinthine old quarter, with its narrow, steep alleyways and lanes and its ancient stone houses, which form a rampart chain along the Onyar. Much of Girona can be appreciated from the outside, but it does contain some important attractions you'll want to see on the inside.

The Jews of Girona form part of its cultural heritage. From 890 to 1492, they were a strong community in the city. It is believed that early settlers from Jerusalem formed the nucleus of the first colony. They were forced to live ghetto style in the Call, their early settlements grouped around the Plaça dels Apòstols. Carrer de la Força was the main artery of the Call. In 1492, the year Columbus landed in America, his patrons, Ferdinand and Isabella, expelled all Jews from Spain, thus ending this once-flourishing colony.

What to See & Do

Catedral, Plaça de la Catedral. ☎ **21-44-26.**

The major attraction of Girona is its magnificent cathedral, reached by climbing a 17th-century baroque staircase of 90 steep steps. The 14th-century cathedral represents many architectural styles, including Gothic and Romanesque, but it is most notably Catalán baroque. The facade that you see as you climb those long stairs dates from the 17th and 18th centuries; from a cornice atop it, there rises a bell tower crowned by a dome with a bronze angel weathervane. Enter the main door of the cathedral and go into the nave, which, at 75 feet, is the broadest in the world of Gothic architecture.

The cathedral contains many works of art, displayed for the most part in its museum. Its prize exhibit is a tapestry of the creation, a unique piece of 11th- or 12th-century Romanesque embroidery depicting humans and animals in the Garden of Eden. The other major work displayed is the 10th-century *Códex del Beatus,* a manuscript containing an illustrated commentary on the Book of the Apocalypse, one of the world's rarest manuscripts.

From the cathedral's Chapel of Hope a door leads to a Romanesque cloister from the 12th and 13th centuries, with an unusual trapezoidal layout. The cloister gallery, with a double colonnade, has a series of biblical scenes that are considered the prize jewel of western Catalán Romanesque art. From the cloister you can view the Torre de Carlemany (Charlemagne's Tower), from the 12th century.

Admission: Cathedral free; cloister and museum 300 ptas. ($2.10).

Open: Cathedral, Tues–Sat 9am–7pm; Sun 9am–2pm; Mon 9am–1pm. Cloister and museum, July–Sept, Tues–Sat 10am–2pm and 4–7pm; Sun 10am–2pm; Oct–June, daily 10am–2pm and 4–6pm.

Museu d'Art, Pujada de la Catedral, 12. ☎ **20-95-36.**

In a former Romanesque and Gothic episcopal palace (Palau Episcopal) next to the cathedral, this museum displays artworks spanning 10 centuries (once housed in the old Diocesan Museum and the Provincial Museum). Stop in the throne room to view the altarpiece of Sant Pere of Púbol by Bernat Martorell and that of Sant Miguel de Crüilles by Lluís Borrassa. Both of these works, from the 15th century, are considered exemplary pieces of Catalán Gothic painting. The museum is also proud of its altar stone of Sant Pere de Roda, which dates from the 10th and 11th centuries; this work in wood and stone, depicting figures and legends, was once covered in embossed silver. The 12th-century *Crüilles Timber* is a unique piece of Romanesque polychrome wood. *Our Lady of Besalù,* from the 15th century, is considered one of the best Virgins carved in alabaster.

Admission: 100 ptas. (70¢) adults; children free.

Open: Mar–Sept, Tues–Sat 10am–7pm; Sun 10am–2pm. Oct–Feb, Tues–Sat 10am–6pm; Sun 10am–2pm.

Banys Arabs, Carrer Ferran el Catòlic. ☎ **21-32-62.**

In the old quarter of the city are the 12th-century Arab baths, an example of Romanesque civic architecture. Visit the *caldarium* (hot bath), with its paved floor, and the *frigidarium* (cold bath), with its central octagonal pool surrounded by pillars that support a prismlike structure in the overhead window. The Moorish baths were heavily restored in 1929, but they give you an idea of what the old ones were like.

Admission: 125 ptas. (90¢)

Open: Tues–Sat 10am–7pm; Sun 10am–1pm.

Museu Arqueològic, Sant Pere de Galligant, Santa Llúcia, 1. ☎ **20-26-32.**

Housed in a Romanesque church and cloister from the 11th and 12th centuries, this museum illustrates the history of the city from the Paleolithic to the Visigothic period, using artifacts discovered in nearby excavations. The monastery itself ranks as one of the best examples of Catalán Romanesque architecture. In the cloister, note some Hebrew inscriptions from gravestones of the old Jewish cemetery.

Admission: 125 ptas. (90¢).

Open: Tues–Sat 10am–1pm and 4:30–7pm; Sun 10am–1pm.

Museu d'História de la Ciutat, Carrer de la Força. ☎ **20-91-60.**

Housed in the old 18th-century Capuchin Convent de Sant Antoni, this collection dates from the time of Puig d'en Roca (Catalonia's oldest prehistoric site) to the present. It includes Girona's (and Spain's) first electric streetlights.

Admission: Free.

Open: Tues–Sat 10am–2pm and 5–7pm; Sun 10am–2pm.

Església de Sant Feliu, Pujada de Sant Feliu. ☎ **20-14-07.**

This 14th- to 17th-century church was built over what may have been the tomb of Feliu of Africa, martyred during Diocletian's persecution at the beginning of the 4th century. Important in the architectural history of Catalonia, the church has pillars and arches in the Romanesque style and a Gothic central nave. The bell tower, one of the Girona skyline's most characteristic features, has eight pinnacles and one central tower, each supported on a solid octagonal base. The main facade of the church is baroque. The interior contains some exceptional works, including a high altarpiece from the 16th century and an alabaster *Reclining Christ* from the 14th century. Notice the eight

Girona & Costa Brava

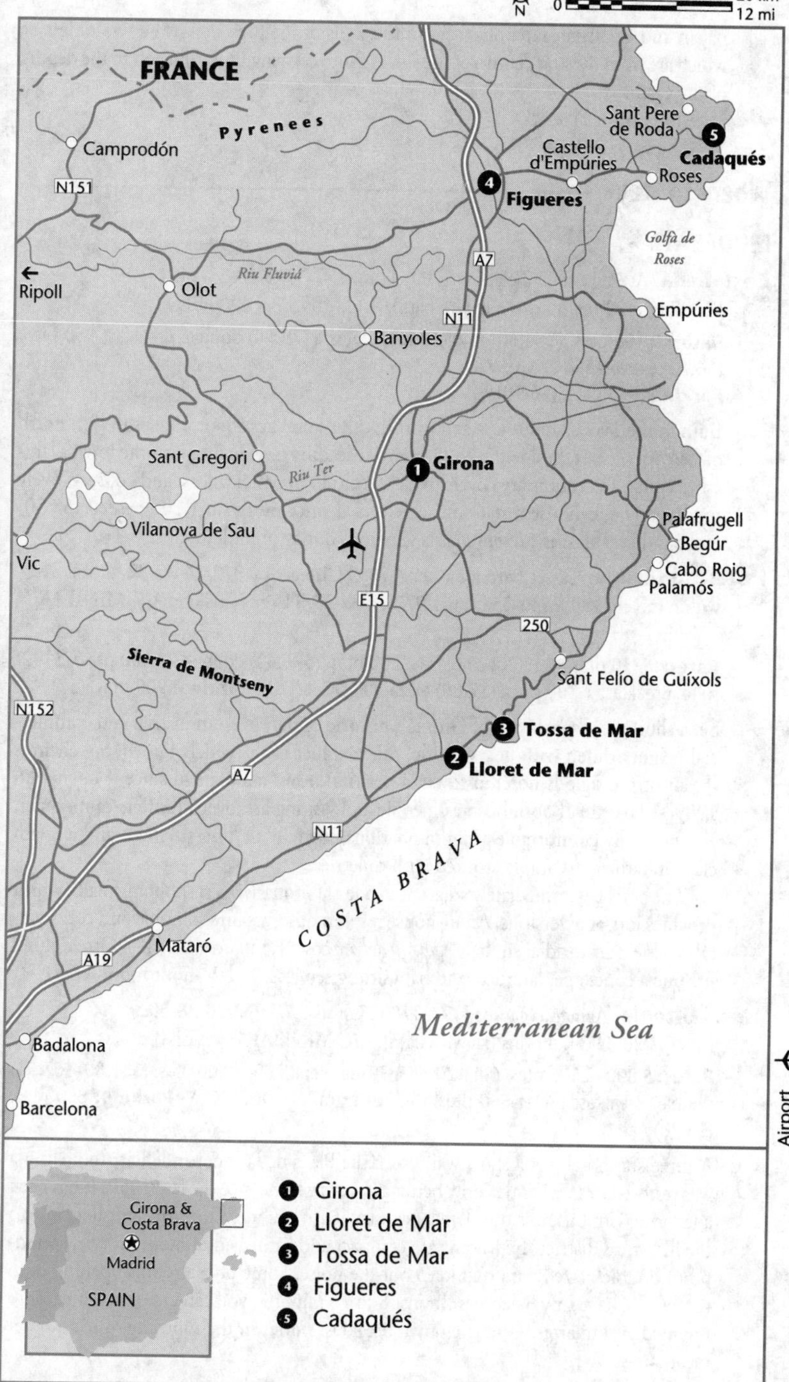

Airport

pagan and Christian sarcophagi set in the walls of the presbytery, the two oldest of which are from the 2nd century. One shows Pluto carrying Proserpina off to the depths of the earth.

Admission: Free.
Open: Daily 8am–8pm.

Where to Stay

MODERATE

Costabella, Avenida de Francia, 61, 17007 Girona. ☎ **972/20-25-24.** Fax 972/20-22-03. 46 rms (all with bath). A/C MINIBAR TV TEL

Rates: 9,100 ptas. ($64.60) single; 11,250 ptas. ($79.90) double. Breakfast 950 ptas. ($6.70) extra. AE, DC, MC, V.
Parking: 975 ptas. ($6.90).

Built in the 1960s, and renovated in 1989, this hotel lies about 2 miles (3 km) north of Girona's center, beside the N-11 highway leading to Figueres, near the town's largest hospital. Bedrooms are comfortable, outfitted in pastel colors, and conservatively modern. The in-house restaurant served fixed-price meals for 1,200 pesetas ($8.50) each, and breakfast is presented as a generous outlay of buffet items.

Hotel Sol Girona, Carrer Barcelona 112, 17003 Girona. ☎ **972/24-32-32,** or toll free within the U.S. **800/336-3542.** Fax 972/24-32-33. 114 rms, 1 suite. A/C MINIBAR TV TEL

Rates: 9,750 ptas. ($69.20) single; 12,200 ptas. ($86.60) double; 20,000 ptas. ($142) suite. Breakfast 1,100 ptas. ($7.80) extra. AE, DC, MC, V. **Parking:** 900 ptas. ($7)

Set a short drive southwest of Girona's historic center, in an industrial and commercial neighborhood with heavy traffic, this member of the widely known Sol chain is the most prestigious hotel in town, a position it has maintained since it opened in 1989. A favorite of both business people and visiting art lovers, it offers calm, quiet, and tastefully comfortable accommodations, many with king-size beds and all with elegant bathrooms amply stocked with toiletries.

The hotel lies immediately adjacent to one of Girona's largest shopping malls, which provides lots of diversions. An in-house restaurant serves international and continental cuisine near an adjacent bar. A *menú del día* costs 1,550 pesetas ($11). Other pluses include a concierge, laundry, and babysitting services, and 24-hour room service.

Hotel Ultonia, Avinguda Jaume I, 22, 17001 Girona. ☎ **972/20-38-50.** Fax 972/20-33-34. 45 rms (all with bath). A/C MINIBAR TV TEL

Rates: 5,800–7,500 ptas. ($41.20–$53.30) single; 8,700–9,500 ptas. ($61.80–$67.50) double. Breakfast buffet 660 ptas. ($4.70) extra. AE, DC, MC, V. **Parking:** 800 ptas. ($5.70) nearby.

A three-star hotel just a short walk from the Plaça de la Independència, the Ultonia was restored in 1993 and is now better than ever. Ever since the late 1950s it has been a favorite with business travelers, but today it attracts more tourists, as it lies close to the historical district. Bedrooms are compact and furnished in modern style; soundproof double-glazed windows keep out the noise. Some of the rooms opening onto the avenue have tiny balconies. In just 8 to 12 minutes, you can cross the Onyar into the medieval quarter. Guests enjoy a breakfast buffet in the morning, but no other meals are served.

Novotel Girona, Carretera del Aeropuerto, 17457 Riudellots de la Selva (Girona). ☎ **972/47-71-00,** or toll free in the U.S. **800/221-4542.** Fax 972/47-72-96. 79 rms, 2 suites. A/C TV TEL **Directions:** Take exit 8 from the A-7 motorway, signposted a few miles west of the Girona city center.

Rates: 9,350 ptas. ($66.40) single; 10,300 ptas. ($73.10) double; 15,000 ptas. ($106.50) suite. Children under 16 free in parents' room. Breakfast buffet 1,250 ptas. ($8.90) extra. AE, DC, MC, V. **Parking:** Free.

Low-slung and modern and set within a sunny, tree-dotted park, this member of the French-based chain offers some of the most consistently reliable accommodations and some of the best value in the region. Located beside the A-7 motorway, just south of the Girona airport and a short drive west of the city center, the Girona offers comfortable and efficient bedrooms with soundproofed windows, large writing tables, and a simple modern decor much appreciated by both families and businesspeople.

The clean and modern restaurant Le Grill serves meals continuously daily from 6am to midnight. Meals are à la carte, averaging 2,500 pesetas ($17.80) person. There's also a bar. Room service is offered from 6am to midnight daily, plus there's concierge and laundry service. Car rentals can be arranged at the hotel, and guests enjoy the outdoor pool set within a garden and the tennis court.

BUDGET

Condal, Joan Maragall, 10, 17002 Girona. ☎ **072/20-44-62.** 39 rms (all with bath).

Rates: 2,500 ptas. ($17.80) single; 4,600 ptas. ($32.70) double. No credit cards.

Located near the rail and bus stations west of the old town, this 1960s hotel is rated third class, and, in the words of one frequent visitor, it is "aggressively simple." As such, it's recommended to bargain hunters only. The lounge and reception area are small, there is no service elevator, and no meals (not even breakfast) are served—but these are minor concerns. The bedrooms are clean and functional, and some of them open onto pleasant views.

Hotel Peninsular, Carrer Nou 3, 17001 Girona. ☎ **972/20-38-00.** Fax 972/21-04-92. 69 rms (all with bath). TEL

Rates: 3,450 ptas. ($24.50) single; 5,300 ptas. ($37.60) double. Breakfast 475 ptas. ($3.40) extra. AE, DC, MC, V.
Parking: 800 ptas. ($5.70) nearby.

Devoid of any significant architectural character, this one-star hotel provides clean but uncontroversial accommodations in a location near the cathedral and the river. Bedrooms are scattered over five different floors, and benefitted from a renovation performed around 1990. The hotel is best selected for short-term stopovers than for prolonged stays. No meals other than breakfast are served.

A NEARBY PLACE TO STAY

★ **Hostal de la Gavina,** Plaça de la Rosaleda, 17248 S'Agaro (Girona). ☎ **972/32-11-00.** Fax 972/32-15-73. 64 rms, 10 suites. A/C MINIBAR TV TEL

Rates: 28,000 ptas. ($198.80) single; 40,000 ptas. ($284) double; 50,000 ptas. ($355) suite. Breakfast 2,000 ptas. ($14.20) extra. AE, DC, MC, V. **Parking:** 1,600 ptas. ($11.40) garage, outside free. **Closed:** Nov–Feb.

Since it was established in the early 1980s, the Hostal de la Gavina has attracted some of the most glamorous persons in the world (such as King Juan Carlos I, Elizabeth

Taylor, and a host of celebrities from northern Europe) to its manicured premises. It lies on a peninsula jutting seaward from the center of S'Agaro, within a thick-walled Iberian villa that was originally built as the private home of the Ansesa family (the owners of the hotel) in 1932. The public rooms, the main restaurant, and most of the accommodations are contained within the resort's main building, which has been much enlarged and modified since its original construction. Many of the public rooms look like the paneled enclaves of a very prosperous and tasteful stylesetter. A large and very modern swimming pool is a short walk away, above the town's public beach. Adjacent to the pool is a beach house, containing a Jacuzzi, a handful of boutiques, and a daytime restaurant.

Dining/Entertainment: The daytime restaurant is Las Conchas, which features arrays of fresh salads, brochettes, and light platters, impeccably served beside the pool. More formal evening meals are served in the main building, in the Candlelight Restaurant. There, an array of well-prepared international specialties costs 6,500 pesetas ($46.20) for a fixed-price meal and might be served on an outdoor patio if the weather justifies it. There are also two bars.

Services: 24-hour room service, hairdresser, massage, laundry/valet, concierge.

Facilities: Two tennis courts, paddle tennis courts, two bars, masses of well-tended gardens, Jacuzzi, swimming pool.

Where to Dine

$ **Bronsoms,** Sant Francesc, 7. ☎ **21-24-93.**

Cuisine: CATALÁN. **Reservations:** Recommended.

Prices: Appetizers 455–750 ptas. ($3.20–$5.30); main courses 750–1,900 ptas. ($5.30–$13.50). Fixed-price menus 1,100 ptas. ($7.80). AE, MC, V.

Open: Lunch, daily 1–4pm; dinner, daily 8:30–11:30pm.

Set in the heart of the old town, within an 1890s building that was originally a private home, this restaurant is considered one of the most consistently reliable in Girona. The subject of recent praise from newspapers as far away as Madrid, the restaurant has been under its present management since 1982, perfecting the art of serving a Catalán-based *cocina del mercado.* Only strictly fresh ingredients are used in dishes that include the frequently ordered house specialties. These include paella; a *suquet de pescados* prepared in the style of the Costa Brava; *arroz negre* (literally, "black rice" tinted with squid ink and studded with shellfish); filet of beef served with your choice of either pepper sauce or Roquefort sauce; and several preparations of Iberian ham.

2 Lloret de Mar

62 miles (100km) S of the French border, 42 miles (68km) N of Barcelona

GETTING THERE • By Train & Bus From Barcelona, take a train to Blanes, then take a bus 5 miles (8km) to Lloret.

• By Car Head north from Barcelona along the A-19.

ESSENTIALS The area code for Lloret de Mar is 972. The tourist information office is at Placa de la Vila, 1 (☎ 972/36-47-35).

Although it has a good half-moon–shaped sandy beach, Lloret is neither chic nor sophisticated, and most of the people who come here are low-income Europeans. The competition for cheap rooms is fierce.

Lloret de Mar has grown at a phenomenal rate from a small fishing village with just a few hotels to a bustling resort with more hotels than anyone could count. And more keep opening up, although there are never enough in July and August. The accommodations are typical of those in the Costa Brava towns, running the gamut from impersonal modern box-type structures to vintage whitewashed, flowerpot-adorned buildings on the narrow streets of the old town. There are even a few pockets of posh, including the Hotel Roger de Flor (see below).

The area has rich vegetation, scenery, and a mild climate.

L'Hostalet del Call, Carrer Batlle i Prats, 4. ☎ **21-26-88.**

Cuisine: CATALÁN. **Reservations:** Recommended.
Prices: Appetizers 400–675 ptas. ($2.80–$4.80); main courses 700–1,300 ptas. ($5–$9.20); fixed-price menu 1,800 ptas. ($12.80). V.
Open: Lunch, Tues–Sun 1–4pm; dinner, Tues–Sat 8–11pm.

Taking its name from the old Jewish ghetto, this intimate restaurant lies near the cathedral in a house that dates from the Middle Ages. Many of its dishes are based on centuries-old recipes, including *fava* (broad beans prepared Sephardic style with spicy lamb). The menu, in English, is changed every two or three months, but features a selection of grilled meats among other dishes. Appetizers are often intriguing, everything perhaps from broccoli with a pink Béchamel sauce to spinach and potato lasagna, from warm calf's tongue to fish mousse. Main dishes are likely to feature cod with raisins and pine seeds, cuttlefish with artichokes, old-style potted rabbit, even pork jaw with almonds.

Where to Stay

Many of the hotels—particularly the three-star establishments—are booked solidly by tour groups. Here are some possibilities if you reserve in advance.

Hotel Excelsior, Passeig Mossèn Jacinto Verdaguer, 16, 17310 Lloret de Mar. ☎ **972/36-61-76.** Fax 972/37-16-54. 45 rms (all with bath). TEL

Rates: July–Sept (including obligatory half board): 6,550 ptas. ($46.50) per person. Oct–June 2,600 ptas. ($18.50) single; 4,575 ptas. ($32.50) double. Breakfast 500 ptas. ($3.60) extra. AE, DC, MC, V. **Parking:** 900 ptas. ($6.40). **Closed:** Oct 31–Mar 20.

This well-managed three-star hotel attracts a beach-oriented clientele from Spain and Northern Europe, many of whom have returned every summer since the hotel opened in 1978. The Excelsior sits almost directly on the beach, rising six floors above the esplanade, and contains an elevator. All but a handful of bedrooms offer either full-frontal or lateral views of the sea, and some have a TV. The furniture is modern and uninspiring, but food in the dining room is well prepared, and clients seem generally content with the services provided. Fixed price meals range from 1,600 to 1,700 pesetas ($11.40 to $12.10); but during midsummer, half-board is obligatory.

Hotel Marsol, Passeig Jacint Verdaguer, 7, 17310 Lloret de Mar. ☎ **972/36-57-54.** Fax 972/37-22-05. 87 rms (all with bath). A/C MINIBAR TV TEL

Rates: 7,700 ptas. ($54.70) single; 9,400 ptas. ($66.70) double. Breakfast 750 ptas. ($5.30) extra. AE, DC, MC, V.

Completely refurbished and vastly improved in 1992, this medium-size hotel opens directly onto beachfront action. Its chief drawing card is its rooftop swimming pool, sauna, and solarium. Favored by an essentially European clientele, it offers sleekly modern bedrooms, each with satellite TV, air conditioning, radio, personal safe, soundproof windows, and minibar. Occupying the ground floor is a cafeteria serving drinks and snacks throughout the town, plus a restaurant, Els Dofins, overlooking a palm-shaded plaza.

★ **Hotel Roger de Flor,** Turó de l'Estelat, s/n, 17310 Lloret de Mar. ☎ **972/36-48-00.** Fax 972/37-16-37. 96 rms, 2 suites (all with bath). TV TEL

Rates: 11,000–12,750 ptas. ($78.10–$90.50) single; 15,550–25,000 ptas. ($110.40–$177.50) double; from 34,000 ptas. ($241.40) suite. Breakfast 1,750 ptas. ($12.40) extra. AE, DC, MC, V. **Parking:** Free.

This much-enlarged older hotel, sections of which are reminiscent of a dignified private villa, is a pleasant diversion from the aging and unimaginative slabs of concrete filling other sections of the resort. Set at the eastern edge of town, within its own verdant park and garden (whose only access is from the Carretera de Tossa, a busy inland boulevard), it offers some of the most pleasant and panoramic views of any hotel in town. Potted geraniums, climbing masses of bougainvillea, and evenly spaced rows of palms add elegance to the combinations of new and old architecture. Bedrooms are high-ceilinged, modern, and simple yet comfortable. The public rooms contain plenty of exposed wood and spill out onto a partially covered terrace that functions as a centerpiece for the dining and drinking facilities.

Dining/Entertainment: The modern and panoramic L'Estelat restaurant, near an airy and comfortable bar, serves international food. Three-course fixed-price menus cost 4,000 pesetas ($28.40) each.

Services: Room service (offered from 8am to 10:30pm), laundry, concierge, babysitting.

Facilities: Car rentals, simple shopping boutique, outdoor swimming pool filled with pumped-in sea water set within the garden.

★ **Hotel Santa Marta,** Playa de Santa Cristina, 17310 Lloret de Mar. ☎ **972/36-49-04.** Fax 972/36-92-80. 76 rms, 2 suites. TEL

Rates: 10,000–15,000 ptas. ($71–$106.50) single; 14,500–25,000 ptas. ($103–$177.50) double; 23,000–40,000 ptas. ($163.30–$284) suite. Breakfast 1,500 ptas. ($10.70) extra. Full-board 15,250–24,500 ptas. ($108.30–$174) per person. AE, DC, MC, V. **Closed:** Dec 23–Jan 31.

This tranquil hotel is a short walk above a crescent-shaped bay favored by swimmers, nestled amid a sunflooded copse of pines. Most rooms offer private balconies overlooking either the sea or a pleasant garden, and about two thirds of them contain minibars, TVs, and air conditioning. Both the public rooms and the bedrooms are attractively paneled and filled with traditional furniture. The hotel lies in a quiet but desirable seaside neighborhood, about 1½ miles (2km) west of the commercial center of town.

Dining/Entertainment: The restaurant Santa Marta (recommended separately below) serves both regional and international cuisine. An airy bar is nearby.

Services: Laundry/valet, concierge, babysitting.

Facilities: Car-rental kiosk, solarium.

Xaine Hotel, Vila, 55, 17310 Lloret de Mar. ☎ **972/36-50-08.** Fax 972/37-11-68. 165 rms (all with bath).

Rates: June–Sept (including obligatory half-board): 3,800–4,600 ptas. ($27–$32.70) single; 6,400–8,400 ptas. ($45.40–$59.60) double. Off-season, 1,870 ptas. ($13.30)

single; 3,200 ptas. ($22.70) double. Breakfast 400 ptas. ($2.80) extra. AE, DC, MC, V. **Closed:** Nov–Apr.

Larger than you might think from a quick glance, this hotel was opened in 1959 within the noisy and congested center of town, about two blocks inland from the beach. Many of its simple but clean bedrooms contain balconies overlooking the commercial center of Lloret. Facilities include an outdoor swimming pool, a sauna, and a restaurant, Raco Catala, which is recommended separately in "Where to Dine" (see below). Laundry service is available.

Where to Dine

$ **Raco Catalá,** in the Xaine Hotel, Vila, 55. ☎ **36-50-08.**

Cuisine: CATALÁN. **Reservations:** Not required.

Prices: Appetizers 600–1,020 ptas. ($4.30–$7.20); main courses 850–3,200 ptas. ($6–$22.70); fixed-price menu 975 ptas. ($6.90).

Open: Lunch, daily 1–2:30pm; dinner, daily 8–11pm. **Closed:** Nov–Apr.

Its location in the commercial heart of Lloret adds to this restaurant's conviviality. In summer, tables with colorful parasols are set out on the sidewalk and on an adjacent terrace. The fixed menu appeals to many beachgoers, who appreciate its good value and ample quantities. A typical menu might include cream-of-mushroom or tomato soup; filet of pork with mashed potatoes; a French-inspired omelet, and, for dessert, flan. The à la carte menu often includes skillfully seasoned versions of Iberian lamb, lobster, or chicken casserole, or the chef's special paella. The view of the passing parade of sunseekers adds greatly to the allure of a meal here. The restaurant, incidentally, lies on the ground floor of the previously recommended Hotel Xaine.

Restaurant Santa Marta, In the Hotel Santa Marta, Playa de Santa Cristina. ☎ **36-49-04.**

Cuisine: INTERNATIONAL. **Reservations:** Recommended.

Prices: Appetizers 900–8,000 ptas. ($6.40–$56.80); main courses 2,000–3,500 ptas. ($14.20–$24.90). AE, DC, MC, V.

Open: Lunch, daily 1:30–3:30pm; dinner, daily 8:30–10:30pm. **Closed:** Dec 23–Jan 31.

Set within a previously recommended hotel lying about 1½ miles (2km) west of the commercial center of town, this pleasantly sunny enclave offers a sweeping view of the beaches and the sea, a pine-forest setting, and well-prepared food. Menu specialties vary with the seasons but might include pâté of wild mushrooms in a special sauce, smoked salmon with hollandaise on toast, médaillons of monkfish served with a mousseline of garlic, a ragoût of giant shrimp with broad beans, a filet of beef Stroganoff, and a regionally inspired cassolette of chicken prepared with cloves.

$ **El Trull,** Cala Canyelles, s/n. ☎ **36-49-28.**

Cuisine: SEAFOOD. **Reservations:** Not required.

Prices: Appetizers 600–1,100 ptas. ($4.30–$7.80); main courses 2,000–3,000 ptas. ($14.20–$21.30); fixed-price menu 1,450 ptas. ($10.30). AE, DC, MC, V.

Open: Lunch, daily 1–4pm; dinner, daily 8–11pm.

Since its establishment in 1975, this restaurant has attracted hordes of Spanish clients, who appreciate the two-mile trek north of Lloret into the nearby hills. Set in the modern suburb of Urbanización Playa Canyelles, El Trull positions its tables within view of a well-kept garden and a (sometimes crowded) swimming pool. Food is acknowledged as some of the best in the neighborhood. Menu items focus on seafood, prepared in the Catalán style, and include fish soup, a fish stew heavily laced with lobster, many variations of hake, monkfish, and clams, and an omelet "surprise." (The waiter will tell you the ingredients if you ask.)

EVENING ENTERTAINMENT

Casino Lloret de Mar, Carretera de Tossa, s/n. ☎ **36-65-12.**

Games of chance include French and American roulette, blackjack, and chemin de fer, among others. There is a restaurant, buffet dining room, bar-boîte, and dance club, along with a swimming pool. Drinks cost around 750 pesetas ($5.30). Bring your passport. The casino lies southwest of Lloret de Mar, beside the coastal road leading to Blanes and Barcelona. Drive or take a taxi at night. Hours are Monday to Friday from 5pm to 4am and Saturday and Sunday from 5pm to 4:30am.

Admission: 1,000 ptas. ($7.10)

Hollywood, Carretera Tossa-Hostalrich, s/n. ☎ **36-74-63.**

This dance club at the edge of town is the place to be and be seen. Look for it on the corner of Carrer Girona. It's open nightly from 11pm to 4am, and drinks cost 700 pesetas ($5).

3 Tossa de Mar

56 miles (90km) N of Barcelona, 7½ miles (12km) NE of Lloret de Mar

GETTING THERE • By Bus Direct bus service is offered from Blanes and Lloret. Tossa de Mar is also on the main Barcelona-Palafruggel route.

• By Car Head north of Barcelona along the A-19.

ESSENTIALS The area code for Tossa de Mar is 972. The tourist information office is at Avinguda El Pelegrí, 25 (☎ 972/34-01-08).

This gleaming white town, with its 12th-century walls and labyrinthine old quarter, fishing boats, and fairly good sands, is the most attractive base for a Costa Brava vacation. It seems to have more joie de vivre than its competitors. The battlements and towers of Tossa were featured in the 1951 Ava Gardner and James Mason movie *Pandora and the Flying Dutchman,* which is still sometimes featured on the late show.

In the 18th and 19th centuries Tossa survived as a port center, growing rich on the cork industry. But that declined in the 20th century, and many of its citizens emigrated to America. Yet in the 1950s, thanks in part to the Ava Gardner movie, tourists began to discover the charms of Tossa and a new industry was born.

To experience these charms, walk through the 12th-century walled town, known as **Vila Vella,** built on the site of a Roman villa from the 1st century A.D. Enter through the Torre de les Hores.

Tossa was once a secret haunt for artists and writers—Marc Chagall called it a blue paradise. It has two main beaches, **Mar Gran** and **La Bauma.** The coast near Tossa—north and south—offers even more possibilities.

As one of few resorts to have withstood exploitation and retained most of its allure, Tossa enjoys a broad base of international visitors—so many, in fact, that it can no longer shelter them all. In spring and fall, finding a room may be a snap, but in summer it's next to impossible unless reservations are made far in advance.

Where to Stay

VERY EXPENSIVE

Grand Hotel Reymar, Platja de Mar Menuda, 17320 Tossa de Mar. ☎ **972/34-03-12.** Fax 972/34-15-04. 136 rms, 20 suites. A/C MINIBAR TV TEL

Rates: June–Sept (including obligatory half board): 14,000 ptas. ($99.40) single; 22,600–24,600 ptas. ($160.50–$174.70) double; 15,500 ptas. ($110.10) per person suite. Off-season (including breakfast): 6,500 ptas. ($46.20) single; 11,000 ptas. ($78.10) double; 13,600 ptas. ($96.60) per person suite. AE, DC, MC, V. **Parking:** 1,000 ptas. ($7.10). **Closed:** Nov–Apr.

Considered a triumph of engineering because of its unusual position on a jagged rock above the edge of the sea, this gracefully contoured building was built in the 1960s and renovated in the early 1990s. A 10-minute walk to the southeast of the historic walls of the old town, the Reymar offers several levels of expansive terraces ideal for sunbathing away from the crowds below, plus a wide variety of indoor/outdoor dining and drinking areas. Each of these has big windows, expansive views, and a clientele devoted to relaxing in the streaming Iberian sunlight. Each bedroom has a balcony, a sea view, a safety-deposit box, a TV with satellite reception, a marble-covered bathroom, and a combination of modern wood-grained and painted furniture.

Dining/Entertainment: The hotel contains four restaurants: the Proa, the Garbi, the Rotonda, and (in midsummer only) La Terraza. In at least two of these, fixed-price lunches and dinners cost 3,500 pesetas ($24.90) each. At least four bars lie scattered amid the terraces and beachfronts. There's also a disco.

Services: 24-hour room service, laundry/valet, concierge, babysitting.

Facilities: Outdoor swimming pool, solarium, car rentals, children's playground, tennis courts.

EXPENSIVE

Mar Menuda, Platja de Mar Menuda, 17320 Tossa de Mar. ☎ **972/34-10-00.** Fax 972/34-00-87. 50 rms.

Rates: 6,300 ptas. ($44.70) single; 11,000 ptas. ($78.10) double. Breakfast 1,075 ptas. ($7.60) extra. AE, DC, MC, V. **Parking:** 950 ptas. ($6.70) garage, free on street. **Closed:** Oct 1–Mar 1.

On the premises of this rustically decorated Mediterranean-style hotel are a pool, tennis courts, a garden, and a big parking lot. A restaurant serves competently prepared meals. Rooms are pleasant and comfortably furnished, all with private baths and 10 with air conditioning, minibars, TVs, and phones (naturally these are booked first).

MODERATE

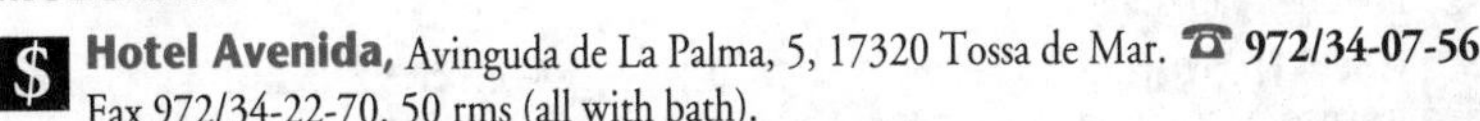

Hotel Avenida, Avinguda de La Palma, 5, 17320 Tossa de Mar. ☎ **972/34-07-56.** Fax 972/34-22-70. 50 rms (all with bath).

Rates: (including half board): 4,500–6,000 ptas. ($32–$42.60) per person. MC, V. **Closed:** Nov–Easter.

This pleasant, clean four-story hotel, located near the village church, about one block from the beach, is one of the best values in town. The lobby level contains a sunny dining room and a modern bar. The comfortable bedrooms, all doubles, have private terraces.

Hotel Diana, Plaza de España, 6, 17320 Tossa de Mar. ☎ **972/34-18-86.** Fax 972/34-11-03. 21 rms (all with bath).

Rates: 3,300–4,500 ptas. ($23.40–$32) single; 5,000–8,300 ptas. ($35.50–$58.90) double. Breakfast 600 ptas. ($4.30) extra. AE, DC, MC, V. **Closed:** Nov–Apr.

Set back from the esplanade, this two-star hotel is a former villa designed in part by students of Gaudí's. It boasts the most elegant fireplace on the Costa Brava. The inner patio—with its towering palms, vines and flowers, and fountains—is almost as popular with guests as the sandy "frontyard" beach. The spacious rooms contain fine furnishings; many open onto private balconies.

Hotel Vora la Mar, Avinguda de La Palma, 14, 17320 Tossa de Mar. ☎ **972/34-03-54.** Fax 972/11-03. 60 rms (all with bath). TEL

Rates: 3,350–4,500 ptas. ($23.80–$32) single; 5,000–7,500 ptas. ($35.50–$53.30) double. Breakfast 600 ptas. ($4.30) extra. AE, DC, MC, V. **Parking:** Free 5 minutes from hotel. **Closed:** Nov–Apr.

On a quiet street a block away from the beach, this hotel was built in the 1950s and renovated in the '70s. It has an outdoor café, a garden, and a dining room. The terrazzo-floored bedrooms are comfortable, many with balconies.

INEXPENSIVE

Hotel Cap d'Or, Passeig de Vila Vella, 1, 17320 Tossa de Mar. ☎ **972/34-00-81.** 11 rms (8 doubles with bath, 3 singles with shower).

Rates: 3,000–4,000 ptas. ($21.30–$28.40) single; 5,200–7,200 ptas. ($36.90–$51.10) double. Breakfast 575 ptas. ($4.10) extra. MC, V. **Closed:** Nov–Mar.

Perched on the waterfront on a quiet edge of town, this 1790s building, originally a fish store, nestles against the stone walls and towers of the village castle. Built of rugged stone itself, the Cap d'Or is like an old country inn and seaside hotel combined. It is both neat and well run. The old-world dining room, with its ceiling beams and ladderback chairs, has a pleasant sea view. Although the hotel is bed and breakfast, it does have a tearoom, offering sandwiches, ice cream, milkshakes, sangría, and coffee daily from 9am to midnight.

$ **L'Hostelet,** Plaça de l'Església, 4, 17320 Tossa de Mar. ☎ **972/34-00-88.** Fax 972/34-18-65. 36 rms (all with bath). TV TEL

Rates: (including breakfast): 4,000 ptas. ($28.40) single; 7,000 ptas. ($49.70) double. AE, DC, MC, V. **Parking:** 800–1,000 ptas. ($5.70–$7.10) nearby. **Closed:** Nov–Apr.

On the same plaza as the Tonet (see below), this modern-looking hotel has an open garden terrace in the front, plus a patio shaded by lemon trees. The hostal is sometimes known as the House of the American Student because of the number of Americans who stay here. All of the rooms are basic, although some are much more inviting than others.

$ **Hotel Neptuno,** La Guardia, 52, 17320 Tossa de Mar. ☎ **972/34-01-43.** Fax 972/34-19-33. 126 rms (all with bath).

Rates: June–Sept (including half board): 4,800 ptas. ($34.10) single; 8,600 ptas. ($61.10) double. Off-season (including breakfast): 2,250 ptas. ($16) single; 5,500 ptas. ($39.10) double. AE, DC, MC, V. **Closed:** Oct–Apr.

A longtime favorite, the Neptuno sits on a quiet residential hillside northwest of Vila Vella, somewhat removed from the seaside promenade. Inside, antiques are mixed with modern furniture, creating a personalized decor; the beamed-ceiling dining room is charming, and the bedrooms are tastefully light-hearted, modern, and sunny. A small swimming pool with its own terraced garden has a view of the sloping forest next door. A longtime favorite with Northern Europeans, who often book it solid during July and August, this hotel sits on a quiet residential hillside near the Vila Romano. Originally built in the 1960s, and renovated and enlarged in the late 1980s, the hotel is attractively removed from the bustle of Tossa de Mar's inner core. Public areas contain a mixture of antiques and modern furniture and a helpful staff. A small swimming pool with its own terraced garden has a view over a neighboring forest. The dining room has a beamed ceiling and bedrooms are tasteful, modern, and sunny.

$ **Hotel Tonet,** Plaça de l'Església, 1, 17320 Tossa de Mar. ☎ **972/34-02-37.** 36 rms (all with bath).

Rates: June–Sept (including half board): 4,125 ptas. ($29.30) single; 7,500 ptas. ($53.30) double. Off-season 2,750 ptas. ($19.50) single; 4,300–4,500 ptas. ($30.50–$32) double. Breakfast 375 ptas. ($2.70) extra. AE, DC, MC, V. **Parking:** 800–1,000 ptas. ($5.70–$7.10) nearby.

Established in the early 1960s, this simple, family-run pension is one of the resort's oldest hotels, built in the earliest days of the region's tourist boom. Renovated since then, it lies on a central plaza surrounded by narrow streets. It maintains the ambience of a country inn, with terraces on its upper floors where guests can relax or have breakfast amid potted vines and other plants. There's a somewhat sleepy bar on the premises where tapas and snacks are served, and a simple dining room for clients taking half board. Bedrooms are rustically simple, with wooden headboards and furniture. Tonet maintains its own brand of well-entrenched Iberian charm.

Where to Dine

$ **Can Tonet,** Plaça de l'Església, 2. ☎ **34-05-11.**

Cuisine: CATALÁN. **Reservations:** Not required.
Prices: Appetizers 625–1,100 ptas. ($4.40–$7.80); main courses 1,400–2,700 ptas. ($9.90–$19.20); *menú del día* 1,650 ptas. ($11.70). AE, DC, MC, V.
Open: Lunch, daily 1–4pm; dinner, daily 7–11pm.

Perched beside one of the most secluded, charming squares of the old town, this restaurant occupies what was originally built in the 1600s as a dormitory for local field hands. Established in 1979, Can Tonet has been one of the best-value and most-popular restaurants in Tossa de Mar ever since, known for its Catalán cuisine and fresh seafood. It has an extensive menu that includes soup Tonet, paella, sole Tonet, Tossa crayfish, grilled shrimp, and *zarzuela* (fish stew). At night the chef keeps the pizza oven going. Diners can eat at outside café tables or in the tavernlike dining room with its old beams and brass chandeliers.

★ **Es Molí,** Carrer Tarull, 5. ☎ **34-14-14.**

Cuisine: CATALÁN. **Reservations:** Recommended.
Prices: Appetizers 700–1,875 ptas. ($5–$13.30); main courses 1,150–3,500 ptas. ($8.20–$24.90); fixed-price menus 2,250–4,500 ptas. ($16–$32). AE, DC, MC, V.
Open: Lunch, daily 1–3:30pm; dinner, daily 7:30–11:30pm.
Closed: Jan 15–Feb 15.

The most beautiful—and the best—restaurant in Tossa is behind the church, set in the courtyard of a stone-walled windmill built in 1856. You'll dine beneath one of three arcades, each facing a three-tiered fountain. There is also a cluster of iron tables near the garden for those who prefer the sunlight. Among the specialties are an elaborately presented platter of local grilled fish, a delightful sole amandine, fisherman's cream soup, salad Es Molí (garnished with seaweed), hazelnut cream soup, hake and shrimp in garlic sauce, crayfish flambéed with Calvados, chef's-style tournedos, and a long list of well-chosen wines. The impeccably dressed waiters serve with a flourish.

Restaurant Bahía, Passeig del Mar, 19. ☎ **34-03-22.**

Cuisine: CATALÁN. **Reservations:** Recommended.
Prices: Appetizers 450–1,000 ptas. ($3.20–$7.10); main courses 850–2,500 ptas. ($6–$17.80); *menú del día* 3,000–3,500 ptas. ($21.30–$24.90). AE, DC, MC, V.
Open: Lunch, daily 1–4pm; dinner, daily 7:30–9pm. **Closed:** Dec 1–15.

Set adjacent to the sea, Bahia is a well-known restaurant with a much-awarded chef and a history of feeding hungry holidaymakers that dates back to its founding in 1953. Menu favorites are for the most part based on time-honored Catalán traditions, and include a *simitomba* (a grilled platter of fish); baked monkfish; a *brandada* of codfish; and an array of grilled fish (including salmonete, dorado, and calamare) whose availability is dependent upon its arrival from local fisherfolk. (Most fish served here are caught locally.)

Evening Entertainment

In Tossa de Mar's fast-changing nightlife, there is little stability or reliability. However, one club that's been in business for a while is the **Ely Club,** Calle Pola (☎ **34-00-09**). Devotees from all over the Costa Brava come here to dance to music that is among the most up to date in the region. Daily hours are 10pm to 4am. In July and August, admission is 1,200 pesetas ($8.50), which includes your first drink. From September to June, admission and your first drink cost only 900 pesetas ($6.40). The Ely Club is in the center of town between the two local cinemas.

4 Figueres

136 miles (219km) N of Barcelona, 23 miles (37km) E of Girona

GETTING THERE • By Train RENFE has hourly train service between Barcelona and Figueres. All trains between Barcelona and France stop here.

• By Bus It's better and faster to take the train if you're coming from Barcelona. But if you're in Cadaqués (see below), there are five daily SARFA buses a day making the 45-minute trip.

• By Car Figueres is a 40-minute ride from Cadaqués. Take the excellent north-south highway, the A-7, either south from the French border at La Jonquera or north from Barcelona, exiting at the major turnoff to Figueres.

ESSENTIALS The area code for Figueres is 972. The tourist information office is at the Plaça del Sol (☎ **972/50-31-55**).

As the heart of Catalonia, Figueres once played a role in Spanish history. Philip V wed Maria Luisa of Savoy here in 1701 in the church of San Pedro, thereby paving the way for the War of the Spanish Succession. But that historical fact is relatively forgotten today: The town is better known as the birthplace of surrealist artist Salvador Dalí in 1904.

There are two reasons for visiting Figueres—one of the best restaurants in Spain and the Dalí Museum.

★ **Teatre Museu Dalím,** Plaça de Gala-Dalí, 5 (☎ **51-17-96**), is filled with works by the late artist. The internationally known Dalí was as famous for his surrealist and often erotic imagery as he was for his flamboyance and exhibitionism. At the Figueres museum you'll find his paintings, watercolors, gouaches, charcoals, and pastels, along with graphics and sculptures, many rendered with seductive and meticulously detailed imagery. His wide-ranging subject matter encompassed everything from putrefaction to castration. You'll see, for instance, *The Happy Horse,* a grotesque and lurid purple beast that the artist painted during one of his long exiles at Port Lligat. A tour of the museum will be an experience. When a catalog was prepared, Dalí said with a perfectly straight face, "It is necessary that all of the people who come out of the museum have false information." The museum is open July through September, Tuesday through Sunday from 11:30am to 1:30pm and 4:30 to 8pm; October through June, Tuesday through Sunday 11am to 1pm and 3:30 to 7pm. Admission is 600 pesetas ($4.30). The museum stands in the center of town beside the Rambla.

Where to Stay

Ampurdán, Antigua Carretera de Francia, s/n (N-II), 17600 Figueres. ☎ **972/50-05-62.** Fax 972/50-93-58. 39 rms (all with bath), 3 suites. A/C TV TEL

Rates: 6,000–7,200 ptas. ($42.60–$51.10) single; 9,100–10,550 ptas. ($64.60–$74.90) double; 14,000–17,000 ptas. ($99.40–$120.70) suite. Breakfast 910 ptas. ($6.50) extra. AE, DC, MC, V. **Parking:** 700 ptas. ($5).

Although the restaurant is a gastronomic landmark (see below), the hotel associated with it provides reasonably priced accommodations for those passing between France and Spain, usually on business. It does not lie near the beach, it does not have a pool, and although rooms are comfortable and distinguished, it is not designed as a place for long-term sojourns. It has three floors of rooms.

$ **Hotel Bon Retorn,** Carretera Nacional IIA, km3, 17600 Figueres. ☎ **972/50-46-23.** Fax 972/67-39-79. 50 rms (all with bath). TV TEL **Directions:** Take the A-17 to exit 4-Figueres south; head toward town on Carretera Nacional IIA or take a taxi from the rail station.

Rates: 5,000 ptas. ($35.50) single; 9,000 ptas. ($63.90) double. Breakfast 700 ptas. ($5) extra. AE, MC, V. **Parking:** 900 ptas. ($6.40).

Located near the edge of the national highway, 1.5 miles (2.5km) south of Figueres, this family-owned hotel features a large and relaxing bar, a children's garden, and a sunny restaurant with an outdoor terrace where fixed-price meals go for 2,000 pesetas ($14.20). The hotel also has a private enclosed garage. The rooms are rustically furnished and comfortable, some with air conditioning and minibars.

Hotel Pirineos, Ronda de Barcelona, 1, 17600 Figueres. ☎ **972/50-03-12.** Fax 972/50-07-66. 53 rms (all with bath) TEL

Rates: 5,000 ptas. ($35.50) single; 6,000 ptas. ($42.60) double. Breakfast 560 ptas. ($4) extra. AE, DC, MC, V.
Parking: Free.

This pleasant hotel, near the main road leading to the center of town, is a five-minute walk from the Dalí Museum. The hotel's restaurant takes up most of the ground floor, and there's also a bar. Many of the comfortable rooms have balconies.

Where to Dine

 **Ampurdán,** Antigua Carretera de Francia, s/n (N-II). ☎ **50-05-62.**
Cuisine: CATALÁN. **Reservations:** Required.
Prices: Appetizers 950–2,500 ptas. ($6.70–$17.80); main courses 2,500–4,000 ptas. ($17.80–$28.40); fixed-price menu 4,100 ptas. ($29.10). AE, DC, MC, V.
Open: Lunch, daily 12:45–3:45pm; dinner, daily 8:30–10:45pm.

At this restaurant, you'll probably have your finest meal in Catalonia. See above for its hotel recommendation. Don't judge the place by its appearance, which is ordinary, if not institutional-looking. But there's nothing ordinary about the cuisine, as all the food-loving French who cross the border to dine here will tell you. This family-run restaurant, half a mile north of the center of town, also gained a reputation early on among U.S. servicemen in the area for subtly prepared game and fish dishes. In time, it was to win devotees in Salvador Dalí (who wrote his own cookbook) and Josep Pla, perhaps the country's greatest 20th-century writer. The appetizers are the finest along the Costa Brava, including such selections as duck foie gras with Armagnac, warm pâté of rape (monkfish) with garlic mousseline, and fish soup with fennel. The outstanding fish dishes include cuttlefish in Catalán sauce, suprême of sea bass with flan made with fennel and anchovy, and filet of red mullet with basil. Among the meat selections are the chef's special roast duck, beef filet in red-wine sauce with onion marmalade, and goose in a delectable mushroom sauce.

$ **Durán,** Carrer Lasauca, 5, 17600 Figueres. ☎ **972/50-12-50.** Fax 972/50-26-09.
Cuisine: CATALÁN. Reservations: Required.
Prices: Appetizers 600–1,600 ptas. ($4.30–$11.40); main courses 1,800–3,200 ptas. ($12.80–$22.70); fixed-price menu 1,600 ptas. ($11.40). AE, DC, MC, V.
Open: Lunch, daily 12:15–3:30pm; dinner, daily 8:15–11:30pm.

This popular place for a top-notch meal in the provinces had Dalí as a loyal patron. You can start with the salad Catalán, made with radishes, boiled egg, ham pâté, tuna fish, tomato, and fresh crisp salad greens. Other specialties include steak with Roquefort, zarzuela (Catalán fish stew), and *filetes de lenguado* à *la naranja* (sole in orange sauce). Like the Ampurdán (see above), the Durán specializes in game. Try, if it's available, the grilled rabbit on a plank, served with white wine. The french fries here, unlike those in most of Spain, are crisp and excellent. Finish off with a rich dessert or at least an espresso.

In Their Footsteps

Salvador Dalí (1904–89). He became the leading exponent of surrealism, depicting irrational imagery of dreams and delirium in a meticulously detailed style. Famous for his eccentricity, he was called "outrageous, talented, relentlessly self-promoting, and unfailingly quotable." At his death at 84, he was the last survivor of the famous *enfants terribles* of Spain (García Lorca and Luis Buñuel being the other two). His partner was the Russian-born Gala, his neurotic and ambitious wife. The first volume of his autobiography was called *The Secret Life of Salvador Dalí,* published in 1942.

Birthplace Figueres

Favorite Haunt Port Lligat on the Costa Brava

You can also stay at the Durán in one of its 67 well-furnished rooms, each with private bath, air conditioning, TV, and phone. A single costs 4,800 pesetas ($34.10), and a double goes for 6,800 pesetas ($48.30). Breakfast is another 650 pesetas ($4.60).

5 Cadaqués

122 miles (196km) N of Barcelona, 19 miles (31km) E of Figueres

GETTING THERE • By Bus Four buses per day from Figueres run to Cadaqués in July and August (off-season, the schedule is curtailed to two or three buses per day). Trip time is 1¼ hours. The service is operated by Estació Autobuses, leaving from Plaça Estació in Figueres. The cost of a one-way trip is 350 pesetas ($2.50), rising to 400 pesetas ($2.80) on Saturday and Sunday.

ESSENTIALS The area code for Cadaqués is 972. The tourist information office is at Cotxe, 2 (☎ **972/25-83-15**).

This little village is still unspoiled and remote, despite the publicity it received when Salvador Dalí lived in the next village of Lligat in a split-level house surmounted by a giant egg. The last resort on the Costa Brava before the French border, Cadaqués is reached by a small winding road, twisting over the mountains from Rosas, the nearest major center. When you get to Cadaqués, you really feel you're off the beaten path. The village winds around half a dozen small coves, with a narrow street running along the water's edge. This street has no railing, so exercise caution.

Scenically, Cadaqués is a knockout—with crystal-blue water; fishing boats on the sandy beaches; old whitewashed houses; narrow, twisting streets; and a 16th-century parish up on a hill.

Where to Stay

$ **Hostal Marina,** Rivera Sant Vincent, 3, 17488 Cadaqués. ☎ **972/25-81-99.** 27 rms (23 with bath).

Rates: 3,500 ptas. ($24.90) single without bath, 4,800 ptas. ($34.10) single with bath; 6,000 ptas. ($42.60) double with bath. Breakfast 500 ptas. ($3.60) extra. AE, MC, V. **Closed:** Nov.

This simple, centrally located hotel near the beach is the oldest in town. It offers clean, no-frills bedrooms at a good price. A fixed-price meal in the flagstone-floored dining room costs 1,600 pesetas ($11.40).

$ **Hostal s'Aguarda,** Carretera de Port Lligat, 28, 17488 Cadaqués. ☎ **972/25-80-82.** Fax 972/25-87-56. 28 rms (all with bath). A/C TV TEL

Rates: (including full board): 7,000 ptas. ($49.70) single; 12,400 ptas. ($88) double. AE, DC, MC, V. **Parking:** Free. **Closed:** Nov.

Situated on the road winding above Cadaqués on the way to Port Lligat, this hostal has a lovely view of the village's harbor and medieval church. Each of the modern, airy accommodations open onto a flower-decked terrace. The rooms have tile floors and simple furniture. Meals are served for 1,650 pesetas ($11.70).

Hotel Playa Sol, Platja Planch, 3, 17488 Cadaqués. ☎ **972/25-81-00.** Fax 972/25-80-54. 50 rms (all with bath). TV TEL

Rates: 9,900–10,000 ptas. ($70.30–$71) single; 11,900–15,900 ptas. ($84.50–$112.90) double. Breakfast 1,000 ptas. ($7.10) extra. AE, DC, MC, V. **Parking:** 1,000 ptas. ($7.10). **Closed:** Jan–Feb 15.

In a relatively quiet section of the port along the bay, this 1950s hotel has, arguably, the best view of the stone church at the distant edge of the harbor. The balconied building is constructed of brick and terra-cotta tiles. Its bedrooms are comfortably furnished. Twenty-five rooms are air-conditioned. The hotel doesn't have a restaurant, but it does offer a cafeteria.

Hotel Port Lligat, Salvador Dalí, 17488 Cadaqués. ☎ **972/25-81-62.**
Fax 972/25-86-43. 30 rms (all with bath). TEL

Rates: (including breakfast): 7,500–10,000 ptas. ($53.30–$71) double. No credit cards. **Closed:** Nov.

Many visitors find the relative isolation of this hotel—at the end of a winding gravel road a half mile outside Cadaqués—to be its most alluring point. The terrace overlooks an idyllic harbor and an unusual house once occupied by Salvador Dalí. The gallery adjoining the reception lobby features a changing series of surrealist paintings. Also on the premises are a swimming pool with cabañas, a restaurant, and a snack bar. The airy bedrooms, all doubles, have tile floors, exposed wood, and balconies.

Where to Dine

Don Quijote, Caridad Seriñana, 5. ☎ **25-81-41.**

Cuisine: CATALÁN. **Reservations:** Recommended.
Prices: Appetizers 750–1,000 ptas. ($5.30–$7.10); main courses 1,800–2,500 ptas. ($12.80–$17.80). AE, DC, MC, V.
Open: Lunch, Tues–Sun 1–4pm; dinner, Tues–Sun 8–11:30pm. **Closed:** Nov–Mar.

Located on the road leading into the village, this intimate bistro has a large vine-covered garden in front. You can dine either inside or al fresco. The à la carte specialties include lamb chops, pepper steak, zarzuela (seafood stew), and gazpacho. The Don Quijote cup, a mixed dessert, is the best way to end a meal.

Es Trull, Port Ditxos, s/n. ☎ **25-81-96.**

Cuisine: SEAFOOD. **Reservations:** Recommended.
Prices: Appetizers 210–925 ptas. ($1.50–$6.60); main courses 780–3,000 ptas. ($5.50–$21.30); fixed-price menus 980–1,500 ptas. ($7–$10.70). MC, V.
Open: Lunch, daily 12:30–4pm; dinner, daily 7:30–11pm. **Closed:** Oct–Easter.

On the harborside street in the center of town, this cedar-shingled cafeteria is named for the ancient olive press that dominates the interior. A filling fixed-price meal is served. According to the chef, if it comes from the sea and can be eaten, he will prepare it with that special Catalán flair. You might, for example, prefer mussels in a marinara sauce or else grilled hake, perhaps various grilled fried fish. Rice dishes are also a specialty, not only paella, but "black rice" colored with squid ink and rice with calamari and shrimp. Natural baby clams are yet another dining delight.

La Galiota, Carrer Narciso Monturiol, 9. ☎ **25-81-87.**

Cuisine: CATALÁN/FRENCH. **Reservations:** Required.
Prices: Appetizers 800–1,400 ptas. ($5.70–$9.90); main courses 1,800–2,500 ptas. ($12.80–$17.80); fixed-price menu 1,600 ptas. ($11.40). AE, DC, MC, V.
Open: Lunch, daily 2–3:30pm; dinner, daily 9–11pm. **Closed:** Mon–Fri in Nov–May.

Dozens of surrealist paintings, including some by Dalí, adorn the walls of this award-winning restaurant, the finest in town. Located on a sloping street below the cathedral, the place has a downstairs sitting room and a dining room converted from what was a private house. The cuisine is not at all pretentious. The secret of the chef is in selecting only the freshest of ingredients and preparing them in a way that enhances—not disguises—their natural flavors. The roast leg of lamb, flavored with garlic, is a specialty. The menu changes with the season but always features the best of French and Catalán fare. The marinated salmon is excellent, as are the sea bass and the sole with orange sauce. For dessert, try the soufflé al Grand Marnier.

$ **Sa Gambina,** Riba Nemeslo Llorens, s/n. ☎ **25-81-27.**

Cuisine: CATALÁN. **Reservations:** Recommended.
Prices: Appetizers 600–1,100 ptas. ($4.30–$7.80); main courses 1,000–2,100 ptas. ($7.10–$14.90); fixed-price menus 1,200–1,500 ptas. ($8.50–$10.70). AE, MC, V.
Open: Lunch, daily noon–4pm; dinner, daily 7–11pm.

This restaurant, with its regional ambience and cavelike dining room, is located on the waterfront and serves reasonably good food at moderate prices. It's been a local favorite since the 1960s. A Catalán salad (tomato, lettuce, peppers, *butifarra,* onions, and olives) is a good choice, as is the paella or the fish soup. The shrimp (*gambas*), for which the place was named, are always reliable. You might also try the fish soufflé.

Evening Entertainment

Es Porró, Portal de la Font, 1. ☎ **25-80-82.**

Although small, Es Porró is popular, thanks to its in-house video shows and warm ambience. At times it becomes a piano bar. It's open daily from 11pm to 4:30am. In the off-season, it is likely to be open only on weekends—check locally. But in midsummer it seems to be thriving every night. Expect to pay around 750 pesetas ($5.30) for a drink.

L'Hostal, Paseo, 8A. ☎ **25-80-00.**

This distinctive place has attracted some of the most glamorous names of the art and music worlds. Some music critics have called it the second-best jazz club in Europe, and it certainly rates as the best club along the coast. It's a Dixieland bar par excellence, run by the most sophisticated entrepreneurial team in town. Habitués still remember when Salvador Dalí escorted Mick Jagger here, much to the delight of Colombian writer Gabriel García Marquez. In fact, the bar's logo, which is not only on the matchbooks but also on the doorstep (in mosaic), was designed by Dalí himself. Heightening the ambience are the dripping candles, the high ceilings, and the heavy Spanish furniture. The best music is usually performed late in the evening. L'Hostal is open daily from noon to 5am. Entrance is free. Beer costs from 350 to 650 pesetas ($2.50 to $4.60); whisky, 750 to 1,000 pesetas ($5.30 to $7.10).

17 Aragón

LANDLOCKED ARAGÓN, WHICH, ALONG WITH NAVARRE FORMS THE NORTHEASTERN quadrant of Spain, is an ancient land. It is composed of three provinces, including Zaragoza; remote Teruel, farther south; and Huesca, in the north as you move toward the Pyrenees. These are also the names of the provinces' major cities. Most of Aragón constitutes terra incognita for the average tourist.

Aragón is one of the most history-rich regions of Spain. You can visit it as an extension of your trip to Castile in the west or an extension of your trek through Catalonia in the east. Huesca, close to the mountains, is ideal for a summer visit, unlike most of Aragón, especially the fiercely hot south—considered Spain's worst climate. Winter is often bitterly cold. Spring and autumn are ideal.

Aragón is known best for two former residents: Catherine of Aragón, who foolishly married Henry VIII of England, and Ferdinand of Aragón, whose marriage to Isabella, queen of Castile and León in the 15th century, led to the unification of Spain.

Aragón is also noted for its notable Mudéjar architecture, which owes a debt to the Muslims, and for its tradition of bull fighting. In September many villages in the region have their own *encierros,* in which bulls run through the streets. What they don't have is the world promotion that Hemingway gave the festival at Pamplona in the neighboring province of Navarre. On the other hand, they aren't plagued with all the wine-drunk foreigners, the curse of the Pamplona festival. In folklore, Aragón is known for a dance, the *jota,* a bounding, leaping dance performed by men and women since at least the 1700s.

Aragón's capital, Zaragoza, is the most visited destination because it lies on the main route between Madrid and Barcelona. If you're driving from Madrid to Barcelona (or vice versa), I suggest a detour to Zaragoza. If you get interested in Aragón there, you may want to stick around to explore this ancient land.

Seeing Aragón

GETTING THERE The easiest way to reach Zaragoza is by plane. Aviaco has several daily weekday flights from both Barcelona and Madrid. International connections are made through either Barcelona or Madrid.

It's also easy to take the train, as RENFE offers frequent service to Zaragoza from both Barcelona and Madrid. The *talgo* express makes the fewest stops. Daily express trains from Madrid continue past Zaragoza to targets in the north, such as Huesca and Jaca, the gateway to the Pyrenees.

Zaragoza is also provided with bus links daily from both Madrid and Barcelona. Once at Zaragoza, you can make bus connections—and sometimes rail—to the chief sightseeing goals in the province.

For motorists, Zaragoza lies on the main auto route between Madrid and Barcelona. The A-68 Basque-Aragón highway links Bilbao with coastal Tarragona in Catalonia, and provides easy access to Zaragoza if you're coming south from Basque country.

A Suggested Route

Days 1–2 Travel to Zaragoza from either Madrid or Barcelona, arriving late in the afternoon. Sample some of the *tascas* (taverns) and nightlife of the city before retiring. In the morning, take a stroll around Zaragoza and visit its major monuments. In the afternoon, if you have a car, consider at least one of the "Easy Excursions" from Zaragoza (see below).

What's Special About Aragón

Great Towns/Villages

- Zaragoza, the provincial capital—vital, alive, and action-packed, with two famous cathedrals.
- Tarazona, known for its Muslim-influenced architecture.
- Daroca, a gem of an Aragonese town that's known for its architecture (some of it Roman).
- Sos del Rey Católico, with its medieval architecture.

A Historic Monastery

- Cartuja de Aula Dei, outside Zaragoza, a 16th-century Carthusian monastery, where the young Goya completed a series of murals.

Religious Shrines

- Catedral de Nuestra Señora del Pilar in Zaragoza, a basilica from the 1500s that draws thousands of pilgrims honoring the tiny statue of the Virgin del Pilar.
- La Seo del Salvador, a Gothic-Mudéjar church, with a rich baroque and Plateresque facade, in Zaragoza.

Parks/Gardens

- Monasterio de Piedra outside Nuévalos—with roaring waterfalls and dancing cascades—everything from a reflecting lake to Diana's bath.

Special Events/Festivals

- Pilar festivities, beginning October 12 in Zaragoza—with bullfights, jota dancing, and processions to extol the Virgin.
- The Folklore Festival of the Pyrenees, from late July to mid-August (odd years) in Jaca, drawing an international array of top-notch music and dance groups.

Day 3 If you're driving, strike out on "the Mudéjar trail," visiting Tarazona to the west of Zaragoza and driving on to Calatayud. If time remains, visit Nuévalos and spend the night at the Monasterio de Piedra (reservation required). If not, there are other accommodations in the area.

Day 4 The next day stop first at Daroca for about two hours of sightseeing, then head north to Sos del Rey Católico for the night.

1 Zaragoza

200 miles (322km) W of Madrid, 190 miles (306km) E of Barcelona

GETTING THERE • By Plane Aviaco has direct flights to Zaragoza from Madrid and Barcelona. From the airport in Zaragoza, you can get a bus to the Plaza de San Francisco. The Iberia office is at Canfranc, 22-24 (☎ **21-82-59**), in Zaragoza.

• By Train From Barcelona, 9 to 12 trains arrive daily, and from Madrid there are 12 per day. The trip takes 3 to 4 hours from Madrid and $4^1/_2$ hours from Barcelona. The RENFE office in Zaragoza is at Calle San Clemente, 13 (☎ **22-65-98**), just off Paseo de la Independencia.

• **By Bus** There is one direct bus a day running between Zaragoza and Barcelona (seven hours away).

• **By Car** Zaragoza is easily reached on the E-90 (A-2) east from Madrid or west from Barcelona.

ESSENTIALS The area code for Zaragoza is 976. The tourist information office is at Torreón de la Zuda–Glorieta Pio XII (☎ **976/39-35-37**), next to the Roman wall.

Zaragoza ("Tha-ra-*go*-tha") is halfway between Madrid and Barcelona. This big provincial capital, the seat of the ancient kingdom of Aragón, is a bustling, prosperous, commercial city of wide boulevards and arcades.

Zaragoza has not one, but two, cathedrals and ranks with Santiago de Compostela in Galicia as a pilgrimage center. According to legend, the Virgin Mary appeared to St. James, patron saint of Spain, on the banks of the Ebro River and ordered him to build a church there.

Zaragoza (Saragossa in English) lies in the center of a rich *huerta.* Its history goes back to the Romans, who called it Caesar Augusta. Today, Zaragoza is a city of more than three quarters of a million people, slightly less than 75% of the population in Aragón.

Some 40,000 students at the University of Zaragoza have brought a new joie de vivre to the once-staid old city. Cafés, theaters, restaurants, music bars, and tascas have boomed in recent years, and more monuments have been restored and opened to the public.

The city's big festivities take place the week of October 12, with top-name bullfighters, religious processions, and general merriment.

What to See & Do

Catedral de Nuestra Señora del Pilar, Plaza de las Catedrales. ☎ **39-74-97.**

This 16th- and 17th-century basilica, on the banks of the Ebro River, is in an almost Oriental style with its domes and towers. Thousands of the faithful travel here annually to pay homage to the tiny statue of the Virgin del Pilar in the Holy Chapel. The name of the cathedral, El Pilar, comes from the pillar upon which the Virgin is supposed to have stood when she asked Santiago (St. James) to build the church.

During the second week of October, the church is a backdrop for an important festival devoted to Our Lady of the Pillar, which combines parades, bullfights, fireworks, flower offerings, and street dancing. Also of interest within the church are frescoes painted by Goya, who was born nearby.

You can also visit the Museo del Pilar, which houses the jewelry collection used to adorn the Pilar statue, as well as sketches by Goya and other artists, including Bayeu. Much of the collection is ancient, including an 18th-century ivory horn.

Admission: Cathedral, free; museum, 100 ptas. (70¢).

Open: Cathedral, Apr–Oct daily 8am–2pm and 4–7pm; winter, daily 9am–2pm and 4–6pm. Museum, daily 9am–2pm and 4–6pm. **Bus:** 22 or 23.

La Seo del Salvador, Plaza de la Seo. ☎ **29-12-38.**

This Gothic-Mudéjar church, built between 1380 and 1550, is more impressive than El Pilar (see above) but has been closed for some time for restoration. Its scheduled reopening is some time in 1995. It has a rich baroque and Plateresque facade and is a particularly fine example of Aragonese Gothic architecture. Among its more important features are the main altar and a fine collection of French and Flemish tapestries from the 15th to the 17th century. The baroque cupolas in the Temple of Pilar were decorated by Goya and Bayeu.

Open: Ask at the tourist office about the church's scheduled reopening. **Bus:** 21, 22, 29, 32, 35, 36, 43, 44, 45.

Palacio de la Aljafería, Aljafería, Calle Los Diputados. ☎ **28-95-28.**

This most unusual sight, a Moorish palace in Aragón, has been restored by the Parliament and preserved as a national monument. Reminiscent of *cordobán* architecture, the palace was built in the 11th century for Moorish kings but has seen considerable alterations and additions since then, particularly when Ferdinand and Isabella lived here.

Admission: Free.

Open: Tues–Sat 10am–2pm and 4–8pm; Sun 10–2pm. **Bus:** 32, 33, or 36.

Museo de Zaragoza, Plaza de los Sitios, 6. ☎ **22-21-81.**

This museum is installed in a 1908 building that has 10 ground-floor rooms devoted to exhibits from the prehistoric to the Muslim period. The Roman legacy (rooms 4 to 8) has sculptures (see the head of Augustus), mosaics, and ceramics. The fine arts section includes paintings by Goya (room 20); see his self-portrait. In the next room you'll find his drawings of *Los Caprichos (The Whims).* Also displayed is a Goya portrait of Carlos IV and his wife. The museum lies directly north of the Paseo de Marino Moreno.

Admission: 250 ptas. ($1.80).

Open: Tues–Sun 9am–2pm. **Bus:** 30, 35, or 40.

Museo Camón Aznar, Espoz y Mina, 23. ☎ **39-73-28.**

One block from El Pilar (see above), occupying a Renaissance palace, this museum has 3 floors and 23 rooms, each filled with artwork. On the second floor is a sketch of María Sarmiento that Velázquez made for his masterpiece *Las Meninas (The Maids of Honor),* which hangs in the Prado in Madrid. The Bayeu brothers (Francisco and Ramón) are represented by several works, as is Goya. His collection includes an important self-portrait, a version of his *Los Caprichos (The Whims), La Tauromaquia (The Tauromachy), Los Desastres de la Guerra (The Disasters of War),* and *Los Disparates (The Follies).*

Admission: 125 ptas. (90¢).

Open: Tues–Sat 10am–1pm; Sun 11am–2pm. **Bus:** 22 or 23.

Museo Pablo Gargallo, Plaza de San Felipe, 3. ☎ **39-20-50.**

The museum honors eponymous sculptor Pablo Gargallo, born in Maella in 1881. It is installed in a beautiful Aragonese Renaissance-style palace (1659) that was declared a national monument in 1963. Gargallo, influential in the art world of the 1920s, is represented by 100 original works, ranging from *Dr. Petit's Fireplace* (1904) to *Great Prophet,* a bronze piece from 1933. The museum is located in the center, a five-minute walk south of El Pilar.

Admission: Free.

Open: Tues–Sat 10am–1pm and 5–9pm; Sun 11am–4pm. **Bus:** 22 or 23.

Where to Stay

MODERATE

Boston, Camino de las Torres, 28, 50008 Zaragoza. ☎ **976/59-91-92.** Fax 976/59-04-46. 297 rms (all with bath) 16 suites. A/C MINIBAR TV TEL **Bus:** 29.

N
0
25 km
15.5 mi
FRANCE
Pyrenees
Sierra de Tendeñera
Pamplona
Anso
Hecho
N330
Toria
Parque Nacional Valle de Ordesa
Viella
Biescas
Benasque
Jaca
N240
Sierra Solana
Sierra Ferrera
Castejón de Sos
Pont de Suert
Ainsa
Sos del Rey Católico
N139
N136
Sierra de Guarda
Graus
A15
Sádaba
Benabarre
E804
Ejea de los Caballeros
Huesca
N240
Barbastro
Tudela
Río Ebro
N420
N123
A68
Tarazona
Borja
Sariñena
Lérida
Río Duero
Zaragoza
Parque Natural Dehesa del Moncayo
Fraga
N234
E90
A2
Calatayud
Cariñena
N221
Belchite
Caspe
E90
N210
Hijar
N232
Doroca
Sierra del Cucalón
Nuévalos
N420
Calamocha
Montalbán
Tortosa
Molina
N234
N232
Villafranca del Cid
Sierra Palomera
Sierra del Pobo
Maestrazgo
A7
Sierra de los Monegros
Balearic Sea
Albarracín
Sierra de Gúder
E15
Teruel
To Mora de Rubielos
Aragón
Madrid
SPAIN
1 Zaragoza
2 Tarazona
3 Calatayud
4 Nuévalos/Piedra
5 Sos del Rey Católico

Rates: Mon–Thurs 11,000 ptas. ($78.10) single; 15,000 ptas. ($106.50) double; suite 21,000 ptas. ($149.10). Fri–Sun 8,000 ptas. ($56.80) single or double; suite 15,000 ptas. ($106.50). Breakfast 950 ptas. ($6.70) extra. AE, DC, MC, V.
Parking: 1,500 ptas. ($10.70).

Set in the heart of Zaragoza's modern business district, a 15-minute walk from the medieval neighborhoods that most foreign visitors search out, this eight-story hotel was opened in 1992. Named in honor of Boston, Massachussetts, where the building's architect earned his degree, it's considered one of the best hotels, and one of the tallest buildings, in town. Many of its public areas are sheathed in layers of beige marble, occasionally accented with wood paneling. Throughout, the style is ultra-modern, even futuristic, strongly infused with postmodern design and American-derived ideas. The in-house restaurant, one floor below the lobby level, is named Niagara, and serves fixed-price meals for around 3,000 pesetas ($21.30). On the premises is a health club with a sauna. Room service is available 24 hours a day.

Gran Hotel, Joaquín Costa 5, 50001 Zaragoza. ☎ **976/22-19-01.** Fax 976/23-67-13. 120 rms, 20 suites. A/C MINIBAR TV TEL

Rates: 11,340 ptas. ($80.50) single; 15,750 ptas. ($111.80) double; from 26,000 ptas. ($184.60) suites. Breakfast 1,200 ptas. ($8.50) extra. AE, DC, MC, V. **Parking:** 1,500 ptas. ($10.70).

Located half a mile south of the cathedral, behind one of the most beautiful Hispano–art deco facades in town, this hotel is considered the most historic and probably the most charming in Zaragoza. Established by King Alphonso XIII in 1929, the Gran offers a domed rotunda for conversation and an array of formal public rooms and conference facilities with crystal chandeliers and classic furniture. Bedrooms have been restored into a neutral, traditional international style, yet they retain the high ceilings and spaciousness of their original design, as well as occasional touches of art deco. A favorite of the business community, the hotel offers excellent service and many hide-aways for quiet drinks and dialogs.

Hemingway, and one of his biographers, A. E. Hotchner, stayed at the Gran when they were in Zaragoza.

Dining/Entertainment: The hotel's restaurants include the very elegant Lion d'Or, where three-course fixed-price lunches and dinners begin at 2,500 pesetas ($17.80) each but can go much higher. Current newspapers are available along with the drinks served in the bar, an enclave that some visitors consider their favorite spot.

Services: 24-hour room service, laundry, concierge.

Hotel Goya, Calle Cinco de Marzo, 5, 50004 Zaragoza. ☎ **976/22-93-31.** Fax 976/23-21-54. 148 rms (all with bath). A/C TV TEL **Bus:** 22.

Rates: 8,860 ptas. ($62.90) single; 13,000–13,650 ptas. ($92.30–$96.90) double. Breakfast 900 ptas. ($6.40) extra. AE, DC, MC, V. **Parking:** 1,100 ptas. ($7.80).

Just off the Paseo de la Independencia, near the Plaza de España in the city center, this hotel (rebuilt in 1986) has excellent bedrooms that in some respects equal the much more expensive accommodations at the Gran (see above). True to its name-sake, the hotel displays copies of Goya's paintings throughout the multilevel lobby, which is decorated in black marble and wood paneling.

Hotel Palafox, Calle Casa Jiménez, s/n. 50004 Zaragoza. ☎ **976/23-77-00.** Fax 976/23-47-05. 180 rms, 4 suites. A/C MINIBAR TV TEL **Bus:** 22.

Rates: 12,800 ptas. ($90.90) single; 16,000 ptas. ($113.60) double; 24,000 ptas. ($170.40) suite. Buffet breakfast 1,200 ptas. ($8.50) extra. AE, DC, MC, V. **Parking:** 1,000 ptas. ($7.10).

Affiliated with the also recommended Hotel Goya, this is a more modern version, with sleek Spanish styling. Considered one of the leading top four hotels of town it looks somewhat like an apartment house. It was inaugurated in 1982 and has been rated five stars by the government. A favorite of business travelers, it is frequently the venue for local events such as fashion shows. A rooftop swimming pool is a magnet during the long, hot Aragonese summer. Bedrooms have sleek traditional styling (often leather armchairs) and are well maintained and comfortable. The hotel restaurant, Puerto Sanco, serves a traditional Aragonese cuisine, with meals costing from 3,500 pesetas ($24.90). Other services and facilities include a sauna, massage, and 24-hour room service.

Rey Alfonso I, Calle Coso, 17-19, 50003 Zaragoza. ☎ **976/39-48-50.**
Fax 976/39-96-40. 117 rms (all with bath). A/C MINIBAR TV TEL **Bus:** 22.

Rates: 10,800 ptas. ($76.70) single; 15,700 ptas. ($111.50). Breakfast 775 ptas. ($5.50) extra. AE, DC, MC, V. **Parking:** 1,000 ptas. ($7.10).

This clean, efficient place is a favorite with businesspeople, who prefer its location in the commercial heart of town. A prominent arcade marks the entrance. The hotel has a popular countertop-service snack bar and, in the basement, a comfortably modern restaurant. A helpful crew of veteran and good-natured doormen help visitors with their luggage. The rooms are furnished with comfortable modern furniture.

INEXPENSIVE

Hotel Oriente, Calle Coso, 11-13, 50003 Zaragoza. ☎ **976/39-80-61.**
Fax 976/39-83-02. 87 rms (all with bath). A/C MINIBAR TV TEL **Bus:** 33.

Rates: 5,300–7,600 ptas. ($37.60–$54) single; 9,500 ptas. ($67.50) double. Breakfast 750 ptas. ($5.30) extra. AE, DC, MC, V. **Parking:** 1,500 ptas. ($10.70).

This Franco era hotel has been completely renovated and given three stars by the government. The lobby has been modernized, and the attractive, comfortable bedrooms have been considerably upgraded. It's in a good location—about one block from the Plaza de España and the Plaza de Salamero.

$ **Hotel Sauce,** Calle Espoz y Mina, 33, 50003 Zaragoza. ☎ **976/39-01-00.**
Fax 976/39-85-97. 20 rms (all with bath). A/C TV TEL **Bus:** 22.

Rates: 4,900 ptas. ($34.80) single; 7,200 ptas. ($51.10) double. Breakfast 500 ptas. ($3.60) extra. AE, MC, V. **Parking:** 900 ptas. ($6.40).

Lying in the historic and artistic old town, right off the Calle de Don Jaime I, this rates as one of the best bargains in a high-priced city. The decor is cozy, the staff helpful. The guest rooms are small but comfortably furnished and well maintained.

Where to Dine

Los Borrachos, Paseo de Sagasta, 64. ☎ **27-50-36.**

Cuisine: SPANISH/INTERNATIONAL. **Reservations:** Recommended.
Prices: Appetizers 850–1,650 ptas. ($6–$11.70); main courses 1,700–4,200 ptas. ($12.10–$29.80). AE, MC, V.
Open: Lunch, daily 1–4pm; dinner, daily 8:30pm–midnight.

Solid and dignified, and committed to preserving a discreet and old-fashioned kind of service, this restaurant occupies a formal set of dining rooms in a location near the heart of town. Menu items may include such dishes as a combination platter of hake with lobster; wild boar with wine sauce; filet of beef with a pepper-cognac sauce; roasted pheasant or rabbit; and an asparagus mousse accented with strips of Serrano ham. This restaurant's name, incidentally, translates as "The Drunkards," and was taken from the characters in a famous Velásquez painting.

$ **Faustino's,** Plaza San Francisco, 3. ☎ **35-68-68.**

Cuisine: ARAGONESE. **Reservations:** Recommended.
Prices: Appetizers 550–750 ptas. ($3.90–$5.30); main courses 900–1,300 ptas. ($6.40–$9.20); *menú del día* 1,495 ptas. ($10.60). AE, DC, MC, V.
Open: Lunch, daily 12:30–5pm; dinner, daily 7pm–1am.

This starkly modern building near the football stadium is on the corner of one of the largest squares in town. At a sidewalk café and a metallic bar, you can choose from a selection of tapas. One flight down you'll find the Bodega, one of Zaragoza's most charming restaurants. The heavy ceiling beams, stone floors, and enormous copper still nestled in the stairwell create a unique ambience. Grilled specialties include veal chops, spicy sausages, entrecôte, and filet of pork. Dessert might be a temptingly caloric slice of whisky-flavored tart. Enjoy an array of local wines, poured from oak-sided casks behind the bar.

Gurrea, San Ignacio de Loyola, 14. ☎ **23-31-61.**

Cuisine: SPANISH. **Reservations:** Recommended.
Prices: Appetizers 800–1,800 ptas. ($5.70–$12.80); main courses 2,000–3,200 ptas. ($14.20–$22.70); fixed-price menu 3,500 ptas. ($24.90). AE, DC, MC, V.
Open: Lunch, daily 1–5pm; dinner, Mon–Sat 9pm–12:30am.

This is probably the most enduring restaurant in Zaragoza, committed to maintaining its reputation for good service, an attractive setting, and a time-honored cuisine. It's a favorite of the lunching business community and the venue, supposedly, of many successfully completed deals. Menu items might include goosemeat terrine, duck with orange sauce, chateaubriand with foie-gras sauce, hake served with fruit sauce, venison meatballs (in season) with truffles, wild mushrooms with goose liver, and filet mignon in curry sauce—plus a succulent array of desserts.

La Mar, Plaza Aragón, 12. ☎ **21-22-64.**

Cuisine: SEAFOOD. **Reservations:** Recommended.
Prices: Appetizers 800–1,100 ptas. ($5.70–$7.80); main courses 950–2,600 ptas. ($6.70–$18.50), fixed-price menu 4,500 ptas. ($32). AE, MC, V.
Open: Lunch, Mon–Sat 1:30–4pm; dinner, Mon–Sat 9pm–midnight.

Established in 1985 within what was originally (1890) a private house, this is considered one of the better seafood restaurants in town. Service is leisurely, and your meal might take more time than you're willing to invest; but if you're in the mood for a prolonged meal, the menu will include a full range of seasonal vegetables; peppers stuffed with seafood mousse; *dorada* cooked in a salt crust; baked sea bream; turbot with clams, grilled hake or monkfish; grilled squid; shellfish soup or shellfish rice; and—if you're not in the mood for fish—grilled beefsteak with several kinds of sauces.

La Rinconada de Lorenzo, Calle La Salle, 3. ☎ **55-51-08.**

Cuisine: ARAGONESE. **Reservations:** Required. **Bus:** 40 or 45.

Prices: Appetizers 650–1,100 ptas. ($4.60–$7.80); main courses 2,700–3,500 ptas. ($19.20–$24.90); fixed-price menu 2,000 ptas. ($14.20). AE, DC, MC, V.
Open: Lunch, daily 1–4pm; dinner, daily 8–11:30pm.

This restaurant, one of the best in town, offers such unusual dishes as fried rabbit with snails. Oven-roasted lamb or lamb hock can be ordered in advance, but lamb skewers are always available. The chef prepares several versions of *migas* (fried breadcrumbs) flavored with a number of different ingredients, including ham. Giant asparagus spears are often served. Even though Zaragoza is inland, fresh fish is always on the menu: hake, grilled sole, sea bream, and salmon, for example. Desserts are all homemade, including rice pudding, chocolate mousse with cream, and fig ice cream with nuts. Red, white, and rosé wines of Aragón help wash everything down smoothly.

Evening Entertainment

Casa Amadico, Jordán de Urriés, 3. ☎ **29-10-41.**

This popular hangout is located near Plaza del Pilar, on one of the smallest streets in the city. Local government workers and businesspeople come here after work for the tasty seafood tapas. Oysters come in three different sizes, or perhaps you'll be tempted by the smoked salmon, lobster, or Serrano ham. It's open Tuesday to Sunday from 1 to 4pm and 7pm to 1am; closed in August. A glass of wine costs 75 ptas. (50¢); tapas range from 100 to 550 ptas. (70¢–$3.90). **Bus:** 22.

Casa Luís, Romea, 8. ☎ **29-11-67.**

This tiled-and-oak bar is one of the more interesting places in the barrio of La Magdalena. The array of tapas served here—some of the best around—includes fresh oysters, shrimp, and razor clams "in little bundles." It's open daily from 1 to 4pm and again from 7pm to midnight. A glass of wine will cost 75 ptas. (50¢); tapas are 100 to 550 ptas. (70¢–$3.90). **Bus:** 22.

El Plata, Cuatro 4 de Agosto, 23. ☎ **29-32-15.**

Located at the Plaza de España, this is one of the last *café-cantantes* left in Spain. The good-sized café, popular with all types of people, has a bar at the entrance and an old, musty stage at the other end of the room. Three times daily a wobbly three-piece orchestra whoops up the tunes, and a scantily dressed dancer comes out to warble a love song and do a couple of bumps and grinds. It's all hilariously simple and authentic. Shows are daily at 3, 8:30, and 10:45pm.

Admission (including first drink): 900 ptas. ($6.40).

Salón Oasis, Boggiero, 28. ☎ **44-10-62.**

This former theater transformed into a cabaret/music hall features a variety of artists who perform to a predominantly local crowd. It's open Tuesday to Thursday from 11pm until the show is over, on Friday from 11pm to 1am and again from 1:30am until the end of the show, and on Saturday from 7 to 10:30pm and 11pm to 1am.

Admission: 1,500 ptas. ($10.70).

Easy Excursions

Goya aficionados (male ones only) can visit the **Cartuja de Aula Dei** (☎ **15-42-11**), a 16th-century Carthusian monastery 7 miles (11km) north of Zaragoza in Montañana. The young Goya, an Aragonese, completed one of his first important commissions here in 1774, a series of 11 murals depicting scenes from the lives of Christ and Mary. In the Napoleonic invasion, the murals suffered badly, but restoration has since been done. In this strictly run Carthusian community, only men are admitted. Visiting times are Wednesday and Saturday from 10am to 1pm and 3 to 7pm. From Zaragoza you can drive or take a local bus. In Zaragoza, bus 28 departs about every half hour to the site (trip time: 20 minutes), a one-way ticket costing 60 pesetas (40¢). Catch the bus at the stop near the Roman walls.

Goya fans—this time male *and* female—can also go east from Zaragoza to the little village of **Fuendetodos,** the birthplace of Goya in 1746. A small two-room cottage in the village (not his actual birthplace, however), was restored in 1985 and turned into a museum, **Casa de Goya,** Zuloaga, 3 (☎ **14-38-30**). You're shown transparencies of his most important works. From April through October, it is open Tuesday through Sunday from 11am to 2pm and 4 to 7pm; November through March, Tuesday through Sunday from 11am to 2pm and 3:30 to 6:30pm. Admission is 300 pesetas ($2.10). From Muel, go 11 miles (18km) to Villanueva del Huerve, then continue east for 5 miles (8km) to Fuendetodos on the C-221. From Zaragoza, Samar Buil, Calle Borao, 13 (☎ **27-61-79**) carries passengers to the village. There are two departures daily (trip time: 45 minutes), a one-way ticket costing 510 pesetas ($3.60).

2 Tarazona

54½ miles (88km) W of Zaragoza, 182 miles (293km) NE of Madrid

GETTING THERE • By Bus From Zaragoza four buses leave daily for Tarazona (1½ hours away).

• By Car Drive west from Zaragoza along the A-68, connecting with the N-122 to Tarazona.

ESSENTIALS The area code for Tarazona is 976. The tourist information office is at Iglesias, 5 (☎ **976/64-00-74**).

To call this town the "Toledo of Aragón" may be a bit much, but it does deserve the name "Mudéjar City." Lying about halfway along the principal route connecting Zaragoza to the province of Soria, it is laid out in tiers above the quays of the Queiles River. Once the kings of Aragón lived here, and before that the place was known to the Romans. You can walk through the old barrio with its tall facades and narrow medieval streets.

Tarazona's major attraction is its Gothic **cathedral,** begun in 1152 but essentially reconstructed in the 15th and 16th centuries. However, the Aragonese Mudéjar style is still much in evidence, especially as reflected by the lantern tower and belfry. Its dome resembles that of the old cathedral in Zaragoza. Daily visiting hours are 11am to 1pm and 4 to 6pm. Admission is free.

The town is also known for its 16th-century **Ayuntamiento (Town Hall),** which has reliefs across its facade depicting the retaking of Granada by Ferdinand and Isabella. The monument stands on Plaza de España in the older upper town, on a hill overlooking the river. Take the Ruta Turística from here up to the church of Santa Magdalena, with a Mudéjar tower that forms the chief landmark of the town's skyline; its mirador opens onto a panoramic view. Continuing up the hill, you reach **La Concepción,** another church with a narrow brick tower.

Where to Stay & Dine

Brujas de Bécquer, Carretera de Zaragoza, s/n, 50500 Tarazona. ☎ **976/64-04-04.** Fax 976/64-01-98. 59 rms (all with bath). TV TEL

Rates: 2,600–4,200 ptas. ($18.50–$29.80) single; 3,825–5,200 ptas. ($27.20–$36.90) double. Breakfast 370 ptas. ($2.60) extra. AE, DC, MC, V. **Parking:** 750 ptas. ($5.30).

Half a mile southeast of town, beside the road leading to Zaragoza, you'll find this unpretentious modern hotel, which was built in 1972 and renovated 20 years later. Rooms are modest but comfortable. The dining room serves fixed-price meals for around 1,200 pesetas ($8.50) each, every day from 1 to 4pm and 8 to 10:30pm. Reservations are almost never needed. The hotel, incidentally, was named in honor of a 19th-century Seville-born patriot (Gustavo Adolfo Bécquer) who praised the beauties of Aragón in some of his poetry.

3 Calatayud

53 miles (85km) W of Zaragoza, 146 miles (235km) NE of Madrid

GETTING THERE • By Train Calatayud lies on the main rail line linking Madrid to Zaragoza. There are 12 trains a day from Madrid, 9 from Zaragoza, and 3 from Barcelona.

• By Bus There are three to four buses a day from Zaragoza ($1^1/_4$ hours away).

• By Car Calatayud is on the E-90 linking Madrid with Zaragoza.

ESSENTIALS The area code for Calatayud is 976. The tourist information office is at Plaza del Fuerte, s/n (☎ **976/88-13-14**).

The Romans founded this town, only to abandon it some time during the 2nd century, and it wasn't until the arrival of the Muslims in the 8th century that it was repopulated. The Moors were routed in 1120 by the conquering Catholic forces, who allowed some of the inhabitants to stay. But they were made virtual slaves and forced to live in a *morería* (Moorish ghetto). Some of the Moorish influence can still be seen in the town. Many 14th- and 15th-century church towers in Calatayud are reminiscent of minarets.

The major attraction of Calatayud is **Santa María la Mayor,** Calle de Opispo Arrué, a brick church built in Aragonese style, with an ornate Plateresque-Mudéjar facade and an exceptionally harmonious octagonal belfry. Nearby, on the Calle Datao, the **Iglesia de San Pedro de los Francos** might be called the leaning tower of Calatayud. This is a fine example of the Mudéjar style.

A walk along the Calle Unión leads to **La Parraguía de San Andrés,** with an elegant and graceful Mudéjar belfry.

Strike a path through the old Moorish quarter up the hill to the ruins of the castle that dominated Qal'at Ayyub (the old Arab name for the town). Once you're there, a panoramic view unfolds.

East of Calatayud, excavations continue to uncover the **Roman city of Bibilis,** lying on the Mérida-Zaragoza highway. It was the birthplace of Roman satirist Martial (ca. A.D. 40–104).

Where to Stay

Hotel Calatayud, Autovia de Aragón Salida, km 237, 50300 Calatayud. ☎ **976/88-13-23.** Fax 976/88-54-38. 63 rms (all with bath). TV TEL

Rates: 4,175 ptas. ($29.60) single; 6,950 ptas. ($49.30) double. Breakfast: 500 ptas. ($3.60) extra. AE, MC, V. **Parking:** 250 ptas. ($1.80).

Of a lackluster lot, this low-slung, modern hotel is your best best in town. Set about a mile (1.6 km) east of Calatayud, on the N-II highway to Zaragoza, the hotel contains acceptable bedrooms with simple furnishings, and a garden. It also offers a popular restaurant and bar, which are the only air-conditioned areas in the entire building. Fixed-price meals cost from 1,600 pesetas ($11.40).

Where to Dine

The restaurant recommended below planned a management change during the lifetime of this edition. Should you find it closed, you can always dine at the Hotel Calatayud recommended above.

Lisboa, Paseo Cortés de Aragón, 10. ☎ **88-25-35.**

Cuisine: ARAGONESE. **Reservations:** Recommended.
Prices: Appetizers 550–750 ptas. ($3.90–$5.30); main courses 1,400–2,500 ptas. ($9.90–$17.80); fixed-price menu 1,200 ptas. ($8.50). AE, DC, MC, V.
Open: Lunch, daily 1–4pm; dinner, Tues–Sun 8:30–11:30pm.

The Lisboa comes as a surprise, offering not only good food at reasonable prices, but also professional service administered in air-conditioned comfort. Try the hake Basque style with baby eels or perhaps the roast lamb Aragón style. The combination of green beans and spicy sausage makes a delectable dish. For dessert, try the specialty, *biscuit glacé.* The Lisboa is in the center near the train station.

An Easy Excursion

From Calatayud, take the N-234 25 miles (40km) southeast to **Daroca.** Once a Roman military outpost known as Agiria, it was eventually taken by the Moors, who called it Kalat-Daruca. Moorish clans fought over the town bitterly, paving the way for its eventual takeover in 1122 by King Alfonso I of Aragón. Daroca is a gem of an Aragonese town, known for its architecture, including Roman, Mudéjar, Romanesque, and Gothic. It is visited mainly for the ruins of its walls, with 114 towers. An attempt in the 15th century to restore them was abandoned because of the enormity of the task. Some of the gates are in better shape, particularly Puerta Baja, flanked by twin towers and bearing the coat-of-arms of Carlos I. Other attractions include a beautiful fountain, Fuente de Veine Caños (20 spouts), lying just outside the walls, and a half-mile tunnel carved into a mountain to carry off flood waters, an unusual feat of engineering for the 16th century.

4 Nuévalos/Piedra

73 miles (118km) W of Zaragoza, 143 miles (230km) E of Madrid

GETTING THERE • By Train From Madrid, train connections reach Alhama de Aragón. Take a taxi from there to the monastery.

• **By Car** From Calatayud, head west along the N-11. At the little town of Ateca, take the left turnoff, which is signposted for Nuévalos and the Monasterio de Piedra. If you're driving from Madrid, turn east at the spa town of Alhama de Aragón. From Zaragoza, turn left at Calatayud and drive 14 miles (22.5km).

ESSENTIALS The area code for Nuévalos/Piedra is 976.

The town of Nuévalos, with its one paved road, isn't much of a lure, but thousands of visitors from all over the world flock to the ★ **Monasterio de Piedra,** called the garden district of Aragón.

Piedra means "rock" in Spanish, and after the "badlands" of Aragón, you expect bleak, rocky terrain. Instead, you have a virtual Garden of Eden, with a 197-foot waterfall. It was here in 1194 that Cistercian monks built a charter house on the banks of the Piedra River. The monks are long gone, having departed in 1835, and their former quarters have been reconstructed and turned into a hotel (see below).

Two pathways, marked in either blue or red, meander through the grounds. Views are offered from any number of levels. Tunnels and stairways date from the 19th century, the work of Juan Federico Mutadas, who created a park here. Slippery steps lead down to an iris grotto, just one of many quiet, secluded retreats. It is said that the original monks inhabited the site because they wanted a "foretaste of paradise." To be honest, they were also escaping the court intrigues at the powerful Monestir de Poblet in Tarragona province. The monastery at Piedra lies only 2 miles (3.2km) from the hillside village of Nuévalos. You can wander through the monastery grounds daily from 9am to 8pm in summer (closed at 5pm in winter) for an admission charge of 775 ptas. ($5.50) adults, 475 ptas. ($3.40) children.

Either for rooms or meals, **Monasterio de Piedra,** 50201 Nuévalos (☎ **84-90-11**), is one of the showplaces of Aragón, and a meal in the great hall is a medieval event. The room has been tastefully decorated and is a perfect backdrop for the good-tasting Aragonese fare. Meals cost from 2,300 pesetas ($16.30), and service is daily from 1 to 4pm and 9pm to midnight. On weekends, the dining room can get crowded. The grounds include a swimming pool; tennis courts; and, naturally, a garden, with little log bridges and masses of flowering plants and trees. The beautifully maintained bedrooms (all doubles), for which you should reserve well in advance, have phones but no other amenities. Some open onto terraces. Singles cost from 6,500 pesetas ($46.20) and doubles from 8,500–9,500 pesetas ($60.40–$67.50)—plus 500 pesetas ($3.60) for breakfast.

5 Sos del Rey Católico

262 miles (422km) N of Madrid, 37 miles (60km) SW of Pamplona

GETTING THERE • **By Bus** From Zaragoza to Sos, 2¼ hours away, there is a daily bus at 6:30pm, returning at 7am the next morning.

• **By Car** From Huesca, take Rte. 240 to Pamplona, but turn south at the cutoff to Sanquesa.

ESSENTIALS The area code for Sos del Rey Católico is 948.

In northern Aragón, Sos del Rey Católico formed one of the Cinco Villas of Aragón, stretching along a 56-mile (90km) frontier with Navarre. The far-distant part of northern Aragón, these villages included Tauste, Ejea, Uncastillo, and Sabada. Despite their small size, they were raised to the status of towns by Philip V, who was grateful for their assistance and loyalty in the War of Spanish Succession (1701–13).

The most visited town is Sos del Rey Católico, so named because it was the birthplace of Ferdinand, El Rey Católico, who was born here in 1452 and later entered the world's history books, especially after his marriage to Isabella of Castile and León. Locals will point out the Palacio de Sada, where the future king allegedly was born. The town is more interesting than its minor monuments, and you can explore it at will, wandering its narrow cobbled streets and stopping at any place that attracts your fancy. The kings of Aragón fortified this village on the border with Navarre with a thick wall. Much of that medieval character has been preserved today—enough so that the village has been declared a national monument.

Where to Stay & Dine

Parador Fernando de Aragón, Sianz de Vicuña, 1, 50680 Sos del Rey Católico. ☎ **948/88-80-11.** Fax 948/88-81-00. 66 rms (all with bath). A/C MINIBAR TV TEL

Rates: 6,400–7,200 ptas. ($45.40–$51.10) single; 8,000–9,000 ptas. ($56.80–$63.90) double. Breakfast 1,100 ptas. ($7.80) extra. AE, DC, MC, V. **Parking:** 600 ptas. ($4.30). **Closed:** Dec–Jan.

This member of the government-owned parador network is considered unusual because of the care that was taken to blend a six-story building into the medieval setting around it. Built in 1975 on much older foundations, it's composed mostly of stone and wood timbers, with lots of interior paneling and antique-looking accessories. Despite its location in the heart of the village, sweeping views open from some of the bedroom windows onto the nearby countryside. Accommodations are dignified, clean, and comfortable. Hearty Aragonese food is served in the restaurant, where *menús del día* cost 3,200 pesetas ($22.70) each. Service is daily from 1 to 4pm and from 8 to 10:30pm.

18

Navarre & La Rioja

THE ANCIENT LAND OF NAVARRE (*NAVARRA* IN SPANISH; *NAFARROA* IN BASQUE) SHARES with France an 81-mile (130km) frontier, with nine crossing points. As such, it is an important link between Iberia and the rest of the continent. Lying east of Castile, Navarre is a single province with a strong Basque tradition.

When the Muslims ruled from Córdoba, Navarre was one of the four Catholic kingdoms of northern Spain. Its history has always been linked to that of its neighbors, the Basques. Basque language and customs are still very important here, but the Navarrese tend to be very conservative, rejecting for the most part the extremists and terrorists of the more radical Basque parties.

As a border region, Navarre has had a rough time in history, and to this day the remains of lonely castles and fortified walled towns bear witness to that. But somehow this kingdom, one of the most ancient on the peninsula, has managed to preserve its own government and identity. Romans, Christians, Muslims, and Jews have all influenced Navarre, and its architecture is as diverse as its landscape. It is also a province rich in folklore. Pagan rites were blended into Christian traditions to form a mythology that lives even today in Navarre's many festivals. Dancers and singers wear the famous red berets; the *jota* is the most celebrated folk dance; and the best-known sport is *pelota*, sometimes called *jai alai* elsewhere in the world.

The Pyrenean scenery of Navarre is unmatched in Spain. However, mountain scenery gives way to rather arid and brown flatlands in the south as the province moves closer to the great Castilian *meseta*. The landscape is dotted with monasteries and churches, dating from the days when it lay on the main pilgrim's path from France to the shrine of St. James in Santiago de Compostela in Galicia.

Navarre is rich in natural attractions, although most foreign visitors miss them when they visit just for the Fiesta de San Fermín in July, the running of the bulls through the streets of Pamplona, Navarre's capital and major city. Even if you do visit just for the festival, try to explore some of the panoramic Pyrenean landscapes.

Adjoining Navarre is La Rioja, the smallest region on mainland Spain—bordered not only by Navarre but by Castile and Aragón. Extending along the Ebro River, this province has far greater influence than its tiny dimensions would suggest, since it is one of the most important wine-growing districts of Europe. The land is generally split into two sections: Rioja Alta, which gets a lot of rainfall and has a mild climate, and Rioja Baja, which is much hotter and more arid, more like Aragón. The capital of the province, Logroño, a city of some 200,000, links the two regions.

In the 1980s long overdue recognition came to La Rioja's vineyards, as its wines gained increasing recognition on the tables of the world. The popularity of the district grows, and, of course, this has led to much tourist activity in the area—mainly by those wishing to visit the wineries.

The smallest *autonomía*, or government department, of Spain, La Rioja boasts only a quarter of a million inhabitants—and a lot of grapes. Its name comes from a river, Río Oja, compressed into one word: Rioja. The Ebro River is the backbone of the district, and major towns cluster in its seven tributary valleys.

The most visited towns are the capital of Logroño and Hang, the latter known for its wineries. Santo Domingo de la Calzada was considered a major stop on the pilgrim's route, and Nájera was once the capital of the kings of Navarre. Now, little more than a village, it lies along the Najerilla River. From that river's valleys comes about a third of all Rioja wine production.

What's Special About Navarre & La Rioja

Great Towns/Villages

- Pamplona, the most important city of the Spanish Pyrenees, immortalized in *The Sun Also Rises.*
- Haro, the best center for visiting La Rioja's famous bodegas and sampling its wines.

Ancient Monuments

- The Monastery of San Salvador of Leyre, 11th-century spiritual center of Navarre, whose crypt is Spain's major piece of Romanesque architecture.
- The Monastery of the Oliva, one of the first Cistercian monasteries built by French monks outside France.

Historic Castles

- Javier Castle, built around the birthplace of St. Francis Xavier, who is said to have converted two million Buddhists to Christianity.
- The castle of the kings of Navarre at Olite—the preferred residence of Navarrese royalty.

Major Cathedrals

- The cathedral at Pamplona, with 14th- and 15th-century Gothic cloisters, built in front of an ancient city wall.
- The 12th-century cathedral at Tudela, in traditional Romanesque-Gothic style—famous for its Doorway of the Last Judgment.

Special Events/Festivals

- Fiesta de San Fermín at Pamplona, with its running of the bulls through the streets. July 6–14.
- The Battle of Wine at Haro, a mock contest in which opposing teams get doused with the intoxicating stuff. June 29.
- The Wine Harvest Festival throughout La Rioja—with dances, parades, music, and bullfights. September 15–30.

Seeing Navarre & La Rioja

GETTING THERE Several flights arrive weekdays, via Aviaco Airlines, from Madrid and Barcelona, from which air connections to the rest of the world can be made. Pamplona also has flights to and from Santander on the northern coast. There is no commercial airport in La Rioja. However, any of the airports at Pamplona, Zaragoza, Bilbao, and even Madrid can be used as a gateway to La Rioja. From one of those cities, you can take either the bus or the train or else drive to La Rioja.

Pamplona has the best rail links to the Basque country to its north, including Irún, from which you can transfer onto French rail lines. Pamplona is also linked by rail to Barcelona and Zaragoza. From Madrid, you can take an overnight express pulling out of Chamartín Station and be in Pamplona in 10 hours.

The best rail link to La Rioja is via Zaragoza (Aragón) or Bilbao in the Basque country. Most visitors, however, take a RENFE-operated *talgo* express from Madrid, going first to Miranda de Ebro, where a change of trains is necessary to reach the capital of Logroño. You can also continue by bus from Miranda de Ebro to the major towns of La Rioja.

Pamplona has bus links with Madrid in the south and San Sebastián in the north, and many other cities as well, including Logroño in La Rioja. You can also take the bus from Irún near the French frontier. The Conda bus company services the Ebro Valley area, including Logroño. For villages in the north of Navarre, take the Montañesa line.

To reach La Rioja by car from Madrid, take Rte. N-1, going east on the A-1 expressway or else east on the N-1 to Miranda de Ebro. You can go on to Logroño via the A-68. If you're north in the Basque country, take the A-68 south from Bilbao to reach La Rioja.

Pamplona can be reached by major toll roads, including the A-68 Basque country–Aragón expressway, which links Bilbao with Tarragona on the Mediterranean coast. Of the major N roads in the district, the most vital link is the east-west Barcelona-Madrid highway, the N-11.

A Suggested Route

The major center for visitors will be Pamplona. If you have a car, you can base yourself in a hotel there and make day trips to check out all the tourist highlights of the province. But if you're dependent on public transportation, you may want to stay in various towns and villages.

Days 1–2 Spend Day 1 in Pamplona. On your second day, drive west to the town of Estella, returning by nightfall to Pamplona.

Day 3 Head south to visit the towns of Olite and Tudela, planning an overnight stopover in either place.

Day 4 Continue east to the town of Sangüesa and visit the Javier Castle and the Monastery of San Salvador of Leyre in its environs.

Day 5 If you have time, drive to Logroño, a province in the west bordering Navarre, and spend the night.

Day 6 Head north to Haro and its wineries. Here you can learn about wine making and sample a vintage yourself.

1 Pamplona (Iruña)

56 miles (90km) SE of San Sebastián, 239 miles (385km) NE of Madrid, 104 miles (167km) NE of Zaragoza

GETTING THERE • By Plane The gateway for air travel to Navarre is Pamplona. The city is served by two weekday Aviaco flights from both Madrid and Barcelona; international connections can be made from either city. Arrivals are at Aeropuerto de Noaín (☎ **31-75-82**), 4 miles (6km) from the city center and accessible only by taxi.

• By Train Three trains a day arrive from Madrid (5 hours away) and three from Barcelona (a 6-hour trip). Pamplona also has connections from San Sebastián in the north (three trains per day; $2^1/_2$ hours) and with Zaragoza in the south (nine per day; 2 hours). For information, call **13-02-02.**

• By Bus Buses connect Pamplona with several major Spanish cities; four to five per day from Madrid ($5^1/_2$ hours away), two per day from Barcelona ($5^1/_2$ hours), nine per day from Zaragoza ($3^1/_2$ hours), and seven per day from San Sebastián ($2^3/_4$ hours).

• **By Car** The A-15 Navarra national highway begins on the outskirts of Pamplona and runs south and joins the A-68, midway between Zaragoza and Logroño. Rte. 240 connects San Sebastián with Pamplona.

ESSENTIALS The area code for Pamplona is 948. The tourist information office is at Duque de Ahumada, 3 (☎ **948/22-07-41**).

It was in 1927 that Ernest Hemingway wrote *The Sun Also Rises.* But the book's glamour remains undiminished for foreigners who read it and then rush off to Pamplona to see the running (encierro) of the bulls during the Fiesta de San Fermín. Attempts to outlaw this world-famed ceremony have failed so far, and it remains a superstar attraction, particularly among aficionados. The riotous festival of San Fermín usually begins on July 6 and lasts through the 14th. Fireworks and Basque flute concerts are only some of the spectacles that give added color to the fiesta, where the wine flows. Nobody sleeps, which is just as well—accommodations are virtually impossible to find. You can bed down in a sleeping bag in an emergency, or, like most, stay up carousing with the drunks around the clock. Those who want to know they'll have a bed after watching the encierro should reserve years in advance at one of the city's handful of hotels or boarding houses or stay in San Sebastián or some other neighboring town and visit Pamplona during the day. After all, one visit to Pamplona will probably be enough to satisfy your curiosity.

Pamplona is more than just a city where an annual festival takes place. Long the most significant town in Spain's Pyrenean region, it was also a major stopover for those traveling either of two frontier roads: the Roncesvalles Pass or the Velate Pass. Once a fortified city, it was for centuries the capital of the ancient kingdom of Navarre.

In its historical core, the Pamplona of legend lives on, but the city has been engulfed by modern real-estate development. The saving grace of "new Pamplona" is La Taconera, a spacious "green lung" of fountain-filled gardens and parkland, lying west of the old quarter, where you will often see students from the University of Navarre.

Pamplona became the capital of Navarre in the 10th century. Its golden age was the reign of Charles III (called "the Noble"), who gave it its cathedral, in which he was eventually buried. Over the years the city has been the scene of many battles, with various factions struggling for control. Those who lived in the old quarter, the Navarrería, wanted to be allied with Castile, whereas those on the outskirts favored a French connection. Obviously, Castile eventually won out, although some citizens of Navarre today want Pamplona to be part of a newly created country of the Basque lands.

What to See & Do

The heart of Pamplona is the **Plaza del Castillo,** built in 1847. It was the former Plaza de Toros (bullring). Expanded in 1932, it is today the seat of the provincial government, which has a certain amount of autonomy. This elegant tree-lined *paseo* becomes a virtual communal bedroom during the Festival of San Fermín.

The narrow streets of the old quarter extend from three sides of the square. The present bullring, the **Plaza de Toros,** lies just east and south of this square alongside the Paseo Hemingway. Running parallel to the east of the square is the **Calle Estafeta,** a narrow street that is the site of the running of the bulls. With its bars and tascas, it attracts university students and is lively all year, even without a festival. During the festival it is the most frequented place in town next to the Plaza del Castillo. The bulls are also run through the barricaded streets of Santo Domingo and Mercaderes.

★ **Fiesta de San Fermín.**

Beginning at noon on July 6 and continuing nonstop through July 14, the running of the bulls is one of the most attended events in Europe, drawing thousands of tourists who overtax the severely limited facilities of Pamplona. Get up early (or don't go to bed in the first place)—the bulls run every day at 8am sharp. To watch, be in position behind the barricades along the Calle Estafeta no later than 6am. Only the able-bodied and sober should plan to run. Women are not permitted to run. (Many defy this ban each year.)

There simply aren't enough beds or bullfight tickets to go around, and scalpers have a field day. Technically, tickets for a good seat in the ring go on sale at 8pm the night before the *corrida* and tickets for standing room go on sale at 4pm on the day of the bullfight. But all of the tickets are sold out, and since it is impossible to obtain them through a travel agent beforehand, tourists have to use scalpers.

The fiesta draws half a million visitors, many of whom camp in the city parks. Temporary facilities are set up, but there are never enough beds. Hotel reservations should be confirmed at least six months beforehand. If you look respectable, some Pamplonicos will probably rent you a room. Expect to pay about 2,000 pesetas ($14.20). If you can't find a room, check your valuables at the bus station on the Calle Conde Oliveto (where there are also showers—free, but cold).

As for bars and restaurants, ignore all of the times given below. Most establishments operate around the clock at this time.

A Couple of Warnings: (1) Some people go to the festival not to watch the bulls but to pick pockets. (2) Don't take needless risks, such as leaping from a building in the hope that friends below will catch you. Many people do this each year, and not all are caught.

Catedral, Plaza de la Catedral.

The most important sight in Pamplona is the cathedral, dating from the late 14th century on the site of a former Romanesque basilica. The present facade, a mix of neoclassical and baroque, was the work of Ventura Rodríguez, architect to Charles III. The interior is Gothic, with lots of fan vaulting. In the center is the alabaster tomb of Charles III and his Castilian wife, Queen Leonor, the work of Flemish sculpture Janin de Lomme in 1416. The 14th- and 15th-century Gothic cloisters are a highlight of the cathedral. The Barbazán Chapel, off the east gallery, is noted for its vaulting. Housed in the cathedral's refectory and kitchen, the Museo Diocesano displays religious objects.

Admission: Cathedral, free; museum 150 ptas. ($1.10).

Open: Mid–May to mid–Oct, daily 8am–2pm and 6:30–8pm. Off-season, daily 8–11:30am and 6–8pm.

Museo de Navarra, Cuesta de Santa Domingo, s/n. ☎ **22-78-31.**

Close to the river, housed in a 16th-century hospital, the Nuestra Señora de la Misericordia, is the major museum of Pamplona. It has rich collections of both Roman artifacts, including some 2nd-century mosaics, and Romanesque art, plus an important Goya portrait of the Marqués de San Adrián. Gothic and Renaissance paintings are on the second floor. Murals from the 13th century are also a highlight.

Admission: 200 ptas. ($1.40).

Open: Tues–Sat 10am–2pm and 5–7pm, Sun 10am–2pm.

Pelota (Jai Alai).

At 3.7 miles (6km) outside Pamplona, at Frontón Euskal-Jai Berri (☎ **33-11-59**), along the Avenida de Francia, you can watch professional pelota (jai alai) being played. Four matches are usually played on game days, and tickets can be purchased at any time during the sets. Betting is for aficionados only.

Admission: Bleachers 1,000–1,500 ptas. ($7.10–$10.70).

Game Times: Thurs and Sat–Sun 4pm.

Where to Stay

During the Festival of San Fermín, prices are two or three times higher than those listed below. In some instances a hotel will commit itself to prices it will charge at *Fiesta* (the original name of *The Sun Also Rises* when it first published in Britain). Other owners charge pretty much what they think they can get, and they can get a lot. Therefore, agree on the price when making a reservation, if you've been able to get a reservation in the first place. At the time of the festival, you can check with the tourist office about getting a room in a private home, as these prices remain reasonable. However, check to see what you're getting. Sometimes a room in a private home translates as sharing space on a dirty floor with 20 other diehard *sanferministas* in a decaying part of town. The locals prefer that you do that instead of joining the drunken revelers who sleep free in their gardens at night as unwanted guests. At other times of the year, Pamplona is a reasonably priced tourist destination.

EXPENSIVE

Hotel Tres Reyes, Jardines de la Taconera 1, 31001 Pamplona. ☎ **948/22-66-00.**
Fax 948/22-29-30. 160 rms, 8 suites. A/C MINIBAR TV TEL

Rates: 13,500 ptas. ($95.90) single; 17,000 ptas. ($120.70) double; 31,000 ptas. ($220.10) suite. Festival, 24,000 ptas. ($170.40) single; 31,000 ptas. ($220.10) double; 50,000 ptas. ($355) suite. Breakfast 1,600 ptas. ($11.40) extra. AE, DC, MC, V. **Parking:** Free outdoors, 1,500 ptas. ($10.70) indoors.

A short walk west of the old town, just two blocks north of the ancient citadel, this is considered one of the finest hotels in town. Modern, with a cement-balconied facade that curves around a pleasant garden, it provides tasteful and airy bedrooms with contemporary furnishings, lots of sunlight, and private baths. Many have balconies, and all are welcome refuges from the intensity of the local festivals.

Dining/Entertainment: The Grill Tres Reyes serves an excellently prepared Basque and Navarre cuisine. There's also a bar from which cocktails are served throughout the lobby, plus an inexpensive cafeteria.

Services: 24-hour room service, laundry, concierge, babysitting, daily exercise classes led by an aerobics instructor.

Facilities: Car rentals; shopping boutiques; health club with sauna, gymnasium, squash courts, and massage facilities; kidney-shaped heated outdoor swimming pool set into a verdant garden.

Iruña Park Hotel, Ronda Ermitagaña, s/n, 31008 Pamplona. ☎ **948/17-32-00.**
Fax 948/17-23-87. 219 rms, 6 suites. A/C MINIBAR TV TEL

Rates: 13,600 ptas. ($96.60) single; 17,000 ptas. ($120.70) double; 30,000 ptas. ($213) suite. Festival, 24,000 ptas. ($170.40) single; 30,000 ptas. ($213) double; 52,000 ptas. ($369.20) suite. Breakfast 1,420 ptas. ($10.10) extra. AE, DC, MC, V. **Parking:** 1,150 ptas. ($8.20).

A short walk west of the Parque de la Ciudadela, behind a facade of mirrored glass and white masonry, this is the largest and most convention-conscious hotel in town. A large staff maintains the blandly furnished but comfortable bedrooms. The public rooms are modern and glossy, with deep armchairs and big windows.

Dining/Entertainment: The Royal Restaurant serves regional and international cuisine as part of full à la carte meals beginning at 3,000 pesetas ($21.30) each. There's also a bar.

Services: Room service (available daily from 7am to 11pm), concierge, babysitting, laundry.

Facilities: Car rentals, business center.

MODERATE

Avenida, Zaragoza, 5, 31000 Pamplona. ☎ **948/24-54-54.** Fax 948/23-23-23. 24 rms (all with bath). MINIBAR TV TEL

Rates: 8,600 ptas. ($61.10) single; 13,400 ptas. ($95.10) double. Festival, 16,500 ptas. ($117.20) single; 25,200 ptas. ($178.90) double. Breakfast 900 ptas. ($6.40) extra. AE, MC, V.

One of the best inns in town, and also one of the newest, this small, well-run place opened in 1989. The guest rooms are well furnished and maintained; some are even better than the inn's three-star rating suggests. Furnishings tend toward the sleek and modern, and local watercolors add a warming touch. Sixteen units are air-conditioned. In the restaurant Leyre, known for its regional cuisine, you can order a full lunch or dinner for 1,500 pesetas ($10.70). There's also a cafeteria on the premises, serving snacks and drinks daily from 7am to 11pm.

Hotel Orhi, Leyre, 7, 31002 Pamplona. ☎ **948/22-85-00.** Fax 948/22-83-18. 55 rms (all with bath). MINIBAR TV TEL **Bus:** 11.

Rates: 9,240 ptas. ($65.60) single; 13,620 ptas. ($96.70) double; Festival, 20,000 ptas. ($142) single; 27,200 ptas. ($193.10) double. Breakfast 550 ptas. ($3.90) extra. AE, DC, MC, V. **Parking:** 80 ptas. ($0.60) nearby in a municipal lot.

Conveniently located in the town center, a few steps from the bus station, the Orhi was built around 1965 and renovated in 1991. It's been consistently popular with bull breeders and with matadors and their fans. Bedrooms are comfortable but simple, with sturdy furniture and high ceilings. A restaurant and a popular bar are on the premises.

Hotel Sancho Ramírez, Calle Sancho Ramírez, 11, 31008 Pamplona. ☎ **948/27-17-12.** Fax 948/17-11-43. 86 rms (all with bath). A/C MINIBAR TV TEL **Bus:** 7.

Rates: 8,000 ptas. ($56.80) single; 12,000 ptas. ($85.20) double. Breakfast 700 ptas. ($5) extra. AE, DC, MC, V.

Built in 1981 and last renovated in 1990, the Sancho Ramírez has quickly drawn business away from its older competitors. Each of the reasonably priced units has a streamlined and contemporary decor; some contain minibars. The hotel restaurant serves a regional cuisine, with meals costing from 2,000 pesetas ($14.20).

Maisonnave, Nueva, 20, 31001 Pamplona. ☎ **948/22-26-00.** Fax 948/22-01-66. 152 rms (all with bath). MINIBAR TV TEL **Bus:** 5, 9, or 10.

Rates: 10,300 ptas. ($73.10) single; 12,900 ptas. ($91.60) double. Breakfast 900 ptas. ($6.40) extra. AE, DC, MC, V. **Parking:** 1,100 ptas. ($7.80).

In the historic old town of Pamplona, west of the Plaza del Castillo and within easy walking distance of the tascas and restaurants, this place is solidly booked for the fiesta. You must reserve at least six months in advance—and then say a prayer. Rooms have been completely renovated, each well furnished, well maintained, and comfortable. The hotel also offers a Navarrese restaurant serving a regional and Spanish national cuisine, with meals beginning at 1,500 pesetas ($10.70).

La Perla, Plaza del Castillo, 1, 31001 Pamplona. ☎ **948/22-77-06.** 67 rms (all with bath), 8 suites.

Rates: 5,500 ptas. ($39.10) single; 8,250–10,900 ptas. ($58.60–$77.40) double. Breakfast 675 ptas. ($4.80) extra. AE, DC, MC, V.

Opened in 1880 and last renovated in 1970, this is not the most prepossessing hotel in town—far from it. But at the festival it becomes the most desirable place to stay, since it opens onto the main square of Pamplona and overlooks Calle Estafeta, the straightaway of the encerrio through which the bulls run. The guest rooms are often furnished with an old-fashioned flair and in days of yore they sheltered everybody from Ernest Hemingway to U.S. Senator Henry Cabot Lodge (d. 1924).

INEXPENSIVE

Residencia Eslava, Plaza Virgen de la O, 7, or Calle Recoletas, 20, 31001 Pamplona. ☎ **948/22-22-70.** Fax 948/22-51-57. 28 rms (all with bath). TV TEL **Bus:** 9.

Rates: 4,500 ptas. ($32) single; 9,500 ptas. ($67.50) double. Festival, 8,000 ptas. ($56.80) single; 15,000 ptas. ($106.50) double. Breakfast 500 ptas. ($3.60) extra. AE, DC, MC, V.

Located right off Plaza de Recoletas, a 10-minute walk from the bus station, this renovated hotel manages to combine the spirit of old and new Spain. Its small living room resembles the drawing room of a distinguished Spanish house. All the average-size guest rooms are tastefully decorated; some have balconies with views of the city walls and the balconies beyond. A cellar lounge offers drinks.

Where to Dine

EXPENSIVE

Alhambra, Calle Bergamín, 7. ☎ **24-50-07.**

Cuisine: NAVARRESE/SPANISH. **Reservations:** Recommended.
Prices: Appetizers 800–1,950 ptas. ($5.70–$13.80); main courses 2,500–3,200 ptas. ($17.80–$22.70). Fixed-price menus 4,100–5,800 ptas. ($29.10–$41.20). AE, DC, MC, V.
Open: Lunch, Mon–Sat 1–3:30pm; dinner, Mon–Sat 9–11pm.

One of the best-known and most stable restaurants in Pamplona, Alhambra, a 16-minute walk from the cathedral, was established shortly after World War II. Since 1985, it has been directed by a well-trained group of new owners. Set within two paneled dining rooms, the restaurant features a complete array of local wines, and regional specialties that include carefully deboned sardines, grilled and served with truffles; grilled filet of hake with local herbs, selected cuts of filet steak with sauces made from local mushrooms and garlic; roasted goat with mountain herbs; and an array of desserts.

Europa, Calle Espoz y Mina, 11. ☎ **22-18-00.**

Cuisine: SPANISH. **Reservations:** Recommended.
Prices: Appetizers 1,100–2,400 ptas. ($7.80–$17); main courses 2,200–3,200 ptas. ($15.60–$22.70); *menú del día* 2,900 ptas. ($20.60). AE, DC, MC, V.
Open: Lunch, Mon–Sat 1–3:30pm; dinner, Mon–Sat 9–11pm.

Known for its creative interpretations of regional recipes, this restaurant occupies several intimate, recently renovated dining rooms within what was originally built in the 1930s as a private house. The chef and culinary artist is Pamplona-born Pilar Idoate, who prepares food based on seasonal availability of ingredients. Examples include baked potatoes stuffed with truffles and minced crayfish; roulades of sole with mountain herbs; filet steaks with Roquefort dressing; and game dishes such as venison and pheasant. Desserts include an orange mousse with a *marquesa de chocolate.*

This restaurant lies in the center of Pamplona, near the Plaza del Castillo.

Hartza, Juan de Labrit, 19. ☎ **22-45-68.**

Cuisine: NAVARRESE. **Reservations:** Recommended.
Prices: Appetizers 800–2,100 ptas. ($5.70–$14.90); main courses 3,200–3,800 ptas. ($22.70–$27). AE, DC, MC, V.
Open: Lunch, Tues–Sun 1:30–3:30pm; dinner, Tues–Sat 9–11:30pm. **Closed:** Aug and 10 days at Christmas.

One of the oldest bodegas in town, this popular and much-honored restaurant has flourished at this location near the bullring since the 1870s. There's a summer garden for outdoor dining, plus a street-level bar, with additional dinner seating upstairs. The portions are generous (and expensive), and specialties change with the season. Menu items might include a steamy, well-seasoned vegetable soup; stuffed peppers; tournedos; hake and eel; and a selection of regional cheeses. The interior is air-conditioned during the hottest summer months.

Josetxo, Plaza Principe de Viana, 1. ☎ **22-20-97.**

Cuisine: BASQUE. **Reservations:** Recommended on weekends.
Prices: Appetizers 1,475–3,475 ptas. ($10.50–$24.70); main courses 1,975–3,975 ptas. ($14–$28.20). AE, DC, V.
Open: Lunch, Mon–Sat 1:30–4pm; dinner, Mon–Sat 9–11:30pm. **Closed:** Holy Week and Aug.

Considered the finest, grandest, and most prestigious restaurant in town, Josexto is run by a civic-minded local family with more than 30 years' experience in the restaurant trade. Specialties vary with the seasons but might include cream-of-crabmeat soup, puff pastry stuffed with shellfish, lobster salad, a panaché of fresh vegetables with Serrano ham, sea bass cooked in white wine, several variations of goose pâté, and several dishes concocted from rabbit and trout. Dessert might be selected from the array of homemade pastries or perhaps a tart of chocolate truffles layered with orange-flavored cream. The restaurant lies beside a busy traffic circle, four blocks south of the Plaza del Castillo.

Las Pocholas, Paseo de Sarasate, 6. ☎ **22-22-14.**

Cuisine: INTERNATIONAL. **Reservations:** Required.
Prices: Appetizers 825–1,300 ptas. ($5.90–$9.20); main courses 1,900–3,200 ptas. ($13.50–$22.70). AE, DC, MC, V.

Open: Lunch, Mon–Sat 1–4pm; dinner, Mon–Sat 9–11pm. **Closed:** Aug.

This restaurant west of the Plaza del Castillo is well known for its good food and elegant air-conditioned dining salons. You can enjoy salt-cured cod with lobster chunks in garlic sauce, sea bass baked in red wine, a champagne-laden filet of sole, seasonal game dishes, a superb roast pork, and temptingly elaborate desserts.

INEXPENSIVE

Estafeta, Estafeta, 57. ☎ **22-16-05.**

Cuisine: NAVARRESE. **Reservations:** Not accepted.

Prices: Appetizers 300–500 ptas. ($2.10–$3.60); main courses 525–1,000 ptas. ($3.70–$7.10); fixed-price menu 950 ptas. ($6.70). No credit cards.

Open: Lunch, Sun–Tues and Thurs–Sat noon–4pm; dinner, Mon–Tues and Thurs–Sat 8:30–11:30pm.

At the festival this self-service cafeteria west of Plaza del Castillo seems to be everybody's favorite budget restaurant. It's cheap and clean. Go as early as possible in the evening—the dishes are cooked at the same time and everything tastes fresher and better the earlier you dine. Drawing everybody from young American students to retired pensioners in Pamplona, the Estafeta is a relaxed, informal place with wholesome and filling food, including fresh hake, salt cod, squid, and trout in the style of Navarre.

Evening Entertainment

Café Iruña, Plaza del Castillo, 44. ☎ **22-42-93.**

This art deco bar and café, dating from 1888, has an outdoor terrace that is popular in summer. The winter crowd is likely to congregate around the bar, ordering combination plates and snacks in addition to drinks. The place thrives as a café/bar daily from 9am to 1am; however, it also becomes more of a restaurant during the lunch hour. Platters of hot food are served to many of the local office workers and day laborers. There is no *menú del día* but a full lunch, served daily from 1 to 3:30pm, costs from 1,500–2,000 pesetas ($10.70–$14.20). Beer goes for 150 pesetas ($1.10) at the bar, slightly more at a table.

Cafeteria El Molino, Bayona, 13. ☎ **25-10-90.**

This cafeteria, centrally located in the commercial Barrio San Juan, doubles as a popular tapas bar. Late in the evening its ambience becomes more youthful, lighthearted, and animated. The huge assortment of tapas includes fried shrimp, squid, anchovies, fish croquettes, and Russian salad. Tapas begin at 125 pesetas (90¢), and most orders don't exceed 175 pesetas ($1.20) although some of the more expensive ones peak at 400 pesetas ($2.80). The cafeteria is open Monday through Saturday from 8am to 1am and Sunday from 9am to 1am.

2 Olite

27 miles (43km) S of Pamplona, 229 miles (369km) N of Madrid

GETTING THERE • **By Train** Olite is connected by rail to Pamplona.

• **By Bus** Three buses a day make the run from Pamplona.

• **By Car** Take the expressway highway, the A-15, directly south from Pamplona.

ESSENTIALS The area code for Olite is 948. The tourist information office is at Castillo Palacio, s/n (☎ **948/74-00-35**).

A historical city, Olite sits in a rich agricultural belt with a Mediterranean climate of short winters and long hot summers. Cornfields and vineyards, along with large villages, pepper the countryside. It is also the center of a wine-making industry carried on by cooperative cellars. These wine merchants hold a local festival each year from September 14 to 18.

What to See & Do

In the 15th century, this "Gothic town" was a favorite address of the kings of Navarre. Charles III put Olite on the map, ordering that a **Castillo Palacio** be built in 1406. The oldest towers and lookouts make visiting it a bit of an adventure. From April through September, hours are Monday through Saturday from 10am to 2pm and 4 to 5pm, Sunday 10am to 2pm; October through March, Monday through Saturday 10am to 2pm and 4 to 5pm, Sunday 10am to 2pm. Admission is 100 pesetas (70¢).

Next to the castle stands the Gothic church of **Iglesia de Santa María la Real,** with its splendid 12th-century doorway decorated with flowers.

Where to Stay & Dine

Parador Principe de Viana, Plaza de los Teobaldos, 2, 31390 Olite.
☎ **948/74-00-00.** Fax 948/74-02-01. 43 rms (all with bath). A/C MINIBAR TV TEL

Rates: 8,800–12,200 ptas. ($62.50–$86.60) single; 11,000–15,250 ptas. ($78.10–$108.30) double. Breakfast 1,350 ptas. ($9.60) extra. AE, DC, MC, V. **Parking:** Free.

This parador in the center of town lies within one of the wings of the Castillo Palacio (see above). Surrounded by watchtowers, thick walls, and massive buttresses, the building is one of the most impressive sights in town. Only 12 accommodations, however, lie within the parador's medieval core, and these sell for a premium over their very comfortable counterparts, which lie a new wing that was added to the castle in 1963 when it became a parador. Regardless of their location within the compound, bedrooms are severely dignified and very clean.

Even if you're visiting just for the day, consider a meal here, which might include a dish such as grilled ribs or rabbit with snails. The chef takes pride in his regional offerings. Meals cost from 3,200 pesetas ($22.70). The restaurant is open daily from 1 to 4pm and 8 to 10:30pm.

Easy Excursions

High up on a mountain of the same name, **Ujúe,** a short drive east along a secondary road from Olite, appears as if from the Middle Ages. Built as a defensive town, it has cobblestoned streets and stone houses clustered around its fortress **Church of Santa María,** dating from the 12th to the 14th century. The heart of King Charles II ("the Bad") was placed to rest here. The church towers open onto views of the countryside, extending to Olite in the west and the Pyrenees in the east.

On the Sunday after St. Mark's Day (April 25), Ujúe is an important pilgrimage center for the people of the area, many of whom wear tunics and go barefoot and carry large crosses. They come to Ujúe to worship Santa María, depicted on a Romanesque statue dating from 1190. It was plated in silver in the second half of the 15th century.

Motorists may want to consider yet another excursion from Olite, to the **Monastero del la Oliva,** 21 miles (34km) south of Olite. It was founded by King García Ramírez in 1164 and is an excellent example of Cistercian architecture. This monastery, one of the first to be constructed by French monks outside of France, once had great influence; its most notable feature is its 14th-century Gothic cloisters. The church dates from the late 12th century and is even more impressive than the cloisters. It has a distinguished portal and two rose windows. Pillars and pointed arches fill its interior. In summer it's open daily from 9am to 8pm; in October through March, it's open daily from 9am to 6pm.

3 Tudela

52 miles (84km) S of Pamplona, 196 miles (316km) N of Madrid

GETTING THERE • By Train Tudela lies on the southern rail line south of Pamplona.

• By Bus In Pamplona Conda buses (☎ **22-10-26**) go to Tudela at the rate of 7 to 9 per day (trip time: 1½ hours). A one-way fare is 770 pesetas ($5.50).

• By Car Take the expressway highway, the A-15, south from Pamplona.

ESSENTIALS The area code for Tudela is 948. The tourist information office is at Carrera Gaztambide, 11 (☎ **948/82-15-39**).

In the center of the food belt of the Ribera or Ebro Valley, the ancient city of Tudela, with a population of only 30,000, is the second largest in Navarre. Lying on the right bank of the Ebro, it had a long history as a city where Jews, Arabs, and Christians lived and worked together. The Muslims made it a dependency of the Caliphate at Córdoba, a period of domination that lasted until 1119. The city had a large Moorish quarter, the *morería,* and many old brick houses are in the Mudéjar style. King Sancho VII ("the Strong"), who defeated the Saracens, chose Tudela as his favorite residence in 1251. It has been a bishopric since the 18th century.

What to See & Do

Begin your exploration at the central Plaza de los Fueros, from where you can wander through a maze of narrow alleys that were laid out during the Moorish occupation. At the square, visit Tudela's most important monument, the **Catedral de Santa Ana,** which is open daily from 9am to 1pm and 5 to 8pm. Constructed in the 12th and 13th centuries, it has an outstanding work of art on its facade, the Doorway of the Last Judgment, with about 120 groups of figures. Creation is depicted, but the artisans showed their true inspiration in showing the horrors of hell. The church contains many Gothic works of art, such as choir stalls from the 1500s. Several chapels are richly decorated, including one dedicated to Our Lady of Hope, with masterpieces from the 15th century. The main altar contains an exceptional retablo painted by Pedro Díaz de Oviedo. The small but choice cloisters, however, are the highlight of the tour. Dating from the 12th and 13th centuries, they contain many Romanesque arches. Capitals on the columns include scenes from the New Testament.

Where to Stay

Hotel Tudela, Avenida Zaragoza, 56, 31500 Tudela. ☎ **948/41-08-02.**
Fax 948/41-09-72. 51 rms (all with bath). A/C MINIBAR TV TEL

Rates: 5,830 ptas. ($41.40) single; 7,420 ptas. ($52.70) double. Breakfast 425 ptas. ($3) extra. AE, DC, MC, V. **Parking:** Free.

Set directly in front of the bullring (Plaza de Toros), this hotel was built in the 1930s, and then tripled in size in two separate stages between 1989 and 1992. Today, with five floors, it's one of the best hotels in town, modern and functional, with a polite staff. The in-house restaurant draws a lively crowd, especially before and after bullfights, and serves well-prepared food. (See separate recommendation in Where to Dine.)

Morase, Paseo de Invierno, 2, 31500 Tudela. ☎ **948/82-17-00.** Fax 948/87-17-04. 11 rms (all with bath). A/C MINIBAR TV TEL

Rates: 4,000 ptas. ($28.40) single; 6,000 ptas. ($42.60) double. Breakfast 750 ptas. ($5.30) extra. AE, DC, MC, V. **Parking:** 1,000 ptas. ($7.10)

Not only is this one of the best places to stay in town, but also it's the leading restaurant (see below). Built in 1963 and completely renovated in 1986, it is small but very comfortable. The guest rooms are furnished in a modern style and have many conveniences.

Where to Dine

Hotel Tudela, Avenida Zaragoza, 56. ☎ **41-08-02.**

Cuisine: NAVARRESE. **Reservations:** Recommended.
Rates: Appetizers 800–1,000 ptas. ($5.70–$7.10); main courses 1,800–2,200 ptas. ($12.80–$15.60); fixed-price menu 1,150 ptas. ($8.20). AE, MC, V.
Open: Lunch, daily 1–4pm; dinner, Mon–Sat 9–11:30pm.

Previously recommended as a place to stay, this is also one of the leading restaurants in the city. It offers typical and fresh products of the Ribera region, along with some magnificent fish and grilled meat. Try the omelet with codfish or the baked monkfish. You can also order beefsteak, followed by homemade pastries and desserts. And sample such wines as Viña Magaña. You can dine in air-conditioned comfort and will find parking on the premises.

Morase, Paseo de Invierno, 2. ☎ **82-17-00.**

Cuisine: NAVARRESE. **Reservations:** Recommended.
Prices: Appetizers 700–1,150 ptas. ($5–$8.20); main courses 950–1,950 ptas. ($6.70–$13.80); *menú del día* 1,950 ptas. ($13.80). AE, DC, MC, V.
Open: Lunch, daily 1–4pm; dinner, Mon–Sat 8pm–midnight. **Closed:** Aug 1–7.

Considered the finest dining room in town, the Morase is a special delight when the first of the asparagus comes in, as the region's product is praised by gastronomes all over Spain. The specialties sound conventional but are well prepared, including a "pastel" of vegetables and hake baked with garlic. The lamb from Navarre is delectable, as is roast pork with herbs or red peppers stuffed with purée of seafood. Set on the banks of the Ebro, the restaurant offers a garden, an air-conditioned dining room, and adequate parking.

4 Sangüesa

253 miles (407km) N of Madrid, 29 miles (47km) SE of Pamplona

GETTING THERE • By Bus Two to three buses bound for Sangüesa leave from Pamplona daily; the trip takes 45 minutes.

• By Car Take the 240, a secondary road, to Sangüesa.

ESSENTIALS The area code for Sangüesa is 948. The tourist information office is at Calle Alfonso el Batallador, 20 (☎ **948/87-03-29**).

On the left bank of the Aragón River, Sangüesa stands at the Aragonese frontier. If after visiting the town, you want to spend the night in the area, drive 9 miles (14.5km) across the border south to Sos del Rey Católico, one of the most charming towns of Aragón; it boasts an excellent parador. With fewer than 5,000 inhabitants, Sangüesa is the largest town on the eastern side of the middle zone of Navarre.

Sangüesa was long a trading center, as mountain sheep passed through on their route to the south of Navarre to spend the winter. Today it is the hub of a large agricultural area, where grapes and cereals are produced on irrigated land. Sangüesa, a "monumental town" in its own right, also serves as base for a number of excursions in the area, including visits to some of Navarre's major attractions, such as the monastery at Leyre and Javier Castle.

Long known to the Romans, Sangüesa was also involved in the battle against Muslim domination in the 10th century. It has known many wars, including occupation by supporters of Archduke Charles of Austria in 1710, and many a skirmish occurred during the Carlist struggles of the 19th century. On several occasions, it has been the seat of the Parliament of Navarre. Pilgrims crossing northern Spain to Santiago de Compostela stopped at Sangüesa.

What to See & Do

Iglesia de Santa María stands at the far end of town beside the river. Begun in the 12th century, it has a doorway from the 12th and 13th centuries that is considered one of the outstanding works of Romanesque art. The south portal, filled with remarkably carved sculptures, is Santa María's most outstanding feature. The vestry contains a 4 1/2-foot-high processional monstrance from the 15th century.

The nearby **Iglesia de Santiago** is a late traditional Romanesque structure from the 12th and 13th centuries. It has a battlemented tower and contains an impressive array of Gothic sculpture, which was discovered under the church only in 1964. Look for the bizarre statue of St. James atop a big conch.

Where to Stay & Dine

$ **Yamaguchy,** Cerretera de Javier, s/n, 31400 Sangüesa, ☎ **948/87-01-27.** Fax 948/87-07-00. 40 rms (all with bath). A/C TEL

Rates: 5,300 ptas. ($37.60) single; 7,600 ptas. ($54) double. Breakfast 900 ptas. ($6.40) extra. AE, MC, V. **Parking:** Free.

The best place to stay (from an extremely limited choice) is this hotel lying 1/4 mile (.40km) outside town on the road to Javier. In summer its most attractive feature is a swimming pool. Bedrooms are in a functional modern style, but they're clean and comfortable.

Meals costing from 1,300 pesetas ($9.20) are available daily from 1 to 4pm and 8 to 10:30pm. The many Navarrese dishes served here include lamb stew and steak. The local wine cellars produce red and rose wines that have won many prizes, and you can sample some of them here.

Easy Excursions

The **Monasterio de San Salvador of Leyre** lies 10 miles (16km) east of Sangüesa, perched on the side of a mountain of the same name, overlooking the Yesa Dam. Of major historical and artistic interest, the main body of the monastery was constructed between the 11th and 15th century on the site of a primitive Pre-Romanesque church;

in time, it became the spiritual center of Navarre. Many kings, including Sancho III, made it their pantheon. Its crypt, consecrated in 1057, ranks as one of the country's major works of Romanesque art.

When the church was reconstructed by the Cistercians in the 13th century, they kept the bays of the old Romanesque church. The 12th-century west portal is outstanding and richly adorned. Called the Porta Speciosa, it is covered with intricate carvings; in one section, Jesus and the disciples are depicted atop mythical creatures. Some of the other artistic treasures of this once-great monastery are displayed at the Museo de Navarra in Pamplona.

When Navarre joined with Aragón, the power of Leyre declined. Finally, in the 19th century, the monastery was abandoned. Not until 1954 did a Benedictine order come here and begin the difficult restoration.

The monastery lies 2$^1/_2$ miles (4km) from Yesa, which itself is on the major road linking Pamplona with Huesca. The church opens daily at 8pm, and vespers are held at 7pm just before the church closes. Admission is free.

At Leyre you'll also find one of the most unusual accommodations in Navarre, the **Hospedería,** Monasterio de Leyre, 31410 Leyre (☎ **948/88-41-00;** fax 948/88-41-37), which is open only from March to October. This two-star inn with 32 rooms (all with private baths and phone) was created from the annexes constructed by the Benedictines in the 1700s. The guest rooms open onto views of the Yesa Reservoir. The rates are 3,900 pesetas ($27.70) for a single and 7,800 pesetas ($55.40) for a double—with breakfast another 700 pesetas ($5). The hotel restaurant serves good Navarrese fare in a rustic setting. A meal is offered daily for 2,500 pesetas ($17.80) from 1 to 4pm and 8 to 10:30pm. AE, DC, MC, V. **Parking:** Free.

The second major excursion possible in the area is to **Castillo de Javier** (☎ **948/88-40-00**), 5 miles (8km) from Sangüesa and dating from the 11th century. It owes its present look to restoration work carried out in 1952. Francisco Javier (Xavier), patron of Navarre, was born here on April 7, 1506. Along with Ignatius Loyola, he founded the order of the Society of Jesus (the Jesuits) in the mid-16th century. The castle houses a magnificent 13th-century crucifix, and thousands of the faithful congregate at Javier on two consecutive Sundays in March. This is one of the most popular pilgrimages in Navarre. Known as the Javierada, it pays homage to Francisco Javier, who was canonized in 1622.

Guided tours of the castle take you through the oratory, the guard chamber, the great hall, and the saint's bedroom. The most interesting art is pointed out on the tour, including a 15th-century fresco called *The Dance of Death.* Hours are daily from 9am to 1pm and 4 to 7pm. Admission is free.

For good and lodging, go the **Hotel El Mesón**, Zona Turistica, s/n, 31411 Javier (☎ **948/88-40-35;** fax 948/88-42-26), which rents eight comfortably furnished bedrooms except from December 15 through February. Rooms cost 5,200 pesetas ($36.90) for a double plus another 500 pesetas ($3.60) for breakfast. With its hotels and terraces, the hotel makes for a tranquil choice. It also offers the best food in the area, a fixed price menu going for 1,600 pesetas ($11.40) and a large à la carte meal tallying up at 3,000 pesetas ($21.30). Parking is free.

5 Logroño

205 miles (330km) N of Madrid, 57 miles (92km) W of Pamplona

GETTING THERE • By Train There are five daily RENFE trains making the 6 to 7½ hour trip from Barcelona and two per day from Madrid (5 hours away). From Bilbao in the north, three trains arrive per day (a 3-hour trip). For information, call **23-17-37**).

• By Bus There are good bus connections from Pamplona four times per day (2 hours away) and from Madrid five a day (5 hours away). For information, call **23-59-83.**

ESSENTIALS The area code is 941. The tourist office is at Calle Miguel Villanueva, 10 (☎ **941/29-12-60**).

The capital of the province of La Rioja, Logroño is also the major distribution center for the area's wines and agricultural products. Because La Rioja is so small, Logroño could be your base for touring all the major attractions of the province. Although much of Logroño is modern and dull, it does have an old quarter known to the pilgrims crossing this region to visit the tomb of St. James at Santiago de Compostela.

What to See & Do

The **Catedral de Santa María de la Redonda,** Plaza del Mercado (☎ **25-76-11**), has vaulting from the 1400s, but the baroque facade dates from 1742. Inside, you can visit its 1762 Chapel of Our Lady of the Angels, built in an octagonal shape with rococo adornments. Constructed on top of an earlier Romanesque church, today's cathedral is known for its broad naves and twin towers. It is open daily from 9am to 1pm and 7 to 9pm.

From the square on which the cathedral sits, walk up Calle de la Sagasta until you reach the 12th-century **Iglesia de Santa María de Palacio,** Marqués de San Nicolás, once part of a royal palace. The palace part dates from 1130, when Alfonso VII offered his residence to the Order of the Holy Sepulchre. Most of what he left is long gone, of course, but there is still a pyramid-shaped spire from the 13th century.

Walk through the heart of Logroño, exploring the gardens of the broad **Paseo del Espolón.** In the late afternoon, all the residents turn out for their paseo.

While in Logroño, you can visit the **Bodegas Olarra**, Poligono Independencia de Cantabria, s/n (☎ **23-52-99**), open Monday to Friday from 10am to 1pm and 4 to 6pm. It produces wines under the Otonal and Olarra labels.

Where to Stay

Hotel Murrieta, Marqués de Murrieta, 1, 26005 Logroño. ☎ **941/22-41-50.** Fax 941/22-32-13. 109 rms (all with bath), 2 suites. TV TEL

Rates: 6,500 ptas. ($46.20) single; 8,500 ptas. ($60.40) double; breakfast 600 ptas. ($4.30) extra. AE, MC, V. **Parking:** Free.

Set at the western border of the historic part of town, a block north of the Gran Vía, this 1980s cement-sided hotel offers comfortable, pristinely decorated rooms, and relatively good value. The public rooms are outfitted with shades of colored marble, deep carpeting, and upholstery, all modernized in 1991 and tasteful.

Efficient and unpretentious, the Murrieta restaurant serves both regional and Spanish food, along with an appealing collection of Rioja wines. Uncomplicated à la carte lunches and dinners cost 1,550 pesetas ($11) in the hotel's cafeteria.

Room service is available from 7:30am to midnight; other extras include laundry, babysitting, and car rentals.

$ **La Numantina,** Calle Sagasta, 4, 26000 Logroño. ☎ **941/25-41-11.** 17 rms (all with bath). TEL

Rates: 2,600 ptas. ($18.50) single; 4,000 ptas. ($28.40) double. AE, MC, V. **Closed:** Dec 24–Jan 8.

Viewed as one of the bargains of town, this rather simple hotel lies on a street central to both the historic core and the commercial district. Its basic rooms are clean and reasonably comfortable. No breakfast is served, but you can buy pastries at a shop across the street.

Paris, Avenida La Rioja, 8, 26000 Logroño. ☎ **941/22-87-50.** 36 rms (all with bath) TEL

Rates: 3,500-3,700 ptas. ($24.90–$26.30) single; 5,700–6,000 ptas. ($40.50–$42.60) double. No credit cards.

One of the town's bargain accommodations lies within what was originally built during the 1920s as a private house. Renovated during the 1980s, it lies near the police station, and attracts many employees of the wine industry who are in Logroño on business. Bedrooms are outfitted in a basic modern style. No meals are served, but many cafés populate the neighborhood.

Where to Dine

Asador La Chata, Carnicerías, 3. ☎ **25-12-96.**

Cuisine: RIOJANA. **Reservations:** Required.
Prices: Appetizers 600–1,450 ptas. ($4.30–$10.30); main courses 1,600–2,000 ptas. ($11.40–$14.20). Fixed-price menu 3,000 ptas. ($21.30). DC, MC, V.
Open: Lunch, daily 1:30–4pm. Dinner, Thurs–Sat 9–11:30pm.

This is probably the most delightful dining choice in Logroño, reeking with ambience and a sense of Old Navarre. Founded in 1821, it occupies a building close to the town's cathedral. Its tactful owners define it as an *asador,* which means that it specializes in wood-roasted meat dishes, in this case in the style of the region. Although lunch is an everyday event, and much patronized by workers in the local wine trade, dinner is served only three evenings a week. Because of the establishment's small size (only 40 seats), advance reservations are essential. Within the wood-paneling dining room, ringed with artifacts of the wine trade, you can enjoy the two house specialties: fresh asparagus prepared with strips of locally cured ham, and *cabrito asado* (roast baby goat with herbs). Meats are succulently tender, having cooked long and slowly before your arrival.

$ **Casa Emilio,** Pérez Galdós, 18. ☎ **25-88-44.**

Cuisine: RIOJANA. **Reservations:** Recommended.
Prices: Appetizers 725–1,350 ptas. ($5.10–$9.60); main courses 900–2,100 ptas. ($6.40–$14.90); *menú del día* 2,700 ptas. ($19.20). AE, DC, MC, V.
Open: Lunch, Mon–Sat 1:30–4pm; dinner, Mon–Sat 9–11:30pm. **Closed:** Aug.

There is an ample bar set at the entrance to the dining room at Casa Emilio, which serves primarily roasts, especially goat and beef. In air-conditioned comfort, you can also enjoy peppers stuffed with codfish or baked hake. From the well-stocked wine cellar come some of the finest Rioja wines. Casa Emilio lies south of the old town, directly west of the major boulevard, Vara de Rey.

Las Cubanas, San Agustín, 17. ☎ **22-00-50.**

Cuisine: RIOJANA. **Reservations:** Recommended.
Prices: Appetizers 600–850 ptas. ($4.30–$6); main courses 1,400–2,200 ptas. ($9.90–$15.60). MC, V.
Open: Lunch, Mon–Sat 1–4pm; dinner, Mon–Fri 9–11:30pm. **Closed:** July 15–30 and Sept 15–30.

In the center of the old town, west of the police station and three minutes from the cathedral, is this family-owned establishment, which succeeds in maintaining a happy balance between quality and price. The cuisine is based on the use of fresh seasonal ingredients. Try the veal with mushrooms, and perhaps finish with the dessert specialty, *leche frita* (fried milk). The restaurant is air-conditioned.

La Merced, Marqués de San Nicolas, 109. ☎ **22-11-66.**

Cuisine: RIOJANA/INTERNATIONAL. **Reservations:** Required.
Prices: Appetizers 800–1,200 ptas. ($5.70–$8.50); main courses 1,800–3,500 ptas. ($12.80–$24.90). AE, DC, MC, V.
Open: Lunch, Mon–Sat 1:15–3:30pm; dinner, Mon–Sat 9–11pm. **Closed:** Aug 1–21.

This restaurant occupies the street level and two upper floors of the 18th-century palace of the Marqués of Covarrubias. Much of the decoration inside is in the original baroque style of the palace. The chefs offer a modern interpretation of regional cuisine. Its collection of wines are especially well represented in the Rioja category. Your meal might include steamed seabass with truffle sauce, roast lamb with potatoes, sweet peppers stuffed with heavily spiced meat, or an array of fresh vegetables of the season. The dessert special is a succulent version of caramelized apples with chocolate sauce and cream.

6 Haro

223 miles (359km) N of Madrid, 30 miles (48km) NE of Logroño

GETTING THERE • **By Train** Eight trains per day make the one-hour run from Logroño to Haro.

• **By Bus** There are seven buses per day running from Logroño to Haro (45 minutes away).

• **By Car** Take the A-68 expressway (south of Logroño) northwest to the turnoff for Haro.

ESSENTIALS The area code for Haro is 941. The tourist information office is at Plaza Hermanos Florentino Rodríguez, s/n (☎ **941/31-27-26**).

Center of the wine tours of the Rioja Alta district, this region has been compared to Tuscany. Come here to taste the wine at the bodegas, as the international wine merchants do every year.

What to See & Do

The town itself deserves a look before you head for the bodegas. Its old quarter is filled with mansions, some from the 16th century; the most interesting ones lie along **Calle del Castillo.** The major architectural monument of town is the 16th-century **Iglesia de San Tomás,** Plaza de la Iglesia, the center of the old quarter. With its wedding-cake tower and Plateresque south portal, the 16th-century church is the major town landmark. The interior is Gothic.

You could spend at least three days touring the wineries in the town, but chances are that a few visits will satisfy your curiosity. The **Bodegas Muga,** Barrio de la Estación, s/n (☎ **31-04-98**), near the rail station, offers tours (usually in Spanish) of its wine cellars. It's open Monday to Friday from 9am to 1pm and 3 to 6pm; it's closed from August 15 to September 15.

You can also visit the **Compañia Vinícola del Norte de España,** Avenida Costa del Vino, 21 (☎ **31-06-50**), which is open Monday to Friday from 9am to 1pm and 3 to 6:30pm; it's closed from mid-August to mid-September. It dates from the 1870s, and its cellars have some vintages more than 100 years old.

Finally, pay a visit to **Rioja Alta,** Avenida Vizcaya, s/n (☎ **31-03-46**), not far from the Muga, which is open Monday to Friday from 11am to 1pm (closed from mid-August to mid-September).

Many of the bodegas are closed in August and the first two weeks in September. If you arrive in Haro when they are closed, settle instead for drinking wine in the tascas that line the streets between Parroquía and Plaza de la Par. After a night spent there, you'll forget all about the bodega tours. Some of the finest wines in Spain are sold at these tascas, along with tapas—all at reasonable prices.

Where to Stay

Los Agustinos, Calle San Agustin, 2, 26200 Haro. ☎ **941/31-13-08.**
Fax 941/30-31-48. 62 rms, 2 suites (all with bath). A/C TV TEL

Rates: 10,240 ptas. ($72.70) single; 12,550 ptas. ($89.10) double; 24,200 ptas. ($171.80) suite. Breakfast 975 ptas. ($6.90) extra. AE, DC, MC, V.

A former Augustinian convent has been turned into a four-star hotel in the center of Haro. Since its restoration and reopening in 1990, it has become the most desirable place to stay in a town that has always had too few accommodations. Owned by a Basque chain of hotels, it lies in a "zone of tranquility." The bedrooms are well appointed and offer much comfort. Good-tasting regional meals, accompanied by selections from a well-stocked cellar of Rioja wines, are offered Tuesday to Sunday for 3,000 pesetas ($21.30).

Iturrimurri, Carretera N-124, km 41, s/n, 26200 Haro. ☎ **941/31-12-13.**
Fax 941/31-17-21. 36 rms (all with bath). A/C MINIBAR TV TEL

Rates: 6,500 ptas. ($46.20) single; 9,900 ptas. ($70.30) double. Breakfast 900 ptas. ($6.40) extra. AE, MC, V. **Parking:** Free.

Lying half a mile southeast of the city on the highway, this is the "second choice" hotel for Haro. The comfortable rooms are attractively furnished, many with impressive views. There is an animated cafeteria, as well as a large dining room serving regional meals for 2,200 pesetas ($15.60). Ample parking facilities are also provided. In summer the garden and the swimming pool are compelling reasons to stay here.

Where to Dine

Beethoven I y II, Santo Tomás, 3-5, ☎ **31-11-81.**

Cuisine: RIOJANA/BASQUE. **Reservations:** Required in summer.
Prices: Appetizers 800–1,600 ptas. ($5.70–$11.40); main courses 1,600–2,000 ptas. ($11.40–$14.20); fixed-price menus 1,600–2,000 ptas. ($11.40–$14.20). MC, V.
Open: Lunch, Wed–Sun 1:30–4pm; dinner, Wed–Mon 9–11:30pm. **Closed:** July 1–15 and Dec.

In the center of town is the premier restaurant of Haro—actually two restaurants, standing beside each other. Both offer good food and value. One of them is a large old house where a bar has been installed. Have a drink here, then perhaps move next door to sample the more modern restaurant, Beethoven II, which was recently renovated. The place is justifiably famous for its platters of wild mushrooms, which owner Carlos Aquirre raises himself. Try the stuffed filet of sole, vegetable stew, or wild pheasant, finishing off with an apple tart. The interior is air-conditioned.

Terete, Arana, 17. ☎ **31-00-23.**

Cuisine: RIOJANA. **Reservations:** Recommended.
Prices: Appetizers 450–850 ptas. ($3.20–$6); main courses 950–1,600 ptas. ($6.70–$11.40); fixed-price menu 1,400 ptas. ($9.90). AE, DC, MC, V.
Open: Lunch, Tues–Sun 1:15–4pm; dinner, Tues–Sat 8–11pm. **Closed:** Oct.

This place has been a *horno asado* (restaurant specializing in roasts) since 1867 and is beloved by locals who dine here on roast suckling pig. The service is discreet, the food both savory and succulent—the kitchen has had a long time to learn the secrets of roasting meats. They are all prepared according to traditional regional recipes. When the fresh asparagus comes in, that is reason enough to dine here. The local peaches in season make the best dessert. Naturally, the finest of Rioja wines are served. Terete is located in the center of Haro.

19

Basque Country

THE BASQUES ARE THE OLDEST TRACEABLE ETHNIC GROUP IN EUROPE. THEIR language, called Euskera, predates any of the commonly spoken Romance languages, and its origins, like that of the Basque race itself, are lost in obscurity. Perhaps the Basques were descended from the original Iberians, who lived in Spain before the arrival of the Celts some 3,500 years ago. Conqueror after conqueror, Roman to Visigoth to Moor, may have driven these people into the Pyrenees, where they stayed and carved out a life for themselves—filled with tradition and customs still practiced to this day.

The region is called Euskadi, which in Basque means "collection of Basques." In a very narrow sense it refers to three provinces of Spain: Guipúzcoa (with its capital San Sebastián, the number-one sightseeing destination in Euskadi), Viscaya (whose capital is industrial Bilbao), and Alava (with its capital at Vitoria). But to Basque nationalists, who dream of forging a new nation that will one day unite all the Basque lands, Euskadi also refers to the northern part of Navarre and three provinces in France, including the famed resort of Biarritz.

The three current Basque provinces occupy the eastern part of the Cantabrian Mountains, between the Pyrenees and the valley of the Nervión. They maintained a large degree of independence until the 19th century, when they finally gave in to control from Castile, which recognized their ancient rights and privileges until 1876.

As a badge of pride, Basques wear a *boina,* a beret of red, blue, or white woolen cloth. Today, more than ever, the wearing of the boina is also a political statement. In recent years, more and more graffiti have appeared. You'll see such slogans as "Euskadi Ta Askatasuna" ("Freedom for Basques") painted virtually everywhere. Most of the people are friendly, hospitable, and welcoming, but a small but violent minority has given the land much bad publicity. Politics, however, rarely needs to concern the foreign traveler intent on having a vacation in these lands, which remain some of the most beautiful in Spain.

Seeing Basque Country

GETTING THERE The three Basque provinces are a major gateway into Spain from Europe via France, and public transportation is excellent. The busiest airport is Sandira, outside Bilbao. There's a smaller airport at Fuenterrabía, about 11 miles (18km) northeast of San Sebastián. If you're already in Spain, domestic connections can be arranged through Iberia Airlines, offering daily service to both Bilbao and Fuenterrabía (an hour away). Planes are small, so reserve far in advance.

The Basque lands are also easily reached by train. The most notable run is RENFE service from Chamartín Station in Madrid, heading for Irún and the French border. Many frontier-bound trains stop at San Sebastián. RENFE also runs trains to Bilbao, plus overnight service from Barcelona to San Sebastián and to Bilbao.

Bus links are also possible from major cities of Spain (see the individual city or town listings for connections).

For those driving from Madrid, access to the Basque country is on the N-1 to Burgos and Miranda de Ebro, then the A-68 to Bilbao (if that is your gateway). If you're coming from France, take the A-8 running inland along the coast to your desired turnoff.

What's Special About Basque Country

Beaches

- Playa de la Concha at San Sebastián, one of Spain's best-loved and most popular stretches of sand.
- Fuenterrabía, the widest sandy stretch of beach in Guipúzcoa province, known for its calm waters.

Great Towns/Villages

- San Sebastián, fashionable Belle Epoque resort, with the Basque coast's choicest sands.
- Fuenterrabía, near the French border, with many well-preserved villas in its medieval quarter.
- Lekeitio, in Vizcaya, an old fishing town, now a resort, visited for its fish restaurants and marine life.
- Ondárroa—for some, the ultimate symbol of the picture-postcard Costa Vasca fishing village.

Pilgrimages

- Guernica, immortalized by Picasso, a living symbol of the federation of Basque towns.
- Loyola, birthplace of St. Ignatius of Loyola, founder of the Jesuit order. His family home is now a monument.

Panoramic Vistas

- Jaizkibel Road, west of Fuenterrabía, winner of the "spectacular at sunset" sweepstakes.
- Costa Vasca, or Basque coast—a string of fishing villages spread along the Bay of Biscay.

Special Events/Festivals

- The International Film Festival at San Sebastián, drawing stars from around the world in September.
- Semana Grande at San Sebastián in mid-August, with fun fairs, fireworks, concerts, and sports competitions.
- Jazzaldia, a jazz festival at San Sebastián, in the second half of July.

A Suggested Route

Most visitors arrive from France, crossing the border at Irún.

Days 1–2 Spend two nights in San Sebastián, enjoying its beaches and lively after-dark tapas crawls through the old quarter. The following day take one or two day trips, such as to Fuenterrabía.

Days 3–4 Leave San Sebastián and spend two nights in one of the little fishing villages along the Costa Vasca, or Basque coast. One of the most desirable places is Ondárroa. Using one of the villages as your center, explore the other ones nearby. Allow time for a morning or an afternoon visit south to Guernica, made famous by Picasso.

Day 5 Bilbao, the "Chicago of Spain," deserves a day. This sturdy bastion of Basque industrial might, however, is surprisingly light in historic monuments.

Day 6 If time remains, journey to Vitoria, the capital of Alava, in the south, the most neglected of the three Basque provinces.

1 San Sebastián (Donostia)

13 miles (21km) W of the French border, 300 miles (483km) N of Madrid, 62 miles (100km) E of Bilbao

GETTING THERE • By Plane From Madrid, Iberia Airlines offers two daily 1-hour flights to San Sebastián, plus one daily flight from Barcelona. The domestic airport is at nearby Fuenterrabía. Phone **54-22-40** for flight information.

• By Train From Madrid, RENFE runs trains to the French border at Irún, many of which stop in San Sebastián (6 to 7 hours away). An overnight train from Paris to Madrid also stops in San Sebastián—just in time for breakfast. (San Sebastián's cafés serve the best croissants south of the Pyrenees.) RENFE also provides overnight train service from Barcelona to San Sebastián and on to Bilbao. For RENFE information, call **28-35-99.**

• By Bus San Sebastián is well linked by a bus network to many of Spain's major cities. Nine to 16 buses a day connect it to Bilbao (1 hour away); one daily bus arrives from Barcelona (a 7-hour trip); five buses run daily from Pamplona (3 hours away). If you're in Madrid, it's more convenient to take a train. These routes are covered by several private bus companies. The tourist office (see below) distributes an information pamphlet outlining various routes, the companies that service these runs, and telephone numbers to call for schedules.

• By Car From Madrid, take the N-1 toll road north to Burgos and Miranda de Ebro, continuing on the A-68 north to Bilbao, then along the A-8 east to San Sebastián and the French border. From Pamplona, the N-240 runs north to Tolosa, where the N-1 route will take you into San Sebastián.

ESSENTIALS The area code for San Sebastián is 943. The tourist information office is at Calle Reina Regente, s/n (☎ **943/48-11-66**).

San Sebastián (Donostia in Basque), ideally situated on a choice spot on the Bay of Biscay, surrounded by green mountains, is the summer capital of Spain, where the Belle Epoque lives on. From June to September the population swells as hundreds of Spanish bureaucrats escape the heat and head for this capital city. A tasteful resort, it has few of the tawdry trappings associated with major beachfront cities. It is also an ideal excursion center for trips to some of the Basque country's most fascinating towns.

Queen Isabella II put San Sebastián on the map as a tourist resort when she spent the summer of 1845 there. In time it became the summer residence of the royal court. On July 8, 1912, Queen María Cristina inaugurated the grand hotel named after her, and the resort became the pinnacle of fashion. In what is now the city hall, built in 1887, a casino opened, and here European aristocrats gambled in safety during World War I.

San Sebastián is the capital of the province of Guipúzcoa, the smallest in Spain, tucked in the far northeastern corner bordering France. It is said that Guipúzcoa has preserved Basque customs better than any other province. Half of the *donostiarras* speak Euskera. It is also a major seat of Basque nationalism, so be advised that protests, sometimes violent, are frequent.

San Sebastián contains an old quarter, **La Parte Vieja,** with narrow streets, hidden plazas, and medieval houses, but it is primarily a modern city of elegant shops, wide boulevards, sidewalk cafés, and restaurants.

La Concha is the most famous beach, where it seems half the population of Spain and France spend their days under striped canopies when they're not dashing into the refreshingly cool waters of the bay. Shell-shaped La Concha is half encircled by a promenade, where crowds mill during the evening. The adjoining beach is the **Playa de Ondarreta.** Its climate is more Atlantic than Mediterranean.

San Sebastián has a good but insufficient choice of hotels in summer, plus an excellent number of Basque restaurants, most of which are expensive. Its chief drawback is overcrowding—it is overpopulated in July, and there is no space at all in August.

Bullfights, art and film festivals, sporting events, and cultural activities keep San Sebastián hopping during the summer season.

What to See & Do

Two weeklong events draw visitors from around the world. In mid-August, San Sebastián stages its annual carnival, **Aste Nagusia,** a joyous celebration of traditional Basque music and dance, along with fireworks, cooking competitions, and sports events. In mid-September, the San Sebastián **International Film Festival** draws luminaries from America and Europe. The actual dates of these festivals vary from year to year, so check with the tourist office.

People come to San Sebastián for fun and to take a promenade along the Paseo de la Concha. The monuments, such as they are, can easily be viewed before lunch.

Museo de San Telmo, Plaza Ignacio Zuloaga, 1 (☎ **48-12-46**), housed in a former Dominican monastery, contains an impressive collection of Basque artifacts dating from unrecorded Iberian times. The display includes works by Zuloaga (*Torreillos en Turégano,* for example), "golden age" artists such as El Greco and Ribera, and a large number of Basque painters. Standing in the old town at the base of Monte Urgull, the museum is open Tuesday to Saturday from 9:30am to 1:30pm and 3:30 to 7pm; Sunday hours are 10:30 to 2pm; and Monday hours are 3:30 to 7pm. Admission is free.

The **Paseo Nuevo** is a wide promenade that almost encircles **Monte Urgull,** one of the two mountains between which San Sebastián is nestled (Monte Igueldo is the other one). A ride along this promenade opens onto panoramic vistas of the Bay of Biscay. The *paseo* comes to an end at the **Palacio del Mar,** Muelle, 34 (☎ **42-49-77**), an oceanographic museum and aquarium. Here you can see the skeleton of the last whale caught in the Bay of Biscay, in 1878. The museum is open daily from 10am to 2pm and 3:30 to 8:30pm; it is closed on Monday from September 15 to May 15. Admission is 250 pesetas ($1.80) for adults and 100 pesetas (70¢) for children.

Other sights include the **Palacio Miramar,** which stands on its own hill opening onto La Concha. In the background is the residential district of Antiguo. Queen María Cristina, after whom the grandest hotel in the north of Spain is named, opened this palace in 1893, but by the turbulent 1930s it had fallen into disrepair. The city

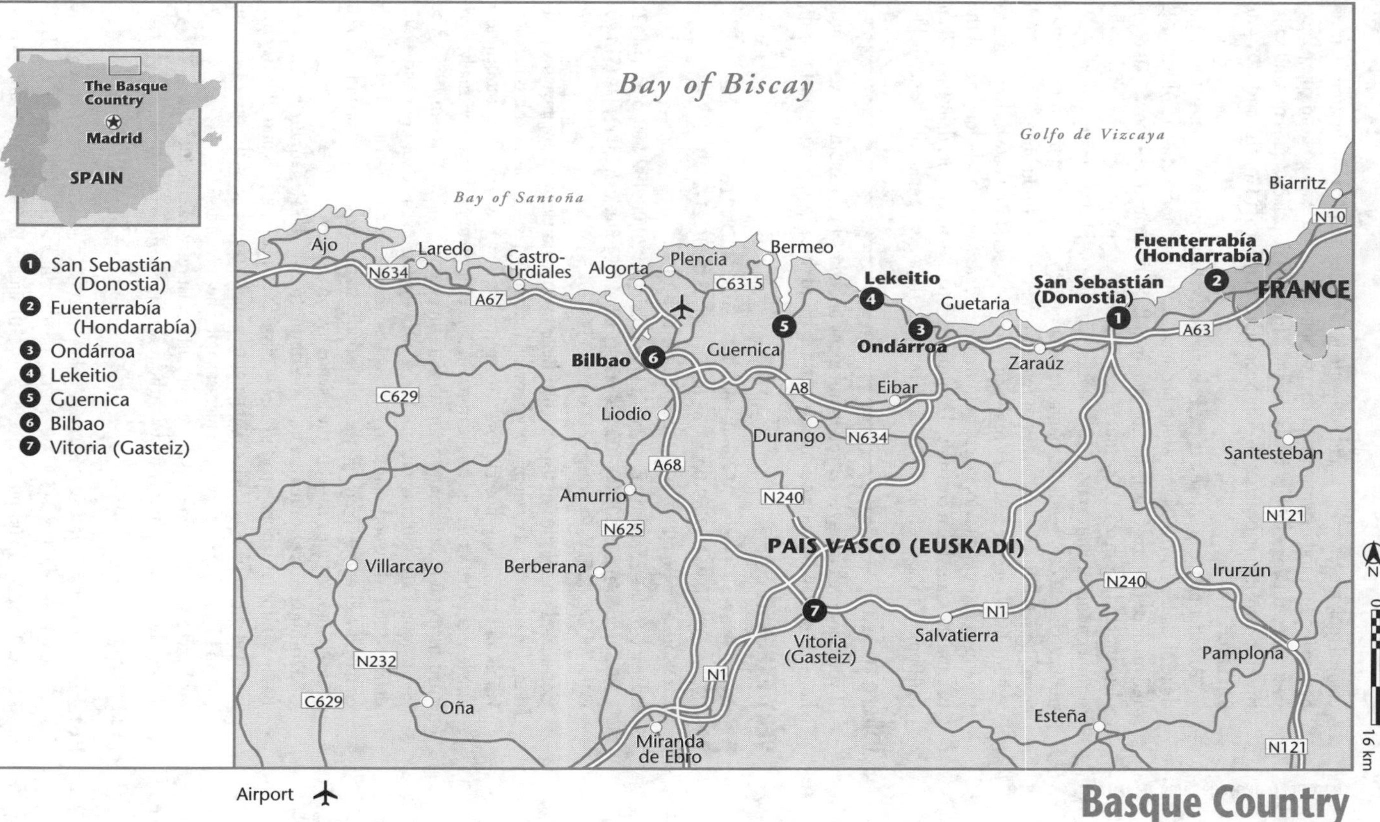

Basque Country

council took it over in 1971, and renovations continue. You can visit in summer from 8am to 8:30pm and in winter from 8am to 5pm. Since you can't go inside the palace, you must settle for a look at the lawns and gardens. The palace stands on land splitting the two major beaches of San Sebastián: Playa de la Concha and Playa de Ondarreta.

Another palace of interest is the **Palacio de Ayete,** which was constructed by the duke of Bailéen in 1878 and which became the summer home of King Alfonso XII and his queen, María Cristina, until their own Palacio Miramar (see above) was completed. Standing in 250,000 square feet of parkland, the palace also served as the summer home of Franco from 1940 until 1975. The residence remains closed to the public, but you can wander through the beautiful grounds in summer from 10am to 5pm. To reach it, take bus no. 19 to Ayete from Plaza de Guipúzcoa.

Finally, to get the best view of the city, for 75 pesetas (50¢) take the funicular to the top of Monte Igueldo, where from the belevedere you get a fabulous view of the bay and the Cantabrian coastline. The funicular operates in summer daily from 10am to 10pm. It's also possible to drive up. In spring the air is scented with honeysuckle.

Where to Stay

If you book well in advance, you'll find many good hotel values, but in season most hoteliers may insist that you take at least half board (breakfast, plus one main meal).

VERY EXPENSIVE

Hotel María Cristina, Paseo República Argentina, 4, 20004 San Sebastián (Donostia). ☎ **943/42-49-00,** or toll free in the U.S. **800/221-2340.** Fax 943/42-39-14. 109 rms, 30 suites. A/C MINIBAR TEL

Rates: 16,200–25,000 ptas. ($115–$177.50) single; 20,000–32,500 ptas. ($142–$230.80) double; suite 80,000–100,000 ptas. ($568–$710). Breakfast 2,000 ptas. ($14.20) extra. AE, DC, MC, V. **Parking:** 2,000 ptas. ($14.20).

Considered one of the most spectacular Belle Epoque hotels in Spain, enviably positioned in the heart of town midway between the bay and Río Urumea, this is the most visible and prestigious hotel in town. It received its first guests in 1912. Set behind a facade of chiseled stone and ornate ironwork, once the preferred hotel of virtually every titled aristocrat in France and Spain, the Cristina was richly remodeled in 1987. The public rooms are opulent with ormolu, Cuban mahogany, acres of onyx and exotic marbles, and rosewood marquetry. The guest rooms are appropriately lavish, with equally lavish rates. Today the clientele includes starlets, film directors, and a crowd of newly monied moguls—but the legends live on anyway.

Dining/Entertainment: The main dining room, the Restaurant Easo, serves Basque and international food in three-course fixed-price lunches and dinners costing from 5,800 pesetas ($41.20). The hotel also contains one of the most beautiful bars in town, the Gritti, where a pianist sometimes performs.

Services: 24-hour room service, babysitting, laundry/valet, concierge.

Facilities: Car rentals (with or without driver), business center.

EXPENSIVE

Hotel de Londres y de Inglaterra, Zubleta, 2, 20007 San Sebastián (Donostia). ☎ **943/42-69-89.** Fax 943/42-00-31. 127 rms, 18 suites. A/C MINIBAR TV TEL

Rates: 13,500–15,200 ptas. ($95.90–$107.90) single; 16,900–19,000 ptas. ($120–

$134.90) double; 22,000–26,000 ptas. ($156.20–$184.60) suite. Breakfast 1,000 ptas. ($7.10) extra. AE, DC, MC, V.

Beside the northern edge of the town's most popular beach, the Playa de la Concha, this venerable 19th-century hotel is one of the most enduring and stylish in town. Views from many of the balconies encompass the beach and a handful of rocky offshore islands. The traditional-style public rooms contain deep armchairs and big windows. Completely renovated in the past few years, the hotel has comfortably conservative guest rooms with a vaguely English decor, individual safes, and private modern bathrooms sheathed with slabs of Spanish marble.

Dining/Entertainment: At La Brasserie Mari Galant, both Basque and international cuisine is served, with meals costing 3,000 to 3,500 pesetas ($21.30–$24.90). A bar lies adjacent to it, and there's also The Swing Bar at street level to attract the sun-worshipping passersby.

Services: Room service (available from 1 to 4pm and from 8:30 to 11pm), laundry/valet, concierge, babysitting, in-house tour operator/travel agent.

Facilities: Outdoor swimming pool, car rentals, easy access to the Kursaal Casino (not affiliated with the hotel).

MODERATE

Hotel San Sebastián, Avenida Zumalacárregui, 20, 20008 San Sebastián. ☎ **943/21-44-00.** Fax 943/21-72-99. 92 rms (all with bath), 2 suites. MINIBAR TV TEL **Bus:** 5.

Rates: 9,200 ptas. ($65.30) single; 14,000 ptas. ($99.40) double; 23,000 ptas. ($163.30) suite. Breakfast buffet 1,200 ptas. ($8.50) extra. AE, DC, MC, V. **Parking:** 1,200 ptas. ($8.50).

Only a short distance from Ondarreta beach, near the edge of the city on the main road to Bilbao and Madrid, this modern hotel has a swimming pool in a pleasant garden, as well as an informal restaurant, a disco, two bars and one coffee bar. The rooms are comfortable and attractively furnished.

Monte Igueldo, Paseo del Faro, s/n, Monte Igueldo, 20008 San Sebastián. ☎ **943/21-02-11.** Fax 943/21-50-28. 125 rms (all with bath). A/C TV TEL **Bus:** Igueldo.

Rates: 8,500–9,400 ptas. ($60.40–$66.70) single; 14,500–16,000 ptas. ($103–$113.60) double. Extra bed 5,000 ptas. ($35.50). Breakfast 980 ptas. ($7) extra. AE, DC, MC, V. **Parking:** Free.

On the top of the mountain overlooking San Sebastián, only a 10-minute drive from the center of town, this first-class hotel perches like a castle. The public rooms, bedrooms, and pool terrace all boast a panoramic view of the Cantabrian coast. Each of the streamlined, modern rooms has a private balcony. Ample parking is provided.

Niza, Zubieta, 56, 20007 San Sebastián. ☎ **943/42-66-63.** Fax 943/42-66-63. 41 rms (all with bath). TV TEL **Bus:** 5 or 6.

Rates: 5,950 ptas. ($42.20) single; 11,650 ptas. ($82.70) double. Breakfast 625 ptas. ($4.40) extra. AE, DC, MC, V.

This charming little hotel, which opens onto the Playa de la Concha, has character and is favored by those who like to be near the beach and the esplanade. It has modern furnishings in the bedrooms and antiques in the public lounges. The petit salon, for example, contains an oriental rug, Directoire chairs, a tall grandfather clock, and a rosewood breakfront. In direct contrast are the basic rooms, with wooden headboards, white walls, and wall-to-wall carpeting. There's a pizzeria in the cellar, plus a bar overlooking the sea.

INEXPENSIVE

Codina, Zumalacárregui, 21, 20008 San Sebastián. ☎ **943/21-22-00.** Fax 943/21-25-23. 77 rms (all with bath). TV TEL **Bus:** 5.

Rates: July–Sept (including half board): 11,250 ptas. ($79.90) single; 14,500 ptas. ($103) double. Oct–June: 7,150 ptas. ($50.80) single; 8,800 ptas. ($62.50) double. Breakfast 750 ptas. ($5.30) extra. AE, DC, MC, V. **Parking:** 1,000 ptas. ($7.10).

Near an attractive residential district and close to a beach, this modern building is designed so that all of the comfortably furnished, compact rooms have a view of the bay. On the wide, busy boulevard you'll find a popular café and bar. A Basque cuisine is served.

$ **Hostal Bahía,** Calle San Martín, 54B, 20007 San Sebastián. ☎ **943/46-92-11.** Fax 943/46-39-14. 59 rms (all with bath). TV TEL **Bus:** 5, 6, 7, 8, or 9.

Rates (including breakfast): 5,900 ptas. ($41.90) single; (Oct–June only); 8,800 ptas. ($62.50) double (July–Sept); 7,700 ptas. ($54.70) double (Oct–June). MC, V.

A good-value little hotel just one block from the beach near a string of other hotels, the Bahía features guest rooms of varying sizes: Some are large enough to contain sofas and armchairs; others fall into the cubicle category. Many North Americans stay at the *hostal* and take public transportation to Pamplona for the running of the bulls.

Residencia Parma, Paseo de Salamanca, 10, 20002 San Sebastián. ☎ **943/42-88-93.** Fax 943/42-40-82. 27 rms (all with bath). TEL **Bus:** 5 or 7.

Rates: 6,500 ptas. ($46.20) single; 9,400–11,600 ptas. ($66.70–$82.40) double. Breakfast 750 ptas. ($5.30) extra. AE, MC, V.

A modern, clean hotel in the center of town, where many of the accommodations have beautiful views of the ocean, the Parma has up-to-date rooms cozily furnished in wood, with good, modern bathrooms. There are also a downstairs snack bar and a pleasant TV lobby, with armchairs and sofas. Breakfast is the only meal served.

Where to Dine

EXPENSIVE

★ **Akelare,** Paseo del Padre Orkolaga, 56. ☎ **21-20-52.**

Cuisine: BASQUE. **Reservations:** Strongly recommended.

Prices: Appetizers 1,500–3,950 ptas. ($10.70–$28); main courses 2,950–4,400 ptas. ($20.90–$31.20); *menú degustación* 6,000 ptas. ($42.60). AE, DC, MC, V.

Open: Lunch, Tues–Sun 1–3:30pm; dinner, Tues–Sat 8:30–11pm. **Closed:** Jan 21–Feb 23, Oct 3–19.

A visit to Akelare is considered essential for any dedicated aficionado of gourmet food in Spain. The preparations of owner/chef Pedro Subijana have influenced a generation of chefs and defined—perhaps more than any other—the entire philosophy of *la nueva cocina vasco* (modern Basque cuisine). Established in 1974, the restaurant lies on the western edge of San Sebastián, within a tile-roofed hexagonal villa originally built as a catering hall for weddings and christenings. Inside, a sweeping view through large windows encompasses the mists and raging currents of the Bay of Biscay far below. The plushly upholstered modern decor, with its hospitable cold-weather fireplace, is an appropriate foil for dishes inspired by the Basque *caserios* (farmsteads).

The perfect beginning to any meal here is puff pastry filled with filets of anchovies, accompanied by a glass of chilled fino sherry. Traditional dishes might include seafood soup in the style of San Sebastián; fish cooked on a griddle with garlic and parsley; beans accompanied by bacon, chorizo, pork ribs, and sausage; baked rice with clams; or a special *marmitako* (fisherman's stew). More innovative are the snails with watercress sauce; a *millefeuille* of scrambled eggs with exotic mushrooms; boiled cabbage stuffed with duckmeat and served with purée of celery; a salad of tomatoes with marinated fresh tuna and twin pepper and tomato sauces; a warm salad of bonito fish served with a basil, lemon, chervil, and vinegar sauce; a ragoût of salt cod; and filet of duck with an assortment of exotic seasonal mushrooms. On occasion, Subijana—who won the 1983 National Prize for Gastronomy, which is awarded to the best chef in Spain—may venture into the dining room to gauge the reaction to his inventions and to offer advice about the day's menu. The name of the restaurant, incidentally, translates from the Basque as "Witches Sabbath."

Arzak, Alto de Miracruz, 21. ☎ **28-55-93.**

Cuisine: BASQUE. **Reservations:** Required.

Prices: Appetizers 1,400–3,800 ptas. ($9.90–$27); main courses 2,600–4,400 ptas. ($18.50–$31.20); fixed-price menu 7,100 ptas. ($50.40). AE, DC, MC, V.

Open: Lunch, Tues–Sun 1–3:30pm; dinner, Tues–Sat 8:30–11pm. **Closed:** June 15–30.

Considered one of the most famous restaurants in the Basque world (an honor it shares with the also-recommended Akelare, see above), this legendary restaurant occupies the lavishly renovated childhood home of owner/chef Juan Mari Arzak. Well known in San Sebastián for his role in preparing a meal for visiting monarch Elizabeth II of Britain (for which he later received an invitation to Buckingham Palace), Arzak combines staples of the Basque culinary legacy with many new creations of his own. Many diners begin their meals with a selection of fresh oysters, or, even more elegant, natural foie gras. Crayfish is regularly featured as an appetizer, as is the chef's special *sopa de pescado* (fish soup). For a main course, consider *merluza* (hake) in a vinaigrette with onions and small squid. On the back of the menu is a list of classic dishes that have won the most praise among visitors since the restaurant's opening—everything from stuffed sweet peppers with a fish mousse to pheasant or partridge. For dessert, the orange flan with cream might just be the best version you've ever had of this classic dish. The restaurant is on the main road leading from the center of town to the French border.

Casa Nicolasa, Calle Aldamar, 4. ☎ **42-17-62.**

Cuisine: BASQUE. **Reservations:** Required.

Prices: Appetizers 1,800–2,200 ptas. ($12.80–$15.60); main courses 2,500–4,000 ptas. ($17.80–$28.40). AE, DC, MC, V.

Open: Lunch, Mon–Sat 1–3:30pm; dinner, Tues–Sat 8:30pm–midnight. **Closed:** 3 weeks in Feb (dates vary).

Some members of those all-male eating clubs (a Basque tradition going back to the 19th century) assured us that Casa Nicolasa serves the best cuisine at San Sebastián. That would be difficult to prove, especially in a city where international food critics have rated Arzak and Akelare even higher (see above). Nevertheless, Casa Nicolasa surfaces very close to the top.

In the heart of the resort, at the edge of Old Town by the Mercado la Brecha, the restaurant features a refined cuisine and service of impeccable standards. Diners are made to feel like guests being served by a proper butler in a part that Sir Anthony Hopkins could play so well. Master chef José Juan Castillo seems to believe that gastronomy should be elevated to a high art—and he does so convincingly here. Devotees of the place have their own favorite dishes among his inventive repertoire, but the menu, of course, is seasonally adjusted to take advantage of the best produce or fresh fish, whatever, in any given month.

The chef, Señor Castillo, is greatly aided by his wife, the gracious Ana María. Many of the dishes served here have stood the test of time; others reflect the free-reign culinary imagination of the 1990s. The foie gras is homemade and is the smoothest, albeit expensive, way to begin a meal here. *Rape* (monkfish) is also prepared in various creative ways, and I have found, is one of the most satisfying main courses. Save room for dessert, as the pastry selections are one of the outstanding features of the kitchen.

When business is at its peak in August and September, the restaurant is likely to open Monday night for dinner as well.

★ **Panier Fleuri,** Paseo de Salamanca, 1. ☎ **42-42-05.**

Cuisine: BASQUE/INTERNATIONAL. **Reservations:** Required.
Prices: Appetizers 1,850–2,200 ptas. ($13.10–$15.60); main courses 2,000–4,200 ptas. ($14.20–$29.80); fixed-price menu 5,275 ptas. ($37.50). AE, DC, MC, V.
Open: Lunch, Thurs–Tues 1–3:30pm; dinner, Mon–Tues and Thurs–Sat 8:30–11pm.
Closed: June 1–24 and Dec 15–Jan 2.

Yet another celebrated restaurant in San Sebastián, this citadel of good cuisine serves Basque dishes with a definite French flavor and flair, typical of the resort of Biarritz across the border in France. The third generation of the Fombedilla family of chefs has had a long time to perfect their cuisine and their special offerings. Service is discreet and elegant, and diners here have a chance to learn why Basque food preparation is regarded as among the finest in Europe.

The setting alone is rewarding, in a formal dining room opening onto the pounding surf at the mouth of the Urumea River.

The female chef, Tatus Fombellida, once won the National Gastronomy Award in Spain, no mean feat, and critics of San Sebastián cuisine claim she's better than ever. Her *faisan* (pheasant) and *becada asada* (roast woodcock) have been hailed as among the finest game dishes at the resort. But, if you don't like game, you'll find an array of other delectable offerings, including, for example, sole baked with spinach and presented with a freshly made hollandaise sauce, similar to what you might find in one of the better restaurants of Florence. Finish off this rich fare with perhaps a lemon sorbet with champagne.

Even better known than the cuisine is the wine cellar, containing many vintage bottles. The wine steward will guide you through an often perplexing selection, including mellow versions of such wines as Remelluri, Barón de Oña, and Viña Albina.

MODERATE

Juanito Kojua, Puerto, 14. ☎ **42-01-80.**

Cuisine: SEAFOOD. **Reservations:** Required.
Prices: Appetizers 1,000–1,500 ptas. ($7.10–$10.70); main courses 1,800–2,800 ptas. ($12.80–$19.90); fixed-price menus 2,600–3,200 ptas. ($18.50–$22.70). AE, DC, MC, V.

Open: Lunch, daily 1–3:30pm; dinner, Mon–Sat 8:30–11:30pm.

This little seafood restaurant in the old town, off Plaza de la Constitución, has no decor to speak of, but it has become famous throughout Spain. There's always a wait, but it's worth it. There are two dining areas on the main floor, behind a narrow bar (perfect for an appetizer while you're waiting for your table), plus one downstairs—all of them air-conditioned in summer. Specialties may include paella, *pisto,* half a *besugo* (sea bream), *rape* (monkfish) *l'americana,* and *lubina* (sea bass). Meats are good, too, but it's best to stick to the fresh fish dishes.

Salduba, Pescadería, 6. ☎ **42-56-27.**

Cuisine: BASQUE. **Reservations:** Recommended.
Prices: Appetizers 1,000–1,400 ptas. ($7.10–$9.90); main courses 1,600–2,200 ptas. ($11.40–$15.60); fixed-price menu 3,500 ptas. ($24.90). AE, DC, MC, V.
Open: Lunch, Mon–Sun 1–4pm; dinner, Mon–Sat 8–11pm. **Closed:** Nov.

Opened shortly after the end of World War II, this well-established restaurant owes much of its popularity to the owners, who oversee the cooking. Specialties include Basque hake; herb-laden fish soup; a confit of duckling; filet of beef; and a platter stacked high with the "fruits of the sea"—as well as succulent beef, veal, and pork dishes and various desserts. There are several dining rooms. Salduba lies on the edge of the old town, a five-minute walk from the beach.

 **Urepel,** Paseo de Salamanca, 3. ☎ **42-40-40.**

Cuisine: BASQUE/INTERNATIONAL. **Reservations:** Required.
Prices: Appetizers 1,400–2,200 ptas. ($9.90–$15.60); main courses 1,700–2,800 ptas. ($12.10–$19.90). AE, DC, MC, V.
Open: Lunch, Mon–Sat 1–3:30pm; dinner, Mon and Wed–Sat 8:30–11pm. **Closed:** June 24–July 20 and Dec 23–Jan 12.

Standing close to one of its major competitors, the equally rewarding Panier Fleuri (see above), Urepel lies near the mouth of the Urumea River. Perhaps its interior is not as elegant as those of the other starred restaurants of San Sebastián, but devotees of this place aren't bothered by that at all. They're here for the cuisine, as only the freshest and best produce along with the finest cuts of meat and the "harvests of the sea" are served here.

The chef demands impeccable ingredients to concoct a menu of traditional Basque fare. The Basque palate, at least according to legend, is the most discriminating in Spain, and few complaints are heard here. The restaurant, lying on two levels at the edge of old town, is the domain of Tomás Almandoz, one of the outstanding chefs in the north of Spain. Seafood dominates the menu, as it should in this region of the world, and it's deftly handled by the kitchen staff. The fish is often served with delicate sauces, and the main courses are made even better by an emphasis on fresh and perfectly prepared vegetables. *Rape* (monkfish), *dorada* (John Dory), and *cigalas* (crayfish) are likely to turn up on the menu, based on fish-market shopping that morning. Somewhat of a rarity in San Sebastián, you can also order goose or duck. One specialty is *pato de caserio fileteado a la naranja* (regional-style duck flavored with oranges).

One local food critic got so carried away with the dessert *carte* and its presentation that she claimed "it would take Velásquez to arrange a pastry so artfully"—a gross exaggeration, of course, but an indication of how highly regarded this place is. I prefer it in the evening instead of lunch. At midday many of the tables are reserved by local business persons and government officials.

BUDGET

$ **La Oka,** Calle San Martín, 43. ☎ **46-38-84.**

Cuisine: BASQUE. **Reservations:** Not required.

Prices: Appetizers 450–650 ptas. ($3.20–$4.60); main courses 650–1,200 ptas. ($4.60–$8.50); fixed-price menu 1,200 ptas. ($8.50). V.

Open: Lunch, Thurs–Tues 1–3:30pm; dinner, Fri–Sat 8:30–11pm. **Closed:** Last three weeks in Dec.

Don't come to La Oka, near the beach in the center of town, looking for glamour. If, on the other hand, you're looking for an inexpensive self-service cafeteria, you might enjoy this place. Some critics, in fact, rate it the best self-service cafeteria in Spain. The diners represent a cross section of the city's office workers. The Basque cooking is hearty and plentiful.

SPECIALTY DINING

In the summer, walk along the **Fishermen's Harbor** in San Sebastián and order a plate of charcoal-broiled sardines. At several bistros, rustic wooden tables and chairs have been placed outside rough-and-tumble restaurants.

Evening Entertainment

The best evening entertainment in San Sebastián is to go tapa-tasting in the old quarter of town. Throughout the rest of Spain this is known as a *tapeo,* or tapas crawl. In San Sebastián it's called a *poteo-ir-de pinchos,* or searching out morsels on cocktail sticks. Groups of young people often spend their evenings on some 20 streets in the old town, each leading toward Monte Urgull, the port, or La Brecha marketplace. The Alameda del Bulervar, the "popular grove," is the most upscale of these streets, the Calle Fermín Calveton one of the most popular. You'll find plenty of these places on your own, but here are some to get you going.

El Astelena, Plaza de la Constitución. ☎ **42-62-75.**

This bar lies in the very heart of San Sebatián, which is the center of many cultural and political events, including protests. The Plaza de la Constitución, lined with houses with tall arcades and balconies, was once the scene of bullfights, and the tapas served in this much-patronized bar are often called *banderillas,* which means "bullfighting darts." They include a favorite Basque specialty, calf's cheek, but you may opt for a cheese croquette. Salt cod with onions and green peppers is the eternal favorite. Tapas range from 250 to 750 pesetas ($1.80–$5.30); drinks begin at 175 pesetas ($1.20). El Astelena is open Tuesday to Sunday from 10am to 1am.

Bar Asador Ganbara, Calle San Jerónimo, 21. ☎ **42-25-75.**

Decorated with a flair in light-colored wood, this place is a tapas lover's delight. The dishes are well prepared, using market-fresh ingredients. Try the house specialty and the chef's pride: small melt-in-your-mouth croissants filled with cheese, egg, bacon, and Serrano ham. Try also the spider crab and prawns with mayonnaise. Tapas run 350–750 pesetas ($2.50–$5.30); drinks from 175 pesetas ($1.20). In addition to its bar service, the establishment also runs a restaurant in a separate section, offering a fixed-price menu at 2,500 pesetas ($17.80) Tuesday through Saturday from 8 to 11:15pm. Calle San Jerónimo runs at right angles to Calle Fermín Calveton. The bar is open Tuesday through Saturday from 10am to 1am.

Casa Alcalde, Mayor, 19. ☎ **42-62-16.**

The tasty tapas served at the Casa Alcalde, just a five-minute walk from the Parque Alderdi Eder, are thinly sliced ham, cheeses, and shellfish dishes. The different varieties are all nearly displayed, and priced from 125 to 225 pesetas (90¢ to $1.60). You can also have full meals in a small restaurant at the back, for 1,500 to 2,200 pesetas. ($10.70 to $15.60). Open daily from 10am to 11pm.

Casa Valles, Reyes Católicos, 10. ☎ **45-22-10.**

The variety of tapas and wines offered here seems endless. Go to hang out with the locals and feast on tidbits guaranteed to spoil your dinner. You'll find it in the center of town behind the cathedral, open Thursday to Tuesday from 8:30 to 11pm (closed in late June and late December). Most tapas cost 125 pesetas (90¢), with a beer going for 140 pesetas ($1). In addition, a *menú del día* is offered for 3,000 pesetas ($21.30).

La Cepa, 31 de Agosto, 7-9. ☎ **42-63-94.**

Many locals say that the best tapas in town are found at La Cepa, on the northern edge of the old town, and the Jabugo ham is one proof of this claim. Try the grilled squid or the salt-cod-and-green-pepper omelet. You can also order dinner here—a daily changing menu costing 2,000 pesetas ($14.20) in the peak summer season but lowered to 1,700 pesetas ($12.10) off season. Tapas begin at 100 pesetas (70¢) but could go up to 1,500 pesetas ($10.70) for a small portion of Jabugo ham. A glass of wine costs 85 pesetas (60¢). The owner, a former bullfighter known as Barberito, is usually on the scene visiting with his many friends, although he is semi-retired. La Cepa is open from Thursday to Tuesday from 11am to midnight.

Easy Excursions

TWO FISHING VILLAGES

One of the reasons for coming to San Sebastián is to use it as a base for touring the environs. Driving is best because bus connections are awkward or nonexistent.

On the east bank of a natural harbor 6.5 miles (10.5km) from San Sebastián, **Pasai Donibane** is one of the most typical of Basque fishing villages. Once it was known by its Spanish name, Pasajes de San Juan. Many visitors come here to dine. The village, with its codfish-packing factories, is on a sheltered harbor; fishing boats are tied up at the wharf. The architecture is appealing: five- and six-story balconied tenementlike buildings in different colors.

Victor Hugo lived here in the summer of 1846 (it hasn't changed much since) at building no. 63 on the narrow main street, San Juan.

In summer, don't take a car into the village. Parking is difficult, the medieval streets are one-way, and the wait at traffic signals is long, for all southbound traffic has to clear the street before northbound motorists have the right of way.

A bus leaves every 15 minutes from the Calle Aldamar in San Sebastián for **Pasajes de San Pedro,** Pasai Donibane's neighboring fishing village. It's also possible to walk from Pasai Donibane. Buses head back to San Sebastián from Pasajes de San Pedro, at a quarter to the hour all day long.

Where to Dine

Txulotxo, San Juan, 82, Pasai Donibane. ☎ **52-39-52.**

Cuisine: BASQUE. **Reservations:** Recommended.

Prices: Appetizers 950–1,400 ptas. ($6.70–$9.90); main courses 1,800–2,200 ptas. ($12.80–$15.60); *menú del día* 1,900 ptas. ($13.50). AE, V.
Open: Lunch, Wed–Mon 1:30–4:30pm; dinner, Wed–Sat and Mon 8:30–11:30pm.
Closed: Oct 15–Nov 15.

Right on the waterfront, this old stone building with a glass-enclosed dining room overlooking the harbor is one of the most authentic and typical of Basque restaurants. The house specialties are made from fish that is delivered daily.

LOYOLA

Surrounded by mountain scenery, Loyola, 34 miles (55km) southwest of San Sebastián, is the birthplace of St. Ignatius, the founder of the Jesuits. He was born in 1491, died in 1556, and was canonized in 1622. The sanctuary at Loyola is the most-visited attraction outside the city.

There are large pilgrimages to Loyola for an annual celebration on St. Ignatius Day, July 31. The activity centers around the **Monastery of San Ignacio de Loyola,** an immense structure built by the Jesuits in the 1700s around the Loyola family manor house near Azpeitia. An International Festival of Romantic Music is held here during the first week of August.

The **basilica** was the work of Italian architect Fontana. Surrounded by a 118-foot-high cupola by Churriguera, it is circular in design.

From 12:30 to 3:30pm daily, visitors can enter the **Santa Casa,** site of the former Loyola manor house, with its 15th-century tower. The rooms in which the saint was born and in which he convalesced have been converted into richly decorated chapels. At the entrance you can rent a tape detailing Loyola's life, and dioramas are shown at the end of the tour.

Six buses a day leave from Plaza Guipúzcoa, 2, San Sebastián, for Loyola (the first departing at 8:30am and the last at 8pm). Buses return about every two hours.

2 Fuenterrabía (Hondarribía)

14 miles (23km) E of San Sebastián, 317 miles (510km) N of Madrid, 11 miles (18km) W of St-Jean-de-Luz (France)

GETTING THERE • By Train Irún is the "end of the line" for trains in northern Spain. East of Irún, you must board French trains. Irún is about 3 miles (4.8km) from Fuenterrabía.

• By Bus Buses running every 15 minutes from San Sebastián connect that city with Fuenterrabía, one hour away.

• By Car Take the A-8 east to the French border, turning toward the coast at the exit sign for Fuenterrabía. Telephone **64-13-02** for information.

ESSENTIALS The area code for Fuenterrabía is 943.

A big seaside resort mand fishing port, Fuenterrabía (Hondarribía in Basque) lies near the French frontier, and for that reason it has been subject to frequent attacks over the centuries. In theory, it was supposed to guard the access to Spain, but sometimes it didn't perform that task too well.

What to See & Do

The most interesting part of town is the **medieval quarter** in the upper market. Some of the villas here date from the early 17th century. The fishing district, in the lower part of town, is called **La Marina:** old homes, painted boats, and the general marine atmosphere attract many visitors. Since restaurants in Fuenterrabía tend to be very expensive, you can fill up here on seafood tapas in the many taverns along the waterfront. The beach at Fuenterrabía is wide and sandy, and many prefer it to the more famous ones at San Sebastián.

Wander for an hour or two around the old quarter, taking in the Calle Mayor, Calle Tiendas y Pampinot, and Calle Obispo. The **Castillo de Carlos V,** standing at the Plaza de las Armas, has been turned into one of the smallest and most desirable paradores in Spain (see below). It's hard to get a room here unless you reserve well in advance, but you can visit the well-stocked bar over the entrance hall.

Sancho Abarca, a king of Navarre in the 10th century, is supposed to have founded the original castle that stood on this spot. The present look owes more to Charles V in the 16th century. You can still see the battle scars on the castle that date from the time of the Napoleonic invasion of Spain.

The most impressive church in the old quarter is the **Iglesia de Santa María,** a Gothic structure that was vastly restored in the 17th century and given a baroque tower. The proxy wedding of Louis XIV and the Infanta María Teresa took place here in June 1660.

If you have a car, you can take some interesting trips in the area, especially to **Cabo Higuer,** a promontory with spectacular views, reached by going 2½ miles (4km) north. Leave by the harbor and beach road. You can see the French coast and the town of Hendaye from this cape.

You can also head west out of town along the **Jaizkibel Road,** which many motorists prefer at sunset. After going three miles (4.8km), you'll reach the shrine of the Virgin of Guadalupe, where a panoramic view unfolds. From here you can see the French Basque coast. Even better views await you if you continue along to the Hostal Jaizkibel. If you stay on this road, you will come to the little fishing village of Pasai Donibane (see the "Easy Excursions" from San Sebastián), 11 miles (18km) away.

Where to Stay

Hotel Pampinot, Kale Nagusia, Calle Mayor, 3, 20280 Fuenterrabía. **☎ 943/64-06-00.** Fax 943/64-51-28. 5 rms (all with bath), 3 suites. TV TEL

Rates: 12,000–14,000 ptas. ($85.20–$99.40) single; 14,000–17,000 ptas. ($99.40–$120.70) double; from 17,000 ptas. ($120.70) suite. Breakfast 1,100 ptas. ($7.80) extra. DC, MC, V. **Closed:** Feb.

If the walls here could talk, they would probably reveal more tales than those of any other hotel in the region. Originally built as an aristocratic mansion in 1587, it sheltered for a night the Infanta María Teresa during her trip toward France and her eventual marriage with the Sun King, Louis XIV. Today, it presents a richly textured stone facade with Renaissance detailing and heraldic symbols to one of the most historic and quiet streets of the old town. Inside, an antique sense of elegance is conveyed by beamed ceilings, exposed stonework, parquet flooring, and ornate ironwork. The guest rooms are traditional and charming, with a mixture of antique and reproduction furniture.

Dining/Entertainment: Although breakfast is the only meal served, the staff can direct you to a choice of nearby eateries.

Services: Laundry, concierge, babysitting.

Facilities: Car rentals.

Jáuregui, San Pedro, 28, 20280 Fuenterrabía. ☎ **943/64-14-00.** Fax 943/64-44-04. 53 rms (all with bath). TV TEL

Rates: 7,400 ptas. ($52.50) single; 10,580 ptas. ($75.10) double. Breakfast 640 ptas. ($4.50) extra. AE, DC, MC, V. **Parking:** 600 ptas. ($4.30).

Opened in 1981 in the center of the old village, this is a good choice for moderately priced accommodations. The modern interior boasts comfortable accessories, and the hotel also has a garage—a definite plus, since parking in Fuenterrabía is virtually impossible. Each of the rooms is well furnished and maintained; thoughtful extras include a hairdryer in each bathroom and a shoeshine machine on each floor. Only breakfast is served.

Parador de Hondarribía, Plaza de Armas, 20280 Fuenterrabía. ☎ **943/64-55-00.** Fax 943/64-21-53. 16 rms (all with bath). TEL

Rates: 11,000 ptas. ($78.10) single; 15,000 ptas. ($106.50) double. Breakfast 1,200 ptas. ($8.50) extra. AE, DC, MC, V. **Parking:** Free.

This beautifully restored 10th-century castle situated on a hill in the center of the old town was once used by Emperor Charles V as a border fortification. The building itself is impressive, and so are the taste and imagination of the restoration: Antiques, old weapons, and standards hang from the high-vaulted ceilings. Some of the comfortable provincial-style rooms open onto the Bay of Biscay. Breakfast is the only meal served. Ample parking is available out front. It's best to reserve well in advance.

Where to Dine

★ **Ramón Roteta,** Villa Alnara. ☎ **64-16-93.**

Cuisine: BASQUE. **Reservations:** Recommended.
Prices: Appetizers 900–2,000 ptas. ($6.40–$14.20); main courses 2,200–3,100 ptas. ($15.60–$22). AE, MC, V.
Open: Lunch, Fri–Wed 1–3:30pm; dinner, Mon–Wed and Fri–Sat 8–11pm.

Named after its owner and founder, this attractively furnished restaurant is considered one of Europe's most consistently respected purveyors of traditional Basque cuisine. Contained within what was originally a 1920s private villa, it lies in the southern outskirts of town, near the local parador and the city limits of Irún. Menu specialties include a terrine of green vegetables and fish served with red-pepper-flavored vinaigrette; baked sea crabs with tiny potatoes and onions; fresh pasta with seafood; and the dessert specialty, a mandarin-orange tart flavored with rose petals. The villa is surrounded by a pleasantly unstructured garden.

Sebastián, Mayor, 7. ☎ **64-01-67.**

Cuisine: BASQUE. **Reservations:** Required.
Prices: Appetizers 750–1,300 ptas. ($5.30–$9.20); main courses 1,300–2,900 ptas. ($9.20–$20.60) fixed-price menus 4,000–4,500 ptas. ($28.40–$32). AE, MC, V.
Open: Lunch, Tues–Sun 1–3:30pm; dinner, Tues–Sat 8:30–11pm. **Closed:** Nov.

Lying within the oldest district of Fuenterrabía, close to the castle, this restaurant offers modern cuisine, well presented and using top-notch ingredients appropriate to the season. On two floors, the milieu is a sheltering one, with thick masonry walls; among them are scattered an array of 18th-century paintings. Try one of the specialties: foie gras of duckling Basque style, terrine of fresh mushrooms, or médaillons of sole and salmon with seafood sauce.

3 Ondárroa

30 miles (48km) W of San Sebastián, 38 miles (61km) E of Bilbao, 265 miles (427km) N of Madrid

GETTING THERE • By Bus From San Sebastián, Ondárroa is serviced by buses that run along the Costa Vasca.

• By Car Head west from Zarauz along the coastal road.

ESSENTIALS The area code for Ondárroa is 94.

Ondárroa is described as a *pueblo típico,* a typical Basque fishing village. It is also the area's largest fishing port. Lying on a spit of land, it stands between a hill and a loop of the Artibay River. Laundry hangs from the windows of the little plant-filled balconied Basque houses, and most of the residents are engaged in canning and fish salting, if not fishing. The local church looks like a ship's prow at one end. Around the snug harbor you'll find many little places to drink and dine after taking a stroll through the village.

Where to Stay

Hotel/Restaurant Vega, Calle Antigua, 8, 48700 Ondárroa. ☎ **94/683-00-02.** 22 rms (5 with bath).

Rates: 2,300 ptas. ($16.30) single without bath; 4,500 ptas. ($32) double without bath; 5,500 ptas. ($39.10) double with bath. Breakfast 450 ptas. ($3.20) extra. AE, V. **Parking:** Free.

In the center of town is a real find, offering comfortable and simple rooms for reasonable prices year round. It is the only hostal of note in town, and the setting is pleasant.

The dining room serves a well-prepared *menú del día* for 1,200 pesetas ($8.50). Veal, fish, fried beef, and fish soup are typical. The restaurant is open daily from 1:30 to 3:30pm and 8 to 11pm (Friday to Wednesday in winter); it's closed for the month of October.

Where to Dine

Restaurant Penalty, Eribera, 32. ☎ **683-00-00.**

Cuisine: SEAFOOD. **Reservations:** Required.
Prices: Appetizers 500–750 ptas. ($3.60–$5.30); main courses 1,800–2,200 ptas. ($12.80–$15.60). No credit cards.
Open: Lunch, Thurs–Tues 1:30–3:30pm; dinner, daily Thurs–Tues 8:30–11:30pm.
Closed: Dec and Jan.

This small restaurant, with a limited number of tables, stands at a crossroads at the edge of town. Meals might include a house recipe for hake that is simply heavenly, plus other fish specialties. The *sopa de pescado* (fish soup) invariably makes a good choice for a beginning to a fine meal.

4 Lekeitio

38 miles (61km) W of San Sebastián, 37 miles (60km) E of Bilbao, 280 miles (451km) N of Madrid

GETTING THERE • By Bus Six buses a day connect Lekeitio with Bilbao (1½ hours away), and four buses a day run from San Sebastián (1½ hours away).

• **By Car** From Ondárroa, take the coastal road northwest along the Costa Vasca.

ESSENTIALS The area code for Lekeitio is 94.

This unspoiled Basque fishing village that everybody talks about is most often visited on a day trip. There are those who consider it "more authentic" than Ondárroa, the more obvious choice. At the foot of Mount Calvario, Lekeitio opens onto a deeply indented bay. Queen Isabella II first gave the town prominence when she spent time here in the 19th century. Fishing may have diminished in recent years, but Lekeitio is still home to some of the Basque coast's trawlers. The island of San Nicolás converts the bay into a naturally protected harbor, a phenomenon that led to the village's growth.

A beach lies across from the harbor, but the one at Carraspio, farther along the bay, is considered safer. Note the **church** from the 15th century "guarding" the harbor. Three tiers of flying buttresses characterize this monument, which has a baroque belfry. Go inside to the third south chapel, of the right nave, to see a remarkable altarpiece, *The Road to Calvary*, which was erected in a flamboyant Gothic style.

The town is noted for its **festivals,** including the feast day of Saints Peter and Paul on June 29, at which a *Kaxarranca,* a Basque folk dance, takes place. A dancer leaps about on top of a trunk carried through the streets by some hearty Basque fishermen. Even better known is the controversial Jaiak San Antolín, or goose festival on September 1 to 8. A gruesome custom, it involves hanging live geese in the harbor. Youths leap from row boats to grab the greased necks of the geese. Both youth and goose are dunked into the water, using a system of pulleys, until the youth cries uncle or the neck of the goose is wrenched off. Perhaps you'll want to skip this one. The candlelit march through the streets, with everyone dressed in white, does not mourn the unfortunate geese but signals the end of the festival.

Where to Dine

Restaurante Egaña, Santa Catalina, 4. ☎ **684-01-03.**

Cuisine: SEAFOOD. **Reservations:** Not required.

Prices: Appetizers 550–750 ptas. ($3.90–$5.30); main courses 750–1,200 ptas. ($5.30–$8.50); *menú del día* 850 ptas. ($6). AE, V.

Open: Lunch, Tues–Sun 1–4pm; dinner, Tues–Sun 8–10:30pm.

In a spacious, breezy dining room on the upper side of the village, devotees of Basque seafood get their fill. The portions are large and generous, and the price is right. The place is unfussy and unpretentious: You are here to eat without frills. The menu depends on the catch of the day. Try the Basque-style hake.

5 Guernica

266 miles (428km) N of Madrid, 52 miles (84km) W of San Sebastián

GETTING THERE • **By Train** From San Sebastián, trains run three times daily to Guernica. Change at Amorebieta.

• **By Bus** Vascongados, Estación de Amara in San Sebastián, runs buses to Bilbao, with connections to Guernica. Inquire at the station.

• **By Car** Guernica is a 20-minute drive beyond Bermeo on the C-6315.

ESSENTIALS The area code for Guernica is 94.

The subject of Picasso's most famous painting (returned to Spain from the United States and displayed at the Thyssen-Bornemisza Museum in Madrid), Guernica, the spiritual home of the Basques and the seat of Basque nationalism, was destroyed in a Nazi air raid on April 26, 1937. It was the site of a revered oak tree, under whose branches Basques had elected their officials since medieval times. No one knows how many died during the 3 1/2 hour attack—estimates range from 200 to 2,000. The bombers reduced the town to rubble, but a mighty symbol of independence had been born.

The town has been attractively rebuilt, close to its former style. The chimes of a church ring softly, and laughing children play in the street. In the midst of this peace, however, you'll suddenly come upon a sign: "Souvenirs . . . Remember."

What to See & Do

The former Basque parliament, the **Casa de Juntas** (or *Juntetxea*), is the principal attraction in the town, containing a historical display of Guernica. It is open daily from 10am to 2pm and 4 to 7pm in summer (to 6pm in winter). Admission is free. Outside are the remains of the ancient communal oak tree, symbol of Basque independence; it was not uprooted by Hitler's bombs. From the train station, head up the Calle Urioste.

Where to Dine

Asador Zaldua, Sabino Arana, 10. ☎ **687-08-71.**

Cuisine: BASQUE. **Reservations:** Required in summer. **Directions:** Lies 5 1/2 miles (9km) north of Guernica.

Prices: Appetizers 850–1,200 ptas. ($6–$8.50); main courses 1,800–3,500 ptas. ($12.80–$24.90); *menú del día* 2,000 ptas. ($14.20). AE, DC, MC, V.

Open: Lunch, daily 1:30–3:30pm; dinner, Mon–Sat 9–11pm. **Closed:** Mid–Dec to Jan 31.

Most of the specialties served here come from the blazing grill, whose turning spits are visible from the dining room. A wide array of seafood and fish is also available, some dishes baked to a flaky goodness in a layer of rock salt. The restaurant lies north of the center of town on the road to Bermeo.

6 Bilbao

246 miles (396km) N of Madrid, 62 miles (100km) W of San Sebastián

GETTING THERE • By Plane Bilbao Airport (**453-13-50**) lies 5 miles (8km) north of the city, near the town of Erandio. From the airport into town take red bus A3247. Flights arrive from Madrid, Barcelona, Alicante, Arrecife, Fuenteventura, Las Palmas, Málaga, Palma, Santiago de Compostela, Sevilla, Tenerife, Valencia, Vigo, Brussels, Frankfurt, Lisbon, London, Milan, Paris, and Zurich. Iberia's main booking office in Bilbao is at Ercilla, 20 (☎ **424-43-00**).

• By Train The RENFE Station, Estación de Abando (☎ **423-86-23**), is on the Hurtado de Amézaga, just off the Plaza de España, in Bilbao. From here, you can catch short-distance trains within the metropolitan area of Bilbao, and long-distance trains to most parts of Spain. From this station, two trains per day run to and from Madrid (6 hours away in the afternoon train, and 7 hours away in the night train); two trains per day run to and from Barcelona (11 hours away), and two trains per day run to and from Galicia (12 hours away). There are also two night trains per week running to and from the Mediterranean Coast: one toward Alicante and Valencia (this train runs daily during peak seasons), and the other toward Málaga (this runs three times per week during peak season).

• **By Bus** PESA, Calle Hurtado de Amézaga (☎ **416-94-79**), at the Estación Abando, operates buses to and from San Sebastián, more than a dozen per day (trip time: 1¼ hours), costing 880 pesetas ($6.20) one way. ANSA, Calle Autonomía, 17 (☎ **444-31-00**), has services from Madrid at the rate of nine buses per day (trip time: 5 hours), a one-way ticket costing 2,950 pesetas ($20.90). It also has four buses per day running to and from Barcelona (trip time: 7 hours), costing 4,760 pesetas ($33.80) for a one-way ticket. If you'd like to explore either Lekeitio or Guernica (see above) by bus, use the services of CAV, Plaza Encarnación, 7 (☎ **433-12-79**). From Monday through Saturday, it operates seven buses per day to Lekeitio and only two on Sunday. Trip time is 45 minutes, a one-way ticket costing 455 pesetas ($3.20). From Monday through Friday it runs ten buses to Guernica (trip time: 45 minutes), a one-way ticket costing 260 pesetas ($1.80). On weekends, only five buses per day go to Guernica.

• **By Car** Bilbao lies beside the A-8, linking the cities of Spain's northern Atlantic seacoast to the western edge of France. It is connected by superhighway to both Barcelona and Madrid.

ESSENTIALS The area code for Bilbao is 94. The tourist information office is at Plaza Arriaga, s/n (☎ **94/416-00-22**). The Post Office is at Alameda de Urquijo, 15. (☎ **422-05-48**).

Bilbao is often described as an "ugly, gray, decaying, smokestack city," and so it is—in part. But it has a number of interesting secrets to reveal, as well as a good-quality cuisine, and it is a rail hub and a center for exploring some of the best attractions in the Basque country if you're dependent on public transport. Most of its own attractions can be viewed in a day.

It is Spain's sixth-largest city, its biggest port (with hundreds of skycranes), the industrial hub of the north, and the political capital of the Basques. Shipping, shipbuilding, and steelmaking have made it prosperous. Many bankers and industrialists live here. Its commercial heart contains skyscrapers and hums with activity. Among cities of the Basque region, it has the highest population (around 450,000); the metropolitan area, including the suburbs and many surrounding towns, takes in one million inhabitants.

Bilbao has a wide-open feeling, extending more than 5 miles (8km) across the valley of the Nervión River, one of Spain's most polluted waterways. Many buildings wear a layer of grime. Some visitors compare Bilbao to England—not the England of hills and vales, but rather the sooty postindustrial sprawl of an English port town. (Because of the interconnected interests of coal and iron, in fact, there has always been English commerce here, and even English schools and pubs.) Surrounding the city's central core are slums and heavily polluting factories. There's a feeling of decay here, not to mention political unrest from the Basque separatist movement. These factors, plus the frequent rainfall, do not place Bilbao on the major touristic maps of Europe or even of Spain.

The city was established by a charter dated June 15, 1300, which converted it from a village (*pueblo*), ruled by local feudal duke Don Diego López de Haro, into a city. Aided by water power and the transportation potential of the Nervión River, it grew and grew, most of its fame and glory coming during the industrial expansion of the

19th century. Many grand homes and villas for industrialists were constructed at that time. (Its wealthiest suburb is Neguri.) The most famous son of Bilbao was Miguel de Unamuno, the writer and educator, more closely associated with Salamanca.

The hardworking Basques of Bilbao, who have a rough-and-ready, no-nonsense approach to life, like to have a good time. *Festivals* often fill the calendar, the biggest and most widely publicized being La Semana Grande, dedicated to the Virgin of Begoña and lasting from mid-August until early September. During this time, the Nervión River is the site of many flotillas and regattas. July 25 brings the festival of Bilbao's patron saint, Santiago (St. James), whereas July 31 is the holiday devoted to the region's patron saint, St. Ignatius.

CITY LAYOUT The River Nervión meanders through Bilbao, whose historic core was built inside one of its loops, with water protecting it on three sides. Most of the important shops; banks, and tourist facilities lie within a short walk of the **Gran Via,** running east-west through the heart of town. The old quarter lies east of the modern commercial center, across the river. It and the shop-flanked Gran Vía on the western edge form an east-west axis upon which are located most of the major attractions.

What to See & Do

Museo de Bellas Artes, Plaza del Museo, 2. ☎ **441-95-36.**

This is considered one of Spain's most important art museums, containing both medieval and modern works, including paintings by Velázquez, Goya, Zurbarán, and El Greco. Among the works of non-Spanish artists are *The Money Changers* by the Flemish painter Quentin Metsys and *The Lamentation Over Christ* by Anthony van Dyck. In its modern wing, the museum contains works by Gauguin, Picasso, Léger, Sorolla, and American Mary Cassatt. The gallery is particularly strong in 19th- and 20th-century Basque artists, the foremost of which is the modern sculptor Chillida, who created a massive piece entitled *Monument to Iron.* If you tire of looking at the art, you can walk in the English-inspired gardens around the museum.

Admission: Free.

Open: Tues–Sat 10am–1:30pm and 4–7:30pm; Sun 10am–2pm.

Euskal Arkeologia, Etnografia Eta Kondaira-Museoa, Cruz, 4. ☎ **415-54-23.**

In the center of the old quarter, south of Calle Esperanza Ascao, this museum—devoted to Basque archeology, ethnology, and history—is contained within a centuries-old Jesuit cloister. Some of the exhibits showcase Basque commercial life during the 16th century. You see everything from ship models to shipbuilding tools, along with reconstructions of rooms illustrating political and social life. Basque gravestones are also on view. You'll also see the equipment used to play the popular Basque game of *pelota.*

Admission: Free.

Open: Tues–Sat 10:30am–1:30pm and 4–7pm; Sun 10:30am–1:30pm.

Casco Viejo [Old Quarter], east side of Nervión River.

Despite Bilbao's establishment around 1300, it is curiously scarce in medieval monuments. It does have this old quarter, however, site of its most intriguing bars and restaurants. The custom is to go here at night and bar-hop, ordering small cups of beer or wine. A small glass of wine is called a *chiquiteo.*

The old quarter of Bilbao is connected by four bridges to the much larger modern section on the opposite bank. A few paces north of the old quarter's center lie the graceful arches, 64 in all, enclosing Plaza Nueva, also called Plaza de los Martires, completed in 1830.

The entire barrio has been declared a national landmark. It originally defined an area around seven streets, but it long ago spilled beyond that limitation. Every Sunday at 8am a flea market is held on the streets of the old quarter. Its most important church is the **Church of St. Nicolás.** Behind this church you'll find an elevator on Calle Esperanza Ascao, which, if working, carries sightseers to the upper town. You can also climb 64 steps from Plaza Unamuno. From there it's a short walk to the **Basílica de Begoña,** built largely in the early 1500s. Inside the dimly lit church, there is a brightly illuminated depiction of the Virgin, dressed in long, flowing robes. She is the patroness of the province. Also displayed are some enormous paintings by Luca Giordano.

While in the old town, you might also visit the **Cathedral of Santiago,** Plaza Santiago, which was originally built in the 14th century, then restored in the 16th century after a fire. The facade was later rebuilt in the 19th century.

To reach the old town on foot, the only way to explore it, take the Puente del Arenal from the Gran Vía, the main street of Bilbao.

Where to Stay

EXPENSIVE

Gran Hotel Ercilla, Ercilla, 37-39, 48011 Bilbao. ☎ **94/410-20-00.** Fax 94/443-93-35. 338 rms, 7 suites. A/C MINIBAR TV TEL

Rates: 14,440 ptas. ($102.50) single; 22,855 ptas. ($162.30) double; 26,900 ptas. ($191) triple; 28,875–49,350 ptas. ($205–$350.40) suite. Breakfast 1,440 ptas. ($10.20) extra. AE, DC, MC, V. **Parking:** 1,550 ptas. ($11).

Soaring high above the buildings surrounding it and located in the heart of Bilbao's business district, this is a tastefully decorated bastion of attentive service and good living. The guest rooms—all with private baths—are conservative and comfortably furnished, usually with coordinated schemes of pink, blue, or earth tones. Completely renovated in 1989 and 1990, the Ercilla is considered one of Bilbao's most desirable hotels, usually the preferred choice of Spanish politicians, movie stars, and journalists away from home.

Dining/Entertainment: The Restaurant Bermeo, specializing in Basque cuisine, is known as one of the best restaurants in Bilbao. See "Where to Dine," below. Adjacent to it is an American-inspired bar (with an English-inspired decor) providing a peaceful haven with its richly grained hardwood paneling. There are also an informal and stylishly modern snack bar, the Ercilla (open daily from 7am to 2am), and a high-tech, high-energy disco, the Bocaccio.

Services: 24-hour room service, concierge, laundry/valet, babysitting.

Facilities: Business center, car-rental, safety-deposit boxes, shopping boutiques.

★ **Hotel López de Haro,** Obispo Orueta 2, 48000 Bilbao. ☎ **94/423-55-00.** Fax 94/423-45-00. 49 rms, 5 suites. A/C MINIBAR TV TEL

Rates: 25,300 ptas. ($179.60) single; 35,650 ptas. ($253.10) double; from 48,300 ptas. ($342.90) suite. Breakfast 1,850 ptas. ($13.10) extra. AE, DC, MC, V. **Parking:** 1,600 ptas. ($11.40).

Behind a discreet facade of chiseled gray stone and filled with English touches, this 1990 six-story hotel maintains an elegance that includes marble flooring, hardwood paneling, and a uniformed staff. The comfortable guest rooms are accessorized with flowered or striped upholstery, modern private bath, and wall-to-wall carpets and/or hardwood floors.

Dining/Entertainment: The hotel's two restaurants are the Club Nautico (recommended below) and El Ambigu Orueta: Both provide gracious havens for good food and service. In El Ambigu, three-course fixed-price meals, served with flair, cost 5,200 pesetas ($36.90) each. A luxurious English-inspired cocktail bar lies nearby.

Services: 24-hour room service, laundry/valet, available limousines, concierge, babysitting.

Facilities: Car rentals.

MODERATE

Avenida, Zumalacárregui, 40, 48007 Bilbao. ☎ **94/412-43-00.** Fax 94/411-46-17. 116 rms (all with bath). TV TEL **Bus:** 48.

Rates: 7,700–8,700 ptas. ($54.70–$61.80) single; 10,900 ptas. ($77.40) double. Breakfast 850 ptas. ($6) extra. AE, MC, V. **Parking:** Free.

For those who want to be away from the center, and don't mind a bus or taxi ride or two, this is a welcoming choice. It lies in the Barrio de Begoña, near one of the major religious monuments of Bilbao, the Basílica de Begoña. Rising five floors, it was built in the late 1960s. Rooms, furnished in a sober, functional modern style, are well kept and maintained. The hotel has a garden and a helpful staff. During special fairs in Bilbao, rates are increased by at least 10%.

BUDGET

Roquefer, Lotería, 2–4, 48005 Bilbao. ☎ **94/415-07-55.** 18 rms (6 with bath).

Rates: 1,700 ptas. ($12.10) single without bath; 2,500 ptas. ($17.80) single with bath; 2,800 ptas. ($19.90) double without bath; 3,500 ptas. ($24.90) double with bath. No credit cards.

If you'd like to live in the old quarter and avoid the high prices of business-client hotels, this is a basic choice, suitable for a stopover. Rooms are simple and furnished in a functional style. You'll be in the center of the tasca-and-restaurant district for nighttime prowls. To reach the hotel, take the bridge, the Puente del Arenal, across the river to the old town.

WHERE TO DINE

Expensive

Guría, Gran Vía de López de Haro, 66. ☎ **441-05-43.**

Cuisine: BASQUE. **Reservations:** Required.
Prices: Appetizers 1,300–3,000 ptas. ($9.20–$21.30); main courses 1,800–4,600 ptas. ($12.80–$32); fixed-price menus 5,800–8,000 ptas. ($41.20–$56.80). AE, DC, MC, V.
Open: Lunch, Mon–Sat 1:30–4pm; dinner, Mon–Sat 8:30pm–midnight. **Closed:** Last week of July; first week of Aug.

One of the most venerated restaurants of Bilbao, the air-conditioned Guría is expensive—and worth it, say its devotees. The chef shows care and concern for his guests, serving only market-fresh ingredients. He is celebrated for his bacalao (codfish), which he prepares in many ways. Try his sea bass with saffron as an alternative or his loin of beef cooked in sherry. A slightly caloric but divine dessert is *espuma de chocolat.*

Restaurant Bermeo, Gran Hotel Ercilla, Ercilla, 37. ☎ **410-20-00.**

Cuisine: BASQUE. **Reservations:** Required.
Prices: Appetizers 1,500–2,850 ptas. ($10.70–$20.20); main courses 1,875–3,675 ptas. ($13.30–$26.10); fixed-price menu 5,500 ptas. ($39.10). AE, DC, MC, V.
Open: Lunch, Sun–Fri 1–4pm; dinner, Mon–Sat 7:30–11pm.

Considered one of the finest hotel restaurants in all of Spain and one of the finest representatives of Basque cuisine anywhere in the world, the Bermeo caters to a clientele of the Basque world's most influential politicians, writers, and social luminaries. Contained within the modern walls of one of Bilbao's tallest hotels, the establishment is decorated in richly conservative glowing wood panels, crisp linens, and copies of 19th-century antiques. The service from the uniformed and formal staff is impeccable. Menu items change with the seasons but might include a salad of lettuce hearts in saffron dressing with smoked salmon, homemade foie gras scented with essence of bay leaves, fresh thistles sautéed with ham, five preparations of codfish, stewed partridge with glazed shallots, and filets of duckling with green peppercorns. For dessert, try the truffled figs or a slice of bilberry pie with cream.

Restaurant Club Nautico, in the Hotel López de Haro, Obispo Orueta, 2. ☎ **423-55-00.**

Cuisine: BASQUE. **Reservations:** Recommended.
Prices: Appetizers 1,250–3,550 ptas. ($8.90–$25.20); main courses 1,850–7,000 ptas. ($13.10–$49.70); fixed-price menus 5,000–10,500 ptas. ($35.50–$74.60). AE, DC, MC, V.
Open: Lunch, Mon–Fri 12:30–3:30pm; dinner, Mon–Sat 7–10:30pm.

Considered one of the finest and most prestigious restaurants in the Basque world, the elegantly decorated Club Nautico lies within a previously recommended hotel. Featuring the cuisine of Alberto Zuluaga, one of the most publicized culinary luminaries of northern Spain, the restaurant offers an impeccably uniformed staff and formal tables set with some of the finest china, crystal, and silverware available. Menu specialties include succulent local artichokes stuffed with foie gras, poached eggs with beluga caviar and oyster sauce, lobster sautéed with artichokes and balsamic vinegar, baked sea bass with béarnaise sauce, sautéed scallops with truffle sauce, and roast beef with a purée of radishes. A superb array of Spanish and international wines are available by either the glass or the bottle.

MODERATE

Matxinbenta, Ladesma, 26. ☎ **424-84-95.**

Cuisine: BASQUE. **Reservations:** Required.
Prices: Appetizers 850–1,600 ptas. ($6–$11.40); main courses 2,000–2,550 ptas. ($14.20–$18.10); *menú del día* 4,000 ptas. ($28.40). AE, DC, MC, V.
Open: Lunch, Mon–Sat 1–4pm; dinner, Mon–Sat 8–11:30pm.

Serving some of the finest Basque food in the city since the 1950s, this restaurant, one block north of the Gran Vía, is popular for business lunches or dinners. Specialties include fresh tuna in piquant tomato sauce and a local version of ratatouille known as *piperada.* You can also order veal cutlets cooked in port wine and finish with a mint-flavored fresh-fruit cocktail. The service is excellent.

INEXPENSIVE

Restaurante Begoña, Virgen de Begoña, s/n. ☎ **412-72-57.**

Cuisine: BASQUE. **Reservations:** Recommended. **Bus:** 48.
Prices: Appetizers 550–1,050 ptas. ($3.90–$7.50); main courses 1,200–2,800 ptas. ($8.50–$19.90). AE, MC, V.
Open: Lunch, Mon–Sat 1:30–3:30pm; dinner, Mon–Sat 9–11pm. **Closed:** Aug.

At this tranquil choice, near the famous Basilica de Begoña, lying on the eastern bank of the river, the chef combines classic dishes with those of the modern repertoire, and he does so in imaginative ways. Specialties include stuffed onions, loin of pork, and sea bass with *fines herbes.* The relation of food quality to price is correct, and the wine cellar offers prestigious vintages at competitive rates. The service is attentive.

7 Vitoria [Gasteiz]

41 miles (66km) S of Bilbao, 71 miles (114km) SW of San Sebastián, 218 miles (351km) N of Madrid

GETTING THERE • By Plane Vitoria Airport (☎ **16-35-00**), five miles (8km) northwest of the town center, has domestic air links to and from Madrid. The sales office for Iberia Airlines is at Avenida de Gasteiz, 50 bis (☎ **22-82-50**) or at the airport. There are air links, via Air Europa, to Málaga, Palma de Majorca, and Tenerife in the Canary Islands. The sales office for Air Europa is at Viajes Halcon, Calle Tomás de Zumarraga, 34 (☎ **24-97-00**), or at the airport.

• By Train From San Sebastián, 16 trains daily make the two-hour trip to Vitoria. For information, call **23-02-02.**

• By Bus From San Sebastián, four buses daily make the 1½ hour trip. Bus connections are also possible through Bilbao (8 to 12 buses daily make the 1-hour trip).

• By Car Take the N-1 north from Madrid to Burgos, cutting northwest until you see the turnoff for Vitoria.

ESSENTIALS The area code for Vitoria is 945. The tourist information office is at Parque de la Florida (% 945/13-13-21).

Quiet and sleepy until the early 1980s, Vitoria was chosen as headquarters of the Basque region's autonomous government. In honor of that occasion, it revived the name Gasteiz, by which it was known when founded in 1181 by King Sancho of Navarre. Far more enduring, however, has been the name Vitoria, a battle site revered by the English. On June 21, 1813, Wellington won here against the occupying forces of Napoleon. A statue dedicated to the Iron Duke stands today on the neoclassical Plaza de la Virgen Blanca.

Shortly after its founding, the city became a rich center for the wool and iron trades, and this wealth paid for the fine churches and palaces in the medieval quarter. Many of the city's buildings are made of gray-gold stone. There is a university, whose students keep the taverns rowdy until the wee hours.

What to See & Do

The most important sight in Vitoria is the **medieval district,** whose Gothic buildings were built on a series of steps and terraces. Most of the streets are arranged in concentric ovals and are named after medieval artisan guilds. The northern end is marked by the Cathedral of Santa María, its southern flank by the Church of San Miguel.

One of the barrio's most interesting streets is **Calle Cuchillaría,** which contains many medieval buildings. You can enter the courtyard at no. 24, the Casa del Cordón, which was constructed in different stages from the 13th to the 16th century. Number 58, the Bendana Palace, built in the 15th century, has a fine ornate staircase set into its courtyard.

The **Cathedral of Santa María** (the "old" cathedral), Calle Fray Zacaras, was built in the 14th century in the Gothic style. It contains a good art collection, with paintings that imitate various schools, including those of van Dyck, Caravaggio, and Rubens, as well as several tombs carved in a highly decorated Plateresque style. Santa María lies at the northern edge of the old town.

This cathedral is not to be confused with the town's enormous "new" cathedral on Avenida Magdalena, just north of the Jardines la Florida and built in a Neo-Gothic style.

The major historic square is the **Plaza de la Virgen Blanca,** a short walk south of the Gothic quarter. Its neoclassical balconies overlook the statue of Wellington. The square is named after the late-Gothic polychrome statue of the Virgen Blanca (the town's patron) that adorns the portico of the 13th-century **Church of San Miguel,** which stands on the square's upper edge. The 17th-century altarpiece inside was carved by Gregoria Hernández.

At **Plaza de España** (also known as Plaza Nueva), a satellite square a short walk away, the student population of Vitoria congregates to drink.

Vitoria has some minor museums, which are free. **Museo de Arqueología de Álava,** Correría, 116 (☎ **14-23-10**), behind a half-timbered facade, exhibits artifacts such as pottery shards and statues that were unearthed from digs in the area. Some of these are from Celto-Iberian days as well as from the Roman era.

The museum is open Tuesday to Friday from 11am to 2pm and 4 to 6:30pm, Saturday from 11am to 2pm.

Museo de Bellas Artes de Álava, Palacio de Agustín, Paseo de Fray Francisco, 8 (☎ **23-17-77**), has a collection of several unusual weapons, a *Crucifixion* and portraits of Saints Peter and Paul by Ribera, and a triptych by the Master of Ávila. It is open Tuesday to Friday from 11am to 2pm and 4 to 6:30pm, Saturday from 11am to 2pm; it's closed in November.

Where to Stay

$ **Achuri,** Rioja, 11, 01005 Vitoria. ☎ **945/25-58-00.** Fax 945/26-40-74. 40 rms (all with bath). TEL

Rates: 3,600 ptas. ($25.60) single; 5,800 ptas. ($41.20) double. Breakfast 375 ptas. ($2.70) extra. DC, V.

This is an attractively priced modern hotel with a welcoming style. A short walk from the train station, it offers tidy and comfortably furnished bedrooms. Breakfast is the only meal available, but you'll find several places serving food in the vicinity.

$ **Hotel Dato,** Eduardo Dato, 28, 01005 Vitoria. ☎ **945/23-23-20.** Fax 945/24-23-22. 14 rms (all with bath). TV TEL

Rates: 3,948 ptas. ($28) single; 4,939 ptas. ($35.10) double. AE, DC, MC, V. **Parking:** Meters on street.

Lying three blocks south of the southern extremity of the old town in the pedestrian zone, this hotel has firmly established itself as the best budget establishment in town.

It has modern decor and amenities but only a few bedrooms—so reservations are wise. No breakfast is served.

Hotel General Álava, Gasteiz, 79, 01009 Vitoria, ☎ **945/22-22-00.** Fax 945/24-83-95. 114 rms, 1 suite (all with bath). TV TEL

Rates: 6,700–7,700 ptas. ($47.60–$54.70) single; 10,400–11,300 ptas. ($73.80–$80.20) double. Suites 20,000 ptas. ($142). Breakfast 750 ptas. ($5.30) extra. AE, DC, MC, V. **Parking:** 800 ptas. ($5.70).

Named after a local hero—a Spanish general who won an important battle against the French in 1815—this hotel is considered one of the best and most comfortably furnished in town. Built in 1975, it attracts scores of business travelers from throughout Spain. It does not maintain a formal restaurant, but rather a well-managed bistro (open only Monday to Friday) where fixed-price menus cost 1,415 pesetas ($10); and where *platos del día* are usually priced between 750 pesetas ($5.30) and 1,300 pesetas ($9.20). The hotel lies a 10-minute walk west of the town center, near the junction of Calle Chile.

Hotel Residencia Gasteiz, Avenida Gasteiz, 45, 01009 Vitoria (Gasteiz). ☎ **945/22-81-00.** Fax 945/22-62-58. 146 rms (all with bath), 4 suites. A/C MINIBAR TV TEL

Rates: Mon–Thurs, 9,600 ptas. ($68.20) single; 14,000 ptas. ($99.40) double; 24,000 ptas. ($170.40) suite. Fri–Sun, room and suite prices reduced 50%. Breakfast buffet 1,200 ptas. ($8.50) extra. AE, DC, MC, V. **Parking:** 1,300 ptas. ($9.20).

Located on the eastern flank of the broad, tree-lined boulevard that circumnavigates the old town, this is the most modern and solidly reliable hotel around. Built in 1982, it was completely renovated in 1994. Although not architecturally distinguished, it serves as the preferred meeting point for the city's business community, offering conservative bedrooms with uncomplicated furnishings and a series of comfortable (albeit undramatic) public rooms.

Dining/Entertainment: The Restaurant Artagnan, specializing in Basque and international cuisine, serves a set menu for 1,750 pesetas ($12.40), with à la carte dinners averaging 3,500 pesetas ($24.90). The restaurant, not the hotel, is closed every Sunday and from August 10 to September 10. There are also an American-inspired bar and a disco.

Services: Room service (available daily from 7am to midnight), laundry, concierge, babysitting.

Facilities: Car rentals.

Where to Dine

As in Bilbao, tasca-hopping before dinner, with the consumption of many small glasses *(chiquiteos)* of beer or wine at many different bars and taverns, is popular and fun. There are a number of places on the Avenida de Gasteiz.

$ **Mesa,** Calle Chile, 1. ☎ **22-84-94.**

Cuisine: BASQUE. **Reservations:** Recommended.

Prices: Appetizers 550–850 ptas. ($3.90–$6); main courses 1,100–1,850 ptas. ($7.80–$13.10); *menús de la casa* 1,700–1,800 ptas. ($12.10–$12.80). AE, MC, V.

Open: Lunch, Thurs–Tues 1–3:30pm; dinner, Thurs–Tues 9–11:30pm. **Closed:** Aug 10–Sept 10.

For price and value, this ranks as one of the most competitive and worthwhile restaurants in town. In air-conditioned comfort you can partake of a number of Basque specialties, none better than the notable merluza (hake), the fish so beloved by Basque chefs. Fresh fish and a well-chosen selection of meats are presented nightly, and the service is attentive.

$ **Oleaga,** Adrinao VI, 16. ☎ **24-54-05.**

Cuisine: BASQUE. **Reservations:** Required.
Prices: Appetizers 800–1,400 ptas. ($5.70–$9.90); main courses 1,200–2,500 ptas. ($8.50–$17.80); fixed-price menu 2,500 ptas. ($17.80). AE, DC, MC, V.
Open: Lunch, Tues–Sun 1–3:30pm; dinner, Tues–Sat 9–11:30pm. **Closed:** Aug 15–Sept 1.

Oleaga's owner, Jesús Oleaga, is a professional restaurateur who pays particular attention to the wines served in his bodega. Many guests come in only for drinks at the stand-up bar. The tapas, called *pinchos* here, make a tasty prelude to a dinner. You can also order one of the most reasonably priced fixed-priced menus in town. In the restaurant, try the stuffed onions filled with minced pork and covered with a green sauce or the foie gras of duckling with grapes and an onion sauce.

El Portalón, Correría, 151. ☎ **14-27-55.**

Cuisine: BASQUE. **Reservations:** Recommended.
Price: Appetizers 725–1,450 ptas. ($5.10–$10.30); main courses 1,350–2,800 ptas. ($9.60–$19.90); fixed-price menu 5,500 ptas. ($39.10). AE, MC, V.
Open: Lunch, Mon–Sat 1–3:30pm; dinner, Mon–Sat 9–11pm. **Closed:** Aug 10–Sept 1.

This is the finest and most interesting restaurant in town. It was originally built in the late 1400s as a tavern and post office near what was, at the time, one of the only bridges leading in and out of Vitoria. Rich with patina and a sense of history, the restaurant prides itself on serving extremely fresh fish from the nearby Gulf of Biscay, always prepared in traditional Basque formulas. Cream and butter are rarely used here. Menu items include a salad of endive with shellfish; vegetarian crêpes; a traditional hake dish known as *merluza koxkera,* ragoûts of fish and/or shellfish; and many variations of monkfish, turbot, lotte, and eel.

Cantabria & Asturias

20

PART OF "GREEN SPAIN," THE PROVINCES OF CANTABRIA AND ASTURIAS ARE HISTORIC old lands filled with attractions ranging from the fishing villages of the Cantabrian and Asturian coastlines to the Picos de Europa, a magnificent stretch of snow-capped mountains.

Cantabria, settled in prehistoric times, was colonized by the Romans. The Muslims were less successful in their invasion. Many Christians, protected by the mountains, found refuge here during the long centuries of Moorish domination. Much religious architecture remains from this period, particularly Romanesque. Cantabria was once part of the Castilla y León district of Spain but is now an autonomous region with its own government.

Most of the tourism is confined to the northern coastal strip, whereas much of the mountainous area inland is poor and depopulated. If you venture away from the coast, which is serviced by buses, you'll usually need a rented car because public transport is inadequate at best. Santander, a rail terminus, makes the best center for touring the province; it also has the most tourist facilities. From Santander, you can reach virtually anywhere in the province in a three-hour drive.

The ancient principality of Asturias lies between Cantabria in the east and Galicia in the west. It reaches its scenic peak in the Picos de Europa, where the first Spanish national park was inaugurated. Asturias is a land for all seasons, with green valleys, fishing villages, and forests.

The coastline of Asturias constitutes one of the major sightseeing attractions of northern Spain. Once called the Costa Verde, it begins in the east at San Vicente de la Barquera and stretches about 88 miles (142km) to Gijón. Allow about six hours to drive it without stopovers. The western coast, beginning at Gijón, goes all the way to Ribadeo, a border town with Galicia—a distance of 112 miles (180km). This rocky coastline studded with fishing villages, and containing narrow estuaries and small beaches, is one of the most spectacular stretches of scenery in Spain. It takes all day to explore.

Asturias is an ancient land, as prehistoric cave paintings in the area demonstrate. Iron Age Celtic tribes resisted the Romans, as Asturians proudly point out even to this day. They also resisted the Moors, who subjugated the rest of Spain. The Battle of Covadonga in 722 represented the Moors' first major setback after their arrival in Iberia some 11 years previously.

The Asturians are still staunchly independent. In 1934 Francisco Franco, seen as a promising young general, arrived with his Moroccan troops to suppress an uprising by miners who had declared an independent Socialist Republic. His Nationalist forces returned again and again to destroy Asturian cities such as Gijón for their fierce resistance during the Spanish Civil War.

Seeing Cantabria & Asturias

GETTING THERE • Cantabria Getting to Cantabria without a car is easy, but once you're there, you may find it difficult to move around, since public transportation is very poor. In this mountainous region, rail lines are few.

The only airport in Cantabria is at Parayas, 4 miles (6.5km) outside Santander. Domestic service from Madrid consists of a morning and an evening flight on Monday through Friday, with only one per day on weekends. Barcelona is also linked to Santander by a daily flight.

What's Special About Cantabria & Asturias

Beaches
- El Sardinero, outside Santander, with golden sands and lots of facilities.
- Laredo, with its long sandy beach opening onto the Bay of Santoña, attracting hordes of people in summer.

Great Towns/Villages
- Santander, the former royal summer residence—a commercial city and stylish resort.
- Santillana del Mar, a gem preserved from the Middle Ages, with mansions built by adventurers using New World gold.
- Oviedo, the capital of Asturias, unique for its Pre-Romanesque architecture.
- Gijón, the major port of Asturias and a summer vacation spot; its old quarter is declared a historic zone.

Scenic Routes
- The coast of Cantabria—with long expanses of sands cleaned by Atlantic tides.
- The Costa Verde, from Unquera to Vegadeo—studded with estuaries and low cliffs, broken by sandy islets.
- The Picos de Europa—the highest range in the Cantabrian Cordillera—snowcapped and split by gorges.

Cave Paintings
- The Cuevas de Altamira—the "Sistine Chapel of prehistoric art."

It's possible to take one of the twice-weekly ferries from Plymouth, England, to Santander. The trip takes 24 hours. For information in Plymouth, phone **752/22-13-21**.

Madrid and Santander are linked by RENFE, with four trains a day. Daily trains also come in from Valladolid. Narrow-gauge FEVE trains link Bilbao and Santander daily, with continuing service to El Ferrol, north of La Coruña in Galicia. You can take the complete journey all the way in about 13 hours or make stopovers along the way. There's an obligatory change of trains at Oviedo.

It's also possible to arrive at Santander by bus, with service from Burgos, Barcelona, and Bilbao. Once at Santander, you can take buses to the villages along the coast.

Santander lies about a day's drive from Madrid. Take the N-1 from Madrid to Burgos, then the 623 north to Santander. From Bilbao in the east, take the 624, cutting north to the coast at the turnoff onto the 623.

Asturias Your gateway to Asturias is likely to be Gijón or Oviedo, either of which can be reached by air from Madrid on Iberia Airlines. Iberia flies into Ranón Airport, 12 miles (19.5km) from Oviedo and 26 miles (42km) from Gijón. After that, it's a long haul by taxi into either city or a sometimes seemingly endless wait for a bus.

Therefore, many visitors opt for the train. From Madrid's Chamartín Station, three trains a day head for both Gijón and Oviedo. The *talgo* departs in the middle of the afternoon, whereas the Costa Verde sleeper express is an overnight train. Figure on about 6½ to 8½ hours to make either trip.

By bus, connections are usually convenient on one of the ALSA buses out of Madrid, about half a dozen daily, leaving early in the morning and late in the evening. You'll be in Oviedo in about 6 hours on this bus. From Oviedo, ALSA buses also connect with other major towns. For example, you can make day trips to nearly all the recommended coastal towns if you time your schedule properly. From Oviedo, you can also take a bus to the Picos de Europa, although a car would be a lot more convenient.

It's a long drive from Madrid to Asturias, a hard day's work. From Cantabria, continue west along the N-634 coastal highway.

A Suggested Route

Cantabria can be part of a car or train ride across the northern rim of Spain. After visiting the Basque country in the east, you can head west to the Cantabrian coastline.

Day 1 Spend the day in Laredo, after a stop for lunch in Castro-Urdiales.

Days 2–3 Spend two nights in Santander. You'll need a day to explore the single most rewarding sightseeing target in the province: the medieval town of Santillana del Mar, with the nearby Cuevas de Altamira.

Day 4 Leave Santander and pay a morning visit to the seaside town of Comillas (to look at the Catalán *modernisme* architecture). Have a seafood lunch farther west at San Vicente de la Barquera, another seaside town. At Unquera, on the border between Cantabria and Asturias, begin a drive into the Picos de Europa. Take the N-621 through scenic landscapes alongside the Deva River until you reach the town of Potes, 24 miles (39km) inland. Stay overnight in or around Potes.

Day 5 Continue your drive through the Picos de Europa, heading for the western section. Plan to spend the night in the Picos district at Cangas de Ons.

Day 6 Take the N-632, a winding but scenic coast road west to Gijón for another overnight stopover.

Day 7 Drive to Oviedo and spend the day exploring the capital of Asturias. Spend the night there.

Day 8 Head west from Oviedo along the N-634 to reach the old port city of Luarca. Have lunch there and, if time is up, conclude your tour and return to Oviedo, where rail and train connections can be made to Madrid. If time permits, continue west along the N-634 coastal road to Ribadeo, a border town between Galicia and Asturias and a possible gateway to the province of Galicia.

1 Laredo

37 miles (60km) W of Bilbao, 30 miles (48km) E of Santander, 265 miles (427km) N of Madrid

GETTING THERE • By Bus Service is available from both Bilbao and Santander (one hour away).

• By Car From Castro-Urdiales, take the coastal route, the N-634, west to Laredo, 16 miles (26km).

ESSENTIALS The area code for Laredo is 942. The tourist information office is at Alameda de Miramar, s/n (☎ **942/60-54-92**).

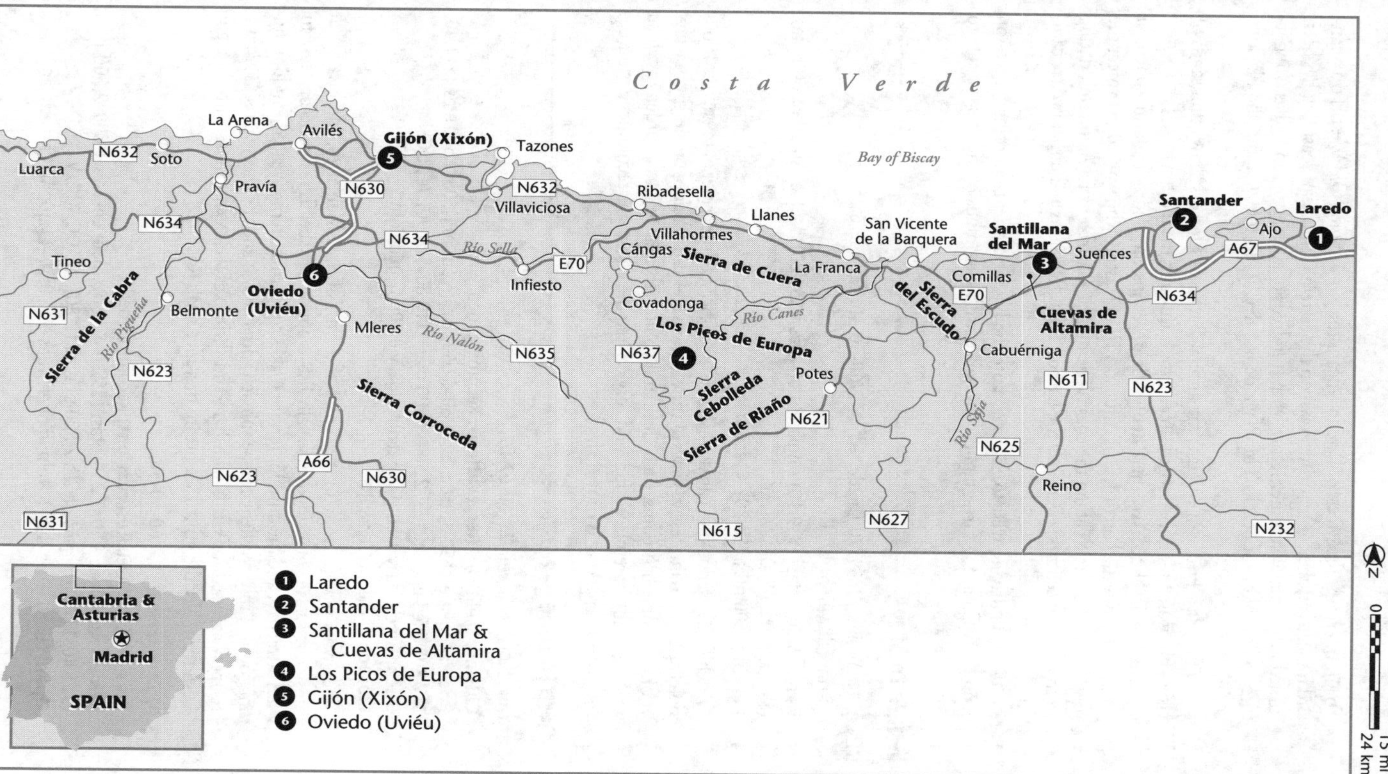

Cantabria & Asturias

To an American "the streets of Laredo" means the gun-slinging Old West. To a Spaniard it means an ancient maritime town on the eastern Cantabrian coast that has been turned into a major summer resort, with hundreds of apartments and villas along its three miles (5km) of beach. The Playa de la Salvé lies to the west and the Playa de Oriñón to the east.

On the last Friday of August, the annual **Battle of Flowers** draws thousands of visitors to watch bloom-adorned floats parade through the old town.

The medieval quarter, the **Puebla Vieja,** retains the traditional atmosphere of Laredo. It was walled on orders of Alfonso VIII of Castile, who wanted to protect the town from pirate raids along the coast. The hillside **Church of La Asunción,** dating from the 13th century, overlooks the harbor. It has five naves and rather bizarre capitals.

If you're driving west to Santoña, note the big monument honoring native son Juan de la Cosa, the cartographer who sailed with Columbus on his first voyage to America.

Where to Stay

Risco, La Arenosa, 2, 39770 Laredo. ☎ **942/60-50-30.** Fax 942/60-50-55.
25 rms (all with bath). TV TEL

Rates: 5,500 ptas. ($39.10) single; 8,000 ptas. ($56.80) double. Breakfast 600 ptas. ($4.30) extra. AE, DC, MC, V.
Parking: 600 ptas. ($4.30). **Closed:** Jan.

On a hillside overlooking Laredo, half a mile southeast of the center of town, this 1960s hotel opens onto impressive views of the old town and also of one of the nearby beaches. It offers simple bedrooms, each clean and comfortable, as well as a garden in which scattered tables are placed for food service (see the restaurant recommendation below). Ample parking is provided.

Where to Dine

Camarote, Vitoria, s/n. ☎ **60-67-07.**

Cuisine: SEAFOOD. **Reservations:** Recommended.
Prices: Appetizers 650–1,050 ptas. (4.60–$7.50); main courses 1,600–2,500 ptas. ($11.40–$17.80); fixed-price menus. 2,500–3,500 ptas. ($17.80–$24.90). AE, DC, MC, V.
Open: Lunch, daily 1:30–4pm; dinner, daily 8:30pm–midnight.
Closed: Sun dinner in winter.

The owner of Camarote (in the center of town) is Felipe Manjarrés, and his chef de cuisine specializes in seafood, especially fish as opposed to shellfish. The decor is tasteful and attractive, and the outdoor terrace makes a pleasant alternative to the indoor dining room. Truly excellent are the spinach with crayfish and the cheese tarts. "Original recipes" are used for salads with ham and shrimp as well as for those with tuna and fresh fruit. Try the grilled sea bream or a filet steak Rossini.

Risco, La Arenosa, 2. ☎ **60-50-30.**

Cuisine: SEAFOOD. **Reservations:** Recommended.
Prices: Appetizers 750–1,050 ptas. ($5.30–$7.50); main courses 1,600–2,500 ptas. ($11.40–$17.80); *menú del día* 2,500 ptas. ($17.80). AE, DC, MC, V.
Open: Lunch, Tues–Sun 1–4pm; dinner, Tues–Sun 8:30–11:30pm. **Closed:** Jan.

This is Laredo's most appealing restaurant, known for its innovative seafood dishes. The chef de cuisine, assisted by a battery of helpers, prepares such items as *en panaché,* marinated salmon with pink peppercorns, scrambled eggs with lobster, and codfish "prepared in the style of the mountains." One of the more unusual dishes is peppers stuffed with minced pig's trotters or crabmeat. For dessert, try a fresh-fruit sorbet. Some tables are set up in the garden, or you can dine in a traditional dining room with views of the sea. The restaurant is on the ground floor of the Risco hotel (see above). During the busy months of July and August, it remains open on Monday.

2 Santander

244 miles (393km) N of Madrid, 72 miles (116km) NW of Bilbao

GETTING THERE • By Plane Daily flights from Madrid and Barcelona land at Aeropuerto de Santander (☎ **25-10-07**), a little more than four miles (6.5km) from the town center, accessible by taxi only.

• By Train There are four trains daily from Madrid (5 hours away). Four trains a day travel from Bilbao (3 hours). For rail information call **28-02-02**.

• By Bus About a dozen buses per day from Bilbao arrive in Santander (3 hours), and there are also four buses per day from Madrid (6 hours).

• By Car The N-634 continues west to Santander, with an N-635 turnoff to reach the resort.

ESSENTIALS The area code for Santander is 942. The tourist information office is at Plaza Porticada, s/n (☎ **942/31-07-08**).

Santander has always been a rival of San Sebastián in the east, although it has never attained the premier status of that Basque resort. It did, however, become a royal residence from 1913 to 1930, after city officials presented an English-style Magdalena Palace to Alfonso XIII and his queen, Victoria Eugenia.

An ancient city, Santander was damaged by a 1941 fire that destroyed the old quarter and most of its dwellings. It was rebuilt along original lines, with wide boulevards, a waterfront promenade, sidewalk cafés, shops, restaurants, and hotels.

The **Music and Dance Festival** in August is considered one of the most important artistic events in Spain (accommodations are very hard to find then). At times, this festival coincides with religious celebrations honoring Santiago, the patron saint of Spain.

Santander is an education center in summer as well. Courses are offered at the once-royal palace, now the Menéndez Pelayo International University. Students and teachers from North America and Europe come here to study and enjoy the area.

Most visitors to Santander head for **El Sardinero,** a resort less than 1.5 miles (2.4km) from the city. Buses and trolleys make the short run between the city center and El Sardinero both day and night. Besides hotels and restaurants, Santander has three beaches, the **Playa de Castaneda,** the **Playa del Sardinero,** and the **Playa de la Concha,** where people stretch out under candy-striped umbrellas.

If these beaches get too crowded, take a 15-minute boat ride to **El Puntal,** a beautiful beach that is not crowded, even in August.

If you don't like crowds or beaches, go up to the lighthouse, a little more than a $1^1/_4$ mile (2km) from El Sardinero, where the views are wide ranging. A restaurant serves both indoor and outdoor snacks. Here you can hike along the green cliffs or loll in the grass.

What to See & Do

Catedral, Somorrostro, s/n. ☎ **22-60-24.**

Greatly damaged in the 1941 fire, this restored fortresslike 13th-century cathedral holds the tomb of historian/writer Marcelino Menéndez y Pelayo (1856–1912), Santander's most illustrious man of letters. The 12th-century crypt with a trio of low-slung aisles, untouched by fire, can be entered through the south portico. The Gothic cloister was restored after the fire. Roman ruins were discovered beneath the north aisle in 1983.

Admission: Free.

Open: Daily 9:30am–12:30pm and 5:30–8:30pm.

Museo Provincial de Prehistoria y Arqueología, Calle Casimiro Sainz, 4. ☎ **20-71-05.**

This museum has some interesting artifacts discovered in the Cantabrian province—not only Roman but also some unusual prehistoric finds. Since it is unlikely that you'll be allowed to visit the Cuevas de Altamira (see Section 3 later in this chapter), come here to see objects and photographs from these prehistoric caves with their remarkable paintings. Some of the displays date from 15,000 years ago.

Admission: Free.

Open: Tues–Sat 10am–1pm and 4–7pm, Sun 11am–2pm.

Museo Municipal de Bellas Artes, Calle Rubío, 6. ☎ **23-94-85.**

Located near the Ayuntamiento (Town Hall), the Municipal Museum of Fine Arts has some interesting Goyas, notably his portrait of Ferdinand VII, commissioned by the city, and his series of etchings called *Disasters of War.* You can also see some of his continuing series of *caprichos* (whims). See also Zurbarán's *Mystic Scene* and an array of works by Flemish, Spanish, and Italian artists, many of them contemporary.

Admission: Free.

Open: Mon–Fri 10:30am–1:30pm and 5:30–8pm, Sat 10am–1pm.

Biblioteca Menéndez y Pelayo, Calle Rubío, 4. ☎ **23-45-34.**

Located in the same building as the Municipal Museum is this 45,000-volume library amassed by Menéndez y Pelayo and left to Santander upon his death in 1912. Guided tours are available. Opposite the building is the Casa Museo, which displays this great man's study and shows how modestly he lived.

Admission: Free.

Open: Mon–Fri 9am–noon.

Where to Stay

Santander is loaded with good-value hotels, from its year-round city hotels to its summer villas at El Sardinero. It gets crowded, so try to reserve well in advance.

IN TOWN

Hotel Ciudad de Santander, Menéndez Pelayo, 13–15, 39006 Santander. ☎ **942/22-79-65.** Fax 942/21-73-03. 60 rms, 2 suites (all with bath). A/C MINIBAR TEL. **Bus:** 5.

Rates: 10,200–12,700 ptas. ($72.40–$90.20) single; 12,750–15,900 ptas. ($90.50–$112.90) double; 16,000–20,000 ptas. ($113.60–$142) suite. Breakfast buffet 900 ptas. ($6.40) extra. AE, DC, MC, V. **Parking:** 600 ptas. ($4.30) outdoors, 1,200 ptas. ($8.50) indoors.

Located about eight blocks north of Santander's busiest seaside promenade (the Paseo de Pereda) in the heart of the city's commercial heartland, this white-sided rectangular hotel was built in 1989, rising five floors. The big-windowed lobby has marble floors, honey-colored wooden paneling, and modern accessories. Bedrooms are monochromatic, reflecting themes similar to that of the lobby, with fully equipped bathrooms and conveniently proportioned writing desks.

Dining/Entertainment: The hotel contains an informal snack bar, plus a stone-and-glass-sheathed restaurant serving three-course fixed-price lunches and dinners costing 1,500 to 2,800 pesetas ($10.70 to $19.90).

Services: Room service (available daily 7am to midnight), laundry/valet, concierge.

Facilities: Car rentals.

Hotel México, Calderón de la Barca, 3, 39002 Santander. ☎ **942/21-24-50.** Fax 942/22-92-38. 35 rms (all with bath). TV TEL

Rates: 4,800 ptas. ($34.10) single; 8,300 ptas. ($58.90) double. Breakfast 500 ptas. ($3.60) extra. MC, V.

Lying only a block from the rail station, this is one of your best budget bets in the heart of the city, ideal for those without transportation who don't want to range far afield of the hotel, especially if they have luggage. The exterior may not be too enticing, but once inside this family-operated inn, the atmosphere improves. Even though in a congested area, street noises seem at a minimum here, and the rooms are well cared for and comfortably furnished. Often they are in the old-fashioned architectural styling of northern Spain, with glassed-in balconies and tall ceilings. Breakfast, the only meal served, is offered in a formal room with Queen Anne chairs and oak wainscoting. The manager speaks English.

AT EL SARDINERO

★ **Hotel Real,** Paseo Pérez Galdós, 28 (El Sardinero), 39005 Santander. ☎ **942/27-25-50.** Fax 942/27-45-73. 115 rms (all with bath), 9 suites. A/C MINIBAR TV TEL **Bus:** 1, 2, 5, or 7.

Rates: 12,600–22,000 ptas. ($89.50–$156.20) single; 18,900–33,000 ptas. ($134.20–$234.30) double; 26,300–95,000 ptas. ($186.70–$674.50) suite. Buffet breakfast 1,250 ptas. ($8.90) extra. AE, DC, MC, V. **Parking:** Free.

Architecturally noteworthy as the first building in the entire region constructed of reinforced concrete, the Real was built in 1917 to house the entourage of courtiers who accompanied King Alfonso XIII on his midsummer vacations to Santander. Purchased and completely renovated by the prestigious HUSA chain in 1987, it is once again considered one of the most elegant hotels in northern Spain, filled with updated reminders of a more gracious age. Located about 2 miles (3km) east of the commercial center of town, near the site of the Royal Palace on a hillside above the Magdalena Beach, the Real contains richly conservative bedrooms, most with views of the sea and all with many comfort-inducing amenities.

Dining/Entertainment: The El Puntal Restaurant serves regional and international three-course fixed-price lunches and dinners costing 4,000 pesetas ($28.40) each.

Nearby lies a cocktail lounge accented with potted palms and high ceilings, and boasting a well-mannered staff.

Services: 24-hour room service, concierge, babysitting, laundry/valet.

Facilities: Car rentals, easy availability of nearby golfing.

Hotel Rhin, Avenida Reina Victoria, 153, 39005 Santander. ☎ **942/27-43-00.** Fax 942/27-86-53. 95 rms (all with bath). A/C TV TEL **Bus:** 1, 2, 5, or 7.

Rates: 5,680–7,650 ptas. ($40.30–$54.30) single; 8,300–11,700 ptas. ($58.90–$83.10) double. Breakfast 575 ptas. ($4.10) extra. AE, DC, MC, V. **Parking:** 800 ptas. ($5.70).

Built in the early 1970s, this hotel has panoramic views of the city's beaches. The rooms are comfortable and clean and cheaper than many of the nearby accommodations. There are a cafeteria and a restaurant on the premises, serving an international cuisine. Laundry service and room service are provided. Although it's at the beach, the hotel is open all year.

Where to Dine

Most visitors to Santander eat at their hotels or boarding houses, which sometimes offer better value for the money and more efficient service than city restaurants. For variety, though, here are a few suggestions.

IN TOWN

Bodega Cigaleña, Daoíz y Velarde, 19. ☎ **21-30-62.**

Cuisine: CANTABRIAN. **Reservations:** Not required. **Bus:** 5.
Prices: Appetizers 650–2,000 ptas. ($4.60–$14.20); main courses 1,200–3,200 ptas. ($8.50–$22.70); fixed-price menu 2,800 ptas. ($19.90). AE, DC, MC, V.
Open: Lunch, Mon–Sat noon–4pm; dinner, Mon–Sat 7:30pm–midnight.
Closed: June 20–July 1; Oct 20–Nov 20.

Popular with the young set of Santander, this Castilian bodega in the city center serves typical regional cuisine in a rustic decor—hanging hams, large wine kegs, and provincial tables. The set menu changes every day. A sample meal might be *sopa de pescado* (fish soup), shellfish paella, the fruit of the season, bread, and wine. The Cigaleña offers a good choice of wines from an old Castilian town near Valladolid. Ask to see its Museo del Vino.

Cañadío, Gómez Oreña, 15. ☎ **31-41-49.**

Cuisine: BASQUE. **Reservations:** Recommended Fri–Sat. **Bus:** 5.
Prices: Appetizers 900–1,800 ptas. ($6.40–$12.80); main courses 1,700–2,800 ptas. ($12.10–$19.90); fixed-price menu 1,500 ptas. ($10.70). AE, DC, MC, V.
Open: Lunch, Mon–Sat 1–4pm; dinner, Mon–Sat 9pm–12:30am. **Closed:** Oct 15–Nov 1.

This pleasant, centrally located restaurant off Plaza Cañadío has a reputation for serving some of the best specialties in the region. Featured may be shrimp flan, hake in *cava* (Catalán champagne) sauce, and escalopes of ham with cheese. The bar, where drinks and light snacks are served, is open daily from 11am to midnight.

AT EL SARDINERO

Piquío, Plaza de las Brisas. ☎ **27-55-03.**

Cuisine: SPANISH. **Reservations:** Recommended. **Bus:** 1, 2, 5, or 7.
Prices: Appetizers 1,200–1,900 ptas. ($8.50–$13.50); main courses 1,800–2,900 ptas. ($12.80–$20.60); fixed-price menu 1,800 ptas. ($12.80). AE, DC, MC, V.
Open: Lunch, daily 1–4pm; dinner, daily 9pm–midnight.

The panoramic view of the public gardens and the beach beyond offered by this restaurant is only one of many reasons to visit it. Specialties include a full array of fish and meat dishes, each well prepared. The chef uses market-fresh ingredients.

La Sardina de Plata, Doctor Fleming, 4. ☎ **27-10-35.**

Cuisine: SEAFOOD. **Reservations:** Required. **Bus:** 1, 2, 5, or 7.
Prices: Appetizers 1,000–1,500 ptas. ($7.10–$10.70); main courses 1,800–3,500 ptas. ($12.80–$24.90); fixed-price menus 1,800–3,500 ptas. ($12.80–$24.90). AE, DC, MC, V.

In a warren of small streets in the center of the old city, this nautically designed restaurant serves an imaginative cuisine highlighted by several delicate sauces. Menu selections might include cheese mousse, beef filet with truffles and cognac, and an unusually seasoned fish salad. There is also an extensive wine list. The service is courteous.

SPECIALTY DINING

In the evening, for a change of pace, walk or take a taxi to the fishing port, where three or four outdoor restaurants specialize in grilled sardines and other freshly caught seafood. Across the street, fishermen might be mending their nets. It's all part of the local color.

Evening Entertainment

Gran Casino del Sardinero, Plaza de Italia. ☎ **27-60-54.**

This is the most exciting nighttime diversion, offering such games as blackjack and chemin de fer. Be sure to bring your passport. The casino serves dinner from 9pm to 1am, costing 2,500 pesetas ($17.80). It's open daily from 7pm to 4am. **Bus:** 1, 2, 5, or 7.

Admission: Free.

Lisboa, Plaza de Italia. ☎ **27-10-20.**

Located within the city casino, this establishment draws all kinds of people—from gamblers taking a break from the tables to visitors looking for action of another sort. Many residents drop in for breakfast. Beer and mixed drinks are served. In summer it's especially crowded. It's open daily from 8:30am to 3:30am. Drinks run from 250 to 700 pesetas ($1.80 to $5). **Bus:** 1, 2, 5, or 7.

3 Santillana del Mar & Cuevas de Altamira

18 miles (29km) SW of Santander; 244 miles (393km) N of Madrid

GETTING THERE • By Bus From Santander, six buses leave the Plaza de las Estaciones daily (trip time: 45 minutes).

• By Car Take the N-611 out of Santander to reach the C-6316 cutoff to Santillana.

ESSENTIALS The area code for Santillana del Mar is 942. The tourist information office is at Plaza Mayor (☎ **942/81-82-51**).

Among the most perfectly preserved medieval villages in Europe and a Spanish national landmark, ★ **Santillana del Mar** was once famous as a place of pilgrimage. A monastery housed the relics of St. Juliana, a martyr in Asia Minor who refused to surrender her virginity to her husband. Pilgrims, especially the grandees of Castile, came to worship at this site. The name Santillana is a contraction of Santa Juliana. The "del Mar" is misleading, as Santillana is not on the water but inland.

Jean-Paul Sartre called Santillana "the prettiest village in Spain," and I wouldn't want to dispute his judgment. In spite of all the tour buses, Santillana still retains its medieval atmosphere and is still very much a village of dairy farmers.

Wander on foot throughout the village, taking in its principal sites, including **Plaza de Ramón Pelayo** (sometimes called Plaza Mayor). Here the Parador de Santillana (see below), named after the hero of the novel by 18th-century French writer Alain-René Lesage, has been installed in the old Barreda Bracho residence.

A 15th-century tower, facing Calle de Juan Infante, is known for its pointed arched doorway. A walk along Calle de las Lindas (Street of Beautiful Women) doesn't live up to its promise, but includes many of the oldest buildings in Santillana and two towers dating from the 14th and 15th centuries. Calle del Ro gets its name from a stream running through town to a central fountain.

Visit the 800-year-old cathedral, the **Colegiata de Santillana,** Calle Santo Domingo, which shelters the tomb of the patron saint of the village, Juliana, and walk through its interesting cloister. Other treasures include 1,000-year-old documents and a 17th-century Mexican silver altarpiece. The cathedral is open daily from 9am to 12:30pm and 4 to 7:30pm. Admission, including entrance to the Convent of the Poor Clares, is 100 pesetas (70¢).

The 400-year-old Convent of the Poor Clares **(Museo Diocesano)** houses a rich art collection that was inspired by a Madrid art professor who encouraged the nuns to collect and restore religious paintings and statues damaged or abandoned during the Spanish Civil War. The collection is constantly growing. It's open daily from 10am to 1pm and 4 to 8pm (closes at 6pm in winter). Admission is 100 pesetas (70¢).

Where to Stay

EXPENSIVE

Parador de Santillana, Plaza de Ramón Pelayo, 11. 39330 Santillana del Mar. ☎ **942/81-80-00.** Fax 942/81-83-91. 56 rms. MINIBAR TV TEL

Rates: 8,800–11,60 ptas. ($62.50–$82.00) single; 11,000–14,500 ptas. ($78.10–$103) double. Breakfast 1,100 ptas. ($7.80) extra. AE, DC, MC, V.

A 400-year-old former palace filled with many beautiful antiques, this parador is one of the most popular in Spain. The public rooms are elegantly informal. The hand-hewn plank floor, the old brass chandeliers, and the refectory tables with their bowls of fresh flowers enhance the atmosphere. Large portraits of knights in armor hang in a gallery. Most of the guest rooms are unusually large, with antiques and windows on two sides; many have views of the garden. The large baths contain all sorts of conveniences, including terry-cloth robes. Note that the third-floor rooms are very small. Four-course evening meals and luncheons are served in the great dining hall, a set meal costing 3,500 pesetas ($24.90).

MODERATE

Hostal-Residencia Emperador, Avenida le Dorat, 12, 39330 Santillana del Mar. ☎ **942/81-80-54.** 5 rms (all with bath).

Rates: 3,200–5,500 ptas. ($22.70–$39.10) single; 3,800–6,500 ptas. ($27–$46.20) double. Breakfast 475 ptas. ($3.40) extra. No credit cards.

This residencia offers simply furnished but clean and reasonably comfortable rooms. For such a modest place, the hospitality is gracious. Because of the Emperador's small size, it can be difficult to get a room from June 15 to September 1.

Hotel Altamira, Calle Cantón, 1, 39330 Santillana del Mar. ☎ **942/81-80-25.** Fax 942/84-01-36. 32 rms (all with bath). TV TEL

Rates: 5,000 ptas. ($35.50) single; 10,000 ptas. ($71) double. Breakfast 500 ptas. ($3.60) extra. AE, DC, MC, V.

This three-star hotel in the center of the village is a 400-year-old former palace. Although not as impressive as the government-run parador (see above), it often takes the overflow in its comfortable, well-maintained guest rooms. At the large restaurant seating 130 and decorated in Castilian style, you can get a complete meal for 1,500 pesetas ($10.70).

Los Infantes, L'Dorat, 1, 39330 Santillana del Mar. ☎ **942/81-81-00.** Fax 942/84-01-03. 50 rms (all with bath). TV TEL

Rates: 3,000–8,000 ptas. ($21.30–$56.80) single; 5,000–11,000 ptas. ($35.50–$78.10) double. Breakfast 500 ptas. ($3.60) extra. AE, DC, MC, V.

This three-star hotel, although not as charming as the Altamira (see above), is a comfortable choice, dating from 1975. Located on the main road leading into the village, the Infantes has successfully kept the old flavor of Santillana: beamed ceilings and lounges furnished with tapestries, antiques, clocks, and paintings. The rooms are pleasant and simple, with wall-to-wall carpeting; two have small balconies.

Where to Dine

Los Blasones, Plaza de la Gándara, s/n. ☎ **81-80-70.**

Cuisine: CANTABRIAN. **Reservations:** Recommended.
Prices: Appetizers 700–1,300 ptas. ($5–$9.20); main courses 1,400–1,800 ptas. ($9.90–$12.80); fixed-price menu 2,000 ptas. ($14.20). AE, MC, V.
Open: Lunch, daily 1–4pm; dinner, daily 8–11pm. **Closed:** Dec–Feb.

Located in the center of town off the Plaza de la Gándara, this bar-cum-restaurant is a local hangout. It's in a rustic building made of stone. Barbecue specialties are featured. The chef's specialty is *solomillo al queso de Treviso* (sirloin with cheese sauce). Try also the grilled hake or the stuffed peppers.

An Easy Excursion

About 1.5 miles (2.5km) from Santillana del Mar are the ★ **Cuevas de Altamira** (☎ **81-80-05**), famous for prehistoric paintings dating from the end of the Ice Age, paintings that have led those caves to be called the "Sistine Chapel of prehistoric art."

These ancient depictions of bison and horses, painted vividly in reds and blacks on the cave ceilings, were not discovered until the late 19th century. Once their authenticity was established, scholars and laypeople alike flocked to see these works of art, which provide a fragile link to our remote ancestors.

Severe damage was caused by the bacteria that so many visitors brought with them; so now the Research Center and Museum of Altamira allows only 20 visitors per day (no children under 13). If you wish to visit, write to this address one year in advance asking permission to see the main cave and specifying the number in your party and the desired date: **Centro de Investigación y Museo de Altamira,** 39330 Santillana del Mar, Cantabria, Spain.

Reservations are not necessary for visits to the nearby **Cave of the Stalactites** and the little admission-free museum at the site, open Monday to Saturday from 10am to 1pm and 4 to 6pm, Sunday from 10am to 1pm. There you can see reproductions of the caves' artwork and buy color slides that show the subtleties of color employed. You'll also see pictures of what the bacteria did to these priceless paintings. To reach the area, you need to go by car or on foot because there is no bus service.

4 Los Picos de Europa

Potes: 71 miles (114km) W of Santander, 247 miles (398km) N of Madrid, Cangas de Onís: 91 miles (147km) W of Santander, 260 miles (419km) N of Madrid

GETTING THERE • By Car By far the best way to see this region is by car. Most drivers head into the region on the N-621 highway, heading southwest from Santander, or on the same highway northeast from the cities of north central Spain (especially León and Valladolid). This highway connects many of the region's best vistas in a straight line. It also defines the region's eastern boundary. If you're driving east from Oviedo, you'll take the N-6312, in which case the first town of any importance will be Cangas de Onís.

• By Bus Travel by bus is much less convenient but possible if you have lots of time and have had your fill of the rich architecture of the Spanish heartland. The region's touristic hubs are the towns of Panes and Potes, both of which receive bus service (two buses per day in summer, one per day in winter) from both Santander and León. More frequent buses (five per day) come from the coastal town of Unquera (which lies along the coastal train lines) to Potes. From Oviedo, there are two buses daily to the district's easternmost town of Cangas; these continue a short distance farther southeast to Covadonga. Within the region, a small local bus runs once a day, according to an erratic schedule, along the northern rim of the Picos, connecting Cangas de Onís with Las Arenas. Frankly, bus service in this region is time consuming.

These mountains are technically part of the Cordillera Cantábrica, which runs parallel to the northern coastline of Spain. In the narrow and vertiginous band known as Los Picos de Europa, they are by far at their most dramatic.

They are the most famous and most legend-riddled mountains in Spain. Rising more than 8,500 feet, they are not considered high by alpine standards, but their proximity to the sea makes their height especially awesome. During the Middle Ages, they were considered passable only with great difficulty. (Much earlier, the ancient Romans constructed a north-south road whose stones are still visible in some places.) The abundance of wildlife, the medieval battles that occurred here, and the dramatically rocky heights have all contributed to the "twice-told tales" that are an essential part of the entire principality of Asturias.

The position of Los Picos defined the medieval borders between Asturias, Santander, and León. Covering a distance of only 24 miles (39km) at their longest point, they are geologically and botanically different from anything else in the region. Thousands of years ago, busy glaciers created massive and forbidding limestone cliffs that today challenge the most dedicated and intrepid rock climbers in Europe.

Even hill climbers should never underestimate the dangers of walking here. Many of the slopes are covered with loosely compacted shale, making good treads and hiking boots necessary. For amateurs, only well-established paths are safe: Setting out on their own for uncharted vistas has left many neophytes stranded. In summer, temperatures can get hot and humid, and sudden downpours sweeping in from the frequently rainy coastline are common in any season. Hiking is not recommended between October and May. Excursions by car and the walking tour contained in Motor Tour 3, below, are possible in any season.

The Picos are divided by swiftly flowing rivers into three regions: From east to west, they are Andara, Urrieles, and Cornion.

Motor Tours

If you have a car, the number and variety of tours within this region are almost endless, but for the purposes of this guide, I have organized the region into three motor tours. Any of them, with their side excursions, could fill an entire day; if you're rushed and omit some of the side excursions, you'll spend half a day.

Motor Tour 1

From Panes to Potes

18 miles (29km); 1 hour

This drive, except for one optional detour, extends entirely along one of the region's best roads, the N-621, which links León and Valladolid to Santander. The drive is most noteworthy for its views of the ravine containing the Deva River, a ravine so steep that direct sunlight rarely penetrates it.

About two-thirds of the way to Potes, signs will point you on a detour to the village of **Lebana,** half a mile off the main road. There you'll find the church of Nuestra Señora de Lebena, built in the 10th century in the Mozarabic style, surrounded by a copse of trees at the base of tall cliffs. Some people consider it the best example of "Arabized" Christian architecture in Europe, with Islamic-inspired geometric motifs. If it isn't open, knock at the door of the first house you see as you enter the village—the home of the guardian, who will unlock the church if she's around. For this, she will expect a tip. If she's not around, content yourself with admiring the church from the outside, noting its spectacular natural setting.

Continuing for about another 5 miles (8km), you'll reach the village of **Potes,** a charming place with well-kept alpine houses against a backdrop of jagged mountains.

EXCURSIONS FROM POTES Two miles (3.2km) southwest of Potes, near Turiano, stands the **Monastery of Santo Toribio de Liébana,** dating from the 17th century. Restored to the style it enjoyed at the peak of its vast power, a transitional Romanesque, it contains what is reputed to be a splinter from the True Cross, brought from Jerusalem in the 8th century by the Bishop of Astorga. The monastery is also famous as the former home of Beatus de Liébana, the 8th-century author of *Commentary on the Apocalypse,* one of medieval Spain's most famous ecclesiastical documents. Today the building remains a functioning monastery. Ring the bell during daylight hours, and one of the brothers will probably let you enter if you are properly attired.

At the end of a winding and breathtakingly beautiful road to the west of Potes lies the **Parador del Río Deva,** where you can spend the night or stop for lunch only. The drive to Fuente-Dé will, for the most part, follow the path of the Deva River. Once you're there, a teleféric will carry you 2,000 feet up to an observation platform above a wind-scoured rock face. In summer the teleféric operates daily in July and August from 9am to 8pm; from September through June hours are daily 10am to 6pm. Round-trip fare is 1,000 pesetas ($7.10). At the top you can walk 3 miles (4.8km) along a footpath to the rustic Refugio de Aliva, open between June 15 and September 15. A few bunks are available for 550 pesetas ($3.90). If you opt for just a meal or a snack at the hostal's simple restaurant, remember to allow enough time to return to the teleféric before its last trip down.

Motor Tour 2

From Potes to Cangas De Onís

93 miles (150km); 4 hours

This tour includes not only the Quiviesa Valley and some of the region's most vertiginous mountain passes, but also some of its most verdant fields and most elevated pastures. You might stop at an occasional village, but most of the time you will be going through deserted countryside. Your route will take you under several tunnels and high above mountain streams set deep into gorges. The occasional belvederes signposted along the way always deliver on their promise of spectacular views.

After a day of vistas, the first really important place you'll reach is **Cangas de Onís,** the westernmost town in the region, where you can get a clean hotel room and a solid meal after a trek through the mountains. The biggest attraction in Cangas de Onís is an ivy-covered **Roman bridge,** lying west of the center, spanning the Sella River. Also of interest is the **Capilla de Santa Cruz,** immediately west of the center. One of the earliest Christian sites in Spain (and probably a holy spot many centuries before that), it was originally built in the 8th century over a Celtic dolmen and rebuilt in the 15th century.

A mile northwest of Cangas de Onís, beside the road leading to Arriondas, stands the Benedictine **Monastery of San Pedro,** in the village of Villanueva. The church that you see was originally built in the 17th century, when it enclosed within its premises the ruins of a much older Romanesque church. Combining a blend of baroque opulence and Romanesque simplicity, it has some unusual carved capitals showing the unhappy end of the medieval King Favila, supposedly devoured by a Cantabrian bear.

Motor Tour 3

From Cangas de Onís to Panes

35 miles (56km); 1 hour

This tour travels along the relatively straight C-6312 from the western to the eastern entrance to the Picos de Europa region. A number of unusual excursions could easily stretch this into an all-day outing.

From Cangas de Onís, heading west about 1 mile (1.6km), you'll reach the turnoff to the **El Buxu Cueva.** Inside the cave are a limited number of prehistoric rock engravings and charcoal drawings, somewhat disappointingly small. Only 25 persons per day are allowed inside (respiration erodes the drawings), so unless you get there early, you won't get in. It's open Tuesday to Sunday, except during November, from 10am to 12:30pm and 4 to 6:30pm. Admission is 150 pesetas ($1.10).

Four miles (6.5km) east, signs point south in the direction of **Covadonga,** revered as the birthplace of Christian Spain, about 6 miles (9.6km) off the main highway. A battle here in A.D. 718 pitted a ragged band of Christian Visigoths against a small band of Muslims. The resulting victory introduced the first niche of Christian Europe into a Moorish Iberia.

The town's most important monument is **La Santa Cueva,** a cave containing the sarcophagus of Pelayo, king of the Visigothic Christians (d. 737) and an enormous Neo-Romanesque basilica, built between 1886 and 1901, commemorating the Christianization of Spain. At the end of the long boulevard that funnels into the base of the church stands a statue of Pelayo.

Return to the highway and continue east. You'll come to the village of Las Estazadas; then after another 7 miles (11km) you'll reach **Las Arenas de Cabrales** (some maps refer to it as Arenas). This is the headquarters of a cheese-producing region whose Cabrales, a blue-veined cheese made from ewe's milk, is avidly consumed throughout Spain.

Drive 3 miles (4.8km) south from Arenas, following signs to the village of **Puente de Poncebos** (known on some maps as Poncebos). Here, the road ends abruptly (except perhaps for four-wheel-drive vehicles). This village is set several miles downstream from the source of Spain's most famous salmon-fishing river, the Cares, which flows from its source near the more southerly village of Cain through deep ravines.

A TREK THROUGH THE DIVINE GORGE Beginning at Poncebos, a footpath has been cut into the ravine on either side of the Cares River. It is one of the engineering marvels of Spain, known for centuries as The Divine Gorge. It crosses the ravine many times over footbridges and sometimes through tunnels chiseled into the rock face beside the water, making a hike along the banks of this river a memorable outing. You can climb up the riverbed from Poncebos, overland to the village of Cain, a total distance of 7 miles (11km). Allow between three and four hours. At Cain, you can take a taxi back to where you left your car in Poncebos if you don't want to retrace your steps.

After your trek up the riverbed, continue your drive on to the village of **Panes,** a distance of 14 miles (22km), to the eastern extremity of the Picos de Europa.

WHERE TO STAY & DINE

Accommodations are extremely limited in these mountain towns. If you're planning an overnight stopover, make sure you have a reservation. Most taverns will serve you food during regular opening hours without a reservation.

Cangas De Onís

La Palmera, Soto de Cangas. ☎ **98/594-00-96.**

Cuisine: ASTURIAN. **Reservations:** Not required.
Prices: Appetizers 700–1,100 ptas. ($5–$7.80); main courses 900–1,900 ptas. ($6.40–$13.50); menús del día 800–1,000 ptas. ($5.70–$7.10). No credit cards.
Open: Lunch, daily 1–4pm; dinner, daily 8pm–midnight.

When the weather is right, you can dine outside here, enjoying some mountain air with the mountain food. Sometimes this place is overrun, but on other occasions you can have a meal in peace. The menu features game from the surrounding mountains, along with filet of beef, lamb chops, and salmon in green sauce. Try the local mountain cheese. La Palmera lies 2 miles (3.2km) east of Cangas de Onís on the road to Covadonga.

Cosgaya

Hotel Del Oso, Carretera Espinama, s/n, 39539. Cosgaya. ☎ **942/73-30-18.**
Fax 942/73-30-36. 36 rms (all with bath). TEL **Directions:** From Potes, take the road signposted to Espinama 9 miles (14.5km) south.

Rates: 6,000 ptas. ($42.60) single; 7,600 ptas. ($54) double. Breakfast 500 ptas. ($3.60) extra. AE, DC, MC, V. **Parking:** Free.

This well-run little hotel is set next to the banks of the Deva River, beside the road leading from Potes to the parador and cablecar at Fuente-Dé. The place is ringed with natural beauty. Its bedrooms are well furnished and maintained, and meals are taken at the Mesón del Oso (see below).

$ **Mesón del Oso,** Carretera Espinama, s/n. ☎ **73-04-18.**

Cuisine: ASTURIAN. **Reservations:** Not required. **Directions:** From Potes, take the route south toward Espinama 9 miles (14.5km).

Prices: Appetizers 550–950 ptas. ($3.90–$6.70); main courses 1,000–1,800 ptas. ($7.10–$12.80). AE, DC, MC, V.

Open: Lunch, daily 1–4pm; dinner, daily 8–11pm. **Closed:** Jan 7–Feb 15.

Open to the public since 1981, this stone-built place is named after the bear that supposedly devoured Favilia, an 8th-century king of Asturias. Here, at the birthplace of the Christian warrior king Pelayo, you can enjoy Liébana cuisine, reflecting the bounty of mountain, stream, and sea. The portions are generous. Try trout from the Deva River; grilled tuna; roast suckling pig; or a mountain stew called *cocida lebaniego,* whose recipe derives from local lore and tradition. Dessert might be a fruit-based tart. There's also an outdoor terrace.

Covadonga

Hotel Pelayo, 33589 Covadonga. ☎ **985/584-60-61.** Fax 985/584-60-54. 43 rms (all with bath), 2 suites. TV TEL **Directions:** Take the road that leads into the national park.

Rates: 4,500–6,250 ptas. ($32–$44.40) single; 7,600–12,000 ptas. ($54–$85.20) double; 10,000–16,000 ptas. ($71–$113.60) suite. AE, MC, V. **Closed:** Dec 12–Feb 1. **Parking:** Free.

There's no street address for this place, but it lies in the shadow of the large 19th-century basilica that dominates the village. The view from its windows takes in a panoramic landscape. Guests come here to enjoy the mountain air, and many pilgrims check in while visiting religious shrines in the area. The place has a somewhat dated, but nevertheless appealing, family atmosphere. The rooms are comfortable and well furnished. The facilities include a parking lot, a garden, and a restaurant offering well-prepared lunch or dinner for 2,200 pesetas ($15.60).

Fuente-Dé

Parador del Río Deva, at 3.5km de Espinama, 39588 Espinama. ☎ **942/73-66-51.** Fax 942/73-02-12. 78 rms (all with bath). TV TEL **Directions:** Drive 16 miles (26km) west of Potes.

Rates: 6,000-7,000 ptas. ($42.60–$49.70) single; 7,500–9,500 ptas. ($53.30–$67.50) double. Breakfast 1,000 ptas. ($7.10) extra. AE, DC, MC, V. **Parking:** Free.

The finest place to stay in the area, this government-run parador opens onto panoramic vistas of the Picos de Europa. Opened in 1975, it lies at the end of the major road through the Liébana region. Hunters in autumn and mountain climbers in summer often fill its attractively decorated and comfortably furnished bedrooms. The place has a pleasant bar, and its restaurant serves good regional cuisine, with a *menú del día* costing 3,000 pesetas ($21.30).

Potes

$ **Restaurant Martín,** Roscabao, s/n. ☎ **942/73-02-33.**

Cuisine: ASTURIAN. **Reservations:** Not required.
Prices: Appetizers 550–750 ptas. ($3.90–$5.30); main courses 1,200–2,000 ptas. ($8.50–$14.20); fixed-price menu 1,000 ptas. ($7.10). V.
Open: Lunch, daily 1–4:30pm; dinner, daily 8:30–11:30pm. **Closed:** Jan.

This family-run establishment in the center of Potes is filled with regional charm and spirit. They prepare garbanzos (chick peas) with bits of chorizo sausage. Other vegetables and the rich produce of the region appear on the seasonally adjusted menu, as well as game from the Picos and fish from the Cantabrian coast. The dessert choices comprise more than a dozen tarts and pastries.

5 Gijón (Xixón)

294 miles (473km) N of Madrid, 119 miles (192km) W of Santander, 18 miles (29km) E of Oviedo

GETTING THERE • By Plane Gijón doesn't have an airport, but there is one at Ranón, 26 miles (42km) away, a facility it also shares with Oviedo-bound passengers.

• By Train Gijón has good rail links and makes a good gateway into Asturias. Three trains a day make the 6½ to 8½-hour trip from Madrid. León is a convenient rail hub for reaching Gijón because nine trains per day make the 2- to 3-hour trip between these cities. You can also take the narrow-gauge FEVE from Bilbao.

• By Bus Six buses a day connect Gijón with Madrid (5½ hours away), and two buses per day run to and from Santander (4½ hours away). Four buses a day go to León (2 hours away).

• By Car From Santander in the east, continue west along the N-634. At Ribadesella, you can take the turnoff to the 632, which is the coastal road that will take you to Gijón. This is the scenic route. To save time, continue on the N-634 until you reach the outskirts of Oviedo, then cut north on the expressway highway to Gijón.

ESSENTIALS The area code for Gijón is 98. The tourist information office is at Marqués de San Estebán, 1 (☎ **98/534-60-46**).

The major port of Asturias and its largest city is not just that: It is also a summer resort and an industrial center rolled into one. As a port, Gijón (pronounced hee-HON) is said to predate the Romans. The Visigoths came through here, and in the 8th century the Moors also made some forays into the area, but none of those would-be conquerors seems to have made much impression on Gijón.

The best part of the city to explore is the barrio of **Cimadevilla,** with its maze of alleys and leaning houses. This section, jutting into the ocean to the north of the new town, spills over an elevated piece of land known as Santa Catalina. Santa Catalina forms a headland at the west end of the **Playa San Lorenzo,** stretching for about 1½ miles (2km); this beach has good facilities and is sandy. After time at the beach you can stroll through the **Parque Isabel la Católica** at its eastern end.

The most exciting time to be in Gijón is on **Asturias Day,** the first Sunday in August. This fiesta is celebrated with parade floats, traditional folk dancing, and lots of music. But summers here tend to be festive even without a festival. Vacationers are fond of patronizing the cider taverns (*chigres*), eating grilled sardines, and joining in sing-alongs in the portside tascas. Be aware that you can get as drunk on cider as you can on beer, maybe somewhat faster.

Gijón is short on major monuments. The city was the birthplace of Gaspar Melchor de Jovellanos (1744–1811), one of Spain's most prominent men of letters, as well as agrarian reformer and liberal economist. Manuel de Godoy, the notorious minister, ordered that Jovellanos be held prisoner for seven years in Bellver Castle on Majorca. In Gijón his birthplace has been restored and turned into the Museo-Casa Natal de Jovellanos, Plaza de Jovellanos, open Tuesday to Saturday from 10am to 2pm and 4 to 8pm. Admission is free.

Where to Stay

EXPENSIVE

Parador El Molino Viejo [Parador de Gijón], Parque Isabel la Católica, s/n, 33203 Gijón. ☎ **98/537-05-11,** or toll free within the U.S. **800/223-1356.** Fax 98/537-02-33. 40 rms. A/C TV TEL **Bus:** 4 or 11.

Rates: 10,400 ptas. ($73.80) single; 13,000 ptas. ($92.30) double. Breakfast 1,100 ptas. ($7.80) extra. AE, DC, MC, V. **Parking:** Free.

Next to the verdant confines of Gijón's most visible park, about half a mile east of the town center and an easy walk from the popular Playa (beach) of San Lorenzo, this is the only parador in the entire province of Asturias. Awarded four stars by the government (which also runs it), it was constructed around the core of an 18th-century cider mill. The parador is surrounded by a garden strewn with tables, beside a stream sheltering colonies of swans, and it contains a cider bar that on weekends is very popular with local residents, a marble-sheathed reception area, and an unpretentious restaurant. The guest rooms are somewhat cramped and surprisingly simple for a four-star hotel; however, they're tastefully restored with well-scrubbed wooden floors, thick shutters, traditional furniture, and larger-than-usual baths.

MODERATE

Begoña, Carretera de la Costa, 44, 33205 Gijón. ☎ **98/514-72-11.** Fax 98/539-82-22. 249 rms (all with bath). TV TEL **Bus:** 4 or 11.

Rates: 7,100–7,800 ptas. ($50.40–$55.40) single; 9,075–9,900 ptas. ($64.40–$70.30) double. Breakfast 600 ptas. ($4.30) extra. AE, V. **Parking:** 1,200 ptas. ($8.50).

This functional modern hotel with much-appreciated parking has rooms that are well furnished and comfortable, plus efficient chamber service to keep everything clean. Regional and national dishes, with many seafood concoctions, are served in the Begoña's restaurant, where meals begin at 1,700 pesetas ($12.10). The hotel lies on the southern outskirts of the new town, one block north of Avenida Manuel Llaneza, the major traffic artery from the southwest.

La Casona de Jovellanos, Plaza de Jovellanos, 1,33201 Gijón. ☎ **98/534-12-64.** Fax 98/535-61-51. 13 rms (all with bath). TV TEL **Bus:** 4 or 11.

Rates: 9,000 ptas. ($63.90) single; 11,000 ptas. ($78.10) double. Breakfast 900 ptas. ($6.40) extra. AE, MC, V. **Parking:** 1,000 ptas. ($7.10) nearby.

This venerable hotel stands on the rocky peninsula that was the site of the oldest part of fortified Gijón, a short distance south of the Parque Santa Catalina. It contains only a few bedrooms, so reservations are imperative. The rooms themselves are attractively furnished and well maintained. The hotel was built on foundations three centuries old. In 1794 the writer, Jovellanos, established the Asturian Royal Institute of Marine Life and Mineralogy here, and it was transformed into a hotel, lying within walking distance of the beach and yacht basin.

Hernán Cortés, Fernández Vallín, 5, 33205 Gijón. ☎ **98/534-60-00.**

Fax 98/535-56-45. 109 rms (all with bath). MINIBAR TV TEL **Bus:** 4 or 11.

Rates: 4,300 ptas. ($30.50) single; 6,800–7,600 ptas. ($48.30–$54) double. Breakfast 600 ptas. ($4.30) extra. AE, DC, MC, V. **Parking:** 1,000 ptas. ($7.10) nearby.

About one block east of Plaza del 6 de Agosto, midway between Playa San Lorenzo and the harbor, the Cortés is one of the finest hotels in town. Although it was recently renovated, its guest rooms still retain a bit of the allure of yesteryear and provide such thoughtful extras as shoeshine equipment. The facilities include a disco, convention rooms, and ample parking. The Cortés doesn't have a restaurant, but it does offer a nighttime cafeteria for snacks and light meals.

Where to Dine

Casa Justo [Chigre Asturianu], Hermanos Feigueroso, 50. ☎ **538-63-57.**

Cuisine: ASTURIAN. **Reservations:** Recommended. **Bus:** 4 or 11.

Prices: Appetizers 550–950 ptas. ($3.90–$6.70); main courses 1,200–2,200 ptas. ($8.50–$15.60). AE, V.

Open: Lunch, daily 1–4pm; dinner, daily 7pm–midnight. **Closed:** 3 weeks in June (dates vary).

Housed within a very old cider press, for years this place has been called Chigre Asturianu, but most locals still call it by its old designation. Renovations have added well-designed dining rooms and kitchens to what used to be a large and drafty building. The cuisine is based primarily on fish and shellfish but with plenty of Asturian regional dishes as well. Try octopus with potatoes, grilled fresh John Dory, or veal chops. There is a full array of wines. Here, too, you can sample that Roquefort-like cheese, Cabrales, made in the Picos de Europa. The Casa Justo lies south of the old town near Campo Sagrada on the road to Pola de Siero.

Casa Tino, Alfredo Truán, 9. ☎ **534-13-87.**

Cuisine: ASTURIAN. **Reservations:** Recommended. **Bus:** 4 or 11.

Prices: Appetizers 650–950 ptas. ($4.60–$6.70); main courses 1,500–2,200 ptas. ($10.70–$15.60); *menú del día* 1,500 ptas. ($10.70). AE. V.

Open: Lunch, Fri–Wed 1:30-3:30pm; dinner, Fri–Wed 8:30–11:30pm. **Closed:** June 17–July 22.

Quality combined with quantity—at reasonable prices—is the hallmark of this restaurant, located near the police station, north of Manuel Llaneza and west of the Paseo de Begoña. Each day the chef prepares a different stew—sometimes fish and sometimes meat. The place is packed with chattering diners every evening, many of them habitués. Sample the white beans of the region cooked with pork, stewed hake, or marinated beefsteak, perhaps finishing with one of the fruit tarts.

Casa Victor, Carmen, 11. ☎ **534-83-10.**

Cuisine: SEAFOOD. **Reservations:** Recommended. **Bus:** 4 or 11.

Prices: Appetizers 650–1,200 ptas. ($4.60–$8.50); main courses 1,800–2,500 ptas. ($12.80–$17.80); fixed-price menu 1,800 ptas. ($12.80). AE, MC, V.

Open: Lunch, daily 1:30–3:30pm; dinner, Mon–Sat 8:30–11:30pm. **Closed:** Thurs in Nov.

Owner and sometime chef Victor Bango is a bit of a legend. He oversees the buying and preparation of the fresh fish for which this place is famous locally. The successful young people of Gijón enjoy the tavernlike atmosphere here, as well as the imaginative dishes—a mousse made from the roe of sea urchins, for example, is all the rage in Asturias these days. Well-chosen wines accompany such other menu items as octopus served with fresh vegetables, many preparations of hake, and grilled steak. Casa Victor is located by the dockyards.

6 Oviedo (Uviéu)

126 miles (203km) W of Santander, 276 miles (444km) N of Madrid

GETTING THERE • **By air** Oviedo doesn't have an airport. The nearest one is at Ranón, 32 miles (51.5km) away, which it shares with Gijón-bound passengers.

• **By Train** From Madrid, there are three trains per day. Call RENFE at **524-33-64** for information.

• **By Bus** From Santander one bus per day makes the 3-hour trip; from Madrid, three buses per day make the 6-hour trip. Call **528-12-00** for schedules.

• **By Car** Take the N-634 across the coast of northern Spain.

ESSENTIALS The area code for Oviedo is 98. The tourist information office is at Plaza de Alfonso II (☎ **98/521-33-85**).

Oviedo is the capital of the province of Asturias on Spain's northern coast, laved by the Bay of Biscay. Despite its high concentration of industry and mining, the area has unspoiled scenery. Only 16 miles (26km) from the coast, Oviedo is very pleasant in summer, when much of Spain is unbearably hot. It also makes an ideal base for excursions along the "Green Coast."

A peaceful city today, Oviedo has had a long and violent history. Razed in the 8th century during the Reconquest, it was rebuilt in an architectural style known as "Asturian Pre-Romanesque," which predated many of the greatest achievements under the Moors. Remarkably, this architectural movement was in flower when the rest of Europe lay under the black cloud of the Dark Ages.

As late as the 1930s Oviedo was suffering violent upheavals. An insurrection in the mining areas on October 5, 1934, led to a seizure of the town by miners, who set up a revolutionary government. The subsequent fighting led to the destruction of many historical monuments. The cathedral was also damaged, and the university was set on fire. Even more destruction came during the Spanish Civil War.

What to See & Do

Oviedo has been rebuilt into a modern city around the Parque de San Francisco. It still contains some historical and artistic monuments, however, the most important being the **cathedral** on the Plaza de Alfonso II (☎ **522-10-33**), a Gothic building begun in 1348 and completed at the end of the 15th century (except for the spire, which dates from 1556). Inside is an altarpiece in the florid Gothic style, dating from the 14th and 15th centuries. The cathedral's 9th-century **Cámara Santa (Holy Chamber)** is famous for the Cross of Don Pelayo, the Cross of the Victory, and the Cross of the Angels, the finest specimens of Asturian art in the world. Admission to the cathedral is free, but admission to the Holy Chamber is 200 pesetas ($1.40) for adults and 100 pesetas ($7.10) for children 10 to 15; children under 10 are free. The cathedral is open daily from 10am to 1pm and 4 to 6pm; the Holy Chamber is open daily from 10am to 1pm and 4 to 6pm. Take bus no. 1.

Behind the cathedral, the **Museo Arqueológico,** Calle San Vicente, 5 (☎ **521-54-05**), in a former convent dating from the 15th century, houses prehistoric relics discovered in Asturias, Pre-Romanesque sculptures, a numismatic display, and old musical instruments. It's open Tuesday to Saturday from 10am to 1:30pm and 4 to 6pm, Sunday from 11am to 1pm. Admission is free.

Standing above Oviedo, on Monte Naranco, are two of the most famous examples of Asturian Pre-Romanesque architecture, the churches of Santa María de Naranco (converted from a 9th-century palace) and San Miguel de Lillo (a once-royal chapel). These structures stand a mile northwest of the center.

Santa María del Naranco (☎ **529-67-55**), originally a palace/hunting lodge of Ramiro I (842-52), offers views of Oviedo and the snowcapped Picos de Europa. Once containing baths and private apartments, it was converted into a church in the 12th century. Intricate stonework depicts hunting scenes, and barrel vaulting rests on a network of blind arches. The open porticoes at both ends were considered 200 years ahead of their time architecturally. The church is open April through September, daily from 10am to 1pm and 3 to 7pm; October through March, daily from 10am to 1pm and 3 to 5pm.

Lying about 100 yards away is **San Miguel de Lillo** (☎ **529-56-85**). It, too, was built by Ramiro I and was no doubt a magnificent specimen of Asturian Pre-Romanesque until 15th-century "architects" marred its grace. The stone carvings that remain, however, are exemplary. Most of the sculpture has been transferred to the archeological museum in town.

San Miguel de Lillo keeps the same hours as Santa María de Naranco (see above). Ask at the tourist office for its 45-minute walking tour from the center of Oviedo to the churches. Also check that the churches will be open at the time of your visit.

Where to Stay

EXPENSIVE

★ **Hotel de La Reconquista,** Gil de Jaz 16, 33004 Oviedo. ☎ **98/524-11-00.** Fax 98/542-11-66. 131 rms, 14 suites. A/C MINIBAR TV TEL **Bus:** 1, 2, or 3.

Rates: 15,800–19,500 ptas. ($112.20–$138.50) single; 19,900–24,400 ptas. ($141.30–$173.20) double; from 38,000 ptas. ($269.80) suite. Buffet breakfast 1,700 ptas. ($12.10) extra. AE, DC, MC, V. **Parking:** 1,325 ptas. ($9.40).

Named after a subject dear to the hearts of the Catholic monarchs (the ejection of the Muslims from Iberia), this is considered one of the most prestigious hotels in Spain. Originally built between 1754 and 1777 as an orphanage and hospital, it received visits from Queen Isabel II in 1858 and a reworking of its baroque stonework during a restoration in 1958. The Reconquista was converted into a hotel in 1973 after the outlay of massive amounts of cash. Despite the growth of the city, it remains the second-largest building in Oviedo today.

Today, the interior boasts a combination of modern and reproduction furniture, as well as a scattering of ecclesiastical paintings and antiques. The spacious guest rooms contain private baths and are outfitted in antique styles, with views of the old town or of a series of elegantly antique interior courtyards. The hotel lies two blocks north of the largest park in the town center, the Campo San Francisco.

Dining/Entertainment: Rey Casto, a cafeteria/restaurant, offers both regional and national dishes, with complete meals costing 5,150 pesetas ($36.60). In addition there is a bar, plus yet another lounge bar with live piano music.

Services: 24-hour room service, concierge, currency exchange, safe deposit boxes, doctor on call, and babysitting upon request.

Facilities: Sauna, hairdresser, shopping boutiques, business center.

MODERATE

Clarín, Caveda, 23, 33002 Oviedo. ☎ **98/522-72-72.** Fax 98/522-80-18. 47 rms (all with bath). MINIBAR TV TEL **Bus:** 1, 2, or 3.

Rates: 8,450 ptas. ($60) single; 11,878 ptas. ($84.30) double. Breakfast 700 ptas. ($5) extra. AE, MC, V.

This recently built modern hotel in the old quarter is noted for its tasteful decor, with comfortable, inviting, and well-maintained rooms. On the premises you'll find a cozy and well-managed cafeteria but no restaurant. The hotel stands right in the middle of the "monumental zone," within walking distance of many of the attractions.

Hotel La Gruta, Alto de Buenavista, s/n, 33006 Oviedo. ☎ **98/523-24-50.** Fax 98/525-31-41. 105 rms (all with bath). TV TEL **Bus:** 1.

Rates: 8,300 ptas. ($58.90) single; 10,900 ptas. ($77.40) double. Breakfast 750 ptas. ($5.30) extra. AE, DC, MC, V. **Parking:** Free.

In this family-run hotel just outside the city limits, the rooms are comfortably furnished, many with views of the surrounding countryside. Amenities include safety deposit boxes. At the on-premises restaurant meals begin at 3,500 pesetas ($24.90).

Hotel Principado, Calle San Francisco, 6, 33003 Oviedo. ☎ **98/521-77-92.** Fax 98/521-39-46. 63 rms (all with bath), 3 suites. MINIBAR TV TEL

Rates: 9,180 ptas. ($65.20) single; 12,750 ptas. ($90.50) double; 14,500 ptas. ($103) suite. Buffet breakfast 950 ptas. ($6.70) extra. AE, DC, MC, V. **Parking:** 700 ptas. ($5).

The well-managed Principado stands opposite the university. Guests have access to an underground parking garage, easing the problem of parking in the center of town. The guest rooms are comfortably furnished and well maintained. The dining room serves nonguests as well as guests. A *menú del día* costs 1,500 pesetas ($10.70). Although built in 1951, the hotel was completely renovated in 1991.

A NEARBY PLACE TO STAY

If you're driving to La Coruña and Santiago de Compostela, you may want to stop in the little town of Cornellana (Salas), 24 miles (39km) west of Oviedo on the route to Luarca.

Hotel La Fuente, Carretera N-634, 33876 Cornellana. ☎ **98/583-40-42.** 19 rms (10 with bath). **Directions:** Take the N-634 west to Cornellana.

Rates: 2,000 ptas. ($14.20) single without bath; 3,850 ptas. ($27.30) double with bath; 5,400 ptas. ($38.30) double with bath. Breakfast 350 ptas. ($2.50) extra. MC, V. **Parking:** Free. **Closed:** Sept 20–Oct 2.

This little inn, located on the N-634, has a sitting room on each floor as well as a bath. Bedrooms are simply furnished but comfortable. In the dining room overlooking the garden you can order a three-course *menú del día* for 1,100 ptas. ($7.80) including bread and wine.

Where to Dine

Casa Conrado, Argülles, 1. ☎ **522-39-19.**

Cuisine: ASTURIAN. **Reservations:** Required. **Bus:** 1.
Prices: Appetizers 950–1,300 ptas. ($6.70–$9.20); main courses 1,500–2,750 ptas. ($10.70–$19.50); fixed-price menu 2,750 ptas. ($19.50). AE, DC, MC, V.
Open: Lunch, Mon–Sat 1–4pm; dinner, Mon–Sat 9pm–midnight. **Closed:** Aug.

Almost as solidly established as the cathedral nearby, this restaurant offers Asturian stews, seafood platters, seafood soups, several preparations of hake, including one cooked in cider, escalopes of veal with champagne, and a full range of desserts. It is a local favorite and a long-established culinary tradition. The service is attentive.

★ $ **Casa Fermín,** Calle San Francisco, 8. ☎ **521-64-52.**

Cuisine: ASTURIAN/INTERNATIONAL. **Reservations:** Recommended. **Bus:** 1 or 2.
Prices: Appetizers 900–1,900 ptas. ($6.40–$13.50); main courses 750–2,500 ptas. ($5.30–$17.80); fixed-price menus 4,500–5,000 ptas. ($32–$35.50). DC, MC, V.
Open: Lunch, Mon–Sat 1–4pm; dinner, Mon–Sat 8:30–11:30pm.

The chef here prepares the best regional cuisine in town in a building near the university and the cathedral. To order its most classic dish, ask for *fabada asturiana,* a bean dish with Asturian black pudding and Avilés ham. A tasty hake cooked in cider is another suggestion. In season (October to March), venison is the specialty. Try also the traditional Cabrales cheese of the province. The Casa Fermín lies directly east of the Parque de San Francisco.

$ **Cabo Peñas,** Melquiades Alvarez, 24. ☎ **522-03-20.**

Cuisine: ASTURIAN. **Reservations:** Not required. **Bus:** 1.
Prices: Appetizers 725–1,600 ptas. ($5.10–$11.40); main courses 825–2,200 ptas. ($5.90–$15.60); fixed-price menu 950 ptas. ($6.70). AE, DC, MC, V.
Open: Lunch, daily 1–4pm; dinner, daily 8pm–midnight.

Considered the most atmospheric place in town, Cabo Peñas, near the train station, is one of the few fast-food places that attract the gastronomes of Oviedo. At the dining room in the rear, diners perch on high stools placed around wood tables. They can begin with tapas before going on to order a *plato del día* (plate of the day). Deli-type cold cuts are featured, including boiled pork shoulder, and the huge steaks are often served with cheese sauce.

El Raitán, Trascorrales, 6. ☎ **521-42-18.**

Cuisine: ASTURIAN. **Reservations:** Recommended. **Bus:** 1.
Prices: Fixed-price menu 3,500 ptas. ($24.90). AE, DC, MC, V.
Open: Lunch only, Mon–Sat 2–5pm.

This place south of the cathedral, serving a set menu, bases all its dishes on regional ingredients, with meals accompanied by wines from La Rioja. A large array of choices is available for each course. Each day the chef presents nine classic regional dishes that change with the season. The place has a tavern setting with overhead beams—atmospheric and intimate.

★ **Trascorrales,** Plaza Trascorrales, 19. ☎ **522-24-41.**

Cuisine: ASTURIAN. **Reservations:** Required. **Bus:** 1.
Prices: Appetizers 950–1,800 ptas. ($6.70–$12.80); main courses 2,000–4,000 ptas. ($14.20–$28.40); fixed-price menu 5,000 ptas. ($35.50). AE, DC, MC, V.
Open: Lunch, Mon–Sat 1:30–3:30pm; dinner, Mon–Sat 8:30pm–midnight.

The cuisine of Fernando Martín, the leading restaurateur of Oviedo, has introduced many new dishes to this city. In spite of the innovations, however, none of the plates has lost its original Asturian base. Each dish is based on ingredients purchased at local markets. Try his gratinée of seafood; bull's-tail stew; or the most expensive item on the menu, bass baked in cider sauce. The orange ice cream makes a good dessert. This timbered building, draped in ivy, rises two floors. It lies in the west central part of town, three blocks south of the cathedral and two blocks west of the busy Avenida Padre Suárez.

21 Galicia

SET ATOP PORTUGAL IN THE NORTHWEST CORNER OF SPAIN, GALICIA IS A RAINSWEPT land of green grass and granite, much of its coastline gouged out by fjordlike inlets. It is a land steeped in Celtic traditions, and in many areas its citizens, called *gallegos*, speak their own language, which they insist is not a dialect of Spanish but a combination of Portuguese and Spanish. Often tossed by Atlantic storms, Galicia consists of four provinces: La Coruña (including Santiago de Compostela), Pontevedra, Lugo, and Ortense.

The Romans, who arrived late, after having conquered practically everything else in Europe, made quite an impression on the monuments of the land. The Roman walls around the city of Lugo and the Tower of Hercules at La Coruña are part of their legacy. The Moors came this way, too, and did a lot of damage along the way. But finding the natives none too friendly and other battlefields more promising, they moved on.

Nothing did more to put Galicia on the tourist map than the Santiago Road. It is the oldest, most traveled, and most famous route on the old continent. To guarantee their place in heaven, pilgrims journeyed to the tomb of Santiago (St. James), patron saint of Spain. They came across the Pyrenees by the thousands, risking their lives along the way. The Pilgrims' Way to Santiago led to the development and spreading of Romanesque art and architecture. The pilgrimage to the shrine lasted until medieval culture itself declined.

Seeing Galicia

GETTING THERE The quickest way to reach Galicia from Madrid is to fly to Labacolla Airport, east of Santiago de Compostela. Iberia offers daily flights from Madrid and also from Bilbao and Barcelona. La Coruña Airport has only one flight a week to Madrid, so it is inconvenient for most schedules.

The train run from Madrid to Galicia takes from 8 to 12 hours, depending on the train and what part of Galicia you have selected as your gateway to the province. The most popular train runs to Santiago de Compostela and La Coruña. A third line runs to Vigo, a port in the south of Galicia, closer to the Portuguese frontier. The Expreso Nocturno contains sleepers.

Bus connections to Galicia are also possible from Madrid. ALSA, a private bus company, serves the route, with connections from Madrid to all the major cities, including La Coruña and Santiago de Compostela.

To reach Galicia by car from Madrid, take the N-VI all the way to La Coruña. If Santiago is your goal, you can cut south before entering La Coruña, taking the expressway highway, the A-9, into Santiago.

A Suggested Route

If you're touring the northern coast of Spain, you'll enter Galicia at the border town of Ribadeo.

Day 1 Take the corniche road along the northwestern coast; exploring the Rías Altas, or fjord district, of Galicia. Spend the night at La Coruña.

Day 2 After visiting the Tower of Hercules in the morning, continue south to Santiago de Compostela, the goal of the medieval pilgrim. Stay overnight there after visiting the old town and the cathedral.

What's Special About Galicia

Beaches

- La Toja's La Lanzada beach, semi-wild and 5 miles (8km) long.
- La Coruña's two beaches: Riazor in town: and—even better—Santa Cristina, a few miles outside.

Great Towns

- Santiago de Compostela, the goal of medieval pilgrims and the legendary site of the tomb of St. James.
- La Coruña, an oldtime Atlantic seaport and the embarkation site of Spain's Invincible Armada.

A Great Cathedral

- The cathedral at Santiago de Compostela, one of the Christian world's most important, with its celebrated Romanesque Pórtico de la Gloria.

Ancient Monument

- The town walls of the provincial capital of Lugo, encircling it since Roman times.

Scenic Drives

- Rías Bajas, the lower country of Galicia—with deep inlets from Muros to La Toja.
- Rías Altas, north-country inlets from Ribadeo to La Coruña—with miles and miles of corniche road scenery.
- Mirador de la Curota—at 1,634 feet, offering panoramic view of four inlets comprising Rías Bajas.

A Historic District

- The old town of Santiago de Compostela, where the Middle Ages live on.

Day 3 Drive to Pontevedra, a provincial capital, for the night, but take the detour along the *rías* of the Rías Bajas country, which many consider the most dramatic fjord scenery in Galicia.

Day 4 Leave Pontevedra after seeing its old quarter and drive northeast to another provincial capital, Lugo, for the night. After a visit to its old Roman walls, you'll find yourself the next morning on the national highway (N-VI) leading back to Madrid.

1 Lugo

314 miles (506km) NW of Madrid; 60 miles (97km) SE of La Coruña

GETTING THERE • By Train Lugo lies on the rail link with Madrid. Two trains per day arrive from La Coruña.

• By Bus Lugo has bus links with most of the major towns in the northwest, including Oviedo, with one per day making the five-hour trip, and Orense, with five per day making the 2½-hour trip.

• By Car The N-VI connects Lugo with La Coruña as well as, at some distance, Madrid.

ESSENTIALS The area code for Lugo is 982. The tourist information office is at Plaza de España, 27 (☎ **982/23-13-61**).

Lugo has known many conquerors. The former Celti-Iberian settlement fell to the Romans, and centuries later the Moors used the land and its people to grow crops for them. Today, Lugo is one of the four provincial capitals of Galicia. It is generally neglected by those taking the Pilgrims' Way to Santiago de Compostela. However, it makes a rewarding detour for a morning or afternoon of sightseeing.

What to See & Do

Lugo, split by the Miño River, is surrounded by a thick 1¼-mile (2km) ★ **Roman wall,** the best preserved in the country. The wall is about 33 feet high and contains a total of 85 round towers; a sentry path can be approached by steps at the various town gates. Your best bet is to enter the old town at Puerto de Santiago, the most interesting of the ancient gates, and begin a most impressive promenade—what may well be one of the highlights of your tour of Galicia.

Along the way you'll come to the **cathedral,** built in 1129 and notable for its trio of landmark towers. Standing at the Plaza Santa María, it has many Romanesque architectural features, such as its nave, but it was subsequently given a Gothic overlay. Further remodeling took place in the 18th century, when many features were added, such as the Chapel of the Wide-Eyed Virgin (Ojos Grandes) at the east end, with a baroque rotunda. The highlight of the cathedral is a 13th-century porch at the north end, which provides shelter for a Romanesque sculpted *Jesus Christ in His Majesty.* The figure rises over a capital and seems to hang in space. At the far end of the transept rise huge wood-built altarpieces in the Renaissance style.

As you wander about—and that is far preferable to going inside many monuments—you'll traverse the cobblestoned, colonnaded medieval streets and interesting squares of the old town, especially behind the cathedral. The 18th-century **Episcopal Palace**—called a *pazo* in Galicia—faces the north side of the cathedral and opens onto Plaza Santa María. From the palace, old alleys behind it lead to a tiny nugget, **Plaza del Campo,** one of the most charming squares of Lugo, flanked with ancient houses and graced with a fountain at its core.

Or from the bishop's palace at the Plaza Santa María, you can take Calle Cantones to Plaza de España, where you will be greeted with the **Ayuntamiento (Town Hall),** built in a flowery rococo style.

From the Town Hall, follow Calle de la Reina north to the **Iglesia de San Francisco,** a church said to have been founded by St. Francis upon his return from a pilgrimage west to the tomb of St. James. The cloister of the church, entered at Plaza de la Soledad, s/n, has been turned into the **Museo Provincial** (☎ **24-21-12**). Many artifacts, including sundials from Celtic and Roman days, are found in this museum, along with folkloric displays. In July and August, it is open Monday through Friday from 10am to 1pm and 4 to 7pm; Saturday 10am to 2pm. From September through June, it is open Monday through Saturday from 10:30am to 2pm and 4:30 to 8:30pm; Sunday 11am to 2pm. Admission is free.

Where to Stay

EXPENSIVE

Gran Hotel Lugo, Avenida Ramón Ferreiro, 21, 27002 Lugo. ☎ **982/22-41-52.**

Fax 982/24-16-60. 156 rms, 12 suites. A/C MINIBAR TV TEL **Bus:** 1, 2, 3, or 4.

Rates: 10,600 ptas. ($75.30) single; 13,250 ptas. ($94.10) double; 18,500 ptas. ($131.40) suite. Breakfast 900 ptas. ($6.40) extra. AE, DC, MC, V. **Parking:** 850 ptas. ($6).

About half a mile west of the ancient city walls in a leafy residential neighborhood, this hotel is large, modern, and generally acknowledged as the best in town. Its guest rooms are conservative and comfortable, with marble and/or tile private baths and restful monochromatic colors.

Dining/Entertainment: The Os Marisqueiros restaurant serves regional and international three-course fixed-price lunches and dinners for 3,000 ptas. ($21.30). Live music is sometimes performed in the Atalaya Bar. Snack 2003 is a coffee shop/snack bar, and La Oca is a combination pizzeria and pub. You can dance the night away at the Chalry Max disco.

Services: Room service (available daily from 8am to midnight), laundry, concierge, babysitting.

Facilities: Business center, car rentals, shopping boutiques, bingo hall.

MODERATE

Méndez Núñez, Raiña, 1, 27002 Lugo. ☎ **982/23-07-11.** Fax 982/22-97-38. 86 rms (all with bath). TEL **Bus:** 1, 2, 3, or 4.

Rates: 4,500–6,000 ptas. ($32–$42.60) single; 6,500–8,500 ptas. ($46.20–$60.40) double. Breakfast 450 ptas. ($3.20) extra. MC, V. **Parking:** 130 ptas. (90¢) per hour in nearby garage.

Just around the corner from Plaza Mayor, this hotel was built in 1888 and named in honor of a then-famous Spanish general who had just won an important battle against revolutionaries in Cuba. Rebuilt and modernized in 1970, the hotel is today considered one of the best-managed in town. Bedrooms are well maintained and comfortable. No meals other than breakfast are served, but many restaurants and cafés lie within the neighborhood. The hotel is especially convenient for exploring the medieval streets of the town's old quarter.

$ **Portón Do Recanto,** La Campiña, 27923 Lugo. ☎ **982/22-34-55.** Fax 982/25-01-07. 23 rms (all with bath). TV TEL

Rates: 5,200 ptas. ($36.90) single; 6,500 ptas. ($46.20) double. Breakfast 400 ptas. ($2.80) extra. **Parking:** Free.

If you're driving, this little hotel 2 miles (3.2km) north of town on the Carretera N 640 is one of your best bets, particularly if you're arriving from neighboring Asturias. The old building has a bit of charm, while the well-maintained bedrooms are filled with modern comforts. You can enjoy the scenery as you dine in the hotel restaurant, which serves regional fare; a complete meal costs 2,000 pesetas ($14.20).

Where to Dine

Campos, Rúa Nova, 4. ☎ **22-07-43.**

Cuisine: GALICIAN. **Reservations:** Recommended. **Bus:** 1, 2, 3, or 4.
Prices: Appetizers 650–1,200 ptas. ($4.60–$8.50); main courses 1,200–2,600 ptas. ($8.50–$18.50); fixed-price menus 1,950–2,250 ptas. ($13.80–$16). AE, DC, MC, V.
Open: Lunch, daily noon–4:30pm; dinner, daily 7:30pm–midnight.

In the old quarter, immediately adjacent to Plaza del Campo, this well-acclaimed restaurant is the creation of Amparo Yañez and his son, Manuel. Together, they offer imaginative combinations of fresh ingredients that are deftly prepared and much appreciated by their loyal clients. Seasonal game dishes, especially local pheasant, are featured along with fresh fish, such as grouper with almonds. The best dessert is fresh local strawberries with honey and cream.

Ferreiros, Rúa Nueva, 1. ☎ **22-97-28.**

Cuisine: GALICIAN. **Reservations:** Recommended. **Bus:** 1, 2, 3, or 4.
Prices: Appetizers 750–1,050 ptas. ($5.30–$7.50); main courses 1,600–2,300 ptas. ($11.40–$16.30); *menú del día* 1,500–1,900 ptas. ($10.70–$13.50). V.
Open: Lunch, Thurs–Tues 1–5pm; dinner, Thurs–Tues 7:30pm–midnight.

In business since the 1920s, this long-time favorite near the cathedral must be doing something right. In fact, it offers well-prepared and old-fashioned regional fare with a certain unpretentious flair. The portions are generous, and the food is fresh. The many shellfish dishes featured are the most expensive items on the menu. You can also order a big slab of rib of beef or monkfish prepared in different ways.

Mesón de Alberto, Cruz, 4. ☎ **22-83-10.**

Cuisine: GALICIAN. **Reservations:** Recommended. **Bus:** 1, 2, 3, or 4.
Prices: Appetizers 650–1,000 ptas. ($4.60–$7.10); main courses 1,600–2,500 ptas. ($11.40–$17.80); fixed-price menu 2,300 ptas. ($16.30). AE, DC, MC, V.
Open: Lunch, Mon–Sat 1–4pm; dinner, Mon–Sat 8pm–midnight.

Alberto García is the culinary star of Lugo, and with good reason. Ably assisted by his wife, Flor, he offers a well-chosen menu of imaginative fish and meat dishes and perhaps the best wine cellar in Lugo. The style of the place is that of a rustic tavern: a stand-up bar serving tapas, plus a handful of dining tables. The overflow is directed either to a somewhat more formal dining room beside the tavern or to the second floor. Try Alberto's salad with eel and an exotic vinegar, monkfish served with a mountain cheese (Cabrales from Asturias), or beefsteak for two, prepared with his "secret" sauce. Mesón de Alberto stands one block north of the cathedral in the old quarter.

2 La Coruña

375 miles (604km) NW of Madrid, 96 miles (155km) N of Vigo

GETTING THERE • By Air There is one flight a week from Madrid to La Coruña Airport. Serviced only by Aviaco, the Aeropuerto de Alvedro (☎ **23-22-40**) lies 6 miles (10km) from the heart of the city.

• By Train From Madrid (via Orense and Zamora), there is express service three times a day ($8^1/_2$ hours). Arrivals are at the La Coruña Station on Calle Joaquín Planelles (☎ **23-03-09**).

• By Bus From Santiago, there's frequent daily bus service leaving from the station on the Calle Caballeros (☎ **23-96-44**). Four buses a day connect Madrid and La Coruña (9 hours).

• By Car La Coruña is reached from Madrid by the N-VI. You can also follow the coastal highway, the N-634, which runs all the way across the northern rim of Spain from San Sebastián in the east.

ESSENTIALS The area code for La Coruña is 981. The tourist information office is at Dársena de la Marina, s/n (☎ **981/22-18-22**).

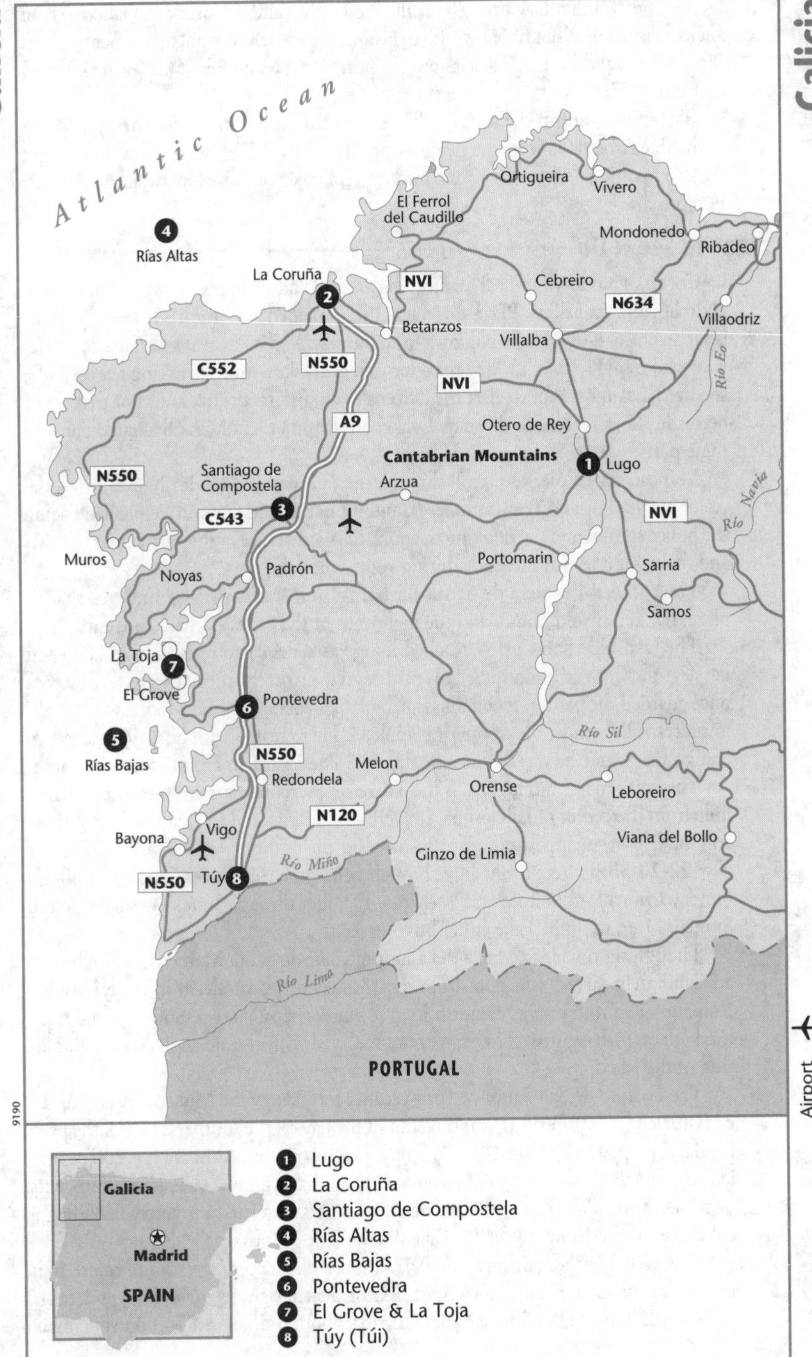

Galicia
15 mi
25.5 km
N
Atlantic Ocean
Rías Altas
La Coruña
El Ferrol del Caudillo
Ortigueira
Vivero
Mondonedo
Ribadeo
Cebreiro
N634
Villaodriz
NVI
Betanzos
Villalba
N550
C552
NVI
A9
Río Eo
Otero de Rey
Cantabrian Mountains
Lugo
N550
Santiago de Compostela
Arzua
Río Navia
C543
NVI
Muros
Noyas
Padrón
Portomarin
Sarria
Samos
La Toja
El Grove
Pontevedra
Río Sil
Rías Bajas
N550
Melon
Redondela
Orense
Leboreiro
N120
Bayona
Vigo
Viana del Bollo
Ginzo de Limia
Río Miño
N550
Túy
Río Lima
PORTUGAL
Airport
9190
Galicia
Madrid
SPAIN
1 Lugo
2 La Coruña
3 Santiago de Compostela
4 Rías Altas
5 Rías Bajas
6 Pontevedra
7 El Grove & La Toja
8 Túy (Túi)

Despite the fact that La Coruña (Corunna in English and A Coruña in Galician) is an ancient city, it does not have a wealth of historical and architectural monuments. Celts, Phoenicians, and Romans all occupied the port, and it is another of the legendary cities that claims Hercules as its founder.

The great event in the history of La Coruña occurred in 1588, when Philip II's Invincible Armada sailed from here to England. Only half of the ships eventually got back to Spain. The following year, Sir Francis Drake and his ships attacked the port in reprisal.

What to See & Do

La Coruña's old town is ideal for strolling around and stopping at any of the historic churches and mansions. **Plaza de María Pita**—named after the 16th-century Spanish Joan of Arc—divides the old town from the new. María Pita was a La Coruña housewife who is said to have spotted the approach of Drake's troops. Risking her own life, she fired a cannon shot to alert the citizens to an imminent invasion. For that act of heroism, she is revered to this day. Drake, on the other hand, is still a hated name in these parts.

You can take a pleasant stroll through the Jardines de Méndez Núñez, lying between the harbor and Los Cantones (Cantón Grande and Cantón Pequeño). Facing the police station and overlooking the port, the gardens are in the very center of town and make for a restful interlude during your sightseeing.

The cobbled **Plazuela de Santa Bárbara** also merits a visit—a tiny tree-shaded plaza, flanked by old houses and the high walls of the Santa Bárbara convent.

The **Jardín de San Carlos,** reached along Paseo del Parrote, dates from 1843 and lies near the Casa de la Cultura. This garden grew up on the site of an old fortress that once guarded the harbor. It contains the tomb of General Sir John Moore, who fought unsuccessfully against the troops of Napoleon. He retreated with his British forces to La Coruña, where he was shot in a final battle. These gardens are an ideal picnic spot.

The city's major monument is the **Torre de Hércules,** a lighthouse more than a mile from the center of La Coruña. It overlooks the city and the sea and was supposedly built by the emperor Trajan (restored in the 1700s). Admission to the tower (☎ **22-20-38**) is free. From July through September, it is open Tuesday through Sunday from 11am to 2pm and 4 to 7pm; October through June, Tuesday through Sunday 11am to 3pm. Take either bus 9 or 13.

The **Iglesia de Santa María del Campo,** Calle de Santa María, is a church with an elaborately carved west door from the 13th century—modeled in the traditional Romanesque-Gothic style. Beneath its rose window you'll see a Gothic portal from the 13th or 14th century. The tympanum is carved with a scene depicting the Adoration of the Magi.

The Castillo de San Antón, a 16th-century fort is now the **Museo Arqueológico e Histórico** (☎ **20-59-94**), standing out in the bay on the southeast side of the peninsula. It is open daily from 10am to 2pm and 4 to 7:30pm. Admission is 200 pesetas ($1.40) for adults; free for children. In addition to having a spectacular location on its own islet, it displays many unusual artifacts from La Coruña province, including a collection of pre-Roman jewelry. Take the no. 3 or 3A bus.

The second-largest port in Spain, La Coruña is also a popular vacation resort, so it gets really crowded in July and August. Riazor Beach, right in town, is a good, fairly wide beach, but the best one is Santa Cristina, about 3 miles (4.8km) outside town.

There's regular round-trip bus service. The best way to go, however, is via the steamer that plies the bay.

Where to Stay

EXPENSIVE

Ciudad de La Coruña, Ciudad Residencial La Torre, Poligono de Adormideras, s/n, 15002 La Coruña. ☎ **981/21-11-00.** Fax 981/22-46-10. 123 rms, 9 suites. A/C MINIBAR TV TEL **Bus:** 3 or 3A.

Rates: 7,700–9,350 ptas. ($54.70–$66.40) single; 9,350–11,550 ptas. ($66.40–$82) double; 14,300–17,600 ptas. ($101.50–$125) suite. Breakfast 800 ptas. ($5.70) extra. AE, DC, MC, V. **Parking:** Free.

On the northwestern tip of the peninsula, surrounded by sea grasses and dunes, this three-star establishment is cordoned off from the apartment-house complexes that surround it by a wide swath of green. Built in the early 1980s, the hotel features a swimming pool, a big-windowed bar, a gym, and a ground-floor restaurant. Each attractively modern guest room contains a kitchenette and a private bath. In the hotel restaurant, fixed-price meals cost 1,800 pesetas ($12.80), and there is also a bar-style cafeteria serving coffee, drinks, and snacks.

Hotel Atlántico, Jardines de Méndez Nuñez, s/n, 15006 La Coruña. ☎ **981/22-65-00.** Fax 981/20-10-71. 195 rms, 2 suites. TV TEL **Bus:** 1, 2, or 3.

Rates: 9,300–11,400 ptas. ($66–$80.90) single; 11,700–14,300 ptas. ($83.10–$101.50) double; 17,000–19,500 ptas. ($120.70–$138.50) suite. Breakfast 800 ptas. ($5.70) extra. AE, DC, MC, V. **Parking:** 900 ptas. ($6.40).

This convenient, comfortable hotel with a contemporary design contrasts with the lavishly ornate 19th-century park surrounding it. Crowds of Galicians promenade here in fine weather. The Atlántico is in the building that also houses the city's casino, a modern restaurant, and a disco. The well-furnished guest rooms, all with private baths, are among the best in town.

Hotel Finisterre, Paseo del Parrote, 20, 15001 La Coruña. ☎ **981/20-54-00.** Fax 981/20-84-62. 120 rms, 7 suites. A/C MINIBAR TV TEL **Bus:** 1, 2, 3, or 5.

Rates: 11,000–13,200 ptas. ($78.10–$93.70) single; 13,800–17,500 ptas. ($98–$124.30) double; 20,400–23,700 ptas. ($144.80–$168.30) suite. Breakfast 1,100 ptas. ($7.80) extra. AE, DC, MC, V. **Parking:** Free.

Immediately above the port, a short walk east of the tourist information office at the edge of the old town, this high-rise hotel is considered the finest and most panoramic in town. Bedrooms are small but comfortable, with wall-to-wall carpeting, lots of exposed wood, brightly contemporary upholsteries, and private baths. The hotel seems to be the preferred choice of business travelers. Although it was built in 1947, it has been remodeled many times since, the latest in 1991.

Dining/Entertainment: La Finisterre restaurant serves à la carte meals beginning at around 4,000 pesetas ($28.40); there's also a bar.

Services: Room service, concierge, babysitting, laundry.

Facilities: Tennis courts, four outdoor swimming pools (two heated for year-round use, one reserved for children), garden, children's nursery, gym and health club, skating rink, sauna, ample opportunities for brisk and invigorating seafront walks, barber/hairdresser, nearby basketball court.

Residencia Riazor, Barrio de la Maza, 29, 15004 La Coruña. ☎ **981/25-34-00.** Fax 981/25-34-04. 176 rms. TV TEL **Bus:** 5, 20, or 22.

Rates: 6,800 ptas. ($48.30) single; 8,600 ptas. ($61.10) double. Breakfast 600 ptas. ($4.30) extra. AE, DC, MC, V. **Parking:** 800 ptas. ($5.70).

This 12-story 1960s hotel is right on the beach and was last renovated in 1993. It has a glass-enclosed lounge on the second floor and a snack bar/cafeteria. The guest rooms are functional and lack style, but they are clean and comfortable and have private baths.

MODERATE

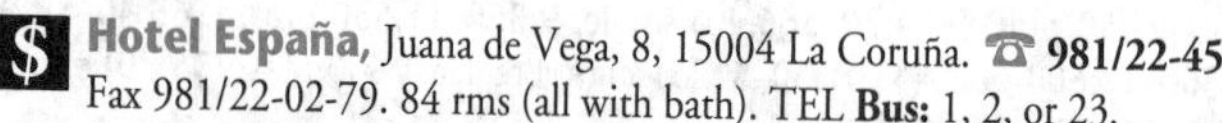

Hotel España, Juana de Vega, 8, 15004 La Coruña. ☎ **981/22-45-06.** Fax 981/22-02-79. 84 rms (all with bath). TEL **Bus:** 1, 2, or 23.

Rates: 3,500–4,500 ptas. ($24.90–$32) single; 5,800–7,800 ptas. ($41.20–$55.40) double. Breakfast 450 ptas. ($3.20) extra. AE, DC, MC, V. **Parking:** 1,000 ptas. ($7.10).

This pleasant hotel, just a few steps from the gazebos and roses of the Jardines de Méndez Núñez, has a narrow reception area, a comfortable series of long sitting rooms; and modern, simply furnished bedrooms. Breakfast is the only meal served. The hotel has a bar and provides laundry service.

INEXPENSIVE

Almirante, Paseo de Ronda, 54, 15011 La Coruña. ☎ **981/25-96-00.** 20 rms (all with bath). TV TEL **Bus:** 7, 14, or 14A.

Rates: 5,500 ptas. ($39.10) double. Breakfast 375 ptas. ($2.70) extra. MC, V. **Parking:** 1,000 ptas. ($7.10).

There are few amenities here—just good, clean rooms, all doubles, at a real bargain price. There is no restaurant, but a continental breakfast will be served on order. Room service is available. The hotel was last renovated in 1993.

Where to Dine

Two or so blocks from the waterfront, there are several restaurants that specialize in Galician cuisine. It is customary to go window shopping for food here. The restaurants along two of the principal streets—Calle de la Estrella and Calle de los Olmos—have display counters in front of their establishments. Most of them charge comparable prices.

Casa Pardo, Novoa Santos, 15. ☎ **28-71-78.**

Cuisine: GALICIAN. **Reservations:** Recommended.
Prices: Appetizers 750–1,500 ptas. ($5.30–$10.70); main courses 1,350–2,200 ptas. ($9.60–$15.60); fixed-price menu 3,000 ptas. ($21.30). AE, DC, MC, V.
Open: Lunch, Mon–Sat 1:30–4pm; dinner, Mon–Sat 9pm–midnight.

Located near the Palacio de Congresos south of the old town, this restaurant is acclaimed as one of the finest dining rooms in the city. Under the direction of Eduardo Pardo, the restaurant offers both a traditional cuisine and innovative seafood dishes. Shellfish and other fish dishes are prepared here with skill, everything from oysters to salmon. Mollusks and crustaceans aren't the only items on the menu—meat and vegetable dishes are also well prepared. Galician turbot is delectable. The kitchen seems always aware of the necessity of securing fresh ingredients—both from field and shore. The first-rate service matches the cuisine. Patrons of this well-entrenched dining room prefer such wines as Terras Gauda and Viña Costeira.

El Coral, Calle Estrella, 2–4. ☎ **22-10-82.**

Cuisine: GALICIAN/SEAFOOD/INTERNATIONAL. **Reservations:** Recommended. **Bus:** 1, 2, 5, or 17.

Prices: Appetizers 1,000–2,000 ptas. ($7.10–$14.20); main courses 1,500–2,800 ptas. ($10.70–$19.90); fixed-price menus 2,500–3,500 ptas. ($17.80–$24.90). AE, DC, MC, V.

Open: Lunch, daily 1–4pm; dinner, daily 9pm–midnight. **Closed:** Sun night except in July–Aug.

This is my favorite and one of the most popular dining spots at the port. In business since 1954, it offers polite service, cleanliness, and Galician cookery prepared with distinction. This restaurant specializes in shellfish, fish, meats, and Galician wines. The chef's specialty is *turbante de mariscos* (shellfish). You might also try the *calamares rellenos* (stuffed squid). A popular main course is *lubina* (sea bass) *al horno,* and the dessert specialty is a rich and fattening *filloas.* A pitcher (1 liter) of Ribero wine makes a good choice, and you can also order Condados and Ríoja wines.

$ **Taverna Pil-Pil,** Paralela a Orillamar, s/n. ☎ **21-27-12.**

Cuisine: GALICIAN. **Reservations:** Recommended. **Bus:** 3 or 3A.

Prices: Appetizers 650–850 ptas. ($4.60–$6); main courses 1,050–1,800 ptas. ($7.50–$12.80). No credit cards.

Open: Lunch, Tues–Sat 1–4:30pm; dinner, Tues–Sat 8pm–12:30am. **Closed:** Sept 15–Oct 15.

In spite of its size, this small tavern has a fine culinary tradition and serves many elegant wines that are moderate in price. Host Luis Moya purchases fresh ingredients, often seafood, and handles them deftly in the kitchen. Try a clam omelet as an appetizer, followed by one of the main courses, perhaps grilled fish, concluding with a velvety-smooth chocolate mousse. The place is on the road leading to the Torre de Hércules.

3 Santiago de Compostela

381 miles (613km) NW of Madrid, 46 miles (74km) S of La Coruña

GETTING THERE • By Plane From Madrid, Iberia has daily flights to Santiago, and there are also daily flights from Barcelona. The only international airport in Galicia is east of Santiago de Compostela at Labacolla (☎ **981/59-74-10** for flight information). It lies 7 miles (11km) from the center on the road to Lugo.

• By Train From La Coruña, 14 trains make the one-hour trip daily. Two trains arrive daily from Madrid after the 8-hour trip. Call **52-02-02** for information.

• By Bus Buses leave on the hour, connecting La Coruña with Santiago ($1^1/_2$ hours). Two buses arrive in Santiago daily from Madrid (8 to 9 hours). Phone **58-77-00** for schedules.

• By Car Take the expressway highway (A-9/E-50) south from La Coruña to reach Santiago. From Madrid, the N-VI runs to Galicia. From Lugo, head south along the N-640.

ESSENTIALS The area code for Santiago de Compostela is 981. The tourist information office is at Rúa del Villar, 43 (☎ **981/58-40-81**).

All roads in Spain used to lead to this northwestern pilgrimage city. In addition to being the third-largest holy city of the Christian world, Santiago de Compostela is both a university town and a marketplace for Galician farmers.

But it was the pilgrims who made the city famous. A pilgrimage to the tomb of the beheaded apostle, St. James, was a high point for the faithful—peasant and prince alike—who journeyed here from all over Europe, often under difficult, sometimes life-threatening conditions.

Santiago de Compostela's link with legend began in A.D. 813, when an urn was discovered containing, it was believed, the remains of St. James. A temple was erected over the spot, but the poor saint wasn't allowed to remain in peace. Wars, a long and mysterious disappearance, and an equally mysterious "rediscovery" followed.

Aside from its religious connections, Santiago de Compostela, with its flagstoned streets, churches, and shrines, is one of the most romantic and historic of Spain's great cities and has been declared a national landmark. It also has the dubious distinction of being the rainiest city in Spain, but the showers tend to arrive and end suddenly. Locals claim that the rain only makes their city more beautiful.

What to See & Do

The highlight at Santiago de Compostela is undoubtedly the cathedral, and you should take at least two hour to see it. Afterward, take a stroll through this enchanting town, which has a number of other interesting monuments as well as many stately mansions along Rúa de Villar and Rúa Nueva.

The ✪ **cathedral,** Plaza del Obradoiro (☎ **58-35-48**), begun in the 11th century, is thought by some to be the crowning achievement of Spanish Romanesque, even though it actually reflects a number of styles. Some of the architecture is spectacular. The Pórtico de la Gloria, carved by Mateo in the late 12th century, ranks among the finest produced in Europe at that time; the altar, with its blend of Gothic simplicity and baroque decor, is also extraordinary. The floor plan of the cathedral resembles a cross. It has three naves and several chapels and cloisters. You can visit the crypt, where a silver urn contains what are believed to be the remains of the Apostle St. James. A cathedral museum displays tapestries and archeological fragments. Next door, the **Palacio de Gelmírez,** an archbishop's palace built during the 12th century, is another outstanding example of Romanesque architecture. Admission to the cathedral is free; to the cloisters it is 300 pesetas ($2.10); to the Palacio de Gelmírez it is 100 pesetas (70¢). Hours for the cathedral are daily from 10am to 1:30pm and 4 to 7:30pm; for the museum, daily from 10:30am to 1:30pm and 4 to 6pm; for the Palacio de Gelmírez, July through September daily from 10:30am to 1:30pm and 4 to 7pm.

Most of the other impressive buildings are also on Plaza del Obradoiro, also called Plaza de España. Next door to the cathedral is **Los Reyes Católicos,** now a parador (see "Where to Stay," below), formerly a royal hospital and, in the 15th century, a pilgrims' hospital. It was designed by Enrique de Egas, Isabella and Ferdinand's favorite architect. Tours (daily from 10am to 1pm and 4 to 7pm; ☎ **58-22-00** for information) visit the cloistered courtyard with its beautiful 16th- to 18th-century fountains and the main chapel with its beamed ceiling.

Monasterio de San Martín Pinario, Plaza de la Immaculada, founded in 899 by monks and rebuilt in the 17th century, remains one of the most important monasteries in Galicia. Its large facade was built in the Compostela baroque style, with massive

Doric columns. The interior has a richly ornamented Churrigueresque high altar and choir stalls that are truly works of art.

One of the most important squares in the old town is **Plaza de la Quintana,** to the left of the cathedral's Goldsmith's Doorway. This is a favorite square with students, who often perch on the flight of broad steps that connect the rear of the cathedral to the walls of a convent. The square is dominated by **Casa de la Canónica,** the former residence of the canon, which has wrought-iron window bars, lending it a rather severe appearance.

South of the square is the Renaissance-style **Plaza de las Platerías (Silversmiths' Square),** which has an elaborate fountain.

Farther afield, visit the Romanesque **Santa María del Sar,** on Calle Castron d'Ouro, half a mile down Calle de Sar, which starts at Patio de Madre. This collegiate church is considered one of the architectural gems of the Romanesque style in Galicia. Its walls and columns are on a 15-degree slant, thought to be attributable to either a fragile foundation or an architect's fancy. Visit the charming cloister with its slender columns. The church is open Monday to Saturday from 10am to 1pm and 4 to 6:30pm. Admission is 500 pesetas ($3.60).

Finally, cap off your day with a walk along **Paseo de la Herradura,** the gardens southwest of the old town, from where you'll have an all-encompassing view of the cathedral and the old city.

Where to Stay

VERY EXPENSIVE

Hostal de Los Reyes Católicos, Plaza de España, 1, 15705 Santiago de Compostela. ☎ **981/58-22-00.** Fax 981/56-30-94. 136 rms. MINIBAR TV TEL **Bus:** 4, 21, 25, 26, 33, or 34.

Rates: 18,400 ptas. ($130.60) single; 23,000 ptas. ($163.30) double. Breakfast 1,200 ptas. ($8.50) extra. AE, DC, MC, V. **Parking:** 1,700 ptas. ($12.10).

This former 16th-century hospital, founded by Ferdinand and Isabella, has been turned into one of the most spectacular hotels in Europe. Next to the cathedral, it also served as a hospital and resting place for pilgrims visiting the tomb of St. James. Even if you don't stay here, you should stop in and see it, but only on a guided tour (see above).

The hotel has four huge open-air courtyards, each with its own covered walk, gardens, and fountains. In addition, there are great halls, French grillwork, copies of paintings by El Greco, and a large collection of antiques. The Gothic chapel is the setting for weekly concerts.

There is a full range of accommodations, everything from Franco's former bedchamber to small rooms. Many of the palatial rooms have ornate canopied beds draped in embroidered red velvet; hand-carved chests, gilt mirrors, and oil paintings—along with private baths—enhance the air of luxury.

Dining/Entertainment: The hotel's formal dining room, Libredon, serves both Galician and international cuisine, with meals costing from 3,500 pesetas ($24.90). There is also an elegant bar.

Services: Room service, laundry, hairdresser.

Facilities: Car rentals.

EXPENSIVE

Hotel Araguaney, Calle Alfredo Brañas, 5, 15701 Santiago de Compostela. ☎ **981/59-59-00.** Fax 981/59-02-87. 60 rms, 5 suites. A/C MINIBAR TV TEL **Bus:** 4, 21, 25, 26, 33, or 34.

Rates: 14,000–17,500 ptas. ($99.40–$124.30) single; 17,500–22,000 ptas. ($124.30–$156.20) double; from 27,000 ptas. ($191.70) suite. Breakfast 2,200 ptas. ($15.60) extra. AE, DC, MC, V. **Parking:** 1,200 ptas. ($8.50).

Located in Santiago's commercial and residential zone, about eight blocks southwest of the cathedral, this is a comfortable hotel whose streamlined walls contain some of the most up-to-date dining, drinking, and conference facilities in town. The modern guest rooms, all with private baths, are quite stylish.

Dining/Entertainment: The Restaurant Luis XVI and the Restaurant 3 Conchas (O'Portón) serve fixed-price lunches and dinners for 3,400 pesetas ($24.10). The comfortable hotel bar offers an array of international drinks and Spanish brandies. The hotel also contains one of the most frequented discos in Galicia.

Services: Room service (available daily from 7am to 4pm and 9pm to midnight), concierge, babysitting, in-house tour operator, laundry/valet.

Facilities: Large and well-maintained swimming pool, sauna, solarium, shopping boutiques, business center, car rentals.

MODERATE

Hotel Compostela, Hórreo, 1, 15702 Santiago de Compostela. ☎ **981/58-57-00.** Fax 981/56-32-69. 99 rms (all with bath), 1 suite. MINIBAR TV TEL **Bus:** 10.

Rates: 8,500 ptas. ($60.40) single; 13,000 ptas. ($92.30) double; 17,000 ptas. ($120.70) triple; 16,500 ptas. ($117.20) suite for two. Breakfast buffet 800 ptas. ($5.70) extra. AE, DC, MC, V.

This hotel is conveniently located just a few short blocks from the cathedral, but it is also, unfortunately, close to the heavily trafficked city center. It has a grand granite facade, which belies the modern interior and bedrooms filled with clean, angular, machine-made furniture. A pleasant dining room and a café/bar are on the premises, offering a fixed-price lunch or dinner for 2,100 pesetas ($14.90). The hotel was completely renewed in 1994.

Hotel del Peregrino, Rosalía de Castro, s/n, 15706 Santiago de Compostela. ☎ **981/52-18-50.** Fax 981/52-17-77. 150 rms (all with bath), 7 suites. MINIBAR TV TEL **Bus:** 1 or 2.

Rates: 10,500–12,400 ptas. ($74.60–$88) single; 15,500 ptas. ($110.10) double; 19,500 ptas. ($138.50) suite. Breakfast buffet 1,200 ptas. ($8.50) extra. AE, DC, MC, V. **Parking:** Free.

This four-star hotel at the edge of town off the main road is preferred by many people traveling to this remote part of Spain. It has a good restaurant, a bar and snack bar, and a rear garden with a swimming pool. The decor is restrained and tasteful; the bedrooms are modern and well furnished.

Hotel Gelmírez, Hórreo, 92, 15702 Santiago de Compostela. ☎ **981/56-11-00.** Fax 981/56-32-69. 138 rms (all with bath). TV TEL **Bus:** 10.

Rates: 5,440–6,800 ptas. ($38.60–$48.30) single; 7,680–9,600 ptas. ($54.50–$68.20) double. Breakfast 600 ptas. ($4.30) extra. AE, DC, MC, V.

This soaring concrete structure near the train station is one of the largest hotels in the region. Built in the early 1970s, it has a comfortable and pleasant interior far more attractive than its plain facade suggests. The guest rooms are furnished in a functional modern style. On the premises is a bistro/cafeteria/bar, offering *platos combinados,* or combination plates, along with a wide array of drinks.

INEXPENSIVE

$ **Hostal Residencia Alameda,** San Clemente, 32, 15705 Santiago de Compostela. ☎ **981/58-81-00.** 20 rms (all with bath). TV TEL **Bus:** 10.

Rates: 2,650 ptas. ($18.80) single without bath, 4,000 ptas. ($28.40) single with bath; 4,500 ptas. ($32) double without bath, 6,000 ptas. ($42.60) double with bath. Breakfast 375 ptas. ($2.70) extra. AE, MC, V. **Parking:** 700 ptas. ($5).

Located on the second floor of a 1970s building in the cathedral district, the Alameda has comfortable, immaculate rooms. The staff here is courteous and efficient. Ample parking is available, adjacent to the hostal. The Alameda serves breakfast only.

$ **Hotel Maycar,** Doctor Teijeiro, 15, 15701 Santiago de Compostela. ☎ **981/56-34-44.** 40 rms (all with bath). TEL **Bus:** 10 from train station.

Rates: 3,000–4,000 ptas. ($21.30–$28.40) single; 4,800–6,000 ptas. ($34.10–$42.60) double. Breakfast 350 ptas. ($2.50) extra. No credit cards.

This simple two-star hotel stands not far from the busy central Plaza de Galicia. The marble-trimmed lobby is unpretentious, and there is an elevator. The rooms are well-maintained but spartan. Breakfast is the only meal served.

$ **Hotel Universal,** Plaza de Galicia, 2, 15706 Santiago de Compostela. ☎ **981/58-58-00.** 54 rms (all with bath). TV TEL

Rates (including breakfast): 3,604–4,664 ptas. ($25.60–$33.10) single; 5,936–7,208 ptas. ($42.10–$51.20) double. AE, DC, MC, V.

Located south of the Fuente de San Antonio, just outside the center of the city, this is a pleasant and comfortable hotel despite its drab concrete facade, built in 1970. It has a modernized lobby, and there is a TV lounge on the premises. The guest rooms are furnished in a simple modern style. Breakfast is the only meal served.

Where to Dine

$ **Alameda,** Porta Faxeira, 15. ☎ **58-66-57.**
Cuisine: GALICIAN. **Reservations:** Recommended in summer.
Prices: Appetizers 650–1,200 ptas. ($4.60–$8.50); main courses 1,800–3,000 ptas. ($12.80–$21.30); fixed-price menus 2,500–3,000 ptas. ($17.80–$21.30). AE, DC, MC, V.
Open: Lunch, daily 1–4:30pm; dinner, daily 8pm–12:30am.

Since 1954 the constant stream of diners, both foreign and local, indicates the popularity of this government-rated two-fork restaurant, located opposite the Parque de Alameda. There is a stylish cafeteria/snack bar on the ground floor, handy for light meals and drinks; guests can sit at sidewalk tables in fair weather. The fare includes many Galician specialties, and the chef is noted for his paella. Start with the caldo gallego (Galician soup) and follow with another regional specialty, *lacón con grelos* (hamhock with greens). The *necoras* (spider crabs) are also a real gourmet delight.

Anexo Vilas, Avenida de Villagarcía, 21. ☎ **59-86-37.**

Cuisine: GALICIAN. **Reservations:** Recommended. **Bus:** 4, 21, or 25.
Prices: Appetizers 1,000–1,500 ptas. ($7.10–$10.70); main courses 2,000–3,500 ptas. ($14.20–$24.90); fixed-price menu 4,500 ptas. ($32). AE, DC, MC, V.
Open: Lunch, Tues–Sun 1–4pm; dinner, Tues–Sun 8pm–midnight.

Although this restaurant is located at the edge of the old quarter, on a drab street off Avenida de Donallo Romero, it's worth seeking out. It looks like a country tavern, and, in fact, the tasca in front is one of the most popular in the area, especially with locals. It's a family-run place with conscientious service. A few of the Galician dishes served here are based on meat (the filet of beef with sherry sauce is especially good), but the real specialties are seafood creations, such as fish soup, hake, and grilled shrimp.

★ **Toñi Vicente,** Calle Rosalía de Castro, 24. ☎ **59-41-00.**

Cuisine: INTERNATIONAL. **Reservations:** Recommended.
Prices: Appetizers 800–1,875 ptas. ($5.70–$13.30); main courses 700–3,300 ptas. ($5–$23.40). Fixed-price meals 2,900–5,500 ptas. ($20.60–$39.10). AE, DC, MC, V.
Open: Lunch, Mon–Sat 1:30–3:30pm; dinner, Mon–Sat 9–11:30pm. **Closed:** Two weeks in Aug.

Set in the heart of town, on two floors of a building erected around 1950, this is considered the most flamboyantly international (and the finest) restaurant in Santiago. Within dining rooms accented with a neoclassical overlay and a color scheme of blue and salmon, you can enjoy the celebrated cuisine of Toñi Vicente. Menu items change with the availability of the ingredients, but are likely to include such dishes as a warm seafood salad with herbs; escalopes of veal with a confit of onions; turbot with chive sauce; unusual preparations of seasonal game dishes, and for dessert, a tart made with Galician pears.

Restaurant Vílas, Rosalía de Castro, 88. ☎ **59-21-70.**

Cuisine: SEAFOOD. **Reservations:** Required.
Prices: Appetizers 1,000–1,800 ptas. ($7.10–$12.80); main courses 1,850–3,200 ptas. ($13.10–$22.70); fixed-price menus 4,500–5,000 ptas. ($32–$35.50). AE, DC, MC, V.
Open: Lunch, Mon–Sat 1–4pm; dinner, Mon–Sat 8:30pm–midnight.

Located on the outskirts of the old town on the road to Pontevedra, this reliable Spanish tavern, housed in a three-story town house, has a devoted clientele, many from industry, politics, and the arts. Beyond the large bar near the entrance and display cases filled with fresh fish, you'll find the baronial stone-trimmed dining room. A wide variety of fish is available—fresh sardines, three different preparations of salmon, a *zarzuela* (seafood stew), and eels. Two kinds of paella are served, and nonfish dishes such as partridge and rabbit also grace the menu. The restaurant was founded in 1915 as a little eating house. Back then, it was on the outskirts of town, but the place was enveloped by the city long ago. It stands on a street named after the illustrious poetess of Galicia. Today, the restaurant is run by the grandsons of the original founders.

La Tacita d'Juan, Hórreo, 31. ☎ **56-32-55.**

Cuisine: GALICIAN. **Reservations:** Recommended. **Bus:** 10.
Prices: Appetizers 450–2,500 ptas. ($3.20–$17.80); main courses 1,200–2,750 ptas. ($8.50–$19.50). AE, DC, MC, V.
Open: Lunch, Mon–Sat 12:30–4pm; dinner, Mon–Sat 8pm–midnight. **Closed:** Dec.

A favorite place for business lunches, five minutes from the train station, this restaurant offers caldo gallego, fish soup, artichokes with ham, Basque-style eels, shellfish cocktail, and a wide array of fish platters. Two special meat courses are the hamhock with greens and *fabada asturiana,* the famous stew of Asturias. The portions are generous, and the service is attentive.

4 Rías Altas

In Norway they're called fjords, in Brittany, *abers;* in Scotland, lochs; and in Galicia, *rías.* These are inlets cut into the Galician coastline by the turbulent Atlantic pounding against its shores. Rías Altas is a relatively modern name applied to all the estuaries on the northern Galicia coast, from Ribadeo (the gateway to Galicia on the border with Asturias) to La Coruña (the big Atlantic seaport of northwest Spain). The part that begins at Ribadeo—part of Lugo province—is also called Marina Lucense. Four estuaries form the Artabro Gulf: La Coruña, Betanzoa, Ares, and Ferrol. All four converge on a single point where Marola crag rises.

From Ribadeo to La Coruña

From Ribadeo, take the corniche road west (N-634) until you reach the Ría de Foz. About 1½ miles (2.5km) south of the Foz-Barreiros highway, perched somewhat in isolation on a hill, stands the Iglesia de San Martín de Mondoñeda, part of a monastery that dates from 1112.

The little town of *Foz* itself is a fishing village and also a summer beach resort. Its beaches are separated by a cliff. You might stop here for lunch.

From Foz cut northwest along the coastal highway (C-642) going through **Burela,** another fishing village. You can make a slight detour south to **Sargadelos,** which is a ceramics center. You can purchase these famous Galician products here much more cheaply than elsewhere in Spain.

Back on the coastal road at Burela, continue west approaching Ría de Vivero and the historic village of *Vivero.* Part of its medieval walls and an old gate, Puerta de Carlos V, have been preserved. The town has many old churches of interest, including the Gothic-style Iglesia San Francisco. Vivero is also a summer resort, attracting vacationers to its beach, the Playa Covas. Vivero also makes a good lunch stop.

The road continues northwest to *Vicedo,* passing such beaches as Xillo and Aerealong. Excellent vistas of the estuary greet you. Oxen can be seen plowing the cornfields.

Driving on, you'll notice the coastline becoming more sawtoothed. Eventually you reach **Ortigueira,** a major fishing village at the head of the ría from which it takes its name. A Celtic Folk Festival is staged here at the end of August.

From here you can continue south along the C-642 to **El Ferrol,** which used to be called El Caudillo, in honor of the late dictator Francisco Franco, who was born here and who used to spend part of his summers in this area. El Ferrol is one of the major shipbuilding centers of Spain, and since the 18th century it has also been a center of the Spanish navy. It's a grimy town, but it lies on one of the most beautiful rías. In spite of its parador, few tourists will want to linger at El Ferrol (also spelled O Ferrol).

From El Ferrol, the road continues south, passing through the small town of **Puentedeume** (also spelled Pontedeume), on the Rías Ares. Historically, it was the center of the counts of Andrade. The last remains of their 14th-century palace can be seen, along with the ruins of a 13th-century castle rising to the east.

Shortly below Betanzos, head west along the N-VI until you reach La Coruña. The entire 150-mile trip from Ribadeo takes at least four hours.

Where to Dine

Nito, Playa de Area, Vivero. ☎ **982/56-09-87.**

Cuisine: SEAFOOD. **Reservations:** Recommended.
Prices: Appetizers 650–1,150 ptas. ($4.60–$8.20); main courses 1,500–2,800 ptas. ($10.70–$19.90); fixed-price menu 1,800 ptas. ($12.80). AE, MC, V.
Open: Lunch, daily 2:30–4pm; dinner, daily 8pm–midnight. **Closed:** Sun night in winter.

Established in the early 1970s, this restaurant lies in the center of the Vivero, only a hundred yards from the beach, with a sweeping view of the Atlantic. It starts serving dinner early for Spain (8pm) but it's strictly for those who like to lunch late, as the first service isn't until 2:30 in the afternoon. The restaurant maintains a balance between its prices and the quality of its ingredients, and you get unpretentious but flavorful food. Shellfish, priced according to weight, is the specialty, but you can also order grilled sea bream, perhaps a house-style beefsteak. Most diners begin their meal with a bowl of *caldo gallego.* A full range of wines also is offered. Diners wishing to eat outside can sit on a garden-view terrace.

From La Coruña to Cape Fisterra

This next drive—called "to the end of the world"—takes you from La Coruña to Cape Fisterra (called Cabo Fisterra on most maps). It's a 90-mile trip that will take at least three hours. For the ancients, Cape Fisterra was the end of the world as they knew it.

This route takes you along **A Costa da Morte** (also called La Costa de la Muerte—The Coast of Death), so called because of the numerous shipwrecks that occurred here.

Leaving La Coruña, take the coastal road west, heading first to the road junction of **Carballo,** a distance of 22 miles (35.5km). From this little town, many of the small coastal harbors will be within an easy drive. **Malpica,** to the northwest, is the most interesting, with its own beach. An offshore seabird sanctuary exists there, and Malpica itself was a former whaling port. From Malpica, continue to the tiny village of **Corme** at Punta Roncudo. This sheltered fishing village draws the summer beach fans, as there are many isolated sand dunes.

From Corme, continue along the circuitous roads to the whitewashed village of **Camariñas,** which stands on the ría of the same name. A road here leads all the way to the lighthouse at Cabo Vilán. Camariñas is known as a village of expert lacemakers, and you'll see the work for sale at many places.

The road now leads to **Mugia,** below which stands the lighthouse at Cabo Touriñan. Continue south to **Corcubion,** a village with a Romanesque church. From here, drive to the "end of the line," **Cabo Fisterra,** for a spectacular view. The sunsets from here are said to be among the most spectacular in the world. The Roman poet Horace said it all: "The brilliant skylight of the sun drags behind it the black night over the fruitful breasts of earth."

5 Rías Bajas

From Cabo Fisterra you can continue south along the C-550 through Muros and Noya to the ✪ Rías Bajas, the four large estuaries facing the Atlantic from Cape Silleiro to

Baiona to Point Louro in Muros. Two of these are in the province of Pontevedra (Pontevedra and Vigo); one is in the province of La Coruña (Muros and Noya); and one (Arousa) divides its shores between the two provinces. The 20-mile (32km) Vigo estuary is the longest, stretching from *Ponte Sampasio* to Baiona.

From Muros to Ribeira

The seaside town of **Muros** has many old houses and a harbor, but **Noya** (also spelled Noia), to the southeast, is more impressive. If you don't have a car but would like to see at least one or two ría fishing villages, you can do so at either Noya or Muros: Both lie on a bus route connecting them with Santiago de Compostela. Eleven buses per day leave from Santiago heading for Noya and nine run to Muros. Some of the tiny little villages and beaches are also connected by bus routes.

Noya is known for its braided straw hats with black bands. It has a number of interesting, handsome old churches, including the 14th-century **Igrexa de Santa María** (with tombstones dating from the 10th century) and the **Igrexa de San Francisco.** A lot of good beaches lie on the northern bank of the ría near Muros. Noya might be your best bet for a lunch stop.

From Noya, the coast road continues west to **Porto do Son.** You can take a detour to Cabo de Corrubedo, with its lighthouse, before continuing on to **Ribeira** at the southern tip. Ribeira is a fishing port and a canning center. At Ribeira you'll see the **Ría de Arousa,** the largest and deepest of the inlets.

From Ribeira, continue east along the southern coastal road to **A Puebla de Caramiñal.** From here, take a signposted route 6 miles (9.6km) inland into the mountains, to admire the most magnificent panorama in all of rías country—the **Mirador de la Curota,** at 1,634 feet. The four inlets of the Rías Bajas can, under the right conditions, be seen from the belvedere. In clear weather you can also view Cape Fistera.

Back on the C-550, drive as far as Padrón, where, it is claimed, the legendary sea vessel arrived bringing Santiago (St. James) to Spain. Padrón was also the home of romantic poet Rosalía de Castro (1837–85), sometimes called the Emily Dickinson of Spain. Her house, the **Casa Museo de Rosalía de Castro,** Carretera de Herbrón (☎ **981/81-12-04**), is open to the public daily from 9am to 2pm and 4 to 8pm. Admission is free. Padrón also makes a good lunch stop.

From Padrón, follow the alleged trail of the body of St. James north along the N-550 to Santiago de Compostela or take the N-550 south to Pontevedra.

Where to Stay & Dine

Ceboleiro II, Galicia, 15, Noya. ☎ **981/82-05-31.** Fax 981/82-44-97.
Cuisine: SEAFOOD. **Reservations:** Not required.
Prices: Appetizers 650–1,200 ptas. ($4.60–$8.50); main courses 1,100–2,850 ptas. ($7.80–$20.20). AE, DC, MC, V.
Open: Lunch, daily 1:30–4pm; dinner, daily 8:30–11:30pm.
Closed: Dec 20–Jan 15.

For about a century, this inn has provided food and accommodations to passersby. Set in the heart of Noya, it is owned and managed by three generations of the Fernandez family. It offers hearty food from the sea, prepared in conservative but flavorful ways that usually correspond to the culinary traditions of Galicia and northern Portugal. The menu almost always includes several versions of hake; shellfish soup, several kinds of rice studded with fish or shellfish; pork and beef dishes, and among other desserts, an apple tart. The establishment also contains 13 simple but comfortable accommodations, each with private bathroom, TV, and telephone. Singles cost from 5,000 to 6,000 pesetas ($35.50 to $42.60); doubles from 8,000 to 9,000 pesetas ($56.80 to $63.90), with breakfast costing an additional 300 pesetas ($2.10) per person.

Chef Rivera, Enlace Parque, 7, Padrón. ☎ **981/81-04-13.**

Cuisine: GALICIAN. **Reservations:** Recommended.
Prices: Appetizers 400–1,800 ptas. ($2.80–$12.80); main courses 975–2,300 ptas. ($6.90–$16.30); fixed-price menus 1,700–2,300 ptas. ($12.10–$16.30). AE, DC, MC, V.
Open: Lunch, daily 1–4pm; dinner, daily 8pm–midnight.
Closed: Sun night in winter.

The name of the owner, to everyone in town, is simply El Chef. The cuisine of chef Rivera is innovative but also based on traditional recipes. His wife, Pierrette, attends to service in the dining room, which resembles an English pub with its dark, warm colors and leather upholstery. Try the shellfish soup or stew or the house-style monkfish. The restaurant is known for its *pimientos de Padrón.* Tiny green peppers are sautéed with olive oil—there's nothing unusual about that; the trick is that about one in five of those peppers is hot. Finish with lemon mousse. The couple also rent 20 simply furnished guest rooms, at 3,200 pesetas ($22.70) for a single and 4,850 pesetas ($34.40) for a double—with breakfast another 275 pesetas ($2).

6 Pontevedra

36 miles (58km) S of Santiago de Compostela; 521 miles (839km) NW of Madrid

GETTING THERE • By Train From Santiago de Compostela in the north, 11 trains per day make the one-hour trip to Pontevedra. RENFE has an office on Calle Gondomar, 3 (☎ **85-13-13**), where you can get information. The actual rail and bus stations (☎ **85-13-13**) for information about transportation in the area), lie half a mile from the center on Alféreces Provisionales.

• By Bus Pontevedra has good links to major Galician cities. From Vigo in the south, the bus traveling time is only 1/2 hour if you take one of the 12 inland expresses leaving from Vigo daily. From Santiago de Compostela in the north, a bus leaves every hour during the day for Pontevedra (1 hour).

• By Bus From Santiago de Compostela, head south along the N-550 to reach Pontevedra.

ESSENTIALS The area code for Pontevedra is 986. The tourist information office is at General Mola, 3 (☎ **986/85-08-14**).

An aristocratic old Spanish town on the Lérez River and the capital of Pontevedra province, the city of Pontevedra still has vestiges of an ancient wall that once encircled the town. In medieval days, the town was called Pontis Veteris (Old Bridge).

Some of the best Gallego seamen lived in Pontevedra in the Middle Ages. Sheltered at the end of the Pontevedra Ría, the city was a bustling port and foreign merchants mingled with local traders, seamen, and fishermen. It was the home of Pedro Sarmiento de Gamboa, the 16th-century navigator and cosmographer who wrote *Voyage to the Magellan Straits.* In the 18th century the Lérez delta silted up and the busy commerce moved elsewhere, mainly to Vigo. Pontevedra entered a period of decline, which may account for its significant old section. Had it been a more prosperous town, the people might have torn down the buildings to rebuild.

The old barrio—a maze of colonnaded squares and cobbled alleyways—lies between Calle Michelena and Calle del Arzobispo Malvar, stretching to Calle Cobián and the river. The old mansions are called pazos, and they speak of former marine glory, since it was the sea that provided the money to build them. Seek out such charming squares as Plaza de la Leña, Plaza de Mugártegui, and Plaza de Teucro.

What to See & Do

In the old quarter, the major attraction is the **Basílica de Santa María in Mayor,** Arzobispo Malvar, with its avocado-green patina, dating from the 16th century. This is a Plateresque church constructed with funds provided by the mariners' guild. Its most remarkable feature is its west front, which was carved to resemble an altarpiece. At the top is a depiction of the Crucifixion.

The **Museo Provincial,** Pasantería, 10 (☎ **85-14-55**), with a hodgepodge of everything from the Pontevedra attic, contains displays ranging from prehistoric artifacts to a still life by Zurbarán. Many of the exhibits are maritime-oriented, and there is also a valuable collection of jewelry. Hours are Tuesday to Sunday from 10:30am to 1:30pm and 4:30 to 8pm. Admission is 200 pesetas ($1.40). The museum opens onto a major square in the old town, the Plaza de Leña (Square of Wood).

Iglesia de San Francisco, Plaza de la Herrería, is another church of note. Its Gothic facade opens onto gardens. It was founded in the 14th century and contains a sculpture of Don Payo Gómez Charino, noted for his part in the 1248 Reconquest of Seville, when it was wrested from Muslim domination.

Directly south, the gardens lead to the 18th-century **Capilla de la Peregrina,** Plaza Peregrina, with a narrow half-moon facade connected to a rotunda and crowned by a pair of towers. It was constructed by followers of the cult of the Pilgrim Virgin, which was launched in Galicia some time in the 17th century.

Where to Stay

EXPENSIVE

Hotel Rías Bajas, Daniel de la Sota, 7, 36001 Pontevedra. ☎ **986/85-51-00.** Fax 986/85-51-00. 93 rms, 7 suites. MINIBAR TV TEL

Rates: 6,600 ptas. ($46.90) single; 10,500 ptas. ($74.60) double; 12,500 ptas. ($88.80) suite. Breakfast 600 ptas. ($4.30) extra. AE, DC, MC, V. **Parking:** 600 ptas. ($4.30).

On a busy street corner near Plaza de Galicia in the commercial center, this 1960s is more comfortable than you might expect, judging from the outside. The largest hotel in town, it is often used for community political meetings and press conferences. The lobby, of stone and wood paneling, has been designed to look like an English club. Bedrooms are comfortable and well maintained, with private baths. The hotel doesn't have a restaurant but does offer a cafeteria.

Hotel Virgen del Camino, Virgen del Camino, 55, 36001 Pontevedra. ☎ **986/85-59-00.** Fax 986/85-09-00. 53 rms. TV TEL

Rates: 5,500 ptas. ($39.10) single; 7,250 ptas. ($51.50) double. Breakfast 600 ptas. ($4.30) extra. AE, MC, V.

On a relatively quiet street off the C-531, at the edge of the suburbs, this balconied stucco hotel contains a comfortable English-style pub as well as spacious, comfortable sitting rooms. The bedrooms have wall-to-wall carpeting and private baths, plus central heating in winter. The best doubles contain separate salons and sitting rooms. Breakfast is the only meal served.

Parador Nacional Casa del Barón, Plaza de Maceda, s/n, 36002 Pontevedra. ☎ **986/85-58-00.** Fax 986/85-21-95. 47 rms. MINIBAR TV TEL

Rates: 7,600 ptas. ($54) single; 11,000 ptas. ($78.10) double. Breakfast 1,100 ptas. ($7.80) extra. AE, DC, MC, V.

The parador is located in the old quarter of Pontevedra, in a well-preserved 16th-century palace near the Basílica de Santa María la Mayor. Built on either 13th- or 14th-century foundations, this hotel became one of Spain's first paradors when it opened in 1955. The interior has been maintained very much as the old *pazo* (manor house) must have looked. It includes a quaint old kitchen, or *lar* (literally "heart"), typical of Galician country houses and furnished with characteristic items. Off the vestibule is a courtyard dominated by a large old stone staircase. Many of the accommodations, all with private baths, are large enough to include sitting areas; the beds are comfortable, the furnishings attractive. Many of the rooms overlook the walled-in formal garden. Both lunch and dinner are served for 3,500 pesetas ($24.90). Most dishes, such as a casserole of shrimp with tomato sauce, are well prepared.

Moderate

Hotel Comercio, Augusto González Besada, 3, 36001 Pontevedra. ☎ **986/85-12-17.** Fax 986/85-99-91. 40 rms (all with bath). A/C TV TEL **Bus:** 14 or 20 from the train station.

Rates: 4,500 ptas. ($32) single; 6,000 ptas. ($42.60) double. Breakfast 450 ptas. ($3.20) extra. AE, DC, V.

This tall hotel, with its modern facade and art deco-inspired café and bar, is an acceptable choice in its price category. The guest rooms are fairly comfortable, but only functional in style. A restaurant serves lunch and dinner for 2,000 pesetas ($14.20).

Where to Dine

Casa Román, Augusto García Sánchez, 12. ☎ **84-35-60.**

Cuisine: SEAFOOD. **Reservations:** Not required.
Prices: Appetizers 950–1,500 ptas. ($6.70–$10.70); main courses 950–3,000 ptas. ($6.70–$21.30); fixed-price menus 3,500–4,000 ptas. ($24.90–$28.40). AE, DC, MC, V.
Open: Lunch, daily 1–4pm; dinner, Mon–Sat 9pm–midnight. **Closed:** Sun night, except in July and Aug.

Known for the quality of its food, this well-established restaurant is on the street level of a brick apartment building in a leafy downtown development known as Campolongo, near Plaza de Galicia. To reach the dining room, you pass through a tavern. In addition to lobster (which you can see in the window), a wide array of fish and shellfish dishes are served here, including sea bass, squid, sole, crab, lobsters, and tuna.

Doña Antonia, Soportales de la Herrería, 9. ☎ **84-72-74.**

Cuisine: GALICIAN. **Reservations:** Required.
Prices: Appetizers 950–1,200 ptas. ($6.70–$8.50); main courses 1,400–2,600 ptas. ($9.90–$18.50); *menú del día* 4,000 ptas. ($28.40). AE, MC, V.
Open: Lunch, Mon–Sat 1:30–4pm; dinner, Mon–Sat 9–11:30pm. **Closed:** Nov.

Without question, Pontevedra's best restaurant is Doña Antonia, located under a stone arcade on one of the town's oldest streets, east of the Jardines Vincenti. You climb one flight to reach the pink-and-white dining room. Menu items include baked suckling lamb, scaloppine with port, rolled filet of salmon, and kiwi sorbet.

7 El Grove & La Toja

395 miles (636km) NW of Madrid; 20 miles (32km) W of Pontevedra; 45 miles (72km) S of Santiago de Compostela

GETTING THERE • By Train The train from Santiago de Compostela goes as far as Vilagarcía de Arousa; take the bus from there.

• By Bus From Pontevedra, buses heading for Ponte Vilagarcía de Arousa stop at La Toja.

• By Car From Pontevedra, take the 550 coastal road east via Sanxenxo. From Santiago de Compostela, take expressway A-9 to Caldas de Reis, turn off onto the 550, and head west to the coast.

ESSENTIALS The area code for El Grove and La Toja is 986.

A summer resort and fishing village, **El Grove** is on a peninsula west of Pontevedra, with some 5 miles (8km) of beaches of varying quality. It juts out into the Ría de Arousa, a large inlet at the mouth of Ulla River. The village, sheltered from Atlantic gales because of its eastern position, has become more commercial than many visitors would like, but it is still renowned for its fine cuisine. A shellfish festival is held here every October.

La Toja (A Toxa in Galician), an island linked to El Grove by a bridge, is a famous spa and the most fashionable resort in Galicia, known for its sports and leisure activities. The casino and the golf course are both very popular. The island is covered with pine trees and surrounded by some of the finest scenery in Spain.

La Toja first became known for health-giving properties when, according to legend, the owner of a sick donkey left it on the island to die. The donkey recovered, and its cure was attributed to the waters of an island spring.

Where to Stay in El Grove

Hotel Amandi, Castelao, 94, 36989 El Grove. ☎ **986/73-19-42.** Fax 986/73-16-43. 30 rms (all with bath). TEL

Rates (including breakfast): 4,850 ptas. ($34.40) single; 9,700 ptas. ($68.90) double. MC, V. **Closed:** Nov.

This stylish and tasteful hotel is a brisk 10-minute walk from the bridge that connects El Grove with La Toja. The rooms, most with TVs, are decorated with antique reproductions; the majority have tiny terraces with ornate cast-iron balustrades and sea views. Breakfast is the only meal served.

Where to Dine in El Grove

La Pousada del Mar, Castelao, 202. ☎ **73-01-06.**

Cuisine: SEAFOOD. **Reservations:** Required in July and Aug.

Prices: Appetizers 600–1,200 ptas. ($4.30–$8.50); main courses 1,200–2,500 ptas. ($8.50–$17.80); fixed-price menu 3,600 ptas. ($25.60). AE, DC, MC, V.

Open: Lunch, daily 1–4pm; dinner, Mon–Sat 8:30pm–midnight. **Closed:** Dec 10–Jan 31.

This warm, inviting place near the bridge leading to La Toja is the best dining spot outside those at the hotels. At times you can watch women digging for oysters in the river in front. The chef, naturally, specializes in fish, including a wide selection of shellfish. Among the specialties are a savory soup, an outstanding shellfish paella, hake Galician style, and fresh grilled salmon. For dessert, try the *flan de la casa.*

Where to Stay in La Toja

Hotel Louxo, 36991 Isla de la A Toxa. ☎ **986/73-02-00.** Fax 986/73-27-91. 115 rms (all with bath). MINIBAR TV TEL

Rates (including breakfast): 13,200 ptas. ($93.70) single; 16,900 ptas. ($120) double. AE, DC, MC, V. **Parking:** Free. **Closed:** Nov–May.

Set on flatlands a few paces from the town's ornate casino is this modern white building, sheltered from the Atlantic winds. It offers clean, stylish, modern accommodations. The many ground-floor public rooms have rows of comfortable seating areas and sweeping views over the nearby tidal flats. The hotel also serves an outstanding menu, with an emphasis on fresh fish. A *menú del día* costs 1,900 pesetas ($13.50).

8 Túy (Túi)

18 miles (29km) S of Vigo; 30 miles (48km) S of Pontevedra

GETTING THERE • By Train Trains run daily for the 1½- to 2-hour trip from Vigo to Túy.

• **By Bus** From Vigo, buses run south to Túy hourly, taking 1 hour.

• **By Car** From Vigo, head south along the A-9 expressway until you see the turnoff for Túy.

ESSENTIALS The area code for Túy is 986. The tourist information office is at Puente Tripes, Avenida de Portugal (☎ **986/60-17-89**).

A frontier town first settled by the Romans, Túy is a short distance from Portugal, located near the two-tiered road-and-rail bridge (over the Miño River) that links the two countries. The bridge was designed by Gustave Eiffel. For motorists coming from Portugal's Valenca do Minho, Túy will be their introduction to Spain.

What to See & Do

The winding streets of the old quarter lead to the **cathedral,** a national art treasure that dominates the *zona monumentale.* The acropolislike cathedral-fortress, built in 1170, wasn't used for religious purposes until the early 13th century. Its principal portal, ogival in style, is exceptional. What is astounding about this cathedral is that later architects respected the original Romanesque and Gothic style and didn't make changes in its design. If you have time, you may want to visit the Romanesque-style **Church of San Bartolomé,** on the outskirts, and the **Church of Santo Domingo,** a beautiful example of Gothic style (look for the bas-reliefs in the cloister). The latter church stands next to the Parque de Santo Domingo. Walls built over Roman fortifications surround Túy.

Where to Stay & Dine

Parador Nacional de San Telmo, Avenida de Portugal, s/n, 36700 Túy. ☎ **986/60-03-09.** Fax 986/60-21-63. 23 rms (all with bath), 1 suite. A/C MINIBAR TV TEL

Rates: 6,800-9,200 ptas. ($48.30–$65.30) single; 8,500–11,500 ptas. ($60.40–$81.70) double; 16,100 ptas. ($114.30) suite. Breakfast 1,100 ptas. ($7.80) extra. AE, DC, MC, V. **Parking:** Free.

Advance reservations are essential if you want to stay in this elegant, fortress-style hacienda located four streets north of the Miño River crossing. Built in 1968, the inn, with its cantilevered roof, was designed to blend in with the architectural spirit of the province, emphasizing local stone and natural woods. Brass chandeliers, paintings by well-known gallegos, and antiques combined with reproductions furnish the public rooms. In the main living room are a large inglenook fireplace, a tall banjo-shaped grandfather clock, hand-knotted rugs, 18th-century paintings, hand-hewn benches, and comfortable armchairs.

The bedrooms are sober in style, but comfortable, and offer views across a colonnaded courtyard to the river and hills. They are furnished with Castilian-style pieces, and the tiled baths are modern. The dignified dining room has a high wooden ceiling and tall windows that offer a fine view of the surrounding hills. Even if you are not a hotel guest, it is worth dining on the regional cuisine served here. The hors d'oeuvres alone consist of almost a dozen little dishes. The fish dishes are excellent, especially (when available) lamprey, as well as salmon, shad, and trout. Homemade cakes are offered for dessert. A complete meal costs 3,500 pesetas ($24.90).

Appendix

A Basic Phrases & Vocabulary

ENGLISH	SPANISH	PRONUNCIATION
Hello	**Buenos días**	*bway*-noss *dee*-ahss
How are you?	**Como está usted?**	*koh*-moh ess-*tah* oo-*steth*
Very well	**Muy bien**	mwee byen
Thank you	**Gracias**	*gra*-theeahss
Good-bye	**Adiós**	ad-*dyohss*
Please	**Por favór**	pohr fah-*bohr*
Yes	**Sí**	see
No	**No**	noh
Excuse me	**Pardóneme**	pahr-*doh*-neh-may
Give me	**Deme**	*day*-may
Where is?	**Donde está?**	*dohn*-day ess-*tah*
the station	**la estación**	la ess-tah-*thyohn*
a hotel	**un hotel**	oon oh-*tel*
a restaurant	**un restaurante**	oon res-tow-*rahn*-tay
the toilet	**el servicio**	el ser-*vee*-the-o
To the right	**A la derecha**	ah lah day-*ray*-chuh
To the left	**A la izquierda**	ah lah eeth-*kysyr*-duh
Straight ahead	**Adelante**	ah-day-*lahn*-tay
I would like	**Quiero**	*kyehr*-oh
to eat	**comer**	ko-*mayr*
a room	**una habitación**	*oo*-nah ah-bee-tah-*thyon*
How much is it?	**Cuánto?**	*kwahn*-toh
The check	**la cuenta**	la *kwen*-tah
When	**Cuándo?**	*kwan*-doh
Yesterday	**Áyer**	ah-*yeyr*
Today	**Hoy**	oy
Tomorrow	**Mañana**	mah-*nyah*-nah
Breakfast	**Desayuno**	deh-sai-*yoo*-noh
Lunch	**Comida**	co-*mee*-dah
Dinner	**Cena**	*thay*-nah

Numbers

1 **uno** (*oo*-noh)
2 **dos** (dose)
3 **tres** (trayss)
4 **cuatro** (*kwah*-troh)
5 **cinco** (*theen*-koh)
6 **sais** (sayss)
7 **siete** (*syeh*-tay)
8 **ocho** (*oh*-choh)
9 **nueve** (*nway*-bay)
10 **diez** (dyeth)
11 **once** (*ohn*-thay)
12 **doce** (*doh*-thay)
13 **trece** (*tray*-thay)
14 **catorce** (kah-*tor*-thay)
15 **quince** (*keen*-thay)
16 **dieciseis** (dyeth-ee-*sayss*)
17 **diecisiete** (dyeth-ee-*sye*-tay)
18 **dieciocho** (dysth-ee-*oh*-choh)
19 **diecinueve** (dyeth-ee-*nyway*-bay)
20 **veinte** (*bayn*-tey)
30 **trienta** (*trayn*-tah)
40 **cuarenta** (kwah-*ren*tah)
50 **cincuenta** (theen-*kween*-tah)
60 **sesenta** (say-*sen*-tah)
70 **setenta** (say-*ten*-tah)
80 **ochenta** (oh-*chan*tah)
90 **noventa** (noh-*ben*tah)
100 **cien** (thyen)

B Menu Savvy

Alliolo Sauce made from garlic and olive oil
Arroz con costra Rice dish of chicken, rabbit, sausages, black pudding, chickpeas, spices, and pork meatballs—everything "hidden" under a layer of beaten egg crust
Arroz empedrado Rice cooked with tomatoes and cod and a top layer of white beans
Bacalao al ajo arriero Cod-and-garlic dish named after Leonese mule drivers
Bacalao al pil-pil Code with garlic and chile peppers
Bacalao a la vizcaina Cod with dried peppers and onion
Bajoques farcides Peppers stuffed with rice, pork, tomatoes, and spices
Butifarra Catalonian sausage made with blood, spices, and eggs
Caldereta Stew or a stew pot
Caldereta extremña Kid or goat stew
Caldo gallego Soup made with cabbage, potatoes, beans, and various meat flavorings (ham, chorizo, spare ribs)
Chanfaina salmantina Rice, giblets, lamb sweetbreads, and pieces of chorizo
Chilindrón Sauce made from tomatoes, peppers, garlic, chorizo, and spicy sausage
Cochifrito navarro Small pieces of fried lamb
Cocido español Spanish stew
Cocido de pelotas Stew of minced meat wrapped in cabbage leaves and cooked with poultry, bacon, chickpeas, potatoes, and spices
El arroz amb feseola i naps Rice with beans and turnips
El caldillo de perro "Dog soup," made with onions, fresh fish, and orange juice
El cocido Madrileña Chickpea stew of Madrid, with potatoes, cabbage, turnips, beef, marrow, bacon, chorizo, and black pudding
El pato a la naranja Duck with orange, an old Valencian dish
Empanada Crusted pie of Galicia, with a variety of fillings
Escudella Catalán version of chickpea stew
Fabada White bean stew of Asturias
Habas a la catalana Stew of broad beans, herbs, and spices
Judías blancas Haricot beans
Judías negras Runner beans
Lacón con grelos Salted ham with turnip tops
La caseolada Potato-and-vegetable stew with bacon and ribs
La salsa verde Green sauce to accompany fish

Las magras con tomate Slices of slightly fried ham dipped in tomato sauce
La trucha a la navarra Trout fried with a piece of ham
La pericana Code, olive oil, dry peppers, and garlic
Mar y cielo "Sea and heaven," made with sausages, rabbit, shrimp, and fish
Merluza a la gallega Galician hake with onions, potatoes, and herbs
Meriuza a la sidra Hake cooked with cider
Morcilla Black sausage akin to black pudding
Paella alicantina Rice dish with chicken and rabbit
Picada Sauce made from nuts, parsley, garlic, saffron, and cinnamon
Pilota Ball made of meat, parsley, bread crumbs, and eggs
Pinchito Small kebab
Pisto manchego Vegetable stew from La Mancha
Pollos a la chilindron Chicken cooked in a tomato, onion, and pepper sauce
Romesco Mediterranean sauce, with olive oil, red pepper, bread, garlic, and maybe cognac
Samfaina Sauce made from tomatoes, eggplant, onions, and zucchini
Sangría Drink made with fruit, brandy, and wine
Sofrito Sauce made from peppers, onions, garlic, tomatoes, and olive oil
Sopas castellanas Bread, broth, ham, and sometimes a poached egg and garlic
Sopa de ajo castellana Garlic soup with ham, bread, eggs, and spices
Tapas Small dishes or appetizers served with drinks at a tavern
Tortilla de patatas Spanish omelet with potatoes
Turrónn Almond paste
Zarzuela Fish stew

C Glossary of Architectural Terms

Alcazaba Moorish fortress
Alcázar Moorish fortified palace
Ayuntamiento Town hall
Azulejo Painted glazed tiles, popular in Mudéjar work and later architecture, especially in Andalusia, Valencia, and Portugal
Barrio (Barri in Catalán) City neighborhood or district
Churrigueresque Floridly ornate baroque style of the late 17th and early 18th centuries in the style of Spanish sculptor and architect José Churriguera (1650–1725)
Ciudadela Citadel
Cortijo Andalusian country house or villa
Granja Farm or farmhouse
Isabeline Gothic Architectural style popular in the late 15th century, roughly corresponding to the English perpendicular
Judería Jewish quarter
Lonja Merchants' exchange or marketplace
Medina Walled center of a Moorish city, traditionally centered around a mosque
Mezquita Mosque
Mirhab Prayer niche in a mosque, by Koranic law facing Mecca
Mirador Scenic overlook or belvedere, or a glassed-in panoramic balcony sheltering its occupants from the wind
Mudéjar Moorish-influenced architecture, usually "Christianized" and adopted as Spain's most prevalent architectural style from the 12th to the 16th century

Plateresque Heavily ornamented Gothic style widely used in Spain and Portugal during the 16th century. Its name derives from the repoussé floral patterns hammered into 16th-century silver (*la plata*), which were imitated in low relief carvings in stone
Plaza de Toros Bullring
Plaza Mayor Square at the center of many Spanish cities, often enclosed, arcaded, and enhanced with cafés and fountains
Puerta Portal or gate
Reja Iron grilles, either those covering the exterior windows of buildings or the decorative dividers in churches
Retablo Carved and/or painted altarpiece

D The Metric System

Length

1 millimeter (mm)	=	.04 inches (*or less than* 1/16 in.)
1 centimeter (cm)	=	.39 inches (*or* just under 1/2 in.)
1 meter (m)	=	39 inches (*or* about 1.1 yards)
1 kilometer (km)	=	.62 miles (*or* about 2/3 of a mile)

To convert kilometers to miles, multiply the number of kilometers by .62. Also use to convert kilometers per hour (kmph) to miles per hour (m.p.h.).
To convert miles to kilometers, multiply the number of miles by 1.61. Also use to convert from m.p.h. to kmph.

Capacity

1 liter (l)	=	33.92 fluid ounces	=	2.1 pints	=	1.06 quarts
	=	.26 U.S. gallon				
1 Imperial gallon	=	1.2 U.S. gallons				

To convert liters to U.S. gallons, multiply the number of liters by .26.
To convert U.S. gallons to liters, multiply the number of gallons by 3.79.
To convert Imperial gallons to U.S. gallons, multiply the number of Imperial gallons by 1.2.
To convert U.S. gallons to Imperial gallons, multiply the number of U.S. gallons by .83.

Weight

1 gram (g)	=	.035 ounces (*or* about a paperclip's weight)
1 kilogram (kg)	=	35.2 ounces
1 metric ton	=	2,205 pounds (1.1 short ton)

To convert kilograms to pounds, multiply the number of kilograms by 2.2.
To convert pounds to kilograms, multiply the number of pounds by .45.

Area

1 hectare (ha)	=	2.47 acres		
1 square kilometer (km^2)	=	247 acres	=	.39 square miles

To convert hectares to acres, multiply the number of hectares by 2.47.
To convert acres to hectares, multiply the number of acres by .41.
To convert square kilometers to square miles, multiply the number of square kilometers by .39.
To convert square miles to square kilometers, multiply the number of square miles by 2.6.

Temperature

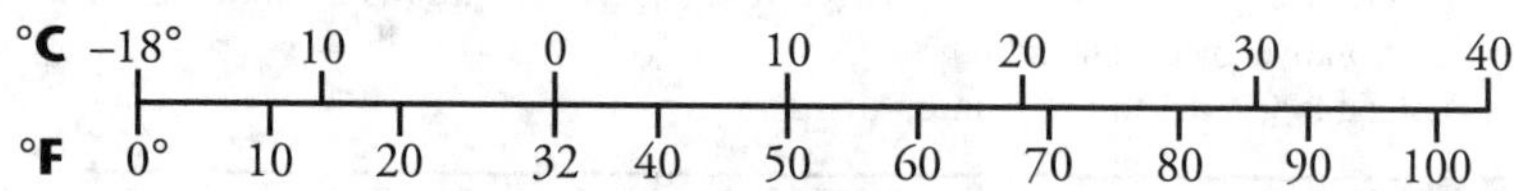

To convert degrees Celsius to degrees Fahrenheit, multiply °C by 9, divide by 5, and add 32 (example: 20°C × 9/5 + 32 = 68°F).
To convert degrees Fahrenheit to degrees Celsius, subtract 32 from °F, multiply by 5, then divide by 9 (example: 85°F - 32 × 5/9 = 29.4°C).

Index

The following Frommer's guides are available from your favorite bookstore, or you can use the order form on the preceding page to request them as part of your membership in Frommer's Travel Book Club.

FROMMER'S COMPLETE TRAVEL GUIDES

(Comprehensive guides to sightseeing, dining and accommodations, with selections in all price ranges—from deluxe to budget)

Title	Code
Acapulco/Ixtapa/Taxco, 2nd Ed.	C157
Alaska '94-'95	C131
Arizona '95	C166
Australia '94-'95	C147
Austria, 6th Ed.	C162
Bahamas '96 (avail. 8/95)	C172
Belgium/Holland/Luxembourg, 4th Ed.	C170
Bermuda '96 (avail. 8/95)	C174
California '95	C164
Canada '94-'95	C145
Caribbean '96 (avail. 9/95)	C173
Carolinas/Georgia, 2nd Ed.	C128
Colorado '96 (avail. 11/95)	C179
Costa Rica, 1st Ed.	C161
Cruises '95-'96	C150
Delaware/Maryland '94-'95	C136
England '96 (avail. 10/95)	C180
Florida '96 (avail. 9/95)	C181
France '96 (avail. 11/95)	C182
Germany '96 (avail. 9/95)	C176
Honolulu/Waikiki/Oahu, 4th Ed. (avail. 10/95)	C178
Ireland, 1st Ed.	C168
Italy '96 (avail. 11/95)	C183
Jamaica/Barbados, 2nd Ed.	C149
Japan '94-'95	C144
Maui, 1st Ed.	C153
Nepal, 3rd Ed. (avail. 11/95)	C184
New England '95	C165
New Mexico, 3rd Ed.	C167
New York State, 4th Ed.	C133
Northwest, 5th Ed.	C140
Portugal '94-'95	C141
Puerto Rico '95-'96	C151
Puerto Vallarta/Manzanillo/Guadalajara, 2nd Ed.	C135
Scandinavia, 16th Ed.	C169
Scotland '94-'95	C146
South Pacific '94-'95	C138
Spain, 16th Ed.	C163
Switzerland, 7th Ed. (avail. 9/95)	C177
Thailand, 2nd Ed.	C154
U.S.A., 4th Ed.	C156
Virgin Islands, 3rd Ed. (avail. 8/95)	C175
Virginia '94-'95	C142
Yucatán '95-'96	C155

FROMMER'S $-A-DAY GUIDES

(Dream Vacations at Down-to-Earth Prices)

Title	Code
Australia on $45 '95-'96	D122
Berlin from $50, 3rd Ed. (avail. 10/95)	D137
Caribbean from $60, 1st Ed. (avail. 9/95)	D133
Costa Rica/Guatemala/Belize on $35, 3rd Ed.	D126
Eastern Europe on $30, 5th Ed.	D129
England from $50 '96 (avail. 11/95)	D138
Europe from $50 '96 (avail. 10/95)	D139
Greece from $45, 6th Ed.	D131
Hawaii from $60 '96 (avail. 9/95)	D134
Ireland on $45 '94-'95	D118
Israel on $45, 15th Ed.	D130
London from $55 '96 (avail. 11/95)	D136
Madrid on $50 '94-'95	D119
Mexico from $35 '96 (avail. 10/95)	D135
New York on $70 '94-'95	D121
New Zealand from $45, 6th Ed.	D132
Paris on $45 '94-'95	D117
South America on $40, 16th Ed.	D123
Washington, D.C. on $50 '94-'95	D120

FROMMER'S COMPLETE CITY GUIDES

(Comprehensive guides to sightseeing, dining, and accommodations in all price ranges)

Amsterdam, 8th Ed.	S176	Minneapolis/St. Paul, 4th Ed.	S159
Athens, 10th Ed.	S174	Montréal/Québec City '95	S166
Atlanta & the Summer Olympic Games '96 (avail. 11/95)	S181	Nashville/Memphis, 1st Ed.	S141
Atlantic City/Cape May, 5th Ed.	S130	New Orleans '96 (avail. 10/95)	S182
Bangkok, 2nd Ed.	S147	New York City '96 (avail. 11/95)	S183
Barcelona '93-'94	S115	Paris '96 (avail. 9/95)	S180
Berlin, 3rd Ed.	S162	Philadelphia, 8th Ed.	S167
Boston '95	S160	Prague, 1st Ed.	S143
Budapest, 1st Ed.	S139	Rome, 10th Ed.	S168
Chicago '95	S169	St. Louis/Kansas City, 2nd Ed.	S127
Denver/Boulder/Colorado Springs, 3rd Ed.	S154	San Antonio/Austin, 1st Ed.	S177
Disney World/Orlando '96 (avail. 9/95)	S178	San Diego '95	S158
Dublin, 2nd Ed.	S157	San Francisco '96 (avail. 10/95)	S184
Hong Kong '94-'95	S140	Santa Fe/Taos/Albuquerque '95	S172
Las Vegas '95	S163	Seattle/Portland '94-'95	S137
London '96 (avail. 9/95)	S179	Sydney, 4th Ed.	S171
Los Angeles '95	S164	Tampa/St. Petersburg, 3rd Ed.	S146
Madrid/Costa del Sol, 2nd Ed.	S165	Tokyo '94-'95	S144
Mexico City, 1st Ed.	S175	Toronto, 3rd Ed.	S173
Miami '95-'96	S149	Vancouver/Victoria '94-'95	S142
		Washington, D.C. '95	S153

FROMMER'S FAMILY GUIDES

(Guides to family-friendly hotels, restaurants, activities, and attractions)

California with Kids	F105	San Francisco with Kids	F104
Los Angeles with Kids	F103	Washington, D.C. with Kids	F102
New York City with Kids	F101		

FROMMER'S WALKING TOURS

(Memorable strolls through colorful and historic neighborhoods, accompanied by detailed directions and maps)

Berlin	W100	Paris, 2nd Ed.	W112
Chicago	W107	San Francisco, 2nd Ed.	W115
England's Favorite Cities	W108	Spain's Favorite Cities (avail. 9/95)	W116
London, 2nd Ed.	W111	Tokyo	W109
Montréal/Québec City	W106	Venice	W110
New York, 2nd Ed.	W113	Washington, D.C., 2nd Ed.	W114

FROMMER'S AMERICA ON WHEELS

(Guides for travelers who are exploring the U.S.A. by car, featuring a brand-new rating system for accommodations and full-color road maps)

Arizona/New Mexico	A100	Florida	A102
California/Nevada	A101	Mid-Atlantic	A103

FROMMER'S SPECIAL-INTEREST TITLES

Arthur Frommer's Branson! P107
Arthur Frommer's New World of Travel (avail. 11/95) P112
Frommer's Caribbean Hideaways (avail. 9/95) P110
Frommer's America's 100 Best-Loved State Parks P109
Frommer's Where to Stay U.S.A., 11th Ed. P102
National Park Guide, 29th Ed. P106
USA Today Golf Tournament Guide P113
USA Today Minor League Baseball Book P111

FROMMER'S BEST BEACH VACATIONS

(The top places to sun, stroll, shop, stay, play, party, and swim—with each beach rated for beauty, swimming, sand, and amenities)

California (avail. 10/95) G100
Florida (avail. 10/95) G101
Hawaii (avail. 10/95) G102

FROMMER'S BED & BREAKFAST GUIDES

(Selective guides with four-color photos and full descriptions of the best inns in each region)

California B100
Caribbean B101
East Coast B102
Eastern United States B103
Great American Cities B104
Hawaii B105
Pacific Northwest B106
Rockies B107
Southwest B108

FROMMER'S IRREVERENT GUIDES

(Wickedly honest guides for sophisticated travelers and those who want to be)

Chicago (avail. 11/95) I100
London (avail. 11/95) I101
Manhattan (avail. 11/95) I102
New Orleans (avail. 11/95) I103
San Francisco (avail. 11/95) I104
Virgin Islands (avail. 11/95) I105

FROMMER'S DRIVING TOURS

(Four-color photos and detailed maps outlining spectacular scenic driving routes)

Australia Y100
Austria Y101
Britain Y102
Canada Y103
Florida Y104
France Y105
Germany Y106
Ireland Y107
Italy Y108
Mexico Y109
Scandinavia Y110
Scotland Y111
Spain Y112
Switzerland Y113
U.S.A. Y114

FROMMER'S BORN TO SHOP

(The ultimate travel guides for discriminating shoppers—from cut-rate to couture)

Hong Kong (avail. 11/95) Z100
London (avail. 11/95) Z101